DogFriendly.com's

Campground and Park Guide
2nd Edition

by
Tara Kain and Len Kain
DogFriendly.com, Inc.

DogFriendly.com's Campground and RV Park Guide
by Tara Kain and Len Kain

DogFriendly.com, Inc.
6454 Pony Express Trail #33-233
Pollock Pines, CA 95726 USA
1-877-475-2275
email: email@dogfriendly.com
http://www.dogfriendly.com

PLEASE NOTE
Although the authors and publisher have tried to make the information as accurate as possible, they do not assume, and hereby disclaim, any liability for any loss or damage caused by errors, omissions, misleading information or potential travel problems caused by this book, even if such errors or omissions result from negligence, accident or any other cause.

CHECK AHEAD
We remind you, as always, to call ahead and confirm that the applicable establishment is still "dog-friendly" and that it will accommodate your pet.

DOGS OF ALL SIZES
If your dog is over 75-80 pounds, then please call the individual establishment to make sure that they allow your dog. Please be aware that establishments and local governments may also not allow particular breeds.

OTHER PARTIES DESCRIPTIONS
Some of the descriptions have been provided to us by our web site advertisers, paid researchers or other parties.

ISBN 13 – 978-0-9795551-1-4
ISBN 10 – 0-9795551-1-6

Printed in the United States of America

Table of Contents

5. Dog-Friendly Highway Campground Guides.................................. 555

6. United States National Park Guide 595

Introduction

DogFriendly.com's guides have helped over one million dog lovers plan vacations and trips with their dogs. This book is a guide for people who want to camp with dogs in tents, RVs, and motor homes. With this book, it is our goal to help you not only find campgrounds for you and your pet but also parks to visit, trails to hike, beaches and other places to enjoy together. We have researched campgrounds and RV parks, U.S. and Canadian Parks, State Parks and Provincial Parks for their detailed pet policies. This goes beyond a statement such as "Pets Allowed, with Restrictions" or "Pets allowed – on leash". These are the types of descriptions most campground guides have regarding pets. People who travel with pets know, however, that this is not the real pet policy. There are many other questions such as

- What additional fees are there for my pet?
- How many dogs may I have in my campsite?
- Are some breeds not allowed at the campground?
- Are there size restrictions on dogs at the campground?
- How many dogs may I have at my campsite?
- Dogs may be allowed in my RV but are they allowed if I camp in a tent? Or in the camping cabins?
- Is there a place to walk my dog? Am I allowed to walk my dog throughout the campground?
- Is there a place to let my dog off-leash? Are there any other pet amenities at the campground?
- If the campground is in a park are dogs allowed on the trails in the park? What other areas of the park are they allowed in?

The book also has highway guides for major highways throughout the U.S. and Canada listing campgrounds in cities along these highways. This will make it easier to find a place for the night. It also has a listing of off-leash dog parks and dog-friendly beaches and a guide to the U.S. National Parks. If you also plan on staying at hotels and other lodging during your travels you might also consider our book "DogFriendly.com's United States and Canada Dog Travel Guide" which looks at these accommodations as well as attractions, stores and outdoor restaurants that allow dogs.

Thank you for selecting DogFriendly.com's Camping and RV Park Guide and we hope you spend less time researching and more time actually going places with your dog. Enjoy your dog-friendly camping.

About Authors Tara and Len Kain

Tara and Len Kain have traveled over 150,000 miles across the U.S. and Canada with their family and dogs in search of some of the best dog-friendly places around. They founded DogFriendly.com in 1998 and have been traveling together with dogs since 1990. Currently, over 1 million people annually visit DogFriendly.com. Tara and Len, along with DogFriendly.com, have been featured in many newspaper articles, on radio and on TV. Tara, Len and their family reside in the California foothills near Sacramento.

Your Comments and Feedback

We value and appreciate your feedback and comments. If you want to recommend a dog-friendly place or establishment, let us know. If you find a place that is no longer dog-friendly, allows small dogs only or allows dogs in smoking rooms only, please let us know. You can contact us using the following information.

Mailing Address and Contact Information:
DogFriendly.com, Inc.
6454 Pony Express Trail #33-233
Pollock Pines, CA 95726 USA
Toll free phone: 1-877-475-2275
email: email@ dogfriendly.com
http://www.dogfriendly.com

How To Use This Guide

General Guidelines

1. Please only travel with a well-behaved dog that is comfortable around other people and especially children. Dogs should also be potty trained and not bark excessively.

2. Always keep your dog leashed unless management specifically tells you otherwise.

3. Campgrounds listed do not allow dogs to be left alone in your campsite unless specified by management. If the establishment does not allow pets to be left alone, try hiring a local pet sitter to watch your dog in the room.

4. Pet policies and management change often. Please always call ahead to make sure an establishment still exists and is still dog-friendly.

5. After purchasing your book, please visit http://www.dogfriendly.com/updates for FREE book updates. We will do our best to let you know which places may no longer be dog-friendly.

Preparation for a Road Trip

A Month Before

If you don't already have one, get a pet identification tag for your dog. It should have your dog's name, your name and phone number. Consider using a cell phone number, a home number and, if possible, the number of where you will be staying.

Get a first aid kit for your dog. It comes in very handy if you need to remove any ticks. The kits are usually available at a pet store, a veterinary office or on the Internet.

If you do not already have a dog harness for riding in the car or motor home, consider purchasing one for your dog's and your own safety. A loose dog can fly into the windshield or into you and injure you or cause you to lose control of the vehicle. Dog harnesses are usually sold at pet stores or on the Internet.

Make a trip to the vet if necessary for the following:

- A current rabies tag for your dog's collar. Also get paperwork with proof of the rabies vaccine.
- Dogs can possibly get heartworm from mosquitoes in the mountains, rural areas or on hikes. Research or talk to your vet and ask him or her if the area you are traveling to has a high risk of heartworm disease. The vet may suggest placing your dog on a monthly heartworm preventative medicine.
- Consider using some type of flea preventative for your dog.
- Make sure your dog is in good health.

Several Days Before

Make sure you have enough dog food for the duration of the trip.

If your dog is on any medication, remember to bring it along.

Some dog owners will also purchase bottled water for the trip, because some dogs can get sick from drinking water they are not used to. Talk to your vet for more information.

If you are visting the desert or another hot envionment be aware that your dogs paws may burn if it is very hot. You may consider boots for your dog if you are planning to spend much time in these environments.

The Day Before

Do not forget to review DogFriendly.com's Etiquette for the Traveling Dog!

Road Trip Day

Remember to pack all of your dog's necessities: food, water, dog dishes, leash, snacks and goodies, several favorite toys, brush, towels for dirty paws, plastic bags for cleaning up after your dog, doggie first aid kit, possibly dog booties if you are venturing to an especially cold or hot region, and bring any medicine your dog might be taking.

Before you head out, put on that doggie seat belt harness.

On The Road

Keep it cool and well ventilated in the vehicle for your dog.

Stop at least every 2-3 hours so your dog can relieve him or herself. Also offer him or her water during the stops.

Never leave your pet alone in a parked car - even in the shade with the window cracked open. According to the Los Angeles SPCA, on a hot day, a car can heat up to 160 degrees in minutes, potentially causing your pet (or child) heat stroke, brain damage, and even death. If you leave your pet in an RV make sure that the windows are open, there is sufficient air flow or you are running fans or A/C.

If your dog needs medical attention during your trip, check the yellow pages phone book in the area and look under Veterinarians. If you do not see an emergency vet listed, call any local vet even during the evening hours and they can usually inform you of the closest emergency vet.

Etiquette for the Traveling Dog

So you have found the perfect getaway spot that allows dogs, but maybe you have never traveled with your dog. Or maybe you are a seasoned dog traveler. But do you know all of your doggie etiquette? Basic courtesy rules, like your dog should be leashed unless a place specifically allows your dog to be leash-free. And do you ask for a paper bowl or cup for your thirsty pooch at an outdoor restaurant instead of letting him or her drink from your water glass?

There are many do's and don'ts when traveling with your best friend. We encourage all dog owners to follow a basic code of doggie etiquette, so places will continue to allow and welcome our best friends. Unfortunately all it takes is one bad experience for an establishment to stop allowing dogs. Let's all try to be on our best behavior to keep and even encourage new places to allow our pooches.

Everywhere...

- Well-Behaved Dogs. Only travel or go around town with a well-behaved dog that is friendly to people and especially children. If your dog is not comfortable around other people, you might consider taking your dog to obedience classes or hiring a professional trainer. Your well-behaved dog should also be potty trained and not bark excessively. We believe that dogs should be kept on leash. If a dog is on leash, he or she is easier to bring under control. Also, many establishments require that dogs be on leash and many people around you will feel more comfortable as well. And last, please never leave your dog alone at a campground, hotel or other establishment unless it is permitted by the management.

- Leashed Dogs. Please always keep your dog leashed, unless management specifically states otherwise. Most establishments (including lodging, outdoor restaurants, attractions, parks, beaches, stores and festivals) require that your dog be on leash. Plus most cities and counties have an official leash law that requires pets to be leashed at all times when not on your property. Keeping your dog on leash will also prevent any unwanted contact with other people that are afraid of dogs, people that do not appreciate strange dogs coming up to them, and even other dog owners who have a leashed dog. Even when on leash, do not let your pooch visit with other people or dogs unless welcomed. Keeping dogs on leash will also protect them from running into traffic, running away, or getting injured by wildlife or other dogs. Even the most well-behaved and trained dogs can be startled by something, especially in a new environment.

- Be Considerate. Always clean up after your dog. Pet stores sell pooper scooper bags. You can also buy sandwich bags from your local grocery store. They work quite well and are cheap!

At Campgrounds or RV Parks...

- Although most RV Parks and many campgrounds allow dogs each has different rules, restrictions and types of dogs that are allowed. Be aware of these rules when you check in and respect them.

- Always assume that a dog must be on leash in a campground. If there is an off-leash area then use that area for your pets off-leash activity.

- Always assume that your dog is not allowed in common areas such as swimming pools, game rooms and general stores unless it is specifically allowed by management.

- Be respectful of your neighbors. Don't assume that they will want to have your dog barking at them or visiting with them. Only leave your dog outside of your vehicle if it is chained or otherwise restrained and you are there to supervise.

- Many campgrounds have designated specific dog walk areas. Walk your dog in the designated areas. Always clean up after your dog.

In Parks...

- Respect the park's leash laws and always clean up after your pet. Those parks that ban dogs cite these two reasons in most cases as to why dogs are not allowed in the park.

- Always assume that another park visitor is not interested in a visit from your dog unless they specifically invite your dog over to them. This is especially true of children.

At Hotels or Other Types of Lodging...

- Unless it is obvious, ask the hotel clerk if dogs are allowed in the hotel lobby. Also, because of health codes, dogs are usually not allowed into a lobby area while it is being used for serving food like continental breakfast. Dogs may be allowed into the area once there is no food being served, but check with management first.

- Never leave your dog alone in the hotel room. The number one reason hotel management does not allow dogs is because some people leave them in the room alone. Some dogs, no matter how well-trained, can cause damage, bark continuously or scare the housekeepers. Unless the hotel management allows it, please make sure your dog is never left alone in the room. If you need to leave your dog in the room, consider hiring a local pet sitter.

- While you are in the room with your dog, place the Do Not Disturb sign on the door or keep the deadbolt locked. Many housekeepers have been surprised or scared by dogs when entering a room.

- In general, do not let your pet on the bed or chairs, especially if your dog sheds easily and might leave pet hair on the furniture. Some very pet-friendly accommodations will actually give you a sheet to lay over the bed so your pet can join you. If your pet cannot resist coming hopping onto the furniture with you, bring your own sheet.

- When your dog needs to go to the bathroom, take him or her away from the hotel rooms and the bushes located right next to the rooms. Try to find some dirt or bushes near the parking lot. Some hotels have a designated pet walk area.

At Outdoor Restaurants...

- Tie your dog to your chair, not the table (unless the table is secured to the ground). If your dog decides to get up and move away from the table, he or she will not take the entire table.

- If you want to give your dog some water, please ask the waiter/waitress to bring a paper cup or bowl of water for your dog. Do not use your own water glass. Many restaurants and even other guests frown upon this.

- Your pooch should lay or sit next to your table. At restaurants, dogs are not allowed to sit on the chairs or tables, or eat off the tables. This type of activity could make a restaurant owner or manager ban dogs. And do not let your pooch beg from other customers. Unfortunately, not everyone loves dogs!

At Retail Stores...

- Keep a close eye on your dog and make sure he or she does not go to the bathroom in the store. Store owners that allow dogs inside assume that responsible dog owners will be entering their store. Before entering a dog-friendly store, visit your local pet store first. They are by far the most forgiving. If your dog does not go to the bathroom there, then you are off to a great start! If your dog does make a mistake in any store, clean it up. Ask the store clerk for paper towels or something similar so you can clean up any mess.

At Festivals and Outdoor Events...

Make sure your dog has relieved himself or herself before entering a festival or event area. The number one reason that most festival coordinators do not allow dogs is because some dogs go to the bathroom on a vendor's booth or in areas where people might sit.

Breed Specific Laws and the Effect of These Laws on Travel With Dogs

There has been a trend in cities, counties, states and provinces towards what is known as Breed-Specific Laws (BSL) in which a municipality bans or restricts the freedoms of dog owners with specific breeds of dogs. These laws vary from place to place and are affecting a greater number of dog owners every year. Most people may think that these laws affect only the "Pit Bull" but this is not always the case. Although the majority of dogs affected are pit-bulls other breeds of dogs as well as mixed breeds that include targeted breeds are also named in the various laws in North America. These laws range from registration requirements and leash or muzzle requirements to extreme laws in which the breed is banned from the municipality outright. Some places may even be permitted to confiscate a visitors dog who unknowingly enters the region with a banned breed.

As of August 29, 2005 the province of Ontario, Canada (including Toronto, Niagara Falls, and Ottawa) passed a very broad breed-specific law banning Pit Bulls and "similar" dogs from the province. The law allows for confiscation of visiting dogs as well as dogs living in Ontario. It is extremely important that people visiting Ontario make sure that they are able to prove that their dog is not a Pit Bull with other documentation. Various cities throughout the U.S. and Canada have muzzle requirements for Pit Bulls and other restrictions on targeted breeds as well. Breed-specific laws do get repealed as well. In October, 2005 the city of Vancouver, BC removed its requirement that Pit Bulls be muzzled in public and now only requires dogs with a known history of aggressiveness to be muzzled.

The breed specific laws usually effect pit bull type dogs but are often vaguely written and may also effect mixed breed dogs that resemble the targeted breeds. These laws are always changing and can be passed by cities, counties and even states and provinces. We recommend that travelers with dogs check into whether they are affected by such laws. You may check www.DogFriendly.com/bsl for links to further information on BSL.

DogFriendly.com does not support breed-specific laws. Most people who take their dogs out in public are responsible and those that choose to train a dog to be viscous will simply choose another breed, causing other breeds to be banned or regulated in the future.

Customs Information for Traveling Between the United States and Canada

If you will be traveling between the United States and Canada, identification for Customs and Immigration is required. U.S. and Canadian citizens traveling across the border need the following:

People

- A passport is now required (or will shortly be required depending on your point of entry) to move between the U.S. and Canada. This is a new policy so be sure to have your passport with you. Children also need a passport of their own now.

Dogs

- Dogs must be free of evidence of diseases communicable to humans when possibly examined at the port of entry.

- Valid rabies vaccination certificate (including an expiration date usually up to 3 years from the actual vaccine date and a veterinarian's signature). If no expiration date is specified on the certificate, then the certificate is acceptable if the date of the vaccination is not more than 12 months before the date of arrival. The certificate must show that the dog had the rabies vaccine at least 30 days prior to entry.

- Young puppies must be confined at a place of the owner's choosing until they are three months old, then they must be vaccinated. They must remain in confinement for 30 days after the vaccination.

Chapter 1

Campgrounds and RV Parks

United States

Alabama

Wind Creek State Park
4325 H 128
Alexander City, AL
256-329-0845 (800-ALAPARK (252-7275))
This park of 1,445 acres, along the shores of a 41,000 acre clear-water reservoir, provides a marina, trails, various habitats, and a variety of land and water activities and recreation. Dogs of all sizes are allowed at no additional fee. Dogs may not be left unattended, and they must be leashed and cleaned up after in camp areas. Dogs are not allowed in or around the cabins, in park buildings, or on the beaches. Dogs are allowed on the trails. The camping and tent areas also allow dogs. There is a dog walk area at the campground. Multiple dogs may be allowed.

Leisure Time Campground
2670 S College Street
Auburn, AL
334-821-2267
Dogs of all sizes are allowed. There are no additional pet fees. Dogs must be leashed and cleaned up after. The camping and tent areas also allow dogs. There is a dog walk area at the campground. Multiple dogs may be allowed.

Circle S Stables, Campground and Steakhouse
454 Seales Road
Beaverton, AL
205-698-9005
This campsite has 20 sites and can accommodate the larger units. There is a bathhouse with hot showers, horse stables, and a steakhouse restaurant. Dogs are allowed in the camp area; they are not allowed in buildings or at the restaurant. Dogs must be leashed and cleaned up after. The camping and tent areas also allow dogs. There is a dog walk area at the campground. Multiple dogs may be allowed.

Blue Springs State Park
2595 H 10
Clio, AL
334-397-4875 (800-ALAPARK (252-7275))
The main feature at this 103 acre park is the crystal clear spring-fed

swimming pools. Dogs are allowed in the park and campground for no additional fee. They must be quiet, well behaved, crated or on no more than a 6 foot leash, and picked up after at all times. Dogs are not allowed in any park buildings or swim areas; however, they are allowed river access. The camp area offers modern to primitive sites, each with a picnic table and grill; comfort stations and a playground are nearby. The camping and tent areas also allow dogs. There is a dog walk area at the campground. Multiple dogs may be allowed.

Good Hope Campground
330 Super Saver Road
Cullman, AL
256-739-1319
Dogs of all sizes are allowed. There are no additional pet fees. Dogs must be leashed and cleaned up after. The camping and tent areas also allow dogs. There is a dog walk area at the campground. Multiple dogs may be allowed.

Dauphin Island Park
109 Bienville Blvd
Dauphin Island, AL
251-861-6972
dauphinisland.org/
This island has many popular features for land and water recreation, but other favorites are the 10 annual fishing rodeos and birding activities. Dogs are allowed throughout the area and at the campground; they are not allowed on the pier or where otherwise noted. Dogs must leashed and cleaned up after at all times. The camp area offers 150 sites with picnic tables, restrooms, showers, a laundry, camp store, and gaming areas. The camping and tent areas also allow dogs. There is a dog walk area at the campground. Multiple dogs may be allowed.

Point Mallard Campground
2600-C Point Mallard Drive
Decatur, AL
256-351-7772
pointmallardpark.com
Dogs of all sizes are allowed. There are no additional pet fees. Dogs must be leashed and cleaned up after. The camping and tent areas also allow dogs. There is a dog walk area at the campground. Multiple dogs may be allowed.

Cheaha Resort State Park
19644 H 281
Delta, AL

800-ALAPARK (252-7275)
Holding the distinction of being the state's oldest continuously operating park, it is also the highest point (at 2,407 feet) in the state offering great scenic views, plus it is surrounded by a national forest. Dogs are allowed in the park and campground for no additional fee. They must be quiet, well behaved, crated or on no more than a 6 foot leash, and under their owner's control at all times. Dogs are not allowed in any park buildings or swim areas-including beaches. The camp areas range from primitive to modern and they may have some or all of the following on site or close by: modern restrooms, full service bathhouses, grills, picnic tables, a restaurant, country store, or playground. The camping and tent areas also allow dogs. There is a dog walk area at the campground. Multiple dogs may be allowed.

Bankhead National Forest
1070 H 33 (Bankhead Ranger District)
Double Springs, AL
205-489-5111
This national forest offers spectacular scenery, 6 different recreation areas-each with their own uniqueness, 153+ miles of trails, and diverse ecosystems that support a large variety of flora and fauna. Dogs of all sizes are allowed at no additional fee. Dogs may not be left unattended, and they must be leashed and cleaned up after. There are several camp areas and they may have all or some of the following: picnic tables, fire rings, restrooms, showers, potable water, a boat launch, or dump station. The camping and tent areas also allow dogs. There is a dog walk area at the campground. There are no electric or water hookups at the campgrounds. Multiple dogs may be allowed.

Lakepoint Resort State Park
104 Lakepoint Drive
Eufaula, AL
334-687-8011 (800-ALAPARK (252-7275))
This scenic 1,220 acre park along the 45,000 acre Lake Eufaula offers a convention center, an 18-hole golf course, and a variety of land and water recreation. Dogs of all sizes are allowed at no additional fee. Dogs may not be left unattended, and they must be leashed and cleaned up after. Dogs are not allowed in park buildings, at the

lodge, or on the trails. The camping and tent areas also allow dogs. There is a dog walk area at the campground. Multiple dogs may be allowed.

Magnolia Springs RV Hideaway
10831 Magnolia Springs H
Foley, AL
800-981-0981
Dogs of all sizes are allowed. There are no additional pet fees. Dogs may not be left unattended outside, and they must be quiet, well behaved, leashed, and cleaned up after. This is an RV only park. There is a dog walk area at the campground. Multiple dogs may be allowed.

Palm Lake RV Park
15810 H 59
Foley, AL
251-970-3773 (888-878-5687)
palmlakerv.com/
Dogs are allowed for no additional fee. They may not be left unattended outside the RV at any time, nor inside unless they will be quiet. Dogs must be leashed and under their owner's control at all times; they are not allowed in or around the Clubhouse, the pool, or common areas. The pet walk areas are well marked and pets must be picked up after promptly. There is a fenced, off-leash doggie play area on site. There is a dog walk area at the campground. 2 dogs may be allowed.

DeSoto Resort State Park
13883 H 89
Fort Payne, AL
256-845-0051 (800-ALAPARK (252-7275))
Sitting on top of beautiful Lookout Mountain surrounded by waterfalls and wildflowers, this popular resort park offers a wide variety of recreational and educational opportunities. Dogs are allowed in the park and campground for no additional fee. They must be quiet, well behaved, crated or on no more than a 6 foot leash, and under their owner's control at all times. Dogs are not allowed in any park buildings or swim areas-including beaches. The campground is temporarily closed for renovations until further notice. The camping and tent areas also allow dogs. There is a dog walk area at the campground. Multiple dogs may be allowed.

Noccalula Falls Park and Campground
1600 Noccalula Road

Gadsden, AL
256-543-7412
Dogs of all sizes are allowed. There are no additional pet fees. Dogs may not be left unattended, and they must be quiet, leashed, and cleaned up after. There are some breed restrictions. The camping and tent areas also allow dogs. There is a dog walk area at the campground. Multiple dogs may be allowed.

River Country Campground
1 River Road
Gadsden, AL
256-543-7111
Dogs of all sizes are allowed. There are no additional pet fees. Dogs must be leashed and cleaned up after. The camping and tent areas also allow dogs. There is a dog walk area at the campground. 2 dogs may be allowed.

Chattahoochee Park
250 Chattahoochee State Park Road
Gordon, AL
334-522-3607 (800-ALAPARK (252-7275))
There are almost 600 land acres and a 22 acre spring-fed lake at this recreational destination. The park also offers handicapped hunting facilities. Dogs are allowed in the park and campground for no additional fee. They must be quiet, well behaved, crated or on no more than a 6 foot leash, and picked up after at all times. Dogs are not allowed in any park buildings or swim areas. They are allowed water access, but they must be kept leashed and close to their human companions (alligators occasionally enter). The camp area offers picnic tables, grills, modern restrooms, and showers. The camping and tent areas also allow dogs. There is a dog walk area at the campground. Multiple dogs may be allowed.

Fort Morgan RV Park
10397 2nd Street
Gulf Shores, AL
251-540-2416
fortmorganrvpark.com/
Located right on Mobile Bay, this RV park offers 20 spacious, private sites on 20 acres. All sites are shaded and on the water front or with ocean views. In addition to providing a bathhouse and a laundry, they also have cable and Wi-Fi available. Dogs are allowed for no additional fee; they must be leashed and under their owner's control at all times. Dogs are

allowed down at the dock and are welcome to take a swim. There are some breed restrictions. The camping and tent areas also allow dogs. There is a dog walk area at the campground. Multiple dogs may be allowed.

Gulf Breeze Resort
19800 Oak Road W
Gulf Shores, AL
251-968-8884
wakefieldenterprises.com
Dogs of all sizes are allowed. There are no additional pet fees. Dogs may not be tied to camp property and they may not be left unattended outside. Dogs must be leashed and cleaned up after, and they are not allowed in the buildings, pavilion, bathrooms, or at the pool. The camping and tent areas also allow dogs. There is a dog walk area at the campground. Multiple dogs may be allowed.

Gulf State Park
20115 H 135
Gulf Shores, AL
251-948-7275 (800-ALAPARK (252-7275))
Over 6,000 recreational acres, white sand beaches, an 18-hole golf course, a 900 acre lake, nature programs, and a lot more have made this a popular destination. Dogs are allowed in the campground only for no additional fee. They must be quiet, well behaved, crated or on no more than a 6 foot leash, and picked up after at all times. Dogs are not allowed in any park buildings or swim areas-including beaches. The recently improved campground offers 496 sites, picnic tables, grills, and modern restrooms. The camping and tent areas also allow dogs. There is a dog walk area at the campground. Multiple dogs may be allowed.

Luxury RV Resort
590 Gulf Shores Parkway
Gulf Shores, AL
251-948-5444 (800-982-3510)
redelephants.com/LuxuryRV.html
Dogs of all sizes are allowed. There are no additional pet fees. Dogs may not be left unattended, and they must be leashed and cleaned up after. This is an RV only park. There is a dog walk area at the campground. Multiple dogs may be allowed.

Cherokee Campground
2800 H 93
Helena, AL
205-428-8339
cherokee.tripod.com

Dogs of all sizes are allowed. There are no additional pet fees. Dogs must be quiet, leashed, and cleaned up after. There is a dog walk area at the campground. Multiple dogs may be allowed.

Monte Sano State Park
5105 Nolen Avenue
Huntsville, AL
256-534-3757 (800-ALAPARK (252-7275))
Sitting nestled among the trees on a lush green bluff, this beautiful 2,400 acre park offers scenic views, a modern playground, and picnic areas. Dogs are allowed in the park and campground for no additional fee. They must be quiet, well behaved, crated or on no more than a 6 foot leash, and picked up after at all times. Dogs may not be left unattended outside, and they are not allowed in any park buildings. The campground offers more than 80 shady campsites. The camping and tent areas also allow dogs. There is a dog walk area at the campground. Multiple dogs may be allowed.

Knox Hill RV Park
252 Old Patton Road
Knoxville, AL
205-372-3911 (877-372-3911)
knoxhillrv.com/pages/1/index.htm
Dogs of all sizes are allowed. There are no additional pet fees. Dogs may not be left unattended, and they must be leashed and cleaned up after. The camping and tent areas also allow dogs. There is a dog walk area at the campground. Multiple dogs may be allowed.

Little Mountain Marina
1001 Murphy Hills Road
Langston, AL
256-582-8211
wakefieldenterprises.com
Dogs of all sizes are allowed. There are no additional pet fees. Dogs may not be left unattended, and they must be quiet, leashed, and cleaned up after. There are some breed restrictions. The camping and tent areas also allow dogs. There is a dog walk area at the campground. 2 dogs may be allowed.

South Sauty Creek Resort
6845 S Sauty Road
Langston, AL
256-582-3367
southsautyresort.com
Dogs of all sizes are allowed. There are no additional pet fees. Dogs may not be left unattended, and they must be leashed and cleaned up

after. This RV park is closed during the off-season. The camping and tent areas also allow dogs. Multiple dogs may be allowed.

Tannehill Ironworks Historical State Park
12632 Confederate Parkway
McCalla, AL
205-477-5711 (800-ALAPARK (252-7275))
tannehill.org/
Once an important iron making area for early settlers, this lively village park now offers many educational and recreational activities. The park has a swap meet every 3rd weekend from March to November, seasonal living history demonstrations, over 45 buildings of the 1800s, direct shopping from local artisans, annual events, and much more. Dogs are allowed in the park and campground for no additional fee. They must be quiet, well behaved, crated or on no more than a 6 foot leash, and picked up after at all times. Dogs are not allowed in any park buildings or swim areas-including beaches. The campground offers 195 improved, first come first serve campsites. The camping and tent areas also allow dogs. There is a dog walk area at the campground. Multiple dogs may be allowed.

Shady Acres Campground
2500 Old Military Road
Mobile, AL
251-478-0013
shadyacresmobile.com
Dogs of all sizes are allowed. There are no additional pet fees. Dogs may not be left unattended outside, and they must be leashed and cleaned up after. There is a dog walk area at the campground. Multiple dogs may be allowed.

Capital City RV Park
4655 Old Wetumpka H (H 231N)
Montgomery, AL
877-271-8026
capitalcityrvpark.net
Dogs of all sizes are allowed. There are no additional pet fees. Dogs may not be left unattended outside, and they must be leashed and cleaned up after. This is an RV only park. There is a dog walk area at the campground. Multiple dogs may be allowed.

Ozark Travel Park
2414 N H 231
Ozark, AL
334-774-3219
ozarktravelpark.com

Dogs of all sizes are allowed. There are no additional pet fees. Dogs may not be left unattended outside, and they must be leashed and cleaned up after. There is a fenced in dog run for off lead. The camping and tent areas also allow dogs. There is a dog walk area at the campground. Multiple dogs may be allowed.

Birmingham South Campground
222 H 33
Pelham, AL
205-664-8832
Dogs of all sizes are allowed. There are no additional pet fees. Dogs must be leashed and cleaned up after. The camping and tent areas also allow dogs. There is a dog walk area at the campground. Dogs are allowed in the camping cabins. Multiple dogs may be allowed.

Oak Mountain State Park
200 Terrace Drive
Pelham, AL
800-ALAPARK (252-7275)
The state's largest park at 9,940 acres offers lush surroundings, abundant land and marine recreation, 50+ miles of hiking trails, a golf course/pro shop, and concessionaires. They are also home to the state's largest wildlife rehabilitation center, and a treetop nature trail. Dogs are allowed in the park and campground for no additional fee. They must be quiet, well behaved, crated or on no more than a 6 foot leash, and picked up after at all times. Dogs are not allowed in any park buildings or swim areas-including beaches. Primitive camping and more than 140 RV and tent sites are available here. Most sites have picnic tables and grills; a camp store, modern restrooms and bathhouses with hot showers are on site. The camping and tent areas also allow dogs. There is a dog walk area at the campground. Multiple dogs may be allowed.

Joe Wheeler State Park
201 McLean Drive
Rogersville, AL
256-247-1184 (800-ALAPARK (252-7275))
In addition to a wide range of land and water recreation, this resort park also offers a restaurant, a gift shop, concessionaires, a playground, a variety of special events throughout the year, and much more. Dogs are allowed in the park and campground for no additional fee. They must be quiet, well behaved, crated or on no

more than a 6 foot leash, and under their owner's control at all times. Dogs are not allowed in any park buildings or swim areas-including beaches. The campground offers 116 shaded, spacious, level sites, each with picnic tables and grills; restrooms and a bathhouse are nearby. The camping and tent areas also allow dogs. There is a dog walk area at the campground. Multiple dogs may be allowed.

Wales West RV Park
13670 Smiley Street
Silverhill, AL
888-569-5337
waleswest.com/rv_main.htm
This modern RV resort is reminiscent of a scenic Welsh vale with some interesting features; they are home to the only authentic Welsh narrow gauge railway in the country, and a 7.5 inch miniature railway-the only one in the area. They also have a 3.5 fresh water lake with a white sandy beach, a nature trail with a waterfall and several crossing dams, and a number of amenities/activities. Dogs are allowed for no additional fee unless pet waste is not cleaned up after and disposed of properly-then there will be additional fees of $10. Dogs must be kept leashed and they may not be left unattended outside unless they will be quiet at all times. Dogs must be current on license and vaccinations-including rabies, and they are not allowed in buildings, the indoor pool, the beach, or on the trains. There are some breed restrictions. There is a dog walk area at the campground. 2 dogs may be allowed.

Blakeley State Historical Park
34745 H 225
Spanish Fort, AL
251-626-0798 (800-ALAPARK (252-7275))
BlakeleyPark.com
In addition to being a significant Civil War area offering several historic sites, annual reenactments, and a recreated 1820s town, this park's bio-diversity is highlighted by seasonal eco-tours aboard the Delta Explorer. Dogs are allowed in the park and campground for no additional fee. They must be quiet, well behaved, crated or on no more than a 6 foot leash, and picked up after at all times. Dogs are not allowed on the boat, in park buildings, or swim areas-including beaches. The campground offers wooded sites, picnic tables, fire rings, and restrooms. The camping

and tent areas also allow dogs. There is a dog walk area at the campground. Multiple dogs may be allowed.

Meaher State Park
5200 Battleship Parkway E
Spanish Fort, AL
251-626-5529 (800-ALAPARK (252-7275))
Set in the scenic wetlands of Mobile Bay, this 1,327 acre park offers a number of land and marine activities, plus there are 2 self-guided nature trials with a boardwalk for better views of the Mobile Delta. Dogs are allowed in the park and campground for no additional fee. They must be quiet, well behaved, crated or on no more than a 6 foot leash, and under their owner's control at all times. Dogs are not allowed in any park buildings or swim areas-including beaches. They are also not allowed at the construction site. Eleven campsites are available at present; a new 56 site campground is under construction and plans to open in fall of 2008. Restrooms, tables, grills, and a dump station are available; there are no showers at present. The camping and tent areas also allow dogs. There is a dog walk area at the campground. Multiple dogs may be allowed.

Talladega National Forest
1001 North Street
Talladega, AL
256-362-2909
fs.fed.us/r8/alabama/aboutus/
This forest provides a variety of camping areas, trails, recreation, and diverse ecosystems that support a large variety of plants, fish, mammals, and bird species. Dogs are allowed at no additional fee. Dogs may not be left unattended outside, and they must be leashed at all times and cleaned up after in the camp areas. Dogs are allowed on the trails. This campground is closed during the off-season. The camping and tent areas also allow dogs. There is a dog walk area at the campground. There are no water hookups at the campground. Multiple dogs may be allowed.

Deer Run RV Park
25629 H 231N
Troy, AL
334-566-6517 (800-552-3036)
deerrunrvpark.com
Dogs of all sizes are allowed. There are no additional pet fees. Dogs

may not be left unattended outside, and please clean up after your pet. They may be off lead only if they are under voice control and will not chase other animals. Dogs are allowed on the trails that wind through the 72 acre park. This is an RV park only. There is a dog walk area at the campground. Multiple dogs may be allowed.

Tuskegee National Forest
125 National Forest Road, Bldg 949
Tuskegee, AL
334-727-2652
fs.fed.us/r8/alabama/aboutus/
This forest provides a variety of camping areas, trails, recreation, and diverse ecosystems that support a large variety of plants, fish, mammals, and bird species. Dogs are allowed at no additional fee. Dogs may not be left unattended, and they must be leashed and cleaned up after in the camp areas. Dogs may be off lead in the forest only if they will not chase and are under voice control. The camping and tent areas also allow dogs. There is a dog walk area at the campground. There are no water hookups at the campground. Multiple dogs may be allowed.

Rickwood Caverns
370 Rickwood Park Road
Warrior, AL
205-647-9692 (800-ALAPARK (252-7275))
This park is home to caverns 260 million years old-and still growing. In addition to the tours, the park has a large seasonal swimming pool, concessionaires, hiking trails, a playground, and gift shop. Dogs are allowed in the park and campground for no additional fee. They must be quiet, well behaved, crated or on no more than a 6 foot leash, and picked up after at all times. Dogs are not allowed in any park buildings, swim areas, or in the cave. There are 13 developed sites (9 can accommodate any size RV), comfort stations with seasonal showers, a dump station, and security patrol. The camping and tent areas also allow dogs. There is a dog walk area at the campground. Multiple dogs may be allowed.

Conecuh National Forest
H 137
Wing, AL
334-222-2555
fs.fed.us/r8/alabama/aboutus/
This forest provides a variety of camping areas, trails, recreation, and

diverse ecosystems that support a large variety of plants, fish, mammals, and bird species. Dogs are allowed at no additional fee. Dogs may not be left unattended, and they must be quiet, well behaved, leashed and cleaned up after in the camp areas. Dogs are allowed on the trails. The camping and tent areas also allow dogs. There is a dog walk area at the campground. There are no water hookups at the campground. Multiple dogs may be allowed.

Alaska

Centennial Campground
8300 Glenn H 1
Anchorage, AK
907-343-6986
muni.org/parks/camping.cfm
Open from May 23 thru September 7, this camp area is close to some great hiking trails and they are only 15 minutes from town. Dogs of all sizes are allowed for no additional fee. Dogs must be quiet, leashed (or confined) at all times, and cleaned up after. This RV park is closed during the off-season. The camping and tent areas also allow dogs. There is a dog walk area at the campground. 2 dogs may be allowed.

Chugach National Forest
3301 C Street
Anchorage, AK
907-743-9500 (877-833-6777)
fs.fed.us/r10/chugach/
This stunning park is America's most northerly national forest with some of the most breathtaking landscape to be found anywhere, and is one of the rare places where active glaciers are still carving valleys. It also has a very diverse topographic landscape with numerous hiking trails, drawing nature and adventurer devotees from all over. Dogs are allowed throughout the park, on the trails, at the glaciers, and in camp areas for no additional fee. Dogs must be leashed when in camp areas or when there other people around, and they may only be off lead if they are under strict voice control. There are about 15 campgrounds and 40 rustic cabins available throughout the forest. Cabins can be reserved; some of the camp areas are first come first served, and it is all pack in,pack out. Cabins are reached mostly by hiking, boat, or plane. The camping and tent

areas also allow dogs. There is a dog walk area at the campground. Dogs are allowed in the camping cabins. There are no electric or water hookups at the campgrounds. Multiple dogs may be allowed.

Chugach State Park
18620 Seward H
Anchorage, AK
907-345-5014
There are number of year round recreational opportunities available here at America's 3rd largest state park at a half a million acres and it draws in naturist and adventurers from all over to explore some of the most diverse topography on earth. Although the park is open year round, the campground is only open from mid-May to mid-September, weather permitting. Dogs are allowed throughout the park, on the trails, and in the camp area for no additional fee. Dogs must be leashed when in camp, and cleaned up after at all times. They suggest caution having pets off lead in the park because of wild animals. The Eklutna Lake campground at mile 26 of the Glenn Highway offers 50 campsites, water, latrines, fire pits, picnic tables, interpretive displays with a telescope, and a picnic shelter. There is also an overflow camp area with 15 sites, and camping at Eagle River and Bird Creek. This RV park is closed during the off-season. The camping and tent areas also allow dogs. There is a dog walk area at the campground. There are no electric or water hookups at the campgrounds. Multiple dogs may be allowed.

Golden Nugget Camper Park
4100 DeBarr Road
Anchorage, AK
907-333-5311 (800-449-2012)
goldennuggetcamperpark.com/
In addition to being centrally located in town, they also provide a number of amenities including Wi-Fi, hot showers, gaming areas, picnic tables, outdoor fire pits, a gift shop, and more. Dogs of all sizes are allowed for no additional fee. Dogs must be well behaved, leashed, and cleaned up after. This RV park is closed during the off-season. The camping and tent areas also allow dogs. There is a dog walk area at the campground. Multiple dogs may be allowed.

Ship Creek Landings RV Park
150 N Ingra Street

Anchorage, AK
907-277-0877 (888-778-7700)
This camp area offers numerous amenities, a great gift shop, touring assistance, and they are located only a few blocks to the downtown area of Alaska's largest city. They are open from May 1st to September 30th. Dogs of all sizes are allowed for no additional fee. Dogs must be friendly, leashed, and cleaned up after. This RV park is closed during the off-season. The camping and tent areas also allow dogs. There is a dog walk area at the campground. Multiple dogs may be allowed.

Border City Motel and RV Park
Mile 1225 Alaska H
Border City, AK
907-774-2205
karo-ent.com/border.htm
This rest and re-supply stop offers guests a motel, camping area, deli, ice creamery, fuels, and large, grassy pull-thru sites. Dogs of all sizes are allowed for no additional fee in the camp area; there is a $50 refundable deposit for the motel's 1 pet-friendly room. They request that heavy shedding dogs be crated in the motel room. Dogs must be leashed and cleaned up after at all times. The camping and tent areas also allow dogs. There is a dog walk area at the campground. Dogs are allowed in the camping cabins. There are no water hookups at the campgrounds.

Big Delta State Historical Park
Mile 274.5 Richardson Highway
Delta Junction, AK
907-269-8400
Being such an important crossroad for a variety of purposes, this park has an extensive and varied history to share via the museum, structures, and equipment that has be preserved or restored. Dogs are allowed for no additional fee. Dogs must be on no more than a 9 foot leash and be cleaned up after; they are not allowed in buildings. Dogs are allowed at the outer tables of the eatery. There are 24 RV campsites in the parking lot development that include restrooms, water, a picnic area, and dump station. There is a dog walk area at the campground. There are no electric or water hookups at the campgrounds. Multiple dogs may be allowed.

Smith's Green Acres
Mile 268 Richardson Highway
Delta Junction, AK
907-895-4369 (800-895-4369)

smithsgreenacres.com/
Open from May to the end of September, this camp area is located at the northern-most end of the Alaska Highway and they offer large sites, modern restrooms, a laundry, and a spacious playground. Dogs of all sizes are allowed for no additional fee. Dogs may not be left unattended on the campsite, and they must be leashed and cleaned up after. Dogs may not be walked by children, digging is not allowed, and they may not be tied to trees. Visitors are requested to walk dogs in provided area. This RV park is closed during the off-season. The camping and tent areas also allow dogs. There is a dog walk area at the campground. 2 dogs may be allowed.

Denali Grizzly Bear Cabins and Campground
231 Parks H
Denali, AK
907-683-2696 (866-583-2696)
denaligrizzlybear.com/
This camp area offers heated cabins, spectacular scenery, a convenience store, gift shop, liquor store, laundry and modern restroom facilities, and a great starting point for exploring the area. They are open from mid-May to mid-September, weather permitting. Dogs of all sizes are allowed for no additional fee in the camp area; they are not allowed in the hotel. Dogs must be well behaved, leashed, and cleaned up after. This RV park is closed during the off-season. The camping and tent areas also allow dogs. There is a dog walk area at the campground. Dogs are allowed in the camping cabins. Multiple dogs may be allowed.

Denali Rainbow Village
M.P. 238.6 George Parks H
Denali, AK
907-683-7777
denalirvpark.com
Dogs of all sizes are allowed. There are no additional pet fees. Dogs must be leashed and cleaned up after. This RV park is closed during the off-season. There is a dog walk area at the campground. Multiple dogs may be allowed.

Denali Riverside RV Park
M.P. 240 George Parks H
Denali, AK
907-388-1748
denaliriversiderv.com
Dogs of all sizes are allowed. There are no additional pet fees. Dogs must be leashed and cleaned up after. This RV park is closed during

the off-season. There is a dog walk area at the campground. Multiple dogs may be allowed.

Riley Creek Campground
Mile 0.5 Denali National Park Road
Denali National Park, AK
907-683-2294 (800-622-7275)
Located in the Denali National Park, this 150 site camp area is the closest to all the amenities; there are flush and vault toilets, potable water, a convenience store, laundry, showers, and a dump station. Dogs are allowed for no additional fee; they may not be left unattended at any time, and they must be under owner's control, leashed, and cleaned up after at all times. Dogs are to be walked on roadways only; they are not allowed on any of the trails. Precaution with pet food is necessary and must be handled like human food. The camping and tent areas also allow dogs. There is a dog walk area at the campground. There are no electric or water hookups at the campgrounds. Multiple dogs may be allowed.

Savage River Campground
Mile 13 Denali National Park Road
Denali National Park, AK
907-683-2294 (800-622-7275)
This 33 site camp area has flush and vault toilets and potable water; there are no other amenities. Their season runs from late May to early September, weather permitting. Dogs are allowed for no additional fee; they may not be left unattended at any time, and they must be under owner's control, leashed, and cleaned up after at all times. Dogs are to be walked on roadways only; they are not allowed on any of the trails. Precaution with pet food is necessary and must be handled like human food. This RV park is closed during the off-season. The camping and tent areas also allow dogs. There is a dog walk area at the campground. There are no electric or water hookups at the campgrounds. Multiple dogs may be allowed.

Teklanika River Campground
Mile 39 Denali National Park Road
Denali National Park, AK
907-683-2294 (800-622-7275)
This 53 site camp area has flush and vault toilets and potable water; there are no other amenities. Their season runs from late May to early September, weather permitting. Dogs are allowed for no additional

fee; they may not be left unattended at any time, and they must be under owner's control, leashed, and cleaned up after at all times. Dogs are to be walked on roadways only; they are not allowed on any of the trails. Precaution with pet food is necessary and must be handled like human food. This RV park is closed during the off-season. The camping and tent areas also allow dogs. There is a dog walk area at the campground. Dogs are allowed in the camping cabins. There are no electric or water hookups at the campgrounds. Multiple dogs may be allowed.

Wonder Lake Campground
Mile 85 Denali National Park Road
Denali National Park, AK
907-683-2294 (800-622-7275)
This 28 site camp area has flush and vault toilets and potable water; there are no other amenities. Their season runs from June 8th to early September, weather permitting, and all sites are walk-in only. Dogs are allowed for no additional fee; they may not be left unattended at any time, and they must be under owner's control, leashed, and cleaned up after at all times. Dogs are to be walked on roadways only; they are not allowed on any of the trails. Precaution with pet food is necessary and must be handled like human food. This RV park is closed during the off-season. The camping and tent areas also allow dogs. There is a dog walk area at the campground. There are no electric or water hookups at the campgrounds. Multiple dogs may be allowed.

Denali National Park and Preserve
PO Box 9
Denali Park, AK
907-683-2294
nps.gov/dena/index.htm
Dogs must be on leash and must be cleaned up after in Denali National Park. Dogs are only allowed on the paved roads and dirt roads. One place to walk is on the road to Savage after mile 15, which is a dirt road and only the park buses are allowed. Access is by car depending on weather. Dogs on leash are allowed in the Denali National Park campgrounds, but they may not be left unattended in the campgrounds. The park features auto touring, camping, and scenery.

Denali RV Park & Motel
Mile 245 Parks H/H 3
Denali Park, AK

907-683-1500 (800-478-1501)
denalirvpark.com/
Offering level sites with easy access and outstanding panoramic views, this park also has Wi-Fi, a laundry, an outdoor cooking area, a gift shop, and hiking trails. Dogs of all sizes are allowed for no additional fee in the camp area; they are not allowed in the motel. Dogs must be leashed and cleaned up after. The camping and tent areas also allow dogs. There is a dog walk area at the campground. Multiple dogs may be allowed.

Chena Hot Springs
56.5 Chena Hot Springs Road
Fairbanks, AK
907-451-8104 (800-478-4681)
chenahotsprings.com/
Although there is a number of activities, attractions, and recreational pursuits at this year round resort, two attractions that are particular favorites are the natural hot springs known for their healing powers, and it is considered to be one of the best places on earth for viewing the Northern Lights. Dogs of all sizes are allowed in the campground; they are not allowed in the resort. Dogs must be quiet, well behaved, leashed, and cleaned up after at all times. The camping and tent areas also allow dogs. There is a dog walk area at the campground. There are no water hookups at the campgrounds. Multiple dogs may be allowed.

Pioneer Park
2300 Airport Way
Fairbanks, AK
907-459-1087
In addition to camping, this riverside theme park is full of native and historical artifacts, a restored gold rush town, museums, a narrow gauge train that runs through the park, a reconditioned Sternwheeler, gaming areas, a reproduced early 1900 Pioneer Hall, an antique carousel, and much more. Dogs are allowed throughout the park; it is up to individual shops whether they may enter; they are allowed to take the train ride. Dogs must be well behaved, leashed, and cleaned up after at all times. The RV park area is open from Memorial Day to Labor Day, but the park office is open year round. This RV park is closed during the off-season. The camping and tent areas also allow dogs. There is a dog walk area at the campground. There are no electric or water hookups at the campgrounds.

Multiple dogs may be allowed.

River's Edge Resort and RV Park
4200 Boat Street
Fairbanks, AK
907-474-0286 (800-770-3343)
riversedge.net/
Open from mid-May to mid-September, this resort sits along the banks of the Chena River and is only moments from the airport and highways. Dogs of all sizes are allowed for no additional fee for the RV park; they are not allowed in the resort. Dogs must be well mannered, leashed, and cleaned up after. This RV park is closed during the off-season. The camping and tent areas also allow dogs. There is a dog walk area at the campground. Multiple dogs may be allowed.

Riverview RV Park
1316 Badger Road
Fairbanks, AK
888-488-6392
alaskaone.com/riverview/
Open from May 15th to September 15th, this park sits on the banks of the Chena River only 10 minutes from Fairbanks or North Pole, and they offer a convenience store, gas station, modern restrooms and showers, a laundry, and a variety of land and water recreation. Dogs must be kept leashed and cleaned up after. This RV park is closed during the off-season. The camping and tent areas also allow dogs. There is a dog walk area at the campground. Multiple dogs may be allowed.

Grand View RV Park
22518 W Glenn H/Milepost 109.5
Glacier View, AK
907-746-4480
grandviewrv.com/
Open from May to the beginning of September, this park offers a great starting point for exploring the area, including one of the few glaciers in Alaska accessible by foot-the Matanuska Glacier and it is only a 15 minute drive away. Dogs of all sizes are allowed for no additional fee. Dogs must be leashed and cleaned up after at all times. This RV park is closed during the off-season. The camping and tent areas also allow dogs. There is a dog walk area at the campground. Multiple dogs may be allowed.

Glacier View Campground
Mile 59 Mccarthy Road
Glennallen, AK
907-554-4490

glacierviewcampground.com/
Surrounded by the Wrangell Mountains, this campground offers scenic views of the Root Glacier, private campsites, an outdoor café (dogs OK outside), a camp store, bike rentals, and more. They are open from Memorial Day to mid-September, weather permitting. Dogs of all sizes are allowed for no additional fee. Dogs must be well behaved, leashed, and cleaned up after. This RV park is closed during the off-season. The camping and tent areas also allow dogs. There is a dog walk area at the campground. There are no electric or water hookups at the campgrounds. Multiple dogs may be allowed.

Moose Horn RV Park
Mile 187.5 Glenn H
Glennallen, AK
907-822-3953
mhrvp.com/
Open from May 15th to September 15th, this camp area offers Wi-Fi at individual sites, a dump station, and a good starting location for enjoying a variety of local activities. Dogs of all sizes are allowed for no additional fee. Dogs must be leashed and cleaned up after at all times. This RV park is closed during the off-season. The camping and tent areas also allow dogs. There is a dog walk area at the campground. Multiple dogs may be allowed.

Northern Lights RV Campground
18 H.7 Glen Highway
Glennallen, AK
907-822-3199
Dogs of all sizes are allowed. There are no additional pet fees. Dogs may not be left unattended, must be leashed, and cleaned up after. This RV park is closed during the off-season. There is a dog walk area at the campground. Multiple dogs may be allowed.

Tolsona Campground
M.P. 173 Glenn H
Glennallen, AK
907-822-3865
tolsona.com
Dogs of all sizes are allowed. There are no additional pet fees. Dogs must be leashed and cleaned up after. This RV park is closed during the off-season. The camping and tent areas also allow dogs. There is a dog walk area at the campground. Multiple dogs may be allowed.

Haines Hitch-up RV Park
851 Main Street/Haines H

Haines, AK
907-766-2882
hitchuprv.com/
In addition to 92 large grassy sites, laundry facilities, hot showers, a gift shop, Wi-Fi, and plenty of wildlife, this camp spot also provides for some outstanding views. They are open from mid-May to mid-September, weather permitting. Dogs of all sizes are allowed for no additional fee; they must have current vaccinations. Dogs may not be left unattended outside, and they must be leashed and cleaned up after. This RV park is closed during the off-season. There is a dog walk area at the campground. 2 dogs may be allowed.

Oceanside RV Park
10 Front Street
Haines, AK
907-766-2437
oceansiderv.com/
This full-service, scenic oceanside camp area is also close to other sites of interest and recreational opportunities. Dogs of all sizes are allowed for no additional fee. Dogs must be leashed and cleaned up after. The camping and tent areas also allow dogs. There is a dog walk area at the campground. Multiple dogs may be allowed.

McKinley RV and Campground
248.5 M.P. George Parks H
Healy, AK
907-683-2379
mtaonline.net/~rvcampak/
Dogs of all sizes are allowed. There are no additional pet fees. Dogs are not to be left unattended except for short periods, and only if the the dog will be quiet and well behaved. Dogs must be leashed and cleaned up after. The camping and tent areas also allow dogs. There is a dog walk area at the campground. Multiple dogs may be allowed.

Heritage RV Park
3550 Homer Spit Road
Homer, AK
907-226-4500 (800-380-7787)
alaskaheritagervpark.com/
This full-service, scenic ocean-side camp area is located next to the famous "Fishing Hole", and they provide visitors with a variety of amenities including free Wi-Fi, an espresso and pastry café, and a ½ mile private beach. Their season is from mid-May to mid-September. Dogs of all sizes are allowed for no additional fee. Dogs must be leashed and cleaned up after at all times.

This RV park is closed during the off-season. There is a dog walk area at the campground. Multiple dogs may be allowed.

Ocean View RV Park
Mile 172.7 at 455 Sterling H/H 1
Homer, AK
907-235-3951
oceanview-rv.com/main.htm
In addition to spectacular views of Kachemak Bay, this beachfront park is also just a short walk to all the sites and activities in town. Their season runs from mid-May to mid-September. Dogs of all sizes are allowed for no additional fee. Dogs must be quiet, leashed, and cleaned up after. This RV park is closed during the off-season. There is a dog walk area at the campground. Multiple dogs may be allowed.

Mendenhall Glacier Campground
Skater's Cabin Road
Juneau, AK
907-586-8800 (877-444-6777)
Located in the Tongass National Forest (the nation's largest forest) in view of Mendenhall Glacier, this scenic lakeside camp area has innumerable recreation and education opportunities, and sites have pads, tables, and fire grills with vault toilets nearby and a central dump station. There is a visitor center here with an exhibit gallery and theater, and they are open May 1st to mid-September, weather permitting. Dogs of all sizes are allowed for no additional fee. Dogs must be leashed and cleaned up after. This RV park is closed during the off-season. The camping and tent areas also allow dogs. There is a dog walk area at the campground. Multiple dogs may be allowed.

Spruce Meadow RV Park
10200 Mendenhall Loop Road
Juneau, AK
907-789-1990
juneaurv.com/homepage.html
Nestled among the woods on Alaskan wetlands, this 47 site campground is only 3½ miles from Juneau's favorite attraction-the Mendenhall Glacier where dogs on leash are also allowed. Dogs of all sizes are allowed for no additional fee throughout the park, on the trails, and at the beach. They must have current vaccinations, license, and health certificates. Dogs may not be left unattended on site at any time-even in the RV. Dogs must be

quiet, leashed and cleaned up after at all times. They ask that dogs be walked in the dog park area. There is a dog walk area at the campground. 2 dogs may be allowed.

Beluga Lookout Lodge and RV Park
929 Mission Avenue
Kenai, AK
800-745-5999
belugalookout.com
Dogs of all sizes are allowed. There are no additional pet fees. Dogs must be leashed and cleaned up after. Dogs may not be tied up outside unattended. This RV park is closed during the off-season. The camping and tent areas also allow dogs. There is a dog walk area at the campground. Multiple dogs may be allowed.

Diamond M Ranch RV and Cabins
48500 Diamond M Ranch Road
Kenai, AK
907-283-9424 (866-283-9424)
diamondmranch.com/
A great base camp for exploring this area that is rich in land and water recreational opportunities, the camp area also has a central fire pit for friendly gatherings, fish cleaning facilities, restrooms with showers, and occasionally moose or caribou pay a visit. Dogs of all sizes are allowed for no additional fee in the RV/tent area; there is an additional fee of $25 for 1 dog; $40 for 2 dogs, and $50 for a maximum of 3 dogs per stay for the cabins. Dogs must be well behaved, leashed, and cleaned up after. The camping and tent areas also allow dogs. There is a dog walk area at the campground. Dogs are allowed in the camping cabins.

Clover Pass Resort and RV Park
105 N Point Higgins Road
Ketchikan, AK
907-247-2234 (800-410-2234)
cloverpassresort.com/
Sitting on the shores of Clover Pass where fishing is only a few steps away, this camp area is also part of a resort with lodging, and a restaurant and bar (dogs not allowed). The campground is open from mid-June to the end of September. Dogs of all sizes are allowed in the RV area for no additional fee; there is an additional fee of $50 per pet per stay for the lodge. Dogs must be well behaved, leashed, and cleaned up after at all times. This RV park is closed during the off-season. There is a dog walk area at the campground. Multiple dogs may be

allowed.

Tongas National Forest
Federal Building, 648 Mission Street
Ketchikan, AK
907-225-3101 (877-444-6777)
fs.fed.us/r10/tongass/
As the nation's largest forest, there is an abundance of marine, bird, and wildlife to view in addition to some spectacular scenery of Southeast Alaska and the Inside Passage. There are innumerable recreational opportunities, and there are also maintained wildlife viewing areas, a Discovery Center, and the Glacier Visitor Center for viewing an active glacier. Dogs of all sizes are allowed throughout the forest for no additional fee. Dogs must be under their owner's control, leashed, and cleaned up after at all times. Many of the camp areas have picnic tables, running water, pit toilets, parking spurs, and dump stations. The cabins have warming stoves, bunk beds, tables, and benches. This RV park is closed during the off-season. The camping and tent areas also allow dogs. There is a dog walk area at the campground. Dogs are allowed in the camping cabins. There are no electric or water hookups at the campgrounds. 2 dogs may be allowed.

Buskin River State Rec Site
Rezanof Drive
Kodiak, AK
907-486-6339
Popular for sports fishing, this primitive camp area provides a handicapped-accessible fishing platform, and Fish and Game operates a weir just outside the park. They usually open the beginning of summer and stay open until September-depending on weather conditions, and sites have picnic tables and fire pits. Dogs of all sizes are allowed for no additional fee. Dogs must be leashed and cleaned up after. This RV park is closed during the off-season. The camping and tent areas also allow dogs. There is a dog walk area at the campground. There are no electric or water hookups at the campgrounds. Multiple dogs may be allowed.

Fort Abercrombie State Historical Park
1623 Mill Bay Road
Kodiak, AK
907-581-5150
Sitting amid a lush maritime forest, this park safeguards what is left of a WWII military installation, and in addition to a lake stocked with trout and grayling, there are also a number of beautiful hiking trails and a variety of recreational pursuits. Dogs of all sizes are allowed throughout the park including the trails leading to the beach for no additional fee. Dogs must be leashed and cleaned up after at all times, and they suggest keeping a special eye on pets because of bears and eagles. Camping consists mostly of tenting areas; RV parking is allowed in the overflow parking area; there are no amenities. This RV park is closed during the off-season. The camping and tent areas also allow dogs. There is a dog walk area at the campground. There are no electric or water hookups at the campgrounds. There are special amenities given to dogs at this campground. 2 dogs may be allowed.

Chena Lake Rec Area
Lake Park Road
North Pole, AK
907-488-1655
Although only open for camping from the Wednesday before Memorial Day through Labor Day, this is a year round destination with more than 2,100 recreational acres, 4½ Km of self-guided nature trails, a well stocked lake, and many on-site amenities. Dogs of all sizes are allowed for no additional fee. Dogs must be on no more than a 6 foot leash and cleaned up after at all times. Dogs are not allowed on swimming beaches. There are 2 camp areas each offering restrooms, potable water, gaming areas, picnic tables, fire rings, sandy beaches, boat launch areas, and more. This RV park is closed during the off-season. The camping and tent areas also allow dogs. There is a dog walk area at the campground. There are no electric or water hookups at the campgrounds. Multiple dogs may be allowed.

Riverview RV Park
1316 Badger Road
North Pole, AK
888-488-6392
riverviewrvpark.net
Dogs of all sizes are allowed. There are no additional pet fees. Dogs may not be left unattended or tied up outside alone. Dogs must be leashed and cleaned up after. This RV park is closed during the off-season. There is a dog walk area at the campground. Multiple dogs may be allowed.

Santaland RV Park
125 St Nicholas Drive
North Pole, AK
907-488-9123
santalandrv.com
Dogs of all sizes are allowed. There are no additional pet fees. Dogs must be leashed and cleaned up after. This RV park is closed during the off-season. The camping and tent areas also allow dogs. There is a dog walk area at the campground. Multiple dogs may be allowed.

Fox Run RV Campground
4466 S. Glenn Highway (Mile 36.3)
Palmer, AK
907-745-6120
This lakeside park offers laundry facilities, boat rentals, Wi-Fi, and close proximity to the activities of town. They are open from May 1st to September 30th. Dogs of all sizes are allowed for no additional fee. Dogs must be leashed and cleaned up after. This RV park is closed during the off-season. The camping and tent areas also allow dogs. There is a dog walk area at the campground. Multiple dogs may be allowed.

Mountain View RV Park
1405 N Smith Road
Palmer, AK
800-264-4582
mtviewrvpark.com
Dogs of all sizes are allowed. There are no additional pet fees. Dogs may not be left unattended at any time, must be leashed, and cleaned up after. Dogs must not be near the neighbors' trees that edge some of the property. This RV park is closed during the off-season. The camping and tent areas also allow dogs. There is a dog walk area at the campground. Multiple dogs may be allowed.

Paxson Inn and RV
Mile 185 Richardson H
Paxson, AK
907-822-3330
Sitting central to several fishing lakes and hiking trails, this camp area also has a full restaurant and bar on site as well as a lodge. There are also modern restrooms, a laundry, and dump station. Dogs of all sizes are allowed at the campground for no additional fee. There is an additional pet fee of $20 per night for a maximum of 1 dog at the lodge. Dogs must be leashed and cleaned

up after. This RV park is closed during the off-season. The camping and tent areas also allow dogs. There is a dog walk area at the campground. 2 dogs may be allowed.

Twin Creek RV Park
7.4 Mitkof H
Petersburg, AK
907-772-3244
twincreekrv.com/RVinAK/index.php
Usually open in either April or May to September (depending on the weather), this scenic waterside park sits nestled among old growth rainforest, and offer guests awesome views and a variety of recreational opportunities. Dogs of all sizes are allowed for no additional fee. Dogs must be leashed and cleaned up after. This RV park is closed during the off-season. The camping and tent areas also allow dogs. There is a dog walk area at the campground. 2 dogs may be allowed.

Williwaw Campground
Mile 4 Portage H
Portage Valley, AK
907-522-8368
Open from Memorial Day weekend to Labor Day weekend and located in the Chugach National Forest, this campground offers 60 sites (restroom facilities nearby), it is close to glacier viewing, Begich, the Boggs Visitor Center, and they have a fish viewing area for spawning salmon. Dogs are allowed for no additional fee. Dogs must be leashed in developed areas, under owner's control/care at all times, and cleaned up after. This RV park is closed during the off-season. The camping and tent areas also allow dogs. There is a dog walk area at the campground. Dogs are allowed in the camping cabins. There are no electric or water hookups at the campgrounds. Multiple dogs may be allowed.

Bear Creek RV Park
33508 Lincoln
Seward, AK
907-224-5725
bearcreekrv.com
Dogs of all sizes are allowed. There are no additional pet fees. Dogs must be leashed and cleaned up after. There is a dog walk area at the campground. Multiple dogs may be allowed.

Miller's Landing
13890 Beach Avenue
Seward, AK
907-224-5739 (866-541-5739)
millerslandingak.com/
Nestled among hundred year old trees, this oceanfront park offers a number of amenities, a variety of land and water recreation, a mile long beach, and an abundance of land and marine life. Dogs of all sizes are allowed for no additional fee. Dogs must be friendly, leashed, and cleaned up after. The camping and tent areas also allow dogs. There is a dog walk area at the campground. There are no water hookups at the campgrounds. Multiple dogs may be allowed.

Stoney Creek RV Park
13760 Leslie Place
Seward, AK
907-224-6465 (877-437-6366)
stoneycreekrvpark.com/
Able to accommodate big rigs, this 15 acre scenic, creek-side park offers 81 large sites, modern facilities, a number of amenities, and they are located only 6 miles from Seward. Their season usually runs from mid-May to mid-September (weather permitting) Tent camping is allowed in selected sites, and only when also camping with a motor home. Dogs of all sizes are allowed for no additional fee. Dogs must be well behaved, leashed, and cleaned up after. This RV park is closed during the off-season. There is a dog walk area at the campground. Multiple dogs may be allowed.

Shuyak Island State Park
Kodiak Archipelago area
Shuyak Island, AK
907-486-6339
Accessible by boat or float plane only, this wilderness park consists of about 47,000 acres, part of which includes a coastal forest and a wide number of sheltered interior waterway great for kayaking.. Dogs are allowed at the park and cabins for no additional fee. Dogs must be leashed and cleaned up after; pets must be inside at night, and they suggest taking extra precautions with a pet because of bears. There are 4 public use cabins available, each will house up to 8 people, and cabin sites have water, 25 pounds of propane, a wood-burning store, firewood that can be split, a gravity shower, some cooking supplies, and bunk beds. This RV park is closed during the off-season. Only one dog is allowed per campsite. There is a dog walk area at the campground. Dogs are allowed in

the camping cabins. There are no electric or water hookups at the campgrounds.

Sitka Sportsman's Association RV Park
5211 Halibut Point Road
Sitka, AK
907-747-6033
This year round camp area also has an indoor shooting range, trap and skeet range, and an archery range. Dogs of all sizes are allowed for no additional fee. Dogs must be well behaved, leashed, and cleaned up after The camping and tent areas also allow dogs. There is a dog walk area at the campground. Multiple dogs may be allowed.

Tongas National Forest /Misty Fjords National Monument
204 Siginaka Way
Sitka, AK
907-225-3101 (877-444-6777)
fs.fed.us/r10/tongass/
As the nation's largest forest, there is an abundance of marine, bird, and wildlife to view in addition to some spectacular scenery of Southeast Alaska and the Inside Passage. There are innumerable recreational opportunities, maintained wildlife viewing areas, a Discovery Center, the Glacier Visitor Center for viewing an active glacier, and they are home to the Misty Fjords National Monument. Dogs of all sizes are allowed throughout the forest for no additional fee. Dogs must be under their owner's control, leashed, and cleaned up after at all times. Many of the camp areas have picnic tables, running water, pit toilets, parking spurs, and dump stations. The cabins have warming stoves, bunk beds, tables, and benches. This RV park is closed during the off-season. The camping and tent areas also allow dogs. There is a dog walk area at the campground. Dogs are allowed in the camping cabins. There are no electric or water hookups at the campgrounds. 2 dogs may be allowed.

Garden City RV Park
1528 State Street/Klondike H/H 2
Skagway, AK
907-983-2378
karo-ent.com/klondikes.htm
Open from May 1st to October 1st, this park is only a short distance to scenic hiking trails and town, and they offers showers, a laundry, a shuttle to town if needed, and mini-golf. Dogs of all sizes are allowed for no additional fee. Dogs must be

leashed and cleaned up after. This RV park is closed during the off-season. The camping and tent areas also allow dogs. There is a dog walk area at the campground. Multiple dogs may be allowed.

Skagway Mountain View RV Park
12th and Broadway
Skagway, AK
907-983-3333
BestofAlaskaTravel.com
Dogs of all sizes are allowed. There are no additional pet fees. Dogs must be leashed and cleaned up after. This RV park is closed during the off-season. The camping and tent areas also allow dogs. There is a dog walk area at the campground.

Kachemak Bay State Park and State Wilderness Park
PO Box 1247
Soldotna, AK
907-262-5581
Accessed only by boat or plane, this is the states first and only wilderness park with about 400,000 acres-abundant with marine, bird, and wildlife, and it offers some very diverse topography of ocean, glaciers, forests, mountains, and valleys. Dogs are allowed throughout the park, on the trails, at the glaciers, cabins, and campgrounds for no additional fee. Dogs must be leashed in developed areas, under their owner's control at all times, and cleaned up after. The camp areas are on a first come first served basis and are located throughout the park; some have been developed and have picnic tables, fireplaces, outhouses, food caches, and tent pads. The cabins are rustic and are rentable on a reservation basis. This RV park is closed during the off-season. The camping and tent areas also allow dogs. There is a dog walk area at the campground. Dogs are allowed in the camping cabins. There are no electric or water hookups at the campgrounds. Multiple dogs may be allowed.

Kenai National Wildlife Refuge
Ski Hill Road
Soldotna, AK
907-262-7021
kenai.fws.gov/index.htm
At almost 2 million acres and home to very diverse habitats for innumerable marine, bird, and wildlife, visitors are able enjoy a wide variety of recreational and educational opportunities. Dogs are allowed throughout the refuge and in camp areas for no additional fee.

Dogs must be leashed when in camp areas, and may be off lead on trails if they are under strict voice control, but they suggest caution because of wild animals. Dogs must be under their owner's control and cleaned up after at all times. Campground areas are located along Swanson River Road, at the Skilak Wildlife Recreation area, and dispersed on various lakes at favored hiking and fishing spots; they are on a first come first served basis. There is water at all the camp areas, and most of them have restrooms. Most of the cabins can be reserved; however, some of them are first come first served. The camping and tent areas also allow dogs. There is a dog walk area at the campground. Dogs are allowed in the camping cabins. There are no electric or water hookups at the campgrounds. Multiple dogs may be allowed.

Klondike RV Park
Funny River Road
Soldotna, AK
907-262-6035 (800-980-6035)
klondikecabins.com/
Nestled among tall pines, only 1 block from the Kenai River and 5 minutes from town, this park offers 27 large grassy and/or treed sites, and modern facilities. The park's season runs from May 15th until about the end of August. Dogs of all sizes are allowed for no additional fee. Dogs must be leashed and cleaned up after. Guests with pets are asked to take dogs to the dog walk area to do their business; it is not allowed in the park. This RV park is closed during the off-season. The camping and tent areas also allow dogs. There is a dog walk area at the campground. Multiple dogs may be allowed.

Alaska Canoe and Campground
35292 Sterling H (M.P.84)
Sterling, AK
907-262-2331
alaskacanoetrips.com
Dogs of all sizes are allowed. There are no additional pet fees. Dogs may not be left unattended, must be leashed, and cleaned up after. Dogs are also allowed to go on the canoe trips. This RV park is closed during the off-season. The camping and tent areas also allow dogs. There is a dog walk area at the campground. Multiple dogs may be allowed.

Moose River RV Park

33190 Sterling H
Sterling, AK
907-260-7829
stayalaska.com/
Offering an espresso cyber-café and a number of other amenities and activities, this modern park is located on the Kenai Peninsula-a fisherman's, hunter's, and nature lover's paradise. Dogs are allowed in the RV camp area only (not in tents) for no additional fee. Dogs must be leashed and cleaned up after. There is a dog walk area at the campground. Multiple dogs may be allowed.

Matanuska Glacier State Recreation Site
Mile 102.2 Glenn H
Sutton, AK
907-745-5151 (800-770-5151)
Unusual because of its blue color (created by ice density and summer light), this park is also home to the state's largest active glacier that is reachable by foot. They are open from May to the end of September, weather permitting. Dogs are allowed at the rec site, on the trails, at the glacier, the campground, and in one cabin. There is neither additional fee nor a set number of dogs for the campground; there is a $50 one time fee for the cabin and only 1 dog is allowed. Dogs must be under their owner's control, leashed, and cleaned up after at all times. The campground is located at mile 101 and there are 12 sites, water, toilets, picnic tables, and fire pits; there is also a large paved rest area for RVs that has a dumpster, interpretive shelter, and a great scenic picnic area. Glacier viewing platforms are accessible on the Edge Nature Trail leading from the campground. This RV park is closed during the off-season. The camping and tent areas also allow dogs. There is a dog walk area at the campground. Dogs are allowed in the camping cabins. There are no electric or water hookups at the campgrounds.

Gateway Salmon Bake and RV Park
1313.1 Alaska H
Tok, AK
907-883-5555
karo-ent.com/toksbake.htm
This scenic, clean camp area offers a number of amenities including a restaurant that specializes in flame-grilled king salmon, reindeer sausage, and buffalo burgers with seasonal outdoor dining. The park is open from May 15th to September 1st. Dogs of all sizes are allowed for

no additional fee. Dogs must be leashed and cleaned up after at all times. Dogs are allowed at the outer tables of the restaurant. This RV park is closed during the off-season. The camping and tent areas also allow dogs. There is a dog walk area at the campground. There are no water hookups at the campgrounds. Multiple dogs may be allowed.

Sourdough Campground
Mile 122.8 Glen H
Tok, AK
907-883-5543
Voted by guests as "Alaska's funniest" camp for their numerous fun activities, they have also become famous for their sourdough pancakes that are made from a starter that began in 1956. They feature an "all you can eat" sourdough pancake buffet daily starting at 7 am. They also offer large wooded sites, showers all year, a laundry, gift shop, an RV/car wash, internet, and a restaurant with seasonal outdoor dining. Dogs of all sizes are allowed for no additional fee. Dogs must be leashed and cleaned up after at all times. Dogs are allowed at the outer tables of the restaurant. The camping and tent areas also allow dogs. There is a dog walk area at the campground. Multiple dogs may be allowed.

Tundra Lodge and RV Park
M.P. 1315 Alaska Hwy
Tok, AK
907-883-7875
Dogs of all sizes are allowed. There are no additional pet fees. Dogs may not be left unattended, must be leashed, and cleaned up after. This RV park is closed during the off-season. The camping and tent areas also allow dogs. There is a dog walk area at the campground. Multiple dogs may be allowed.

Bear Paw RV and Tent Park
101 N Harbor Drive
Valdez, AK
907-835-2530
Dogs of all sizes are allowed. There are no additional pet fees. Dogs must be leashed and cleaned up after This RV park is closed during the off-season. The camping and tent areas also allow dogs. There is a dog walk area at the campground. Multiple dogs may be allowed.

Blueberry Lake Campground
Mile 23 Richardson H
Valdez, AK
907-262-5581

Located on 192 scenic acres, this park has 25 camp sites near plenty of hiking areas; there are toilets and water on site. Their season runs from the beginning of May to the end of September, weather permitting. Dogs of all sizes are allowed for no additional fee. Dogs must be leashed and cleaned up after. Private contractors operate the campground; their phone for campground reservations is 907-835-4778. This RV park is closed during the off-season. The camping and tent areas also allow dogs. There is a dog walk area at the campground. There are no electric or water hookups at the campgrounds. Multiple dogs may be allowed.

Eagle's Rest
139 Pioneer Drive
Valdez, AK
907-835-2373 (800-553-7275)
eaglesrestrv.com/
This park is a great base camp for exploring the unspoiled beauty of Prince William Sound and the lush and majestic surrounding area. There are numerous multi-use trails, and if a bit more adventure is desired, the park can book glacier tours, fishing trips, and much more. Depending on the weather, they usually open the end of April, beginning of March and close sometime in October (open weekends only after Labor Day). Dogs of all sizes are allowed for no additional fee. Dogs must be leashed and cleaned up after at all times. This RV park is closed during the off-season. There is a dog walk area at the campground. Multiple dogs may be allowed.

Arizona

Mountain View RV Ranch
2843 E Frontage Road
Amando, AZ
520-398-9401
mtviewrvranch.com
Dogs of all sizes are allowed. There are no additional pet fees. Dogs must be quiet, well behaved, leashed, and cleaned up after. The camping and tent areas also allow dogs. There is a dog walk area at the campground. Dogs are allowed in the camping cabins. Multiple dogs may be allowed.

La Hacienda RV Resort

1797 W 28th Avenue
Apache Junction, AZ
480-982-2808
lahaciendarv.com
One dog up to 60 pounds, or 2 dogs up to 10 pounds each are allowed. There are no additional pet fees. Dogs may not be left unattended outside, and they must be quiet, well behaved, leashed, and cleaned up after. There are some breed restrictions. There is a dog walk area at the campground.

Lost Dutchman State Park
6109 N. Apache Trail
Apache Junction, AZ
480-982-4485
This park is located at the base of the Superstition Mountains, and there are many year round recreational activites and trails to explore. Dogs are allowed at no additional fee. Dogs may not be left unattended, and they must be leashed and cleaned up after. The camping and tent areas also allow dogs. There is a dog walk area at the campground. There are no electric or water hookups at the campground. Multiple dogs may be allowed.

Mesa/Apache Junction KOA
1540 S Tomahawk Road
Apache Junction, AZ
480-982-4015 (800-562-3404)
koa.com
Dogs of all sizes are allowed, and there are no additional pet fees for tent or RV sites. There is a $25 refundable deposit for the cabins and only 2 dogs are allowed. Dogs may not be left unattended, and they must be leashed and cleaned up after. There are some breed restrictions. The camping and tent areas also allow dogs. There is a dog walk area at the campground. Dogs are allowed in the camping cabins. Multiple dogs may be allowed.

Superstition Sunrise
702 S Meridian
Apache Junction, AZ
480-986-4524
azrvresort.com
This park is mostly close to 55 or older, no children. Dogs of all sizes are allowed. There are no additional pet fees. Dogs must be leashed and cleaned up after. There is a fenced in area for off lead. Dogs must be walked in the designated pet areas only, and not to the office or other non-pet areas. There is a dog walk area at the campground. Multiple dogs may be allowed.

Weaver's Needle Travel Trailor Resort
250 S Tomahawk Road
Apache Junction, AZ
480-982-3683
weaversneedle.com
Dogs of all sizes are allowed. There are no additional pet fees. Dogs must be leashed and cleaned up after, and there is a fenced in dog park on site. Dogs must be walked in designated areas for pets only and not in the rest of the park where campers do not have dogs. There is a dog walk area at the campground.

Ash Fork RV Park
783 W Old Route 66
Ash Fork, AZ
928-637-2521
Dogs of all sizes are allowed. There are no additional pet fees. Dogs must be leashed and cleaned up after. The camping and tent areas also allow dogs. There is a dog walk area at the campground. Multiple dogs may be allowed.

Benson KOA
180 W Four Feathers
Benson, AZ
520-586-3977 (800-562-6823)
koa.com
Dogs of all sizes are allowed, and there are no additional pet fees for tent or RV sites. There is a $5 one time fee per pet for the cabins. Dogs may not be left unattended outside, and they must be leashed and cleaned up after. The camping and tent areas also allow dogs. There is a dog walk area at the campground. Dogs are allowed in the camping cabins. 2 dogs may be allowed.

Butterfield RV Resort and Observatory
251 S Ocotillo
Benson, AZ
520-586-4400
rv-resort.com
Dogs of all sizes are allowed. There are no additional pet fees. Dogs must be leashed and cleaned up after. There is a fenced in area for dogs where they can be off lead. There is a dog walk area at the campground. Multiple dogs may be allowed.

Kartchner Caverns State Park
2980 S H 90
Benson, AZ
520-586-2283
The guided cave tours are a main attraction at this park and reservations for the caves are suggested. Other attractions at this

park include the Discovery Center, interactive displays, an amphitheater, and a variety of hiking trails. Dogs are allowed at no additional fee. Dogs must be leashed and cleaned up after. Dogs are not allowed in the Discovery Center or other park buildings. The camping and tent areas also allow dogs. There is a dog walk area at the campground. There are no water hookups at the campground. Multiple dogs may be allowed.

Black Canyon City KOA
19600 E St Joseph Road
Black Canyon City, AZ
623-374-5318
koa.com
Dogs of all sizes are allowed. There are no additional pet fees. Dogs may not be left unattended, and they must be quiet, leashed, and cleaned up after. There are some breed restrictions. The camping and tent areas also allow dogs. There is a dog walk area at the campground. Multiple dogs may be allowed.

Trails End RV Park
983 Finney Flat Road
Camp Verde, AZ
928-567-0100
trailsend-rvpark.com
Dogs of all sizes are allowed. There are no additional pet fees. Dogs must be leashed and cleaned up after. There is a dog walk area at the campground. 2 dogs may be allowed.

Zane Grey RV Park
4500 E H 260
Camp Verde, AZ
928-567-4320 (800-235-0608)
zanegreyrvpark.com/
This beautifully landscaped RV park is close to several attractions in the area, and they offer large clean restrooms, showers, spa, laundry facilities, and propane. Dogs of all sizes are allowed for no additional fee. Dogs may not be left alone at any time, and they must be leashed and cleaned up after. There is a dog walk area at the campground. Multiple dogs may be allowed.

Buena Tierra RV Park and Campground
1995 S Cox Road
Casa Grande, AZ
520-836-3500
campgroundbuenatierra.com
Dogs of all sizes are allowed. There are no additional pet fees. Dogs may not be left unattended outside or left out at night. Dogs must be

quiet, well behaved, leashed, and cleaned up after. The camping and tent areas also allow dogs. There is a dog walk area at the campground. Multiple dogs may be allowed.

Palm Creek Golf and RV Resort
1110 N Hennes Road
Casa Grande, AZ
800-421-7004
palmcreekgolf.com
Dogs up to 55 pounds are allowed. There are no additional pet fees. This is a 55 or over park, and one person can be 41 or over. There is a pet section where dogs are allowed, and they are allowed in the park model rentals. Dogs must be on no more than a 6 foot leash, except in the dog runs, and they must be cleaned up after. There is a dog walk area at the campground. 2 dogs may be allowed.

Lo Lo Mai Springs Outdoor Resort
11505 Lo Lo Mai Road
Cornville, AZ
928-634-4700
lolomai.com/
Abundant springs in this area provides lush foliage creating a rich oasis for recreation in the high desert. Amenities offered at this campground include hot showers, a spring fed pond, clean restrooms, a heated swimming pool, Jacuzzi, convenience store, club house, children's playground, ball and game courts, and a variety of recreational pursuits. Dogs of all sizes are allowed. There is a $3 per night per pet additional fee for the campground or the cabins. Dogs are not allowed in the cottages. Dogs must be leashed and cleaned up after. Dogs are allowed throughout the park, but not at the pool or in buildings. The camping and tent areas also allow dogs. There is a dog walk area at the campground. Dogs are allowed in the camping cabins. 2 dogs may be allowed.

Dead Horse Ranch State Park
675 Dead Horse Ranch Road
Cottonwood, AZ
928-634-5283
This park along the Verde River Greenway, shares a unique ecosystem, in that their Cottonwood/Willowriparian gallery forest is one of less than 20 riparian type zones in the world. There are also many trails to explore. Dogs are allowed at no additional fee. Dogs may not be left unattended, and they must be leashed and cleaned up after. Dogs are not allowed in park

buildings or ramadas. The camping and tent areas also allow dogs. There is a dog walk area at the campground. Multiple dogs may be allowed.

Coconino National Forest
1824 S Thompson Street
Flagstaff, AZ
928-527-3600
fs.fed.us/r3/coconino/
This diverse forest, of 1,821,495 acres, offers alpine tundra, pine forest, high mountain desert and a variety of land and water recreation. Dogs of all sizes are allowed at no additional fee. Dogs may not be left unattended, and they must be leashed at all times, and cleaned up after in camp areas. The camping and tent areas also allow dogs. There is a dog walk area at the campground. There are no electric or water hookups at the campground. Multiple dogs may be allowed.

Flagstaff KOA
5803 N H 89
Flagstaff, AZ
928-526-9926 (800-562-3524)
flagstaffkoa.com
Dogs of all sizes are allowed. There are no additional pet fees. Dogs may not be left unattended outside, and they must be leashed and cleaned up after. The camping and tent areas also allow dogs. There is a dog walk area at the campground. Dogs are allowed in the camping cabins. Multiple dogs may be allowed.

Woody Mountain Campground and RV Park
2727 W H 66
Flagstaff, AZ
928-774-7727
woodymountaincampground.com
Dogs of all sizes are allowed. There are no additional pet fees. Dogs may not be left unattended, and they must be quiet, leashed, and cleaned up after. This RV park is closed during the off-season. The camping and tent areas also allow dogs. There is a dog walk area at the campground. 2 dogs may be allowed.

Eagle View RV Resort
9605 N Fort McDowell Road
Fort McDowell, AZ
480-836-5310
eagleviewresort.com
Dogs of all sizes are allowed. There are no additional pet fees. Dogs must be leashed and cleaned up after. There is a dog walk area at the campground. Multiple dogs may be allowed.

Grand Canyon National Park
Hwy 64
Grand Canyon, AZ
928-638-7888
nps.gov/grca/
The Grand Canyon, located in the northwest corner of Arizona, is considered to be one of the most impressive natural splendors in the world. It is 277 miles long, 18 miles wide, and at its deepest point, is 6000 vertical feet (more than 1 mile) from rim to river. The Grand Canyon has several entrance areas, but the most popular is the South Rim. Dogs are not allowed in most areas of the North Rim of the Park. On the North Rim, the only trail that dogs are allowed on is the bridle trail from the lodge to the North Kaibab Trail (but not on the North Kaibab Trail). Dogs are not allowed on any trails below the rim, but leashed dogs are allowed on the paved rim trail. This dog-friendly trail is about 2.7 miles each way and offers excellent views of the Grand Canyon. Remember that the elevation at the rim is 7,000 feet, so you or your pup may need to rest more often than usual. Also, the weather can be very hot during the summer and can be snowing during the winter, so plan accordingly. And be sure you or your pup do not get too close to the edge! Feel like taking a tour- Well-behaved dogs are allowed on the Geology Walk. This is a one hour park ranger guided tour and consists of a leisurely walk along a 3/4 mile paved rim trail. They discuss how the Grand Canyon was created and more. The tour departs at 11am daily (weather permitting) from the Yavapai Observation Station. Pets are allowed in the Grand Canyon's Mather Campground in Grand Canyon Village (reservations 877-444-6777), the Desert View Campground 26 miles east of the village (no reservations), and, for RVs, the Trailer Village in Grand Canyon Village. Trailer Village has full hookups and sites for trailers up to 50 feet. It is less than one mile from the rim and the village. Their advanced reservation number is 888-297-2757 and you can call 928-638-2631 for same day reservations. Dogs must be leashed at all times in the campgrounds and may not be left unattended. There are kennels available at the South Rim. Its hours are 7:30 am to 5 pm. To make kennel reservations or for other kennel information call 928-

638-0534. The Grand Canyon park entrance fee is currently $25.00 per private vehicle, payable upon entry to the park. Admission tickets are for 7 days.

Holbrook/Petrified Forest KOA
102 Hermosa Drive
Holbrook, AZ
928-524-6689 (800-562-3389)
koa.com
Dogs of all sizes are allowed. There are no additional pet fees. Dogs must be leashed and cleaned up after. The camping and tent areas also allow dogs. There is a dog walk area at the campground. Multiple dogs may be allowed.

Mountain View RV Park
99 W Vista Lane
Huachuca, AZ
800-772-4103
mountainviewrvpark.com
Dogs of all sizes are allowed. There are no additional pet fees. Dogs may not be left unattended outside, and they must be leashed and cleaned up after. There are some breed restrictions. The camping and tent areas also allow dogs. There is a dog walk area at the campground. Multiple dogs may be allowed.

Kaibab Campervillage
Forest Road #461
Jacob Lake, AZ
928-643-7804
kaibabcampervillage.com
Dogs of all sizes are allowed. There are no additional pet fees. Dogs may not be left unattended, and they must be leashed and cleaned up after. This RV park is closed during the off-season. The camping and tent areas also allow dogs. There is a dog walk area at the campground. Multiple dogs may be allowed.

Kingman KOA
3820 N Roosevelt
Kingman, AZ
928-757-4397 (800-562-3991)
koa.com
Dogs of all sizes are allowed. There are no additional pet fees. There is, however, a $20 refundable deposit for the cabins. Dogs must be leashed and cleaned up after. There are some breed restrictions. The camping and tent areas also allow dogs. There is a dog walk area at the campground. Dogs are allowed in the camping cabins. Multiple dogs may be allowed.

Cattail Cove State Park
P. O. Box 1990

Lake Havasu City, AZ
928-855-1223
This 2,000 acre park offers a beach, boat ramp, an amphitheater, 61 campsites, and a variety of year around land and water recreation. If you have your own watercraft, there are an additional 28 campsites along the water's edge. Dogs of all sizes are allowed at no additional fee. Dogs must be leashed at all times, and cleaned up after. Dogs may not be left unattended at any time. The camping and tent areas also allow dogs. There is a dog walk area at the campground. Multiple dogs may be allowed.

Islander RV Resort
751 Beachcomer Blvd
Lake Havasu City, AZ
928-680-2000
islanderrvresort.com
Dogs of all sizes are allowed. There is a $1 per night per pet additional fee. Dogs are not allowed to be left unattended outside, and they must be leashed and cleaned up after. This is an adult only park. There are some breed restrictions. There is a dog walk area at the campground. 2 dogs may be allowed.

Lake Havasu State Park
699 London Bridge Road
Lake Havasu City, AZ
928-855-2784
This park is home to the Mohave Sunset Walking Trail and the Arroyo-Camino Interpretive Garden that showcases the variety of life in and around the park. Dogs are allowed at no additional fee. Dogs must be leashed, cleaned up after, and water and shade must be provided. The camping and tent areas also allow dogs. There is a dog walk area at the campground. Multiple dogs may be allowed.

Double Adobe
5057 W Double Adobe Road
McNeal, AZ
520-364-4000
doubleadobe.com
Dogs of all sizes are allowed. There are no additional pet fees. Dogs must be well behaved, leashed, and cleaned up after. The camping and tent areas also allow dogs. There is a dog walk area at the campground. Multiple dogs may be allowed.

Mesa Spirit
3020 E Main Street
Mesa, AZ
480-832-1770
mesaspirit.com

Dogs of all sizes are allowed. There are no additional pet fees. Dogs must be quiet, well behaved, leashed and cleaned up after. Dogs must remain in the pet section of the campground. At least one person must be 55 years or older to stay at this resort. There is a dog walk area at the campground. 2 dogs may be allowed.

Silveridge RV Resort
8265 E Southern
Mesa, AZ
480-373-7000 (800-354-0054)
silveridge.com
Dogs of all sizes are allowed. There are no additional pet fees. Dogs must be leashed and cleaned up after, and they must stay in the pet section of the campground. At least one person must be 55 or older to stay at this resort. There is a dog walk area at the campground. Multiple dogs may be allowed.

Munds Park RV Resort
17550 Munds Ranch Road
Munds Park, AZ
928-286-1309
mundsparkrv.com
Dogs of all sizes are allowed. There are no additional pet fees. Dog may be off lead on the trails with voice command, and be leashed and cleaned up after when in the park. This RV park is closed during the off-season. The camping and tent areas also allow dogs. There is a dog walk area at the campground. Multiple dogs may be allowed.

Page-Lake Powell Campground
849 S Copper Mine Road
Page, AZ
928-645-3374
pagecampground.com
Dogs of all sizes are allowed. There are no additional pet fees. Dogs may not be left unattended outside, and they must stay off the grass, be leashed and cleaned up after. The camping and tent areas also allow dogs. There is a dog walk area at the campground. Multiple dogs may be allowed.

Wahweap RV Park and Campground
100 S Lake Shore Drive
Page, AZ
888-486-4679
lakepowell.com
Dogs of all sizes are allowed. There are no additional pet fees. Dogs may not be left unattended, and they must be leashed and cleaned up after. There is also a lodge on

site where pets are allowed in the standard rooms. There is a dog walk area at the campground. Multiple dogs may be allowed.

Buckskin Mountain State Park
5476 H 95
Parker, AZ
928-667-3231
This scenic campground sits along an 18-mile stretch of the Colorado River between Parker Dam and Headgate Dam. The park has different activities planned throughout the year. There are ranger led hikes, weekly speakers, ice cream socials, boating safety classes, and campfire programs. They also offer basketball and volleyball courts, a playground, clothing boutique, restaurant, camp store, arcade, restrooms, and a gas dock. Dogs of all sizes are allowed for no additional fee. They may not be left unattended at any time, and they must be leashed at all times, and cleaned up after. Dogs are not allowed in the cabaña area or on the beach from the day use area to the cabañas. At the River Island area, dogs are allowed in the water, but must be kept on right side of boat ramp. Well behaved dogs on lead are allowed on the variety of trails and throughout the rest of the park. The camping and tent areas also allow dogs. There is a dog walk area at the campground. Multiple dogs may be allowed.

Patagonia Lake State Park
400 Patagonia Lake Road
Patagonia, AZ
520-287-6965
This park has a variety of water and land recreation, trails, and the Sonoita Creek State Natural Area is now open to the public. Dogs are allowed at no additional fee. Dogs may not be left unattended, they must be on no more than a 6 foot leash, and be cleaned up after. Dogs are not allowed in the public swim areas. The camping and tent areas also allow dogs. There is a dog walk area at the campground. Multiple dogs may be allowed.

Covered Wagon RV Park
6540 N Black Canyon H
Phoenix, AZ
602-242-2500
Dogs of all sizes are allowed. There is a $1 per night per pet additional fee. Dogs may not be left unattended, and they must be leashed and cleaned up after. There are some breed restrictions. The

camping and tent areas also allow dogs. There is a dog walk area at the campground. Multiple dogs may be allowed.

Desert Sands RV Park
22036 N 27th Avenue
Phoenix, AZ
623-869-8186
desertsandsrvpark.com
Dogs of all sizes are allowed. There are no additional pet fees. Dogs may not be left unattended, and they must be leashed and cleaned up after. There are some breed restrictions. There is a dog walk area at the campground. Multiple dogs may be allowed.

Desert Shadows RV Resort
19203 N 29th Avenue
Phoenix, AZ
623-869-8178 (800-595-7290)
arizonarvresorts.com
Dogs of all sizes are allowed. There are no additional pet fees. Dogs are to be walked along the path just outside the front gate, and they must be leashed and cleaned up after. This is an adult resort and at least one person must be 55 or older. Dogs are not allowed in the park models. There are some breed restrictions. There is a dog walk area at the campground. 2 dogs may be allowed.

Destiny RV Resort
416 N Citrus Road
Phoenix, AZ
623-853-0537
destinyrv.com
Dogs of all sizes are allowed, but there can only be 2 average sized dogs or 3 if all small. There are no additional pet fees. Dogs are not allowed to be tied to the trees or tables, and may not be left unattended outside. Dogs must be on no more than a 6 foot leash and cleaned up after. There is a fenced in area for off lead, and there is a Bark Park about 4 miles from the resort. There are some breed restrictions. There is a dog walk area at the campground.

Pioneer RV Resort
36408 N Black Canyon H
Phoenix, AZ
800-658-5895
arizonarvresort.com
Dogs of all sizes are allowed. There are no additional pet fees. Dogs must be leashed and cleaned up after. There are some breed restrictions. There is a dog walk area at the campground. This is a 55 plus

park so one person must be 55 or older. 2 dogs may be allowed.

Tonto National Forest
2324 E. McDowell Road
Phoenix, AZ
602-225-5200
The fifth largest forest in the US with almost 3 million acres offers a wide range of ecosystems, habitats and spectacular scenery. It also supports a large variety of plants, animals, and recreation. Dogs of all sizes are allowed at no additional fee. Dogs may not be left unattended, and they must have current rabies, shot records, and license. Dogs must be leashed at all times and cleaned up after in camp areas. Dogs are allowed on the trails. The camping and tent areas also allow dogs. There is a dog walk area at the campground. There are no electric or water hookups at the campground. Multiple dogs may be allowed.

Picacho Peak RV Resort
17065 E Peak Lane
Picacho, AZ
520-466-7841
picachopeakrv.com
Dogs of all sizes are allowed. There are no additional pet fees. Dogs may not be left unattended outside, and they must have up to date shots, and be leashed and cleaned up after. This is an adults only park. There are some breed restrictions. There is a dog walk area at the campground. 2 dogs may be allowed.

Picacho Peak State Park
Picacho Peak Road
Picacho, AZ
520-466-3183
This park has a variety of trails varying in length and difficulty. The trails are open from 8 am to sunset. Dogs are allowed at no additional fee. Dogs may not be left unattended, they must be on no more than a 6 foot leash, and be cleaned up after. Dogs are not allowed on the advanced trails. The camping and tent areas also allow dogs. There is a dog walk area at the campground. There are no water hookups at the campground. Multiple dogs may be allowed.

Granite Basin Yavapai Campground/Prescott National Forest
Iron Springs Road
Prescott, AZ
928-443-8000

Granite Mountain Wilderness is very popular due to its proximity to Prescott (only 20 minutes by paved road) and the unique experience it offers for hikers among huge granite boulders and varying trails, rock formations, and the spectacular view of the surrounding area. Dogs of all sizes are allowed for no additional fee, and they are allowed to go everywhere their owners can go except public buildings. Dogs may only be left for short periods on the campsite if they will be quiet and well behaved, and they must be leashed and cleaned up after. The camping and tent areas also allow dogs. There is a dog walk area at the campground. There are no electric or water hookups at the campgrounds. Multiple dogs may be allowed.

Prescott National Forest
344 S Cortez Street
Prescott, AZ
928-443-8000
fs.fed.us/r3/prescott/
This forest of over a million acres provides spectacular scenery, a rich cultural history, and diverse ecosystems that support a large variety of plants, animals, and recreation. Dogs of all sizes are allowed at no additional fee. Dogs may not be left unattended, and they must be leashed and cleaned up after. Dogs are allowed on the trails. This campground is closed during the off-season. The camping and tent areas also allow dogs. There is a dog walk area at the campground. Multiple dogs may be allowed.

Willow Lake RV and Camping Park
1617 Heritage Park Road
Prescott, AZ
928-445-6311
Dogs of all sizes are allowed. There are no additional pet fees. Dogs must be leashed and cleaned up after. The camping and tent areas also allow dogs. There is a dog walk area at the campground. Multiple dogs may be allowed.

B-10 Campground
615 Main
Quartzsite, AZ
928-927-4393
Dogs of all sizes are allowed. There are no additional pet fees. Dogs must be leashed and cleaned up after. There are some breed restrictions. This RV park is closed during the off-season. There is a dog walk area at the campground. Multiple dogs may be allowed.

Roper Lake State Park
101 E. Roper Lake Road
Safford, AZ
928-428-6760
This park has 2 camping sections, and offers a model Indian village, land and water recreation, and a natural hot spring. Dogs are allowed at no additional fee. Dogs may not be left unattended, and they must be leashed and cleaned up after. Dogs are not allowed in park buildings or on the beach, but they are allowed on the trails. The camping and tent areas also allow dogs. There is a dog walk area at the campground. Dogs are allowed in the camping cabins. Multiple dogs may be allowed.

Rancho Sedona RV Park
135 Bear Wallow Lane
Sedona, AZ
928-282-7255
ranchosedona.com
Dogs of all sizes are allowed. There is a $1 per night per pet additional fee, and there are discounts for AAA or Good Sam members. Dogs may not be left unattended outside, and they must be quiet, leashed, and cleaned up after. There is a dog walk area at the campground. Multiple dogs may be allowed.

Fool Hollow Lake Recreation Area
1500 N Fool Hollow Lake Road
Show Low, AZ
928-537-3680
Nestled among 100 foot pine trees along a lake at 6300 feet, this rec area offers an impressive list of weekend activities May through September such as parades, car shows, festivals, concerts, rodeos, and more, in addition to a variety of land and water recreation. Dogs are allowed throughout the park for no additional fee, and on the trails, as long as they are on lead at all times, and cleaned up after. The campground offers 123 camping sites, a dump station, fish cleaning station, boat ramps, picnic tables, picnic ramadas, grills, playgrounds, private showers and restrooms. The camping and tent areas also allow dogs. There is a dog walk area at the campground. Multiple dogs may be allowed.

Apache-Sitgreaves National Forest
309 S Mountain Avenue
Springerville, AZ
928-333-4301
fs.fed.us/r3/asnf/
Two forests were combined creating over 2 million acres of spectacular

scenery, hundreds of miles of trails, a variety of recreational pursuits, and more areas of water than any other Southwestern National Forest. Dogs of all sizes are allowed at no additional fee. Dogs may not be left unattended, and they must be leashed and cleaned up after. Dogs are allowed on the trails. The camping and tent areas also allow dogs. There is a dog walk area at the campground. There are no electric or water hookups at the campground. Multiple dogs may be allowed.

Lyman Lake State Park
On H 180/191 11 miles E of St Johns
St Johns, AZ
928-337-4441
This park shares the ancient historic Pueblo Trail, and offers many sites of interest and villages of the Hopi people. Dogs of all sizes are allowed, and there are no additional pet fees for tent or RV sites. There is a $5 one time additional pet fee for the cabins. Dogs must be leashed and cleaned up after. The camping and tent areas also allow dogs. There is a dog walk area at the campground. Dogs are allowed in the camping cabins. Multiple dogs may be allowed.

Supai and the Havasupai Reservation
P. O. Box 10/Indian Road 18
Supai, AZ
928-448-2141
havasupaitribe.com/index.htm
Want to take your dog down to the Colorado River in the Grand Canyon but, of course, this is not allowed by the National Park Service. Instead, just down river from Grand Canyon National Park is the Havasupai Indian Reservation, which shares the Canyon with the National Park. And here, your dog may enter the canyon with you. The strikingly beautiful, secluded canyon sits at the west end of the Grand Canyon and is accessible only by foot, horseback, or helicopter. The entrance fee is $35 per person, and everything is carry in/carry out, or pack animals can be hired. Only a limited number of persons may visit the Havasu Canyon at a time, so advance inquiry is suggested. There is a large parking lot about 64 miles from the turn-off onto Indian Road 18 where visitors may park at Hualapai Hilltop. This is a trailhead with no services. Here you may

start the 8 mile hike to the Supai Village in the canyon where there is a small café, lodge, general store, museum, and a post office that is the only office to still receive mail via Pony Express. The trail is moderately difficult and starts off steep with switchbacks for about the first 1 1/2 miles with narrow canyon passages before it levels out. The name Havasupai means 'People-Of-The Blue-Green-Waters' and the Havasu Creek is a year round spring-fed stream that will astonish visitors with the 4 powerful main waterfalls and deeply colored turquoise pools that it supplies. You first pass Supai Falls as you are nearing the village; then Navajo Falls is about 1 1/2 miles past the village. Just before you reach the campground about 2 miles past the village is the very popular, spectacular double waterfall of the Havasu Falls with a great swimming hole. Then, about 2 miles past the campground is Mooney Falls with the highest drop of 200 feet, but also the most difficult to access. The hiking trails of the Reservation include the hike in from Hualapai Hilltop to the village, to the camp area, and from the campgrounds to the Colorado River which is about 8 miles from the camp area. There is no hiking allowed in Cataract Canyon or off the main trails. Dogs of all sizes are allowed for no additional fees. Dogs must be under their owner's control, and leashed and cleaned up after at all times. Dogs may not be left unattended at any time, and dog owners accept full responsibility for their pet. Dogs are allowed to take the helicopter ride in for about $25 for a small to medium dog; it may be more for a large dog. Their website is www.airwesthelicopters.com. Dogs are not allowed at the lodge or in the village buildings. Campers must pack all supplies and refuge in and out of the canyon. The camp area is primitive but rich with lush vegetation and shade trees. Amenities include spring water (treat or purify first), composting toilets, picnic tables, and night security during tourist season. The fee for tent camping is $10 per person, and no additional pet fee is required. There are no electric or water hookups at the campgrounds. 2 dogs may be allowed.

Tombstone RV Park
MM 315 H 80
Tombstone, AZ
800-348-3829
tombstone-rv.com
Dogs of all sizes are allowed. There

are no additional pet fees. Dogs may be walked in the park, but they must be taken to the dog walk areas to do their business, and cleaned up after. There is a dog walk area at the campground. Multiple dogs may be allowed.

Catalina State Park
11570 N Oracle Road
Tucson, AZ
520-628-5798
This scenic desert recreational park has a variety of attractions plus an archaeological site to explore and there are 8 trails of varying length and difficulty. Dogs are allowed at no additional fee. Dogs must be leashed and cleaned up after. Dogs are not allowed at the Pusch Ridge Wilderness area, but they are allowed on trails. The camping and tent areas also allow dogs. There is a dog walk area at the campground. Multiple dogs may be allowed.

Coronado National Forest
5700 N Sabino Canyon Road
Tucson, AZ
520-388-8300
fs.fed.us/r3/coronado/
This forest, with elevations ranging from 3000 feet to 10,720 feet, covers more than 1.7 million acres over twelve widely scattered mountain ranges. The rugged mountains rise from the desert floor, and are known as the "sky islands". There is recreation during all seasons. Dogs of all sizes are allowed at no additional fee. Dogs may not be left unattended, and they must be leashed and cleaned up after. Dogs are allowed on the trails, but they are not allowed in the Push Ridge Wilderness Area. The camping and tent areas also allow dogs. There is a dog walk area at the campground. There are no electric or water hookups at the campground. Multiple dogs may be allowed.

Crazy Horse RV Park
6660 S Craycroft
Tucson, AZ
520-574-0157
crazyhorserv.com
Dogs of all sizes are allowed. There is $1 per night per pet additional fee for daily rates; $5 by the week, and $15 by the month. Dogs must be walked in designated areas only, and they must be leashed and cleaned up after. Dogs may be left in the RV only if air conditioned. Tucson pet ordinance prohibits dogs from being left in an auto or tied up at any time. There is a dog walk area at the

campground. 2 dogs may be allowed.

Prince of Tucson RV Park
3501 N Freeway
Tucson, AZ
520-887-3501
princeoftucsonrvpark.com
Dogs of all sizes are allowed. There are no additional pet fees for the first two dogs, thereafter the fee is $2 per night per pet. Dogs may not be left unattended outside, and they must be leashed and cleaned up after. Tucson pet ordinance prohibits dogs from being left in an auto or tied up at any time. There are some breed restrictions. There is a dog walk area at the campground. Multiple dogs may be allowed.

Alamo Lake State Park
Alamo Road
Wenden, AZ
928-669-2088
This recreational park has one of Arizona'a best fishing holes, and there is more than enough to interest nature lovers also with a wide variety of flora and fauna. Dogs are allowed at no additional fee. Dogs may not be left unattended, and they must be leashed and cleaned up after. Dogs are allowed on the trails. The camping and tent areas also allow dogs. There is a dog walk area at the campground. Multiple dogs may be allowed.

Flintstones Bedrock City
Junction 64 and 180
Williams, AZ
928-635-2600
bedrockcityaz.com
Dogs of all sizes are allowed. There are no additional pet fees. Dogs may be off leash at the site if the dog is well behaved and will stay on the site regardless of what passes by. They must be on leashed when walked and dogs must be cleaned up after. The camping and tent areas also allow dogs. There is a dog walk area at the campground. Multiple dogs may be allowed.

Grand Canyon/Williams KOA
5333 H 64
Williams, AZ
928-635-2307 (800-562-5771)
koa.com
Dogs of all sizes are allowed. There are no additional pet fees. Dogs may not be left unattended, and they must be quiet, leashed, and cleaned up after. There are some

breed restrictions. This RV park is closed during the off-season. The camping and tent areas also allow dogs. There is a dog walk area at the campground. Dogs are allowed in the camping cabins. Multiple dogs may be allowed.

Kaibab National Forest
Railroad Blvd
Williams, AZ
928-635-8200
fs.fed.us/r3/kai/
This picturesque forest of 1.6 million acres borders both the north and south rims of the Grand Canyon. It is the largest contiguous ponderosa pine forest in US and its diverse ecosystems support a large variety of plants, fish, mammals, bird species, and recreation. Dogs of all sizes are allowed at no additional fee. Dogs may not be left unattended except for shore periods, and they must be leashed and cleaned up after in camp areas. Dogs may be off lead on the trails if no one is around, they will not chase wildlife, and are under strict voice command. The camping and tent areas also allow dogs. There is a dog walk area at the campground. Dogs are allowed in the camping cabins. There are no electric or water hookups at the campground. Multiple dogs may be allowed.

Williams/Circle Pines KOA
1000 Circle Pines Road
Williams, AZ
928-635-2626 (800-562-9379)
circlepineskoa.com
Dogs of all sizes are allowed. There are no additional pet fees. Dogs may not be left unattended outside, and they must be leashed and cleaned up after. Dogs must be crated when left in a cabin. There are some breed restrictions. The camping and tent areas also allow dogs. There is a dog walk area at the campground. Dogs are allowed in the camping cabins. Multiple dogs may be allowed.

Homolovi Ruins State Park
Honahanie Road
Winslow, AZ
928-289-4106
This archeological recreational park explores the rich Native American history. There is a book store as well as the exhibits, and several trails. Dogs are allowed at no additional fee. Dogs must be leashed and cleaned up after. Dogs are not allowed in any of the buildings. The camping and tent areas also allow

dogs. There is a dog walk area at the campground. Multiple dogs may be allowed.

Cocopah RV & Golf Resort
6800 Strand Avenue
Yuma, AZ
928-343-9300
cocopahrv.com
Dogs of all sizes are allowed. There are no additional pet fees. Dogs must be walked in designated pet areas only, and they must be leashed and cleaned up after. Dogs are not allowed in the golf course area. This is an adult only resort. There is a dog walk area at the campground. 2 dogs may be allowed.

Shangri-la RV Resort
10498 N Frontage Road
Yuma, AZ
877-742-6474
shangrilarv.com
Dogs of all sizes are allowed. There are no additional pet fees. Dogs must be walked in the designated pet areas only, and they must be leashed and cleaned up after. There are some breed restrictions. There is a dog walk area at the campground. 2 dogs may be allowed.

Westwind RV and Golf Resort
9797 E 32nd Street
Yuma, AZ
928-342-2992
westwindrvgolfresort.com
Dogs of all sizes are allowed. There are no additional pet fees. Dogs are also allowed in the park models in the pet section only. Dogs must stay in the designated pet areas only to be walked, and are not allowed at the office or other non-pet areas. Dogs may not be left unattended, and they must be leashed and cleaned up after. There are some breed restrictions. There is a dog walk area at the campground. 2 dogs may be allowed.

Arkansas

Fort Smith/Alma KOA
3539 N H 71
Alma, AR
479-632-2704 (800-562-2703)
koa.com
Dogs of all sizes are allowed. There are no additional pet fees. Dogs must be leashed and cleaned up after, and they may not be on the

playground. There is only 1 pet friendly cabin. There are some breed restrictions. The camping and tent areas also allow dogs. There is a dog walk area at the campground. Dogs are allowed in the camping cabins.

Speedway RV Park
1005 Heber Springs (H 14W/H 25S)
Batesville, AR
870-251-1008
speedwayrvpark.com/
Dogs of all sizes are allowed. There are no additional pet fees. Dogs must be leashed and cleaned up after. The camping and tent areas also allow dogs. There is a dog walk area at the campground. 2 dogs may be allowed.

I 30 Travel Park
19719 I-30
Benton, AR
501-778-1244
Dogs of all sizes are allowed. There are no additional pet fees. Dogs may not be left unattended, and they must be leashed and cleaned up after. There is a dog walk area at the campground. Multiple dogs may be allowed.

DeGray Lake Resort State Park
2027 State Park Entrance Road
Bismarck, AR
501-865-2801
degray.com/
This resort park sits on the 13,800 acre DeGray Lake and in addition to all the resort amenities; there is an abundance of recreational opportunities-including a championship golf course and full service marina. Dogs are allowed throughout the park and in the campground; they are not permitted in buildings or public swim areas. Dogs must be leashed and under the immediate control/care of owner at all times. The campground offers 113 sites along the shoreline or nestled in shaded wooded areas and offer picnic tables, grills, restrooms, showers, and dump stations. The camping and tent areas also allow dogs. There is a dog walk area at the campground. Multiple dogs may be allowed.

Denton Ferry RV Park
740 Denton Ferry Road
Cotter, AR
800-275-5611
whiteriver.net/dentonrv
Dogs of all sizes are allowed. There are no additional pet fees. Dogs must be quiet, leashed, and

cleaned up after. There is a dog walk area at the campground.

Eureka Springs KOA
15020 H 187S
Eureka Springs, AR
479-253-8036 (800-562-0536)
eurekaspringskoa.com
Dogs of all sizes are allowed. There are no additional pet fees. Dogs must be leashed and cleaned up after. This RV park is closed during the off-season. The camping and tent areas also allow dogs. There is a dog walk area at the campground. Multiple dogs may be allowed.

Wanderlust RV Park
468 Passion Play Road
Eureka Springs, AR
479-253-7385
wanderlust-rvpark.com
Dogs of all sizes are allowed. There are no additional pet fees. Dogs must be leashed and cleaned up after. This RV park is closed during the off-season. The camping and tent areas also allow dogs. There is a dog walk area at the campground. Multiple dogs may be allowed.

Cedar Hollow RV Park
76 MC Road 8110
Flippin, AR
870-453-8643
billyhill.com/cedarhollowrv
Dogs of all sizes are allowed. There are no additional pet fees. Dogs must be leashed and cleaned up after. There is a dog walk area at the campground. Multiple dogs may be allowed.

Harrison Village Campground
2364 H 65S
Harrison, AR
870-743-3388
Dogs of all sizes are allowed. There are no additional pet fees. Dogs must be leashed and cleaned up after. There are some breed restrictions. The camping and tent areas also allow dogs. There is a dog walk area at the campground. Multiple dogs may be allowed.

Cloud Nine RV Park
136 Cloud Nine Drive
Hot Springs, AR
501-262-1996
cloudninerv.com
Dogs of all sizes are allowed. There are no additional pet fees. Dogs must be leashed and cleaned up after. There are some breed restrictions. The camping and tent areas also allow dogs. There is a dog walk area at the campground.

Multiple dogs may be allowed.

Hot Springs National Park
101 Reserve Street
Hot Springs, AR
501-624-3383
nps.gov/hosp
Known for its curative waters, people have come from all over the world to experience the wonderful effects of thermal bathing, and to enjoy the beauty and recreation available in the area. Dogs are allowed throughout the park and in the camp area. Dogs must be leashed and cleaned up after at all times. The camp sites are available first come, first served and they provide picnic tables and a grill; water and restrooms are nearby, as is a dump station. The camping and tent areas also allow dogs. There is a dog walk area at the campground. There are no electric or water hookups at the campgrounds. Multiple dogs may be allowed.

Hot Springs National Park KOA
838 McClendon Road
Hot Springs, AR
501-624-5912 (800-562-5903)
hotspringskoa.com
Dogs of all sizes are allowed. There are no additional pet fees. Dogs must be leashed and cleaned up after. The camping and tent areas also allow dogs. There is a dog walk area at the campground. Dogs are allowed in the camping cabins. Multiple dogs may be allowed.

Lake Catherine State Park
1200 Catherine Park Road
Hot Springs, AR
501-844-4176 (888-287-2757)
Almost 2,000 acres of lakes add to the recreation at this state park. There are a variety of activities, recreation, and trails to explore. Dogs of all sizes are allowed at no additional fee. Dogs may not be left unattended, and they must be leashed and cleaned up after. Dogs are not allowed in buildings or on the beaches, but they are allowed on the trails. The camping and tent areas also allow dogs. There is a dog walk area at the campground. Multiple dogs may be allowed.

Lake Hamilton RV Resort
3027 Albert Pike
Hot Springs, AR
501-767-4400
lakehamiltonrvresort.com
Dogs of all sizes are allowed. There are no additional pet fees. Dogs may not be left unattended, and they must

be leashed and cleaned up after. Outside pens or kennels are not allowed, and dogs must be walked in designated pet areas only. There is a dog walk area at the campground. Multiple dogs may be allowed.

Ouachita National Forest
H 270
Hot Springs, AR
501-321-5202 (877-444-6777)
fs.fed.us/r8/ouachita/
Located in Oklahoma and Arkansas with 5 ranger districts and over 1.8 million acres, this forest provides a variety of camping areas, trails, recreation, and diverse ecosystems that support a large variety of flora, fauna, and industry. Dogs are allowed at no additional fee. Dogs may not be left unattended, and they must be leashed and cleaned up after in the camp areas. They suggest not letting dogs off lead in the forest because of snakes and other wild animals. The camp areas are varied and may have some or all of the following: accessible flush toilets, showers, picnic areas, dump stations, boat launch, interpretive trails, a playground, amphitheater, and lakeside sites. The camping and tent areas also allow dogs. There is a dog walk area at the campground. Multiple dogs may be allowed.

Jacksonport State Park
205 Avenue Street
Jacksonport, AR
870-523-2143 (888-287-2757)
Located along the White River, this park is home to the Tunstall Riverwalk Trail, and a variety of water and land recreation. Dogs of all sizes are allowed at no additional fee. Dogs may not be left unattended, and they must be leashed and cleaned up after. Dogs are allowed on the trails. The camping and tent areas also allow dogs. There is a dog walk area at the campground. Multiple dogs may be allowed.

Dogwood Springs Jasper Resort
P.O. Box 157/On H 7 one mile N
Jasper, AR
870-446-2163
jasperandnewtoncountyresorts.com
Well behaved dogs of all sizes are allowed at no additional fee for the tent or RV sites. There is a $10 per night per pet additional fee for the cabins, plus a $50 refundable deposit that is refundable by mail 7 days after checkout. Dogs may not

be left unattended at any time, and they must be quiet, leashed at all times, and cleaned up after. Your visitors may not have a dog on the property or in their vehicle on the property, for any reason, at anytime. The camping and tent areas also allow dogs. There is a dog walk area at the campground. Dogs are allowed in the camping cabins. Multiple dogs may be allowed.

Moro Bay State Park
6071 H 600
Jersey, AR
870-463-8555 (888-287-2757)
This park is one of the most popular fishing and water sport areas in the state and offers a variety of land and water recreational opportunities. Well behaved, quiet, dogs of all sizes are allowed at no additional fee. Dogs must be leashed and cleaned up after. Dogs are not allowed in the buildings, but they are allowed on the trails. The camping and tent areas also allow dogs. There is a dog walk area at the campground. Multiple dogs may be allowed.

Pecan Grove RV Park
1518 Barton Springs Road
Lake Village, AR
512-472-1067
Dogs of all sizes are allowed. There are no additional pet fees. Dogs must be leashed and cleaned up after. Long term guests are allowed one dog up to 15 pounds. There is a dog walk area at the campground. 2 dogs may be allowed.

America's Best Campground
7037 I 55
Marion, AR
870-739-4801 (888-857-4801)
campmemphis.com
Dogs of all sizes are allowed. There are no additional pet fees. Dogs must be leashed and cleaned up after. The camping and tent areas also allow dogs. There is a dog walk area at the campground. Multiple dogs may be allowed.

Memphis KOA
7037 I-55 Marion
Marion, AR
870-739-4801 (800-562-3240)
koa.com/where/ar/04142/
In addition to being central to many local attractions, this park also provides free Wi-Fi, seasonal weekend dinners and pancake breakfasts, gaming courts, planned activities, and a children's playground. This park also has a fenced pet playground. Dogs are

allowed for no additional fee in the campground; there is an additional fee of $2 per night per pet for the cabins. Only 2 dogs are allowed per cabin; there may be more than 2 dogs per site in the RV/tent area. Dogs may not be left unattended outside, and they may only be left alone inside if they will be quiet. Dogs must be on no more than a 6 foot leash and cleaned up after at all times. There are some breed restrictions. The camping and tent areas also allow dogs. There is a dog walk area at the campground. Dogs are allowed in the camping cabins. There are special amenities given to dogs at this campground.

Morrilton/Conway KOA
30 Kamper Lane
Morrilton, AR
501-354-8262 (800-562-9038)
koa.com
Dogs of all sizes are allowed. There are no additional pet fees. Dogs may not be left unattended outside, and they must be leashed and cleaned up after. This RV park is closed during the off-season. The camping and tent areas also allow dogs. There is a dog walk area at the campground. Dogs are allowed in the camping cabins. Multiple dogs may be allowed.

Petit Jean State Park
1285 Petit Jean Mountain Road
Morrilton, AR
501-727-5441
petitjeanstatepark.com/
Rich in legend and lore, this enchanting forested park has several blazed trails taking visitors through a number of its distinctive natural features. Dogs are allowed throughout the park, in the camp area, and at one of the cabins. There is a $40 one time additional pet fee for the cabins. Dogs may not be left unattended; they must have proof of rabies vaccinations, be disease and bug free, and dogs in heat are not allowed. Dogs may not be tied to trees, park property, or anchored to the ground. There are 125 campsites with picnic tables, grills, modern bathhouses, lantern holders, and a dump station. The camping and tent areas also allow dogs. There is a dog walk area at the campground. Dogs are allowed in the camping cabins.

White Buffalo Resort
418 White Buffalo Trail
Mountain Home, AR
870-425-8555

whitebuffaloresort.com/
Dogs of all sizes are allowed at no additional fee for the tent or RV sites. There is a $10 per night per pet additional fee for the cabins. Dogs may not be left unattended outside or in the cabins or tents. Dogs are not allowed on the furniture in the cabins. Dogs may only be left in an RV if they will be quiet and well behaved. The camping and tent areas also allow dogs. There is a dog walk area at the campground. Dogs are allowed in the camping cabins. 2 dogs may be allowed.

Fiddler's Valley RV Resort
234 Oak Avenue
Mountain View, AR
870-269-5700 (877-784-1482)
Dogs of all sizes are allowed. There are no additional pet fees. Dogs may not be left unattended outside, and they must be quiet, leashed, and cleaned up after. There is a dog walk area at the campground. Multiple dogs may be allowed.

Ozark RV Park
1022 Park Avenue
Mountain View, AR
870-269-2542
ozarkrvpark.com
Dogs of all sizes are allowed. There are no additional pet fees. Dogs must be leashed and cleaned up after. This RV park is closed during the off-season. The camping and tent areas also allow dogs. There is a dog walk area at the campground. Multiple dogs may be allowed.

Crater of Diamonds State Park
201 State Park Road
Murfreesboro, AR
870-285-3113
craterofdiamondsstatepark.com/
Among the many geological wonders of this state, this park is home to the only diamond producing area that is open to the public and what visitors find-they get to keep, regardless of the value. There are also miles of wooded trails, a seasonal waterpark, educational opportunities, and historic buildings/artifacts. Dogs are allowed throughout the park and in the campground; they are not permitted in buildings, in public swim areas, or to be left unattended. Dogs must be leashed and under the immediate control/care of owner at all times. The camp area offers 59 sites, a modern bathhouse with hot showers, a laundry, and a dump

station. The camping and tent areas also allow dogs. There is a dog walk area at the campground. Multiple dogs may be allowed.

Burns Park Campground
4101 Arlene Laman Drive
North Little Rock, AR
501-771-0702
Dogs of all sizes are allowed. There are no additional pet fees. Dogs must have up to date shot records, and be cleaned up after. Dogs must be leashed while in the park, but there is a dog park with large fenced in areas about a mile and a half away. The camping and tent areas also allow dogs. There is a dog walk area at the campground. Multiple dogs may be allowed.

Little Rock North/Jct I 40 KOA
7820 Crystal Hill Road
North Little Rock, AR
501-758-4598 (800-562-4598)
koa.com
Dogs of all sizes are allowed. There are no additional pet fees. Dogs may not be left unattended outside, and they must be leashed and cleaned up after. There is a fenced dog area. There is only 1 pet friendly cabin. The camping and tent areas also allow dogs. There is a dog walk area at the campground. Dogs are allowed in the camping cabins. Multiple dogs may be allowed.

Crowley's Ridge State Park
2092 H 168N
Paragould, AR
870-573-6751 (888-287-2757)
Sitting atop forested hills, this park offers interpretive programs throughout the year as well as a variety of land and water recreation. Dogs of all sizes are allowed at no additional fee. Dogs may not be left unattended, and they must be leashed and cleaned up after. Dogs are not allowed in buildings or at the group facilities, but they are allowed on the trails. The camping and tent areas also allow dogs. There is a dog walk area at the campground. Multiple dogs may be allowed.

Old Davidson State Park
7953 H 166S
Pocohontas, AR
870-892-4708 (888-287-2757)
This historical park offers exhibits, interpretive tours, and a variety of land and water recreation. Well behaved, quiet dogs of all sizes are allowed at no additional fee. Dogs must be leashed at all times, and be cleaned up after. Dogs are not

allowed in buildings or in the lake, but they may wade by the edge on leash. Dogs are allowed on the trails. The camping and tent areas also allow dogs. There is a dog walk area at the campground. Multiple dogs may be allowed.

Ozark-St. Francis National Forest
605 W Main Street
Russellville, AR
479-964-7200
fs.fed.us/oonf/ozark/
These are two separate forest areas have their own unique qualities, but they both offer a wide variety of land and water recreation. Ouachita also has the tallest mountain in the state, and an incredible living underground cave. Dogs of all sizes are allowed at no additional fee. Dogs may not be left unattended, and they must be leashed and cleaned up after. Dogs are not allowed in the swim areas, but they are allowed on the trails. This campground is closed during the off-season. The camping and tent areas also allow dogs. There is a dog walk area at the campground. There are no water hookups at the campground. Multiple dogs may be allowed.

Buffalo National River
170 Ranger Road
St Joe, AR
870-439-2502
nps.gov/buff
One of the few undammed rivers in the lower 48 states, this 135 mile free flowing river park has 3 designated wilderness areas within its borders, and numerous recreational and educational opportunities. Dogs are allowed throughout the park and in the campground; they are not allowed on the trails. Dogs may not be left unattended, and they must be leashed and under the immediate control/care of owner at all times. There are 13 campgrounds available; some of them have potable water and comfort stations. The camping and tent areas also allow dogs. There is a dog walk area at the campground. There are no electric or water hookups at the campgrounds. Multiple dogs may be allowed.

Devil's Den State Park
11333 W H 74
West Fork, AR
479-761-3325
There are a number of educational as well as recreation opportunities at this lush mountain park. There are many miles of hiking and multiple

use trails, places to explore above and below ground, and a beautiful stone dam creating the 8 acre Lake Devil. Dogs are allowed throughout the park and in the campground for no additional fee; they are not permitted in buildings or public swim areas. Dogs must have proof of inoculations, be leashed, and under the immediate control/care of owner at all times. Camp areas are varied and may have some or all of the following: comfort stations, a seasonal swimming pool and café, or a park store. Backpacking campers must obtain a free backcountry permit at the visitor center prior to camping. The camping and tent areas also allow dogs. There is a dog walk area at the campground. Multiple dogs may be allowed.

Tom Sawyer's Mississippi River RV Park
1286 S 8th Street
West Memphis, AR
870-735-9770
Dogs of all sizes are allowed. There are no additional pet fees. Dogs must be quiet, well behaved, leashed, and cleaned up after. Dogs are also welcome to swim at the river. The camping and tent areas also allow dogs. There is a dog walk area at the campground. Multiple dogs may be allowed.

Wiederkehr Wine Cellars RV Park
3324 Swiss Family Drive
Wiederkehr Village, AR
479-468-9463 (800-622-WINE (9463))
wiederkehrwines.com/rvpark.html
This RV park is located in the largest and oldest winery in mid-America. In addition to their beautiful setting, they offer a long list of fine wines and a gift shop. Dogs are allowed for no additional fee; they must be kept leashed and cleaned up after. The camping and tent areas also allow dogs. There is a dog walk area at the campground. 2 dogs may be allowed.

Village Creek State Park
201 County Road 754
Wynne, AR
870-238-9406 (888-287-2757)
Interpretive programs and exhibits inform visitors of the natural and cultural heritage of this unique park. There are several miles of trails, and a variety of land and water recreation. Dogs of all sizes are allowed at no additional fee. Dogs may only be left unattended for

short periods, and only if they will be quiet and well behaved. Dogs must be cleaned up after. Dogs are not allowed in the water or in buildings, but they are allowed on the trails. The camping and tent areas also allow dogs. There is a dog walk area at the campground. Multiple dogs may be allowed.

Sherwood Forest RV Park & Campground
216 MC Road 5042
Yellville, AR
870-449-3452
arksherwoodforestrvpark.com
Dogs of all sizes are allowed. There are no additional pet fees. Dogs may not be left unattended, and they must be leashed and cleaned up after. The camping and tent areas also allow dogs. There is a dog walk area at the campground. Dogs are allowed in the camping cabins. Multiple dogs may be allowed.

California

Albion River Campground and Fishing Village
34500 H 1
Albion, CA
7 0 7-937-0606
albionrivercampground.com/
Located along side the Albion River on the beautiful Mendocino coast, this campground offers a variety of recreational pursuits, a small store, restaurant, a boat dock, and a nice sandy beach. Some other amenities include on-site RV rentals, picnic tables, fire rings, showers and restrooms. Dogs of all sizes are allowed for an additional fee of $2 per pet. Dogs must be leashed and cleaned up after at all times, and they may not be left unattended on the camp site or in a vehicle. There is a steep hill down from Highway 1 to the campground. Dogs are allowed throughout the park and on the beach. The camping and tent areas also allow dogs. There is a dog walk area at the campground. Multiple dogs may be allowed.

Canyon RV Park at Featherly
24001 Santa Ana Canyon Road
Anaheim, CA
714-637-0210
canyonrvpark.com/about.htm
This RV only park is situated on the Santa Ana River surrounded by mature cottonwood and sycamore

trees. They have 140 RV hookup sites. Other amenities include a pool, playground, laundry, acres of wilderness and trees, bike trails, and an amphitheater. This park is about 14 miles from Disneyland. Well-behaved leashed dogs are welcome for an additional $1 per day. Please clean up after your pets. There are some breed restrictions. There is a dog walk area at the campground. Multiple dogs may be allowed.

Green Valley Campground
Green Valley Lake Road
Arrowbear, CA
909-337-2444 (877-444-6777)
This 36 site campground is located in the San Bernardino National Forest. RVs up to 22 feet are allowed. The lake offers fishing, swimming and boating. Trails are located nearby. Dogs of all sizes are allowed for no additional fee. Dogs may not be left unattended outside, and they must be on no more than a 6 foot leash at all times, and cleaned up after. Dogs are allowed on the trails. This campground is closed during the off-season. The camping and tent areas also allow dogs. There is a dog walk area at the campground. There are no water hookups at the campgrounds. Multiple dogs may be allowed.

Crab Flats Campground
Forest Road 3N16
Arrowbear Lake, CA
909-337-2444
This San Bernardino National Forest campground is located at an elevation of 6,200 feet in tall pine, oak and cedar trees. It is a popular campsite and off-highway vehicle staging area. Off-road and hiking trails are located near this campground. Tent and small RV sites are available, with a maximum RV length of 15 feet. Sites are available on a first-come, first-served basis. Pets on leash are allowed and please clean up after them. Dogs are allowed on the trails. From Green Valley Road exit turn left and go about 4 miles to the Crab Flats Campground sign at Forestry (dirt road). Turn left and go about 4.5 miles. The camping and tent areas also allow dogs. There is a dog walk area at the campground. There are no electric or water hookups at the campgrounds. Multiple dogs may be allowed.

Lake Lopez Recreation Area
Campground
6820 Lopez Drive

Arroyo Grande, CA
805-788-2381
This campground has 354 campsites which overlook the lake or are nestled among oak trees. This lake is popular for fishing, camping, boating, sailing, water skiing, canoeing, bird-watching and miles of hiking trails ranging from easy to strenuous. The marina allows dogs on their boat rentals for an extra $20 fee. Other amenities at the marina include a guest laundry, grocery store and tackle shop. Dogs must be leashed at all times and people need to clean up after their pets. There is an additional fee of $2 per night per pet. Dogs are not allowed in the water, but they are allowed on the trails. Reservations for the campsites are accepted. The camping and tent areas also allow dogs. There is a dog walk area at the campground. Multiple dogs may be allowed.

Auburn Gold Country RV (formally KOA)
3550 KOA Way
Auburn, CA
530-885-0990 (866-820-8362)
auburngoldcountryrvpark.com
Dogs of all sizes are allowed for no additional fee at this recreational park. Dogs may not be left unattended, and they must be leashed and cleaned up after. They are not allowed in the pool or playground areas, or in park buildings. There are some breed restrictions. The camping and tent areas also allow dogs. There is a dog walk area at the campground. Multiple dogs may be allowed.

Hole in the Wall Campground
Black Canyon Road
Baker, CA
760-928-2562
nps.gov/moja
This desert park, located in the scenic Mojave National Preserve, offers various recreational pursuits to its visitors. Dogs of all sizes are allowed. There are no additional pet fees. Dogs must be on no more than a 6 foot leash and cleaned up after. Dogs must be brought in at night, and they are allowed on the trails on lead. The camping and tent areas also allow dogs. There is a dog walk area at the campground. There are no electric or water hookups at the campgrounds. Multiple dogs may be allowed.

Mohave National Preserve
Campgrounds

Black Canyon Road
Baker, CA
760-252-6101
nps.gov/moja/mojareca.htm
This park offers two family campgrounds with elevations ranging from 4,400 feet to 5,600 feet. The campgrounds offer tent camping and one camp offers spaces for RVs. The campsites are usually booked during deer hunting season. Spaces are available on a first-come, first-served basis. Dogs of all sizes are allowed at no additional fee. Dogs must be leashed in camp and cleaned up after. Dogs may be off lead only if they are under voice control and will not chase. Dogs are allowed on the trails, and can even go in the visitor's center. Contact the park for campground locations and more details. The camping and tent areas also allow dogs. There is a dog walk area at the campground. There are no electric or water hookups at the campgrounds. Multiple dogs may be allowed.

Bakersfield Palms RV Resort
250 Fairfax Road
Bakersfield, CA
661-366-6700 (888-725-6778 (888-PALMSRV))
palmsrv.com
This RV only park offers various recreational pursuits, and ready access to other nearby attractions. Dogs of all sizes are allowed. There are no additional pet fees. Dogs may not be left unattended outside, and they must be leashed and cleaned up after. There is a dog walk area at the campground. Multiple dogs may be allowed.

Orange Grove RV Park
1452 S Edison Road
Bakersfield, CA
661-366-4662
orangegrovervpark.com/
This RV park is on a 40 acre orange grove about eight miles east of Highway 99. Site amenities include pull-thru sites with up to 50 amp service. Other amenities include a rig and car wash, a children's playground, oranges available from December through March, a swimming pool, laundry facilities, propane, TV/group meeting room and a country store. Well-behaved, leashed dogs are welcome. There are no pet fees. Please clean up after your pet. The camping and tent areas also allow dogs. There is a dog walk area at the campground. Multiple dogs may be allowed.

Banning Stagecoach KOA
1455 S San Gorgonio
Banning, CA
951-849-7513 (800-562-4110)
koa.com/where/ca/05450/
Wide grassy sites, great mountain views, and a year around swimming pool and children's playground are just a few of the amenities here. Additionally, they are close to several casinos and one of the largest prime outlets in the country. Dogs are allowed for no additional fee. Tethered dogs may not be left unattended, and they must be quiet, on no more than a 6 foot leash, and be cleaned up after at all times. There are some breed restrictions. The camping and tent areas also allow dogs. There is a dog walk area at the campground. Multiple dogs may be allowed.

Rainbow Basin Natural Area
Fossil Bed Road
Barstow, CA
760-252-6060
blm.gov/ca/barstow/basin.html
This park offers a diverse landscape of hills, canyons, washes, multi-colored rock walls, and mesas that are ever changing in color and light. The park has geological and paleontological importance, an auto tour of an Area of Critical Environmental Concern, and a variety of recreational activities to pursue. Dogs are allowed throughout the park and on the trails. Dogs must be under owner's immediate control, leashed, and cleaned up after at all times. Camping is permitted only at Owl Canyon on a first come first served basis, and each site has a table, shelter, and campfire grates. Pit toilets are located in the campground. There is no potable water. The camping and tent areas also allow dogs. There is a dog walk area at the campground. There are no electric or water hookups at the campgrounds. Multiple dogs may be allowed.

Lupine/Cedar Bluff Campground
County Road 222 on South side of Bass Lake
Bass Lake, CA
559-877-2218 (877-444-6777)
This campground is next to Bass Lake in the Sierra National Forest. It is at an elevation of 3,400 feet and offers shade from dense pine, oak and cedar frees. There are 113 campsites for tent and RV camping. RVs up to 40 feet are allowed, and amenities include piped water, flush toilets, picnic tables and grills. The

campground is open all year. A .5 mile trail called The Way of the Mono Trail, is located near this campground. Dogs are allowed at the campgrounds, on trails and in the water but only at non-designated swimming beaches. Pets must be leashed and please clean up after them. Dogs may not be left unattended outside, and they are not allowed on the beach. Check in at the Bass Lake Campground office before heading to your campsite. The office is located at the west end of the lake near Recreation Point. The camping and tent areas also allow dogs. There is a dog walk area at the campground. There are no electric or water hookups at the campgrounds. Multiple dogs may be allowed.

Country Hills RV Park
14711 Manzanita Park Road
Beaumont, CA
951-845-5919 (800-203-5662)
countryhillsrv.com/
This country like park is close to many local attractions and offers a variety of services and recreational opportunities. Dogs of all sizes are allowed for an additional $1 per night per pet. Dogs may not be left unattended outside, and left inside only if they will be well behaved and physically comfortable. Dogs must be leashed and cleaned up after. No Pit Bulls are allowed. This is an RV only park. There are some breed restrictions. There is a dog walk area at the campground. 2 dogs may be allowed.

Holloway's RV Park
398 Edgemoor Road
Big Bear Lake, CA
909-8666-5706 (800-448-5335)
bigbearboating.com/
This RV park offers large level sites with a nice view of Big Bear Lake. RV sites offer tables, barbecues, and TV cable. Park amenities include a small convenience store, restrooms, showers, laundry room, playground with horseshoes, basketball and boat rentals. Dogs are allowed at the campgrounds and on the boat rentals. Pets must be leashed and please clean up after them. There is a dog walk area at the campground. 2 dogs may be allowed.

Pineknot Campground
Bristlecone
Big Bear Lake, CA
909-866-3437 (800-280-CAMP

(2267))
fs.fed.us/r5/sanbernardino/
This 52 site campground is part of the San Bernardino National Forest. It is located at an elevation of 7,000 feet. RV spaces have a maximum length of 45 feet. Amenities include water, flush toilets and picnic areas. Pets must be on leash and cannot be left unattended. Please clean up after your pets. The campground is on Bristlecone near Summit Blvd. Call to make a reservation. The camping and tent areas also allow dogs. There is a dog walk area at the campground. There are no electric or water hookups at the campgrounds. Multiple dogs may be allowed.

Serrano Campground
4533 N Shore Drive
Big Bear Lake, CA
909-866-3437 (877-444-6777)
This camp area is situated among tall pines on the North Shore of Bear Lake, and some of their new facilities include showers, toilets, and telephones. Dogs of all sizes are allowed. There are no additional pet fees. Dogs may not be left unattended, and they must be leashed and cleaned up after. The camping and tent areas also allow dogs. There is a dog walk area at the campground. Multiple dogs may be allowed.

Big Pine Creek Campground
Glacier Lodge Road
Big Pine, CA
760-873-2500 (877-444-6777)
This 36 site campground is located in the Inyo National Forest at an elevation of 7,700 feet. Amenities include water and space for RVs. For hiking, the trailheads for the Big Pine Canyon Trails are located here. The fee for a campsite is $13. Pets must be leashed while in the campground and please clean up after your pets. They may be off lead in the back country if they are under voice command. Dogs may not be left unattended outside, and only left inside if they will be comfortable, quiet, and well behaved. This campground is closed during the off-season. The camping and tent areas also allow dogs. There is a dog walk area at the campground. There are no electric or water hookups at the campgrounds. Multiple dogs may be allowed.

Glacier Lodge RV Park
Glacier Lodge Road
Big Pine, CA
760-938-2837

This campground offers tent camping and some RV spaces with full hookups. Amenities include a general store and nearby hiking and fishing. Dogs are also allowed in the cabins for an extra $15 per pet per stay. The Big Pine Canyon trailheads are located here which offer miles of dog-friendly on or off-leash hiking trails. Pets must be leashed in the campground and please clean up after them. This RV park is closed during the off-season. The camping and tent areas also allow dogs. There is a dog walk area at the campground. Dogs are allowed in the camping cabins. Multiple dogs may be allowed.

Grandview Campground
White Mountain Road
Big Pine, CA
760-873-2500
This campground is in Bristlecone Pine Forest, at 8,600 feet, in the White Mountain area of Inyo National Forest. There are no services or water available here. Dogs of all sizes are allowed at no additional fee. Dogs may not be left unattended, and they must be leashed and cleaned up after. When out of camp, on the trails, dogs may be off lead if no one is around, and they are under voice control. This campground is closed during the off-season. The camping and tent areas also allow dogs. There is a dog walk area at the campground. There are no electric or water hookups at the campgrounds. Multiple dogs may be allowed.

Big Sur Campground and Cabins
47000 H 1
Big Sur, CA
831-677-2322
This tent and RV campground is set amongst redwood trees along the Big Sur River. Camp amenities include some pull-thru sites, a general store, playground, basketball court and more. Well-behaved leashed dogs of all sizes are allowed in the tent, RV sites, and the tent cabins, but not in the hardwood cabins or around them. There is an additional fee of $5 per night per pet for the tent or RV sites. There is an additional fee of $15 per night per pet for the tent cabins. Pets must be attended at all times. People need to clean up after their pets. They are located about 5 miles from the dog-friendly Pfieffer Beach and 2.5 miles from Big Sur Station. The camping and tent areas also allow dogs. There is a dog walk area at the

campground. Dogs are allowed in the camping cabins. Multiple dogs may be allowed.

Fernwood at Big Sur
47200 H 1
Big Sur, CA
831-667-2422
fernwoodbigsur.com/
Home to a famous and rare Albino Redwood tree, this park provides historic sites, river campsites, a store, tavern and planned events. One of the many trails here ends at Pfeiffer Falls, a 60-foot high waterfall. Dogs of all sizes are allowed for an additional fee of $5 per night per pet for the tent or RV sites, and an additional fee of $10 per night per pet for the tent cabins. Dogs may not be left unattended, and they must be leashed and cleaned up after. Dogs are allowed on the trails unless otherwise marked. The camping and tent areas also allow dogs. There is a dog walk area at the campground. Dogs are allowed in the camping cabins.

Ventana Big Sur Campground
28106 H 1
Big Sur, CA
831-667-2712
ventanacampground.com/
This 40 acre campground, located in a redwood tree lined canyon, offers 80 camp sites nestled among the trees and along the edge of the stream. RV's are limited to 22 feet. Well-behaved, quiet, leashed dogs of all sizes are allowed, maximum of two dogs per site. People need to clean up after their pets. There is a $5 per night pet fee per dog. This campground is closed during the off-season. The camping and tent areas also allow dogs. There is a dog walk area at the campground. There are no electric or water hookups at the campgrounds. 2 dogs may be allowed.

Four Jeffrey Campground
South Lake Road
Bishop, CA
760-873-2500 (877-444-6777)
This 106 site campground is located in the Inyo National Forest at an elevation of 8,100 feet. Amenities include water, space for RVs and a dump station. For hiking, the Bristlecone Pine Forest is located nearby and offers many dog-friendly trails. The fee for a campsite is $14. Pets must be leashed while in the campground and please clean up after your pets. Dogs must be quiet

and friendly. This campground is closed during the off-season. The camping and tent areas also allow dogs. There is a dog walk area at the campground. There are no electric or water hookups at the campgrounds. Multiple dogs may be allowed.

Upper Jamison Creek Campground
310 Johnsville Road
Blairsden, CA
530-836-2380
This campground is located in the scenic Sierra Plumas Eureka State Park at the foot of Eureka Mountain. Dogs of all sizes are allowed at no additional fee. Dogs may not be left unattended, and they must be quiet, leashed, and cleaned up after. Dogs are not allowed on the trails; they are allowed on Jamison Trail Road or in the back country on lead. This campground is closed during the off-season. The camping and tent areas also allow dogs. There is a dog walk area at the campground. There are no electric or water hookups at the campgrounds. Multiple dogs may be allowed.

Blythe / Colorado River KOA
14100 Riviera Drive
Blythe, CA
760-922-5350 (800-562-3948)
koa.com/where/ca/05451/
In addition to over 300 sites, an arcade, year around pool and spa, a laundry, and recreation center, this park offers a boat landing/launching area and a gas station. The park is also home to a large, fenced dog park for letting the pooches run free. Dogs are allowed for no additional fee. Dogs may not be left unattended outside, and they may only be left alone inside if they will be quiet. Dogs must be kept on no more than a 6 foot leash (except in off-lead area) and cleaned up after at all times. There are some breed restrictions. The camping and tent areas also allow dogs. There is a dog walk area at the campground. Multiple dogs may be allowed.

Collis Mayflower Park
4980 Colorado River Road
Blythe, CA
760-922-4665 (800-234-PARK (7275))
This scenic recreational park features 152 camp sites, a day use picnic area, gaming areas, a boat launch, restrooms, showers, and a dump station. Spaces are available on a first come first served basis, although reservations can be made. Dogs of all sizes are welcome for an

additional $1 per pet per day; there is no pet fee if the stay is a week or longer. Dogs must be under owner's control, and be leashed and cleaned up after at all times. The camping and tent areas also allow dogs. There is a dog walk area at the campground. Multiple dogs may be allowed.

Reynolds Riviera Resort
14100 Riviera Drive
Blythe, CA
760-922-5350
reynoldsresorts.com/Riviera.htm
Located along the Colorado River, this park offers more than 300 full service sites and park models, a heated pool, spa, laundry facilities, an arcade, and a community center. Dogs of all sizes are welcome for no additional fee. They are allowed throughout the park. Dogs must be under owner's immediate control, and leashed and cleaned up after at all times. The camping and tent areas also allow dogs. There is a dog walk area at the campground. Multiple dogs may be allowed.

Bodega Bay RV Park
2001 H 1
Bodega Bay, CA
707-875-3701 (800-201-6864)
bodegabayrvpark.com/index.html
Steeped in history and a natural beauty, this park is the only full service park in the area, and they offer 72 sites on 51/2 wind-protected acres. Some features include Wi-Fi, a restaurant, hot showers and restrooms, a laundry, dump station, gaming courts, and they are host to various celebrations and events throughout the year. Dogs of all sizes are allowed for no additional fee. Dogs must be friendly, well behaved, leashed and cleaned up after. Pit Bulls are not allowed. There is a dog walk area at the campground. 2 dogs may be allowed.

Bodega Dunes Campground
3095 H 1
Bodega Bay, CA
707-875-3483 (800-444-7275)
This campground is located in one of the largest beach parks in the state, and offers miles of hiking trails, whale-watching sites, various nature habitats, and a variety of land and water recreation. Dogs of all sizes are allowed. There are no additional pet fees. Dogs must be on no more than a 6 foot leash at all times and cleaned up after. Dogs must be inside at night, and they are not allowed on beach adjacent to the

campground or on trails. The camping and tent areas also allow dogs. There is a dog walk area at the campground. There are no electric or water hookups at the campgrounds. Multiple dogs may be allowed.

Doran Regional Park Campgrounds
201 Doran Beach Road
Bodega Bay, CA
707-875-3540
Walk to the beach from your campsite! There are over 100 campsites in this park which features 2 miles of sandy beach. There is a dump station for RVs. Dogs are allowed for an additional fee of $1 per night per pet. Dogs must be on no more than a 6 foot leash at all times, and proof of a rabies vaccination is required. They may not be left unattended unless they will be quiet and well behaved. The number for reservations is 707-565-CAMP(2267). The camping and tent areas also allow dogs. There is a dog walk area at the campground. There are no electric or water hookups at the campgrounds. Multiple dogs may be allowed.

Porto Bodega Marina and RV Park
1500 Bay Flat Road
Bodega Bay, CA
707-875-2354
This RV park offers 58 RV sites and is located along 16 acres of the bay near a marina where there are a variety of recreation and hiking opportunities available. There is also a sports fishing center on site that allows dogs to go on their boats. Dogs are allowed for no additional fee. Dogs must be well behaved, under owner's control, and leashed and cleaned up after at all times. There is a dog walk area at the campground. Multiple dogs may be allowed.

Westside Regional Park Campground
2400 Westshore Road
Bodega Bay, CA
707-875-3540
This park offers 38 campsites. Fishing is the popular activity at this park. Dogs are allowed but must be on a 6 foot or less leash at all times, and proof of a rabies vaccination is required. There is an additional $1 per night per pet. Dogs may not be left unattended outside unless they will be quiet and well behaved. The camping and tent areas also allow dogs. There is a dog walk area at the campground. There are no

electric or water hookups at the campgrounds. Multiple dogs may be allowed.

Sweetwater Summit Regional Park
3218 Summit Meadow Road
Bonita, CA
619-472-7572 (877-565-3600)
This park offers spectacular views from the summit, various habitats to explore, and offers a wide variety of recreational pursuits. Dogs of all sizes are allowed for an additional $1 per night per pet, and they must have current tags, rabies, and shot records. Dogs may not be left unattended at any time, and they must be on no more than a 6 foot leash and cleaned up after. Dogs are not allowed on the trails, but they may be walked on the payment and along side the roads on leash. The camping and tent areas also allow dogs. There is a dog walk area at the campground. Multiple dogs may be allowed.

Culp Valley Primitive Camp, Anza Borrego State Park
Off Montezuma Valley Road/HS 22
Borrego Springs, CA
760-767-5311
Located in the Anza Borrego park, this park allows dogs of all sizes at no additional fee. Dogs may not be left unattended at any time, and they must be on no more than a 6 foot leash, and cleaned up after. Dogs are not allowed on the hiking trails; they may be walked on paved or dirt roads, or in the camp area. The camping and tent areas also allow dogs. There is a dog walk area at the campground. There are no electric or water hookups at the campgrounds. Multiple dogs may be allowed.

Lake San Antonio Campground
2610 San Antonio Road
Bradley, CA
805-472-2311 (888-588-2267)
lakesanantonio.net/
Lake San Antonio is a premier freshwater recreation area, located just 20 miles inland from California's beautiful Central Coast. Lake San Antonio offers year-round activities including picnicking, camping, fishing, hiking, swimming, boating and water-skiing. Dogs of all sizes are allowed at no additional fee. Dogs must be on no more than a 7 foot leash and be cleaned up after. Dogs are allowed on the trails. The camping and tent areas also allow dogs. There is a dog walk area at the campground. 2 dogs may be allowed.

Honeymoon Flat
P. O. Box 631/Twin Lakes Road
Bridgeport, CA
760-932-7070
This campground is in the Twin Lakes Recreation Area of the Sierra Nevada Mountain Range, and there are a variety of recreational pursuits. Dog of all sizes are allowed at no additional fee. Dogs must be leashed in the camp areas, and cleaned up after at all times. Dogs may be off lead when hiking if they are under voice control, however, they may not be off lead at any time on the Robinson Head Creek Trail. This campground is closed during the off-season. The camping and tent areas also allow dogs. There is a dog walk area at the campground. There are no electric or water hookups at the campgrounds. Multiple dogs may be allowed.

Silver Lake Campground
Forest Road 24N29X/Silver Lake
Bucks Lake, CA
530-283-0555
This tent only campground is located in the Plumas National Forest and offers 8 campsites and vault toilets. There is no water available. Campsites are on a first-come, first-served basis. The trailhead for the Gold Lake Trail is located at this campground. In the campground dogs must be on leash. On the trails, dogs on leash or off-leash but under direct voice control are allowed. Dogs may not be left unattended. From the turn-off, travel 6.4 miles on Road 24N29X, a gravel road. This campground is closed during the off-season. The camping and tent areas also allow dogs. There is a dog walk area at the campground. There are no electric or water hookups at the campgrounds. Multiple dogs may be allowed.

Flying Flags RV Park and Campground
180 Avenue of the Flags
Buellton, CA
805-688-3716
flyingflags.com/
This award winning campground offers beautiful landscaped grounds, grassy pull-thru sites with up to 50 amp service, Wi-Fi, a guest laundry, convenience store, snack bar, pool, spa, and playground. Up to 2 dogs are allowed at no additional fee. If there are more than 2 dogs, then there is a $2 per night per pet fee. Dogs must be leashed at all times and cleaned up after. Dogs may not

be left unattended outside, and they are not allowed in the pool area, playground, or in buildings. There are some breed restrictions. The camping and tent areas also allow dogs. There is a dog walk area at the campground.

McArthur-Burney Falls Memorial State Park
24898 H 89
Burney, CA
530-335-2777 (800-444-PARK (7275))
Formed from volcanic activity, this park also has a rich natural and cultural history, and the park's showcase is the beautiful 129 foot Burney Falls flowing from springs at 100 million gallons a day. There is a variety of land and water recreation and activities to pursue, exhibits, and the park now has Wi-Fi service. Dogs of all sizes are allowed for no additional fee. Dogs are not allowed on the trails or on the beach. Dogs must be under their owner's control at all times, and be leashed and cleaned up after. There are 128 family campsites and 7 primitive sites. Amenities include picnic tables, restrooms, showers, and a dump station. The camping and tent areas also allow dogs. There is a dog walk area at the campground. There are no electric or water hookups at the campgrounds. Multiple dogs may be allowed.

Sierra Trails RV Park
21282 H 14N
California City, CA
877-994-7999
sierratrailsrv.com/
This RV only park offers shade trees, cement patios, lawns, barbecue grills and picnic tables at each site, a heated pool in summer, a rec room, restrooms with showers and a laundry. Dogs of all sizes are allowed at no additional fee. Dogs may not be left unattended outside, and they must be leashed at all times, and cleaned up after. They ask that you walk your pet along the outside of the park, and in another area close by. There are some breed restrictions. Multiple dogs may be allowed.

Napa County Fairgrounds Campground
1435 Oak Street
Calistoga, CA
707-942-5111
Located at the fairgrounds, this campground offers 46 RV/tent sites. RV sites are parallel in the parking

lot and tent sites are located on an adjacent lawn. RV sites have full hookups (some have sewer). Other amenities include restrooms, showers, potable water and disabled accessible. Dogs are allowed but must be on a 10 foot or less leash. Dogs must be well behaved, and please clean up after your pet. For reservations call 707-942-5221. The camping and tent areas also allow dogs. There is a dog walk area at the campground. Multiple dogs may be allowed.

Lake Moreno County Park
2550 Lake Moreno Drive
Campo, CA
858-565-3600
This park of just over 3,200 acres has the distinction because of it's location to have the characteristics of desert, coastal and mountain habitats. It is home to a vast variety of plants, birds, and wildlife. There is a good variety of land and water recreation, many hiking trails including a piece of the Pacific Crest Trail, and they also provide boat rentals; dogs are allowed on the boats. Dogs of all sizes are allowed for camping for an additional fee of $1 per night per pet. Dogs must be leashed and cleaned up after at all times. They are allowed throughout the park and on the trails; they are not allowed at the cabins. The camp area offers 86 individual sites (58 with hook-ups) cozily situated in a majestic grove of oak trees. Some of the amenities include a playground, picnic table, barbecues, and restrooms. The camping and tent areas also allow dogs. There is a dog walk area at the campground. Multiple dogs may be allowed.

New Brighton State Beach
1500 Park Avenue
Capitola, CA
831-464-6330 (800-444-7275)
Rich in natural and cultural history, this park also has various marine and land habitats to explore and a variety of recreational opportunities. Dogs of all sizes are allowed. There are no additional pet fees. Dogs may not be left unattended outside, and they must be on no more than a 6 foot leash at all times, and cleaned up after. Dogs are allowed to walk on the beach. The camping and tent areas also allow dogs. There is a dog walk area at the campground. 2 dogs may be allowed.

San Elijo State Beach Campground
2050 Coast H

Cardiff, CA
760-753-5091 (800-444-7275)
This campground offers RV sites with limited hookups. RVs up to 26 feet can use the hookup sites and RVs up to 35 feet are allowed. They offer both inland and ocean view spaces. While dogs are not allowed at this beach, you can walk to the dog-friendly Cardiff State Beach. The beach is about 1 mile south of Cardiff. Dogs may not be left unattended, and they must be leashed and cleaned up after. There are some breed restrictions. The camping and tent areas also allow dogs. There is a dog walk area at the campground. 2 dogs may be allowed.

Carmel by the River RV Park
27680 Schulte Road
Carmel, CA
831-624-9329
carmelrv.com/CarmelRVpark.htm
This RV park is located right next to the river. Amenities include hookups, a basketball court, recreation room and dog walk area. Per Monterey County's Ordinance, the maximum length per stay from April through September is 14 days and from October through March is 8 weeks. Well-behaved quiet dogs of all sizes are allowed, up to a maximum of three pets. Pets must be kept on a short leash and never left unattended in the campsite or in your RV. People need to clean up after their pets. There is a $2 per night per dog pet fee. The owners have dogs that usually stay at the office. There is a dog walk area at the campground. Multiple dogs may be allowed.

Valencia Travel Resort
27946 Henry Mayo Drive (H 126)
Castaic, CA
661-257-3333
This full service park offers a pool, store, laundry room, meeting room, planned activities, and a variety of recreation. Dogs of all sizes are allowed. There are no additional pet fees. Dogs may not be left unattended outside unless they will be quiet and well behaved. They must be leashed, and cleaned up after. There is also an off-lead dog run area at this RV only park. There are some breed restrictions. There is a dog walk area at the campground. Multiple dogs may be allowed.

Palm Springs Oasis RV Resort
36-100 Date Palm Drive
Cathedral City, CA
800-680-0144

Amidst spectacular views, this parks' amenities include a clubhouse, 2 swimming pools, a spa, an 18 hole executive golf course, and tennis courts to name just a few. Dogs of all sizes are allowed. There are no additional pet fees. Dogs may not be left unattended, and they must be leashed and cleaned up after. The camping and tent areas also allow dogs. There is a dog walk area at the campground. Multiple dogs may be allowed.

The Lakes RV and Golf Resort
1024 Robetson Blvd
Chowchilla, CA
866-665-6980
thelakesrv.com/about.htm
This luxury resort offers many amenities in addition to a wide variety of recreational opportunities. Dogs of all sizes are allowed at no additional fee. Dogs may not be left unattended outside, and they must be quiet, well behaved, on no more than a 6 foot leash, and cleaned up after. Dogs are not allowed in the green belt or pool/spa areas. This campground is closed during the off-season. There is a dog walk area at the campground. Multiple dogs may be allowed.

San Diego Metro
111 N 2nd Avenue
Chula Vista, CA
619-427-3601 (800-562-9877)
koa.com/where/ca/05112/
Only minutes from world class attractions, this resort campground also offers landscaped grounds, 65 feet pull-thru sites with 50 amp, cable TV, swimming pool, hot tub, sauna, and a variety of planned activities and recreation. Dogs of all sizes are allowed for no additional fee. There is a $50 refundable pet deposit for the cabins. Dogs must be under owner's control and visual observation at all times. Dogs must be quiet, well behaved, and be on no more than a 6 foot leash at all times, or otherwise contained. Dogs may not be left unattended outside the owner's camping equipment, and must be brought inside at night. There are some breed restrictions. The camping and tent areas also allow dogs. There is a dog walk area at the campground. Multiple dogs may be allowed.

Funtime RV Park, Cabins and Campground
6035 Old H 53
Clear Lake, CA

707-994-6267
funtimervparks.com/
This family campground offers more than 60 sites and tent camping areas for large groups with plenty of shade trees, and many sites are on the waterfront. Some of the amenities include a private beach, swimming pool, barbecues, gaming courts/areas, a boat launch, laundry facilities, hot showers, and picnic tables. They will allow 2 dogs per site provided they are current on all shots and attended to at all times. Dogs must always be leashed and cleaned up after. They are allowed throughout the park, but they are not allowed in cabins, on the beach, docks, or fishing pier. There are some breed restrictions. The camping and tent areas also allow dogs. There is a dog walk area at the campground. 2 dogs may be allowed.

Island RV Park
12840 Island Drive
Clearlake Oaks, CA
707-998-3940
islandrvpark.com/
Located on a small island in Clear Lake (you will cross a bridge to get to the island), this RV park offers 30 full hookup sites and 4 tent sites. Amenities include laundry facilities, boat ramps and docks and hot showers. Well-behaved leashed dogs are allowed. Please clean up after them. They do not accept credit cards. The camping and tent areas also allow dogs. There is a dog walk area at the campground.

Cloverdale KOA
1166 Asti Ridge Road
Cloverdale, CA
707-894-3337 (800-562-4042)
koa.com/where/ca/05275/
This park is nestled among 100-year-old oak, eucalyptus and evergreen trees, and some of the amenities include a hillside pool and spa, nature trail, pond, gymnastics playground, and various land and water recreation. Dogs of all sizes are allowed for no additional fee. Dogs must be under owner's control and visual observation at all times. Dogs must be quiet, well behaved, and be on no more than a 6 foot leash at all times, or otherwise contained. Dogs may not be left unattended outside the owner's camping equipment. There are some breed restrictions. The camping and tent areas also allow dogs. There is a dog walk area at the campground. Dogs are allowed in the camping

cabins. Multiple dogs may be allowed.

Yosemite South / Coarsegold KOA
34094 H 41
Coarsegold, CA
559-683- 7855 (800-562-7606)
koa.com/where/ca/05449/
There are 30 scenic acres to explore at this park; they also have a playground, gaming areas, a seasonal outdoor theater and swimming pool, Wi-Fi, and cable TV. Dogs are allowed for no additional fee. Dogs may not be left unattended, and they must be on no more than a 6 foot leash and cleaned up after at all times. There is a $250 fine for unauthorized dogs in cabins. There are some breed restrictions. There is a dog walk area at the campground. 2 dogs may be allowed.

Jellystone Park
14117 Bottle Rock Road
Cobb, CA
707-928-4322 (866-928-4322)
jellystonecobbmtn.com/
A family-style resort, this fun campground offers a seasonal paddle boat pond, swimming pool, gaming areas, a playground, outdoor movies, theme weekends, go cart bikes, a camp store, and kids (or adults) can have fun making their own stuffed animal. Dogs are allowed for an additional fee of $3 per night per pet. They may not be left unattended at any time, and they must be leashed and cleaned up after at all times. There are some breed restrictions. The camping and tent areas also allow dogs. There is a dog walk area at the campground. Multiple dogs may be allowed.

Sonora Bridge Campground
Sonora Bridge Road
Coleville, CA
760-932-7070
Dogs of all sizes are allowed. There are no additional pet fees. Dogs may not be left unattended, and they must be leashed and cleaned up after. Dogs may be off lead on the trails only if they will respond to voice command and will not chase wildlife. Dogs are not allowed on the trails that go into Yosemite. This campground is closed during the off-season. The camping and tent areas also allow dogs. There is a dog walk area at the campground. There are no electric or water hookups at the campgrounds. Multiple dogs may be allowed.

49er RV Ranch
23223 Italian Bar Road
Columbia, CA
209-532-4978 (800-446-1333)
49rv.com/
This RV only park is located within a short distance to the dog-friendly Columbia State Historic Park. Park amenities offers full hookups, cable TV, a store, laundry, propane and a modem hookup in the store. Dogs of all sizes are allowed for no additional fee. They ask you take your pet to the pet walk area to do their business, and that you clean up after your pet at all times. Dogs may not be left unattended, and they must be well behaved, and leashed. There is a dog walk area at the campground. Multiple dogs may be allowed.

Rolling Hills Casino
2657 Barham Avenue
Corning, CA
530-528-3500 (888-331-6400)
There are 50 RV sites at this Casino RV park offering security patrol, showers and laundry facilities, not to mention the full range of dining and entertainment opportunities of the casino. Dogs are allowed for no additional fee; they must be leashed and cleaned up after at all times. The casino also provides an air conditioned doggy day care facility for no additional charge that is open from 9 am to 9 pm daily. There is a dog walk area at the campground. Multiple dogs may be allowed.

Woodson Bridge State Recreation Area
25340 South Avenue
Corning, CA
530-839-2112 (800-444-7275)
This beautiful oak wooded park sits along the Sacramento River, and is home to one of the last remaining riparian habitats in California. Fishing and birding are popular here, as are a variety of land and water recreation, and there is easy access to a boat launch ramp across the road. Dogs are allowed for no additional fee. They must be on no more than a 6 foot leash and be cleaned up after at all times. Dogs may be at your campsite and on paved areas only; they are not allowed on the trails. On the east side of the park there are 37 family campsites and a group campsite; the west bank has a boat-in campsite. They are on a first come first served basis when not on reservations. Some the amenities

include fire rings, a laundry, restrooms, and showers. The camping and tent areas also allow dogs. There is a dog walk area at the campground. There are no electric or water hookups at the campgrounds. Multiple dogs may be allowed.

Crescent City KOA
4241 H 101N
Crescent City, CA
707-464-5744 (800-562-5754)
koa.com/where/ca/05102/
This 17 acre campground has 10 acres of camping in the redwood forest. It offers ice cream socials, pancake breakfasts, movie nights, hay rides, snack bar, bike rentals and a maximum pull-thru length of 60 feet with 50 amp service. Dogs of all sizes are allowed for no additional fee. Dogs must be under owner's control and visual observation at all times. Dogs must be quiet, well behaved, and be on no more than a 6 foot leash at all times, or otherwise contained. Dogs may not be left unattended outside the owner's camping equipment. There are some breed restrictions. The camping and tent areas also allow dogs. There is a dog walk area at the campground. Dogs are allowed in the camping cabins. Multiple dogs may be allowed.

De Norte Coast Redwoods State Park
7 miles S of Crescent City off H 101
Crescent City, CA
707-464-6101, ext. 5064
This predominately old growth coastal forest park is known for its steep topography and lush natural setting, and they offer guided tours, exhibits, and a variety of recreational pursuits. Dogs of all sizes are allowed. There are no additional pet fees. Dogs must be leashed and cleaned up after. Dogs are not allowed on the nature trails, but they are allowed on the beach on lead. No swimming, due to high danger, is allowed. This campground is closed during the off-season. The camping and tent areas also allow dogs. There is a dog walk area at the campground. There are no electric or water hookups at the campgrounds. Multiple dogs may be allowed.

Jedediah Smith Redwoods State Park
9 miles east of Crescent City on Highway 199.
Crescent City, CA
707-464-6101, ext. 5112
This predominately old growth

coastal forest of redwoods is home to the last major free flowing river in California. The park is abundant with animal and plant life and offers a variety of interpretive programs, guided tours, and recreational pursuits. Dogs of all sizes are allowed. There are no additional pet fees. Dogs must be leashed and cleaned up after. Dogs are not allowed on the trails, but they are allowed on the beach on lead. The camping and tent areas also allow dogs. There is a dog walk area at the campground. There are no electric or water hookups at the campgrounds.

Mill Creek Campground
1375 Elk Valley Road
Crescent City, CA
707-464-9533 (800-444-PARK (7275))
nps.gov/redw/camping.html
This park is located in a second growth Redwood forest, and offers guided walks, campfire programs, and a variety of recreational pursuits. Dogs of all sizes are allowed. There are no additional pet fees. Dogs must be on no more than a 6 foot leash and cleaned up after. Dogs are not allowed on the beach. They are allowed on the trails unless otherwise marked. This campground is closed during the off-season. The camping and tent areas also allow dogs. There is a dog walk area at the campground. There are no electric or water hookups at the campgrounds. Multiple dogs may be allowed.

Crowley Lake Campground
Crowley Lake Drive
Crowley Lake, CA
760 873-2503
This campground is located in open high desert country at 7,000 feet and has 47 tent and RV sites available. Please note that there are no trees and the winds can be strong. The area overlooks Crowley Lake which is a popular site for fishing. The campground is usually open from late April until the end of October. Camp amenities include 4 pit toilets and pull-thru trailer spaces. All sites are first-come, first-served. This campsite is managed by the BLM (Bureau of Land Management), and there is a $5 per night camping fee. Dogs are allowed at no additional fee, but please keep them under control, and leashed in camp. The closest convenience stores are located in Mammoth Lakes, about 10 miles north of the campground or at a very small store in the Crowley Lake area. After exiting H 395, go

west through the Crowley Lake community for about 2 miles. At Crowley Lake Drive turn north and go about 2 miles. This campground is closed during the off-season. The camping and tent areas also allow dogs. There is a dog walk area at the campground. There are no electric or water hookups at the campgrounds.

Doheny State Beach Park
25300 Dana Point Harbor Drive
Dana Point, CA
949-496-6172 (800-444-PARK (7275))
This park, nestled among the trees on the ocean, offers exhibits, various other programs, and a variety of land and water recreation. Dogs of all sizes are allowed. There are no additional pet fees. Dogs must be leashed and cleaned up after. Dogs are not allowed on the beach. The camping and tent areas also allow dogs. There is a dog walk area at the campground. There are no electric or water hookups at the campgrounds. Multiple dogs may be allowed.

Death Valley National Park Campgrounds
H 190
Death Valley, CA
760-786-3200 (800-365-CAMP (2267))
nps.gov/deva/pphtml/camping.html
There are 10 campgrounds to choose from at this park, ranging from 196 feet below sea level to 8,200 feet above sea level. The Emigrant campground, located at 2,100 feet, offers tent camping only. This free campground offers 10 sites with water, tables and flush toilets. The Furnace Creek campground, located at 196 feet below sea level has 136 sites with water, tables, fireplaces, flush toilets and a dump station. Winter rates are $18 per night and less for the summertime. There are no hookups and some campgrounds do not allow generators. The Stovepipe Wells RV Campground is managed by the Stovepipe Wells Resort and offers 14 sites with full hookups but no tables or fireplaces. See our listing in Death Valley for more information about this RV park. About half of the campgrounds are open all year. Pets must be leashed and attended at all times. Please clean up after your pets. Dogs are not allowed on any trails in Death Valley National Park, but they can walk along

roads. Pets are allowed up to a few hundred yards from the paved and dirt roads. The camping and tent areas also allow dogs. There is a dog walk area at the campground. Multiple dogs may be allowed.

Stovepipe Wells Village Campgrounds and RV Park
H 190
Death Valley, CA
760-786-2387
stovepipewells.com/
In addition to the motel, this establishment also offers a campground and RV park with full hookups. The main building has a restaurant, saloon, gift shops and swimming pool. They are located in the Death Valley National Park. Well-behaved leashed dogs are allowed for no additional fee in the camp area and there is no set number of dogs. There is a $20 refundable deposit for the motel, and only 2 dogs are allowed. Dogs are allowed in public areas only, and they are not allowed on the trails or in the canyon areas. The camping and tent areas also allow dogs. There is a dog walk area at the campground.

Cuyamaca Ranch State Park Campgrounds
12551 H 79
Descanso, CA
760-765 -0755 (800-444-PARK (7275))
This scenic park has two family campgrounds, and some of the amenities include a picnic table, fire ring, barbecue, restrooms with pay showers, and water located near each site. Campsites are $20 per night May 15 through September 15, and $15 the rest of the season. There is an eight person maximum per site. You may bring your own padlock if you wish to lock the cabin during your stay. Dogs are allowed at no additional fee, but restricted to the campgrounds, picnic areas, paved roads, and the Cuyamaca Peak Fire Road. Dogs must be leashed and cleaned up after. They may not be left unattended at any time. This park is located about 15 miles south of the town of Julian. The camping and tent areas also allow dogs. Dogs are allowed in the camping cabins. There are no electric or water hookups at the campgrounds. Multiple dogs may be allowed.

Lawsons Landing Campground
137 Marine View Dr
Dillon Beach, CA
707-878-2726

lawsonslanding.com/camping.htm
This campground is located along the sand dunes a short distance from the Pacific Ocean and Tomales Bay. There are rest rooms but no shower facilities and there are dump stations. Dogs on leash are allowed in the campground and on the beach. There are no electric or water hookups at the campsite. During wet times the campground may be closed so for information on current conditions call 707-878-2443.

Dinkey Creek Campground
Dinkey Creek Road
Dinkey Creek, CA
559-297-0706 (877-444-6777)
This campground is next to Dinkey Creek in the Sierra National Forest. The campground is on a large sandy flat above the river and shaded by cedar and pine trees at an elevation of 5,400 feet. There are 128 tent and RV sites. RVs up to 35 feet are allowed. Amenities include piped water, flush toilets, picnic tables and grills. There are several trails that start at this campground. Dogs are allowed at the campgrounds, on trails, and in the water, but only at non-designated swimming beaches. Pets must be leashed and please clean up after them. Dogs must be quiet and well behaved. This campground is closed during the off-season. The camping and tent areas also allow dogs. There is a dog walk area at the campground. There are no electric or water hookups at the campgrounds. Multiple dogs may be allowed.

Rocky Rest Campground
H 49
Downieville, CA
530-288-3231
This 10 site campground is located at the Yuba River District in the Tahoe National Forest at a 2,200 foot elevation. Amenities include piped water and vault toilets. The North Yuba trailhead is located at this campground. Pets must be leashed in the campsite and please clean up after your pets. Dogs are not allowed to be left unattended outside. This campground is closed during the off-season. The camping and tent areas also allow dogs. There is a dog walk area at the campground. There are no electric or water hookups at the campgrounds. Multiple dogs may be allowed.

Casini Ranch Family Campground
22855 Moscow Road
Duncans Mills, CA

707-865-2255 (800-451-8400)
casiniranch.com
This beautiful family campground lies along the Russian River, offers great scenery, fishing, trails, and a variety of recreation. Dogs of all sizes are allowed for an additional $1 per night per pet. Dogs may not be left unattended, and they must be quiet, leashed at all times, and cleaned up after. Dogs must be inside at night, and they are not allowed in the livestock areas. Dogs are allowed on the trails on lead. The camping and tent areas also allow dogs. There is a dog walk area at the campground. Multiple dogs may be allowed.

Railroad Park Resort
100 Railroad Park Road
Dunsmuir, CA
530-235-4440
rrpark.com/rvpark/
This RV park is located at the foot of the grand Castle Crags, and their features/amenities include a swimming hole, a game room, flush toilets, hot showers, laundry facilities, and a group barbecue pit. Dogs of all sizes are allowed for no additional fee. Dogs must be friendly, leashed, and cleaned up after. This RV park is closed during the off-season. The camping and tent areas also allow dogs. There is a dog walk area at the campground. Multiple dogs may be allowed.

Desert Trails RV Park and Golf Course
225 Wake Avenue
El Centro, CA
760-352-PARK (7275)
deserttrailsrv.com/
Each season brings a variety of recreational activities at this park. It is a bird watchers haven in the winter months. Some of the features/amenities here include a pool and spa, laundry and restroom facilities, cable TV, a recreation room, and a 9-hole executive golf course. Dogs of all sizes are allowed for no additional fee, and there is a special dog run for canine visitors. Dogs must be well mannered, and leashed and cleaned up after at all times. Dogs are not allowed on the golf course. There are some breed restrictions. There is a dog walk area at the campground. 2 dogs may be allowed.

Sunland RV Resorts
1740 Seven Oaks Road
Escondido, CA

760-740-5000 (800-331-3556)
sunlandrvresorts.com
This lushly landscaped resort park is a favorite family and pet-friendly retreat, and they have a pet walking and play area, many amenities, and a variety of recreational opportunities. Dogs of all sizes are allowed for an additional $3 per night per pet. Dogs must be leashed at all times, and cleaned up after. Dogs are not allowed in buildings or the pool area. There are some breed restrictions. There is a dog walk area at the campground. There are special amenities given to dogs at this campground. 2 dogs may be allowed.

Eureka KOA
4050 N H 101
Eureka, CA
707-822-4243 (800-562-3136)
koa.com/where/ca/05122/
Located along Humboldt Bay in the heart of the giant redwood country, this well-kept park offers a maximum length pull-thru of 70 feet with 50 amp service. Some amenities include cable TV, two playgrounds, a swimming pool, family hot tub, adults-only hot tub, horseshoe pits, rental bikes, a camp store, and ice cream socials during the summer months. Dogs of all sizes are allowed for an additional fee of $3 per night per pet. Dogs must be under owner's control and visual observation at all times. Dogs must be quiet, well behaved, and be on no more than a 6 foot leash at all times, or otherwise contained. Dogs may not be left unattended outside the owner's camping equipment. There are some breed restrictions. The camping and tent areas also allow dogs. There is a dog walk area at the campground. Dogs are allowed in the camping cabins. Multiple dogs may be allowed.

Big Bear Shores RV Resort and Yacht Club
40751 North Shore Lane
Fawnskin, CA
909-866-4151
bigbearshores.com
This gated resort offers a fully equipped private health club in addition to other recreational pursuits. Dogs of all sizes are allowed at an additional $10 per night per pet. Dogs may not be left unattended outside, and not left inside unless they will be quiet and well behaved. Dogs must be leashed and cleaned up after. Dogs are allowed on the trails. There is a dog

walk area at the campground. 2 dogs may be allowed.

Hanna Flat Campground
Rim of the World Drive
Fawnskin, CA
909-382-2790 (877-444-6777)
This 88 site campground, of tall pines, wildflowers and wild roses, is located in the San Bernardino National Forest at an elevation of 7,000 feet. RVs up to 40 feet are allowed. Amenities include picnic tables, fire rings, paved parking, flush toilets and trash dumpster. The Hanna Flat Trailhead is located at this camp. Pets on leash are allowed and please clean up after them. Dogs may not be left unattended. To get there take Highway 18 to Big Bear Lake Dam. Go straight, do not cross over the dam. Highway 18 becomes Highway 38. Go the Fawnskin Fire Station and turn left onto the Rim of the World Drive. Go about 2.5 miles on a dirt road to the campsite. This campground is closed during the off-season. The camping and tent areas also allow dogs. There is a dog walk area at the campground. There are no electric or water hookups at the campgrounds. Multiple dogs may be allowed.

Holcomb Valley Campground
40971 North Shore Drive
Fawnskin, CA
909-866-3437
This tent and RV campground is located in the historic Holcomb Valley about a mile from the Belleville Ghost Town. See our listing under Big Bear Lake for more information about the ghost town. There is no water at the campsite. Camp amenities include toilets. The sites are on a first-come, first-served basis. Pets are allowed but must be leashed at all times, picked up after, and they cannot be left unattended. Watch out for rattlesnakes, especially during the warm summer months. The campground is located in the San Bernardino National Forest. Dogs are allowed on the trails on lead. The camping and tent areas also allow dogs. There is a dog walk area at the campground. There are no electric or water hookups at the campgrounds. Multiple dogs may be allowed.

Beals Point Campground
7806 Folsom-Auburn Road
Folsom, CA
916-988-0205 (800-444-PARK (7275))
This park, located on shores of

Folsom Lake, offers miles of hiking trails, and a wide variety of recreational opportunities. Dogs of all sizes are allowed. There are no additional pet fees. Dogs must be on no more than a 6 foot leash and cleaned up after. Dogs are not allowed at the main swimming beaches. Dogs are allowed on the trails. The camping and tent areas also allow dogs. There is a dog walk area at the campground. There are no electric or water hookups at the campgrounds. Multiple dogs may be allowed.

French Meadows Reservoir Campground
Mosquito Ridge Road
Foresthill, CA
530-367-2224
Located in the Tahoe National Forest, this 75 site campground is at an elevation of 5,300 feet. The campground is next to the French Meadows Reservoir. Camp amenities include piped water and flush/vault toilets. Pets are allowed but must be leashed in the campground. The campsite is located 36 miles east of Foresthill on Mosquito Ridge Road. Call to make a reservation. Dogs are allowed on the trails. This campground is closed during the off-season. The camping and tent areas also allow dogs. There is a dog walk area at the campground. There are no electric or water hookups at the campgrounds. Multiple dogs may be allowed.

Robinson Flat Campground
Foresthill Divide Road
Foresthill, CA
530-367-2224
This campground is located at an elevation of 6,800 feet in the Tahoe National Forest, near the Little Bald Mountain Trail. The campground offer 14 sites (7 family sites and 7 equestrian sites) on a first-come, first-served basis. Amenities include well water and vault toilets. There is no fee. Pet must be on leash in the campground. Please clean up after your pets. To get there, go 28 miles from Foresthill on Foresthill Divide Road to Robinson Flat. This campground is closed during the off-season. The camping and tent areas also allow dogs. There is a dog walk area at the campground. There are no electric or water hookups at the campgrounds. Multiple dogs may be allowed.

East Fork Campground

Salmon River Road
Forks of Salmon, CA
530-468-5351
This Klamath National Forest campground has 9 camp sites with no water but there are vault toilets. There is no charge for a camp site. Hiking from the East Fork Campground provides access to the lakes in the Caribou Basin, Rush Creek, and Little South Fork drainages. The campground is located 27 miles southwest of Callahan next to the East and the South Forks of the Salmon River. It sits at a 2,600 foot elevation. Dogs of all sizes are allowed at no additional fee. Dogs may not be left unattended outside, except for short periods, and only if they will be quiet and well behaved. Dogs must be leashed in camp and cleaned up after. Dogs are allowed on the trails, and they may be off lead on the trails if they will respond to voice command. This campground is closed during the off-season. The camping and tent areas also allow dogs. There is a dog walk area at the campground. There are no electric or water hookups at the campgrounds. Multiple dogs may be allowed.

Dolphin Isle Marina
32399 Basin Drive
Fort Bragg, CA
707-964-4113 (866-964-4113)
dolphinisle.com/
This lush vacation spot features beautiful views of the Noyo River, and they offer a full service marina, a deli with patio dining, a store, free wireless internet service, and RV camping. The camp area offers showers and a laundry room. Dogs of all sizes are allowed for no additional fee. They are allowed throughout the park and at the deli patio dining area. Dogs must be well behaved, leashed and cleaned up after. This RV park is closed during the off-season. There is a dog walk area at the campground. Multiple dogs may be allowed.

Pomo RV Park and Campground
17999 Tregoning Lane
Fort Bragg, CA
707-964-3373
infortbragg.com/pomorvpark
This small scenic park offers a good variety of recreational opportunities. They have a "major holiday dog policy", wherein dogs must remain on the owners campsite only. No walking of dogs in the park is allowed on major holidays and dogs may not be left alone on campsites for any

reason. Dogs of all sizes are allowed for an additional $1 per night per dog. Dogs must be leashed and cleaned up after. There are some breed restrictions. The camping and tent areas also allow dogs. There is a dog walk area at the campground. Multiple dogs may be allowed.

Bridge Flat Campground
Scott River Road
Fort Jones, CA
530-468-5351 (877-444-6777)
This Klamath National Forest campground offers 4 camp sites with no water but there are vault toilets. There are no fees. Popular activities include hiking and fishing. The campground is open from May to October. The Kelsey Trail begins at this camp site. The campground is located on the Scott River approximately 17 miles from Fort Jones towards the town of Scott Bar, at a 2,000 foot elevation. Dogs must be on lead at all times in developed sites. They may be off lead on the trails if they are under voice control. Dogs may not be left unattended outside, except for short periods. This campground is closed during the off-season. The camping and tent areas also allow dogs. There is a dog walk area at the campground. There are no electric or water hookups at the campgrounds. Multiple dogs may be allowed.

Millerton Lake State Recreation Area
47597 Road 145 (campground) 5290 Millerton Road (day use)
Friant, CA
559-822-2332
This popular park offers lush rolling hills and over 40 miles of shoreline allowing for ample recreational opportunities. Dogs of all sizes are allowed. There are no additional pet fees. Dogs must be on no more than a 6 foot leash and cleaned up after. Dogs are not allowed in park buildings, on trails, or on most beaches. Dogs may be walked in the campgrounds, along the shoreline, or on the side of the roads on lead. The camping and tent areas also allow dogs. There is a dog walk area at the campground. Multiple dogs may be allowed.

Benbow Valley RV Resort and Golf Course
7000 Benbow Drive
Garberville, CA
707-923-2777 (866) BENBOWRV (236-2697))
benbowrv.com
This beautiful full service resort

offers many amenities in addition to a wide variety of recreation. Dogs of all sizes are allowed for an additional $3 per night per pet. Dogs may not be left unattended outside, and left inside only if they will be quiet and well behaved. Dogs must be on no more than a 6 foot leash and be cleaned up after. They are also adjacent to a state park where there are several hiking trails. This is an RV only park. This campground is closed during the off-season. There is a dog walk area at the campground. 2 dogs may be allowed.

Richardson Grove Campground
750 H 101
Garberville, CA
70 7-247-3380
redwoodfamilycamp.com/
This well kept camp area also offers a chapel on site and a variety of family and age-appropriate church camps. Some of the amenities include a general store, high-speed internet, a laundry, showers, and restrooms. Dogs of all sizes are allowed for no additional fee. They must have a current license and proof of vaccinations. Dogs must be under owner's immediate control, and leashed and cleaned up after at all times. Pets may not be left unattended on site, and they must be walked in the designated areas only. Although sites are on a first come first served basis, reservations are suggested between June 1st and October 1st. The camping and tent areas also allow dogs. There is a dog walk area at the campground. Multiple dogs may be allowed.

Panther Flat Campground
Mile Post 16.75 H 199
Gasquet, CA
707-442-1721 (877-444-6777)
This campground is located in the Smith River National Recreation Area and is part of the Six Rivers National Forest. The campground offers 39 tent and RV sites. RVs up to 40 feet are allowed. Amenities include flush restrooms, pay shower, potable water, picnic tables, grills, fishing, and sites with river and scenic views. Pets on leash are allowed at no additional fee, and please clean up after them. Dogs are allowed on the trails in the National Forest on lead but not on State Park trails. The camping and tent areas also allow dogs. There is a dog walk area at the campground. There are no electric or water

hookups at the campgrounds. Multiple dogs may be allowed.

El Capitan State Beach
10 Refugio Beach Road
Goleta, CA
805-968-1033 (800-444-PARK (7275))
Set among sycamores and oaks along El Capitán Creek, this park offers rocky tide pools, a sandy beach, and a variety of land and water recreation. Dogs of all sizes are allowed at no additional fee. Dogs may not be left unattended at any time, and they must be leashed and cleaned up after. Dogs are not allowed on the beach. The camping and tent areas also allow dogs. There is a dog walk area at the campground. There are no electric or water hookups at the campgrounds. 2 dogs may be allowed.

Kirk Creek Campground
H 1
Gorda, CA
831-385-5434
Located in the Los Padres National Forest, this campground is situated on an open bluff 100 feet above sea level and offers great views of the ocean and coastline. The beach is reached by hiking down from the campgrounds. The Kirk Creek trailhead is also located at the campground and leads to the Vicente Flat Trail which offers miles of hiking trails. Dogs are allowed in the campgrounds, on the hiking trails, and on the beach, but they must be leashed. Dogs must be cleaned up after. Be aware that there are large amounts of poison oak on the trails. RVs up to 30 feet are permitted. The campground is located about 25 miles south of Big Sur. There is no additional fee for pets, but dogs must have proof of rabies vaccinations and current shot records. Dogs may not be left unattended outside, and left inside an RV only if they will be quiet and comfortable. The camping and tent areas also allow dogs. There is a dog walk area at the campground. There are no electric or water hookups at the campgrounds. 2 dogs may be allowed.

Plaskett Creek Campground
H 1
Gorda, CA
831-385-5434 (877-444-6677)
Located in the Los Padres National Forest, this tent and RV campground is nestled among large Monterey Pine trees. The campsites are within

walking distance of the dog-friendly Sand Dollar Beach. Dogs of all sizes are allowed at no additional fee. Dogs may not be left unattended outside, and left inside only if they will be quiet and comfortable. Dogs must be leashed in the campgrounds, on trails, on the beach, and have proof of current shots. The campground is about 5 miles south of the Kirk Creek and about 30 miles south of Big Sur. The camping and tent areas also allow dogs. There is a dog walk area at the campground. There are no electric or water hookups at the campgrounds. 2 dogs may be allowed.

Lakes Basin Campground
County Road 519
Graeagle, CA
530-836-2575 (877-444-6777)
Glaciers formed the special geological features of this park that is located in the Plumas National Forest, and it is known for it's spectacular scenery and numerous clear lakes. Amenities include water, vault toilets and trailer space. Located at this campground is the trailhead for the Grassy Lake Trail. In the campground dogs must be on leash. On the trails, dogs on leash or off-leash, but under direct voice control, are allowed. Owners must clean up after their pets. This campground is closed during the off-season. The camping and tent areas also allow dogs. There is a dog walk area at the campground. There are no electric or water hookups at the campgrounds. Multiple dogs may be allowed.

Gualala Point Regional Park Campgrounds
42401 Coast H 1
Gualala, CA
707-785-2377
This dog-friendly park offers sandy beaches, hiking trails and 20 campsites. RVs are permitted and there is a dump station. Dogs are allowed but must be on a 6 foot or less leash at all times, be cleaned up after, and have proof of rabies vaccination. There is an additional fee of $1 per night per pet. Reservations are taken by telephone at 707-565-CAMP(2267). The camping and tent areas also allow dogs. There is a dog walk area at the campground. There are no electric or water hookups at the campgrounds. Multiple dogs may be allowed.

Dawn Ranch Lodge
16467 H 116

Guerneville, CA
707-869-0656
fifes.com/
Located on 15 acres and among redwood trees, this guest ranch offers individual cabins, cottages and tent camping. Amenities include a pool, volleyball court, gym and onsite massages. Well-behaved dogs of all sizes are allowed in the campsites, cabins, and cottages for an additional fee of $50 per stay. Dogs are allowed on the trails nearby and on the beach. This campground is closed during the off-season. There is a dog walk area at the campground. 2 dogs may be allowed.

Norcross Campground
Elk Creek Road
Happy Camp, CA
530-493-1777
This 6 site campground is located in the Klamath National Forest at an elevation of 2,400 feet. Amenities include vault toilets. The campground is open from May to October. This campground serves as a staging area for various trails that provide access into the Marble Mountain Wilderness. The trails are used by hikers and horseback riders. Dogs must be leashed in the campground. On trails, pets must be either leashed or off-leash but under direct voice control. Please clean up after your pets. Dogs may not be left unattended outside your unit, except for short periods. The campsite is located 16 miles south of Happy Camp on Elk Creek Road. This campground is closed during the off-season. The camping and tent areas also allow dogs. There is a dog walk area at the campground. There are no electric or water hookups at the campgrounds. Multiple dogs may be allowed.

Hat Creek Campground
H 89
Hat Creek, CA
530-336-5521 (877-444-6777)
This campground is located in the Lassen National Forest at an elevation of 4,300 feet. The camp offers 75 campsites. Camp amenities include water, fire rings, picnic tables and restrooms. Most sites are available on a first-come, first-served basis. Some sites can be reserved. Dogs on leash are allowed at the campground and on trails. Please clean up after your dog. Dogs must be quiet, well behaved, and have current shot records. This campground is closed

during the off-season. The camping and tent areas also allow dogs. There is a dog walk area at the campground. There are no electric or water hookups at the campgrounds. Multiple dogs may be allowed.

Casa de Fruta, RV Orchard Resort
10031 Pacheco Pass H
Hollister, CA
408-842-9316 (800-548-3813 (Information))
casadefruta.com/VISIT_accom.aspx
This RV park is located at a popular roadside orchard resort which features a fruit stand, store, 24 hour restaurant, zoo, rock shop, gold panning, children's train ride, children's playground and picnic areas. Amenities at the RV park include full hookups, pull-thru sites, shady areas, TV hookups and seasonal tent sites. Well-behaved leashed dogs are allowed. Dogs may not be left unattended. There is a $3 per night pet fee per pet. Please clean up after your pets. The resort is located on Highway 152/Pacheco Pass, two miles east of the Highway 156 junction. The camping and tent areas also allow dogs. There is a dog walk area at the campground. Multiple dogs may be allowed.

Bolsa Chica State Beach Campground
Pacific Coast H
Huntington Beach, CA
714-377-5691 (800-444-7275)
Most RVs can be accommodated at this campground, just let them know when making a reservation if your RV is over 25 feet. Tent camping is not allowed. Pets on leash are allowed and please clean up after them. While dogs are not allowed on this state beach, they are allowed on several miles of paved trails that follow the coast. Dogs are also allowed at the adjacent Huntington Dog Beach. The campground is located on the Pacific Coast Highway between Golden West to Warner Avenue. There is a dog walk area at the campground.

Huntington By the Sea
21871 Newland
Huntington Beach, CA
714-536-8316 (800-439-3486)
huntingtonbythesea.com
If you love the beach and everything about it, then you will love this RV park, which also provides a host of amenities. Dogs of all sizes are allowed. There are no additional pet fees. Dogs may not be left unattended outside, and they must

be leashed and cleaned up after. This is an RV only park. There are some breed restrictions. There is a dog walk area at the campground. Multiple dogs may be allowed.

Goodale Creek Campground
Aberdeen Cutoff Road
Independence, CA
760-872-5000
This campground is located at a 4,000 foot elevation on a volcanic flow, next to Goodale Creek. It offers great views of the Sierra Nevada Mountains. There are 62 tent and RV sites available, 5 pit toilets, picnic tables and campfire rings/stands. The campground is usually open from late April to the end of October. There are no fees, no hookups and no drinking water. All sites are on a first-come, first-served basis. Be aware of rattlesnakes in the area, especially during the summer months. The closest convenience stores are located in the towns of Independence and Big Pine. Dogs are allowed at the campground, but please keep them under control, and they must be leashed and cleaned up after. Dogs are allowed on the trails on lead. The camping and tent areas also allow dogs. There is a dog walk area at the campground. There are no electric or water hookups at the campgrounds. Multiple dogs may be allowed.

Indian Wells RV Resort
47-340 Jefferson Street
Indio, CA
800-789-0895
This RV only resort offers many amenities such as three swimming pools, two spas, shuffleboard courts, basketball courts, pavilion with gas grills, billiards, horseshoes, fitness area, library, modem hookup, putting green, laundry facility, computer center and even a dog run. Site amenities include full hook-ups with 50 amp service, electric, water, sewer, paved pad and patio, and phone service for stays of 30 days or longer. Well-behaved leashed dogs are welcome. Please clean up after your pet. There is no pet fee. Dogs may not be left unattended outside. There is a dog walk area at the campground. Multiple dogs may be allowed.

Brannan Island KOA
922 W Brannan Island Road
Isleton, CA
916-777-5588 (800-562-9105)
koa.com/where/ca/05447/
There is a full service marina, free

Wi-Fi, plenty of shady sites, gaming courts, a rec room with a big screen TV and lots more to be enjoyed at this campground. Dogs are allowed for no additional fee. Dogs may not be left unattended outside, and they may only be left alone inside if they will be quiet. Dogs must be on no more than a 6 foot leash and cleaned up after at all times. The camping and tent areas also allow dogs. There is a dog walk area at the campground. There are special amenities given to dogs at this campground. 2 dogs may be allowed.

Salt Point State Park
2050 H 1
Jenner, CA
707-847-3221
Enjoy panoramic views and the dramatic sounds of the surf at this park that offers a variety of sights and recreational activities. This park is also home to one of the first underwater parks in California. Dogs of all sizes are allowed at the campgrounds and in any of the developed areas. Dogs are not allowed on the trails or on the beaches, and they must be inside at night. There is no additional pet fee. Dogs must be leashed and cleaned up after at all times. Campsites are all equipped with a fire ring, picnic tables, and a food locker except for the overflow camping area. There is drinking water and restrooms, but there are no showers or a dump station. The camping and tent areas also allow dogs. There is a dog walk area at the campground. There are no electric or water hookups at the campgrounds. Multiple dogs may be allowed.

Stillwater Cove Regional Park
Campgrounds
22455 H 1
Jenner, CA
707-847-3245
This 210 acre park offers 17 campsites. RVs are permitted and there is a dump station. The park also features a small beach, great views of the Pacific Ocean, picnic tables and restrooms. Dogs are allowed but must be on a 6 foot or less leash and proof of a rabies vaccination is required. There is an additional fee of $1 per night per pet. Please clean up after your pet. The camping and tent areas also allow dogs. There is a dog walk area at the campground. There are no electric or water hookups at the campgrounds. Multiple dogs may

be allowed.

Redwood Meadow Campground
Off Mountain Road 50 on Western Divide H/M 107
Johnsondale, CA
559-539-2607 (877-444-6777)
This campground is located in the Sequoia National Forest at an elevation of 6,100 feet. It is across the road from the Trail of a Hundred Giants. The campground offers 15 tent and small RV sites. RVs up to 16 feet are allowed. Vault toilets are located at the camp. Ideal camping is from May to October. Pets must be on no more than a 6 foot leash and attended to at all times. Please clean up after your pet. The campsite is located about 45 miles northwest of Kernville. This campground is closed during the off-season. The camping and tent areas also allow dogs. There is a dog walk area at the campground. There are no electric or water hookups at the campgrounds. Multiple dogs may be allowed.

Lake Cuamaca
15027 H 79
Julian, CA
760-765-0515 (877-581-9904)
lakecuyamaca.org/
This campground has 40 RV sites, 14 tent sites, and 2 cabins located next a popular fishing lake. There is a 3.5 mile trail surrounding the lake. Dogs on leash are welcome both in the campground and on the trail, but they are not allowed in the water and must stay at least 50 feet from the shore. Dogs are, however, allowed to go on the rental boats. People must clean up after their pets. The camping and tent areas also allow dogs. There is a dog walk area at the campground. Dogs are allowed in the camping cabins. Multiple dogs may be allowed.

Pinezanita Trailer Ranch and
Campground
4446 H 79
Julian, CA
760-765-0429
pinezanita.com/
They have a fishing pond which is stocked with blue gill and catfish. You can find fishing tackle and bait in the Campground Registration Office. Dogs are not allowed in the cabins, but they are welcome to stay with you at your RV, trailer, or campsite. There is a $2 per day per pet charge. Pets must be on a 6 foot or shorter leash at all times. Noisy pets are cause for eviction. Carry plastic bags or a pooper scooper and pick up

after your pet. The camping and tent areas also allow dogs. There is a dog walk area at the campground. Multiple dogs may be allowed.

Stagecoach Trails RV Equestrian and Wildlife Resort
7878 Great Southern Overland Stage Route of 1849
Julian, CA
760-765-2197 (877-TWO CAMP (896-2267))
stagecoachtrails.com
This scenic desert resort park has an historical, natural, cultural history to share in addition to many amenities and recreational pursuits. Dogs of all sizes are allowed at no additional fee. Dogs may not be left unattended, and they must be quiet, well behaved, leashed, and cleaned up after. Dogs are allowed on the trails unless otherwise indicated. This is an RV only park. There is a dog walk area at the campground. Multiple dogs may be allowed.

William Heise County Park
4945 Heise Park Road
Julian, CA
760-765-0650 (877-565-3600)
Dogs of all sizes are allowed for an additional $1 per night per pet, and they must have current tags, rabies, and shot records. Dogs may not be left unattended at any time, and they must be on no more than a 6 foot leash and cleaned up after. Dogs are not allowed on the trails, but they may be walked on the payment and along side the roads on leash. The camping and tent areas also allow dogs. There is a dog walk area at the campground. There are no water hookups at the campgrounds. Multiple dogs may be allowed.

June Lake RV Park
155 Crawford Avenue
June Lake, CA
760-648-7967
This full service campground is located between June Lake and Gulf Lake in the June Lake area. The campground is within walking distance of both lakes. There are full hook ups, cable TV, and a laundry room. This is an RV campground only; tent camping is not allowed. There are no public bathrooms or showers. Dogs are allowed, they must be on a leash at all times. Dogs must be picked up after. The campground is open from April through October annually.

Pine Cliffs Resort
P.O. Box 38

June Lake, CA
760-648-7558
Pine Cliff Resort RV park is located right on June Lake. It is a full-service campground with a general store, propane, a laundry and showers. Dogs are allowed in the campground in RVs and in tents. They must be leashed and cleaned up after.

Silver Lake Resort
6957 H 158
June Lake, CA
760-648-7572
This resort, located on the shore of Silver Lake, offers great views and amenities that include a general store, cafe, showers, restrooms, laundry room and picnic area. Well-behaved dogs of all sizes are allowed at no additional fee. Dogs must be leashed, and walked outside of the park, and please clean up after your pet in the Sierra National Forest. The resort is open from the end of April to mid-October. This is an RV only park. This campground is closed during the off-season. The camping and tent areas also allow dogs. There is a dog walk area at the campground. Multiple dogs may be allowed.

Clear Lake State Park
5300 Soda Bay Road
Kelseyville, CA
707-279-4293 (800-444-7275)
This park offers 149 campsites for RV or tent camping, and is located along the shores of California's largest freshwater lake. Amenities include picnic tables, restrooms, showers and grills. While dogs are not allowed on the trails or the swimming beaches at this park, they are allowed in the campgrounds and in the water at non-designated swim areas. One of the non-designated swim beaches is located between campgrounds 57 and 58. Pets must be on leash at all times, and please clean up after them. The park is located 3.5 miles northeast of Kelseyville. The camping and tent areas also allow dogs. There is a dog walk area at the campground. There are no electric or water hookups at the campgrounds. Multiple dogs may be allowed.

Edgewater Resort and RV Park
6420 Soda Bay Road
Kelseyville, CA
707-279-0208 (800-396-6224)
edgewaterresort.net/
This resort is located in a natural

park-like setting with plenty of shade trees in a protected cove on the shores of California's largest natural lake. Some of the amenities include a lakefront clubhouse, cable TV, a general store, a fish cleaning station, gaming areas, spotless restrooms, showers and laundry facilities, picnic tables, barbecues, and fire pits. Well behaved dogs of all sizes are allowed for an additional fee of $2.50 per night per pet for RV and tent camping, and an additional $10 per night per pet for the cabins. Dogs will receive a 'guest at Edgewater Resort' locater tag, and they must be current on all their shots, be friendly, under owner's immediate control, and leashed and quickly cleaned up after at all times. Dogs may not be left outside alone or unattended anywhere in the park, and they may only be left alone in the cabin if they are kenneled. Dogs are allowed throughout the park and at the beach; they may even go for a supervised off-leash swim if they are under good voice command. They are not allowed in the general store, clubhouse, or the gated pool area, but there is fresh water for thirsty canine visitors outside the store. Dogs must always be brought inside at night. The camping and tent areas also allow dogs. There is a dog walk area at the campground. Dogs are allowed in the camping cabins. 2 dogs may be allowed.

Rivernook Campground
14001 Sierra Way
Kernville, CA
760-376-2705
gocampingamerica.com/rivernook/
This park is nestled in 60 wooded acres along the scenic Kern River and offers a variety of land and water recreation. Dogs of all sizes are allowed. There are no additional pet fees. Dogs may not be left unattended outside, and left inside only if they will be quiet, well behaved, and physically comfortable. Dogs must be leashed and cleaned up after. The camping and tent areas also allow dogs. There is a dog walk area at the campground. Multiple dogs may be allowed.

San Lorenzo Campground and RV Park
1160 Broadway
King City, CA
831-385-5964
This campground is located in the dog-friendly San Lorenzo Park where leashed dogs are allowed on the hiking trails. Camp amenities include

grassy tent sites, shaded RV spaces, an information center and museum, a walking trail along the river, laundry facilities, a putting green, playground, internet access kiosk, restrooms, and showers. Well-behaved leashed dogs of all sizes are allowed in the campground. Pets must be attended at all times. People need to clean up after their pets. There is a $2 per night per pet fee. Dogs are allowed on the trails, on roads, and at a place on the other side of the levy. The camping and tent areas also allow dogs. There is a dog walk area at the campground. 2 dogs may be allowed.

Mystic Forest RV Park
15875 H 101
Klamath, CA
707-482-4901
mysticforestrv.com/
This scenic camp area offers a natural environment with lots of shade trees and grass. Some of the amenities include a gift shop, small store, a club house, recreation room, a laundry, showers and restrooms, lots of hiking trails, and an 18-hole miniature golf course. Dogs of all sizes are allowed for no additional fee. Dogs must be under owner's immediate control, leashed, cleaned up after, and they may not be left unattended in vehicles or outside. Dogs are allowed throughout the park and on the trails. The camping and tent areas also allow dogs. There is a dog walk area at the campground. 2 dogs may be allowed.

Sunland RV Resort - San Diego
7407 Alvarado Road
La Mesa, CA
619-469-4697 (877-787-6386)
sdrvresort.com/default.asp
In addition to an abundance of land and water recreation, this beautiful RV park offers all the amenities of a luxury resort. Dogs of all sizes are allowed for an additional fee of $3 per night per pet. Dogs may not be left unattended outside, and they must be leashed and cleaned up after. Dogs are not allowed in the buildings. This is an RV only park. There are some breed restrictions. There is a dog walk area at the campground. 2 dogs may be allowed.

Little Beaver Campground, Feather River District
off Forest Road 120/La Porte Road
La Porte, CA
530-534-6500 (877-444-6777)

This campground is located at the Little Grass Valley Reservoir Recreation Area in the Plumas National Forest. There are 120 campsites, some of which offer prime lakeside sites. Amenities include water, flush toilets, trailer space, and an RV dump station. Dogs are allowed in the campgrounds, on trails and in the water. In the campground dogs must be on leash. On the trails, dogs on leash or off-leash but under direct voice control are allowed. Dogs may not be left unattended outside. Please clean up after your pet. This campground is closed during the off-season. The camping and tent areas also allow dogs. There is a dog walk area at the campground. There are no electric or water hookups at the campgrounds. Multiple dogs may be allowed.

Samuel P. Taylor State Park
8889 Sir Francis Drake Blvd
Lagunitas, CA
415-488-9897 (800-444-PARK (7275))
This park is home to a unique contrast of coastal redwood groves, open grassland and flowers. Amenities include water, tables, grills, flush toilets and showers. Dogs of all sizes are allowed at no additional fee. While dogs are not allowed on the hiking trails, they are allowed on the bike trail that runs about six miles through the park. The path is nearly level and follows the Northwest Pacific Railroad right-of-way. The trail is both paved and dirt and it starts near the park entrance. Dogs are also allowed in the developed areas like the campgrounds. Pets must be leashed, and please clean up after your pet. Dogs may not be left unattended. The camping and tent areas also allow dogs. There is a dog walk area at the campground. There are no electric or water hookups at the campgrounds. Multiple dogs may be allowed.

North Shore Campground
Torrey Road
Lake Arrowhead, CA
909-337-2444 (877-444-6777)
This 27 site campground is located in the San Bernardino National Forest at 5,300 feet. RVs up to 22 feet are allowed and there are no hookups. The trailhead for the North Shore National Recreation Trail is located at this campground. Pets on leash are allowed at no additional

fee, and please clean up after them. Dogs are allowed on the trails. The camp is located near the north shore of Lake Arrowhead, about two miles northeast of the village. To get there from the Lake Arrowhead Marina, go east on Torrey Road. At the first left, take the dirt road to Forest Road 2N25 to the trailhead. This campground is closed during the off-season. The camping and tent areas also allow dogs. There is a dog walk area at the campground. There are no electric or water hookups at the campgrounds. Multiple dogs may be allowed.

Antlers RV Park and Campground
20682 Antlers Road
Lakehead, CA
530-238-2322 (800-642-6849)
antlersrvpark.com/
This camping area is located on beautiful Shasta Lake, and they provide some fun activities such as movies Tuesday thru Sunday, Monday night bingo, and a Sunday all-you-can-eat pancake breakfast. Other amenities include a playground, ball field/courts, a horseshoe pit, a convenience store with a great deck providing scenic views, a pool, laundry facilities, picnic tables, fire pits, a snack bar, hot showers, and lake access. Dogs of all sizes are allowed for no additional fee. Dogs must be leashed and cleaned up after at all times. The camping and tent areas also allow dogs. There is a dog walk area at the campground. 2 dogs may be allowed.

Castle Crags State Park
Castle Creek Road
Lakehead, CA
530-235-2684 (800-444-7275)
Named for 6,000-feet tall glacier-polished crags, this park features a variety of land and water recreation, activities, and interpretive and campfire programs are offered in summer. Dogs are allowed for no additional fee. They must be under their owner's control at all times, be on no more than a 6 foot leash, and cleaned up after. Dogs are not permitted on the trails, except for the campground/river trail to the picnic area, or in park buildings, and they must be inside a vehicle or tent at night. The park provides 76 developed campsites and six environmental campsites, each with a table, stove and food storage locker; restrooms and showers are nearby. The camping and tent areas also allow dogs. There is a dog walk

area at the campground. There are no electric or water hookups at the campgrounds. Multiple dogs may be allowed.

Lakeshore Inn and RV
20483 Lakeshore Drive
Lakehead, CA
530-238-2003
shastacamping.com/camping.html
This campground has tall pine and oak trees and overlooks Shasta Lake. Septic and cable TV are available at some of the sites. Other amenities include a large swimming pool, mini store, gift shop, playground, picnic area, video game room, showers, guest laundry, dump station and handicap bathrooms. Well-behaved dogs are welcome. Pets should be quiet and please clean up after them. There is a $1 per day per pet fee. Dogs may not be left unattended, and they must be leashed at all times. Dogs are allowed on the trails. The camping and tent areas also allow dogs. There is a dog walk area at the campground. Multiple dogs may be allowed.

Shasta Lake RV Resort and Campground
20433 Lakeshore Drive
Lakehead, CA
530-238-2370 (800-3-SHASTA (374-2782))
shastarv.com/
This RV resort and campground is located on Lake Shasta. The campground is on Shasta-Trinity National Forest land. RVs up to 60 feet are allowed. Amenities include hot showers, swimming pool, private boat dock, playground, grocery store, and more. Well-behaved leashed dogs are allowed for an additional $1 per night per pet. Please clean up after your pets. There are some breed restrictions. The camping and tent areas also allow dogs. There is a dog walk area at the campground. 2 dogs may be allowed.

Konocti Vistat Casino Resort and Marina
2755 Mission Rancheria Road
Lakeport, CA
707-262-1900 (800-FUN-1950 (386-1950))
kvcasino.com
Located on beautiful, historic Clear Lake, this RV park sits along a casino that has its own 90 slip marina, and there are several recreational activities to explore. Dogs of all sizes are allowed at no additional fee. Dogs may not be left

unattended, and they must be leashed and cleaned up after. Dogs are not allowed in the hotel or casino. This is an RV only park. There is a dog walk area at the campground. Multiple dogs may be allowed.

Lake Jennings County Park
10108 Bass Road
Lakeside, CA
619-443-2004 (877-565-3600)
This popular park offers great scenery, an amphitheater, various programs and exhibits, and a wide variety of recreational pursuits. Dogs of all sizes are allowed for an additional $1 per night per pet, and they must have current tags, rabies, and shot records. Dogs may not be left unattended at any time, and they must be on no more than a 6 foot leash and cleaned up after. Dogs are not allowed on the trails, but they may be walked on the payment and along side the roads on leash. The camping and tent areas also allow dogs. There is a dog walk area at the campground. Multiple dogs may be allowed.

Glass Creek Campground
H 395
Lee Vining, CA
760-873-2408
This 50 site campground is located in the Inyo National Forest at an elevation of 7,600 feet. It is located near several trails. The fee for a campsite is $14. The sites are available on a first-come, first-served basis. Pets must be leashed while in the campground and please clean up after them. The campground is located between Lee Vining and Mammoth Lakes on Highway 395. It is at the intersection of the highway and the Crestview CalTrains Maintenance Station, about one mile north of the Crestview Rest Area. This campground is closed during the off-season. The camping and tent areas also allow dogs. There is a dog walk area at the campground. There are no electric or water hookups at the campgrounds. Multiple dogs may be allowed.

Lundy Canyon County Park Campground
Lundy Lake Road, Mono Lake
Lee Vining, CA
760-932-5440
This park, in the Mono Lake area, offers hikers a variety of trails and recreational pursuits. There are also trails to enter the Ansel Adams and

Hoover Wildernesses. Dogs of all sizes are allowed. There are no additional pet fees. Dogs must be leashed at all times and cleaned up after. Dogs are allowed on the trails on lead. This campground is closed during the off-season. The camping and tent areas also allow dogs. There is a dog walk area at the campground. There are no electric or water hookups at the campgrounds. Multiple dogs may be allowed.

Lakeview Terrace Resort
Trinity Dam Blvd
Lewiston, CA
530-778-3803
lakeviewterraceresort.com/
This resort overlooks Lewiston Lake and features an RV park and cabin rentals. RV spaces feature pull-thru sites, tables and barbecues. Most of the pull-thru sites offer a lake view. Other amenities include a laundry facility, restrooms and showers. Well-behaved quiet leashed dogs are welcome, up to two pets per cabin or RV. Pets are not allowed in the swimming pool area and cannot not be left alone at any time, either in your RV or at the cabins. Please clean up after your pet. There is no pet fee if you stay in an RV space, but there is a $10 per day fee for pets in the cabins. Dogs may not be left unattended in the cabins, or outside your RV. There are some breed restrictions. There is a dog walk area at the campground. 2 dogs may be allowed.

Blue Lake Campground
Forest Service Road 64
Likely, CA
530-233-5811
This campground is located along Blue Lake at a 6,000 foot elevation in the Modoc National Forest. There are 48 RV and tent sites, several of which are located directly on the lake. RVs up to 32 feet are allowed. There is a $7 per vehicle fee. Amenities include picnic tables, fire pits, vault toilets and piped water. A boat ramp is located near the campground. Rowboats, canoes and low powered boats are allowed on the lake. The 1.5 mile Blue Lake National Recreation Trail begins at this campsite. Dogs on leash are allowed at the campgrounds, on trails and in the water. There are no additional pet fees. Please clean up after your pets. This campground is closed during the off-season. The camping and tent areas also allow dogs. There is a dog walk area at the campground. There are no electric or

water hookups at the campgrounds. Multiple dogs may be allowed.

Mill Creek Falls Campground
Mill Creek Road
Likely, CA
530-233-5811
This campground is located in the Modoc National Forest at an elevation of 5,700 feet. There are 19 RV and tent sites. There is a $6 per night fee. Amenities include picnic tables, fire pits, vault toilets and drinking water. The Clear Lake Trail begins here and provides access into the South Warner Wilderness. Dogs on leash are allowed at the campgrounds, on trails and in the water. Please clean up after your pets. To get there from the town of Likely, go 9 miles east on Co. Rd. #64. Then go northeast on West Warner Road for 2.5 miles. Go east on Mill Creek access road for 2 more miles. This campground is closed during the off-season. The camping and tent areas also allow dogs. There is a dog walk area at the campground. There are no electric or water hookups at the campgrounds. Multiple dogs may be allowed.

Van Damme State Park
8125 N H 1
Littleriver, CA
707-937-5804 (800-444-PARK (7275))
Covering almost 2000 acres of beach and uplands on the Mendocino Coast, this park offers a variety of camp sites; some are on a first come first served basis, but reservations are suggested. The park offers a visitor center, Wi-Fi, showers, restrooms, picnic areas, and a dump station. Dogs of all sizes are allowed for no additional fee. Dogs may be on paved roads, fire roads, on the beach, and in the campground area; they are not allowed on the trails. Dogs must be under owner's immediate control, and leashed and cleaned up after at all times. The camping and tent areas also allow dogs. There is a dog walk area at the campground. There are no electric or water hookups at the campgrounds. Multiple dogs may be allowed.

Del Valle Regional Park
7000 Del Valle Road
Livermore, CA
510-562-2267
ebparks.org/parks/delval.htm
This park of almost 4,000 acres sits along a lake surrounded by rolling hills. It is a popular area for nature study, a variety of land and water recreation, and for hiking. It also serves as an entrance to the Ohlone Wilderness Trail. Dogs of all sizes are allowed for an additional $2 per night per pet, and they must have current tags, rabies, and shot records. Dogs may not be left unattended at any time, and they must be on no more than a 6 foot leash and cleaned up after. Dogs are not allowed on the beach. The gates at this park close each night at 10 pm. There are some breed restrictions. This campground is closed during the off-season. The camping and tent areas also allow dogs. There is a dog walk area at the campground. There are no electric hookups at the campgrounds. Multiple dogs may be allowed.

Stockton/Lodi (formally KOA)
2851 East Eight Mile Road
Lodi, CA
209-334-0309 (800-562-1229)
stknlodirv.com/
This campground offers a store, a host of amenities, planned activities, and various land and water recreation. Dogs of all sizes are allowed at no additional fee. Dogs may not be left unattended, and they must be on no more than a 6 foot leash. Dogs must be taken to the dog walk area to do their "business", and be cleaned up after at all times. There are some breed restrictions. The camping and tent areas also allow dogs. There is a dog walk area at the campground. Multiple dogs may be allowed.

Lone Pine Campground
Whitney Portal Road
Lone Pine, CA
760-876-6200 (877-444-6777)
This 43 site campground is located in the Inyo National Forest at an elevation of 6,000 feet. Water is available at the site. There is a $12 fee per campsite. Pets must be leashed while in the campground. Please clean up after your pets. Dogs may not be left unattended. Dogs may be off lead on the trails if they are under good voice control. The camping and tent areas also allow dogs. There is a dog walk area at the campground. There are no electric or water hookups at the campgrounds. Multiple dogs may be allowed.

Tuttle Creek Campground
Horseshoe Meadows Road
Lone Pine, CA

760-876-6200
This campground is located at 5,120 feet and is shadowed by some of the most impressive peaks in the Sierra Nevada Mountain Range. The camp is located in an open desert setting with a view of Alabama Hills and Mt. Whitney. There are 85 tent and RV sites, but no potable water. Amenities include 9 pit toilets, stream water, barbecues, fire rings and picnic tables. All sites are based on a first-come, first-served basis. This campground is managed by the BLM (Bureau of Land Management). Pets on leash are allowed and please clean up after them. Dogs may not be left unattended. They may be off lead on the trials if they are under good voice control. To get there go 3.5 miles west of Lone Pine on Whitney Portal Road. Then go 1.5 miles south on Horseshoe Meadows Road and follow the sign to the campsite. This campground is closed during the off-season. The camping and tent areas also allow dogs. There is a dog walk area at the campground. There are no electric or water hookups at the campgrounds. Multiple dogs may be allowed.

Whitney Portal Campground, Inyo National Forest
Whitney Portal Road
Lone Pine, CA
760-876-6200 (877-444-6777)
This camp area at 8,000 feet, is located in a national forest, and offers a wide variety of both land and water recreational opportunities. Dogs of all sizes are allowed at no additional fee. Dogs may not be left unattended, and they must be on no more than a 6 foot leash, and cleaned up after. Dogs are allowed on the trails up to the trail camp. This campground is closed during the off-season. The camping and tent areas also allow dogs. There is a dog walk area at the campground. There are no electric or water hookups at the campgrounds. Multiple dogs may be allowed.

Wildrose Campground
On Corner of H 395 and H 136
Lone Pine, CA
760-786-3200
nps.gov/deva/pphtml/camping.html
Wildrose is a free campground at 4,100 feet in the Panamint Mountains and is not accessible to vehicles over 25 feet in length. Dogs of all sizes are allowed. There are no additional pet fees. Dogs may not be left unattended outside, and they must be leashed and cleaned up

after. Dogs are not allowed off the main road or along side the main road if being walked. Dogs must remain by the vehicle otherwise, and they are not allowed on the trails. The camping and tent areas also allow dogs. There is a dog walk area at the campground. There are no electric or water hookups at the campgrounds. Multiple dogs may be allowed.

Fraser Flat Campground
Fraser Flat Road
Long Barn, CA
209-586-3234
At an elevation of 4,800 feet this campground offers forested sites on the South Fork of the Stanislaus River. There are 34 tent and RV sites with a maximum RV length of 22 feet. There are no hookups. Amenities include piped water, vault toilets, picnic tables and grills. All sites are on a first-come, first-served basis. Pets on leash are allowed and please clean up after them. This campground is located in the Stanislaus National Forest. To get there, drive 3 miles north of Highway 108 at Spring Gap turnoff (Fraser Flat Road). This RV park is closed during the off-season. The camping and tent areas also allow dogs. There is a dog walk area at the campground. There are no electric or water hookups at the campgrounds. Multiple dogs may be allowed.

Kenneth Hahn State Rec Area
4100 S La Cienega
Los Angeles, CA
323-298-3660
In 1932 this area hosted the 10th Olympiad, and again in 1984 Los Angeles hosted the Olympics with athletes from 140 nations, so as a reminder, 140 trees were planted here to commemorate this event. Other park features/amenities include large landscaped areas, picnic sites, barbecues, playgrounds, a fishing lake, lotus pond/Japanese Garden, gaming fields/courts, and several miles of hiking trails. Dogs are allowed throughout the park and on the trails. Dogs of all sizes are allowed for no additional fee. Dogs must be well behaved, leashed, and cleaned up after. There is primitive camping allowed. The camping and tent areas also allow dogs. There is a dog walk area at the campground. There are no electric or water hookups at the campgrounds. Multiple dogs may be allowed.

Lost Hills RV Park (formally KOA)

14831 Warren Street
Lost Hills, CA
661-797-2719 (800-562-2793)
Dogs of all sizes are allowed for no additional fee at this RV only park. Dogs must be leashed and cleaned up after. There are some breed restrictions. There is a dog walk area at the campground. Multiple dogs may be allowed.

Leo Carrillo State Park
Campground
35000 Pacific Coast H (H 1)
Malibu, CA
818-880-0350 (800-444-PARK (7275))
This campground offers tent and RV camping near the dog-friendly (leashes only and certain sections only) beach, tide pools, marine viewing, interpretive programs, and a variety of recreational activities. The campsites are located on the inland side of Highway 1. You can walk to the beach along a road that goes underneath the highway. Dogs on leash are allowed in the campgrounds and on a certain section of the beach. Please clean up after you pets. Dogs are not allowed in the rocky tide pool area, or on the back country trails. The camping and tent areas also allow dogs. There is a dog walk area at the campground. There are no electric or water hookups at the campgrounds. Multiple dogs may be allowed.

Malibu Beach RV Park
25801 Pacific Coast H
Malibu, CA
310-456-6052 (800-622-6052)
maliburv.com/
This ocean park provide many amenities, some of which are a rec room, video game room, an outdoor game room, marine life viewing, hiking trails, and various other land and water recreational activities. Dogs of all sizes are allowed for an additional fee of $3 per night per pet. Dogs may not be left unattended, and they must be leashed at all times, and cleaned up after. This is an RV only park. There are some breed restrictions. There is a dog walk area at the campground. 2 dogs may be allowed.

Convict Lake Campground
HCR - 79, Box 204
Mammoth Lakes, CA
760-924-5771 (877-444-6777)
convictlakeresort.com/
Located at the Convict Lake Resort,

this camp area offers 88 sites; 25 of which can be reserved. Some of the amenities include fire rings, water, flush toilets, a dump, and showers. Dogs of all sizes are allowed for no additional fee. Dogs must be on no more than a 6 foot leash, and be cleaned up after. They are allowed on the trails. This RV park is closed during the off-season. The camping and tent areas also allow dogs. There is a dog walk area at the campground. There are no electric or water hookups at the campgrounds. Multiple dogs may be allowed.

Lake George Campground
Lake George Road
Mammoth Lakes, CA
760-924-5500
This 16 site campground is located in the Inyo National Forest at an elevation of 9,000 feet. It is located near several trails. The fee for a campsite is $14. The sites are available on a first-come, first-served basis. Pets must be leashed while in the campground and please clean up after them. Dogs may be off lead on the trails only if they are under voice control. To get there from the intersection of Main Street and Hwy 203, take Lake Mary Road to the left. Go past Twin Lakes. You'll see a road that goes off to the left (Lake Mary Loop Rd). Go past this road, you'll want the other end of the loop. When you come to another road that also says Lake Mary Loop Rd, turn left. Then turn right onto Lake George Road and follow it to the campground. This campground is closed during the off-season. The camping and tent areas also allow dogs. There is a dog walk area at the campground. There are no electric or water hookups at the campgrounds. Multiple dogs may be allowed.

Lake Mary Campground
Lake Mary Loop Road
Mammoth Lakes, CA
760-924-5500
This 48 site campground is located in the Inyo National Forest at an elevation of 8,900 feet. It is located near several trails. The fee for a campsite is $14. The sites are available on a first-come, first-served basis. Pets must be leashed while in the campground and please clean up after them. Dogs may be off lead on the trails if they will respond to voice command. From Hwy 203, take Lake Mary Road to the left. Pass Twin Lakes and then you'll come to Lake Mary. Turn left onto Lake Mary Loop Road. This campground is closed

during the off-season. The camping and tent areas also allow dogs. There is a dog walk area at the campground. There are no electric or water hookups at the campgrounds. Multiple dogs may be allowed.

Mammoth Mountain RV Park
P.O. Box 288/H 203
Mammoth Lakes, CA
760-934-3822 (800-582-4603)
This RV park offers over 160 tent sites and RV sites with full hookups. Amenities include dump stations, restrooms with hot showers, laundry rooms, picnic tables, indoor heated swimming pool and spa, children's play area and RV supplies. Site rates range from $21 to $34 per night. Rates are subject to change. Pets are welcome but need to be leashed at all times and cannot be left unattended outside, and left inside only if they will be physically comfortable and quiet. There is a $3 per night per pet fee. They are located within walking distance of shops and restaurants. The RV park is open year round. There are some breed restrictions. The camping and tent areas also allow dogs. There is a dog walk area at the campground. Multiple dogs may be allowed.

New Shady Rest Campground
Sawmill Cutoff Road
Mammoth Lakes, CA
760-924-5500 (877-444-6777)
This 94 site campground is located in the Inyo National Forest at an elevation of 7,800 feet. It is located near several trails. Amenities include water, flush toilets, fire ring, showers, interpretive programs, and a visitors' center. The fee for a campsite is $13. The sites are available on a first-come, first-served basis. Pets must be leashed while in the campground and please clean up after them. This campground is closed during the off-season. The camping and tent areas also allow dogs. There is a dog walk area at the campground. There are no electric or water hookups at the campgrounds. Multiple dogs may be allowed.

Red Meadows Campground
Off H 203
Mammoth Lakes, CA
760-924-5500
This 56 site campground is located in the Inyo National Forest at an elevation of 7,600 feet. It is near the dog-friendly Devil's Postpile National Monument and hiking trails including the John Muir Trail. Amenities include water. The fee for a campsite

is $15, and sites are available on a first-come, first-served basis. Pets must be leashed while in the campground and please clean up after them. From Highway 395, drive 10 miles west on Highway 203 to Minaret Summit. Then drive about 7 miles on a paved, narrow mountain road. This campground is closed during the off-season. The camping and tent areas also allow dogs. There is a dog walk area at the campground. There are no electric or water hookups at the campgrounds. Multiple dogs may be allowed.

Twin Lakes Campground, Inyo National Forest
Lake Mary Road
Mammoth Lakes, CA
760-924-5500
This forest campground located at 8,600 feet offers great scenery amid a variety of recreational activities and pursuits. Dogs of all sizes are allowed. There are no additional pet fees. Dogs may not be left unattended, and they must be leashed and cleaned up after. Dogs are allowed on the trails unless otherwise marked. This campground is closed during the off-season. The camping and tent areas also allow dogs. There is a dog walk area at the campground. There are no electric or water hookups at the campgrounds. Multiple dogs may be allowed.

Manchester Beach/Mendocino Coast KOA
44300 Kinney Road
Manchester, CA
707-882-2375 (800-562-4188)
koa.com/where/ca/05182/
There is a variety of land and water recreation at this park located on a spectacular five-mile stretch of sand beach on the Mendocino Coast. Dogs of all sizes are allowed for no additional fee. Dogs must be under owner's control and visual observation at all times. Dogs must be quiet, well behaved, and be on no more than a 6 foot leash at all times, or otherwise contained. Dogs may not be left unattended outside the owner's camping equipment. There are some breed restrictions. The camping and tent areas also allow dogs. There is a dog walk area at the campground. Dogs are allowed in the camping cabins. 2 dogs may be allowed.

Grover Hot Springs State Park
3415 Hot Springs Road

Markleeville, CA
530-694-2248
You will find a variety of weather and recreation at this park that is known for its mineral hot springs. Dogs of all sizes are allowed. There are no additional pet fees. Dogs may not be left unattended, and they must be leashed at all times, and cleaned up after. Dogs are not allowed in the pool area, and guests or their dogs are not allowed in the meadows. The camping and tent areas also allow dogs. There is a dog walk area at the campground. There are no electric or water hookups at the campgrounds. Multiple dogs may be allowed.

Indian Creek Campground
Indian Creek Road
Markleeville, CA
775-885-6000
Surrounded by pine trees at 5,600 feet, this park covers 160 acres used for recreational pursuits. Dogs of all sizes are allowed. There are no additional pet fees. Dogs may not be left unattended, and they must be leashed at all times, and cleaned up after. Dogs are allowed on the trails. This campground is closed during the off-season. The camping and tent areas also allow dogs. There is a dog walk area at the campground. There are no electric or water hookups at the campgrounds.

Fowlers Campground
H 89
McCloud, CA
530-964-2184
This campground has 39 sites available on a first come first served basis. Water and vault toilets are on site. Dogs of all sizes are allowed for no additional fee; they must be leashed and cleaned up after at all times when in a developed site, and in areas where posted. Dogs are not allowed in the wilderness area at the base of Mt Shasta. This RV park is closed during the off-season. The camping and tent areas also allow dogs. There is a dog walk area at the campground. There are no electric or water hookups at the campgrounds. Multiple dogs may be allowed.

McGee Creek Campground
McGee Creek Road
McGee Creek, CA
760-873-2500 (877-444-6777)
This 28 site campground is located in the Inyo National Forest at an elevation of 7,600 feet. The campsite is in an open area and adjacent to McGee Creek. Amenities include water, flush toilets and space for

RVs. For hiking, the McGee Creek Trail is located within a few miles of the campground. The fee for a campsite is $15. Pets must be leashed while in the campground and please clean up after your pets. This campground is closed during the off-season. The camping and tent areas also allow dogs. There is a dog walk area at the campground. There are no electric or water hookups at the campgrounds. Multiple dogs may be allowed.

Casper Beach RV Park and Campground
14441 Point Cabrilla
Mendocino, CA
707-964-3306
casparbeachrvpark.com%2F
This RV park is located in one of the most picturesque coastal regions anywhere in the US, with such amenities as an arcade, an onsite grocery & novelty store, and host to a variety of land and water recreation. Dogs of all sizes are allowed for an additional fee of $2 per night per per pet. Dogs must be very friendly, quiet, well behaved, leashed, and cleaned up after. The camping and tent areas also allow dogs. There is a nice dog-friendly beach right across from the campground where you can walk your leashed dog. The campground is about five miles north of Mendocino. 2 dogs may be allowed.

Navarro River Redwoods State Park
H 128
Mendocino, CA
707-895-3141
Paralleling the Navarro River and Highway 128 is this 673 acre park that offers outstanding natural beauty, walking paths through redwood groves, and access to the Pacific Ocean. Camping is on a first come first served basis at the 25 developed sites and the 10 beach sites. There are restrooms but no drinking water available. Dogs of all sizes are allowed for no additional fee, and they are allowed throughout the park, on the trails, and on the beach. Dogs must be leashed at all times and be cleaned up after. This RV park is closed during the off-season. The camping and tent areas also allow dogs. There is a dog walk area at the campground. There are no electric or water hookups at the campgrounds. Multiple dogs may be allowed.

Yosemite/Mariposa KOA
6323 H 140

Midpines, CA
209-966-2201 (800-562-9391)
koa.com/where/ca/05195/
Nestled in the pines, close to Yosemite, this campground offers such amenities as 43 foot pull-thru sites with 50 amp service, cable TV, swimming pool, mini golf, planned activities, and guided tours. Dogs of all sizes are allowed for an additional pet fee of $2 per night per pet. Dogs must be under owner's control and visual observation at all times. Dogs must be quiet, well behaved, and be on no more than a 6 foot leash at all times, or otherwise contained. Dogs may not be left unattended outside the owner's camping equipment, and must be brought inside at night. There are some breed restrictions. The camping and tent areas also allow dogs. There is a dog walk area at the campground. Multiple dogs may be allowed.

Butte Lake, Lassen Volcanic National Park
PO Box 100,
Mineral, CA
530-595-4444 (877-444-6777)
nps.gov/lavo/pphtml/camping.html
This park, at 6,100 feet, sits amid a variety of landscapes and recreational pursuits. Dogs of all sizes are allowed. There are no additional pet fees. Dogs may not be left unattended outside, and they must be leashed and cleaned up after. Dogs are allowed only on paved roads, and in the developed areas of the campground. Dogs are not allowed on the trails. The campsite is located 17 miles from Old Station on Highway 44 East, then 6 miles south on a dirt road. This campground is closed during the off-season. The camping and tent areas also allow dogs. There is a dog walk area at the campground. There are no electric or water hookups at the campgrounds. Multiple dogs may be allowed.

Lassen Volcanic National Park Campgrounds
36050 H 36
Mineral, CA
530-595-4444
This park offers many campgrounds, with the largest campground having 179 sites. Trailers up to 35 feet are permitted, and all sites are on a first-come, first-served basis. Pets must be leashed and attended at all times. Please clean up after your pet. Dogs must be well behaved, and

have current shot records. Dogs are permitted on established roadways, in campgrounds, picnic areas, and in other developed areas. Dogs are not allowed on any trails or hikes in this park, but see our Lassen National Forest listing for nearby dog-friendly hiking, sightseeing and additional camping. This campground is closed during the off-season. The camping and tent areas also allow dogs. There is a dog walk area at the campground. There are no electric or water hookups at the campgrounds. Multiple dogs may be allowed.

Marina Dunes RV Park
3330 Dunes Dr
Marina, CA 93933 (Monterey)
831-384-6914
marinadunesrv.com
This RV park is located right on the sand dunes and a 10 minute walk to the beach. It is about 10 minutes north of Monterey and 15 minutes from Carmel.

Coyote Valley RV Resort
9750 Monterey Rd
Morgan Hill, CA
408-463-8400
coyotevalleyresort.com
This RV campground is located near golfing and only about 15 minutes from downtown San Jose. It offers Wi-Fi, an exercise room, cable TV and a fenced and double-gated dog park. There are some breed restrictions.

Parkway Lakes RV Park
100 Ogier Avenue
Morgan Hill, CA
408-779-0244
This 110 RV space park offers a pool, mini mart, Wi-Fi, club house, laundry, showers, and more. Dogs of all sizes are allowed for an additional fee of $1 per night per pet. Dogs must be leashed and cleaned up after. There is an area just outside the park for walking your pet. There are some breed restrictions. The camping and tent areas also allow dogs. 2 dogs may be allowed.

Moss Landing KOA
7905 Sandholdt Road
Moss Landing, CA
831-633-6800 (800-562-3390)
koa.com/where/ca/05448/
A nature lover's paradise, this park located in the Monterey Bay Sanctuary offers a number of onsite amenities and activities plus access to one of the states largest coastal wetlands. Dogs are allowed for no additional fee. Dogs may not be left

unattended outside, and they may only be left alone inside if they will be quiet. Dogs must be on no more than a 6 foot leash and cleaned up after at all times. There are some breed restrictions. The camping and tent areas also allow dogs. There is a dog walk area at the campground. Multiple dogs may be allowed.

Lake Siskiyou Camp Resort
4239 W. A. Barr Rd
Mount Shasta, CA
530-926-2618 (888-926-2618)
lakesis.com/
This recreational and camping area sits on 250 forested acres along side a pristine 430 acre sailing lake. There is a large grocery/deli/gift shop and marina, and the campground has 360 overnight sites, laundry facilities, a dump station, restrooms with showers, free family outdoor movies, and a rec hall. Dogs of all sizes are allowed for an additional fee of $2 per day per pet. Dogs must be leashed and cleaned up after at all times, and they may not be left unattended on a camp site. Dogs are allowed throughout the park, except they are not allowed in the lodging (rentals), picnic areas, or the beach. This RV park is closed during the off-season. The camping and tent areas also allow dogs. There is a dog walk area at the campground. Multiple dogs may be allowed.

Lake Isabella RV Resort
11936 H 178
Mountain Mesa, CA
800-787-9920
lakeisabellarv.com/home.htm
This picturesque, RV only park, is located along Lake Isabella, and amenities include more than 40 miles of open shoreline, a full service marina, and a pool. Dogs of all sizes are allowed for an additional $1 per night per pet. Dogs may not be left unattended outside, and they must be brought in at night, leashed, and cleaned up after. There are some breed restrictions. There is a dog walk area at the campground. 2 dogs may be allowed.

Putah Creek Resort
7600 Knoxville Road
Napa, CA
707-966-0794
This park of many mini-peninsulas along Lake Berryessa allows for lots of accessible shoreline along with land and water recreation. Dogs of all sizes are allowed for an additional $2 per night per pet. Dogs may only be left unattended on your site if they

have secure water and food, will be quiet, and well behaved. Dogs must be leashed at all times and cleaned up after. There are some breed restrictions. The camping and tent areas also allow dogs. There is a dog walk area at the campground. Multiple dogs may be allowed.

Moabi Regional Park Campgrounds
Park Moabi Road
Needles, CA
760-326-3831
This park has a campground with 35 RV sites with full hookups, 120 sites with partial hookups, and unlimited tent sites. The sites are situated in the main section of the park and along 2.5 miles of shoreline. The park is located on the banks of the Colorado River and is popular for camping, fishing, boating, swimming and water skiing. Dogs can go into the water but they strongly advise against it because there are so many fast boats in the water. Dogs must be leashed and please clean up after them. There is an additional fee of $1 per night per pet. The camping and tent areas also allow dogs. There is a dog walk area at the campground. Multiple dogs may be allowed.

Needles KOA
5400 National Old Trails H
Needles, CA
760-326-4207 (800-562-3407)
koa.com/where/ca/05366/
This desert oasis park offers 90 foot pull-thru sites with 50 amp service, LP gas, snack bar, swimming pool, and guided tours. Dogs of all sizes are allowed for no additional fee. Dogs must be under owner's control and visual observation at all times. Dogs must be quiet, well behaved, and be on no more than a 6 foot leash at all times, or otherwise contained. Dogs may not be left unattended outside the owner's camping equipment, and must be brought inside at night. Dogs are not allowed in the pool area or buildings. There are some breed restrictions. The camping and tent areas also allow dogs. There is a dog walk area at the campground. Dogs are allowed in the camping cabins. Multiple dogs may be allowed.

Lodgepole Campground
Lake Valley Reservoir
Nevada City, CA
916-386-5164
This 35 site campground is located

in the Tahoe National Forest and is managed by PG&E. The campsite is located at an elevation of 5,800 feet. Pets must be leashed in the campground must be cleaned up after. There is a $1 per night per pet additional fee. To get there from I-80, take the Yuba Gap exit for .4 miles. Go around Lake Valley Reservoir for 1.2 miles. Then take right fork 2.5 miles. This campground is closed during the off-season. The camping and tent areas also allow dogs. There is a dog walk area at the campground. There are no electric or water hookups at the campgrounds. 2 dogs may be allowed.

South Yuba Campground
North Bloomfield Road
Nevada City, CA
919-985-4474
This campground has 16 sites for tents or RVs. Camp amenities include picnic tables, fire grills, piped water, pit toilets and garbage collection. The cost per site is $5 per night with a 14 day maximum stay, and are on a first-come, first-served basis. The South Yuba River Recreation Area is located about 10 miles northeast of Nevada City. Once turned on North Bloomfield Road, drive 10 miles to the South Yuba Recreation Area. From the one lane bridge at Edwards Crossing, go about 1.5 miles on a dirt/gravel road to the campground and trailhead. Trailers and motorhomes should take Highway 49 and then turn right at the junction of Tyler Foote Road. At the intersection of Grizzly Hill Road turn right and proceed to North Bloomfield Road. Dogs of all sizes are allowed at no additional fee. Dogs may not be left unattended outside, and they must be leashed and cleaned up after. Dogs are allowed on the trails. This campground is closed during the off-season. The camping and tent areas also allow dogs. There is a dog walk area at the campground. There are no electric or water hookups at the campgrounds. Multiple dogs may be allowed.

Selby Campgrounds
Soda Lake Road
New Cuyama, CA
661-391-6000
Primitive camping is available at this campground which is located at the base of the Caliente Mountains and near the dog-friendly Caliente Mountain Access Trail. There are 5 picnic tables and 4 fire pits, but no shade trees. There is no garbage

pickup service, electricity or drinking water. Leave vehicles along the edge of the road, do not drive to your chosen campsite. Be aware of rattlesnakes in the area. Dogs on leash are allowed. Dogs may not be left unattended, and please clean up after your dog. The campground is about 14 miles west of New Cuyama off Hwy 166, on Soda Lake Road. There will be signs. Dogs are not allowed at Painted Rock at any time. This campground is closed during the off-season. The camping and tent areas also allow dogs. There is a dog walk area at the campground. There are no electric or water hookups at the campgrounds. Multiple dogs may be allowed.

Newport Dunes RV Park
1131 Back Bay Drive
Newport Beach, CA
949-729-3863
newportdunes.com
This waterfront resort features lush grounds, many amenities, and a variety of land and water recreation. Dogs of all sizes are allowed for an additional $2 per night per pet for the nightly fee, and an additional $5 per night per pet for the weekly fee. Dogs may not be left unattended, and they must be leashed and cleaned up after. Dogs are not allowed on the beach or anywhere on the sand. There are some breed restrictions. The camping and tent areas also allow dogs. There is a dog walk area at the campground. 2 dogs may be allowed.

Novato RV Park
1530 Armstrong Avenue
Novato, CA
415-897-1271 (800-733-6787)
novatorvpark.com/
Nestled in a quiet country setting just minutes from all the attractions of the bay cities, this park offers modern amenities, and various recreation. Dogs of all sizes are allowed. There are no additional pet fees. Dogs may not be left unattended outside, and they must be quiet, well behaved, leashed, and cleaned up after. This is an RV only park. There is a dog walk area at the campground. Multiple dogs may be allowed.

Anthony Chabot Regional Park
9999 Redwood Road
Oakland, CA
510-562-2267
ebparks.org/parks/anchabot.htm
With almost 5,000 acres this beautiful park features an amphitheater, naturalist-led campfire

programs, a marksmanship range, and a full range of activities and recreation. Dogs of all sizes are allowed for an additional $2 per night per pet. Dogs may not be left unattended, and they must be leashed, and cleaned up after at all times. Dogs are not allowed on the beach. The gates at this park close at 10 pm. The camping and tent areas also allow dogs. There is a dog walk area at the campground. Multiple dogs may be allowed.

North Beach Campground, Pismo State Beach Park
555 Pier Avenue
Oceano, CA
805-489-1869 (800-444-7275)
Close to the ocean, sitting inland behind the dunes, is a beautiful campground offering a variety of land and water recreation. Dogs of all sizes are allowed. There are no additional pet fees. Dogs may not be left unattended, and they must be leashed and cleaned up after. Dogs are allowed on the trails on lead. The camping and tent areas also allow dogs. There is a dog walk area at the campground. There are no electric or water hookups at the campgrounds. Multiple dogs may be allowed.

Pacific Dunes RV Resort
1025 Silver Spur Place
Oceano, CA
760-328-4813 (888-908-7787)
Walk to the dog-friendly sand dunes and beach from this campground. Well-behaved leashed dogs are welcome in the tent sites and RV spaces. Please clean up after your pet. There is no pet fee, and dogs are allowed on the trails. The RV sites are pull-thru or back-in with 50 amp service, water, electric, sewer hookups, cable TV and a picnic table. Other campground amenities include a volleyball court, pool table, basketball courts, horseback riding, barbecue facilities, bicycle and walking paths, general store, laundry facilities, lighted streets, restrooms/showers, modem hookup and a clubhouse. The camping and tent areas also allow dogs. There is a dog walk area at the campground. Multiple dogs may be allowed.

Guajome County Park
3000 Guajome Lake Road
Oceanside, CA
858-565-3600
Rich in natural and cultural history, this historic 557 acre park features a wide diversity of plant, bird, and

wildlife, spring-fed lakes, scenic picnic areas, trails, a gazebo and an enclosed pavilion that overlooks the lake. There is a variety of land and water recreational opportunities to explore. Dogs of all sizes are allowed for an additional fee of $1 per pet. Dogs must have current tags or shot records, be on no more than a 6 foot leash, and be cleaned up after. Dogs must remain in developed and paved areas; they are not allowed on the trails. The camp area has 35 developed sites, restrooms, hot showers, fire rings, and a dump station. There are 4 sites that will accommodate larger trailers. The camping and tent areas also allow dogs. There is a dog walk area at the campground. Multiple dogs may be allowed.

Paradise by the Sea RV Resort
1537 S Coast H
Oceanside, CA
760-439-1376
paradisebythesearvresort.com/
Set between the beautiful Pacific Ocean and historic Highway 101, this park features beach and pool swimming, a rec room, hot showers, restroom and laundry facilities, and a convenience store. Dogs of all sizes are allowed for an additional fee of $1 per night per pet. Dogs may not be left unattended, and they must be leashed and cleaned up after. Dogs are not allowed on the beach. This is an RV only park. There are some breed restrictions. There is a dog walk area at the campground. Multiple dogs may be allowed.

Wheeler Gorge Campground
17017 Maricopa Highway
Ojai, CA
805-640-1977 (877-444-6777)
This campground is located on a year round stream and is shaded by trees running the length of the camp area. There are vault toilets and potable water, and each site has a table, barbecue, and fire ring. A variety of land and water recreation activities are available, and there are interpretive and campfire nature presentations offered in the summer. Dogs of all sizes are allowed for no additional pet fee. Dogs must be under owner's control at all times, and be leashed and cleaned up after. The camping and tent areas also allow dogs. There is a dog walk area at the campground. Multiple dogs may be allowed.

Big Basin Redwoods State Park
21600 Big Basin Way

Old Creek, CA
831-338-8860 (800-444-PARK
(7275))
bigbasin.org
This park is California's oldest park
and is home to the largest
continuous stand of ancient coast
redwoods south of the bay area. It
offers a wide variety of recreation
and other activities. Dogs of all sizes
are allowed. There are no additional
pet fees. Dogs may not be left
unattended at any time, and they
must be leashed and cleaned up
after. Dogs are allowed in the picnic
area, the campground area, on
paved roads, and the North escape
road only. Dogs are not allowed
anywhere at Rancho del Oso or on
any other trails or interior roads.
They must be kept in the RV or tent
at night. Check at Park Headquarters
for scheduled guided "dog walks",
which are informative group hikes
that give dog owners a chance to
take their dogs along while learning
about redwood ecology and park
history. The camping and tent areas
also allow dogs. There is a dog walk
area at the campground. There are
no electric or water hookups at the
campgrounds. Multiple dogs may be
allowed.

Cave Campground
H 89
Old Station, CA
530-336-5521 (877-444-6777)
This campground is located in the
Lassen National Forest near the
Subway Cave where you and your
pooch can explore an underground
lava tube. The camp is at an
elevation of 4,300 feet and offers 46
campsites. Camp amenities include
water, fire rings, picnic tables and
restrooms. Most sites are available
on a first-come, first-served basis.
Some sites can be reserved. Dogs
on leash are allowed at the
campground and on trails. Please
clean up after your dog. Dogs must
be quiet, well behaved, and have
current shot records. This
campground is closed during the off-
season. The camping and tent areas
also allow dogs. There is a dog walk
area at the campground. There are
no electric or water hookups at the
campgrounds. Multiple dogs may be
allowed.

Olema Ranch Campground
10155 H 1
Olema, CA
415-663-8001 (800-655-CAMP
(2267))
olemaranch.com

This full service park features both
natural forest and open meadow
camp sites, a laundry, rec hall,
store, Post Office, and a wide
variety of activities and recreation.
Dogs of all sizes are allowed for an
additional $1 per night per pet.
Dogs must be on no more than an 8
foot leash at all times and cleaned
up after. The camping and tent
areas also allow dogs. There is a
dog walk area at the campground.
Multiple dogs may be allowed.

Walker Pass Campground
H 178
Onyx, CA
661-391-6000
This BLM (Bureau of Land
Management) campground has 11
walk-in sites for Pacific Crest Trail
hikers and two sites are available
for vehicles. Drinking water is
available from spring through fall.
Hitching racks and corrals are
available for horses. There are no
reservations or fees but donations
are accepted. Dogs are allowed but
need to be on leash while in the
campground. They are allowed on
the trails. The camping and tent
areas also allow dogs. There is a
dog walk area at the campground.
There are no electric or water
hookups at the campgrounds.
Multiple dogs may be allowed.

Collins Lake
7530 Collins Lake Road
Oregon House, CA
530-692-1600 (800-286-0576)
collinslake.com/
This is a popular 1600 acre lake
and recreation area with a wide
range of land and water recreation
and activities. Some of the
features/amenities include a big
sandy swimming beach with beach
volleyball, picnic areas, a
playground, general store, boat
launch, a marina with rentals, and
lakeside camping. The camp areas
have tables, fire pits, and showers.
Dogs of all sizes are allowed for an
additional fee of $2 per night per
pet. Dogs must be under owner's
control, well mannered, leashed,
and cleaned up after at all times.
Dogs may not be left unattended,
and they are not allowed on the
swim beach or on the playground.
The camping and tent areas also
allow dogs. There is a dog walk
area at the campground. Multiple
dogs may be allowed.

Elk Prairie Campground
127011 Newton B. Drury Scenic

Parkway
Orick, CA
707-464-6101 (800-444-PARK
(7275))
This campground is located in Prairie
Creek Redwoods State Park. While
dogs are not allowed on any park
trails or the beach, they are allowed
at this campground. There are 75 RV
or tent sites which are next to a
prairie and old growth redwood
forest. RVs must be less than 27
feet. Camp amenities include
restrooms, showers, fire pits, dump
station and bear-proof lockers.
Located just north of the
campground is Cal Barrel Road.
Dogs can walk on or along this 3
mile gravel road. There are not too
many cars that travel along this road.
Pets must be on no more than a 6
foot leash and attended to at all
times. Please clean up after your pet.
The camping and tent areas also
allow dogs. There is a dog walk area
at the campground. There are no
electric or water hookups at the
campgrounds. 2 dogs may be
allowed.

Gold Bluffs Beach Campground
Davidson Road
Orick, CA
707-464-6101
nps.gov/redw/camping.html
This campground is located in Prairie
Creek Redwoods State Park. While
dogs are not allowed on any park
trails, they are allowed at this
campground and the adjoining
beach. There are 29 tent sites and
25 RV sites at the beach. RVs must
be less than 24 feet long and 8 feet
wide. All sites are on a first-come,
first-served basis. Camp amenities
include restrooms, solar showers
and fire pits. Pets must be leashed
and attended at all times. Please
clean up after your pets. Dogs are
not allowed on any established trails.
They are allowed in parking lots, the
campground, picnic areas, paved
roads, and must stay within 100 feet
of the roads. Although the
campground is open year round, call
ahead, as sometimes the roads are
closed for repairs. The camping and
tent areas also allow dogs. There is
a dog walk area at the campground.
There are no electric or water
hookups at the campgrounds.
Multiple dogs may be allowed.

Black Butte Lake Recreation Area
19225 Newville Road
Orland, CA
530-865-4781 (877-444-6777)
Located on Stony Creek, this popular

recreation area features a 4,460 surface acre lake with 40 miles of shoreline, and during the spring nature puts on a wonderful display of wildflowers. Some of the features/amenities include 3 self-guided nature trails, interpretive programs, well maintained picnic facilities, a playground, and a variety of land and water recreational activities. Dogs of all sizes are allowed for no additional fee. Dogs must be under their owner's control at all times, and be leashed and cleaned up after. Dogs are not allowed at the beach. There are two campgrounds available at the lake. Some of the amenities include drinking water, picnic tables, fire pits, phones, and restrooms with showers. The camping and tent areas also allow dogs. There is a dog walk area at the campground. There are no electric hookups at the campgrounds. Multiple dogs are allowed.

Buckhorn Recreation Area
19225 Newville Road
Orland, CA
530-865-4781 (877-444-6777)
This picturesque park, snuggled in the foothills of north-central California along Black Butte Lake, offers a variety of recreational pursuits and an interpretive trail. Next door is a 75-acre all-terrain park. Dogs of all sizes are allowed at no additional fee. Dogs must be on no more than a 6 foot leash at all times in the camp and trail areas. Dogs may be off lead at the backside of the lake only if they are under voice command. The camping and tent areas also allow dogs. There is a dog walk area at the campground. There are no electric or water hookups at the campgrounds. Multiple dogs may be allowed.

Oroville State Wildlife Area
945 Oroville Dam Blvd West
Oroville, CA
530-538-2236
Just outside the city limits sits this wildlife area of almost 12,000 acres of riparian forest bordered by 12 miles of river channels. The area is popular for fishing, birding, and hiking. Dogs of all sizes are allowed for no additional fee. Dogs must be under their owner's control, and leashed and cleaned up after at all times. Primitive camping is allowed; there are restrooms and drinking water available. The camping and tent areas also allow dogs. There is a dog walk area at the campground.

There are no electric or water hookups at the campgrounds. Multiple dogs may be allowed.

Spenceville Wildlife and Recreation Area
Larkin Road
Oroville, CA
530-538-2236
Fishing and birding are popular at this 11,448 acre park of mostly foothill oak trees and grasslands with creeks and springs found throughout. Dogs of all sizes are allowed for no additional fee. They must be under their owner's control at all times, and be leashed and cleaned up after. The camp area is very primitive and provides a vault toilet. The camping and tent areas also allow dogs. There is a dog walk area at the campground. There are no electric or water hookups at the campgrounds. Multiple dogs may be allowed.

Evergreen RV Park
2135 N Oxnard Blvd
Oxnard, CA
805-485-1936
Dogs are welcome at this 90 space RV park for an additional pet fee of $1 per night per pet. The fee is $15 per pet if paying monthly. Dogs may not be left outside unattended, and they must be leashed and cleaned up after at all times. There is a dog walk area at the campground. Multiple dogs may be allowed.

Lake Nacimiento Resort RV and Campgrounds
10625 Nacimiento Lake Drive
Paso Robles, CA
805-238-3256 (800-323-3839)
nacimientoresort.com/
This campground offers a variety of amenities and land and water recreation. Dogs are allowed around and in the lake at this campground, but be careful about letting your dog get too far into the water, as there are many boats on the lake. They are also allowed on trails. Pets must be on no more than a 6 foot leash, cleaned up after, and attended at all times. There is a $10 per day charge for dogs. Proof of your dogs' rabies vaccination is required. The camping and tent areas also allow dogs. There is a dog walk area at the campground. Multiple dogs may be allowed.

South Fork Campground
Big Rock Creek Road/Forest Road 4N11A

Pearblossom, CA
661-296-9710
This 21 site campground is located in the Angeles National Forest at an elevation of 4,500 feet. There are both tent and small RV sites up to 16 feet. Amenities include vault toilets. There are many hiking trails nearby including one which leads to the dog-friendly Devil's Punchbowl County Park. Well behaved dogs on leash are allowed and please clean up after them. Dogs may not be left unattended outside, and only left inside if they will be quiet and comfortable. The camping and tent areas also allow dogs. There is a dog walk area at the campground. There are no electric or water hookups at the campgrounds. Multiple dogs may be allowed.

Lake Perris Campgrounds
17801 Lake Perris Drive
Perris, CA
951-657-0676 (800-444-7275)
This campground offers 434 campsites including two RV areas with full hookups. While dogs are not allowed in the lake or within 100 feet of the water, they are allowed on miles of trails including the bike trail that loops around the lake. Pets must be on no more than a 6 foot leash, and please clean up after them. Dogs may not be left unattended. The camping and tent areas also allow dogs. There is a dog walk area at the campground. Multiple dogs may be allowed.

Luiseno Campground, Lake Perris State Rec Area
17801 Lake Perris Drive
Perris, CA
951-940-5603 (800-444-PARK (7275))
This campground sits among the white sands and blue waters of Lake Perris and offers a wide variety of land and water recreation. Animals must be leashed (6 foot or less leash), caged, or in a tent, motor home, or vehicle at all times, and can not be left unattended. Visitors are responsible for clean-up after their pets. No body contact with the water is allowed, and dogs may not be on the trails or the beach. The camping and tent areas also allow dogs. There is a dog walk area at the campground. Multiple dogs may be allowed.

Butano State Park Campground
Off H 1 4.5 miles SE of Pescadero
Pescadero, CA
650-879-2040 (800-444-7275)

The campground can accept RVs up to 27 feet, and camp amenities include picnic tables, water and vault toilets. While dogs are not allowed on the park trails, they are allowed in the campground, picnic area, all paved roads, and on miles of fire roads. Mountain biking is also allowed on the fire roads. Pets must be on a 6 foot or less leash at all times. Please clean up after them. The camping and tent areas also allow dogs. There is a dog walk area at the campground. There are no electric or water hookups at the campgrounds. Multiple dogs may be allowed.

San Francisco North/Petaluma KOA
20 Rainsvile Road
Petaluma, CA
707-763-1492 (800-562-1233)
koa.com/where/ca/05330/
Just north of the Golden Gate, this scenic country-style campground offers tours of the city, a petting farm, a full recreational program, swimming pool, hot tub, cable TV, and a snack bar. Friendly dogs of all sizes are allowed for no additional fee. Dogs must be under owner's control and visual observation at all times. Dogs must be quiet, well behaved, and be on no more than a 6 foot leash at all times, or otherwise contained. Dogs may not be left unattended outside the owner's camping equipment, and must be brought inside at night. There are some breed restrictions. The camping and tent areas also allow dogs. There is a dog walk area at the campground. Multiple dogs may be allowed.

Pine Flat Lake Rec Area
28100 Pine Flat Road
Piedra, CA
559-488-3004
This park of 120 acres is located on the Kings River below Pine Flat Dam, has 5 day use areas in addition to the camp area, and offers a variety of recreational pursuits. Dogs of all sizes are allowed at no additional fee. Dogs may not be left unattended, and they must be on no more than a 6 foot leash at all times, and cleaned up after. Dogs are allowed on the trails. The camping and tent areas also allow dogs. There is a dog walk area at the campground. There are no electric or water hookups at the campgrounds. Multiple dogs may be allowed.

Yogi Bear's Jellystone Park Camp-Resort of Pine Grove

13026 Tabeaud Road
Pine Grove, CA
209-296-4650 (877-I-GO-YOGI (446-9644))
goldcountryjellystone.com/
Located in the heart of Gold Country in heavily wooded surroundings, this fun park offers theme weekends, a seasonal swimming pool, mini golf, a gift shop, and an arcade/activity room. Additionally, they will soon be adding a snack bar, a kiddy splash-pad with spray features, and laundry facilities. Dogs are allowed for no additional fee. They must be leashed and cleaned up after at all times, and they are not allowed in any of the rental units. The camping and tent areas also allow dogs. There is a dog walk area at the campground. Multiple dogs may be allowed.

Laguna Campground
Sunrise H
Pine Valley, CA
619-445-6235 (877-444-6777)
This 104 site campground is located in the Cleveland National Forest. It is located at an elevation of 5,600 feet and offers both tent and RV sites. RVs up to 40 feet are allowed. Flush toilets are available at this campground. Pets must be on no more than a 6 foot leash at all times, cleaned up after, and contained at night. There are no additional pet fees. The camping and tent areas also allow dogs. There is a dog walk area at the campground. There are no electric or water hookups at the campgrounds. Multiple dogs may be allowed.

Boulder Flat,
21 miles east of Pinecrest on Highway 108
Pinecrest, CA
209-965-3434
This camp area is located in the Brightman Recreation Area in a forested area along the Stanislaus River. Dogs of all sizes are allowed. There are no additional pet fees. Dogs must be well behaved, leashed in camp, and cleaned up after. Dogs may be off lead on the trails if they are under voice command and will not chase wildlife. Please refrain from taking pets to beach areas to prevent contamination. This campground is closed during the off-season. The camping and tent areas also allow dogs. There is a dog walk area at the campground. There are no

electric or water hookups at the campgrounds. Multiple dogs may be allowed.

Pinecrest Lake
Pinecrest Lake Road
Pinecrest, CA
209-965-3434
Located in a timbered setting at an elevation of 5,600 feet, this scenic park offers interpretive programs and a variety of land and water recreation. Dogs of all sizes are allowed. There are no additional pet fees. Dogs must be quiet, well behaved, leashed, and cleaned up after. No dogs allowed in Day Use Area (between Pinecrest Lake Road/Pinecrest Avenue and the boat launch and the fishing pier) from May 15 to September 15. This campground is closed during the off-season. The camping and tent areas also allow dogs. There is a dog walk area at the campground. There are no electric or water hookups at the campgrounds. Multiple dogs may be allowed.

Olive Grove Campground
4780 Piru Canyon Road
Piru, CA
805-521-1500
lake-piru.org/
Located at Lake Piru, this campground allows well-behaved leashed dogs in the developed campgrounds, but not in the water. However, dogs are allowed on a boat on the water. The Marina rents pontoon boats and dogs are allowed on the rentals. Campsite amenities including laundry facilities, showers, water, picnic areas and dumping stations. Five of the RV sites have hookups. There is a $2 per day pet fee, and dogs must have current shot records. Please clean up after your pets. Dogs may not be left unattended outside. The camping and tent areas also allow dogs. There is a dog walk area at the campground. Multiple dogs may be allowed.

Pismo Coast Village RV Park
165 S Dolliver Street
Pismo Beach, CA
805-773-1811
pismocoastvillage.com/
This 26 acre RV park is located right on the dog-friendly Pismo State Beach. There are 400 full hookup sites each with satellite TV. RVs up to 40 feet can be accommodated. Nestled right on the beach and beautifully landscaped, park amenities include a general store,

arcade, guest laundry, guest modem access in lobby, heated pool, bicycle rentals and miniature golf course. The maximum stay is 29 consecutive nights. Well-behaved leashed dogs of all sizes are allowed, up to a maximum of three pets. People need to clean up after their pets. There is no pet fee. Dogs may not be left unattended outside. This RV only campground is open all year. There are some breed restrictions. There is a dog walk area at the campground. Multiple dogs may be allowed.

49er Village RV Resort
18265 H 49
Plymouth, CA
800-339-6981
49ervillage.com
Nestled in the Sierra foothills, this park offers spacious, shady sites on tree-lined streets, 2 swimming pools-one year round-heated, an indoor whirlpool spa, and an on-site Deli-Espresso Cafe and Gift Shop, which is open daily at 7 a.m. Up to 3 dogs of any size are allowed for the RV section, and there is no additional fee or deposit. There are 2 pet friendly cabins; 1 dog is allowed in the studio, and up to 2 dogs are allowed in the one bedroom. There is a $100 per pet refundable deposit. Dogs may not be left unattended in the cottages or outside. Dogs must be leashed and cleaned up after. This is an RV only park. There is a dog walk area at the campground. Dogs are allowed in the camping cabins.

Ice House Resort
Forest Road 3
Pollock Pines, CA
530-644-2348
Located in the El Dorado National Forest at 5,500 feet, this scenic park offers a variety of recreational opportunities. Dogs of all sizes are allowed. There are no additional pet fees. Dogs may not be left unattended outside, and they must be leashed and cleaned up after. This campground is closed during the off-season. The camping and tent areas also allow dogs. There is a dog walk area at the campground. There are no electric or water hookups at the campgrounds. 2 dogs may be allowed.

Sly Park Campground
4771 Sly Park Road
Pollock Pines, CA
530-644-2792 (866-SLY-PARK (759-7275))
The wooded Sly Park Recreation

Area offers 159 campsites at an elevation of 3,500 feet. Site amenities include a table, barbecue and fire ring. Camp amenities include water, vault toilets, and a dump station at the park entrance. Pets on leash are allowed in the campground and on trails including the 8 to 9 mile trail which surround the lake. Dogs are not allowed in the lake. There is an additional fee of $2 per night per pet. Although open year round, call first in winter as snow causes road closures. The camping and tent areas also allow dogs. There is a dog walk area at the campground. There are no electric or water hookups at the campgrounds. Multiple dogs may be allowed.

Wench Creek Campground
Ice House Road/Forest Road 3
Pollock Pines, CA
530-644-2349
This campground is located in the El Dorado National Forest next to Union Valley Reservoir and offers 100 tent and RV campsites. Camp amenities include restrooms, water, swimming, bicycling, and hiking. Dogs are allowed in the campground, on the trails, and in the water. Pets should be leashed and please clean up after them. Dogs are not allowed to go into Desolation Valley. This campground is closed during the off-season. The camping and tent areas also allow dogs. There is a dog walk area at the campground. There are no electric or water hookups at the campgrounds. Multiple dogs may be allowed.

Sequoia National Forest
1839 South Newcomb Street
Porterville, CA
559-784-1500 (877-444-6777)
fs.fed.us/r5/sequoia/recreation/
Named for the world's largest tree, this forest is home to 38 groves of the giant sequoias, as well as impressive granite monoliths, glacier torn canyons, lush meadows, and rushing rivers. There are also several features/attractions here, some of which include; a 50 mile auto route (Kings Canyon Scenic Byway) that descends into one of North America's deepest canyons; several lookout stations-including the highest lookout (Bald Mountain) in the southern Sierra Nevadans; there are 3 National Recreation Trails, 45 miles of the Pacific Crest National Scenic Trail, and more than 800 miles of

maintained roads/over a 1,000 miles of trails. There is a wide variety of year round land and water recreational opportunities. Your dog is welcome here at Sequoia National Forest (not to be confused with the less than dog-friendly Sequoia National Park). Dogs must be friendly, well behaved, on no more than a 6 foot leash, cleaned up after, and inside an enclosed vehicle or tent at night. Dogs may go on all the trails and throughout the park; they are not allowed on developed swimming beaches or in park buildings. There are more than 50 developed campgrounds, reserved- and first come first served sites that offer a wide variety of different altitudes/features/amenities; all have vault or flush toilets. If you plan to make your own camp, be sure to obtain a campfire permit. The camping and tent areas also allow dogs. There is a dog walk area at the campground. There are no electric or water hookups at the campgrounds. 2 dogs may be allowed.

Grasshopper Flat Campground
Grizzley Flat Road (Road 112)
Portola, CA
530-836-2575 (877-444-6777)
This park on Lake Davis in the Sequoia National Forest offers varied habitats, ecosystems, and a wide variety of land and water recreation. Dogs may not be left unattended, and they must be leashed at all times and cleaned up after. Dogs are allowed on the trails unless otherwise marked, and in developed areas. Dogs are not allowed in any park buildings. This campground is closed during the off-season. The camping and tent areas also allow dogs. There is a dog walk area at the campground. Multiple dogs may be allowed.

Potrero County Park
24800 Potrero Park Drive
Potrero, CA
619-478-5212 (877-565-3600)
Dotted with hundred-year-old coastal oak trees and rich in natural and cultural history, this park at 2,600 feet, offers a wide variety of habitats and recreational activities. Dogs of all sizes are allowed for an additional $1 per night per pet, and they must have current tags, rabies, and shot records. Dogs may not be left unattended at any time, and they must be on no more than a 6 foot leash and cleaned up after. Dogs are not allowed on the trails, but they may be walked on the payment and

along side the roads on leash. The camping and tent areas also allow dogs. There is a dog walk area at the campground. Multiple dogs may be allowed.

Buck's Lake Recreation Area
Bucks Lake Road
Quincy, CA
530-283-0555 (877-444-6777)
This recreation area of 1,827 acres sits at an elevation of over 5,100 feet and provides a wide variety of year round land and water recreational activities. There are several businesses surrounding the 103,000 acre-feet Buck's Lake, with an assortment of services available. The park also offers 4 boat launch areas and access to the Pacific Crest Trail. Dogs of all sizes are allowed for no additional fee. Dogs must be leashed and cleaned up after. They are not allowed in the public swim areas; they are allowed on the trails. There are about 63 camp sites on a first come first served basis and 3 group sites that can be reserved, each with piped water and restroom facilities with the exception of Lower Bucks Lake. This RV park is closed during the off-season. The camping and tent areas also allow dogs. There is a dog walk area at the campground. There are no electric or water hookups at the campgrounds. Multiple dogs may be allowed.

Pioneer RV Park
1326 Pioneer Road
Quincy, CA
530-283-0796 (888-216-3266)
campingfriend.com/pioneerrvpark/
This pet-friendly RV park is located in the Sierra Nevada Mountains between Lassen National Park and Lake Tahoe. They have over 60 sites on 6.5 acres. RV sites have long wide pull-thru sites, picnic tables, 30 or 50 amp service, and satellite TV. Tent campers are also welcome. Other amenities include a laundry room, LP gas, rec room with DSL and WI-FI, big screen TV, books exchange and a ping-pong table. They are located about 1.5 miles from downtown Quincy and right next to a county park which has an Olympic size swimming pool and a playground. Well-behaved leashed dogs of all sizes are allowed. There is a covered dog kennel available for your use and a dog wash area. People need to clean up after their pets. There is no pet fee. There is a large area outside the park for walking your pet. The camping and tent areas also allow dogs. Multiple

dogs may be allowed.

Dos Picos County Park
17953 Dos Picos Park Road
Ramona, CA
760-789-2220 (877-565-3600)
This park, located in a small valley sheltered by nearby mountains, is full of plant and animal life, and offers various trails and recreational pursuits. Dogs of all sizes are allowed for an additional $1 per night per pet, and they must have current tags, rabies, and shot records. Dogs may not be left unattended at any time, and they must be on no more than a 6 foot leash and cleaned up after. Dogs are not allowed on the trails, but they may be walked on the payment and along side the roads on leash. The camping and tent areas also allow dogs. There is a dog walk area at the campground. Multiple dogs may be allowed.

Mountain Gate RV Park
14161 Holiday Road
Redding, CA
530-283-0769 (888-216-3266)
mt-gatervpark.com/
This RV park's amenities include full RV hookups, lighted grounds, large pull-thru sites, a convenience store, video rentals, cable TV, pool, rec room with pool table, email station, laundry, showers, restrooms, dump station, easy I-5 access, and an off lead, fenced pet area. Well-behaved leashed dogs are allowed. Please clean up after your pets. There is an additional fee of $1 per night per pet. The park is located 7 miles north of Redding. There are some breed restrictions. There is a dog walk area at the campground. There are special amenities given to dogs at this campground. Multiple dogs may be allowed.

Redding RV Park
11075 Campers Court
Redding, CA
530-241-0707 (800-428-2089)
campingfriend.com/reddingrvpark/
This scenic RV only park offers 110 paved, landscaped sites, barbecues, swimming pools, laundry facilities, a recreation room with pool tables, a convenience store, and a dump station. Dogs of all sizes are welcome for no additional fee. Dogs must be well behaved, and leashed and cleaned up after at all times. There is a dog walk area at the campground. Multiple dogs may be allowed.

Sacramento River RV Resort
6596 Riverland Drive
Redding, CA
530-365-6402
sacramentoriverrvresort.com
This is an RV only park located along the Sacramento River. No number or size restrictions are set on dogs for a one or two night stay, and there is no additional fee. For stays of one week or longer, there can be no more than 2 dogs and they can not be over 25 pounds, also for no additional fee. Dogs must be leashed and cleaned up after. There are some breed restrictions. There is a dog walk area at the campground.

Dean Creek Resort
4112 Redwood Drive
Redway, CA
707-923-2555
deancreekresort.com/
Located on the Eel River, this campground is located just 3 miles from the Avenue of the Giants attraction. Riverfront sites are available for both RVs and tent camping. Many of the RV sites have full hookups with 50 amp service available. All sites have picnic tables and barbecue grills. Other amenities include a pool, spa, sauna, coin laundry, mini-mart, meeting room, game room, playground, and restrooms. Pets are allowed but must be leashed at all times. There is an additional $1.50 per night per pet fee for the tent or RV sites. There is a $6 per night per pet additional fee for the motel rooms. Dogs may not be left unattended at any time. There are some breed restrictions. The camping and tent areas also allow dogs. There is a dog walk area at the campground. 2 dogs may be allowed.

Fossil Falls Campground
Cinder Road
Ridgecrest, CA
760-384-5400
This park, rich in prehistoric and modern history, features a rugged and primitive landscape as a result of ancient volcanic activity. Dogs of all sizes are allowed. There are no additional pet fees. Dogs must be leashed at all times and cleaned up after. Dogs are allowed on the trails; take caution around the cliff areas. The camping and tent areas also allow dogs. There is a dog walk area at the campground. There are no electric or water hookups at the campgrounds. Multiple dogs may be allowed.

Dogwood Campground
H 18
Rimforest, CA
909-337-2444 (877-444-6777)
This 93 site campground is located in the San Bernardino National Forest at 5,600 feet. RVs up to 22 feet are allowed. Amenities include water, showers, and a dump station. The camp is located less than a mile from Rimforest and 3 miles from Lake Arrowhead. Pets on leash are allowed at no additional fee, and please clean up after them. Dogs are allowed on the trails. This campground is closed during the off-season. The camping and tent areas also allow dogs. There is a dog walk area at the campground. There are no electric or water hookups at the campgrounds. Multiple dogs may be allowed.

Cal Expo RV Park
1600 Exposition Blvd
Sacramento, CA
916-263-3000 (877-CAL-EXPO (225-3976))
calexpo.com/html/rvpark.asp
Centrally located amid an abundance of attractions and recreational opportunities, this park also provides a laundry room, private restroom and showers, and 24 hour security. Dogs of all sizes are allowed. There are no additional pet fees. Dogs may not be left unattended outside, and only inside if they will be physically comfortable, quiet, and well behaved. Dogs must be leashed at all times, and cleaned up after. This is an RV only park. There is a dog walk area at the campground. 2 dogs may be allowed.

Laguna Seca Campground
1025 Monterey H 68
Salinas, CA
831-755-4895 (888-588-2267)
The popular Laguna Seca raceway is the highlight of this park. The park also offers a rifle range and an OHV and Off-Highway Motocross Track. Dogs are not permitted on any of the tracks including the OHV area. Dogs on leash are allowed at the RV and tent campgrounds, and on hiking trails. There is an additional fee of $2 per night per pet. RV sites are paved and offer up to 30 amp service. Tent sites are dirt pads with showers, telephones and a playground within walking distance. Camping fees are subject to change depending on events that are being held at the raceway. Call ahead for rates and reservations. The camping and tent areas also allow dogs. There is a

dog walk area at the campground. 2 dogs may be allowed.

San Clemente State Beach
3030 El Avenida Del Presidente
San Clemente, CA
949-492-3156 (800-444-PARK (7275))
Set among the sandstone cliffs on the ocean, this park is home to many species of land and marine life. The park offers interpretive exhibits and programs and a variety of recreational activities. Dogs of all sizes are allowed. There are no additional pet fees. Dogs may not be left unattended, and they must be well behaved, on no more than a 6 foot leash, and cleaned up after. Dogs must be brought inside at night. Dogs are not allowed on the trails or on the beach. The camping and tent areas also allow dogs. There is a dog walk area at the campground. Multiple dogs may be allowed.

Campland on the Bay
2211 Pacific Beach Drive
San Diego, CA
800-422-9386
campland.com/
This RV park is located on Mission Bay, across the water from Sea World. They offer beach front, bay view or primitive sites. Amenities include boat slips, a boat launch, store with a market, game room and a laundry room. Dogs of all sizes are allowed for an additional fee of $3 per night per pet. They must be leashed and please clean up after them. Dogs may not be left unattended outside, and they are not allowed on the beach. The camping and tent areas also allow dogs. There is a dog walk area at the campground. 2 dogs may be allowed.

Santee Lakes Recreation Preserve
9310 Fanita Parkway
San Diego, CA
619-596-3141
santeelakes.com
This large park, also a prime bird habitat, offers 2 swimming pools, a spa, 7 scenic lakes-stocked, a laundry with shower facilities, a clubhouse, watercraft rentals, 5 playgrounds including the Kiwanis Playground for children with disabilities, and miles of paved trails. Dogs of all sizes are allowed for an additional fee of $1 per night per pet. Dogs may not be left unattended outside, and they must be leashed and cleaned up after.

Dogs are allowed ONLY on the pet walks around lakes 6 and 7 and in the campground. Dogs are not allowed in any of the day use areas. The camping and tent areas also allow dogs. There is a dog walk area at the campground. 2 dogs may be allowed.

East Shore RV Park
1440 Camper View Road
San Dimas, CA
909-599-8355 (800-809-3778)
eastshorervpark.com/
This family RV park offers over 500 full hookup paved sites including some pull-thru sites. Site amenities include a grassy area, view sites, and full hookups with 20, 30 or 50 amp service. Park amenities include picnic areas, children's playground, laundry room, swimming pool, general store and market, video rentals, basketballs and volleyballs, email station, restrooms and 24 hour check-in. Well-behaved dogs are allowed in the RV park, but not in the tenting area. Pets must be leashed and please clean up after them. There is a $2 per day pet fee. Dogs may not be left unattended. This RV park is open year-round. There is a dog walk area at the campground. Multiple dogs may be allowed.

Candlestick RV Park
650 Gilman Avenue
San Francisco, CA
415-822-2299 (800-888-CAMP (2267))
gocampingamerica.com/candlestick
This modern park is next to it's namesake stadium and near local Bay-Area attractions. It has shuttles to downtown San Francisco, a game room, and laundry. Dogs of all sizes are allowed. There are no additional pet fees. Dogs may not be left unattended outside, and may only be left inside if they will be quiet and comfortable. Dogs must be leashed and cleaned up after. Dogs are not allowed in buildings. The RV park sits along side a state park with miles of trails, and dogs are allowed on the trails except where indicated. The camping and tent areas also allow dogs. There is a dog walk area at the campground. Multiple dogs may be allowed.

Betabel RV Park
9664 Betabel Road
San Juan Bautista, CA
831-623-2202 (800-278-7275)
betabel.com/
Located about 5 miles south of Gilroy, this RV park is set in the quiet

countryside. Amenities include 30 or 50 amp service, a mini mart, seasonally heated pool, propane, club/meeting rooms, satellite TV, restrooms, showers and handicapped access. Well-behaved leashed dogs of all sizes are allowed at no additional fee. People need to clean up after their pets. There is no pet fee. Dogs may not be left unattended outside, and they may only be left inside your unit for a short time if they will be quiet and comfortable. There is a large park across from the office where dogs can run off lead if they are well behaved and under voice control. The camping and tent areas also allow dogs. There is a dog walk area at the campground. 2 dogs may be allowed.

Mission Farms RV Park & Campground
400 San Juan Hollister Road
San Juan Bautista, CA
831-623-4456
Thanks to one of our readers for recommending this campground. Close to the highway, but quiet with lots of shade trees, this RV only park offers pull thru sites, big rig access, cable TV, and laundry. The camp sites are $28 per night. There is a $2 per night per pet fee for each small dog, and there is a $4 per night per pet fee for medium to large dogs. Dogs may not be left unattended, and they must be leashed and cleaned up after. There is a dog walk area at the campground. Multiple dogs may be allowed.

El Chorro Regional Park Campground
H 1
San Luis Obispo, CA
805-781-5930
This campground offers 62 campsites for tent or RV camping. Some of the RV spaces are pull-thru sites and can accommodate RVs up to 40 feet. All sites are available on a first-come, first-served basis. Use the self-registration envelopes upon arrival. There are several hiking trails to choose from at this park, from hiking on meadows to walking along a creek. There is an additional fee of $2 per night per pet. Dogs must be leashed at all times on the trails and in the campground. Please clean up after your pets. This park is home to the Dairy Creek Golf Course and features a day use area, barbecue facilities, volleyball courts, an off leash dog park (with two separate areas - one for smaller pets and one

for larger pets), horseshoe pits, a botanical garden, softball fields and various hiking trails. The camping and tent areas also allow dogs. There is a dog walk area at the campground. Multiple dogs may be allowed.

Cachuma Lake Rec Area
H 154
Santa Barbara, CA
805-686-5054
cachuma.com
This modern Santa Barbara park is well known for its natural beauty and a variety of recreational opportunities. Dogs of all sizes are allowed for an additional fee of $3 per night per dog. Dogs may not be left unattended, and they must have current rabies and shot records. Dogs must be quiet, well behaved, leashed at all times, and cleaned up after. Dogs may not be closer than 50 feet to the shore. The camping and tent areas also allow dogs. There is a dog walk area at the campground. Multiple dogs may be allowed.

Santa Margarita KOA
4765 Santa Margarita Lake Road
Santa Margarita, CA
805-438-5618 (800-562-5619)
koa.com/where/ca/05224/
Set in a rural setting with panoramic vistas, other amenities offered are 40 foot pull-thru sites with 30 amp, LP gas, swimming pool, and planned activities. Dogs of all sizes are allowed for no additional fee. Dogs must be under owner's control and visual observation at all times. Dogs must be quiet, well behaved, and be on no more than a 6 foot leash at all times, or otherwise contained. Dogs may not be left unattended outside the owner's camping equipment, and must be brought inside at night. In the cabins, dogs must remain in their carriers at all times. There are some breed restrictions. The camping and tent areas also allow dogs. There is a dog walk area at the campground. Dogs are allowed in the camping cabins. 2 dogs may be allowed.

Santa Margarita Lake Regional Park Camping
4695 Santa Margarita Lake Road
Santa Margarita, CA
805-781-5930
Primitive boat-in sites are available at this park. This lake is popular for fishing, boating and hiking. Swimming is not allowed at the lake because it is a reservoir which is

used for city drinking water. There is a seasonal swimming pool at the park. Hiking can be enjoyed at this park which offers miles of trails, ranging from easy to strenuous. Dogs must be leashed at all times and people need to clean up after their pets. There is an additional fee of $2 per night per pet. Dogs are allowed on the trails. The camping and tent areas also allow dogs. There is a dog walk area at the campground. There are no electric or water hookups at the campgrounds. Multiple dogs may be allowed.

Spring Lake Regional Park Campgrounds
5585 Newanga Avenue
Santa Rosa, CA
707-785-2377
This 320 acre regional park with a 72 acre lake, offers 27 campsites and miles of easy walking trails. RVs are permitted and there is a dump station. Dogs are allowed at an additional $1 per night per pet. They must be on a 6 foot or less leash and proof of a rabies vaccination is required. Dogs are not allowed around the swimming lagoon area. For reservations call 707-565-CAMP (2267). To get to the campground, take Hoen Avenue east, cross Summerfield Road, left at the stop sign (Newanga Avenue) into park. This campground is closed during the off-season. The camping and tent areas also allow dogs. There is a dog walk area at the campground. There are no electric or water hookups at the campgrounds. Multiple dogs may be allowed.

Lake Henshaw Resort
26439 H 76
Santa Ysabel, CA
760-782-3487
lakehenshawresort.com/
Lake Henshaw Resort, located at a lake which rests at the foot of the Palomar Mountains, is a great place for fishermen of all levels. Some of the amenities include a sparkling pool and spa, children's playground, grocery store with all your fishing needs, clubhouse, laundry facilities, and restaurant. Dogs of all sizes are allowed at an additional $2 per night per pet. Dogs are not allowed on the furniture in the cabins and they may not be left unattended. Dogs are allowed to walk along the lakeshore and to go in the water. The camping and tent areas also allow dogs. There is a dog walk area at the campground. Dogs are allowed in the camping cabins. Multiple dogs may

be allowed.

Santa Cruz Ranch RV Park
917 Disc Drive
Scotts Valley, CA
831-438-1288 (800-546-1288)
santacruzranchrv.com
This RV Park is located just off
Highway 17 5 miles from Santa Cruz
and 20 miles from San Jose in Scotts
Valley. It has a tent area and a dog
walk area. Dogs are welcome in the
campground.

Bakersfield KOA
5101 E Lerdo H
Shafter, CA
661-399-3107 (800-562-1633)
koa.com/where/ca/05381/
Some of this park's amenities are
free morning coffee, a swimming
pool, and large pull thru grass sites
with shade trees. Dogs of all sizes
are allowed at no additional fee.
Dogs may not be left unattended for
long periods, and they must be well
behaved, leashed and cleaned up
after. There are some breed
restrictions. The camping and tent
areas also allow dogs. There is a
dog walk area at the campground.
Multiple dogs may be allowed.

Mount Shasta KOA
900 N Mt Shasta Blvd
Shasta City, CA
530-926-4029 (800-562-3617)
koa.com/where/ca/05108/
There is a variety of land, water, and
air recreation at this scenic alpine
park. The campground also offers 80
foot pull-thru sites with 50 amp,
cable, LP gas, snack bar, and
swimming pool. Dogs of all sizes are
allowed for no additional fee. Dogs
must be under owner's control and
visual observation at all times. Dogs
must be quiet, well behaved, and be
on no more than a 6 foot leash at all
times, or otherwise contained. Dogs
may not be left unattended outside
the owner's camping equipment.
There are some breed restrictions.
The camping and tent areas also
allow dogs. There is a dog walk area
at the campground. Dogs are
allowed in the camping cabins.
Multiple dogs may be allowed.

Hirz Bay Campground
Gilman Road
Shasta Lake, CA
530-275-1587 (877-444-6777)
This campground is located in the
Shasta-Trinity National Forest at an
elevation of 1,100 feet. The
campground offers 37 tent and RV
campsites. RVs up to 30 feet are

allowed. Amenities include drinking
water, accessible restrooms, flush
toilets and boat ramp. Fishing,
swimming and boating are popular
activities at the campground. The
camp is open year round. Dogs are
allowed in the lake, but not at the
designated swimming beaches.
Pets must be leashed and please
clean up after them. The camping
and tent areas also allow dogs.
There is a dog walk area at the
campground. There are no electric
or water hookups at the
campgrounds. Multiple dogs may
be allowed.

Camp Edison at Shaver Lake
42696 Tollhouse Road
Shaver Lake, CA
559-841-3134
This campground is located at
Shaver Lake in the Sierra National
Forest and is managed by Southern
California Edison. There are 252
campsites with electricity and free
cable TV. Amenities include picnic
tables, restroom with heated
showers, a guest laundry, marina
and a general store. Dogs are
allowed at the campgrounds, on
trails and in the water but only at
non-designated swimming beaches.
Pets must be leashed and please
clean up after them. There is a $5
per night per pet fee. Dogs may not
be left unattended, and they must
be brought inside at night. The
camping and tent areas also allow
dogs. There is a dog walk area at
the campground. Multiple dogs may
be allowed.

Dorabelle Campground
Dorabella Street
Shaver Lake, CA
559-297-0706 (877-444-6777)
This campground is next to Shaver
Lake in the Sierra National Forest.
Some of the sites have lake views
and all of the sites have shade from
dense pines trees. The camp is at
an elevation of 5,500 feet. There
are 68 tent and RV sites, and RVs
up to 40 feet are allowed. Amenities
include water, vault toilets, picnic
tables and grills. Be sure to bring
some mosquito repellant. There are
several trails here that provide
access around the lake. Dogs are
allowed at the campgrounds, on
trails and in the water but only at
non-designated swimming beaches.
Pets must be leashed and please
clean up after them. Dogs may not
be left unattended. This
campground is closed during the
off-season. The camping and tent

areas also allow dogs. There is a
dog walk area at the campground.
There are no electric or water
hookups at the campgrounds.
Multiple dogs may be allowed.

Placerville KOA
4655 Rock Barn Road
Shingle Springs, CA
530-676-2267 (800-562-4197)
koa.com/where/ca/05429/
Located close to other attractions,
this park offers 110 foot pull-thru
sites with 50 amp service, a store,
petting zoo, playground, pond,
swimming pool, sauna/spa, cable,
Wi-Fi, and more. Dogs of all sizes
are allowed for no additional fee.
Dogs must be under owner's control
and visual observation at all times.
Dogs must be quiet, well behaved,
and be on no more than a 6 foot
leash at all times, or otherwise
contained. Dogs may not be left
unattended outside the owner's
camping equipment, and must be
brought inside at night. There is a
fenced in dog run area where your
pet may be off lead. There are some
breed restrictions. The camping and
tent areas also allow dogs. There is
a dog walk area at the campground.
There are special amenities given to
dogs at this campground. Multiple
dogs may be allowed.

Mt Lassen/Shingletown KOA
7749 KOA Road
Shingletown, CA
530-474-3133 (800-562-3403)
koa.com/where/ca/05147/
Located at an elevation of 3,900 feet,
this twelve acre campground offers
both tent and RV sites in the pines.
The maximum length for pull-thru
sites is 60 feet. Sites have 30 amp
service available. Other amenities
include LP gas, free modem
dataport, snack bar, swimming pool
during the summer, and a deli. Dogs
of all sizes are allowed for no
additional fee. Dogs must be under
owner's control and visual
observation at all times. Dogs must
be quiet, well behaved, and be on no
more than a 6 foot leash at all times,
or otherwise contained. Dogs may
not be left unattended outside the
owner's camping equipment. There
is a large field where dogs may be
off lead if they are well trained, and
under voice command. There are
some breed restrictions. This
campground is closed during the off-
season. The camping and tent areas
also allow dogs. There is a dog walk
area at the campground. Multiple
dogs may be allowed.

D. L. Bliss State Park
H 89
South Lake Tahoe, CA
530-525-9529 (800-444-7275)
This park, at 6,200 feet, offers an impressive panoramic view of Lake Tahoe and the Tahoe Valley and a variety of recreational opportunities. Dogs are allowed in the parks at no additional fee. However, they must be kept on a leash during the day and in an enclosed vehicle or tent at night. Due to the possible danger to wildlife and other park visitors, dogs are not permitted on the trails, beaches or in the Vikingsholm area. The camping and tent areas also allow dogs. There is a dog walk area at the campground. There are no electric or water hookups at the campgrounds. Multiple dogs may be allowed.

Encore Tahoe Valley RV Resort
1175 Melba Drive
South Lake Tahoe, CA
877-717-8737
Located in South Lake Tahoe, this campground sits among towering pines and mountain vistas, and some of their amenities include volleyball and tennis courts, seasonal heated outdoor pool, pool table, playground, video game center, general store, laundry facilities, modem hookups and even a dog run. Well-behaved leashed (at all times) dogs are welcome. Please clean up after your pet. There is no pet fee. Dogs may not be left unattended. The camping and tent areas also allow dogs. There is a dog walk area at the campground. Multiple dogs may be allowed.

Fallen Leaf Campground
Fallen Leaf Lake Road
South Lake Tahoe, CA
530-543-2600 (877-444-6777)
This campground is at a 6,377 foot elevation and is located in the Lake Tahoe Management Basin Unit of the National Forest. The camp offers 250 sites and 17 are available on a first-come, first-served basis. The maximum RV length allowed is 40 feet. Amenities include water, flush toilets, fire rings, picnic tables and barbecues. There are miles of trails which begin at or near this campground. Pets on leash are allowed at no additional fee, but not at the beach; they are allowed to swim in the lake. Please clean up after your pets. Dogs are allowed on the trails. Access to the campgrounds is on a rough paved

road. A regular passenger car will make it, but go slow. This campground is closed during the off-season. The camping and tent areas also allow dogs. There is a dog walk area at the campground. There are no electric or water hookups at the campgrounds. Multiple dogs may be allowed.

Lake Tahoe-South Shore KOA
760 North Highway 50
South Lake Tahoe, CA
530-577-3693 (800-562-3477)
koa.com/where/ca/05148/
Surrounded by tall pines with a creek running through, this campground offers a variety of land and water recreation with amenities that include cable TV, 60 foot pull-thru sites with 30 amp, LP gas, Wi-Fi, swimming pool, and tours. Dogs of all sizes are allowed for an additional fee of $4 per night per pet. Dogs must be under owner's control and visual observation at all times. Dogs must be quiet, well behaved, and be on no more than a 6 foot leash at all times, or otherwise contained. Dogs may not be left unattended outside the owner's camping equipment. There are some breed restrictions. This campground is closed during the off-season. The camping and tent areas also allow dogs. There is a dog walk area at the campground. Multiple dogs may be allowed.

Letts Lake Campground
Forest Road M10
Stonyford, CA
530-934-3316
This campground is located in the Mendocino National Forest and is next to a 35 acre lake. Water-based activities include non-motorized boating, trout fishing and swimming. There are 44 campsites and camp amenities include toilets, fire rings, water and trailer space. The access road and camps are suitable for 16 to 20 foot camping trailers. The campground is at an elevation of 4,500 feet. There is a $10 per day campsite fee. Prices are subject to change. Dogs on leash are allowed at the campground, on trails and in the water at non-designated swimming areas only. The camp is located 19 miles west of Stonyford. This campground is closed during the off-season. The camping and tent areas also allow dogs. There is a dog walk area at the campground. There are no electric or water hookups at the campgrounds. Multiple dogs may be allowed.

Goumas Campground, Eagle Lake
477-050 Eagle Lake Road
Susanville, CA
530-257-4188 (877-444-6777)
This primitive campground, at 5,600 feet and near Eagle Lake, offers great scenery and a host of recreational pursuits. Dogs of all sizes are allowed. There are no additional pet fees. Dogs must be on no more than a 6 foot leash at all times in the camp areas, but they may be off lead on the trails if they are under voice command and well behaved. Please clean up after your pet. This campground is closed during the off-season. The camping and tent areas also allow dogs. There is a dog walk area at the campground. There are no electric or water hookups at the campgrounds. Multiple dogs may be allowed.

Merrill Campground, Eagle Lake
477050 Eagle Lake Road
Susanville, CA
530-257-4188 (877-444-6777)
Located at the south end of Eagle Lake at 5,100 feet, this park offers great scenery and a variety of land and water recreation. Dogs of all sizes are allowed. There are no additional pet fees. Dogs may not be left unattended, and they must be leashed and cleaned up after. Dogs are allowed on the trails. This campground is closed during the off-season. The camping and tent areas also allow dogs. There is a dog walk area at the campground. There are no water hookups at the campgrounds. Multiple dogs may be allowed.

Meeks Bay Campground
H 89
Tahoe City, CA
530-543-2600 (877-444-6777)
This campground is at 6,225 feet elevation and is located in the Lake Tahoe Management Basin Unit of the National Forest. The camp offers 40 tent and RV sites. The maximum RV length allowed is 20 feet. Amenities include water, flush toilets, fire rings, picnic tables and barbecues. Pets on leash are allowed but not at the beach. Please clean up after your pets. Dogs are allowed on the trails. The camp is about 10 miles south of Tahoe City, located near D.L. Bliss State Park. This campground is closed during the off-season. The camping and tent areas also allow dogs. There is a dog walk area at the campground. There are no electric or water

hookups at the campgrounds. Multiple dogs may be allowed.

D. L. Bliss State Park
H 89/South Lake Tahoe
Tahoma, CA
530-525-7277 (800-444-7275)
Donated by the D. L. Bliss family in 1929, this park of 744 acres displays the grandeur of the mountain building processes of Mother Earth and offers visitors spectacular views of the surrounding area and deep into the lake. Dogs of all sizes are only allowed in developed areas, picnic grounds, and on paved roads. They are not allowed on the trails, beaches, or in the Vikingsholm area, and they must be inside a tent or vehicle from the hours of 10 pm to 6 am. Dogs must be under their owner's control at all times, be on no more than a 6 foot leash, and be cleaned up after. There are 268 family campsites and a group camp between the D.L. Bliss State Park and Emerald Bay, reserved-or on a first come/first serve basis and the sites each have a table, cupboard, and stove. There are restrooms and hot showers nearby. This RV park is closed during the off-season. The camping and tent areas also allow dogs. There is a dog walk area at the campground. There are no electric or water hookups at the campgrounds. Multiple dogs may be allowed.

Emerald Bay State Park
H 89/South Lake Tahoe
Tahoma, CA
530-541-3030 (800-444-7275)
A National Natural Landmark, this beautiful state park is rich in its natural beauty, history, and geology, and features Vikingsholm, one of the best examples of Scandinavian architecture in the western hemisphere. The park is also home to Lake Tahoe's only island, Fannette Island, and there are a variety of recreational opportunities to pursue. Dogs of all sizes are allowed in developed areas, picnic grounds, and on paved roads. They are not allowed on the trails, beaches, or in the Vikingsholm area, and they must be inside a tent or vehicle from the hours of 10 pm to 6 am. Dogs must be under their owner's control at all times, be on no more than a 6 foot leash, and be cleaned up after. There are 268 family campsites and a group camp between the D.L. Bliss State Park and Emerald Bay, reserved-or on a first come/first serve basis and the sites each have a table, cupboard,

and stove. There are restrooms and hot showers nearby. This RV park is closed during the off-season. The camping and tent areas also allow dogs. There is a dog walk area at the campground. There are no electric or water hookups at the campgrounds. Multiple dogs may be allowed.

General Creek Campground
West Shore Lake Tahoe
Tahoma, CA
530-525-7982 (800-444-7275)
This park is located in the Sugar Pine Point State Park, offering various habitats to explore, miles of trails, and a variety of land and water recreation. Dogs of all sizes are allowed at no additional fee. Dogs must be kept on a leash no longer than six feet and under control at all times. They are not permitted in buildings or beaches. Dogs are allowed on all paved trails. Dogs must be confined to a vehicle or tent from 10:00 p.m. to 6:00 a.m. This campground is closed during the off-season. The camping and tent areas also allow dogs. There is a dog walk area at the campground. Multiple dogs may be allowed.

Pechanga RV Resort
45000 Pechanga Parkway
Temecula, CA
951-587-0484 (877-997-8386)
pechangarv.com/index.asp
This RV only resort is located at the Pechanga Casino. They offer 168 sites with 20, 30 and 50 amp service, cable TV, 25 pull-thru sites, 3 internet access stations, a heated pool, two spas, and an attractive patio area with a full barbecue adjoining the recreation room. Well behaved, friendly dogs are allowed for no additional fee. Dogs may not be left unattended, and they must be leashed and cleaned up after. If dogs are not cleaned up after, they will ask visitors to leave. There are some breed restrictions. There is a dog walk area at the campground. 2 dogs may be allowed.

Vail Lake Wine Country RV Resort
38000 H 79 S
Temecula, CA
951-303-0173 (866-VAIL LAKE (824-5525))
This RV resort is located in the country, about 15 minutes from Interstate 15. There are several hiking trails throughout the RV park where you can walk with your dog. There is no additional pet fee. Dogs

may not be left unattended, and they must be leashed and cleaned up after. There is a dog walk area at the campground. 2 dogs may be allowed.

Azalea Campground, Kings Canyon National Park
Grant Tree Road
Three Rivers, CA
559-565-3708
This scenic park, located at 6,500 feet in the Kings Canyon National Park, offers a variety of recreational pursuits. Dogs of all sizes are allowed. There are no additional pet fees. Dogs must be leashed at all times and cleaned up after. Dogs are not allowed on the hiking trails, and must stay in the camp area or on the roads. The camping and tent areas also allow dogs. There is a dog walk area at the campground. There are no electric or water hookups at the campgrounds. Multiple dogs may be allowed.

Potwisha Campground, Sequoia and Kings Canyon Nat'l Park
47050 Generals H (H 198)
Three Rivers, CA
559-565-3341
nps.gov/seki
Located in a National Forest, this park offers spectacular scenery, varied habitats and elevations, and a wide variety of land and water recreation. Dogs of all sizes are allowed at no additional fee. Dogs may not be left unattended at any time. Keep in mind that dogs are not permitted on park trails and it may be too hot to leave them in the car. It is highly suggested that dogs are not brought to the park in summer as temperatures reach over 110 degrees, and there is poison oak, snakes, and ticks. Dogs are not allowed in the water or on any of the trails. Dogs may be walked in the campground, on walkways or roadways only. Dogs must be leashed at all times and cleaned up after. The camping and tent areas also allow dogs. There is a dog walk area at the campground. There are no electric or water hookups at the campgrounds. 2 dogs may be allowed.

Sequoia and Kings Canyon National Park Campgrounds
47050 General H
Three Rivers, CA
559-565-3341
nps.gov/seki/pphtml/camping.html
This park offers many campgrounds which range in elevation from 2,100

feet to 7,500 feet. The Lodgepole, Dorst, Grant Grove and Atwell Mill campgrounds are located near giant sequoia groves. The Lodgepole campground, located at 6,700 foot elevation, is one of the largest camps and offers 250 sites. Tent and RV camping is available, with a maximum RV length of 35 feet. Amenities at this campground include a guest laundry, deli, market, gift shop, pay showers, flush toilets and more. Some of the campgrounds are open all year. Pets must be leashed and attended at all times. Please clean up after your pet. Keep in mind that dogs are not permitted on park trails and it may be too hot to leave them in the car. Please see our listings in the towns of Johnsondale and Hume for details about nearby dog-friendly hiking, sightseeing and additional camping. A couple of the camp areas are not accessible to RV's, so research ahead. The camping and tent areas also allow dogs. There is a dog walk area at the campground. There are no electric or water hookups at the campgrounds. Multiple dogs may be allowed.

Eagles Nest RV Park
634 County Road 97A
Tionesta, CA
530-664-2081
eaglesnestrvpark.com/
This RV park is located 24 miles south of the town of Tulelake and 2 miles off Highway 139. Amenities include 20 full hookup pull-thru sites, showers, restrooms, a guest laundry, clubhouse with pool table, satellite TV, and a book exchange. Grassy tent sites are also available. Well-behaved leashed dogs are welcome for no additional fee. Please clean up after your pets. This campground is closed during the off-season. The camping and tent areas also allow dogs. There is a dog walk area at the campground. Multiple dogs may be allowed.

East Fork Campground
Rock Creek Canyon Road
Tom's Place, CA
760-873-2500 (877-444-6777)
This 133 site campground is located in the Inyo National Forest at an elevation of 9,000 feet. Amenities include water, flush toilet, picnic tables and space for RVs. For hiking, there are several trailheads nearby including the Hilton Lakes and Little Lakes Valley trails. The fee for a campsite is $15. Pets must be leashed while in the campground and please clean up after them. Dogs

may not be left unattended outside. This campground is closed during the off-season. The camping and tent areas also allow dogs. There is a dog walk area at the campground. There are no electric or water hookups at the campgrounds. Multiple dogs may be allowed.

Emerald Forest of Trinidad
753 Patrick's Point Drive
Trinidad, CA
707-677-3554 (888-677-3800)
cabinsintheredwoods.com/
This well kept campground covers 12 acres of redwood forest and is less than a mile from Trinidad Bay. Some of the amenities include a gift shop, playground, an arcade, laundry facilities, an outdoor pavilion with barbecues, gaming areas, and a dump station. Dogs are allowed in 2 of the cabins for an additional fee of $10 per stay per pet, and 1 medium dog or 2 small dogs (15 pound limit each) are allowed per cabin. Dogs are not allowed in the tent area. There is no additional pet fee for RV camping or size restrictions. Dogs may not be left unattended, and they must be leashed and cleaned up after at all times. There is a dog walk area at the campground. Dogs are allowed in the camping cabins.

Patrick's Point State Park
4150 Patrick's Point Drive
Trinidad, CA
707-677-3570
Located in the heart of the coastal redwood country, this park is a mix of dense forests and wildflower filled meadows. They feature a recreated Yurok Village, a Native American Plant Garden, fully developed picnic areas with barbecues and restrooms, and interpretive programs in the summer. Dogs are allowed for no additional fee. They are allowed at the lagoons, and in developed and paved areas only; they are not allowed on the trails or the beaches. Dogs must be inside an enclosed vehicle or tent at night, be on no more than a 6 foot leash, and cleaned up after. There are three family campgrounds with a total of 124 campsites; they each have a table, stove, cupboard, and water and restrooms nearby. Group campsites are also available. The camping and tent areas also allow dogs. There is a dog walk area at the campground. There are no electric or water hookups at the campgrounds. Multiple dogs may

be allowed.

Clark Springs Campground
Off H 3
Trinity Center, CA
530-623-2121 (877-444-6777)
This campground is located in the Shasta-Trinity National Forest at an elevation of 2,400 feet. The campground offers 21 tent and RV campsites. RVs up to 25 feet are allowed, and amenities include a swimming beach, boat ramp, drinking water, picnic sites, wheelchair access and flush toilets. Fishing, swimming, boating and hiking are popular activities at the campground. The Trinity Lakeshore trailhead is located here. Dogs are allowed on the trails and in the lake water but only on non-designated swimming areas. Pets must be leashed at all times in camp, and please clean up after them. Dogs may be off lead on the trails only if they are under strict voice control, and they will not chase. This campground is closed during the off-season. The camping and tent areas also allow dogs. There is a dog walk area at the campground. There are no electric or water hookups at the campgrounds. Multiple dogs may be allowed.

Hayward Flat Campground
H 3
Trinity Center, CA
530-623-2121 (877-444-6777)
This campground is located on the west side of the East Fork arm of Trinity Lake in the Shasta-Trinity National Forest. The campground is at an elevation of 2,400 feet and offers 94 tent and RV campsites. RVs up to 40 feet are allowed, and amenities include drinking water and flush toilets. Fishing, swimming and boating are popular activities at the campground. Dogs may not be left unattended outside. Pets must be leashed at all times in the camp areas, and please clean up after them. Dogs may be off lead on the trails if they are under strict voice command and will not chase. This campground is closed during the off-season. The camping and tent areas also allow dogs. There is a dog walk area at the campground. There are no electric or water hookups at the campgrounds. Multiple dogs may be allowed.

Wyntoon Resort
60260 H 3
Trinity Center, CA
530-266-3337 (800-715-3337)
wyntoonresort.com/

This 90 acre wooded resort is located at the north end of Lake Trinity and offers both RV and tent sites. The RV sites are tree shaded with 30 or 50 amp service, and will accommodate RVs up to 60 feet. Tent sites are located under pine and cedar trees and have picnic tables and barbecues. Other camp amenities include a swimming pool, clubhouse, snack bar, ping pong, showers and laundry facilities. Well-behaved leashed pets are always welcome. Please clean up after your pet. There is a $1 per day pet fee. Dogs may not be left unattended. The camping and tent areas also allow dogs. There is a dog walk area at the campground. Multiple dogs may be allowed.

Lakeside Campground
Off H 89
Truckee, CA
530-587-3558 (877-444-6777)
This 30 site campground is located in the Tahoe National Forest at an elevation of 5,741 feet. Camp amenities include vault toilets. There is no water. Sites are $13 per night. The campground is located next to the reservoir and activities include fishing and swimming. Pets are allowed at no additional fee, and they must be leashed in the campground. Dogs must be cleaned up after. They may be off lead on the trails only if they are under voice control. This campground is closed during the off-season. The camping and tent areas also allow dogs. There is a dog walk area at the campground. There are no electric or water hookups at the campgrounds. 2 dogs may be allowed.

Logger Campground, Truckee District
9646 Donner Pass Road
Truckee, CA
530-587-3558
fs.fed.us/r5/tahoe
Located high in the northern Sierra Nevada mountain range, this park offers great scenery, interpretive exhibits, miles of trails, and a variety of recreation. Dogs of all sizes are allowed. There are no additional pet fees. Dogs must be leashed in the camp areas, and cleaned up after. Dogs may be off lead on the trails if they are under voice control. This campground is closed during the off-season. The camping and tent areas also allow dogs. There is a dog walk area at the campground. There are no electric or water hookups at the campgrounds. Multiple dogs may be

allowed.

Indian Well Campground
1 Indian Well
Tulelake, CA
530-667-8100
nps.gov/labe/pphtml/camping.html
This campground, located in the Lava Beds National Monument, offers 40 campsites for tents and small to medium sized RVs. Amenities include water and flush toilets. Campsites are available on a first-come, first-served basis. Pets must be on no more than a 6 foot leash and attended at all times. Please clean up after your pet. Dogs may not be left unattended. Dogs are not allowed on any trails or hikes in this park, but see our Modoc National Forest listings in this region for nearby dog-friendly hiking, sightseeing and additional camping. The camping and tent areas also allow dogs. There is a dog walk area at the campground. There are no electric or water hookups at the campgrounds. Multiple dogs may be allowed.

Medicine Lake Campground
Forest Service Road 44N38
Tulelake, CA
530-233-5811
This campground is located on the shores of Medicine Lake at a 6,700 foot elevation in the Modoc National Forest. There are 22 RV and tent sites. RVs up to 22 feet are allowed, and amenities include picnic tables, fire pits, vault toilets and potable water. Dogs on leash are allowed at the campgrounds and in the water. Please clean up after your pets. There is a $7 per vehicle fee. This campground is closed during the off-season. The camping and tent areas also allow dogs. There is a dog walk area at the campground. There are no electric or water hookups at the campgrounds. Multiple dogs may be allowed.

29 Palms RV Resort
4949 Desert Knoll
Twentynine Palms, CA
760-367-3320
29palmsgolf.com/
This RV resort is located less than 10 minutes from the Joshua Tree National Park visitor center. RV sites include shade trees, and they can accommodate large motorhomes and trailers. Park amenities include a recreation hall, fitness room, tennis courts, shuffle board, heated indoor pool, laundry, showers, and restrooms. You can

stay for a day, a week, or all winter. Pets on leash are welcome. There is no pet fee, just clean up after your dog. They also provide a fenced-in dog run area. Dogs may not be left unattended outside. The camping and tent areas also allow dogs. There is a dog walk area at the campground. There are special amenities given to dogs at this campground. Multiple dogs may be allowed.

Joshua Tree National Park Campgrounds
74485 National Park Drive
Twentynine Palms, CA
760-367-5500 (800-365-CAMP (2267))
nps.gov/jotr/pphtml/camping.html
There are nine campgrounds at this park which range from 3,000 foot to 4,500 foot elevations. Many have no fees and offer pit toilets. Only a few of the campgrounds offer water and flush toilets. Generators are not allowed between the hours of 10pm and 6am, and they are only allowed for 3 two hour periods each day. Dogs of all sizes are allowed at no additional fee. Dogs may not be left unattended, and they must be leashed and cleaned up after. Dogs are not allowed on the trails, but they are allowed on all paved roads, and the paved trail by the Visitor's Center. The camping and tent areas also allow dogs. There is a dog walk area at the campground. There are no electric or water hookups at the campgrounds. Multiple dogs may be allowed.

Cow Mountain Recreation Area/Ukiah Field Office
2550 North State Street
Ukiah, CA
707-468-4000
blm.gov/ca/ukiah/cowmtn.html
Dogs are allowed at the North Cow Mountain portion of this recreation area off Mill Creek Road; the South area is mostly for off-road vehicles. Dogs of all sizes are allowed for no additional fee. Dogs must be under their owner's control at all times, and leashed and cleaned up after. Campsites are on a first-come, first-served basis and some of the amenities include tables, barbecues, fire grates, and pit toilets; there is no potable water. The camping and tent areas also allow dogs. There is a dog walk area at the campground. There are no electric or water hookups at the campgrounds. Multiple dogs may be allowed.

Lake Mendocino Recreation Area
1160 Lake Mendocino Drive
Ukiah, CA
707-462-7581 (877-444-6777)
lakemendocino.com/camping.htm
Created by the construction of the
Coyote Dam, this beautiful lake
recreation area is set among rolling
hills and oak groves near the
headwaters of the Russian River
offering plenty of hiking trails. The
lake has more than 1,800 surface
acres, and there is a wide variety of
land and water recreational
opportunities. Dogs of all sizes are
allowed for no additional fee. Dogs
must be on no more than a 6 foot
leash and be cleaned up after. Dogs
are allowed throughout the park and
on the trails. There are 3 main
campgrounds (offering more than
200 campsites) each with different
features; 2 of them have pay
showers, 2 shares an amphitheater,
1 has an 18-hole golf course, and all
have potable water, picnic tables,
and a fire ring. Most sites can be
reserved up to 240 days in advance
at the 877-444-6777 number. The
camping and tent areas also allow
dogs. There is a dog walk area at the
campground. There are no electric or
water hookups at the campgrounds.
Multiple dogs may be allowed.

Pine Acres Resort
5328 Blue Lakes Road
Upper Lake, CA
707-275-2811
bluelakepineacres.com/
This well kept mountain resort sits
along a regularly stocked spring-fed
lake, and each of the RV sites has a
scenic lake view. Some of the
features/amenities include a country
store, tackle shop, boat launch, hot
showers, and restrooms. Dogs are
allowed for an additional $5 per night
per pet. Dogs are allowed throughout
the park, except they are not allowed
in the tent area or in rooms or
cottages. Dogs must be leashed and
cleaned up after at all times. There is
a dog walk area at the campground.
Multiple dogs may be allowed.

Sunset Campground
County Road 301/Forest Road M1
Upper Lake, CA
916-386-5164
This campground is located in the
Mendocino National Forest and is
managed by Pacific Gas and
Electric. Camp amenities include 54
tables, 54 stoves, 12 toilets, water,
trailer spaces and 27 grills. The
Sunset Nature Trail Loop begins at
this campground. There is a $12 fee

per campsite and an extra $1 per
night per pet fee. Dogs on leash are
allowed and please clean up after
them. This campground is closed
during the off-season. The camping
and tent areas also allow dogs.
There is a dog walk area at the
campground. There are no electric
or water hookups at the
campgrounds. 2 dogs may be
allowed.

Midway RV Park
4933 Midway Road
Vacaville, CA
707-446-7679 (866-446-7679)
midwayrvpark.com/
Located in a beautiful rural setting,
this park offers a pool, Wi-Fi,
laundry, pull-thru sites, sewer hookups, and is centrally located to
several attractions. Dogs of all sizes
are allowed for an additional $1 per
night per pet. Dogs may not be left
unattended outside, and they must
be leashed and cleaned up after.
This is an RV only park. There are
some breed restrictions. There is a
dog walk area at the campground.
Multiple dogs may be allowed.

Vineyard RV Park
4985 Midway Road
Vacaville, CA
707-693-8797 (866-447-8797)
This nicely landscaped park offers a
large enclosed dog walk area, a rec
room, Wi-Fi, laundry room, pool,
and a variety of activities and
recreation. Dogs of all sizes are
allowed for an additional $1 per
night per pet by the day, or for an
additional $5 per night per pet by
the week. Dogs may not be left
unattended outside, and they must
be leashed and cleaned up after.
This is an RV only park. There are
some breed restrictions. There is a
dog walk area at the campground.
There are special amenities given
to dogs at this campground. 2 dogs
may be allowed.

Vallecito Regional Park
37349 County Route S-2
Vallecito, CA
760-765-1188 (877-565-3600)
Rich in natural and cultural history,
this park has been called a beautiful
oasis in the desert. It offers a wide
variety of recreational pursuits.
Dogs of all sizes are allowed for an
additional $1 per night per pet, and
they must have current tags, rabies,
and shot records. Dogs may not be
left unattended at any time, and
they must be on no more than a 6
foot leash and cleaned up after.

Dogs are not allowed on the trails,
but they may be walked on the
payment and along side the roads on
leash. This campground is closed
during the off-season. The camping
and tent areas also allow dogs.
There is a dog walk area at the
campground. There are no electric or
water hookups at the campgrounds.
Multiple dogs may be allowed.

Acorn Campground
2713 Hogan Dam Road
Valley Springs, CA
209-772-1343 (877-444-6777)
This campground, along New Hogan
Lake on the Calaveras River,
features an amphitheater, an
interpretive trail, hiking trails, and
various recreation opportunities.
Dogs of all sizes are allowed. There
are no additional pet fees. Dogs
must be on no more than a 6 foot
leash and cleaned up after. Dogs are
allowed on the trails, but they are not
allowed at Wrinkle Cove. The
camping and tent areas also allow
dogs. There is a dog walk area at the
campground. There are no electric or
water hookups at the campgrounds.
2 dogs may be allowed.

Lake Casitas Recreation Area
11311 Santa Ana Road
Ventura, CA
805-649-2233
lakecasitas.info/
Along side the lake or up on the
hillside nestled among the trees,
there are over 400 camp sites to
choose from here. Visitors will find a
variety of concessions throughout
the park, including a seasonal
waterpark. All camp sites offer picnic
tables and fire rings with children's
playgrounds close by; restrooms and
showers are located by the front gate
and towards the back of the park.
Reservations can be made for camp
sites at 805-649-1122. Dogs of all
sizes are allowed. There is a $1.50
per pet fee for day use, and a $3
additional fee per pet per night for
camping. Dogs must be under
owner's immediate control, leashed,
and cleaned up after at all times.
Dogs are allowed throughout the
park, but they must be kept at least
50 feet away from the water. The
camping and tent areas also allow
dogs. There is a dog walk area at the
campground. Multiple dogs may be
allowed.

Ventura Beach RV Resort
800 W Main Street
Ventura, CA
805-643-9137

venturabeach-rvresort.com/
This camping resort offers 144 paved sites, all with a grassy area, picnic tables, shade trees, and fire rings. Some of the amenities include a children's playground, laundry facilities, a pool and spa, family activities, gaming tables/courts, an arcade, bike rentals, restrooms and showers, and Wi-Fi. Dogs of all sizes are allowed for an additional $2 per night per pet, and they must have a current rabies certificate. Dogs may not be left unattended outside at any time, and they must be leashed and cleaned up after. Pit Bulls are not allowed. The camping and tent areas also allow dogs. There is a dog walk area at the campground. Multiple dogs may be allowed.

Victorville/Inland Empire KOA
16530 Stoddard Wells Road
Victorville, CA
760-245-6867 (800-562-3319)
koa.com/where/ca/05114/
A shady get-away in the high desert, this park offers a maximum pull-thru of 75 feet with 30 amp, LP gas, seasonal swimming pool, several planned activities, and bike rentals. Dogs of all sizes are allowed for no additional fee. Dogs must be under owner's control and visual observation at all times. Dogs must be quiet, well behaved, and be on no more than a 6 foot leash at all times, or otherwise contained. Dogs may not be left unattended outside the owner's camping equipment, and must be brought inside at night. Only dogs that are house trained are allowed in the cabins, and they must not be left inside unattended. There are some breed restrictions. The camping and tent areas also allow dogs. There is a dog walk area at the campground. Dogs are allowed in the camping cabins.

Horse Creek Campgrounds
Horse Creek(Lake Kaweah), H 198
Visalia, CA
559-597-2301 (800-444-CAMP (2267))
Located on the Kaweah River in the foothills of the central Sierra Nevada Mountains, this park offers interpretive and hiking trails and a variety of land and water recreation. Dogs of all sizes are allowed. There are no additional pet fees. Dogs must be leashed and cleaned up after. Dogs are allowed on the trails. The camping and tent areas also allow dogs. There is a dog walk area at the campground. There are no electric or water hookups at the

campgrounds. Multiple dogs may be allowed.

Visalia/Fresno South KOA
7480 Avenue 308
Visalia, CA
559-651-0544 (800-562-0540)
koa.com/where/ca/05180/
Amenities include old time charm, a good location, 65 foot pull-thru sites with 50 amp service, cable, LP gas, snack bar, and swimming pool. Dogs of all sizes are allowed for no additional fee. Dogs must be under owner's control and visual observation at all times. Dogs must be quiet, well behaved, and be on no more than a 6 foot leash at all times, or otherwise contained. Dogs may not be left unattended outside the owner's camping equipment, and must be brought inside at night. There is a fenced-in dog area where your pets may be off lead. There are some breed restrictions. The camping and tent areas also allow dogs. There is a dog walk area at the campground. There are special amenities given to dogs at this campground. Multiple dogs may be allowed.

Mount Madonna County Park
7850 Pole Line Road
Watsonville, CA
408-355-2201
From the towering redwoods to the Monterey Bay, this 3,688 acre park offers great scenery, interpretive exhibits and programs, an amphitheater, access to an extensive 14 mile trail system, a self-guided nature trail, and a variety of recreation. Dogs of all sizes are allowed at no additional fee. Dogs must be on no more than a 6 foot leash, and cleaned up after. Dogs must be in confined areas at night. The camping and tent areas also allow dogs. There is a dog walk area at the campground. 2 dogs may be allowed.

Santa Cruz/Monterey Bay KOA
1186 San Andreas Road
Watsonville, CA
831-722-0551 (800-562-7701)
koa.com/where/ca/05113/
This scenic family resort along the coast of Monterey Bay offers a long list of amenities, planned activities, and land and water recreation. Dogs of all sizes are allowed for no additional fee. Dogs must be under owner's control and visual observation at all times. Dogs must be quiet, well behaved, and be on no more than a 6 foot leash at all

times, or otherwise contained. Dogs may not be left unattended outside the owner's camping equipment, and must be brought inside at night. Dogs are not allowed in the lodge or the play areas. There are some breed restrictions. The camping and tent areas also allow dogs. There is a dog walk area at the campground. Dogs are allowed in the camping cabins. Multiple dogs may be allowed.

Sunset State Beach
201 Sunset Beach Road
Watsonville, CA
831-763-7062 (800-444-PARK (7275))
parks.ca.gov/park_list.asp
Dogs of all sizes are allowed. There are no additional pet fees. Dogs may not be left unattended at any time, and they must be leashed and cleaned up after. Dogs are not allowed on the beach. This campground is closed during the off-season. The camping and tent areas also allow dogs. There is a dog walk area at the campground. There are no electric or water hookups at the campgrounds. 2 dogs may be allowed.

Shasta Trinity National Forest Campgrounds
P.O.Box 2303/H 3
Weaverville, CA
530-286-2666 (877-444-6777)
campersonline.com/
There are 19 campgrounds here with sites along rivers, lakes, or nestled among the trees, and a variety of services/amenities are available depending on the site locations. Dogs of all sizes are welcome for no additional pet fees. Dogs must be under owner's immediate control, and be leashed and cleaned up after at all times. Dogs are allowed on the trails but not on the beaches. The camping and tent areas also allow dogs. There is a dog walk area at the campground. Multiple dogs may be allowed.

Sidney Gulch RV Park
504 N Main Street/H 299
Weaverville, CA
530-623-6621 (800-554-1626)
This 4.9 acre park offers 40 level sites in a mountain setting, and some of the amenities include showers and restrooms, laundry facilities, and a recreation room with a full kitchen. Dogs of all sizes are allowed for no additional pet fee. Dogs must be leashed and cleaned up after, and they may not be left unattended on

site at any time. Dogs are allowed throughout the park, but not in buildings. The camping and tent areas also allow dogs. There is a dog walk area at the campground. Multiple dogs may be allowed.

Isabella Lake KOA
15627 H 178
Weldon, CA
760-378-2001 (800-562-2085)
koa.com/where/ca/05106/index.htm
Located near the dog-friendly Isabella Lake, this campground offers both tent sites and RV spaces. Well-behaved leashed dogs of all sizes are allowed. People need to clean up after their pets. There is no pet fee. Site amenities include a maximum length pull-thru of 40 feet and 30 amp service available. Other amenities include LP gas, an entrance gate, free modem dataport, snack bar and a seasonal swimming pool, playground, and adult pub. There are some breed restrictions. The camping and tent areas also allow dogs. There is a dog walk area at the campground. Multiple dogs may be allowed.

Giant Redwoods RV & Camp
455 Boy Scout Camp Road
P.O. Box 222
Myers Flat (Weott), CA
707-943-3198
giantredwoodsrvcamp.com
This campground is located in the middle of the Avenue of the Giants region in coastal California. It is surrounded by the Humboldt Redwoods State Park. This 23 acre park is located on a river and is a family campground. They welcome your pet as well. There are 82 sites, 14 which have full hookups, 44 with partial hookups and 33 pull through sites are available. There are hot showers and restrooms, a laundry, RV supplies, a playground and a rec hall. There is an additional pet fee of $2 per day per pet and $3 per day per child over 3 years old. From 101 North or South take the Myers Flat exit to the campground. Multiple dogs may be allowed.

Humboldt Redwoods State Park Campgrounds
17119 Avenue of the Giants
(H 254) Weott, CA
707-946-2409 (800-444-PARK (7275))
There are several campgrounds located in this park including Albee

Creek, Burlington and Hidden Springs Campgrounds. Tent and RV sites are available. Camp amenities include picnic tables, fire rings, showers and flush toilets. While dogs are not allowed on the trails, they are allowed in the campgrounds and on miles of fire roads and access roads. These paths are used mainly for mountain biking, but dogs are allowed too. There are both steep and gently sloping fire roads. Some of the fire roads are located next to the Albee Creek Campground. Pets must be on no more than a 6 foot leash, and cleaned up after. There is no additional pet fee, but dogs must have proof of their shots. Dogs must be quiet, well behaved, and inside at night. They are not allowed in park buildings. The park is located about 45 miles south of Eureka and 20 miles north of Garberville The camping and tent areas also allow dogs. There is a dog walk area at the campground. There are no electric or water hookups at the campgrounds. Multiple dogs may be allowed.

Sacramento Metropolitan KOA
3951 Lake Road
West Sacramento, CA
916-371-6771
koa.com/where/ca/05151/
This camping area, located close to many other attractions and the state capitol, offer such amenities as 65 foot pull-thru sites with 50 amp service, cable, phone, swimming pool, bike rentals, and planned activities. Up to 3 dogs of all sizes are allowed for no additional fee at the tent or RV sites. There is an additional fee of $10 per night per pet for the cabins, and only 2 dogs are allowed. Guests who own any of the known aggressive breeds must sign a waiver. Dogs must be under owner's control and visual observation at all times. Dogs must be quiet, well behaved, and be on no more than a 6 foot leash at all times, or otherwise contained. Dogs may not be left unattended outside the owner's camping equipment, and must be brought inside at night. The camping and tent areas also allow dogs. There is a dog walk area at the campground. Dogs are allowed in the camping cabins.

Westport Beach RV and Camping
37700 N H 1
Westport, CA

707-964-2964
westportbeachrv.com/
This 30 acre camping area offers several camp areas that immerse visitors in the natural beauty that is unique to the Mendocino Coast. There is a large sandy beach; beach site campers may build their own fire on the beach, and sites along the creek offer picnic tables and fire rings at each site. There is a coin laundry, phone/internet hookup, showers, restrooms, gaming areas/courts, a playground, and club house. Dogs of all sizes are allowed for an additional $2 per night per pet. We suggest that RVs approach Westport from the south on Highway 1. Dogs must be leashed and cleaned up after at all times. Dogs are allowed on the beach and throughout the park. The camping and tent areas also allow dogs. There is a dog walk area at the campground. Multiple dogs may be allowed.

Brandy Creek RV Campground
P. O. Box 188
Whiskeytown, CA
530-246-1225 (800-365-CAMP (2267))
nps.gov/whis/pphtml/camping.html
This campground is part of the Whiskeytown National Recreation Area which allows dogs on trails, in the lake and on non-swimming beaches only. The camp offers paved parking spots for RVs along an access road. There are no hookups, and generators are allowed, but not during the quiet time which is usually from 10pm to 6am. All sites are on a first-come, first-served basis. Dogs must be leashed, or crated, and attended at all times. Please clean up after your pet. The campground is open all year. The camping and tent areas also allow dogs. There is a dog walk area at the campground. There are no electric or water hookups at the campgrounds. Multiple dogs may be allowed.

Oak Bottom Campgrounds
Oak Bottom Road
Whiskeytown, CA
530-359-2269 (800-365-CAMP (2267))
nps.gov/whis/pphtml/camping.html
This campground offers tent sites next to Whiskeytown Lake. The campground is part of the Whiskeytown National Recreation Area which allows dogs on trails, in the lake and on non-swimming

beaches only. The camp also offers RV sites. Generators are allowed but not during the quiet time which is usually from 10pm to 6am. During the summer reservations are required and during the winter sites are on a first-come, first-served basis. Dogs must be leashed at all times while in the camp areas. Dogs may be off lead on trails only if they will respond to voice command and will not chase. Please clean up after your pet. Dogs may not be left unattended. The camping and tent areas also allow dogs. There is a dog walk area at the campground. There are no electric or water hookups at the campgrounds. Multiple dogs may be allowed.

Nadelos Campground
Chemise Mountain Road
Whitehorn, CA
707-825-2300
blm.gov/ca/
This campground offers 8 walk-in tent sites ranging from 50 to 300 feet from the parking lot. The sites are shaded by Douglas fir trees and are set along a small mountain stream. Campground amenities include picnic tables, vault toilets, drinking water and fire rings. Day use parking for the dog-friendly Chemise Mountain Trail is located at this campground. Sites are $8 per day with a maximum of 14 days per stay. Pets are allowed but must be leashed in the campground. If off leash on the trails, they must respond to voice command and not chase wildlife. Dogs may not be left unattended. To get there, take Highway 101 to Redway. Go west on Briceland/Shelter Cove Road for 22 miles and then head south on Chemise Mountain Road for 1.5 miles. Travel time from Highway 101 is about 55 minutes. The camping and tent areas also allow dogs. There is a dog walk area at the campground. There are no electric or water hookups at the campgrounds. Multiple dogs may be allowed.

Wailaki Campground
Chemise Mountain Road
Whitehorn, CA
707-825-2300
blm.gov/ca/
This campground offers 13 tent and trailer sites along a small mountain stream amidst large Douglas fir trees. Large RVs are not recommended on the roads to this campground. Day use parking for the dog-friendly Chemise Mountain Trail is located at this campground. Camp

amenities include picnic tables, grills, water and restrooms. Sites are $8 per day with a maximum of 14 days per stay. Pets are allowed but must be leashed in the campground. If off leash on the trails, they must respond to voice command and not chase wildlife. Dogs may not be left unattended. To get there, take Highway 101 to Redway, go west on Briceland/Shelter Cove Road for 22 miles, and then head south on Chemise Mountain Road for 2 miles. Travel time from Highway 101 is about 55 minutes. This campground is closed during the off-season. The camping and tent areas also allow dogs. There is a dog walk area at the campground. There are no electric or water hookups at the campgrounds. Multiple dogs may be allowed.

Lake Skinner Campground
37101 Warren Road
Winchester, CA
951-926-1541 (800-234-PARK (7275))
The campground is located in a 6,040 acre park which features a lake, hiking/interpretive trails, equestrian trails, seasonal swimming pool, launch ramps, boat rentals, and a camp store. Dogs are allowed on the trails and in the campgrounds, but not in the lake or within 50 feet of the lake. Dogs must be on a 6 foot or less leash and please clean up after them. There is an additional fee of $2 per night per pet. The camping and tent areas also allow dogs. There is a dog walk area at the campground. Multiple dogs may be allowed.

Barstow/Calico KOA
35250 Outer H 15
Yermo, CA
760-254-2311 (800-562-0059)
koa.com/where/ca/05233/
This campground is located in a desert setting about 3.5 miles from the dog-friendly Calico Ghost Town. RV site amenities include a maximum pull-thru length of 70 feet and 50 amp service. Other camp amenities include a seasonal swimming pool, free modem dataport, LP gas, snack bar, pavilion/meeting room, and dog walking area. Dogs of all sizes are allowed for no additional fee. Dogs must be under owner's control and visual observation at all times. Dogs must be quiet, well behaved, and be on no more than a 6 foot leash at all times or otherwise contained. Dogs

may not be left unattended outside the owner's camping equipment. Dogs are not allowed in the pool or playground areas, and may not be tied to trees. There are some breed restrictions. The camping and tent areas also allow dogs. There is a dog walk area at the campground. Multiple dogs may be allowed.

Barstow/Calico KOA
35250 Outer H 15
Yermo, CA
760-254-2311 (800-562-0059)
koa.com/where/ca/05233/
In a convenient location midway between Los Angeles and Las Vegas, this KOA provides easy access to dozens of desert attractions and activities. Amenities include 70 foot pull-thru sites with 50 amp, LP Gas, modem dataport, snack bar, and a swimming pool. Dogs of all sizes are allowed for no additional fee. Dogs must be under owner's control and visual observation at all times. Dogs must be quiet, well behaved, and be on no more than a 6 foot leash at all times, or otherwise contained. Dogs may not be left unattended outside the owner's camping equipment, and must be brought inside at night. Dogs are not allowed in the pool area, buildings, or playgrounds, and they may not be tied to trees. There are some breed restrictions. The camping and tent areas also allow dogs. There is a dog walk area at the campground. Multiple dogs may be allowed.

Bridalveil Creek Campground
Glacier Point Road
Yosemite, CA
209/372-0200
This 110 site camp area is about 45 minutes south of the Yosemite Valley at an altitude of 7,200 feet, and all sites are on a first-come, first-served basis; each site has a fire ring, picnic table, and a food storage locker. There is potable water and flush toilets in camp, and a Laundromat and showers nearby. Dogs are allowed here and at 7 more of the 13 campgrounds in Yosemite for no additional pet fee. Dogs may not be left unattended while tied in a campsite, and they must be leashed and cleaned up after at all times. They are not allowed in any group camp areas, on any hiking trails, beaches, in the backcountry, or in public buildings. This RV park is closed during the off-season. The camping and tent areas also allow dogs. There is a dog walk area at the

campground. There are no electric or water hookups at the campgrounds. Multiple dogs may be allowed.

Crane Flat Campground
Big Oak Flat and Tioga Roads
Yosemite National Park, CA
209-372-0200 (877-444-6777)
Next to the Big Tree Groves and only 17 miles from the Yosemite Valley, it is suggested that you get an early reservation as this popular camp site usually fills up well in advance. It sits at an altitude of 6,200 feet and offers 166 campsites; each site has a fire ring, picnic table, and a food storage locker. There is potable water and flush toilets in camp, and a Laundromat and showers nearby. Dogs are allowed here and at 7 more of the 13 campgrounds in Yosemite for no additional pet fee. Dogs may not be left unattended while tied in a campsite, and they must be leashed and cleaned up after at all times. They are not allowed in any group camp areas, on any hiking trails, beaches, in the backcountry, or in public buildings. For reservations call 877-444-6777. This RV park is closed during the off-season. The camping and tent areas also allow dogs. There is a dog walk area at the campground. There are no electric or water hookups at the campgrounds. Multiple dogs may be allowed.

Hodgdon Meadow Campground
Big Oak Flat Road
Yosemite National Park, CA
800-388-2733 (877-444-6777)
Only 25 miles from the Yosemite Valley at an elevation of 4,872 feet, this camp area offers 105 camp sites; each site has a fire ring, picnic table, and a food storage locker. There is potable water and flush toilets in camp, and a Laundromat and showers in the valley. Dogs are allowed here and at 7 more of the 13 campgrounds in Yosemite for no additional pet fee. Dogs may not be left unattended while tied in a campsite, and they must be leashed and cleaned up after at all times. They are not allowed in any group camp areas, on any hiking trails, beaches, in the backcountry, or in public buildings. For reservations call 877-444-6777. The camping and tent areas also allow dogs. There is a dog walk area at the campground. There are no electric or water hookups at the campgrounds. Multiple dogs may be allowed.

Tuolumne Meadows Campground
Tioga Road

Yosemite National Park, CA
800-388-2733 (877-444-6777)
This beautiful open meadow area offers 314 campsites at 8,600 feet altitude, and half of the sites can be reserved; the other half is on a first come first served basis. Each site has a fire ring, picnic table, and a food storage locker with potable water, flush toilets, and a dump station in camp, and groceries, laundry and showers nearby. Dogs are allowed here and at 7 more of the 13 campgrounds in Yosemite for no additional pet fee. Dogs may not be left unattended while tied in a campsite, and they must be leashed and cleaned up after at all times. They are not allowed in any group camp areas, on any hiking trails, beaches, in the backcountry, or in public buildings. For reservations call 877-444-6777. This RV park is closed during the off-season. The camping and tent areas also allow dogs. There is a dog walk area at the campground. There are no electric or water hookups at the campgrounds. Multiple dogs may be allowed.

Upper Pines Campground
East Yosemite Valley
Yosemite National Park, CA
800-388-2733 (877-444-6777)
This 238 site campground is located inside the Yosemite Valley. Reservations are required during the busy seasons. Potable water, fire pits, a dump station, showers, and restrooms are available. Dogs are allowed here and at 7 more of the 13 campgrounds in Yosemite for no additional pet fee. Dogs may not be left unattended while tied in a campsite, and they must be leashed and cleaned up after at all times. They are not allowed on any hiking trails, beaches, in the backcountry, or in public buildings. For reservations call 877-444-6777. The camping and tent areas also allow dogs. There is a dog walk area at the campground. There are no electric or water hookups at the campgrounds. Multiple dogs may be allowed.

Wawona Campground
Highway 41
Yosemite National Park, CA
209-375-9531 (877-444-6777)
Located along the south fork of the Merced River, this camp area sits at 4,000 feet and offers 100 campsites; each site has a picnic table and fire pit. There is drinking water, flush toilets, a dump station,

and groceries available in the camp area. Dogs are allowed here and at 7 more of the 13 campgrounds in Yosemite for no additional pet fee. Dogs may not be left unattended while tied in a campsite, and they must be leashed and cleaned up after at all times. They are not allowed in any group camp areas, on any hiking trails, beaches, in the backcountry, or in public buildings. For reservations call 877-444-6777. The camping and tent areas also allow dogs. There is a dog walk area at the campground. There are no electric or water hookups at the campgrounds. Multiple dogs may be allowed.

White Wolf Campground
Tioga Road
Yosemite National Park, CA
209-379-1899
Sitting at an elevation of 8,000 feet, this campground lies between the Tuolumne River and Tioga Road and offers 87 camp sites on a first come first served basis; each site has a picnic table, food storage locker, and a fire pit; drinking water and flush toilets are available within the camp area. Dogs are allowed here and at 7 more of the 13 campgrounds in Yosemite for no additional pet fee. Dogs may not be left unattended while tied in a campsite, and they must be leashed and cleaned up after at all times. They are not allowed in any group camp areas, on any hiking trails, beaches, in the backcountry, or in public buildings. This RV park is closed during the off-season. The camping and tent areas also allow dogs. There is a dog walk area at the campground. There are no electric or water hookups at the campgrounds. Multiple dogs may be allowed.

Yosemite Creek Campground
Tioga Road/H 120
Yosemite National Park, CA
209-379-1899
This tent-camping only park sits at 7,700 feet, offers 75 camp sites available on a first come first served basis, and provides easy access for fishing in its namesake creek. The 5 mile access road from Tioga Road is not suitable for RVs or large trailers, and all water obtained on site must be treated or boiled before use. Each site has a picnic table, food storage locker, and a fire pit; pit toilets are located in camp. Dogs are allowed here and at 7 more of the 13 campgrounds in Yosemite for no additional pet fee. Dogs may not be

left unattended while tied in a campsite, and they must be leashed and cleaned up after at all times. They are not allowed in any group camp areas, on any hiking trails, beaches, in the backcountry, or in public buildings. This RV park is closed during the off-season. There is a dog walk area at the campground. There are no electric or water hookups at the campgrounds. Multiple dogs may be allowed.

Tree of Heaven Campground,
Klamath National Forest
1312 Fairlane Road
Yreka, CA
530-468-5351 (877-444-6777)
This park features great river access, a Birding Nature Trail and various recreation. Dogs of all sizes are allowed. There are no additional pet fees. Dogs must be leashed and cleaned up after. Dogs are allowed on the trails. The camping and tent areas also allow dogs. There is a dog walk area at the campground. There are no electric or water hookups at the campgrounds. Multiple dogs may be allowed.

Yacaipa Regional Park
33900 Oak Glen Road
Yucaipa, CA
909-790-3127
Sitting on 885 acres in the foothills of the San Bernardino Mountains, this park offers a wide variety of land and water recreation. Dogs of all sizes are allowed for an additional $1 per night per pet. Dogs must be leashed and cleaned up after. The camping and tent areas also allow dogs. There is a dog walk area at the campground. Multiple dogs may be allowed.

Camp at the Cove
760 H 50
Zephyr Cove, NV
775-589-4907 (800-23-TAHOE (238-2463))
zephyrcove.com
Located in spectacular scenery, this award winning resort campground offers a wide variety of amenities and recreational opportunities. Dogs of all sizes are allowed at no additional fee for tent or RV sites. There is a $15 per night per pet additional fee for the cabins. Dogs may not be left unattended outside, or in a tent. They may be left in an RV if they will be quiet and well behaved. Dogs are not allowed on the beach or in the buildings. The camping and tent areas also allow dogs. There is a dog walk area at the campground.

Dogs are allowed in the camping cabins. Multiple dogs may be allowed.

Zephyr Cove RV Park and Campground
760 H 50
Zephyr Cove, NV
775-589-4922 (800-23-TAHOE (238-2463))
This campground is located within minutes of South Lake Tahoe and Stateline. RV site amenities include telephone lines, cable TV, picnic tables, fire rings, bear proof lockers, barbecues, and spectacular scenery. There is also a restaurant, coffee bar, general store and gift shop, and a full service marina. RVs up to 40 feet can be accommodated. Tent sites are either drive-in or walk-in sites, some of which offer lake views. Well-behaved dogs on leash are allowed for no additional fee for the tent or RV sites. There is an additional fee of $15 per night per pet for the cabins. Dogs may not be left unattended in the cabins. Dogs must be leashed and cleaned up after, and they are not allowed on the beach. The camping and tent areas also allow dogs. There is a dog walk area at the campground. Dogs are allowed in the camping cabins. Multiple dogs may be allowed.

Colorado

Alamosa KOA
6900 Juniper Avenue
Alamosa, CO
719-589-9757 (800-562-9157)
koa.com
Dogs of all sizes are allowed, however there can only be up to 3 dogs at tent and RV sites, and up to 2 dogs at the cabins. There are no additional pet fees. Dogs may not be left unattended at the cabins or outside, and they must be leashed and cleaned up after. There are some breed restrictions. The camping and tent areas also allow dogs. There is a dog walk area at the campground. Dogs are allowed in the camping cabins.

Navajo State Park
1526 County Road 982 (Box 1697)
Arboles, CO
970-883-2208 (800-678-2267)
This scenic park touts a reservoir

with over 15,000 acres, and offers a variety of land and water recreation in addition to the geological and historical points of interest. Dogs of all sizes are allowed at no additional fee. Dogs may not be left unattended, and they must be on no more than a 6 foot leash, and be cleaned up after. The camping and tent areas also allow dogs. There is a dog walk area at the campground. Dogs are allowed in the camping cabins. Multiple dogs may be allowed.

Denver Meadows RV Park
2075 Potomac Street
Aurora, CO
303-364-9483 (800-364-9487)
denvermeadows.com/
Dogs of all sizes are allowed. There are no additional pet fees. Dogs may not be left unattended outside, and they must be leashed and cleaned up after. This is an RV only park. There are some breed restrictions. There is a dog walk area at the campground. Multiple dogs may be allowed.

Aspen Basalt Campground
20640 H 82
Basalt, CO
800-567-2773
Dogs of all sizes are allowed. There are no additional pet fees. Dogs may not be left unattended outside, and must be leashed and cleaned up after. There is a dog walk area at the campground. 2 dogs may be allowed.

Blue Spruce Cabins and RV Park
1875 County Road 500
Bayfield, CO
970-884-2641
Dogs of all sizes are allowed. There are no additional pet fees. Dogs may not be left out at night, or outside unattended. Dogs must be leashed and cleaned up after. There are some breed restrictions. This RV park is closed during the off-season. The camping and tent areas also allow dogs. There is a dog walk area at the campground. 2 dogs may be allowed.

Vallecito Resort
13030 County Road 501
Bayfield, CO
970-884-9458
vallecitoresort.com
Dogs of all sizes are allowed. There are no additional pet fees. Dogs must be leashed and cleaned up after. There are some breed restrictions. This RV park is closed

during the off-season. The camping and tent areas also allow dogs. There is a dog walk area at the campground. Dogs are allowed in the camping cabins. 2 dogs may be allowed.

Tiger Run RV Resort
85 Tiger Run Road
Breckenridge, CO
800-895-9594
tigerrunresort.com
Dogs of all sizes are allowed. There are no additional pet fees. Dogs must be leashed and cleaned up after. There is a dog walk area at the campground. Multiple dogs may be allowed.

Arrowhead Point Camping Resort
33975 H 24N
Buena Vista, CO
719-395-2323
arrowheadpointresort.com
Dogs of all sizes are allowed. There are no additional pet fees. Dogs must be leashed and cleaned up after. There are some breed restrictions. This RV park is closed during the off-season. The camping and tent areas also allow dogs. There is a dog walk area at the campground. Multiple dogs may be allowed.

Buena Vista KOA
27700 H 303
Buena Vista, CO
719-395-8318 (800-562-2672)
koa.com
Dogs of all sizes are allowed, and there are no additional pet fees for tent or RV sites. There is a $5 per night per pet additional fee for cabins. There can be up to 3 dogs at tent or RV sites, but only up to 2 dogs at the cabins. Dogs may not be left unattended, and they must be leashed and cleaned up after. There are some breed restrictions. This RV park is closed during the off-season. The camping and tent areas also allow dogs. There is a dog walk area at the campground. Dogs are allowed in the camping cabins.

Bonny Lake State Park
32300 Yuma County Road 2
Burlington, CO
970-354-7306
Dogs of all sizes are allowed. There are no additional pet fees. Dogs must be on no more than a 6 foot leash, and be cleaned up after. Dogs are allowed on the trails and at the beach, but not at the swim areas. The camping and tent areas also allow dogs. There is a dog walk area

at the campground. There are no water hookups at the campground. Multiple dogs may be allowed.

Fort Gorge RV Park
45044 H 50W
Canon City, CO
719-275-5111
fortgorge.com
Dogs of all sizes are allowed. There are no additional pet fees. Dogs may not be left unattended, and must be leashed and cleaned up after. The camping and tent areas also allow dogs. There is a dog walk area at the campground. Dogs are allowed in the camping cabins. Multiple dogs may be allowed.

Royal Gorge/Canon City KOA
559 County Road 3A
Canon City, CO
719-275-6116 (800-562-5689)
royalgorgekoa.net
Dogs of all sizes are allowed. There are no additional pet fees. Dogs may not be left unattended at the cabins, and they must be leashed and cleaned up after. This RV park is closed during the off-season. The camping and tent areas also allow dogs. There is a dog walk area at the campground. Dogs are allowed in the camping cabins. Multiple dogs may be allowed.

Yogi Bear Jellystone Park
43595 H 50
Canon City, CO
719-275-2128 (800-341-4471)
royalgorgejellystone.com
Dogs of all sizes are allowed. There are no additional pet fees. Dogs may not be left unattended except for short periods. Dogs must be well behaved, quiet, leashed, and cleaned up after. There are some breed restrictions. This RV park is closed during the off-season. The camping and tent areas also allow dogs. There is a dog walk area at the campground. Multiple dogs may be allowed.

Castle Rock Campground
6527 S I 25
Castle Rock, CO
303-681-3169 (800-387-9396)
castlerockcampground.com
Dogs of all sizes are allowed. There are no additional pet fees. Dogs must be well behaved, leashed, and cleaned up after. They also have lodges (deluxe cabins) where your dog is allowed at no extra fee. The camping and tent areas also allow dogs. There is a dog walk area at the campground. Dogs are allowed

in the camping cabins. Multiple dogs may be allowed.

Gambler's Edge RV Park
605 Lake Gultch Road
Central City, CO
303-582-9345
gamblersedgervpark.com
Dogs of all sizes are allowed. There are no additional pet fees. Dogs must be leashed and cleaned up after. There are some breed restrictions. There is a dog walk area at the campground. 2 dogs may be allowed.

Steamboat Lake State Park
61105 Rural County Road 129
Clark, CO
970-879-3922
This park sits in a lush forest setting at 8,100 feet, and offers wonderful scenery of green valleys and alpine wildflowers. A park for all seasons, there is an abundance of activities and recreation to enjoy, such as hiking, fishing, swimming, boating, and skiing. Dogs of all sizes are allowed for no additional fee. Dogs must be on no more than a 6 foot leash and cleaned up after at all times. Dogs are allowed throughout the park and on the trails; they are not allowed on the swim beach. The campground offers 198 sites, and some of the amenities include a visitor's center, an amphitheater, a marina with store, campfires, barbecue grills, tables, coin operated laundry, hot showers (even in winter), and a dump station. Although the camp areas are closed in winter, there are 18 sites for RVs at the marina. The State Park daily vehicle pass is not included in your reservation and must be purchased separately at the park. The camping and tent areas also allow dogs. There is a dog walk area at the campground. There are no water hookups at the campgrounds. Multiple dogs may be allowed.

Colorado River State Park
700 32 Road
Clifton, CO
970-434-3388
This is an unusual park in that there are five separate areas along the Colorado River for this park, each with their own special recreational features. From Island Acres on the east, down to the river at Fruita, there is a variety of scenery, a wildlife area, and varied activities such as hiking, biking, picnicking, fishing, swimming, and more, to greet visitors. The 3 middle sections

of the park are for day use only, and at each end there is camping. Dogs of all sizes are allowed for no additional fee. Dogs must be on no more than a 6 foot leash and cleaned up after at all times. Dogs are allowed throughout the park and on the trails; they are not allowed on the swim beach. The campgrounds are in the Island Acres (I-70 at exit 47) and Fruita (I-70 at exit 19) areas, and they offer flush toilets, laundry facilities, coin-operated hot showers, barbecues, campfires, a dump station, firewood for sale, and vending machines. Camping fees may be reduced in winter, and an Aspen Leaf day use pass is required in addition to applicable camping fees. The camping and tent areas also allow dogs. There is a dog walk area at the campground. Multiple dogs may be allowed.

RV Ranch at Grand Junction
3238 E I 70 Business Loop
Clifton, CO
970-434-6644
rvranches.com
One dog of any size is allowed. There are no additional pet fees. Dogs must be leashed and cleaned up after. There are some breed restrictions. The camping and tent areas also allow dogs. There is a dog walk area at the campground.

Fountain Creek RV Park
3023 W Colorado Avenue
Colorado Springs, CO
719-633-2192
fountaincreekrvpark.com
Dogs of all sizes are allowed. There are no additional pet fees. Dogs may not be left unattended, and must be leashed and cleaned up after. The camping and tent areas also allow dogs. There is a dog walk area at the campground. Multiple dogs may be allowed.

Garden of the Gods Campground
3704 W Colorado Avenue
Colorado Springs, CO
719-475-9450
coloradocampground.com
Dogs of all sizes are allowed. There are no additional pet fees. Dogs must be quiet, leashed, and cleaned up after. The camping and tent areas also allow dogs. There is a dog walk area at the campground. Multiple dogs may be allowed.

Cortez Mesa Verde KOA
27432 E H 160
Cortez, CO
970-565-9301 (800-562-3901)

cortezkoa.com
Dogs of all sizes are allowed. There are no additional pet fees. Dogs may not be left unattended at the cabins or outside, and they must be leashed and cleaned up after. There are some breed restrictions. This RV park is closed during the off-season. The camping and tent areas also allow dogs. There is a dog walk area at the campground. Dogs are allowed in the camping cabins. Multiple dogs may be allowed.

Cotopaxi Arkansas River KOA
21435 H 50
Cotopaxi, CO
719-275-9308 (800-562-2686)
koa.com
Dogs of all sizes are allowed, and there are no additional pet fees for tent or RV sites. There is a $5 per night per pet additional fee for the cabins or motel. Dogs must be quiet, well behaved, be on no more than a 6 foot leash, and cleaned up after. Dogs may not be left unattended at any time. There are some breed restrictions. This RV park is closed during the off-season. The camping and tent areas also allow dogs. There is a dog walk area at the campground. Dogs are allowed in the camping cabins. Multiple dogs may be allowed.

Craig KOA
2800 E H 40
Craig, CO
970-824-5105 (800-562-5095)
koa.com
Dogs of all sizes are allowed. There are no additional pet fees. Dogs must be leashed and cleaned up after. The camping and tent areas also allow dogs. There is a dog walk area at the campground. Dogs are allowed in the camping cabins. Multiple dogs may be allowed.

Crawford State Park
40468 H 92 N
Crawford, CO
970-921-5721 (800-678-2267)
Water recreation, fishing, and hiking are the main attractions at this scenic park. Dogs of all sizes are allowed at no additional fee. Dogs may not be left unattended, and they must be on no more than a 6 foot leash, and cleaned up after. Dogs are not allowed in buildings, or on the swim or ski beaches. The camping and tent areas also allow dogs. There is a dog walk area at the campground. Multiple dogs may

be allowed.

Cripple Creek/Colorado Springs W KOA
2576 County Road 81
Cripple Creek, CO
719-689-3376 (800-562-9152)
cripplecreekkoa.com
Dogs of all sizes are allowed. There are no additional pet fees. Dogs may not be left unattended at the cabins or outside. Dogs must be quiet, be on no more than a 6 foot leash, and cleaned up after. This RV park is closed during the off-season. The camping and tent areas also allow dogs. There is a dog walk area at the campground. Dogs are allowed in the camping cabins. Multiple dogs may be allowed.

Rio Grande National Forest
13308 W H 160
Del Norte, CO
719-852-5941 (800-678-2267)
fs.fed.us/r2/riogrande/
With 4 ranger districts and over a million acres, this forest provides a variety of camping areas and trails. The diverse ecosystems support a large variety of plant, fish, mammal, and bird species. Dogs are allowed at no additional fee. Dogs may not be left unattended, and they must be leashed and cleaned up after in the camp areas. Dogs are allowed on the trails. The camping and tent areas also allow dogs. There is a dog walk area at the campground. Multiple dogs may be allowed.

Grand Mesa, Uncompahgre and Gunnison National Forests
2250 H 50
Delta, CO
970-874-6600
fs.fed.us/r2/gmug/
With more than 3 million acres of public land, there is a variety of recreational pursuits. Dogs of all sizes are allowed. There are no additional pet fees. Dogs must be leashed and cleaned up after. Dogs are allowed on the trails. This campground is closed during the off-season. The camping and tent areas also allow dogs. There is a dog walk area at the campground. There are no electric or water hookups at the campground. Multiple dogs may be allowed.

Dinosaur National Monument
4545 E H 40
Dinosaur, CO
970)374-3000
nps.gov/dino/
This park is the largest quarry of the

Jurassic Period dinosaur bones ever found, and gives this 200,000+ acre, visually striking park its name. The Quarry visitor's Center is now closed, but the monument is open with much to see; there are exhibits, fossil displays, ranger led programs (in summer), many trails to explore, 2 self-guided auto tours offering spectacular scenery, and plenty of land and water recreation. The Canyon Area Visitor Center in Dinosaur, Colorado, is open daily from 8:00 a.m. to 4:00 p.m. through Labor Day; then to October 31 they are closed on the weekends, and closed from November 1st to April 30th. The park is open year round for auto touring, weather permitting; roads are not maintained and are closed when there is snow. Dogs of all sizes are allowed for no additional fee. Dogs may not be left unattended, and they must be leashed and cleaned up after at all times. Dogs are not allowed on the trails at this park or in any of the park buildings. They may get out of the vehicle when stopping along side the road on the auto tour, but may not walk along trails to get to overlooks. The Green River Campground, just 5 miles east of the Quarry, is on a first-come, first-served basis. Some of the amenities include picnic tables, fireplaces and wood for sale, drinking water, modern restrooms, and fishing. There are also campfire circle ranger talks through the summer. There are no electric or water hookups at the campgrounds. Multiple dogs may be allowed.

Mueller State Park
21045 H 67S
Divide, CO
719-687-2366 (800-678-2267)
Extending over 5,000 acres across some of the most beautiful land in the state, this park is a popular wildlife area and a joy for photographers and sightseers. For the hiker/mountain biker/horseback rider, there are more than 55 miles of scenic, year round, multi-use trails. Dogs of all sizes are allowed for no additional fee. Dogs are not allowed in the backcountry or on the nature trails; they may be walked on paved roads only. Dogs must be on no more than a 6 foot leash, and be cleaned up after. The campground is in a forested setting at 9,500 feet and offer panoramic views, 132 sites, and some tent walk-in sites. Some of the amenities include a Camper Services Building, modern restrooms, coin operated showers and laundry,

campfires, barbecue grills, and a dump station. Some services are not available in winter. The camping and tent areas also allow dogs. There is a dog walk area at the campground. There are no water hookups at the campgrounds. Multiple dogs may be allowed.

Dolores River RV Park
18680 H 145
Dolores, CO
970-882-7761
doloresriverrv.com
Dogs of all sizes are allowed, and there are no additional pet fees for tent or RV sites. There may be a small one time fee for pets in cabins. This RV park is closed during the off-season. The camping and tent areas also allow dogs. There is a dog walk area at the campground. Dogs are allowed in the camping cabins. Multiple dogs may be allowed.

Alpen Rose RV Park
27847 H 550N
Durango, CO
970-247-5540
alpenroservpark.com
Dogs of all sizes are allowed. There are no additional pet fees. Dogs may not be left unattended outside, and must be quiet, leashed, and cleaned up after. There are a couple of dog sitters on site that will take care of your dog with walks, food and water, and play time for $10 per day per dog. This RV park is closed during the off-season. There is a dog walk area at the campground. There are special amenities given to dogs at this campground. Multiple dogs may be allowed.

Durango East KOA
30090 H 160
Durango, CO
970-247-0783 (800-562-0793)
koa.com
Dogs of all sizes are allowed. There are no additional pet fees. Dogs may not be left unattended, and they must be quiet, well behaved, leashed and cleaned up after. There are some breed restrictions. This RV park is closed during the off-season. The camping and tent areas also allow dogs. There is a dog walk area at the campground. Dogs are allowed in the camping cabins. Multiple dogs may be allowed.

Durango North KOA
13391 County Road 250

Durango, CO
970-247-4499 (800-562-0793)
koa.com
Dogs of all sizes are allowed. There are no additional pet fees. Dogs may not be left unattended, and they must be leashed and cleaned up after. This RV park is closed during the off-season. The camping and tent areas also allow dogs. There is a dog walk area at the campground. Dogs are allowed in the camping cabins. 2 dogs may be allowed.

San Juan National Forest
15 Burnett Court
Durango, CO
970-247-4874
fs.fed.us/r2/sanjuan/
With over 2 and a half million acres, and home to the Anasazi Heritage Center, there are historical and geological interests as well as a variety of recreational pursuits. Dogs are allowed at no additional fee. Dogs may not be left unattended, and they must be leashed and cleaned up after. Dogs are allowed on the trails, and they may be off lead in the forest if they are under voice control. This campground is closed during the off-season. The camping and tent areas also allow dogs. There is a dog walk area at the campground. There are no water hookups at the campground. Multiple dogs may be allowed.

United Campground of Durango
1322 Animas View Road
Durango, CO
970-247-3853
unitedcampground.com
Dogs of all sizes are allowed. There are no additional pet fees. Dogs may not be in the buildings, or at the pool, nor left unattended. Dogs must be leashed at all times, and must be cleaned up after. This RV park is closed during the off-season. The camping and tent areas also allow dogs. There is a dog walk area at the campground. Multiple dogs may be allowed.

Elk Meadow Lodge and RV Resort
1665 H 66
Estes Park, CO
970-586-5342
elkmeadowrv.com
Dogs of all sizes are allowed. There are no additional pet fees. Dogs may not be left unattended, and they must be quiet, leashed, and cleaned up after. There are some breed restrictions. This RV park is closed during the off-season. The camping and tent areas also allow dogs.

There is a dog walk area at the campground. Multiple dogs may be allowed.

Estes Park KOA
2051 Big Thompson Avenue
Estes Park, CO
970-586-2888 (800-562-1887)
estespark-koa.com
Dogs of all sizes are allowed. There are no additional pet fees. Dogs may not be left unattended, and they must be leashed and cleaned up after. There may only be up to 2 dogs in the cabins. There are some breed restrictions. This RV park is closed during the off-season. The camping and tent areas also allow dogs. There is a dog walk area at the campground. Dogs are allowed in the camping cabins. Multiple dogs may be allowed.

Manor RV Park
815 Riverside Drive
Estes Park, CO
970-586-3251
manorrvparkandmotel.com
Dogs of all sizes are allowed. There are no additional pet fees. Dogs must be quiet, leashed, and cleaned up after. This RV park is closed during the off-season. There is a dog walk area at the campground. Multiple dogs may be allowed.

Mary's Lake Campground
2120 Mary's Lake Road
Estes Park, CO
970-586-4411
maryalakecampground.com
Dogs of all sizes are allowed. There are no additional pet fees. Dogs must be leashed and cleaned up after. This RV park is closed during the off-season. The camping and tent areas also allow dogs. There is a dog walk area at the campground. Multiple dogs may be allowed.

Yogi Bear Jellystone Park
5495 H 36
Estes Park, CO
970-586-4230 (800-722-2928)
jellystoneofestes.com
Dogs of all sizes are allowed. There are no additional pet fees. Dogs must be well behaved, quiet, leashed, and cleaned up after. This RV park is closed during the off-season. The camping and tent areas also allow dogs. There is a dog walk area at the campground. Multiple dogs may be allowed.

Arapaho Roosevelt National Forest
2150 Center Avenue, Building E
Fort Collins, CO
970-498-2770
fs.fed.us/r2/arnf
This park covers 22 million acres of forest and grassland in 5 states. There are about 50 campgrounds, but only 2 are open all year, and only 3 have electric hook-ups. Dogs of all sizes are allowed. There are no additional pet fees. Dogs are not allowed in any buildings, and on some of the trails as marked. Dogs must be leashed and cleaned up after. The Arapaho Roosevelt National Forest surrounds the Rocky Mountain National Park, and the National Park doesn't allow dogs in most areas. The camping and tent areas also allow dogs. There is a dog walk area at the campground. There are no water hookups at the campground. Multiple dogs may be allowed.

Fort Collins KOA Lakeside
1910 N Taft Hill
Fort Collins, CO
970-484-9880 (800-562-9168)
heronlakerv.com
Dogs of all sizes are allowed. Dogs must be leashed and cleaned up after. There are some breed restrictions. This RV park is closed during the off-season. The camping and tent areas also allow dogs. There is a dog walk area at the campground. Multiple dogs may be allowed.

Colorado Springs South KOA
8100 Bandley Drive
Fountain, CO
719-382-7575 (800-562-8609)
coloradospringskoa.com
Dogs of all sizes are allowed, and there are no additional pet fees for tent or RV sites. There is a $3 per night per pet additional fee for cabins. Dogs may not be left unattended in the cabins or outside, and they must be leashed and cleaned up after. There are some breed restrictions. The camping and tent areas also allow dogs. There is a dog walk area at the campground. Dogs are allowed in the camping cabins. Multiple dogs may be allowed.

Mountain RV Resort
607 H 340
Fruita, CO
970-858-3155
Dogs of all sizes are allowed, but there can only be up to 3 small dogs or 2 large dogs per site. There are no additional pet fees. Dogs must be leashed and cleaned up after. There are some breed

restrictions. There is a dog walk area at the campground.

Glenwood Canyon Resort
1308 County Road 129
Glenwood Springs, CO
970-945-6737 (800-970-6737)
glenwoodcanyonresort.com/
Located on the banks of the Colorado River, this park offers some of the prettiest scenery in the state, and some great land and water recreational opportunities. Amenities include picnic tables, fire pits, restrooms, showers, laundry facilities, and a recreation room. Dogs of all sizes are allowed. There is a $5 per night per pet additional fee. Dogs must be leashed and cleaned up after. Dogs are allowed throughout the park and on the trails, but they are not allowed in park buildings. The camping and tent areas also allow dogs. There is a dog walk area at the campground. Multiple dogs may be allowed.

Rock Gardens RV Resort and Campground
1308 County Road 129
Glenwood Springs, CO
800-958-6737
glenwoodcanyonresort.com
Dogs of all sizes are allowed. There are no additional pet fees. Dogs must be leashed and cleaned up after. This RV park is closed during the off-season. The camping and tent areas also allow dogs. There is a dog walk area at the campground. Multiple dogs may be allowed.

White River National Forest
900 Grand Avenue
Glenwood Springs, CO
970-945-2521
fs.fed.us/r2/whiteriver/
With over 2 million acres and 8 wilderness areas, this forest provides a variety of camping areas and trails. The diverse ecosystems support a large variety of plants, fish, mammals, bird species, and recreation. Dogs are allowed at no additional fee. Dogs may not be left unattended, and they must be leashed and cleaned up after in the camp areas. Dogs are not allowed in some of the wilderness areas. This campground is closed during the off-season. The camping and tent areas also allow dogs. There is a dog walk area at the campground. Multiple dogs may be allowed.

Dakota Ridge RV Park
17800 W Colfax
Golden, CO

800-398-1625
dakotaridgerv.com
Dogs of all sizes are allowed. There is a $1 per night per pet additional fee. Dogs must be quiet, leashed, and cleaned up after. Dogs may not be put in outside pens, or be left unattended outside. There are some breed restrictions. There is a dog walk area at the campground. Multiple dogs may be allowed.

Genesee Park/Chief Hosa Campground
27661 Genesee Drive
Golden, CO
303-526-1324
chiefhosa.com/
This is Denver's largest mountain park with 2,341 acres of trees, wildlife, recreation, and popular hiking trails. There is even a Braille Trail with interpretive signs in Braille. Some of the amenities include picnic areas, charcoal grills, a volleyball court, softball field, and a scenic overlook along I 70 where you can view the resident buffalo herd. They are open daily from 5 am to 11 pm. Dogs of all sizes are allowed. Dogs must be leashed and cleaned up after at all times. They are allowed throughout the park and on the trails; they are not allowed in park buildings. The Chief Hosa Campground was dubbed 'America's First Motor-Camping Area when it opened in 1913, and sits at 7,700 feet altitude. There are 61 sites, and amenities include gaming courts, showers, restrooms, and a dump station. This campground will not be open to concert camping. There is a $1 per night per pet additional fee for camping. This RV park is closed during the off-season. The camping and tent areas also allow dogs. There is a dog walk area at the campground. Multiple dogs may be allowed.

Jackson Lake State Park
26363 County Road 3
Goodrich, CO
970-645-2551 (800-678-2267)
This park has been referred to as an "oasis in the plains", and there are a variety of recreational pursuits offered all year. Quiet and well behaved dogs of all sizes are allowed at no additional fee. Dogs may not be left unattended, and they must be on no more than a 6 foot leash, and be cleaned up after. Dogs are not allowed on the swim or ski beaches, or in buildings. Dogs are allowed on the trails. There is an off-leash area and a pond where dogs

can swim at the North end of the park. The camping and tent areas also allow dogs. There is a dog walk area at the campground. Multiple dogs may be allowed.

Gunnison KOA
105 County Road 50
Gunnison, CO
970-641-1358 (800-562-1248)
koa.com
Dogs of all sizes are allowed, but there can only be 1 large or 2 small dogs per site. There are no additional pet fees. Dogs may not be left unattended, and they must be leashed at all times, and cleaned up after. This RV park is closed during the off-season. The camping and tent areas also allow dogs. There is a dog walk area at the campground. Dogs are allowed in the camping cabins.

Lake Fork Resort and RV Park
940 Cove Road
Gunnison, CO
970-641-3564
This resort offers 12 RV sites, fire pits, a store, playground, horseshoe pits, and a wide range of land and water recreational opportunities. Dogs of all sizes are allowed for no additional fee for tent or RV sites. There is a $5 per night per pet additional fee for the cabins. Not all the cabins are pet friendly. Dogs must be leashed and cleaned up after at all times. The camping and tent areas also allow dogs. There is a dog walk area at the campground. Dogs are allowed in the camping cabins. Multiple dogs may be allowed.

Mesa RV Resort
36128 W H 50
Gunnison, CO
970-641-3186
mesarvresort.com
Dogs of all sizes are allowed. There are no additional pet fees. Dogs must be quiet, leashed, and cleaned up after. This RV park is closed during the off-season. The camping and tent areas also allow dogs. There is a dog walk area at the campground. Multiple dogs may be allowed.

La Junta KOA
26680 H 50
La Junta, CO
719-384-9580 (800-562-9501)
koa.com
Dogs of all sizes are allowed. There are no additional pet fees. Dogs must be quiet, be on no more than

a 6 foot leash, and cleaned up after. There are some breed restrictions. The camping and tent areas also allow dogs. There is a dog walk area at the campground. Dogs are allowed in the camping cabins. Multiple dogs may be allowed.

Fort Collins KOA
6670 N H 287
LaPorte, CO
970-493-9758 (800-562-2648)
koa.com
Dogs of all sizes are allowed. There are no additional pet fees. Dogs must be leashed and cleaned up after. Dogs are not allowed at the playground, the camp kitchen, or the bathrooms. This RV park is closed during the off-season. The camping and tent areas also allow dogs. There is a dog walk area at the campground. Dogs are allowed in the camping cabins. Multiple dogs may be allowed.

Eleven Mile State Park
4229 County Road 92
Lake George, CO
719-748-3401 (800-678-2267)
Great fishing, hiking, waterfront camping, and various water and land recreation make this a popular park. Dogs of all sizes are allowed at no additional fee. Dogs may not be left unattended, and they must be on no more than a 6 foot leash, and be cleaned up after. Dogs are not allowed in the water anywhere. Dogs are allowed on the trails. The camping and tent areas also allow dogs. There is a dog walk area at the campground. There are no water hookups at the campground. Multiple dogs may be allowed.

Limon KOA
575 Colorado Avenue
Limon, CO
719-775-2151 (800-562-2129)
koa.com
Dogs of all sizes are allowed. There are no additional pet fees. Dogs must be leashed and cleaned up after. There are some breed restrictions. This RV park is closed during the off-season. The camping and tent areas also allow dogs. There is a dog walk area at the campground. Dogs are allowed in the camping cabins. Multiple dogs may be allowed.

Chatfield State Park
11500 N Roxborough Park Road
Littleton, CO
303-791-7275
This beautiful, multi-functional park

offers resource education, diverse ecosystems, an expansive trail system It is a great retreat for camping, picnicking, hiking/biking, birding, boating and fishing. This park is also one of the most popular hot-air balloon launch areas on the Front Range. Dogs of all sizes are allowed for no additional fee. Dogs must be on no more than a 6 foot leash, and cleaned up after at all times. The exception is when dogs are used in hunting, field trials, or while being trained on lands open to such use. Dogs may be anywhere throughout the park, except they are not allowed on any swim beach, water-ski beach, or in park buildings. There are 4 camping areas with 197 sites that are within walking distance to the lake. Amenities include picnic sites with tables and grills (also picnic sites throughout the park), flush toilets, showers, laundry, firewood, centrally located water, and a dump station. Camping permits are required in addition to the day-use park pass. The camping and tent areas also allow dogs. There is a dog walk area at the campground. Multiple dogs may be allowed.

St. Vrain State Park
3525 H 119
Longmont, CO
303-678-9402
Dogs of all sizes are allowed. There are no additional pet fees. Dogs must be leashed and cleaned up after. The camping and tent areas also allow dogs. There is a dog walk area at the campground. Multiple dogs may be allowed.

Johnson's Corner RV Retreat
3618 SE Frontage Road
Loveland, CO
970-669-8400
johnsonscornercampgrnd.com
Dogs of all sizes are allowed. There is a $1 per night per pet additional fee. Dogs must be leashed and cleaned up after. There is a dog walk area at the campground. Multiple dogs may be allowed.

Echo Basin Ranch
43747 Co. Rd M
Mancos, CO
970-533-7000 (800-426-1890)
echobasin.com/rvpark.html
Dogs of all sizes are allowed. There are no additional pet fees. Dogs must be leashed or crated at all times, and be cleaned up after. This RV park is closed during the off-season. The camping and tent areas also allow dogs. There is a dog walk

area at the campground. 2 dogs may be allowed.

Mesa Verde RV Resort
35303 H 160
Mancos, CO
970-533-7421 (800-776-7421)
mesaverdervresort.com/
Dogs of all sizes are allowed. There are no additional pet fees. Dogs must be leashed and cleaned up after. Dogs are not allowed in buildings or the pool area. The camping and tent areas also allow dogs. There is a dog walk area at the campground. Multiple dogs may be allowed.

Morefield Campground
34879 H 160
Mancos, CO
800-449-2288
visitmesaverde.com
Dogs of all sizes are allowed, and there are no additional pet fees for tent or RV sites. There is a $25 per night per pet additional fee for the lodge. Dogs may not be left unattended at the lodge at any time. Dogs must be leashed and cleaned up after. Dogs may not be left outside unattended, and they are not allowed in the buildings or on the trails. This RV park is closed during the off-season. The camping and tent areas also allow dogs. There is a dog walk area at the campground. Multiple dogs may be allowed.

Elk Creek Campgrounds
0581 County Road 241
New Castle, CO
970-984-2240 (800-562-3240)
elkcreekcamping.com
Dogs of all sizes are allowed, and there are no additional pet fees for tent or RV sites. There is a $5 per night per pet additional fee for cabins. Dogs may not be left unattended, and they must be leashed and cleaned up after. There is a small fenced in area for off lead. This RV park is closed during the off-season. The camping and tent areas also allow dogs. There is a dog walk area at the campground. 2 dogs may be allowed.

Stagecoach State Park
25500 R County Road 14
Oak Creek, CO
970-736-2436
Located south of Steamboat Springs in the fertile Yampa Valley, this park boasts a 780 acre reservoir with a full service marina,

and offers a wide variety of land and water recreation and activities. There are a couple of great trails to walk your dog, and they are allowed at no additional fee. Dogs must be on no more than a 6 foot leash and cleaned up after. Dogs are allowed on the trails, but they are not allowed on the swim beach. There are 92 campsites located in 4 separate campgrounds. Some of the amenities include picnic areas, restrooms, a dump station, campfires, and barbecue grills. The State Park daily vehicle pass is not included in your reservation and must be purchased separately at the park. The camping and tent areas also allow dogs. There is a dog walk area at the campground. There are no water hookups at the campgrounds. Multiple dogs may be allowed.

Ouray KOA
225 County Road 23
Ouray, CO
970-325-4736 (800-562-8026)
koa.com
Dogs of all sizes are allowed. There are no additional pet fees. Dogs may not be left unattended at the cabins or outside, and they are not allowed in the buildings. Dogs must be quiet, well behaved, be on no more than a 6 foot leash, and cleaned up after. There are some breed restrictions. This RV park is closed during the off-season. The camping and tent areas also allow dogs. There is a dog walk area at the campground. Dogs are allowed in the camping cabins. Multiple dogs may be allowed.

Elk Meadows River Resort
5360 E H 160
Pagosa Springs, CO
970-264-5482 (866-264-5482)
elkmeadowsresort.com
Dogs of all sizes are allowed. There are no additional pet fees. Dogs may not be left unattended outside unless they will be quiet and well behaved, and they must be leashed and cleaned up after. This is an RV and rental cabins park. This RV park is closed during the off-season. There is a dog walk area at the campground. Dogs are allowed in the camping cabins. Multiple dogs may be allowed.

Lake Pueblo
640 Reservoir Road
Pueblo, CO
719-561-9320 (800-678-2267)
There are over 9,000 acres at this scenic park, 2 full service marinas, a swim beach/waterpark, miles of

hiking trails, and a variety of land and water recreation. Dogs of all sizes are allowed at no additional fee. Dogs may not be left unattended, and they must be on no more than a 6 foot leash, and be cleaned up after. Dogs are not allowed on the swim beach. The camping and tent areas also allow dogs. There is a dog walk area at the campground. There are no water hookups at the campground. Multiple dogs may be allowed.

Pike and San Isabel National Forests
2840 Kachina Drive
Pueblo, CO
719-545-8737
fs.fed.us/r2/psicc/
This forest, with it's nearly 3 million acres, unique ecosystem, flora and fauna, is one of the most diverse forest in the U.S. Campgrounds are seasonal, however the park is open year round. Dogs of all sizes are allowed. There are no additional pet fees. Dogs are allowed on the trails. Dogs must be leashed and cleaned up after. This campground is closed during the off-season. The camping and tent areas also allow dogs. There is a dog walk area at the campground. There are no water hookups at the campground. Multiple dogs may be allowed.

Pueblo KOA
4131 I 25N
Pueblo, CO
719-542-2273 (800-562-7453)
koa.com
Dogs of all sizes are allowed. There are no additional pet fees. Dogs may not be left unattended, and they must be leashed and cleaned up after. The camping and tent areas also allow dogs. There is a dog walk area at the campground. Dogs are allowed in the camping cabins. Multiple dogs may be allowed.

Ridgeway State Park
28555 H 550
Ridgeway, CO
970-626-5822 (800-678-2267)
This park offers a sandy swim beach, a full service marina, and is known as a very accessible recreation area for people with disabilities. Dogs of all sizes are allowed at no additional fee for tent or RV sites. There is a $10 daily additional pet fee for the yurts. Dogs may not be left unattended outside, and they must be on no more than a 6 foot leash, and be cleaned up after. Dogs are not allowed in public swim areas, but they are allowed on the trails. The

camping and tent areas also allow dogs. There is a dog walk area at the campground. Dogs are allowed in the camping cabins. 2 dogs may be allowed.

Rifle Falls State Park
575 H 325
Rifle, CO
970-625-1607 (800-678-2267)
Visitors will enjoy the unusual scenery and tropical feel of this park as a result of the waterfalls and the mist they create for vegetation. Dogs of all sizes are allowed at no additional fee. Dogs may not be left unattended, and they must be on no more than a 6 foot leash, and be cleaned up after. Dogs are not allowed on the swim beach or at Harvey Gap, but they are allowed on the trails. The camping and tent areas also allow dogs. There is a dog walk area at the campground. Multiple dogs may be allowed.

Silver Summit RV Park
640 Mineral Street
Silverton, CO
970-387-0240
silversummitrvpark.com
Dogs of all sizes are allowed. There are no additional pet fees. Dogs may not be left unattended, and they must be quiet, leashed, and cleaned up after. This RV park is closed during the off-season. There is a dog walk area at the campground. Multiple dogs may be allowed.

Paonai State Park
On H 133
Somerset, CO
970-921-5721 (800-678-2267)
This small primitive park offers wildflowers in abundance and a small lake for recreation. There is no drinking water available here, so bring your own. Dogs of all sizes are allowed at no additional fee. Dogs may not be left unattended, and they must be leased and cleaned up after. Dogs are not allowed in public swim areas. Dogs are allowed on the trails. The camping and tent areas also allow dogs. There is a dog walk area at the campground. There are no electric or water hookups at the campground. Multiple dogs may be allowed.

Jellystone Park
22018 H 6
Sterling, CO
970-522-2233 (866-964-4232)
buffalohillscampground.com

Dogs of all sizes are allowed. There are no additional pet fees. Dogs must be well behaved, quiet, leashed, and cleaned up after. For those on the road in the off season, they have electric only hook-ups. This RV park is closed during the off-season. The camping and tent areas also allow dogs. There is a dog walk area at the campground. 2 dogs may be allowed.

Denver East/Strasburg KOA
1312 Monroe
Strasburg, CO
303-622-9274 (800-562-6538)
koa.com
Dogs of all sizes are allowed, and there are no additional pet fees for tent or RV sites. There is a $4 per night per pet additional fee for the cabins. Dogs are greeted at check in with a dog biscuit. Dogs may not be left unattended at the cabins or outside, and they must be leashed and cleaned up after. The camping and tent areas also allow dogs. There is a dog walk area at the campground. Dogs are allowed in the camping cabins. There are special amenities given to dogs at this campground. Multiple dogs may be allowed.

Town Park Campground
500 E Colorado Avenue
Telluride, CO
970-728-2173
This campground is located at the Town Park in Telluride, (refer to our listing under Telluride Town Park) a 36 acre landscaped public park and festival grounds bustling with year around activities. Dogs of all sizes are allowed throughout the park and on the trails in the summer. They are not allowed at the event center during festivals or other planned events. Dogs must be leashed at all times, and cleaned up after. Camping is on a cash/money order, first come first served basis, and during the season they fill up fast on the weekends. Dogs are allowed for no additional fee. There are 28 vehicle campsites and 5 primitive sites, coin-operated showers, and toilet facilities. This RV park is closed during the off-season. The camping and tent areas also allow dogs. There is a dog walk area at the campground. There are no electric or water hookups at the campgrounds. Multiple dogs may be allowed.

Ute Mountain Casino RV Resort
3 Weeminuche Drive
Towaoc, CO

970-565-6544 (800-889-5072)
utemountaincasino.com/
This RV park is along side the state's first Tribal gaming facility; the largest casino in the 4 corners area. Some of the amenities of the camp area include a convenience store, restrooms, showers, laundry facilities, sauna, indoor pool, wading pool, cable, a game room, and playground. Dogs of all sizes are allowed for no additional fee. Dogs must be leashed and cleaned up after at all times. This RV park is closed during the off-season. The camping and tent areas also allow dogs. There is a dog walk area at the campground. Multiple dogs may be allowed.

North Park/Gould/Walden KOA
53337 H 14
Walden, CO
970-723-4310 (800-562-3596)
koa.com
Dogs of all sizes are allowed. There are no additional pet fees. Dogs may not be left unattended, and they must be leashed and cleaned up after. This RV park is closed during the off-season. The camping and tent areas also allow dogs. There is a dog walk area at the campground. Dogs are allowed in the camping cabins. Multiple dogs may be allowed.

Fort Collins North/Wellington KOA
4821 E County Road 70/Owl Canyon Road
Wellington, CO
970-568-7486 (800-562-8142)
koa.com
Dogs of all sizes are allowed. There are no additional pet fees. Dogs must be leashed and cleaned up after. The camping and tent areas also allow dogs. There is a dog walk area at the campground. Dogs are allowed in the camping cabins. Multiple dogs may be allowed.

Grape Creek RV Park
56491 H 69
Westcliffe, CO
719-783-2588
coloradovacation.com/camp/grape
Dogs of all sizes are allowed. There are no additional pet fees. Dogs must be leashed and cleaned up after. There is only one dog friendly cabin. This RV park is closed during the off-season. The camping and tent areas also allow dogs. There is a dog walk area at the campground. Dogs are allowed in the camping cabins. Multiple dogs may be allowed.

Prospect RV Park
11600 W 44th Avenue
Wheat Ridge, CO
303-424-4414
prospectrv.com
Dogs of all sizes are allowed. There are no additional pet fees. Dogs must be leashed and cleaned up after. There are some breed restrictions. There is a dog walk area at the campground. Multiple dogs may be allowed.

Connecticut

Brialee RV and Tent Park
174 Laurel Lane
Ashford, CT
860-429-8359 (800-303-2267)
brialee.com
Dogs of all sizes are allowed. There are no additional pet fees. Dogs must be leashed and under your control at all times and must be cleaned up after. The camping and tent areas also allow dogs. There is a dog walk area at the campground. 2 dogs may be allowed.

American Legion and Peoples State Forests
West River Road
Barkhamsted, CT
860-379-2469
This forest park is a year round land and water recreational destination that feature cultural and historic sites, more than 11 miles of hiking trails, a seasonal museum, a lighthouse, and they are also participants in the state forest Letterboxing. Dogs are permitted for no additional pet fee. Dogs are allowed at the picnic areas and on the hiking trails; they are not allowed in park buildings. Dogs must be under their owner's control at all times, and be leashed and cleaned up after. Only one dog is allowed per campsite. The camp area offers 30 wooded sites with picnic tables, showers, restrooms, a dump station, and reservations are accepted from April 20th through Columbus Day. The phone number for the campground office (May-September) is 860-379-0922. This RV park is closed during the off-season. The camping and tent areas also allow dogs. There is a dog walk area at the campground. There are no electric or water hookups at the campgrounds.

Acron Acres Campground
135 Lake Road
Bozrah, CT
860-859-1020
acornacrescampsites.com
Dogs of all sizes are allowed. There are no additional pet fees. Dogs must be quiet, well behaved, leashed and cleaned up after. There are some breed restrictions. The camping and tent areas also allow dogs. There is a dog walk area at the campground. 2 dogs may be allowed.

Odetah Campground
38 Bozrah Street Extension
Bozrah, CT
860-889-4144
odetah.com
Dogs of all sizes are allowed to stay in the campground but are not allowed to leave your camp site. There are no additional pet fees. Dogs must be well behaved, quiet, and kept leashed. There is a dog walk area at the campground. Multiple dogs may be allowed.

Lone Oak Campsites
360 Norfolk
E Canaan, CT
860-824-7051
loneoakcampsites.com
Dogs of all sizes are allowed. There are no additional pet fees. Dogs must be leashed, cleaned up after, and have proof of rabies shots. There is a dog walk area at the campground. Multiple dogs may be allowed.

Aces High RV Park
301 Chesterfield Road
East Lyme, CT
860-739-8858
aceshighrvpark.com
Well behaved dogs of all sizes are allowed. There are no additional pet fees. Dogs are not allowed in other people's sites and they also have a separate swim area for them. Dogs must be quiet, leashed and cleaned up after. There is a dog walk area at the campground. Multiple dogs may be allowed.

Stateline Camp Resort
1639 Hartford Pike
Killingly, CT
860-774-3016
resortcamplands.com
Dogs of all sizes are allowed, however some breeds are not. There is a $3 per night per pet additional fee. Dogs must be well behaved, quiet, leashed, and cleaned up after. Dogs are not to be left unattended.

The camping and tent areas also allow dogs. There is a dog walk area at the campground. Multiple dogs may be allowed.

Water's Edge Family Campground
271 Leonard Bridge Road
Lebanon, CT
860-642-7470
watersedgecampground.com
Dogs of all sizes are allowed. There are no additional pet fees. Dogs must be leashed and cleaned up after. Dogs are allowed in the camping cabins. 2 dogs may be allowed.

Ross Hill Park
170 Ross Hill Road
Lisbon, CT
860-376-9606 (800-308-1089)
rosshillpark.com/
Pets of all sizes are allowed. There are no additional pet fees. Dogs allowed on leash only, and fecal matter MUST BE CLEANED UP IMMEDIATELY. Failure to pick up after your pet will result in eviction. Pets are not allowed in the swimming area. This RV park is closed during the off-season. The camping and tent areas also allow dogs. There is a dog walk area at the campground. 2 dogs may be allowed.

Hemlock Hill Camp Resort
118 Hemlock Hill Road
Litchfield, CT
860-567-2267
hemlockhillcamp.com
One dog of any size per site is the usual allowance, however two dogs are allowed if they are both under 25 pounds. Pit Bulls, Rottweilers, and some other breeds are not allowed. Dogs must have proof of rabies shots. The camping and tent areas also allow dogs. There is a dog walk area at the campground.

Mystic KOA
118 Pendleton Hill Road
North Stonington, CT
860-599-5101 (800-562-3451)
koa.com/where/ct/07119/
Ocean cooled breezes add to the ambiance of this scenic camp area located on a treed hill with great views. They offer free Wi-Fi, 2 seasonal pools, mini-golf, a large jumping pillow, an outdoor cinema, cable TV, and plenty of campfire fun. Dogs are allowed for no additional fee in the RV/tent area; there is one time fee of $15 for the cabins. Dogs may not be left unattended, and they must be on no more than a 6 foot leash and cleaned up after at all

times. There are some breed restrictions. The camping and tent areas also allow dogs. There is a dog walk area at the campground. Dogs are allowed in the camping cabins. Multiple dogs may be allowed.

Seaport Campground
Old Campground Road
Old Mystic, CT
860-536-4044
seaportcampground.com/
This scenic family camp area features spacious sites, free internet, a store, laundry, pool-but beaches are close by too, a fishing pond, mini-golf, planned activities, and live entertainment. There is no additional pet fee for 1 dog; it is $5 per day extra if there is a 2nd dog. One dog is allowed in tents with permission from the management, and they may not be left alone in a tent at any time. Dogs may not be left outside alone, and they must be leashed and cleaned up after at all times. Guests must have proof of current rabies inoculation for their pet. This RV park is closed during the off-season. The camping and tent areas also allow dogs. There is a dog walk area at the campground. 2 dogs may be allowed.

Strawberry Park Resort
Campground
42 Pierce Road
Preston, CT
860-886-1944
strawberrypark.net
Dogs of all sizes are allowed, but some breeds are not. There are no additional pet fees. Dogs must remain on your site and are not to be walked or carried around the campground. The camping and tent areas also allow dogs. Multiple dogs may be allowed.

Salem Farms Campground
39 Alexander Road
Salem, CT
860-859-2320
salemfarmscampground.com
Dogs of all sizes are allowed. There are no additional pet fees. Dogs must be leashed, are not allowed to be on the grass areas, and must be cleaned up after. The camping and tent areas also allow dogs. There is a dog walk area at the campground. 2 dogs may be allowed.

Witch Meadow Lake Campground
139 Witch Meadow Road
Salem, CT
860-859-1542

witchmeadowcampground.com/
Dogs of all sizes are allowed. There are no additional pet fees. Dogs may not be left unattended, and they must be leashed and cleaned up after. Dogs must be kept on the campsite or walked on the dog walk trail at the back of the campground. There are some breed restrictions. This RV park is closed during the off-season. The camping and tent areas also allow dogs. There is a dog walk area at the campground. Multiple dogs may be allowed.

Del-Aire Campground
704 Shenipsit Road
Tolland, CT
860-875-8325
Dogs of all sizes are allowed. There are no additional pet fees. Dogs must be well behaved, quiet, leashed, and cleaned up after. Dogs may not be left on site unattended. The camping and tent areas also allow dogs. There is a dog walk area at the campground. Multiple dogs may be allowed.

Pachaug State Forest Chapman Area
H 49/ P. O. Box 5
Voluntown, CT
860-376-4075 (866-287-2757)
This state forest is home to miles and miles of multi-use year round trails, a beautiful walk through a rare Rhododendron Sanctuary (blooms early July), a scenic overlook, a stocked fishing pond, and the park also partakes in Letterboxing. Dogs are allowed throughout the park and the campground for no additional fee. Dogs must be under their owner's control, be well behaved, leashed, and cleaned up after at all times. Two camping areas offer 40 wooded sites on a first come first served basis, and only one dog is allowed per campsite. The camp areas provide water, fireplaces and pit toilets. This RV park is closed during the off-season. The camping and tent areas also allow dogs. There is a dog walk area at the campground. There are no electric or water hookups at the campgrounds.

Beaver Pines Campground
1728 H 198
Woodstock, CT
860-974-0110
beaverpinescampground.com/
Dogs of all sizes are allowed at no additional fee. Dogs may not be left unattended, and they must have current rabies and shot records. Dogs must be leashed and cleaned

up after. There are some breed restrictions. This RV park is closed during the off-season. The camping and tent areas also allow dogs. There is a dog walk area at the campground. Multiple dogs may be allowed.

Delaware

Lums Pond State Park
1068 Howell School Road
Bear, DE
302-368-6989 (877-987-2757)
destateparks.com/lpsp/lpsp.asp
This park of over 1,700 acres with a 200 surface acre lake, offers sports facilities, and a variety of land and water recreation. Dogs of all sizes are allowed at no additional fee. Dogs may not be left unattended, and they must be quiet, be on no more than a 6 foot leash, and be cleaned up after. Dogs are not allowed in buildings, in picnic areas, or on the trails. However, just past this park on Buck's Jersey Road, there is an off leash training area for dogs. This campground is closed during the off-season. The camping and tent areas also allow dogs. There is a dog walk area at the campground. There are no water hookups at the campground. Multiple dogs may be allowed.

Killens Pond State Park
5025 Killens Pond Road
Felton, DE
302-284-3412 (877-987-2757)
destateparks.com/kpsp/kpsp.htm
This resort type park features an all new water park, a variety of hiking trails, nature study, and land and water recreation. Dogs of all sizes are allowed at no additional fee. Dogs may not be left unattended, and they must be on no more than a 6 foot leash, and be cleaned up after. Dogs are not allowed in the buildings, but they are allowed on the trails. The camping and tent areas also allow dogs. There is a dog walk area at the campground. Multiple dogs may be allowed.

G and R Campground
4075 Gun and Rod Club Road
Houston, DE
302-398-8108
gnrcampground.com
Dogs of all sizes are allowed, and there are no additional pet fees for the tent or RV sites. There is a $15

per night per pet additional fee for the cabin rentals, and there are only 2 pets per cabin allowed. Dogs must be quiet and well behaved. Dogs may not be left unattended, must be leashed, and cleaned up after. There are some breed restrictions. The camping and tent areas also allow dogs. There is a dog walk area at the campground. Dogs are allowed in the camping cabins.

Trap Pond State Park
33587 Bald Cypress Lane
Laurel, DE
302-875-2392 (877-987-2757)
destateparks.com/tpsp/tpsp.htm
Trap Pond State Park offers an opportunity to explore a wetland forest and its inhabitants on both land and water and a variety of recreational activities and pursuits. Dogs of all sizes are allowed at no additional fee. Dogs may not be left unattended, and they must be leashed and cleaned up after. Dogs are not allowed in buildings. This campground is closed during the off-season. The camping and tent areas also allow dogs. There is a dog walk area at the campground. Multiple dogs may be allowed.

Cape Henlopen State Park
42 Cape Henlopen Drive
Lewes, DE
302-645-8983 (1-877-98 PARKS (72757))
destateparks.com/chsp/chsp.htm
A main year round land and water recreation destination with a variety of activities, concerts, and special events, this 129-acre barrier island park also has various scenic seaside trails, or nature trails through the pines to an observation tower, and an 18 hold disc golf course. Dogs of all sizes are allowed for no additional pet fee. Dogs must be quiet, well behaved, under their owner's control, leashed, and cleaned up after at all times. Dogs must have proof of currents shots, and they may not be left unattended at any times. Dogs are allowed throughout the park, on the trails, and on the surf-fishing beaches; they are not allowed on swim beaches. The camp area offers 150 spacious sites, drinking water, restrooms, showers, a laundry, playing fields, and a dump station. This RV park is closed during the off-season. The camping and tent areas also allow dogs. There is a dog walk area at the campground. There are no electric

hookups at the campgrounds. Multiple dogs may be allowed.

Tall Pines Camping Resort
29551 Persimmon Road
Lewes, DE
302-684-0300
tallpines-del.com
Dogs of all sizes are allowed. There are no additional pet fees. Dogs must be quiet, well behaved, and are not to be left unattended. They must be leashed and cleaned up after. The camping and tent areas also allow dogs. There is a dog walk area at the campground. Multiple dogs may be allowed.

Holly Lake Campsites
32087 Hollly Lake Road
Millsboro, DE
302-945-3410
hollylakecampsites.com/
Dogs of all sizes are allowed. There are no additional pet fees. Dogs may not be left unattended outside and they must be quiet, well behaved, leashed and cleaned up after. Dogs are allowed on the trails. This RV park is closed during the off-season. The camping and tent areas also allow dogs. There is a dog walk area at the campground. Multiple dogs may be allowed.

Delaware Motel and RV Park
235 S. Dupont Highway
New Castle, DE
302-328-3114
Dogs of all sizes are allowed. There are no additional pet fees. Dogs must be well behaved and not left unattended at any time. There is a dog walk area at the campground. Multiple dogs may be allowed.

Big Oaks Family Campground
35567 Big Oaks Lane
Rehoboth Beach, DE
302-645-6838
bigoakscamping.com
Dogs of all sizes are allowed in the campground area but not in the rentals. There are no additional pet fees. Dogs must be on a 6 foot or shorter leash and cleaned up after. The camping and tent areas also allow dogs. There is a dog walk area at the campground. Multiple dogs may be allowed.

Delaware Seashore State Park
130 Coastal H
Rehoboth Beach, DE
302-539-7202 (877-987-2757)
destateparks.com/dssp/dssp.asp
This park, being on the coast, offers a wide variety of water related

activities. Dogs of all sizes are allowed at no additional fee. Dogs may not be left unattended, and they must be on no more than a 6 foot leash, and be cleaned up after. Dogs are not allowed in public swim areas or buildings. Dogs are allowed on the beach at the North end, at T-Box Road, Conquest Road, and the 3 Rs. The camping and tent areas also allow dogs. There is a dog walk area at the campground. Multiple dogs may be allowed.

Florida

Wekiwa Springs State Park
1800 Wekiwa Circle
Apopka, FL
407-884-2008 (800-326-3521)
There are many water and land activities year round at this park, and they have interpretive programs at their amphitheater, a nature center, and 13 miles of multi-use trails. Dogs of all sizes are allowed at no additional fee. Dogs may not be left unattended, and they must have current rabies and shot records. Dogs must be on no more than a 6 foot leash, and be cleaned up after. Dogs are not allowed in buildings, at the beach, the springs, the top of the slope, or on the boardwalk trails. Dogs are allowed on the other trails. The camping and tent areas also allow dogs. There is a dog walk area at the campground. Multiple dogs may be allowed.

Sunshine Key RV Resort
38801 Overseas H
Big Pine Key, FL
305-872-2217 (800-852-0348)
Dogs of all sizes are allowed. There are no additional pet fees. Dogs must be leashed and cleaned up after. The camping and tent areas also allow dogs. There is a dog walk area at the campground. Multiple dogs may be allowed.

Horseshoe Cove RV Resort
5100 60th Street & Caruso Road
Bradenton, FL
941-758-5335
Dogs up to about 75 pounds are allowed. There are no additional pet fees. Dogs must be leashed and cleaned up after. There are some breed restrictions. There is a dog walk area at the campground. 2 dogs may be allowed.

Lake Manatee State Park
20007 H 64E
Bradenton, FL
941-741-3028 (800-326-3521)
This park,set along 3 miles of lake shoreline, offers both land and water recreation. Well behaved dogs of all sizes are allowed at no additional fee. Dogs may not be left unattended for more than 30 minutes at a time, and they must have current rabies and shot records. Dogs must be on no more than a 6 foot leash, and be cleaned up after. Dogs are not allowed in buildings, public swimming areas, or by the boat ramps. Dogs are allowed on the trails. The camping and tent areas also allow dogs. There is a dog walk area at the campground. Multiple dogs may be allowed.

Sarasota North Resort
800 K Road
Bradenton, FL
800-678-2131
Dogs of all sizes are allowed. There are no additional pet fees. Dogs must be leashed and cleaned up after. The camping and tent areas also allow dogs. There is a dog walk area at the campground. Multiple dogs may be allowed.

Chattahoochee/Tallahassee W KOA
2309 Flat Circle Road
Chattahoochee, FL
850-442-6657 (800-562-2153)
koa.com
Dogs of all sizes are allowed. There are no additional pet fees. Dogs may not be left unattended outside, and they must be well behaved, leashed, and cleaned up after. There are some breed restrictions. The camping and tent areas also allow dogs. There is a dog walk area at the campground. Dogs are allowed in the camping cabins. Multiple dogs may be allowed.

Falling Waters State Rec Area
1130 State Park Road
Chipley, FL
850-638-6130 (800-326-3521)
Features of this park are the Sink Hole Trail that takes you along a boardwalk to Florida's highest waterfall, the butterfly garden, and interpretive programs held in their amphitheater. Well behaved dogs of all sizes are allowed at no additional fee. Dogs must have current rabies and shot records, be on no more than a 6 foot leash, and be cleaned up after. Dogs are not allowed in

buildings, in the lake, or on the boardwalk to the waterfall. The camping and tent areas also allow dogs. There is a dog walk area at the campground. Multiple dogs may be allowed.

Lake Louisa State Park
7305 H 27
Clermont, FL
352-394-3969 (800-326-3521)
Lake Louisa has 6 lakes, is a part of a chain of 13 lakes connected by the Palatlakaha River, has over 20 miles of hiking trails, and a variety of land and water activities. Dogs of all sizes are allowed at no additional fee. Dogs must have current rabies and shot records, be on no more than a 6 foot leash, and be cleaned up after. Dogs are not allowed in or around buildings, but they are allowed on the trails. The camping and tent areas also allow dogs. There is a dog walk area at the campground. Multiple dogs may be allowed.

Rock Crusher Canyon Park
275 S Rock Crusher Road
Crystal River, FL
352-795-1313
rccrvpark.com
Dogs of all sizes are allowed. There are no additional pet fees. Dogs must be leashed and cleaned up after. The camping and tent areas also allow dogs. There is a dog walk area at the campground. Multiple dogs may be allowed.

Florida Camp Inn
48504 H 27
Davenport, FL
863-424-2494
Dogs of all sizes are allowed. There are no additional pet fees. Dogs may not be left unattended, and they must be leashed and cleaned up after. The camping and tent areas also allow dogs. There is a dog walk area at the campground. Multiple dogs may be allowed.

Camping on the Gulf
1005 Emerald Coast Parkway
Destin, FL
877-226-7485
campgulf.com
Dogs of all sizes are allowed. There are no additional pet fees. Dogs may not be left unattended outside, and they must be leashed and cleaned up after. There is a large fine levied for dogs on the beach. The camping and tent areas also allow dogs. There is a dog walk area at the campground. 2 dogs may be allowed.

Destin RV Beach Resort
362 Miramar Beach Drive
Destin, FL
877-737-3529
destinrvresort.com
Dogs of all sizes are allowed. There are no additional pet fees. Dogs must be leashed and cleaned up after. The dogs may be walked on the grass just outside of the park. 2 dogs may be allowed.

Henderson Beach State Park
17000 Emerald Coast Parkway
Destin, FL
850-837-7550 (800-326-3521)
Land and water recreation is offered here with about 6000 feet of white sandy beaches, a boardwalk, and nature trails. Quiet and well behaved dogs of all sizes are allowed at no additional fee. Dogs may not be left unattended at any time, and they must have current rabies and shot records. Dogs must be on no more than a 6 foot leash, and be cleaned up after. Dogs are not allowed in buildings, on the beach, or on the Boardwalk. Dogs are allowed on all the trails. The camping and tent areas also allow dogs. There is a dog walk area at the campground. Multiple dogs may be allowed.

Greenfield Village RV Park
1015 H 542W
Dundee, FL
863-439-7409
Dogs of all sizes are allowed. There are no additional pet fees. Dogs may not be left unattended outside, and they must be leashed and cleaned up after. This is a 55 years or older park. There are some breed restrictions. There is a dog walk area at the campground. 2 dogs may be allowed.

Koreshan State Historic Site
Corner of H 41 and Corkscrew Road
Estero, FL
239-992-0311 (800-326-3521)
Guided or self-guided tours are offered here as well as a variety of recreational pursuits. Dogs of all sizes are allowed at no additional fee. Dogs may not be left unattended for more than 15 minutes if outside, and they must have current rabies and shot records. Dogs must be on no more than a 6 foot leash, and be cleaned up after. Dogs are not allowed in buildings, but they are allowed on the trails. The camping and tent areas also allow dogs. There is a dog walk area at the campground. Multiple dogs may be

allowed.

Fort Clinch State Park
2601 Atlantic Avenue
Fernandina Beach, FL
904-277-7274 (800-326-3521)
This park is home to one of the most well preserved 19th century forts in America, and offers deep woods, white sandy beaches, a living history program, and a variety of recreation and trails. Dogs of all sizes are allowed at no additional fee. Dogs may not be left unattended, and they must have current rabies and shot records. Dogs must be on no more than a 6 foot leash, and be cleaned up after. Dogs are not allowed in buildings or on the beaches, but they are allowed on the trails. The camping and tent areas also allow dogs. There is a dog walk area at the campground. Multiple dogs may be allowed.

Beverly Beach Campground
2816 N Ocean Shore Blvd
Flagler Beach, FL
800-255-2706
beverlybeachcampground.com
Dogs of all sizes are allowed. There are no additional pet fees. Dogs must be quiet, leashed, and cleaned up after. Dogs may not be left unattended outside. They ask that dogs be walked just outside of the park, and they are allowed at the beach. The camping and tent areas also allow dogs. Multiple dogs may be allowed.

Bulow Plantation RV Resort
3345 Old Kings Road S
Flagler Beach, FL
800-782-8569
rvonthego.com
Dogs of all sizes are allowed. There are no additional pet fees. Dogs must be quiet, well behaved, leashed, and cleaned up after. There are some breed restrictions. The camping and tent areas also allow dogs. There is a dog walk area at the campground. Multiple dogs may be allowed.

Gamble Rogers Memorial State Recreation Area
3100 S A1A (Ocean Shore Blvd)
Flagler Beach, FL
386-517-2086 (800-326-3521)
This park is tucked between the Intracoastal Waterway and the Atlantic Ocean with the beach being the popular draw, and there is a nature trail and boat ramp also. Dogs of all sizes are allowed at no

additional fee. Dogs may not be left unattended, and they must have current rabies and shot records. Dogs must be on no more than a 6 foot leash, and be cleaned up after. Dogs are not allowed in buildings or on the beach, but they are allowed on the trails. The camping and tent areas also allow dogs. There is a dog walk area at the campground. Multiple dogs may be allowed.

Indian Creek RV Resort
17340 San Carlos Blvd
Fort Myers Beach, FL
800-828-6992
sunresorts.com
Dogs of all sizes are allowed. There are no additional pet fees. Dogs may not be left unattended outside, and they must be leashed and cleaned up after. There are some breed restrictions. There is a dog walk area at the campground. 2 dogs may be allowed.

Jonathan Dickinson State Park
16450 SE Federal H (H 1)
Hobe Sound, FL
772-546-2771 (800-326-3521)
This park is Florida's first federally designated Wild and Scenic River, and is home to abundant wildlife in 13 natural communities. Dogs of all sizes are allowed at no additional fee. Dogs may not be left unattended, and they must have current rabies and shot records. Dogs must be on no more than a 6 foot leash, and be cleaned up after. Dogs are not allowed in buildings or any public swimming areas. The camping and tent areas also allow dogs. There is a dog walk area at the campground. Multiple dogs may be allowed.

Blackwater River State Park
7720 Deaton Bridge Road
Holt, FL
850-983-5363 (800-326-3521)
This park was certified as a Registered State Natural Feature for their preserving and representation of the natural history of Florida. Dogs of all sizes are allowed at no additional fee. Dogs may not be left unattended, and they must have current rabies and shot records. Dogs must be on no more than a 6 foot leash, and be cleaned up after. Dogs are not allowed in buildings or at the beaches. Dogs are allowed on the trails, including the Chain O'Lakes Trail. The camping and tent areas also allow dogs. There is a dog walk area at the campground. Multiple dogs may be allowed.

Little Talbot Island State Park
12157 Heckscher Drive
Jacksonville, FL
904-251-2320 (800-326-3521)
This park has scenic, historical, biological, and geological sites to explore. They have introduced a new interpretive program of a self-guided auto tour of the area. Dogs of all sizes are allowed at no additional fee. Dogs may not be left unattended, and they must have current rabies and shot records. Dogs must be on no more than a 6 foot leash, and be cleaned up after. Dogs are not allowed in buildings, on beaches, or in the waterways. Dogs are allowed on the trails. The camping and tent areas also allow dogs. There is a dog walk area at the campground. Multiple dogs may be allowed.

Juno Ocean Walk RV Resort
900 Juno Ocean Walk
Juno Beach, FL
561-622-7500
junobeachrvresort.com
Dogs of all sizes are allowed. There is a $3 per night per pet additional fee. Dogs must be friendly, well behaved, leashed, and cleaned up after. There is a dog walk area at the campground. Multiple dogs may be allowed.

John Pennekamp Coral Reef State Park
H 1, MM 102.5
Key Largo, FL
305-451-1202 (800-326-3521)
pennekamppark.com/
This campground is located at Americas first undersea park where they offer boat tours, rentals, guided nature walks, and 47 full service tent and RV sites with restrooms and hot showers. Dogs are not allowed in buildings or on the boat tours. Dogs of all sizes are allowed at no additional fee. Dogs may not be left unattended outside the camping unit, and they must be quiet, well behaved, leashed and cleaned up after. Dogs are not allowed at this park for day use because they may not be left in vehicles in the parking lot. The camping and tent areas also allow dogs. There is a dog walk area at the campground. Multiple dogs may be allowed.

Key Largo Kampground and Marina
Mile Marker 101.5
Key Largo, CA
305-451-1431 (800-KAMP-OUT)
keylargokampground.com
This campground is located on 40

acres along the Atlantic Ocean. It is one mile south of the entrance to John Pennekamp State Park. Also nearby are boat charters and diving activities. Multiple dogs may be allowed.

Riptide R/V Park & Motel
97680 Overseas Highway
Key Largo, FL 33037
305-852-8481 (877-853-71330)
riptidervparkfloridakeys.com
This campground is located near the waters of the Florida Keys in Key Largo. It is located at mile marker 97.2 on the Overseas Highway. Dogs are allowed in the RV campground but are not allowed in the motel. Multiple dogs may be allowed.

Boyd's Key West Campground
6401 Maloney Avenue
Key West, FL
305-294-1465
boydscampground.com
Dogs of all sizes are allowed. There are no additional pet fees. Dogs may not be left unattended outside, and they must be leashed and cleaned up after. There are some breed restrictions. The camping and tent areas also allow dogs. There is a dog walk area at the campground. Multiple dogs may be allowed.

Encore Tropical Palms
2650 Holiday Trail
Kissimmee, FL
800-647-2567
Dogs of all sizes are allowed. There are no additional pet fees. Dogs must be quiet, well behaved, leashed, and cleaned up after. There is a dog walk area at the campground. Multiple dogs may be allowed.

Kissimmee KOA
2643 Happy Camper Place
Kissimmee, FL
407-396-2400 (800-562-7791)
kissorlando.com
Dogs of all sizes are allowed. There are no additional pet fees. Dogs may not be left unattended outside, and they must be quiet, leashed, and cleaned up after. The camping and tent areas also allow dogs. There is a dog walk area at the campground. Multiple dogs may be allowed.

Sanlan Ranch Campground
3929 H 98S
Lakeland, FL
863-665-1726
sanlan.com

Dogs of all sizes are allowed. There is $.50 per night per pet additional fee. Dogs may not be left unattended outside, and they must be leashed and cleaned up after. Dogs must stay out of the water because of alligators. The camping and tent areas also allow dogs. There is a dog walk area at the campground. 2 dogs may be allowed.

Suwannee River State Park
20185 County Road 132
Live Oak, FL
386-362-2746 (800-326-3521)
Rich in scenery, history, and recreation, this park offers 5 different trails and panoramic views of the great river. Dogs of all sizes are allowed at no additional fee. Dogs may not be left unattended, and they must have current rabies and shot records. Dogs must be on no more than a 6 foot leash, and be cleaned up after. Dogs are not allowed in buildings or public swim areas, but they are allowed on the trails. The camping and tent areas also allow dogs. There is a dog walk area at the campground. Multiple dogs may be allowed.

Jellystone Park
1051 SW Old St. Augustine Road
Madison, FL
800-347-0174
jellystoneflorida.com
Dogs of all sizes are allowed. There are no additional pet fees. Dogs must be leashed and cleaned up after. Dogs are not allowed in public areas or the beach. The camping and tent areas also allow dogs. There is a dog walk area at the campground. Multiple dogs may be allowed.

Florida Caverns State Park
3345 Caverns Road (H 166)
Marianna, FL
850-482-9598 (800-326-3521)
As well as having a variety of year round recreational activities, this park offers the only guided cave tours in Florida. Dogs of all sizes are allowed at no additional fee. Dogs may not be left unattended, and they must have current rabies and shot records. Dogs must be on no more than a 6 foot leash, and be cleaned up after. Dogs are not allowed in buildings, any public swimming areas, or on the cave tours. The camping and tent areas also allow dogs. There is a dog walk area at the campground. Multiple dogs may be allowed.

Sebastian Inlet State Park
9700 S A1A
Melbourne Beach, FL
321-984-4852 (800-326-3521)
This park offers premier saltwater fishing, 3 miles of beaches, a boat dock, and a variety of land and water recreation. Dogs of all sizes are allowed at no additional fee. Dogs may not be left unattended, and they must have current rabies and shot records. Dogs must be on no more than a 6 foot leash, and be cleaned up after. Dogs are not allowed in buildings, on the beaches, on the jetty, or catwalks. Dogs are allowed on the trails, and there is a small area at the cove where they may go in the water as long as they are still on lead. The camping and tent areas also allow dogs. There is a dog walk area at the campground. Multiple dogs may be allowed.

Flamingo Lake RV Resort
3640 Newcomb Road
N Jacksonville, FL
904-766-0672
flamingolake.com
Dogs of all sizes are allowed. There are no additional pet fees. Dogs may not be left unattended outside, and they must be leashed and cleaned up after. There are some breed restrictions. There is a dog walk area at the campground. Multiple dogs may be allowed.

Collier-Seminole State Park
20200 E Tamiami Trail
Naples, FL
239-394-3397 (800-326-3521)
This park displays wildlife and vegetation typical of the Everglades, a forest of tropical trees, and is a National Historic Mechanical Engineering Landmark site. Dogs of all sizes are allowed at no additional fee. Dogs may not be left unattended outside, and they must have current rabies and shot records. Dogs must be on no more than a 6 foot leash, and be cleaned up after. Dogs are not allowed in buildings, on canoe rentals, or on any of the trails. Dogs may be walked around the camp area. The camping and tent areas also allow dogs. There is a dog walk area at the campground. Multiple dogs may be allowed.

Hitching Post RV Resort
100 Barefoot Williams Road
Naples, FL
239-774-1259
Dogs of all sizes are allowed. There are no additional pet fees. Dogs

must be quiet, leashed, and cleaned up after. This RV park is closed during the off-season. The camping and tent areas also allow dogs. There is a dog walk area at the campground. Multiple dogs may be allowed.

Lake San Marino RV Resort
1000 Wiggins Pass
Naples, FL
239-597-4202
lakesanmarino.com
Dogs of all sizes are allowed. There are no additional pet fees. Dogs may not be tied up or left unattended outside, and they must be leashed and cleaned up after. They do have an off lead dog park on site. This a 55 years or older park. There are some breed restrictions. There is a dog walk area at the campground. There are special amenities given to dogs at this campground. 2 dogs may be allowed.

North Fort Myers RV Resort
(Pioneer Village)
7974 Samville Road
North Fort Myers, FL
239-543-3303 (877-897-3757)
rvonthego.com
Dogs of all sizes are allowed. There are no additional pet fees. Dogs must be leashed and cleaned up after. The camping and tent areas also allow dogs. There is a dog walk area at the campground. Multiple dogs may be allowed.

Paradise Island RV Resort
2121 NW 29th Court
Oakland Park, FL
954-485-1150
paradiserv.com
Dogs of all sizes are allowed. There are no additional pet fees. Dogs may not be left unattended outside at any time, and they must be well behaved, leashed, and cleaned up after. There is also a Bark Park about 20 minutes from the resort. There are some breed restrictions. There is a dog walk area at the campground. Multiple dogs may be allowed.

Silver River State Park
1425 NE 58th Avenue
Ocala, FL
352-236-7148 (800-326-3521)
This park has dozens of springs, 15 miles of trails, 14 distinct natural communities, a pioneer cracker village, the Silver River Museum and an Environmental Education Center. Dogs of all sizes are

allowed at no additional fee. Dogs may not be left unattended, and they must have current rabies and shot records. Dogs must be on no more than a 6 foot leash, and be cleaned up after. Dogs are not allowed in or around any buildings, and dogs should not be down by the river because of alligators. The camping and tent areas also allow dogs. There is a dog walk area at the campground. Multiple dogs may be allowed.

Big Cypress National Preserve
33100 Tamiami Trail East
Ochopee, FL
239-695-1201
nps.gov/bicy/index.htm
This recreational paradise offers day use, camping, canoeing, kayaking, hiking, bird-watching opportunities, interpretive programs, and self guided nature walks. Dogs of all sizes are allowed for no additional fee. Dogs must be leashed at all times and cleaned up after. Dogs are allowed anywhere in the front country and the campgrounds, but they are not allowed on trails or on any of the boardwalks. The camping and tent areas also allow dogs. There is a dog walk area at the campground. There are no water hookups at the campgrounds. 2 dogs may be allowed.

Blue Spring State Park
2100 W French Avenue
Orange City, FL
386-775-3663 (800-326-3521)
Blue Spring, a scenic recreation area, is also a designated manatee refuge because the warm waters in winter create a perfect habitat for the growing population of West Indian Manatees. Dogs of all sizes are allowed at no additional fee. Dogs may not be left unattended for more than 30 minutes at a time, and they must have current rabies and shot records. Dogs must be on no more than a 6 foot leash, and be cleaned up after. Dogs are not allowed in buildings or on the beaches. Dogs are allowed on the trails. The camping and tent areas also allow dogs. There is a dog walk area at the campground. Multiple dogs may be allowed.

Deland/Orange City KOA
1440 E Minnesota Avenue
Orange City, FL
386-775-3996 (800-562-7857)
theockoa.com
Dogs of all sizes are allowed. There are no additional pet fees. Dogs may

not be left unattended, and they must be leashed and cleaned up after. There are some breed restrictions. The camping and tent areas also allow dogs. There is a dog walk area at the campground. Multiple dogs may be allowed.

Grand Lake RV & Golf Resort
4555 W H 318
Orange Lake, FL
352-591-3474
grandlakeresort.com
Dogs of all sizes are allowed. There are no additional pet fees. Dogs must be leashed when walking around the resort and cleaned up after, but may be off lead on own site if well behaved and under voice command. The camping and tent areas also allow dogs. There is a dog walk area at the campground. Multiple dogs may be allowed.

Orlando SE/Lake Whippoorwill KOA
12345 Narcoossee Road
Orlando, FL
407-277-5075 (800-562-3969)
koa.com
Dogs of all sizes are allowed. There are no additional pet fees. Dogs may not be left unattended, and they must be leashed and cleaned up after. The camping and tent areas also allow dogs. There is a dog walk area at the campground.

Daytona North RV Resort
1701 H 1
Ormond Beach, FL
877-277-8737
rvonthego.com
Dogs of all sizes are allowed. There are no additional pet fees. Dogs must be leashed and cleaned up after. The camping and tent areas also allow dogs. There is a dog walk area at the campground. Multiple dogs may be allowed.

Tomoka State Park
2099 N Beach Street
Ormond Beach, FL
386-676-4050 (800-326-3521)
This park protects a variety of wildlife habitats and endangered species and over 160 bird species. It boasts a nature trail, a museum, and a variety of land and water recreation. Dogs of all sizes are allowed at no additional fee. Dogs may not be left unattended, and they must have current rabies and shot records. Dogs must be on no more than a 6 foot leash, and be cleaned up after. Dogs are not allowed in buildings or on the beach. Dogs are allowed on the trails. The camping and tent

areas also allow dogs. There is a dog walk area at the campground. Multiple dogs may be allowed.

Oscar Scherer State Park
1843 S Tamiami Trail
Osprey, FL
941-483-5956 (800-326-3521)
Special events, campfire programs, guided tours, and 15 miles of trails add to the year round recreation offered here. Dogs of all sizes are allowed at designated pet sites for no additional fee. Dogs may not be left unattended, and they must have current rabies and shot records. Dogs must be leashed, and cleaned up after. Dogs are not allowed by the creek, but they are allowed on the trails. The camping and tent areas also allow dogs. There is a dog walk area at the campground. Multiple dogs may be allowed.

Clearwater/Tarpon Springs KOA
37061 H 19N
Palm Harbor, FL
727-937-8412 (800-562-8743)
koa.com
Dogs of all sizes are allowed. There are no additional pet fees. Dogs may not be left unattended outside, and they must be well behaved, leashed, and cleaned up after. There are some breed restrictions. There is a dog walk area at the campground. Dogs are allowed in the camping cabins. 2 dogs may be allowed.

Emerald Coast RV Beach Resort
1957 Allison Avenue
Panama City Beach, FL
800-232-2478
rvresort.com
Dogs of all sizes are allowed. There are no additional pet fees. Dogs may not be left unattended outside, and they must be leashed and cleaned up after. Dogs are not allowed in any of the buildings. There are some breed restrictions. There is a dog walk area at the campground. 2 dogs may be allowed.

Raccoon River Campground
12209 Hutchison Blvd
Panama City Beach, FL
877-234-0181
floridacamping.com
Dogs of all sizes are allowed. There are no additional pet fees. Dogs must be leashed and cleaned up after. There are some breed restrictions. There is a dog walk area at the campground. Multiple dogs may be allowed.

Highland Woods
850/900 NE 48th Street
Pompano Beach, FL
866-340-0649
mhchomes.com
Dogs of all sizes are allowed. There are no additional pet fees. Dogs may not be left unattended, and they must be leashed and cleaned up after. There is a dog walk area at the campground. Multiple dogs may be allowed.

Daytona Beach Campground
4601 Clyde Morris Blvd
Port Orange, FL
386-761-2663
rvdaytona.com
Dogs of all sizes are allowed. There are no additional pet fees. Dogs may not be left unattended outside or in tents, and they must be quiet, leashed, and cleaned up after. There is a dog walk area just outside of the park. There are some breed restrictions. The camping and tent areas also allow dogs. Multiple dogs may be allowed.

Encore RV Resort
16905 NW H 225
Reddick, FL
352-591-1723
Dogs of all sizes are allowed. There are no additional pet fees. Dogs may not be left unattended outside, and they must be leashed and cleaned up after. The camping and tent areas also allow dogs. There is a dog walk area at the campground. Multiple dogs may be allowed.

Buttonwood Bay RV Resort
10001 H 27S
Sebring, FL
863-655-1122
buttonwoodbay.com
Dogs of all sizes are allowed. There are no additional pet fees. Dogs must be leashed and cleaned up after. There are some breed restrictions. There is a dog walk area at the campground. 2 dogs may be allowed.

Highlands Hammock State Park
5931 Hammock Road
Sebring, FL
863-386-6094 (800-326-3521)
This park offers a variety of recreational pursuits, nine trails, special events, and an elevated boardwalk that traverses an old-growth cypress swamp. Dogs of all sizes are allowed at no additional fee. Dogs may not be left unattended, and they must have

current rabies and shot records. Dogs must be on no more than a 6 foot leash, and be cleaned up after. Dogs are not allowed in buildings or on any of the elevated boardwalk trails. Dogs are allowed on the other trails. The camping and tent areas also allow dogs. There is a dog walk area at the campground. Multiple dogs may be allowed.

Ocala National Forest
17147 E H 40
Silver Springs, FL
352-625-2520 (877-444-6777)
This National forest offers interesting geological and historical sites to explore, a wide abundance of land and water recreation, and a variety of trails, including a portion of the Florida National Scenic Trail. Dogs of all sizes are allowed at no additional fee. Dogs may not be left unattended, they must have current rabies and shot records, be on no more than a 6 foot leash, and be cleaned up after. Dogs are not allowed in public swim areas, buildings, or any day use areas. Dogs are allowed on all the trails except for the short interpretive trails. The camping and tent areas also allow dogs. There is a dog walk area at the campground. Multiple dogs may be allowed.

Ochlockonee River State Park
429 State Park Road
Sopchoppy, FL
850-962-2771 (800-326-3521)
This park is where the Ochlockonee and Dead rivers intersect and flow into the Gulf of Mexico. This allows a variety of year round recreation including both freshwater and saltwater fishing. Dogs of all sizes are allowed at no additional fee. Dogs may not be left unattended outside at any time, and can only be left in your camping unit for no more than 30 minutes. Dogs must have current rabies and shot records, be on no more than a 6 foot leash, and be cleaned up after. Dogs are not allowed in buildings, in swim areas, or in the water. Dogs are allowed on the trails. The camping and tent areas also allow dogs. There is a dog walk area at the campground. Multiple dogs may be allowed.

Anastasia State Park Campgrounds
Anastasia Park Drive
St Augustine, FL
904-461-2033
This campsite offers electric and water hookups at each camp site. RVs under 40 feet can be

accommodated. Pets are allowed at the campground, in day use areas and on the 1/2 mile nature trail and the old quarry walk. Pets are not allowed on the beach, in playgrounds, bathing areas, cabins, park buildings, or concession facilities. Pets cannot be tied to trees, tables, bushes, or shelter facilities. Dogs tied at a campsite cannot be left unattended for more than 30 minutes. Dogs must be on a 6 foot or less leash and people are required to clean up after their pets. During the park's quiet hours, usually from 11pm to 8am, your pets must be inside your camping unit. To get there from I-95, take exit 311 (old exit 94). Go east on State Road 207. Turn right on State Road 312. Turn left on A1A. Go about 1.5 miles north to the main park entrance, which is on the right after your pass The Surf Station.

St. Augustine Beach KOA
525 West Pope Road
St Augustine, FL
904-471-3113
koa.com/where/fl/09205/
This campground is located on Anastasia Island. Both RV and tent sites are available. Campground amenities include a year round swimming pool, fishing, bicycle rentals, maximum length pull-thru of 70 feet, Cable TV, modem dataport, and 50 amp service available. Pets are welcome at the campground but not in the cabins. There is no extra pet fee. This KOA has a dog walk area. The campground is open year round.

Stagecoach RV Park
2711 County Road 208
St Augustine, FL
904-824-2319
Dogs of all sizes are allowed. There are no additional pet fees. Dogs must be leashed and cleaned up after. It is suggested to book 8 to 12 months in advance for the winter months. There are some breed restrictions. There is a dog walk area at the campground. Multiple dogs may be allowed.

Fort Myers/Pine Island KOA
5120 Stringfellow Road
St James City, FL
239-283-2415 (800-562-8505)
pineislandkoa.com
Dogs of all sizes are allowed. There is a $5 per night per pet additional fee. Dogs may not be left unattended outside, and only inside if they will be quiet and well

behaved. Dogs must be leashed and cleaned up after. The camping and tent areas also allow dogs. There is a dog walk area at the campground. Dogs are allowed in the camping cabins. Multiple dogs may be allowed.

Sugarloaf Key/Key West KOA
251 H 939
Sugarloaf Key, FL
305-745-3549 (800-562-7731)
koa.com
Dogs of all sizes are allowed. There are no additional pet fees. Dogs may not be left unattended outside, and they must be leashed and cleaned up after. The camping and tent areas also allow dogs. There is a dog walk area at the campground. Dogs are allowed in the camping cabins. Multiple dogs may be allowed.

Markham Park
16001 W H 84
Sunrise, FL
954-389-2000
broward.org/parks/mk.htm
Home to a series of interlocking lakes have made this a popular park for a number of recreational activities. The park also has a swimming pool complex, concessionaires, gaming fields/courts, multi-use trails, an observatory, model airplane field, target range, and more. Dogs are allowed for no additional fee, but they must be registered at the time of check-in. Dogs must be on no more than a 6 foot leash, be cleaned up after at all times, and they are not allowed in designated swim areas, on the athletic fields, or where otherwise posted. There are 86 tent and RV sites available at the camp area, and they offer 24 hour security, modern restrooms and showers, picnic tables, and grills. The camping and tent areas also allow dogs. There is a dog walk area at the campground. 2 dogs may be allowed.

Apalachicola National Forest
11152 NW State Road 20
Tallahassee, FL
850-643-2282 (877-444-6777)
This National Forest offers a wide variety of year round land and water recreation, interpretive exhibits, and 85 miles of various types of trails. Dogs of all sizes are allowed at no additional fee. Dogs may not be left unattended, and they must have current rabies and shot records. Dogs must be on no more than a 6 foot leash, and be cleaned up after in

the camp area. Dogs are allowed on the trails. The camping and tent areas also allow dogs. There is a dog walk area at the campground. There are no water hookups at the campground. Multiple dogs may be allowed.

Big Oak RV Park
4024 N Monroe Street
Tallahassee, FL
850-562-4660
bigoakrvpark.com
Dogs of all sizes are allowed. There are no additional pet fees. Dogs must be quiet, well behaved, leashed, and cleaned up after. There is a dog walk area at the campground. Multiple dogs may be allowed.

Hillsborough River State Park
15402 H 301 N
Thonotosassa, FL
813-987-6771 (800-326-3521)
Take a tour of a replica of an 1837 fort from the Second Seminole War, walk The Wetlands Restoration Trail, or enjoy the variety of land and water recreation at this park. Dogs of all sizes are allowed at no additional fee. Dogs may not be left unattended, and they must have current rabies and shot records. Dogs are not allowed in buildings, at the pool, or on canoe rentals. Dogs are allowed on the trails but they must be in designated dog areas at all times. The camping and tent areas also allow dogs. There is a dog walk area at the campground. Multiple dogs may be allowed.

Stephen Foster Folk Culture Center State Park
P. O. Drawer G/ US 41 N
White Springs, FL
386-397-2733 (800-326-3521)
This beautiful recreational nature park offers a museum, a Craft Square, miles of trails, and special events throughout the year. Dogs of all sizes are allowed at no additional fee. Dogs may not be left unattended, and they must have current rabies and shot records. Dogs must be on no more than a 6 foot leash, and be cleaned up after. Dogs are not allowed in buildings, but they are allowed on the trails. The camping and tent areas also allow dogs. There is a dog walk area at the campground. Multiple dogs may be allowed.

Suwannee Valley Campground
786 N W Street
White Springs, FL

866-397-1667
suwanneevalleycampground.com
Dogs of all sizes are allowed, and there are no additional pet fees for tent or RV sites. There is a $50 one time pet fee for cabins. Dogs must have up to date shot records, and be leashed and cleaned up after. The camping and tent areas also allow dogs. There is a dog walk area at the campground. Dogs are allowed in the camping cabins. 2 dogs may be allowed.

East Haven RV Park
4320 Dundee Road
Winter Haven, FL
863-324-2624
easthavenrvpark.com
One dog of any size is allowed. There are no additional pet fees. Dogs may not be left unattended, and they must be leashed and cleaned up after. There are some breed restrictions. The camping and tent areas also allow dogs. There is a dog walk area at the campground.

Georgia

Holiday Harbor
5989 Groover's Landing
Acworth, GA
770-974-2575
Dogs of all sizes are allowed. There are no additional pet fees. Dogs must be leashed and cleaned up after. This is an RV only park with cabin rentals, but there is only one pet friendly cabin. The camping and tent areas also allow dogs. There is a dog walk area at the campground. Dogs are allowed in the camping cabins. Multiple dogs may be allowed.

Harvest Moon RV Park
1001 Poplar Springs Road
Adairsville, GA
770-773-7320
harvestmoonrvpark.us
Dogs of all sizes are allowed. There are no additional pet fees. Dogs may not be left unattended outside, and they must be leashed and cleaned up after. There are some breed restrictions. There is a dog walk area at the campground. 2 dogs may be allowed.

Mistletoe State Park
3723 Mistletoe Road
Appling, GA
706-541-0321 (800-864-PARK

(7275))
gastateparks.org/info/mistletoe/
This 1,920 acre peninsula park on a 7,200 acre lake, offers a wide variety of land and water activities and recreation. Dogs of all sizes are allowed at no additional fee. Dogs may not be left unattended, and they must be leashed and cleaned up after. Dogs are not allowed around the cabin areas, however, they are allowed on the trails. The camping and tent areas also allow dogs. There is a dog walk area at the campground. Multiple dogs may be allowed.

Trackrock Campground and Cabins
4887 Trackrock Camp Road
Blairsville, GA
706-745-2420
trackrock.com
Dogs of all sizes are allowed. There are no additional pet fees. Dogs must be quiet, leashed, and cleaned up after. The camping and tent areas also allow dogs. There is a dog walk area at the campground. Multiple dogs may be allowed.

Vogel State Park
7485 Vogel State Park Road
Blairsville, GA
706-745-2628 (800-864-7275)
gastateparks.org/info/vogel/
This 233 acre park with a 20 acre lake is one of the oldest and most popular parks in the state. It offers a museum, 17 miles of hiking trails with access to the Appalachian Trail nearby, and a variety of land and water recreation. Dogs of all sizes are allowed at no additional fee. Dogs may not be left unattended, and they must be leashed and cleaned up after. Dogs are not allowed in public swim areas or in buildings. Dogs are allowed on the trails. The camping and tent areas also allow dogs. There is a dog walk area at the campground. Multiple dogs may be allowed.

Blythe Island Regional Park
6616 Blythe Island H (H 303)
Brunswick, GA
912-279-2812
This is a marina park that is close to other hydro attractions and offers a variety of land and water recreation. Dogs of all sizes are allowed at no additional fee. Dogs may not be left unattended, and they must be leashed and cleaned up after. Dogs are not allowed on the beaches or in buildings. Dogs are allowed on the trails. The camping and tent areas also allow dogs. There is a dog walk

area at the campground. Multiple dogs may be allowed.

Calhoun KOA
2523 Redbud Road NE
Calhoun, GA
706-629-7511 (800-562-7512)
koa.com
Dogs of all sizes are allowed. There are no additional pet fees. Dogs may not be left unattended outside or in the cabins, and they must be quiet, leashed, and cleaned up after. The camping and tent areas also allow dogs. There is a dog walk area at the campground. Dogs are allowed in the camping cabins. Multiple dogs may be allowed.

Allatoona Landing Marine Resort
24 Allatoona Landing Road
Cartersville, GA
770-974-6089
allatoonalandingmarina.com/
Dogs of all sizes are allowed. There are no additional pet fees. Dogs may not be left unattended outside, and they must be leashed and cleaned up after. There are some breed restrictions. The camping and tent areas also allow dogs. There is a dog walk area at the campground. Multiple dogs may be allowed.

Carterville/Cassville-White KOA
800 Cass-White Road NW
Cartersville, GA
770-382-7330 (800-562-2841)
koa.com
Dogs of most all sizes are allowed; ex-large dogs are not. There are no additional pet fees. Dogs must be leashed and cleaned up after. There are some breed restrictions. The camping and tent areas also allow dogs. There is a dog walk area at the campground. Multiple dogs may be allowed.

Red Top Mountain State Park
50 Lodge Road
Cartersville, GA
770-975-4226 (800-864-PARK (7275))
gastateparks.org/info/redtop/
This popular park of 1,562 acres along the 12,000-acre Lake Allatoona, offers over 15 miles of hiking trails, an interpretive center, and a wide variety of land and water recreation. Dogs of all sizes are allowed at no additional fee. Dogs may not be left unattended, and they must be leashed and cleaned up after. Dogs are not allowed in public swim areas or in buildings. Dogs are allowed on the trails. The camping and tent areas also allow dogs.

There is a dog walk area at the campground. Multiple dogs may be allowed.

Fort Mountain State Park
181 Fort Mountain Park Road
Chatsworth, GA
706-422-1932 (800-864-7275)
gastateparks.org/info/fortmt/
There is a myriad of recreational activities available at this 3,712 acre park that is also home to interesting ancient sites, some of the most scenic trails in the state, and a seasonal mountain lake. Dogs are allowed throughout the park and in the campground (2+ dogs) for no additional fee. There is a $40 one time fee per pet for the cabin, and only 2 dogs are allowed. Dogs must be current on all vaccinations, licensed, flea/tic free, and in good health. Dogs must be on no more than a 6 foot leash, cleaned up after, and may not be left unattended. The campground offers about 80 campsites, picnic tables, grills, and restrooms. The camping and tent areas also allow dogs. There is a dog walk area at the campground. Dogs are allowed in the camping cabins.

Moccasin Creek State Park
3655 H 197
Clarkesville, GA
706-947-3194 (800-864-PARK (7275))
gastateparks.org/info/moccasin/
This scenic 32 acre park along the 2,800-acre Lake Burton, offers a wildlife observation tower, trails with access to the Appalachian Trail, and a variety of land and water activities and recreation. Dogs of all sizes are allowed at no additional fee. Dogs may not be left unattended, and they must be on no more than a 6 foot leash, and cleaned up after. Dogs are not allowed in public swim areas or in buildings. Dogs are allowed on the trails. The camping and tent areas also allow dogs. There is a dog walk area at the campground. Multiple dogs may be allowed.

Leisure Acres Campground
3840 W Moreland Road
Cleveland, GA
888-748-6344
leisureacrescampground.com
Dogs of all sizes are allowed. There are no additional pet fees. Dogs must be leashed and cleaned up after. The camping and tent areas also allow dogs. There is a dog walk area at the campground.

Multiple dogs may be allowed.

Cordele KOA
373 Rockhouse Road E
Cordele, GA
229-273-5454 (800-562-0275)
koa.com
Dogs of all sizes are allowed, and there are no additional pet fees for tent or RV sites. There is a limit of 1 dog under 15 pounds for the cabins. Dogs must be leashed, cleaned up after, and in at night. The camping and tent areas also allow dogs. There is a dog walk area at the campground.

Veterans Memorial State Park
2459A H 280W
Cordele, GA
229-276-2371 (800-864-PARK (7275))
This park of more than 1,300 acres on Lake Blackshear was established as a memorial to U.S. veterans, featuring a museum with artifacts from the Revolutionary War through the Gulf War. The park offers a variety of activities and recreation. Dogs of all sizes are allowed at no additional fee. Dogs may not be left unattended, and they must be on no more than a 6 foot leash, and be cleaned up after. Dogs are allowed on the trails. The camping and tent areas also allow dogs. There is a dog walk area at the campground. Multiple dogs may be allowed.

Amicalola Falls State Park and Lodge
418 Amicalola Falls State Park Road
Dawsonville, GA
706-265-4703 (800-864-7275)
gastateparks.org/info/amicalola/
True to its Cherokee word meaning "tumbling waters", the 729 foot falls at this park are the highest cascading falls east of the Mississippi, and there are numerous trails for exploring this beautiful mountain recreational destination. The park is also host to many special events throughout the year. Dogs are allowed throughout the park and in the campground (2+ dogs) for no additional fee. There is a $40 one time fee per pet for the cabin, and only 2 dogs are allowed. They are not allowed in the Lodge or in any park buildings. Dogs must be leashed and under their owner's control at all times. The camp area offers 24 sites, 14 cottages (2-pet friendly), picnic areas, restrooms, concessionaires, and a dump station. The camping and tent areas also allow dogs. There is a dog walk area

at the campground. Dogs are allowed in the camping cabins.

River Vista Mountain Village
960 H 246
Dillard, GA
888-850-PARK (7275)
rvmountainvillage.com/
Up to 3 dogs of all sizes are allowed. There are no additional pet fees for tent or RV sites. There is a $10 per night per pet additional fee for the cabins, and only 2 dogs are allowed. Dogs may not be left unattended outside or in the cabins. Dogs must be on no more than a 6 foot leash and cleaned up after. The camping and tent areas also allow dogs. There is a dog walk area at the campground. Dogs are allowed in the camping cabins.

Bobby Brown State Park
2509 Bobby Brown State Park Road
Elberton, GA
706-213-2046 (800-864-PARK (7275))
Rich in natural and cultural history, this 655 acre park, on the shores of the 70,000-acre Clarks Hill Lake, offers a variety of land and water recreation. Dogs of all sizes are allowed at no additional fee. Dogs may not be left unattended except for short periods, they must be on no more than a 6 foot leash, and be cleaned up after. Dogs are not allowed in the yurt area, however, they are allowed on the trails. The camping and tent areas also allow dogs. There is a dog walk area at the campground. Multiple dogs may be allowed.

Twin Oaks RV Park
305 H 26E
Elko, GA
478-987-9361
twinoaksrvpark.com
Dogs of all sizes are allowed. There are no additional pet fees. Dogs must be leashed and cleaned up after. The camping and tent areas also allow dogs. There is a dog walk area at the campground. 2 dogs may be allowed.

Stephen C. Foster State Park
17515 H 177
Fargo, GA
912-637-5274 (800-864-7275)
gastateparks.org/info/scfoster/
Some of the most interesting and breathtaking scenery can be found at this park with its moss-laced cypress trees canopying the black waters below, and in addition to a range of recreational activities and the 1.5

mile Trembling Earth Nature Trail, there are environmental and educational programs provided. Dogs are allowed throughout the park and in the campground (2+ dogs) for no additional fee. There is a $40 one time fee per pet for the cabin, and only 2 dogs are allowed. Dogs are not allowed in buildings or on the boats. Dogs should not be close to the edge of waterways because of alligators. The campground offers 66 sites, restrooms, an amphitheater, a dump station, and some food, drinks, and ice can be obtained at the park office. The camping and tent areas also allow dogs. There is a dog walk area at the campground. Dogs are allowed in the camping cabins.

Indian Springs State Park
678 Lake Clark Road
Flovilla, GA
770-504-2277 (800-864-PARK (7275))
gastateparks.org/info/indspr/
Thought to be the oldest state park in the nation, and home to a "healing" spring, this park offers a variety of land and water recreation. Dogs of all sizes are allowed at no additional fee. Dogs must be on no more than a 6 foot leash, and be cleaned up after. Dogs are not allowed in buildings or in the cabin area, however, they are allowed on the trails. The camping and tent areas also allow dogs. There is a dog walk area at the campground. Multiple dogs may be allowed.

Forsyth KOA
414 S Frontage Road
Forsyth, GA
478-994-2019 (800-562-8614)
koa.com
Dogs of all sizes are allowed. There are no additional pet fees. Dogs may not be left unattended outside, and they must be leashed, cleaned up after, and inside at night. The camping and tent areas also allow dogs. There is a dog walk area at the campground. Dogs are allowed in the camping cabins. Multiple dogs may be allowed.

Chattahoochee-Oconee National Forest
1755 Cleveland H
Gainesville, GA
770-297-3000
fs.fed.us/conf/
This forest has 7 district offices, 2 visitor centers, almost 900,000 acres, and diverse ecosystems that

support a large variety of plants, fish, mammals, bird species, and year round recreation. Dogs of all sizes are allowed at no additional fee. Dogs may not be left unattended, and they must be leashed at all times, and be cleaned up after. The camping and tent areas also allow dogs. There is a dog walk area at the campground. Multiple dogs may be allowed.

Hart State Park
330 Hart State Park Road
Hartwell, GA
706-376-8756 (800-864-PARK (7275))
gastateparks.org/info/hart/
This scenic park of 147 acres on Lake Hartwell offers a variety of land and water activities and recreation. Dogs of all sizes are allowed at no additional fee. Dogs must be on no more than a 6 foot leash, and be cleaned up after. Dogs are allowed on the trails. The camping and tent areas also allow dogs. There is a dog walk area at the campground. Multiple dogs may be allowed.

Unicoi State Park
1788 H 356
Helen, GA
706-878-3982 (800-864-PARK (7275))
gastateparks.org/info/unicoi/
This park offers programs that focus on its historical, natural, cultural, and recreational resources. Dogs of all sizes are allowed at no additional fee. Only 2 dogs are allowed in the cabins. Dogs may not be left unattended outside, and they must be on no more than a 6 foot leash, and be cleaned up after. Dogs are allowed on the trails, but not in the lodge. The camping and tent areas also allow dogs. There is a dog walk area at the campground. Dogs are allowed in the camping cabins.

Georgia Mountain
1311 Music Hall Road
Hiawassee, GA
706-896-4191
georgia-mountain-fair.com
Dogs of all sizes are allowed. There are no additional pet fees. Dogs are not allowed in the fair area, and they must be leashed and cleaned up after. The RV sites are open all year, but the tent sites are seasonal. The camping and tent areas also allow dogs. There is a dog walk area at the campground. Multiple dogs may be allowed.

High Falls State Park

76 High Falls Park Drive
Jackson, GA
478-993-3053 (800-864-7275)
gastateparks.org/info/highfall/
Steeped in American history, this
1,050 acre park with 650 lake acres
offers waterfalls, scenic trails, and a
variety of land and water recreation.
Dogs of all sizes are allowed at no
additional fee. Dogs must be on no
more than a 6 foot leash, and be
cleaned up after. The camping and
tent areas also allow dogs. There is
a dog walk area at the campground.
Multiple dogs may be allowed.

Jekyll Island Campground
1197 Riverview Drive
Jekyll Island, GA
866-658-3021
Dogs of all sizes are allowed. There
are no additional pet fees. Dogs
must be leashed and cleaned up
after. The camping and tent areas
also allow dogs. There is a dog walk
area at the campground. Multiple
dogs may be allowed.

Jacksonville N/Kingsland KOA
2970 Scrubby Buff Road
Kingsland, GA
912-729-3232 (800-562-5220)
koa.com
Dogs of all sizes are allowed. There
are no additional pet fees. Dogs may
not be left unattended outside, and
they must be leashed and cleaned
up after. The camping and tent areas
also allow dogs. There is a dog walk
area at the campground. Dogs are
allowed in the camping cabins.
Multiple dogs may be allowed.

Eagle's Roost RV Resort
5465 Mill Store Road
Lake Park, GA
229-559-5192
eaglesroostresort.com
Dogs of all sizes are allowed. There
are no additional pet fees. Dogs
must be leashed and cleaned up
after. The camping and tent areas
also allow dogs. There is a dog walk
area at the campground. Multiple
dogs may be allowed.

Valdosta/Lake Park KOA
5300 Jewel Futch Road
Lake Park, GA
229-559-9738 (800-562-2124)
koa.com
Dogs of all sizes are allowed, and
there are no additional pet fees for
tent or RV sites. There is a $25 one
time additional pet fee for the cabin
and park models. Dogs may not be
left unattended outside or in rentals,
and they must be leashed and

cleaned up after. The camping and
tent areas also allow dogs. There is
a dog walk area at the campground.
Dogs are allowed in the camping
cabins. Multiple dogs may be
allowed.

Elijah Clark State Park
2959 McCormick H
Lincolnton, GA
706-359-3458 (800-864-PARK
(7275))
gastateparks.org/info/elijah/
Rich in American history, this 447
acre park with a 70,000 acre lake
offers a variety of land and water
recreation. Dogs of all sizes are
allowed at no additional fee. Dogs
may not be left unattended unless
quiet and well behaved; they must
be on no more than a 6 foot leash,
and cleaned up after. Dogs are not
allowed in buildings or on the
beaches. Dogs are allowed on the
trails. This campground is closed
during the off-season. The camping
and tent areas also allow dogs.
There is a dog walk area at the
campground. Multiple dogs may be
allowed.

Brookwood RV Park
1031 Wylie Road SE
Marietta, GA
877-727-5787
atlantarvpark.com
Dogs of all sizes are allowed. There
are no additional pet fees. Dogs
must be leashed and cleaned up
after. There is a dog walk area at
the campground. Multiple dogs may
be allowed.

Atlanta South RV Resort
281 Mount Olive Road
McDonough, GA
770-957-2610
atlantasouthrvresort.com
Dogs of all sizes are allowed. There
are no additional pet fees. Dogs
must be leashed and cleaned up
after. The camping and tent areas
also allow dogs. There is a dog
walk area at the campground.
Multiple dogs may be allowed.

Brookwood RV Park
Rt 5, Box 3107; on Pulaski
Excelsior
Metter, GA
888-636-4616
bkwdrv.com
Dogs of all sizes are allowed. There
are no additional pet fees. Dogs
must be leashed and cleaned up
after. There is a dog walk area at
the campground. Multiple dogs may
be allowed.

General Coffee State Park
46 John Coffee Road
Nicholls, GA
912-384-7082 (800-864-PARK
(7275))
gastateparks.org/info/gencoffee/
Rich in agricultural history, and host
to a cypress swamp of rare and
endangered plants, this park offers
an amphitheater, history and nature
programs, and a variety of land and
water recreation. Dogs of all sizes
are allowed at no additional fee.
Dogs may not be left unattended,
and they must be on no more than a
6 foot leash, and be cleaned up after
in camp areas. Dogs are not allowed
in the buildings, however, they are
allowed on the trails. The camping
and tent areas also allow dogs.
There is a dog walk area at the
campground. Multiple dogs may be
allowed.

Sugar Mill Plantation RV Park
4857 McMillan Road
Ochlocknee, GA
229-227-1451
Dogs of all sizes are allowed. There
are no additional pet fees. Dogs may
not be left unattended outside, and
they must be leashed and cleaned
up after. There are some breed
restrictions. The camping and tent
areas also allow dogs. There is a
dog walk area at the campground.
Multiple dogs may be allowed.

Pine Mountain Campground
8804 Hamilton Road
Pine Mountain, GA
706-663-4329
camppinemountain.com
Dogs of all sizes are allowed. There
are no additional pet fees. Dogs may
not be left unattended, and they must
be leashed and cleaned up after.
There are some breed restrictions.
The camping and tent areas also
allow dogs. There is a dog walk area
at the campground. Multiple dogs
may be allowed.

Roosevelt State Park
2970 H 190E
Pine Mountain, GA
706-663-4858 (800-864-PARK
(7275))
gastateparks.org/info/fdr/
This historical park of 9,049 acres
offers spectacular views, 37 miles of
hiking trails, an amphitheater and a
wide variety of recreational pursuits.
Dogs of all sizes are allowed at no
additional fee. Dogs may not be left
unattended, and they must be on no
more than a 6 foot leash, and

cleaned up after. Dogs are not allowed in the cottage area, at the group camp, or at the pool. Dogs are allowed on the trails. The camping and tent areas also allow dogs. There is a dog walk area at the campground. Multiple dogs may be allowed.

Fort McAllister State Historic Park
3894 Fort McAllister Road
Richmond Hill, GA
912-727-2339 (800-864-PARK
(7275))
This park, rich in American history and along the Colonial Coast Birding Trail, offers a Civil War museum, an Earthwork Fort, and a variety of recreational pursuits. Dogs of all sizes are allowed at no additional fee. Dogs may not be left unattended, and they must be on no more than a 6 foot leash, and be cleaned up after. Dogs are not allowed in any of the buildings, however, they are allowed on the trails. The camping and tent areas also allow dogs. There is a dog walk area at the campground. Multiple dogs may be allowed.

Savannah South KOA
4915 H 17
Richmond Hill, GA
912-756-3396 (800-562-8741)
koa.com
Dogs of all sizes are allowed. There are no additional pet fees. Dogs must be leashed and cleaned up after. The camping and tent areas also allow dogs. There is a dog walk area at the campground. Multiple dogs may be allowed.

Waterway RV Park
70 H 17
Richmond Hill, GA
912-756-2296
Dogs up to 75 pounds are allowed. There are no additional pet fees. Dogs may not be left unattended, and they must be leashed and cleaned up after. Dogs are not allowed to swim in the river because of alligators. There are some breed restrictions. There is a dog walk area at the campground. 2 dogs may be allowed.

Cloudland Canyon State Park
122 Cloudland Canyon Park Road
Rising Farm, GA
706-657-4050 (800-864-7275)
gastateparks.org/info/cloudland/
Rugged geology and beautiful vistas make this one of the most scenic parks in the state, and a variety of trails and recreation are available for

your use. Dogs of all sizes are allowed at no additional fee. Dogs may not be left unattended, and they must be quiet, well behaved, leashed and cleaned up after. Dogs are not allowed in buildings. Dogs are allowed on the trails. The camping and tent areas also allow dogs. There is a dog walk area at the campground. Multiple dogs may be allowed.

Holiday Trav-L-Park
1653 Mack Smith Road
Rossville, GA
706-891-9766
chattacamp.com
Dogs of all sizes are allowed. There are no additional pet fees. Dogs may not be left unattended outside, must be on no more than a 6 foot leashed, and be cleaned up after. The camping and tent areas also allow dogs. There is a dog walk area at the campground. 2 dogs may be allowed.

Hard Labor Creek State Park
Knox Chaple Road
Rutledge, GA
706-557-3001 (800-864-PARK
(7275))
gastateparks.org/info/hardlabor/
Although best known for its golf course, there are a wide variety of land and water activities and recreation offered at this state park. Dogs of all sizes are allowed at no additional fee. Dogs must be leashed, and cleaned up after in camp areas. Dogs are not allowed in or around cottage areas or on the beach. Dogs are allowed on the trails. The camping and tent areas also allow dogs. There is a dog walk area at the campground. Multiple dogs may be allowed.

Skidaway Island State Park
52 Diamond Causeway
Savannah, GA
912-598-2300 (800-864-PARK
(7275))
gastateparks.org/info/skidaway/
This 588 acre barrier island park along the Colonial Coast Birding Trail, offers observation towers, an interpretive center, and a variety of recreational pursuits. Dogs of all sizes are allowed at no additional fee. Dogs may not be left unattended, and they must be leashed and cleaned up after. Dogs are not allowed in buildings or in the pool area. The camping and tent areas also allow dogs. There is a dog walk area at the campground. Multiple dogs may be allowed.

Dynasty Canine Training Facility and RV Park
3554 H 21N
Springfield, GA
912-754-4834
dynastyrvpark.com
Dogs of all sizes are allowed. There are no additional pet fees. Dogs may not be left unattended outside, and they must be in at dusk. Dogs must be quiet, well behaved, leashed, and cleaned up after. The Park provides wading pools for your pets in the summer, and there are 2 fenced in areas where dogs can be off lead. The camping and tent areas also allow dogs. There is a dog walk area at the campground. There are special amenities given to dogs at this campground. Multiple dogs may be allowed.

Stone Mountain Park
H 78E
Stone Mountain, GA
800-385-9807
stonemountainpark.com
Dogs of all sizes are allowed. There are no additional pet fees. Dogs are not allowed on the Lazer Lawn, walk up trails, posted areas, nor at any of the attractions or special events. Dogs may not be left unattended, and they must be leashed and cleaned up after. The camping and tent areas also allow dogs. There is a dog walk area at the campground. Multiple dogs may be allowed.

Tallulah Gorge State Park
338 Jane Hurt Yarn Drive
Tallulah Falls, GA
706-754-7970 (800-864-7275)
At 2 miles long and about 1000 feet wide, there is some spectacular scenery to view from the many trails and gorge lookouts at this 2,689 acre park; there are interpretive programs, a gift shop, a 63 acre seasonal lake with beaches, and a variety of special events held throughout the year. Dogs are allowed throughout the park and in the campground for no additional fee. Dogs are not allowed on the gorge floor, on any trails accessing the gorge, or on the bridge to (or on) the Suspension Bridge; they are allowed on the rim trails. Dogs must be leashed and cleaned up after at all times. The camp area offers 50 sites, picnic tables, gaming areas, restrooms, and a dump station. This RV park is closed during the off-season. The camping and tent areas also allow dogs. There is a dog walk area at the campground. 2 dogs may be

allowed.

Agirama RV Park
1392 Windmill Road
Tifton, GA
229-386-3344 (800-767-1875)
agrirama.com
Dogs of all sizes are allowed. There are no additional pet fees. Dogs may not be left unattended outside, and they must be leashed and cleaned up after. This park is along side an 1870's working village. Dogs are not allowed in any of the Museum of Agriculture or village buildings. There is a dog walk area at the campground. 2 dogs may be allowed.

Amy's South Georgia RV Park
4632 Union Road
Tifton, GA
229-386-8441
amysrvpark.com
Dogs of all sizes are allowed. There are no additional pet fees. Dogs may not be left unattended outside, and they must be in at night, leashed, and cleaned up after. The camping and tent areas also allow dogs. There is a dog walk area at the campground. Multiple dogs may be allowed.

Lookout Mountain/Chattanooga West KOA
930 Mountain Shadows Drive
Trenton, GA
706-657-6815 (800-562-1239)
lookoutmountainkoa.com
Dogs of all sizes are allowed. There are no additional pet fees. Dogs must be leashed and cleaned up after. There are some breed restrictions. The camping and tent areas also allow dogs. There is a dog walk area at the campground. Dogs are allowed in the camping cabins. Multiple dogs may be allowed.

River's End Campground
915 Polk Street
Tybee Island, GA
912-786-5518
riversendcampground.com
Dogs of all sizes are allowed. There are no additional pet fees. Dogs may not be left unattended, or at the beach at any time, and they must be leashed and cleaned up after. The camping and tent areas also allow dogs. There is a dog walk area at the campground. Multiple dogs may be allowed.

Idaho

Dent Acres Rec Area
P. O. Box 48/ Well Bench Road
Ahsahka, ID
208-476-1261 (877-444-6777)
This 677 acre park located on the Dworshak Reservoir offers a variety of land and water recreation. Dogs of all sizes are allowed at no additional fee. Dogs may not be left unattended outside, and they must be leashed and cleaned up after. Dogs are not allowed on the swim beach or in buildings. Dogs are allowed on the trails. This campground is closed during the off-season. The camping and tent areas also allow dogs. There is a dog walk area at the campground. Multiple dogs may be allowed.

City of Rocks National Reserve
3035 S Elba Almo Road
Almo, ID
208-824-5519 (866-634-3246)
This scenic park holds geologic and historic significance in that it is home to some of the oldest rocks in America (some over 60 stories high), so rock climbing is popular here. Dogs of all sizes are allowed at no additional fee. Dogs may not be left unattended, and they must be on no more than a 6 foot leash, and be cleaned up after. Dogs must not be allowed to dig, especially at the staging/climbing areas. Dogs are allowed on the trails. The camping and tent areas also allow dogs. There is a dog walk area at the campground. There are no electric or water hookups at the campground. Multiple dogs may be allowed.

Massacre Rocks State Park
3592 Park Lane
American Falls, ID
208-548-2672 (866-634-3246)
This 1000 acre park is rich in geological and cultural history, and is home to a variety plant and animal life. It is situated on the Snake River and offers a visitor center, about 10 miles of hiking trails, a self-guided nature trail, boat launch area, seasonal weekend campfire programs, and they are host to special events held throughout the year. Dogs of all sizes are allowed for no additional fee. Dogs may not be left unattended outside and may only be left inside the camp unit if they

will be quiet and comfortable. Dogs must be leashed and cleaned up after at all times. The campground offers 40 camp sites, 4 cabins, restrooms, and hot showers. Dogs are allowed in one of the cabins-also, for no additional charge. The camping and tent areas also allow dogs. There is a dog walk area at the campground. Dogs are allowed in the camping cabins. There are no water hookups at the campgrounds. 2 dogs may be allowed.

Craters of the Moon National Monument
H 20/26/93 18 miles SW of Arco
Arco, ID
208-527-3257
nps.gov/crmo
The landscape is so surreal here that an Oregon-bound pioneer in the early 1800's described this area as the 'the Devil's Vomit'. Roughly the size of Rhode Island, these young lava flows are visible from space, and the Visitor's Center is replete with information and exhibits. The park offers interpretive programs/signage, and a 7 mile scenic loop drive. Dogs are allowed in the park for no addition fee, but they must remain on the paved roads or in the camp areas. They are not allowed on the trails or back country. Dogs must be leashed and cleaned up after. Among the lava formations beyond the visitor center, is a 52 site campground available on a first come, first serve basis. Some of the amenities include water (except during off season), restrooms, grills and picnic tables. The camping and tent areas also allow dogs. There is a dog walk area at the campground. There are no electric or water hookups at the campgrounds. Multiple dogs may be allowed.

Farragut State Park
13550 E H 54
Athol, ID
208-683-2425
With over 4,000 acres and home to the largest lake in the state, this biologically diverse park offers a variety of nature study, and land and water recreation. This park also has exhibits about their part as a Navel Training Center in WWII. Dogs of all sizes are allowed at no additional fee. Dogs may not be left unattended, and they must be quiet, well behaved, leashed and cleaned up after. Dogs are not allowed on the beach or in buildings. Dogs are allowed on the trails. The camping and tent areas also allow dogs.

There is a dog walk area at the campground. Dogs are allowed in the camping cabins. Multiple dogs may be allowed.

Silverwood RV Park and Campground
27843 N H 95
Athol, ID
208-683-3400, Ext 139
silverwoodthemepark.com/rv.html
This RV park and campground has 126 sites in a beautifully wooded park setting, and sits adjacent to the Silverwood Theme Park/Boulder Beach Water Park - the Northwest's largest theme park. Some of the amenities here include a convenience store, volleyball courts, horseshoe pits, laundry facilities, showers/restrooms, picnic areas, and discounted admission tickets to the theme/water park. Dogs may be left inside your RV unit if they will be quiet, comfortable, and they are checked on regularly. There is no additional pet fee, and dogs must be leashed and cleaned up after at all times. This RV park is closed during the off-season. The camping and tent areas also allow dogs. There is a dog walk area at the campground. Multiple dogs may be allowed.

On the River RV Park
6000 Glenwood
Boise, ID
208-375-7432
camplan.com/ontheriver
Dogs up to 35 pounds are allowed. There are no additional pet fees but there may be a deposit required. Dogs must be leashed and cleaned up after. The camping and tent areas also allow dogs. There is a dog walk area at the campground. Multiple dogs may be allowed.

Copper Creek Campground
Forest Road 2517
Bonner's Ferry, ID
208-267-5561
Located 1 mile south of Eastport, this primitive 16 unit campsite offers 3 handicap sites, potable water, and pit toilets. Nearby is the Copper Falls self-guided nature trail that takes visitors to a spectacular outlook over the falls; the best viewing is in the spring. Dogs of all sizes are allowed. There are no additional pet fees. Dogs must be leashed and cleaned up after. The camping and tent areas also allow dogs. There is a dog walk area at the campground. There are no electric or water hookups at the campgrounds. Multiple dogs may be allowed.

Ambassador RV Resort
615 S Mead Parkway
Caldwell, ID
888-877-8307
ambassadorrvresort.com
Dogs of all sizes are allowed. There are no additional pet fees. Dogs must be quiet, leashed, and cleaned up after. Dogs may not be left unattended outside. There are some breed restrictions. There is a dog walk area at the campground. Multiple dogs may be allowed.

Coeur D'Alene KOA
10588 E Wolf Lodge Bay Road
Coeur D'Alene, ID
208-664-4471 (800-562-2609)
koa.com
Dogs of all sizes are allowed. There are no additional pet fees. Dogs must be quiet, leashed, and cleaned up after. This RV park is closed during the off-season. The camping and tent areas also allow dogs. There is a dog walk area at the campground. Dogs are allowed in the camping cabins. Multiple dogs may be allowed.

Blackwell Island RV Resort
800 S Marina Way
Coeur d'Alene, ID
208-665-1300
idahorvpark.com
Dogs of all sizes are allowed. There are no additional pet fees. Dogs must be leashed and cleaned up after. This RV park is closed during the off-season. There is a dog walk area at the campground. Multiple dogs may be allowed.

Idaho Panhandle National Forest
3815 Schreiber Street
Coeur d'Alene, ID
208-765-7223
fs.fed.us/ipnf/
This forest of 2.5 million acres has more than 3,300 miles of hiking trails, and the various ecosystems support a large variety of plants, fish, mammals, bird species, and recreation. Dogs of all sizes are allowed at no additional fee. Dogs may not be left unattended, and they must be leashed and cleaned up after. Dogs are allowed on the trails. The camping and tent areas also allow dogs. There is a dog walk area at the campground. Dogs are allowed in the camping cabins. Multiple dogs may be allowed.

Priest Lake State Park
3140 Indian Creek Park Road
Coolin, ID

208-443-6710
idahoparks.org/parks/priest.html
Steeped in history, this scenic park offers a variety of habitats, trails, and land and water recreation. Dogs of all sizes are allowed at no additional fee. Dogs may not be left unattended, and they must be quiet, be on no more than a 6 foot leash, and cleaned up after. Dogs are not allowed in the public swim area, but they are allowed at their own designated swim area and on the trails. The camping and tent areas also allow dogs. There is a dog walk area at the campground. Dogs are allowed in the camping cabins. There are no water hookups at the campground. Multiple dogs may be allowed.

Anderson Camp
S Tipperary
Eden, ID
888-480-9400
andersoncamp.com
Dogs of all sizes are allowed. There are no additional pet fees. Dogs may not be left unattended, and must be quiet, leashed, and cleaned up after. The camping and tent areas also allow dogs. There is a dog walk area at the campground. Dogs are allowed in the camping cabins. Multiple dogs may be allowed.

Three Island Crossing
1083 S Three Island Park Drive
Glenn's Ferry, ID
208-366-2394 (866-634-3246)
This 613 acre park sits at an elevation of almost 2,500 feet on the Snake River, and it was one of the most famous river crossing areas on the historic pioneer trail. Some of the features/amenities here include an interpretive center, educational programs, historic artifacts, a self-guided tour, picnic areas, hiking trails, and a variety of other recreational pursuits. Dogs of all sizes are allowed for no additional fee. Dogs are allowed around the park and on the trails. Dogs must be well behaved, leashed and cleaned up after. The campground offers about 100 sites, with showers, flush toilets, a group shelter, and a dump station. Reservations are available from April 1st to October 31st, and is on a first come, first served basis in the off season. The camping and tent areas also allow dogs. There is a dog walk area at the campground. Multiple dogs may be allowed.

Bear Den RV Park
16967 H 95S

Grangeville, ID
208-983-2383
beardenrvresort.com/
Dogs of all sizes are allowed. There are no additional pet fees. When out walking with your pet, they must be on a leash. Dogs may be off leash on site if they are under voice command and will not chase. Dogs must be cleaned up after at all times. There is a dog walk area at the campground. Multiple dogs may be allowed.

Nez Perce National Forest
1005 H 13
Grangeville, ID
208-983-1950
fs.fed.us/r1/nezperce/
This diverse forest of 2.2 million acres provides spectacular scenery, a rich cultural history, and diverse ecosystems that support a large variety of plants animals, and recreation. Dogs of all sizes are allowed at no additional fee. Dogs may not be left unattended, and they must be leashed and cleaned up after in camp areas. Dogs are allowed on the trails except in winter when they are not allowed on the ski trails. The camping and tent areas also allow dogs. There is a dog walk area at the campground. There are no electric or water hookups at the campground. Multiple dogs may be allowed.

Hagerman RV Village
18049 H 30
Hagerman, ID
208-837-4906
Dogs of all sizes are allowed. There are no additional pet fees. Dogs must be quiet, well behaved, leashed, and cleaned up after. They are allowed in the cabins, but they may not be left unattended there, and they are not allowed on the furniture. The camping and tent areas also allow dogs. There is a dog walk area at the campground. Multiple dogs may be allowed.

High Adventure River Tours RV Park
1211 E 2350 S
Hagerman, ID
208-837-9005 (800-286-4123)
Scenic tours, river rafting, Dutch oven cooking, and even fresh produce in season are offered here. Well behaved dogs of all sizes are allowed at no additional fee. Dogs must be well behaved, leashed, and cleaned up after. Dogs are not allowed in the buildings, but they are allowed on the trails. The camping and tent areas also allow dogs. There is a dog walk area at the

campground. There are no electric or water hookups at the campground. Multiple dogs may be allowed.

Boise National Forest
3833 H 21
Idaho City, ID
208-373-4100 (877-444-6777)
fs.fed.us/r4/boise/
This forest has 6 ranger districts, over 2 million acres, and diverse ecosystems that support a large variety of plants, fish, mammals, bird species, and year round recreation. Dogs of all sizes are allowed at no additional fee. Dogs may not be left unattended, and they must be leashed and cleaned up after. Dogs are not allowed on the furniture in the cabins, or in any other park buildings. Dogs are allowed on the trails. This campground is closed during the off-season. The camping and tent areas also allow dogs. There is a dog walk area at the campground. Dogs are allowed in the camping cabins. There are no electric or water hookups at the campground. Multiple dogs may be allowed.

Caribou-Targhee National Forest
3659 East Ririe Highway
Idaho Falls, ID
208-524-7500
These 2 forests were joined in the year 2000, creating 6 ranger districts, over 3 million acres, and diverse ecosystems that support a large variety of plants, animals and year round recreation. Dogs of all sizes are allowed at no additional fee. Dogs may not be left unattended, and they must be leashed and cleaned up after. Dogs are not allowed on the West Mink Trail, but they are allowed on the other trails. This campground is closed during the off-season. The camping and tent areas also allow dogs. There is a dog walk area at the campground. There are no electric or water hookups at the campground. Multiple dogs may be allowed.

Targhee-Caribou National Forest
1405 Hollipark Drive
Idaho Falls, ID
208-524-7500
These 2 forests were joined in the year 2000, creating 7 ranger districts, over 3 million acres, and diverse ecosystems that support a large variety of plants, fish, mammals, bird species, and year round recreation. Dogs of all sizes

are allowed at no additional fee. Dogs may not be left unattended, and they must be leashed and cleaned up after. Dogs are not allowed on the West Mink Trail, but they are allowed on the other trails. This campground is closed during the off-season. The camping and tent areas also allow dogs. There is a dog walk area at the campground. There are no electric or water hookups at the campground. Multiple dogs may be allowed.

Henry's Lake State Park
3917 E 5100 N
Island Park, ID
208-558-7532
idahoparks.org/parks/henrys.html
This high mountain lake park offers beautiful scenery and a variety of land and water recreational pursuits. Dogs of all sizes are allowed at no additional fee. Dogs may not be left unattended, and they must be on no more than a 6 foot leash, and be cleaned up after. Dogs are not allowed in buildings, but they are allowed on the trails. This campground is closed during the off-season. The camping and tent areas also allow dogs. There is a dog walk area at the campground. Multiple dogs may be allowed.

Twin Falls/Jerome KOA
5431 H 93
Jerome, ID
208-324-4169 (800-562-4169)
koa.com
Dogs of all sizes are allowed. There are no additional pet fees, but they request that if you rented a cabin with a dog that you sweep the cabin out before you leave. Dogs may not be left unattended, must be leashed, and cleaned up after. There are some breed restrictions. This RV park is closed during the off-season. The camping and tent areas also allow dogs. There is a dog walk area at the campground. Dogs are allowed in the camping cabins. Multiple dogs may be allowed.

Sawtooth National Rec Area
5 N Fort Canyon Road
Ketchum, ID
208-837-9005
fs.fed.us/r4/sawtooth/
Located in the Sawtooth National Forest, this recreational area provides a wide variety of year round land and water activities. Dogs of all sizes are allowed at no additional fee. Dogs may not be left unattended, and they must be leashed and cleaned up after. Dogs

are allowed on the trails. The camping and tent areas also allow dogs. There is a dog walk area at the campground. There are no electric or water hookups at the campground. Multiple dogs may be allowed.

Smiley Creek Lodge
HC 64, Box 9102/ 37 miles N of Ketchum on H 75
Ketchum, ID
208-774-3547 (877-774-3547)
ruralnetwork.net/~smileyck/
Dogs of all sizes are allowed. There are no additional pet fees. Dogs may not be left unattended outside, and they must be leashed and cleaned up after. The camping and tent areas also allow dogs. There is a dog walk area at the campground. Multiple dogs may be allowed.

Wood River Campground/Sawtooth National Forest
12 Miles N of Ketchum on H 75
Ketchum, ID
208-726-7672
Dogs of all sizes are allowed. There are no additional pet fees. Dogs must be leashed and cleaned up after. This RV park is closed during the off-season. The camping and tent areas also allow dogs. Multiple dogs may be allowed.

Hells Gate State Park
4832 Hells Gate State Park
Lewiston, ID
208-799-5015 (866-634-3246)
This park offers shady campsites on the Snake River along the deepest river gorge in North America, an interpretive plaza, a discovery center, tours, and various recreation. Dogs of all sizes are allowed at no additional fee. Dogs may not be left unattended, and they must be leashed at all times, and cleaned up after. Dogs are not allowed on the beach or in buildings, but they are allowed on the trails. The camping and tent areas also allow dogs. There is a dog walk area at the campground. Dogs are allowed in the camping cabins. Multiple dogs may be allowed.

Riverfront Gardens RV Park
MM 210.5 H 95
Lucile, ID
208-628-3777
This is an RV only park. Dogs of all sizes are allowed at no additional fee. Dogs must be leashed and cleaned up after. There is a dog walk area at the campground. Multiple dogs may be allowed.

Payette National Forest
102 W Lake Street
McCall, ID
208-634-0700
fs.fed.us/r4/payette/
From the deepest river gorge in North America to elevations of almost 9,500 feet, this diverse forest of 2.3 million acres supports a large variety of plants, fish, mammals, bird species, and recreation. Dogs of all sizes are allowed at no additional fee. Dogs may not be left unattended, and they must be leashed and cleaned up after in camp areas. Dogs are not allowed in any buildings, but however they are allowed on the trails. This campground is closed during the off-season. The camping and tent areas also allow dogs. There is a dog walk area at the campground. There are no electric or water hookups at the campground. Multiple dogs may be allowed.

Ponderosa State Park
Miles Standish Road
McCall, ID
208-634-2164 (866-634-3246)
This scenic 1500+ acre park sits at an elevation of just over 5000 feet, and it covers most of a 1000-acre peninsula on Payette Lake. The park offers a wide variety of year round land and water recreation, wildlife viewing, guided walks, picnicking, and seasonal evening campfire programs. There are both dirt and hard path multi-use trails, and a nature store and visitor center. Dogs of all sizes are allowed for no additional fee. Dogs must be well behaved, leashed, and cleaned up after at all times. Dogs are allowed throughout the park and on the trails. They are not allowed on the beaches or in the park at all in the winter. Campsites can be reserved from Thursday prior to Memorial Day through Labor Day, and are on a first come first served basis during off-season, weather permitting. Amenities include restrooms, showers, picnic tables, and a dump station. This RV park is closed during the off-season. The camping and tent areas also allow dogs. There is a dog walk area at the campground. Multiple dogs may be allowed.

Boise Meridian RV Resort
184 Pennwood
Meridian, ID
877-894-1357
Dogs of all sizes are allowed. There

are no additional pet fees. Dogs may not be left unattended, or tied to the trees or other campsite furnishings. Dogs must be leashed and cleaned up after. There are some breed restrictions. There is a dog walk area at the campground. 2 dogs may be allowed.

The Playground RV Park
1680 Overland Road
Meridian, ID
208-887-1022
playgroundrv.com
Dogs of all sizes are allowed. There are no additional pet fees. Dogs must be leashed and cleaned up after. There is a dog walk area at the campground. Multiple dogs may be allowed.

Montpelier Creek KOA
28501 H 89N
Montpelier, ID
208-847-0863 (800-562-7576)
koa.com
Dogs of all sizes are allowed. There are no additional pet fees. Dogs must be leashed and cleaned up after. This RV park is closed during the off-season. The camping and tent areas also allow dogs. There is a dog walk area at the campground. Dogs are allowed in the camping cabins. 2 dogs may be allowed.

Ro VelDo Cabins and Campgrounds
20925 H J5T
Moravia, ID
641-437-4084
roveldo.com/
Dogs of all sizes are allowed. There are no additional pet fees for tent or RV sites. There is a $50 one time additional pet fee for the cabins, which are open all year. Dogs must be quiet, well behaved, leashed, and cleaned up after. This RV park is closed during the off-season. The camping and tent areas also allow dogs. There is a dog walk area at the campground. Multiple dogs may be allowed.

Bruneau Dunes State Park
27608 Sand Dunes Road
Mountain Home, ID
208-366-7919 (866-634-3246)
This park is home to the tallest single-structured sand dune in North America at a height of 470 feet, and this high mountain desert park offers lakes, prairies, and marshlands to explore. There is a wide variety of land and water recreation and activities, a nature store, a 5 mile hiking trail that will present visitors with stunning views, interpretive

programs, and star/space viewing at Idaho's only public observatory. Dogs of all sizes are allowed for no additional fee. Dogs must be under their owner's control, and be leashed and cleaned up after at all times. Dogs are allowed on all the trails. Camping is available year round on a first-come, first-served basis (weather conditions permitting). The campground offers one of the longest camping seasons of the state parks. Amenities include restrooms, showers, a group shelter, a dump station, and lots of shade trees. The camping and tent areas also allow dogs. There is a dog walk area at the campground. Multiple dogs may be allowed.

Mountain Home KOA
220 E 10th N
Mountain Home, ID
208-587-5111 (800-562-8695)
koa.com
Dogs of all sizes are allowed. There are no additional pet fees. Dogs must be leashed and cleaned up after. This RV park is closed during the off-season. The camping and tent areas also allow dogs. There is a dog walk area at the campground. Dogs are allowed in the camping cabins. Multiple dogs may be allowed.

Mountain Home RV Park
2295 American Legion Blvd
Mountain Home, ID
208-890-4100
Dogs of all sizes are allowed. There are no additional pet fees. Dogs must be quiet, well behaved, and cleaned up after. Dogs may be off lead if they are under voice control. There is a dog walk area at the campground. Multiple dogs may be allowed.

Clearwater National Forest
83544 H 12
Orofino, ID
208-476-4541
fs.fed.us/r1/clearwater/
This forest has 4 ranger districts, 1.8 million acres, and has diverse ecosystems that support a large variety of plants, fish, mammals, bird species as well as year round recreation. Dogs of all sizes are allowed at no additional fee. Dogs may not be left unattended, and they must be leashed, and cleaned up after in camp areas, and especially on the beaches. Dogs are not allowed in swim areas or in buildings. Dogs are allowed on the trails. This campground is closed during the off-

season. The camping and tent areas also allow dogs. There is a dog walk area at the campground. Dogs are allowed in the camping cabins. There are no electric or water hookups at the campground. Multiple dogs may be allowed.

Dworshak State Park
P. O. Box 2028/Freeman Creek Road
Orofino, ID
208-476-5994 (866-634-3246)
This 850, acre park located on shores of Dworshak Reservoir, offers a variety of activities and land and water recreation. Dogs of all sizes are allowed at no additional fee. Dogs may not be left unattended, and they must be leashed at all times, and cleaned up after. Dogs are not allowed in the buildings or on the beaches. Dogs are allowed on the trails. The camping and tent areas also allow dogs. There is a dog walk area at the campground. Dogs are allowed in the camping cabins. Multiple dogs may be allowed.

Bear Lake State Park
P. O. Box 297
Paris, ID
208-847-1757 (866-634-3246)
This 966 acre park sits at an elevation of 5,900 feet, and with Bear Lake at 20 miles long and 8 miles wide, there is a wide variety of year round land and water recreation. There are various programs and activities hosted by the park, and they also offer group shelters, boat ramps, and picnicking. Dogs of all sizes are allowed for no additional fee. Dogs are not allowed in the North Beach day use area, but they are allowed down by the beach that is adjacent to the campground. Dogs must be friendly, leashed, and cleaned up after. The campground is located on the east side of the lake and offer 47 individual sites, plus three (3) group campsites. This RV park is closed during the off-season. The camping and tent areas also allow dogs. There is a dog walk area at the campground. There are no water hookups at the campgrounds. Multiple dogs may be allowed.

Kellogg/Silver Valley KOA
801 N Division Street
Pinehurst, ID
208-682-3612 (800-562-0799)
kelloggsilvervalleykoa.com
Dogs of all sizes are allowed. There are no additional pet fees. There is

a $50 refundable deposit (or have credit card on file) for the cabin rentals. Dogs must be well behaved, may not be left unattended, must be leashed at all times, and cleaned up after. There is a fenced in dog run on site. This RV park is closed during the off-season. The camping and tent areas also allow dogs. There is a dog walk area at the campground. Dogs are allowed in the camping cabins. 2 dogs may be allowed.

Heyburn State Park
1291 Chatcolet Road
Plummer, ID
208-686-1308 (866-634-3246)
This park of about 5,500 acres with 2,300 acres of lake is rich in natural and cultural history. The park offers an interpretive center along with a wide variety of land and water activities and recreation. Dogs of all sizes are allowed at no additional fee. Dogs may not be left unattended except for short periods, and then only if they will be quiet and well behaved. Dogs must be on no more than a 6 foot leash, and be cleaned up after. Dogs are allowed on the trails. This campground is closed during the off-season. The camping and tent areas also allow dogs. There is a dog walk area at the campground. Dogs are allowed in the camping cabins. Multiple dogs may be allowed.

Pocatello KOA
9815 W Pocatello Creek Road
Pocatello, ID
208-233-6851 (800-562-9175)
koa.com
Dogs of all sizes are allowed. There are no additional pet fees. Dogs may not be left unattended, must be leashed, and cleaned up after. The camping and tent areas also allow dogs. There is a dog walk area at the campground. Multiple dogs may be allowed.

Canyon Pines Resort
10 Barn Road
Pollock, ID
208-628-4006
canyonpinesrv.com
Dogs of all sizes are allowed. There are no additional pet fees. Dogs may not be left unattended, and must be leashed and cleaned up after. The camping and tent areas also allow dogs. There is a dog walk area at the campground. Multiple dogs may be allowed.

Suntree RV Park
350 N Idahline Road

Post Falls, ID
208-773-9982
Dogs of all sizes are allowed. There is a $1 per night per pet additional fee. Dogs may not be left unattended, and they must be quiet, well behaved, leashed, and cleaned up after. There is a dog walk area at the campground. 2 dogs may be allowed.

Heald's Haven RV Park and Campground
22 Heald Haven Drive
Salmon, ID
208-756-3929
This campground offers clean, grassy sites with shade trees, and easy pull-thru sites. Some of the amenities include drinking water, fire rings, restrooms, showers, handicap access, and a dump station. They are open for self-contained visitors only in the winter. Dogs of all sizes are welcome for no additional fee. Dogs must be well behaved, leashed, and cleaned up after. This RV park is closed during the off-season. The camping and tent areas also allow dogs. There is a dog walk area at the campground. Multiple dogs may be allowed.

Salmon River RV Park
111 Whitetail Drive
Salmon, ID
208-894-4549
salmonriverrvp.com/
Dogs of all sizes are allowed. There are no additional pet fees. Dogs may not be left unattended outside, and they must be quiet, well behaved, leashed, and cleaned up after. This is an RV only park. There is a dog walk area at the campground. Multiple dogs may be allowed.

Salmon-Challis National Forest
1669 H 93
Salmon, ID
208-879-4100
fs.fed.us/r4/sc/
This forest has 7 ranger districts, is home to the largest wilderness area in the US with over 4.3 million acres, and has diverse ecosystems that support a large variety of plants, animals, and year round recreation. Dogs of all sizes are allowed at no additional fee. Dogs may not be left unattended outside, and they must be leashed and cleaned up after. Dogs are not allowed in buildings, but they are allowed on the trails. This campground is closed during the off-season. The camping and tent areas also allow dogs. There is a dog walk area at the campground.

There are no electric or water hookups at the campground. Multiple dogs may be allowed.

Bear Lake North RV Park
220 N Main
St Charles, ID
208-945-2941
bearlakenorth.com
Dogs of all sizes and numbers are allowed at RV sites, however only 1 dog up to 20 pounds is allowed at the cabins. There is a $1.50 per night per pet additional fee. Dogs may not be left unattended at the cabins, and they are not allowed on the beds or in the loft. The camping and tent areas also allow dogs. There is a dog walk area at the campground. Dogs are allowed in the camping cabins.

Carmela Winery Golf Course and RV Park
1294 W Madison
Stanley, ID
208-366-2773
Dogs of all sizes are allowed at no additional fee. Dogs may only be left inside your RV for short periods, and only if they will be quiet and well behaved. Dogs must be leashed and cleaned up after. The park has an adjoining 65 acres nearby where your dog may run off lead if they are trained and will obey voice command. The camping and tent areas also allow dogs. There is a dog walk area at the campground. Multiple dogs may be allowed.

Sawthooth National Forest
2647 Kimberly Road E.
Twin Falls, ID
208-737-3200 (800-260-5970)
fs.fed.us/r4/sawtooth/
In addition to archaeological and historical sites and interests, this forest of more than a million acres has diverse ecosystems support a large variety of plants, animals, and recreation. Dogs of all sizes are allowed at no additional fee. Dogs may not be left unattended, and they must be leashed and cleaned up after. Dogs are allowed on the trails. This campground is closed during the off-season. The camping and tent areas also allow dogs. There is a dog walk area at the campground. There are no electric or water hookups at the campground. Multiple dogs may be allowed.

Hells Canyon Jet Boat Trips and Lodging
1 mile S of White Bird on Old H 95

White Bird, ID
800-469-8757
Dogs of all sizes are allowed. There are no additional pet fees. Dogs must be leashed and cleaned up after. Dogs may be left on site on leash, but please inform the office as to how long you will be gone and if you will be on the 6 hour jet boat tour. There is a motel on site that has one pet-friendly room, also at no additional fee for a pet, however, only 1 dog is allowed in the motel room at a time. The camping and tent areas also allow dogs. There is a dog walk area at the campground.

Winchester Lake State Park
Forest Road
Winchester, ID
208-924-7563 (866-634-3246)
This 418 acre park, with 103 lake acres, is popular for nature study, fishing, and hiking, and offers a variety of land and water activities and recreation. Dogs of all sizes are allowed at no additional fee. Dogs may not be left unattended, and they must be well behaved, leashed and cleaned up after. Dogs are not allowed in the buildings, but they are allowed on the trails. The park has one pet-friendly yurt available. The camping and tent areas also allow dogs. There is a dog walk area at the campground. 2 dogs may be allowed.

Illinois

O'Connells' Yogi Bear Jellystone Park Camp Resort
970 Greenwing Road
Amboy, IL
815-857-3860 (800-FOR-YOGI (367-9644))
rvonthego.com
Dogs of all sizes are allowed. There are no additional pet fees. Dogs must be leashed and cleaned up after. This RV park is closed during the off-season. The camping and tent areas also allow dogs. There is a dog walk area at the campground. Multiple dogs may be allowed.

Apple River Canyon State Park
8763 E Canyon Road
Apple River, IL
815-745-3302
Flowing waters and glacial sweeps designed this forested park leaving colorful canyons, massive cliffs, an abundance of flora and fauna, and

there are 5 trails through the park to explore it all. Dogs are allowed throughout the park and camp areas for no additional fee. Dogs must be leashed and cleaned up after at all times. Camp sites are primitive and they are first come first served. Camping permits are required and can be gotten at the park office. Tables, grills, and accessible drinking water are available. The camping and tent areas also allow dogs. There is a dog walk area at the campground. There are no water hookups at the campgrounds. Multiple dogs may be allowed.

Benton KOA
1500 N DuQuoin Street
Benton, IL
618-439-4860 (800-562-8619)
bentonkoa.com
Dogs of all sizes are allowed, and there are no additional pet fees for tent or RV sites. There is a $5 one time additional pet fee for the cabins. Dogs may not be left unattended, and they must be leashed and cleaned up after. This RV park is closed during the off-season. The camping and tent areas also allow dogs. There is a dog walk area at the campground. Dogs are allowed in the camping cabins. 2 dogs may be allowed.

Kankakee River State Park
5314 West Rt. 102
Bourbonnais, IL
815-933-1383
Rich in prehistoric, natural, and cultural heritage, this 4000 acre park offers a wide range of land and water recreation, and there are several miles of year round trails that follow along both sides of the river and into canyon and waterfall areas. Dogs are allowed throughout the park, on the trails, and in the campground for no additional fee. Dogs must be leashed and cleaned up after. The campgrounds total more than 250 sites and offer seasonal concessionaires, restrooms, showers, picnic tables, grills, and a dump station. The camping and tent areas also allow dogs. There is a dog walk area at the campground. There are no water hookups at the campgrounds. Multiple dogs may be allowed.

Casey KOA
1248 E 1250th Road
Casey, IL
217-932-5319 (800-562-9113)
koa.com
Dogs of all sizes are allowed. There

are no additional pet fees. Dogs may not be left unattended or placed in outside pens. Dogs must be leashed and cleaned up after. There are some breed restrictions. This RV park is closed during the off-season. The camping and tent areas also allow dogs. There is a dog walk area at the campground. Multiple dogs may be allowed.

Cave-In-Rock State Park
#1 New State Park Road
Cave-In-Rock, IL
618-289-4325
A long and notorious history, a secluded 55 foot wide cave, spectacular fall foliage, 60 foot high cliffs, rugged bluffs, colorful trails, and more can be explored at this 204 acre riverside park. Dogs are allowed for no additional fee. Dogs must be leashed and cleaned up after at all times, and they are not allowed in swim areas. Thirty-four campsites are located on the north side of the park. They can accommodate larger rigs, and offer showers, restrooms, firewood, grills, and a dump station. Camping permits are required and can be obtained from the site superintendent or the campground host. The camping and tent areas also allow dogs. There is a dog walk area at the campground. There are no water hookups at the campgrounds. Multiple dogs may be allowed.

Jim Edgar Panther Creek State Park
10149 H 11
Chandlerville, IL
217-452-7741
There is a wide variety of trails in this park. Dogs of all sizes are allowed. There are no additional pet fees. Dogs must be on no more than a 10 foot leash and be cleaned up after. The camping and tent areas also allow dogs. There is a dog walk area at the campground. Multiple dogs may be allowed.

Fox Ridge State Park
18175 State Park Road
Charleston, IL
217-345-6416
Every season brings a special beauty to this 2,064 acre park of thick woods, lush valleys, and abundant plant, bird, and wildlife, but it is especially popular for its trail system; it's easy-on, easy-off with dramatic scenery, 18 wooden bridges, plenty of rest areas, a fitness trail, and a stairway to

"Eagle's Nest" of 144 steps to a deck overlooking the valley and river below. Dogs are allowed throughout the park, in the camp area, and on the trails. Dogs may not be left unattended at any time, and they must be leashed and cleaned up after. The campground provides showers, restrooms, tables, grills, drinking water, and dump stations; playgrounds and gaming fields/courts are nearby. The camping and tent areas also allow dogs. There is a dog walk area at the campground. There are no water hookups at the campgrounds. Multiple dogs may be allowed.

Double J Campground
9683 Palm Road
Chatham, IL
217-483-9998
doublejcampground.com
Dogs of all sizes are allowed. There are no additional pet fees. Dogs may not be left unattended or tied up outside alone. Dogs must be quiet, leashed, and cleaned up after. This RV park is closed during the off-season. The camping and tent areas also allow dogs. There is a dog walk area at the campground. Multiple dogs may be allowed.

Kankakee South KOA
425 E 6000 Road
Chebanse, IL
815-939-4603 (800-562-4192)
koa.com/where/il/13144/
Dogs of all sizes are allowed. There are no additional pet fees. Dogs may not be left unattended, and must be leashed and cleaned up after. There are some breed restrictions. This RV park is closed during the off-season. The camping and tent areas also allow dogs. There is a dog walk area at the campground. Dogs are allowed in the camping cabins. Multiple dogs may be allowed.

Weldon Springs State Park
1159 500 North RR 2
Clinton, IL
217-935-2644
Dogs of all sizes are allowed. There are no additional pet fees. Dogs may not be left unattended, they must be on no more than a 10 foot leash, and be cleaned up after. Dogs are allowed on the trails, but they are not allowed in the pet free zones. The camping and tent areas also allow dogs. There is a dog walk area at the campground. There are no water hookups at the campground. Multiple dogs may be allowed.

Arglye Lake State Park
640 Argyle Park Road
Colchester, IL
309-776-3422
Dogs of all sizes are allowed. There are no additional pet fees. Dogs may not be left unattended, they must be on no more than a 10 foot leash, and be cleaned up after. Dogs are allowed on the trails. The camping and tent areas also allow dogs. There is a dog walk area at the campground. There are no water hookups at the campground. Multiple dogs may be allowed.

Clinton Lake State Park
H 14
DeWitt, IL
217-935-8722
Dogs of all sizes are allowed. There are no additional pet fees. Dogs may not be left unattended, they must be on no more than a 10 foot leash, and be cleaned up after. Dogs are allowed on the trails. The camping and tent areas also allow dogs. There is a dog walk area at the campground. Multiple dogs may be allowed.

Camp Lakewood
1217 W Rickelman
Effingham, IL
217-342-6233
camplakewoodcampground.com
Dogs of all sizes are allowed. There are no additional pet fees. Dogs must be quiet, leashed, and cleaned up after. This RV park is closed during the off-season. There is a dog walk area at the campground. Multiple dogs may be allowed.

Burnidge and Paul Wolff Forest Preserve
38W235 Big Timber Road
Elgin, IL
630-232-5980
Rolling hills, scenic panorama views, several watersheds feeding Tyler Creek and 590 acres to explore make this a popular recreational destination. Dogs are allowed throughout the park and in the campground; they must be leashed and cleaned up after at all times. Although the park is open all year, camping is seasonal, and the camp area has a stocked fishing pond, picnic areas, restrooms, a pad, and a dump station. This RV park is closed during the off-season. The camping and tent areas also allow dogs. There is a dog walk area at the campground. There are no water hookups at the campgrounds. Multiple dogs may be allowed.

Eagle Creek State Recreation Area
Road 2025 N
Findlay, IL
217-756-8260
Stretched along 250 miles of Lake Shelbyville shoreline with plenty of recreational opportunities, this park has large expanses of maintained indigenous woodlands, 3 nature trails plus a 12 mile backpacking trail, a 110 foot earthen embankment dam built as flood control and water supply, and a resort in the park. Campers are welcome to enjoy the pool at the resort for $5 per day, and there is also a restaurant on site. Dogs are allowed throughout the park, on the trails, and in the campgrounds for no additional fee; they are not allowed at the resort. Dogs may not be left alone at any time, and they must be leashed and cleaned up after. The campground offers restrooms, showers, water, picnic tables, and fire blocks. This RV park is closed during the off-season. The camping and tent areas also allow dogs. There is a dog walk area at the campground. There are no water hookups at the campgrounds. Multiple dogs may be allowed.

Palace Campground
11357 H 20W
Galena, IL
815-777-2466
palacecampground.com
Dogs of all sizes are allowed. There are no additional pet fees. Dogs may not be left unattended, must be leashed, and cleaned up after. This RV park is closed during the off-season. The camping and tent areas also allow dogs. There is a dog walk area at the campground. Dogs are allowed in the camping cabins. Multiple dogs may be allowed.

Holiday Acres Camping Resort
7050 Epworth
Garden Prairie, IL
815-547-7846
holidayacres.net
Dogs of all sizes are allowed, but there can only be one dog in the cabins. There are no additional pet fees. Dogs must be well behaved, leashed, and cleaned up after. The camping and tent areas also allow dogs. There is a dog walk area at the campground. Dogs are allowed in the camping cabins.

Yogi Bear Campground
RR 1 Timberline Road

Goodfield, IL
309-965-2224
jellystonegoodfield.com
Dogs of all sizes are allowed. There are no additional pet fees. Dogs must be quiet, leashed, and cleaned up after. The camping and tent areas also allow dogs. There is a dog walk area at the campground. 2 dogs may be allowed.

Ferne Clyffe State Park
On H 37 one mile S of Goreville
Goreville, IL
618-995-2411
Dogs of all sizes are allowed. There are no additional pet fees. Dogs may not be left unattended, and they must be quiet, well behaved, be on no more than a 10 foot leash, and be cleaned up after. Dogs are allowed on the trails, but not in any buildings. The camping and tent areas also allow dogs. There is a dog walk area at the campground. There are no water hookups at the campground. Multiple dogs may be allowed.

Pere Marquette State Park
Route 100, P.O. Box 158/Great River Road
Grafton, IL
618-786-3323
Touted for its brilliant fall colors, the majestic bald eagles in the winter, and blazed trails through lush forests to lofty bluffs, this 8000 acre park also has an abundance of bird and wildlife, and a variety of recreational pursuits. Dogs are allowed throughout the park; they are not allowed in cabins. Dogs must be leashed and cleaned up after at all times. The camp area has restrooms, showers, grills, tables, drinking water, and a dump station. The camping and tent areas also allow dogs. There is a dog walk area at the campground. There are no water hookups at the campgrounds. Multiple dogs may be allowed.

MGM Lakeside Campground
3133 W Chain of Rocks
Granite City, IL
618-797-2820
Dogs of all sizes are allowed. There are no additional pet fees. Dogs must be leashed and cleaned up after. The camping and tent areas also allow dogs. There is a dog walk area at the campground. Multiple dogs may be allowed.

Northeast/I 270/Granite City KOA
3157 Chain of Rocks Road
Granite City, IL
618-931-5160 (800-562-5861)

koa.com
Dogs of all sizes are allowed, and there are no additional pet fees for tent or RV sites. There is a $2.50 per night per pet additional fee for the cabins. Dogs must be quiet, well behaved, leashed, and cleaned up after. There are some breed restrictions. This RV park is closed during the off-season. The camping and tent areas also allow dogs. There is a dog walk area at the campground. Dogs are allowed in the camping cabins. Multiple dogs may be allowed.

Old Blanding Tavern and Campground
6846 S River Road
Hanover, IL
815-591-3346 (866-722-5454)
Twenty campsites are available at this beautifully landscaped retreat which also offers modern restrooms and showers, a bait shop, arcade, and a full bar and restaurant. Dogs are allowed for no additional fee. Dogs must be kept leashed at all times as there are other dogs on site, and cleaned up after at all times. Dogs are not allowed in the rental trailers. The camping and tent areas also allow dogs. There is a dog walk area at the campground. Multiple dogs may be allowed.

Shawnee National Forest
Ridge Road
Harrisburg, IL
800-699-6637
fs.fed.us/
This national forest has 14 campgrounds, and one of them has electric hookups. The pet policy applies to all the campgrounds. Dogs of all sizes are allowed. There are no additional pet fees. Dogs may not be left unattended, they must have a current rabies certificate and shot records, be leashed at all times, and be cleaned up after. Dogs are allowed on the trails. The camping and tent areas also allow dogs. There is a dog walk area at the campground. There are no water hookups at the campground. Multiple dogs may be allowed.

Evening Star Camping Resort
23049 H 136
Havana, IL
309-562-7590
eveningstarcamp.com
Dogs of all sizes are allowed. There are no additional pet fees. Dogs must be quiet, leashed, and cleaned up after. The camping and tent areas also allow dogs. There is a dog walk

area at the campground. 2 dogs may be allowed.

Trail of Tears State Park
3240 State Forest Road (Southern Region)
Jonesboro, IL
618-833-4910
Rich in Native American history and covering 5,114 acres, this working forest is managed for timber plus other resources, and although it has some of the most rugged terrain in the state, there is a wide variety of educational and recreational opportunities available. Dogs are allowed throughout the park and on all the trails. Dogs must be kept leashed and cleaned up after. Tent camping with vehicle access and backpack camping is all that is available at this park, and some have picnic areas, water, and restrooms. The camping and tent areas also allow dogs. There is a dog walk area at the campground. There are no electric or water hookups at the campgrounds. Multiple dogs may be allowed.

Lake Ke-aqua-na State Park
8542 Lake Road
Lena, IL
815-369-4282
This park has many year round recreational activities in and around the 715 acre park and 40 acre lake. Dogs of all sizes are allowed. There are no additional pet fees. Dogs may not be left unattended, and they must be quiet, leashed, and cleaned up after. Dogs are allowed on the trails, but not at the beach. The camping and tent areas also allow dogs. There is a dog walk area at the campground. There are no water hookups at the campground. Multiple dogs may be allowed.

Lena KOA
10982 W H 20
Lena, IL
815-369-2612 (800-562-5361)
lenakoa.com
Dogs of all sizes are allowed, and there are no additional pet fees for tent or RV sites. There is a $2 per night per pet additional fee for the cabins, and only 2 dogs are allowed. Dogs must be leashed and cleaned up after. There are some breed restrictions. This RV park is closed during the off-season. The camping and tent areas also allow dogs. There is a dog walk area at the campground. Dogs are allowed in the camping cabins.

Moraine View State Recreation Area
27374 Moraine View Park Road
Leroy, IL
309-724-8032
With 1,687 recreational acres, wooded and meadow areas, a 158 acre stocked lake, multi-use year round trails, a convenient location, and more have made this a popular fun destination. Dogs are allowed throughout the park, on the trails, and in the campground for no additional fee; they are not allowed in the lake. Dogs must be on no more than a 10 foot leash and cleaned up after at all times. Developed or primitive campsites are available with water, restrooms, and showers; a dock, boat launch, and concessionaires are nearby. The camping and tent areas also allow dogs. There is a dog walk area at the campground. There are no water hookups at the campgrounds. Multiple dogs may be allowed.

Rock Cut State Park
7318 Harlem Road
Loves Park, IL
815-885-3311
This park offers about 40 miles of hiking, 23 miles of mountain biking, and about 14 miles of equestrian trails. Dogs of all sizes are allowed. There are no additional pet fees. Dogs may not be left unattended, and they must be leashed and cleaned up after. Dogs are allowed on marked trails. The camping and tent areas also allow dogs. There is a dog walk area at the campground. There are no water hookups at the campground. Multiple dogs may be allowed.

Giant City State Park
235 Giant City Road
Makanda, IL
618-457-4836
The spectacular natural beauty of this park makes it a popular recreational and educational destination, and there are a number of nature and interpretive trails, and a new visitor center with exhibits. Dogs are allowed throughout the park; they must be leashed and cleaned up after. Campgrounds are well-kept and provide restrooms, showers, and water. There is also an equestrian and primitive camp area. The camping and tent areas also allow dogs. There is a dog walk area at the campground. There are no water hookups at the campgrounds. Multiple dogs may be allowed.

Lehman's Lakeside RV Resort
19609 Harmony Road
Marengo, IL
815-923-4533
lehmansrv.com
Dogs of all sizes are allowed. There are no additional pet fees. Dogs must be leashed and cleaned up after. This RV park is closed during the off-season. There is a dog walk area at the campground. Multiple dogs may be allowed.

Lincoln Trail State Park
1685 1350th Road
Marshall, IL
217-826-2222
This 1,023-acre park is home to a variety of flora and is rich in wildlife. There are many scenic and historic sites, and activities year round. Dogs of all sizes are allowed. There are no additional pet fees. Dogs may not be left unattended except for very short periods, and may only be left in unit if it poses no danger to the animal. Dogs must be leashed and cleaned up after. Dogs are allowed on the trails. The camping and tent areas also allow dogs. There is a dog walk area at the campground. There are no water hookups at the campground. Multiple dogs may be allowed.

Fort Massac State Park
1308 E. 5th Street
Metropolis, IL
618-524-4712
Rich in cultural, American, and natural history, this 1,450 acre historic park has a replica of an 1802 American fort with an outline of the previous 1757 French fort, and in addition to varied recreational pursuits, there are interpretive programs, reenactments, and a visitor center. Dogs are allowed throughout the park and in the camp area for no additional fee. Dogs must be leashed and cleaned up after at all times. Fifty campsites are available with restrooms, showers, a dump station, and picnic areas and playgrounds are close by. The camping and tent areas also allow dogs. There is a dog walk area at the campground. There are no water hookups at the campgrounds. Multiple dogs may be allowed.

Jellystone Park
8574 Millbrook Road
Millbrook, IL
800-438-9644
jellystonechicago.com
Dogs of all sizes are allowed. There is a $3 per night per pet additional

fee for tent and RV spaces, and $5 per night per pet for cabin rentals. Dogs are not allowed in trailor or park models. Dogs may not be left unattended, must be leashed, and cleaned up after. The camping and tent areas also allow dogs. There is a dog walk area at the campground. Dogs are allowed in the camping cabins. Multiple dogs may be allowed.

Horseshoe Lake-Alexander State Park
21204 Promise Land Road
Miller City, IL
618-776-5689
Dogs of all sizes are allowed. There are no additional pet fees. Dogs may not be left unattended, and they must be leashed and cleaned up after. Dogs on lead are allowed on the trails. The camping and tent areas also allow dogs. There is a dog walk area at the campground. Multiple dogs may be allowed.

Kickapoo State Recreation Area
10906 Kickapoo Park Road
Oakwood, IL
217-442-4915
From a scarred wasteland to a lush recreational environment is this park's success story; there are 22 deep water ponds, miles of trails, abundant bird, flora, and fauna. Dogs are allowed throughout the park, in the camp area, and on the trails for no additional fee. Dogs may not be left unattended at any time, and they must be leashed and cleaned up after. The campground provides showers, restrooms, tables, grills, drinking water, and dump stations; camping permits are required before entering the campgrounds. The camping and tent areas also allow dogs. There is a dog walk area at the campground. There are no water hookups at the campgrounds. Multiple dogs may be allowed.

Lowden State Park
1411 N River Road
Oregon, IL
815-732-6828
Although already one of the most picturesque areas along Rock Creek, the stand out feature here is a 50 foot tall Native American bust sitting high up on the bluffs and considered to be the 2nd largest concrete monolithic statue in the world. Dogs are allowed throughout the park and in the camp area for no additional fee. Dogs must be leashed and cleaned up after at all

times. The campground has restrooms, a shower building, dump stations, and seasonal concessionaires. Camping permits are required and can be obtained at the park office. The camping and tent areas also allow dogs. There is a dog walk area at the campground. There are no water hookups at the campgrounds. Multiple dogs may be allowed.

Lincoln's New Salem State Historic Site
15588 History Lane
Petersburg, IL
217-632-4000
lincolnsnewsalem.com/
One of America's premiere historic sites, this 700 acre living history, educational, and recreational destination offers a number of activities, special events, a country store, a seasonal restaurant, a Theater in the Park, and a lot more. Dogs are allowed throughout the park, on the trails, and in the camp area for no additional fee. Dogs may not be left unattended at any time, and they must be leashed and cleaned up after. Campsites are first come, first served, and a camping permit is required that can be obtained at the camp office. Restrooms, showers, and a dump station are on site. The camping and tent areas also allow dogs. There is a dog walk area at the campground. There are no water hookups at the campgrounds. 2 dogs may be allowed.

Pyramid State Park
1562 Pyramid Park Road
Pinckneyville, IL
618-357-2574
Stand out features of this 19,701 acre, forested park are the many lakes and ponds that are found throughout and the scenic trails that allow their exploration. Dogs are allowed throughout the park and in the camp areas. Dogs must be leashed, cleaned up after at all times, and they are not allowed in public swim areas. Camping is allowed in designated areas only and water and a dump station are located by the site office. The camping and tent areas also allow dogs. There is a dog walk area at the campground. There are no electric or water hookups at the campgrounds. Multiple dogs may be allowed.

Pine Lakes Resort
RR3 Box 3077
Pittsfield, IL

877-808-7436
pinelakesresort.com
Dogs of all sizes are allowed, and there are no additional pet fees for tent or RV sites. There is a $5 per night per pet additional fee for cottages. Dogs may not be left unattended except for short periods, and they must be leashed and cleaned up after. The camping and tent areas also allow dogs. There is a dog walk area at the campground. Dogs are allowed in the camping cabins. Multiple dogs may be allowed.

Beaver Dam State Park
14548 Beaver Dam Road
Plainview, IL
217-854-8020
Dogs of all sizes are allowed. There are no additional pet fees. Dogs must be leashed and cleaned up after. This campground is closed during the off-season. The camping and tent areas also allow dogs. There is a dog walk area at the campground. Multiple dogs may be allowed.

Springfield KOA
4320 KOA Road
Rochester, IL
217-498-7002 (800-562-7212)
koa.com
Dogs of all sizes are allowed. There are no additional pet fees. Dogs must be quiet, leashed, and cleaned up after. This RV park is closed during the off-season. The camping and tent areas also allow dogs. There is a dog walk area at the campground. Dogs are allowed in the camping cabins.

Rock Island KOA
2311 78th Avenue W
Rock Island, IL
309-787-0665 (888-562-4502)
riqckoa.com
Dogs of all sizes are allowed. There are no additional pet fees. Dogs must be leashed and cleaned up after. The camping and tent areas also allow dogs. There is a dog walk area at the campground. Dogs are allowed in the camping cabins. Multiple dogs may be allowed.

River's Edge Campground
12626 N Meridian
Rockton, IL
815-629-2526
riversedgecampground.com
Dogs of all sizes are allowed. There are no additional pet fees. Dogs may not be left unattended, must be leashed, and cleaned up after. This

RV park is closed during the off-season. The camping and tent areas also allow dogs. There is a dog walk area at the campground. Multiple dogs may be allowed.

Mississippi Palisades State Park
16327A H 84
Savanna, IL
815-273-2731
As well as all the recreational activities this 2,500 acre park has to offer, it has some interesting geological sites to explore ear round. This park is also rich in Native American history. Dogs of all sizes are allowed. There are no additional pet fees. Dogs may not be left unattended, and they must be leashed and cleaned up after. Stay on designated trails. The camping and tent areas also allow dogs. There is a dog walk area at the campground. There are no water hookups at the campground. Multiple dogs may be allowed.

Chain O' Lakes State Park
8916 Wilmot Road
Spring Grove, IL
847-587-5512
Offering 488 miles of shoreline, this 2,793 acre park sits near an adjoining 3,230 acre conservation area in the state's largest concentration of natural lakes. There are multiple bird and wildlife habitats, a wide array of year round land and water recreation, seasonal concessionaires, and 80 acres in the park's bog area has been set aside as a nature preserve. Dogs are allowed throughout the park and in the camp areas; they are not allowed in cabin areas. Dogs must be leashed and cleaned up after at all times. Campsites are located throughout the park and offer picnic tables, grills, showers, and restrooms. Sites are first come first served with a limited number of sites available for reservations. The camping and tent areas also allow dogs. There is a dog walk area at the campground. Multiple dogs may be allowed.

Windy City Campground
18701 S 80th Avenue
Tinley Park, IL
708-720-0030
windycitycampground.com
Dogs of all sizes are allowed. There are no additional pet fees. Dogs may not be left outside unattended, and may only be left inside if they will be comfortable and quiet. Dogs must be leashed and cleaned up

after. This RV park is closed during the off-season. There is a dog walk area at the campground. 2 dogs may be allowed.

Chicago Northwest KOA
8404 S Union Road
Union, IL
815-923-4206 (800-562-2827)
chicagonwkoa.com
Dogs of all sizes are allowed. There are no additional pet fees. Dogs may not be left unattended, they must be on no more than a 6 food leash, and cleaned up after. There are some breed restrictions. This RV park is closed during the off-season. The camping and tent areas also allow dogs. There is a dog walk area at the campground. Multiple dogs may be allowed.

Hickory Hollow Campground
757 N 3029 Road
Utica, IL
815-667-4996
hickoryhollowcg.com
Dogs of all sizes are allowed. There are no additional pet fees. Dogs may not be tied to trees or other campground property, and they must be leashed and cleaned up after. This RV park is closed during the off-season. The camping and tent areas also allow dogs. There is a dog walk area at the campground. 2 dogs may be allowed.

LaSalle/Peru KOA
756 N 3150th Road
Utica, IL
815-667-4988 (800-562-9498)
koa.com
Dogs of all sizes are allowed. There are no additional pet fees. Dogs may not be left unattended at the cabins, and they must be leashed and cleaned up after. This RV park is closed during the off-season. The camping and tent areas also allow dogs. There is a dog walk area at the campground. Dogs are allowed in the camping cabins. Multiple dogs may be allowed.

Starved Rock State Park
H 178
Utica, IL
815-667-4726
Rich in Native American lore, colonial history, and recreation, this park offers 13 miles of blazed trails, and unusual beauty from the glacial and stream erosion activity that created its 18 canyons and striking waterfall and rock formations. Dogs are allowed throughout the park and in the camp area for no additional fee.

Dogs must be leashed and cleaned up after. Camp sites are reserveable and first come first served; there are flush and pit toilets, water, showers, a playground, a camp store, and a dump station. Permits are required and may be obtained from the park office or permit booth, and the campgrounds close during firearm deer season. This RV park is closed during the off-season. The camping and tent areas also allow dogs. There is a dog walk area at the campground. There are no water hookups at the campgrounds. Multiple dogs may be allowed.

Fossil Rock Recreation Area
24615 W Strip Mine Road
Wilmington, IL
815-476-6784
Dogs of all sizes are allowed. There are no additional pet fees. Dogs must be leashed and cleaned up after. There are some breed restrictions. The camping and tent areas also allow dogs. There is a dog walk area at the campground. 2 dogs may be allowed.

Wolf Creek State Park
Wolf Creek Road
Windsor, IL
217-459-2831
Stretched along 250 miles of Lake Shelbyville shoreline with plenty of recreational opportunities, this park also has large expanses of maintained indigenous woodlands, 7 hiking trails, and a 110 foot earthen embankment dam built as flood control and water supply. Dogs are allowed throughout the park, on the trails, and in the campgrounds for no additional fee. Dogs may not be left alone at any time, and they must be leashed and cleaned up after. Campsites can be reserved at Lick Creek; most others are first come first served. The camp areas have restrooms, showers, picnic tables, and dump station. This RV park is closed during the off-season. The camping and tent areas also allow dogs. There is a dog walk area at the campground. There are no water hookups at the campgrounds. Multiple dogs may be allowed.

Hide-A-Way Lakes
8045 Van Emmons Road
Yorkville, IL
630-553-6323
hideawaylakes.com
Dogs of all sizes are allowed. There are no additional pet fees. Dogs must be quiet, well behaved, leashed, and cleaned up after. The

camping and tent areas also allow dogs. There is a dog walk area at the campground. Multiple dogs may be allowed.

Indiana

Chain O' Lakes State Park
2355 E 75S
Albion, IN
260-636-2654 (866-6CAMPIN (622-6746))
This park has a nature center with regular programs, many hiking trails, and 8 connecting lakes you can paddle through. Dogs of all sizes are allowed. There are no additional pet fees. Dogs must be on no more than a 6 foot leash and be cleaned up after. Dogs are allowed on all the trails. The camping and tent areas also allow dogs. There is a dog walk area at the campground. There are no water hookups at the campground. Multiple dogs may be allowed.

Oakhill Family Campground
4450 N 50W
Angola, IN
260-668-7041
oakhillcamp.com
Dogs of all sizes are allowed. There are no additional pet fees. Dogs must be leashed and cleaned up after. The camping and tent areas also allow dogs. There is a dog walk area at the campground. 2 dogs may be allowed.

Pokagon State Park
450 Lane 100 Lake James
Angola, IN
260-833-2012 (866-6CAMPIN (622-6746))
This park has several natural lakes, a nature center, and a seasonal toboggan run. Dogs are allowed at no additional fee. Dogs may not be left unattended at any time, and they must be leashed and cleaned up after. Dogs are not allowed at the group camping area or in any of the buildings. Dogs are not allowed on the beach from Memorial Day through Labor Day. The camping and tent areas also allow dogs. There is a dog walk area at the campground. There are no water hookups at the campground. Multiple dogs may be allowed.

Auburn/Fort Wayne North KOA
5612 County Road 11A

Auburn, IN
260-925-6747 (800-562-7518)
koa.com
Dogs of all sizes are allowed. There are no additional pet fees. Dogs must be quiet, well behaved, leashed, and cleaned up after. The camping and tent areas also allow dogs. There is a dog walk area at the campground. Multiple dogs may be allowed.

Prophetstown State Park
4112 E State Road 4
Battle Ground, IN
765-567-4919 (866-622-6746)
This park's historical and geological setting allow visitors to step back in time with a recreated Native American village and a 1920's era living history farm. Dogs of all sizes are allowed at no additional fee. Dogs may not be left unattended, and they must be on no more than a 6 foot leash, and be cleaned up after. Dogs are allowed on the trails. The camping and tent areas also allow dogs. There is a dog walk area at the campground. Multiple dogs may be allowed.

Hoosier National Forest
811 Constitution Avenue
Bedford, IN
812-275-5987
fs.fed.us/r9/hoosier/
This national forest offers 200,000 acres of spectacular scenery, miles of trails, a 1939 lookout tower, several historic sites, and diverse ecosystems that support a large variety of flora, fauna, and recreation. Dogs of all sizes are allowed at no additional fee. Dogs may not be left unattended at any time, and they must be leashed and cleaned up after. The campgrounds run from primitive to developed areas with comfort stations and picnic areas. The camping and tent areas also allow dogs. There is a dog walk area at the campground. There are no water hookups at the campgrounds. Multiple dogs may be allowed.

Lake Monroe Village
8107 S Fairfax
Bloomington, IN
812-824-2267
lakemonroevillage.com
Dogs of all sizes are allowed. There are no additional pet fees. Dogs must be leashed and cleaned up after. The camping and tent areas also allow dogs. There is a dog walk area at the campground. Dogs are allowed in the camping cabins.

Multiple dogs may be allowed.

Monroe Lake Park
4850 H 446S
Bloomington, IN
812-837-9546 (866-6CAMPIN (622-6746))
in.gov/dnr/parklake/6739.htm
Recreationalist, naturalist, and sports enthusiast will all find activities to do at this 23,952 acre park with a 10,750 acre lake. Dogs are allowed throughout the park and in the campground for no additional fee. They must have proof of current vaccinations, be well mannered, and quiet during quiet hours. Dogs must be kept on no more than a 6 foot leash except when in a camper, tent or vehicle, and be cleaned up after at all times. Dogs are not allowed on the beach, and they may not be left unattended at any time. The campground has over 300 sites with comfort stations, a fishing pier with a gas dock, playgrounds, a camp store, and a dump station. The camping and tent areas also allow dogs. There is a dog walk area at the campground. There are no water hookups at the campgrounds. Multiple dogs may be allowed.

Ouabache State Park
4930 H 201E
Bluffton, IN
260-824-0926 (866-6CAMPIN (622-6746))
in.gov/dnr/parklake/6701.htm
This park offers a variety of land and water recreational activities, and naturalist programs during the summer months. Dogs are allowed throughout the park and in the campground for no additional fee. They must have proof of current vaccinations, be well mannered, and quiet during quiet hours. Dogs must be kept on no more than a 6 foot leash except when in a camper, tent or vehicle, and be cleaned up after at all times. Dogs are not allowed at the pool or in buildings, and they may not be left unattended at any time. The campground offers over a 100 sites with comfort stations, potable water, timber-form playgrounds, a swimming pool, playing fields/courts, and a dump station. The camping and tent areas also allow dogs. There is a dog walk area at the campground. There are no water hookups at the campgrounds. Multiple dogs may be allowed.

Charlestown State Park
3000 State Park Drive
Charlestown, IN

812-256-5600 (866-622-6746)
Dogs of all sizes are allowed. There are no additional pet fees. Dogs may not be left unattended, and they must be leashed and cleaned up after. Dogs are allowed on the trails. The camping and tent areas also allow dogs. There is a dog walk area at the campground. Multiple dogs may be allowed.

Indiana Dunes State Park
1600 North 25 E
Chesterton, IN
219-926-1952 (866-6CAMPIN (622-6746))
Located near Lake Michigan, this park offers a nature/interpretive center, group shelters, and access to the Calumet hiking trail. Dogs are allowed in the campground for no additional fee. They must have proof of current vaccinations, be well mannered, and quiet during quiet hours. Dogs must be kept on no more than a 6 foot leash except when in a camper, tent or vehicle, and be cleaned up after at all times. Dogs are not allowed on the swim beach, and they may not be left unattended at any time. The campground offers picnic areas, modern comfort stations, vault toilets, playgrounds, a camp store, and potable water. The camping and tent areas also allow dogs. There is a dog walk area at the campground. There are no water hookups at the campgrounds. Multiple dogs may be allowed.

Broadview Lake Campground
4850 Broadview Road
Colfax, IN
765-324-2622
Dogs of all sizes are allowed. There are no additional pet fees. Dogs must be quiet, leashed, and cleaned up after. This RV park is closed during the off-season. There is a dog walk area at the campground. Multiple dogs may be allowed.

Woods N Waters Kampground
8855 S 300 W
Columbus, IN
812-342-1619
woodsnwaters.com
Dogs of all sizes are allowed. There are no additional pet fees. Dogs may not be left unattended, must be leashed, and cleaned up after. The camping and tent areas also allow dogs. There is a dog walk area at the campground. Multiple dogs may be allowed.

O'Bannon Woods State Park
7240 Old Forest Road
Corydon, IN
812-738-8232 (866-6CAMPIN (622-6746))
This 26,000 acre park is called one of the 7 hidden jewels of the Indiana parks because of it's beauty and seclusion. Dogs are allowed at no additional fee. Dogs must be on no more than a 6 foot leash and be cleaned up after. Dogs are not allowed in the buildings. This campground is closed during the off-season. The camping and tent areas also allow dogs. There is a dog walk area at the campground. There are no water hookups at the campground. Multiple dogs may be allowed.

Crawfordsville KOA
1600 Lafayette Road
Crawfordsville, IN
765-362-4190 (800-562-4191)
crawfordsvillekoa.com
Dogs of all sizes are allowed. There are no additional pet fees. Dogs may not be left unattended in the cabins or outside alone. Dogs must be leashed and cleaned up after. This RV park is closed during the off-season. The camping and tent areas also allow dogs. There is a dog walk area at the campground. Dogs are allowed in the camping cabins. Multiple dogs may be allowed.

Elkhart Campground
25608 County Road 4
Elkhart, IN
574-264-2914
elkhartcampground.com
Dogs of all sizes are allowed. There are no additional pet fees. Dogs must be quiet, leashed, and cleaned up after. If you have dogs in one of the cabins they request you sweep out the cabin before you leave. Dogs must be leashed and cleaned up after. This RV park is closed during the off-season. The camping and tent areas also allow dogs. There is a dog walk area at the campground. Dogs are allowed in the camping cabins. 2 dogs may be allowed.

Oak Lake Campground
5310 E 900N
Fair Oaks, IN
219-345-3153
Dogs of all sizes are allowed, however there can only be one large dog, or two small dogs per site. There are no additional pet fees. Dogs must be quiet, leashed, and cleaned up after. This RV park is closed during the off-season. There

is a dog walk area at the campground.

Jellystone Park
140 Lane, 201 Barton Lake
Freemont, IN
260-833-1114 (800-375-6063)
jellystonesbest.com
Dogs of all sizes are allowed. There are no additional pet fees. Dogs may not be left unattended, must be leashed, and cleaned up after. This RV park is closed during the off-season. The camping and tent areas also allow dogs. There is a dog walk area at the campground. 2 dogs may be allowed.

Amishville RV Park
844 E 900 S
Geneva, IN
260-589-3536
amishville.com
Dogs of all sizes are allowed. There are no additional pet fees. Dogs must be quiet, well behaved, leashed, and cleaned up after. This RV park is closed during the off-season. The camping and tent areas also allow dogs. There is a dog walk area at the campground. Multiple dogs may be allowed.

South Bend East KOA
50707 Princess Way
Granger, IN
574-277-1335 (800-562-2470)
koa.com
Dogs of all sizes are allowed, and there are no additional pet fees for tent or RV sites. There is a $50 cash only refundable deposit for the cabins. Dogs must be leashed and cleaned up after. This RV park is closed during the off-season. The camping and tent areas also allow dogs. There is a dog walk area at the campground. Dogs are allowed in the camping cabins. Multiple dogs may be allowed.

Heartland Resort
1613 W 300N
Greenfield, IN
317-326-3181
heartlandresort.com
Dogs of all sizes are allowed. There are no additional pet fees. Dogs must be quiet, well behaved, may not be left unattended, and must be leashed and cleaned up after. Dogs are not allowed in the buildings or at the beach. The camping and tent areas also allow dogs. There is a dog walk area at the campground. 2 dogs may be allowed.

Indianapolis KOA

5896 W 200 N
Greenfield, IN
317-894-1397 (800-562-0531)
koa.com/where/in/14149.htm
Dogs of all sizes are allowed. There are no additional pet fees. Dogs may not be left unattended in the cabins, and they must be leashed and cleaned up after. This RV park is closed during the off-season. The camping and tent areas also allow dogs. There is a dog walk area at the campground. Dogs are allowed in the camping cabins. Multiple dogs may be allowed.

S & H Campground
2573 W 100N
Greenfield, IN
317-326-3208
shcampground.com
Dogs of all sizes are allowed. There are no additional pet fees. Dogs must be leashed and cleaned up after. The camping and tent areas also allow dogs. There is a dog walk area at the campground. Multiple dogs may be allowed.

Twin Mills Camping Resort
1675 W H 120
Howe, IN
260-562-3212
rvinthesun.com
Dogs of all sizes and numbers are allowed, and there are no additional pet fees for tent or RV sites. There is a $25 per stay additional fee for cabins or rentals, and only 2 dogs 10 pounds or under are allowed. There must be proof of insurance for known aggressive breeds. Dogs must be leashed and cleaned up after. This RV park is closed during the off-season. The camping and tent areas also allow dogs. There is a dog walk area at the campground. Dogs are allowed in the camping cabins.

Shakamak State Park
6265 W H 48
Jasonville, IN
812-665-2158 (866-6CAMPIN (622-6746))
in.gov/dnr/parklake/6688.htm
Plenty of water activities are available here with three man-made lakes that cover 400 acres and a family aquatic center. Dogs are allowed in the campground for no additional fee. They must have proof of current vaccinations, be well mannered, and quiet during quiet hours. Dogs must be kept on no more than a 6 foot leash except when in a camper, tent or vehicle, and be cleaned up after at all times.

Dogs are not allowed on the swim beach, and they may not be left unattended except inside an RV if they are quiet. The campground offers modern restrooms, a playground, fishing pier, potable water, and a dump station. The camping and tent areas also allow dogs. There is a dog walk area at the campground. There are no water hookups at the campgrounds. Multiple dogs may be allowed.

Yogi Bear Campground
5964 S H 109
Knightstown, IN
765-737-6585 (800-I-GO-YOGI (446-9644))
jellystoneindy.com
Dogs of all sizes are allowed. There are no additional pet fees. Dogs must be friendly, well behaved, leashed, and cleaned up after. The camping and tent areas also allow dogs. There is a dog walk area at the campground. Dogs are allowed in the camping cabins. Multiple dogs may be allowed.

Whitewater Memorial Park
1418 S State Road 101
Liberty, IN
765-458-5565 (866-622-6746)
This historical and scenic park offers a 200 acre lake and a variety of land and water recreation. Dogs of all sizes are allowed at the tent and RV sites at no additional fee. There may only be one dog in the cabins, and there are only 2 pet friendly cabins. Dogs may not be left unattended, and they must be on no more than a 6 foot leash, and be cleaned up after. Dogs are allowed on the trails. The camping and tent areas also allow dogs. There is a dog walk area at the campground. Dogs are allowed in the camping cabins. There are no water hookups at the campground.

Lincoln State Park
On H 162 3 miles W of Santa Claus
Lincoln City, IN
812-937-4710 (866-6CAMPIN (622-6746))
This park is a natural living history park. Dogs of all sizes are allowed. There are no additional pet fees. Dogs may not be left unattended, and they must be on no more than a 6 foot leash, and be cleaned up after. Dogs are allowed on the trails, but not on the beach. The camping and tent areas also allow dogs. There is a dog walk area at the campground. Multiple dogs may be allowed.

Clifty Falls State Park

2221 Clifty Drive
Madison, IN
812-273-8885 (877-622-6746)
Great scenic hiking and a beautiful water fall offer year round beauty at this park. Dogs of all sizes are allowed. There are no additional pet fees. Dogs may not be left unattended, and they must be leashed and cleaned up after. Dogs are not allowed at the pool or in the buildings. The camping and tent areas also allow dogs. There is a dog walk area at the campground. There are no water hookups at the campground.

Turkey Run State Park
8121 E Park Road
Marshall, IN
765-597-2635 (866-622-6746)
The natural geologic wonders, a Nature Center and Planetarium, great trails, and variety of land and water recreation brings visitors to this park. Dogs of all sizes are allowed at no additional fee. Dogs may not be left unattended, and they must be on no more than a 6 foot leash, and be cleaned up after. Dogs are not allowed in the nature center or in the lake, but they are allowed on the trails. The camping and tent areas also allow dogs. There is a dog walk area at the campground. There are no water hookups at the campground. Multiple dogs may be allowed.

Michigan City Campground
601 N H 421
Michigan City, IN
800-813-2267
michigancitycampground.com
Dogs of all sizes are allowed. There are no additional pet fees. Dogs may not be left unattended, must be leashed, and cleaned up after. The camping and tent areas also allow dogs. There is a dog walk area at the campground. 2 dogs may be allowed.

Elkhart Co/Middlebury Exit KOA
52867 H 13
Middlebury, IN
574-825-5932 (800-562-5892)
koa.com
Dogs of all sizes are allowed. There are no additional pet fees. Dogs may not be left unattended at the cabins, and they must be leashed and cleaned up after. This RV park is closed during the off-season. The camping and tent areas also allow dogs. There is a dog walk area at the campground. Dogs are allowed in the camping cabins. Multiple dogs may

be allowed.

Spring Mill State Park
3333 H 60 E
Mitchell, IN
812-849-4129 (866-6CAMPIN)
in.gov/dnr/parklake/6685.htm
In addition to numerous recreational opportunities, this park is also home to an 1800's pioneer village, a memorial for Virgil "Gus" Grissom (the second man in space), 3 nature preserves, several trails, and historic sites. Dogs are allowed in the campground for no additional fee. They must have proof of current vaccinations, be well mannered, and quiet during quiet hours. Dogs must be kept on no more than a 6 foot leash except when in a camper, tent or vehicle, and be cleaned up after at all times. Dogs are not allowed in the Pioneer Village, and they may not be left unattended at any time. The campground offers modern facilities, showers, picnic tables, grills, a playground, camp store, and a dump station. The camping and tent areas also allow dogs. There is a dog walk area at the campground. There are no water hookups at the campgrounds. Multiple dogs may be allowed.

Indiana Beach Camp Resort
5224 E Indiana Beach Road
Monticello, IN
574-583-4141 (800-583-5306)
inbeachcamping.com/
Located on beautiful Lake Shafer, this major recreation destination is the largest privately owned campground in the country, and in addition to a family water park, they offer a long list of amenities and activities. The campground has a variety of site options and may have some or all of the following: picnic tables, grills, cable TV, a laundry, camp store, fire rings, modern comfort stations, hot showers, and concessionaires. Dogs are allowed throughout the campground and park; they are not allowed in buildings, playgrounds, or recreation areas. Dogs must be on no more than a 10 foot leash and cleaned up after at all times. Dogs may not be left unattended at any time, and they are not to be walked by children. There are some breed restrictions. This RV park is closed during the off-season. The camping and tent areas also allow dogs. There is a dog walk area at the campground. 2 dogs may be allowed.

Jellystone Park
2882 N West Shafer Drive
Monticello, IN
574-583-8646 (888-811-YOGI (9644))
jellystoneindianabeach.com
Dogs of all sizes are allowed. There are no additional pet fees. Dogs may not be left unattended, must be leashed, and cleaned up after. Pit Bulls are not allowed. This RV park is closed during the off-season. The camping and tent areas also allow dogs. There is a dog walk area at the campground. 2 dogs may be allowed.

Brown County State Park
1405 H 46
Nashville, IN
812-988-6406 (866-6CAMPIN (622-6746))
in.gov/dnr/parklake/6725.htm
As the state's largest park, visitors will find plenty of recreational and educational activities to pursue here. Dogs are allowed in the campground for no additional fee. They must have proof of current vaccinations, be well mannered, and quiet during quiet hours. Dogs must be kept on no more than a 6 foot leash except when in a camper, tent or vehicle, and be cleaned up after at all times. Dogs may not be left unattended at any time. The campground offers hundreds of sites, picnic areas, comfort stations, playgrounds, a seasonal pool, playing fields/courts, a camp store, and dump station. The camping and tent areas also allow dogs. There is a dog walk area at the campground. There are no water hookups at the campgrounds. Multiple dogs may be allowed.

Westward Ho Campground
4557 E H 46
Nashville, IN
812-988-0008
gowestwardho.com
Dogs of all sizes are allowed. There are no additional pet fees. Dogs may not be tied up alone outside, they must be leashed at all times, and cleaned up after. This RV park is closed during the off-season. There is a dog walk area at the campground. Multiple dogs may be allowed.

Mini Mountain Campground
32351 H 2
New Carlisle, IN
574-654-3307
minimountaincampground.com
Dogs of all sizes are allowed. There

are no additional pet fees. Dogs must have shot records, may not be left unattended, and must be leashed and cleaned up after. Although this is mostly a seasonal campground, they have a few RV sites open in the winter for those traveling through. This RV park is closed during the off-season. The camping and tent areas also allow dogs. There is a dog walk area at the campground. Multiple dogs may be allowed.

Summit Lake State Park
5993 N Messick Road
New Castle, IN
765-766-5873 (866-622-6746)
With over 2,500 acres and a large lake, this park offers a variety of nature study and land and water recreation. Dogs of all sizes are allowed at no additional fee. Dogs may not be left unattended, and they must be on no more than a 6 foot leash, and be cleaned up after. Dogs are not allowed on the beaches or in buildings, but they are allowed on the trails. The camping and tent areas also allow dogs. There is a dog walk area at the campground. Multiple dogs may be allowed.

Walnut Ridge Campground
408 County Road 300W
New Castle, IN
877-619-2559
walnutridgerv.com
Dogs of all sizes are allowed. There are no additional pet fees. Dogs must be leashed and cleaned up after. This RV park is closed during the off-season. The camping and tent areas also allow dogs. There is a dog walk area at the campground. Multiple dogs may be allowed.

Harmonie State Park
3451 Harmonie State Park Road
New Harmony, IN
812-682-4821 (866-6CAMPIN (622-6746))
This park has a natural resources education center, and many trails for hiking, walking, and biking. Dogs of all sizes are allowed. There are no additional pet fees. Dogs must be on no more than a 6 foot leash and cleaned up after. Dogs are not allowed at the pool or in the buildings, but they are allowed on the trails. The camping and tent areas also allow dogs. There is a dog walk area at the campground. There are no water hookups at the campground. Multiple dogs may be allowed.

Natural Springs Resort

500 S Washington Street
New Paris, IN
888-330-5771
naturalspringsresort.com
Dogs of all sizes are allowed. There is a $3 per night per pet additional fee. Dogs must be leashed and cleaned up after. This RV park is closed during the off-season. There is a dog walk area at the campground. Multiple dogs may be allowed.

Potato Creek State Park
25601 H 4
North Liberty, IN
574-656-8186 (866-6CAMPIN (622-6746))
in.gov/dnr/parklake/6697.htm
There are a variety of habitats rich with bird, marine, and wildlife for visitors to explore at this park. This is a popular park for year round activities and reservations are suggested. Dogs are allowed in the campground for no additional fee. They must have proof of current vaccinations, be well mannered, and quiet during quiet hours. Dogs must be kept on no more than a 6 foot leash except when in a camper, tent or vehicle, and be cleaned up after at all times. Dogs are not allowed on the swim beach, and they may not be left unattended at any time. There is a beach area where dogs are allowed. The campground offers over 300 sites, comfort stations, pit toilets, playgrounds, potable water, a general store, and dump station. The camping and tent areas also allow dogs. There is a dog walk area at the campground. There are no water hookups at the campgrounds. Multiple dogs may be allowed.

Camp Yogi Jellystone Park
1916 N 850 E
Pierceton, IN
574-594-2124
campyogi.net
Dogs of all sizes are allowed, however there can only be 2 large or up to 3 small pets per site. There are no additional pet fees. Dogs may not be left unattended, must be leashed, and cleaned up after. There are some breed restrictions. This RV park is closed during the off-season. The camping and tent areas also allow dogs. There is a dog walk area at the campground.

Jellystone Park
7719 Redwood Road
Plymouth, IN

574-936-7851
jellystoneparkplymouth.com
Dogs of all sizes are allowed. There are no additional pet fees. Dogs may not be left unattended, must be leashed at all times, and cleaned up after. This RV park is closed during the off-season. The camping and tent areas also allow dogs. There is a dog walk area at the campground. Dogs are allowed in the camping cabins. Multiple dogs may be allowed.

Yogi Bear Campground
5300 Old Porter Road
Portage, IN
219-762-7757
campjellystone-portage.com
Dogs of all sizes are allowed. There are no additional pet fees. Dogs are not allowed in the rentals, must be leashed, and cleaned up after. This RV park is closed during the off-season. The camping and tent areas also allow dogs. There is a dog walk area at the campground. Multiple dogs may be allowed.

Indiana Dunes National Lakeshore
1100 North Mineral Springs Road
Porter, IN
219-926-7561 (866-6CAMPIN (622-6746))
indianaoutfitters.com/dunes.html
The dunes, the nature center, trails, and special programs throughout the year make this an interesting place to visit. Dogs of all sizes are allowed. There are no additional pet fees. Dogs must be on no more than a 6 foot leash and be cleaned up after. From October 1st to April 30th dogs are allowed at West Beach, Camel, Dunbar, and Lakeview. They are allowed at all through the year at Central Beach and Mount Baldie. The camping and tent areas also allow dogs. There is a dog walk area at the campground. There are no water hookups at the campground. Multiple dogs may be allowed.

Caboose Lake Campground
3657 H 24
Remington, IN
877-600-CAMP (2267)
cabooselake.com
Dogs of all sizes are allowed. There are no additional pet fees. Dogs must be quiet, well behaved, not left unattended at any time, leashed, and cleaned up after. There are some breed restrictions. The camping and tent areas also allow dogs. There is a dog walk area at the campground. Multiple dogs may be allowed.

Richmond KOA
3101 Cart Road
Richmond, IN
756-962-1219 (800-562-0611)
richmondinkoa.com
Dogs of all sizes are allowed, and there are no additional pet fees for tent or RV sites. Two dogs up to 50 pounds are allowed at the cabins also at no additional fee. Dogs may not be left unattended, and they must be leashed and cleaned up after. This RV park is closed during the off-season. The camping and tent areas also allow dogs. There is a dog walk area at the campground. Dogs are allowed in the camping cabins.

Lake Rudolph Campground
78 N Holiday Blvd
Santa Claus, IN
877-478-3657
lakerudolph.com
Dogs of all sizes are allowed. There are no additional pet fees. Dogs must be leashed and cleaned up after. This RV park is closed during the off-season. The camping and tent areas also allow dogs. There is a dog walk area at the campground. Multiple dogs may be allowed.

Jellystone Park
4577 W H 56
Scottsburg, IN
812-752-4062 (800-437-0566)
campindiana.com
Dogs of all sizes are allowed. There are no additional pet fees. Dogs may not be left unattended, must be leashed, and cleaned up after. The camping and tent areas also allow dogs. There is a dog walk area at the campground. Multiple dogs may be allowed.

McCormick's Creek State Park
250 McCormicks Creek Park Road
Spencer, IN
812-829-2235 (866-6CAMPIN (622-6746))
In addition to the recreational activities, this park touts beautiful waterfalls and some unique limestone formations. Dogs of all sizes are allowed. There are no additional pet fees. Dogs may not be left unattended, and they must be on no more than a 6 foot leash, and be cleaned up after. Dogs are not allowed at the pool, the group camping area, or the hotel. The camping and tent areas also allow dogs. There is a dog walk area at the campground. There are no water hookups at the campground. Multiple dogs may be allowed.

Terre Haute KOA
5995 E Sony Drive
Terre Haute, IN
812-232-2457 (800-562-4179)
koa.com/where/in/14115/ccwu/
Dogs of all sizes are allowed. There is a $5 one time fee for pets. Dogs must be leashed and cleaned up after. The camping and tent areas also allow dogs. There is a dog walk area at the campground. Dogs are allowed in the camping cabins. Multiple dogs may be allowed.

Old Mill Run Park
8544 W 690N
Thorntown, IN
765-436-7190
oldmillrun.com
Dogs of all sizes are allowed. There are no additional pet fees. Dogs may not be left unattended or tied up alone outside. Dogs must be leashed and cleaned up after. This RV park is closed during the off-season. The camping and tent areas also allow dogs. There is a dog walk area at the campground. Dogs are allowed in the camping cabins.

Versailles State Park
1387 E H 50
Versailles, IN
812-689-6424 (866-622-6746)
A 230 acre lake and a variety of land and water recreation are offered at this park. Dogs of all sizes are allowed at no additional fee. Dogs may not be left unattended, and they must be on no more than a 6 foot leash, and be cleaned up after. Dogs are not allowed in the lake or at the group camps, but they are allowed on the trails. The camping and tent areas also allow dogs. There is a dog walk area at the campground. There are no water hookups at the campground. Multiple dogs may be allowed.

Shades State Park
7751 S 890 W
Waveland, IN
765-435-2810 (866-622-6746)
A variety of habitats create a nature lover's paradise here, and it has become a favorite among hikers and canoeists. Dogs of all sizes are allowed at no additional fee. Dogs may not be left unattended, and they must be on no more than a 6 foot leash, and be cleaned up after. Dogs are not allowed in buildings, but they are allowed on the trails. This campground is closed during the off-season. The camping and

tent areas also allow dogs. There is a dog walk area at the campground. There are no electric or water hookups at the campground. Multiple dogs may be allowed.

Tippecanoe River State Park
4200 N H 35
Winamac, IN
574-946-3213 (866-622-6746)
This park along the Tippecanoe River offers a variety of land and water recreation. Dogs of all sizes are allowed at no additional fee. Dogs may not be left unattended, and they must be leased and cleaned up after. Dogs are not allowed in public swim areas or in buildings. Dogs are allowed on the trails. The camping and tent areas also allow dogs. There is a dog walk area at the campground. There are no water hookups at the campground. Multiple dogs may be allowed.

Iowa

Des Moines West KOA
3418 L Avenue
Adel, IA
515-834-2729 (800-562-2181)
koa.com
Dogs of all sizes are allowed. There are no additional pet fees. Dogs must be leashed and cleaned up after. There are some breed restrictions. The camping and tent areas also allow dogs. There is a dog walk area at the campground. Multiple dogs may be allowed.

Indian Hills RV Park
100 H 34E
Albia, IA
800-728-4286
indianhillsinn.com
Dogs of all sizes are allowed, and there are no additional pet fees for tent or RV sites. There is a $6 per night per pet additional fee for rooms at the inn, and they are in the smoking rooms. Dogs may not be left unattended, must be well behaved, leashed and cleaned up after. There is a dog walk area at the campground. 2 dogs may be allowed.

Adventureland Campground
2600 Adventureland Drive
Altoona, IA
512-265-7384
Dogs of all sizes are allowed. There

are no additional pet fees. Dogs may not be left unattended, must be quiet, well behaved, leashed, and cleaned up after. The camping and tent areas also allow dogs. There is a dog walk area at the campground. 2 dogs may be allowed.

Amana Colonies RV Park
3890 C Street
Amana, IA
319-622-7622 (800-579-2294)
amanarv.com/
Located in the heart of the historic Amana Colonies, of which the entire 2700 acres of villages are listed as a National Historic Landmark, this 60 acre campground offers a number of amenities. There are modern, accessible restrooms with showers, over 500 sites with picnic tables/fire rings, 4 dump stations, laundry facilities, free Wi-Fi, and a camp store. Dogs are allowed for no additional fee; they must be leashed and cleaned up after at all times. This RV park is closed during the off-season. The camping and tent areas also allow dogs. There is a dog walk area at the campground. Multiple dogs may be allowed.

Amana Colony RV Park
#39 38th Avenue
Amana, IA
319-622-7616
amanacolony.com
Dogs of all sizes are allowed. There are no additional pet fees. Dogs must be leashed and cleaned up after. This RV park is closed during the off-season. The camping and tent areas also allow dogs. There is a dog walk area at the campground. Multiple dogs may be allowed.

Bellevue Butterfly Garden
21466 429th Avenue
Bellevue, IA
563-872-4019
There are 2 separate tracts to this 770 acre park-each with their own special features: On the south edge of town on H 52 sits the Nelson unit with great views of the river, and 2 miles further on H 52 is the Dyas unit where camping is available. Dogs are allowed in the park and campground areas for no additional fee; they must be on no more than a 6 foot leash and picked up after at all times. The campground offers half the sites for first come first served; the other half can be reserved. There are modern restrooms, showers, and a dump station on site. The camping and tent areas also allow dogs. There is a dog walk area at the

campground. There are no water hookups at the campgrounds. Multiple dogs may be allowed.

Lake Darling State Park
111 Lake Darling Road
Brighton, IA
319-694-2323 (877-IAPARKS (427-2757))
This beautiful park of 1,417 acres with a 302-acre lake, offers various recreational pursuits. Along the parks many trails you will see a variety of plant, animal and bird species. Dogs of all sizes are allowed at no additional fee. Dogs may not be left unattended, and they must be leashed and cleaned up after. Dogs are not allowed in public swim areas or in buildings. Dogs are allowed on the trails. The camping and tent areas also allow dogs. There is a dog walk area at the campground. Dogs are allowed in the camping cabins. There are no water hookups at the campground. Multiple dogs may be allowed.

Black Hawk Park
2410 W Lonetree Road
Cedar Falls, IA
319-266-6813
This large park offers a variety of activities and recreation. Dogs of all sizes are allowed at no additional fee. Dogs may not be left unattended at any time, and they must be quiet, be on no more than a 6 foot leash, and cleaned up after. Dogs are allowed on the trails, but not on the playground. The camping and tent areas also allow dogs. There is a dog walk area at the campground. Dogs are allowed in the camping cabins. Multiple dogs may be allowed.

Clear Lake State Park
6490 S Shore Drive
Clear Lake, IA
641-357-4212 (877-IAPARKS (427-2757))
This 55 acre park sits along the southeast shore of the beautiful 3,643-acre Clear Lake. It offers a variety of land and water recreational pursuits. Dogs of all sizes are allowed at no additional fee. Dogs may not be left unattended, and they must be quiet, leashed, and cleaned up after. Dogs are not allowed on the beach. Dogs are allowed on the trails. The camping and tent areas also allow dogs. There is a dog walk area at the campground. There are no water hookups at the campground. Multiple dogs may be allowed.

Oakwood RV Park
5419 240th Street
Clear Lake, IA
641-357-4019
Dogs of all sizes are allowed. There are no additional pet fees. Dogs must be quiet, well behaved, leashed, and cleaned up after. There are some breed restrictions. This RV park is closed during the off-season. There is a dog walk area at the campground. Multiple dogs may be allowed.

Skip A Way RV Park
3825 Harding Road
Clermont, IA
563-423-7338
skipawayresort.com
Dogs of all sizes are allowed. There are no additional pet fees. Dogs may not be left unattended outside your unit, must be leashed, and cleaned up after. Dogs can be walked down by the lake and also go for a swim. The camping and tent areas also allow dogs. There is a dog walk area at the campground. Multiple dogs may be allowed.

Interstate RV Park
8448 Fairmont
Davenport, IA
563-386-7292
Dogs of all sizes are allowed. There are no additional pet fees. Dogs may not be left unattended, must be leashed, and cleaned up after. Dogs are not allowed at the playground or pool areas. There are some breed restrictions. There is a dog walk area at the campground. Multiple dogs may be allowed.

Nine Eagles State Park
Del Miller Road
Davis City, IA
641-442-2855 (877-IAPARKS (427-2757))
Although a favorite among picnickers for its shady lakeside picnic areas, this 1,100 acre park with a 64 acre lake has a wide variety of recreational pursuits, several miles of hiking trails, and beautiful stands of old forest. Dogs are allowed for no additional fees; they must be on no more than a 6 foot leash and picked up after at all times. Dogs are not allowed on the beach or in the water. The campground has 68 sites in 3 areas, picnic tables, fire rings, restrooms, showers, a playground, and a dump station. The camping and tent areas also allow dogs. There is a dog walk area at the campground. There are no water

hookups at the campgrounds. Multiple dogs may be allowed.

Iowa State Fair Campground
E 30th Street and University Avenue
Des Moines, IA
515-262-3111 ext. 284 (800-545-FAIR (3247))
The campground offers hundreds of sites, 3 large bathhouses, and 3 dump stations-all scenically located on 160 acres of wooded hills. Campsites are first come, first served except during fair time when reservations are accepted only if staying for the entire 15 days of the fair. The campground is open mid-April to mid-July and September to mid-October for non-Fair camping. Dogs are allowed for no additional fee; they must be kept on no more than a 6 foot leash or in the RV, and picked up after at all times. This RV park is closed during the off-season. There is a dog walk area at the campground. Multiple dogs may be allowed.

Backbone State Park
1347 129th Street
Dundee, IA
563-924-2527 (877-IAPARKS (427-2757))
The state's first-and still most significant state park, this 2,000+ acre forested recreation area features a large lake and a spring-fed trout fishing stream, 21 miles of year around multi-use trails, concessionaires, and a popular area for rock climbers. Dogs are allowed for no additional fees; they must be on no more than a 6 foot leash and picked up after at all times. Dogs are not allowed on the beach. The campground offers 125 sites, picnic tables, restrooms, showers, a playground, and a dump station. The camping and tent areas also allow dogs. There is a dog walk area at the campground. There are no water hookups at the campgrounds. Multiple dogs may be allowed.

Riverview Canoes and Camping
26070 Hawk Drive
Farmington, IA
319-878-3715
riverviewhunting.com/camp.htm
Dogs of all sizes are allowed. There are no additional pet fees. Dogs may not be left unattended unless they will be quiet and well behaved. Dogs must be leashed and cleaned up after. This RV park is closed during the off-season. The camping and tent areas also allow dogs. There is a dog walk area at the campground.

Dogs are allowed in the camping cabins. Multiple dogs may be allowed.

Springbrook State park
2437 160th Road
Guthrie Center, IA
641-747-3591 (877-IAPARKS (427-2757))
This beautiful park is located along a lake shore and offers 12 miles of hiking/nature trails and a variety of land and water recreation. Dogs of all sizes are allowed at no additional fee. Dogs may not be left unattended, and they must be leashed at all times, and cleaned up after. Dogs are not allowed on beaches or in buildings. Dogs are allowed on the trails. The camping and tent areas also allow dogs. There is a dog walk area at the campground. There are no water hookups at the campground. Multiple dogs may be allowed.

Waubonsie State Park
2585 Waubonsie Park Road
Hamburg, IA
712-382-2786 (877-IAPARKS (427-2757))
Born of glacial activity with a long rich natural and cultural history, this beautiful park has some unique features for a northern park. The park also has several miles of hiking and equestrian trails-plus a separate interpretive trail, and some of the prettiest seasonal landscape of any of the state's parks. Dogs are allowed for no additional fees; they must be on no more than a 6 foot leash and picked up after at all times. They request dogs be kept off the equestrian trail and away from the horses. The campground has 40 sites, picnic tables, modern restrooms, showers, a playground, and a dump station. The camping and tent areas also allow dogs. There is a dog walk area at the campground. There are no water hookups at the campgrounds. Multiple dogs may be allowed.

Beed's Lake State Park
1422 165th Street
Hampton, IA
641-456-2047 (877-IAPARKS (427-2757))
This popular park provides a beautiful backdrop for a wide range of land and water activities, recreation and scenic trails. Dogs of all sizes are allowed at no additional fee. Dogs may not be left unattended, and they must be leashed and cleaned up after. Dogs

are not allowed on the beach or in buildings. Dogs are allowed on the trails. This campground is closed during the off-season. The camping and tent areas also allow dogs. There is a dog walk area at the campground. Multiple dogs may be allowed.

Prairie Rose State Park
680 H M47
Harlan, IA
712-773-2701 (877-IAPARKS (427-2757))
Noted as being one of the most attractive areas in the state, this 422 acre park features a popular 218 acre lake, about 7 miles of multi-purpose trails, and an interpretive trail. Dogs are allowed for no additional fee; they must be on no more than a 6 foot leash and picked up after at all times. Dogs are not allowed on the sandy part of the beach. The campground has 95 sites in 2 areas, picnic tables, fire rings, restrooms, showers, a playground, and a dump station. The camping and tent areas also allow dogs. There is a dog walk area at the campground. Multiple dogs may be allowed.

Lake Ahquabi State Park
1650 118th Avenue
Indianola, IA
515-961-7101 (877-IAPARKS (427-2757))
Ahquabi translates to "resting place" and seems appropriate for this scenic, serene 770 acre park. The park has a modern boat ramp, several fishing jetties, a handicapped fishing pier, concessionaires, and trails-including one that goes around the entire lake. Dogs are allowed for no additional fees; they must be on no more than a 6 foot leash and picked up after at all times. The campground offers 141 sites, picnic tables, fireplaces, modern restrooms, showers, a playground, and 2 dump stations. The camping and tent areas also allow dogs. There is a dog walk area at the campground. There are no water hookups at the campgrounds. Multiple dogs may be allowed.

Devonian Fossil Gorge
2850 Prairie Du Chien Road NE
Iowa City, IA
319-338-3543 ext. 6300 (877-444-6777)
An historic flood in the early 90's uncovered ancient bedrock and fossils that visitors can now see close up here. It is a major recreation

destination for numerous land and water activities. Dogs are allowed for no additional fee; they must be well behaved, on no more than a 6 foot leash, and picked up after at all times. The park offers 3 separate camp areas with more than 500 sites. They may have all or some of the following: picnic tables, grills, modern restrooms/showers, a playground, disc golf, a boat launch, fish cleaning station, potable water, swim areas, interpretive/hiking trails, and dump stations. The camping and tent areas also allow dogs. There is a dog walk area at the campground. Multiple dogs may be allowed.

Kellogg RV Park
1570 H 224
Kellogg, IA
641-526-8535
Dogs of all sizes are allowed. There are no additional pet fees. Dogs must be quiet, well behaved, leashed, and cleaned up after. This RV park is closed during the off-season. The camping and tent areas also allow dogs. There is a dog walk area at the campground. Multiple dogs may be allowed.

Rock Creek State Park
5628 Rock Creek E
Kellogg, IA
641-236-3722 (877-IAPARKS (427-2757))
This park provides a haven for many different species of birds and wildlife. In addition it is a popular recreational area with a variety of activities. Dogs of all sizes are allowed at no additional fee. Dogs may not be left unattended, and they must be leashed and cleaned up after. Dogs are not allowed in public swim areas or buildings. Dogs are allowed on the trails. The camping and tent areas also allow dogs. There is a dog walk area at the campground. There are no water hookups at the campground. Multiple dogs may be allowed.

Brushy Creek Rec Area
3175 290th Street
Lehigh, IA
515-543-8298 (877-IAPARKS (427-2757))
This park, with over 6,000 acres located along a creek and the Des Moines River, offers about 50 miles of multi-use trails and a variety of land and water recreation. Dogs of all sizes are allowed at no additional fee. Dogs may not be left unattended, and they must be leashed and cleaned up after in

camp area. Dogs may be off lead on the trails only if they are under strict voice command and will not chase. Dogs are not allowed on the beach. The camping and tent areas also allow dogs. There is a dog walk area at the campground. Multiple dogs may be allowed.

Ledges State Park
1515 P Avenue
Madrid, IA
515-432-1852 (877-IAPARKS (427-2757))
Born of glacial activity and rich in natural and cultural history, this park is popular for the beauty of its canyons and bluffs and its scenic trails with overlooks. The park also has a recreational lake, a river for stream fishing, and historical/memorial sites. Dogs are allowed for no additional fees; they must be on no more than a 6 foot leash and picked up after at all times. The campground has 94 sites, picnic tables, modern restrooms, showers, a playground, and a dump station. The camping and tent areas also allow dogs. There is a dog walk area at the campground. There are no water hookups at the campgrounds. Multiple dogs may be allowed.

Maquoketa Caves State Park
10970 98th Street
Maquoketa, IA
563-652-5833 (877-IAPARKS (427-2757))
The caves are a geological highlight at this unique park; there are also 6 miles of scenic trails and a rich culture and natural history to explore. Dogs are allowed for no additional fees; they must be on no more than a 6 foot leash (unless being actively used in hunting or in a training exercise in a designated dog trail area) and picked up after at all times. The campground has 29 sites, picnic tables, restrooms, showers, a playground, and a dump station. The camping and tent areas also allow dogs. There is a dog walk area at the campground. There are no water hookups at the campgrounds. Multiple dogs may be allowed.

Shady Oaks RV and Campground
2370 Shady Oaks Road
Marshalltown, IA
641-752-2946
bigtreehouse.net/shadyoaks.html
Dogs of all sizes are allowed. There are no additional pet fees. Dogs may not be left unattended, and

they must be leashed and cleaned up after. This RV park is closed during the off-season. The camping and tent areas also allow dogs. There is a dog walk area at the campground. Multiple dogs may be allowed.

Spook Cave and Campground
13299 Spook Cave Road
McGregor, IA
563-873-2144
spookcave.com/
Although the cave (toured by boat) is the highlight of this park, there is plenty of recreation topside. The campground has picnic tables, fire rings, restrooms, showers, a laundry, game room/fields, a playground, store, and a dump station. Dogs are allowed throughout the park for no additional fee; however, they are not allowed inside the cave or at the beach/swim areas. Dogs may not be left unattended at any time, and they must be leashed and under their owner's control at all times. This RV park is closed during the off-season. The camping and tent areas also allow dogs. There is a dog walk area at the campground. Multiple dogs may be allowed.

Emerson Bay and Lighthouse
Emerson Street
Milford, IA
712-337-3211 (877-IAPARKS (427-2757))
This park provides a variety of habitats, trails, and land and water recreation. Dogs of all sizes are allowed at no additional fee. Dogs may not be left unattended unless they will be quiet, well behaved, and comfortable. Dogs must be leashed and cleaned up after. Dogs are not allowed in public swim areas or buildings. Dogs are allowed on the trails. The camping and tent areas also allow dogs. There is a dog walk area at the campground. There are no water hookups at the campground. Multiple dogs may be allowed.

Wilson Island Rec Area
32801 Campground Lane
Missouri Valley, IA
712-642-2069 (877-IAPARKS (427-2757))
This secluded park offers a variety of land and water recreation and is home to an abundance of bird and wildlife. Dogs of all sizes are allowed at no additional fee. Dogs may not be left unattended, and they must be leashed and cleaned up after. Dogs are not allowed in the Wildlife

Refuge, in public swim areas, or buildings. Dogs are allowed on the trails. The camping and tent areas also allow dogs. There is a dog walk area at the campground. There are no water hookups at the campground. Multiple dogs may be allowed.

Old Threshers Campground
405 E Threshers Road
Mount Pleasant, IA
319-385-8937
oldthreshers.org/index.cfm
Dogs of all sizes are allowed. There are no additional pet fees. Dogs may not be left unattended, and they must be leashed and cleaned up after. This RV park is closed during the off-season. The camping and tent areas also allow dogs. There is a dog walk area at the campground. Multiple dogs may be allowed.

Wildcat Den State Park
1884 Wildcat Den Road
Muscatine, IA
563-263-4337 (877-IAPARKS (427-2757))
The highlights here are the park's trails that offer interesting terrains of scenic bluffs and rock outcroppings that give visitors some fantastic views of the area. The park is also home to the Pine Creek Grist Mill and it is listed on the National Register of Historic Places. Dogs are allowed for no additional fees; they must be on no more than a 6 foot leash (unless being actively used in hunting or in a training exercise in a designated dog trail area) and picked up after at all times. The campground has 28 sites, picnic tables, restrooms, showers, a playground, and a dump station. The camping and tent areas also allow dogs. There is a dog walk area at the campground. There are no electric or water hookups at the campgrounds. Multiple dogs may be allowed.

Rolling Acres RV Park
1601 E 36th Street
Newton, IA
641-792-2428
rollingacresrvpark.com
Dogs of all sizes are allowed. There are no additional pet fees. Dogs must be well behaved, leashed and cleaned up after. This RV park is closed during the off-season. The camping and tent areas also allow dogs. There is a dog walk area at the campground. Multiple dogs may be allowed.

Colony Country Campground

1275 Forever Green Road
North Liberty, IA
319-626-2221
colonycountry.com/
Dogs of all sizes are allowed. There are no additional pet fees. Dogs must be leashed and cleaned up after. This RV park is closed during the off-season. The camping and tent areas also allow dogs. There is a dog walk area at the campground. Multiple dogs may be allowed.

Lewis and Clark State Park
21914 Park Loop
Onawa, IA
712-423-2829 (877-IAPARKS (427-2757))
This historic park is home to a full-sized reproduction of Lewis and Clark's keelboat, "Discovery" and, in addition to commemorative events with period reenactments, it hosts a variety of land and water recreation. Dogs of all sizes are allowed at no additional fee. Dogs may not be left unattended, and they must be leashed and cleaned up after. Dogs are not allowed on beaches or in buildings. Dogs are allowed on the trails. The camping and tent areas also allow dogs. There is a dog walk area at the campground. There are no water hookups at the campground. Multiple dogs may be allowed.

On-Ur-Wa RV Park
1111 28th Street
Onawa, IA
712-423-1387
onurwarvpark.com
Dogs of all sizes are allowed. There are no additional pet fees, and your pets are met with a biscuit at check in. Dogs must be leashed and cleaned up after. This RV park is closed during the off-season. There is a dog walk area at the campground. There are special amenities given to dogs at this campground. Multiple dogs may be allowed.

Onawa/Blue Lake KOA
21788 Dogwood Avenue
Onawa, IA
712-423-1633 (800-562-4182)
koa.com
Dogs of all sizes are allowed. There are no additional pet fees. Dogs must be quiet, well behaved, leashed, and cleaned up after. Dogs may not be left unattended. This RV park is closed during the off-season. The camping and tent areas also allow dogs. There is a dog walk area at the campground.

Dogs are allowed in the camping cabins. Multiple dogs may be allowed.

Terribles Lakeside Casino
777 Casino Drive
Osceola, IA
541-342-9511 (877-477-LAKE (5253))
Dogs of all sizes are allowed. There are no additional fees for the tent, RV sites, or the hotel. Dogs may not be left unattended unless they will be quiet and well behaved. Dogs must be crated if left in the motel room unattended. The camping and tent areas also allow dogs. There is a dog walk area at the campground. 2 dogs may be allowed.

Stone State park
5001 Talbot Road
Sioux City, IA
712-255-4698 (877-IAPARKS (427-2757))
The highlight of this park is the Dorothy Pecaut Nature Center; it has a children's discovery area, a 400 gallon aquarium, interpretive displays and more. This is also a great park for picnics and they have about 20 miles of multi-use trails that offers a number of impressive views. Dogs are allowed for no additional fees; they must be on no more than a 6 foot leash and picked up after at all times. The campground has 30 sites, picnic tables, restrooms, showers, a playground, and a dump station. This RV park is closed during the off-season. The camping and tent areas also allow dogs. There is a dog walk area at the campground. Dogs are allowed in the camping cabins. There are no water hookups at the campgrounds. Multiple dogs may be allowed.

Hunt's Cedar River Campground
1231 306th Street
Tipton, IA
563-946-2431
Dogs of all sizes are allowed. There are no additional pet fees. Dogs must be quiet, in your unit at night, leashed, and cleaned up after. This RV park is closed during the off-season. The camping and tent areas also allow dogs. There is a dog walk area at the campground. Multiple dogs may be allowed.

McIntosh Woods State Park
1200 East Lake Street
Ventura, IA
641-829-3847 (877-IAPARKS (427-2757))
Nestled along the shores of the

beautiful 3,684 acre Clear Lake, this 60 acre park has become a popular boating and water recreation destination. Dogs are allowed for no additional fee; they must be on no more than a 6 foot leash and picked up after at all times. The campground has 95 sites in 2 areas, picnic tables, fire rings, restrooms, showers, a playground, and a dump station. The camping and tent areas also allow dogs. There is a dog walk area at the campground. Dogs are allowed in the camping cabins. There are no water hookups at the campgrounds. Multiple dogs may be allowed.

George Wyth State Park
3659 Wyth Road
Waterloo, IA
319-232-5505 (877-IAPARKS (427-2757))
This beautiful park is unique in having several water areas for a variety of activities. It also offers several miles of various trails with connecting links to other larger trails. Dogs of all sizes are allowed at no additional fee. Dogs may not be left unattended, and they must be leashed and cleaned up after. Dogs are not allowed on beaches or in buildings. Dogs are allowed on the trails. The camping and tent areas also allow dogs. There is a dog walk area at the campground. There are no water hookups at the campground. Multiple dogs may be allowed.

Walnut Woods State Park
3155 Walnut Woods Drive
West Des Moines, IA
515-285-4502 (877-IAPARKS)
Located along the Raccoon River, this 260 acre park features a large old stand of black walnut trees, shady picnic areas along the river, a bird (blind) viewing area, and about 2½ miles of trails. Dogs are allowed for no additional fees; they must be on no more than a 6 foot leash and picked up after at all times. Dogs are not allowed at the lodge. The campground offers 23 shaded sites, modern restrooms, picnic tables, fireplaces, and a dump station. The camping and tent areas also allow dogs. There is a dog walk area at the campground. Multiple dogs may be allowed.

West Liberty KOA
1961 Garfield Avenue
West Liberty, IA
319-627-2676 (800-562-7624)
koa.com

Dogs of all sizes are allowed. There are no additional pet fees. Dogs may not be left unattended, and must be leashed and cleaned up after. The camping and tent areas also allow dogs. There is a dog walk area at the campground. Dogs are allowed in the camping cabins. Multiple dogs may be allowed.

Kansas

Covered Wagon RV Resort
803 Buckeye
Abilene, KS
785-263-2343
coveredwagonrvpark.com
Dogs of all sizes are allowed. There are no additional pet fees. Dogs must be leashed and cleaned up after. The camping and tent areas also allow dogs. There is a dog walk area at the campground. Multiple dogs may be allowed.

Bourquin's RV Park
155 E Willow
Colby, KS
785-462-3300
colbycamp.com
Dogs of all sizes are allowed. There are no additional pet fees. Dogs may not be left unattended outside, and they must be leashed and cleaned up after. The camping and tent areas also allow dogs. There is a dog walk area at the campground. Multiple dogs may be allowed.

Gunsmoke Trav-L-Park
11070 108 Road
Dodge City, KS
620-227-8247
gunsmokervpark.com
Dogs of all sizes are allowed. There are no additional pet fees. Dogs may not be tied up or left unattended outside at any time. Dogs must be well behaved, leashed, and cleaned up after. Dogs may not be walked in the tent or pool areas, and they are not allowed in the buildings. This RV park is closed during the off-season. There is a dog walk area at the campground. Multiple dogs may be allowed.

Watersports Campground
500 E Cherry
Dodge City, KS
620-225-8044
watersportscampground.com
Dogs of all sizes are allowed. There

are no additional pet fees. Dogs may not be left unattended except for very short periods, and they must be cleaned up after. Dogs may be off lead if they are friendly, well behaved, and they will stay by the side of owner. The camping and tent areas also allow dogs. There is a dog walk area at the campground. Multiple dogs may be allowed.

Deer Grove RV Park
2873 SE H 54
El Dorado, KS
316-321-6272
Dogs of all sizes are allowed. There are no additional pet fees. Dogs may not be left unattended outside, and they must be leashed and cleaned up after. The camping and tent areas also allow dogs. There is a dog walk area at the campground. Multiple dogs may be allowed.

El Dorado State Park
618 NE Bluestem Road
El Dorado, KS
316-321-7180
The largest park in the state spreads along the shores of the El Dorado Reservoir and offer a full range of recreational pursuits. I addition it boasts an amphitheater and 7 different trails. Dogs of all sizes are allowed at no additional fee. Pets must be restrained by a camper, cage, hand-held leash, or tethered chain no longer than 10 feet at all times. Dogs may not be left unattended unless quiet and very well behaved. For cabin visitors, dogs may be tied up outside, and at night they must be crated. They are not allowed on swimming beaches, or in swimming areas that are delineated by buoys/markers, or in public buildings or structures. Dogs are allowed on the trails. The camping and tent areas also allow dogs. There is a dog walk area at the campground. Multiple dogs may be allowed.

Cimarron National Grassland
242 East Highway 56
Elkhart, KS
620-697-4621
fs.fed.us/r2/psicc/cim/
There are 108,175 scenic acres at this natural area with an abundance of flora, fauna, and recreation. A 50 mile auto tour through here stops at 11 unique places and offers 6 points of interest; it starts at the intersection of Hwy 56 and Morton Street. Dogs are allowed throughout the park and at the campground for no additional fee. Dogs must be picked up after

and leashed (the only exception being during hunting season). The established campground is 4 miles east of Hwy 27 on the gravel road FS700, south of the river. They offer picnic tables, grills, and restrooms. Dispersed primitive camping is available in the park except at the Cimarron Recreation Area, the Cottonwood and Middle Spring Picnic Grounds, and Point of Rocks. The camping and tent areas also allow dogs. There is a dog walk area at the campground. There are no electric or water hookups at the campgrounds. Multiple dogs may be allowed.

Emporia RV Park
1601 W H 50
Emporia, KS
620-343-3422
emporiarvpark.com
Dogs of all sizes are allowed. There are no additional pet fees. Dogs must be leashed and cleaned up after. There is a dog walk area at the campground. Multiple dogs may be allowed.

Crawford State Park
I Lake Road
Farlington, KS
620-362-3671
Rich in history and spectacular scenery, this 500-acre park, with a 150 acre lake and 2 archaeological sites, offers an array of recreational pursuits. Pets must be restrained by a camper, cage, hand-held leash, or tethered chain no longer than 10 feet at all times. Dogs may not be left unattended outside. They are not allowed on swimming beaches, or in swimming areas that are delineated by buoys or other markers, or in public buildings or structures. Dogs are allowed on the trails. This campground is closed during the off-season. The camping and tent areas also allow dogs. There is a dog walk area at the campground. There are no water hookups at the campground. Multiple dogs may be allowed.

All Seasons RV Campground
15520 W Maple Street
Goddard, KS
316-722-1154
Dogs of all sizes are allowed. There are no additional pet fees. Dogs may not be left unattended, and they must be leashed and cleaned up after. The camping and tent areas also allow dogs. There is a dog walk area at the campground. 2 dogs may be allowed.

Goodland KOA
1114 E H 24
Goodland, KS
785-890-5701 (800-562-5704)
koa.com
Dogs of all sizes are allowed. There are no additional pet fees. Dogs must be well behaved, leashed, and cleaned up after. There are some breed restrictions. This RV park is closed during the off-season. The camping and tent areas also allow dogs. There is a dog walk area at the campground. Dogs are allowed in the camping cabins. Multiple dogs may be allowed.

Topeka KOA
3366 KOA Road
Grantville, KS
785-246-3419 (800-562-8717)
koa.com
Dogs of all sizes are allowed. There are no additional pet fees. There is a pet waiver to sign if the dog(s) are any of the known aggressive breeds. Dogs must be quiet, leashed and cleaned up after. This RV park is closed during the off-season. The camping and tent areas also allow dogs. Dogs are allowed in the camping cabins. Multiple dogs may be allowed.

Spring Lake RV Resort
1308 S Spring Lake Road
Halstead, KS
316-835-3443
springlakervresort.com/
Considered one of the largest RV parks in the state with 93 acres and 180 sites, this camp area offers many standard amenities, plus playing fields/courts, a mini-golf course, playground, a large pool, fishing sites, gospel concerts, planned activities, and more. Dogs are allowed for no additional fee. Dogs must be short leashed and cleaned up after. The camping and tent areas also allow dogs. There is a dog walk area at the campground. Multiple dogs may be allowed.

Cottonwood Grove RV Campground
101 E Lincoln Blvd
Hesston, KS
620-327-4173
cottonwoodgrove.com/
Dogs of all sizes are allowed. There are no additional pet fees. Dogs must be quiet, well behaved, leashed, and cleaned up after. The camping and tent areas also allow dogs. There is a dog walk area at the campground. Multiple dogs may be allowed.

Elk City State Park
4825 Squaw Peak Road
Independence, KS
620-331-6295
Dense woodlands, blue streams, and a variety of scenic trails make this a popular recreational destination. Pets must be restrained by a camper, cage, hand-held leash, or tethered chain no longer than 10 feet at all times. Dogs may not be left unattended outside, and they must be well taken care of. They are not allowed on swimming beaches, or in swimming areas that are delineated by buoys or other markers, or in public buildings or structures. Dogs are allowed on the trails. The camping and tent areas also allow dogs. There is a dog walk area at the campground. Multiple dogs may be allowed.

Owl's Nest RV Campground
1912 Old H 40
Junction City, KS
785-238-0778
owlsnestcampground.com
Dogs of all sizes are allowed. There are no additional pet fees. Dogs must be leashed and cleaned up after. There is a dog walk area at the campground. Multiple dogs may be allowed.

Lawrence/Kansas City KOA
1473 H 40
Lawrence, KS
785-842-3877 (800-562-3708)
koa.com
Dogs of all sizes are allowed. There are no additional pet fees. Dogs may not be left unattended outside or in the cabins, and they must be quiet, be on no more than a 6 foot leash, and cleaned up after. There are some breed restrictions. The camping and tent areas also allow dogs. There is a dog walk area at the campground. Dogs are allowed in the camping cabins. Multiple dogs may be allowed.

Rutlader Outpost and RV Park
33565 Metcalf
Louisburg, KS
866-888-6779
rutladeroutpost.com
Dogs of all sizes are allowed. There are no additional pet fees. Dogs must be leashed and cleaned up after. There is a dog walk area at the campground. Multiple dogs may be allowed.

Tuttle Creek State Park
5800A River Pond Road

Manhattan, KS
785-539-7941
Numerous trails, an 18 hole disc golf course, excellent fishing, and a variety of other land and water recreation greet visitors at this park. Pets must be restrained by a camper, cage, hand-held leash, or tethered chain no longer than 10 feet at all times. Dogs may not be left unattended outside. They are not allowed on swimming beaches, or in swimming areas that are delineated by buoys or other markers, or in public buildings or structures. Dogs are allowed on the trails. The camping and tent areas also allow dogs. There is a dog walk area at the campground. Multiple dogs may be allowed.

Milford State Park
8811 State Park Road
Milford, KS
785-238-3014
This resort like park sits along the shores of the largest lake in the state, and offer a multi- purpose trail system, a full service marina and yacht club, and various water and land recreation. Dogs of all sizes are allowed at no additional fee. Pets must be restrained by a camper, cage, hand-held leash, or tethered chain no longer than 10 feet at all times. Dogs may not be left unattended outside. They are not allowed on swimming beaches, or in swimming areas that are delineated by buoys/markers, or in public buildings or structures. Dogs are allowed on the trails. The camping and tent areas also allow dogs. There is a dog walk area at the campground. Multiple dogs may be allowed.

Praire Dogs State Park
P.O. Box 431
Norton, KS
785-877-2953
This park offers a variety of recreation, historical interpretation programs, a 1.4 mile nature trail, and is home to a thriving prairie dog colony. Pets must be restrained by a camper, cage, hand-held leash, or tethered chain no longer than 10 feet at all times. Dogs must be well behaved, and may not be left unattended outside. They are not allowed on swimming beaches, or in swimming areas that are delineated by buoys or other markers, or in public buildings or structures. Dogs are allowed on the trails, and they may be off lead in the wildlife area if they will not chase and are under

voice command. The camping and tent areas also allow dogs. There is a dog walk area at the campground. Multiple dogs may be allowed.

High Plains Camping
462 H 83
Oakley, KS
785-672-3538
highplainscamping.com
Dogs of all sizes are allowed. There are no additional pet fees. Dogs may not be left unattended outside, and they must be leashed and cleaned up after. The camping and tent areas also allow dogs. There is a dog walk area at the campground. Multiple dogs may be allowed.

Salina KOA
1109 W Diamond Drive
Salina, KS
785-827-3182 (800-562-3126)
koa.com
Dogs of all sizes and numbers are allowed at the tent or RV sites. Two dogs of any size are allowed at the cabins. There are no additional pet fees. Dogs may not be left unattended, and they must be leashed and cleaned up after. This RV park is closed during the off-season. The camping and tent areas also allow dogs. There is a dog walk area at the campground. Dogs are allowed in the camping cabins.

Scott State Park
520 W Scott Lake Drive
Scott City, KS
620-872-2061
Rich in natural and cultural history, this 1,020 acre park offers a wide variety of activities and environs, plus they are home to El Cuartelejo- the northernmost pueblo in the country. Dogs are allowed at the park and in the campground for no additional fee. Dogs must be restrained by a camper, kennel, a hand-held leash, or on a tethered chain no longer than 10 feet. They are not allowed in public buildings or structures, or on swimming beaches/areas. The camp area offers 55 utility/100 primitive campsites, picnic tables, grills, 3 modern shower buildings, vault toilets, and a playground. The camping and tent areas also allow dogs. There is a dog walk area at the campground. Multiple dogs may be allowed.

Pine Haven Retreat
217 E H 50
St John, KS

620-549-3444
Dogs of all sizes are allowed. There are no additional pet fees. Dogs may not be left unattended, and they must be leashed and cleaned up after. There are some breed restrictions. The camping and tent areas also allow dogs. There is a dog walk area at the campground. 2 dogs may be allowed.

Webster State Park
1210 Nine Road
Stockton, KS
785-425-6775
This park covers 880 acres along the shores of Webster Reservoir, and a wide variety of land and water recreation is available. Dogs of all sizes are allowed at no additional fee. Pets must be restrained by a camper, cage, hand-held leash, or tethered chain no longer than 10 feet at all times. Dogs may not be left unattended outside. They are not allowed on swimming beaches, or in swimming areas that are delineated by buoys/markers, or in public buildings or structures. Dogs are allowed on the trails. The camping and tent areas also allow dogs. There is a dog walk area at the campground. Multiple dogs may be allowed.

Capital City RV Park
1949 SW 49th Street
Topeka, KS
785-862-5267
capitalcityrvpark.com
Dogs of all sizes are allowed. There are no additional pet fees. Dogs may not be left unattended, and they must be leashed and cleaned up after. The camping and tent areas also allow dogs. There is a dog walk area at the campground. Multiple dogs may be allowed.

Cross Timbers State Park
144 H 105
Toronto, KS
620-637-2213
This park, with over 1000 acres and with access to a 2,800 acre reservoir, offers a variety of trails, recreational pursuits, and some of the most diverse flora and fauna in the state. Dogs of all sizes are allowed at no additional fee. Pets must be restrained by a camper, cage, hand-held leash, or tethered chain no longer than 10 feet at all times. Dogs may not be left unattended unless they will be quiet and very well behaved. They are not allowed on swimming beaches, or in swimming areas that are delineated

by buoys/markers, or in public buildings or structures. Dogs are allowed on the trails. The camping and tent areas also allow dogs. There is a dog walk area at the campground. Multiple dogs may be allowed.

WaKeeney KOA
I 70 S. Frontage Road, Box 170
WaKeeney, KS
785-743-5612 (800-562-2761)
koa.com
Dogs of all sizes are allowed, and there are no additional pet fees for tent or RV sites. There is a $25 refundable deposit for the cabins, and dogs may not be left unattended there. Dogs must be well behaved, leashed, and cleaned up after. There are some breed restrictions. This RV park is closed during the off-season. The camping and tent areas also allow dogs. There is a dog walk area at the campground. Dogs are allowed in the camping cabins. There are special amenities given to dogs at this campground. Multiple dogs may be allowed.

USI RV Park
2920 E 33rd
Wichita, KS
316-838-8699
usirvpark.com
Dogs of all sizes are allowed. There is a pet waiver to sign at check in and there are no additional pet fees. Dogs are not allowed in any of the buildings, and they may not be left unattended. Dogs must be quiet, leashed, and cleaned up after. There is a dog walk area at the campground. Multiple dogs may be allowed.

Winfield City Lake
10348 141st Road
Winfield, KS
620-221-5635
This major recreation destination offers an abundance of land and water activities. Permits are required for entrance to the park and/or for camping; they are available at the lake office from 8 AM to 8 PM or at the City Hall on 9th Avenue. Dogs are allowed for no additional fee; they must be leashed and under their owner's control at all times. Pets may not be tied to trees. The camping and tent areas also allow dogs. There is a dog walk area at the campground. Multiple dogs may be allowed.

Winfield Fairgrounds
1105 W 9th Avenue/H 160

Winfield, KS
620-221-5525
The campground here offers a variety of sites in woods and natural settings. Dogs are allowed for no additional fee; they must be kept leashed and cleaned up after at all times. The camping and tent areas also allow dogs. There is a dog walk area at the campground. 2 dogs may be allowed.

Kentucky

Holts Campground
2351 Templin Ave (H 1430)
Bardstown, KY
502-348-6717
bardstown.com/~pholt/
Dogs of all sizes are allowed. There are no additional pet fees. Dogs must be leashed and cleaned up after. The camping and tent areas also allow dogs. There is a dog walk area at the campground. Multiple dogs may be allowed.

My Old Kentucky Home State Park
501 E Stephen Foster Avenue/H 150
Bardstown, KY
502-348-3502 (888-459-7275)
Years before Daniel Boone brought fame to this area it was explored and surveyed by Dr. Walker who built the state's first cabin at this site. The 12 acre site is dedicated to the state's early pioneers, and they offers picnicking areas, a gift store, snack bar and a seasonal 9-hole mini-golf course. Dogs are allowed on the grounds; they are not allowed in buildings or on the golf course. Dogs must be licensed, current on inoculations, leashed, and cleaned up after at all times. The camp area offers 39 sites, picnic tables, showers, restrooms, and a dump station. A grocery store and laundry are located across the street. The camping and tent areas also allow dogs. There is a dog walk area at the campground. Multiple dogs may be allowed.

Lago Linda Hideaway Campground
850 Black Ridge Road
Beattyville, KY
606-464-2876
lagolinda.com/
Dogs of all sizes are allowed. There are no additional pet fees. Dogs may not be left unattended outside or in the cabins, and they must be

leashed and cleaned up after. There are 2 pet-friendly cabins. Dogs are to stay off the furniture in the cabins, and they are not allowed in other park buildings or on other people's camp sites. The camping and tent areas also allow dogs. There is a dog walk area at the campground. Dogs are allowed in the camping cabins. 2 dogs may be allowed.

Old Kentucky RV Park
1142 Paint Lick Road
Berea, KY
859-986-1150
ohkentuckycampground.com
Dogs of all sizes are allowed. There are no additional pet fees. Dogs must be quiet, well behaved, leashed, and cleaned up after. The camping and tent areas also allow dogs. There is a dog walk area at the campground. Multiple dogs may be allowed.

Beech Bend Park & Splash Lagoon Family Campground
798 Beech Bend Road
Bowling Green, KY
270-781-7634
beechbend.com
Dogs of all sizes are allowed. There are no additional pet fees. Dogs must be quiet, well behaved, leashed, and cleaned up after. The camping and tent areas also allow dogs. There is a dog walk area at the campground. Multiple dogs may be allowed.

Bowling Green KOA
1960 Three Springs Road
Bowling Green, KY
270-843-1919 (800-562-2458)
koa.com
Dogs of all sizes are allowed, and there are no additional pet fees for tent or RV sites. There is a $5 per night per pet additional fee for the cabins. Dogs may not be left unattended outside or in the cabins, and they must be leashed and cleaned up after. The camping and tent areas also allow dogs. There is a dog walk area at the campground. Dogs are allowed in the camping cabins. Multiple dogs may be allowed.

General Burnside State Park
8801 S H 27
Burnside, KY
606-561-4104 (888-459-PARK (7275))
Scenic views, an 18 hole golf course, and a variety of activities and recreational pursuits are offered in the park. Dogs of all sizes are

allowed at no additional fee. Dogs may not be left unattended, and they must be leashed and cleaned up after. Dogs are not allowed on the golf course. This campground is closed during the off-season. The camping and tent areas also allow dogs. There is a dog walk area at the campground. Multiple dogs may be allowed.

Kamptown RV Resort
4124 Rockcastle Road
Cadiz, KY
270-522-7976
kamptown.com
Dogs of all sizes are allowed. There are no additional pet fees. Dogs must be cleaned up after. Dogs may be off lead if they are under control of owner and they are well behaved. This RV park is closed during the off-season. The camping and tent areas also allow dogs. There is a dog walk area at the campground. Multiple dogs may be allowed.

Kentucky Lakes / Prizer Point KOA
1777 Prizer Point Road MM 55
Cadiz, KY
270-522-3762 (800-562-3701)
koa.com/where/ky/17146/
There is an abundance of land and water recreational activities for children and adults available at this campground, and soon a Kamp K-9 off leash dog play area will be available too. Dogs are allowed for no additional fee in the RV/tent area; there is a $50 one time fee for 1 dog and $25 for each additional dog in the cabins. Dogs may not be left unattended outside or in the cabins, and they may only be left alone inside RVs if they will be quiet. Dogs must be on no more than a 6 foot leash and cleaned up after at all times. There are some breed restrictions. This RV park is closed during the off-season. The camping and tent areas also allow dogs. There is a dog walk area at the campground. Dogs are allowed in the camping cabins. Multiple dogs may be allowed.

Prizer Point Marina and Resort
1777 Prizer Point Road
Cadiz, KY
270-522-3762
prizerpoint.com
Dogs of all sizes are allowed, and there are no additional pet fees for tent or RV sites. There is a $25 one time fee for 1 dog and $5 for each dog thereafter for the lodge. The campsites are seasonal, but the lodge is open year around. Dogs

may not be left unattended at any time, or tied up outside alone. Dogs must be leashed and cleaned up after. This RV park is closed during the off-season. The camping and tent areas also allow dogs. There is a dog walk area at the campground. Multiple dogs may be allowed.

Paducah/I 24/Kentucky Lake KOA
4793 H 62
Calvert City, KY
270-395-5841 (800-562-8540)
koa.com
Dogs of all sizes are allowed at the tent or RV sites, and there can be up to 3. There can only be 2 dogs up to 25 pounds each in the cabins. There are no additional pet fees. Dogs may not be left unattended, and they must be leashed and cleaned up after. This RV park is closed during the off-season. The camping and tent areas also allow dogs. There is a dog walk area at the campground. Dogs are allowed in the camping cabins.

General Butler State Resort Park
1608 H 227
Carrollton, KY
502-732-4384 (866-462-8853)
In addition to historic sites, numerous recreational activities, and planned events, this resort park features a great lookout over the Kentucky and Ohio Rivers. Dogs are allowed throughout the park and in the camp area; they are not allowed in the lodge, cabins or on the golf course. Dogs must be licensed, current on inoculations, leashed, and cleaned up after at all times. The campground offers 111 sites, picnic tables, grills, and a playground. Restrooms, showers, and a laundry are nearby. The camping and tent areas also allow dogs. There is a dog walk area at the campground. Multiple dogs may be allowed.

Crystal Onyx Cave and
Campground Resort
363 Prewitts Knob Road
Cave City, KY
270-773-2359
crystalonyxcave.com
Dogs of all sizes are allowed. There are no additional pet fees. Dogs may not be left unattended outside, and they must be well behaved, and cleaned up after. Dogs may be off lead only if they are under voice command and will not chase. This RV park is closed during the off-season. The camping and tent areas also allow dogs. There is a

dog walk area at the campground. 2 dogs may be allowed.

Jellystone Park
1002 Mammoth Cave Road
Cave City, KY
270-773-3840 (800-523-1854)
jellystonemammothcave.com
Dogs of all sizes are allowed. There are no additional pet fees. Dogs must be leashed and cleaned up after. There are some breed restrictions. The camping and tent areas also allow dogs. There is a dog walk area at the campground. Dogs are not allowed in the camping cabins. Multiple dogs may be allowed.

Louisville Metro KOA
900 Marriott Drive
Clarksville, IN
812-282-4474 (800-562-4771)
koa.com
Dogs of all sizes are allowed. There are no additional pet fees. Dogs may not be left unattended outside, and they must be leashed and cleaned up after. The camping and tent areas also allow dogs. There is a dog walk area at the campground. Dogs are allowed in the camping cabins. Multiple dogs may be allowed.

Columbus-Belmont State Park
350 Park Road
Columbus, KY
270-677-2327 (888-459-7275)
Steeped in colonial history with a pivotal role in the War Between the States, this is an educational as well as a recreational park. In addition to a long list of amenities and activities, this park also features various living history events, reenactments, and artifacts from the colonial era. Dogs are allowed on the grounds; they are not allowed in buildings. Dogs must be licensed, current on inoculations, leashed, and cleaned up after at all times. The camp area sits along the cliffs on the river and offers 38 sites with picnic tables, grills, fire rings, a playground, restrooms, showers, a dump station, and concessionaires. The camping and tent areas also allow dogs. There is a dog walk area at the campground. Multiple dogs may be allowed.

Corbin KOA
171 E City Dam Road
Corbin, KY
806-528-1534 (800-562-8132)
corbinkoa.com
Up to 3 dogs are allowed at the RV sites, 2 dogs at the tent sites, and 1 dog in the cabins. There are no

additional pet fees. Dogs may not be left unattended, and must be leashed and cleaned up after. The camping and tent areas also allow dogs. There is a dog walk area at the campground. Dogs are allowed in the camping cabins.

Cumberland Falls State Resort Park
7351 H 90
Corbin, KY
606-528-4121 (800-325-0063)
This park, known as the "Niagara of the South", has an impressive waterfall, but only on the night of a full moon over the waterfall can you see the Moonbow, a phenomenon not found anywhere else in the Western Hemisphere. There is also a variety of trails and recreation available. Dogs of all sizes are allowed at no additional fee. Dogs may not be left unattended outside, and they must be leashed and cleaned up after. Dogs are not allowed in buildings, but they can be on the trails. The camping and tent areas also allow dogs. There is a dog walk area at the campground. Multiple dogs may be allowed.

Three Springs Campground
595 Campground Road
Corinth, KY
859-806-3030
threesprings.net/_wsn/page2.html
Dogs of all sizes are allowed. There are no additional pet fees. Dogs must be leashed and cleaned up after. Dogs may be unleashed on your site if they are under voice command, will stay on the site, and will not chase. The camping and tent areas also allow dogs. There is a dog walk area at the campground. Dogs are allowed in the camping cabins. Multiple dogs may be allowed.

Grand Trails RV Park
205 S Mulberry
Corydon, IN
812-738-9077
grandtrailsrvpark.com
Dogs of all sizes are allowed, and there are no additional pet fees for tent or RV sites. There is a $25 refundable pet deposit for the cabins. Dogs may not be tied to anything belonging to the campground, and they may not be tied up alone outside. Dogs must be leashed at all times, and cleaned up after. The camping and tent areas also allow dogs. There is a dog walk area at the campground. Dogs are allowed in the camping cabins. Multiple dogs may be allowed.

Cincinnati South KOA
3315 Dixie H
Crittenden, KY
859-428-2000 (800-562-9151)
koa.com
Dogs of all sizes are allowed. There are no additional pet fees. Dogs must be leashed and cleaned up after. There are some breed restrictions. This RV park is closed during the off-season. The camping and tent areas also allow dogs. There is a dog walk area at the campground. Multiple dogs may be allowed.

Kingdom Come State Park
502 Park Road
Cumberland, KY
606-589-2479
This park sits at a 2,700 feet elevation and preserves almost 1,300 acres of unspoiled wilderness. There are 4 mountain top overlooks, 14 hiking trails, and this park is home to some of the most impressive rock formations in the state. Dogs are allowed throughout the park; they are not allowed in the lodge. Dogs must be licensed, current on inoculations, leashed, and cleaned up after at all times. Primitive camping is available year around and sites are reservable. Restrooms and the gift shop are open from April 1st to October 31st. The camping and tent areas also allow dogs. There is a dog walk area at the campground. There are no electric or water hookups at the campgrounds. Multiple dogs may be allowed.

Pennyrile Forest State Park
20781 Pennyrile Lodge Road
Dawson Springs, KY
270-797-3421 (800-325-1711)
This park is a back-to-nature hideaway, offering interpretive programs, an 18-hole par-72 golf course, 7 easy to difficult hiking trails, and a variety of recreational pursuits. Dogs of all sizes are allowed at no additional fee. Dogs may not be left unattended unless they will be quiet and well behaved. Dogs must be leashed and cleaned up after. Dogs are allowed on the trails, but not in any park buildings. The camping and tent areas also allow dogs. There is a dog walk area at the campground. Multiple dogs may be allowed.

Eddy Creek Marina Resort
7612 H 93S
Eddyville, KY

270-388-2271
eddycreek.com/rvpark.htm
Dogs of all sizes are allowed. There are no additional pet fees for the camping area. There is a $100 refundable pet deposit for the lodge. Dogs must be leashed and cleaned up after. Dogs are allowed on the trails. This RV park is closed during the off-season. The camping and tent areas also allow dogs. There is a dog walk area at the campground. Multiple dogs may be allowed.

North Fork Park
14500 Falls of Rough Road
Falls of Rough, KY
270-257-8139
This park along Rough River Lake offers a variety of land and water recreation. Dogs of all sizes are allowed at no additional fee. Dogs may not be left unattended, and they must be on no more than a 6 foot leash, and cleaned up after. Dogs are not allowed on the beaches. This campground is closed during the off-season. The camping and tent areas also allow dogs. There is a dog walk area at the campground. Multiple dogs may be allowed.

Rough River State Resort Park
450 Lodge Road
Falls of Rough, KY
270-257-2311 (800-325-1713)
This park, overlooking a 5,000 acre lake, offers a wide range of activities and land and water recreation. Dogs of all sizes are allowed at no additional fee. Dogs may not be left unattended, and they must be leashed and cleaned up after. Dogs are allowed on the trails. The camping and tent areas also allow dogs. There is a dog walk area at the campground. Multiple dogs may be allowed.

Kincaid Lake State Park
565 Kincaid Park Road
Falmouth, KY
859-654-3531 (888-459-PARK (7275))
This scenic park, located along a 183-acre lake, offers mini golf, hiking trails, a 9 hole golf course, and a variety of land and water recreation. Dogs of all sizes are allowed at no additional fee. Dogs may not be left unattended, and they must be leashed and cleaned up after. Dogs are not allowed in public swim areas or in buildings. Dogs are allowed on the trails. The camping and tent areas also allow dogs. There is a dog walk area at the campground. Multiple dogs may be allowed.

Elkhorn Campground
165 N Scruggs Lane
Frankfort, KY
502-695-9154
Dogs of all sizes are allowed, but dogs over 60 pounds must wear a harness lead. There are no additional pet fees. Dogs may not be left unattended, must be quiet, well behaved, leashed, and cleaned up after. Although they mostly close down in winter, they do have a few RV sites available for those traveling through. There are some breed restrictions. This RV park is closed during the off-season. The camping and tent areas also allow dogs. There is a dog walk area at the campground. Multiple dogs may be allowed.

Franklin KOA
2889 Scottsville Road
Franklin, KY
270-586-5622 (800-562-5631)
koa.com
Dogs of all sizes are allowed. There are no additional pet fees. Dogs must be leashed and cleaned up after. The camping and tent areas also allow dogs. There is a dog walk area at the campground. Dogs are allowed in the camping cabins. Multiple dogs may be allowed.

Land Between the Lakes
100 Van Morgan Drive
Golden Pond, KY
270-924-2000 (877-444-6777)
lbl.org/Home.html
Although there are numerous recreational activities at this 170,000 acre peninsula park offering over 300 miles of undeveloped shoreline, there are several historical and environmental education opportunities as well. Dogs are allowed throughout the park; they must be licensed, current on inoculations, and cleaned up after at all times. Dogs may only be off leash during authorized field trials and hunts. All pets must have owner's name and address on their collars. Hundreds of campsites are available in 3 areas of the park; some are available for reservation. The campgrounds have all or some of the following: picnic tables, fire rings, restrooms, showers, a playground, playing fields and courts, fishing pier, and a dump station. This RV park is closed during the off-season. The camping and tent areas also allow dogs. There is a dog walk area at the campground. Multiple dogs may be allowed.

Greenbow Lake State Park
965 Lodge Road
Greenup, KY
606-473-7324 (800-325-0083)
Rich in natural and cultural history, this park offers 25 miles of nature trails and a host of land and water recreation year round. Dogs of all sizes are allowed at no additional fee. Dogs may not be left unattended, and they must be leashed and cleaned up after. Dogs are not allowed in buildings, however, they are allowed on the trails. This campground is closed during the off-season. The camping and tent areas also allow dogs. There is a dog walk area at the campground. Multiple dogs may be allowed.

Kenlake State Resort Park
542 Kenlake Road
Hardin, KY
270-474-2211 (800-325-0143)
For quiet relaxation, active recreation, or as a business retreat, this park offers nature trails, and a wide array of land and water activities year round. Dogs of all sizes are allowed at no additional fee. Dogs may not be left unattended, and they must be leashed and cleaned up after. Dogs are not allowed in buildings. Dogs are allowed on the trails. This campground is closed during the off-season. The camping and tent areas also allow dogs. There is a dog walk area at the campground. Multiple dogs may be allowed.

Ohio County Park and Campground
2300 H 69N
Hartford, KY
270-298-4466
ohiocountypark.net
Dogs of all sizes are allowed. There are no additional pet fees. Dogs may not be left unattended, must be well behaved, leashed, and cleaned up after. The camping and tent areas also allow dogs. There is a dog walk area at the campground. 2 dogs may be allowed.

John James Audubon State Park
3100 H 41 N
Henderson, KY
270-826-2247
This beautiful park celebrates the renowned artist and naturalist John James with the largest collection of his works in the world. Because this is a nature preserve dogs are only allowed in the campground, on the . 9 mile Eagle Glen Pet Trail, and in

the parking lot area. Dogs must be leashed and picked up after. The camp area offers 69 sites, showers, restrooms, picnic tables, grills, a playground, and a dump station. This RV park is closed during the off-season. The camping and tent areas also allow dogs. There is a dog walk area at the campground. Multiple dogs may be allowed.

Horse Cave KOA
109 Knob Hill Road
Horse Cave, KY
270-786-2819 (800-562-2809)
koa.com
Dogs of all sizes are allowed. There are no additional pet fees. Dogs must be leashed and cleaned up after. The camping and tent areas also allow dogs. There is a dog walk area at the campground. Dogs are allowed in the camping cabins. Multiple dogs may be allowed.

Lake Cumberland State Park
5465 State Park Road
Jamestown, KY
270-343-3111 (800-325-1709)
This park offers panoramic views of the 60,000 acre lake that is considered one of best in the Eastern US for boating and fishing. It also provides interpretive programs, scenic trails and a variety of land and water recreation. Dogs of all sizes are allowed at no additional fee. Dogs may not be left unattended, and they must be leashed and cleaned up after. Dogs are not allowed in buildings. Dogs are allowed on the trails. This campground is closed during the off-season. The camping and tent areas also allow dogs. There is a dog walk area at the campground. Multiple dogs may be allowed.

Kentucky Horse Park Campground
4089 Iron Works Parkway
Lexington, KY
859-259-4257
There are many amenities at this beautiful park and a variety of activities and recreational pursuits. Dogs of all sizes are allowed at no additional fee. Dogs may not be left unattended, and they must be on no more than a 6 foot leash, and cleaned up after. The camping and tent areas also allow dogs. There is a dog walk area at the campground. Multiple dogs may be allowed.

Barren River Lake State Resort
1149 State Park Road
Lucas, KY
270-646-2151 (800-325-1709)

This beautiful park curves around the 10,000-acre lake, providing spectacular views and sunsets. It also offers nature trails, a regulation 18 hole golf course and a wide variety of land and water recreation. Dogs of all sizes are allowed at no additional fee. Dogs may not be left unattended, and they must be quiet, well behaved, leashed and cleaned up after. Dogs are not allowed in buildings. Dogs are allowed on the trails. This campground is closed during the off-season. The camping and tent areas also allow dogs. There is a dog walk area at the campground. Multiple dogs may be allowed.

Mammoth Cave National Park
1 Mammoth Cave Parkway
Mammoth Cave, KY
270-758-2180
nps.gov/maca/
Home to the longest cave system in the world with 365 miles currently explored, this park also shares some great places up top as well. More than 70 miles of forested trails lead visitors through a variety of habitats and scenery. Dogs are allowed throughout the park and the campgrounds; they are not allowed in buildings or on the cave tours. Dogs must be under their owner's control at all times. There are 3 developed campgrounds and several primitive sites along backcountry rivers, and they offer some or all of the following: potable water, grills, picnic tables, restrooms, showers, a camp store, laundry, and/or a dump station. The camping and tent areas also allow dogs. There is a dog walk area at the campground. There are no electric or water hookups at the campgrounds. Multiple dogs may be allowed.

Clay County Campground
83 Crawfish Road
Manchester, KY
606-598-3449
claycocampground.com
Dogs of all sizes are allowed. There are no additional pet fees. Dogs must be well behaved, leashed, and cleaned up after. Only one dog at a time can be in the cabins. This RV park is closed during the off-season. The camping and tent areas also allow dogs. There is a dog walk area at the campground. Dogs are allowed in the camping cabins.

Cumberland Gap National Historical Park
H 25E South
Middleboro, KY
606-248-2817
nps.gov/cuga/
Rich in natural and cultural history, this park is commemorated as the "doorway to the West", as it marks a major break in the formidable Appalachian Mountains. Within the park you will find a number of recreational pursuits and over 70 miles of trails. Dogs of all sizes are allowed at no additional fee. Dogs may not be left unattended unless they will be quiet and well behaved. Dogs must be leashed and cleaned up after. Dogs are allowed on the trails. The camping and tent areas also allow dogs. There is a dog walk area at the campground. There are no water hookups at the campground. Multiple dogs may be allowed.

Poppy Mountain Campground
8030 H 60E
Morehead, KY
606-780-4192
Dogs of all sizes are allowed. There are no additional pet fees. Dogs may not be in the stage area, and they must be leashed and cleaned up after. This RV park is closed during the off-season. The camping and tent areas also allow dogs. There is a dog walk area at the campground. Multiple dogs may be allowed.

Twin Knobs Rec Area
2375 Kentucky H
Morehead, KY
606-784-6428 (877-444-6777)
This recreation area, located on a 700-acre wooded peninsula, offers interpretive programs and land and water recreation. Dogs must be leashed and cleaned up after. Dogs are allowed on the trails, but not in the public swimming areas. This campground is closed during the off-season. The camping and tent areas also allow dogs. There is a dog walk area at the campground. There are no water hookups at the campground. Multiple dogs may be allowed.

Carter Caves State Resort Park
344 Caveland Drive
Olive Hill, KY
606-286-4411
Beneath this beautiful park with 26 miles of wooded nature trails lies a maze of caverns. Five of the 20 caves found here have been prepared for tours. Dogs are allowed throughout the park and camp area; they are not allowed on the cave tours or in the lodge or cottages. Dogs must be under their owner's control at all times. The camp area offers 89 sites, a dump station, restrooms, and showers. This RV park is closed during the off-season. The camping and tent areas also allow dogs. There is a dog walk area at the campground. Multiple dogs may be allowed.

Duck Creek RV Park & Campground
2540 John Puryear Drive
Paducah, KY
270-415-0404
duckcreekrvpark.com/
Dogs of all sizes are allowed. There are no additional pet fees. Dogs must be leashed and cleaned up after. The camping and tent areas also allow dogs. There is a dog walk area at the campground. Multiple dogs may be allowed.

Eagle Falls Resort
11251 H 90
Parker's Lake, KY
888-318-2658
eaglefallsresort.com
Dogs of all sizes are allowed, and there are no additional pet fees for tent or RV sites. There is a $10 per night per pet additional fee for the resort. Dogs must be leashed and cleaned up after. The camping and tent areas also allow dogs. There is a dog walk area at the campground. Multiple dogs may be allowed.

Jenny Wiley State Resort Park
75 Theatre Court
Prestonsburg, KY
606-889-1790 (800-325-0142)
Although known as a showcase for the performing arts, this park also offers numerous educational and recreational opportunities. Dogs are allowed throughout the park and in the campground; they are not allowed in the lodge or cabins. Dogs must be leashed and cleaned up after. The camp area offers 117 sites, restrooms, showers, a store, and a dump station. This RV park is closed during the off-season. The camping and tent areas also allow dogs. There is a dog walk area at the campground. Multiple dogs may be allowed.

Renfro Valley KOA
Red Foley Road, H 25
Renfro Valley, KY
606-256-2474 (800-562-2475)
koa.com
Dogs of all sizes are allowed. There are no additional pet fees. Dogs may not be left unattended outside except

for very short periods, and they must be leashed and cleaned up after. There are some breed restrictions. The camping and tent areas also allow dogs. There is a dog walk area at the campground. Dogs are allowed in the camping cabins.

Renfro Valley RV Park
Renfro Valley Entertainment Center
Renfro Valley, KY
606-256-2638 (800-765-7464)
renfrovalley.com
Dogs of all sizes are allowed. There are no additional pet fees. Dogs must be well behaved, leashed, and cleaned up after. There is a dog walk area at the campground. Multiple dogs may be allowed.

Ft. Boonesborough State Park
4375 Boonesborough Road/H 627
Richmond, KY
859-527-3131
Established by Daniel Boone as the state's 2nd settlement, this is a true working pioneer fort where many resident craftspersons help give visitors a glimpse of what early settlement life was like. There is also a self guided interpretive trail showcasing native plants, and prehistoric, geological, and historic sites. Dogs are allowed in the park and campground; they are not allowed in the fort. Dogs must be leashed and cleaned up after. The campground offers 167 sites, showers, restrooms, a laundry, and a grocery store. The camping and tent areas also allow dogs. There is a dog walk area at the campground. Multiple dogs may be allowed.

Russell Springs KOA
1440 H 1383
Russell Springs, KY
270-866-5616 (800-562-5617)
koa.com
Dogs of all sizes are allowed. There are no additional pet fees. Dogs must be quiet, leashed, and cleaned up after. This RV park is closed during the off-season. The camping and tent areas also allow dogs. There is a dog walk area at the campground. Multiple dogs may be allowed.

Carr Creek State Park
2086 Smithboro Road
Sassafras, KY
606-642-4050 (888-459-7275)
Featuring the longest lakefront sand beach in the Kentucky State Park system, this park offers a full service marina, and a variety of land and water recreation. Dogs of all sizes

are allowed at no additional fee. Dogs must have current tags and shot records, be leashed at all times, and cleaned up after. Dogs are not allowed on the beach or in park buildings. This campground is closed during the off-season. The camping and tent areas also allow dogs. There is a dog walk area at the campground. Multiple dogs may be allowed.

Louisville South KOA
2433 H 44E
Shepherdsville, KY
502-543-2041 (800-562-1880)
louisvillesouthkoa.com
Dogs of all sizes are allowed. There are no additional pet fees. Dogs may not be left unattended, and they must be leashed and cleaned up after. The camping and tent areas also allow dogs. There is a dog walk area at the campground. Dogs are allowed in the camping cabins. Multiple dogs may be allowed.

Natural Bridge State Resort Park
2135 Natural Bridge Road
Slade, KY
606-663-2214 (800-325-1710)
In addition to stellar scenery and the natural sandstone arch the park is named for, this recreational destination also offers a variety of land and water activities, planned events, educational opportunities, and a restaurant. Dogs are allowed in the parking lot and at the campground; they are not allowed on the trails. Dogs must be leashed and cleaned up after at all times. The campground has 94 sites (12 that are primitive), and offer restrooms, showers, and a dump station. This RV park is closed during the off-season. The camping and tent areas also allow dogs. There is a dog walk area at the campground. Multiple dogs may be allowed.

Big Bone Lick State Park
3380 Beaver Road
Union, KY
859-384-3522 (888-459-PARK (7275))
Visitors will get to experience a bit of pre-history at this park that has a boardwalk through recreated grasslands leading to a diorama showing the struggles of the woolly mammoths, giant sloth, bison, and others. There is also a thriving buffalo herd on site. Dogs are allowed throughout the grounds and campground for no additional fee.

Dogs must be current on all shots, leashed, and under their owner's control. The campground has 62 campsites and offers tables, grills, a swimming pool, playground, restrooms, showers, a grocery store, laundry facilities, and a dump station. This RV park is closed during the off-season. The camping and tent areas also allow dogs. There is a dog walk area at the campground. Multiple dogs may be allowed.

Daniel Boone National Forest
1700 Bypass Road/H 1958
Winchester, KY
859-745-3100
fs.fed.us/r8/boone/
This working forest features a rich cultural and natural history, more than 707,000 acres of beautiful rugged scenery, over 600 miles of trails, and an abundance of recreational opportunities. Dogs are allowed throughout the forest; they are not allowed in forest buildings. Dogs must be on no more than a 6 foot leash and cleaned up after at all times. Dogs may not be left unattended, and they are not allowed in beach swimming areas. Developed and primitive camping is available throughout the forest and may have some or all of the following: picnic tables, grills, drinking water, restrooms, showers, boating access, and/or a dump station. The camping and tent areas also allow dogs. There is a dog walk area at the campground. There are no water hookups at the campgrounds. Multiple dogs may be allowed.

Louisiana

Natalbany Creek Campground
30218 H 16
Amite, LA
985-747-9909
natalbanycreekcampground.com
Dogs of all sizes are allowed. There are no additional pet fees. Dogs may not be left unattended outside, and they must be leashed and cleaned up after. The camping and tent areas also allow dogs. There is a dog walk area at the campground. Multiple dogs may be allowed.

Cypress Black Bayou Recreation Area
135 Cypress Park Dr
Benton, LA

318-965-0007
cypressblackbayou.com/
There are plenty of recreational activities here with a great swimming place and a lush environment for camping and hiking. The nature center provides a variety of educational opportunities. Dogs are allowed throughout the park and at the campground; they are not allowed at the zoo, in or around the cabins, or at the main swimming beach. Dogs are allowed at the "doggy beach" area. Dogs must be leashed and cleaned up after. There are 73 campsites with 2 large comfort stations with showers; primitive camping is also available. The camping and tent areas also allow dogs. There is a dog walk area at the campground. Multiple dogs may be allowed.

Cash Point Landing
215 Cash Point Landing
Bossier City, LA
318-742-4999
cashpointlanding.com/
Dogs of all sizes are allowed. There are no additional pet fees. Dogs must be quiet, well behaved, leashed, and cleaned up after. Dogs may be off lead on your site if they are under voice control and will not chase. This is an RV only park. There is a dog walk area at the campground. Multiple dogs may be allowed.

St. Bernard State Park
501 St. Bernard Parkway
Braithwaite, LA
504-682-2101 (888-677-7823)
Wetlands meet woodlands at this recreational park with several man-made lagoons, a natural trail, and an abundance of bird and wildlife. Dogs are allowed throughout the park and in the campground for no additional fee. Dogs are not allowed in public swim areas, buildings, in the cabins, or on the walkways to the cabins. Dogs must be on no more than a 6 foot leash and under their owner's control at all times. The campground offers restrooms, showers, a playground, picnic tables, grills, and dump station. The camping and tent areas also allow dogs. There is a dog walk area at the campground. Multiple dogs may be allowed.

Bayou Wilderness RV Resort
201 St Claire Road
Carencro, LA
337-896-0598
bwrvr.com
Dogs of all sizes are allowed. There

are no additional pet fees. Dogs must be leashed and cleaned up after. There is a dog walk area at the campground. Multiple dogs may be allowed.

Jimmy Davis State Park (AKA-Caney Creek Lake State Park
1209 State Park Road
Chatham, LA
888-677-2263 (877-226-7652)
This peninsula park offers an interesting history, fishing, trails, and a host of land and water recreation. Dogs of all sizes are allowed at no additional fee. Dogs may not be left unattended, and they must be leashed at all times, and cleaned up after. Dogs are not allowed on the beach or in park buildings. Dogs are allowed on the trails. The camping and tent areas also allow dogs. There is a dog walk area at the campground. Multiple dogs may be allowed.

Red River Recreation Area
1 Recreation Park Road (Colfax Rec Area)
Colfax, LA
318-352-7446 (800-352-7446)
redriverwaterway.com
This major recreational destination offers land and marine activities for the whole family and is popular for naturalists, historians, and sports enthusiasts as well. There are 19 parks throughout the recreation area, each with its own special draw. Dogs are allowed throughout the parks and campgrounds for no additional fee; they must be on no more than a 6 foot leash and be cleaned up after. Dogs must display a current rabies inoculation tag to enter the park. The camp areas offer modern restrooms, showers, picnic tables on concrete, a fire ring, grill, lantern post, playground, a floating dock, and dump stations. The camping and tent areas also allow dogs. There is a dog walk area at the campground. Multiple dogs may be allowed.

Grand Bayou Resort
Rt 5, Box 11250
Coushatta, LA
877-932-3821
grandbayouresort.com
Dogs of all sizes are allowed. There are no additional pet fees. Dogs must be leashed and cleaned up after. The camping and tent areas also allow dogs. There is a dog walk area at the campground. Multiple dogs may be allowed.

Poverty Point Reservoir State Park
1500 Poverty Point Parkway
Delhi, LA
318-878-7536 (800-474-0392)
In addition to an abundance of fish, bird, and wildlife, this park features a 2,700 acre lake with a full service marina and concessionaires. Dogs are allowed throughout the park and in the campground for no additional fee. Dogs are not allowed in public swim areas, buildings, on their porches, in the cabins, or on the walkways to the cabins. Dogs must be on no more than a 6 foot leash and under their owner's control at all times. The campsite offers picnic areas, a playground, restrooms, and a dump station. The camping and tent areas also allow dogs. There is a dog walk area at the campground. Multiple dogs may be allowed.

Baton Rouge KOA
7628 Vincent Road
Denham Springs, LA
225-664-7281 (800-562-5673)
koa.com
Dogs of all sizes are allowed. There are no additional pet fees. Dogs may not be left unattended outside, and they must be leashed and cleaned up after. There are some breed restrictions. The camping and tent areas also allow dogs. There is a dog walk area at the campground. Multiple dogs may be allowed.

Lake Bistineau State Park
103 State Park Road
Doyline, LA
318-745-3503 (888-677-2478)
This park offers visitors a 30 acre lake, numerous recreational and educational opportunities, about 10 miles of scenic woodland trails and more. Dogs are allowed throughout the park and in the campground for no additional fee. Dogs are not allowed in public swim areas, buildings, on their porches, in the cabins, or on the walkways to the cabins. Dogs must be on no more than a 6 foot leash and under their owner's control at all times. The camp area offers comfort stations, showers, picnic areas, a playground, and dump station. The camping and tent areas also allow dogs. There is a dog walk area at the campground. Multiple dogs may be allowed.

Lake D'arbonne State Park
3628 Evergreen Road
Farmerville, LA
888-677-5200 (877-226-7652)
lastateparks.com/default.htm
This serene 665 acre park with a

lake of more than 15,000 acres puts its focus on natural beauty and offers a wide variety of land and water recreation. Dogs of all sizes are allowed at no additional fee. Dogs may not be left unattended, and they must be leashed and cleaned up after. Dogs are not allowed in buildings or in the screened in areas. Dogs are allowed on the trails. The camping and tent areas also allow dogs. There is a dog walk area at the campground. Multiple dogs may be allowed.

Kincaid Lake Rec Area
Valentine Lake Road
Gardner, LA
318-793-9427 (877-226-7652)
A variety of colorful trees add to the beauty of this park that offers miles of various scenic trails and a host of land and water recreation. The park is located in the Kisatchie National Forest in the Calcasieu district. Dogs of all sizes are allowed at no additional fee. Dogs may not be left unattended, and they must be leashed and cleaned up after. Dogs are allowed on the trails. The camping and tent areas also allow dogs. There is a dog walk area at the campground. Multiple dogs may be allowed.

Grand Isle State Park
Admiral Craik Drive
Grand Isle, LA
985-787-2550 (888-787-2559)
This popular barrier island park is a common fishing area with more than 280 species noted, and it's also a great place for birding and numerous recreational opportunities. Dogs are allowed throughout the park and in the campground for no additional fee. Dogs are not allowed in public swim areas, buildings, on their porches, in the cabins, or on the walkways to the cabins. Dogs must be on no more than a 6 foot leash and under their owner's control at all times. The camp area offers a comfort station, picnic areas, and dump station. The camping and tent areas also allow dogs. There is a dog walk area at the campground. Multiple dogs may be allowed.

New Orleans/Hammond KOA
14154 Club Deluxe Road
Hammond, LA
985-542-8094 (800-562-9394)
koa.com
Dogs of all sizes are allowed. There are no additional pet fees. Dogs may not be left unattended outside, and they must be leashed and cleaned

up after. There is a fenced in dog park for dogs to be off-leash. The camping and tent areas also allow dogs. There is a dog walk area at the campground. There are special amenities given to dogs at this campground. Multiple dogs may be allowed.

Lake Claiborne State Park
225 State Park Road
Homer, LA
888-677-2524 (877-226-7652)
lastateparks.com/default.htm
This park with a pristine lake of over 6,000 acres, offers scenic trails, long sandy beaches, and a variety of land and water activities and recreation. Dogs of all sizes are allowed at no additional fee. Dogs must be well behaved, be on no more than a 5 foot leash and cleaned up after. Dogs are not allowed in buildings; they are allowed on the trails. The camping and tent areas also allow dogs. There is a dog walk area at the campground. Multiple dogs may be allowed.

Acadian Village RV Park
200 Greenleaf Drive
Lafayette, LA
337-981-2364 (800-962-9133)
acadianvillage.org/index.htm
This recreated 1800's Cajun village with 11 authentic homes displays remarkable examples of Acadian workmanship. Dogs are allowed throughout the grounds and in the camp area for no additional fee. Dogs must be leashed and cleaned up after. The campground offers 40 tree-shaded sites with restroom facilities (closes at 4 pm daily) and dump sites. Fees must be paid in advance at the General Store located in the village. The camping and tent areas also allow dogs. There is a dog walk area at the campground. 2 dogs may be allowed.

Jellystone Park
4200 Luke Powers Road
Lake Charles, LA
337-433-1114 (877-433-2400)
jellystonelcla.com
Dogs of all sizes are allowed. There are no additional pet fees. Dogs must be leashed and cleaned up after. The camping and tent areas also allow dogs. There is a dog walk area at the campground. Multiple dogs may be allowed.

Sam Houston Jones State Park
107 Sutherland Road

Lake Charles, LA
337-855-2665 (888-677-7264)
Named after one of the state's folk heroes, this 1,087 acre park offers a scenic natural park with an abundance of bird and wildlife, a mixed pine and hardwood forest, numerous waterways, and picturesque hiking trails to explore it all. Dogs are allowed throughout the park and in the campground for no additional fee. Dogs are not allowed in public swim areas, buildings, in the cabins, or on the walkways to the cabins. Dogs must be on no more than a 6 foot leash and under their owner's control at all times. The campground offers restrooms, showers, a playground, and dump station. The camping and tent areas also allow dogs. There is a dog walk area at the campground. Multiple dogs may be allowed.

Lake Fausse Pointe State Park
5400 Levee Road/Park Road 169
Martinville, LA
337-229-4764 (888-677-7200)
This 6,000 acre recreational destination shares a long diverse cultural and natural history with visitors as well. Dogs are allowed throughout the park and in the campground for no additional fee. Dogs are not allowed in public swim areas, buildings, on their porches, in the cabins, or on the walkways to the cabins. Dogs must be on no more than a 6 foot leash and under their owner's control at all times. The campground offer sites from primitive to full service. The camping and tent areas also allow dogs. There is a dog walk area at the campground. Multiple dogs may be allowed.

Caney Lakes Rec Area
194 Caney Lake Road
Minden, LA
318-927-2061
fs.fed.us/r8/kisatchie/caney-rd/
This park offers a variety of landscapes, from the National Sugar Cane Recreation Trail to two completely different types of lakes for recreation. Dogs of all sizes are allowed at no additional fee. Dogs may not be left unattended, and they must be leashed and cleaned up after. Dogs are allowed on the trails. The camping and tent areas also allow dogs. There is a dog walk area at the campground. Multiple dogs may be allowed.

Kisatchie National Forest
2500 Shreveport H/H 71
Pineville, LA

318-473-7160
Covering 604,000 acres in 7 parishes and overseen by 5 Ranger Districts, this working forest offers numerous recreational, sporting, educational, and naturalist activities. Dogs are allowed throughout the forest and in the camp areas for no additional fees. Dogs must be leashed and under their owner's control at all times. The camp areas are varied and may offer some or all of the following: lakeside sites, picnic tables, lantern posts, fire rings, grills, flush or vault toilets, or potable water. The camping and tent areas also allow dogs. There is a dog walk area at the campground. There are no water hookups at the campgrounds. Multiple dogs may be allowed.

Cajun Country Campground
4667 Relle Lane
Port Allen, LA
800-264-8554
Dogs of all sizes are allowed. There are no additional pet fees. Dogs must be leashed and cleaned up after. There is a dog walk area at the campground. Multiple dogs may be allowed.

Jellystone Park
46049 H 445
Robert, LA
985-542-1507 (800-349-YOGI (9644);)
jellystonela.com/
A family-style entertainment resort, this fun park offers unlimited use of mini-golf, pedal boats, canoes, and kayaks, plus they have a fishing pond, game room, playing fields/courts, a seasonal cartoon café, swimming pools, a store, and laundry facilities. Dogs of all sizes are allowed for no additional fee. They must be leashed and cleaned up after at all times. There are some breed restrictions. The camping and tent areas also allow dogs. There is a dog walk area at the campground. Multiple dogs may be allowed.

Lafayette KOA
537 Apollo Road
Scott, LA
337-235-2739 (800-562-0809)
koa.com
Dogs of all sizes are allowed. There are no additional pet fees. Dogs may not be left unattended outside, and they must be leashed and cleaned up after. The camping and tent areas also allow dogs. There is a dog walk area at the campground. Multiple dogs may be allowed.

Shreveport/Bossier KOA
6510 W 70th Street
Shreveport, LA
318-687-1010 (800-562-1232)
koa.com
Dogs of all sizes are allowed. There are no additional pet fees. Dogs may not be left unattended outside, and they must be leashed and cleaned up after. There are some breed restrictions. The camping and tent areas also allow dogs. There is a dog walk area at the campground. Dogs are allowed in the camping cabins. Multiple dogs may be allowed.

Fausse Point State Park and Canoe Trail
5400 Levee Road/PR-169
St Martinville, LA
337-229-4764 (888-677-7200)
In addition to a wide range of land and water recreational activities at this 6,000 acre site, there are also cultural, natural, and historical educational opportunities. Dogs are allowed throughout the park and in the campground for no additional fee. They are also allowed on boat and canoe rentals. Dogs are not allowed in public swim areas, buildings, on their porches, in the cabins, or on the walkways to the cabins. Dogs must be on no more than a 6 foot leash and under their owner's control at all times. The campground offers more than 100 serviced and primitive sites with modern restrooms and a dump station. The camping and tent areas also allow dogs. There is a dog walk area at the campground. There are no water hookups at the campgrounds. Multiple dogs may be allowed.

Bayou Boeuf RV Park
11791 H 165 N
Sterlington, LA
318-665-2405
Dogs of all sizes are allowed. There are no additional pet fees. Dogs must be quiet, well behaved, leashed, and cleaned up after. The camping and tent areas also allow dogs. There is a dog walk area at the campground. Multiple dogs may be allowed.

Hidden Ponds RV Park
1207 Ravia Road
Sulphur, LA
337-583-4709
hiddenpondsrvpark.com
Dogs of all sizes are allowed. There are no additional pet fees. Dogs

may not be left unattended outside, and they must be leashed and cleaned up after. There is a dog walk area at the campground. Multiple dogs may be allowed.

River View RV Park and Resort
100 River View Parkway
Vidalia, LA
318-336-1400
riverviewrvpark.com/
Dogs of all sizes are allowed. There are no additional pet fees. Dogs must be leashed and cleaned up after. The camping and tent areas also allow dogs. There is a dog walk area at the campground. Multiple dogs may be allowed.

Chicot State Park
3469 Chicot Park Road
Ville Platte, LA
337-363-2403 (888-677-2442)
This recreational destination covers more than 6,400 acres and offers a clear water lake and extensive multi-use trails to explore. Dogs are allowed throughout the park and in the campground for no additional fee. Dogs are not allowed in public swim areas, buildings, on their porches, in the cabins, or on the walkways to the cabins. Dogs must be on no more than a 6 foot leash and under their owner's control at all times. The camp areas range from primitive to serviced sites and offer picnic areas, a playground, a fishing pier, and comfort stations. The camping and tent areas also allow dogs. There is a dog walk area at the campground. Multiple dogs may be allowed.

Cheniere Lake Park
104 Cheniere Lake Road
West Monroe, LA
318-387-2383
This recreational destination offers a variety of land and water activities, an abundance of bird, marine, and wildlife, and a beautiful natural environment to explore. Dogs are allowed in the park and camp area for no additional fee. Dogs must be leashed and cleaned up after at all times. The camp area offers a laundry and modern bath facilities. The camping and tent areas also allow dogs. There is a dog walk area at the campground. Multiple dogs may be allowed.

Maine

Balsam Woods
112 Pond Road
Abbot, ME
207-876-2731
balsamwoods.com
Dogs of all sizes are allowed. There are no additional pet fees. Dogs must be leashed and cleaned up after. This RV park is closed during the off-season. The camping and tent areas also allow dogs. There is a dog walk area at the campground. Dogs are allowed in the camping cabins. Multiple dogs may be allowed.

Walnut Grove Campground
599 Gore Road
Alfred, ME
207-324-1207
walnutgrovecampground.net
Dogs of all sizes are allowed. There are no additional pet fees. Dogs must be leashed and cleaned up after. Visitor pets are not allowed. Dogs must have current rabies records. This RV park is closed during the off-season. Only one dog is allowed per campsite. The camping and tent areas also allow dogs. There is a dog walk area at the campground.

Hemlock Grove Campground
1299 Portland Road
Arundel, ME
207-985-0398
hemlockgrovecampground.com/
Dogs of all sizes are allowed. There are no additional pet fees. Dogs can be left unattended only if they are quiet, well behaved, and comfortable with owner's absence. They must be left in the tent or RV. Dogs must be leashed at all times and cleaned up after. This RV park is closed during the off-season. The camping and tent areas also allow dogs. There is a dog walk area at the campground. 2 dogs may be allowed.

Paul Bunyan Campground
1862 Union Street
Bangor, ME
207-941-1177
paulbunyancampground.com
Dogs of all sizes are allowed. There are no additional pet fees. Dogs must be leashed and cleaned up after. This RV park is closed during the off-season. The camping and tent areas also allow dogs. There is a dog walk area at the campground.

Spruce Valley Campground
136 County Road
Bar Harbor, ME
207-288-5139
barharborkoa.com
Dogs of all sizes are allowed. There are no additional pet fees. Dogs may not be left unattended, must be leashed, and cleaned up after. This RV park is closed during the off-season. The camping and tent areas also allow dogs. There is a dog walk area at the campground. Multiple dogs may be allowed.

Beaver Dam Campground
551 H 9
Boothbay, ME
207-698-2267
beaverdamcampground.com
Dogs of all sizes are allowed. There are no additional pet fees. Dogs may not be left unattended, must be leashed at all times, and cleaned up after. Dogs are not allowed at the playground or the beach. This RV park is closed during the off-season. The camping and tent areas also allow dogs. There is a dog walk area at the campground. Multiple dogs may be allowed.

Little Ponderosa Campground
159 Wiscasset Road
Boothbay, ME
207-633-2700
littleponderosa.com
Dogs of all sizes are allowed. There are no additional pet fees. Dogs may not be left unattended unless they are well behaved and will be quiet, and then only inside your unit for short periods. Dogs must be leashed and cleaned up after. This RV park is closed during the off-season. The camping and tent areas also allow dogs. There is a dog walk area at the campground. Multiple dogs may be allowed.

Shore Hills Campground
553 Wiscaffet Road
Boothbay, ME
207-633-4782
shorehillscampground.com
Dogs of all sizes are allowed. There are no additional pet fees. Dogs may not be left unattended, must be leashed, and cleaned up after. This RV park is closed during the off-season. The camping and tent areas also allow dogs. There is a dog walk area at the campground. Multiple dogs may be allowed.

Camden Hills State Park
280 Belfast Road
Camden, ME
207-236-3109
This park is a year round recreational destination providing cross-country skiing in winter and more than 30 miles of hiking trails that can be accessed from 5 major trailheads at other parts of the year, and there is a scenic auto drive up Mount Battie for some fantastic views. Dogs must be well behaved under their owner's control, leashed, and cleaned up after at all times. They are very strict about pets being on leash and dogs may not be left unattended. The 107 site campground offers hot showers, picnic areas, and flush toilets. This RV park is closed during the off-season. The camping and tent areas also allow dogs. There is a dog walk area at the campground. There are no electric or water hookups at the campgrounds. Multiple dogs may be allowed.

Skowhegan/Canaan
18 Cabin Row
Canaan, ME
207-474-2858
smorefuncampground.com
Dogs of all sizes are allowed and they are allowed in the cabins with a credit card on file. There are no additional pet fees. Dogs must be quiet and well behaved. Dogs may not be left unattended, must be leashed, and cleaned up after. Dogs are not allowed in the buildings, the pavilion, the pool or playground. This RV park is closed during the off-season. The camping and tent areas also allow dogs. There is a dog walk area at the campground. Dogs are allowed in the camping cabins.

Lake Pemaquid Camping
100 Twin Cove Lane
Damariscotta, ME
207-563-5202
lakepemaquid.com
Dogs of all sizes are allowed. There are no additional pet fees. Dogs must be quiet, leashed, and cleaned up after. This RV park is closed during the off-season. The camping and tent areas also allow dogs. There is a dog walk area at the campground. Dogs are allowed in the camping cabins. Multiple dogs may be allowed.

Cobscook Bay State Park
RR#1
Dennysville, ME
207-726-4412
This peninsula park offers visitors excellent vantage points to view the

ebb and flow of the tides of Whiting Bay, scenic hiking trails, groomed x-country trails in winter, and it is a popular clamming destination as well. Dogs of all sizes are allowed for no additional fee. Dogs may not be left unattended at any time, and they must be on no more than a 4 foot leash and cleaned up after. Dogs must be quiet and well mannered. There are more than 100 secluded, well maintained sites, and most of the campsites are located along the water's edge. There are picnic sites, restrooms, and hot showers available. This RV park is closed during the off-season. The camping and tent areas also allow dogs. There is a dog walk area at the campground. There are no electric or water hookups at the campgrounds. 2 dogs may be allowed.

Peaks-Kenny State Park
401 State Park Road
Dover-Foxcroft, ME
207-564-2003
Dogs of all sizes are allowed. There are no additional pet fees. Dogs may not be left unattended, and they must be leashed and cleaned up after at all times. Dogs are not allowed on the beach, the gravel, in the water, or the picnic areas. Dogs can be on the grass at the beach area and on all the trails. This campground is closed during the off-season. The camping and tent areas also allow dogs. There is a dog walk area at the campground. There are no electric or water hookups at the campground. Multiple dogs may be allowed.

Freeport/Durham KOA
82 Big Skye Lane
Durham, ME
207-688-4288 (888-562-5609)
freeportkoa.com
Dogs of all sizes are allowed, and there are no additional pet fees for tent or RV sites. There is a $10 one time additional pet fee for cabin rentals. Dogs must be quiet, leashed, and cleaned up after. There are some breed restrictions. This RV park is closed during the off-season. The camping and tent areas also allow dogs. There is a dog walk area at the campground. Dogs are allowed in the camping cabins. Multiple dogs may be allowed.

Lamoine State Park
23 State Park Road
Ellsworth, ME
207-667-4778 (207-287-3824 (out of state res.))
Dogs of all sizes are allowed. There

are no additional pet fees. Dogs may not be left unattended at any time, and they must be quiet, be on no more than a 4 foot leash, and be cleaned up after. Dogs may be off lead on your own site if they will stay on site, and they are well behaved and under voice command. There are no dump stations at this park. This campground is closed during the off-season. The camping and tent areas also allow dogs. There is a dog walk area at the campground. There are no electric or water hookups at the campground. Multiple dogs may be allowed.

Cedar Haven Campground
39 Baker Road
Freeport, ME
207-865-6254
campmaine.com/cedar haven
Well behaved dogs of all sizes are allowed. There are no additional pet fees. Dogs may not be left unattended, must be leashed, and cleaned up after. There is a pond for dogs to swim in at which time they can be off lead if they are under voice control. No excessive barking is allowed. This RV park is closed during the off-season. The camping and tent areas also allow dogs. There is a dog walk area at the campground. Dogs are allowed in the camping cabins.

Lily Bay State Park
Lily Bay Road
Greenville, ME
207-695-2700
Dogs of all sizes are allowed. There are no additional pet fees. Dogs may not be left unattended, and they must be leashed and cleaned up after. Dogs are allowed on all of the trails. This park has 2 campgrounds, and one usually closes up for the season earlier than the other. This campground is closed during the off-season. The camping and tent areas also allow dogs. There is a dog walk area at the campground. There are no electric or water hookups at the campground. Multiple dogs may be allowed.

Paul Bunyan's Wheeler Stream Campground
2202 H 2
Hermon, ME
207-848-7877
Dogs of all sizes are allowed. There are no additional pet fees. Dogs may not be left unattended, must be leashed, and cleaned up after. This

RV park is closed during the off-season. The camping and tent areas also allow dogs. There is a dog walk area at the campground. Multiple dogs may be allowed.

Pumpkin Patch
149 Billings Road
Hermon, ME
207-848-2231
pumpkinpatchry.com
Dogs of all sizes are allowed, and they are greeted here with a bone or other doggy treat when they come. There are no additional pet fees. Dogs must be leashed and cleaned up after. There are some breed restrictions. This RV park is closed during the off-season. The camping and tent areas also allow dogs. There is a dog walk area at the campground. There are special amenities given to dogs at this campground. Multiple dogs may be allowed.

Red Barn Campground
602 Main Road
Holden, ME
207-843-6011
redbarnmaine.com
Dogs of all sizes are allowed. There are no additional pet fees. Dogs may not be left unattended, be leashed, and cleaned up after. Dogs may not be in any of the buildings. This RV park is closed during the off-season. The camping and tent areas also allow dogs. There is a dog walk area at the campground. Multiple dogs may be allowed.

My Brother's Place Campground
659 North Street
Houlton, ME
207-532-6739
mainerec.com/mybro.html
Dogs of all sizes are allowed, however the cabins will only accept 1 dog up to 50 pounds. There are no additional pet fees. Dogs may not be left unattended, must be leashed, and cleaned up after. This RV park is closed during the off-season. The camping and tent areas also allow dogs. There is a dog walk area at the campground. Dogs are allowed in the camping cabins.

Red Apple Campground
111 Sinnott Road
Kennebunkport, ME
207-967-4927
redapplecampground.com
Dogs of all sizes are allowed. There are no additional pet fees. Dogs may not be left unattended, must be leashed, and cleaned up after. This

RV park is closed during the off-season. The camping and tent areas also allow dogs. There is a dog walk area at the campground. Multiple dogs may be allowed.

Katahdin Shadows Campground and Cabins
H 157
Medway, ME
207-746-9349
katahdinshadows.com
Dogs of all sizes are allowed. There are no additional pet fees. Dogs may not be left unattended, must be leashed, and cleaned up after. This campground is open through the winter and closes for only one month in April. This RV park is closed during the off-season. The camping and tent areas also allow dogs. There is a dog walk area at the campground. Dogs are allowed in the camping cabins. Multiple dogs may be allowed.

Naples Campground
295 Sebago Road
Naples, ME
207-693-5267
naplescampground.com
Dogs of all sizes are allowed. There are no additional pet fees. Dogs must be friendly, not left unattended, be leashed, and cleanded up after. Dogs are not allowed in the rentals. This RV park is closed during the off-season. The camping and tent areas also allow dogs. There is a dog walk area at the campground. 2 dogs may be allowed.

Lakeside Pines Campground
54 Lakeside Pines Road
North Bridgton, ME
207-647-3935
lakesidecamping.com
Dogs of all sizes are allowed. There are no additional pet fees. Dogs must be up to date on their shots. Some breeds are not allowed. Dogs are not allowed in the rentals or on the beach. Dogs must be leashed and cleaned up after. This RV park is closed during the off-season. The camping and tent areas also allow dogs. There is a dog walk area at the campground. Multiple dogs may be allowed.

Beaver Brook Campground
RFD 1 Box 1835 Wilson Pond Roa
North Monmouth, ME
207-933-2108
beaver-brook.com
Dogs of all sizes are allowed. There are no additional pet fees. Dogs must be leashed and cleaned up

after. Dogs can be off leash to go swimming at the lake as long as they are under owner's control. This RV park is closed during the off-season. The camping and tent areas also allow dogs. There is a dog walk area at the campground. 2 dogs may be allowed.

Hid'n Pines Family Campground
8 Cascade Road
Old Orchard Beach, ME
207-934-2352
hidnpines.com
A maximum of two dogs are allowed. There is a pet policy to sign at check in and there is a $1 per day additional pet fee per dog. Dogs may not be left unattended at any time and must be leashed and cleaned up after. Dogs are not allowed in the pool or bathroom areas. This RV park is closed from Labor Day to the beginning of May. There is a dog walk area at the campground.

Powder Horn Family Camping Resort
48 Cascade Road
Old Orchard Beach, ME
207-934-4733
mainecampgrounds.com
Dogs of all sizes are allowed. There is a pet policy to sign at check in and there are a $1 per day additional pet fee. Dogs may not be left unattended at any time, and they are not allowed at the tents, buildings, or common areas. This RV park is open from Mother's Day weekend until Columbus Day.

Wild Acres Family Camping Resort
179 Saco Avenue
Old Orchard Beach, ME
207-934-2535
mainecamping.com
Dogs of all sizes are allowed. There are no additional pet fees. There is a pet policy to sign at check in and there are no additional fees. Dogs may not be left unattended, be leashed, and cleaned up after. This RV park is closed during the off-season. The camping and tent areas also allow dogs. There is a dog walk area at the campground. Multiple dogs may be allowed.

Orr's Island Campground
44 Bond Point Road
Orrs Island, ME
207-833-5595
orrsisland.com/contact.htm
This full-service coastal campground offers 70 open or wooded sites for RV camping only.

One dog is allowed per site for no additional fee. Dogs must be quiet, leashed, cleaned up after, and they may not be left unattended at any time. They are allowed throughout the park and on the trails. This RV park is closed during the off-season. There is a dog walk area at the campground.

Meadowbrook Camping
33 Meadowbrook Road
Phippsburg, ME
207-443-4967
meadowbrookme.com
Dogs of all sizes are allowed. There are no additional pet fees. Dogs may not be left unattended, must be leashed, and cleaned up after. Dogs are not allowed in the rentals. The camping and tent areas also allow dogs. There is a dog walk area at the campground. Multiple dogs may be allowed.

Blueberry Pond Camping
218 Poland Range Road
Pownal, ME
207-688-4421
blueberrycampground.com
Dogs of all sizes are allowed. There are no additional pet fees. Dogs must be well behaved, leashed, and cleaned up after. This RV park is closed during the off-season. The camping and tent areas also allow dogs. There is a dog walk area at the campground. Dogs are allowed in the camping cabins. Multiple dogs may be allowed.

Bradbury Mountain State Park
528 Hallowell Road/H9
Pownal, ME
207-688-4712
Home to a wide variety of flora and fauna, this 590 acre forested park also features many recreational opportunities, great views from the summit, and a variety of multi-use trails. Dogs are allowed for no additional pet fee. Dogs must be well behaved, on no more than a 4 foot leash, cleaned up after at all times, and never be left unattended. Dogs are allowed throughout the park and on the trails; they are not allowed on the beaches. The camp area offers 41 sites, restrooms, a playground, ball fields, picnic tables, and grills. The camping and tent areas also allow dogs. There is a dog walk area at the campground. There are no electric or water hookups at the campgrounds. Multiple dogs may be allowed.

Rangeley Lake State Park

South Shore Drive
Rangeley, ME
207-864-3858
Dogs of all sizes are allowed. There are no additional pet fees. Dogs may not be left unattended, and they must be well behaved, leashed at all times, and be cleaned up after. Dogs are allowed on all the trails in the park. This campground is closed during the off-season. The camping and tent areas also allow dogs. There is a dog walk area at the campground. There are no electric or water hookups at the campground. Multiple dogs may be allowed.

Augusta/Gardiner KOA
30 Mallard Drive
Richmond, ME
207-582-5086 (800-562-1496)
koa.com
Dogs of all sizes are allowed. There are no additional pet fees. There is only one pet friendly cabin available, so early booking would be advised. Dogs must be leashed and cleaned up after. There are some breed restrictions. This RV park is closed during the off-season. The camping and tent areas also allow dogs. There is a dog walk area at the campground. Dogs are allowed in the camping cabins. Multiple dogs may be allowed.

Camden Hills RV Resort
30 Applewood Road
Rockport, ME
207-236-2498
camdenhillsrv.com
Dogs of all sizes are allowed. There are no additional pet fees. Dogs may not be left unattended, must be leashed, and cleaned up after. This RV park is closed during the off-season. There is a dog walk area at the campground. 2 dogs may be allowed.

Megunticook Campground
On H 1
Rockport, ME
207-594-2428
campgroundbythesea.com
Dogs of all sizes are allowed. There are no additional pet fees. Dogs must be quiet and well behaved. Dogs may not be left unattended, must be leashed, and cleaned up after. There are some breed restrictions. This RV park is closed during the off-season. The camping and tent areas also allow dogs. There is a dog walk area at the campground. Dogs are allowed in the camping cabins. Multiple dogs may be allowed.

KOA Saco/Portland South
814 Portland Road
Saco, ME
207-282-0502 (800-562-1886)
sacokoa.com
Dogs of all sizes are allowed, and there are no additional pet fees for tent or RV sites. There is a $15 one time fee plus a $100 refundable pet deposit for cabin rentals. Dogs may not be left unattended, must be leashed, and cleaned up after. This RV park is closed during the off-season. The camping and tent areas also allow dogs. There is a dog walk area at the campground. Dogs are allowed in the camping cabins. Multiple dogs may be allowed.

Bayley's Camping Resort
275 Pine Point Road
Scarborough, ME
207-883-6043
bayleys-camping.com
Dogs of all sizes are allowed. There is a pet policy to sign at check in and there are no additional pet fees. Dogs may not be left unattended, must be leashed, and cleaned up after. This RV park has many special weekends and events such has Father's Day and Halloween. This RV park is closed during the off-season. The camping and tent areas also allow dogs. There is a dog walk area at the campground. Multiple dogs may be allowed.

Wassamki Springs
56 Soco Street
Scarborough, ME
207-839-4276
wassamkisprings.com
Well behaved dogs of all sizes are allowed. There are no additional pet fees. Dogs may not be left unattended, must be leashed, and cleaned up after. There are some breed restrictions. This RV park is closed during the off-season. There is a dog walk area at the campground. 2 dogs may be allowed.

Old Quarry Campground
130 Settlement Road
Stonington, ME
207-367-9877
This camp area gives access to the Maine shoreline and plenty of hiking opportunities. They also offer dog friendly kayak rentals. There are hot showers, a laundry, Wi-Fi (fee), swimming pond, and a camp store in the campground. Responsible owners are allowed to bring their

dogs for no additional fee. Dogs must be quiet, well behaved, leashed, and cleaned up after at all times. The camping and tent areas also allow dogs. There is a dog walk area at the campground. There are no electric or water hookups at the campgrounds. 2 dogs may be allowed.

Timberland Acres Campground
57 Bar Harbor
Trenton, ME
207-667-3600
Dogs of all sizes are allowed. There are no additional pet fees. Dogs may not be left unattended, must be leashed, and cleaned up after. This RV park is closed during the off-season. The camping and tent areas also allow dogs. There is a dog walk area at the campground. 2 dogs may be allowed.

Mt Blue State Park
299 Center Hill Road
Weld, ME
207-585-2347
Dogs of all sizes are allowed. There are no additional pet fees. Dogs may not be left unattended at any time, and they must be leashed and cleaned up after. Dogs are not allowed on Webb Beach, or anywhere on the sand, but they may go up to the tree line at the beach. Dogs are allowed on leash throughout the park, and at the boat launch area for swimming. The camping and tent areas also allow dogs. There is a dog walk area at the campground. There are no electric or water hookups at the campground. 2 dogs may be allowed.

Sea-Vu Campground
1733 Post Road
Wells, ME
207-646-7732
sea-vucampground.com
Dogs of all sizes are allowed. There are no additional pet fees. Dogs must be leashed and cleaned up after. This RV park is closed during the off-season. The camping and tent areas also allow dogs. There is a dog walk area at the campground. Multiple dogs may be allowed.

Well Beach Resort
1000 Post Road
Wells, ME
207-646-7570
wellsbeach.com
Dogs of all sizes are allowed. There are no additional pet fees for 2 pets per site. There is a $7 per night per pet additional fee if over 2 dogs.

Dogs must be leashed and cleaned up after. This RV park is closed during the off-season. There is a dog walk area at the campground. Multiple dogs may be allowed.

Augusta West Lakeside Resort
183 Holmes Brook Lane
Winthrop, ME
207-377-9993
Dogs of all sizes are allowed. There is a $4 per pet per stay additional fee. Dogs may not be left unattended, must be leashed, and cleaned up after. Dogs are also not allowed at the beach or the pool. This RV park is closed during the off-season. The camping and tent areas also allow dogs. There is a dog walk area at the campground. 2 dogs may be allowed.

Libby's Oceanside Camp
725 York Street
York Harbor, ME
207-363-4171
libbysoceancamping.com
Dogs of all sizes are allowed. There are no additional pet fees. Dogs must be leashed and cleaned up after. Dogs are allowed to go to the beach before 8AM and after 6PM. This RV park is closed during the off-season. The camping and tent areas also allow dogs. There is a dog walk area at the campground. 2 dogs may be allowed.

Maryland

Assateague Island National Seashore
7206 National Seashore Lane
Assateague Island, MD
410-641-1441 (877-444-6777)
nps.gov/asis/
This undeveloped barrier island park allots visitors educational as well as numerous land, water, and seaside recreational opportunities. Dogs are allowed in the Maryland portion of the National Seashore for day and overnight use for no additional fee. Dogs are allowed on the many unguarded beaches on the Maryland portion of the National Seashore. They are not allowed in the Maryland State Park, on the Virginia part of the island-(even in a vehicle), or north of the State Park to the Ocean City inlet. They may not be on life-guarded beaches or on nature trails. Dogs may not be left unattended, and they must be on no more than a

6 foot leash and cleaned up after at all times. The camp area includes chemical toilets, cold-water showers, picnic tables, grills, and water. The camping and tent areas also allow dogs. There is a dog walk area at the campground. There are no electric or water hookups at the campgrounds. Multiple dogs may be allowed.

Frontier Town
8428 Stephen Decatur H
Berlin, MD
410-641-0880
frontiertown.com
Friendly dogs of all sizes are allowed. There are no additional pet fees. Dogs may not be left unattended, must be leashed, and cleaned up after. Dogs are not allowed in the rentals. There are some breed restrictions. This RV park is closed during the off-season. The camping and tent areas also allow dogs. There is a dog walk area at the campground. 2 dogs may be allowed.

Fort Frederick State Park
11100 Fort Frederick Road
Big Pool, MD
301-842-2155 (888-432-CAMP (2267))
Restored to its original 1758 appearance, this site was the states frontier defense during the French and Indian War. There are interpretive activities depicting the historical significance of this site, a number of water and land recreational pursuits, and the Western Maryland Rail Trail is only a 1/ 2 mile from the fort. Dogs are allowed in the park for no additional fee; they are not allowed inside the fort, park buildings, or the picnic areas. Dogs are allowed on the trails, in other areas of the park, and at the campground. They must be leashed and cleaned up after at all times. The camp area offers a camp store and 29 primitive first come first serve sites with fire rings, tables, and portable toilets. The camping and tent areas also allow dogs. There is a dog walk area at the campground. There are no electric or water hookups at the campgrounds. Multiple dogs may be allowed.

Little Bennet Regional Park
23701 Frederick Road
Clarksburg, MD
301-972-9222
This scenic park of 3,600 acres and 20 miles of trails offers a variety of

activities and recreational pursuits. Dogs of all sizes are allowed at no additional fee. Dogs may not be left unattended, and they must be on no more than a 6 foot leash, and be cleaned up after. This campground is closed during the off-season. The camping and tent areas also allow dogs. There is a dog walk area at the campground. There are no water hookups at the campground. Multiple dogs may be allowed.

Cherry Hill Park
9800 Cherry Hill Road
College Park, MD
800-801-6449
cherryhillpark.com
Dogs of all sizes are allowed. There are no additional pet fees. Dogs must be well behaved, not be left unattended, be leashed, and cleaned up after. The camping and tent areas also allow dogs. There is a dog walk area at the campground. Multiple dogs may be allowed.

Patapsco Valley State Park
8020 Baltimore National Pike
Ellicott City, MD
410-461-5005 (888-432-CAMP (2267))
This scenic park of 14,000 acres runs along 32 miles of shoreline, and features the world's longest multiple-arched stone railroad bridge, a 300 foot suspension bridge, a variety of trails, and various land and water recreation. Dogs of all sizes are allowed at no additional fee. Dogs may not be left unattended outside, and they must be leashed and cleaned up after. Dogs are not allowed to use the trails at the main entrance of the park or to be in developed areas. They are allowed only on marked trails, on the road, or just outside the park. This campground is closed during the off-season. The camping and tent areas also allow dogs. There is a dog walk area at the campground. Multiple dogs may be allowed.

Greenridge State Forest
28700 Headquarters Drive NE
Flintstone, MD
301-478-3124
The second largest forest in the state, this 44,000-acre oak-hickory forest offers a variety of trails, various land and water recreation, and some scenic lookout points. Dogs of all sizes are allowed at no additional fee. Dogs may not be left unattended, they must be leashed, and cleaned up after in camp areas. Dogs are allowed on the trails. This

campground is closed during the off-season. The camping and tent areas also allow dogs. There is a dog walk area at the campground. There are no electric or water hookups at the campground. Multiple dogs may be allowed.

Rocky Gap State Park
12500 Pleasant Valley Road NE
Flintstone, MD
301-722-1480 (888-432-CAMP (2267))
A popular recreation destination, this 3,000+ acre park has a 243 acre lake surrounded by rugged, forested mountains, offers breathtaking views, and a variety of land and water activities. There are interpretive programs, areas for special events, and easy to challenging trails including a 4 ½ mile trail that encircles the lake and a mile-long gorge trail. Dogs are allowed on the trails, throughout the park, and in designated camp areas; they are not allowed on the beach. Dogs must be leashed and cleaned up after at all times. There are 278 campsites with restrooms, showers, a game room, laundry, camp store, fire rings, and a dump station is close by. This RV park is closed during the off-season. The camping and tent areas also allow dogs. There is a dog walk area at the campground. There are no water hookups at the campgrounds. Multiple dogs may be allowed.

Morris Meadows
1523 Freeland Road
Freeland, MD
410-329-6636
morrismeadows.us
Dogs of all sizes are allowed. There are no additional pet fees. Dogs must have current shot records, may not be left unattended, and must be on no more than a 6 foot leash and cleaned up after. There are some breed restrictions. The camping and tent areas also allow dogs. There is a dog walk area at the campground. 2 dogs may be allowed.

Big Run State Park
349 Headquarters Lane
Grantsville, MD
301-895-5453 (888-432-CAMP (2267))
This park of about 300 acres offers land and water recreation, but by being surrounded by the Savage River State Forest, visitors are offered an even wider variety of options. Dogs of all sizes are allowed at no additional fee. Dogs may not be left unattended, and they must be

leashed and cleaned up after. Dogs are allowed on the trails. The camping and tent areas also allow dogs. There is a dog walk area at the campground. There are no electric or water hookups at the campground. Multiple dogs may be allowed.

Savage River State Forest
127 Headquarters Lane
Grantsville, MD
301-895-5759
Over 12,000 acres of this 54,000 acre forest has been designated wildlands. It is the largest facility in the state forest system, it preserves an important watershed area, and there are a variety of trails (maps available at the office) and recreational opportunities. Dogs of all sizes are allowed throughout the park, in the camp area, and on the trails. There is no additional pet fee. Dogs must be leashed and cleaned up after at all times. Fifty-two primitive, self-registering roadside campsites with fire rings and picnic tables are available on a first come first served basis. The camping and tent areas also allow dogs. There is a dog walk area at the campground. There are no water hookups at the campgrounds. Multiple dogs may be allowed.

Susquehanna State Park
4122 Wilkinson Road
Havre de Grace, MD
410-557-7994 (888-432-2267)
Rich in historical significance and recreational opportunities, this forested, river valley park offers a variety of trails to explore, a working grist mill, and an archery range. Dogs of all sizes are allowed throughout the park for no additional fee. Dogs must be leashed and cleaned up after at all times. Dogs are not allowed in picnic or historic areas or at the cabins. The campground offers 69 sites with picnic tables, grills, comfort stations, hot showers, a playground, and an amphitheater. This RV park is closed during the off-season. The camping and tent areas also allow dogs. There is a dog walk area at the campground. There are no water hookups at the campgrounds. 2 dogs may be allowed.

Susquehanna State Park
3318 Rocks Chrome Hill Road
Jarrettsville, MD
410-557-7994 (888-432-CAMP (2267))

A variety of land and water recreation, and a wide range of trails varying in length and difficulty greet visitors at this park. Dogs of all sizes are allowed at no additional fee. Dogs may not be left unattended, and they must be on no more than a 10 foot leash, and be cleaned up after. Dogs are not allowed in picnic areas or buildings. Dogs are allowed on the trails. This campground is closed during the off-season. The camping and tent areas also allow dogs. There is a dog walk area at the campground. There are no water hookups at the campground. Multiple dogs may be allowed.

Duncan's Family Campground
5381 Sands Beach Road
Lothian, MD
410-741-9558
duncansfamilycampground.com
Dogs of all sizes are allowed. There are no additional pet fees. Dogs must be quiet, leashed, and cleaned up after. Dogs may not be left tied up at the site. The camping and tent areas also allow dogs. There is a dog walk area at the campground. Multiple dogs may be allowed.

Washington DC - NE KOA
768 Cecil Avenue N
Millersville, MD
410-923-2771 (800-562-0248)
koa.com
Dogs of all sizes are allowed. There are no additional pet fees. Dogs may not be left unattended, must be leashed, and cleaned up after. Dogs are not allowed at the lodge. This RV park is closed during the off-season. The camping and tent areas also allow dogs. There is a dog walk area at the campground. Dogs are allowed in the camping cabins. Multiple dogs may be allowed.

Roaring Point
2360 Nanticoke Wharf Road
Nanticoke, MD
410-873-2553
roaringpoint.com
Dogs of all sizes are allowed. There are no additional pet fees. Dogs must be well behaved, not left unattended, be leashed, and cleaned up after. This RV park is closed during the off-season. The camping and tent areas also allow dogs. There is a dog walk area at the campground.

Elk Neck State Park
4395 Turkey Point Road
North East, MD
410-287-5333 (888-432-CAMP

(2267))
This peninsula park is home to the Turkey Point Lighthouse, and offers a diversified topography for a variety of activities and recreation. Dogs of all sizes are allowed at no additional fee. Dogs may not be left unattended outside, and they must be leashed and cleaned up after. Dogs are not allowed on the beach, in buildings, or in day use areas. Dogs are allowed in the NE loop, at the "Y" pet area, and on the trails. The camping and tent areas also allow dogs. There is a dog walk area at the campground. Multiple dogs may be allowed.

Garrett State Forest
222 Herrington Lane
Oakland, MD
301-334-2038
This forest displays a wide variety of trees, abundant wildlife, glimpses of beaver ponds and cranberry bogs and provides various land and water recreation. Dogs of all sizes are allowed at no additional fee. Dogs may not be left unattended, and they may be off lead if they are well behaved and under voice control. Dogs are allowed on the trails. The camping and tent areas also allow dogs. There is a dog walk area at the campground. There are no electric or water hookups at the campground. Multiple dogs may be allowed.

Potomac State Forest
1431 Potomac Camp Road
Oakland, MD
301-334-2038
Mountains and valleys, forests and streams, overlooks displaying great views, primitive camping, and a variety of land and water recreational opportunities (including a 3-D archery range) are all available at this 11,535 acre forest, which also has the highest point of any other state forest at 3,220 feet. Dogs are allowed throughout the park, on the trails, and for overnight camping. Dogs must be under strict voice control or leashed, and cleaned up after at all times. Primitive camping is allowed at pre-existing campsites; new forging of campsites is prohibited. The camping and tent areas also allow dogs. There is a dog walk area at the campground. There are no electric or water hookups at the campgrounds. Multiple dogs may be allowed.

Swallow Falls State Park
222 Harrington Lane
Oakland, MD
301-387-6938 (888-432-CAMP

(2267))
Hike through old growth forest at this mountain park that is home to Maryland's highest waterfall, and some of the states most breathtaking scenery. Dogs are not allowed in the day use area or on the trails between the Saturday before Memorial Day and Labor Day. Dogs may not be left unattended outside, and they must be leashed and cleaned up after. This campground is closed during the off-season. The camping and tent areas also allow dogs. There is a dog walk area at the campground. Multiple dogs may be allowed.

Ocean City Campground
105 70th Street
Ocean City, MD
410-524-7601
occamping.com
Dogs of all sizes are allowed. There are no additional pet fees. Pets must be on a leash and exercised outside of the campground property. Dogs must be leashed and cleaned up after. Pets cannot be left unattended inside or outside of camper at any time. No pets in tents or RV's without air conditioning. The camping and tent areas also allow dogs. Multiple dogs may be allowed.

Tuckahoe State Park
13070 Crouse Mill Road
Queen Anne, MD
410-820-1668 (888-432-CAMP (2267))
This park offers a 60 acre lake, 20 miles of scenic multi-use trails, and an arboretum that encompasses 500 acres of park land with almost three miles of surfaced walkways featuring tagged native species of trees and shrubs. Dogs of all sizes are allowed at no additional fee. Dogs must be on leash, and when in camp, cleaned up after. Dogs are allowed on the trails, but not in the lake area. This campground is closed during the off-season. The camping and tent areas also allow dogs. There is a dog walk area at the campground. There are no water hookups at the campground. Multiple dogs may be allowed.

Point Lookout State Park
11175 Point Lookout Road
Scotland, MD
301-872-5688 (888-432-CAMP (2267))
Rich in folk lore, historical significance, recreation, and educational opportunities, this

beautiful peninsula park has much to offer. Dogs are allowed throughout the park and at certain designated areas for no additional fee. Although dogs are not allowed on the public swim beach, they are allowed on the "Pet Beach". Dogs are permitted in Malone Circle, Tulip Loop, Hoffman's Loop, Green's Point Loop, on the pavement part of the causeway, and on the beach (north of causeway) to the entrance of Tanner's Creek. Dogs are not allowed at picnic areas, day use areas, or on other trails. Dogs must be leashed and cleaned up after at all times. The campground offers a variety of camp sites, grills, picnic tables, a camp store, and a dump station. The camping and tent areas also allow dogs. There is a dog walk area at the campground.

Pocomoke River State Forest and Park
3461 Worcester Highway/H113
Snow Hill, MD
401-632-2566
888-432-CAMP (2267)
There is a long list of water and land recreational opportunities here in addition to being an ecology school-room with its stand of loblolly pine, the cypress swamps that border the Pocomoke River, and for the wide variety of plant, animal, bird life that make their home here. Dogs of all sizes are allowed for no additional fee at Milburn Landing; they are not allowed at Shad Landing. Only registered campers are to have pets in the park; day use only is not allowed. Dogs must be leashed and cleaned up after. The camp areas all have picnic tables and fire rings with hot water showers, flush toilets, a laundry tub, playground, and a dump station close by. The camping and tent areas also allow dogs. There is a dog walk area at the campground. There are no water hookups at the campgrounds. 2 dogs may be allowed.

Deep Creek Lake State Park
898 State Park Road
Swanton, MD
301-387-5563 (888-432-CAMP (2267))
This year round park offers an educational/interpretive center with hands on exhibits, trails varying from moderate to difficult, and a variety of land and water recreation. Dogs of all sizes are allowed at no additional fee. Dogs may not be left unattended, and they must be leashed and cleaned up after. Dogs

124

are not allowed in picnic, swim areas, or in buildings. Dogs are allowed on the trails. This campground is closed during the off-season. The camping and tent areas also allow dogs. There is a dog walk area at the campground. There are no water hookups at the campground. Multiple dogs may be allowed.

Taylors Island Family Campground
4362 Bay Shore Road
Taylors Island, MD
410-397-3275
Dogs of all sizes are allowed. There are no additional pet fees. Dogs may not be left unattended except for short periods, and they must be quiet, well behaved, leashed, and cleaned up after. The camping and tent areas also allow dogs. There is a dog walk area at the campground. Multiple dogs may be allowed.

Catoctin Mountain Park
6602 Foxville Road
Thurmont, MD
301-663-9388
nps.gov/cato/
This 5,810-acre hardwood forest park comes complete with rushing streams, scenic vistas, and a variety of recreational pursuits. Dogs of all sizes are allowed at no additional fee. Dogs may not be left unattended, and they must be quiet, be on no more than a 6 foot leash, and be cleaned up after. Dogs are allowed at Owens Creek Campground and on the trails. They are not allowed in camps 1, 2 and 4, the youth camp, or in the Adirondack backcountry shelters. Dogs are also not allowed at the waterfall in the adjoining state park, or left in the car at that location. This campground is closed during the off-season. The camping and tent areas also allow dogs. There is a dog walk area at the campground. There are no electric or water hookups at the campground. Multiple dogs may be allowed.

Grambrill State Park
14039 Catoctin Hollow Road
Thurmont, MD
301-271-7574 (888-432-CAMP (2267))
Some points of interests at this park of over 1,100 acres include 3 native stone scenic overlooks, a good variety of trails, interpretive programs, and a nature center. Dogs of all sizes are allowed at no additional fee. Dogs may not be left unattended, and they must be leashed and cleaned up after. Dogs

are allowed on the trails and throughout the park, unless otherwise posted. This campground is closed during the off-season. The camping and tent areas also allow dogs. There is a dog walk area at the campground. There are no water hookups at the campground. Multiple dogs may be allowed.

Fort Whaley
11224 Dale Road
Whaleysville, MD
410-641-9785
fortwhaley.com
Dogs of all sizes are allowed. There are no additional pet fees. Dogs must be well behaved, leashed, and cleaned up after. Dogs may only be left inside of your unit if there is air conditioning on and if they will be quiet. The camping and tent areas also allow dogs. There is a dog walk area at the campground. Multiple dogs may be allowed.

KOA Hagerstown/Snug Harbor
11759 Snug Harbor Lane
Williamsport, MD
301-223-7571
hagerstownkoa.com
Dogs of all sizes are allowed. There are no additional pet fees. Dogs must be quiet, be on no more than a 6 foot leash, and be cleaned up after. This RV park is closed during the off-season. The camping and tent areas also allow dogs. There is a dog walk area at the campground. Dogs are allowed in the camping cabins. Multiple dogs may be allowed.

Yogi Bear Jellystone Park
16519 Lappans Road
Williamsport, MD
800-421-7116
jellystonemaryland.com
Dogs of all sizes are allowed. There are no additional pet fees. Dogs must be leashed and cleaned up after. Dogs are not allowed at the cabins. The camping and tent areas also allow dogs. There is a dog walk area at the campground. 2 dogs may be allowed.

Ramblin Pines Campground
801 Hoods Mill Road
Woodbine, MD
410-795-5161 (800-550-8733)
ramblinpines.com
Dogs of all sizes are allowed. There are no additional pet fees. Dogs may not be left unattended, and they must be leashed and cleaned up after. There is a fenced in dog run area where pets may be off

lead. There are some breed restrictions. The camping and tent areas also allow dogs. There is a dog walk area at the campground. Multiple dogs may be allowed.

Massachusetts

Otter River State Forest
86 Winchendon Road
Baldwinville, MA
978-939-8962
Dogs of all sizes are allowed. There are no additional pet fees. Dogs may not be left unattended, and they must be leashed and cleaned up after. Dogs are allowed on all of the trails, but they are not allowed in the water. This campground is closed during the off-season. The camping and tent areas also allow dogs. There is a dog walk area at the campground. There are no electric or water hookups at the campground. Multiple dogs may be allowed.

Coldbrook Resort and Campground
864 Old Coldbrook Road
Barre, MA
978-355-2090
coldbrookcountry.com/
Dogs of all sizes are allowed. There is a $5 per night per pet additional fee. Dogs may not be left unattended, and they must be leashed and cleaned up after. This RV park is closed during the off-season. The camping and tent areas also allow dogs. There is a dog walk area at the campground. 2 dogs may be allowed.

Circle Farm
131 Main Street
Bellingham, MA
508-966-1136
hometown.aol.com/cgfrmcamp
Well behaved dogs of all sizes are allowed. There are no additional pet fees. Dogs must be quiet, leashed, and cleaned up after. Multiple dogs may be allowed.

Bay View Campgrounds
260 McArthur Blvd
Bourne, MA
508-759-7610
bayviewcampgrounds.com
Dogs of all sizes are allowed. There are no additional pet fees. Dogs must be quiet, leashed, cleaned up after, and not left unattended at any time. There is a dog walk area at the campground. Multiple dogs may be

allowed.

Bourne Scenic Park Campground
370 Scenic Highway
Bourne, MA
508-759-7873
bournescenicpark.com
Dogs of all sizes are allowed. There are no additional pet fees. Dogs must be quiet, leashed, and cleaned up after. Multiple dogs may be allowed.

Nickerson State Park Campgrounds
Route 6A
Brewster, MA
508-896-3491
state.ma.us/dem/parks/nick.htm
This state park has 1900 acres of land and offers over 400 campsites. Your dog is welcome at the campgrounds, but they ask that your dog never be left unattended. Dogs are also allowed on the hiking trails, and paved trails. Dogs are not allowed in the pond or on public beaches. However, you can take your dog to an uncrowded beach, where there are not many other people. Dogs must be leashed and you must have proof of your dog's rabies vaccination.

Mohawk Trail State Forest
On H 2
Charlemont, MA
413-339-5504
Dogs of all sizes are allowed. There are no additional pet fees. Dogs may not be left unattended, they must have current rabies certificate and shot records, be leashed, and cleaned up after. Dogs are allowed on all the trails. This campground is closed during the off-season. The camping and tent areas also allow dogs. There is a dog walk area at the campground. Dogs are allowed in the camping cabins. There are no electric or water hookups at the campground. Multiple dogs may be allowed.

Walker Island Family Camping Resort
27 Route 20
Chester, MA
413-354-2295
walkerisland.com
Dogs of all sizes are allowed. There are no additional pet fees. Dogs may not be left unattended, and they must be quiet, friendly, leashed, and cleaned up after. Dogs must have proof of current shots. Dogs are not allowed in the pool area, or in buildings. This RV park is closed during the off-season. The camping

and tent areas also allow dogs. There is a dog walk area at the campground. Multiple dogs may be allowed.

Clarksburg State Park
1199 Middle Road
Clarksburg, MA
413-664-8345
Dogs of all sizes are allowed. There are no additional pet fees. Dogs may not be left unattended, and they must have a current rabies certificate and shot records. Dogs must be quiet during quiet hours, leashed, and cleaned up after. Dogs are allowed on the trails, but not on the beach or in the swim area. Although the campground is seasonal, the park is open year round. This campground is closed during the off-season. There is a dog walk area at the campground. Dogs are allowed in the camping and tent areas. There are no electric or water hookups at the campground. Multiple dogs may be allowed.

Camper's Haven
184 Old Wharf Road
Dennisport, MA
508-398-2811
campershaven.com/
One dog of any size is allowed during their off season, which begins after Labor Day. There are no additional pet fees. Dogs must be quiet, leashed, cleaned up after, and not left unattended.

Massasoit State Park
1361 Middleboro
E Taunton, MA
508-822-7405
Dogs of all sizes are allowed. There are no additional pet fees. Dogs may not be left unattended, they must have current rabies certificate and shot records, be quiet, well behaved, leashed, and cleaned up after. Dogs are allowed on the trails. This campground is closed during the off-season. The camping and tent areas also allow dogs. There is a dog walk area at the campground. There are no water hookups at the campground. Multiple dogs may be allowed.

Cape Cod Camp Resort
176 Thomas Landers Road
East Falmouth, MA
508-548-1458
resortcamplands.com
Dogs of all sizes are allowed. There is a $4 per night per pet additional fee and there must be proof of

shots; either tags or paperwork. Dogs must be cleaned up after, leashed, and not left unattended at any time. There are some breed restrictions. Multiple dogs may be allowed.

Jellystone Park
290 Glen Charlie Road
East Wareham, MA
508-291-2267
mapleparkfamilycampground.com
A family-style entertainment resort, this fun campground features 400 campsites on 600 wooded acres with hiking trails, kayak/paddle boat rentals, a game room, daily activities, theme weekends, and soon to come- an indoor pool and water park. Dogs are allowed for an additional fee of $5 per night per pet. Dogs may not be left unattended outside, and they may only be left alone inside if they will be quiet. They must be leashed and cleaned up after at all times. Although dogs are not allowed on the swim beach, there is a doggy beach area on site. There are some breed restrictions. This RV park is closed during the off-season. The camping and tent areas also allow dogs. There is a dog walk area at the campground. Multiple dogs may be allowed.

Erving State Forest
Laurel Lake Road
Erving, MA
978-544-3939
Dogs of all sizes are allowed. There are no additional pet fees. Dogs may not be left unattended, they must have current rabies certificate and shot records, be leashed, and cleaned up after. Dogs are allowed on all of the trails, but not on the beach. This campground is closed during the off-season. The camping and tent areas also allow dogs. There is a dog walk area at the campground. There are no electric or water hookups at the campground. Multiple dogs may be allowed.

Normandy Farms
72 West Street
Foxboro, MA
508-543-7600
normandyfarms.com
This large, full-service RV campground has it all, including an indoor and outdoor pool, restaurant with outdoor seating and a clubhouse. It's kind of like a hotel for your RV. There is also a new off-leash dog park. Well behaved dogs of all sizes are allowed. There are no additional pet fees. Dogs must be

quiet, leashed, cleaned up after, and not left unattended at any time. Multiple dogs may be allowed.

Daughters of the American Revolution (DAR) State Forest
78 Cape Street
Goshen, MA
413 268-7098
With an original donation of 1,020 acres by the Daughters of the American Revolution, this park has now grown to almost 1,800 acres and has become a popular year round recreational destination with such features as the Upper and Lower Highland Lakes, miles and miles of scenic multi-use trails, and a fire tower that gives clear day views into 5 states. Dogs of all sizes are allowed for no additional fee. Dogs must be on no more than a 10 foot leash, be cleaned up after, and have proof of current rabies inoculation. Dogs are not allowed on the sandy beach area. The camp area is available with reservations from mid-May through mid-October, and on a first-come/first-served basis during the off-season. The 51 site campground sits above a scenic wetland where wildlife sighting is common, and accessible restrooms, water, and a dump station are available. The camping and tent areas also allow dogs. There is a dog walk area at the campground. 2 dogs may be allowed.

Prospect Mountain Campground
1349 Main Road (H 57)
Granville, MA
888-550-4PMC (762)
prospectmtncampground.com/
Dogs of all sizes are allowed. There are no additional pet fees. Dogs may not be left unattended outside, and left inside only for short periods. There is a day kennel close by for your pet when you will be gone longer. Dogs must be leashed and cleaned up after. This RV park is closed during the off-season. The camping and tent areas also allow dogs. There is a dog walk area at the campground. Multiple dogs may be allowed.

Wompatuck State Park
Union Street
Hingham, MA
781-749-7160
Dogs of all sizes are allowed. There are no additional pet fees. Dogs may not be left unattended, they must have current rabies certificate and shot records, be leashed, and cleaned up after. Dogs are allowed

on all the trails. This campground is closed during the off-season. The camping and tent areas also allow dogs. There is a dog walk area at the campground. There are no water hookups at the campground. Multiple dogs may be allowed.

Hidden Valley Campground
15 Scott Road (Box700)
Lanesborough, MA
413-447-9419
Only one dog is allowed for the local residents, however, out of town travelers with 2 dogs are allowed if they are both small. They are allowed in the RV area only, not the campsites. Dogs must be quiet, be on a 6 foot max leash, cleaned up after, and not left unattended at any time. There are some breed restrictions.

Mount Greylock State Reservation
Rockwell Road, P.O. Box 138
Lanesborough, MA
413-499-4262 (877-I-CAMP-MA (877-422-6762))
PLEASE NOTE: Roads are closed at this park for the 2007/8 seasons for updates and repairs so many places are not available by car; the visitor center and trails will remain open. Tent camping is allowed during the reconstruction period and reservations are required. There are limited services; potable water is not available, but solar composting toilets are provided. The camping and tent areas also allow dogs. There is a dog walk area at the campground. There are no electric or water hookups at the campgrounds. 2 dogs may be allowed.

October Mountain State Forest
317 Woodland Road
Lee, MA
413-243-1778
Dogs of all sizes are allowed. There are no additional pet fees. Dogs may not be left unattended, they must have current rabies certificate and shot records, be on no more than a 10 foot leash, and be cleaned up after. Dogs are allowed on all the trails, but they are not allowed in any buildings. This campground is closed during the off-season. The camping and tent areas also allow dogs. There is a dog walk area at the campground. There are no electric or water hookups at the campground. Multiple dogs may be allowed.

Boston Minuteman Campground

264 Ayer Road
Littleton, MA
877-677-0042
minutemancampground.com
Well behaved dogs of all sizes are allowed. There are no additional pet fees. Dogs must be quiet, leashed, and cleaned up after. There is a dog walk area at the campground. Multiple dogs may be allowed.

KOA
438 Plymouth Street
Middleboro, MA
508-947-6435 (800-562-3046)
bostonsouthkoa.net
Dogs of all sizes are allowed. There are no additional pet fees. Dogs may not be left unattended, must be quiet at night, be leashed, and cleaned up after. This RV park is closed during the off-season. The camping and tent areas also allow dogs. There is a dog walk area at the campground. Multiple dogs may be allowed.

Sunset View Farms
57 Town Farm Road
Monson, MA
413-267-9269
sunsetview.com
Dogs of all sizes are allowed. There are no additional pet fees. Dogs must have current rabies shots, be leashed, and cleaned up after. Dogs may not be left unattended. 2 dogs may be allowed.

Harold Parker State Forest
305 Middleton Road
North Andover, MA
978-686-3391
Dogs of all sizes are allowed. There are no additional pet fees. Dogs may not be left unattended, they must have current rabies certificate and shot records, be quiet, leashed, and cleaned up after. Dogs are allowed on all the trails. This campground is closed during the off-season. The camping and tent areas also allow dogs. There is a dog walk area at the campground. There are no electric or water hookups at the campground. Multiple dogs may be allowed.

Pine Acres Family Camping Resort
203 Bechan Road
Oakham, MA
508-882-9509
pineacresresort.com
Dogs of all sizes are allowed. There is a $2 per night per pet additional fee. Dogs must be leashed and cleaned up after. The camping and tent areas also allow dogs. There is a dog walk area at the campground. 2 dogs may be allowed.

Pittsfield State Forest
1041 Cascade Street
Pittsfield, MA
413-442-8992
Dogs of all sizes are allowed. There are no additional pet fees. Dogs may not be left unattended, they must have a current rabies certificate and shot records, be on no more than a 10 foot leash, and be cleaned up after. Dogs are allowed on all of the trails, but not at the swimming area. This campground is closed during the off-season. The camping and tent areas also allow dogs. There is a dog walk area at the campground. There are no electric or water hookups at the campground. Multiple dogs may be allowed.

Peppermint Park Camping Resort
169 Grant Street
Plainfield, MA
413-634-5385
peppermintpark.net
Dogs of all sizes are allowed. There is a $10 per night per pet additional fee and dogs must have proof of up to date shots. Dogs must be leashed, cleaned up after, and can not be left unattended. The camping and tent areas also allow dogs. There is a dog walk area at the campground. Multiple dogs may be allowed.

Ellis Haven Family Campground
531 Furnace Road
Plymouth, MA
508-746-0803
elllishaven.com
Dogs of all sizes are allowed. There is a $2 per night additional fee for a dog. Dogs may not be left unattended outside, and they must be leashed and cleaned up after. This RV park is closed during the off-season. Only one dog is allowed per campsite. The camping and tent areas also allow dogs. There is a dog walk area at the campground.

Winter Island Park
50 Winter Island Road
Salem, MA
978-745-9430
mass.gov/dcr/listing.htm
This is a marine recreational park, and dogs of all sizes are allowed to camp in your RV but not in a tent. There are no additional pet fees. Dogs may not be left unattended outside, and may only be left inside your unit if it will not cause a danger to the animal. They must have a current rabies certificate and shot records. Dogs must be quiet during quiet hours, leashed, and cleaned up

after. Dogs are allowed on the trails, but not on the beach or in the buildings. Although the campground is seasonal, the park is open year round from 7 am to 10 pm. This campground is closed during the off-season. There is a dog walk area at the campground. There are no electric or water hookups at the campground. 2 dogs may be allowed.

Rusnik Campground
115 Lafayette Road
Salisbury, MA
978-462-9551
rusnik.com
Well behaved dogs of all sizes are allowed. There are no additional pet fees. Dogs must be quiet, leashed, and cleaned up after. Multiple dogs may be allowed.

Peter's Pond Park
185 Cotuit Road
Sandwich, MA
508-477-1775
peterspond.com
Dogs of all sizes are allowed in the RV section only. There is one street where they park all the RVs. There are no additional pet fees. Dogs must be leashed and cleaned up after. There is a dog walk area at the campground. Multiple dogs may be allowed.

Shawme-Crowell State Forest
42 Main Street
Sandwich, MA
508-888-0351
Dogs of all sizes are allowed. There are no additional pet fees. Dogs may not be left unattended, they must have current rabies certificate and shot records, be leashed, and cleaned up after. Dogs are allowed on all of the trails. The forest is open from 8am to 8pm daily. The camping and tent areas also allow dogs. There is a dog walk area at the campground. There are no electric or water hookups at the campground. Multiple dogs may be allowed.

Savoy Mountain State Forest
Central Shaft Road
Savoy, MA
413-663-8469
mass.gov/dcr/listing.htm
Dogs of all sizes are allowed. There are no additional pet fees. Dogs may not be left unattended, and they must have a current rabies certificate and shot records. Dogs must be quiet during quiet hours, be leashed, and cleaned up after. This

campground is closed during the off-season. The camping and tent areas also allow dogs. There is a dog walk area at the campground. There are no electric or water hookups at the campground. Multiple dogs may be allowed.

Country Aire Campground
1753 Mohaw Trail
Shelburne Falls, MA
413-625-2996
countryairecampground.com
Well behaved dogs of all sizes are allowed. There are no additional pet fees. Dogs must be quiet, leashed, cleaned up after, and not left unattended. Multiple dogs may be allowed.

Myles Standish State Forest
1941 Cranberry Road
South Carver, MA
508-866-2526
mass.gov/dcr/listing.htm
Dogs of all sizes are allowed. There are no additional pet fees. Dogs may not be left unattended, and they must have a current rabies certificate and shot records. Dogs must be quiet during quiet hours, be leashed, and cleaned up after. Dogs are allowed on the trails, but not on the beach or swim areas, and not in the buildings. This campground is closed during the off-season. The camping and tent areas also allow dogs. There is a dog walk area at the campground. There are no electric or water hookups at the campground. Multiple dogs may be allowed.

Jellystone Park
30 River Road
Sturbridge, MA
508-347-9570
jellystonessturbridge.com
Dogs of all sizes are allowed. There are no additional pet fees. The camping and tent areas also allow dogs. There is a dog walk area at the campground. Multiple dogs may be allowed.

Wells State Park
159 Walker Pond Road
Sturbridge, MA
508-347-9257
Dogs of all sizes are allowed. There are no additional pet fees. Dogs may not be left unattended, they must have a current rabies certificate and shot records, be leashed at all times, and cleaned up after. Dogs are allowed on all the trails, but not on the beach. This campground is closed during the off-season. The camping and tent areas also allow

dogs. There is a dog walk area at the campground. There are no electric or water hookups at the campground. Multiple dogs may be allowed.

Oak Haven Family Campground
22 Main Street
Wales, MA
413-245-7148
oakhavencampground.com
Dogs of all sizes are allowed. There are no additional pet fees. Dogs must have current rabies records, be leashed, and cleaned up after. 2 dogs may be allowed.

Waquoit Bay National Estuarine Research Reserve
149 Waquoit H/H 28
Waquoit, MA
508-457-0495 (877-422-6762)
waquoitbayreserve.org/
Located on the south shore of Cape Cod and accessible by boat only, this 330 acre park and research reserve is one of the last undeveloped coastal properties on the cape with barrier beaches, an oak and pine forest, coastal salt ponds, marshlands, and uplands. Dogs of all sizes are allowed for no additional fee. Dogs must be leashed, cleaned up after, and have proof of current rabies inoculation. Dogs are not allowed on the beaches at any time because of endangered birds. Primitive camping is allowed with prior camping permits and reservations through Reserve America. The camp area has composting toilets in the summer, and potable water is not available. The camping and tent areas also allow dogs. There is a dog walk area at the campground. There are no electric or water hookups at the campgrounds. 2 dogs may be allowed.

Summit Hill Campground
34 Old Middlefield
Washington, MA
413-623-5761
summithillcampground.com
Dogs of all sizes are allowed. There are no additional pet fees, and rabies shots and licenses must be up to date. There is a dog walk area at the campground. 2 dogs may be allowed.

KOA-Webster/Sturbridge
106 Douglas Road
Webster, MA
508-943-1895 (800-562-1895)
webstercamp.com
Dogs of all sizes are allowed. There are no additional pet fees. Dogs

must be leashed and cleaned up after. There are some breed restrictions. This RV park is closed during the off-season. The camping and tent areas also allow dogs. There is a dog walk area at the campground. Multiple dogs may be allowed.

The Old Sawmill Campground
Box 377 Longhill Road
West Brookfield, MA
508-867-2427
oldsawmillcampground.com
Dogs of all sizes are allowed. There are no additional pet fees. Dogs must be leashed and cleaned up after. 2 dogs may be allowed.

Wyman's Beach Family Camping
48 Wyman's Beach Road
Westford, MA
978-692-6287
wymanscamping.com
Well behaved dogs of all sizes are allowed. There are no additional pet fees. Dogs must remain in one's own site and be leashed at all times. There is a dog walk area close by that you can drive to. Dogs are allowed in the camping cabins. Multiple dogs may be allowed.

Horseneck Beach State Reservations
On H 88
Westport Point, MA
508-636-8817
mass.gov/dcr/listing.htm
This park is popular because of it's almost 2 miles of beaches and it's salt marsh. Dogs of all sizes are allowed. There are no additional pet fees. Dogs may not be left unattended, and they must have a current rabies certificate and shot records. Dogs must be quiet during quiet hours, be leashed, and cleaned up after. Dogs are allowed on the trails, but not on the beach, in the buildings, or at the sand dunes. This campground is closed during the off-season. The camping and tent areas also allow dogs. There is a dog walk area at the campground. There are no water hookups at the campground. Multiple dogs may be allowed.

White Birch Campground
214 North Street
Whately, MA
800-244-4941
Dogs of all sizes are allowed. There are no additional pet fees. Dogs must be quiet, leashed, and cleaned up after. Multiple dogs may be allowed.

Michigan

Sequoia Campgrounds
2675 Gady Road
Adrian, MI
517-264-5531
sequoiacamping.com
Dogs of all sizes are allowed. There are no additional pet fees. Dogs must be leashed and cleaned up after. The camping and tent areas also allow dogs. There is a dog walk area at the campground. 2 dogs may be allowed.

Hungry Horse Campground
2016 142nd Avenue
Allegan, MI
616-681-9843
hungryhorsecampground.com
Dogs of all sizes are allowed. There are no additional pet fees. Dogs must be leashed and cleaned up after. This RV park is closed during the off-season. There is a dog walk area at the campground. Multiple dogs may be allowed.

Campers Cove RV Park
505 Long Rapids Road
Alpena, MI
989-356-3708
camperscovecampground.com
Dogs of all sizes are allowed. There are no additional pet fees. Dogs must be quiet, well behaved, leashed and cleaned up after. There are some breed restrictions. The camping and tent areas also allow dogs. There is a dog walk area at the campground. Multiple dogs may be allowed.

Au Gres City Park
522 Park Street
Au Gres, MI
989-876-8310
Dogs of all sizes are allowed. There are no additional pet fees. Dogs must be leashed and cleaned up after. This RV park is closed during the off-season. The camping and tent areas also allow dogs. There is a dog walk area at the campground. Multiple dogs may be allowed.

Fort Custer Recreation Area
5163 Fort Custer Drive
Augusta, MI
269-731-4200 (800-447-2757)
Covering over 3,000 acres of farm country, forests, and prairie, this park also has 3 lakes, a river, and more than 25 miles of year round multi-use

trails. In the winter there are specially planned dog sledding events. Dogs are allowed throughout the park, on the trails, and in the camp area for no additional fee. Dogs may not be left unattended at any time, and they must be quiet, on no more than a 6 foot leash, and cleaned up after at all times. Dogs are not allowed on the sand at the beach, but they may be on the grassy areas. The camp area offers 219 modern grassy or paved sites with picnic tables and fire pits/grills. The camping and tent areas also allow dogs. There is a dog walk area at the campground. There are no water hookups at the campgrounds. Multiple dogs may be allowed.

Bay City State Recreation Area
3582 State Park Drive
Bay City, MI
989-684-3020 (800-447-2757)
In addition to year round educational and recreational opportunities, this park is also home to a 3 acre enclosed playground, 3 observation towers, boardwalks, viewing platforms, and more than 7 miles of trails to explore it all. Dogs are allowed for no additional pet fee; they must be current on vaccinations and rabies shots. Dogs may not be left unattended in a vehicle, camper, or a campsite at any time, and they must be quiet, on no more than a 6 foot leash, and cleaned up after at all times. Dogs may not be left outside tied up alone and they are not allowed in park buildings or at swim beaches. The campground offers 193 sites and modern facilities. The camping and tent areas also allow dogs. There is a dog walk area at the campground. Dogs are allowed in the camping cabins. Multiple dogs may be allowed.

Chain-O-Lakes Campground
7231 S H 88
Bellaire, MI
231-533-8432
chainolakescamp.com
Dogs of all sizes are allowed. There are no additional pet fees. Dogs must be friendly, be on leash, and cleaned up after. Dogs may not be left unattended at any time. The camping and tent areas also allow dogs. There is a dog walk area at the campground. Dogs are allowed in the camping cabins. Multiple dogs may be allowed.

Wayne County Fairgrounds and RV Park
10871 Quirk Road

Belleville, MI
734-697-7002
waynecountyfair.net
Dogs of all sizes are allowed. There are no additional pet fees. Dogs must be leashed and cleaned up after. This RV park is closed during the off-season. There is a dog walk area at the campground. Multiple dogs may be allowed.

Grand Rouge Campgrounds
6400 W River Drive
Belmont, MI
616-361-1053
michcampgrounds.com/grandrogue/
This quiet family camp area offers 110 spacious, wooded and grassy sites with waterside settings, and they have planned activities in addition to a long list of land and water recreational opportunities. Dogs are allowed throughout the grounds; they are not allowed on swim beaches, on the watercraft rentals, or on the campground "tour train". Dogs must be well mannered, leashed, and cleaned up after at all times. This RV park is closed during the off-season. The camping and tent areas also allow dogs. There is a dog walk area at the campground. 2 dogs may be allowed.

House of David Travel Trailer Park
1019 E Empire
Benton Harbor, MI
269-927-3302
Dogs of all sizes are allowed. There are no additional pet fees. Dogs must be leashed and cleaned up after. There are some breed restrictions. The camping and tent areas also allow dogs. There is a dog walk area at the campground. Dogs are allowed in the camping cabins. 2 dogs may be allowed.

Vacation Trailer Park
2080 Benzie H
Benzonia, MI
231-882-5101
vacationtrailer.com
Dogs of all sizes are allowed. There are no additional pet fees. Dogs must be quiet, well behaved, and leashed and cleaned up after. The camping and tent areas also allow dogs. There is a dog walk area at the campground. Multiple dogs may be allowed.

Brimley State Park
9200 W 6 Mile Road
Brimley, MI
906-248-3422 (800-44PARKS (447-2757))

This park is located along the shore of Whitefish Bay. Its activities include land and water recreation and an explorer program. Dogs of all sizes are allowed at no additional fee. Dogs may not be left unattended, they must be on no more than a 6 foot leash, and be cleaned up after. Dogs are not allowed on the beach, on any sand, or in buildings. This campground is closed during the off-season. The camping and tent areas also allow dogs. There is a dog walk area at the campground. There are no water hookups at the campground. Multiple dogs may be allowed.

Fuller's Resort and Campground
1622 E Clearlake Road
Buchanan, MI
269-695-3785
fullersresort.com
Dogs of all sizes are allowed. There are no additional pet fees. Dogs must be leashed, cleaned up after, and are not allowed on the beach. There are some breed restrictions. The camping and tent areas also allow dogs. There is a dog walk area at the campground. Multiple dogs may be allowed.

Traverse City KOA
9700 H 37
Buckley, MI
231-269-4562 (800-562-0280)
traversecity.koa.com
Dogs of all sizes are allowed. There are no additional pet fees. Dogs must be leashed and cleaned up after. Dogs are not allowed at the lodge or rentals. There are some breed restrictions. This RV park is closed during the off-season. The camping and tent areas also allow dogs. There is a dog walk area at the campground. Multiple dogs may be allowed.

Woodchip Campground
7501 Burlingame SW
Byron Center, MI
616-878-9050
woodchipcampground.com
Dogs of all sizes are allowed. There are no additional pet fees. Dogs must be leashed and cleaned up after. There are some breed restrictions. The camping and tent areas also allow dogs. There is a dog walk area at the campground. Multiple dogs may be allowed.

Camp Cadillac
10621 E 34th Road (Boon Road)
Cadillac, MI
231-775-9724

campcadillac.com
One dog of any size or 2 small dogs are allowed. There are no additional pet fees. Dogs must be leashed and cleaned up after. The camping and tent areas also allow dogs. There is a dog walk area at the campground.

Huron-Manistee National Forest
1755 S. Mitchell Street (Forest Supervisor)
Cadillac, MI
231-723-2211 (800-821-6263)
fs.fed.us/r9/hmnf/
Rich in history and spectacular scenery with 5 ranger districts and almost a million acres, this forest provides a variety of camping areas, trails, recreation, and diverse ecosystems that support a large variety of plants, fish, mammals, and bird species. They are also home to the Nordhouse Dunes Natural Area. Dogs of all sizes are allowed throughout the forest for no additional fee; they must be under owner's control, be on no more than a 6 foot leash, and cleaned up after at all times. Dogs are not permitted on beaches. The camping and tent areas also allow dogs. There is a dog walk area at the campground. There are no electric or water hookups at the campgrounds. Multiple dogs may be allowed.

Nuron-Manistee National Forest
1755 S Mitchell Street
Cadillac, MI
616-775-2421 (877-444-6777)
fs.fed.us/r9/hmnf/index.shtml
These 2 forests combined have over a million acres and there is ample outdoor recreation year round. Dogs are allowed at no additional fee. Dogs may not be left unattended, they must be leashed, and they are not allowed on the beaches. This campground is closed during the off-season. The camping and tent areas also allow dogs. There is a dog walk area at the campground. Multiple dogs may be allowed.

Albert E. Sleeper State Park
6573 State Park Road
Caseville, MI
989-856-4411 (800-447-2757)
Visitors can enjoy both sunrises and sunsets on the bay at this 723 acre year round park of ancient forest dunes, wetlands, sandy beaches, and woods. Dogs are allowed for no additional pet fee; they must be current on vaccinations and rabies shots. Dogs may not be left unattended in a vehicle, camper, or a campsite at any time, and they must

be quiet, on no more than a 6 foot leash, and cleaned up after at all times. Dogs may not be left outside tied up alone and they are not allowed in any park buildings (including cabins) or at swim beaches. They request that dogs be walked on the outer side of groomed ski trails in the winter. The campground offers 223 modern and semi-modern sites, modern facilities, and a playground. This RV park is closed during the off-season. The camping and tent areas also allow dogs. There is a dog walk area at the campground. There are no water hookups at the campgrounds. Multiple dogs may be allowed.

Evergreen Park, Sanilac County
4731 Van Dyke
Cass City, MI
989-872-6600
sanilaccountyevergreenpark.com
Dogs of all sizes are allowed. There are no additional pet fees. Dogs must be leashed and cleaned up after. The camping and tent areas also allow dogs. There is a dog walk area at the campground. 2 dogs may be allowed.

Lakeside Camp Park
13677 White Creek Avenue
Cedar Springs, MI
616-696-1735
lakesidecamppark.com
Dogs of all sizes are allowed. There are no additional pet fees. Dogs must be leashed and cleaned up after. There are some breed restrictions. The camping and tent areas also allow dogs. There is a dog walk area at the campground. 2 dogs may be allowed.

Cedarville RV
634 Grove Street
Cedarville, MI
906-484-3351 (800-906-3351)
cedarvillervpark.com
Dogs of all sizes are allowed. There are no additional pet fees. Three dogs can be accepted if they are all small. Dogs may not be left unattended, must be leashed, and cleaned up after. The camping and tent areas also allow dogs. There is a dog walk area at the campground.

Irish Hills Campground
16230 US H 12
Cement City, MI
517-592-6751
irishhillskampground.com
Dogs of all sizes are allowed. There are no additional pet fees. Dogs

must be leashed and cleaned up after. The camping and tent areas also allow dogs. There is a dog walk area at the campground. Multiple dogs may be allowed.

Cheboygan State Park
4490 Beach Road
Cheboygan, MI
231-798-3711 (800-44PARKS (447-2757))
A variety of year round recreational activities, beautiful beaches and trails greet visitors at this park. Well behaved dogs are allowed at no additional fee. Dogs may not be left unattended, and they must be leashed and cleaned up after. Dogs are not allowed in public swim areas or in buildings. Dogs are allowed on the trails. This campground is closed during the off-season. The camping and tent areas also allow dogs. There is a dog walk area at the campground. There are no water hookups at the campground. Multiple dogs may be allowed.

Waterloo Recreation Area
16345 McClure Road
Chelsea, MI
734-475-8307 (800-447-2757)
This recreation area provides over 20,000 acres with 47 miles of hiking trails, 11 lakes, glacial topography, and an abundance of flora and fauna. No alcohol is allowed here from April 15 through Labor Day. The Sugarloaf camp area is seasonal, but the Portage area is open all year. Dogs of all sizes are allowed at no additional fee. Dogs may not be left unattended at any time, including in automobiles, and they must have a current rabies certificate and shot records. Dogs must be quiet, well behaved, be on no more than a 6 foot leash, and be cleaned up after. Dogs are allowed on the trails, and at the picnic areas. Dogs are not allowed in buildings, day use areas, at the beaches or in the water. The camping and tent areas also allow dogs. There is a dog walk area at the campground. There are no water hookups at the campground. Multiple dogs may be allowed.

Waffle Farm Camp
790 N Union City Road
Coldwater, MI
517-278-4315
wafflefarm.com
Dogs of all sizes are allowed. There are no additional pet fees. Dogs must be quiet, well behaved, and in your unit by 11PM. Dogs must be kept leashed and cleaned up after.

This RV park is closed during the off-season. The camping and tent areas also allow dogs. There is a dog walk area at the campground. Multiple dogs may be allowed.

Fort Wilkins Historic State Park
15223 H 41
Copper Harbor, MI
906-482-0278 (800-447-2757)
A living history park, there are costumed docents bringing to life the history of the area and the importance of the outpost here in protecting the copper resources, and they are also home to one of the first lighthouses on Lake Superior. Dogs are allowed for no additional pet fee; they must be current on vaccinations and rabies shots. Dogs may not be left unattended in a vehicle, camper, or a campsite at any time, and they must be quiet, on no more than a 6 foot leash, and cleaned up after at all times. Dogs may not be left outside tied up alone, and they are not allowed in any park buildings or at swim beaches. There are 159 sites with modern facilities, showers, picnic tables, grills, and dump stations. This RV park is closed during the off-season. The camping and tent areas also allow dogs. There is a dog walk area at the campground. There are no water hookups at the campgrounds. Multiple dogs may be allowed.

Covert / South Haven KOA
39397 H 140
Covert, MI
269-764-0818 (800-562-9304)
koa.com/where/mi/22228/
Some of the amenities at this campground include a large seasonal swimming pool, theme weekends, pancake breakfasts, planned activities, nature trails, free Wi-Fi, and a coffee bar. Dogs are allowed for no additional fee in the RV/tent area; there is an additional one time pet fee of $5 for the cabins. Dogs may not be left unattended, and they must be on no more than a 6 foot leash and cleaned up after at all times. There are some breed restrictions. This RV park is closed during the off-season. The camping and tent areas also allow dogs. There is a dog walk area at the campground. Dogs are allowed in the camping cabins. 2 dogs may be allowed.

Bewabic State Park
1933 US Highway 2 W (720 Idlewild Rd.)
Crystal Falls, MI

906-875-3324 (800-44-PARKS (447-2757))
This recreational park has among it's amenities access to Fortune Lake for boating, swimming and fishing. Dogs of all sizes are allowed. There are no additional pet fees. Dogs may not be left unattended at any time, including in automobiles, and they must have a current rabies certificate and shot records. Dogs must be quiet, well behaved, be on no more than a 6 foot leash, and be cleaned up after. Dogs are allowed on the trails, and at the picnic areas. Dogs are not allowed in buildings, day use areas, at the beaches or in the water. This campground is closed during the off-season. The camping and tent areas also allow dogs. There is a dog walk area at the campground. There are no water hookups at the campground. Multiple dogs may be allowed.

Oak Shores Campground
86882 County Road 215
Decatur, MI
269-423-7370
michcampgrounds.com/oakshores
Dogs of all sizes are allowed. There are no additional pet fees. Dogs may not be left unattended, must be leashed, and cleaned up after. The camping and tent areas also allow dogs. There is a dog walk area at the campground. Multiple dogs may be allowed.

Walnut Hills
7685 Lehring
Durand, MI
989-634-9782
michcampgrounds.com/walnuthills
Dogs of all sizes are allowed. There are no additional pet fees. Dogs must be quiet and may not be left unattended. They must be on no more than a 6 foot leash and cleaned up after. Dogs can not be in the campground building, the beach, or the lake. This RV park is closed during the off-season. The camping and tent areas also allow dogs. There is a dog walk area at the campground. Multiple dogs may be allowed.

Tawas Point State Park
686 Tawas Beach Road
East Tawas, MI
989-362-5041 (800-447-2757)
Sitting on 183 scenic acres at the end of a sand spit and is home to the last remaining Victorian era styled lighthouse on the Great Lakes. Dogs are allowed for no

additional pet fee; they must be current on vaccinations and rabies shots. Dogs may not be left unattended in a vehicle, camper, or a campsite at any time, and they must be quiet, on no more than a 6 foot leash, and cleaned up after at all times. Dogs may not be left outside tied up alone and they are not allowed in park buildings, at swim beaches, or on the nature trail. They are allowed on the paved trail to the lighthouse. The camp area offers 193 sites, modern restroom facilities, showers, and a dump station. This RV park is closed during the off-season. The camping and tent areas also allow dogs. There is a dog walk area at the campground. There are no water hookups at the campgrounds. 2 dogs may be allowed.

Emmett KOA
3864 Breen Road
Emmett, MI
810-395-7042 (888-562-5612)
emmettkoa.com
Dogs of all sizes are allowed. There are no additional pet fees. Dogs must be quiet, well behaved, not left unattended, and leashed and cleaned up after. Dogs are not allowed in the lake. This RV park is closed during the off-season. The camping and tent areas also allow dogs. There is a dog walk area at the campground. Multiple dogs may be allowed.

Sleeping Bear Dunes National Lakeshore
9922 Front Street
Empire, MI
231-326-5134
nps.gov/slbe/
There are educational as well as recreational opportunities at this beautiful peninsula park with 35 miles of coastline, islands to explore, a 7-mile info-drive of 12 interpretive stops, spectacular views, and the popular dunes. Although dogs are not allowed on the dunes, and some of the beaches, they are allowed throughout the rest of the park and on the trails for no additional fee. Dogs must be on no more than a 6 foot leash (even when in the water) and cleaned up after at all times. The campground is located 10 miles south of empire at 5685 Lake Michigan Road, Honor, MI, 49646 and offers modern facilities. The camping and tent areas also allow dogs. There is a dog walk area at the campground. Multiple dogs may be allowed.

Snow Lake Campground
644 E Snows Lake Road
Fenwick, MI
989-248-3224
snowlakekamground.com
Dogs of all sizes are allowed. There are no additional pet fees. Dogs may not be left unattended, must be leashed, and cleaned up after. There are some breed restrictions. The camping and tent areas also allow dogs. There is a dog walk area at the campground. Multiple dogs may be allowed.

Frankenmuth Jellystone Park
1339 Weiss Street
Frankenmuth, MI
989-652-6668
frankenmuthjellystone.com
Dogs of all sizes are allowed. There are no additional pet fees. Dogs may not be left unattended, must be leashed, and cleaned up after. The camping and tent areas also allow dogs. There is a dog walk area at the campground. Multiple dogs may be allowed.

Fayette Historic State Park
13700 13.25 Lane
Garden, MI
906-644-2603 (800-447-2757)
Home to an historic town-site that was once a lively industrial community, this scenic waterside park also has a rich cultural history to share with visitors. Dogs are allowed for no additional pet fee; they must be current on vaccinations and rabies shots. Dogs may not be left unattended in a vehicle, camper, or a campsite at any time, and they must be quiet, on no more than a 6 foot leash, and cleaned up after at all times. Dogs may not be left outside tied up alone, and they are not allowed in any park buildings or at swim beaches. There are 61 sites at the campground with vault toilets and pump water. The camping and tent areas also allow dogs. There is a dog walk area at the campground. There are no water hookups at the campgrounds. Multiple dogs may be allowed.

Gaylord KOA
5101 Campfires Parkway
Gaylord, MI
989-939-8723 (800-562-4146)
koa.com
Dogs of all sizes are allowed. There are no additional pet fees. Dogs may not be left unattended, must be leashed, and cleaned up after. This RV park is closed during the off-

season. The camping and tent areas also allow dogs. There is a dog walk area at the campground. Dogs are allowed in the camping cabins. Multiple dogs may be allowed.

Grand Haven State Park
1001 S Harbor Drive
Grand Haven, MI
616-847-1309 (800-447-2757)
Sitting on sandy shores of Lake Michigan and the Grand River, this beautiful 48 acre park offers great views and a variety of land and water recreation. Dogs are allowed for no additional pet fee; they must be current on vaccinations and rabies shots. Dogs may not be left unattended in a vehicle, camper, or a campsite at any time, and they must be quiet, on no more than a 6 foot leash, and cleaned up after at all times. Dogs may not be left outside tied up alone and they are not allowed in any park buildings or on the beach. The campground offers 174 sites, modern facilities, a store, and free Wi-Fi in the day use area. This RV park is closed during the off-season. The camping and tent areas also allow dogs. There is a dog walk area at the campground. There are no water hookups at the campgrounds. Multiple dogs may be allowed.

Yogi Bear's Jellystone Park Camp-Resort
10990 H 31N
Grand Haven, MI
616-842-9395 (800-828-1453)
ghjellystone.com/
This resort like park offers a wide variety of activities and recreational pursuits. Dogs of all sizes are allowed at no additional fee. Dogs may not be left unattended, and they must be quiet, well behaved, leashed and cleaned up after. Dogs are not allowed on the playground. This campground is closed during the off-season. The camping and tent areas also allow dogs. There is a dog walk area at the campground. 2 dogs may be allowed.

Warner Camp on Lester Lake
60 55th Street
Grand Junction, MI
269-434-6844
warnercamp.com
Dogs of all sizes are allowed. There are no additional pet fees. Dogs must be leashed and cleaned up after, and are not allowed on the beach. This RV park is closed during the off-season. The camping

and tent areas also allow dogs. There is a dog walk area at the campground. Dogs are allowed in the camping cabins. Multiple dogs may be allowed.

Apple Creek Campground
11185 Orban Road
Grass Lake, MI
517-522-3467
applecreekrv.com
Dogs of all sizes are allowed. There are no additional pet fees. Dogs may not be left unattended, must be leashed, and cleaned up after. This RV park is closed during the off-season. The camping and tent areas also allow dogs. There is a dog walk area at the campground. Multiple dogs may be allowed.

Hartwick Pines State Park
4216 Ranger Road
Grayling, MI
989-348-7068 (800-447-2757)
This scenic 9, 672 acre park is one of the state's largest, and it offers a variety of habitats for numerous wildlife, plenty of land and water recreation, and a 49 acre old growth pine forest. Dogs are allowed for no additional pet fee; they must be current on vaccinations and rabies shots. Dogs may not be left unattended in a vehicle, camper, or a campsite at any time, and they must be quiet, on no more than a 6 foot leash, and cleaned up after at all times. Dogs may not be left outside tied up alone and they are not allowed in any park buildings or at swim beaches. There is a 100 site modern campground with picnic tables, grills, and a playground. This RV park is closed during the off-season. The camping and tent areas also allow dogs. There is a dog walk area at the campground. Multiple dogs may be allowed.

Jellystone Park
370 W 4 Mile Road
Grayling, MI
989-348-2157
campfirememories.net
Dogs of all sizes are allowed. There are no additional pet fees. Dogs must be well behaved, be leashed, and cleaned up after. This RV park is closed during the off-season. The camping and tent areas also allow dogs. There is a dog walk area at the campground. Multiple dogs may be allowed.

McLain State Park
18350 H 203
Hancock, MI

906-482-0278 (800-447-2757) Centrally located in the Keweenaw Peninsula, this beautiful park on Lake Superior offers a wide variety of year round recreational opportunities. Dogs are allowed for no additional pet fee; they must be current on vaccinations and rabies shots. Dogs may not be left unattended in a vehicle, camper, or a campsite at any time, and they must be quiet, on no more than a 6 foot leash, and cleaned up after at all times. Dogs may not be left outside tied up alone, and they are not allowed in any park buildings or at swim beaches. There are 98 sites with modern facilities, showers, picnic tables, grills, and dump stations. The camping and tent areas also allow dogs. There is a dog walk area at the campground. There are no water hookups at the campgrounds. Multiple dogs may be allowed.

Wilson State Park
910 N 1st Street
Harrison, MI
989-539-3021
Dogs of all sizes are allowed. There are no additional pet fees. Dogs may not be left unattended at any time, including in automobiles, and they must have a current rabies certificate and shot records. Dogs must be quiet, well behaved, be on no more than a 6 foot leash, and be cleaned up after. Dogs are allowed on the trails, and at the picnic areas. Dogs are not allowed in buildings, day use areas, at the beaches or in the water. This campground is closed during the off-season. The camping and tent areas also allow dogs. There is a dog walk area at the campground. There are no water hookups at the campground. Multiple dogs may be allowed.

Harrisville State Park
248 State Park Road
Harrisville, MI
989-724-5126 (800-447-2757)
Nestled among pine and cedar trees on the shores of Lake Huron, this 107 acre park is the state's oldest and it offers a variety of recreational and educational opportunities in addition to annual events. Dogs are allowed for no additional pet fee; they must be current on vaccinations and rabies shots. Dogs may not be left unattended in a vehicle, camper, or a campsite at any time, and they must be quiet, on no more than a 6 foot leash, and cleaned up after at all times. Dogs may not be left outside

tied up alone and they are not allowed in any park buildings (including cabins) or at swim beaches. The camp area offers 195 sites with picnic tables, fire rings, and modern facilities. The camping and tent areas also allow dogs. There is a dog walk area at the campground. There are no water hookups at the campgrounds. Multiple dogs may be allowed.

Oak Grove Resort
2011 Ottawa Beach Road
Holland, MI
616-399-9230
oakgroveresort.com
Dogs of all sizes are allowed. There is a $3 per night per dog additional fee. Dogs must be leashed and cleaned up after. The camping and tent areas also allow dogs. There is a dog walk area at the campground. Multiple dogs may be allowed.

Jellystone Park
2201 E H 68
Indian River, MI
231-238-8259
jellystoneindianriver.com/
This family-style entertainment campground offers a full activity program, theme weekends, mini-golf, an outdoor theater, a camp store and goodie shop, a Michigan shaped swimming pool, playing fields/courts, a game room, and a lot more. Dogs are allowed for no additional fee. They must be leashed and cleaned up after at all times, and they are not allowed at the pool, playground, or in buildings. This RV park is closed during the off-season. The camping and tent areas also allow dogs. There is a dog walk area at the campground. Multiple dogs may be allowed.

Ottawa National Forest
E6248 H 2
Ironwood, MI
906-932-1330
fs.fed.us/r9/ottawa/
Located in the western upper peninsula of Michigan, there are 5 ranger districts and almost a million acres with a variety of camping areas, hundreds of miles of trails and shoreline, year round recreation, and diverse ecosystems that support a large variety of plants, fish, mammals, and bird species. Dogs of all sizes are allowed throughout the forest for no additional fee; they must be under their owner's control, be on no more than a 6 foot leash, and cleaned up

after at all times. Dogs are not permitted on beaches or in the wilderness. There are 22 accessible campgrounds for a variety of camping choices; most are near water and have beaches, and they all have picnic tables, fire grates, toilet facilities, and potable water is available at most. The camping and tent areas also allow dogs. There is a dog walk area at the campground. There are no water hookups at the campgrounds. Multiple dogs may be allowed.

Greenwood Campgrounds
2401 Hilton Road
Jackson, MI
517-522-8600
greenwoodacrescampground.com
Dogs of all sizes are allowed. There are no additional pet fees. Dogs must be leashed and cleaned up after. This RV park is closed during the off-season. The camping and tent areas also allow dogs. There is a dog walk area at the campground. Multiple dogs may be allowed.

Sleepy Hollow State Park
7835 E Price Road
Laingsburg, MI
517-483-4277 (800-447-2757)
A 410 acre lake, river tributaries, open fields, woods, over 16 miles of hiking trails, educational activities, year round recreational opportunities, and more are offered at this 2,678 acre park (also a popular migration stop). Dogs of all sizes are allowed for no additional fee. Dogs must be on no more than a 6 foot leash and cleaned up after at all times; they are not allowed on the beach. The camp area offers 181 sites, modern facilities, concessionaires, and a store. This RV park is closed during the off-season. The camping and tent areas also allow dogs. There is a dog walk area at the campground. There are no water hookups at the campgrounds. 2 dogs may be allowed.

Lakeport State Park
7605 Lakeshore Road
Lakeport, MI
810-327-6765
Dogs of all sizes are allowed. There are no additional pet fees. Dogs may not be left unattended at any time, including in automobiles, and they must have a current rabies certificate and shot records. Dogs must be quiet, well behaved, be on no more than a 6 foot leash, and be cleaned up after. Dogs are allowed on the

trails, and at the picnic areas. Dogs are not allowed in buildings, day use areas, at the beaches or in the water. This campground is closed during the off-season. The camping and tent areas also allow dogs. There is a dog walk area at the campground. There are no water hookups at the campground. Multiple dogs may be allowed.

Lansing Campground
5339 S Aurelius Road
Lansing, MI
517-393-3200
Dogs of all sizes are allowed. There are no additional pet fees. Dogs must be well behaved, leashed, and cleaned up after. This RV park is closed during the off-season. There is a dog walk area at the campground. Multiple dogs may be allowed.

Hoyles Marina and Campground
135 S Linwood Beach Road
Linwood, MI
989-697-3153
hoylesmarina.com
Dogs of all sizes are allowed. There are no additional pet fees. Dogs may be off leash in some areas as long as there is control by owner and your dog will not run after people or pets, otherwise they must be leashed and cleaned up after. Dogs must be quiet, especially at night, and be well behaved. Dogs may not be left unattended. The camping and tent areas also allow dogs. There is a dog walk area at the campground. Multiple dogs may be allowed.

Ludington State Park
8800 H 116
Ludington, MI
231-843-2423 (800-447-2757)
With almost 3,000 acres nestled between Hamlin Lake and Lake Michigan offering an outdoor interpretive facility, beaches, sand dunes, marshlands, and forests, this park affords for a variety of educational and recreational opportunities. Dogs are allowed for no additional pet fee; they must be current on vaccinations and rabies shots. Dogs may not be left unattended in a vehicle, camper, or a campsite at any time, and they must be quiet, on no more than a 6 foot leash, and cleaned up after at all times. Dogs may not be left outside tied up alone and they are not allowed in any park buildings or at swim beaches. The park has seasonal concessionaires, a store, free Wi-Fi (near main headquarters),

and more than 350 campsites from rustic to modern with showers and restrooms. The camping and tent areas also allow dogs. There is a dog walk area at the campground. There are no water hookups at the campgrounds. Multiple dogs may be allowed.

Nordhouse Dunes Natural Area
W Numberg Road
Ludington, MI
231-723-2211
Located in the Manistee Forest, this 3,450 acre park features the largest area of wind blown sand dunes and interdunal wetlands neighboring fresh water than anywhere else in the world, and among the wooded and open dunes are miles and miles of trails to explore this unique ecosystem. Dogs are welcome throughout the park; they are not allowed on beaches. Dogs may not be left unattended at any time, and they must be leashed and cleaned up after at all times. Wilderness camping is permitted, and although there are restroom facilities, there is no potable water. There are unofficial campsites on Green Road just before the wilderness that is sometimes used by small RV's and trailers. The camping and tent areas also allow dogs. There is a dog walk area at the campground. There are no electric or water hookups at the campgrounds. 2 dogs may be allowed.

Mackinaw City/Mackinac Island KOA
566 Trailsend Road
Mackinaw City, MI
231-436-5643 (800-562-1738)
koa.com
Dogs of all sizes are allowed. There are no additional pet fees, but there can only be one pet per adult per site. Dogs may not be left unattended, must be leashed, and cleaned up after. Dogs are not allowed in the cabins, tents, or pop ups. There are some breed restrictions. This RV park is closed during the off-season. There is a dog walk area at the campground.

Mackinaw Mill Creek Camping
9730 H 23
Mackinaw City, MI
231-436-5584
campmackinaw.com
Dogs of all sizes are allowed. There are no additional pet fees. Dogs must be leashed and cleaned up after, and they are not allowed on the beach. The camping and tent

areas also allow dogs. There is a dog walk area at the campground. Multiple dogs may be allowed.

Lake Gogebic State Park
N 9995 H 64
Marenisco, MI
906-842-3341 (800-44-PARKS (447-2757))
This recreational park has about a mile of lake frontage on the largest inland lake in the Upper Peninsula. Dogs of all sizes are allowed. There are no additional pet fees. Dogs may not be left unattended at any time, including in automobiles, and they must have a current rabies certificate and shot records. Dogs must be quiet, well behaved, be on no more than a 6 foot leash, and be cleaned up after. Dogs are allowed on the trails, and at the picnic areas. Dogs are not allowed in buildings, day use areas, at the beaches or in the water. This campground is closed during the off-season. The camping and tent areas also allow dogs. There is a dog walk area at the campground. There are no water hookups at the campground. Multiple dogs may be allowed.

Tri-Lakes Trails Campground
219 Perrett Road
Marshall, MI
269-781-2297
There are plenty of land and water recreational opportunities at this 300 acre park that offers wooded areas of virgin timber, 3 scenic lakes, and trails that wind through a variety of landscapes. Dogs of all sizes are allowed for no additional fee. Dogs must be leashed and cleaned up after at all times. This RV park is closed during the off-season. The camping and tent areas also allow dogs. There is a dog walk area at the campground. Multiple dogs may be allowed.

Jellystone Park
8239 W Hazel
Mears, MI
231-873-4502
silverlakejellystone.com
Dogs of all sizes are allowed. There are no additional pet fees. Dogs may not be left unattended, must be leashed, and cleaned up after. This RV park is closed during the off-season. The camping and tent areas also allow dogs. There is a dog walk area at the campground. Multiple dogs may be allowed.

Silver Lake State Park
9679 W State Park Road

Mears, MI
231-873-3083 (800-447-2757)
This scenic park offers almost 3000 acres of mature forests, dunes, a large sandy beach, and more than 4 miles of shoreline. Dogs are allowed for no additional pet fee; they must be current on vaccinations and rabies shots. Dogs may not be left unattended in a vehicle, camper, or a campsite at any time, and they must be quiet, on no more than a 6 foot leash, and cleaned up after at all times. Dogs may not be left outside tied up alone and they are not allowed in any park buildings or at swim beaches. The campground offers 200 sites, picnic tables, grills, and modern facilities. This RV park is closed during the off-season. The camping and tent areas also allow dogs. There is a dog walk area at the campground. There are no water hookups at the campgrounds. Multiple dogs may be allowed.

Yankee Springs Recreation Area
2104 Briggs Road S
Middleville, MI
269-795-9081 (800-44-PARKS (447-2757))
Providing a long list of seasonal land and water recreational opportunities, this 5,200 acre, year round park also offers 9 lakes and 30 miles of hiking trails. Dogs are allowed for no additional pet fee; they must be current on vaccinations and rabies shots. Dogs may not be left unattended in a vehicle, camper, or a campsite at any time, and they must be quiet, on no more than a 6 foot leash, and cleaned up after at all times. Dogs may not be left outside tied up alone and they are not allowed in any park buildings or at swim beaches. There are 2 campsites; the modern camp area has a boat access site/launch, and the other camp area is a rustic setting at Deep Lake. This RV park is closed during the off-season. The camping and tent areas also allow dogs. There is a dog walk area at the campground. There are no water hookups at the campgrounds. Multiple dogs may be allowed.

Valley Plaza Resort
5215 Bay City Road
Midland, MI
989-496-2159
valleyplazaresort.com
One dog of any size is allowed. There are no additional pet fees. Dogs must be well behaved, leashed, and cleaned up after. This RV park is closed during the off-

season. The camping and tent areas also allow dogs. There is a dog walk area at the campground.

Harbortown RV Resort
14931 La Plaisance
Monroe, MI
734-384-4700
harbortownrv.com
Dogs of all sizes are allowed. There are no additional pet fees. Dogs may not be left unattended, must be leashed, and cleaned up after. The camping and tent areas also allow dogs. There is a dog walk area at the campground. Multiple dogs may be allowed.

Moscow Maples RV Park
8291 E Chicago
Moscow, MI
517-688-9853
moscowmaples.com
Dogs of all sizes are allowed. There are no additional pet fees. Dogs may not be left unattended, must be leashed, and cleaned up after. This RV park is closed during the off-season. The camping and tent areas also allow dogs. There is a dog walk area at the campground. Multiple dogs may be allowed.

Pictured Rocks National Lakeshore
Sand Point Road
Munising, MI
906-387-3700
nps.gov/piro/
Forty miles of lakeshore compliment this park that features sandy beaches, waterfalls, forests, lakes, picturesque sandstone cliffs, and an abundance of year round land and water recreational opportunities. Dogs are allowed for no extra fee at the Little Beaver Campground; at the Beaver Basin Outlook in the parking lot and on the road; at the Miner's Castle picnic/overlook and beach area; at the Miner's Falls picnic area and parking lot; at Sand Point to the base of the cliff and on the beach, and on the trail to Munising Falls. They are not allowed anywhere else. Dogs must be on no more than a 6 foot leash and cleaned up after. Campsites are first come first served and provide a fire grate, tent pad, picnic table, and solar powered wells for water and vault toilets are nearby. This RV park is closed during the off-season. The camping and tent areas also allow dogs. There is a dog walk area at the campground. There are no electric or water hookups at the campgrounds. 2 dogs may be allowed.

Wandering Wheels Campground
E10102 H 28E
Munising, MI
906-387-3315
wanderingwheelscampground.net
Dogs of all sizes are allowed. There are no additional pet fees. Dogs must be leashed and cleaned up after. This RV park is closed during the off-season. The camping and tent areas also allow dogs. There is a dog walk area at the campground. Dogs are allowed in the camping cabins. Multiple dogs may be allowed.

Hoffmaster State Park
6585 Lake Harbor Road
Muskegon, MI
231-798-3711 (800-447-2757)
This park sits nestled among forest covered dunes and offers almost 3 miles of one of the best beaches on the coast in addition to a variety of year round educational and recreational opportunities. Dogs are allowed for no additional pet fee; they must be current on vaccinations and rabies shots. Dogs may not be left unattended in a vehicle, camper, or a campsite at any time, and they must be quiet, on no more than a 6 foot leash, and cleaned up after at all times. Dogs may not be left outside tied up alone and they are not allowed in any park buildings or on the beach. The campground offers 293 sites and modern facilities. This RV park is closed during the off-season. The camping and tent areas also allow dogs. There is a dog walk area at the campground. There are no water hookups at the campgrounds. Multiple dogs may be allowed.

Muskegon
3500 N Strand
Muskegon, MI
231-766-3900 (800-562-3902)
koa.com
Dogs of all sizes are allowed. There are no additional pet fees. Dogs may not be left unattended, must be leashed, and cleaned up after. Dogs are allowed at the backside of the lake. There are some breed restrictions. This RV park is closed during the off-season. The camping and tent areas also allow dogs. There is a dog walk area at the campground. Multiple dogs may be allowed.

Newberry KOA
13724 H 28
Newberry, MI

906-293-5762 (800-562-5853)
koa.com
Dogs of all sizes are allowed. There are no additional pet fees. Dogs may not be left unattended, must be leashed, and cleaned up after. This RV park is closed during the off-season. The camping and tent areas also allow dogs. There is a dog walk area at the campground. Dogs are allowed in the camping cabins. Multiple dogs may be allowed.

Leelanau State Park
15310 N Lighthouse Point Road
Northport, MI
231-386-5422
True to its Native American translation meaning "A Land of Delight", there are more than 1,300 scenic acres at this peninsula park. Dogs are allowed for no additional pet fee; they must be current on vaccinations and rabies shots. Dogs may not be left unattended in a vehicle, camper, or a campsite at any time, and they must be quiet, on no more than a 6 foot leash, and cleaned up after at all times. Dogs may not be left outside tied up alone and they are not allowed on swimming beaches. The campground offers 57 rustic sites with picnic tables and a fire ring. This RV park is closed during the off-season. The camping and tent areas also allow dogs. There is a dog walk area at the campground. There are no electric or water hookups at the campgrounds. Multiple dogs may be allowed.

W. J. Hayes State Park
1220 Wamplers Lake Road
Onsted, MI
517-467-7401 (800-447-2757)
Located in the Irish Hills surrounded by inland lakes, this is one of the state's oldest parks, and it provides a good variety of land and water recreational opportunities. Dogs are allowed throughout the park, campground, and at the cabins for no additional fee. Dogs must be on no more than a 6 foot leash and cleaned up after at all times. The campground offers reservable sites and modern facilities. This RV park is closed during the off-season. The camping and tent areas also allow dogs. There is a dog walk area at the campground. Dogs are allowed in the camping cabins. Multiple dogs may be allowed.

Porcupine Mountains Wilderness State Park
33303 Headquarters Road

Ontonagon, MI
906-885-5275 (800-447-2757)
The state's largest park at 60,000 acres, it is also one of the last remaining large wilderness areas in the Midwest, and in addition to all the recreation available, there are several educational opportunities also. Dogs are allowed for no additional pet fee; they must be current on vaccinations and rabies shots. Dogs may not be left unattended in a vehicle, camper, or a campsite at any time, and they must be quiet, on no more than a 6 foot leash, and cleaned up after at all times. Dogs may not be left outside tied up alone, and they are not allowed in park buildings or at swim beaches. The camp areas range from rustic to modern with showers, restrooms, and dump stations. The camping and tent areas also allow dogs. There is a dog walk area at the campground. There are no water hookups at the campgrounds. Multiple dogs may be allowed.

Huron National Forest
5761 North Skeel Avenue/Huron Shores Ranger District
Oscoda, MI
800-821-6263
fs.fed.us/r9/hmnf/
Located east of Manistee but combined for management purposes, they share 5 ranger districts and almost a million acres with a variety of camping areas, some 330 miles of trails, year round recreation, and diverse ecosystems that support a large variety of plants, fish, mammals, and bird species. Dogs of all sizes are allowed throughout the forest for no additional fee; they must be under their owner's control, be on no more than a 6 foot leash, and cleaned up after at all times. Dogs are not permitted on beaches. The camp areas offer restrooms, fire rings, picnic tables, and potable water. The camping and tent areas also allow dogs. There is a dog walk area at the campground. There are no electric or water hookups at the campgrounds. Multiple dogs may be allowed.

Oscoda KOA
3591 Forest Road
Oscoda, MI
989-739-5115 (800-562-9667)
koa.com
Dogs of all sizes are allowed. There are no additional pet fees. Dogs must be leashed and cleaned up

after. This RV park is closed during the off-season. The camping and tent areas also allow dogs. There is a dog walk area at the campground. Multiple dogs may be allowed.

Tahquamenon Falls State Park
41382 W H 123
Paradise, MI
906-492-3415 (800-447-2757)
This park is mostly undeveloped woods, but it is quite popular because of its beautiful and dramatic waterfalls. Dogs are allowed for no additional pet fee; they must be current on vaccinations and rabies shots. Dogs may not be left unattended in a vehicle, camper, or a campsite at any time, and they must be quiet, on no more than a 6 foot leash, and cleaned up after at all times. Dogs may not be left outside tied up alone and they are not allowed in park buildings or at swim beaches. Dogs are allowed on all the trails and at the upper and lower falls. The campsites range from rustic to modern with flush toilets, showers, fire rings, picnic tables, and a dump station. There are also concessionaires on site and an eatery at the upper falls. The camping and tent areas also allow dogs. There is a dog walk area at the campground. There are no water hookups at the campgrounds. 2 dogs may be allowed.

Charles Mears State Park
400 W Lowell Street
Pentwater, MI
231-869-2051 (800-447-2757)
Located on the shores of Lake Michigan, this park offers year round recreational opportunities, an interpretive trail, and sand blown dune areas that gives visitors great views of the surrounding area. Dogs are allowed for no additional pet fee; they must be current on vaccinations and rabies shots. Dogs may not be left unattended in a vehicle, camper, or a campsite at any time, and they must be quiet, on no more than a 6 foot leash, and cleaned up after at all times. Dogs may not be left outside tied up alone and they are not allowed in any park buildings or at swim beaches. The camp area has 175 sites, modern facilities, a store, and free Wi-Fi. This RV park is closed during the off-season. The camping and tent areas also allow dogs. There is a dog walk area at the campground. There are no water hookups at the campgrounds. Multiple dogs may be allowed.

Monroe Co/Toledo North KOA
US 23 at Summerfield Road
Petersburg, MI
734-856-4972 (800-562-7646)
monroekoa.com
Dogs of all sizes are allowed. There is a $5 per night per pet additional fee. Dogs are not allowed in the rentals. Dogs may not be left unattended, must be leashed, and cleaned up after. There are some breed restrictions. This RV park is closed during the off-season. The camping and tent areas also allow dogs. There is a dog walk area at the campground. Multiple dogs may be allowed.

Petoskey KOA
1800 N H 31
Petoskey, MI
231-347-0005 (800-562-0253)
koa.com
Dogs of all sizes are allowed. There are no additional pet fees. Dogs may not be left unattended, must be leashed, and cleaned up after. Dogs are allowed in the cabins but not the park models. This RV park is closed during the off-season. The camping and tent areas also allow dogs. There is a dog walk area at the campground. Dogs are allowed in the camping cabins. Multiple dogs may be allowed.

Pinckney Recreation Area
8555 Silver Hill Road
Pinckney, MI
734-426-4913 (800-447-2757)
This 11,000 park offers a wide variety of land and water recreation, gaming courts/fields, concessionaires, a designated wildlife watching site, and a lot more. Dogs of all sizes are allowed through most of the park, on the trails, and in the campground. Dogs may not be left unattended at any time, either in the park or in a vehicle. Dogs must be quiet, well behaved, under their owner's control at all times, and leashed and cleaned up after. There are a few different camping areas, with the largest having 186 sites. Sites are reservable and there are restrooms, showers, and sanitation stations available. This RV park is closed during the off-season. The camping and tent areas also allow dogs. There is a dog walk area at the campground. There are no water hookups at the campgrounds. Multiple dogs may be allowed.

Pleasant Lake County Park & Campground
1000 Styles Road

Pleasant Lake, MI
517-467-2300
There are 69 modern campsites available at this 22 acre park that provides a variety of land and water recreation, and a good starting point to numerous other attractions and events. Dogs of all sizes are allowed for no additional fee. Dogs are allowed in the camp area only; they are not allowed on the beach or in the water. This RV park is closed during the off-season. The camping and tent areas also allow dogs. There is a dog walk area at the campground. 2 dogs may be allowed.

Duggans Family Campground
2941 Port Austin Road
Port Austin, MI
989-738-5160
duggansfamilycampground.com
Dogs of all sizes are allowed. There are no additional pet fees. Dogs must be quiet and well behaved. Dogs may not be left unattended, must be leashed, and cleaned up after. This RV park is closed during the off-season. The camping and tent areas also allow dogs. There is a dog walk area at the campground. Multiple dogs may be allowed.

Port Crescent State Park
1775 Port Austin Road
Port Austin, MI
989-738-8663
In a setting of sand, surf, and trees this recreation destination also has a wooden boardwalk that follows along the shoreline affording some excellent scenic vistas. Dogs are allowed for no additional pet fee; they must be current on vaccinations and rabies shots. Dogs may not be left unattended in a vehicle, camper, or a campsite at any time, and they must be quiet, on no more than a 6 foot leash, and cleaned up after at all times. Dogs may not be left outside tied up alone and they are not allowed in any park buildings (including cabins) or at swim beaches; they are allowed at the Buccaneer Den Beach. The campground offers 137 sites and modern facilities. This RV park is closed during the off-season. The camping and tent areas also allow dogs. There is a dog walk area at the campground. There are no water hookups at the campgrounds. Multiple dogs may be allowed.

Roberts Roost Campsite
3121 Gook Road

Quesnel, MI
250-747-2015 (888-227-8877)
robertsroostcampsite.ca/
In addition to the wide variety of land and water recreation here, the beauty of Dragon Lake is upstaged only by its exquisite gardens, scenic walking paths, and expansive green lawns. Of special note is the "Heart Garden"; a perfect place for some quiet repose or special occasions. Dogs of all sizes are allowed for no additional fee. Dogs must be leashed and cleaned up after. This RV park is closed during the off-season. The camping and tent areas also allow dogs. There is a dog walk area at the campground. Multiple dogs may be allowed.

Whitefish Hill RV Park
8455 H 2
Rapid River, MI
800-476-6515
whitefishhill.com
Dogs of all sizes are allowed. There are no additional pet fees for the RV or camp sites, however there is a $50 refundable pet deposit for any of their rentals. Dogs must be leashed and cleaned up after. The camping and tent areas also allow dogs. There is a dog walk area at the campground. Multiple dogs may be allowed.

Coloma/St Joseph KOA
3527 Coloma Road
Riverside, MI
269-849-3333
koa.com
Dogs of all sizes are allowed. There are no additional pet fees. Dogs may not be left unattended, must be leashed, and cleaned up after. There are some breed restrictions. This RV park is closed during the off-season. The camping and tent areas also allow dogs. There is a dog walk area at the campground. Dogs are allowed in the camping cabins. 2 dogs may be allowed.

Higgins Lake / Roscommon KOA
3800 W. Federal H
Roscommon, MI
989-275-8151 (800-562-3351)
koa.com/where/mi/22229/
This wooded park sits along a 10,000 acre lake-once voted the 6th most beautiful lake in the world by National Geographic. Great for swimming with its sandy shallow shores, it is also a favorite among snorkelers, anglers, and boating enthusiasts. Free Wi-Fi, a snack bark, an extreme 25 foot Rock climbing wall, outdoor movies, and

much more are also available. Dogs are allowed for no additional fee with a credit card on file, and there is a pet policy to sign at check in. Dogs may not be left unattended, and they must be on no more than a 6 foot leash and cleaned up after at all times. There are some breed restrictions. This RV park is closed during the off-season. The camping and tent areas also allow dogs. There is a dog walk area at the campground. Multiple dogs may be allowed.

North Higgins Lake State Park
11747 N Higgins Lake Drive
Roscommon, MI
989-821-6125 (800-44PARKS (447-2757))
This park was once the world's largest seedling nursery which led in part to a large population of animals, birds, trees and plants. Dogs of all sizes are allowed at no additional fee. Dogs may not be left unattended, they must be on no more than a 6 foot leash, and cleaned up after. Dogs are allowed on the trails, but they are not allowed on the beach, in buildings, or on ski trails in winter. This campground is closed during the off-season. The camping and tent areas also allow dogs. There is a dog walk area at the campground. There are no water hookups at the campground. Multiple dogs may be allowed.

Back Forty Ranch
5900 S Water Road
Rothbury, MI
231-894-4444 (800-368-2535)
doublejj.com
Dogs of all sizes are allowed. There are no additional pet fees for RV spaces, however there is a $25 per night per pet additional fee for the Back 40 Cabins plus a $100 refundable deposit. Dogs may not be left unattended except for short periods and if they will be well behaved in owner's absence. Dogs must be leashed and cleaned up after. The camping and tent areas also allow dogs. There is a dog walk area at the campground. Dogs are allowed in the camping cabins. Multiple dogs may be allowed.

Van Buren State Park
23960 Ruggles Road
South Haven, MI
269-637-2788 (800-447-2757)
There are 400 recreational acres at this park with a mile of sandy beach on shores of Lake Michigan, and a highlight of this park is the high

dunes. Dogs are allowed for no additional pet fee; they must be current on vaccinations and rabies shots. Dogs may not be left unattended in a vehicle, camper, or a campsite at any time, and they must be quiet, on no more than a 6 foot leash, and cleaned up after at all times. Dogs may not be left outside tied up alone and they are not allowed in any park buildings or at swim beaches. The campground offers 220 sites, modern restroom facilities, picnic tables, fire pits, and a playground. This RV park is closed during the off-season. The camping and tent areas also allow dogs. There is a dog walk area at the campground. There are no water hookups at the campgrounds.

St. Ignace/Mackinac Island KOA
1242 H 2 W
St Ignace, MI
906-643-9303 (800-562-0534)
koa.com
Dogs of all sizes are allowed. There are no additional pet fees. Dogs may not be left unattended, must be leashed, and cleaned up after. This RV park is closed during the off-season. The camping and tent areas also allow dogs. There is a dog walk area at the campground. Dogs are allowed in the camping cabins. Multiple dogs may be allowed.

Big Bend Family Campground
513 Conrad Road
Standish, MI
989-653-2267
bigbendcamp.com
Dogs of all sizes are allowed. There are no additional pet fees. Dogs can go in the river and the lake, otherwise they must be leashed at all times and cleaned up after. This RV park is closed during the off-season. The camping and tent areas also allow dogs. There is a dog walk area at the campground. Dogs are allowed in the camping cabins. Multiple dogs may be allowed.

River Ridge Resort
22265 8 mile Road
Stanwood, MI
877-287-4837
riverridgeresort.com
Dogs of all sizes are allowed. There is a $3 per night per dog additional fee. Dogs must be leashed and cleaned up after. There is a dog walk area at the campground. Multiple dogs may be allowed.

Leisure Lake Campground
505 S Warner Road
Sumner, MI
989-875-4689 (877-975-4689)
Dogs of all sizes are allowed. There are no additional pet fees. Dogs must be quiet, not left unattended, leashed and cleaned up after. Dogs are not allowed at the beach area of the lake, but they are allowed at the east end. This RV park is closed during the off-season. The camping and tent areas also allow dogs. There is a dog walk area at the campground. Multiple dogs may be allowed.

Holiday Park Campground
4860 H 31S
Traverse City, MI
231-938-4410
Dogs of all sizes are allowed. There are no additional pet fees. Dogs must be leashed and cleaned up after. This RV park is closed during the off-season. The camping and tent areas also allow dogs. There is a dog walk area at the campground. Multiple dogs may be allowed.

Interlochen State Park
On Michigan H 137
Traverse City, MI
231-276-9511 (800-447-2757)
Covering 200 acres sitting between two popular swimming and fishing lakes, this is the state's first park and it provides a variety of land and water recreation. Dogs are allowed for no additional pet fee; they must be current on vaccinations and rabies shots. Dogs may not be left unattended in a vehicle, camper, or a campsite at any time, and they must be quiet, on no more than a 6 foot leash, and cleaned up after at all times. Dogs may not be left outside tied up alone and they are not allowed in any park buildings or at swim beaches. The camp areas range from rustic to modern with showers, restrooms, and dump stations. This RV park is closed during the off-season. The camping and tent areas also allow dogs. There is a dog walk area at the campground. There are no water hookups at the campgrounds. Multiple dogs may be allowed.

Traverse City State Park
1132 H 32N
Traverse City, MI
231-922-5270 (800-447-2757)
Great views, sugary sand, mixed forests, and a variety of year round land and water recreational opportunities are available at this 47

acre urban park. Dogs are allowed for no additional fee. Dogs must be under their owner's control, leashed, and cleaned up after at all times (mutt mitts are supplied). Although dogs are not allowed at the swim beach, there is an area at the southern end of the beach where dogs may go. There is one small, posted area in the park where dogs are not allowed. Set among the woods, the seasonal campground offers 343 sites with modern bathhouse facilities, picnic tables, and grills. The camping and tent areas also allow dogs. There is a dog walk area at the campground. There are no water hookups at the campgrounds. Multiple dogs may be allowed.

Cadillac Woods Campground
23163 H 115
Tustin, MI
231-825-2012
campthewoods.com
Dogs of all sizes are allowed. There are no additional pet fees. Dogs may not be left unattended, must be leashed and cleaned up after. Dogs are allowed off leash at your site if the dog will not chase people or pets, and will stay on the site. The camping and tent areas also allow dogs. There is a dog walk area at the campground. Dogs are allowed in the camping cabins. Multiple dogs may be allowed.

Highland Recreation Area
5200 E Highland Road
White Lake, MI
248-889-3750 (800-44PARKS (447-2757))
There are a variety of trails at this park of about 5,900 acres, with 4 lakes, a doggy trail, and activities for all seasons. Dogs of all sizes are allowed at no additional fee. Dogs may not be left unattended, they must be on no more than a 6 foot leash, and be cleaned up after. Dogs are allowed on marked trails, but they are not allowed in public swim areas or in buildings. This campground is closed during the off-season. The camping and tent areas also allow dogs. There is a dog walk area at the campground. There are no electric or water hookups at the campground. Multiple dogs may be allowed.

Traverse Bay RV Resort
5555 H 72E
Williamsburg, MI
231-938-5800
traversebayrv.com

Dogs of all sizes are allowed. There are no additional pet fees. Dogs must be leashed and cleaned up after. This RV park is closed during the off-season. There is a dog walk area at the campground. 2 dogs may be allowed.

Circle S Campground
15247 Trowbridge Road
Wolverine, MI
231-525-8300
This camp area offers a variety of land and water recreational opportunities, a camp store, laundry, and a playground. Dogs of all sizes are allowed for no additional pet fee. Dogs must be friendly, leashed, and cleaned up after. The camping and tent areas also allow dogs. There is a dog walk area at the campground. There are no water hookups at the campgrounds. Multiple dogs may be allowed.

Detroit/Greenfield KOA
6680 Bunton Road
Ypsilanti, MI
734-482-7222 (800-562-7603)
koa.com
Dogs of all sizes are allowed. There are no additional pet fees. Dogs must be leashed and cleaned up after, and may not go in the lake. This RV park is closed during the off-season. The camping and tent areas also allow dogs. There is a dog walk area at the campground. Multiple dogs may be allowed.

Dutch Treat Camping
10300 Gordon Street
Zeeland, MI
616-772-4303
dutchtreatcamping.com
Dogs of all sizes are allowed. There are no additional pet fees. Dogs may not be left unattended, must be well behaved, leashed, and cleaned up after. The camping and tent areas also allow dogs. There is a dog walk area at the campground. Multiple dogs may be allowed.

Minnesota

Big Island State Park
19499 780th Avenue
Albert Lea, MN
507-379-3403 (866-85PARKS (857-2757))
Highlights of this park include a 118 forested island, a glacial esker in

the northeast area of the park, and the migratory waterfowl that frequent here. There are also miles of trails, and a number of recreational and educational opportunities. Dogs are allowed throughout the park and in the campground for no additional fee. Dogs may not be left unattended, they must be kept on no more than a 6 foot leash, and cleaned up after at all times. Dogs are not allowed in buildings, cabins, or in beach areas. Campsites include forested or prairie settings with picnic areas, restrooms, showers, and a dump station. The camping and tent areas also allow dogs. There is a dog walk area at the campground. There are no water hookups at the campgrounds. Multiple dogs may be allowed.

Whitewater State Park
19041 H 74
Altura, MN
507-932-3007 (866-85PARKS (857-2757))
This popular park offers easy-to-challenging hiking trails. Dogs of all sizes are allowed at no additional fee. Dogs may not be left unattended, and they must be leashed and cleaned up after. Dogs are not allowed in public swim areas or buildings. Dogs are allowed on the trails. The camping and tent areas also allow dogs. There is a dog walk area at the campground. There are no water hookups at the campground. Multiple dogs may be allowed.

Beaver Trails Campground and RV Park
21943 630th Avenue
Austin, MN
507-584-6611
beavertrials.com
Dogs of all sizes are allowed. There are no additional pet fees. Dogs must be leashed and cleaned up after. There are some breed restrictions. This RV park is closed during the off-season. The camping and tent areas also allow dogs. There is a dog walk area at the campground. Dogs are allowed in the camping cabins. Multiple dogs may be allowed.

Glendalough State Park
25287 Whitetail Lane
Battle Lake, MN
218-864-0110 (866-85PARKS (857-2757))
There are 6 lakes at this park creating a wide variety of marine recreation and great fishing. The

park is also home to two wildlife observation areas, a Heritage Fishery, and during migratory times it is a prime waterfowl staging arena. Dogs are allowed throughout the park and in the campground for no additional fee. Dogs may not be left unattended, they must be kept on no more than a 6 foot leash, and cleaned up after at all times. Dogs are not allowed in buildings or on beach areas. Tent camping only is allowed, and campsites are dispersed in wooded areas about 200 to 500 feet from the parking lot. There are seasonal flush toilets, showers, and a dump station; vault toilets are available year around. The camping and tent areas also allow dogs. There is a dog walk area at the campground. There are no electric or water hookups at the campgrounds. 2 dogs may be allowed.

Bemidji KOA
510 Brightstar Road NW
Bemidji, MN
218-444-7562 (800-562-1742)
koa.com
Dogs of all sizes are allowed, and there are no additional pet fees for tent or RV sites. There is a $5 per pet per stay additional fee for the lodge and cabins. Dogs must be on no more than a 6 foot leash, and be cleaned up after. This RV park is closed during the off-season. The camping and tent areas also allow dogs. There is a dog walk area at the campground. Dogs are allowed in the camping cabins. Multiple dogs may be allowed.

Crow Wing State Park
3124 State Park Road
Brainard, MN
218-825-3075 (866-857-2757)
This scenic park offers an interpretive exhibit, 18 miles of hiking trails, and a variety of recreation. Dogs of all sizes are allowed at no additional fee. Dogs may not be left unattended except for very short periods, and they must be on no more than a 6 foot leash, and cleaned up after. Dogs are allowed on the trails, except for the ski trails in winter. The camping and tent areas also allow dogs. There is a dog walk area at the campground. There are no water hookups at the campground. Multiple dogs may be allowed.

Lake Byllesby Regional Park
7650 Echo Point Road
Cannon Falls, MN
507-263-4447 (866-857-2757)

This beautiful park, located along Lake Byllesby Reservoir, offers a variety of year round land and water recreation. Dogs of all sizes are allowed at no additional fee. Dogs may not be left unattended, and they must be on no more than a 6 foot leash, and cleaned up after. Dogs may not be tied to trees, plants, buildings, or park equipment. Dogs are allowed on the trails. This campground is closed during the off-season. The camping and tent areas also allow dogs. There is a dog walk area at the campground. Multiple dogs may be allowed.

Jay Cooke State Park
500 E H 210
Carlton, MN
218-384-4610 (866-85PARKS (866-857-2757))
Hikers and naturalists find this park a "must visit". In addition to spectacular scenic trails, a swinging suspension bridge, and a historic cemetery to explore, there are a variety of recreational opportunities here. Dogs are allowed throughout the park and in the campground for no additional fee. Dogs may not be left unattended, they must be kept on no more than a 6 foot leash, and cleaned up after at all times. Dogs are not allowed in buildings, cabins, camper cabins, tours or on beach areas. The camp areas offer a variety of settings and may have all or some of the following; flush or vault toilets, picnic tables, fire rings, potable water, and a seasonal dump station. The camping and tent areas also allow dogs. There is a dog walk area at the campground. There are no water hookups at the campgrounds. Multiple dogs may be allowed.

Chippewa National Forest
Norway Beach Road
Cass Lake, MN
218-335-8600
Steeped in a rich history and culture, this 1.6 million acre forest with 1300 lakes provides a variety of camping areas, miles of trails, recreation pursuits, and diverse ecosystems that support a large variety of plants and animals. Dogs are allowed at no additional fee. Dogs may not be left unattended, and they must be leashed and cleaned up after in the camp areas. This campground is closed during the off-season. The camping and tent areas also allow dogs. There is a dog walk area at the campground.

There are no water hookups at the campground. Multiple dogs may be allowed.

Stonypoint Resort
5510 H 2 NW
Cass Lake, MN
507-584-6611
stonyptresortcasslake.com
Dogs of all sizes are allowed. There is a $2 per night per pet additional fee. Dogs must be well behaved, house trained, leashed, and cleaned up after. This RV park is closed during the off-season. The camping and tent areas also allow dogs. There is a dog walk area at the campground. Dogs are allowed in the camping cabins. Multiple dogs may be allowed.

Cloquet/Duluth KOA
1381 Carlton Road
Cloquet, MN
218-879-5726 (800-562-9506)
koa.com
Dogs of all sizes are allowed. There are no additional pet fees. Dogs must be leashed and cleaned up after. This RV park is closed during the off-season. The camping and tent areas also allow dogs. There is a dog walk area at the campground. Dogs are allowed in the camping cabins. 2 dogs may be allowed.

Lake Shetek State Park
163 State Park Road
Currie, MN
507-763-3256 (866-85PARKS (857-2757))
This 1,100 acre park, born of glacial activity, is rich in natural and cultural history and offer 14 miles of hiking trails. It also houses an interpretive trail over a causeway to Loon Island (a bird sanctuary) and a variety of land and water recreation. Dogs of all sizes are allowed at no additional fee. Dogs may not be left unattended, and they must be on no more than a 6 foot leash at all times, and cleaned up after. Dogs are not allowed on beaches or in buildings. Dogs are allowed on trails. There is a shoreline access for dogs to go swimming. The camping and tent areas also allow dogs. There is a dog walk area at the campground. There are no water hookups at the campground. Multiple dogs may be allowed.

Lake Winnibigoshish Rec Area and Dam
County Road 9
Deer River, MN
218-326-6128 (877-444-6777)

This park is on a premier fishing lake with a dam built by the Corp of Engineers (on National Register of Historical Places), and offers spectacular views, abundant plant and wildlife, and various recreational pursuits. Dogs of all sizes are allowed at no additional fee. Dogs may not be left unattended unless they will be quiet and well behaved, and then only for a short time. Dog must be on no more than a 6 foot leash, and cleaned up after. Dogs are allowed on the trails. This campground is closed during the off-season. The camping and tent areas also allow dogs. There is a dog walk area at the campground. There are no water hookups at the campground. Multiple dogs may be allowed.

Long Lake Campsite
17421 W Long Lake Road
Detroit Lakes, MN
218-847-8920
Dogs of all sizes are allowed. There are no additional pet fees. Dogs must be quiet, well behaved, leashed, and cleaned up after. Dogs may not be on the beach. This RV park is closed during the off-season. There is a dog walk area at the campground. Multiple dogs may be allowed.

Indian Point Campground
7000 Polaski Street
Duluth, MN
218-628-4977 (800-982-2453)
indianpointcampground.com/
Close to the base of Spirit Mountain on the St. Louis River, this park-like campground offers 70 roomy campsites with free Wi-Fi, picnic tables, modern restrooms, coin operated showers, a laundry, hiking/birding trails, environmental programs, and more. Dogs are allowed for no additional fee; they must be leashed and under owner's care. This RV park is closed during the off-season. The camping and tent areas also allow dogs. There is a dog walk area at the campground. Multiple dogs may be allowed.

Superior National Forest
8901 Grand Avenue Place
Duluth, MN
218-626-4300
fs.fed.us/r9/forests/superior/
This forest of over 3 million acres provides a variety of camping areas, trails, recreation, and diverse ecosystems. Dogs are allowed at no additional fee. Dogs may not be left unattended, and they must be leashed and cleaned up after in the camp areas. Dogs are not allowed on the beach or in buildings. This campground is closed during the off-season. The camping and tent areas also allow dogs. There is a dog walk area at the campground. There are no water hookups at the campground. Multiple dogs may be allowed.

Chester Woods Campground
8378 H 14 E
Eyota, MN
507-285-7050
Located at the headwaters of Bear Creek, this 1330 park offers a 113 acre lake, hard surface and primitive trails, a fishing pier, and a wide variety of recreational activities. An annual or daily permit is required and can be purchased at the park entrance. Comfort stations, potable water, and a dump station are on site. Dogs are allowed throughout the park and in the campground for no additional fee. They must be quiet, leashed, and under owner's care at all times. This RV park is closed during the off-season. The camping and tent areas also allow dogs. There is a dog walk area at the campground. There are no water hookups at the campgrounds. Multiple dogs may be allowed.

Flying Goose Campground
2521 115th Street
Fairmont, MN
507-235-3458
flyinggoosecampground.com
Dogs of all sizes are allowed. There are no additional pet fees. Dogs may not be left unattended, and must be leashed and cleaned up after. This RV park is closed during the off-season. The camping and tent areas also allow dogs. There is a dog walk area at the campground. Multiple dogs may be allowed.

Sherwood Forest Campground
PO box 548
Gilbert, MN
218-748-2221 (800-403-1803)
This popular park provides a variety of land and water recreational pursuits. Dogs of all sizes are allowed at no additional fee. Dogs may not be left unattended at any time; they must be quiet, well behaved, be leashed, and cleaned up after. Dogs are allowed on the trails. Dogs are not allowed on beaches or in buildings. This campground is closed during the off-season. The camping and tent areas also allow dogs. There is a dog walk area at the campground. Multiple dogs may be allowed.

Buffalo River State Park
565 155th Street S
Glyndon, MN
218-498-2124 (866-85PARKS (857-2757))
This is a prairie lover's paradise with trails that meander thru one of the state's largest and best remnant prairies. There are plenty of birds and wildlife, a forest path and interpretive programs. Dogs are allowed throughout the park and in the campground for no additional fee. Dogs may not be left unattended, but they must be kept on no more than a 6 foot leash, and cleaned up after at all times. Dogs are not allowed in buildings, on tours, or in beach areas. There are 44 campsites and reservations are recommended in summer. There are seasonal flush toilets, showers, and dump station; vault toilets are available year around. The camping and tent areas also allow dogs. There is a dog walk area at the campground. There are no water hookups at the campgrounds. Multiple dogs may be allowed.

Pokegama Lake and Dam
34385 H 2
Grand Rapids, MN
218-326-6128 (877-444-6777)
This scenic park lies along the Mississippi River and offers a variety of activities and recreation. Dogs of all sizes are allowed at no additional fee. Dogs may not be left unattended unless they will be quiet and well behaved, and only then for short periods. Dogs must be on no more than a 6 foot leash, and cleaned up after. This campground is closed during the off-season. The camping and tent areas also allow dogs. There is a dog walk area at the campground. There are no water hookups at the campground. Multiple dogs may be allowed.

Greenwood Campground
13797 190th Street E
Hastings, MN
651-437-5269
Dogs of all sizes are allowed. There are no additional pet fees. Dogs must be quiet, leashed, and cleaned up after. This RV park is closed during the off-season. There is a dog walk area at the campground. 2 dogs may be allowed.

Albert Lea/Austin KOA

84259 County Road 46
Hayward, MN
507-373-5170 (800-562-5196)
koa.com
Dogs of all sizes are allowed. There are no additional pet fees. Dogs must be well behaved, leashed, and cleaned up after. This RV park is closed during the off-season. The camping and tent areas also allow dogs. There is a dog walk area at the campground. Dogs are allowed in the camping cabins. Multiple dogs may be allowed.

St Croix State Park
30065 St Croix Park Road
Hinckley, MN
320-384-6591 (866-85PARKS (857-2757))
With over 34,000 acres along 2 great rivers, this scenic park offers a fire tower, miles of multi-use trails, and a variety of land and water recreation. Dogs may not be left unattended, and they must be on no more than a 6 foot leash and be cleaned up after. Dogs are not allowed on ski trails in the winter or in buildings. Dogs are allowed on the trails. The camping and tent areas also allow dogs. There is a dog walk area at the campground. There are no water hookups at the campground. Multiple dogs may be allowed.

Voyageurs National Park
3131 H 53
International Falls, MN
218-283-6600
nps.gov/voya/
This is the only inland water-based park in the National Park system and it's maze of waterways allows visitors to explore this beautiful park from a whole different avenue. Dogs are allowed in developed areas, along park roads, at boat landings, and campsites only; they are not allowed on any of the trails in the park or inside buildings. Dogs must be kept leashed, and they may not be left unattended at any time. There are more than 200 developed campsites dispersed through the park. All the campsites are accessible only by water, and there are watercraft rental companies in the area that will allow dogs on the various watercrafts. Although free, a camping permit is required and can be obtained at any of the visitor centers or self-registration stations. This RV park is closed during the off-season. The camping and tent areas also allow dogs. There is a dog walk area at the campground. There are no electric or water hookups at the campgrounds.

Multiple dogs may be allowed.

Father Hennepin State Park
41294 Father Hennepin Park Road
Isle, MN
320-676-8763 (866-85PARKS (857-2757))
A large sandy beach, panoramic views, a hardwood forest, and a rocky shoreline all greet the hiker at this 316 acre recreational park. Dogs of all sizes are allowed at no additional fee. Dogs may not be left unattended; they must be quiet, well behaved, be on no more than a 6 foot leash, and cleaned up after. Dogs are allowed on the trails. Dogs are not allowed in swim areas or in buildings. The camping and tent areas also allow dogs. There is a dog walk area at the campground. There are no water hookups at the campground. Multiple dogs may be allowed.

Jackson KOA
2035 H 71N
Jackson, MN
507-847-3825 (800-562-5670)
koa.com
Dogs of all sizes are allowed, and there are no additional pet fees for the tent or RV sites. There is a $5 one time additional pet fee for cabin rentals. Dogs must be leashed and cleaned up after. This RV park is closed during the off-season. The camping and tent areas also allow dogs. There is a dog walk area at the campground. Dogs are allowed in the camping cabins. Multiple dogs may be allowed.

Split Rock Creek State Park
336 50th Avenue
Jasper, MN
507-348-7908 (866-85PARKS (857-2757))
This 1,303 acre park provides a variety of habitats for birds and wildlife, interpretive exhibits, self guided trails, and various land and water recreational pursuits. The off-season phone number is 507-283-1307. Dogs of all sizes are allowed at no additional fee. Dogs may not be left unattended, and they must be on no more than a 6 foot leash, and cleaned up after. Dogs are allowed on the trails. This campground is closed during the off-season. The camping and tent areas also allow dogs. There is a dog walk area at the campground. There are no water hookups at the campground. Multiple dogs may be allowed.

Minneapolis Southwest KOA
3315 W 166th Street
Jordan, MN
952-492-6440 (800-562-6317)
koa.com
Dogs of all sizes are allowed. There is a $1 per night per pet additional fee. There is an additional refundable pet deposit of $50 for the cabin rentals. Dogs must be leashed and cleaned up after. This RV park is closed during the off-season. The camping and tent areas also allow dogs. There is a dog walk area at the campground. Dogs are allowed in the camping cabins. 2 dogs may be allowed.

Charles Lindbergh State Park
1615 Lindbergh Drive S/H 52
Little Falls, MN
320-616-2525 (866-85PARKS (857-2757))
In addition to being host to the home of Charles Lindbergh, Sr., this park has lakeside picnic sites, several miles of trails, and a stone water tower. Dogs are allowed throughout the park and in the campground for no additional fee. Dogs may not be left unattended, they must be kept on no more than a 6 foot leash, and cleaned up after at all times. Dogs are not allowed in buildings or in beach areas. The campground has seasonal flush toilets, showers, and a dump station; vault toilets are available year around. This RV park is closed during the off-season. The camping and tent areas also allow dogs. There is a dog walk area at the campground. There are no water hookups at the campgrounds. 2 dogs may be allowed.

Blue Mounds State Park
1410 161st Street
Luverne, MN
507-283-1307 (866-85PARKS (857-2757))
This recreational park is full of natural surprises like the 100 foot straight-up Sioux quartzite cliff, a bison herd, and an historic site with a mystery. They also offer an interpretive center and 13 miles of hiking trails. Dogs of all sizes are allowed at no additional fee. Dogs may not be left unattended, and they must be on no more than a 6 foot leash, and cleaned up after. Dogs are not allowed on beaches or in buildings. Dogs are allowed on trails. The camping and tent areas also allow dogs. There is a dog walk area at the campground. There are no water hookups at the campground. Multiple dogs may be allowed.

143

Minneopa State Park
54497 Gadwall Road
Mankato, MN
507-389-5464 (866-85PARKS (857-2757))
Named in the Dakota language meaning "water falling twice", this beautiful park features a walking trail that surrounds the falls, then goes down to the grasslands below via a limestone stairway. Dogs are allowed throughout the park and in the campground for no additional fee. Dogs may not be left unattended, they must be kept on no more than a 6 foot leash, and cleaned up after at all times. Dogs are not allowed in buildings or in beach areas. The campground offers 61 sites, modern restrooms, and showers. The camping and tent areas also allow dogs. There is a dog walk area at the campground. There are no water hookups at the campgrounds. Multiple dogs may be allowed.

Minneapolis Northwest KOA
10410 Brockton
Maple Grove, MN
763-420-2255 (800-562-0261)
koa.com
Dogs of all sizes are allowed. There are no additional pet fees. Dogs may not be tied up outside alone, must be leashed, and cleaned up after. There are some breed restrictions. This RV park is closed during the off-season. The camping and tent areas also allow dogs. There is a dog walk area at the campground. 2 dogs may be allowed.

Savanna Portage State Park
55626 Lake Place
McGregor, MN
218-426-3271 (866-85PARKS (857-2757))
This 15,818 acre park is home to 4 fishing lakes, a river, and several miles of year round trails-including the scenic Continental Divide Trail. Dogs are allowed throughout the park and in the campground for no additional fee. Dogs may not be left unattended, they must be kept on no more than a 6 foot leash, and cleaned up after at all times. Dogs are not allowed in buildings, camper cabins, or on beaches. The campground offers over 60 sites with seasonal flush toilets, showers, and dump station; vault toilets are available year around. The camping and tent areas also allow dogs. There is a dog walk area at the campground. There are no water hookups at the campgrounds.

River Terrace Park
1335 River Street W
Monticello, MN
763-295-2264
Dogs of all sizes are allowed. There are no additional pet fees unless staying monthly. Dogs must be quiet, well behaved, leashed, and cleaned up after. This RV park is closed during the off-season. The camping and tent areas also allow dogs. There is a dog walk area at the campground. Multiple dogs may be allowed.

Moorhead/Fargo KOA
4396 28th Avenue S
Moorhead, MN
218-233-0671 (800-562-0271)
koa.com
Dogs of all sizes are allowed. There are no additional pet fees. Dogs must be well behaved, may not be left unattended, must be leashed, and cleaned up after. This RV park is closed during the off-season. The camping and tent areas also allow dogs. There is a dog walk area at the campground. Dogs are allowed in the camping cabins. Multiple dogs may be allowed.

Flandrau State Park
1300 Summit Avenue
New Ulm, MN
507-233-9800 (866-85PARKS (957-2757))
This popular park lies along the Big Cottonwood River and offers a scenic diverse terrain, 8 miles of trails, an interpretive exhibit, and a variety of land and water recreation. Dogs of all sizes are allowed at no additional fee. Dogs may not be left unattended, and they must be on no more than a 6 foot leash, and cleaned up after. Dogs are allowed on the trails, except the ski trails in winter. Dogs are not allowed by the pool or in buildings. The camping and tent areas also allow dogs. There is a dog walk area at the campground. There are no water hookups at the campground. Multiple dogs may be allowed.

Mille Lacs Kathio State Park
15066 Kathio State Park Road
Onamia, MN
320-532-3524 (866-85PARKS (857-2757))
A National Historic Landmark, this area holds a rich cultural and archaeological history and is shared through a variety of interpretive and nature programs. The park has a 100 foot observation/fire tower,

multi-use year around trails, and an abundance of wildlife. Dogs are allowed throughout the park and in the campground for no additional fee. Dogs may not be left unattended, they must be kept on no more than a 6 foot leash, and cleaned up after at all times. Dogs are not allowed in buildings, cabins, camper cabins, or in beach areas. There are pull-thru, walk-in, and backpacking campsites with seasonal flush toilets and showers; vault toilets are available all year. The camping and tent areas also allow dogs. There is a dog walk area at the campground. There are no water hookups at the campgrounds. 2 dogs may be allowed.

Big Stone Lake State Park
35889 Meadowbrook State Park Road
Ortonville, MN
320-839-3663 (866-85PARKS (857-2757))
This 986 acre park offers an Environmental Education Center and various land and water recreation. Dogs of all sizes are allowed at no additional fee. Dogs may not be left unattended; they must be quiet, well behaved, be on no more than a 6 foot leash, and cleaned up after. Dogs are allowed on the trails. Dogs are not allowed on beaches or in buildings. The off-season phone number is 320-734-4450. This campground is closed during the off-season. The camping and tent areas also allow dogs. There is a dog walk area at the campground. There are no water hookups at the campground. Multiple dogs may be allowed.

Hope Oak Knoll Campground
9545 County Road 3
Owatonna, MN
507-451-2998
Dogs of all sizes are allowed. There are no additional pet fees. Dogs may not be left unattended, and must be leashed and cleaned up after. This RV park is closed during the off-season. The camping and tent areas also allow dogs. There is a dog walk area at the campground. Multiple dogs may be allowed.

Big Pines
501 S Central
Park Rapids, MN
218-732-4483
Dogs of all sizes are allowed. There are no additional pet fees. Dogs must be leashed and cleaned up after. This RV park is closed during

the off-season. The camping and tent areas also allow dogs. There is a dog walk area at the campground. Multiple dogs may be allowed.

Itasca State Park
36750 Main Park Drive
Park Rapids, MN
218-266-2100 (866-85PARKS (857-2757))
As Minnesota's oldest state park, there is a rich blend of natural and cultural history here. The park is National Register Historic District and offers a variety of trails, interpretive exhibits and programs, tours, and plenty of recreational pursuits. Dogs of all sizes are allowed at no additional fee. Dogs may not be left unattended at any time; they must be quiet, well behaved, be on no more than a 6 foot leash or crated at all times, and cleaned up after. Dogs are allowed on the trails, except the ski trails in winter. Dogs are not allowed on beaches or in buildings. This campground is closed during the off-season. The camping and tent areas also allow dogs. There is a dog walk area at the campground. There are no water hookups at the campground. Multiple dogs may be allowed.

Forestville/Mystery Cave State Park
Route 2, Box 128/H 118
Preston, MN
507-352-5111 (866-85-PARKS (857-2757))
You will see natural wonders below and above ground at this historic park including a restored 1800's village, an interpretive exhibit, tours, nature programs, and a variety of recreational pursuits. Dogs of all sizes are allowed at no additional fee. Dogs may not be left unattended at any time; they must be quiet, well behaved, be on no more than a 6 foot leash or crated at all times, and cleaned up after. Dogs are allowed on the trails, except the ski trails in winter. Dogs are not allowed on beaches or in buildings. The camping and tent areas also allow dogs. There is a dog walk area at the campground. There are no water hookups at the campground. Multiple dogs may be allowed.

Mystery Cave State Park
21071 H 118
Preston, MN
507-352-5111 (866-85PARKS (866-857-2757))
Naturalist and recreationalist alike can both enjoy the beauty above and

below at this park. There are seasonal tours of the Mystery Cave, special events, educational opportunities, and some interesting geological and historical sites to explore above ground. Dogs are allowed throughout the park and in the campground for no additional fee. Dogs may not be left unattended, they must be kept on no more than a 6 foot leash, and cleaned up after at all times. Dogs are not allowed in buildings, cabins, on tours, in beach areas, or in the cave. The camp area offers restrooms, showers, potable water, and a dump station. The camping and tent areas also allow dogs. There is a dog walk area at the campground. There are no water hookups at the campgrounds. Multiple dogs may be allowed.

Old Barn Resort
Rt 3 Box 57
Preston, MN
507-467-2512 ext 1 (800-552-2512)
barnresort.com/
This popular recreation area has some unique features, like a three season indoor pool, access to the 60 mile Root River State Trail, caves, a museum, beautiful scenery and abundant wildlife. Pets are welcome, at no additional fee, if they are kept on a leash, cleaned up after and are quiet so as not to disturb other campers. They are not allowed in the pool or in any part of the buildings on the grounds including the barn itself. Pets may not be left at campsites unattended. This campground is closed during the off-season. The camping and tent areas also allow dogs. There is a dog walk area at the campground. Multiple dogs may be allowed.

Dakotah Meadows RV Park
2341 Park Place
Prior Lake, MN
952-445-8800
dakotahmeadows.com
Dogs of all sizes are allowed. There are no additional pet fees. Dogs must be leashed and cleaned up after. There is a dog walk area at the campground. Multiple dogs may be allowed.

Rochester/Marion KOA
5232 65th Avenue SE
Rochester, MN
507-288-0785 (800-562-5232)
rochesterkoa.com
Dogs of all sizes are allowed. There are no additional pet fees. Dogs must be leashed and cleaned up

after. There are some breed restrictions. This RV park is closed during the off-season. The camping and tent areas also allow dogs. There is a dog walk area at the campground. Multiple dogs may be allowed.

Tettegouche State Park
5702 H 61
Silver Bay, MN
218-226-6365 (866-85PARKS (866-857-2757))
Located near the north shore of Lake Superior on the Baptism River, this park is noted for its spectacular 60 foot high falls, scenic overlooks, great bird-watching (Peregrine Falcons frequent the area), the inland lakes, and miles of 4-season trails. Dogs are allowed throughout the park and in the campground for no additional fee. Dogs may not be left unattended, they must be kept on no more than a 6 foot leash, and cleaned up after at all times. Dogs are not allowed in buildings, cabins, or in beach areas. Camp site vary and they may have all or some of the following; flush or vault toilets, showers, drive-in and walk-in sites, and potable water. The camping and tent areas also allow dogs. There is a dog walk area at the campground. There are no electric or water hookups at the campgrounds. Multiple dogs may be allowed.

St Cloud Campground
2491 2nd Street SE/H 8/47
St Cloud, MN
320-251-4463 (800-690-7045)
stcloudcampground.com/
In addition to providing a wide variety of recreational activities, this 102 site campground also offers a market, laundry, modern restrooms with hot showers, a gas station, and Wi-Fi. Dogs are allowed for no additional fee; they must be leashed and cleaned up after. Dogs are not allowed in buildings or in the pool area. The camping and tent areas also allow dogs. There is a dog walk area at the campground. 2 dogs may be allowed.

William O'Brien State Park
16821 O'Brien Trail N
St Croix, MN
651-433-0500 (866-85PARKS (857-2757))
Set along the banks of the St Croix River, this picturesque park offers several miles of multi-use trails (12 miles hiking), interpretive exhibits, naturalist programs, and a variety of land and water recreation. Dogs of

all sizes are allowed at no additional fee. Dogs may not be left unattended, and they must be on no more than a 6 foot leash, and cleaned up after. Dogs are allowed on the trails, except the ski trails in winter. Dogs are not allowed in swim areas or in buildings. The camping and tent areas also allow dogs. There is a dog walk area at the campground. There are no water hookups at the campground. Multiple dogs may be allowed.

Glacial Lakes State Park
25022 County Road 41
Starbuck, MN
320-239-2860 (866-85PARKS (857-2757))
Born from glacial activity, this park is home to a wide variety of plants, birds, and wildlife, and provides a variety of trails, an interpretive exhibit and various recreational pursuits. Dogs of all sizes are allowed at no additional fee. Dogs may not be left unattended; they must be quiet, well behaved, be on no more than a 6 foot leash or crated at all times, and cleaned up after. Dogs are allowed on the trails, except the ski trails in winter. Dogs are not allowed in swim areas or in buildings. Dogs may not be tied to the trees or other park equipment. The camping and tent areas also allow dogs. There is a dog walk area at the campground. There are no water hookups at the campground. Multiple dogs may be allowed.

Interstate State Park
P. O. Box 254/H 8
Taylors Falls, MN
651-465-5711 (866-85PARKS (857-2757))
Unique geology intrigues visitors at this state park. At least 10 different lava flows are exposed in the park along with two distinct glacial deposits. The park also offers an interpretive exhibit and various trails and recreation. Dogs of all sizes are allowed at no additional fee. Dogs may not be left unattended at any time; they must be quiet, well behaved, be on no more than a 6 foot leash or crated at all times, and cleaned up after. Dogs are allowed on the trails, except the ski trails in winter. Dogs are not allowed on beaches or in buildings. The camping and tent areas also allow dogs. There is a dog walk area at the campground. There are no water hookups at the campground. Multiple dogs may be allowed.

Fortune Bay Resort Casino RV Park
1430 Bois Forte Road
Tower, MN
218-753-2611 (800-555-1714)
Resting on the shores of what has been touted as one of the 10 most scenic lakes in the country sits this resort that offers a wide range of amenities and activities above the average RV park. In addition to the activities and dining options of the casino, there is a golf course, Heritage Center, and a full service marina. Dogs are allowed in the camp area for no additional fee. Dogs must be kept leashed, and they are not allowed at the hotel, on the golf course, or public swim areas. Although dogs are allowed throughout the grounds, there is a specific trail for doing their "business". The camping and tent areas also allow dogs. There is a dog walk area at the campground. Multiple dogs may be allowed.

Gooseberry Falls
3206 H 61 E
Two Harbors, MN
218-834-3855 (866-85PARKS (866-857-2757))
Popular for its exceptionally beautiful waterfalls, the river gorge, scenic trails, and the view of Lake Superior, this park also offers self-guided tour information from the visitor center, a nature store, and a variety of recreational activities. Dogs are allowed throughout the park and in the campground for no additional fee. Dogs may not be left unattended, they must be kept on no more than a 6 foot leash, and cleaned up after at all times. Dogs are not allowed in buildings. The camp area offers 70 sites, potable water, restrooms, and a dump station. This RV park is closed during the off-season. The camping and tent areas also allow dogs. There is a dog walk area at the campground. There are no electric or water hookups at the campgrounds. 2 dogs may be allowed.

Split Rock Lighthouse State Park
3755 Split Park Lighthouse/H 61
Two Harbors, MN
218-226-6377 (866-85PARKS (866-857-2757))
Featuring 2,075 scenic acres and well known for it's historic lighthouse, this lakeside park offers a variety of recreational activities and special events. Dogs are allowed throughout the park and in the campground for no additional

fee. Dogs may not be left unattended, they must be kept on no more than a 6 foot leash, and cleaned up after at all times. Dogs are not allowed at or by historical buildings, at the lighthouse or on the sandy beach; they are allowed at the pebble beach area. The camp area offers backpack (½ to 2 miles from parking lot) and cart-in (about 2000 feet from parking lot) camping; wheeled carts are available. There are flush and vault toilets, potable water, and seasonal showers. This RV park is closed during the off-season. The camping and tent areas also allow dogs. There is a dog walk area at the campground. There are no electric or water hookups at the campgrounds. Multiple dogs may be allowed.

Kiesler's Campground
14360 H 14E
Waseca, MN
800-533-4642
kieslers.com
Dogs of all sizes are allowed. There are no additional pet fees. Dogs may not be left unattended. Dogs must be quiet, well behaved, leashed, and cleaned up after. This RV park is closed during the off-season. The camping and tent areas also allow dogs. There is a dog walk area at the campground. Multiple dogs may be allowed.

Lac Qui Parle State Park
14047 20th Street NW
Watson, MN
320-734-4450 (866-85PARKS (857-2757))
The Dakota Indians called this the "lake that speaks" because it is a stop over for thousands of migratory Canada geese and other waterfowl. The park offers a variety of land and water recreation. Dogs of all sizes are allowed at no additional fee. Dogs may not be left unattended, and they must be quiet, well behaved, on no more than a 6 foot leash, and cleaned up after. Dogs are allowed on the trails. The camping and tent areas also allow dogs. There is a dog walk area at the campground. Multiple dogs may be allowed.

Treasure Island Resort and Casino
5630 Sturgeon Lake Road
Welch, MN
888-777-5668, ext.2334
This site offers plenty of dining and entertainment choices at the resort and casino, and 95 RV spaces with modern restrooms, showers, laundry

facilities, fire pits, and a dump station. Dogs are allowed in camp area for no additional fee; they are not allowed in the casino or hotel. Dogs must be leashed and picked up after at all times. This RV park is closed during the off-season. There is a dog walk area at the campground. Multiple dogs may be allowed.

St Paul East KOA
568 Cottage Grove
Woodbury, MN
651-436-6436 (800-562-3640)
stpaulkoa.com
Dogs of all sizes are allowed. There are no additional pet fees. Dogs must be quiet, well behaved, leashed, and cleaned up after. There are some breed restrictions. This RV park is closed during the off-season. The camping and tent areas also allow dogs. There is a dog walk area at the campground. Dogs are allowed in the camping cabins. Multiple dogs may be allowed.

Mississippi

Tombigbee National Forest
H 15S
Ackerman, MS
662-285-3264
This 66,600 acre forest provides a variety of camping areas, trails, recreation, and diverse ecosystems that support a large variety of plants, fish, mammals, and bird species. Dogs are allowed at no additional fee. Dogs may not be left unattended, and they must be leashed and cleaned up after in the camp areas. Dogs are allowed on the trails. This campground is closed during the off-season. The camping and tent areas also allow dogs. There is a dog walk area at the campground. There are no electric or water hookups at the campground. Multiple dogs may be allowed.

Hollywood Casino RV Park
711 Hollywood Blvd
Bay St Louis, MS
228-467-9257 (866-758-2591)
hollywoodcasinobsl.com./rv/
In addition to all the entertainment and dining options of a 24-hour casino plus a championship golf course, this RV park has a number of its own amenities to offer. There are 100 sites with cable TV, Wi-Fi, picnic tables, grills, a laundry, restrooms,

showers, 24 hour security, and more. Dogs are allowed for no additional fee; they must be leashed and picked up after at all times. There is a dog walk area at the campground. Multiple dogs may be allowed.

Swinging Bridge RV Park
100 Holiday Rambler Lane
Bryam, MS
800-297-9127
Dogs of all sizes are allowed. There are no additional pet fees. Dogs may not be left unattended outside, and they must be leashed and cleaned up after. There are some breed restrictions. There is a dog walk area at the campground. Multiple dogs may be allowed.

Movietown RV Park
109 Movietown Drive
Canton, MS
601-859-7990
movietownrv.com/rvpark.htm
Dogs of all sizes are allowed. There are no additional pet fees. Dogs may not be left unattended outside, and they must be quiet, well behaved, leashed and cleaned up after. The camping and tent areas also allow dogs. There is a dog walk area at the campground. Multiple dogs may be allowed.

Twitley Branch Camping Area
9200 Hamrick Road
Collinsville, MS
601-626-8068
Dogs are allowed at no additional fee. Dogs may not be left unattended unless they will be quiet and very well behaved, and they may not be left outside unattended at any time. Dogs must be leashed and cleaned up after. Dogs are not allowed on the beach or in the buildings. The camping and tent areas also allow dogs. There is a dog walk area at the campground. Multiple dogs may be allowed.

Mimosa Landing Campground
501 Rustique Brick Drive
Columbia, MS
866-736-9700
mimosalanding.com
Dogs of all sizes are allowed. There are no additional pet fees. Dogs must be leashed and cleaned up after. There is a dog walk area at the campground. 2 dogs may be allowed.

Lake Lowndes State Park
3319 Lake Lowndes Road
Columbus, MS

662-328-2110
This scenic park sits along a 150 acre lake, and offers a wide array of land and water activities and recreation. It also hosts an amphitheater and a nature trail. Dogs are allowed at no additional fee. Dogs may not be left unattended outside, and they must be leashed and cleaned up after. Dogs are allowed on the trails. The camping and tent areas also allow dogs. There is a dog walk area at the campground. Multiple dogs may be allowed.

Bienville National Forest
3473 H 35S
Forest, MS
601-469-3811
This working forest of 178,000 acres provides a variety of camping areas, trails, recreation, and diverse ecosystems that support a large variety of plants, fish, mammals, and bird species. Dogs are allowed at no additional fee. Dogs may not be left unattended, and they must be leashed and cleaned up after in the camp areas. This campground is closed during the off-season. The camping and tent areas also allow dogs. There is a dog walk area at the campground. Multiple dogs may be allowed.

Little Creek Ranch
181 County Road 345
Glen, MS
662-287-0362
littlecreek.ms/
Dogs of all sizes are allowed. There are no additional pet fees. Dogs must be quiet, well behaved, leashed, and cleaned up after. The camping and tent areas also allow dogs. There is a dog walk area at the campground. Multiple dogs may be allowed.

Gulf Islands National Seashore
3500 Park Road
Gulf Breeze, FL
228-875-9057 ext. 100
nps.gov/guis/
As the country's largest national seashore, visitors will find an abundance of recreational and educational activities here. There are interpretive programs, historic sites, sugar white beaches, and an abundance of flora, fauna and birds. Dogs are allowed in most areas of the park. They are not allowed on the beach on the Florida side; nor are they allowed on the federally designated wilderness islands, Horn or Petit Bois Islands, or the

designated swim beach on West Ship Island on the Mississippi side. Dogs are not allowed in buildings, and they must be on no more than a 6 foot leash, and picked up after at all times. Dogs are not allowed to be left in cars. There are 2 campgrounds with sites available first come/first served. There are picnic tables, grills, restrooms, showers, potable water, and a dump station. The camping and tent areas also allow dogs. There is a dog walk area at the campground. Multiple dogs may be allowed.

Paul B Johnson State Park
319 Geiger Lake Road
Hattiesburg, MS
601-582-7721 (800-GO-PARKS (467-2757))
home.mdwfp.com/parks.aspx
The mixture of trees here creates a beautiful natural wonderland to explore. In addition, the park offers a gaming room, a well stocked 300 acre lake, and a disc golf course. Fishing licenses are available at the park. Dogs are allowed for no additional fee; they must be on no more than a 6 foot leash and picked up after at all times. Dogs are not allowed in cabins, buildings, or on the beach. Camping is available by reservation only. There are 150 campsites, picnic tables, grills, restrooms, bathhouses, a private swim beach, and a dump station. The camping and tent areas also allow dogs. There is a dog walk area at the campground. Multiple dogs may be allowed.

Chewalla Lake Rec Area
Higdon/Chewalla Road
Holly Springs, MS
601-236-6550
Once a special place for Native Americans, this beautiful recreation area now offers it's tranquil, scenic ambiance to visitors from all over. There is a 260 lake with an accessible fishing pier, a boat/mooring dock, and a swimming beach. Dogs are allowed for no additional fee; they must be on no more than a 6 foot leash and picked up after at all times. Dogs are not allowed on the beach. The campground has 42 sites, modern restrooms with showers, potable water, and a dump station. This RV park is closed during the off-season. The camping and tent areas also allow dogs. There is a dog walk area at the campground. Multiple dogs may be allowed.

Wall Doxey State Park
3946 H 7S
Holly Springs, MS
662-252-4231 (800-GOPARKS (467-2757))
This park sits along a 60-acre spring-fed lake, and offers an abundance of outdoor recreation and activities. Dogs of all sizes are allowed at no additional fee. Dogs may not be left unattended except for short periods and only if they will be quiet and well behaved. Dogs must be leashed and cleaned up after. Dogs are allowed on the trails. The camping and tent areas also allow dogs. There is a dog walk area at the campground. Multiple dogs may be allowed.

J.P. Coleman State Park
613 County Road 321
Iuka, MS
662-423-6515 (800-GO-PARKS (467-2757))
home.mdwfp.com/parks.aspx
Although a popular park for all kinds of water sports, many visitors like to explore the surrounding wilderness. There is a pool, kiddy pool, and mini golf available seasonally. Dogs are allowed for no additional fee; they must be on no more than a 6 foot leash and picked up after at all times. Dogs are not allowed in cabins or in any park buildings. The campground has 86 sites, picnic tables, grills, restrooms, hot showers, a laundry, and potable water. The camping and tent areas also allow dogs. There is a dog walk area at the campground. There are no water hookups at the campgrounds. Multiple dogs may be allowed.

Holly Springs National Forest
100 W Capital Street, Suite 1141
Jackson, MS
662-236-6550
This forest's biodiversity offers a wide range of habitats for migratory and resident bird and wildlife plus it offers numerous land and water recreational activities. Although the main office is located in Jackson and there are several entrances to the forest; camping facilities with amenities is located just out of Holly Springs at the Lake Center exit from H 78. Dogs are allowed for no additional fee; they must be leashed and under their owner's control at all times. Campsites range from primitive to modern with picnic tables, fire rings, and comfort stations. This RV park is closed during the off-season. The camping

and tent areas also allow dogs. There is a dog walk area at the campground. There are no electric or water hookups at the campgrounds. Multiple dogs may be allowed.

LeFleur's Bluff State Park
2140 Riverside Drive
Jackson, MS
601-987-3923 (800-GOPARKS (467-2757))
Rich in cultural heritage, this 305 acre park features a nine-hole golf course with a driving range, a variety of trails, and various land and water activities and recreation. Dogs of all sizes are allowed at no additional fee. Dogs may not be left unattended, and they must be leashed and cleaned up after. Dogs are not allowed in the playground area. Dogs are allowed on the trails. The camping and tent areas also allow dogs. There is a dog walk area at the campground. Multiple dogs may be allowed.

J.P. Coleman State Park
613 County Road 321
Luka, MS
662-423-6515 (800-GO-PARKS (467-2757))
home.mdwfp.com/parks.aspx
Although a popular park for all kinds of water sports, many visitors like to explore the surrounding wilderness. There is a pool, kiddy pool, and mini golf available seasonally. Dogs are allowed for no additional fee; they must be on no more than a 6 foot leash and picked up after at all times. Dogs are not allowed in cabins or in any park buildings. The campground has 86 sites, picnic tables, grills, restrooms, hot showers, a laundry, and potable water. The camping and tent areas also allow dogs. There is a dog walk area at the campground. There are no water hookups at the campgrounds. Multiple dogs may be allowed.

Nanabe Creek Campground
1933 Russell Mount Gilliad Road
Meridian, MS
601-485-4711
Dogs of all sizes are allowed. There are no additional pet fees. Dogs must be leashed, cleaned up after, and walked in designated pet areas. The camping and tent areas also allow dogs. There is a dog walk area at the campground. Multiple dogs may be allowed.

Roosevelt State Park
2149 H 13 S
Morton, MS

601-732-6316 (800-GOPARKS (467-2757))
This picturesque park provides a panoramic view of the Bienville National Forest. It also provides a wide variety of recreational pursuits and numerous trails. Dogs of all sizes are allowed at no additional fee. Dogs may not be left unattended, and they must be quiet, well behaved, leashed and cleaned up after. Dogs are not allowed in buildings, but they are allowed on the trails. The camping and tent areas also allow dogs. There is a dog walk area at the campground. Multiple dogs may be allowed.

Natchez State Park
230 - B Wickcliff Road
Natchez, MS
601-442-2658 (800-GO-PARKS (467-2757))
home.mdwfp.com/parks.aspx
This park's well-stocked lake produced the state's largest catch of a Big Mouth Bass, plus they offer a number of trails, a scenic auto tour, a playground, boat launch, historic sites, and more. Dogs are allowed for no additional fee; they must be on no more than a 6 foot leash and picked up after at all times. Dogs are not allowed in cabins or park buildings. The campground has 58 sites, picnic tables, grills, restrooms, hot showers, and a dump station. The camping and tent areas also allow dogs. There are no water hookups at the campgrounds. Multiple dogs may be allowed.

Holly Springs National Forest
1000 Front Street
Oxford, MS
662-236-6550
This forest provides a variety of camping areas, trails, recreation, and diverse ecosystems that support a large variety of plants, fish, mammals, and bird species. Dogs are allowed at no additional fee. Dogs may not be left unattended, and they must be leashed and cleaned up after in the camp areas. Dogs are not allowed on the beach, however, they are allowed on the trails. The camping and tent areas also allow dogs. There is a dog walk area at the campground. Multiple dogs may be allowed.

Jellystone Park
143 Campgrounds Road
Pelahatchie, MS
601-854-6859 (866-433-9644)
jellystonems.com/
A family-style fun resort, this

campground features a water park, a sandy beach, game room, fishing pier, a convenience store, Wi-Fi, an outdoor theater, gaming courts/fields, planned activities, theme weekends, and a restaurant. Dogs are allowed for no additional fee; they must be quiet, on no more than a 6 foot leash, and cleaned up after-even in the designated dog walk area. Dogs must be quiet, well behaved, and they are not allowed in buildings, the beach, and pool or playground areas. Pets may not be left unattended outside at any time. There are some breed restrictions. This RV park is closed during the off-season. The camping and tent areas also allow dogs. There is a dog walk area at the campground. 2 dogs may be allowed.

Frog Level RV Park
1532 H 16W
Philadelphia, MS
601-650-0044
froglevelrv.com
Dogs of all sizes are allowed. There are no additional pet fees. Dogs must be leashed and cleaned up after, and they can be walk just outside of the park. There are some breed restrictions. Multiple dogs may be allowed.

Grand Gulf Military Park
12006 Grand Gulf Road
Port Gibson, MS
601-437-5911
Located at a 400 acre historic military park (see listing under attractions), this camp area has 42 RV sites plus tenting areas; they offer an upper and lower camp area, picnic tables, a small picnic pavilion, a bathhouse, and laundry facilities. Dogs are allowed for no additional fee; they must be leashed and cleaned up after at all times. The camping and tent areas also allow dogs. There is a dog walk area at the campground. Multiple dogs may be allowed.

Grand Casino RV Resort
13615 Old H 61N
Robinsonville, MS
800-946-4946
Dogs of all sizes are allowed in selected areas. There are no additional pet fees. Dogs may not be left unattended outside, and they must be leashed and cleaned up after. This is an RV only park. There is a dog walk area at the campground. Multiple dogs may be allowed.

Delta National Forest
20380 H 61
Rolling Fork, MS
662-873-6256
fs.fed.us/r8/mississippi/delta/
This 60,000 acre forest is the only bottomland hardwood ecosystem in the National Forest System. Delta National Forest supports various important natural habitats and offers a variety of trails and recreation. Dogs of all sizes are allowed at no additional fee. Dogs may not be left unattended, and they must be leashed and cleaned up after. Dogs are allowed on the trails. The camping and tent areas also allow dogs. There is a dog walk area at the campground. There are no electric or water hookups at the campground. Multiple dogs may be allowed.

John W Kyle State Park
4235 State Park Road
Sardis, MS
662-487-1345 (800-GOPARKS (467-2757))
This scenic park sits along the picturesque Sardis Reservoir, and offers a wide variety of land and water activities and recreation. Dogs of all sizes are allowed at no additional fee. Dogs may not be left unattended except for short periods, and they must be quiet, well behaved, leashed, and cleaned up after. Dogs are allowed on the trails. The camping and tent areas also allow dogs. There is a dog walk area at the campground. Multiple dogs may be allowed.

Tishomingo State Park
MP 304 Natchez Trace Parkway
Tishomingo, MS
662-438-6914 (800-GO-PARKS (467-2757))
home.mdwfp.com/parks.aspx
Rich in natural and cultural history, this park shows occupation back as far as 7000 BC. Part of the Natchez Trace Parkway runs through the park; plus they offer special yearly events, playgrounds, playing fields, a museum/interpretive center, a swinging bridge, disc golf, rock climbing, and a compass course. Dogs are allowed for no additional fee; they must be on no more than a 6 foot leash and picked up after at all times. Dogs are not allowed in cabins, buildings, or on the beach. The campground offers lakeside sites and tent camping in a wooded area overlooking the lake. There are picnic tables, grills, restrooms, showers, a laundry, and a dump station on site. The camping and tent

areas also allow dogs. There is a dog walk area at the campground. Multiple dogs may be allowed.

Natchez Trace Parkway
MP 266 Natchez Trace Parkway
Tupelo, MS
800-305-7417
nps.gov/natr
Sharing hundreds of years of cultural and natural history, this Parkway details the history of this old Indian trail, it's development and growth, and commemorates the people and places that played a part in it. This All American Road and National Scenic Byway is 444 miles long; mile zero starts at Natchez and there are several other entry points available. Dogs are allowed throughout the park and in the camp areas for no additional fee. Dogs must be under their owner's control at all times. Camp areas are first come, first served and offer no amenities. They are located at mileposts 54 (Rocky Springs), milepost 193 (Jeff Busby), and milepost 385 (Meriwether Lewis) of the Natchez Trace Parkway. The camping and tent areas also allow dogs. There is a dog walk area at the campground. There are no electric or water hookups at the campgrounds. Multiple dogs may be allowed.

Rivertown Campground
5900 H 61S
Vicksburg, MS
601-630-9995
rivertown-campground.com
Dogs of all sizes are allowed. There are no additional pet fees. Dogs may not be left unattended, and they must be quiet, well behaved, leashed, and cleaned up after. There is a dog walk area at the campground. Multiple dogs may be allowed.

Vicksburg Battlefield
4407 N Frontage Road
Vicksburg, MS
601-636-2025
Dogs of all sizes are allowed. There are no additional pet fees. Dogs must be leashed and cleaned up after. The camping and tent areas also allow dogs. There is a dog walk area at the campground. Multiple dogs may be allowed.

Lake Lincoln State Park
2573 Sunset Road
Wesson, MS
601-643-9044 (800-GOPARKS (467-2757))
This scenic park is shaded by towering hardwood trees. The park offers easy access to several nearby

attractions and a variety of land and water recreation and trails. Dogs of all sizes are allowed at no additional fee. Dogs may not be left unattended, and they must be leashed and cleaned up after. Dogs are not allowed on beaches or in buildings. Dogs are allowed on the trails. The camping and tent areas also allow dogs. There is a dog walk area at the campground. Multiple dogs may be allowed.

Missouri

Arrow Rock State Historical Park
P.O. Box 1
Arrow Rock, MO
660-837-3330 (877-422-6766)
Steeped in American history, this park offers "living history" reenactments, guided walking tours and land and water recreation. Dogs of all sizes are allowed at no additional fee. Dogs may not be left unattended, and they must be on no more than a 10 foot leash, and be cleaned up after. Dogs are not allowed in buildings, but they are allowed on the trail. The camping and tent areas also allow dogs. There is a dog walk area at the campground. There are no water hookups at the campground. Multiple dogs may be allowed.

Branson KOA
1025 Headwaters Road
Branson, MO
417-334-7450 (800-562-4177)
bransonkoa.com
Dogs of all sizes are allowed. There are no additional pet fees. Dogs may not be left unattended outside, and they must be quiet, leashed, and cleaned up after. There are some breed restrictions. This RV park is closed during the off-season. The camping and tent areas also allow dogs. There is a dog walk area at the campground. Dogs are allowed in the camping cabins. Multiple dogs may be allowed.

Branson Shenanigan RV Park
3675 Keeter Street
Branson, MO
417-334-1920
bransonrvparks.com/
Dogs of all sizes are allowed. There are no additional pet fees. Dogs may not be left outside unattended. Dogs must be quiet, well behaved,

leashed, and cleaned up after. This RV park is closed during the off-season. The camping and tent areas also allow dogs. There is a dog walk area at the campground. Multiple dogs may be allowed.

Branson Stagecoach RV Park
5751 H 165
Branson, MO
417-335-8185
bransonstagecoachrv.com
Dogs of all sizes are allowed, and there are no additional pet fees for tent or RV sites. There is a $25 refundable deposit for the cabins, and only 2 dogs up to 20 pounds are allowed. Dogs must be leashed and cleaned up after. There are some breed restrictions. The camping and tent areas also allow dogs. There is a dog walk area at the campground. Dogs are allowed in the camping cabins.

Cooper Creek Campground
471 Cooper Creek Road
Branson, MO
417-334-5250
coopercreekresort.com
Dogs of all sizes are allowed, and there are no additional pet fees for tent or RV sites. There is a $7 per night per pet additional fee for the cabins. Dogs must be leashed and cleaned up after. The camping and tent areas also allow dogs. There is a dog walk area at the campground. Dogs are allowed in the camping cabins. Multiple dogs may be allowed.

Roaring River State Park
Rt 4 Box 4100
Cassville, MO
417-847-2539 (877-422-6766)
This park's geology adds breathtaking beauty, diverse plant life, and unusual rock formations to a wide array of land and water activities and recreation. Dogs of all sizes are allowed at no additional fee. Dogs may not be left unattended, and they must be on no more than a 10 foot leash, and be cleaned up after. Dogs are not allowed in buildings, but they are allowed on the trails. The camping and tent areas also allow dogs. There is a dog walk area at the campground. There are no water hookups at the campground. Multiple dogs may be allowed.

Cottonwoods RV Park
5170 Oakland Gravel Road
Columbia, MO
573-474-2747

Dogs of all sizes are allowed. There are no additional pet fees. Dogs may not be left unattended, and must be leashed and cleaned up after. There is a dog walk area at the campground. There are special amenities given to dogs at this campground. Multiple dogs may be allowed.

Finger Lakes State Park
1505 E Peabody Road
Columbia, MO
573-443-5315 (877-422-6766)
This 1,131-acre park was once a coal mining operation, and now visitors enjoy wildflowers, rolling hills and running streams, in addition to a variety of recreational pursuits. Dogs of all sizes are allowed at no additional fee. Dogs may not be left unattended, and they must be on no more than a 10 foot leash, and be cleaned up after. Dogs are not allowed on the beach or in buildings. It is suggested that dogs be walked on the trails in the Rocky Fork Conservation area next to the park because Finger Lakes is an off-road ATV park for which the trails are used. The camping and tent areas also allow dogs. There is a dog walk area at the campground. There are no water hookups at the campground. Multiple dogs may be allowed.

Eagle Ridge RV Park
22708 W 182nd Street
Eagleville, MO
660-867-5518
eagleville.com/eagleridge.html
Dogs of all sizes are allowed. There are no additional pet fees. Dogs must be leashed and cleaned up after. The camping and tent areas also allow dogs. There is a dog walk area at the campground. Multiple dogs may be allowed.

Majestic Oaks Park
8 Majestic Oaks Road
Eldon, MO
573-365-1890
majesticoakspark.com/
In addition to hundreds of wonderful shady oak trees, this family campground offers numerous activities and amenities; there is a camp store, game and TV room, modern restrooms, a pool, gaming fields and courts, and a playground on site. Dogs are allowed for no additional fee. Dogs must be leashed and cleaned up after; they are not allowed in the pool area. This RV park is closed during the off-season. The camping and tent areas also

allow dogs. There is a dog walk area at the campground. Multiple dogs may be allowed.

St Louis West KOA
18475 Old H 66
Eureka, MO
636-257-3018 (800-562-6249)
koa.com
Dogs of all sizes are allowed. There are no additional pet fees. Dogs may not be left unattended outside, and they must be leashed and cleaned up after. Dogs must be crated at all times when they are in a cabin. This RV park is closed during the off-season. The camping and tent areas also allow dogs. There is a dog walk area at the campground. Dogs are allowed in the camping cabins. Multiple dogs may be allowed.

Trailside RV Park
1000 R.D. Mize Road
Grain Valley, MO
816-229-2267
trvpark.com
Dogs of all sizes are allowed. There are no additional pet fees. Dogs must be well behaved, leashed, and cleaned up after. The camping and tent areas also allow dogs. There is a dog walk area at the campground. Multiple dogs may be allowed.

Mark Twain Cave and Campgrounds
300 Cave Hollow Road
Hannibal, MO
573-221-1656
marktwaincave.com
Dogs of all sizes are allowed. There are no additional pet fees. Dogs must be leashed and cleaned up after. There are some breed restrictions. The camping and tent areas also allow dogs. There is a dog walk area at the campground. Multiple dogs may be allowed.

Interstate RV Park
On Old H 40
Higginsville, MO
800-690-2267
interstatervpark.com
Dogs of all sizes are allowed. There are no additional pet fees. Dogs must be leashed and cleaned up after. The camping and tent areas also allow dogs. There is a dog walk area at the campground. Multiple dogs may be allowed.

Trail of Tear State Park
429 Moccasin Springs
Jackson, MO
573-334-1711 (877-422-6766)

This park, of almost 3,500 acres along the Mississippi River, is a memorial to the forced relocation of several Cherokee tribes and has interpretive exhibits about their journeys. The park now provides a wide variety of land and water activities and recreation. Dogs of all sizes are allowed at no additional fee. Dogs must be leashed and cleaned up after, and they are not allowed in buildings. Dog are allowed on the trails. The camping and tent areas also allow dogs. There is a dog walk area at the campground. Multiple dogs may be allowed.

Joplin KOA
4359 H 43
Joplin, MO
417-623-2246 (800-562-5675)
koa.com
Dogs of all sizes are allowed. There are no additional pet fees. Dogs must be leashed and cleaned up after. The camping and tent areas also allow dogs. There is a dog walk area at the campground. Dogs are allowed in the camping cabins. Multiple dogs may be allowed.

Lake of the Ozarks State Park
403 H 134
Kaiser, MO
573-348-2694 (877-422-6766)
mostateparks.com/lakeozark.htm
A major recreational destination, this 17,626+ acre park sits nestled in an undeveloped cove on the shores of one of the state's largest lakes. Dogs are allowed throughout the park and in the campground for no additional fee. Dogs may not be left unattended, they must be on no more than a 10 foot leash, and cleaned up after at all times. They must be current on their shots and license. Dogs are not allowed in buildings or beaches, and they must be inside at night. The campground has over 230 shady sites; they offer modern restrooms, showers, picnic tables, grills, a laundry, potable water, and a dump station. The camping and tent areas also allow dogs. There is a dog walk area at the campground. There are no water hookups at the campgrounds. 2 dogs may be allowed.

Water's Edge
72 Marina Way
Kimberling City, MO
417-739-5377
watersedgetr.com
Dogs of all sizes are allowed, and there are no additional pet fees for tent or RV sites. There is a $50

refundable deposit for the cabins, and only 1 small dog is allowed. Dogs may not be left unattended, must be leashed, and cleaned up after. Dogs may swim at the lake, but not in the public swim area. The camping and tent areas also allow dogs. There is a dog walk area at the campground. Dogs are allowed in the camping cabins.

Thousand Hills State Park
2431 H 157
Kirksville, MO
660-665-6995 (877-422-6766)
This 3,215-acre park with a 573 acre lake features an interpretive shelter that displays the park's petroglyphs and offers an array of activities and recreation. Dogs of all sizes are allowed at no additional fee. Dogs must be leashed and cleaned up after. Dogs must be quiet, well behaved, and may not be left unattended outside or inside for long periods. Dogs are allowed on the trails. The camping and tent areas also allow dogs. There is a dog walk area at the campground. There are no water hookups at the campground. Multiple dogs may be allowed.

Riverview RV Park
398 Woodriver Road
Lake Ozark, MO
573-365-1122 (866-242-0851)
riverviewrvparkllc.com
Dogs of all sizes are allowed. There are no additional pet fees. Dogs must be quiet, well behaved, leashed, and cleaned up after. There are some breed restrictions. This RV park is closed during the off-season. The camping and tent areas also allow dogs. There is a dog walk area at the campground. Multiple dogs may be allowed.

Watkins Woolen Mill State Park and State Historic Site
26600 Park Road N
Lawson, MO
816-580-3387
Dedicate to preserving its history with a restored seasonal living history farm, this 1500+ acre park also provides numerous recreational opportunities for the whole family. Dogs are allowed throughout the park and in the campground for no additional fee. Dogs may not be left unattended, and they must be on no more than a 10 foot leash, and cleaned up after at all times. Dogs are not allowed in buildings, at beaches, in public swim areas, or on the historic grounds. The

campground offers more than 100 sites with picnic tables, grills, lantern hooks, comfort stations, a laundry, and a dump station. The camping and tent areas also allow dogs. There is a dog walk area at the campground. There are no water hookups at the campgrounds. 2 dogs may be allowed.

Onondaga Cave State Park
7556 H H
Leasburg, MO
573-245-6576 (800-334-6946)
mostateparks.com/onondaga.htm
The cave here is listed as a National Natural Landmark, but visitors will find plenty of natural beauty above ground also. An overlook gives a great view of the Meramec River, plus there hiking trails and numerous recreational opportunities. Dogs are allowed throughout the park and in the campground for no additional fee. Dogs may not be left unattended, and they must be on no more than a 10 foot leash, and cleaned up after at all times. Dogs are not allowed in the cave, buildings, at beaches, or in public swim areas. The camp area offers modern restrooms, hot showers, a laundry, an amphitheater, a playground, and a dump station. The camping and tent areas also allow dogs. There is a dog walk area at the campground. 2 dogs may be allowed.

Bennett Spring State Park
26250 H 64A
Lebanon, MO
417-532-4338 (877-422-6766)
Home of the 4th largest natural spring in the state, this scenic park has a history of mills of one form or another, and now it provides naturalist programs and ample recreational opportunities. Dogs of all sizes are allowed at no additional fee. Dogs may not be left unattended, and they must be quiet, well behaved, be on no more than a 10 foot leash, and cleaned up after. Dogs are not allowed in buildings, but they are allowed on the trails. There are some breed restrictions. The camping and tent areas also allow dogs. There is a dog walk area at the campground. Multiple dogs may be allowed.

Ozark Trails RV Park and Campground
4171 East US Hwy 54
Linn Creek, MO
573-346-5490
ozarktrailsrvpark.com/

This family campground offers numerous activities and amenities; there is a camp store, game room, modern restrooms, a pool, gaming fields and courts, 2 scenic hiking trails, and a playground on site. Dogs are allowed for no additional fee. Dogs must be leashed and cleaned up after; they are not allowed in the pool area. The camping and tent areas also allow dogs. There is a dog walk area at the campground. Multiple dogs may be allowed.

Long Branch Lake State Park
28615 Visitors Center Road
Macon, MO
660-773-5229 (877-422-6766)
mostateparks.com/longbranch.htm
A great destination for water enthusiasts as well as nature lovers, this park of over 1,800 acres offers a variety of recreational pursuits. Dogs of all sizes are allowed at no additional fee. Dogs may not be left unattended outside, and they must be on no more than a 10 foot leash, and be cleaned up after. Dogs are not allowed on the beach, but they are allowed on the trails. The camping and tent areas also allow dogs. There is a dog walk area at the campground. There are no water hookups at the campground. 2 dogs may be allowed.

Van Meter State Park
Route 1, Box 47
Miami, MO
660-886-7537
mostateparks.com/vanmeter.htm
In addition to numerous recreational pursuits, this 1,104+ acre park is also home to several historic sites, a fresh water marsh, and a rich cultural heritage. Dogs are allowed throughout the park and in the campground for no additional fee. Dogs may not be left unattended, they must be on no more than a 10 foot leash, cleaned up after at all times, and be current on their shots and license. Dogs are not allowed in buildings or on beaches, and they must be inside at night. Pet disposal bags are available from the camp host. The campground offers basic sites available on a first-come, first-served basis. There are restrooms, a seasonal shower-house, picnic tables, grills, and potable water. The camping and tent areas also allow dogs. There is a dog walk area at the campground. There are no water hookups at the campgrounds. 2 dogs may be allowed.

Lazy Day Campground

214 H J
Montgomery City, MO
573-564-2949
lazydaycampground.net
Dogs of all sizes are allowed. There are no additional pet fees. Dogs must be leashed and cleaned up after. The camping and tent areas also allow dogs. There is a dog walk area at the campground.

Kansas City East/Oak Grove KOA
303 NE 3rd
Oak Grove, MO
816-690-6660 (800-562-7507)
koa.com
Dogs of all sizes are allowed. There are no additional pet fees. Dogs must be quiet, leashed, and cleaned up after. There are some breed restrictions. The camping and tent areas also allow dogs. There is a dog walk area at the campground. Multiple dogs may be allowed.

Osage Beach RV Park
3949 Campground Drive
Osage Beach, MO
573-348-3445
osagebeachrvpark.com
Dogs of all sizes are allowed. There are no additional pet fees. Dogs may not be left unattended, must be leashed, and cleaned up after. This RV park is closed during the off-season. There is a dog walk area at the campground. Dogs are not allowed in the camping cabins. 2 dogs may be allowed.

Ozark RV Park
320 N 20th Street
Ozark, MO
417-581-3203
Dogs of all sizes are allowed. There are no additional pet fees. Dogs must be leashed and cleaned up after. There is a dog walk area at the campground. Multiple dogs may be allowed.

Jellystone Park
5300 Foxcreek Road
Pacific, MO
636-938-5925 (800-861-3020)
eurekajellystone.com
Dogs of all sizes are allowed. There are no additional pet fees. Dogs may not be left unattended, must be leashed, and cleaned up after. This RV park is closed during the off-season. The camping and tent areas also allow dogs. There is a dog walk area at the campground. Multiple dogs may be allowed.

Perryville/Cape Girardeau KOA
89 KOA Lane

Perryville, MO
573-547-8303 (800-562-5304)
koa.com
Dogs of all sizes are allowed, and there are no additional pet fees for tent or RV sites. There is a $5 one time fee per pet for the cabins. Dogs may not be left unattended outside, and they must leashed and cleaned up after. This RV park is closed during the off-season. The camping and tent areas also allow dogs. There is a dog walk area at the campground. Dogs are allowed in the camping cabins. 2 dogs may be allowed.

Lebanon KOA
18376 Campground Road
Phillipsburg, MO
417-532-3422 (800-562-3424)
koa.com
Dogs of all sizes are allowed. There are no additional pet fees. Dogs must be leashed and cleaned up after. There are some breed restrictions. This RV park is closed during the off-season. The camping and tent areas also allow dogs. There is a dog walk area at the campground. Multiple dogs may be allowed.

Pomme de Terre State Park
HC 77, Box 890
Pittsburg, MO
417-852-4291 (877-422-6766)
This park sits on both sides of Pomme de Terre Lake, and offer a full service marina, large beaches, trails, and various recreation. Dogs of all sizes are allowed at no additional fee. Dogs may not be left unattended, and they must be on no more than a 10 foot leash, and be cleaned up after. Dogs may not be in the buildings or on the beaches, but the are allowed on the trails. The camping and tent areas also allow dogs. There is a dog walk area at the campground. There are no water hookups at the campground. Multiple dogs may be allowed.

Basswood Country RV Resort
15880 Inter Urban Road
Platte City, MO
816-858-5556
basswoodresort.com
Dogs of all sizes are allowed. There are no additional pet fees. Dogs may not be left unattended, must be quiet, leashed, and cleaned up after. There is a dog walk area at the campground. Multiple dogs may be allowed.

Hayti/Portageville KOA
2824 MO State E Outer Road
Portageville, MO
573-359-1580 (800-562-1508)
koa.com
Dogs of all sizes are allowed. There are no additional pet fees. Dogs must be leashed and cleaned up after. There are some breed restrictions. This RV park is closed during the off-season. The camping and tent areas also allow dogs. There is a dog walk area at the campground. Multiple dogs may be allowed.

Battle of Athens State Historical Park
RR1, Box 26, H CC
Revere, MO
660-877-3871 (800-334-6946)
mostateparks.com/athens.htm
This park offers exhibits and tours interpreting the battle of the northernmost Civil War battle which took place here. In addition, the park offers a variety of trails and recreational pursuits. Dogs of all sizes are allowed at no additional fee. Dogs may not be left unattended, and they must be on no more than a 10 foot leash, and be cleaned up after. Dogs are not allowed in the buildings, but they are allowed on the trails. The camping and tent areas also allow dogs. There is a dog walk area at the campground. There are no water hookups at the campground. Multiple dogs may be allowed.

Rock Port KOA
1409 H 136W
Rock Port, MO
660-744-5485 (800-562-5415)
rockportkoa.com
Dogs of all sizes are allowed. There are no additional pet fees. Dogs in the cabins must be housebroken. Dogs must be well behaved, leashed, and cleaned up after. This RV park is closed during the off-season. The camping and tent areas also allow dogs. There is a dog walk area at the campground. Dogs are allowed in the camping cabins. Multiple dogs may be allowed.

Mark Twain National Forest
401 Fairgrounds Road
Rolla, MO
573-364-4621
fs.fed.us/r9/forests/marktwain/
This scenic park supports a variety of habitats, trails, and year round land and water activities. Dogs of all sizes are allowed at no additional fee. Dogs must be leashed at all times in the camp area, and cleaned up after.

Dogs may only be left unattended for short periods, and only if the dog will be quiet and well behaved. Dogs are allowed on the trails. This campground is closed during the off-season. The camping and tent areas also allow dogs. There is a dog walk area at the campground. There are no water hookups at the campground. Multiple dogs may be allowed.

Lewis and Clark State Park
801 Lake Crest Blvd
Rushville, MO
816-579-5564 (800-334-6946)
This 200 acre park along the shores of Lewis and Clark Lake, offer an interesting history as well as a variety of land and water recreation. Dogs of all sizes are allowed at no additional fee. Dogs may not be left unattended or in vehicles, and they must be on no more than a 10 foot leash, and be cleaned up after. Dogs are not allowed in swim areas or on public beaches. Dogs may not be left outside at night, and they must have ID tags. Dogs are allowed on the trails unless otherwise marked. The camping and tent areas also allow dogs. There is a dog walk area at the campground. There are no water hookups at the campground. Multiple dogs may be allowed.

Springfield KOA
5775 W Farm Road 140
Springfield, MO
417-831-3645 (800-562-1228)
koa.com
Dogs of all sizes are allowed. There are no additional pet fees. Dogs may not be tied up or left unattended outside, and they must be leashed and cleaned up after. The camping and tent areas also allow dogs. There is a dog walk area at the campground. Dogs are allowed in the camping cabins. Multiple dogs may be allowed.

Traveler's Park Campground
425 S Trailview Road
Springfield, MO
417-866-4226
Dogs of all sizes are allowed. There are no additional pet fees. Dogs must be quiet, leashed, and cleaned up after. This RV park is closed during the off-season. There is a dog walk area at the campground. 2 dogs may be allowed.

Sundermeier RV Park
111 Transit Street
St Charles, MO
636-940-0111

sundermeierrvpark.com
Dogs of all sizes are allowed. There are no additional pet fees. Dogs must be leashed and cleaned up after. There are some breed restrictions. There is a dog walk area at the campground. Multiple dogs may be allowed.

Beacon RV Park
822 S Belt H
St Joseph, MO
816-279-5417
Dogs of all sizes are allowed. There are no additional pet fees. Dogs may not be left unattended at any time, must be well behaved, leashed, and cleaned up after. There is a dog walk area at the campground. Multiple dogs may be allowed.

Stanton/Meramec KOA
74 H 'W'
Stanton, MO
573-927-5215 (888-562-4498)
koa
Dogs of all sizes are allowed. There are no additional pet fees. Dogs may not be left unattended, and they must be leashed and cleaned up after. This RV park is closed during the off-season. The camping and tent areas also allow dogs. There is a dog walk area at the campground. Dogs are allowed in the camping cabins. Multiple dogs may be allowed.

Mark Twain State Park
20057 State Park Office Road
Stoutsville, MO
573-565-3440 (877-422-6766)
This historical park, located on Mark Twain Lake, offers a variety of habitats, trails, and land and water recreation. Dogs of all sizes are allowed at no additional fee. Dogs may not be left unattended, and they must be on no more than a 6 foot leash, and be cleaned up after. Dogs are not allowed on the beach or in buildings. Dogs are allowed on the trails. The camping and tent areas also allow dogs. There is a dog walk area at the campground. There are no water hookups at the campground. Multiple dogs may be allowed.

Merramec State Park
115 Meramec Park Drive
Sullivan, MO
573-468-6072 (877-422-6766)
mostateparks.com/meramec.htm
Although the topside of this 6,896 acre riverside park has its own stunning beauty, there are even

more spectacular scenes below, and tours are available for Fisher Cave. There are numerous recreational and educational activities, and large aquariums displaying the aquatic life of the river. Dogs are allowed throughout the park and in the campground for no additional fee. Dogs may not be left unattended, they must be on no more than a 10 foot leash, cleaned up after at all times, and current on shots and license. Dogs are not allowed in buildings, on beaches, and they must be inside at night. Pet disposal bags are available from the camp host. The campground offers picnic tables, grills, restrooms, showers, potable water, a laundry, and a dump station. The camping and tent areas also allow dogs. There is a dog walk area at the campground. 2 dogs may be allowed.

Three Forks KOA
15 KOA Road
Three Forks, MO
406-285-3611 (800-562-9752)
koa.com
Dogs of all sizes are allowed. There are no additional pet fees. Dogs may not be left outside unattended, and they must be quiet and well behaved. Dogs must be leashed and cleaned up after. This RV park is closed during the off-season. The camping and tent areas also allow dogs. There is a dog walk area at the campground. Multiple dogs may be allowed.

Jellystone Park
P O BOX 818
Van Buren, MO
573-323-4447 (888-763-5628)
currentriverjellystone.com/
Located in a rural setting with 950 feet of riverfront, this family-style fun resort features a swimming pool, a playground, an arcade/rec room, a convenience store, restaurant, dock and launch ramp, cable TV, laundry facilities, and free Wi-Fi. Dogs are allowed for no additional fee. Dogs must be quiet; they may not be left unattended at any time, and they must be leashed and cleaned up after. This RV park is closed during the off-season. The camping and tent areas also allow dogs. There is a dog walk area at the campground. Multiple dogs may be allowed.

Onyx Mountain Caverns
404 Watercrest Drive
Van Buren, MO
573-762-3341 (877-444-6777)
pulaskicountyweb.com/onyxcave/

Offering numerous recreational and educational activities, this park's main attractions are it's two exceptional scenic riverways. In addition, there are more than 300 caves and springs, and this is the first national park designated to protect a wild river system. Dogs are allowed throughout the park and in the campground for no additional fee. Dogs may not be left unattended, they must be on no more than a 10 foot leash, cleaned up after at all times, and be current on shots/license. Dogs are not allowed in buildings, on beaches or in public swim areas, and they must be inside at night. There are 100's of camp sites-reservable and on a first come first basis; comfort stations and potable water are on site. The camping and tent areas also allow dogs. There is a dog walk area at the campground. There are no water hookups at the campgrounds. 2 dogs may be allowed.

Pin Oak Creek RV Park
1302 H 8AT
Villa Ridge, MO
636-451-5656
pinoakcreekrvpark.com
Dogs of all sizes are allowed. There is a pet policy to sign at check in, and there are no additional pet fees. Dogs may not be left unattended or tied up outside alone. Dogs must be leashed and cleaned up after. The camping and tent areas also allow dogs. There is a dog walk area at the campground. Multiple dogs may be allowed.

Lake Wappapello State Park
HC 2, Box 102
Williamsville, MO
573-297-3232 (877-422-6766)
This park of over 1,800 acres, nestled by a lake and surrounded by Ozark forests, provides a variety of habitats, trails, and land and water recreation. Dogs of all sizes are allowed at no additional fee. Dogs may not be left unattended, and they must be leashed and cleaned up after in camp areas. Dogs are not allowed on the beach, in buildings, or tied to park trees. Dogs are allowed on the trails. For cabin visitors, dogs may be tied up outside, and at night they must be crated. Cabins are seasonal. The camping and tent areas also allow dogs. There is a dog walk area at the campground. There are no water hookups at the campground. Multiple dogs may be allowed.

Montana

Rivers Edge Resort
22 S Frontage Road E
Alberton, MT
406-722-3338
riversedge.cc/
Dogs of all sizes are allowed. There are no additional pet fees. Dogs may not be left unattended outside, and they must be leashed and cleaned up after. There is also a motel on site that will allow up to 2 dogs per room with a $25 refundable deposit. The camping and tent areas also allow dogs. There is a dog walk area at the campground. Multiple dogs may be allowed.

Alder/Virginia City KOA
2280 H 287
Alder, MT
406-842-5677 (800-562-1898)
koa.com
Dogs of all sizes are allowed. There are no additional pet fees. Dogs must be quiet, leashed, and cleaned up after. There are some breed restrictions. The camping and tent areas also allow dogs. There is a dog walk area at the campground. Multiple dogs may be allowed.

Fort Ponderosa Campground
568 Arminton Road
Belt, MT
406-277-3232
fortponderosa.com
Dogs of all sizes are allowed. There are no additional pet fees. Dogs must be leashed and cleaned up after. This RV park is closed during the off-season. The camping and tent areas also allow dogs. There is a dog walk area at the campground. Multiple dogs may be allowed.

Big Arm State Park
425 Big Arm Road
Big Arm, MT
406-849-5255
The phone numbers at the parks are subject to change each year, but 406-752-5501 is the year round contact number. All the Montana state parks are along a shoreline and this park of over 500 acres offers a variety of land and water recreation. Dogs of all sizes are allowed. There are no additional pet fees. Dogs may not be left unattended, they must be on no more than a 10 foot leash, and be

cleaned up after. Dogs are allowed on the trails. This campground is closed during the off-season. The camping and tent areas also allow dogs. There is a dog walk area at the campground. There are no electric or water hookups at the campground. Multiple dogs may be allowed.

Big Timber KOA
693 H 10 East
Big Timber, MT
406-932-6569
bigtimberkoa.com
Dogs of all sizes are allowed, and there are no additional pet fees for tent or RV sites. Up to three medium to small dogs or up to 2 large dogs are allowed at tent or RV sites. Only one dog is allowed in the cabins and there is an additional $5 fee per night. Dogs may not be left unattended, must be quiet, leashed, and cleaned up after. There are some breed restrictions. This RV park is closed during the off-season. The camping and tent areas also allow dogs. There is a dog walk area at the campground. Dogs are allowed in the camping cabins.

Wayfarers State Park
8600 H 35
Bigfork, MT
406-837-4196
Some parks discontinue phone service and get new numbers the following season, but 406-752-5501 is a non-changing number for park information. This scenic park located on Flathead Lake offers a variety of land and water recreation. Dogs of all sizes are allowed at no additional fee. Dogs may not be left unattended, and they must be quiet, well behaved, be on no more than a 10 foot leash, and be cleaned up after. Dogs are not allowed in public swim areas, but they are allowed on the trails. This campground is closed during the off-season. The camping and tent areas also allow dogs. There is a dog walk area at the campground. There are no water hookups at the campground. Multiple dogs may be allowed.

Yellow Bay State Park
17215 Eastshore
Bigfork, MT
406-752-5501
This scenic park, sitting in the heart of sweet cherry orchards with a wide sandy beach area, creates a rather beautiful setting for visitors and a variety of land and water recreation. Dogs of all sizes are allowed at no additional fee. Dogs may not be left

unattended, and they must be quiet, well behaved, be on no more than a 10 foot leash, and be cleaned up after. Dogs are not allowed in public swim areas, but they are allowed on the trails. This campground is closed during the off-season. The camping and tent areas also allow dogs. There is a dog walk area at the campground. There are no electric or water hookups at the campground. Multiple dogs may be allowed.

Billings KOA
547 Garden Avenue
Billings, MT
406-252-3104 (800-562-8546)
koa.com
Dogs of all sizes are allowed. There are no additional pet fees. Dogs must be well behaved, leashed, and cleaned up after. This RV park is closed during the off-season. The camping and tent areas also allow dogs. There is a dog walk area at the campground. Multiple dogs may be allowed.

Custer National Forest
1310 Main Street
Billings, MT
406-657-6200 (877-444-6777)
fs.fed.us/r1/custer/
This forest of nearly 1.3 million acres, of which almost half is designated wilderness, provides spectacular scenery, a rich cultural history, and diverse ecosystems that support a large variety of plants, fish, mammals, bird species, and year round recreation. Dogs of all sizes are allowed at no additional fee. Dogs may not be left unattended, and they must be leashed and cleaned up after. Dogs are not allowed in public swim areas, but they are allowed on the trails. This campground is closed during the off-season. The camping and tent areas also allow dogs. There is a dog walk area at the campground. There are no electric or water hookups at the campground. Multiple dogs may be allowed.

Yellowstone River Campground
309 Garden Avenue
Billings, MT
406-259-0878
yellowstonerivercampground.com
Dogs of all sizes are allowed. There are no additional pet fees. Dogs must be leashed and cleaned up after. This RV park is closed during the off-season. The camping and tent areas also allow dogs. There is a dog walk area at the campground. Multiple dogs may be allowed.

Bozeman KOA
81123 Gallatin Road
Bozeman, MT
406-587-3030 (800-562-3036)
koa.com
Dogs of all sizes are allowed. There are no additional pet fees. Dogs must be leashed and cleaned up after. The camping and tent areas also allow dogs. There is a dog walk area at the campground. Dogs are allowed in the camping cabins. Multiple dogs may be allowed.

Sunrise Campground
31842 Frontage Road
Bozeman, MT
877-437-2095
Dogs of all sizes are allowed. There are no additional pet fees. Dogs may not be tied up outside alone, and they may not be left unattended unless they will be quiet, well behaved, and comfortable. Dogs must be leashed, cleaned up after, and brought in at night. This RV park is closed during the off-season. The camping and tent areas also allow dogs. There is a dog walk area at the campground. Multiple dogs may be allowed.

Butte KOA
1601 Kaw Avenue
Butte, MT
406-782-8080 (800-562-8089)
koa.com
Dogs of all sizes are allowed. There are no additional pet fees. Dogs must be quiet, leashed, and cleaned up after. This RV park is closed during the off-season. The camping and tent areas also allow dogs. There is a dog walk area at the campground. Dogs are allowed in the camping cabins. Multiple dogs may be allowed.

Choteau KOA
85 H 221
Choteau, MT
406-466-2615 (800-562-4156)
koa.com
Dogs of all sizes are allowed. There are no additional pet fees. Dogs must be leashed and cleaned up after. This RV park is closed during the off-season. The camping and tent areas also allow dogs. There is a dog walk area at the campground. Dogs are allowed in the camping cabins. Multiple dogs may be allowed.

Deer Lodge KOA
330 Park Street
Deer Lodge, MT

406-846-1629 (800-562-1629)
koa.com
Dogs of all sizes are allowed. There are no additional pet fees. Dogs may not be left unattended at any time, must be leashed, and cleaned up after. This RV park is closed during the off-season. The camping and tent areas also allow dogs. There is a dog walk area at the campground. Dogs are allowed in the camping cabins. Multiple dogs may be allowed.

Bannack State Park
4200 Bannack Road
Dillon, MT
406-834-3413
Some parks discontinue phone service and get new numbers the following season, but 406-752-5501 is a non-changing number for park information. This park, located on Grasshopper Creek, is a registered historic landmark, and offers a variety of land and water recreation. Dogs of all sizes are allowed at no additional fee. Dogs may not be left unattended, and they must be quiet, well behaved, be on no more than a 10 foot leash, and be cleaned up after. Dogs are not allowed in public swim areas, but they are allowed on the trails. This campground is closed during the off-season. The camping and tent areas also allow dogs. There is a dog walk area at the campground. There are no electric or water hookups at the campground. Multiple dogs may be allowed.

Deerlodge (Beaverhead) National Forest
420 Barrett Street
Dillon, MT
406-683-3900
fs.fed.us/r1/bdnf/
This is a year round diverse recreational and working forest covering over 3 million acres in eight counties. Dogs are allowed at no additional fee. Dogs may not be left unattended, and they must be leashed and cleaned up after. Dogs are allowed on the trails, and they may be off lead in the forest as long as there is voice control. This campground is closed during the off-season. The camping and tent areas also allow dogs. There is a dog walk area at the campground. Dogs are allowed in the camping cabins. There are no electric or water hookups at the campground. Multiple dogs may be allowed.

Dillon KOA
735 Park Street

Dillon, MT
406-683-2749 (800-562-2751)
koa.com
Dogs of all sizes are allowed. There are no additional pet fees. Dogs must be leashed and cleaned up after. Dogs are not allowed on the beds in the cabins. There are some breed restrictions. The camping and tent areas also allow dogs. There is a dog walk area at the campground. Dogs are allowed in the camping cabins. Multiple dogs may be allowed.

Ennis Village RV
5034 H 287
Ennis, MT
866-682-5272
ennisrv.com
Dogs of all sizes are allowed. There are no additional pet fees. Dogs must be leashed and cleaned up after. This RV park is closed during the off-season. The camping and tent areas also allow dogs. There is a dog walk area at the campground. Multiple dogs may be allowed.

Fairmont RV Park
1700 Fairmont Road
Fairmont, MT
406-797-3505 (866-797-3505)
fairmontrvresort.com/
Dogs of all sizes are allowed. There are no additional pet fees. Dogs may not be left unattended outside, and they must be leashed and cleaned up after. Dogs are also allowed at the teepee sites at no additional fee. This RV park is closed during the off-season. The camping and tent areas also allow dogs. There is a dog walk area at the campground. Multiple dogs may be allowed.

Finley Point State Park
3000 S Finley Point
Finley Point, MT
406-887-2715
Some parks discontinue phone service and get new numbers each season, but 406-752-5501 is a non-changing number for park information. This small, 16 site park, sits in a secluded pine forest on Flathead Lake, and offers a variety of water and land recreation. Dogs of all sizes are allowed at no additional fee. Dogs may not be left unattended, and they must be quiet, well behaved, be on no more than a 10 foot leash, and be cleaned up after. Dogs are not allowed in public swim areas, but they are allowed on the trails. This campground is closed during the off-season. The camping and tent areas also allow dogs.

There is a dog walk area at the campground. There are no electric or water hookups at the campground. Multiple dogs may be allowed.

Bighorn Canyon National Rec Area
5 Avenue B from H 313
Fort Smith, MT
406-666-2412
fs.fed.us/r2/bighorn/
There are over 189,000 acres of wilderness in this forest, with 1,500 miles of trails, and there are several ways to enter. An additional ranger station is at 2013 Eastside 2nd Street, Sheridan, WY 82801, 307-674-2600. Dogs are allowed at no additional fee, and they are allowed on all the trails. Dogs may not be left unattended, and they must be leashed and cleaned up after. The camping and tent areas also allow dogs. There is a dog walk area at the campground. There are no electric or water hookups at the campground. Multiple dogs may be allowed.

Rocky Mountain Campground
14 Gardine
Gardiner, MT
877-534-6931
rockymountaincampground.com
Dogs of all sizes are allowed. There are no additional pet fees. Dogs must be leashed and cleaned up after. This RV park is closed during the off-season. The camping and tent areas also allow dogs. There is a dog walk area at the campground.

7th Ranch RV Camp
7th Ranch & Reno Creek Road
Garryowen, MT
800-371-7963
historicwest.com
Dogs of all sizes are allowed. There are no additional pet fees. Dogs must be quiet, well behaved, leashed, and cleaned up after. This RV park is closed during the off-season. The camping and tent areas also allow dogs. There is a dog walk area at the campground. Multiple dogs may be allowed.

Cottonwood Inn
45 First Avenue NE
Glasgow, MT
800-321-8213
cottonwoodinn.net
Dogs of all sizes are allowed. There are no additional pet fees. Dogs may not be left unattended, and must be well behaved, leashed, and cleaned up after. This RV park is closed during the off-season. There

is a dog walk area at the campground. Multiple dogs may be allowed.

Makoshika State Park
1301 Synder Avenue
Glendive, MT
406-542-5500
As the states largest park at 11634 acres, visitors will find an abundance of recreation as well as educational opportunities. Part of the state's Dinosaur Trail runs through this "Badlands" park, plus they offer a rifle and archery range, a Folf course, and an Amphitheater. Dogs are allowed at no additional fee; they may not be left unattended, and they must be quiet, be on no more than a 10 foot leash, and cleaned up after. The campground offers picnic tables, fire rings, grills, potable water, and vault toilets. The camping and tent areas also allow dogs. There is a dog walk area at the campground. There are no electric or water hookups at the campgrounds. Multiple dogs may be allowed.

Acklley Lake State Park
4600 Giant Srings Road
Great Falls, MT
406-454-5840
This park of 160 acres offers a variety of land and water recreation. Dogs of all sizes are allowed. There are no additional pet fees. Dogs may not be left unattended, they must be on no more than a 10 foot leash, and be cleaned up after. Dogs are allowed on the trails. The camping and tent areas also allow dogs. There is a dog walk area at the campground. There are no electric or water hookups at the campground. Multiple dogs may be allowed.

Dick's RV Park
1403 11th Street SW
Great Falls, MT
406-452-0333
dicksrvpark.com
Dogs of all sizes are allowed. There are no additional pet fees. Dogs must be leashed at all times, and cleaned up after. The camping and tent areas also allow dogs. There is a dog walk area at the campground. Multiple dogs may be allowed.

Great Falls KOA
1500 51st Street S
Great Falls, MT
406-727-3191 (800-562-6584)
koa.com
Dogs of all sizes are allowed. There are no additional pet fees. Dogs may not be left unattended, must be

leashed, and cleaned up after. The camping and tent areas also allow dogs. There is a dog walk area at the campground. Dogs are allowed in the camping cabins. Multiple dogs may be allowed.

Lewis and Clark National Forest
1101 15th Street N.
Great Falls, MT
406-791-7700
fs.fed.us/r1/lewisclark/about/
This forest covers almost 2 million acres, reaches over 9000 feet, has a designated Natural Research area of over 10,000 acres, the National Historic Trail Interpretive Center, and a variety of trails. Dogs are allowed at no additional fee. Dogs may not be left unattended, and they must be leashed and cleaned up after. Dogs are not allowed in public swim areas or buildings. Dogs are allowed on the trails. The camping and tent areas also allow dogs. There is a dog walk area at the campground. Multiple dogs may be allowed.

Bitterroot National Forest
1801 N 1st Street
Hamilton, MT
406-363-7100 (877-444-6777)
fs.fed.us/r1/bitterroot/
This forest of 1.6 million acres has 4 ranger districts, more than 1,600 miles of multi-use trails, and very diverse ecosystems that support a large variety of plants, fish, mammals, bird species, as well as recreational pursuits. Dogs are allowed at no additional fee. Dogs may not be left unattended, and they must be well behaved, leashed and cleaned up after in the camp areas. Dogs may be off lead in the forest if they are under voice command and will not chase the wildlife. This campground is closed during the off-season. The camping and tent areas also allow dogs. There is a dog walk area at the campground. Dogs are allowed in the camping cabins. There are no water hookups at the campground. Multiple dogs may be allowed.

Hardin KOA
RR 1
Hardin, MT
406-665-1635 (800-562-1635)
koa.com
Dogs of all sizes are allowed. There are no additional pet fees. Dogs must be leashed and cleaned up after. There are some breed restrictions. This RV park is closed during the off-season. The camping and tent areas also allow dogs.

There is a dog walk area at the campground. Multiple dogs may be allowed.

Madison Arm Resort
5475 Madison Arm Road
Hebgen Lake, MT
406-646-9328
madisonarmresort.com/rvpark.htm
Popular for fishing and water activities, this lakeside resort area sits only 8 miles from Yellowstone Park and an easy trek to numerous other sites of interest, dining, shopping, and entertainment. Dogs are allowed for no additional fee. They must be leashed and cleaned up after at all times while in camp and on the trails. Dogs are not allowed in buildings or on the swimming beach, but they are allowed in the water from other areas. This RV park is closed during the off-season. The camping and tent areas also allow dogs. There is a dog walk area at the campground. Multiple dogs may be allowed.

Helena Campground
5820 N Montana Avenue
Helena, MT
406-458-4714
helenacampgroundrvpark.com
Dogs of all sizes are allowed. There are no additional pet fees. Dogs may not be left unattended outside, and they must be quiet, be on no more than a 6 foot leash, and be cleaned up after. This RV park is closed during the off-season. The camping and tent areas also allow dogs. There is a dog walk area at the campground. 2 dogs may be allowed.

Helena National Forest
2880 Skyway Drive
Helena, MT
406-449-5201
fs.fed.us/r1/helena/
This recreational and working forest covers almost a million acres and straddles the Continental Divide creating very diverse geology and topography regions. Dogs are allowed at no additional fee. Dogs must be leashed when in the camp area and when on the trails if there are other visitors present. They may be off leash only if they are well behaved, will not chase, and are under voice control. The camping and tent areas also allow dogs. There is a dog walk area at the campground. There are no electric or water hookups at the campground. Multiple dogs may be

allowed.

Timber Wolf Resort
9105 H 2E
Hungry Horse, MT
406-387-9653
timberwolfresort.com/
Dogs of all sizes are allowed. There is a $3 per night per pet additional fee for the tent or RV sites. There is a $10 per night per pet additional fee for the cabins. Dogs may not be left unattended, and they must be leashed at all times, and cleaned up after. Dogs are allowed on the trails. The camping and tent areas also allow dogs. There is a dog walk area at the campground. Dogs are allowed in the camping cabins. Multiple dogs may be allowed.

Cooney State Park
Boyd County Road
Joliet, MT
406-445-2326
This park is one of the most popular parks in south central Montana, and it provides a variety of land and water recreation. Dogs of all sizes are allowed at no additional fee. Dogs may not be left unattended, and they must be leashed and cleaned up after. Dogs are not allowed at the Marshall Cove campground, on swim beaches, or in buildings. Dogs are allowed on the trails. This campground is closed during the off-season. The camping and tent areas also allow dogs. There is a dog walk area at the campground. There are no water hookups at the campground. Multiple dogs may be allowed.

Hell Creek State Park
H 59/25 miles north of Jordon
Jordon, MT
406-234-0900
This park is located on Fort Peck Lake, and provides a variety of water and land recreation. Dogs are allowed at no additional fee. Dogs may not be left unattended, and they must be leashed and cleaned up after. This campground is closed during the off-season. The camping and tent areas also allow dogs. There is a dog walk area at the campground. There are no electric or water hookups at the campground. Multiple dogs may be allowed.

Flathead National Forest
1935 3rd Ave. E
Kalispell, MT
406-758-5200
fs.fed.us/r1/flathead/
This year round forest provides

natural resources in addition to a wide variety of recreational pursuits. Dogs are allowed at no additional fee. Dogs may not be left unattended outside, and may be left inside only if it presents no danger to the animal. Dogs must be quiet, well behaved, leashed and cleaned up after. Dogs are not allowed on the public beach, the picnic areas, or on cross-country ski trails. Dogs may be off lead in the forest as long as they are under voice control. Dogs must be on lead in Jewel Basin, and they are allowed on the hiking trails. There is one dog friendly cabin available in Star Meadows. This campground is closed during the off-season. The camping and tent areas also allow dogs. There is a dog walk area at the campground. There are no electric or water hookups at the campground. Multiple dogs may be allowed.

Lake Mary Ronan State Park
490 N Meridian
Kalispell, MT
406-849-5082
Camping, fishing, swimming, and walking the trails are the popular pastimes at this park. Dogs are allowed at no additional fee. Dogs may not be left unattended, and they must be leashed and cleaned up after. Dogs are not allowed in buildings or in public swim areas, but they are allowed on the trails. This campground is closed during the off-season. The camping and tent areas also allow dogs. There is a dog walk area at the campground. There are no electric or water hookups at the campground. Multiple dogs may be allowed.

Flathead Lake State Park
490 N Meridian
Kallispell, MT
406-844-3066 (406-751-4577 (reservations))
All the Montana state parks are along a shoreline and this park of almost 130 acres, and considered the most private, offers a variety of land and water recreation. Dogs of all sizes are allowed at no additional fee. Dogs may not be left unattended, they must be quiet, well behaved, on no more than a 10 foot leash, and be cleaned up after. Dogs are not allowed at public swim areas, but they are allowed on the trails. This campground is closed during the off-season. The camping and tent areas also allow dogs. There is a dog walk area at the campground. There are no electric or water hookups at the campground. Multiple

dogs may be allowed.

West Shore State Park
9264 H 93S
Lakeside, MT
406-844-3066
Some parks discontinue phone service and get new numbers the following season, but 406-752-5501 is a non-changing number for park information. This secluded park sits along Flathead Lake and provides a variety of land and water recreation. Dogs of all sizes are allowed at no additional fee. Dogs may not be left unattended, and they must be quiet, well behaved, be on no more than a 10 foot leash, and be cleaned up after. Dogs are not allowed in public swim areas, but they are allowed on the trails. The camping and tent areas also allow dogs. There is a dog walk area at the campground. There are no water hookups at the campground. Multiple dogs may be allowed.

Pelican RV Park
11360 S Frontage
Laurel, MT
406-628-4324
Dogs of all sizes are allowed, and there are no additional pet fees for tent or RV sites. There is a $10 one time fee for up to 2 dogs, and a $20 one time fee for 3 dogs at the motel. Dogs must be leashed and cleaned up after. The camping and tent areas also allow dogs. There is a dog walk area at the campground. Multiple dogs may be allowed.

Kootenai National Forest
1101 Hwy. 2 West
Libby, MT
406-293-6211
fs.fed.us/r1/kootenai/
This forest is open year round, and it provides a wealth of natural resources and an abundance of recreational activities. There are lookouts that can be rented, and dogs are allowed there. Dogs are allowed at no additional fee. Dogs may not be left unattended, and they must be leashed and cleaned up after. Dogs are not allowed on the beaches or in buildings, but they are allowed on the trails. Canoe Gultch campground is located at 12557 H 37. This campground is closed during the off-season. The camping and tent areas also allow dogs. There is a dog walk area at the campground. There are no water hookups at the campground.

Livingston/Paradise Valley KOA

163 Pine Creek Road
Livingston, MT
406-222-0992 (800-562-2805)
koa.com
Dogs of all sizes are allowed. There are no additional pet fees. Dogs may not be left unattended, must be leashed, and cleaned up after. This RV park is closed during the off-season. The camping and tent areas also allow dogs. There is a dog walk area at the campground. Dogs are allowed in the camping cabins. Multiple dogs may be allowed.

Medicine Rocks State Park
1 Mile west on County Road from Milepost 10/H 7
Miles City, MT
406-234-0900
Once a scared site of "big medicine" and a hunting ground for peoples of the past, this 320 acre park now delights visitors with its unique ancient sandstone monoliths and an abundance of wildlife. Dogs are allowed at no additional fee; they may not be left unattended, and they must be quiet, be on no more than a 10 foot leash, and cleaned up after. Dogs are not allowed in public swim areas. There are about a dozen camp sites, and grills/fire rings, potable water, picnic tables, and vault toilets are available. The camping and tent areas also allow dogs. There is a dog walk area at the campground. There are no electric or water hookups at the campgrounds. Multiple dogs may be allowed.

Miles City KOA
1 Palmer Street
Miles City, MT
406-232-3991 (800-562-3909)
koa.com
Dogs of all sizes are allowed. There are no additional pet fees. Dogs may not be tied up outside unless an adult is present, and they can only be left in your RV if they will be quiet and comfortable. Dogs must be well behaved, leashed, and cleaned up after. There are some breed restrictions. This RV park is closed during the off-season. The camping and tent areas also allow dogs. There is a dog walk area at the campground. Multiple dogs may be allowed.

Beavertail Hill State Park
3201 Spurgin Road
Missoula, MT
406-542-5500
Some parks discontinue phone service and get new numbers the following season, but 406-752-5501

is a non-changing number for park information. This park, along Flathead Lake, offers a variety of land and water recreation, and a one hour walking nature trail. Dogs of all sizes are allowed at no additional fee. Dogs may not be left unattended, and they must be quiet, well behaved, be on no more than a 10 foot leash, and be cleaned up after. Dogs are not allowed in public swim areas or buildings, but they are allowed on the trails. This campground is closed during the off-season. The camping and tent areas also allow dogs. There is a dog walk area at the campground. There are no water hookups at the campground. Multiple dogs may be allowed.

Jellystone Park
9900 Jellystone Drive
Missoula, MT
406-543-9400 (800-318-9644)
campjellystonemt.com
Dogs of all sizes are allowed. There are no additional pet fees. Dogs must be leashed and cleaned up after. This RV park is closed during the off-season. The camping and tent areas also allow dogs. There is a dog walk area at the campground. 2 dogs may be allowed.

Lolo National Forest
Building 24, Fort Missoula
Missoula, MT
406-329-3750
fs.fed.us/r1/lolo/
With 5 ranger districts, and over 2 million acres, this forest provides a variety of camping areas and trails. The diverse ecosystems support innumerable plant, fish, mammal, and bird species. Dogs are allowed at no additional fee. Dogs must be leashed and cleaned up after in the camp areas. The camping and tent areas also allow dogs. There is a dog walk area at the campground. Multiple dogs may be allowed.

Missoula KOA
3450 Tina Avenue
Missoula, MT
406-549-0881 (800-562-5366)
koa.com
Dogs of all sizes are allowed. There are no additional pet fees. Dogs may not be left unattended, must be leashed, and cleaned up after. The camping and tent areas also allow dogs. There is a dog walk area at the campground. Dogs are allowed in the camping cabins. Multiple dogs may be allowed.

Painted Rocks State Park
Secondary H 473
Missoula, MT
406-542-5500
Located on the Painted Rocks Reservoir, this 293 acre forested park sits at 4,700 feet altitude and they offer several recreational activities. Dogs are allowed at no additional fee; they may not be left unattended, and they must be quiet, be on no more than a 10 foot leash, and cleaned up after. Dogs are not allowed in public swim areas. The campground has about 25 sites with picnic tables, fire rings, grills, potable water, vault toilets, and a boat ramp. The camping and tent areas also allow dogs. There is a dog walk area at the campground. There are no electric or water hookups at the campgrounds.

Polson/Flathead KOA
200 Irvine Flats Road
Polson, MT
406-883-2151 (800-562-2130)
polsonkoa.com
Dogs of all sizes are allowed. There are no additional pet fees. Dogs may not be left unattended, must be leashed, and cleaned up after. This RV park is closed during the off-season. The camping and tent areas also allow dogs. There is a dog walk area at the campground. 2 dogs may be allowed.

Red Lodge KOA
7464 H 212
Red Lodge, MT
406-446-2364 (800-562-7540)
koa.com
Dogs of all sizes and numbers are allowed, and they must be quiet and well behaved. There are no additional pet fees for tent or RV sites. Only one dog is allowed in the cabins with no additional fee. Dogs may not be tied up outside alone, and can only be left in your RV if it is cool. Dogs may not be left unattended, must be leashed, and cleaned up after. This RV park is closed during the off-season. The camping and tent areas also allow dogs. There is a dog walk area at the campground. Dogs are allowed in the camping cabins.

Lewis and Clark RV Park
Box 369, Front Street
Shelby, MT
406-434-2710
Dogs of all sizes are allowed. There are no additional pet fees. Dogs must be quiet, leashed, and cleaned up after. Dogs may not be

left unattended. The camping and tent areas also allow dogs. There is a dog walk area at the campground. 2 dogs may be allowed.

St Mary/East Glacier
106 W Shore Road
St Mary, MT
406-732-4122 (800-562-1504)
goglacier.com
Dogs of all sizes are allowed. There are no additional pet fees. Dogs may be left for short periods, and someone in the office needs to know the dog is unattended. Dogs must be leashed and cleaned up after. There are some breed restrictions. This RV park is closed during the off-season. The camping and tent areas also allow dogs. There is a dog walk area at the campground. Dogs are allowed in the camping cabins. Multiple dogs may be allowed.

Campground St Regis
44 Frontage Road
St Regis, MT
406-649-2470
campgroundstregis.com
Dogs of all sizes are allowed. There are no additional pet fees. Dogs must be leashed and cleaned up after. This RV park is closed during the off-season. The camping and tent areas also allow dogs. There is a dog walk area at the campground. Multiple dogs may be allowed.

Nugget Campground
E of Stop Sign on Main Street
St Regis, MT
888-800-0125
Dogs of all sizes are allowed. There are no additional pet fees. Dogs must be leashed and cleaned up after. The camping and tent areas also allow dogs. There is a dog walk area at the campground. Dogs are allowed in the camping cabins. Multiple dogs may be allowed.

Townsend / Canyon Ferry Lake KOA
81 Silos Road
Townsend, MT
406-266-3100 (800-562-5904)
koa.com/where/mt/26164/
A popular and major recreation destination, this waterside park offers a rec room with a pool table, Wi-Fi, a playground, convenience store, and a seasonal restaurant. Dogs are allowed for no additional fee. Dogs may not be left unattended, and they must be on no more than a 6 foot leash and cleaned up after at all times. There are some breed restrictions. The camping and tent areas also allow dogs. There is a

dog walk area at the campground. Dogs are allowed in the camping cabins. Multiple dogs may be allowed.

Glacier Campground
MM 152 H 2, 1 mile W of W Glacier
West Glacier, MT
406-387-5689
glaciercampground.com
Dogs of all sizes are allowed. There are no additional pet fees. Dogs must be quiet, well behaved, leashed, and cleaned up after. Dogs may not be left unattended at any time. This RV park is closed during the off-season. The camping and tent areas also allow dogs. There is a dog walk area at the campground. Dogs are allowed in the camping cabins. Multiple dogs may be allowed.

Glacier National Park
On H 2 (Going to the Sun Road)
West Glacier, MT
406-888-7800
nps.gov/glac/home.htm
This forest covers more than a million acres and provides recreation for all seasons. Dogs are allowed at no additional fee. Dogs may not be left unattended, and they must be leashed and cleaned up after. Dogs are allowed in developed areas only and on the main road through the park. Dogs are not allowed in the back country or on any of the trails. The camping and tent areas also allow dogs. There is a dog walk area at the campground. There are no electric or water hookups at the campground. Multiple dogs may be allowed.

West Glacier KOA
355 Half Moon Flats Road
West Glacier, MT
406-387-5341 (800-562-3313)
koa.com
Dogs of all sizes are allowed. There are no additional pet fees. Dogs must be well behaved, quiet, leashed, and cleaned up after. Dogs may not be left unattended. There is a local dog sitter available. This RV park is closed during the off-season. The camping and tent areas also allow dogs. There is a dog walk area at the campground. Dogs are allowed in the camping cabins. Multiple dogs may be allowed.

Hibernation Station
212 Gray Wolf Avenue
West Yellowstone, MT
406-646-4200 (800-580-3557)
hibernationstation.com/

This cabin village is only steps from the west entrance to Yellowstone Park and numerous other sites of interest, dining, shopping, and entertainment activities. Dogs are allowed in the cabins for an additional fee of $10 per night per pet; there is no additional pet fee for the campground area. Dogs are not allowed in the pool area; they may not be left alone in the cabins, and they must be leashed and picked up after at all times. The camping and tent areas also allow dogs. There is a dog walk area at the campground. Dogs are allowed in the camping cabins. 2 dogs may be allowed.

Lionshead RV Resort
1545 Targhee Pass H
West Yellowstone, MT
406-646-7662
lionsheadrv.com
Dogs of all sizes are allowed. There are no additional pet fees. Dogs must be leased and cleaned up after. This RV park is closed during the off-season. The camping and tent areas also allow dogs. There is a dog walk area at the campground. Multiple dogs may be allowed.

Madison Arm Resort
5475 Madison Arm Road
West Yellowstone, MT
406-646-9328
madisonarmresort.com/
Dogs of all sizes are allowed. There are no additional pet fees. Dogs may not be left unattended, and they must be leashed at all times, and cleaned up after. This RV park is closed during the off-season. The camping and tent areas also allow dogs. There is a dog walk area at the campground. 2 dogs may be allowed.

Yellowstone Grizzly RV Park
210 S Electric Street
West Yellowstone, MT
406-646-4466
grizzlyrv.com
Dogs of all sizes are allowed. There are no additional pet fees. Dogs must be quiet, well behaved, leashed, and cleaned up after. Dogs may not be left unattended. There is a forest nearby where they can run if they are under voice command. This RV park is closed during the off-season. The camping and tent areas also allow dogs. There is a dog walk area at the campground. Dogs are allowed in the camping cabins. Multiple dogs may be allowed.

Whitefish/Kalispell N KOA
5121 H 93D
Whitefish, MT
406-862-4242 (800-562-8734)
koa.com
Dogs of all sizes are allowed. There are no additional pet fees. Dogs must leashed and cleaned up after. Dogs may be left unattended if they will be quiet. The camping and tent areas also allow dogs. There is a dog walk area at the campground. Dogs are allowed in the camping cabins. Multiple dogs may be allowed.

Lewis and Clark Caverns State Park
1455 H 2E
Whitehall, MT
406-287-3541
Montana's first state park is home to one of the most highly decorated limestone caverns in the Northwest, and the park offers a variety of hiking trails, a visitor center and an amphitheater. Dogs of all sizes are allowed at no additional fee. Dogs may not be left unattended, and they must be leashed and cleaned up after. Dogs are not allowed in food service areas, in the caverns, or on guided tours. Dogs may be in the Visitor's Center if they are not busy. As of 2006 they will be offering 2 kennels free of charge for visitors who would like to take the caverns tour. Dogs are allowed on the other trails. This campground is closed during the off-season. The camping and tent areas also allow dogs. There is a dog walk area at the campground. Dogs are allowed in the camping cabins. There are no electric or water hookups at the campground. Multiple dogs may be allowed.

Pipestone RV Park
41 Bluebird Lane
Whitehall, MT
406-287-5224
pipestonervpark.com
Dogs of all sizes are allowed. There are no additional pet fees. Dogs must be quiet, well behaved, leashed, and cleaned up after. Dogs may not be left unattended. The camping and tent areas also allow dogs. There is a dog walk area at the campground. Multiple dogs may be allowed.

Holter Lake Recreation Area
Recreation Road
Wolf Creek, MT
406-494-5059
All the Montana state parks are along a shoreline and this park of

offers a variety of land and water recreation. Dogs of all sizes are allowed. There are no additional pet fees. Dogs may not be left unattended, they must be on no more than a 10 foot leash, and be cleaned up after. Dogs are not allowed on the beach but they are allowed on the trails. The camping and tent areas also allow dogs. There is a dog walk area at the campground. There are no electric or water hookups at the campground. Multiple dogs may be allowed.

Nebraska

Eugene T. Mahoney State Park
28500 W Park H
Ashland, NE
402-944-2523
This modern resort park offers many amenities including a family aquatic center, a 70-foot observation tower, and a wide variety of land and water activities and recreation. Dogs of all sizes are allowed at no additional fee. Dogs may not be left unattended outside, or in the cabin unless crated. Dogs must be leashed and cleaned up after. Dogs are not allowed in park buildings, but they are allowed on the trails. The state reservation phone number is 402-471-1414. The camping and tent areas also allow dogs. There is a dog walk area at the campground. Dogs are allowed in the camping cabins. Multiple dogs may be allowed.

Chimney Rock Pioneer Crossing
On County Road 75 @ H 92
Bayard, NE
305-586-1988
chimneyrockpioneerxing.com
Dogs of all sizes are allowed. There are no additional pet fees. The camping and tent areas also allow dogs. There is a dog walk area at the campground. Multiple dogs may be allowed.

Flying Bee Ranch
6755 County Road 42
Bayard, NE
888-534-2341
flyingbee-ranch.com/
Dogs of all sizes are allowed. There are no additional pet fees for the tent or RV sites. There is an $8 per night per pet additional fee for the cabins. Dogs may not be left unattended unless they will be quiet and well

behaved. Dogs must be leashed and cleaned up after. The camping and tent areas also allow dogs. There is a dog walk area at the campground. Dogs are allowed in the camping cabins. Multiple dogs may be allowed.

Eagle Canyon Hideaway
1086 Lakeview W Road
Brule, NE
866-866-5253
eagle-canyon.com
Dogs of all sizes are allowed. There are no additional pet fees. Dogs must be quiet, leashed, and cleaned up after. The camping and tent areas also allow dogs. There is a dog walk area at the campground. Dogs are allowed in the camping cabins. Multiple dogs may be allowed.

Chadron State Park
15951 H 385
Chadron, NE
308-432-6167
This scenic 972 acre park at an elevation of 5000 feet sits inside the Nebraska National Forest and offers a variety of land and water activities and recreation. Dogs of all sizes are allowed at no additional fee. Dogs may not be left unattended at any time, and they must be on no more than a 6 foot leash, and be cleaned up after. Dogs are allowed on the trails. The state reservation phone number is 402-471-1414. The camping and tent areas also allow dogs. There is a dog walk area at the campground. Dogs are allowed in the camping cabins. There are no water hookups at the campground. Multiple dogs may be allowed.

Nebraska National Forest
125 N Main Street
Chadron, NE
308-432-0300
fs.fed.us/r2/nebraska/
Comprised of 3 national grasslands, 2 national forests, and home to the oldest national tree nursery, this forest provides diverse ecosystems that support a large variety of plants, fish, mammals, bird species, and year round recreation. Dogs of all sizes are allowed at no additional fee. Dogs may not be left unattended, and they must be leashed and cleaned up after. Dogs are allowed on the trails. The camping and tent areas also allow dogs. There is a dog walk area at the campground. There are no water hookups at the campground.

Multiple dogs may be allowed.

Fort Robinson State Park
3200 H 20
Crawford, NE
308-665-2900
This historically rich park of over 22,000 acres is home to their own herds of buffalo and longhorn. The park offers an interpretive museum as well as a variety of land and water activities and recreation. Dogs of all sizes are allowed at no additional fee. Dogs may not be left unattended at any time, and they must be on no more than a 6 foot leash, and be cleaned up after. Dogs are not allowed in buildings, but they are allowed on the trails. The state reservation phone number is 402-471-1414. The camping and tent areas also allow dogs. There is a dog walk area at the campground. Dogs are allowed in the camping cabins. There are no water hookups at the campground. Multiple dogs may be allowed.

Lewis and Clark State Rec Area
54731 897 Road (H 121)
Crofton, NE
402-388-4169
With over 9,000 acres along the states' 2nd largest lake, this park offers a wide variety of land and water activities and recreation. Dogs of all sizes are allowed at no additional fee. Dogs may not be left unattended at any time, and they must be on no more than a 6 foot leash, and be cleaned up after. Dogs are not allowed on the furniture in the cabins, on the beaches, or other park buildings. Dogs are allowed on the trails. The state reservation phone number is 402-471-1414. The camping and tent areas also allow dogs. There is a dog walk area at the campground. Dogs are allowed in the camping cabins. There are no water hookups at the campground. Multiple dogs may be allowed.

Grand Island KOA
904 South B Road
Doniphan, NE
402-886-2249 (800-562-0850)
koa.com
Dogs of all sizes are allowed, and there are no additional pet fees for tent or RV sites. There is a $5 per night per pet additional fee for the cabins. Dogs may not be left unattended, and they must be quiet, leashed, and cleaned up after. Dogs are not allowed in the buildings or the playground, and they must be in at night. This RV park is closed

during the off-season. The camping and tent areas also allow dogs. There is a dog walk area at the campground. Dogs are allowed in the camping cabins. Multiple dogs may be allowed.

Mormon Island State Rec Area
7425 S H 281
Doniphan, NE
308-385-6211
This park is home to a spectacular gathering each spring of hundreds of thousands of sandhill cranes (the world's largest concentration)and serves as a link in the "Chain of Lakes". Dogs of all sizes are allowed at no additional fee. Dogs may not be left unattended, and they must be on no more than a 6 foot leash, and be cleaned up after. The camping and tent areas also allow dogs. There is a dog walk area at the campground. There are no water hookups at the campground. Multiple dogs may be allowed.

Gallagher Canyon State Recreation Area
1 East Park Drive
Elwood, NE
308-785-2685
This park is popular for its great scenery and water activities. There are 24 recreational land acres and a 400 acre reservoir. Dogs are allowed for no additional fee. They must be well behaved, on no more than a 6 foot leash, crated, or otherwise restricted at all times, and cleaned up after. Dogs are not allowed in food service areas, public buildings, or on designated swimming beaches. There are 72 primitive campsites available with several picnicking areas. The camping and tent areas also allow dogs. There is a dog walk area at the campground. There are no electric or water hookups at the campgrounds. Multiple dogs may be allowed.

Johnson Lake State Rec Area
1 E. Park Drive 25A
Elwood, NE
308-785-2685
This fairly small park borders a 2,000 plus acre lake and provides a variety of land and water recreation. Dogs of all sizes are allowed at no additional fee. Dogs may not be left unattended unless they are crated and comfortable, and they must be on no more than a 6 foot leash, and be cleaned up after. Dogs are not allowed in park buildings. The state reservation phone number is 402-471-1414. The camping and tent

areas also allow dogs. There is a dog walk area at the campground. There are no water hookups at the campground. Multiple dogs may be allowed.

Rock Creek Station State Historic Park
57426 710th Road
Fairbury, NE
402-729-5777
This park is rich in it's history and provides an excellent interpretive center in addition to a variety of hiking trails, activities and recreational pursuits. Well behaved dogs of all sizes are allowed at no additional fee. Dogs must be on no more than a 6 foot leash, and be cleaned up after. Dogs are not allowed in buildings, but they are allowed on the trails. The state reservation phone number is 402-471-1414. The camping and tent areas also allow dogs. There is a dog walk area at the campground. There are no water hookups at the campground. Multiple dogs may be allowed.

Windmill State Recreation Area
2625 Lowell Road
Gibbon, NE
308-468-5700
Highlights at this park include an interesting collection of antique windmills, 154 recreational land acres, and 5 ponds totaling 14 acres. Dogs are allowed for no additional fee. They must be well behaved, on no more than a 6 foot leash, crated, or otherwise restricted at all times, and cleaned up after. Dogs are not allowed in food service areas, public buildings, or on designated swimming beaches. All campers must register; there are 89 sites with picnic tables and grills. Potable water, modern restrooms, showers, a laundry, and a dump station are close by. The camping and tent areas also allow dogs. There is a dog walk area at the campground. There are no water hookups at the campgrounds. Multiple dogs may be allowed.

Gothenburhg KOA
1102 S Lake Avenue
Gothenburg, NE
308-537-7387 (800-562-1873)
koa.com
Dogs of all sizes are allowed. There are no additional pet fees. Dogs may not be left unattended, and must be leashed and cleaned up after. There are some breed restrictions. This RV park is closed

during the off-season. The camping and tent areas also allow dogs. There is a dog walk area at the campground. Dogs are allowed in the camping cabins. Multiple dogs may be allowed.

Pine Grove RV Park
23403 Mynard Road
Greenwood, NE
402-994-3550
Dogs of all sizes are allowed. There are no additional pet fees. With the exception of an off lead area, dogs must be leashed. Dogs must be quiet and cleaned up after. The camping and tent areas also allow dogs. There is a dog walk area at the campground. Multiple dogs may be allowed.

Linoma Beach Resort
17106 S 255th Street
Gretna, NE
402-332-4500
linomabeach.com
Dogs of all sizes are allowed. There are no additional pet fees. Dogs may not be left unattended outside, and they must be leashed and cleaned up after. Dogs must stay within the campers area, and they are not allowed on the beaches at any time. Barking dogs are not allowed. This is an RV only park. This RV park is closed during the off-season. There are no water hookups at the campgrounds. 2 dogs may be allowed.

West Omaha KOA
14601 H 6
Gretna, NE
402-332-3010 (800-562-1632)
koa.com
Dogs of all sizes are allowed. There are no additional pet fees. Dogs must be leashed and cleaned up after. There are some breed restrictions. This RV park is closed during the off-season. The camping and tent areas also allow dogs. There is a dog walk area at the campground. Dogs are allowed in the camping cabins. Multiple dogs may be allowed.

Kimball KOA
4334 Link 53E
Kimball, NE
308-235-4404 (800-562-4785)
koa.com
Dogs of all sizes are allowed. There are no additional pet fees. Dogs may not be left unattended, and they must be leashed and cleaned up after. This RV park is closed during the off-season. The camping and tent areas

also allow dogs. There is a dog walk area at the campground. Dogs are allowed in the camping cabins. Multiple dogs may be allowed.

Twin Pines RV Camp
1508 S H 71
Kimball, NE
308-235-3231
Dogs of all sizes are allowed. There are no additional pet fees. Dogs may not be left unattended, and they must be leashed and cleaned up after. The camping and tent areas also allow dogs. There is a dog walk area at the campground. Multiple dogs may be allowed.

Camp A Way
200 Camper's Circle
Lincoln, NE
866-719-2267
campaway.com
Dogs of all sizes are allowed. There are no additional pet fees. Dogs may not be left unattended, and they must be leashed and cleaned up after. The camping and tent areas also allow dogs. There is a dog walk area at the campground. Multiple dogs may be allowed.

Conestoga State Recreation Area
SW 98th Street and W Pioneers Blvd
Lincoln, NE
402-796-2362
With a 230 acre lake and 486 acres of land, visitors will find a number of recreational opportunities at this park. Dogs are allowed for no additional fee. They must be well behaved, on no more than a 6 foot leash, crated, or otherwise restricted at all times, and cleaned up after. Dogs are not allowed in food service areas, public buildings, or on designated swimming beaches. The campground offers 57 non-designated sites; potable water and a dump station are on site. The camping and tent areas also allow dogs. There is a dog walk area at the campground. There are no electric or water hookups at the campgrounds. Multiple dogs may be allowed.

Pawnee State Recreation Area
3800 NW 105th Street
Lincoln, NE
402-796-2362
There are 1,800 recreational acres at this park with a 740 acre lake and several miles of trails to explore it all. Dogs are allowed for no additional fee. They must be well behaved, on no more than a 6 foot leash, crated, or otherwise restricted at all times, and cleaned up after. The exception

being during hunting season and owners must have voice control. Dogs are not allowed in food service areas, public buildings, or on designated swimming beaches. There are almost 200 campsites with modern restrooms, showers, potable water, and a dump station. The camping and tent areas also allow dogs. There is a dog walk area at the campground. There are no water hookups at the campgrounds. Multiple dogs may be allowed.

Rockford State Recreation Area
3019 Apple Street
Lincoln, NE
402-471-5566
Water activities are a favorite pastime at this park that is home to a 150 acre lake. Dogs are allowed for no additional fee. They must be well behaved, on no more than a 6 foot leash, crated, or otherwise restricted at all times, and cleaned up after. The exception being during hunting season and owners must have voice control. Dogs are not allowed in food service areas, public buildings, or on designated swimming beaches. There are over 100 campsites with picnic areas and potable water. The camping and tent areas also allow dogs. There is a dog walk area at the campground. There are no water hookups at the campgrounds. Multiple dogs may be allowed.

Fort McPherson Campground
12567 Valley View Road
Maxwell, NE
308-582-4320
fortmcphersoncampground.com
Dogs of all sizes are allowed. There are no additional pet fees. Dogs may be off lead when there is no one else around and if they are under voice control. Otherwise dogs must be leashed and cleaned up after. Dogs may not be left unattended. There is 1 cabin and a ranch house that sleeps 6, that is also pet friendly. This RV park is closed during the off-season. The camping and tent areas also allow dogs. There is a dog walk area at the campground. Dogs are allowed in the camping cabins. Multiple dogs may be allowed.

Memphis State Recreation Area
County Road D
Memphis, NE
402-471-5566
Visitors can enjoy a number of activities at this 163 acre park with

a 48 acre stocked lake that only allows electric or non-powered boats. Dogs are allowed for no additional fee. They must be well behaved, on no more than a 6 foot leash, crated, or otherwise restricted at all times, and cleaned up after. Dogs are not allowed in food service areas, public buildings, or on designated swimming beaches. The camp area offers 150 sites scattered among the trees; there are picnic tables, grills, potable water and a dump station. The camping and tent areas also allow dogs. There is a dog walk area at the campground. There are no electric or water hookups at the campgrounds. Multiple dogs may be allowed.

Lake Minatare State Recreation Area
Stonegate Road
Minatare, NE
308-783-2911
There are a number of recreational opportunities at this 2,970 acre park complete with a 2,158 acre lake. This site also has a federal waterfowl refuge and is home to the state's only lighthouse. Dogs are allowed for no additional fee. They must be well behaved, on no more than a 6 foot leash, crated, or otherwise restricted at all times, and cleaned up after. Dogs are not allowed in food service areas, public buildings, or on designated swimming beaches. The campground has 160 sites with picnic tables and grills. Potable water, modern restrooms, showers, a laundry, and a dump station are close by. This RV park is closed during the off-season. The camping and tent areas also allow dogs. There is a dog walk area at the campground. There are no water hookups at the campgrounds. Multiple dogs may be allowed.

Niobrara State Park
89261 522nd Avenue
Niobrara, NE
402-85 7-3373
This park of over 1,600 acres offers opportunities for nature study in addition to providing an interpretive center, more than 14 miles of trails, and a wide range of land and water recreation. Dogs of all sizes are allowed at no additional fee. Dogs may not be left unattended outside, and they must be on no more than a 6 foot leash, and be cleaned up after. Dogs are not allowed on the furniture or bed in the cabins, and they must be placed in a crate if left inside. Dogs are not allowed in the pool area, but they are allowed on the

trails. The state reservation phone number is 402-471-1414. The camping and tent areas also allow dogs. There is a dog walk area at the campground. Dogs are allowed in the camping cabins. There are no water hookups at the campground. Multiple dogs may be allowed.

TahaZouka Park Campground
2201 South 13th Street
Norfolk, NE
402-844-2000
Located in a lush 99 acre recreational park, this campground sits tucked among the trees between the Elkhorn River and a sizable lagoon with a bridge, an accessible fishing area, and water fountains. There are modern restrooms, showers, picnic tables, grills, potable water, and a dump station. Dogs are allowed for no additional fee; they must be leashed (or otherwise restrained), and picked up after at all times. This RV park is closed during the off-season. The camping and tent areas also allow dogs. There is a dog walk area at the campground. There are no electric or water hookups at the campgrounds. Multiple dogs may be allowed.

Holiday Trav-L-Park
601 Halligan Drive
North Platte, NE
308-534-2265
holidayparkne.com
Dogs of all sizes are allowed. There are no additional pet fees. Dogs may not be left unattended at any time, and they must be leashed and cleaned up after. The camping and tent areas also allow dogs. There is a dog walk area at the campground. Multiple dogs may be allowed.

Lake Maloney State Rec Area
301 E State Farm Road
North Platte, NE
308-535-8025
This recreational park sits along a 1000 acre lake. Dogs of all sizes are allowed at no additional fee. Dogs must be leashed and cleaned up after. The camping and tent areas also allow dogs. There is a dog walk area at the campground. There are no water hookups at the campground. Multiple dogs may be allowed.

Lake Ogallala State Rec Area
1475 H 61N
Ogallala, NE
308-284-8800
This modern park is located in a shady spot below the Kingsley Dam

Hydroelectric Plant, and offers both land and water recreation. Dogs of all sizes are allowed at no additional fee. Dogs may not be left unattended, and they must be leashed and cleaned up after. Dogs are allowed on the trails. The camping and tent areas also allow dogs. There is a dog walk area at the campground. There are no water hookups at the campground. Multiple dogs may be allowed.

Glenn Cunningham Lake Park
8660 Lake Cunningham Road
Omaha, NE
402-444-4FUN (4386)
This lush tree-shaded 1438+ acre park along the lake, offers scenic picnic areas, hiking trails and paths along the shores, a playground, and a number of land and water recreation. Dogs are allowed for no additional fee. They must be well behaved, on no more than a 6 foot leash, crated, or otherwise restricted at all times, and cleaned up after. Dogs are not allowed in food service areas, public buildings, or on designated swimming beaches. The camp area offers wooded and lakeside sites. The camping and tent areas also allow dogs. There is a dog walk area at the campground. There are no water hookups at the campgrounds. Multiple dogs may be allowed.

Willow Creek State Recreation Area
54876 852 Road
Pierce, NE
402-329-4053
This 933 acre park offers a 700 acre lake with 7 handicapped fishing piers, miles of trails, and an archery field course. Dogs are allowed for no additional fee. They must be well behaved, on no more than a 6 foot leash, crated, or otherwise restricted at all times, and cleaned up after. Dogs are not allowed in food service areas, public buildings, or on designated swimming beaches. All campers must register; the campground has over 100 sites with picnic tables and grills. Potable water, modern restrooms, showers, a laundry, playgrounds, and a dump station are close by. The camping and tent areas also allow dogs. There is a dog walk area at the campground. There are no water hookups at the campgrounds. Multiple dogs may be allowed.

Ponca State Park
88090 Spur 26E

Ponca, NE
402-755-2284
This picturesque park, rich in history, is home to one of the state's most comprehensive outdoor/environmental education programs, and provides a variety of outdoor recreation. Dogs of all sizes are allowed at no additional fee. Dogs may not be left unattended in the cabins, and they must be leashed at all times, and cleaned up after. Dogs are not allowed in the pool area or buildings, and they may be left tied outside only if they will be quiet and well behaved. Dogs are allowed on the trails. The state reservation phone number is 402-471-1414. The camping and tent areas also allow dogs. There is a dog walk area at the campground. Dogs are allowed in the camping cabins. There are no water hookups at the campground. Multiple dogs may be allowed.

Buffalo Point RV Park and Motel
8175 H 30
Potter, NE
308-879-4400
Dogs of all sizes are allowed. There are no additional pet fees. Dogs must be quiet, leashed, and cleaned up after. There is also a motel on site that allowes dogs. The camping and tent areas also allow dogs. There is a dog walk area at the campground. Dogs are allowed in the camping cabins. Multiple dogs may be allowed.

Scottsbluff/Chimney Rock KOA
180037 KOA Drive
Scottsbluff, NE
308-635-3760
koa.com
Dogs of all sizes are allowed. There are no additional pet fees. Dogs may not be left unattended, and they must be quiet, leashed, and cleaned up after. Dogs may not be tied to the trees or tables. This RV park is closed during the off-season. The camping and tent areas also allow dogs. There is a dog walk area at the campground. Dogs are allowed in the camping cabins. Multiple dogs may be allowed.

Fishberry Campground
5 miles N of Valentine on H 83
Valentine, NE
866-376-1662
fishberrycampground.com
Dogs of all sizes are allowed. There are no additional pet fees. Dogs must be quiet, well behaved, leashed, and cleaned up after. Sites

are available by reservation only after November 1st. The camping and tent areas also allow dogs. There is a dog walk area at the campground. Multiple dogs may be allowed.

Double Nickel Campground
905 Road S
Waco, NE
402-728-5558
Dogs of all sizes are allowed. There are no additional pet fees. Dogs may not be left unattended outside, and they must be leashed and cleaned up after. This RV park is closed during the off-season. The camping and tent areas also allow dogs. There is a dog walk area at the campground.

Two Rivers State Recreation Area
27702 F Street
Waterloo, NE
402-359-5165
Five sandpit lakes with 320 acres, 302 land acres, numerous amenities and recreational activities, beautiful scenery, and several great walking paths have made this a popular destination. Dogs are allowed for no additional fee. They must be well behaved, on no more than a 6 foot leash, crated, or otherwise restricted at all times, and cleaned up after. The exception being during hunting season and owners must have voice control. Dogs are not allowed in food service areas, public buildings, or on designated swimming beaches. There are 5 separate camp areas and they may have all or some of the following: picnic tables, grills, fire rings, pit/vault toilets, modern restrooms, showers, potable water, a playground, stores, concessionaires, and/or a dump station. This RV park is closed during the off-season. The camping and tent areas also allow dogs. There is a dog walk area at the campground. There are no water hookups at the campgrounds. Multiple dogs may be allowed.

Wood River Motel and RV Park
11774 S H 11
Wood River, NE
308-583-2256
Dogs of all sizes are allowed, and there are no additional pet fees for tent or RV sites. There is a motel on site, and there is a $5 per night per pet additional fee. Dogs may not be left unattended in the motel room or outside, and they must be leashed and cleaned up after. The camping and tent areas also allow dogs. There is a dog walk area at the

campground. Multiple dogs may be allowed.

Nevada

Berlin-Ichthyosaur State Park
HC 61 Box 61200
Austin, NV
775-964-2440
parks.nv.gov/bi.htm#SITES
Once a mining area, this park sits at about 7,000 feet and came into being to protect and display North America's richest concentration and largest known Ichthyosaur fossils. It also oversees the old mining town of Berlin and the Diana Mine. There is an extensive sign/trail system that tells the history and features of this Registered Natural Landmark, a nature trail, and viewing windows at the Fossils Shelter. Dogs of all sizes are allowed for no additional fee. Dogs must be well mannered, be on no more than a 6 foot leash, and be cleaned up after. They are allowed throughout the park and on the trails; they are not allowed in park buildings. The camping and tent areas also allow dogs. There is a dog walk area at the campground. There are no electric or water hookups at the campgrounds.

Baileys Hot Springs RV Park
6 miles N of Beatty on H 95
Beatty, NV
775-553-2395
Visitors come from all over to enjoy the hot springs here. Dogs of all sizes are allowed at no additional fee. Dogs must be leashed and cleaned up after. There are some breed restrictions. The camping and tent areas also allow dogs. There is a dog walk area at the campground. Multiple dogs may be allowed.

Lake Mead RV Village
268 Lakeshore Road
Boulder City, NV
702-293-2540
lakemeadrvvillage.com/
Offering beautiful views, this RV park, conveniently located to a variety of attractions, also offers a convenience store, laundry facility, 2 boat launches, and a variety of land and water recreation. Dogs of all sizes are allowed at no additional fee. Dogs may not be left unattended at any time, and they must be quiet, well behaved, leashed at all times, and cleaned up

after. This is an RV only park. There is a dog walk area at the campground. 2 dogs may be allowed.

Fiesta RV Resort
3190 H 95
Bullhead City, AZ
800-982-1750
Dogs of all sizes are allowed. There are no additional pet fees. Dogs must be walked out of the park and be leashed and cleaned up after. Dogs must be quiet and well behaved. There is a dog walk area at the campground. Multiple dogs may be allowed.

Silver View RV Resort
1501 Gold Rush Road
Bullhead City, AZ
928-763-5500
silverviewrvresort.com
With spectacular views from the bluffs overlooking the Colorado River, this 5 star resort offers a mini mart and deli, clubhouse, swimming pool/Jacuzzi, and laundry. Two dogs under 40 pounds or one dog over 40 pounds is allowed at no additional fee. Dogs may not be left unattended outside, and they must be leashed and cleaned up after. Dogs are not allowed on the grass areas. There is a dog run on site where pets may be off lead. There are some breed restrictions. The camping and tent areas also allow dogs. There is a dog walk area at the campground.

Beaver Dam State Park
P. O. Box 985
Caliente, NV
775-726-3564
parks.nv.gov/bd.htm
This remote, primitive 2,393-acre park features deep canyons, pine forests, a flowing stream, numerous beaver dams, hiking, and interpretive trails. Due to flood damage and dangerous conditions, it is strongly advised to check conditions before going to the dam site and the exposed mud flats behind the dam. Dogs of all sizes are allowed at no additional fee. Dogs must be leashed and cleaned up after. Dogs are allowed on the trails. The camping and tent areas also allow dogs. There is a dog walk area at the campground. There are no electric hookups at the campgrounds. 2 dogs may be allowed.

Washoe Lake State Park
4855 East Lake Blvd
Carson City, NV
775-687-4319

parks.nv.gov/wl.htm
This scenic park features a wetlands area with a viewing tower, an interpretive display, nature study and bird watching, hiking, horseback riding, water sports, boat launches, 2 comfort stations with showers, and access to trails and trailheads. Dogs of all sizes are allowed. There are no additional pet fees. Dogs may not be left unattended outside, and they must be leashed and cleaned up after. Dogs may be off lead when other people are not around and they are under voice control. Dogs are allowed on the beach and trails. The camping and tent areas also allow dogs. There is a dog walk area at the campground. There are no electric or water hookups at the campgrounds. Multiple dogs may be allowed.

Dayton State Park
P. O. Box 1478
Dayton, NV
775-687-5678
parks.nv.gov/dsp.htm
The Carson River flows through this park giving visitors fishing opportunities and water activities. The park also offers hiking trails, an interpretive trail, a historic site and various recreation. Dogs of all sizes are allowed at no additional fee. Please keep dogs on a leash in populated areas and clean up after them. Dogs may not be left unattended outside, and they are not allowed in the pavilon area or on the lawns. The camping and tent areas also allow dogs. There is a dog walk area at the campground. There are no electric or water hookups at the campgrounds. Multiple dogs may be allowed.

Double Dice RV Park
3730 Idaho Street
Elko, NV
775-738-5642 (888-738-3423)
This RV park offers 140 sites with amenities that include 30 or 50 amp electric, instant phone, 43 channel TV, 75 pull-thru sites for rigs up to 65 feet, a game room, laundry room, free email/web center, and showers. Tent sites are also available. Well-behaved leashed dogs are welcome. Please clean up after your pets. There is a $1 per night per pet additional fee. Dogs must be leashed, and taken to the dog run to relieve themselves. They are not allowed on the grass. Dogs may not be left outside, and they may be left inside only if they will be quiet and comfortable. The camping and tent areas also allow dogs. There is a

dog walk area at the campground. Multiple dogs may be allowed.

Wild Horse State Recreation Area
HC 31, Box 26/H 225
Elko, NV
775-758-6493
parks.nv.gov/wh.htm
Located on the northeast shore of Wild Horse Reservoir, this park is popular for camping, picnicking, hunting, fishing, boating, and hiking. The park also offers a boat launch, showers and a dump station. Dogs of all sizes are allowed. There are no additional pet fees. Dogs must be well behaved, on no more than a 6 foot leash, and cleaned up after. The camping and tent areas also allow dogs. There is a dog walk area at the campground. There are no electric or water hookups at the campgrounds. Multiple dogs may be allowed.

Cave Lake State Park
P. O. Box 151761
Ely, NV
775-728-4467
parks.nv.gov/cl.htm
This park, along a 32 acre reservoir at 7,300 feet, offers outstanding views, opportunities for nature study and photography, a boat launch, interpretive presentations, winter programs, hiking trails, and more. Dogs of all sizes are allowed at no additional fee. Dogs must be leashed and cleaned up after. Dogs are not allowed in buildings. They are allowed on the trails. The camping and tent areas also allow dogs. There is a dog walk area at the campground. There are no electric or water hookups at the campgrounds. Multiple dogs may be allowed.

Ely Koa
H 93
Ely, NV
775-289-3413 (800-562-3413)
koa.com/where/nv/28106/
Well landscaped grounds and location make this a popular park, with amenities that include 85 foot pull-thru sites with 50 amp service, cable TV, LP gas, and Wi-Fi. Dogs of all sizes are allowed for no additional fee, and there is a pet waiver to sign. There is a $25 refundable pet deposit for the cabins. Dogs must be under owner's control and visual observation at all times. Dogs must be quiet, well behaved, and be on no more than a 6 foot leash at all times, or otherwise contained. Dogs

may not be left unattended outside the owner's camping equipment, and must be brought inside at night. Dogs are not allowed on the grass except by the dog walk. There are some breed restrictions. The camping and tent areas also allow dogs. There is a dog walk area at the campground. Dogs are allowed in the camping cabins. Multiple dogs may be allowed.

Ward Charcoal Ovens State Historic Park
P. O. Box 151761
Ely, NV
775-728-4460
parks.nv.gov/ww.htm
Although mostly known for its historic six beehive-shaped charcoal ovens, this park also offers outstanding geologic sites, trails consisting of several miles of different views and ecotypes, and various other recreation. Dogs of all sizes are allowed at no additional fee. Dogs may not be left unattended outside, and left inside only if they will be quiet and comfortable. Dogs must be on no more than a 6 foot leash and be cleaned up after. Dogs are allowed on the trails. The camping and tent areas also allow dogs. There is a dog walk area at the campground. There are no electric or water hookups at the campgrounds. Multiple dogs may be allowed.

Las Vegas KOA at Circus Circus
500 Circus Circus Drive
Las Vegas, NV
702-733-9707 (800-562-7270)
koa.com/where/nv/28138/
Located on the Las Vegas Strip, this RV mostly park offers 80 foot pull-thru sites with 50 amp service, LP Gas, Wi-Fi, snack bar, swimming pool, hot tub, sauna, and guided tours. Dogs of all sizes are allowed for no additional fee. Dogs must be under owner's control and visual observation at all times. Dogs must be quiet, well behaved, and be on no more than a 6 foot leash at all times, or otherwise contained. Dogs may not be left unattended outside the owner's camping equipment, and must be brought inside at night. There are some breed restrictions. There is a dog walk area at the campground. Multiple dogs may be allowed.

Oasis Las Vegas RV Resort
2711 W Windmill Lane
Las Vegas, NV
800-566-4707
oasislasvegasrvresort.com

This premier RV park offers beautifully landscaped sites, beachfront family pool and waterfalls, adult pool and spa, 18-hole putting course, fitness center, store, restaurant, and a variety of recreational pursuits. Dogs of all sizes are allowed at no additional fee. Dogs may not be left unattended at any time, and they must be leashed and cleaned up after at all times. There is a $50 fine if the dogs are not picked up after. Dogs are not allowed in the non-pet section of the park. There is a fenced in dog run area where they may be off lead, but still must be cleaned up after. This is an RV only park. There are some breed restrictions. There is a dog walk area at the campground. There are special amenities given to dogs at this campground. 2 dogs may be allowed.

Big Bend of the Colorado
P. O. Box 32850
Laughlin, NV
702-298-1859
parks.nv.gov/bb.htm
Located on the shores of the Colorado River, this desert park offers a variety of land and water recreation. Dogs of all sizes are allowed at no additional fee. Dogs must be on no more than a 6 foot leash and be cleaned up after. The camping and tent areas also allow dogs. There is a dog walk area at the campground. There are no electric or water hookups at the campgrounds. 2 dogs may be allowed.

Don Laughlin's Riverside RV Resort
1650 S Casino Drive
Laughlin, NV
702-298-2535 (800-227-3849)
This RV only park, located across the street from the Riverside Resort Hotel, offers 740 full hookup RV sites. Amenities include laundry facilities, showers, and 24 hour security. Well-behaved leashed dogs are allowed. Please clean up after your pets. There is no pet fee. Dogs may not be left unattended outside, and left inside only if they will be quiet and comfortable. There is a dog walk area at the campground. Multiple dogs may be allowed.

Rye Patch State Recreation Area
2505 Rye Patch Reservoir Road
Lovelock, NV
775-538-7321
parks.nv.gov/rp.htm
Rich in natural and cultural history, this park along a 22-mile long reservoir, offers archaeological sites,

and a variety of land and water recreation. Dogs of all sizes are allowed at no additional fee. Dogs may not be left unattended outside, and they must be on no more than a 6 foot leash, and cleaned up after. The camping and tent areas also allow dogs. There is a dog walk area at the campground. There are no electric or water hookups at the campgrounds. Multiple dogs may be allowed.

Silver City RV Resort
3165 H 395N
Minden, NV
775-267-3359 (800-997-6393)
silvercityrvresort.com
This RV campground offers a covered pool and spa, fish pond, fitness club, store, laundry facilities, gaming, and various other recreational pursuits. Dogs of all sizes are allowed for an additional $1 per night per pet. Dogs may not be left unattended outside, and they must be leashed and cleaned up after. This is an RV only park. There are some breed restrictions. There is a dog walk area at the campground. 2 dogs may be allowed.

Valley of Fire State Park
P. O. Box 515/ Valley of Fire Road
Overton, NV
702-397-2088
parks.nv.gov/vf.htm
Unusual red sandstone formations mark this park with a facinating array of shapes, and they offer interpretive exhibits, numerous trails, historic sites, various recreation, and a visitor's center. Dogs of all sizes are allowed at no additional fee. Dogs may not be left unattended outside, and they must be leashed and cleaned up after. Dogs are allowed on the trails. The camping and tent areas also allow dogs. There is a dog walk area at the campground. There are no electric or water hookups at the campgrounds. Multiple dogs may be allowed.

Lakeside Casino RV Park
5870 S Homestead Road
Pahrump, NV
775-751-7770 (888-558-5253)
terribleherbst.com
This lushly landscaped RV resort offers historic old west charm among its many amenities which include watercraft rentals, laundry facilities, swimming lagoon, swimming pool and Jacuzzi. Dogs of all sizes are allowed. There are

no additional pet fees. Dogs may not be left unattended outside, and left inside if they will be quiet and comfortable. They must be leashed and cleaned up after. Dogs are not allowed in the lake, on the beach, or in the pool area. This is an RV only park. There are some breed restrictions. There is a dog walk area at the campground. 2 dogs may be allowed.

Cathedral Gorge State Park
P. O. Box 176
Panaca, NV
775-728-4460
parks.nv.gov/cg.htm
This park sits at 4,800 feet in a long, narrow valley and offers several trails to explore the cathedral spires and cave-like formations, including a 4 mile loop trail for accessing more remote areas. At Miller Point Overlook, there are excellent views of the canyon, and the visitor center offers interpretive displays and related information. Popular activities include nature study, photography, ranger programs, camping, hiking and picnicking. Dogs of all sizes are allowed for no additional fee. Dogs must be well mannered, be on no more than a 6 foot leash, and be cleaned up after. They are allowed throughout the park and on the trails; they are not allowed in park buildings. The camping and tent areas also allow dogs. There is a dog walk area at the campground. There are no electric or water hookups at the campgrounds. Multiple dogs may be allowed.

Echo Canyon State Park
HC 74, Box 295
Pioche, NV
775-962-5103
parks.nv.gov/ec.htm
This 1080-acre park, with a 65 acre reservoir, supports a good variety of plant and animal life. It offers a rich archeological and agricultural history to explore in addition to various recreational pursuits. Dogs of all sizes are allowed at no additional fee. Dogs must be leashed in the camp area, and cleaned up after. Dogs are allowed on the trails. The camping and tent areas also allow dogs. There is a dog walk area at the campground. There are no electric or water hookups at the campgrounds. Multiple dogs may be allowed.

Spring Valley State Park
HC74, Box 201
Pioche, NV
775-962-5102

parks.nv.gov/sv.htm
This high desert park, along a 65 acre reservoir, offers a rich cultural history in addition to a variety of amenities and recreational pursuits. Dogs of all sizes are allowed for no additional fee. Dogs may not be left unattended, except for short periods, and then only if they will be quiet and well behaved. Dogs must be on no more than a 6 foot leash and cleaned up after. When there are not a lot of people around, dogs may be off lead if they are under voice control and will not chase. The camping and tent areas also allow dogs. There is a dog walk area at the campground. There are no electric or water hookups at the campgrounds. Multiple dogs may be allowed.

Bonanza Terrace RV Park
4800 Stoltz Road
Reno, NV
775-329-9624
bonanzaterracervpark.com/
This RV park is located two miles north of downtown Reno off Highway 395. The Bonanza Casino is across the street from the RV park. RV sites include a gravel parking pad, up to 50 amp electric, water, sewer and phone line. RVs up to 40 feet are welcome. Well-behaved, leashed, and quiet pets accompanied by their owner are welcome. There is a $1 per night pet fee. Please clean up after your pet. Dogs may not be left unattended outside. There are some breed restrictions. There is a dog walk area at the campground. Multiple dogs may be allowed.

Reno RV Park
735 Mill Street
Reno, NV
775-323-3381 (800-445-3381)
This RV park is located about 4 blocks from the casinos. They offer restrooms, showers, 24 hour security, electric gates, propane available, recreation area, picnic area and more. Well-behaved leashed dogs are welcome. Please clean up after your pets. There is no pet fee. Dogs may not be left unattended. The camping and tent areas also allow dogs. There is a dog walk area at the campground. Multiple dogs may be allowed.

Fort Churchill State Historic Park
1000 H 95A
Silver Springs, NV
775-577-2345
parks.nv.gov/fc.htm
Rich in American history, this park offers a visitor's center with exhibits

and artifacts, hiking, historic and environmental education, and access to the Carson River for canoeing. Dogs of all sizes are allowed at no additional fee. Dogs may not be left unattended for long periods, and only then if they will be quiet and well behaved. Dogs must be on no more than a 6 foot leash, or crated, and cleaned up after. Dogs are allowed on the trails unless otherwise marked. The camping and tent areas also allow dogs. There is a dog walk area at the campground. There are no electric or water hookups at the campgrounds. Multiple dogs may be allowed.

Silver Springs Beach
1971 Fir Street
Silver Springs, NV
775-577-2226
parks.nv.gov/lah.htm#CAMP
This park, located in the high desert of the Lahontan State Rec Area along a 17 mile reservoir, offers a variety of amenities and recreational opportunities. Dogs of all sizes are allowed at no additional fee. Dogs must be on no more than a 6 foot leash and cleaned up after. Dogs are allowed to go to the beach and on the trails. The camping and tent areas also allow dogs. There is a dog walk area at the campground. There are no electric or water hookups at the campgrounds. 2 dogs may be allowed.

Rivers Edge RV Park
1405 S Rock Blvd
Sparks, NV
775-358-8533 (800-621-4792)
Dogs of all sizes are allowed. There are no additional pet fees. Dogs may not be left unattended outside, and they must be leashed and cleaned up after. Dogs are allowed on the trails. This is an RV only park. There is a dog walk area at the campground. Multiple dogs may be allowed.

South Fork State Recreation Area
353 Lower South Fork Unit 8
Spring Creek, NV
775-744-4346
parks.nv.gov/sf.htm
Surrounded by 2,200 acres of wildlife-filled meadow lands and rolling hills, this park, with a 1,650 acre reservoir, is popular for hunting, boating, hiking, winter sports, and wildlife viewing. Friendly dogs of all sizes are allowed for no additional fee. Dogs must be on no more than a 6 foot leash and be

cleaned up after. The camping and tent areas also allow dogs. There is a dog walk area at the campground. There are no electric or water hookups at the campgrounds. Multiple dogs may be allowed.

Gold Ranch Casino and RV Resort
320 Gold Ranch Road
Verdi, NV
877-792-6789
goldranchrvcasino.com
A few miles from Reno, nestled among the trees of the Sierra Nevada mountain range, this modern, luxury resort offers a 24 hour convenience store, an Arco gas station, clean showers, laundry facilities, clubhouse, heated pool/spa, and wide pull-thru sites. Dogs of all sizes are allowed. There are no additional pet fees. Dogs may not be left unattended outside, and they must be leashed and cleaned up after. This is an RV only park. There is a dog walk area at the campground.

Reno / Boomtown KOA
2100 I-80 W Garson Road
Verdi, NV
775-345-2444 (888-562-5698)
koa.com/where/nv/28136/
Located adjacent to the Boomtown Casino, visitors can find plenty of entertainment, dining options, and a variety of recreation. There is a 30,000 foot family fun center and the worlds first 3D motion, all digital theater also on site. Dogs are allowed for no additional fee. Dogs may not be left unattended, and they must be on no more than a 6 foot leash and cleaned up after at all times. There are some breed restrictions. There is a dog walk area at the campground. There are special amenities given to dogs at this campground. Multiple dogs may be allowed.

Virginia City RV Park
355 N 'F' Street
Virginia City, NV
775-847-0999 (800-889-1240)
Located just two blocks from downtown Virginia City, this park offers 50 RV sites, and amenities include phone equipped spaces, showers, swimming pool, tennis courts park access, onsite market and deli, video rentals, laundry facility, slot machines and tent camping. Well-behaved leashed dogs are allowed. Please clean up after your pets, and do not leave them unattended. Reservations are accepted for busy periods. The park

is open all year. The camping and tent areas also allow dogs. There is a dog walk area at the campground. 2 dogs may be allowed.

Wendover KOA
651 N Camper Drive
West Wendover, NV
775-664-3221 (800-562-8552)
koa.com/where/nv/28130/
Located just 10 miles from the world-famous Bonneville Salt Flats and next to 2 casinos, this oasis park offers large pull-thru sites, seasonal heated outdoor pool, mini golf, a grocery and souvenir shop, laundry and much more. Dogs of all sizes are allowed for no additional fee. Dogs must be under owner's control and visual observation at all times. Dogs must be quiet, well behaved, and be on no more than a 6 foot leash at all times, or otherwise contained, and cleaned up after. Dogs may not be left unattended outside the owner's camping equipment or alone in the cabins, and they must be brought inside at night. There are some breed restrictions. The camping and tent areas also allow dogs. There is a dog walk area at the campground. Dogs are allowed in the camping cabins. Multiple dogs may be allowed.

Model T RV Park
1130 W Winnemucca Blvd
Winnemucca, NV
775-623-2588 (800-645-5658)
modelt.com/rvpark.htm
This RV only park is located in town within walking distance of many services. Amenities include laundry facilities, a seasonal pool, restrooms and showers. Well-behaved leashed pets are allowed. There is no pet fee, just please clean up after your pet. The RV park is part of the Model T Casino and Winnemucca Quality Inn. There is a dog walk area at the campground. Multiple dogs may be allowed.

New Hampshire

Bear Brook State Park
157 Deerfield Road
Allenstown, NH
603-485-9874
With more than 10,000 acres, this is the states largest developed park offering more than 40 miles of scenic trails, and a wide array of land and water recreation and activities for all

ages and interests. Dogs of all sizes are allowed for no additional fee. Dogs must be well behaved, leashed, cleaned up after, and owners are responsible for them at all times. Dogs may not be left unattended in any vehicle, camper, carrier, or enclosure at any time. Dogs are allowed on the trails and in the campground, but not in the day use areas or on the beach. Nestled alone the shore of Beaver Pond, the camp area has 93 reservation only sites (603-271-3628), 2 first come, first served sites, and is located 5 miles from the day use area. There are showers, laundry facilities, and a camp store on site. This RV park is closed during the off-season. The camping and tent areas also allow dogs. There is a dog walk area at the campground. There are no electric or water hookups at the campgrounds. 2 dogs may be allowed.

Jellystone Park
35 Jellystone Park
Ashland, NH
603-968-9000
jellystonenh.com
Dogs of all sizes are allowed. There are no additional pet fees. Dogs must have a valid rabies certificate, can not be left unattended, and must be leashed and cleaned up after. This RV park is closed during the off-season. The camping and tent areas also allow dogs. There is a dog walk area at the campground. Multiple dogs may be allowed.

Davidson's Countryside
Campgrounds
100 Schofield Road
Bristol, NH
603-744-2403
worldpath.net/~davcamp/
Dogs of all sizes are allowed. There are no additional pet fees. Dogs must be well behaved, leashed, and cleaned up after. This RV park is closed during the off-season. The camping and tent areas also allow dogs. There is a dog walk area at the campground. Multiple dogs may be allowed.

Russell Pond Campground
Tripoli Road
Campton, NH
603-528-8721 (877-444-6777)
Located in the White Mountain National Forest, this camp area offers 86 first-come, first-served sites with flush toilets, coin-op showers, and sinks with hot water.

Dogs of all sizes are allowed for no additional pet fee. Dogs must be well behaved, under owner's control, leashed, and cleaned up after at all times. This RV park is closed during the off-season. The camping and tent areas also allow dogs. There is a dog walk area at the campground. There are no electric or water hookups at the campgrounds. Multiple dogs may be allowed.

Terrace Pines Campground
110 Terrace Pine
Center Ossipee, NH
603-539-6210
terracepines.com
Dogs of all sizes are allowed. There are no additional pet fees. Dogs may not be left unattended, must be leashed, and cleaned up after. This RV park is closed during the off-season. The camping and tent areas also allow dogs. There is a dog walk area at the campground. Dogs are allowed in the camping cabins. Multiple dogs may be allowed.

Jigger Johnson Campground
Kancamagus Highway
Conway, NH
603-528-8721 (877-444-6777)
Located in the White Mountain National Forest, this camp area offers 76 sites on a first-come, first-served basis, picnic tables, coin-op showers, and flush toilets. Dogs of all sizes are allowed for no additional pet fee. Dogs must be well behaved, under owner's control, leashed, and cleaned up after at all times. This RV park is closed during the off-season. The camping and tent areas also allow dogs. There is a dog walk area at the campground. There are no electric or water hookups at the campgrounds. Multiple dogs may be allowed.

Circle 9 Ranch
39 Windymere Drive
Epsom, NH
603-736-9656
circle9ranch.com
Dogs of all sizes are allowed. There are no additional pet fees. Dogs must be leashed at all times and be cleaned up after. There is a dog walk area at the campground. Multiple dogs may be allowed.

Fransted Family Campground
974 Profile Road
Franconia, NH
603-823-5675
franstedcampground.com
Dogs of all sizes are allowed. There are no additional pet fees. Dogs may

not be left unattended, must be leashed, and cleaned up after. There are some breed restrictions. This RV park is closed during the off-season. Only one dog is allowed per campsite. The camping and tent areas also allow dogs. There is a dog walk area at the campground.

Danforth Bay Camping Resort
196 Shawtown Road
Freedom, NH
603-539-2069
danforthbay.com
Dogs of all sizes are allowed. There are no additional pet fees. Dogs must have current shot records, and be leashed and cleaned up after. Dogs are not allowed at the pool or beach. There are some breed restrictions. This RV park is closed during the off-season. The camping and tent areas also allow dogs. There is a dog walk area at the campground. 2 dogs may be allowed.

Dolly Copp Family and Barns Field Group Campground
H 16
Gorham, NH
603-528-8721 (877-444-6777)
Located in the White Mountain National Forest, this camp area offers 176 sites (69 are on a first-come, first-served basis), picnic tables, and flush toilets. Dogs of all sizes are allowed for no additional pet fee. Dogs must be well behaved, under owner's control, leashed, and cleaned up after at all times. This RV park is closed during the off-season. The camping and tent areas also allow dogs. There is a dog walk area at the campground. There are no electric or water hookups at the campgrounds. Multiple dogs may be allowed.

Moose Brook State Park
Jimtown Road
Gorham, NH
603-466-3860
Located in an area of unsurpassed scenery, this park offers many trails, fishing from the brook that flows through the park, and a variety of other recreational opportunities. The season for the day use area is from about the end of June to about the first week in September from 10 am to 5pm. Dogs of all sizes are allowed for no additional fee. Dogs must be well behaved, leashed, cleaned up after, and owners are responsible for them at all times. Dogs may not be left unattended in any vehicle, camper, carrier, or enclosure at any

time. Dogs are allowed on the trails and at the campground; they are not allowed on any beaches or picnic areas. The 59 site campground includes 6 first come, first served sites, and the rest are available by reservation only. There are a variety of camp sites with restrooms, showers, and a camp store close by. The number for campground reservations is 603-271-3628. This RV park is closed during the off-season. The camping and tent areas also allow dogs. There is a dog walk area at the campground. There are no electric or water hookups at the campgrounds. 2 dogs may be allowed.

Wakeda Campground
294 Exeter Road
Hampton Falls, NH
603-772-5274
wakedacampground.com
Dogs of all sizes are allowed. There are no additional pet fees. Dogs may not be left unattended, must be leashed, and cleaned up after. This RV park is closed during the off-season. The camping and tent areas also allow dogs. There is a dog walk area at the campground. Dogs are allowed in the camping cabins. Multiple dogs may be allowed.

Mile-Away Campground
41 Old West Hockington Road
Henniker, NH
603-428-7616
mileaway.com
Dogs of all sizes are allowed. There are no additional pet fees. Dogs must be leashed and cleaned up after. This RV park is closed during the off-season. The camping and tent areas also allow dogs. There is a dog walk area at the campground. Multiple dogs may be allowed.

Lantern Resort Motel and Campground
571 Presidential H
Jefferson, NH
603-586-7151
thelanternresort.com
Dogs of all sizes are allowed. There are no additional pet fees. Dogs must be leashed and cleaned up after. Dogs may be left inside your unit for short periods if they will be quiet and well behaved. Dogs are not allowed at the motel. This RV park is closed during the off-season. The camping and tent areas also allow dogs. There is a dog walk area at the campground.

Multiple dogs may be allowed.

White Mountain National Forest
719 Main Street
Laconia, NH
603-528-8721
fs.fed.us/r9/white
Dogs of all sizes are allowed. There are no additional pet fees. Dogs may not be left unattended, and they must be quiet, leashed, and cleaned up after. Dogs are allowed on most trails in the forest. There is a trail map that can be ordered ahead or at seen at the entrances of the park. Since there is private and state owned land, where dogs are not allowed, in the park, they request adherence to the map. There are 22 campgrounds in this national forest. The camping and tent areas also allow dogs. There is a dog walk area at the campground. There are no electric or water hookups at the campground. Multiple dogs may be allowed.

Mountain Lake Campground
485 Prospect Street
Lancaster, NH
603-788-4509
mtnlakecampground.com
Dogs of all sizes are allowed. There is a $2 per night per pet additional fee, and dogs must have current rabies and shot records. Dogs must be leashed and cleaned up after. There are some breed restrictions. This RV park is closed during the off-season. The camping and tent areas also allow dogs. There is a dog walk area at the campground. 2 dogs may be allowed.

Roger's Campground
10 Roger's Campground Road
Lancaster, NH
603-788-4885
rogerscampground.com
Dogs of all sizes are allowed. There are no additional pet fees. Dogs must be leashed and cleaned up after. Dogs are not allowed at the motel or other rentals. This RV park is closed during the off-season. The camping and tent areas also allow dogs. There is a dog walk area at the campground. Multiple dogs may be allowed.

Handcock Campground
Kancamagus Highway
Lincoln, NH
603-528-8721 (877-444-6777)
Located in the White Mountain National Forest, this camp area offers 56 sites, and in summer sites are on a first-come, first-served basis. Winter reservations are

accepted from December 5th to April 15th, and they plow here in the winter. They offer picnic tables, vault and flush toilets, and a variety of land and water recreation. Dogs of all sizes are allowed for no additional pet fee. Dogs must be well behaved, under owner's control, leashed, and cleaned up after at all times. The camping and tent areas also allow dogs. There is a dog walk area at the campground. There are no electric or water hookups at the campgrounds. Multiple dogs may be allowed.

KOA Littleton/Lisbon
2154 Route 302
Lisbon, NH
603-838-5525 (800-562-5836)
littletonkoa.com
Dogs of all sizes are allowed. There are no additional pet fees. Dogs may not be left unattended, must be well behaved, leashed, and cleaned up after. There are some breed restrictions. This RV park is closed during the off-season. The camping and tent areas also allow dogs. There is a dog walk area at the campground. Multiple dogs may be allowed.

Crazy Horse Campground
788 Hiltop Road
Littleton, NH
603-444-2204
ucampnh.com/crazyhorse
Dogs of all sizes are allowed. There are no additional pet fees. Dogs must have current rabies record, be leashed, and cleaned up after. The camping and tent areas also allow dogs. There is a dog walk area at the campground. 2 dogs may be allowed.

Mi-te-jo Campground
111 Mi-te-jo Road
Milton, NH
603-652-9022
mi-te-jo.com
Dogs of all sizes are allowed. There are no additional pet fees. Dogs may not be left unattended, must be leashed, and cleaned up after. Dogs are not allowed on the ball field, the playground, or the beach. This RV park is closed during the off-season. The camping and tent areas also allow dogs. There is a dog walk area at the campground. 2 dogs may be allowed.

Pine Woods Campground
65 Barrett Place
Moultonborough, NH
603-253-6251
bearspinewoodscampground.com

Dogs of all sizes are allowed. There are no additional pet fees. Dogs may not be left unattended, must be leashed, and cleaned up after. Dogs are allowed to go to the lake about a 15 minute walk away. This RV park is closed during the off-season. The camping and tent areas also allow dogs. There is a dog walk area at the campground. Multiple dogs may be allowed.

Friendly Beaver Campground
Old Coach Road
New Boston, NH
603-487-5570
friendlybeaver.com
Dogs of all sizes are allowed. There are no additional pet fees. Dogs must be leashed, cleaned up after, and brought in after dark. The camping and tent areas also allow dogs. There is a dog walk area at the campground. Multiple dogs may be allowed.

Twin Tamarack Family Camping
431 Twin Tamarack Road
New Hampton, NH
603-279-4387
ucampnh.com/twintamarack
Dogs of all sizes are allowed. There are no additional pet fees. Dogs may not be left unattended, must be leashed, and cleaned up after. There are some breed restrictions. This RV park is closed during the off-season. The camping and tent areas also allow dogs. There is a dog walk area at the campground. Multiple dogs may be allowed.

Mt. Sunapee State Park
Off Route 103 between Newbury and Goshen
Newbury, NH
603-763-5561
This beautiful lakeside park features wooded, natural settings and is a major year round recreation destination for a number of activities. Dogs of all sizes are allowed for no additional fee. They must be well behaved, leashed, cleaned up after, and owners are responsible for them at all times. Dogs may not be left unattended in any vehicle, camper, carrier, or enclosure at any time. Pets are permitted at the campground and throughout the park (except during the Arts/Crafts festival), but not in picnic areas, at the beach, or the ski area during the ski operating season. The campground has 5 refurbished lean-to sites available by reservation (603-271-3628) with more lean-to sites in development.

There are pit toilets and water on site, and flush toilets and showers are at the State Beach a mile away. This RV park is closed during the off-season. There is a dog walk area at the campground. There are no electric or water hookups at the campgrounds. 2 dogs may be allowed.

Crow's Nest Campground
529 S Main Street
Newport, NH
603-863-6170
crowsnestcampground.com/
A location along a scenic river, 120 grassy, wooded, or riverfront sites, a store, laundry, rec hall, and all the amenities for a great camping experience, have made this park a popular camping and recreation destination. Dogs of all sizes are allowed for no additional pet fee. Dogs may not be left unattended, and they must be leashed and cleaned up after at all times. Dogs must be quiet, well behaved, and have proof of current rabies inoculation. The camping and tent areas also allow dogs. There is a dog walk area at the campground. Multiple dogs may be allowed.

Beach Camping Area
776 White Mountain H
North Conway, NH
603-447-2723
ucampnh.com/thebeach
Dogs of all sizes are allowed. There is a $2 per night per pet additional fee. Dogs may not be left unattended, must be leashed, and cleaned up after. Dogs are not allowed at the river. This RV park is closed during the off-season. The camping and tent areas also allow dogs. There is a dog walk area at the campground. Multiple dogs may be allowed.

Saco River Camping
1550 White Mountain H
North Conway, NH
603-356-3360
sacorivercampingarea.com
Dogs of all sizes are allowed. There is a $2 per night per pet additional fee. Dogs may not be left unattended, and must be leashed and cleaned up after. Dogs are not allowed at the beach or pool, the playground, or the office. There are some breed restrictions. This RV park is closed during the off-season. The camping and tent areas also allow dogs. There is a dog walk area at the campground. 2 dogs may be allowed.

Jacob's Brook
46 Highbridge Road
Orford, NH
603-353-9210
jacobsbrookcampground.com
Dogs of all sizes are allowed. There are no additional pet fees. Normally only 2 dogs are allowed per site, but more may be accepted if you let them know in advance. Dogs must be well behaved, leashed, and cleaned up after. This RV park is closed during the off-season. The camping and tent areas also allow dogs. There is a dog walk area at the campground.

Pine Acres Family Campground
74 Freetown Road
Raymond, NH
603-895-2519
pineacresrvresort.com
Dogs of all sizes are allowed. There are no additional pet fees. Dogs may not be left unattended, must be leashed and cleaned up after. Dogs are not allowed at the beach or the pavilion This RV park is closed during the off-season. The camping and tent areas also allow dogs. There is a dog walk area at the campground. Multiple dogs may be allowed.

Shir-roy Camping
100 Athol Road
Richmond, NH
603-239-4768
Dogs of all sizes are allowed. There are no additional pet fees. Dogs may not be left unattended, must be leashed, and cleaned up after. This RV park is closed during the off-season. The camping and tent areas also allow dogs. There is a dog walk area at the campground. Multiple dogs may be allowed.

Woodmore Family Campground
21 Woodmore Drive
Rindge, NH
603-899-3362
woodmorecampground.com
Dogs of all sizes are allowed. There are no additional pet fees. Dogs must be quiet, well behaved, leashed, and cleaned up after. Dogs may not be left unattended. This RV park is closed during the off-season. The camping and tent areas also allow dogs. There is a dog walk area at the campground. Dogs are allowed in the camping cabins. Multiple dogs may be allowed.

Timberland Camping Area
809 H 2

Shelburne, NH
603-466-3872
ucampnh.com/timberland
Dogs of all sizes are allowed. There are no additional pet fees. Dogs must be leashed and cleaned up after. There are some breed restrictions. The camping and tent areas also allow dogs. There is a dog walk area at the campground. 2 dogs may be allowed.

Tamworth Camping
194 Depot Road
Tamworth, NH
603-323-8031
tamworthcamping.com/
Dogs of all sizes are allowed. There are no additional pet fees. Dogs must have current rabies and shot records, and be leashed and cleaned up after. There is a river nearby where you can take your pet. This RV park is closed during the off-season. The camping and tent areas also allow dogs. There is a dog walk area at the campground. Multiple dogs may be allowed.

KOA Twin Mountain
372 H 115
Twin Mountain, NH
603-846-5559 (800-562-9117)
twinmtnkoa.com
Dogs of all sizes are allowed. There are no additional pet fees. Dogs must be leashed and cleaned up after. This RV park is closed during the off-season. The camping and tent areas also allow dogs. There is a dog walk area at the campground. 2 dogs may be allowed.

Pillsbury State Park
Clemac Trail/Pillsbury State Park Road
Washington, NH
603-863-2860
Ponds, wetlands, woods, a diversity of habitats, a network of multi-use trails that also connect up with the 51 mile Mt. Monadnock/Mt. Sunapee Trail, historic niches, and a bit of seclusion make this a popular exploring area. Dogs of all sizes are allowed for no additional fee. Dogs must be well behaved, leashed, cleaned up after, and owners are responsible for them at all times. Dogs may not be left unattended in any vehicle, camper, carrier, or enclosure at any time. Dogs are allowed on the trails and in the campground, but not in picnic areas or on the beach. The camp area has 34 sites by reservation only (603-271-3628), 7 first come, first served sites, and there are pit

toilets, water, a playground, and firewood available. The camping permits here may also be used at the Sunapee State Park for free day use. This RV park is closed during the off-season. The camping and tent areas also allow dogs. There is a dog walk area at the campground. There are no electric or water hookups at the campgrounds. 2 dogs may be allowed.

Cold Springs RV and Camp Resort
62 Barnard Hill Road
Weare, NH
603-529-2528
coldspringscampresort.com
Dogs of all sizes are allowed. There is a $2 per night per pet additional fee. Dogs must be quiet, well behaved, leashed, and cleaned up after. Dogs are not allowed at the beach or pool. Visitor dogs are not allowed. This RV park is closed during the off-season. The camping and tent areas also allow dogs. There is a dog walk area at the campground. Multiple dogs may be allowed.

Pine Haven Campground
29 Pine Haven Campground Road
Wentworth, NH
603-786-2900 (800-370-PINE (7463))
Nestled in the Baker River Valley amid the shade of tall white pines with 3000 feet of river frontage, this camp area offers a wide variety of recreational pursuits. They also have Wi-Fi, cable TV, a rec hall, playing fields/courts, a heated pool, a camp store, showers, and a laundry room. Dogs are allowed for no additional pet fee with advance notice. They must be leashed and cleaned up after at all times. Dogs must be quiet, well behaved, and they may not be left unattended at any time. Dogs are not allowed in buildings or at the pool. There are some breed restrictions. This RV park is closed during the off-season. The camping and tent areas also allow dogs. There is a dog walk area at the campground. 2 dogs may be allowed.

Forest Lake Campground
331 Keene Road
Winchester, NH
603-239-4267
ucampnh.com/forestlake
Dogs of all sizes are allowed. There are no additional pet fees. Dogs must be leashed and cleaned up after. There are some breed restrictions. This RV park is closed

during the off-season. The camping and tent areas also allow dogs. There is a dog walk area at the campground. Multiple dogs may be allowed.

KOA Woodstock
1001 Eastside Road
Woodstock, NH
603-745-8008 (800-562-9736)
koa.com
Dogs of all sizes are allowed. There are no additional pet fees. Dogs must be leashed and cleaned up after. This RV park is closed during the off-season. The camping and tent areas also allow dogs. There is a dog walk area at the campground. Dogs are allowed in the camping cabins. Multiple dogs may be allowed.

New Jersey

Shady Pines Camping Resort
443 S 6th Avenue
Absecon Highlands, NJ
609-652-1516
One dog of any size is allowed. There are no additional pet fees. Dogs must be leashed and cleaned up after. The camping and tent areas also allow dogs. There is a dog walk area at the campground.

Panther Lake Camping Resort
6 Panther Lake Road/H 206
Andover, NJ
973-347-4440 (800-543-2056)
One hundred and sixty acres, a variety of land and water recreation, hiking trails, a 45-acre lake, and only 50 miles from New York City, make this a popular get-a-way. Dogs of all sizes are allowed for no additional fee, and they must be leashed and cleaned up after at all times. Dogs are allowed throughout the park, but they are not allowed in the rental units. This RV park is closed during the off-season. The camping and tent areas also allow dogs. There is a dog walk area at the campground. 2 dogs may be allowed.

Buena Vista Camping Park
775 Harding Highway
Buena, NJ
856-697-5555
bvcp.com
Dogs of all sizes are allowed, however some breeds are not. There are no additional pet fees. Dogs must be well behaved, quiet,

leashed, and cleaned up after. The camping and tent areas also allow dogs. There is a dog walk area at the campground. Multiple dogs may be allowed.

Holly Shores Campground
491 Shore Road
Cape May, NJ
609-886-4474 (877- 49-HOLLY (494-6559))
hollyshores.com/index.html
Themed weekends, Wi-Fi, a camp store, planned activities, an adult pool and hot tub, a kiddie pool, golf cart and canoe rentals, seasonal tasty food events on weekends, and more can all be enjoyed at this campground. They are also home to a ¾ acre, fenced dog park with grass, sanitary stations, water and benches. One dog is allowed for no extra fee; there is an added fee of $8 per night per pet for each additional dog. Dogs are not allowed in buildings, and they must be quiet, well mannered, leashed and cleaned up after at all times. There are some breed restrictions. The camping and tent areas also allow dogs. There is a dog walk area at the campground. Multiple dogs may be allowed.

Pomona Campground
Oak Drive
Cape May, NJ
609-965-2123
Dogs of all sizes are allowed. There are no additional pet fees. Dogs must be well behaved, quiet, leashed, and cleaned up after. The camping and tent areas also allow dogs. There is a dog walk area at the campground. Multiple dogs may be allowed.

Seashore Campsites
720 Seashore Road
Cape May, NJ
609-884-4010
seashorecampsites.com
Dogs of all sizes are allowed. There are no additional pet fees. Dogs must be leashed, cleaned up after, and not left unattended. The camping and tent areas also allow dogs. There is a dog walk area at the campground. Multiple dogs may be allowed.

Big Timber Lake Camping Resort
116 Swainton-Goshen Road
Cape May Courthouse, NJ
609-465-4456
bigtimberlake.com
Dogs of all sizes are allowed. There are no additional pet fees. Dogs

may not be left unattended, and they must be leashed and cleaned up after. This RV park is closed during the off-season. The camping and tent areas also allow dogs. There is a dog walk area at the campground. Multiple dogs may be allowed.

Timberlane Campground
117 Timberlane Road
Clarksboro, NJ
856-423-6677
timberlanecampground.com
Dogs of all sizes are allowed. There are no additional pet fees. Dogs may not be left unattended, and they must be quiet, leashed, and cleaned up after. The camping and tent areas also allow dogs. There is a dog walk area at the campground. Multiple dogs may be allowed.

Holly Acres RV Park
218 S Frankfurt Avenue
Egg Harbor, NJ
609-965-3387 (888-2RV-CAMP)
Dogs of all sizes are allowed. There are no additional pet fees. Dogs may not be left unattended outside, and they must be quiet, well behaved, leashed and cleaned up after. There are some breed restrictions. This RV park is closed during the off-season. There is a dog walk area at the campground. Multiple dogs may be allowed.

Yogi Bear Tall Pines
49 Beal Road
Elmer, NJ
800-252-2890
tallpines.com
Dogs of all sizes are allowed, some breeds are not. There are no additional pet fees. Dogs must be leashed, cleaned up after, and not left unattended. This RV park is closed during the off-season. The camping and tent areas also allow dogs. There is a dog walk area at the campground. Dogs are allowed in the camping cabins.

Turkey Pond Swamp Campground
200 Georgia Road
Freehold, NJ
732-842-4000
Dogs of all sizes are allowed. There are no additional pet fees. Dogs may not be left unattended except for short periods, and they must be quiet, leashed, and cleaned up after. The camping and tent areas also allow dogs. There is a dog walk area at the campground. Multiple dogs may be allowed.

Beaver Hill Campground

120 Big Springs Road
Hamburg, NJ
973-827-0670
Dogs of all sizes are allowed. There is a $1 per night per pet additional fee. Dogs must be leashed, cleaned up after, and not left unattended. The camping and tent areas also allow dogs. There is a dog walk area at the campground. Multiple dogs may be allowed.

Butterfly Camping Resort
360 Butterfly Road
Jackson, NJ
732-928-2107
butterflycamp.com
Dogs of all sizes are allowed, some breeds are not. There are no additional pet fees. Dogs must be leashed and cleaned up after. The camping and tent areas also allow dogs. There is a dog walk area at the campground. 2 dogs may be allowed.

Tip Tam Camping Resort
301 Brewer's Bridge Road
Jackson, NJ
877-TIP-TAM1
tiptam.com
Dogs of all sizes are allowed, however some breeds are not. There are no additional pet fees. Dogs must remain on your own site, be leashed, and cleaned up after. The camping and tent areas also allow dogs. 2 dogs may be allowed.

Liberty Harbor RV Park
11 Marin Blvd
Jersey City, NJ
201-387-7500
libertyharborrv.com/
Dogs of all sizes are allowed. There are no additional pet fees. Dogs must be leashed, cleaned up after, and not be left unattended. There is a dog walk area at the campground. Multiple dogs may be allowed.

Whipporwill Campground
810 S Shore Road
Marmora, NJ
609-390-3458
campwhippoorwill.com
Dogs of all sizes are allowed. There are no additional pet fees. Dogs must be quiet and well behaved. They are allowed to be off lead on your site if they will stay regardless of what goes by. Dogs must otherwise be leashed and cleaned up after. The camping and tent areas also allow dogs. There is a dog walk area at the campground. Multiple dogs may be allowed.

Winding River Campground
6752 Weymouth Road
Mays Landing, NJ
609-625-3191
windingrivercamping.com
Dogs of all sizes are allowed. There are no additional pet fees. Dogs must be quiet, leashed, cleaned up after, and have current shot records. The camping and tent areas also allow dogs. There is a dog walk area at the campground. 2 dogs may be allowed.

Yogi Bear's Jellystone Park
1079 12th Avenue
Mays Landing, NJ
609-476-2811 (800-355-0264)
atlanticcityjellystone.com
Dogs of all sizes are allowed. There are no additional pet fees. Dogs must have a valid rabies certificate, be well behaved, leashed, and cleaned up after. The camping and tent areas also allow dogs. There is a dog walk area at the campground. 2 dogs may be allowed.

Cedar Ridge Campground
205 River Road
Montague, NJ
973-293-3512
cedarridgecampground.com/
One dog of any size is allowed. There are no additional pet fees. Dogs may not be left unattended at any time, and they must be leashed and cleaned up after. Dogs must be licensed and have up to date shot records. There are some breed restrictions. This RV park is closed during the off-season. The camping and tent areas also allow dogs. There is a dog walk area at the campground.

Timberline Lake
345 H 679
New Gretna, NJ
609-296-7900
timberlinelake.com
Well behaved dogs of all sizes are allowed. There are no additional pet fees. Dogs must be friendly, leashed, and cleaned up after. All dogs must have recent shot records. The camping and tent areas also allow dogs. There is a dog walk area at the campground. 2 dogs may be allowed.

Ocean View Resort
2555 H 9
Ocean View, NJ
609-624-1675
ovresort.com
Dogs of all sizes are allowed. There are no additional pet fees. Dogs

must be leashed and cleaned up after. There is a dog walk area at the campground. 2 dogs may be allowed.

Pine Haven Camping Resort
2339 H 9
Ocean View, NJ
609-624-3437
rvinthesun.com
Dogs of all sizes are allowed. There are no additional pet fees. Dogs must be leashed and cleaned up after. The camping and tent areas also allow dogs. Multiple dogs may be allowed.

Four Seasons Family Campground
158 Woodstown Road
Pilesgrove, NJ
856-769-3635 (888-372- CAMP (2267))
fourseasonscamping.com/
Dogs of all sizes are allowed. There are no additional pet fees. Dogs may not be left unattended outside, and they must be leashed and cleaned up after. Dogs are not allowed on the beach or at the playground, and they are not allowed in or around the cabin areas. Dogs must be licensed and have current shot records. The camping and tent areas also allow dogs. There is a dog walk area at the campground. Multiple dogs may be allowed.

Pine Cone Resort
340 Georgia Road
Pine Cone, NJ
732-462-2230
pineconenj.com
Dogs up to about 75 pounds are allowed; some breeds are not. There are no additional pet fees. Dogs must be leashed, cleaned up after, and not left unattended. Only one dog is allowed per campsite. The camping and tent areas also allow dogs. There is a dog walk area at the campground.

Blueberry Hill RV Park
283 Clarks Landing Road/H624
Port Republic, NJ
609-652-1644
blueberryhillrvpark.com/
This family shore-side RV park offers shaded or sunny, well-maintained groomed sites, various events throughout the year, gaming courts, modern restrooms, an ice cream and coffee shop, a store, laundry, and more. Dogs are allowed for no additional fee. Dogs must be well behaved, leashed, and cleaned up after. Dogs are not allowed at the playground. This RV park is closed

during the off-season. The camping and tent areas also allow dogs. There is a dog walk area at the campground. Multiple dogs may be allowed.

Pleasant Acres Farm Campground
61 DeWitt Road
Sussex, NJ
973-875-4166 (800-722-4166)
pleasantacres.com/
From a working 300 acre farm to a modern, award-winning campground (sorry, no tent sites), this recreation destination gives visitors a back-to-nature, rural farm experience with many common (and uncommon) amenities included in the rates. Dogs of all sizes are allowed for no additional fee. Dogs must be quiet, well behaved, leashed, and cleaned up after (except in the fenced dog exercise area). Dogs may not be left unattended at any time. There is a dog walk area at the campground. Multiple dogs may be allowed.

Atlantic City North Family Campground
Stage Road
Tuckerton, NJ
609-296-9163
Dogs of all sizes are allowed. There are no additional pet fees. Dogs may not be left unattended outside or in the cabins, and they must be leashed and cleaned up after. This RV park is closed during the off-season. The camping and tent areas also allow dogs. There is a dog walk area at the campground. Dogs are allowed in the camping cabins. Multiple dogs may be allowed.

Sea Pirate Campground
Bay side of H 9, Box 271
West Creek, NJ
609-296-7400 (800-822-CAMP (2267))
sea-pirate.com/
Up to two dogs of any size are allowed at the tent and RV sites at no additional fee. Basic Cabins and 2 Room Basic Cabins allow one pet at $5 per night with a $200 security deposit. Dogs may not be left unattended, and they must be leashed and cleaned up after. This RV park is closed during the off-season. The camping and tent areas also allow dogs. There is a dog walk area at the campground. Dogs are allowed in the camping cabins.

New Mexico

Alamogordo Roadrunner Campground
412 24th Street
Alamogordo, NM
877-437-3003
roadrunnercampground.com
Dogs of all sizes are allowed. There are no additional pet fees. Dogs may not be left unattended outside, and they must be leashed and cleaned up after. The camping and tent areas also allow dogs. There is a dog walk area at the campground. Multiple dogs may be allowed.

Lincoln National Forest
1101 New York Avenue
Alamogordo, NM
505-434-7200
fs.fed.us/r3/lincoln/
Home of Smokey Bear, this forest of over a million acres has diverse ecosystems that support a large variety of plants, fish, mammals, bird species, and recreation. Dogs of all sizes are allowed at no additional fee. Dogs may not be left unattended, and they must be leashed and cleaned up after in camp areas. Dogs may be off lead in the forest if they are well trained and under voice control. Dogs are allowed on the trails. The camping and tent areas also allow dogs. There is a dog walk area at the campground. There are no electric or water hookups at the campground. Multiple dogs may be allowed.

Oliver Lee Memorial State Park
409 Dog Canyon Road
Alamogordo, NM
505-437-8284 (888-NMPARKS 667-2757))
This oasis in the desert features historical exhibits and guided tours of a fully restored 19th century ranch house. Dogs of all sizes are allowed at no additional fee. Dogs may not be left unattended outside, and they must be, quiet, well behaved, leashed and cleaned up after. Dogs are allowed on the trails. The camping and tent areas also allow dogs. There is a dog walk area at the campground. Multiple dogs may be allowed.

Albuquerque Central KOA
12400 Skyline Road NE
Albuquerque, NM
505-296-2729 (800-562-7781)
koa.com
Dogs of all sizes are allowed. There are no additional pet fees. Dogs may not be left unattended outside, and they must be well behaved, leashed, and cleaned up after. There are some breed restrictions. The camping and tent areas also allow dogs. There is a dog walk area at the campground. Dogs are allowed in the camping cabins. Multiple dogs may be allowed.

Enchanted Trails
14305 Central
Albuquerque, NM
505-831-6317
www:enchantedtrails.com
Dogs of all sizes are allowed. There are no additional pet fees. Dogs may not be left unattended outside, and they must be leashed and cleaned up after. There is a dog walk area at the campground. Multiple dogs may be allowed.

High Desert RV Park
13000 W Frontage Road SW
Albuquerque, NM
866-839-9035
highdesertrvpark.com
Dogs of all sizes are allowed. There are no additional pet fees. Dogs may not be penned or left unattended outside, and they must be leashed and cleaned up after. There is a dog walk area at the campground. Multiple dogs may be allowed.

Ruins Road RV Park
312 Ruins Road
Aztec, NM
505-334-3160
ruinsroadrvpark.com/
Dogs of all sizes are allowed. There are no additional pet fees. Dogs may not be left unattended outside, and they must be leashed and cleaned up after. The camping and tent areas also allow dogs. There is a dog walk area at the campground. Multiple dogs may be allowed.

Albuquerque N/Bernalillo KOA
555 S Hill Road
Bernalillo, NM
505-867-5227 (800-562-3616)
koa.com
Dogs of all sizes are allowed. There are no additional pet fees. Dogs may not be left unattended, and they must be quiet, leashed, and cleaned up after. Dogs may not be on the grass, in the store, the bathrooms, or the cafe. There is a fenced area for off lead. The camping and tent areas also allow dogs. There is a dog walk

area at the campground. Dogs are allowed in the camping cabins. Multiple dogs may be allowed.

Coronado State Park
106 Monument Road
Bernalillo, NM
505-980-8256
Named after the conquistador they believed passed through here looking for the 7 golden cities of Cibola, this 210 acre park is also home to the pueblo ruins of Kuana. The reconstructed kiva, visitor center, and interpretive trail tells the story of the ancient agriculturists who once thrived along these banks of the Rio Grande River. Dogs of all sizes are allowed for no additional fee. Dogs must be leashed and cleaned up after. The camp area offers great views of the Sandia mountains and the Rio Grande Valley, sheltered picnic areas, and restrooms. The camping and tent areas also allow dogs. There is a dog walk area at the campground. Multiple dogs may be allowed.

Caballo Lake State Park
Box 32; On H 187
Caballo, NM
505-743-3942 (888-NMPARKS (677-2757))
Main attractions here are the migration of Bald and Golden Eagles and 2 cactus gardens, in addition to a variety of land and water recreation. Dogs of all sizes are allowed at no additional fee. Dogs must be leashed and cleaned up after, and they are allowed on the trails. The camping and tent areas also allow dogs. There is a dog walk area at the campground. Multiple dogs may be allowed.

Percha Dam State Park
Box 32; on H 187
Caballo, NM
505-743-3942 (888-NMPARKS (677-2757))
This 80 acre park along the Rio Grande offers fishing and hiking, nature study, and a variety of land and water recreation. Dogs of all sizes are allowed at no additional fee. Dogs may not be left unattended, and they must be leashed and cleaned up after. Dogs are allowed on the trails. The camping and tent areas also allow dogs. There is a dog walk area at the campground. Multiple dogs may be allowed.

Brantley Lake State Park
Capitan Reef Road

Carlsbad, NM
505-457-2384 (888-NMPARKS (677-2757))
With 3000 land acres and 4000 lake acres, this park offers a variety of recreational pursuits and planned activities throughout the year. Dogs of all sizes are allowed at no additional fee. Dogs must be leashed and cleaned up after in the camp areas. Dogs may be off lead in the primitive areas if they are under voice control. The camping and tent areas also allow dogs. There is a dog walk area at the campground. Multiple dogs may be allowed.

Windmill RV Park
3624 National Parks H (H 62/180N)
Carlsbad, NM
505-887-1387 (888-349-7275)
windmillrvpark.com/
Dogs of all sizes are allowed. There are no additional pet fees. Dogs may not be left unattended outside, and they must be leashed and cleaned up after. This is an RV only park. There is a dog walk area at the campground. Multiple dogs may be allowed.

Valley of Fires Recreation Area
P. O. Box 871
Carrizozo, NM
505-648-2241
This park sits along side what is considered the youngest lava flow in the continental US (125 square miles), and although it may appear desolate from a distance, an amazing amount of plant, animal, and bird life typical of the Chihuahuan desert flourish here. An interpretive trail starts at the group shelter and leads visitors through the lava flow on a paved walkway. Dogs are allowed in the park and on the trails, but they caution to stay on paved trails. There is no additional pet fee. Dogs must be under their owner's control at all times, and be leashed and cleaned up after. There are 19 campsites at the recreation area with picnic shelters, tables, grills, and potable water at each site. There is a full facility bathroom and showers in the camp area, and vault toilets throughout the park. The camping and tent areas also allow dogs. There is a dog walk area at the campground. There are no electric or water hookups at the campgrounds. Multiple dogs may be allowed.

Turquoise Trail Campground and RV Park

22 Calvary Road
Cedar Crest, NM
505-281-2005
This camp area features cool mountain camping with wooded sites, an archeological museum, a playground, laundry, restrooms, and hiking access to the National Forest. The camping and tent areas also allow dogs. There is a dog walk area at the campground. Multiple dogs may be allowed.

Little Creek Resort
2631 S H 84/64
Chama, NM
505-756-2382
littlecreekresort.com
Dogs of all sizes are allowed. There are no additional pet fees. Dogs may not be left unattended outside, and they must be leashed and cleaned up after. The camping and tent areas also allow dogs. There is a dog walk area at the campground. Dogs are allowed in the camping cabins.

Rio Chama RV Park
182 N H 17
Chama, NM
505-756-2303
Dogs of all sizes are allowed. There are no additional pet fees. Dogs must be leashed and cleaned up after. This RV park is closed during the off-season. There is a dog walk area at the campground. 2 dogs may be allowed.

Canyon de Chelly National Monument
Box 588, On H 7 3 miles from Chinle
Chinle, NM
928-674-5500
nps.gov/cach
A long and rich cultural and spiritual history echoes with more than 1,500 years of habitation reflected in the numerous pictographs, petroglyphs, and from the ruins of those who once made their homes here. It is still sustaining a living community of the Navajo people, and you must have a guide to enter canyon areas. However, there are 2 paved auto routes totaling 43 miles that stop at numerous spectacular viewpoints above the canyon, and your pet is welcome to get out at these viewpoints. Dogs are not allowed on tours or on the trails. Dogs of all sizes are welcome for no additional fee, and they may not be left unattended at any time. Dogs must be leashed and cleaned up after at all times. The campground facilities include restrooms, picnic tables, water, and a dump station. Water is

not available in the winter months. The camping and tent areas also allow dogs. There is a dog walk area at the campground. There are no electric or water hookups at the campgrounds. Multiple dogs may be allowed.

Red Rock State Park
P. O. Box 10
Church Rock, NM
505-722-3839
Born from pre-historic times, the spectacular red cliffs that border the park on three sides add to the ancient feeling of the area, and the museum at the park offers a glimpse of the past through interpretations of the unique cultures of the Native Americans of the region. The park's elevation is 6600 to 7000 feet, covers 640 acres, and is known as the 'Gateway to Zuni' (one of the 7 cities of Cibola sought by the Spanish). They also hold several festivals and events throughout the year. Dogs of all sizes are allowed for no additional fee. Dogs are allowed on the trails, and they must be leashed and cleaned up after at all times. The park is home to a large campground with picnic areas, restrooms, and showers. The camping and tent areas also allow dogs. There is a dog walk area at the campground. Multiple dogs may be allowed.

Clayton Lake State Park
141 Clayton Road
Clayton, NM
505-374-8808 (800-NMPARKS (667-2757))
Rolling grasslands, volcanic rocks, and sandstone bluffs all characterize this 471 acre park with a 170 surface acre lake, but the real pull here is the internationally significant dinosaur trackway that contains more than 500 footprints dating back more than 100 million years. Many have been preserved and identified, and a boardwalk trail with extensive signage tells of the ancient visitors here. The park is also home to a variety of plant/bird/animal life, and land and water recreation. Dogs of all sizes are allowed for no additional fee. Dogs must be leashed and cleaned up after at all times. The camp area offers 33 sites, a playground area, restrooms, showers, water, and picnic tables. The camping and tent areas also allow dogs. There is a dog walk area at the campground. Multiple dogs may be allowed.

Pancho Villa State Park
400 W H 9
Columbus, NM
505-531-2711
This 60 acre park with an elevation of just over 4,000 feet, shares the history of Pancho Villa, and of the armed invasion he lead against the nation. Extensive historical exhibits/buildings are on the grounds and in the museum/visitor center-the US Customs House-built in 1902, about the invasion and his pursuit by General Pershing. There are also a variety of other recreational pursuits, and great hiking opportunities. Dogs of all sizes are allowed for no additional pet fee. Dogs are allowed on all the trails and throughout the park; they are not allowed in the museum or park buildings. Dogs must be leashed and cleaned up after at all times. The camp area offer 62 sites, with picnic shelters, restrooms, showers, a playground, and a dump station. The camping and tent areas also allow dogs. There is a dog walk area at the campground. Multiple dogs may be allowed.

Conchas Lake State Park
Box 967; On H 104
Conchas Dam, NM
505-868-2270 (888-NMPARKS (667-2757))
This park offers ancient sites, one of the largest lakes in New Mexico, and a variety of land and water recreation. Dogs of all sizes are allowed at no additional fee. Dogs may not be left unattended, they must be quiet, be on no more than a 10 foot leash and be cleaned up after. The camping and tent areas also allow dogs. There is a dog walk area at the campground. Multiple dogs may be allowed.

Little Vineyard
2901 E Pine
Deming, NM
505-546-3560
littlevineyardrvpark.com
Dogs of all sizes are allowed. There are no additional pet fees. Dogs must be leashed and cleaned up after. There is a dog walk area at the campground. Multiple dogs may be allowed.

Roadrunner RV Park
2849 E Pine Street
Deming, NM
505-546-6960
zianet.com/roadrunnerrv
Dogs of all sizes are allowed. There are no additional pet fees. Dogs

must be quiet, leashed, and cleaned up after. There is a dog walk area at the campground. Multiple dogs may be allowed.

Rockhound State Park
P. O. Box 1064
Deming, NM
505-546-6182 (888-NMPARKS (667-2757))
This park is a favorite for rockhounds, and it also has trails varying in difficulty and elevations that offer breathtaking scenery. Dogs of all sizes are allowed at no additional fee. Dogs may not be left unattended, and they must be on no more than a 10 foot leash, and be cleaned up after. Dogs are allowed on the trails. The camping and tent areas also allow dogs. There is a dog walk area at the campground. Multiple dogs may be allowed.

Cimmarron Canyon State Park
2959 H 64
Eagle Nest, NM
505-377-6271 (888-NMPARKS (677-2757))
This high mountain park of over 33,000 acres is also part of the Colin Neblett Wildlife Area, and offers a variety of nature study and recreation. Dogs of all sizes are allowed at no additional fee. Dogs may not be left unattended, and they must be on no more than a 10 foot leash and be cleaned up after. Dogs are allowed on the trails. The camping and tent areas also allow dogs. There is a dog walk area at the campground. Multiple dogs may be allowed.

Elephant Butte Lake
Box 13; H 195/171
Elephant Butte, NM
505-744-5421 (888-NMPARKS (667-2757))
Scenic Elephant Butte Lake can be described as educational, recreational and pre-historic. Dogs of all sizes are allowed at no additional fee. Dogs may not be left unattended, and they must be leashed and cleaned up after. Dogs are allowed on the trails. The camping and tent areas also allow dogs. There is a dog walk area at the campground. Multiple dogs may be allowed.

Downs RV Park
5701 H 64
Farmington, NM
505-325-7094
Dogs of all sizes are allowed. There are no additional pet fees. Dogs may

not be left unattended outside, and they must be leashed and cleaned up after. The camping and tent areas also allow dogs. There is a dog walk area at the campground. Multiple dogs may be allowed.

City of Rocks State Park
P. O. Box 50
Faywood, NM
505-536-2800
It took the earth millions of years to develop the rock formations that give this park it's name, and there are only 6 other places in the world where they exist. Evidence of ancient cultures now intermingles with the state's first park observatory. Along with a variety of plant/animal/bird life, and recreational opportunities, amenities include a visitor center, picnic sites, Star Parties, interpretive exhibits, and hiking trails. Dogs of all sizes are allowed for no additional fee. Dogs are allowed on all the trails, but not in park buildings. Dogs must be leashed and cleaned up after. The campground offers 52 developed sites and 10 electrical sites. Amenities include restrooms, showers, and picnic tables. The camping and tent areas also allow dogs. There is a dog walk area at the campground. Multiple dogs may be allowed.

Sumner Lake State Park
HC 64, Box 125
Fort Sumner, NM
505-355-2541 (888-NMPARKS (667-2757))
This historical park is popular for water activities and nature study. Dogs of all sizes are allowed at no additional fee. Dogs may not be left unattended, and they must be leashed and cleaned up after. The camping and tent areas also allow dogs. There is a dog walk area at the campground. Multiple dogs may be allowed.

Coal Mine Canyon Campground
1800 Lobo CanyonRoad
Grants, NM
505-287-8833
Located in the Mt. Taylor District of the Cibola National Forest, this small 17 site campground also has its own short nature trail. Some of the amenities include picnic areas, restrooms, and a large deep communal sink. Dogs of all sizes are allowed for no additional fee. Dogs are allowed on the trails, but because of cactus and desert life, they caution you to keep your dog on the trails. Dogs must be leashed and

cleaned up after. This RV park is closed during the off-season. The camping and tent areas also allow dogs. There is a dog walk area at the campground. There are no electric or water hookups at the campgrounds. Multiple dogs may be allowed.

Coyote Creek State Park
Box 477, MM 17 H 434
Guadalupita, NM
505-387-2328 (888-NMPARKS (667-2757))
This scenic park is surround by forests of spruce, pine, and fields of wildflowers, and the creek is considered to be the best stocked in the state. Dogs of all sizes are allowed at no additional fee. Dogs may not be left unattended, and they must be quiet, be on no more than a 10 foot leash, and be cleaned up after. Dogs are allowed on the trails. The camping and tent areas also allow dogs. There is a dog walk area at the campground. Multiple dogs may be allowed.

Morphy Lake State Park
Box 477; Morphy Lake Road
Guadalupita, NM
505-387-2328 (888-NMPARKS (677-2757))
This secluded, pack-in/out park with a well stocked lake, is reached by foot or a high clearance vehicle. There is no drinking water available, and it is suggested to check road conditions before going. Dogs of all sizes are allowed at no additional fee. Dogs may not be left unattended, and they must be on no more than a 10 foot leash at all times, and be cleaned up after. Dogs are allowed on the trails. This campground is closed during the off-season. The camping and tent areas also allow dogs. There is a dog walk area at the campground. There are no electric or water hookups at the campground. Multiple dogs may be allowed.

Fenton Lake State Park
455 Fenton Lake Road
Jemez Springs, NM
505-829-3630 (888-NMPARKS (667-2757))
This park, surrounded by pine forest with a 35 acre lake, sits at an elevation of 7900 feet, and offers a variety of recreation for all seasons. Dogs of all sizes are allowed at no additional fee. Dogs may not be left unattended, and they must be leashed and cleaned up after. Dogs are allowed on the trails. The

camping and tent areas also allow dogs. There is a dog walk area at the campground. There are no water hookups at the campground. Multiple dogs may be allowed.

Hacienda RV and Rally Resort
740 Stern Drive
Las Cruces, NM
888-686-9090
haciendarv.com
Dogs of all sizes are allowed. There are no additional pet fees. Dogs must be leashed and cleaned up after. There is a fenced in area where dogs may be off lead. There is a dog walk area at the campground. Multiple dogs may be allowed.

The Coachlight Inn and RV Park
301 S Motel Blvd
Las Cruces, NM
505-526-3301
zianet.com/coachlight
Dogs of all sizes are allowed. There are no additional pet fees for the RV sites. There is an additional $5 per night per pet fee for small dogs at the inn, and an additional $10 per night per pet fee for medium to large dogs. There are only 2 dogs allowed per room, and no more than 3 for the RV area. This is an RV only park. There is a dog walk area at the campground.

Storrie Lake State Park
HC 33, Box 109 #2
Las Vegas, NM
505-425-7278 (888-NMPARKS (667-2757))
This park with 1,100 acres of lake surface, offers a wide variety of water recreation, an interesting history, and plenty of trails. Dogs of all sizes are allowed at no additional fee. Dogs may not be left unattended, and they must be on no more than a 10 foot leash, and be cleaned up after. Dogs are allowed on the trails. This campground is closed during the off-season. The camping and tent areas also allow dogs. There is a dog walk area at the campground. Multiple dogs may be allowed.

Ute Lake State Park
1800 540 Loop
Logan, NM
505-487-2284 (888-NMPARKS (667-2757))
Nature study, round-the-clock fishing, scenic trails, and a variety of land and water recreation make this a popular park. Dogs of all sizes are allowed at no additional fee. Dogs may not be left unattended, and they must be leashed and cleaned up

after. Dogs are allowed on the trails unless otherwise marked. The camping and tent areas also allow dogs. There is a dog walk area at the campground. Multiple dogs may be allowed.

Heron Lake State Park
Box 159; MM 6 H 95
Los Ojos, NM
505-588-7470 (888-NMPARKS (667-2757))
Ideal for both winter and summer sports at 7200 feet, this scenic park also has a trail that leads to a suspension bridge that crosses the river. Dogs of all sizes are allowed at no additional fee. Dogs may not be left unattended, and they must be leashed and cleaned up after. Dogs are allowed on the trails. The camping and tent areas also allow dogs. There is a dog walk area at the campground. Multiple dogs may be allowed.

Maxwell National Wildlife Refuge
P. O. Box 276/Lake Road 13
Maxwell, NM
505-375-2331
The park was established as a feeding and resting area for over 200 species of migratory birds. There has been more than 400 acres of agricultural fields planted with food for them. There is also roughly 2200 acres of short-grass prairie, 900 acres of lakes, and 200 acres of woodlands or other lands. Interpretive/environmental programs are available upon request, and there is a variety of land and water recreational opportunities plus primitive camping on the west side of Lake 13. Dogs of all sizes are allowed for no additional fee. Dogs are allowed on the trails unless otherwise marked, and they must be leashed and cleaned up after. The primitive campsite is seasonal and has a 3 day stay limit. Restrooms are located at the entrance road leading into Lake 13. This RV park is closed during the off-season. The camping and tent areas also allow dogs. There is a dog walk area at the campground. There are no electric or water hookups at the campgrounds. Multiple dogs may be allowed.

Manzano Mountains State Park
HC66, Box 202
Mountainair, NM
505-847-2820 (888-NMPARKS (667-2757))
This park of 160 acres at 7600 foot altitude has a wide variety of trees and is an important bird fly zone. The park will also provide a field check list for the birds. Dogs of all sizes are allowed at no additional fee. Dogs may not be left unattended, and they must quiet, well behaved, be on no more than a 10 foot leash, and be cleaned up after. Dogs are allowed on the trails. This campground is closed during the off-season. The camping and tent areas also allow dogs. There is a dog walk area at the campground. There are no water hookups at the campground. Multiple dogs may be allowed.

Chaco Culture National Historical Park
County Road 7950
Nageezi, NM
505-786-7014
nps.gov/chcu/
At one time this area was a thriving and sophisticated administrative center for ancient urban peoples, and now these sites are sacred homeland to the Pueblo, Hopi, and Navajo Nations. Most of the park and cultural sites are self guided, and there are hiking trails that will take visitors to a variety of sites, petroglyphs/historic inscriptions, and vistas. Trails are day use only, and a free hiking permit is required. There are few amenities here, so go prepared. Dogs are allowed for no additional fee. Dogs are not allowed inside sites, ruins, or park buildings. Dogs are also not allowed on the short (200 yard) trails to some of the more famous ruins and would have to stay in the parking lot area. They are allowed on leash on the backcountry trails which are 3 to 7 miles long. These trails also have ruins and petroglyths. Dogs would have to remain outside of any ruins that you would enter along these trails. Dogs must be leashed and cleaned up after. Gallo Campground offers 48 sites on a first come, first served basis in a rugged, ancient feeling environment; RVs over 30 feet cannot be provided for. There is a picnic table and fire grate with a grill at each site, and there is non-potable water, restrooms, a dump station, and drinking water at the visitor center. This RV park is closed during the off-season. The camping and tent areas also allow dogs. There is a dog walk area at the campground. There are no electric or water hookups at the campgrounds.

Navajo Lake State Park

1448 H 511 (#1)
Navajo Dam, NM
505-632-2278
Sitting at an altitude of 6,100 feet, this 21,000 acre park is home to the state's 2nd largest lake at almost 16,000 acres. They offer a variety of land and water recreation and services, interpretive exhibits/signage, a full service marina, a wheelchair accessible fishing area, several hiking trails, 7 day use areas, camping, and a visitor center. Dogs are allowed throughout the park and on the trails. There is no additional pet fee. Dogs may not be left unattended at any time, and they must be leashed and cleaned up after at all times. The camp areas offer 246 developed sites; some of the amenities include picnic areas, restrooms, showers, a playground, and a dump station. Many of the camp sites are along the lake. The camping and tent areas also allow dogs. There is a dog walk area at the campground. Multiple dogs may be allowed.

Oasis State Park
1891 Oasis Road
Portales, NM
505-356-5331 (888-NMPARKS (667-2757))
This park of 193 acres, set among the cottonwood trees and shifting sand dunes, offers a small fishing lake and more than 80 species of birds. Dogs of all sizes are allowed at no additional fee. Dogs may not be left unattended outside or for long periods inside, and they must be on no more than a 10 foot leash, and be cleaned up after. Dogs are not allowed in the water, but they are allowed on the trails. The camping and tent areas also allow dogs. There is a dog walk area at the campground. Multiple dogs may be allowed.

Bluewater Lake State Park
Box 3419/ at end of H 412
Prewitt, NM
505-876-2391 (877-664-7787)
This year round recreational park offers great fishing, a wide variety of birds, a visitor's center, and plenty of hiking trails. Dogs are allowed at no additional fee. Dogs must be leashed and cleaned up after. Dogs are allowed on the trails. The camping and tent areas also allow dogs. There is a dog walk area at the campground. There are no water hookups at the campground. Multiple dogs may be allowed.

Leasburg Dam State Park
P.O. Box 6
Radium Springs, NM
505-524-4068 (888-NMPARKS (667-2757)
This park along the Rio Grande offers a variety of land and water recreation. Dogs of all sizes are allowed at no additional fee. Dogs may not be left unattended, and they must be leashed and cleaned up after. Dogs are allowed on the trails. The camping and tent areas also allow dogs. There is a dog walk area at the campground. There are no water hookups at the campground. Multiple dogs may be allowed.

Ancient Way Outpost Campground
4018 H 53
Ramah, NM
505-783-4612
elmorro-nm.com/
This RV park also offers free Wi-Fi, furnished log cabins, an historic café that serves snacks or hearty, American, New Mexican and Vegetarian specialties, and a great location for exploring the many legendary sites close by, including the legendary seven cities of gold (Cibola) that Spanish explorers once sought. Dogs of all sizes are allowed for no additional fee for tent or RV sites. There is a $10 one time additional pet fee for the cabins. There is a mesa behind the park with many trails to walk your pooch. Although not allowed inside the café, there is a bench out front on the porch where you can sit, or get food to go. Dogs must be well behaved, and leashed and cleaned up after in camp and on the trails. The camping and tent areas also allow dogs. There is a dog walk area at the campground. Dogs are allowed in the camping cabins.

El Morrow National Monument
HC 61 Box 43/Monument Drive
Ramah, NM
505-783-4226
nps.gov/elmo
Located at an elevation of over 7,000 feet, this monument boasts a massive mesa-point that rises 200 feet above the valley floor with a 1/2 mile loop trail leading to an historic pool, and more than 2000 inscriptions and petroglyphs. If you continue to the top of the mesa for a 2 mile round trip hike, you will be met with breathtaking views and the ancestral Puebloan ruins. Dogs are allowed on the trails, but they must stay on the trails, and be leashed and under their owner's control at all

times. Dogs must be cleaned up after in the campground area, the park, and on the trails. Pets are not permitted in the visitor center, but they ask that you stop there first before going in to get directions/instructions. There is a picnic area at the visitor center where pets are allowed. The campground has 9 primitive sites on a first come, first served basis. Amenities include picnic tables, fire pits, water, and pit toilets. Water is shut off in the winter when camping is available for no cost. The camping and tent areas also allow dogs. There is a dog walk area at the campground. There are no electric or water hookups at the campgrounds. Multiple dogs may be allowed.

Sugarlite Canyon State Park
HCR 63, Box 386
Raton, NM
505-445-5607 (800-NMPARKS (667-2757))
This park is 3,600 acres of wildflower filled meadows (butterfly paradise), heavily wooded mountains, and interesting geological features such as the giant volcanic Caprock. There is also a 120 acre surface lake, the Coal Camp Interpretive Trail, various scenic trails to hike, a visitor center, and a variety of land and water recreation. Dogs of all sizes are allowed for no additional fee. Dogs are allowed on all the trails-except ski trails in winter and they must be leashed and cleaned up after. The campground offers 2 camp areas with 40 developed sites plus 12 with electric, restrooms, showers, tables, grills, and water. The camping and tent areas also allow dogs. There is a dog walk area at the campground. Multiple dogs may be allowed.

River Ranch
1501 W Main (H 38)
Red River, NM
505-754-2293
riverranch.com/
Dogs of all sizes are allowed. There are no additional pet fees. Dogs may not be left unattended outside, and they must be quiet, well behaved, leashed and cleaned up after. This RV park is closed during the off-season. The camping and tent areas also allow dogs. There is a dog walk area at the campground. Multiple dogs may be allowed.

Rustys RV Ranch

22 Estrella Parkway
Rodeo, NM
505-557-2526
www.caballoresort.com/home.htm
Dogs of all sizes are allowed. There are no additional pet fees. Dogs may not be left unattended outside, and they must be leashed in camp, and cleaned up after. Dogs may be off lead on the trails if they are under voice command and will not chase wildlife. The camping and tent areas also allow dogs. There is a dog walk area at the campground. Multiple dogs may be allowed.

Bottomless Lakes State Park
HC 12, Box 1200 (H 409)
Roswell, NM
505-624-6058 (800-NMPARKS (667-2757))
Although thought to be 'bottomless', the deepest of the several small lakes here is Lea Lake at 90 feet, and it is the only lake that swimming is allowed in. The lakes are set among high red bluffs offering a good variety of land and water recreational opportunities. Amenities include paddle boat rentals in summer, a visitor center, a large day-use and picnic area with a playground, and a host of hiking trails. Dogs of all sizes are allowed for no additional fee. Dogs may not be left unattended at any time, including at the campground. Dogs must be quiet, on no more than a 10 foot leash, and be cleaned up after. Spacious campsites are located at both the Lea Lake Rec area and along the lower lakes. Developed camping with vault toilets and fresh water are offered at the lower lakes, and full hook-ups with hot showers and modern restrooms at Lea Lake. A dump station is also available. The camping and tent areas also allow dogs. There is a dog walk area at the campground.

Red Barn RV Park
2806 E 2nd Street
Roswell, NM
505-623-4897 (877-800-4897)
Dogs of all sizes are allowed. There are no additional pet fees. Dogs must be leashed and cleaned up after. There is a dog walk area at the campground. Multiple dogs may be allowed.

Town and Country RV Park
331 W Brasher Road
Roswell, NM
505-624-1833
townandcountryrvpark.com
Dogs of all sizes are allowed. There

are no additional pet fees. Dogs may not be tied up or left unattended outside, and they must be leashed and cleaned up after. The camping and tent areas also allow dogs. There is a dog walk area at the campground. Multiple dogs may be allowed.

Hyde Memorial State Park
740 Hyde Park Road
Santa Fe, NM
505-983-7175 (888-NMPARKS (677-2757))
Located in the Sangre de Cristo Mountains at 8500 feet, this park offers beautiful scenery, quiet settings, and year round recreation. Dogs of all sizes are allowed at no additional fee. Dogs may not be left unattended, and they must be leashed and cleaned up after. Dogs are allowed on the trails. This campground is closed during the off-season. The camping and tent areas also allow dogs. There is a dog walk area at the campground. Multiple dogs may be allowed.

Rancheros de Santa Fe
736 Old Las Vegas H
Santa Fe, NM
800-426-9259
rancheros.com
Dogs of all sizes are allowed. There are no additional pet fees. Dogs may not be left unattended, and they must be quiet, leashed, and cleaned up after. There is a fenced in Doggy Corral for off lead. The camping and tent areas also allow dogs. There is a dog walk area at the campground. Dogs are allowed in the camping cabins. Multiple dogs may be allowed.

Santa Fe National Forest
1474 Rodeo Road
Santa Fe, NM
505-438-7840
fs.fed.us/r3/sfe/
This forest of 1.6 million acres at an altitude of over 13,000 feet. It offers diverse ecosystems that support a large variety of plants, fish, mammals, bird species, and recreation. Dogs of all sizes are allowed at no additional fee. Dogs may not be left unattended, and they must be leashed and cleaned up after. Dogs are allowed on the trails. The camping and tent areas also allow dogs. There is a dog walk area at the campground. There are no electric or water hookups at the campground. Multiple dogs may be allowed.

Santa Fe Skies RV Park
14 Browncastle Ranch
Santa Fe, NM
505-473-5946
santafeskiesrvpark.com
Dogs of all sizes are allowed. There are no additional pet fees. Dogs must be cleaned up after. Dogs may be off leash if they are friendly and under owner's control. Dogs must be quiet and well behaved. There is a dog walk area at the campground. Multiple dogs may be allowed.

Trailer Ranch RV Resort
3471 Cerrillos
Santa Fe, NM
505-471-9970
trailerranch.com
Dogs of all sizes are allowed. There are no additional pet fees. Dogs must be quiet, well behaved, leashed, and cleaned up after. This is a 55 plus resort so at least one of the campers must be 55 or older. There are some breed restrictions. There is a dog walk area at the campground. Multiple dogs may be allowed.

Santa Rosa Campground
2136 Historic H 66
Santa Rosa, NM
505-472-3126
santarosacampground.com
Dogs of all sizes are allowed. There are no additional pet fees. Dogs may be walked anywhere in the park, but they must be taken to the dog walk to relieve themselves. Dogs must be leashed and cleaned up after. The camping and tent areas also allow dogs. There is a dog walk area at the campground. Dogs are allowed in the camping cabins. Multiple dogs may be allowed.

Santa Rosa Lake State Park
P.O. Box 384
Santa Rosa, NM
505-472-3110 (888-NMPARKS (667-2757))
With 500 land acres and 3,800 lake acres, this park offers a variety of land and water recreation and nature study. Dogs of all sizes are allowed at no additional fee. Dogs may not be left unattended, and they must be on no more than a 10 foot leash, and be cleaned up after. Dogs are allowed on the trails. The camping and tent areas also allow dogs. There is a dog walk area at the campground. Multiple dogs may be allowed.

Gila National Forest
3005 Camino Del Bosque
Silver City, NM
505-388-8201
www2.srs.fs.fed.us/r3/gila/
This forest has 6 ranger districts, covers 3.3 million acres, and has diverse ecosystems that support a large variety of plants, fish, mammals, bird species, and recreation. Dogs of all sizes are allowed at no additional fee. Dogs may not be left unattended, and they must be leashed and cleaned up after. Dogs are not allowed at the cliff dwellings or on the trail to the dwellings, however, they are allowed on the other trails unless marked. The camping and tent areas also allow dogs. There is a dog walk area at the campground. There are no electric or water hookups at the campground. Multiple dogs may be allowed.

Valley View RV Park
401 E Sumner Avenue
Sumner, NM
505-355-2380
Dogs of all sizes are allowed. There are no additional pet fees. Dogs may not be left unattended outside, and they must be leashed and cleaned up after. This park only closes for the first 2 weeks in January each year. There is a dog walk area at the campground. Multiple dogs may be allowed.

Carson National Forest
208 Cruz Alta
Taos, NM
505-758-6200
fs.fed.us/r3/carson/
This forest has 6 ranger districts, covers 1.5 million acres, is home to the states highest mountain at 13,161 feet, and it's diverse ecosystems support a large variety of plants, animals, and recreation. Dogs of all sizes are allowed at no additional fee. Dogs may not be left unattended, and they must be leashed and cleaned up after. Dogs are allowed on trails. The camping and tent areas also allow dogs. There is a dog walk area at the campground. There are no electric or water hookups at the campground. Multiple dogs may be allowed.

Enchanted Moon RV Park and Campground
HC 71 Box 59
Taos, NM
505-758-3338
emooncampground.com/
Dogs of all sizes are allowed. There

are no additional pet fees. Dogs must be leashed and cleaned up after. This RV park is closed during the off-season. The camping and tent areas also allow dogs. There is a dog walk area at the campground.

Orilla Verde Rec Area
Intersection of SH 570 and SH 68
Taos, NM
505-758-8851
The park is located along the Rio Grande within the steep walls of the Rio Grande Gorge, and because of the evidence of ancient cultures and the diversity of the area, it is popular among vacationers, nature enthusiasts, and anthropologist. The Taos Valley Overlook is about 900 feet above the park and offers stunning views of the gorge and Sangre de Cristo Mountains. Great fishing, whitewater rafting, picnicking, and hiking are just a few of the recreational opportunities. Dogs of all sizes are allowed for no additional fee. Dogs are allowed on the trails, and they must be well behaved, leashed, and cleaned up after. There are five campgrounds, each with tables, fire grills, restrooms, shelters, and drinking water. Primitive camping is only allowed at designated sites. The camping and tent areas also allow dogs. There is a dog walk area at the campground. Multiple dogs may be allowed.

Wild Rivers Recreation Area
1120 Cerro Road
Taos, NM
505-770-1600
Located at the confluence of the Rio Grand and Red Rivers, this recreation area also includes an 800 foot deep volcanic canyon (the Gorge) that features diverse ecosystems, and many trails from easy to difficult to explore. There is a wide variety of plants (even 500 year old trees), animals, and bird life, and land and water recreation, including the Wild Rivers Backcountry Byway, a 13 mile, paved road that allows visitors access to several scenic views and recreational spots. Some of the amenities include a picnic area, grills, drinking water, restrooms, and a visitor center. Dogs of all sizes are allowed for no additional fee. Dogs are allowed on the trails and throughout the park; they are not allowed in buildings. Dogs must be under their owner's control at all times, and they must be leashed and cleaned up after. Dogs are not permitted on Big Arsenic Trail or in any freshwater springs.

Camping is available at 5 developed campgrounds, each with tables, grills, drinking water, and bathrooms. Four other trails will take visitors to primitive river campsites The camping and tent areas also allow dogs. There is a dog walk area at the campground. Multiple dogs may be allowed.

El Vado Lake State Park
Box 367; El Vado State Park Road
Tierra Amarilla, NM
505-588-7247 (888-NMPARKS (667-2757))
With over 1700 land acres and a lake with 3200 acres, this park has a variety of nature study and land and water recreation. Dogs of all sizes are allowed at no additional fee. Dogs may not be left unattended, and they must be on no more than a 10 foot leash, and be cleaned up after. Dogs are allowed on the trails. The camping and tent areas also allow dogs. There is a dog walk area at the campground. There are no water hookups at the campground. Multiple dogs may be allowed.

Cibola National Forest
11776 H 337
Tijeras, NM
505-346-3900
fs.fed.us/r3/cibola/
This forest has 6 ranger districts, almost 2 million acres with 5 wilderness areas, and diverse ecosystems that support a large variety of plants, animals, and recreation. Dogs of all sizes are allowed at no additional fee. Dogs may not be left unattended, and they must be leashed and cleaned up after. Dogs are not allowed in buildings, but they are allowed on the trails. The camping and tent areas also allow dogs. There is a dog walk area at the campground. There are no electric or water hookups at the campground. Multiple dogs may be allowed.

Cielo Vista RV Resort
501 S Broadway
Truth or Consequences, NM
505-894-3738
Dogs of all sizes are allowed. There are no additional pet fees. Dogs may not be left unattended, and they must be quiet, well behaved, be on no more than a 6 foot leash, and cleaned up after. There is a dog walk area at the campground. Multiple dogs may be allowed.

Mountain Road RV Park

1700 Mountain Road
Tucumcari, NM
505-461-9628
mountainroadrvpark.com
Dogs of all sizes are allowed. There are no additional pet fees. Dogs may be walked anywhere in the park, but they must be taken to one of the dog walks to relieve themselves. Dogs may not be left unattended outside, and they must be leashed and cleaned up after. The camping and tent areas also allow dogs. There is a dog walk area at the campground. Multiple dogs may be allowed.

Villanueva State Park
P. O. Box 40
Villanueva, NM
505-421-2957 (888-NMPARKS (667-2757))
A scenic, riverside canyon park, there are a variety of land and water recreational pursuits and places to explore. Dogs of all sizes are allowed at no additional fee. Dogs may not be left unattended, and they must be on no more than a 10 foot leash, and be cleaned up after. Dogs are not allowed in buildings, but they are allowed on the trails. This campground is closed during the off-season. The camping and tent areas also allow dogs. Dogs are allowed in the camping cabins. Multiple dogs may be allowed.

White City Resort
17 Carlsbad Caverns Highway
White's City, NM
800-228-3767
whitecity.com/
Dogs of all sizes are allowed. There are no additional pet fees for the tent or RV sites. There is a $10 per night per pet additional fee for the Walnut Inn. Dogs must be quiet, well behaved, leashed, and cleaned up after. The camping and tent areas also allow dogs. There is a dog walk area at the campground. Multiple dogs may be allowed.

New York

Keywaydin State Park
45165 H 12
Alexandria, NY
315-482-3331
nysparks.state.ny.us/
Dogs of all sizes are allowed. There are no additional pet fees. Dogs may not be left unattended, they must have a current rabies certificate and

shot records, be well behaved, on no more than a 6 foot leash, and be cleaned up after. Dogs are allowed on the trails, but not in the picnic or bathroom areas. This campground is closed during the off-season. The camping and tent areas also allow dogs. There is a dog walk area at the campground. There are no water hookups at the campground. Multiple dogs may be allowed.

Woodland Hills Campground
386 Foghill Road
Austerlitz, NY
518-392-3557
whcg.net
Dogs of all sizes are allowed. There are no additional pet fees. Dogs must be quiet, leashed, and cleaned up after. The camping and tent areas also allow dogs. There is a dog walk area at the campground. Multiple dogs may be allowed.

Alps Family Campground
1928 State H 43
Averill Park, NY
518-674-5565
Dogs of all sizes are allowed. There are no additional pet fees. Dogs must have proof of rabies shots, be leashed, cleaned up after, and not left unattended. The camping and tent areas also allow dogs. There is a dog walk area at the campground. Multiple dogs may be allowed.

Hickory Hill Farm Camping Resort
7531 H 13/Mitchellsville Road
Bath, NY
607-776-4345 (800-760-0947)
hickoryhillcampresort.com/
This full service family camping resort has all the extras for family fun including 2 pools, playing courts/fields, an 18 hole mini-golf course, internet access, hiking trails, a store, and lots more. Dogs are allowed for no additional fee for tent or RV camping. In a rental unit, the fees are $20 per unit per stay, and please have proof of current vaccinations. Dogs may not be left alone at any time at a campsite or in a rental, and they must be leashed and cleaned up after at all times. This RV park is closed during the off-season. The camping and tent areas also allow dogs. There is a dog walk area at the campground. Dogs are allowed in the camping cabins.

Lake Erie State Park
5905 Lake Road
Brocton, NY
716-792-9214 (800-456-CAMP (2267))

With ¾ of a mile of beach and great lake views, this family camp area also offers hiking and biking trails with cross-country ski trails in winter, a nature trail, playground, concessionaire, picnic pavilions, and a variety of land and water recreation. Dogs of all sizes are allowed for no additional fee. Dogs must be crated or on a leash not more than 10 feet, and they are not allowed in swim areas, public buildings, or on cross-country ski trails. Dogs must be cleaned up after. The camp area has 97 campsites with tables, fire pits, showers, restrooms, and dump stations. This RV park is closed during the off-season. The camping and tent areas also allow dogs. There is a dog walk area at the campground. Dogs are allowed in the camping cabins. There are no water hookups at the campgrounds. Multiple dogs may be allowed.

Genesee Country Campgrounds
40 Flinthill Road
Caledonia, NY
585-538-4200
geneseecountrycampgrounds.com
Dogs of all sizes are allowed. There are no additional pet fees. Dogs must be leashed and cleaned up after. The camping and tent areas also allow dogs. There is a dog walk area at the campground. Dogs are allowed in the camping cabins. 2 dogs may be allowed.

Lake Lauderdale Campground
744 Country Route 61
Cambridge, NY
518-677-8855
lakelauderdalecampground.com
Dogs of all sizes are allowed. There are no additional pet fees. Dogs must be well behaved, leashed, and cleaned up after. Dogs are not to be left unattended. The camping and tent areas also allow dogs. There is a dog walk area at the campground. Multiple dogs may be allowed.

Clarence Fahnestock State Park
1498 H 301
Carmel, NY
845-225-7207 (800-456-2267)
There are plenty of land and water recreational opportunities, camping, and many scenic hiking trails at this 14,000+ acre recreational destination, including a piece of the Appalachian Trail. Dogs are allowed in designated camp areas and on the trails; there are no additional pet fees. Dogs must be on no more than a 10 foot leash and be cleaned

up after. Dogs are not allowed on the beach or picnic areas. The campground has 80 campsites, each with a picnic table and fire ring, and restrooms and showers are nearby. They also show movies for the campers on Saturday evenings. Dogs are allowed in campsites 70 through 81. This RV park is closed during the off-season. The camping and tent areas also allow dogs. There is a dog walk area at the campground. There are no electric or water hookups at the campgrounds. 2 dogs may be allowed.

Letchworth State Park
1 Letchworth State Park
Castile, NY
585-493-3600 (800-456-2267)
This multi-faceted park provides opportunities for a wide range of year round activities and recreation, and is considered the "Grand Canyon of the East" with 3 major waterfalls, 600 foot high cliffs along the river flanked by lush forests, 70 miles of incredible hiking trails, plenty of food options, and a museum/visitor center that provides the history of the area. Dogs must have proof of rabies inoculation and there are no additional pet fees. Dogs must be crated or leashed (6 foot) and cleaned up after. They are not allowed in buildings, cabins or cabin areas, or swim areas. Dogs are allowed throughout the rest of the park and on the trails. The campground area has a camp store, playground, pool, showers, restrooms, laundry, recreation hall, playing fields, and a dump station. There is also a primitive camp area in the lower falls area. This RV park is closed during the off-season. The camping and tent areas also allow dogs. There is a dog walk area at the campground. There are no water hookups at the campgrounds. Multiple dogs may be allowed.

Catskill State Park
On Highways 28, 23 and 23A
Catskill Area, NY
845-256-3000 (800-456-CAMP (2267))
Covering 700,000 acres of some of the most complex natural areas anywhere in East, this park offers good multi-use trails, numerous plant, animal, and bird habitats, a fish hatchery, and year round land and water recreation. Dogs are allowed for no additional fee. Dogs may be off lead in open forested land if they are under very good voice control, but they must be leashed on

trails and in common or camp areas. Dogs are not allowed in park buildings. There are several campgrounds available here, including the popular Bear Spring Mountain Campground. Camp areas include picnic tables, grills, and restrooms. This RV park is closed during the off-season. The camping and tent areas also allow dogs. There is a dog walk area at the campground. Multiple dogs may be allowed.

High Falls Park Campground
34 Cemetery Road
Chateaugay, NY
518-497-3156
highfallspark.com
Dogs of all sizes are allowed. There are no additional pet fees. Dogs must be kept leashed and cleaned up after. The camping and tent areas also allow dogs. There is a dog walk area at the campground. Multiple dogs may be allowed.

Chenango Valley State Park
153 State Park Road
Chenango Forks, NY
607-648-5251
nysparks.state.ny.us
Dogs of all sizes are allowed. There are no additional pet fees. Dogs may not be left unattended, they must have a current rabies certificate and shot records. Dogs must be quiet, leashed, and cleaned up after. Dogs are allowed on the trails, but not on the beach or in the water. Although the campground is seasonal, the park is open year round. This campground is closed during the off-season. The camping and tent areas also allow dogs. There is a dog walk area at the campground. Dogs are allowed in the camping cabins. Multiple dogs may be allowed.

Cedar Point State Park
36661 Cedar Point State Park Drive
Clayton, NY
315-654-2522 (800-456-CAMP (2256))
Not to be confused with Cedar Point County Park in Long Island, this park is one of the state's oldest parks and is a popular spot for a variety of water and land recreational activities. It sits on a jut of land on the St Lawrence River, and there are also great views of ocean-going vessels from the overlook area. Dogs must have proof of rabies inoculation and there are no additional pet fees. Dogs must be crated or leashed (6 foot) and cleaned up after. They are not allowed in buildings, picnic, or

swim areas. Dogs are allowed throughout the rest of the park and on trails. The large scale camping area features 175 sites with restrooms, hot showers, picnic tables, fire pits, gaming fields, and a dump station. This RV park is closed during the off-season. The camping and tent areas also allow dogs. There is a dog walk area at the campground. Multiple dogs may be allowed.

Grass Point State Park
36661 Cedar Point State Park Drive
Clayton, NY
315-686-4472
nysparks.state.ny.us/
Dogs of all sizes are allowed. There are no additional pet fees. Dogs may not be left unattended, they must have a current rabies certificate and shot records, be well behaved, on no more than a 6 foot leash, and be cleaned up after. Dogs are allowed on the trails, but not in the picnic or bathroom areas. This campground is closed during the off-season. The camping and tent areas also allow dogs. There is a dog walk area at the campground. There are no water hookups at the campground. Multiple dogs may be allowed.

Merry Knoll 1000 Islands Campground
38115 H 12E
Clayton, NY
315-686-3055
merryknollcampground.com
Dogs of all sizes are allowed. There are no additional pet fees. Dogs must be quiet, leashed, and cleaned up after. The camping and tent areas also allow dogs. There is a dog walk area at the campground. Multiple dogs may be allowed.

Glimmerglass State Park
1527 H 31
Cooperstown, NY
607-547-8662 (800-456-CAMP (2267))
Sitting alongside Otsego Lake, this scenic woodland park is home to a variety of plant, bird, and wildlife and offers a variety of year round recreation, multi-use trails, a Beaver Pond Nature Trail, a covered bridge, food concessions, and a mansion. Dogs are allowed throughout the park and on the trails except on the beach or in park buildings. Dogs may not be left alone at any time, they must be on no more than a 6 foot leash, and be cleaned up after at all times. There

must be currant proof of rabies inoculation for camping. The camp area offers 37 well-maintained sites with modern restrooms, showers, tables, fire pits, charcoal grills, and a playground. This RV park is closed during the off-season. The camping and tent areas also allow dogs. There is a dog walk area at the campground. There are no electric or water hookups at the campgrounds. 2 dogs may be allowed.

KOA Cooperstown
565 Ostrander Road
Cooperstown, NY
315-858-0236 (800-562-3402)
koa.com
Dogs of all sizes are allowed. There are no additional pet fees. Dogs are allowed at the cabins but must be kept off the beds. There is a large field where dogs can run off leash if they will come to your command. Otherwise dogs must be leashed and cleaned up after. Dogs may not be left unattended except for short periods, and only if the dog is well behaved and comfortable with a short absence. This RV park is closed during the off-season. The camping and tent areas also allow dogs. There is a dog walk area at the campground. Dogs are allowed in the camping cabins. Multiple dogs may be allowed.

Shadowbrook Campground
2149 County H 31
Cooperstown, NY
607-264-8431
cooperstowncamping.com
Dogs of all sizes are allowed, however some breeds are not. There are no additional pet fees. Dogs must be leashed and cleaned up after. The camping and tent areas also allow dogs. There is a dog walk area at the campground. 2 dogs may be allowed.

Alpine Lake RV Resort
78 Heath Road
Corinth, NY
518-654-6260
alpinelakervresort.com
Dogs of all sizes are allowed, however some breeds are not. There are no additional pet fees. Dogs must have proof of rabies shots, be leashed, and cleaned up after. The camping and tent areas also allow dogs. There is a dog walk area at the campground. 2 dogs may be allowed.

Sugar Creek Glen Campground
11288 Poagf Hole Road

Dansville, NY
585-335-6294
sugarcreekglencampground.com
Dogs of all sizes are allowed. There is a pet policy to sign at check in and there are no additional pet fees. Dogs must not be left unattended for very long periods, and only if they are quiet and well behaved. Dogs must be leashed and cleaned up after. The camping and tent areas also allow dogs. There is a dog walk area at the campground. Dogs are allowed in the camping cabins. Multiple dogs may be allowed.

Black River Bay Campground
16129 Foster Park Road (Box541)
Dexter, NY
315-639-3735
blackriverbaycamp.com
Dogs of all sizes are allowed, however only 2 dogs are allowed per site or 3 dogs are OK if they are all small. There are no additional pet fees. Dogs must be leashed and cleaned up after. The camping and tent areas also allow dogs. There is a dog walk area at the campground.

Schroon River Resort
969 E Schroon River Road
Diamond Point, NY
518-623-3954
adirondackadventureresorts.com
Dogs of all sizes are allowed. There are no additional pet fees. Current shot records and proof of insurance is required for some breeds. Dogs must be leashed and cleaned up after. The camping and tent areas also allow dogs. There is a dog walk area at the campground. Multiple dogs may be allowed.

Cedar Point County Park
Stephen Hands Path
East Hampton, NY
631-852-7620
There are 607 recreational acres here with great views of the bay, an historic lighthouse, nature trails, outer beach access with permit, and a general store and snack bar. One dog of any size is allowed for no additional fee, but they must have current proof of rabies inoculation, leashed (maximum-6 foot), and cleaned up after at all times. Dogs may not be left unattended at any time, and they must be current in license from their home state. The camp areas offer picnic tables, fire rings, a children's playground, restrooms, and free use of recreational equipment. This RV park is closed during the off-season. The camping and tent areas also allow

dogs. There is a dog walk area at the campground. There are no electric or water hookups at the campgrounds.

Fair Haven Beach State Park
14985 Park Road
Fair Haven, NY
315-947-5205
nysparks.state.ny.us
Dogs of all sizes are allowed. There are no additional pet fees. Dogs may not be left unattended, they must have a current rabies certificate and shot records, be on no more than a 6 foot leash, and be cleaned up after. Dogs are allowed on the trails, but they are not allowed on any sandy areas, at the beach, or in the water. Although the campground is seasonal, some cabins remain open all year. This campground is closed during the off-season. The camping and tent areas also allow dogs. There is a dog walk area at the campground. Dogs are allowed in the camping cabins. There are no water hookups at the campground. Multiple dogs may be allowed.

KOA Canandaigua/Rochester
5374 FarmingtonTownline Road
Farmington, NY
585-398-3582 (800-562-0533)
koa.com
Dogs of all sizes are allowed. There is no additional pet fee for RV or tent sites, however there is a $25 refundable pet deposit when renting the cabins. Dogs may not be left unattended; they must be quiet, well behaved, leashed, and cleaned up after. There are some breed restrictions. This RV park is closed during the off-season. The camping and tent areas also allow dogs. There is a dog walk area at the campground. Dogs are allowed in the camping cabins. Multiple dogs may be allowed.

Watch Hill Campground
by Otis Pike High Dunes
Fire Island, NY
631-567-6664
This tent camping area offers 26 family sites and 1 group site, and permits are needed if camping in the back country that is accessible from here. Dogs are not allowed in the back country during plover nesting season. The camp area has a 188 slip marina, interpretive programs, a store, restaurant, restrooms and showers, and a self-guided nature tour. Dogs may not be left unattended at any time, and

they must be leashed (6 foot) and cleaned up after at all times. This RV park is closed during the off-season. The camping and tent areas also allow dogs. There is a dog walk area at the campground. There are no electric or water hookups at the campgrounds. 2 dogs may be allowed.

Black Bear Campground
197 Wheeler Road
Florida, NY
845-651-7717
blackbearcampground.com
Dogs of all sizes are allowed, however some breeds are not. There are no additional pet fees. Dogs must be well behaved, leashed, and cleaned up after. The camping and tent areas also allow dogs. There is a dog walk area at the campground. Dogs are allowed in the camping cabins. 2 dogs may be allowed.

KOA Unadilla/Oneonta
242 Union Church Road
Franklin, NY
607-369-9030 (800-562-9032)
koaunadilla.com
Dogs of all sizes are allowed. There are no additional pet fees. Dogs may not be left unattended, and must be leashed and cleaned up after. This RV park is closed during the off-season. The camping and tent areas also allow dogs. There is a dog walk area at the campground. 2 dogs may be allowed.

Lake George Resort
427 Fortsville Road
Gansevoort, NY
518-792-3519 (800-340-6867)
adirondackadventureresorts.com
Dogs of all sizes are allowed. There are no additional pet fees. Proof of up to date shots and insurance papers for some breeds is required. Dogs must be leashed and cleaned up after. The camping and tent areas also allow dogs. There is a dog walk area at the campground. Multiple dogs may be allowed.

Jellystone Park
50 Bevier Road
Gardiner, NY
845-255-5193
lazyriverny.com
Dogs of all sizes are allowed. There are no additional pet fees. Dogs must be quiet at night, be leashed, and cleaned up after. This RV park is closed during the off-season. There is a dog walk area at the campground. 2 dogs may be allowed.

Yogi Bear Jellystone Park at Crystal Lake
111 East Turtle Lake Road
Garrattsville, NY
607-965-8265 (800-231-1907)
cooperstownjellystone.com
Dogs of all sizes are allowed, except in the rentals. There is no fee if there are only 2 dogs; if there are more, it is $1.50 per night per pet additional fee. Dogs must have a current rabies certificate, be leashed, and cleaned up after. Dogs are not allowed at the pool, pavilion, playground, the rentals, or in the buildings. This RV park is closed during the off-season. The camping and tent areas also allow dogs. There is a dog walk area at the campground. Multiple dogs may be allowed.

Nickerson Park Campground
378 Stryker Road
Gilboa, NY
607-588-7327
nickersonparkcampground.com/
Dogs of all sizes are allowed. There are no additional pet fees. Dogs must be quiet, well behaved, leashed, and cleaned up after. This establishment also shares the New York trail system. The camping and tent areas also allow dogs. There is a dog walk area at the campground. Multiple dogs may be allowed.

KOA Niagara Falls
2570 Grand Island Blvd
Grand Island, NY
716-773-7583 (800-562-0787)
koaniagarafalls.com
Dogs of all sizes are allowed. There are no additional pet fees. Dogs must be friendly, well behaved, leashed, and cleaned up after. This RV park is closed during the off-season. The camping and tent areas also allow dogs. There is a dog walk area at the campground. Multiple dogs may be allowed.

Sarasota Springs Resort
265 Brigham Road
Greenfield Center, NY
518-893-0537
adirondackadventureresorts.com
Dogs of all sizes are allowed. There are no additional pet fees. Dogs must have proof of shots, be leashed, and cleaned up after. The camping and tent areas also allow dogs. There is a dog walk area at the campground. Multiple dogs may be allowed.

Whispering Pines Campsites and RV Park

550 Sand Hill Road
Greenfield Center, NY
518-893-0416
This full service family camping resort sits on 75 acres with towering pines, 2 stream-fed ponds and a trout brook, an in-ground pool, store, playgrounds, rec hall and game room/courts, laundry, hot showers, hi-speed internet access, and a full activity calendar. Dogs of all sizes are allowed for $1 per pet and proof of rabies inoculation. Dogs must be well mannered, leashed, and cleaned up after at all times. Dogs are not allowed in swim areas or in park buildings. This RV park is closed during the off-season. The camping and tent areas also allow dogs. There is a dog walk area at the campground. Multiple dogs may be allowed.

Skyway Camping Resort
99 Mountain Dale Road
Greenfield Park, NY
845-647-5747
skywaycamping.com
Dogs of all sizes are allowed, however some breeds are not. There are no additional pet fees. Dogs must be leashed and cleaned up after. The camping and tent areas also allow dogs. There is a dog walk area at the campground. 2 dogs may be allowed.

Eastern Long Island Kampgrounds
On Queen Street
Greenport, NY
631-477-0022
greenport.com/kampground
Dogs of all sizes are allowed, however some breeds are not. There are no additional pet fees. Dogs must have proof of rabies shots. Dogs must be leashed, cleaned up after, and not left unattended. The camping and tent areas also allow dogs. There is a dog walk area at the campground. 2 dogs may be allowed.

Catskill Forest Preserve/North South Lake
County H 18
Haines Falls, NY
518-357-2234
This park offers a variety of seasonal nature programs, land and water recreation, historic sites, stunning vistas, and the highest waterfall in the state, the double-tiered Kaaterskill Falls. Dogs with valid rabies inoculation papers are welcome. Dogs may not be left unattended anywhere, and they must be quiet, well mannered,

leashed (no more than 6 foot), and cleaned up after at all times. Dogs are not permitted on Lake George Islands, the beach, picnic areas, or park buildings. The campground features 7 camping loops with 219 sites, gaming areas, modern restrooms, hot showers, a boat launch for non-motorized craft, 2 picnic areas with tables and grills, and a dump station. The phone number for the campground is 518-589-5058. This RV park is closed during the off-season. The camping and tent areas also allow dogs. There is a dog walk area at the campground. There are no electric or water hookups at the campgrounds. Multiple dogs may be allowed.

Association Island RV Resort & Marina
Snowshoe Road
Henderson Harbor, NY
315-938-5655
associationislandresort.com
Dogs of all sizes are allowed, however some breeds are not. There are no additional pet fees. Dogs must be leashed, cleaned up after, and have proof of rabies shots. The camping and tent areas also allow dogs. There is a dog walk area at the campground. Multiple dogs may be allowed.

KOA Herkimer
800 Mohawk Street
Herkimer, NY
315-891-7355 (800-562-0897)
koa.com/where/ny/32224/
Dogs of all sizes are allowed. There are no additional pet fees. Dog must be leashed and cleaned up after. This RV park is closed during the off-season. The camping and tent areas also allow dogs. There is a dog walk area at the campground. Multiple dogs may be allowed.

Spruce Row Campground and RV Resort
2271 Kraft Road
Ithaca, NY
607-387-9225 (800-456-CAMP (2267))
sprucerow.com/
This resort hosts several events throughout the year, and offer guests camp sites on a first come first served basis, a huge pool, recreation room, camp store, picnic areas, playing fields, restrooms and showers. Dogs of all sizes are allowed for no additional fee, and proof of current rabies inoculation is required. Dogs must be quiet, crated or leashed, and cleaned up after at

all times. Dogs are not allowed at the pool, playground, or in the store. This RV park is closed during the off-season. The camping and tent areas also allow dogs. There is a dog walk area at the campground. Multiple dogs may be allowed.

Liberty Harbor RV Park
11 Marin Blvd
NYC - Jersey City, NJ
201-387-7500
libertyharborrv.com/
Dogs of all sizes are allowed. There are no additional pet fees. Dogs must be leashed, cleaned up after, and not be left unattended. There is a dog walk area at the campground. Multiple dogs may be allowed.

Lake George RV Park
74 State H 149
Lake George, NY
518-792-3775
lakegeorgervpark.com
Dogs of all sizes are allowed. There are no additional pet fees. Dogs must be leashed, cleaned up after, and not left unattended. The camping and tent areas also allow dogs. There is a dog walk area at the campground. 2 dogs may be allowed.

KOA Lake George/Saratoga
564 Lake Avenue
Lake Luzerne, NY
518-696-2615 (800-562-2618)
lakegeorgekoa.com
Dogs of all sizes are allowed. There are no additional pet fees. Dogs must be leashed and cleaned up after. There are some breed restrictions. This RV park is closed during the off-season. The camping and tent areas also allow dogs. There is a dog walk area at the campground. Multiple dogs may be allowed.

Nickerson Beach Campground
880 Lido Blvd
Lido Beach, NY
516-571-7700
licamping.com/camps/nassaub.htm
This campground has been newly renovated and offer gaming courts, a "Fun Zone" kids center, skating park, beach showers and cabanas, an enclosed dog run, 2 pools, a kiddie pool, modern restrooms, and new benches and grills. For more information on the campgrounds, call 516-571-7701 through March 30th, and during camping season call the number listed above. Dogs of all sizes are allowed for no additional fee. Dogs may be in the campground

area, parking lot, or at the dog run. Dogs are not allowed on the beach or trails. Dogs may not be left unattended at any time, and they must be leashed (except in dog run) and cleaned up after. The camping and tent areas also allow dogs. There is a dog walk area at the campground. 2 dogs may be allowed.

Jellystone Park
601 County Road 16
Mexico, NY
315-963-7096 (800-248-7096)
jellystoneny.com
One dog of any size is allowed, some breeds are not. There are no additional pet fees. Dogs must be walked in the pet walk area only, not around the park. Dogs may not be left unattended and must be leashed and cleaned up after. This RV park is closed during the off-season. The camping and tent areas also allow dogs. There is a dog walk area at the campground.

Meadow-Vale Campsites
505 Gilbert Lake Road
Mount Vision, NY
607-293-8802 (800-701-8802)
meadow-vale.com
Dogs of all sizes are allowed, however some breeds are not. There are no additional pet fees. Dogs must be leashed and cleaned up after. The camping and tent areas also allow dogs. There is a dog walk area at the campground.

KOA Natural Bridge/Watertown
6081 State H 3
Natural Bridge, NY
315-644-4880 (800562-4780)
aticamping.com
Dogs of all sizes are allowed. There are no additional pet fees. Dogs must be leashed and cleaned up after. This RV park is closed during the off-season. The camping and tent areas also allow dogs. There is a dog walk area at the campground. Multiple dogs may be allowed.

Kellystone Park
51 Hawkins Road
Nineveh, NY
607-639-1090
kellystonepark.net
Dogs of all sizes are allowed, however some breeds are not. There are no additional pet fees. Dogs must be quiet, well behaved, leashed, and cleaned up after. The camping and tent areas also allow dogs. There is a dog walk area at the campground. Multiple dogs may

be allowed.

Jellystone Park
5204 Youngers Road
North Java, NY
585-457-9644 (800-232-4039)
wnyjellystone.com
Dogs of all sizes are allowed. There are no additional pet fees unless staying in the pet friendly Boo Boo Chalets. Then there would be an additional $25 per unit. Dogs must be quiet, well behaved, leashed and cleaned up after. Dogs may not be left unattended. This RV park is closed during the off-season. The camping and tent areas also allow dogs. There is a dog walk area at the campground. Dogs are allowed in the camping cabins. 2 dogs may be allowed.

Battle Row Campground
Claremont Road
Old Bethpage, NY
516-572-8690
licamping.com/camps/battle.htm
This camp area is located at the Old Bethpage County Park with large grassy lawns, surrounded by woods, and is the only park in the county that allows tent camping. Camping begins the first Friday in April and ends the last Sunday in November. Dogs are allowed throughout the park; there is no additional pet fee. Dogs must be well mannered, leashed, and cleaned up after at all times. This RV park is closed during the off-season. The camping and tent areas also allow dogs. There is a dog walk area at the campground. 2 dogs may be allowed.

Bowman Lake State Park
745 Bilven Sherman Road
Oxford, NY
607-334-2718
Dogs of all sizes are allowed. There are no additional pet fees. Dogs may not be left unattended and they must have a current rabies certificate and shot record. Dogs must be quiet, well behaved, on no more than a 6 foot leash, and be cleaned up after. Dogs are allowed on the trails, but not on the beach or in any of the buildings. The camping and tent areas also allow dogs. There is a dog walk area at the campground. There are no electric or water hookups at the campground. Multiple dogs may be allowed.

Fire Island National Seashore
120 Laurel Street
Patchogue, NY
631-661-4876

nps.gov/fiis/
Land taxi service isn't available on this 30 mile long, ½ mile wide barrier island. It is home to the tallest lighthouse in the U.S.; 80% of it's over 19,500 acres is undeveloped public park land, and it has a special environment nurturing a diverse selection of plants, animals, birds, marine life, and even people. Land and water recreation, dining, an active nightlife, and shopping opportunities abound here. The best way to arrive on the island is by watercraft; however parking is available in parking lot # 5 at the end of the Causeway. Although dogs are not allowed in the lighthouse or other park buildings, they are allowed to enjoy the miles of boardwalks, trails, beaches, and self-guided nature walks. Dogs may not be in life-guarded areas of the beach, picnic or wildlife habitat areas, and they must be on no more than a 6 foot leash in the park area and cleaned up after at all times. Dogs must be well behaved and not left unattended at any time or tied to any park facilities. The campground (seasonal) has 26 sand sites, and is only a short walk to the visitor center, beach, and marina. Amenities here include a summer lifeguard, general store, showers and restrooms, water, grills, a snack bar, and a Tiki Bar. Wilderness camping is year round, and a permit is required. (Certain areas are restricted to dogs during the summer. Check for updates prior to arrival.) The camping and tent areas also allow dogs. There is a dog walk area at the campground. There are no electric or water hookups at the campgrounds. 2 dogs may be allowed.

KOA Newburgh/NYC North
119 Freetown Highway
Plattekill, NY
845-564-2836 (800-562-7220)
newburghkoa.com
Dogs of all sizes are allowed. There are no additional pet fees. Dogs must be leashed and cleaned up after. This RV park is closed during the off-season. The camping and tent areas also allow dogs. There is a dog walk area at the campground. Dogs are allowed in the camping cabins. Multiple dogs may be allowed.

Plattsburgh RV Park
7182 H 9N
Plattsburgh, NY
518-563-3915
plattsburghrvpark.com

Dogs of all sizes are allowed. There are no additional pet fees. Dogs must be well behaved and under control of owner. Dogs must be leashed and cleaned up after. The camping and tent areas also allow dogs. There is a dog walk area at the campground. Dogs are allowed in the camping cabins. Multiple dogs may be allowed.

Brennan Beach RV Resort
80 Brennan's Beach Road
Pulaski, NY
315-298-2242
brennanbeach.com
Dogs of all sizes are allowed. There are no additional pet fees. Dogs must be leased and cleaned up after. The camping and tent areas also allow dogs. There is a dog walk area at the campground. 2 dogs may be allowed.

Selkirk Sores State Park
7101 H 3
Pulaski, NY
315-298-5737
nysparks.state.ny.us
Dogs of all sizes are allowed. There are no additional pet fees. Dogs may not be left unattended, and they must have a current rabies certificate and shot record, be on no more than a 6 foot leash, and be cleaned up after. Dogs are allowed on the trails and at the beach. This campground is closed during the off-season. The camping and tent areas also allow dogs. There is a dog walk area at the campground. Dogs are allowed in the camping cabins. There are no water hookups at the campground. Multiple dogs may be allowed.

Pope Haven Campgrounds
11948 Pope Road
Randolph, NY
716-358-4900
popehaven.com
Dogs of all sizes are allowed. There are no additional pet fees. Dogs must have proof of rabies shots, and be leashed and cleaned up after. They must also be quiet and well behaved. The camping and tent areas also allow dogs. There is a dog walk area at the campground. Multiple dogs may be allowed.

Delta Lake State Park
8797 H 46
Rome, NY
315-337-04670 (800-456-CAMP (2267))
Located on a fairly flat peninsula on the Delta Reservoir, this scenic park

offers hiking and nature trails, and a variety of year round activities and recreation. Dogs are allowed (for no fee) throughout the park and on the trails except not in swim areas. Dogs may not be left alone at any time, they must be crated or on no more than a 6 foot leash, and be cleaned up after at all times. Currant proof of rabies inoculation is required. The camp area offers about 100 sites, many on the lake front, and there is a picnic table and fire ring at each site with restrooms, showers, and recreation areas nearby. There is also a dump station and boat launch. This RV park is closed during the off-season. The camping and tent areas also allow dogs. There is a dog walk area at the campground. There are no electric or water hookups at the campgrounds. Multiple dogs may be allowed.

Whip-O-Will Family Campsite
644 H 31
Roundtop, NY
518-622-3277
whip-o-willcampsites.com
Dogs of all sizes are allowed. There are no additional pet fees. Dogs must be kept under control, on a leash, and cleaned up after. The camping and tent areas also allow dogs. There is a dog walk area at the campground. Multiple dogs may be allowed.

Allegany State Park
2373 ASP, Route 1, Suite 3
Salamanca, NY
716-354-9121 (800-456-2267)
The states largest park, it is a popular year round recreational destination with more than 65,000 acres of forests, over 70 miles of hiking trails, a nature trail, scenic drives with roadside wildlife viewing, and a museum/visitor center. Dogs must have proof of rabies inoculation and there are no additional pet fees. Dogs must be crated or leashed (6 foot) and cleaned up after. They are not allowed in buildings, cabins, bathing areas, or cross country ski areas. Dogs are allowed throughout the rest of the park and on the trails. The campground area has a camp store, playground, pool, showers, restrooms, laundry, playing fields, boat launch, a dump station, and more. This RV park is closed during the off-season. The camping and tent areas also allow dogs. There is a dog walk area at the campground. There are no water hookups at the campgrounds. Multiple dogs may be allowed.

Saranac Lake Islands
58 Bayside Drive
Saranac Lake, NY
518-897-1309 (800-456-CAMP (2267))
This park provides many miles of boating recreation with direct access to other lakes through a set of locks that raises and lowers vessels through to the next water level. Dogs are welcome for no additional fee, but they must have proof of current rabies inoculation. Dogs may not be left unattended anywhere, and they must be quiet, well mannered, leashed (no more than 6 foot), and cleaned up after at all times. Dogs are not permitted on Lake George Islands, the beach, picnic areas, or in park buildings. The camping area offers 87 primitive sites with fireplaces, picnic tables, and restrooms. 2 dogs may be allowed.

KOA Saugerties/Woodstock
882 H212
Saugerties, NY
845-246-4089 (800-562-4081)
koa.com
Dogs of all sizes are allowed. There are no additional fees for site rentals, however there is a $4 per night per pet additional fee for the cabins. Dogs must be leashed and cleaned up after. There are some breed restrictions. This RV park is closed during the off-season. The camping and tent areas also allow dogs. There is a dog walk area at the campground. Dogs are allowed in the camping cabins. Multiple dogs may be allowed.

Cayuga Lake State Park
2678 Lower Lake Road
Seneca Falls, NY
315-568-5163 (800-456-CAMP (2267))
Nestled among trees with a large lawn area in front facing an expansive view of the lake, this park offers a long list of amenities and year round land and water recreation. Dogs of all sizes are allowed for no additional fee, and owners must have proof of rabies inoculation if camping. Dogs may not be left unattended in cabins or campsites, and they must be leashed (6 foot) and cleaned up after. They are not allowed in swim areas or the playground. Dogs are allowed throughout the rest of the park and on the trails. The camp area offers 50 sites with fireplaces, children's and adult recreation areas, a nature trail, ice machines, restrooms with

showers, and laundry facilities. This RV park is closed during the off-season. The camping and tent areas also allow dogs. There is a dog walk area at the campground. Dogs are allowed in the camping cabins. There are no water hookups at the campgrounds. Multiple dogs may be allowed.

Blydenburgh County Park
New Mill Road
Smithtown, NY
631-854-3713
In addition to providing a long list of land and water recreational pursuits and some nice hiking areas, this 627 acre park holds some historic interests, and they are home to an off leash dog area located in the south area of the park. Dogs are allowed throughout the park and at the camp area for no additional fee; they must be registered at the time of entry, and may not be left unattended at the campsite. Dogs must be sociable, current on all vaccinations-proof required, and under their owner's control at all times. Dogs must be leashed on no more than a 6 foot leash when not in the designated off-lead area, and they are not allowed in picnic areas, designated swim areas, or comfort stations. From about mid-October to mid-May the camp area is open Thursday to Sunday, and from mid-May to early October they are open 7 days a week. During the off-season only self-contained campers are allowed; there is no water services, and tents are not allowed. The camping and tent areas also allow dogs. There is a dog walk area at the campground. 2 dogs may be allowed.

South Shore RV Park
7867 Lake Road
Sodus Point, NY
315-483-8679
southshorervpark.com
Dogs of all sizes are allowed. There are no additional pet fees. Dogs must be quiet, leashed, and cleaned up after. Dogs must not be left unattended at any time, especially in the cabins. The camping and tent areas also allow dogs. There is a dog walk area at the campground. Dogs are allowed in the camping cabins. Multiple dogs may be allowed.

Camp Chautauqua Camping Resort
3900 Westlake Road
Stow, NY
716-789-3435

campchautauqua.com
Dogs of all sizes are allowed. There are no additional pet fees. Shot records must be up to date, and dogs must be kept under owner's control and be quiet during the night. The camping and tent areas also allow dogs. There is a dog walk area at the campground. 2 dogs may be allowed.

Swan Lake Camplands
106 Fulton Road
Swan Lake, NY
845-292-4781
swanlakecamplands.com
Dogs of all sizes are allowed. There are no additional pet fees. Dogs must be leashed and cleaned up after. The camping and tent areas also allow dogs. There is a dog walk area at the campground. Dogs are allowed in the camping cabins. Multiple dogs may be allowed.

Long Point State Park-Thousand Islands
7495 State Park Road
Three Mile Bay, NY
315-649-5258 (800-456-CAMP (2267))
This peaceful park, located on a grassy, semi-wooded peninsula on Lake Ontario, provides a sheltered harbor for boats and a variety of land and water recreational activities. Dogs must have proof of rabies inoculation and there are no additional pet fees. Dogs must be crated or leashed (6 foot) and cleaned up after. They are not allowed in picnic areas. Dogs are allowed throughout the rest of the park and on trails. The camp area offers picnic tables, a children's playground, restrooms, and showers. This RV park is closed during the off-season. The camping and tent areas also allow dogs. There is a dog walk area at the campground. Multiple dogs may be allowed.

Glen Hudson Campsite
564 River Road
Thurman, NY
518-623-9871
Nestled along the banks of the Hudson River, this RV park offers a camping store, laundry, showers, rec hall, and a variety of land and water recreation. Dogs of all sizes are allowed for no additional fees. Dogs must be well behaved, leashed, and cleaned up after at all times. This RV park is closed during the off-season. There is a dog walk area at the campground. 2 dogs may be allowed.

Taughannock Falls State Park
2221 Taughannock Park Road
Trumansburg, NY
607-387-6739 (800-456-2267)
Taller than Niagara Falls by 33 feet, the namesake waterfall of this park plunges 215 feet over craggy cliffs towering nearly 400 feet above the gorge providing spectacular views from lookout points or along the multi-use trails, and there are planned activities like tours and concerts during the summer season. Dogs must have proof of rabies inoculation and there are no additional pet fees. Dogs may not be left unattended in cabins, and they must be leashed (6 foot) and cleaned up after. They are not allowed in buildings or swim areas. Dogs are allowed throughout the rest of the park and on the trails. Camp areas have picnic areas with tables and fireplaces, hot showers, flush toilets, a playground, concession stand, and a dump station. This RV park is closed during the off-season. The camping and tent areas also allow dogs. There is a dog walk area at the campground. Dogs are allowed in the camping cabins. There are no water hookups at the campgrounds. 2 dogs may be allowed.

Turning Stone RV Park
5065 State H 365
Verona, NY
315-361-7275
turningstone.com
Dogs of all sizes are allowed. There are no additional pet fees. Dogs must be leased and cleaned up after. If your dog will remain next to you and not chase other dogs or people, it can be off leash on your own site. There is a dog walk area at the campground. Multiple dogs may be allowed.

Verona Beach State Park
6541 Lakeshore Road S
Verona Beach, NY
315-762-4463 (800-456-2267)
Open for year round activities and recreation, this lake-shore park is also home to one of the most diverse aquatic habitats in the region with a great nature walk through the "Woods and Wetlands" trail. Dogs are allowed (for no fee) throughout the park and on the trails except not in swim areas or in park buildings. Dogs may not be left alone at any time, they must be on no more than a 6 foot leash, and be cleaned up after at all times. Currant proof of rabies inoculation is required. There

is a 1000 acre area across from the park where dogs may be off lead if they are under very good voice control and will not chase other wildlife. The shaded camp area offers 45 sites with a view of the lake, picnic areas, restrooms, showers, a playground, recreation room, and a concession stand. This RV park is closed during the off-season. The camping and tent areas also allow dogs. There is a dog walk area at the campground. There are no electric or water hookups at the campgrounds. Multiple dogs may be allowed.

Daggett Lake Campsites & Cabins
660 Glen Athol Rd
Warrensburg, NY
518-623-2198
daggettlake.com
Friendly, well behaved, leashed, pets are welcome with a copy of their rabies certificate in the campground, all vaccinations plus flea prevention in the cabins. No charge for pets in the campground, $50 fee for housekeeping cottages. This campground is the home of the "Dog Beach" where dogs can go off leash if they're under voice control. 400 acres with hiking and mountain biking trails, canoe, kayak, and rowboat rentals, and a sandy swim beach for people.

Schroon River Campsites
74 State H 149
Warrensburg, NY
518-623-2171
lakegeorgervpark
Dogs of all sizes are allowed. There are no additional pet fees. Dogs must be well behaved, cleaned up after, and not left unattended. The camping and tent areas also allow dogs. There is a dog walk area at the campground. Multiple dogs may be allowed.

Lakeside Beach State Park
Lakeside, H 18
Waterport, NY
585-682-4888
nysparks.state.ny.us/
Dogs of all sizes are allowed. There are no additional pet fees. Dogs may not be left unattended, they must have a current rabies certificate and shot records, be on no more than a 6 foot leash, and be cleaned up after. Dogs are allowed on the trails, but when in the campground they must stay in camping loops that are designated for pets. This campground is closed during the off-season. The camping

and tent areas also allow dogs. There are no water hookups at the campground. Multiple dogs may be allowed.

KOA Watkins Glen/Corning
1710 H 414
Watkins Glen, NY
607-535-7404 (800-562-7430)
watkinsglenkoa.com
Dogs of all sizes are allowed. There are no additional pet fees. Dogs may not be left unattended, and must be leashed and cleaned up after. This RV park is closed during the off-season. The camping and tent areas also allow dogs. There is a dog walk area at the campground. 2 dogs may be allowed.

Watkins Glen State Park
South end of Seneca Lake
Watkins Glen, NY
607-535-4511 (800-456-2267)
This park is famous for an amazing gorge stone path that descends 400 feet past 200 foot cliffs and winds under and through waterfalls, lush greenery, and sculptured rocks created by its 19 cascading waterfalls. Although dogs are not allowed on the Gorge Trail, there are several other scenic trails here, and a variety of land and water recreation year round. Dogs of all sizes are allowed for no additional fee; however there must be written proof of rabies inoculation. Dogs must be well behaved, crated or on no more than a 6 foot leash, and cleaned up after at all times. The camp area offers an Olympic-size pool, gaming fields, picnic areas, food, restrooms, showers, a gift shop, playground, and a dump station. This RV park is closed during the off-season. The camping and tent areas also allow dogs. There is a dog walk area at the campground. There are no water hookups at the campgrounds. Multiple dogs may be allowed.

KOA Westfield/Lake Erie
8001 H 5
Westfield, NY
716-326-3573 (800-562-3973)
koa.com
Dogs of all sizes are allowed. There are no additional pet fees. Dogs may not be left unattended, and must be leashed and cleaned up after. This RV park is closed during the off-season. The camping and tent areas also allow dogs. There is a dog walk area at the campground. Dogs are allowed in the camping cabins. Multiple dogs may be allowed.

KOA Lake Placid/Whiteface Mountain
77 Foxfarm Road
Wilmington, NY
518-946-7878 (800-562-0368)
koacampground.com
Dogs of all sizes are allowed in the camp and RV sites, but only one dog up to 40 pounds is allowed in the cabin. There are no additional pet fees. Dogs may not be left unattended and must have a valid rabies certificate. They must be leashed and cleaned up after. There are some breed restrictions. This RV park is closed during the off-season. The camping and tent areas also allow dogs. There is a dog walk area at the campground. Dogs are allowed in the camping cabins.

Jellystone Park at Birchwood Acres
85 Martinfeld Road, Box 482
Woodridge, NY
845-434-4743 (800-552-4724)
nyjellystone.com
One dog of any size is allowed, except in the rentals or lodge. Dogs may not be left unattended, must be leashed, and cleaned up after. There are some breed restrictions. This RV park is closed during the off-season. The camping and tent areas also allow dogs. There is a dog walk area at the campground.

KOA Niagara Falls N/Lewiston
1250 Pletcher Road
Youngstown, NY
716-754-8013 (800-562-8715)
niagarafallsnorthkoa.com
Dogs of all sizes are allowed. There are no additional pet fees. Dogs may not be left unattended, and must be leashed and cleaned up after. There are some breed restrictions. This RV park is closed during the off-season. The camping and tent areas also allow dogs. There is a dog walk area at the campground. Dogs are allowed in the camping cabins. Multiple dogs may be allowed.

North Carolina

Morrow Mountain State Park
49104 Morrow Mountain Road
Albemarle, NC
704-982-4402
Rich in natural and cultural history, this park offers an exhibit hall and a historic site, an amphitheater, 15 miles of blazed hiking trails, and a wide variety of land and water activities and recreation. Dogs of all sizes are allowed at no additional fee. Dogs may not be left unattended, and they must be on no more than a 6 foot leash, and be cleaned up after. Dogs are not allowed in buildings, however they are allowed on the trails. The camping and tent areas also allow dogs. There is a dog walk area at the campground. There are no electric or water hookups at the campground. Multiple dogs may be allowed.

Jordan Lake State Park
280 State Park Road
Apex, NC
919-362-0586
Rich in ancient American history and home to one of the largest summertime homes of the bald eagle, this park offers educational and interpretive programs, a variety of trails, and various recreation. Dogs of all sizes are allowed at no additional fee. Dogs may not be left unattended, and they must be on no more than a 6 foot leash, and cleaned up after. The camping and tent areas also allow dogs. There is a dog walk area at the campground. Multiple dogs may be allowed.

Bear Creek RV Park
81 S Bear Creek Road
Asheville, NC
828-253-0798
ashevillevearcreek.com
Dogs of all sizes are allowed. There are no additional pet fees for the first two dogs. For more than 2 dogs, there is a $5 per night per pet additional fee. Dogs must be leashed and cleaned up after. The camping and tent areas also allow dogs. There is a dog walk area at the campground. Multiple dogs may be allowed.

Pisgah National Forest
1001 Pisgah H (H276)
Asheville, NC
828-877-3350
cs.unca.edu/nfsnc/
This forest's diverse ecosystems support a large variety of trails, plants, fish, mammals, bird species, recreation, and is also home to the Looking Glass Falls. Dogs of all sizes are allowed at no additional fee. Dogs may not be left unattended, and they must be leashed and cleaned up after. Dogs are not allowed in buildings, however, they are allowed on the trails. Dogs are not allowed on the trails in the Great Smokey

Mountains National Forest that adjoins the park. The camping and tent areas also allow dogs. There is a dog walk area at the campground. There are no electric or water hookups at the campground. Multiple dogs may be allowed.

Moonshine Creek Campground
27 Moonshine Creek Trail
Balsam, NC
828-586-6666
moonshinecreekcampground.com
Dogs of all sizes are allowed. There are no additional pet fees. Dogs must be leashed and cleaned up after. This RV park is closed during the off-season. The camping and tent areas also allow dogs. There is a dog walk area at the campground. Multiple dogs may be allowed.

Creekside Mountain Camping
24 Chimney View Road
Bat Cave, NC
800-248-8118
creeksidecamping.com
Dogs of all sizes are allowed. There are no additional pet fees. Dogs may not be left unattended, and they must be quiet, leashed, and cleaned up after. The camping and tent areas also allow dogs. There is a dog walk area at the campground. 2 dogs may be allowed.

Julian Price Memorial Park
Blue Ridge Parkway Milepost 297
Blowing Rock, NC
828-295-7591 (877-444-6777)
blueridgeparkway.org/
This is the largest of the camp areas along the parkway and they offer numerous recreational opportunities and hiking trails of varying length and difficulty, picnic grounds, interpretive programs, an amphitheater, and it sits adjacent to Price Lake. Although most camps sites are on a first come first served basis, some sites are available for reservations. Dogs are allowed throughout the park and on the trails. Dogs must be well behaved, under owner's control, on no more than a 6 foot leash, and cleaned up after at all times. This RV park is closed during the off-season. The camping and tent areas also allow dogs. There is a dog walk area at the campground. There are no electric or water hookups at the campgrounds. Multiple dogs may be allowed.

Boone KOA
123 Harmony Mountain Lane
Boone, NC
828-264-7250 (800-562-2806)

koa.com
Dogs of all sizes are allowed. There are no additional pet fees. Dogs may not be left unattended, and they must be leashed and cleaned up after. This RV park is closed during the off-season. The camping and tent areas also allow dogs. There is a dog walk area at the campground. Dogs are allowed in the camping cabins. Multiple dogs may be allowed.

Mount Mitchell State Park
2388 H 128
Burnsville, NC
828-675-4611
In addition to being the highest point east of the Mississippi with outstanding views, this 1,855 acre park also offers a number of scenic trails, an observation tower, an interpretive center, concessionaires, and picnic areas with tables and grills. There is also a 9 site, tents only camping area on a first come first served basis. Dogs are allowed throughout the park and on the trails; they are not allowed in park buildings. Dogs must be leashed and cleaned up after at all times. This RV park is closed during the off-season. The camping and tent areas also allow dogs. There is a dog walk area at the campground. There are no electric or water hookups at the campgrounds. There are special amenities given to dogs at this campground. Multiple dogs may be allowed.

Asheville West KOA
309 Wiggins Road
Candler, NC
828-665-7015 (800-562-9015)
koa.com
Dogs of all sizes are allowed. There are no additional pet fees. Dogs must be leashed and cleaned up after. There are some breed restrictions. The camping and tent areas also allow dogs. There is a dog walk area at the campground. Dogs are allowed in the camping cabins. Multiple dogs may be allowed.

Carolina Beach State Park
1010 State Park Road
Carolina Beach, NC
910-458-8206
ncparks.gov/Visit/main.php
This 761 acre park was started to preserve and educate the public of its unique intra-coastal waterway and to provide recreation; there are miles of trails through a variety of habitats with some unusual inhabitants- including the Venus flytrap, and

various events and interpretive programs. Dogs are allowed for no additional fee; they must have proof of currant rabies inoculation. Dogs may not be left unattended and are to be confined to vehicles or tents during quiet hours. They must be well behaved, on no more than a 6 foot leash, and cleaned up after at all times. Dogs are not allowed in any park buildings or swimming areas. The campground offers 83 first come first served sites in a wooded setting with picnic tables and grills at each site; restrooms, showers, water, and a dump station are nearby. The camping and tent areas also allow dogs. There is a dog walk area at the campground. There are no electric or water hookups at the campgrounds. Multiple dogs may be allowed.

Black Forest Family Camping Resort
100 Summer Road
Cedar Mountain, NC
828-884-2267
blackforestcampground.com
Dogs of all sizes are allowed. There are no additional pet fees. Dogs must be leashed and cleaned up after. This RV park is closed during the off-season. The camping and tent areas also allow dogs. There is a dog walk area at the campground. Multiple dogs may be allowed.

Carowinds Camp Wilderness Resort
14523 Carowinds Blvd
Charlotte, NC
704-588-2600 (800-888-4386)
In addition to being located at a major amusement park, this campground offers a number of amenities including Wi-Fi, a pool, gaming areas, a laundry, free shuttle to the park, and more. Dogs are allowed for no additional pet fee. Dogs are allowed in tents and there is a dog walk area. Multiple dogs may be allowed.

McDowell Nature Preserve Campground
15222 York Road
Charlotte, NC
704-583-1284
In addition to providing a number of exhibits and environment/educational programs about this 108 acre preserve, they also offer a variety of land and water recreation, a gift shop, gardens, hiking trails, and more. Dogs are allowed for no additional fee. Dogs may not be left

unattended outside at any time, and they must be kept leashed and cleaned up after. The camp area offers picnic areas and restrooms. The camping and tent areas also allow dogs. There is a dog walk area at the campground. Multiple dogs may be allowed.

Cherokee/Great Smokies KOA
92 KOA Campground Road
Cherokee, NC
828-497-9711 (800-562-7784)
cherokeekoa.com
Dogs of all sizes are allowed. There are no additional pet fees. Dogs may not be left unattended, and they must be leashed and cleaned up after. The camping and tent areas also allow dogs. There is a dog walk area at the campground. Dogs are allowed in the camping cabins. Multiple dogs may be allowed.

Happy Holiday RV Park
1553 Wolftown Road
Cherokee, NC
828-497-7250
happyholidaycherokee.com
Dogs of all sizes are allowed. There are no additional pet fees. Dogs may not be left unattended outside, and they must be leashed and cleaned up after. This RV park is closed during the off-season. The camping and tent areas also allow dogs. There is a dog walk area at the campground. Dogs are allowed in the camping cabins. Multiple dogs may be allowed.

Yogi in the Smokies
317 Galamore Bridge Road
Cherokee, NC
828-497-9151 (877-716-6711)
jellystone-cherokee.com
Dogs of all sizes are allowed. There are no additional pet fees. Dogs may not be left unattended, must be quiet, leashed, and cleaned up after. This RV park is closed during the off-season. The camping and tent areas also allow dogs. There is a dog walk area at the campground. Multiple dogs may be allowed.

Fleetwood RV Racing Camping Resort
6600 Speedway Blvd
Concord, NC
704-455-4445
rvingusa.com
Dogs of all sizes are allowed. There are no additional pet fees. Dogs may not be left unattended outside, and they must be leashed and cleaned up after. There is a dog walk area at the campground. Multiple dogs may

be allowed.

Pettigrew State Park
2252 Lake Shore Road
Creswell, NC
252-797-4475
There are over 1,200 land acres with 16,000 acres of water at this scenic park that offers a rich natural history, a wide variety of recreational and educational activities, and several great hiking trails. Dogs are welcome for no additional fee throughout the park, on the trails, and in the camp area. Campsite are first come first served, and each site has a picnic table and grill with seasonally provided restrooms, showers, and water. The camping and tent areas also allow dogs. There is a dog walk area at the campground. There are no electric or water hookups at the campgrounds. Multiple dogs may be allowed.

Hanging Rock State Park
State Road 2015
Danbury, NC
336-593-8480
Picturesque cascades and waterfalls, high rock cliffs, 18 miles of trails, and spectacular views are all located here. In addition, the park hosts an interactive interpretive center and a variety of land and water activities and recreation. Dogs of all sizes are allowed at no additional fee. Dogs may not be left unattended, and they must be on no more than a 6 foot leash, and be cleaned up after. Dogs are not allowed in swim areas or in buildings. Dogs are allowed on the trails. The camping and tent areas also allow dogs. There is a dog walk area at the campground. There are no electric or water hookups at the campground. Multiple dogs may be allowed.

Jones Lake State Park
4117 H 242N
Elizabethtown, NC
910-588-4550
This 2,208-acre park is a nature lover's delight, and offers educational and interpretive programs as well as a variety of trails and recreational pursuits. Dogs of all sizes are allowed at no additional fee. Dogs may not be left unattended, and they must be on no more than a 6 foot leash, and cleaned up after. Dogs are not allowed in swim areas, however they are allowed on the trails. There is only one site that has an electric hook-ups. The camping and tent areas also allow dogs. There is a dog walk area at the

campground. There are no electric or water hookups at the campground. Multiple dogs may be allowed.

Holiday Trav-L-Park Resort
9102 Coast Guard Road
Emerald Isle, NC
252-354-2250
htpresort.com
Dogs of all sizes are allowed. There is a $5 per night per pet additional fee. Dogs must be leashed and cleaned up after. This RV park is closed during the off-season. There is a dog walk area at the campground. Multiple dogs may be allowed.

Enfield/Rocky Mount KOA
101 Bell Acres
Enfield, NC
252-445-5925 (800-562-5894)
koa.com
Dogs of all sizes are allowed, and there are no additional pet fees for tent or RV sites. There is a $2 per night per pet additional fee for the cabins. Dogs may not be left unattended in the cabins or outside, and they must be leashed and cleaned up after. There are some breed restrictions. The camping and tent areas also allow dogs. There is a dog walk area at the campground. Dogs are allowed in the camping cabins. Multiple dogs may be allowed.

Lakewood RV Resort
915 Ballenger Road
Flat Rock, NC
888-819-4200
lakewoodrvresort.com
Dogs of all sizes are allowed. There are no additional pet fees. Dogs are not allowed at any of the rentals, the clubhouse, or in any of the buildings. Dogs may not be left unattended, and they must be leashed and cleaned up after. There is a dog walk area at the campground. 2 dogs may be allowed.

Jellystone Park
170 Rutledge Road
Fletcher, NC
828-654-7873 (800-368-3209)
rutledgelake.com/
Located on the shores of Rutledge Lake in a wooded setting, this family-style resort offers a beautiful nature trail, pedal boat/canoe rentals, a heated swimming pool, theme weekends, a laundry, and a country store. Dogs are allowed for no additional fee. Dogs may not be

left unattended outside, and they may only be left alone inside if they will be quiet. They must be leashed and cleaned up after at all times, and they are not allowed in any of the rental units. Dogs are not allowed on the beach or at the playground. There are some breed restrictions. The camping and tent areas also allow dogs. There is a dog walk area at the campground. 2 dogs may be allowed.

Charlotte/Fort Mill KOA
940 Gold Hill Road
Fort Mill, NC
803-548-1148 (888-562-4430)
charlottekoa.com
Dogs of all sizes are allowed. There are no additional pet fees. Dogs may not be left unattended, and they must be leashed and cleaned up after. The camping and tent areas also allow dogs. There is a dog walk area at the campground. Multiple dogs may be allowed.

Frisco Woods Campground
53124 H 12
Frisco, NC
800-948-3942
outer-banks.com/friscowoods
Dogs of all sizes are allowed. There is an additional $5 one time fee per pet. Dogs may not be left unattended, and they must be leashed and cleaned up after. This RV park is closed during the off-season. The camping and tent areas also allow dogs. There is a dog walk area at the campground. Dogs are allowed in the camping cabins. Multiple dogs may be allowed.

Merchants Millpond State Park
71 H 158E/Millpond Road
Gatesville, NC
252-357-1191
A rare ecological setting of coastal pond and southern swamp forest gives this park the look of an enchanted forest and it provides a wide variety of habitats for wildlife, an abundance of land and water recreation, educational opportunities, and more. Dogs are allowed throughout the park and on the trails; they are also allowed on the canoe rentals. Dogs may not be left alone at any time, and they must be well mannered, on no more than a 6 foot leash, and cleaned up after at all times. The camp sites are first come first served and each have picnic tables and grills with seasonally supplied water, restroom, and showers. The camping and tent areas also allow dogs. There is a

dog walk area at the campground. There are no electric or water hookups at the campgrounds. Multiple dogs may be allowed.

Cape Lookout National Seashore
131 Charles Street
Harkers Island, NC
252-728-2250
nps.gov/calo/
Although isolated, the natural and historic features provide an incentive to visit Cape Lookout. It offers interpretive programs, a lighthouse complex, and a variety of land and water activities and recreation. This park is either reached by private boat or by ferry. One of three ferries runs all year, the Local Yocal Ferry. Dogs may ride the ferry for an additional $6 fee per pet and dogs must be leashed at all times. Dogs of all sizes are allowed at no additional fee. Dogs may not be left unattended, and they must be on no more than a 6 foot leash, and cleaned up after. The camping and tent areas also allow dogs. There is a dog walk area at the campground. There are no electric or water hookups at the campground. 2 dogs may be allowed.

Hatteras Sands
57316 Eagle Pass Road
Hatteras Village, NC
252-986-2422
hatterassands.com
Dogs of all sizes are allowed. There is a $2 per night per pet additional fee. Dogs may not be left unattended, and they must be leashed and cleaned up after. This RV park is closed during the off-season. The camping and tent areas also allow dogs. There is a dog walk area at the campground. Dogs are allowed in the camping cabins. Multiple dogs may be allowed.

Kerr Lake State Rec Area
6254 Satterwhite Point Road
Henderson, NC
252-438-7791
This park touts a 50,000-acre man-made lake with many miles of wooded shoreline and provides a variety of land and water recreation areas, woodlands, trails, and wildlife habitats. Dogs of all sizes are allowed at no additional fee. Dogs may not be left unattended, and they must be on no more than a 6 foot leash at all times, and cleaned up after. Dogs are not allowed in buildings, but they are allowed on the trails. The camping and tent areas also allow dogs. There is a dog walk

area at the campground. Multiple dogs may be allowed.

Nantahala National Forest
2010 Flat Mountain Road
Highlands, NC
828-526-3765
This forest, the largest in the state with over half a million acres, provides over 600 miles of hiking trails, diverse ecosystems that support a large variety of plants, fish, mammals, bird species, and various recreational pursuits. Dogs of all sizes are allowed at no additional fee. Dogs may not be left unattended, and they must be leashed and cleaned up after. Dogs are not allowed in buildings, however, they are allowed on the trails. Dogs are not allowed on the trails in the Great Smokey Mountains National Forest that adjoin the park. The camping and tent areas also allow dogs. There is a dog walk area at the campground. There are no electric or water hookups at the campground. Multiple dogs may be allowed.

Medoc Mountain State Park
1541 Medoc State Park Road/ H 1322
Hollister, NC
252-586-6588
This park is home to a large variety of plant and animal life and offers educational and interpretive programs, 7 different trails, and various recreational pursuits. Dogs of all sizes are allowed at no additional fee. Dogs may not be left unattended except for short periods, and they must be on no more than a 6 foot leash, and cleaned up after. Dogs are not allowed in buildings, but they are allowed on the trails. The camping and tent areas also allow dogs. There is a dog walk area at the campground. Multiple dogs may be allowed.

Linville Falls Campground
Blue Ridge Parkway mile 316.4
Linville Falls, NC
828-765-7818 (877-444-6777)
blueridgeparkway.org/
Although the smallest campground along the parkway, it is one of the most popular with sites all along the waterfront and it is home to one of the most famous waterfalls in the Blue Ridge. The falls offer a spectacular view as they cascade into a deep lush gorge, and trails lead to views of both the upper and lower falls. Dogs are allowed throughout the park and on the

trails. Dogs must be well behaved, under owner's control, on no more than a 6 foot leash, and cleaned up after at all times. This RV park is closed during the off-season. The camping and tent areas also allow dogs. There is a dog walk area at the campground. There are no electric or water hookups at the campgrounds. Multiple dogs may be allowed.

Crabtree Meadows Campground
Blue Ridge Parkway, Milepost 339.5
Little Switzerland, NC
828-765-6082
blueridgeparkway.org/
This 250 acre recreation area has a restaurant, gift shop, large picnic area, nature walks, and a campground with 71 tent and 22 RV sites on a first come first served basis. One of the best viewing times here is in early summer when wildflowers blaze vast lawns of color, and there is a 70 foot falls for those that can do the 2.5 mile (round trip) strenuous hike. Dogs are allowed throughout the park and on the trails. Dogs must be well behaved, under owner's control, on no more than a 6 foot leash, and cleaned up after at all times. This RV park is closed during the off-season. The camping and tent areas also allow dogs. There is a dog walk area at the campground. There are no electric or water hookups at the campgrounds. Multiple dogs may be allowed.

Cape Hatteras National Seashore
1401 National Park Drive
Manteo, NC
252-473-2111
nps.gov/caha/
This park offers a captivating combination of natural and cultural resources. The park is rich in maritime history, is stretched over 70 miles of barrier islands and offers a variety of recreational pursuits. Dogs of all sizes are allowed at no additional fee. Dogs may not be left unattended, and they must be on no more than a 6 foot leash or crated, and cleaned up after. Dogs are not allowed in public swim areas, however, they are allowed on the trails. The camping and tent areas also allow dogs. There is a dog walk area at the campground. There are no electric or water hookups at the campground. 2 dogs may be allowed.

Buck Creek Campground
2576 Toms Creek Road
Marion, NC
828-724-4888

buckcreekcampground.com
Dogs up to 100 pounds are allowed. There are no additional pet fees. Dogs may not be left unattended outside, and they must be leashed and cleaned up after. There are some breed restrictions. This RV park is closed during the off-season. There is a dog walk area at the campground. Multiple dogs may be allowed.

Jellystone Park at Hidden Valley Campground
1210 Deacon Drive
Marion, NC
828-652-7208
jellystonemarion.com/
Dogs of all sizes are allowed. There are no additional pet fees. Dogs must be leashed and cleaned up after. This RV park is closed during the off-season. The camping and tent areas also allow dogs. There is a dog walk area at the campground. Multiple dogs may be allowed.

Lake Meyers RV Resort
2862 H 64W
Mocksville, NC
336-492-7736
rvinthesun.com
Dogs of all sizes are allowed. There are no additional pet fees. Dogs may not be left unattended outside, and they must be quiet, leashed, and cleaned up after. The camping and tent areas also allow dogs. There is a dog walk area at the campground. Multiple dogs may be allowed.

Croatan National Forest
141 E Fisher Street
New Bern, NC
252-393-7352
This park, called the "Land of Many Ecosystems", has various habitats providing for some unusual plant life and a wide range of birds and wildlife. The park also provides interpretive trails, hiking trails and recreational pursuits. Dogs may not be left unattended, and they must be leashed and cleaned up after. Dogs are allowed on the trails. The camping and tent areas also allow dogs. There is a dog walk area at the campground. Multiple dogs may be allowed.

New Bern
1565 B Street
New Bern, NC
252-638-2556 (800-562-3341)
koa.com
Dogs of all sizes are allowed. There are no additional pet fees. Dogs must be leashed and cleaned up

after. There are 2 fenced in areas for off lead. There are some breed restrictions. The camping and tent areas also allow dogs. There is a dog walk area at the campground. Dogs are allowed in the camping cabins. Multiple dogs may be allowed.

Goose Creek Resort
350 Red Barn Road
Newport, NC
866-839-2628
goosecreekcamping.com
Dogs of all sizes are allowed. There are no additional pet fees. Dogs must be leashed and cleaned up after. There are some breed restrictions. There is a dog walk area at the campground. Multiple dogs may be allowed.

Long Beach Campground
5011 E Oak Island Drive
Oak Island, NC
910-278-5737
Dogs of all sizes are allowed. There are no additional pet fees. Dogs must be leashed and cleaned up after. Dogs are allowed at the beach. The camping and tent areas also allow dogs. There is a dog walk area at the campground. Multiple dogs may be allowed.

Rivercamp USA
2221 Kings Creek Road
Piney Creek, NC
336-359-2267
rivercampusa.com
Dogs of all sizes are allowed. There are no additional pet fees. Dogs may not be left unattended outside, and they must be quiet, leashed, and cleaned up after. This RV park is closed during the off-season. The camping and tent areas also allow dogs. There is a dog walk area at the campground. Multiple dogs may be allowed.

Pilot Mountain State Park
1792 Pilot Knob Park Road
Pinnacle, NC
336-352-2355
Dedicated as a National Natural Landmark, this park offers a wide variety of land and water recreational activities. In addition, it has educational and interpretive programs and many miles of scenic hiking trails. Dogs of all sizes are allowed at no additional fee. Dogs may not be left unattended, and they must be on no more than a 6 foot leash, and cleaned up after. Dogs are allowed on the trails. This campground is closed during the

off-season. The camping and tent areas also allow dogs. There is a dog walk area at the campground. There are no electric or water hookups at the campground. Multiple dogs may be allowed.

William B. Umstead State Park
8801 Glenwood Avenue
Raleigh, NC
919-571-4170
Offering educational as well as a wide variety of land and water recreation, this 5,577 acre park has 2 sections with easy access from I 40 and H 70, and provides a "natural" respite from city life. The park is open year round but campers are only allowed from mid-March to mid-December, Thursday 8 am through Monday at 1 pm. Dogs are allowed throughout the park for no additional fee; they are not allowed in boats, buildings, or group camps. Dogs must be on no more than a 6 foot leash and cleaned up after at all times. Campsites are first come first served and offer shaded sites with tables and grills, and drinking water, restrooms, and showers are nearby. This RV park is closed during the off-season. The camping and tent areas also allow dogs. There is a dog walk area at the campground. There are no electric or water hookups at the campgrounds. Multiple dogs may be allowed.

Stone Mountain State Park
3042 Frank Parkway
Roaring Gap, NC
336-957-8185
Designated as a National Natural Landmark in 1975, this park is home to a magnificent 600-foot granite dome, 16 miles of scenic trails, and a variety of recreational pursuits. Dogs of all sizes are allowed at no additional fee. Dogs may not be left unattended, and they must be on no more than a 6 foot leash at all times, and cleaned up after. Dogs are not allowed in buildings, however, they are allowed on the trails. The camping and tent areas also allow dogs. There is a dog walk area at the campground. Multiple dogs may be allowed.

Camp Hatteras Campground
24798 H 12
Rodanthe, NC
252-987-2777
camphatteras.com
Dogs of all sizes are allowed. There is a $2 per night additional pet fee for up to 3 dogs. Dogs are not allowed in the clubhouse, and they may not be

tied to cars, porches, or tables. Dogs may not be left unattended outside, and they must be leashed and cleaned up after. The camping and tent areas also allow dogs. There is a dog walk area at the campground. Multiple dogs may be allowed.

Cape Hatteras KOA
25099 H 12
Rodanthe, NC
252-987-2307 (800-562-5268)
capehatteraskoa.com
Dogs of all sizes are allowed, and there are no additional pet fees for tent or RV sites. There is a $5 one time pet fee for the cabins. Dogs may not be left unattended, and must be leashed and cleaned up after. This RV park is closed during the off-season. The camping and tent areas also allow dogs. There is a dog walk area at the campground. Dogs are allowed in the camping cabins. Multiple dogs may be allowed.

Four Paws Kingdom
335 Lazy Creek Drive
Rutherfordton, NC
828-287-7324
4pawskingdom.com
Dogs of all sizes are allowed, however some breeds are not. There are no additional pet fees, and dogs must be cleaned up after. There are 2 park areas where your dog can run off leash; one for the large dogs and one for the smaller dogs. There is a pond dedicated for dogs and a bath house with a dog grooming area. The camping and tent areas also allow dogs. There is a dog walk area at the campground. Dogs are allowed in the camping cabins. 2 dogs may be allowed.

Gorges State Park
17762 Rosman H
Sapphire, NC
828-966-9099
Although a fairly new park still in development, there is much to enjoy, including waterfalls plunging through rocky river gorges, overlooks, and easy to difficult trails. Primitive backpack camping is available with a 2.7 mile hike to the camp area. Dogs are allowed throughout the park and on the trails. Dogs may not be left unattended, and they must be on no more than a 6 foot leash, and cleaned up after. The camping and tent areas also allow dogs. There is a dog walk area at the campground. There are no electric or water hookups at the campgrounds. Multiple dogs may be allowed.

Selma/Smithfield KOA
428 Campground Road
Selma, NC
919-965-5923 (800-562-5897)
koa.com
Dogs of all sizes are allowed. There are no additional pet fees. Dogs may not be left unattended outside, and they must be in at night. Dogs must be quiet, leashed, and cleaned up after. The camping and tent areas also allow dogs. There is a dog walk area at the campground. Multiple dogs may be allowed.

Cliffs of the Neuse State Park
345A Park Entrance Road
Seven Springs, NC
919-778-6234
Rich in geological and biological history, this park offers a museum, educational and interpretive programs, and a variety of recreational pursuits. Dogs of all sizes are allowed at no additional fee. Dogs may not be left unattended, and they must be on no more than a 6 foot leash, and cleaned up after. Dogs are not allowed in the swim areas or in buildings, however, they are allowed on the trails. The camping and tent areas also allow dogs. There is a dog walk area at the campground. There are no electric or water hookups at the campground. Multiple dogs may be allowed.

Wildlife Woods Campground
4582 Beaver Blvd
Sherrills Ford, NC
704-483-5611
Dogs of all sizes are allowed. There are no additional pet fees. Dogs may not be left unattended, and they must be leashed and cleaned up after. There are some breed restrictions. The camping and tent areas also allow dogs. There is a dog walk area at the campground. Multiple dogs may be allowed.

Doughton Park Campground
Blue Ridge Parkway Milepost 239.2
Sparta, NC
336-372-8568
blueridgeparkway.org/
Located at one of the parkways largest developed areas, this camp area offers 110 tent and 25 RV first come first served sites, a picnicking and concession area, service station, an information center, and a short stroll away is the Wildcat Rocks Overlook and kiosk. There are also more than 30 miles of trails

of varying difficulty and a variety of recreation available. Dogs are allowed throughout the park and on the trails. Dogs must be well behaved, under owner's control, on no more than a 6 foot leash, and cleaned up after at all times. This RV park is closed during the off-season. The camping and tent areas also allow dogs. There is a dog walk area at the campground. There are no electric or water hookups at the campgrounds. Multiple dogs may be allowed.

Statesville KOA
162 KOA Lane
Statesville, NC
704-873-5560 (800-562-5705)
koa.com
Dogs of all sizes are allowed. There are no additional pet fees. Dogs may not be left unattended, and they must be quiet, leashed, and cleaned up after. There are some breed restrictions. The camping and tent areas also allow dogs. There is a dog walk area at the campground. Multiple dogs may be allowed.

Shallotte/Brunswick Beaches KOA
7200 KOA Drive
Sunset Beach, NC
910-579-7562 (888-562-4240)
koa.com
Dogs of all sizes are allowed. There are no additional pet fees. Dogs may not be left unattended, and they must be up to date on shots, leashed, and cleaned up after. The camping and tent areas also allow dogs. There is a dog walk area at the campground. Multiple dogs may be allowed.

Asheville East KOA
2708 H 70 E
Swannanoa, NC
828-686-3121 (800-562-5907)
koa.com/where/nc/33116/
Dogs of all sizes are allowed. There are no additional pet fees. Dogs may not be left unattended, and they must be quiet, leashed, and cleaned up after. The camping and tent areas also allow dogs. There is a dog walk area at the campground. Dogs are allowed in the camping cabins. Multiple dogs may be allowed.

Mama Gerties Hideaway Campground
15 Uphill Road
Swannanoa, NC
828-686-4258
mamagerties.com
Dogs of all sizes are allowed, and there are no additional pet fees for tent or RV sites. There is a $5 per

night per pet additional fee for the cabins. Dogs may not be left unattended, and they must be quiet, well behaved, leashed, and cleaned up after. There are some breed restrictions. The camping and tent areas also allow dogs. There is a dog walk area at the campground. Dogs are allowed in the camping cabins. 2 dogs may be allowed.

Yogi Bear's Jellystone Park Resort @ Daddy Joe's
626 Richard Wright Road
Tabor City, NC
910-653-2155 (877-668-8586)
taborcityjellystone.com
Dogs of all sizes are allowed. There are no additional pet fees. Dogs must be leashed and cleaned up after. The camping and tent areas also allow dogs. There is a dog walk area at the campground. Multiple dogs may be allowed.

Lake Norman State Park
159 Inland Sea Lane
Troutman, NC
704-528-6350
Located along the state's largest manmade lake, this park supports a wide variety of plant and animal life, provides educational and interpretive programs, and various land and water activities. Dogs of all sizes are allowed at no additional fee. Dogs may not be left unattended, and they must be on no more than a 6 foot leash, and cleaned up after. Dogs are not allowed in public swim areas or buildings, and they must be in your unit at night. Dogs are allowed on the trails. This campground is closed during the off-season. The camping and tent areas also allow dogs. There is a dog walk area at the campground. There are no electric or water hookups at the campground. Multiple dogs may be allowed.

Uwharrie National Forest
789 H 24/27E
Troy, NC
910-576-6391
cs.unca.edu/nfsnc/
This forest's diverse ecosystems support a large variety of plants, fish, mammals, bird species, trails, and recreation. Dogs of all sizes are allowed at no additional fee. Dogs may not be left unattended, and they must be leashed and cleaned up after. Dogs are not allowed in buildings. Dogs are allowed on the trails. The camping and tent areas also allow dogs. There is a dog walk area at the campground. There are no water hookups at the

campground. Multiple dogs may be allowed.

Fayetteville/Wade KOA
6250 Wade Stedman Road
Wade, NC
910-484-5500 (800-562-5350)
koa.com
Dogs of all sizes are allowed, and there are no additional pet fees for tent or RV sites. There is a $4 nightly pet fee for the cabins and pets are only allowed in one cabin, so be sure and call ahead. Leashed pets are allowed to be walked throughout the campground which also has a fenced off-leash area. Dogs may not be left unattended, and must be quiet, leashed, and cleaned up after. The camping and tent areas also allow dogs. Multiple dogs may be allowed.

Falls Lake State Park
13304 Creedmoor Road (H 50)
Wake Forest, NC
919-676-1027
This park of 26,000 acres of woodlands with a 12,000-acre lake, offers educational and interpretive programs, trails with access to the Mountains-to-Sea Trail, and a variety of land and water activities and recreation. Dogs of all sizes are allowed at no additional fee. Dogs may not be left unattended, and they must be on no more than a 6 foot leash, and cleaned up after. Dogs are not allowed in swim areas or in buildings, however, they are allowed on the trails. The camping and tent areas also allow dogs. There is a dog walk area at the campground. Multiple dogs may be allowed.

Mount Pisgah Campground
Blue Ride Parkway Milepost 408.6
Waynesville, NC
828-648-2644 (877-444-6777)
blueridgeparkway.org/
Once part of the Vanderbilt estate, this camp area offers seclusion, the highest and coolest location on the Parkway, an interesting example of a southern Appalachian bog and its ecosystems, an extensive trail system, and outstanding views. Dogs are allowed throughout the park and on the trails. Dogs must be well behaved, under owner's control, on no more than a 6 foot leash, and cleaned up after at all times. This RV park is closed during the off-season. The camping and tent areas also allow dogs. There is a dog walk area at the campground. There are no electric or water

hookups at the campgrounds. Multiple dogs may be allowed.

North Dakota

Turtle River State Park
3084 Park Avenue
Arvilla, ND
701-594-4445 (800-807-4723)
ndparks.com/parks/trsp.htm
Turtle River offers 784 acres in a scenic wooded valley along a popular stocked river. There are year around trails and recreation. Dogs are allowed for no additional fee. They must be well behaved, kept in a secure enclosure or on a leash no more than 6 feet, and cleaned up after at all times. Dogs are not allowed in buildings, designated swim areas, playgrounds, or where posted, and they may not be tied to trees or plants or left unattended. The campground offers 125 sites, picnic tables, fire pits, comfort stations, showers, a playground, an amphitheatre, a park store, and a dump station. This RV park is closed during the off-season. The camping and tent areas also allow dogs. There is a dog walk area at the campground. There are no water hookups at the campgrounds. Multiple dogs may be allowed.

Bismarck KOA
3720 Centennial Road
Bismarck, ND
701-222-2662 (800-562-2636)
koa.com
Dogs of all sizes are allowed. There are no additional pet fees. Dogs must be leashed and cleaned up after. This RV park is closed during the off-season. The camping and tent areas also allow dogs. There is a dog walk area at the campground. Dogs are allowed in the camping cabins. Multiple dogs may be allowed.

Lake Metigoshe State Park
#2 Lake Metigoshe State Park
Bottineau, ND
701-263-4651 (800-807-4723)
ndparks.com/parks/lmsp.htm
Translated from the Chippewa to mean "clear water lake surrounded by oaks" is a good description for one of the states most popular parks. There are 1,551 acres for recreation, nature viewing, hiking, photography, and more. Dogs are allowed for no additional fee. They must be well

behaved, kept in a secure enclosure or on a leash no more than 6 feet, and cleaned up after at all times. Dogs are not allowed in buildings, designated swim areas, playgrounds, or where posted, and they may not be tied to trees or plants or left unattended. The campground offers 130 sites, picnic tables, fire pits, comfort stations, showers, a playground, an amphitheater, and a dump station. This RV park is closed during the off-season. The camping and tent areas also allow dogs. There is a dog walk area at the campground. Dogs are allowed in the camping cabins. There are no water hookups at the campgrounds. Multiple dogs may be allowed.

Governor's RV Park and Campground
2050 Governor's Drive
Casselton, ND
701-347-4524 (888-847-4524)
governorsinnnd.com/
Dogs of all sizes are allowed. There are no additional pet fees for the tent or RV sites. There is a $9 per night per pet additional fee for the hotel, which is open year around. Dogs may not be left unattended outside, and they must be leashed and cleaned up after. Dogs may be kenned when out of the hotel room if they will be quiet. This RV park is closed during the off-season. The camping and tent areas also allow dogs. There is a dog walk area at the campground. 2 dogs may be allowed.

Icelandic State Park
13571 H 5
Cavalier, ND
701-265-4561 (800-807-4723)
ndparks.com/parks/isp.htm
Water sports/activities are a favorite at this 912 acre park. The park has a Pioneer Heritage Center, restored historic buildings, and it is also home to the Gunlogson Homestead and Nature Preserve. Dogs are allowed for no additional fee. They must be well behaved, kept in a secure enclosure or on a leash no more than 6 feet, and cleaned up after at all times. Dogs are not allowed in buildings, at the beach, playgrounds, or where posted, and they may not be tied to trees or plants or left unattended. The campground offers 159 sites, picnic tables, fire pits, comfort stations, showers, a playground, an amphitheater, and a dump station. This RV park is closed during the off-season. The camping and tent areas also allow dogs.

There is a dog walk area at the campground. There are no water hookups at the campgrounds. Multiple dogs may be allowed.

Grahams Island State Park
152 S. Duncan Road
Devils Lake, ND
701-766-4015 (800-807-4723)
ndparks.com/parks/DLSP.htm
This scenic park of over 1,100 acres on the shores of Devil's Lake offers an activity center, miles of trails, and a variety of land and water recreation. Dogs of all sizes are allowed at no additional fee. Dogs may not be left unattended anywhere, including vehicles, and they must have current tags and rabies shot records. Dogs must be quiet, well behaved, on no more than a 6 foot leash or crated, and be cleaned up after. Dogs may not be tied to any native vegetation or camp property, and digging is not allowed. Dogs are not allowed in public swim areas, the playground, or any buildings. Dogs are allowed on the trails, except the ski trails in winter. There are some breed restrictions. The camping and tent areas also allow dogs. There is a dog walk area at the campground. There are no water hookups at the campground. Multiple dogs may be allowed.

Woodland Resort
1012 Woodland Drive
Devils Lake, ND
701-662-5996
woodlandresort.com
Dogs of all sizes are allowed. There are no additional pet fees for tent or RV sites. There is a $10 per night per pet, or $50 per week per pet, additional fee for the lodge, motel, or cabins. Dogs may not be left unattended, and they must be leashed and cleaned up after. The camping and tent areas also allow dogs. There is a dog walk area at the campground. Dogs are allowed in the camping cabins. Multiple dogs may be allowed.

Patterson Lake Recreation Area
H 10
Dickinson, ND
701-456-2056
This recreation area offers 1,438 acres on an 819 acre lake that offers 26 miles of shoreline. In addition to a number of recreations, this park is also host to concerts and other special events. Dogs are allowed; they must be leashed and picked up after at all times. Dogs

are not allowed on the beach. The campground has more than 60 sites, picnic tables, restrooms, and a playground. The camping and tent areas also allow dogs. There is a dog walk area at the campground. 2 dogs may be allowed.

International Peace Garden
RR 1, Box 116/H 3
Dunseith, ND
701-263-4390 (888-432-6733)
peacegarden.com
Located at the amazing one-of-a-kind 2,339 acre International Peace Garden Park (please see Attractions), this camp area features a beautiful setting, modern comfort stations with showers, a gift shop, an emergency weather shelter for periods of extreme weather, and a dump station. Campsites are first come, first served. Dogs are allowed for no additional fee; they must be leashed and cleaned up after at all times. The camping and tent areas also allow dogs. There is a dog walk area at the campground. 2 dogs may be allowed.

Lewis and Clark State Park
4904 119th Road NW
Epping, ND
701-859-3071 (800-807-4723)
ndparks.com/parks/LCSP.htm
This 490 acre park on the shores of Lake Sakakawea offers an extensive trail system and a variety of land and water recreation. Dogs of all sizes are allowed at no additional fee. Dogs may not be left unattended anywhere, including vehicles, and they must have current tags and rabies shot records. Dogs must be quiet, well behaved, on no more than a 6 foot leash or crated, and be cleaned up after. Dogs may not be tied to any native vegetation or camp property, and digging is not allowed. Dogs are not allowed in public swim areas, the playground, or any buildings. Dogs are allowed on the trails, except the ski trails in winter. The camping and tent areas also allow dogs. There is a dog walk area at the campground. There are no water hookups at the campground. Multiple dogs may be allowed.

Lindenwood Campground
1905 Roger Maris Drive S
Fargo, ND
701-232-3987
In addition to camp amenities such as picnic tables, fire pits, modern restrooms and showers, and scenic hiking trails, this popular wooded campground is also home to a

Universal Playground-accessible to all children and it is the only playground of this scale in the region. Dogs are allowed throughout the park; they must be leashed and under their owner's control. This RV park is closed during the off-season. The camping and tent areas also allow dogs. There is a dog walk area at the campground. Multiple dogs may be allowed.

Fort Ransom State Park
5981 Walt Hjelle Parkway/H 3715
Fort Ransom, ND
701-973-4331 (800-807-4723)
ndparks.com/parks/frsp.htm
There are 887 recreational acres at this popular forested park located along the Sheyenne River. The park safeguards the states homesteading heritage with a farmstead on site, and it is located on a state designated Scenic Byway and Backways. Dogs are allowed for no additional fee. They must be well behaved, kept in a secure enclosure or on a leash no more than 6 feet, and cleaned up after at all times. Dogs are not allowed in buildings, designated swim areas, playgrounds, or where posted, and they may not be tied to trees or plants or left unattended. The campground offers picnic tables, fire pits, comfort stations, vault toilets, showers, a playground, an amphitheater, and a dump station. The camping and tent areas also allow dogs. There is a dog walk area at the campground. There are no water hookups at the campgrounds. Multiple dogs may be allowed.

Fort Stevenson State Park
1252 A 41st Avenue NW
Garrison, ND
701-337-5576 (800-807-4723)
ndparks.com/parks/fssp.htm
This 438 acre park on Lake Sakakawea offers an arboretum, prairie dog town, interpretive trails, planned activities, and various land and water recreation. Dogs of all sizes are allowed at no additional fee. Dogs may not be left unattended anywhere, including vehicles, and they must have current tags and rabies shot records. Dogs must be quiet, well behaved, on no more than a 6 foot leash or crated, and be cleaned up after. Dogs may not be tied to any native vegetation or camp property, and digging is not allowed. Dogs are not allowed in public swim areas, the playground, or any buildings. Dogs are allowed on the trails, except the ski trails in winter.

This campground is closed during the off-season. The camping and tent areas also allow dogs. There is a dog walk area at the campground. There are no water hookups at the campground. Multiple dogs may be allowed.

Indian Hills Resort
7302 14th Street NW
Garrison, ND
701-743-4122
indianhillsnd.com
Dogs of all sizes are allowed. There are no additional pet fees. Dogs may not be left unattended, and they must be quiet, well behaved, leashed and cleaned up after. Dogs may be off lead when no other people are around and you have them under voice control. This RV park is closed during the off-season. The camping and tent areas also allow dogs. There is a dog walk area at the campground. Multiple dogs may be allowed.

Grand Forks Campground
4796 S 42nd Street
Grand Forks, ND
701-772-6108
grandforkscampground.com
Dogs of all sizes are allowed. There are no additional pet fees. Dogs must be leashed and cleaned up after. There are some breed restrictions. This RV park is closed during the off-season. The camping and tent areas also allow dogs. There is a dog walk area at the campground. Multiple dogs may be allowed.

Frontier Fort Campground
1838 3rd Avenue SE
Jamestown, ND
701-252-7492
Dogs of all sizes are allowed. There are no additional pet fees. Dogs must be quiet, well behaved, leashed, and cleaned up after. The camping and tent areas also allow dogs. There is a dog walk area at the campground. Multiple dogs may be allowed.

Jamestown Campground
3605 80th Avenue
Jamestown, ND
701-252-6262
gocampingamerica.com
Dogs of all sizes are allowed. There are no additional pet fees. Dogs must be quiet, well behaved, leashed and cleaned up after. This RV park is closed during the off-season. The camping and tent areas also allow dogs. There is a

dog walk area at the campground. Multiple dogs may be allowed.

Lakeside Marina
223 E Lakeside Road
Jamestown, ND
701-252-1183
co.stutsman.nd.us/cntyparks.html
Located on the east side of the 2,095 acre Jamestown Reservoir with 45 miles of shoreline, this scenic camp area offers a variety of recreation, concessionaires, showers, a playground, fishing pier, and more. Quiet dogs are allowed for no additional fee; they must be leashed and cleaned up after at all times. Dogs are not allowed in the swimming beach area. This RV park is closed during the off-season. The camping and tent areas also allow dogs. There is a dog walk area at the campground. Multiple dogs may be allowed.

Pelican Point
8310 28th Street SE
Jamestown, ND
701-252-1451
co.stutsman.nd.us/cntyparks.html
Located on the west side of the 2,095 acre Jamestown Reservoir with 45 miles of shoreline, this scenic camp area offers a variety of recreation, concessionaires, showers, a playground, fishing pier, and more. Dogs are allowed for no additional fee; they must be leashed and cleaned up after at all times. Dogs are not allowed in the swimming beach area. This RV park is closed during the off-season. The camping and tent areas also allow dogs. There is a dog walk area at the campground. Multiple dogs may be allowed.

Fort Abraham Lincoln State Park
4480 Ft. Lincoln Road
Mandan, ND
701-667-6340 (800-807-4723)
ndparks.com/parks/flsp.htm
In preserving the rich military and cultural heritage of this 1,006 acre park, there are reconstructed 1575-1781 earth-lodges from the Mandan tribe and reconstructed historic buildings of this fort that Lt. Col. George Custer rode from to the Little Big Horn. Throughout the summer there are interpretive programs and special events. Dogs are allowed for no additional fee. They must be well behaved, kept in a secure enclosure or on a leash no more than 6 feet, and cleaned up after at all times. Dogs are not allowed in buildings, designated swim areas, playgrounds,

or where posted, and they may not be tied to trees or plants or left unattended. The campground offers 95 sites, picnic tables, fire pits, comfort stations, showers, a playground, an amphitheater, and a dump station. The camping and tent areas also allow dogs. There is a dog walk area at the campground. There are no water hookups at the campgrounds. Multiple dogs may be allowed.

Sully Creek State Recreation Area
Off E River Road South
Medora, ND
701-667-6340 (800-807-4723)
ndparks.com/parks/scsp.htm
This 80 acre park sets deep in the North Dakota badlands along the states only designated scenic river-giving canoeing visitors interesting views of this unique area. There is also access to the 120 mile long Maah Daah Hey Trail. Dogs are allowed for no additional fee. They must be well behaved, kept in a secure enclosure or on a leash no more than 6 feet, and cleaned up after at all times. Dogs are not allowed in buildings, designated swim areas, playgrounds, or where posted, and they may not be tied to trees or plants or left unattended. The campground has 33, first come first served sites and vault toilets. This RV park is closed during the off-season. The camping and tent areas also allow dogs. There is a dog walk area at the campground. There are no electric or water hookups at the campgrounds. Multiple dogs may be allowed.

Theodore Roosevelt National Park
Park Road (South Unit)
Medora, ND
701-623-4730 ext. 3417 (800-807-4723)
nps.gov/thro/
The Little Missouri River Badlands sets a colorful background for this park that memorializes the country's 26th President's long-lasting contributions for resource conservation. His first home (the Maltese Cross Cabin) is also located at the park. The North Unit is on H 85. Dogs are allowed for no additional fee in the campground, the picnic areas, at the overlooks along side the road, and in parking areas. Dogs are not allowed on the trails; they must be leashed and under their owner's control at all times. Campsites are available on a first come, first served basis; there are 2 camp areas (126 sites) plus an

equestrian campsite. There are picnic tables, grills, restrooms, and potable water provided. The camping and tent areas also allow dogs. There is a dog walk area at the campground. There are no electric or water hookups at the campgrounds.

Casa Motel and Campground
1900 H 2 and H 52 Bypass
Minot, ND
701-852-2352
There are 13 first come, first served sites at this camp area. Dogs are allowed in the campground for no additional fee; they are not allowed in the motel. Dogs must be leashed and under their owner's control. This RV park is closed during the off-season. The camping and tent areas also allow dogs. There is a dog walk area at the campground. Multiple dogs may be allowed.

KOA - Minot
5261 H 52E
Minot, ND
701-839-7400 (800-562-7421)
koa.com
Dogs of all sizes are allowed. There are no additional pet fees. Dogs must be leashed and cleaned up after. This RV park is closed during the off-season. The camping and tent areas also allow dogs. There is a dog walk area at the campground. Multiple dogs may be allowed.

Roughrider Campground
500 54th Street NW
Minot, ND
701-852-8442
minot.com/~roughrid
Dogs of all sizes are allowed. There are no additional pet fees. Dogs may not be left unattended, and must be leashed and cleaned up after. This RV park is closed during the off-season. There is a dog walk area at the campground. Multiple dogs may be allowed.

Spirit Lake Casino and Resort
7889 H 57
St Michael, ND
701-766-4747
spiritlakecasino.com
Dogs of all sizes are allowed, and there are no additional pet fees for tent or RV sites. There is a $25 per stay per pet additional fee for the lodge. Dogs must be leashed and cleaned up after. The camping and tent areas also allow dogs. There is a dog walk area at the campground. Multiple dogs may be allowed.

Campground at Red River Valley Fair
1201 Main Ave W
West Fargo, ND
701-282-2200 (800-456-6408)
Located on the grounds of the Red River Valley Fair, this campground has 12 asphalt pads/68 gravel sites on a first come first served basis; picnic tables, restrooms, and showers. Dogs are allowed on site; they must be well behaved, leashed or otherwise restrained, and picked up after at all times. This RV park is closed during the off-season. The camping and tent areas also allow dogs. There is a dog walk area at the campground. Multiple dogs may be allowed.

Prairie Acres RV Park
13853 H 2W
Williston, ND
701-572-4860
Dogs of all sizes are allowed. There are no additional pet fees. Dogs may not be left unattended, and must be leashed and cleaned up after. This RV park is closed during the off-season. There is a dog walk area at the campground. Multiple dogs may be allowed.

Ohio

Stonelick State Park
3294 Elk Lake Road
Afton, OH
513-734-4323
Dogs of all sizes are allowed. There are no additional pet fees. Dogs may not be left unattended at any time, they must be on no more than a 6 foot leash, and be cleaned up after. Dogs must be walked in the designated pet section of the park, and they are not allowed on the beaches, or in any of the park buildings. Dogs must be quiet and well behaved. The camping and tent areas also allow dogs. There is a dog walk area at the campground. 2 dogs may be allowed.

Portage Lakes State Park Campground
5031 Manchester Road
Akron, OH
330-644-2220
The campground at this state park offers 74 sites with no electric hookups. Campground amenities include vault latrines, a dump station and nearby hiking trails. Up to two

dogs per pet campsite are allowed and they must be leashed and cleaned up after.

Pymatuning State Park Campground
6260 Pymatuning Lake Road
Andover, OH
440-293-6030
The campground at this state park offers tent and trailer camping with 349 sites with electrical hookups and 21 sites with no electricity. Campground amenities include heated shower houses, flush toilets, laundry facilities, playgrounds, basketball and volleyball courts, and nearby hiking trails. Up to two dogs per pet campsite are allowed and they must be leashed and cleaned up after.

Strouds Run State Park Campground
11661 State Park Road
Athens, OH
740-592-2302
The campground at this state park offers 75 non-electric camp sites for tents or trailers. Campground amenities include toilets, waste drains, picnic tables, fire rings and nearby hiking trails and lake. Up to two dogs per pet campsite are allowed and they must be leashed and cleaned up after.

Paint Creek State Park Campground
14265 US Route 50
Bainbridge, OH
937-365-1401
The campground at this state park offers 195 sites with electric hookups. Campground amenities include hot showers, flush toilets, laundry facilities, a dump station and nearby hiking trails and swimming. Up to two dogs per pet campsite are allowed and they must be leashed and cleaned up after.

Pike Lake State Park
1847 Pike Lake Road
Bainbridge, OH
740-493-2212
The campground at this state park offers 80 sites with electric hookups. Campground amenities include toilets, tables, fire rings, camp store, a dump station and nearby hiking trails. Up to two dogs per pet campsite are allowed and they must be leashed and cleaned up after.

Clearwater Lake Campgrounds
2845 State Route 50
Batavia, OH
513-625-9893
country-campers.com/
This campground offers over 65 sites with full hookups and tent sites along the lake. Amenities include a bath and laundry house, playground, shelter and fishing lake. Pets are welcome but need to be leashed and cleaned up after. The campground is open from the beginning of April through the end of October.

East Fork State Park
2837 Old State Park
Batavia, OH
513-724-6521
dnr.state.oh.us/parks/lodging/
Dogs of all sizes are allowed. There are no additional pet fees. Dogs may not be left unattended, and they must have a current rabies certificate and shot records. Dogs must be quiet during quiet hours, be well behaved, on no more than a 6 foot leash, and be cleaned up after. Dogs are allowed on the trails, but not on the beach or in the water. Dogs must stay in the pet designated areas. This campground is closed during the off-season. The camping and tent areas also allow dogs. There is a dog walk area at the campground. 2 dogs may be allowed.

Baylor Beach Park Family Camping
8725 Manchester Avenue SW
Baylor, OH
888-922-9567
baylorbeachpark.com
Dogs up to about 60 pounds are allowed. There are no additional pet fees. Dogs must be leashed and cleaned up after. Dogs are not allowed at the waterpark or the beach. There are some breed restrictions. This RV park is closed during the off-season. The camping and tent areas also allow dogs. There is a dog walk area at the campground. 2 dogs may be allowed.

Jellystone Park
6500 Black Road
Bellville, OH
419-886-CAMP (2267)
jellystonemansfield.com
Dogs of all sizes are allowed. There are no additional pet fees. Dogs must be leashed and cleaned up after. There are some breed restrictions. This RV park is closed during the off-season. The camping and tent areas also allow dogs. There is a dog walk area at the campground. Dogs are allowed in the camping cabins. 2 dogs may be allowed.

Barkcamp State Park Campground
65330 Barkamp Road
Belmont, OH
740-484-4064
The campground at this state park offers 125 shaded and sunny sites with electrical hookups. Campground amenities include hot showers, tables, fire rings, two wheelchair accessible sites, a dump station and nearby hiking trails and lake. Up to two dogs per pet campsite are allowed and they must be leashed and cleaned up after.

Top O' The Caves Campground
26780 Chapel Ridge Road
Bloomingdale, OH
800-967-2434
topothecaves.com
Dogs of all sizes are allowed, and there are no additional pet fees for tent or RV sites which are open only for the season. There is a $25 one time fee per pet additional fee for the cabins, which are open all year. Dogs must be leashed and cleaned up after. This RV park is closed during the off-season. The camping and tent areas also allow dogs. There is a dog walk area at the campground. Dogs are allowed in the camping cabins. 2 dogs may be allowed.

Muskingum River State Park
7924 Cutler Lake Road
Blue Rock, OH
740-674-4794
The campground at this state park offers 20 sites and pets are allowed in the camping area at Ellis. Campground amenities water, toilets, fire rings, and picnic tables. Up to two dogs per pet campsite are allowed and they must be leashed and cleaned up after.

Dayton KOA
7796 Wellbaum Road
Brookville, OH
937-833-3888 (800-562-3317)
daytonkoa.com
Dogs of all sizes are allowed. There are no additional pet fees. Dogs must be quiet, well behaved, leashed, and cleaned up after. There are some breed restrictions. This RV park is closed during the off-season. The camping and tent areas also allow dogs. There is a dog walk area at the campground. Dogs are allowed in the camping cabins. Multiple dogs may be allowed.

Buckeye Lake/Columbus East KOA
4460 Walnut Road
Buckeye Lake, OH

740-928-0706 (800-562-0792)
koa.com
Dogs of all sizes are allowed. There are no additional pet fees. Dogs may not be left unattended, be on no more than a 6 foot leash, and cleaned up after. There is a large fenced in area where dogs can run off lead. There are some breed restrictions. This RV park is closed during the off-season. The camping and tent areas also allow dogs. There is a dog walk area at the campground. 2 dogs may be allowed.

Butler/Mohican KOA
6918 Bunker Hills Road S
Butler, OH
419-883-3314 (800-562-8719)
butlermohican.koa.com
Dogs of all sizes are allowed. There is a $5 per pet per stay additional fee. Dogs must be well behaved, leashed, and cleaned up after. There are some breed restrictions. This RV park is closed during the off-season. The camping and tent areas also allow dogs. There is a dog walk area at the campground. Dogs are allowed in the camping cabins. Multiple dogs may be allowed.

Wolf Run State Park Campground
16170 Wolf Run Road
Caldwell, OH
740-732-5035
The campground at this state park offers 71 sites with electrical hookups and 67 without electric. Campground amenities include showers, toilets, laundry facilities and nearby hiking trails. Up to two dogs per pet campsite are allowed and they must be leashed and cleaned up after.

Hillview Acres Campground
66271 Wolfs Den Road
Cambridge, OH
740-439-3348
Amenities include water and electrical hookups, dump station, free showers, playgrounds, nearby hiking and a camping cabin. The campground is open from mid-April to the end of October. Pets are welcome but must be leashed and cleaned up after. There are no pet fees.

Spring Valley Campground
8000 Dozer Road
Cambridge, OH
740-439-9291
Dogs of all sizes are allowed. There are no additional pet fees. Dogs must be leashed and cleaned up

after. The camping and tent areas also allow dogs. There is a dog walk area at the campground. Multiple dogs may be allowed.

Forest Haven Campground
2342 Walnut Creek Road
Chillicothe, OH
740-774-1203
foresthavencampground.com/
This campground is open year round and offers spacious shaded sites. Both full hookup and primitive sites are available. Campground amenities include flush toilets, hot showers, TV/VCR/Video rentals, laundry facility, two playgrounds, bike rentals, swim area, camp store, paddle boats, small fishing lake, horseshoe pit, game room, dump station, book exchange, Halloween camp out, basketball court, Internet access and tent rentals. Pets are allowed but need to be leashed and cleaned up after. There is no pet fee.

Great Seal State Park Campground
635 Rocky Road
Chillicothe, OH
866-644-6727
The campground at this state park offers 15 campsites with pressurized water, vault latrines, a playground and a shelterhouse. The campground is located adjacent to Sugarloaf Mountain. Amenities include nearby hiking trails. Up to two dogs per campsite are allowed and they must be leashed and cleaned up after. To get there from Columbus, take U.S. 23 South through Circleville 17 miles to the Delano Exit. Follow the signs to the park. The park is located 3 miles east off of U.S. 23.

A.W. Marion State Park Campground
7317 Warner-Huffer Road
Circleville, OH
740-869-3124
The campground at this state park offers 58 wooded sites for tents and trailers. Twenty-nine of the sites have electrical hookups. Campground amenities include toilets, water and nearby hiking trails. Up to two dogs per pet campsite are allowed and they must be leashed and cleaned up after.

Hueston Woods State Park Campground
6301 Park Office Road
College Corner, OH
513-523-6347
The campground at this state park

offers 252 sites with electrical hookups and 236 sites with no electric. Campground amenities include showers, flush toilets, laundry, a trailer waste station and nearby hiking trails. Up to two dogs per pet campsite are allowed and they must be leashed and cleaned up after.

Evergreen Lake Park Campground
703 Center Road
Conneaut, OH
440-599-8802
evergreenlake.com
This 70 acre campground offers over 250 campsites with water and electric hookups, many with full hookups. Amenities include flush toilets, sinks, hot showers, tables, fire rings, public phones, RV parts and service department, snack bar, pizza shop, pool tables, video games, playgrounds, Sunday Church services, shuffleboard, tetherball, horseshoe pits, sand volleyball court and mini golf. Pets are allowed but need to be leashed and cleaned up after. There is no pet fee. The campground is open from the beginning of May to mid-October.

Mosquito Lake State Park Campground
1439 State Route 305
Cortland, OH
330-637-2856
The campground at this state park offers 234 sites of which 218 sites have electric hookups. The majority of camp sites are located in a mature forest and the rest of the sites offer lakeshore access and vistas. Campground amenities include a shower building, flush toilets and nearby hiking trails and swimming. Up to two dogs per pet campsite are allowed and they must be leashed and cleaned up after.

Miami Whitewater Forest Campground
various entrances
Crosby, OH
513-521-PARK
hamiltoncountyparks.org
Open from the beginning of March to late October, this campground offers 46 electric sites which cost about $18 per night per site. Campground amenities include parking pads, fire rings, picnic tables, shower building, dump facility and nearby hiking trails. Pets are allowed but must be on a 6 foot or less leash, under control, and picked up after. Pooper scooper dispensers are located at each trailhead and are available from the

Park District Rangers. To get to the park, take I-74 to Dry Fork Road exit, turn right on Dry Fork Road, turn right on West Road to the park entrance. The park is also accessible from Route 128 to Mt. Hope Road.

Alum Creek State Park
Campgrounds
3615 S. Old State Road
Delaware, OH
740-548-4631
The campground at this state park offers 289 woody and sunny sites with electric hookups. Many of the sites also offer water and sewer hookups. Campground amenities include heated showers, toilets and nearby hiking trails. Up to two dogs per pet campsite are allowed and they must be leashed and cleaned up after.

Crosscreek Camping Resort
3190 S Old State
Delaware, OH
740-549-2267
alumcreek.com
Dogs of all sizes are allowed. There are no additional pet fees. Dogs may not be left unattended at any time, must be leashed, and cleaned up after. Proof of liability insurance is required if the dog is on the list for aggressive breeds. They are open all year, but with limited services after Thanksgiving. The camping and tent areas also allow dogs. There is a dog walk area at the campground. Multiple dogs may be allowed.

Delaware State Park Campground
5202 US 23 North
Delaware, OH
740-369-2761
The campground at this state park offers 211 tent and trailer sites with electric hookups. Campground amenities include flush toilets, showers, laundry facilities, dump station, and nearby hiking trails and swimming areas. Up to two dogs per pet campsite are allowed and they must be leashed and cleaned up after. To get there from Columbus, go north on US 23. Go 5 miles north of the city of Delaware and the park entrance is on the east side of the road at the traffic light.

Indian Creek Camping Resort
4710 Lake Road E
Deneva, OH
440-466-8191
indiancreekresort.com
Dogs of all sizes are allowed. There are no additional pet fees. Dogs must be well behaved, leashed, and

cleaned up after. Dogs may be left for short periods if they will be quiet. They are open in winter without water. The camping and tent areas also allow dogs. There is a dog walk area at the campground. Multiple dogs may be allowed.

Beaver Creek State Park
Campground
12021 Echo Dell Road
East Liverpool, OH
330-385-3091
The campground at this state park offers 53 sites with no electric hookups. Campground amenities include tables, fire rings, pit latrines, a dump station and nearby hiking trails. Up to two dogs per pet campsite are allowed and they must be leashed and cleaned up after.

Canton/East Sparta KOA
3232 Downing Street SW
East Sparta, OH
330-484-3901
koa.com/where/OH/35155.htm
Pull through sites up to 50 feet are available as well as 50 amp service. Amenities include a seasonal swimming pool, modem dataport (fee), LP gas (fee) and mini golf (fee). This campground has horseback rides for adults and older kids and ponies for younger children. It also has paddleboats and 3 acre fishing lake. There are a number of weekend events throughout the year. The campground is near the Pro Football Hall of Fame in Canton. The RV park is open all year. Pets are welcome but are not allowed in the cottages. There are no pet fees. To get to the campground from Interstate 77 take the Fohl Rd exit (Exit 99), go three miles west and one mile south on Sherman Church Rd.

Harrison Lake State Park
Campground
26246 Harrison Lake Road
Fayette, OH
419-237-2593
The campground at this state park offers 199 campsites of which 144 have electric hookups. Amenities include showers, flush toilets, a dump station and nearby hiking trails. They have designated sites for campers with pets and offer self-serve "mutt mitts" for cleaning up after your pooch. Up to two dogs per campsite are allowed and they must be leashed and cleaned up after. To get there from Toledo, take

U.S. 20 West through Fayette to County Road 27. Turn left and drive 2 miles to the park.

Geneva State Park Campground
4499 Padanarum Road
Geneva, OH
440-466-8400
The campground at this state park offers 88 shaded or sunny sites with electric hookups. Campground amenities include showers, flush toilets and nearby hiking trails. Up to two dogs per pet campsite are allowed and they must be leashed and cleaned up after. To get there from Cleveland, take Interstate 90 east to Route 534 north. The park entrance is six miles north on Route 534, on the left.

Indian Creek Camping Resort
4710 Lake Road East
Geneva-on-the-Lake, OH
440-466-8191
indiancreekresort.com/
This 110 acre campground offers tent sites and RV sites with full hookups. Big rigs are welcome. Campground amenities include restrooms, heated adult pool for people 21 years and older, heated family pool, coin guest laundry, playground, game room, 18 hole miniature golf, church services, lounge and more. Pets are allowed but need to be kept on a leash, cleaned up after and not left attended. There are no pet fees.

Burr Oak State Park Campground
10220 Burr Oak Lodge Road
Glouster, OH
740-767-3570
The campground at this state park offers 100 non-electric sites for campers. Campground amenities include showers, flush toilets, a dump station and nearby hiking trails and lake. Up to two dogs per pet campsite are allowed and they must be leashed and cleaned up after.

Smoke Rise Ranch Resort Camping
6751 Hunterdon Road
Glouster, OH
740-767-2624
smokeriseranch.com
This working cattle ranch offers a campground with both tent and RV sites. Sites with no hookups are about $16 per night. Sites with electricity and water hookups are about $20 per night. Rates include two adults and two children. There is a $8 fee per additional person. Dogs are welcome in the campground but need to be leashed and cleaned up

after. Pets are not allowed in the cabins.

Rocky Fork State Park
9800 North Shore Drive
Hillsboro, OH
937-393-4284 (866-644-6727)
Dogs of all sizes are allowed. There are no additional pet fees. Dogs may not be left unattended, and they must be leashed and cleaned up after. Dogs are allowed on the trails, but not at the beach swim area. The camping and tent areas also allow dogs. There is a dog walk area at the campground. There are no water hookups at the campground. 2 dogs may be allowed.

Lazy Dog Camp Resort & Noah's Ark Animal Farm
1527 McGiffins Road
Jackson, OH
800-282-2167
noahsarkanimalfarm.net
Dogs of all sizes are allowed at the tent and RV sites. Small dogs only, under 15 pounds are allowed at the cabins. There are no additional pet fees. Dogs must be leashed and cleaned up after. Dogs are not allowed at the lake, nor at the Noah's Ark Animal Farm. The camping and tent areas also allow dogs. There is a dog walk area at the campground. Dogs are allowed in the camping cabins.

Kelleys Island State Park Campground
Division Street
Kelleys Island, OH
419-746-2546
The family campground at this state park offers 82 electric sites and 45 non-electric sites. Campground amenities include showers, flush toilets, a dump station, volleyball court, playground, beaches and six miles of hiking trails. Pets are welcome in the designated pet camp sites. Up to two dogs per campsite are allowed and they must be leashed and cleaned up after. There is a $1 per pet fee. To get there you will need to take a ferry to the island. Kelleys Island Ferry Boat Line operates year round, weather permitting, and offers passenger and limited vehicle service from Marblehead, Ohio to the island. Leashed pets are welcome on the ferry. Once on Kelleys Island, go west on E. Lakeshore Drive and turn right on Division Street. The park is at the end of Division Street on the right.

East Harbor State Park
1169 N Buck Road
Lakeside-Marblehead, OH
866-644-6727
There are many recreational activities to enjoy at this park as it is located along the shores of Lake Erie and it has the largest campground in the Ohio Park System. Dogs of all sizes are allowed. There are no additional pet fees. Dogs may not be left unattended at any time, they must be on no more than a 6 foot leash, and be cleaned up after. Dogs must be walked in the pet designated areas of the park. Dogs must be quiet, well behaved, and have current rabies and shot records. The camping and tent areas also allow dogs. There is a dog walk area at the campground. There are no water hookups at the campground. 2 dogs may be allowed.

Indian Lake State Park Campground
12774 State Route 235 N
Lakeview, OH
937-843-2717
The campground at this state park offers 441 tent and trailer sites, most of which have electrical hookups. Campground amenities include heated shower houses, flush toilets, laundry facility and nearby hiking trails and swimming area. Up to two dogs per pet campsite are allowed and they must be leashed and cleaned up after. To get there from Columbus, take U.S. 33 towards Marysville. The park is about an hour and 15 minutes northwest on U.S. 33.

Lancaster RV Campground
2151 W Fair Avenue
Lancaster, OH
740-653-2261
lancastercampground.com
Dogs of all sizes are allowed. There are no additional pet fees. Dogs must be leashed and cleaned up after. This RV park is closed during the off-season. The camping and tent areas also allow dogs. There is a dog walk area at the campground. Multiple dogs may be allowed.

Palmerosa Campground
19217 Keifel Road
Laurelville, OH
740-385-3799
palmerosa.com
This horseman's campground is located next to Hocking Hills State Forest and offers both RV sites with

electric hookups and primitive camp sites. You are welcome with or without horses. Camp amenities include hot showers, outhouses, picnic tables, dump facilities, and a small tack and gift shop. Pets are welcome but need to be leashed and under control, and cleaned up after. There is a $5 one time per stay pet fee per pet.

Salt Creek Retreats
17549 Crawford Road
Laurelville, OH
614-397-3422
saltcreekretreats.com
These vacation rentals are located near the Hocking Hills area. They offer one cabin rental and one yurt rental (rustic with no electricity or plumbing). Both rentals are furnished. The cabin has air conditioning and a gas furnace. Depending on the season and day of the week, rates for the cabin range from about $90 to $125 per night for up to four people. Yurt rates range from $50 to $65 per night for up to six people. Extra people can be accommodated if they bring their own tent. There is a $10 charge per night per extra person. Pets and children are welcome. There is a $15 one time per stay pet fee. Rental rates are subject to change. Call for details about payment.

Lock 30 RV Campground Resort
45529 Middle Beaver Road
Lisbon, OH
330-424-9197
ohiorvcamp.com/rates.htm
This campground offers RV sites with full hookups with extra space around your site. Amenities include picnic tables, fire rings, hiking and biking trails, vending machines, game room, book exchange, playground, toddler playground, basketball, volleyball, horseshoes, bathrooms with showers, private fishing lake, river access, private dog swim area and hiking paths to the actual un-restored Lock 30 of the historic Sandy & Beaver Canal. Pets are welcome but need to be leashed and cleaned up after. There is no extra pet fee.

Caveman Retreats Campgrounds and Cabin Rentals
18693 State Route 664S
Logan, OH
740-385-9485
This campground is on 20 wooded acres and situated on a working Christmas tree farm. They have primitive tent sites, electric hookup

sites and furnished rustic cabins. Camp amenities include restrooms, picnic tables and fire rings. Pets are allowed and there is a $10 per night pet fee if you stay in one of the rustic cabins. Pets need to be leashed and cleaned up after. Camping sites start at about $18 per night and rustic cabins start at about $90 per night.

Hocking Hills State Park
Campground
19852 State Route 664 South
Logan, OH
740-385-6842
The campground at this state park offers 159 electric sites with 20 to 50 amp electric hookups and 13 non-electric sites. All sites have a paved pad for up to a 50 foot unit. Campground amenities include heated showers, flush toilets, laundry facility, camp store, swimming pool, playgrounds, a volleyball court and nearby hiking trails. Up to two dogs per campsite are allowed and they must be leashed and cleaned up after. To get there from Columbus, take U.S. 33 East through Lancaster to Logan and exit onto State Route 664 South.

Scenic View Family Campground
29150 Pattor Road
Logan, OH
740-385-4295 (866-592-6149)
scenicviewcampground.net
Dogs of all sizes are allowed. There are no additional pet fees. Dogs must be leashed and cleaned up after. There are some breed restrictions. This RV park is closed during the off-season. There is a dog walk area at the campground. 2 dogs may be allowed.

Salt Fork State Park Campgrounds
14755 Cadiz Road
Lore City, OH
740-439-3521
The campground at this state park offers 212 sites all with electrical hookups. Campground amenities include heated shower houses, flush toilets, a dump station and nearby hiking trails. Up to two dogs per pet campsite are allowed and they must be leashed and cleaned up after.

Camp Toodik
7700 Twp Road 462
Loudonville, OH
800-322-2663
camptoodik.com/
This family campground is located in the foothills of the Appalachian Mountains in Holmes County. They offer both tent and RV sites with full

hookups and pull-thru sites. Amenities include canoe and kayak rentals, heated swimming pool, fishing in the river or pond, walking trails, miniature golf, shuttleboard, sand volleyball, horseshoes, playground, game room, recreation hall, picnic shelter and laundry room. Pets are welcome but need to be leashed, cleaned up after and are not allowed in the cabins or cottages. There are no pet fees. Dogs are also allowed in the canoe rentals. The campground is located off I-71. Take exit #173.

Mohican Campground
3058 State Route 3 South
Loudonville, OH
419-994-2267
mohicancamp.com/Campgrounds
This campground offers full hookup sites and primitive camping sites with picnic tables and fire rings. Pets are allowed at the campground but must be leashed and cleaned up after. Pets are not allowed in the pavilion, patio, or any public buildings. Pets are strictly not allowed in or near the cabins (guide or service dogs are exempted from this regulation). There is a $2 per night per pet fee.

Mohican State Park Campground
3116 State Route 3
Loudonville, OH
419-994-4290
The campground at this state park offers 120 sites with electricity, fire rings and picnic tables. Full hookups are available at 33 sites. Campground amenities include showers, flush toilets, a dump station and nearby hiking trails. Up to two dogs per pet campsite are allowed and they must be leashed and cleaned up after.

Cutty's Sunset Camping Resort
8050 Edison Street NE
Louisville, OH
330-935-2431
cuttyssunset.com
Dogs of all sizes are allowed. There are no additional pet fees. Dogs must be leashed and cleaned up after. This RV park is closed during the off-season. The camping and tent areas also allow dogs. There is a dog walk area at the campground. 2 dogs may be allowed.

Malabar Farm State Park
Campground
4050 Bromfield Road
Lucas, OH
419-892-2784

The campground at this state park offers 15 primitive camp sites with no electric hookups. Campground amenities include restrooms, a dump station and nearby hiking trails. Up to two dogs per pet campsite are allowed and they must be leashed and cleaned up after.

Jellystone Park
3392 H 82
Mantua, OH
330-562-9100 (800-344-9644)
jellystoneohio.com
Dogs of all sizes are allowed. There are no additional pet fees. Dogs must be leashed and cleaned up after. Dogs are not allowed in the rentals or at the beach. This RV park is closed during the off-season. The camping and tent areas also allow dogs. There is a dog walk area at the campground. Multiple dogs may be allowed.

Lake Hope State Park Campground
27331 State Route 278
McArthur, OH
740-596-5253

Mary Jane Thurston State Park
Campground
1-466 State Route 65
McClure, OH
419-832-7662
The campground at this state park offers 35 sites with no electric hookups. Fifteen of the sites are for walk-in tent camping only. Campground amenities include restrooms, a nearby dump station and nearby hiking trails. Up to two dogs per campsite are allowed and they must be leashed and cleaned up after.

Scenic Hills RV Park
4483 TR 367
Millersburg, OH
330-893-3607
scenichillsrvpark.com
Located in the heart of Amish country, this RV park offers over 80 full hookups, 40 pull thru sites, modem hookup, dump station available, fire rings, picnic tables and open sites on a grassy hilltop. Pets are welcome but need to be leashed, cleaned up after and not left unattended. The park is located one mile east of Berlin, 500 feet south on TR 367/Hiland Road.

Mount Gilead State Park
Campground
4119 State Route 95
Mount Gilead, OH
419-946-1961

The campground at this state park is set in a scenic pine forest and offers 59 sites with electrical hookups. Campground amenities include a camp store, fire rings, picnic tables, waste water drains, toilets and hiking trails. Up to two dogs per pet campsite are allowed and they must be leashed and cleaned up after.

Deer Creek State Park
20635 Waterloo Road
Mount Sterling, OH
740-869-3508 (866-644-6727)
Dogs of all sizes are allowed. There are no additional pet fees. Dogs may not be left unattended, and they must be on no more than a 6 foot leash, and be cleaned up after. Dogs are not allowed on the swim beach, in any of the buildings, or on the trails. The camping and tent areas also allow dogs. There is a dog walk area at the campground. There are no water hookups at the campground. 2 dogs may be allowed.

Indian Springs Campground
3306 Stateline Road
N Bend, OH
513-353-9244
indianspringcampground.com
Dogs of all sizes are allowed. There are no additional pet fees. Dogs must be leashed, and cleaned up after. There are some breed restrictions. The camping and tent areas also allow dogs. There is a dog walk area at the campground. 2 dogs may be allowed.

Clay's Park Resort
13190 Patterson Road
N Lawrence, OH
800-860-4FUN (386)
clayspark.com
Dogs of all sizes are allowed. There are no additional pet fees. Dogs must be leashed and cleaned up after. Dogs may not be tied up outside unattended. There are some breed restrictions. This RV park is closed during the off-season. The camping and tent areas also allow dogs. There is a dog walk area at the campground. 2 dogs may be allowed.

Dillon State Park Campground
5265 Dillon Hills Drive
Nashport, OH
740-453-4377
The campground at this state park offers 195 sites and 183 of them have electrical hookups. There are also walk-in sites which offer primitive camping. Campground amenities include showers, flush toilets, a dump station, guest laundry, store with groceries, nearby hiking trails. Up to two dogs per pet campsite are allowed and they must be leashed and cleaned up after.http://www.dnr.state.oh.us/parks/parks/dillon.htm

Punderson State Park Campground
11755 Kinsman Road
Newbury, OH
440-564-2279
The campground at this state park, once a former Indian village, offers 196 sites with electrical hookups. Five of the sites have full hookups with electricity, water and sewer service. Campground amenities include showers, flush toilets and nearby hiking and swimming. Up to two dogs per pet campsite are allowed and they must be leashed and cleaned up after.

Maumee Bay State Park Campground
1400 State Park Road
Oregon, OH
419-836-7758
The campground at this state park offers 252 sites with electric hookups. Campground amenities include showers, flush toilets, playground equipment and nearby hiking trails. Up to two dogs per pet campsite are allowed and they must be leashed and cleaned up after.

Kool Lakes Family RV park
12990 H 282
Parkman, OH
440-548-8436
koollakes.com
Dogs of all sizes are allowed. There are no additional pet fees. Dogs must be leashed and cleaned up after. Dogs are not allowed at the beach or in the water. This RV park is closed during the off-season. There is a dog walk area at the campground. Multiple dogs may be allowed.

Toledo East/Stony Ridge KOA
24787 Luckey Road
Perrysburg, OH
419-837-6848 (800-562-6831)
koa.com
Dogs of all sizes are allowed. There are no additional pet fees. Dogs must be leashed and cleaned up after. This RV park is closed during the off-season. The camping and tent areas also allow dogs. There is a dog walk area at the campground. There are special amenities given to dogs at this campground.

Multiple dogs may be allowed.

Stonelick State Park Campground
2895 Lake Drive
Pleasant Plain, OH
513-625-7544
The campground at this state park offers 115 sites with electrical hookups. Campground amenities include showers, flush toilets, camp store, laundry facilities, a dump station and nearby hiking trails. Up to two dogs per pet campsite are allowed and they must be leashed and cleaned up after.

Cedarlane RV Park
2926 NE Catawba Road
Port Clinton, OH
419-797-9907
cedarlanervpark.com
Dogs of all sizes are allowed. There are no additional pet fees. Dogs may not be left unattended, must be leashed, and cleaned up after. This RV park is closed during the off-season. The camping and tent areas also allow dogs. There is a dog walk area at the campground. 2 dogs may be allowed.

East Harbor State Park Campground
Route 269
Port Clinton, OH
419-734-4424
The campground at this state park is the largest in the Ohio State Park system. It offers 365 sites with electric hookups and 205 with no electric. Campground amenities include showers, flush toilets, dump station, camp store and nearby hiking trails. Up to two dogs per pet campsite are allowed and they must be leashed and cleaned up after. To get there from Cleveland, take State Route 2 West to State Route 269 North. The park is located on State Route 269. To get there from Port Clinton, go east on Route 163 to Route 269 north.

Shade Acres RV Campground
1810 W. Catawba Road
Port Clinton, OH
419-797-4681
shadeacres.com
RV sites include water and electric service, picnic tables, fire rings, shade and a concrete patio. Amenities include a small playground. Pets are allowed in the RV sites but not in the tent camping sites. There is no pet fee.

Sleepy Hollows Family Camping
2817 E. Harbor Road
Port Clinton, OH

419-734-3556
sleepyhollowscampground.com/
This campground offers tent sites and RV sites, some of which have electric hookups. Amenities include wooded sites, picnic tables, fire rings, dump station, firewood sales and a boat storage area. Pets are allowed but you will need to register your pet at the office. Pets must be leashed and cleaned up after. The RV park is open from mid-May to mid-October. They are located four miles east of Port Clinton on State Route 163.

Shawnee State Park Campground
4404 State Route 125
Portsmouth, OH
740-858-6652
The campground at this state park offers 103 tent and trailer sites with electrical hookups. Campground amenities include heater shower houses, flush toilets, laundry facilities, a dump station and nearby hiking trails and swimming. Up to two dogs per pet campsite are allowed and they must be leashed and cleaned up after.

Fox's Den Campground
140 Conlan Road
Put-in-Bay, OH
419-285-5001
This campground offers over 60 sites with water and electric hookups. Amenities include a laundry facility, camp store, showers, fire rings and dump station. Pets are allowed but need to be leashed and cleaned up after.

OakDale Camp
4611 State Route 235 South
Quincy, OH
937-585-6232
oakdalecamp.com/
This campground offers over 100 campsites with water and electric at each site. Amenities include a shower house with flush toilets, dump stations, trees and wildlife. Pets are welcome, but must be quiet and kept on a leash. There are no pet fees. They are open from April 1 to October 1.

Country Acres Campground
9850 Minyoung Road
Ravenna, OH
866-813-4321
countryacrescamping.com
Dogs of all sizes are allowed. There are no additional pet fees. Dogs must be quiet, may not be left unattended, must be leashed, and cleaned up after. This RV park is

closed during the off-season. The camping and tent areas also allow dogs. There is a dog walk area at the campground. Multiple dogs may be allowed.

West Branch State Park Campground
5708 Esworthy Road
Ravenna, OH
330-296-3239
The campground at this state park offers 103 sites, 50 of which have 50 amp electric hookups. Campground amenities include heated showers, flush toilets, laundry facilities, a trailer dump station and nearby hiking trails. Up to two dogs per pet campsite are allowed and they must be leashed and cleaned up after.

Forked Run State Park Campground
63300 State Route 124
Reedsville, OH
740-378-6206
The campground at this state park offers 80 electric sites and 100 non-electric sites. Campground amenities include showers, a dump station and nearby hiking trails and lake. Up to two dogs per pet campsite are allowed and they must be leashed and cleaned up after.

Middle Ridge Campground
HC 65, Box 4965 (on Middle Ridge Road)
Ronmey, OH
304-822-8020
middleridgecampground.com
Dogs of all sizes are allowed. There are no additional pet fees. Dogs may not be left unattended, must be quiet, well behaved, leashed, and cleaned up after. This RV park is closed during the off-season. The camping and tent areas also allow dogs. There is a dog walk area at the campground. Multiple dogs may be allowed.

Camper Village RV Park
One Cedar Point Drive
Sandusky, OH
419-627-2106
This RV park is located at Cedar Point Amusement Park. The campground offers over 200 camp sites. There are 111 electric only sites and 97 full hookup sites. Tent camping or ground fires are not permitted. Amenities include restrooms, shower facilities, guest laundry, picnic tables and camping supply store. Pets are allowed but must be on leash and not left

unattended. Pets can be boarded at Cedar Point's Pet Check during park operating hours for $10 per day during the day only.

Shelby/Mansfield KOA
6787 Baker 47
Shelby, OH
419-347-1392 (888-562-5607)
shelbymansfieldkoa.com
Dogs of all sizes are allowed. There are no additional pet fees. Dogs may not be left unattended at any time, must be on no more than a 6 foot leash, and be cleaned up after. There are some breed restrictions. This RV park is closed during the off-season. The camping and tent areas also allow dogs. There is a dog walk area at the campground. Multiple dogs may be allowed.

South Bass Island State Park Campground
Catawba Avenue
South Bass Island, OH
419-285-2112
The campground at this state park offers 125 non-electric camp sites and 10 full service sites with electric, water and sewer hookups. Amenities include showers, flush toilets and a dump station. This 32 acre state park does not allow dogs on the beach and does not really have any hiking trails. Up to two dogs per campsite are allowed and they must be leashed and cleaned up after. There is a $1 per pet fee. To get there you will need to take a ferry to South Bass Island. Miller Boat Line departs from Catawba and Jet Express departs from Port Clinton. Both ferries go to the island and both allow leashed dogs. Jet Express requires that dogs stay on the outside deck. While both ferries offer passenger transportation, Miller Boat Line also offers limited vehicle service. Once on the island, you can either drive your own car or rent a dog-friendly golf cart. From the village, take Catawba Avenue until you reach the park.

Top O' The Caves Camping
26780 Chapel Ridge Road
South Bloomingville, OH
800-967-2434
topothecaves.com/
This 60 acre resort offers the largest campground in the Hocking Hills. They are surrounded by dog-friendly state parks (dogs on leash) which you can walk to from your site. They have both tent camping and full RV hookups. Each site includes a picnic table and fire ring. Resort amenities

include two modern shower houses with hot water, a large swimming pool, kids playground, mini golf, large game arcade, gift shop, laundry facilities and Sunday worship services. Pets are welcome and there are no pet fees. Please keep your dog leashed and clean up after them. The resort also offers cabins rentals that allow dogs. The resort is located on Chapel Ridge Road, near Highway 374.

Buck Creek State Park
1901 Buck Creek Lane
Springfield, OH
937-322-5284 (866-644-6727)
Dogs of all sizes are allowed. There are no additional pet fees. Dogs may not be left unattended, and they must be leashed and cleaned up after. Dogs are not allowed in the water at the swimming area, or any of the sandy areas on the beach, the picnic areas, or in any of the buildings. Dogs must stay in the designated pet areas. The camping and tent areas also allow dogs. There is a dog walk area at the campground. There are no water hookups at the campground. 2 dogs may be allowed.

Enon Beach Campground
2401 Enon Road
Springfield, OH
937-882-6431
Dogs of all sizes are allowed. There are no additional pet fees. Dogs may not be left unattended, must be leashed, and cleaned up after. Dogs may go to the lake, but not be on the beach area. The camping and tent areas also allow dogs. There is a dog walk area at the campground. Multiple dogs may be allowed.

Winton Woods Campground
Winton Road
Springfield Township, OH
513-521-PARK
hamiltoncountyparks.org
Open from late February to early November, this campground offers 100 sites with full and electric hookups. Prices range from $18 to $26 per night. Campground amenities include picnic tables, fire rings, access to a heated shower building, dump station, laundry room, playground, camp store and nearby hiking trails. A 3 night stay is required on holidays. Pets are allowed but must be on a 6 foot or less leash, under control, and picked up after. Pooper scooper dispensers are located at each trailhead and are available from the Park District

Rangers. To get to the park, take I-275 to the Winton Road-Forest Park exit, and head south on Winton Road to the park entrances on left and right. The park is also accessible via the Ronald Reagan-Cross County Highway. Take the Winton Road exit, and head north on Winton Road to the park entrances on the left and right.

Grand Lake Saint Marys State Park Campground
834 Edgewater Drive
St Marys, OH
419-394-3611
The campground at this state park offers 210 sites of which 142 have electricity. Campground amenities include flush toilets, laundry, showers, a dump station, and the lake for recreation. Up to two dogs per pet campsite are allowed and they must be leashed and cleaned up after. To get there from Columbus, head west on Route 33 to St. Marys (33 becomes 29 at St. Marys). Stay on the four lane road to Route 364, then go south to 703. Take 730/364 East to the park entrance.

Lake Loramie State Park Campground
834 Edgewater Drive
St Marys, OH
419-394-3611
The campground at this state park offers 161 sites with electric hookups. Campground amenities include shaded waterfront sites, showers, flush toilets, a dump station, nearby hiking trails and swimming areas. Up to two dogs per pet campsite are allowed and they must be leashed, and are not allowed inside any buildings.

Mar-Lynn Lake Park
187 State Route 303
Streetsboro, OH
330-650-2552
mar-lynn.com
This campground offers full hookup sites, water and electric only sites, pull thru sites and rustic tent sites. Pets are welcome but not in the cabins. Dogs must be leashed, cleaned up after and cannot be left unattended.

Pleasant View
12611 Township Road 218
Van Buren, OH
419-299-3897
pleasantviewcampground.com
Dogs of all sizes are allowed. There are no additional pet fees. Dogs

must be well behaved, leashed, and cleaned up after. This RV park is closed during the off-season. The camping and tent areas also allow dogs. There is a dog walk area at the campground. Multiple dogs may be allowed.

Van Buren State Park Campgrounds
12259 Township Rd. 218
Van Buren, OH
419-832-7662
This park offers a campground with 40 non-electric sites and a multi-use campground for general and horse camping with 38 non-electric sites. Camp amenities include tables, pit toilets, and hiking trails. There are certain designated sites for campers with pets. Up to two dogs per campsite are allowed and they must be leashed and cleaned up after.

Wapakoneta/Lima S KOA
14719 Cemetery Road
Wapakoneta, OH
419-738-6016 (800-562-9872)
wapakonetaohkoa.com
Dogs of all sizes are allowed. There are no additional pet fees. Dogs must be leashed and cleaned up after. There are some breed restrictions. This RV park is closed during the off-season. The camping and tent areas also allow dogs. There is a dog walk area at the campground. Multiple dogs may be allowed.

Caesar Creek State Park
8750 E H 74
Waynesville, OH
513-897-3055 (866-644-6727)
Dogs of all sizes are allowed. There are no additional pet fees. Dogs may not be left unattended, they must be on no more than a 6 foot leash, and be cleaned up after. Dogs must stay in the pet section of the campground. The camping and tent areas also allow dogs. There is a dog walk area at the campground. There are no water hookups at the campground. Multiple dogs may be allowed.

Findley State Park Campground
25381 State Route 58
Wellington, OH
440-647-4490
The campground at this state park offers 272 both sunny and shaded sites with no electric hookups. Campground amenities include showers, flush toilets, laundry facilities, dump station, game room, fully stocked camp store, recreation area with sand volleyball, a basketball court, two horseshoe pits

and nearby hiking trails. Up to two dogs per pet campsite are allowed and they must be leashed and cleaned up after. To get there from Cleveland, take Interstate 480 west to Route 10 west and continue to Route 20 west. Then go to Route 58 south and go ten miles. The park is 2.5 miles south of Wellington on the east side of the road.

Riverside Whistler Camping and Cabins
8018 Mons Road
Whistler, OH
604-905-5533
whistlercamping.com
Dogs of all sizes are allowed. There is a $2.50 per night per pet additional fee for the tent and RV sites, and for the one pet friendly cabin. Dogs may not be left unattended at any time, especially inside the RVs in the summer. Dogs must be leashed and cleaned up after. The camping and tent areas also allow dogs. There is a dog walk area at the campground. Dogs are allowed in the camping cabins. Multiple dogs may be allowed.

Beechwood Acres Camping Resort
855 Yankee Road
Wilmington, OH
937-289-2202
beechwoodacres.com
This campground is located near Cowan State Park which allows dogs on the hiking trails. Camp amenities include tent and RV sites with hookups, heated swimming pool, game room, bike rentals, onsite convenience store, showers, laundry facilities, playground and golf cart train rides for children. Pets are welcome but need to be leashed and cleaned up after. Pets are not allowed in the cabins. There is a $1 per day pet fee.

Cowan Lake State Park
1750 Osborn Road
Wilmington, OH
937-382-1096
Dogs of all sizes are allowed. There are no additional pet fees. Dogs may not be left unattended, they must be quiet, well behaved, be on no more than a 6 foot leash, and be cleaned up after. Dogs must be walked in designated pet areas only. The camping and tent areas also allow dogs. There is a dog walk area at the campground. There are no water hookups at the campground. 2 dogs may be allowed.

John Bryan State Park Campground

3790 State Route 370
Yellow Springs, OH
937-767-1274
The campground at this state park offers 10 sites with electrical hookups and 89 sites without electric. Campground amenities include some shaded sites, picnic tables, fire rings, toilets, drinking water, a dump station and nearby hiking trails. Up to two dogs per pet campsite are allowed and they must be leashed and cleaned up after.

Oklahoma

Lake Murray State Park/Tucker Tower Nature Center
3323 Lodge Road
Ardmore, OK
580-223-6600 (800-257-0322)
Nestled along the shores of Lake Murray, this is the state's oldest and largest park. As a resort park it offers an abundance of recreational, educational, and sporting activities. Dogs are allowed throughout the park, in the cabins and the campground for no additional fee. Dogs must be quiet, well behaved, and be on no more than a 10 foot leash or crated. Owners must show proof of current inoculations-including rabies. Dogs may not be left unattended in any way as to cause harm, and they are not allowed in park buildings, designated swim beaches, or where noted. Dogs must be picked up after at all times. There are 8 camp areas offering 450 sites, 56 cottages, picnic tables, restrooms, showers, a grocery store, restaurant, snack bar, and a playground. The camping and tent areas also allow dogs. There is a dog walk area at the campground. Dogs are allowed in the camping cabins. Multiple dogs may be allowed.

Osage Hills State Park
H 60 W
Bartlesville, OK
918-336-4141 (800-654-8240)
Once an Osage Indian settlement, this 1,100+ acre park now offers repose, abundant recreation, educational opportunities, and hiking and nature trails. Dogs are allowed throughout the park, in the camp areas, and in the cabins where up to 2 dogs are allowed per cabin. Dogs must remain off the

furniture in the cabins and there may be a deposit required. Dogs must be current on vaccinations, leashed, and under their owner's control. The camp sites offer comfort stations, picnic areas, playing fields/courts, a swimming pool, and concessionaires. The camping and tent areas also allow dogs. There is a dog walk area at the campground. Dogs are allowed in the camping cabins. Multiple dogs may be allowed.

Riverside RV Resort
11211 SE Adams Blvd
Bartlesville, OK
888-572-1241
resortrv.com
Dogs of all sizes are allowed. There are no additional pet fees. Dogs may not be left unattended outside, and they must be leashed and cleaned up after. There is an 11 mile city maintained walking/biking trail that passes by this resort. There is a dog walk area at the campground. Multiple dogs may be allowed.

Beaver Dunes State Park
H 270
Beaver, OK
580-625-3373 (800-654-8240)
This 520 acre park has 300 acres of sand dunes, perfect for off-roading, hiking and biking. Dogs of all sizes are allowed at no additional fee. Dogs may not be left unattended, and they must be on no more than a 10 foot leash, and be cleaned up after. Dogs are allowed on the trails. This campground is closed during the off-season. The camping and tent areas also allow dogs. There is a dog walk area at the campground. Dogs are allowed in the camping cabins. Multiple dogs may be allowed.

Beavers Bend State Resort Park
P. O. Box 10/H 259A
Broken Bow, OK
580-494-6300 (800-435-5514)
beaversbend.com/
This is one of the state's most popular major recreation destinations and offered numerous amenities and activities, a heritage center, museum, gift shop, golf course, and more. Dogs are allowed in the park and camp areas for no additional fee; they are not allowed in the lodge. Dogs may not be left unattended at any time, and they must be well mannered, leashed, and under their owner's control at all times. There are 50 RV sites and 150 tent sites provided. Comfort stations, picnic

areas, a dump station, and concessionaires are on site. The camping and tent areas also allow dogs. There is a dog walk area at the campground. Dogs are allowed in the camping cabins. Multiple dogs may be allowed.

El Reno West KOA
301 S Walbaum Road
Calumet, OK
405-884-2595 (800-562-5736)
koa.com
Dogs of all sizes are allowed. There are no additional pet fees. Dogs must be leashed and cleaned up after. This RV park is closed during the off-season. The camping and tent areas also allow dogs. There is a dog walk area at the campground. Dogs are allowed in the camping cabins. Multiple dogs may be allowed.

Elk City/Clinton KOA
Clinton Lake Road
Canute, OK
580-592-4409 (800-562-4149)
koa@cottonball.com
Dogs of all sizes are allowed, and there are no additional pet fees for tent or RV sites. There is a $5 per night per pet additional fee for the cabins. Dogs may not be tied to the trees or left unattended,and they must be quiet, well behaved, leashed, and cleaned up after. There are some breed restrictions. The camping and tent areas also allow dogs. There is a dog walk area at the campground. Dogs are allowed in the camping cabins. Multiple dogs may be allowed.

Tulsa Northeast KOA
19605 E Skelly Drive
Catoosa, OK   -7635
918-266-4227 (800-562-7657)
koa.com
Dogs of all sizes are allowed. There are no additional pet fees. Dogs must be leashed and cleaned up after. There are some breed restrictions. The camping and tent areas also allow dogs. There is a dog walk area at the campground. Dogs are allowed in the camping cabins. Multiple dogs may be allowed. 918-283-8876

Bell Cow Lake Equestrian Campground and Trails
Lake Road
Chandler, OK
405-258-1460
Dogs of all sizes are allowed. There are no additional pet fees. Dogs may not be left unattended, and they must

be leashed and cleaned up after. Dogs are not allowed in the swim area. This RV park is closed during the off-season. The camping and tent areas also allow dogs. There is a dog walk area at the campground. Multiple dogs may be allowed.

Oak Glen RV Park
3 1/2 miles East of Chandler on H 66
Chandler, OK
800-521-6681
oakglenrvpark.com
Dogs of all sizes are allowed. There are no additional pet fees. Dogs must be leashed and cleaned up after. The camping and tent areas also allow dogs. There is a dog walk area at the campground. Multiple dogs may be allowed.

Checotah/Henryetta KOA
On I 40 @Pierce Road (HC 68, Box750)
Checotah, OK
918-473-6511 (800-562-7510)
koa.com
Dogs of all sizes are allowed, and there are no additional pet fees for tent or RV sites. There is a $5 one time additional pet fee for cabins. Dogs must be leashed and cleaned up after. There are some breed restrictions. The camping and tent areas also allow dogs. There is a dog walk area at the campground. Dogs are allowed in the camping cabins. Multiple dogs may be allowed.

Oklahoma City East KOA
6200 S Choctaw Road
Choctaw, OK
405-391-5000 (800-562-5076)
koa.com
Dogs of all sizes are allowed. There are no additional pet fees. Dogs may not be left unattended outside, and they must be leashed and cleaned up after. There are some breed restrictions. The camping and tent areas also allow dogs. There is a dog walk area at the campground. Multiple dogs may be allowed.

Clayton Lake State Park
HC 60 Box 33-10/ H 271
Clayton, OK
918-569-7981 (800-654-8240)
This park of over 500 acres has a 95 acre lake and offers a variety of land and water recreation. Dogs of all sizes are allowed at no additional fee. Dogs may not be left unattended, and they must be leashed and cleaned up after. However, if there are no other

people around and your dog will respond to voice command, they may be off lead when out of the camp area. Dogs are allowed on the trails. The camping and tent areas also allow dogs. There is a dog walk area at the campground. Dogs are allowed in the camping cabins.

Colbert KOA
411 Sherrard Street
Colbert, OK
580-296-2485 (800-562-2485)
koa.com
Dogs of all sizes are allowed. There are no additional pet fees. Dogs may not be left unattended at the cabins or outside, and they must be leashed and cleaned up after. There are some breed restrictions. The camping and tent areas also allow dogs. There is a dog walk area at the campground. Dogs are allowed in the camping cabins. Multiple dogs may be allowed.

Dreamweaver RV Resort
110 Kay Star Trail
Davis, OK
580-369-3399 (866-969-CAMP (2267))
Dogs of all sizes are allowed. There are no additional pet fees. Large dogs must be leashed; smaller dogs may be off lead if they are well behaved and under voice control. Dogs may not be left unattended, and they must be friendly and cleaned up after. There is a creek nearby where dogs are also allowed. There is a dog walk area at the campground. Multiple dogs may be allowed.

Elk Creek RV Park
317 E 20th
Elk City, OK
580-225-7865
Dogs of all sizes are allowed. There are no additional pet fees. Dogs may not be left unattended outside, and they must leashed and cleaned up after. Dogs must be quiet, and in at night. The camping and tent areas also allow dogs. There is a dog walk area at the campground. Multiple dogs may be allowed.

Jellystone Park Eufaula
610 Lake Shore Drive
Eufaula, OK
918-689-YOGI (9644) (800-558-2954 (code 205))
jellystoneok.com/
A family oriented campground, this fun resort sits along the shores of one of the largest lakes in the area and offers a swimming pool, 2 swim

beaches, paddle boats, mini-golf, an outdoor theater, theme weekends, a coffee and sandwich/pizza shop, and much more. Dogs are allowed for no additional fee. They must be leashed and cleaned up after at all times, and they are not allowed in any of the rental units. Dogs are allowed on the beach. The camping and tent areas also allow dogs. There is a dog walk area at the campground. Multiple dogs may be allowed.

Twin Bridges State Park
14801 S H 137
Fairland, OK
918-540-2545 (800-654-8240)
This small park is known for its fishing and offers a variety of recreational pursuits. Well behaved dogs of all sizes are allowed at no additional fee. Dogs may not be left unattended, and they must be leashed at all times, and be cleaned up after. Dogs are allowed on the trails. The camping and tent areas also allow dogs. There is a dog walk area at the campground. There are no water hookups at the campground. Multiple dogs may be allowed.

Alabaster Caverns State Park
H 50 A
Freedom, OK
580-621-3381
This 200 acre park is home to the largest, public natural gypsum cave in the world, and above ground is a beautiful natural park to explore. Dogs are allowed throughout the park and in the campground for no additional fee. Dogs must be well behaved, and be on no more than a 10 foot leash or crated. Owners must show proof of current inoculations-including rabies. Dogs may not be left unattended in any way as to cause harm, and they are not allowed in park buildings, on cave tours, designated swim beaches, or where noted. Dogs must be picked up after at all times. The camp area offers 20 sites, picnic tables, grills, restrooms, a gift shop, and gaming areas. The camping and tent areas also allow dogs. There is a dog walk area at the campground. Multiple dogs may be allowed.

Marval Resort
Marval Lane
Gore, OK
800-340-4280
marvalresort.com
Dogs of all sizes are allowed, and there are no additional pet fees for tent or RV sites. There is a $20 one

time additional pet fee for the cabins. Dogs may not be left unattended, and they must be on no more than a 10 foot leash, and cleaned up after. The camping and tent areas also allow dogs. There is a dog walk area at the campground. Dogs are allowed in the camping cabins. Multiple dogs may be allowed.

Water's Edge RV and Cabin Resort
446714 E 355th
Grand Lake Towne, OK
918-782-1444 (866-990-1444)
watersedgerv.com/
Dogs of all sizes are allowed. There are no additional pet fees. Dogs may be off leash only if they are good under voice command. Dogs must be quiet, well behaved, and cleaned up after. This is an RV only park. The camping and tent areas also allow dogs. There is a dog walk area at the campground. Multiple dogs may be allowed.

Bear's Den Resort
25301 H 59
Grove, OK
918-786-6196
bearsdenresort.com
Dogs of all sizes are allowed. There are no additional pet fees. Dogs may not be left unattended, and they must be quiet, well behaved, leashed, and cleaned up after. The camping and tent areas also allow dogs. There is a dog walk area at the campground. 2 dogs may be allowed.

Cedar Oaks RV Resort
1550 83rd Street NW
Grove, OK
800-880-8884
cedaroaksrv.com
Dogs of all sizes are allowed. There are no additional pet fees. Dogs may not be left unattended, and they must be leashed and cleaned up after. There is a fenced in area for off lead. There is a dog walk area at the campground. Multiple dogs may be allowed.

Red Rock Canyon State Park
H 281 S
Hinton, OK
405-542-6344 (800-654-8240)
This canyon park adds rock climbing to their other recreational activities, and it is a great place for hiking and exploring. Well behaved dogs of all sizes are allowed at no additional fee. Dogs may not be left unattended, and they must have current rabies and shot records.

Dogs must be on no more than a 10 foot leash at all times. Dogs are allowed on the trails. The camping and tent areas also allow dogs. There is a dog walk area at the campground. Multiple dogs may be allowed.

Big Cedar Adventure Park
21823 H 63
Hodgen, OK
918-651-3271
big-cedar.net/
Dogs of all sizes are allowed. There are no additional pet fees for tent or RV sites. There is an additional one time pet fee of $20 for each 1 to 3 days stay for the 1 pet friendly cabin. Dogs may not be left unattended, and they must be leashed and cleaned up after. The camping and tent areas also allow dogs. There is a dog walk area at the campground. Dogs are allowed in the camping cabins. Multiple dogs may be allowed.

Black Mesa State Park and Nature Preserve
H 325
Kenton, OK
580-426-2222
Rich in pre-historic ambiance, visitors can journey with the fossil prints of dinosaurs, walk thru a petrified forest, explore geological features, stroll a nature preserve, or take a view from the state's highest elevation at almost 5,000 feet. Dogs are allowed in the park, nature preserve, and camp areas for no additional fee. Dogs must be leashed, under their owner's control, and cleaned up after at all times. There are 64 campsites available with a comfort station, picnic areas, a playground, and dump station. The camping and tent areas also allow dogs. There is a dog walk area at the campground. Multiple dogs may be allowed.

Quartz Mountain Arts and Nature Park
H 44 A
Lone Wolf, OK
580-563-2238
quartzmountain.org/
This major land and water recreational park also offers educational, cultural, and naturalist opportunities. Dogs must be quiet, well behaved, and be on no more than a 10 foot leash. Owners must show proof of current inoculations-including rabies. Dogs may not be left unattended in any way as to cause harm, and they are not

allowed in park buildings, designated swim beaches, or where noted. Dogs must be picked up after at all times. There are a variety of camp areas and they may have some or all of the following: restrooms, showers, picnic tables, dump stations, boat ramps, and grocery store. The camping and tent areas also allow dogs. There is a dog walk area at the campground. Multiple dogs may be allowed.

Ardmore/Marietta KOA
Oswalt Road (Rt 1, Box 640)
Marietta, OK
580-276-2800 (800-562-5893)
koa.com
Dogs of all sizes are allowed. There are no additional pet fees. Dogs must be quiet, leashed, and cleaned up after. The camping and tent areas also allow dogs. There is a dog walk area at the campground. Dogs are allowed in the camping cabins. Multiple dogs may be allowed.

Lake Thunderbird State Park
13101 Alameda Drive
Norman, OK
405-360-3572 (800-654-8240)
Home to a 6,000 acre lake, this 1,874 acre park also features nature and interpretive trails, a nature center with ongoing programs and events, and a restaurant. Dogs are allowed throughout the park and in the campground for no additional fee. Dogs must be quiet, well behaved, and be on no more than a 10 foot leash or crated. Owners must show proof of current inoculations-including rabies. Dogs may not be left unattended in any way as to cause harm, and they are not allowed in park buildings, designated swim beaches, or where noted. Dogs must be picked up after at all times. The campground has 447 serviced sites, primitive campsites, restrooms, showers, picnic tables, a playground, concessionaires, and a gift shop. There are some breed restrictions. The camping and tent areas also allow dogs. There is a dog walk area at the campground. Multiple dogs may be allowed.

Abe's RV Park
12115 N I 35 Service Road
Oklahoma City, OK
405-478-0278
Dogs of all sizes are allowed. There are no additional pet fees. Dogs must be leashed and cleaned up after. There are some breed restrictions. There is a dog walk area at the campground. Multiple dogs may be allowed.

Rockwell RV Park
720 S Rockwell
Oklahoma City, OK
405-787-5992
rockwellrvpark.com
Dogs of all sizes are allowed. There are no additional pet fees. Dogs must be leashed and cleaned up after. The camping and tent areas also allow dogs. There is a dog walk area at the campground. Multiple dogs may be allowed.

Walnut Creek State Park
209th W Ave
Prue, OK
918-865-4991 (800-654-8240)
Located on the 26,300 acre Keystone Lake, this 1,429 acre park offers a wide range of land and water recreation. Dogs are allowed throughout the park and in the campground for no additional fee. Dogs must be quiet, well behaved, and be on no more than a 10 foot leash or crated. Owners must show proof of their dogs current inoculations-including rabies. Dogs may not be left unattended in any way as to cause harm, and they are not allowed in park buildings, designated swim beaches, or where noted. Dogs must be picked up after at all times. The campground has 172 sites, a playground, playing fields, restrooms with showers, and picnic tables. The camping and tent areas also allow dogs. There is a dog walk area at the campground. Multiple dogs may be allowed.

Sallisaw KOA
1908 Power Drive
Sallisaw, OK
918-775-2792 (800-562-2797)
sallisawkoa.com
Dogs of all sizes are allowed. There are no additional pet fees. Dogs may not be penned or left unattended outside, and they must be leashed and cleaned up after. The camping and tent areas also allow dogs. There is a dog walk area at the campground. Dogs are allowed in the camping cabins. Multiple dogs may be allowed.

Keystone State Park
1926 State Hwy 151
Sand Springs, OK
918-865-4991 (800-654-8240)
Located on the 26,000+ acre Keystone Lake, this 714 acre park offers a full service marina, a seasonal restaurant and café, gift shop, grocery store, a fitness trail, and a wide range of land and water

recreation. Dogs are allowed throughout the park, in the cabins (2), and in the campground (2+) for no additional fee. Dogs must be quiet, well behaved, and be on no more than a 10 foot leash or crated. Owners must show proof of their dogs current inoculations-including rabies. Dogs may not be left unattended in any was as to cause harm, and they are not allowed in park buildings, designated swim beaches, or where noted. Dogs must be picked up after at all times. The camp area offers 154 sites, 22 lakeview cabins, a playground, picnic tables, showers, and restrooms. The camping and tent areas also allow dogs. There is a dog walk area at the campground. Dogs are allowed in the camping cabins.

Ato Z Guest Ranch
64599 Ashby Road
Smithville, OK
580-244-3729
atozguestranch.com/sites.asp
Dogs of all sizes are allowed. There are no additional pet fees. Dogs may not be left unattended, and they must be leashed and cleaned up after. They request guests do not walk dogs on the trails with the horses. The camping and tent areas also allow dogs. There is a dog walk area at the campground. Multiple dogs may be allowed.

Arbuckle RV Resort
700 Charles Cooper Memorial Road
Sulphur, OK
580-622-6338
arbucklereresort.com/
Dogs of all sizes are allowed. There are no additional pet fees. Dogs may not be left unattended outside, and they must be quiet, well behaved, leashed, and cleaned up after. This is an RV mostly park, but they do have a few places for tents. There are some breed restrictions. The camping and tent areas also allow dogs. There is a dog walk area at the campground. Multiple dogs may be allowed.

Chickasaw National Rec Area
1008 W Second Street
Sulphur, OK
580-622-7236 (877-444-6777)
nps.gov/chic/
Evidence points to this being a popular area for repose and hunting for hundreds of years due to its abundance of flora and fauna and numerous mineral springs. Dogs are allowed in the park and campground; they are prohibited at all the

swimming area along Travertine Creek, the Nature Center, and the on all the trails east of the Nature Center. Dogs must be leashed and under their owner's control at all times. The camp areas offer various settings and amenities. The camping and tent areas also allow dogs. There is a dog walk area at the campground. There are no water hookups at the campgrounds. Multiple dogs may be allowed.

Mingo RV Park
801 N Mingo
Tulsa, OK
800-932-8824
mingorvpark.com
Dogs of all sizes are allowed. There are no additional pet fees. Dogs must be leashed and cleaned up after. There is a dog walk area at the campground. 2 dogs may be allowed.

Tulsa Warrior Campground
5131 S Union
Tulsa, OK
800-426-3199
Dogs of all sizes are allowed. There are no additional pet fees. Dogs may not be left unattended at any time, and they must be leashed and cleaned up after. There is a dog walk area at the campground. Multiple dogs may be allowed.

Water's Edge RV Resort
446714 E 355th
Vinita, OK
918-782-1444
watersedgerv.com
Dogs of all sizes are allowed. There are no additional pet fees. Dogs must be leashed and cleaned up after. This RV park is closed during the off-season. The camping and tent areas also allow dogs. There is a dog walk area at the campground. Multiple dogs may be allowed.

Roman Nose State Resort Park
H 8 A
Watonga, OK
580-623-4215
Dogs of all sizes are allowed. There are no additional pet fees. Dogs may not be left unattended, and they must be well behaved, be on no more than a 10 foot leash, and cleaned up after. The camping and tent areas also allow dogs. There is a dog walk area at the campground. Dogs are allowed in the camping cabins. Multiple dogs may be allowed.

GW Exotic Animal Park Campground and Cabins

RR2 Box 67/On H 17
Wynnewood, OK
405-665-5197
gwpark.org/
Located at one of the most amazing exotic animal parks in the country, this park is home to hundreds of wild, rare, and exotic animals showcased in their own habitats. They offer cabins, tent, and RV camp areas. Dogs are allowed in all the camp areas for a $25 refundable deposit per pet per stay. They are not allowed anywhere inside the animal compound. Dogs must be leashed and cleaned up after at all times. The camping and tent areas also allow dogs. There is a dog walk area at the campground. Dogs are allowed in the camping cabins. Multiple dogs may be allowed.

Oregon

Albany/Corvallis KOA
33775 Oakville Road S
Albany, OR
541-967-8521 (800-562-8526)
koa.com
Dogs of all sizes are allowed. There are no additional pet fees. Dogs must be quiet, well behaved, be on no more than a 6 foot leash, and be cleaned up after. There are some breed restrictions. The camping and tent areas also allow dogs. There is a dog walk area at the campground.

Oregon Trails West RV Park
42534 N Cedar Road
Baker City, OR
888-523-3236
Dogs of all sizes are allowed. There are no additional pet fees. Dogs must be quiet, leashed and cleaned up after. Dogs may not be left unattended. The camping and tent areas also allow dogs. There is a dog walk area at the campground. Multiple dogs may be allowed.

Wallowa-Whitman National Forest
1550 Dewey Avenue
Baker City, OR
541-523-6391
fs.fed.us/r6/w-w/
These forests were combined creating 2.3 million acres of spectacular scenery, hundreds of miles of trails, and diverse ecosystems that support a large variety of plants, animals, and recreation. Dogs of all sizes are

allowed at no additional fee. Dogs may not be left unattended, and they must be leashed and cleaned up after in camp areas. Dogs are allowed on the trails. This campground is closed during the off-season. The camping and tent areas also allow dogs. There is a dog walk area at the campground. Multiple dogs may be allowed.

Bandon by the Sea RV Park
49612 H 101
Bandon, OR
541-347-5155
bandonbythesearvpark.com
Dogs of all sizes are allowed. There are no additional pet fees. Dogs must be well behaved, leashed, and cleaned up after. Dogs may be left in your RV only if they will be comfortable and quiet, and they are not allowed at the club house. There is a dog walk area at the campground. Multiple dogs may be allowed.

Bullards Beach State Park
52470 H 101
Bandon, OR
541-347-2209 (800-452-5687)
oregonstateparks.org/park_71.php
This is a large, family-oriented park nestled among the pines along the Coquille River, and offers an historic lighthouse with tours (seasonal) as well as various recreational pursuits. When visiting the park you can bring your binoculars for viewing the wildlife refuge just across the river. Dogs of all sizes are allowed at no additional fee. Dogs may not be left unattended except for short periods, and only if they will be quiet and well behaved. Dogs must be on no more than a 6 foot leash, and cleaned up after. Dogs are allowed on the trails. The camping and tent areas also allow dogs. There is a dog walk area at the campground. Multiple dogs may be allowed.

Deschutes National Forest
1001 SW Emkay Drive
Bend, OR
541-383-5300
fs.fed.us/r6/centraloregon/
Rich in natural and cultural history, this forest is home to the Newberry National Volcanic Monument, 8 wilderness areas and hundreds of miles of trails. The park also offers many diverse scenic and recreational opportunities. Dogs of all sizes are allowed at no additional fee. Dogs must be leashed and cleaned up after. This campground is closed during the off-season. The camping

and tent areas also allow dogs. There is a dog walk area at the campground. Multiple dogs may be allowed.

Sisters/Bend KOA
67667 H 20W
Bend, OR
541-549-3021 (800-562-0363)
koa.com
Dogs of all sizes are allowed. There are no additional pet fees. Dogs must be leashed and cleaned up after. This RV park is closed during the off-season. The camping and tent areas also allow dogs. There is a dog walk area at the campground. Multiple dogs may be allowed.

At Rivers Edge RV Park
98203 S Bank Chetco River Road
Brookings, OR
541-469-3356 (888-295-1441)
atriversedge.com/
Dogs of all sizes are allowed. There are no additional pet fees. Dogs may not be left unattended unless they will be quiet and well behaved. Dogs must be leashed and cleaned up after. Dogs may be off lead on your site only if they are under voice command and will not chase. The camping and tent areas also allow dogs. There is a dog walk area at the campground. 2 dogs may be allowed.

Harris Beach State Park
1655 H 101N
Brookings, OR
541-469-2021 (800-452-5687)
oregonstateparks.org/park_79.php
This park sits along the coastline making marine mammal watching a favorite here. The park also offers interpretive events, nature programs, trails, and a variety of land and water recreation. Dogs of all sizes are allowed at no additional fee. Dogs may not be left unattended; they must be on no more than a 6 foot leash or crated, and cleaned up after. Dogs are allowed on the trails. Dogs are not allowed in buildings. The camping and tent areas also allow dogs. There is a dog walk area at the campground. Multiple dogs may be allowed.

Whaleshead Beach Resort
19921 Whaleshead Road
Brookings, OR
541-469-7446 (800-943-4325)
whalesheadresort.com/
Located in a unique ocean side resort in a forested setting, this scenic RV park features terraced spacious sites, private decks, a

market and gift store, clean restrooms and showers, a laundry, and a restaurant/lounge is also on the property. Dogs of all sizes are allowed for no additional fee, and they must be declared at the time of registration. Dogs must be well behaved, and leashed and cleaned up after at all times. Dogs are also welcome at the resort in the cabins for an additional per night fee, and they are allowed on the beach under voice control or on a 6 foot leash. There is a dog walk area at the campground. Multiple dogs may be allowed.

Cannon Beach RV Resort
340 Elk Creek Road
Cannon Beach, OR
800-847-2231
cbrvresort.com
Dogs of all sizes are allowed. There are no additional pet fees. Dogs may not be left unattended, and they must be well behaved, leashed, and cleaned up after. There is a dog walk area at the campground. Multiple dogs may be allowed.

Sea Ranch RV Park and Stables
415 1st Street
Cannon Beach, OR
503-436-2815
searanchrv.com
Dogs of all sizes are allowed. There is a $2 per night per pet additional fee. Dogs may not be left unattended, and they must be leashed and cleaned up after. Dogs must be friendly to other animals because there are a variety of animals on site, including a free range bunny population. The camping and tent areas also allow dogs. There is a dog walk area at the campground. Multiple dogs may be allowed.

Cascade Locks/Portland East KOA
841 NW Forest Lane
Cascade Locks, OR
541-374-8668 (800-562-8698)
koa.com
Dogs of all sizes are allowed. There are no additional pet fees. Dogs may not be left unattended at any time, must be leashed, and cleaned up after. There are some breed restrictions. This RV park is closed during the off-season. The camping and tent areas also allow dogs. There is a dog walk area at the campground. Dogs are allowed in the camping cabins. Multiple dogs may be allowed.

Port of Cascade Locks and Marine Park
355 WaNaPa Street
Cascade Locks, OR
541-374-8619
portofcascadelocks.org/
The Marine Park here is a 23-acre scenic paradise, perfect for picnics, camping, weddings and outdoor events for groups up to 1000 people. This park is also home to the Sternwheeler Columbia Gorge and the Cascade Locks Historical Museum. They offer a visitors' center, gift shop, 37-slip marina, public boat launch, a playground, RV accommodations, a recently remodeled Gorge Pavilion, and a foot bridge that accesses the adjacent three-acre Thunder Island. Although dogs are not allowed on any of the boats here, they are allowed in the camp area and around the park. Dogs must be leashed and cleaned up after at all times. The camping and tent areas also allow dogs. There is a dog walk area at the campground. 2 dogs may be allowed.

Medford/Gold Hill KOA
12297 Blackwell Road
Central Point, OR
541-855-7710 (800-562-7608)
koa.com/where/or/37109/
Dogs of all sizes are allowed. There are no additional pet fees. Dogs must be quiet, well behaved, leashed, and cleaned up after. Dogs may not be left unattended, and may be left outside alone only if they are in an enclosed pen. There are some breed restrictions. The camping and tent areas also allow dogs. There is a dog walk area at the campground. Dogs are allowed in the camping cabins. Multiple dogs may be allowed.

Charleston Marina RV Park
63402 King Fisher Road
Charleston, OR
541-888-2548
charlestonmarina.com/rvpark.htm
Dogs of all sizes are allowed. There are no additional pet fees. Dogs may not be left unattended, and they must be leashed and cleaned up after. This RV park is closed during the off-season. The camping and tent areas also allow dogs. There is a dog walk area at the campground. Multiple dogs may be allowed.

Lucky Loggers RV Park
250 E Johnson
Coos Bay, OR
541-267-6003

Dogs of all sizes are allowed. There are no additional pet fees. Dogs must be leashed and cleaned up after. There is a dog walk area at the campground. Multiple dogs may be allowed.

Sunset Bay State Park
89814 Cape Arago
Coos Bay, OR
541-888-4902 (800-452-5687)
This picturesque park, along the Oregon coast, features sandy beaches sheltered by towering sea cliffs, interpretive and nature programs, a network of hiking trails, and a variety of land and water recreation. Dogs of all sizes are allowed at no additional fee, and they must have current tags, rabies, and shot records. Dogs may not be left unattended; they must be on no more than a 6 foot leash, and cleaned up after. Dogs are allowed on the trails except where marked. Dogs are not allowed in Shore Acres. The camping and tent areas also allow dogs. There is a dog walk area at the campground. Multiple dogs may be allowed.

Siuslaw National Forest
4077 SW Research Way
Corvallis, OR
541-750-7000
fs.fed.us/r6/siuslaw/
This very diverse and productive forest of over 630,000 acres has unique and varying ecosystems to explore and offers a wide variety of land and water recreation. Dogs of all sizes are allowed at no additional fee. Dogs may not be left unattended, and they must be leashed and cleaned up after. Dogs are not allowed in public swim areas or buildings. Dogs are allowed on the trails. The camping and tent areas also allow dogs. There is a dog walk area at the campground. There are no water hookups at the campground. Multiple dogs may be allowed.

Crater Lake National Park
P.O. Box 7/S Entrance Road
Crater Lake, OR
541-594-2211
nps.gov/crla/
This beautiful and historical lake park is a very diverse area. It is almost 90% wilderness and supports a large variety of plants, fish, mammals, bird species, and recreation. Dogs of all sizes are allowed at no additional fee. Dogs may not be left unattended, and they must be leashed and cleaned up after. Dogs

are not allowed in buildings or in the Rim Village area in the winter. Dogs are allowed on the trails. This campground is closed during the off-season. The camping and tent areas also allow dogs. There is a dog walk area at the campground. Multiple dogs may be allowed.

Madras/Culver KOA
2435 SW Jericho Lane
Culver, OR
541-546-3046 (800-562-1992)
koa.com
Dogs of all sizes are allowed, and there are no additional pet fees for up to 2 dogs. If there are more than 2 dogs, the fee is $2 per night per pet. Dogs must be leashed and cleaned up after. There are some breed restrictions. This RV park is closed during the off-season. The camping and tent areas also allow dogs. There is a dog walk area at the campground. Multiple dogs may be allowed.

The Cove Palisades State Park
7300 SW Jordan Road
Culver, OR
541-546-3412 (800-452-5687)
oregonstateparks.org/park_32.php
This high desert park features a myriad of water and land recreational opportunities, 10 miles of hiking trails, a designated off-leash area for your dog, historic sites, and special events and programs throughout the year. Dogs of all sizes are allowed at no additional fee. Dogs may not be left unattended, and they must be on no more than a 6 foot leash and cleaned up after. Dogs are not allowed in any of the swim areas, in buildings, or where posted as such. Dogs are allowed on the trails. The camping and tent areas also allow dogs. There is a dog walk area at the campground. There are special amenities given to dogs at this campground. Multiple dogs may be allowed.

Detroit Lake State Recreation Area
44000 N Santiam H SE
Detroit, OR
503-854-3346 (800-452-5687)
oregonstateparks.org/park_93.php
This scenic park sits along a beautiful 400-foot-deep lake located in the Cascade Mountains. It features nature programs, interpretive tours and exhibits, various special events, and a variety of land and water recreation. Dogs of all sizes are allowed at no additional fee. Dogs may not be left

unattended, and they must be on no more than a 6 foot leash, and cleaned up after. Dogs are allowed on the trails. This campground is closed during the off-season. The camping and tent areas also allow dogs. There is a dog walk area at the campground. Multiple dogs may be allowed.

Diamond Lake RV Park
3500 Diamond Lake Loop
Diamond Lake, OR
541-793-3318
diamondlakervpark.com
Dogs of all sizes are allowed, but only 2 large or 3 small dogs are allowed per site. There are no additional pet fees. Dogs must be leashed and cleaned up after. This RV park is closed during the off-season. There is a dog walk area at the campground.

Premier RV Resorts
33022 Van Duyn Road
Eugene, OR
541-686-3152 (888-701-8451)
premierrvresorts.com
Dogs of all sizes are allowed. There are no additional pet fees. Dogs must be leashed and cleaned up after. There is a small fenced in area for off lead. There is a dog walk area at the campground. Multiple dogs may be allowed.

Shamrock RV Village
4531 Franklin Blvd
Eugene, OR
541-747-7473
Dogs of all sizes are allowed. There are no additional pet fees. Dogs must be leashed and cleaned up after. There are some breed restrictions. There is a dog walk area at the campground. Multiple dogs may be allowed.

Portland Fairview RV Park
21401 NE Sandy Blvd
Fairview, OR
503-661-1047
portlandfairviewrv.com
Dogs of all sizes are allowed. There are no additional pet fees. Dogs must be quiet, friendly, well behaved, leashed, and cleaned up after. Dogs may not be left unattended outside. There are some breed restrictions. There is a dog walk area at the campground. Multiple dogs may be allowed.

Rolling Hills RV Park
20145 NE Sandy Blvd
Fairview, OR
503-666-7282

Dogs of all sizes are allowed. There are no additional pet fees. Dogs may not be left unattended or chained outside alone. Dogs must be leashed and cleaned up after. There are some breed restrictions. There is a dog walk area at the campground. Multiple dogs may be allowed.

Jessie M Honeyman Memorial State Park
84505 H 101S
Florence, OR
541-997-3641 (800-452-5687)
This park has the second largest overnight camping area in the state and features two miles of sand dunes, two natural freshwater lakes, an ATV area, interpretive and nature programs, and a variety of land and water recreation. Dogs of all sizes are allowed at no additional fee. Dogs may not be left unattended, and they must be on no more than a 6 foot leash, and cleaned up after. Dogs are allowed on the trails, but they are not allowed in buildings or yurts. The camping and tent areas also allow dogs. There is a dog walk area at the campground. Multiple dogs may be allowed.

Mercer Lake Resort
88875 Bay Berry Lane
Florence, OR
800-355-3633
mloregon.com/
Dogs of all sizes are allowed. There is a $5 per night per pet additional fee. Dogs may not be left unattended, and they must be leashed and cleaned up after. This is an RV only park. There is a dog walk area at the campground. 2 dogs may be allowed.

Four Seasons RV Resort
96526 N Bank Road
Gold Beach, OR
800-248-4503
fourseasonsrv.com
Dogs of all sizes are allowed. There are no additional pet fees. Dogs must be leashed and cleaned up after. There is a dog walk area at the campground. 2 dogs may be allowed.

Indian Creek Resort
94680 Jerry's Flat Road
Gold Beach, OR
541-247-7704
indiancreekresort.net
Dogs of all sizes are allowed, and there are no additional pet fees for tent or RV sites. There is a $20 one time additional pet fee for cabins. Dogs may not be left unattended

outside, and they must be leashed and cleaned up after. Dogs must be quiet and well behaved. The camping and tent areas also allow dogs. There is a dog walk area at the campground. Dogs are allowed in the camping cabins. 2 dogs may be allowed.

Turtle Rock RV Resort
28788 Hunter Creek Loop
Gold Beach, OR
541-247-9203
turtlerockresorts.com
Dogs of all sizes are allowed. There are no additional pet fees for one pet, either at the tent and RV sites or the cabins. For more than one dog there is a $4 per night per pet additional fee for the tent and RV sites, and a $15 per night per pet additional pet fee for the cabins. Dogs must be leashed and cleaned up after. The camping and tent areas also allow dogs. There is a dog walk area at the campground. Dogs are allowed in the camping cabins. Multiple dogs may be allowed.

Valley of the Rouge State Park
I 5 AT Exit 45B
Gold Hill, OR
541-582-1118 (800-452-5687)
This scenic park sits along the river made famous by novelist and avid fisherman Zane Grey. It offers a self-guided interpretive walking trail, nature programs, and a variety of land and water recreation. Dogs of all sizes are allowed at no additional fee. Dogs may not be left unattended, be on no more than a 6 foot, and cleaned up after in camp areas. Dogs are allowed on the trails, and they may be off lead there if they will not chase and they are under voice command. The camping and tent areas also allow dogs. There is a dog walk area at the campground. Multiple dogs may be allowed.

Jack's Landing RV Resort
247 NE Morgan Lane
Grants Pass, OR
541-472-1144
jackslandingrv.com
Dogs of all sizes are allowed. There are no additional pet fees. Dogs may not placed in outdoor pens or be left unattended. They may be left in the RV if comfortable and quiet. Dogs must be leashed and cleaned up after. There is a dog walk area at the campground. Multiple dogs may be allowed.

Siskiyou National Forest
2164 NE Spalding Avenue
Grants Pass, OR
541-471-6500 (877-444-6777)
fs.fed.us/r6/rogue-siskiyou/
Rogue River and Siskiyou National Forests were combined creating 1.8 million acres of spectacular scenery, hundreds of miles of trails, and diverse ecosystems that support a large variety of plants, animals, and recreation. Dogs of all sizes are allowed at no additional fee. Dogs may not be left unattended, and they must be leashed and cleaned up after in camp areas. Dogs are allowed off lead in the forest if they will not chase and if they are under strict voice control. This campground is closed during the off-season. The camping and tent areas also allow dogs. There is a dog walk area at the campground. Multiple dogs may be allowed.

Astoria/Seaside KOA
1100 Northwest Ridge Road
Hammond, OR
503-861-2606 (800-562-8506)
astoriakoa.com
Dogs of all sizes are allowed. There is a $2 per night per pet additional fee. Dogs may not be left unattended, must be leashed, and cleaned up after. There are some breed restrictions. The camping and tent areas also allow dogs. There is a dog walk area at the campground. Dogs are allowed in the camping cabins. 2 dogs may be allowed.

Fort Stevens State Park
100 Peter Ierdale
Hammond, OR
503-861-1671 (800-452-5687)
Born out of the need for military defense this historic park offers programs and exhibits on its history, a nature/visitor center, several trails, various habitats, and a variety of land and water recreation. Dogs of all sizes are allowed at no additional fee. Dogs may not be left unattended, and they must be on no more than a 6 foot leash, and cleaned up after. Dogs are allowed off lead on South Beach, and they are allowed on the trails. The camping and tent areas also allow dogs. There is a dog walk area at the campground. Multiple dogs may be allowed.

Blue Heron RV Park
6930 Copco Road
Hornbrook, OR
530-475-3270
klamathranchresort.com

Dogs of all sizes are allowed. There is a $1 per night per pet additional fee. Dogs must be leashed and cleaned up after. There is a dog walk area at the campground. Multiple dogs may be allowed.

Malheur National Forest
431 Patterson Bridge Road
John Day, OR
541-575-3000
fs.fed.us/r6/malheur/
This 1.7 million acre forest offers spectacular scenery, hundreds of miles of trails, and diverse ecosystems that support a large variety of plants, animals, and recreation. Dogs of all sizes are allowed at no additional fee. Dogs may not be left unattended, and they must be leashed and cleaned up after. This campground is closed during the off-season. The camping and tent areas also allow dogs. There is a dog walk area at the campground. There are no electric or water hookups at the campground. Multiple dogs may be allowed.

Park at the River
59879 Wallowa Lake H
Joseph, OR
541-432-8800
eaglecapchalets.com
Dogs of all sizes are allowed. There are no additional pet fees. Dogs may not be left unattended, and must be well behaved, leashed, and cleaned up after. Dogs are not allowed at any of the rentals. There is a dog walk area at the campground. Multiple dogs may be allowed.

Fremont- Winema National Forest
2819 Dahlia Street
Klamath Falls, OR
541-883-6714
fs.fed.us/r6/frewin/
The Fremont-Winema National Forests were combined creating 2.3 million acres of spectacular scenery, hundreds of miles of trails, and diverse ecosystems that support a large variety of plants, animals, and recreation. Dogs of all sizes are allowed at no additional fee. Dogs may not be left unattended, and they must be leashed and cleaned up after in camp areas. Dogs may be off lead in the forest if they will not chase and they are under voice control. Dogs are not allowed in buildings. This campground is closed during the off-season. The camping and tent areas also allow dogs. There is a dog walk area at the campground. There are no electric or water hookups at the campground.

Multiple dogs may be allowed.

Klamath Falls KOA
3435 Shasta Way
Klamath Falls, OR
541-884-4644 (800-562-9036)
koa.com
Dogs of all sizes are allowed. There are no additional pet fees. Dogs may not be left unattended, and they must be leashed and cleaned up after. There is a large fenced in area where dogs may run off lead. The camping and tent areas also allow dogs. There is a dog walk area at the campground. Multiple dogs may be allowed.

LaPine State Park
15800 State Recreation Road
LaPine, OR
541-536-2071 (800-452-5687)
oregonstateparks.org/park_41.php
This park, home to the oldest tree in Oregon aged about 500 years, offers access to 2 rivers, 10 miles of trails, a museum, and a variety of land and water recreation. Dogs of all sizes are allowed at no additional fee. Dogs may not be left unattended, and they must be on no more than a 6 foot leash, and cleaned up after. Dogs are allowed on trails unless otherwise marked. The camping and tent areas also allow dogs. There is a dog walk area at the campground. Multiple dogs may be allowed.

Fremont-Winema National Forest
1301 S G Street
Lakeview, OR
541-947-2151
fs.fed.us/r6/frewin/
The Fremont-Winema National Forests were combined creating 2.3 million acres of spectacular scenery, hundreds of miles of trails, and diverse ecosystems that support a large variety of plants, animals, and recreation. Dogs of all sizes are allowed at no additional fee. Dogs may not be left unattended, and they must be leashed and cleaned up after. This campground is closed during the off-season. The camping and tent areas also allow dogs. There is a dog walk area at the campground. There are no electric or water hookups at the campground. Multiple dogs may be allowed.

Bandon/Port Orford KOA
46612 H 101
Langlois, OR
541-348-2358 (800-562-3298)
koa.com

Dogs of all sizes are allowed. There are no additional pet fees. Dogs must be leashed and cleaned up after. There are some breed restrictions. The camping and tent areas also allow dogs. There is a dog walk area at the campground. 2 dogs may be allowed.

Premier RV Resort
31958 Bellinger Scale Road
Lebanon, OR
541-259-0070
Dogs of all sizes are allowed. There are no additional pet fees. Dogs may not be left unattended, and must be leashed and cleaned up after. There is a fenced dog run area for off lead. There is a dog walk area at the campground. Multiple dogs may be allowed.

Willamette National Forest
57600 McKenzie H
McKenzie Bridge, OR
541-822-3381
fs.fed.us/r6/willamette/
This forest has over a million and a half acres of high mountains, cascading streams, narrow canyons, and diverse ecosystems that support a large variety of plants, animals, and recreation. Dogs of all sizes are allowed at no additional fee. Dogs may not be left unattended, and they must be leashed and cleaned up after in camp. Dogs may be off lead on the trails only if they will not chase, and if they are under strict voice command. The camping and tent areas also allow dogs. There is a dog walk area at the campground. There are no electric or water hookups at the campground. Multiple dogs may be allowed.

Rogue River National Forest
333 W 8th Street
Medford, OR
541-858-2200 (877-444-6777)
fs.fed.us/r6/rogue-siskiyou/
Rogue River and Siskiyou National Forests were combined creating 1.8 million acres of spectacular scenery, hundreds of miles of trails, and diverse ecosystems that support a large variety of plants, animals, and recreation. Dogs of all sizes are allowed at no additional fee. Dogs may not be left unattended, and they must be leashed and cleaned up after in camp areas. Dogs are allowed off lead in the forest if they will not chase and if they are under strict voice control. This campground is closed during the off-season. The camping and tent areas also allow dogs. There is a dog walk area at the

campground. There are no water hookups at the campground. Multiple dogs may be allowed.

Memaloose State Park
Box 472
Mosier, OR
541-478-3008 (800-452-5687)
This oasis like park offers interpretive exhibits and events, nature programs, various day and night programs and a variety of land and water recreation. Dogs of all sizes are allowed at no additional fee. Dogs may not be left unattended unless they will be quiet and well behaved, and they must be on no more than a 6 foot leash, and cleaned up after. Dogs are allowed on the trails unless otherwise marked, and they may be off lead on trails if they are under strict voice command. This campground is closed during the off-season. The camping and tent areas also allow dogs. There is a dog walk area at the campground. Multiple dogs may be allowed.

On the River Golf & RV Resort
111 Whitson Lane
Myrtle Creek, OR
541-679-3505
ontherivergolf-rv.com/
Dogs of all sizes are allowed. There are no additional pet fees. Dogs may not be left unattended outside, and they must be leashed and cleaned up after. There are some breed restrictions. The camping and tent areas also allow dogs. There is a dog walk area at the campground. Multiple dogs may be allowed.

Netarts Bay RV Park and Marina
2260 Bilyeu Avenue
Netarts, OR
503-842-7774
netartsbay.com
Dogs of all sizes are allowed. There are no additional pet fees. Dogs must be leashed and cleaned up after. There are some breed restrictions. There is a dog walk area at the campground. 2 dogs may be allowed.

Beverly Beach State Park
198 NE 123rd Street
Newport, OR
541-265-9278 (800-452-5687)
This forest-sheltered campground sits along the Oregon coast providing a long sandy seashore to explore. It provides nature programs, trails, interpretive programs, and a variety of recreational pursuits. Dogs of all sizes are allowed at no additional

fee. Dogs may not be left unattended, and they must be on no more than a 6 foot leash, and cleaned up after. Dogs are allowed on trails unless otherwise marked. The camping and tent areas also allow dogs. There is a dog walk area at the campground. Multiple dogs may be allowed.

Oregon Dunes KOA
68632 H 101
North Bend, OR
541-756-4851 (800-562-4236)
koa.com
Dogs of all sizes are allowed. There are no additional pet fees. Dogs must be leashed and cleaned up after, and walked by an adult. Dogs are not allowed to be left unattended outside, but they may be left in your auto or RV if they will be comfortable and quiet. The camping and tent areas also allow dogs. There is a dog walk area at the campground. Multiple dogs may be allowed.

Lincoln City KOA
5298 NE Park Lane
Otis, OR
541-994-2961 (800-562-2791)
koa.com
Dogs of all sizes are allowed. There is a pet policy to sign at check in and there are no additional pet fees. Dogs must be leashed and cleaned up after. There are some breed restrictions. The camping and tent areas also allow dogs. There is a dog walk area at the campground. Multiple dogs may be allowed.

Cape Kiwanda RV Resort
33305 Cape Kiwanda Drive
Pacific City, OR
503-965-6230
capekiwandarvpark.com
Dogs of all sizes are allowed. There are no additional pet fees. Dogs must be leashed and cleaned up after. There is a dog walk area at the campground. Multiple dogs may be allowed.

Umatilla National Forest
2517 SW Hailey Avenue
Pendleton, OR
541-278-3716
fs.fed.us/r6/uma/
This forest of nearly 1.4 million acres provides spectacular scenery, a rich cultural history, and diverse ecosystems that support a large variety of plants, animals, and recreation. Dogs of all sizes are allowed at no additional fee. Dogs may not be left unattended; they

must be quiet, well behaved, be on no more than a 6 foot leash, and cleaned up after in camp areas. Dogs are allowed on the trails. This campground is closed during the off-season. The camping and tent areas also allow dogs. There is a dog walk area at the campground. Dogs are allowed in the camping cabins. There are no electric or water hookups at the campground. Multiple dogs may be allowed.

Port Orford RV Village
2855 Port Orford Loop
Port Orford, OR
541-332-1041 (800-332-1041)
portorfordrv.com/
In addition to being close to many points of interest, this RV park features a rec room with a full kitchen, showers, heated bathrooms, a car wash area, fish cleaning station, cable TV, and laundry facilities. Dogs of all sizes are welcome for no additional fee. Dogs must be friendly as there are other animals in residence. Dogs may be left inside an RV unit only if they will be quiet and well behaved; they are not allowed to be left unattended outside at any time. Dogs must be leashed and cleaned up after. The camping and tent areas also allow dogs. There is a dog walk area at the campground. Multiple dogs may be allowed.

Jantzen Beach RV Park
1503 N Hayden Island Drive
Portland, OR
503-289-7626
jantzenbeachrv.com/
One dog of any size is allowed. There are no additional pet fees. Dogs may not be left unattended outside, and they must be leashed and cleaned up after. This is an RV only park. There are some breed restrictions. There is a dog walk area at the campground.

Ochoco National Forest
3160 SE 3rd Street
Prineville, OR
541-416-6500 (877-444-6777)
The Ochoco and Deschutes Forests were combined creating 2.5 million acres of spectacular scenery, hundreds of miles of trails, diverse ecosystems and recreation. Dogs of all sizes are allowed at no additional fee. Dogs may not be left unattended, and they must be leashed and cleaned up after in camp areas. Dogs may be off lead in the forest on the trails if they will not chase wildlife and if they are under

strict voice control. Dogs are not allowed in buildings. This campground is closed during the off-season. The camping and tent areas also allow dogs. There is a dog walk area at the campground. There are no electric or water hookups at the campground. Multiple dogs may be allowed.

Prineville Reservoir State Park
19020 SE Parkland Drive
Prineville, OR
541-447-4363 (800-452-5687)
oregonstateparks.org/park_34.php
This park and reservoir offer a wide variety of land and water recreation, nature programs, trails, and interpretive events and tours. Dogs of all sizes are allowed at no additional fee. Dogs may not be left unattended, and they must be on no more than a 6 foot leash, and cleaned up after. Dogs are not allowed in cabins or in the cabin area. Dogs are allowed on the trails. The camping and tent areas also allow dogs. There is a dog walk area at the campground. Multiple dogs may be allowed.

Rising River RV Park
5579 Grange Road
Roseburg, OR
541-679-7256
Dogs of all sizes are allowed. There are no additional pet fees. Dogs may not be left unattended outside, and they must be leashed and cleaned up after. There are some breed restrictions. There is a dog walk area at the campground. 2 dogs may be allowed.

Umpqua National Forest
2900 Stewart Parkway
Roseburg, OR
541-750-7000 (877-444-6777)
fs.fed.us/r6/umpqua/
This forest of almost a million acres is home to one of the largest developed recreational facilities within the Forest Service. It offers a diverse topography that provides for a wide variety of habitats, naturescapes and recreational activities. Dogs of all sizes are allowed at no additional fee. Dogs may not be left unattended; they must be quiet, well behaved, be on no more than a 6 foot leash, and cleaned up after in camp areas. Dogs are allowed on the trails, but they say to use caution on the horse and ATV trails. The camping and tent areas also allow dogs. There is a dog walk area at the campground. There are no electric or water

hookups at the campground. Multiple dogs may be allowed.

Premier RV Resorts
4700 H 22
Salem, OR
503-364-7714 (503-364-7714)
premierresorts.com
Dogs of all sizes are allowed. There are no additional fees. Dogs must be quiet, well behaved, leashed, and cleaned up after. Dogs may not be left unattended outside. There is a dog walk area at the campground. Multiple dogs may be allowed.

Salem Campground
3700 Hager's Grove Road
Salem, OR
503-581-6736 (800-826-9605)
salemrv.com
Dogs of all sizes are allowed. There are no additional pet fees. Dogs must be leashed and cleaned up after. There are some breed restrictions. There is a dog walk area at the campground. 2 dogs may be allowed.

Mount Hood National Forest
16400 Champion Way
Sandy, OR
503-668-1700
fs.fed.us/r6/mthood/
This beautiful forest of more than a million acres offers hundreds of miles of trails, interpretive programs, and diverse ecosystems that support a large variety of plants, animals, and recreation. Dogs of all sizes are allowed at no additional fee. Dogs may not be left unattended, and they must be leashed and cleaned up after. Dogs are allowed on the trails. This campground is closed during the off-season. The camping and tent areas also allow dogs. There is a dog walk area at the campground. There are no electric or water hookups at the campground.

Champoeg State Heritage Area
Champoeg Road
St Paul, OR
503-678-1251, ext 221 (800-452-5687)
Located on the banks of the Willamette River, this scenic park has a rich historic past, and offers historic tours, living history demonstrations, nature and history programs, and a wide variety of land and water activities. Dogs of all sizes are allowed at no additional fee. Dogs may not be left unattended, and they must be on no

more than a 6 foot leash, and cleaned up after. Dogs are not allowed in buildings. There is a large off-leash area located at the west end of the park for your pet to run. The camping and tent areas also allow dogs. There is a dog walk area at the campground. There are special amenities given to dogs at this campground. Multiple dogs may be allowed.

Hi-Way Haven RV Park
609 Fort McKay Road
Sutherlin, OR
541-459-4557 (800-552-5699)
hiwayhaven.com/
This nicely kept RV only park offers amenities such as a picnic area, barbecue facilities, a recreation room, a convenience store, planned activities, and more, but they also offer another rare treat. The park is built on the site of a drive in theater and is licensed to show classic films, which they usually do on Saturday night for no additional charge. Dogs of all sizes are allowed for no additional fee, and they offer 2 large dog walk/exercise areas. Dogs may not be left alone outside at any time, and may be left in your unit only if they will be quiet and well behaved. Your dog's food and water may not be left outside, and dogs are not allowed on the lawn just in front of the movie screen, but they can be in your vehicle if you pull up to watch the movie. There is a dog walk area at the campground. 2 dogs may be allowed.

Edgewater RV Resort and Marina
1400 60th Avenue
Sweet Home, OR
541-818-0431 (866-695-0932)
edgewateroregon.com
Located along the shores of Foster Lake, this lush recreation area offers 49 sites, Wi-Fi, cable TV, picnic tables, fire pits, laundry facilities, gaming areas, ice cream socials, and during special planned events they offer a pet check-up and walking service. Well behaved dogs are allowed for no additional fee; they must be leashed and under their owner's control. Dogs are allowed in the lake-preferably on a long leash. The camping and tent areas also allow dogs. There is a dog walk area at the campground. Multiple dogs may be allowed.

Cape Lookout State Park
13000 Whiskey Creek Road W
Tillamook, OR
503-842-4981 (800-452-5687)

This lush coastal forest park offers spectacular views, marine watching, hiking trails, interpretive tours, historic programs, and a variety of recreational pursuits. Dogs of all sizes are allowed at no additional fee. Dogs may not be left unattended, and they must be on no more than a 6 foot leash, and cleaned up after. Dogs are allowed on trails unless otherwise marked. The camping and tent areas also allow dogs. There is a dog walk area at the campground. Multiple dogs may be allowed.

RV Park of Portland
6645 SW Nyberg Road
Tualatin, OR
503-692-0225 (800-856-2066)
rvparkofportland.com/
Dogs of all sizes are allowed, but only 1 dog may be over 40 pounds, and St. Bernards are not allowed. There are no additional pet fees. Dogs may not be left unattended outside, and they must be leashed and cleaned up after. There are some breed restrictions. There is a dog walk area at the campground.

Waldport/Newport KOA
1330 NW Pacific Coast H
Waldport, OR
541-563-2250 (800-562-3443)
koa.com
Dogs of all sizes are allowed. There are no additional pet fees. Dogs must be on no more than a 6 foot leash(retractable leashes are not allowed), and cleaned up after. There are some breed restrictions. The camping and tent areas also allow dogs. There is a dog walk area at the campground. There are special amenities given to dogs at this campground. Multiple dogs may be allowed.

Mt Hood Village
65000 E H 26
Welches, OR
800-255-3069
mhcrv.com
One dog of any size is allowed, and there are no additional pet fees for tent or RV sites. There is a $10 one time additional pet fee for the cabin. Dogs must be quiet, well behaved, leashed, and cleaned up after. There are some breed restrictions. The camping and tent areas also allow dogs. There is a dog walk area at the campground. Dogs are allowed in the camping cabins.

Grants Pass/Redwood Hwy KOA
13370 Redwood H

Wilderville, OR
541-476-6508 (800-562-7566)
koa.com/where/or/37106/
Dogs of all sizes are allowed. There are no additional pet fees. Dogs may not be tied to the picnic tables, and they must be leashed and cleaned up after. Dogs must be taken to the specified dog walk area to do their business. There are some breed restrictions. The camping and tent areas also allow dogs. There is a dog walk area at the campground. Multiple dogs may be allowed.

The Marina RV Resort
End of Marina Way
Winchester Bay, OR
541-271-0287
marinarvresort.com
Dogs of all sizes are allowed. There are no additional pet fees. Dogs may not be left unattended, and they must be well behaved, leashed and cleaned up after. There is a dog walk area at the campground. Multiple dogs may be allowed.

Pennsylvania

Union Canal Campground and the Swatara Creek Water Trail
1929 Blacks Bridge Road
Annville, PA
717-838-9580
This recreation destination offers canoe rentals (dogs allowed), a trail that follows the river, an 18-hole chip and putt golf course, and camping. Dogs are allowed in the camp area for no additional pet fee. Dogs must be quiet, well behaved, leashed, and cleaned up after at all times. This RV park is closed during the off-season. The camping and tent areas also allow dogs. There is a dog walk area at the campground. 2 dogs may be allowed.

Locust Lake State Park
Burma Road/H 1006
Barnesville, PA
570-467-2404
A mountain lake surrounded by beautiful forests with plenty of recreation, easy to difficult hiking trails, and a lot more are all offered at this 1,089 acre park. Dogs of all sizes are allowed for an additional $2 per pet per stay. Visitors are not allowed to bring dogs for day use when the campground is open from early April to mid-October; they are

allowed in the park from mid-October to the beginning of April. Dogs must be well behaved, under their owner's control, leashed or crated, and cleaned up after at all times (exceptions during hunting season). Dogs must be licensed with proof of vaccinations. Aggressive dogs are not allowed. Dogs may not be left unattended outside at any time and if in a vehicle-for very short times. Dogs must stay on selected pet routes/trails and areas; they may not be in designated swim areas, park buildings, or in the campground area. Trail maps allowing dogs can be obtained at the park office. The camp area has nice wooded sites with a parking pad, fire rings, picnic tables, and modern restrooms, showers, playgrounds, and a dump station are nearby. This RV park is closed during the off-season. The camping and tent areas also allow dogs. There is a dog walk area at the campground. There are no water hookups at the campgrounds.

Bellefonte/State College KOA
2481 Jacksonville Road
Bellefonte, PA
814-355-7912 (814-355-7912)
koa.com
Dogs of all sizes are allowed. There are no additional pet fees. Dogs must be leashed and cleaned up after. This RV park is closed during the off-season. The camping and tent areas also allow dogs. There is a dog walk area at the campground. Dogs are allowed in the camping cabins. Multiple dogs may be allowed.

Lackawanan State Park
N Abington Road/H 407
Benton, PA
570-945-3239 (888-PA-PARKS (727-2757))
This 1,411 acre park with a 198 acre lake offers modern facilities, year round land and water recreation, environmental education, and trails that wander through a variety of scenic landscapes. Dogs of all sizes are allowed for an additional $2 per pet per stay. Dogs must be well behaved, under their owner's control, leashed or crated, and cleaned up after at all times (exceptions during hunting season). Dogs must be licensed and have proof of all vaccinations. Aggressive dogs are not allowed. Dogs may not be left unattended outside at any time and may only be left alone in a vehicle for VERY short periods. Dogs must stay on selected pet routes/trails and

areas; they may not be in designated swim areas or in park buildings. The campground has modern sites, washhouses with hot showers, children's play areas, and some small fishing ponds close by. There is also a dump station available. The camping and tent areas also allow dogs. There is a dog walk area at the campground. There are no water hookups at the campgrounds. 2 dogs may be allowed.

Sun Valley Campground
451 Maple Grove Road
Bowmansville, PA
717-445-6262
sunvalleycamping.com
Dogs of all sizes are allowed. There are no additional pet fees. Dogs must be leashed and cleaned up after. This RV park is closed during the off-season. The camping and tent areas also allow dogs. There is a dog walk area at the campground. Multiple dogs may be allowed.

Kinzua East KOA
Klondike Road, Kinzua Heights
Bradford, PA
814-368-3662 (800-562-3682)
kinzuacamping.com
One dog of any size is allowed. There are no additional pet fees. Dogs may not be left unattended, must be leashed, and cleaned up after. There are some breed restrictions. This RV park is closed during the off-season. The camping and tent areas also allow dogs. There is a dog walk area at the campground.

Western Village RV Park
200 Greenview Drive
Carlisle, PA
717-243-1179
westernvillagervpark.com
Dogs of all sizes are allowed. There are no additional pet fees. Dogs may not be left unattended, must be leashed, and cleaned up after. Dogs are not allowed on other guests' sites. There is a dog walk area at the campground. Multiple dogs may be allowed.

Twin Bridge Meadow Campground
1345 Twin Bridges Road
Chambersburg, PA
717-369-2216
Dogs of all sizes are allowed. There are no additional pet fees. Dogs may not be left unattended, must be leashed, and cleaned up after. There are some breed restrictions. This RV park is closed during the off-season. The camping and tent areas also

allow dogs. There is a dog walk area at the campground. 2 dogs may be allowed.

Timberland Campground
117 Timber Lane
Clarksboro, NJ
856-423-6677
timberlanecampground.com
Dogs of all sizes are allowed. There are no additional pet fees. Dogs must be quiet and well behaved. Dogs may not be left unattended, must be leashed, and cleaned up after. The camping and tent areas also allow dogs. There is a dog walk area at the campground. Multiple dogs may be allowed.

Hidden Springs Campground
815 Beans Cove Road
Clearville, PA
814-767-9676
Dogs of all sizes are allowed. There are no additional pet fees. Dogs must be quiet, leashed, and cleaned up after. This RV park is closed during the off-season. The camping and tent areas also allow dogs. There is a dog walk area at the campground. Multiple dogs may be allowed.

Philadelphia/West Chester KOA
1659 Embreeville Road
Coatsville, PA
610-486-0447 (800-562-1726)
koa.com
Well behaved and friendly dogs of all sizes are allowed. There are no additional pet fees. Dogs may not be left unattended, must be leashed, and cleaned up after. This RV park is closed during the off-season. The camping and tent areas also allow dogs. There is a dog walk area at the campground. Multiple dogs may be allowed.

Camperland at Conneaut Lake Park
12382 Center Street
Conneaut Lake, PA
814-382-7750
This full service family campground offers a long list of amenities, activities, attractions, and events at this recreational destination, plus they have an ice cream parlor on site. Dogs are allowed throughout the resort; there is no additional fee. Dogs may not be left unattended, and they must be leashed and cleaned up after at all times. There are some breed restrictions. This RV park is closed during the off-season. There is a dog walk area at the campground. 2 dogs may be allowed.

Cook Forest State Park
River Road
Cooksburg, PA
814-744-8407 (888-PA-PARKS (727-2757))
Famous for its "Forest Cathedral" of virgin white pine and hemlock stands that resulted in it being listed as a National Natural Landmark, this 7,000+ acre park offers an array of land and water recreation and 27 blazed trails. Dogs must be quiet, well behaved, under their owner's control, leashed or crated, and cleaned up after at all times. Dogs must be licensed and have proof of all vaccinations. Aggressive dogs are not allowed. Dogs may not be left unattended outside at any time and may only be left alone in a vehicle for VERY short times. Dogs must stay on selected pet routes/trails and areas; they may not be in designated swim areas or in park buildings, and pet food may not be left outside. The camp areas have picnic tables, fire rings, restrooms, showers, laundry facilities, and a dump station. Dogs are allowed in the Ridge Campground only. This RV park is closed during the off-season. The camping and tent areas also allow dogs. There is a dog walk area at the campground. There are no electric or water hookups at the campgrounds. 2 dogs may be allowed.

Hickory Run Camping Resort
285 Greenville Road
Denver, PA
717-336-5564
hickoryruncampingresort.com
Dogs of all sizes are allowed. There are no additional pet fees. Dogs must be leashed and cleaned up after. They can be left in your unit if they are well behaved, and there is sufficient cooling. This RV park is closed during the off-season. The camping and tent areas also allow dogs. There is a dog walk area at the campground. Multiple dogs may be allowed.

Keystone State Park
1150 Keystone Park Road
Derry, PA
724-668-2939
Dogs of all sizes are allowed. There is a $2 per night per pet additional fee. Pets are to be walked in designated walking areas of the campground and on designated pet walkways when accessing other areas of the park from the campground. Dogs must be leashed, under physical control at all times,

and cleaned up after. Pet food must remain inside the camping unit, and dogs must have current shot records and a rabies certificate, be quiet, and well behaved. Dogs are allowed on the trails and day use areas, but they are not allowed on the beach, in any swim areas, or in any of the buildings. Dogs may not be left unattended except for very short periods; then they must be left inside your unit, weather permitting. Dogs are allowed on the trails. This campground is closed during the off-season. The camping and tent areas also allow dogs. There is a dog walk area at the campground. There are no water hookups at the campground. 2 dogs may be allowed.

Delaware Water Gap KOA
233 Hollow Road
E Stroudsburg, PA
570-223-8000 (800-562-0375)
koa.com
Dogs of all sizes are allowed. There are no additional pet fees. Dogs must be leased and cleaned up after. There are some breed restrictions. This RV park is closed during the off-season. The camping and tent areas also allow dogs. There is a dog walk area at the campground. Multiple dogs may be allowed.

Mountain Vista Campground
50 Taylor Drive
E Stroudsburg, PA
570-223-0111
mountainvistacampground.com
Dogs of all sizes are allowed. There are no additional pet fees. Dogs must be well behaved, leashed, and cleaned up after. This RV park is closed during the off-season. The camping and tent areas also allow dogs. There is a dog walk area at the campground. Multiple dogs may be allowed.

Otter Lake Camp Resort
4805 Marshall's Creek Road
E Stroudsburg, PA
570-223-0123
otterlake.com
Dogs of all sizes are allowed. There are no additional pet fees. Dogs may not be left unattended, must be leashed, and cleaned up after. The camping and tent areas also allow dogs. There is a dog walk area at the campground. Multiple dogs may be allowed.

Hershey Conewago Campground
1590 Hershey Road
Elizabethtown, PA

717-367-1179
hersheyconewago.com
Dogs of all sizes are allowed. There are no additional pet fees. Dogs may not be left unattended at any time, must be leashed, and cleaned up after. This RV park is closed during the off-season. The camping and tent areas also allow dogs. There is a dog walk area at the campground. Multiple dogs may be allowed.

French Creek State Park
843 Park Road
Elverson, PA
610-582-9680 (888-PA-PARKS (727-2757))
With 2 beautiful lakes and almost 40 miles of well-marked trails, this beautifully forested 7,339 acre park offers a wide variety of educational and recreational opportunities. Dogs of all sizes are allowed for an additional $2 per pet per stay. Dogs must be well behaved, under their owner's control, leashed or crated, and cleaned up after at all times (exceptions during hunting season). Dogs must be licensed and have proof of all vaccinations. Aggressive dogs are not allowed. Dogs may not be left unattended outside at any time and may only be left alone in a vehicle for VERY short periods. Dogs must stay on selected pet routes/trails and areas; they may not be in designated swim areas or in park buildings. Trail maps allowing dogs can be obtained at the park office. The campground offers 201 modern, wooded sites with flush toilet facilities and showers close by. The camping and tent areas also allow dogs. There is a dog walk area at the campground. There are no water hookups at the campgrounds. 2 dogs may be allowed.

Knoebel's Campground
Route 487
Elysburg, PA
800-ITS-4FUN
knoebels.com/family-vacation.asp
This campground is located next to the Knoebel's Amusement Park which is the largest free admission amusement park in the country. Dogs are allowed at your RV or tent site. Pets are not allowed in the cabins but leashed dogs are allowed in the amusement park.

Lyman Run State Park
454 Lyman Run Road
Galeton, PA
814-435-5010

Dogs of all sizes are allowed. There is a $2 per night per pet additional fee. Pets are to be walked in designated walking areas of the campground and on designated pet walkways when accessing other areas of the park from the campground. Dogs must be leashed, under physical control at all times, and cleaned up after. Pet food must remain inside the camping unit, and dogs must have current shot records and a rabies certificate, be quiet, and well behaved. Dogs are allowed on the trails and day use areas, but they are not allowed on the beach, in any swim areas, or in any of the buildings. Dogs may not be left unattended except for very short periods; then they must be left inside your unit, weather permitting. Dogs are allowed on the trails. This campground is closed during the off-season. The camping and tent areas also allow dogs. There is a dog walk area at the campground. There are no water hookups at the campground. 2 dogs may be allowed.

Mountain Creek Campground
349 Pine Grove Road
Gardners, PA
717-486-7681
mtncreekcg.com
Dogs of all sizes are allowed. There are no additional pet fees. Dogs must be quiet, well behaved, leashed, and cleaned up after. This RV park is closed during the off-season. The camping and tent areas also allow dogs. There is a dog walk area at the campground. Multiple dogs may be allowed.

Artillery Ridge Camping Resort
610 Taneytown Road
Gettysburg, PA
717-334-1288 (866-932-2674)
artilleryridge.com/
There is a long list of amenities, activities, attractions, and events here to enjoy, but a highlight is the largest Battlefield diorama in the US with over 800 feet of display of Gettysburg and of the battle fought there. Dogs are allowed throughout the resort; there is no additional fee. Dogs must be leashed and cleaned up after. This RV park is closed during the off-season. The camping and tent areas also allow dogs. There is a dog walk area at the campground. Multiple dogs may be allowed.

Drummer Boy Camping Resort
1300 Hanover Road

Gettysburg, PA
800-293-2808
drummerboycamping.com
Dogs of all sizes are allowed. There are no additional pet fees. Dogs may not be left unattended, must be leashed, and cleaned up after. They are also not allowed to be tied up outside alone or be in any of the buildings. This RV park is closed during the off-season. The camping and tent areas also allow dogs. There is a dog walk area at the campground. 2 dogs may be allowed.

Gettysburg Campground
2030 Fairfield Road/H 116
Gettysburg, PA
717-334-3304 (888 879-2241)
gettysburgcampground.com/
This full service family campground offers a long list of amenities, activities, attractions, and events at this recreational destination, plus they have an ice cream parlor on site. Dogs are allowed throughout the resort; there is no additional fee. Dogs must be leashed and cleaned up after at all times. This RV park is closed during the off-season. The camping and tent areas also allow dogs. There is a dog walk area at the campground. Multiple dogs may be allowed.

Gettysburg/Battlefield KOA
20 Knox Road
Gettysburg, PA
717-642-5713 (800-562-1869)
gettysburgkoa.com
Dogs of all sizes are allowed, and there are no additional pet fees for tent or RV sites. There is a $10 one time pet fee for cabin rentals. Dogs may not be left unattended at any time, must be leashed, and cleaned up after. This RV park is closed during the off-season. The camping and tent areas also allow dogs. There is a dog walk area at the campground. Dogs are allowed in the camping cabins. Multiple dogs may be allowed.

Round Top Campground
180 Night Road
Gettysburg, PA
717-334-9565
roundtopcamp.com
Dogs of all sizes are allowed. There are no additional pet fees. Dogs may not be left unattended, must be leashed, and cleaned up after. Dogs are not allowed in the rentals. The camping and tent areas also allow dogs. There is a dog walk area at the campground. Multiple dogs may be

allowed.

Promised Land State Park
Park Avenue
Greentown, PA
570-676-3428 (888-PA-PARKS (727-2757))
This scenic 3,000 acre park includes natural areas, forests, 2 lakes, several small streams, waterfalls, and about 50 miles of hiking trails in the park and the surrounding state forest. Dogs of all sizes are allowed for an additional $2 per pet per stay. Dogs must be well behaved, under their owner's control, leashed or crated, and cleaned up after at all times (exceptions during hunting season). Dogs must be licensed and have proof of all vaccinations. Aggressive dogs are not allowed. Dogs may not be left unattended outside at any time and may only be left alone in a vehicle for VERY short periods. Dogs must stay on selected pet routes/trails and areas; they may not be in designated swim areas or in park buildings. There are 4 modern to rustic campgrounds with picnic tables, fire pits, restrooms, and hot showers. This RV park is closed during the off-season. The camping and tent areas also allow dogs. There is a dog walk area at the campground. There are no water hookups at the campgrounds. 2 dogs may be allowed.

Codorus State Park
1066 Blooming Grove Rd
Hanover, PA
717-637-2418
dcnr.state.pa.us/stateparks
Dogs of all sizes are allowed. There is a $2 per night per pet additional fee. Dogs are to be leashed and under physical control at all times. Pet food must remain inside the camping unit, and pet waste must be disposed of quickly and properly. Pets are to be walked in designated walking areas of the campground and on designated pet walkways when accessing other areas of the park from the campground. Dogs are not permitted in swimming areas or inside buildings, they must have current rabies certificate and shot records, be quiet, and well behaved. Dogs may not be left unattended except for very short periods, and then they must be inside, weather permitting. Dogs on lead are allowed on the trails. There are some breed restrictions. This campground is closed during the off-season. The camping and tent

areas also allow dogs. There is a dog walk area at the campground. There are no water hookups at the campground. 2 dogs may be allowed.

Raccoon Creek State Park
3000 State Route 18
Hookstown, PA
724-899-2200
Dogs of all sizes are allowed. There is a $2 per night per pet additional fee. Pets are to be walked in designated walking areas of the campground and on designated pet walkways when accessing other areas of the park from the campground. Dogs must be leashed, under physical control at all times, and cleaned up after. Pet food must remain inside the camping unit, and dogs must have current shot records and a rabies certificate, be quiet, and well behaved. Dogs are allowed on the trails and day use areas, but they are not allowed on the beach, in any swim areas, or in any of the buildings. Dogs may not be left unattended except for very short periods; then they must be left inside your unit, weather permitting. Dogs are allowed on all the trails. This campground is closed during the off-season. The camping and tent areas also allow dogs. There is a dog walk area at the campground. There are no water hookups at the campground. 2 dogs may be allowed.

Hershey Highmeadow Campground
1200 Matlock Road
Hummelstown, PA
717-534-8999
hersheycamping.com
Dogs of all sizes are allowed. There are no additional pet fees. Dogs must be leashed and cleaned up after. There is a dog walk area at the campground. Multiple dogs may be allowed.

Penn Roosevelt
Stone Creek Road
Huntingdon, PA
814-667-1800
Dogs of all sizes are allowed. There is a $2 per night per pet additional fee. Pets are to be walked in designated walking areas of the campground and on designated pet walkways when accessing other areas of the park from the campground. Dogs must be leashed, under physical control at all times, and cleaned up after. Pet food must remain inside the camping unit, and dogs must have current shot records

and a rabies certificate, be quiet, and well behaved. Dogs are allowed on the trails and day use areas, but they are not allowed on the beach, in any swim areas, or in any of the buildings. Dogs may not be left unattended except for very short periods; then they must be left inside your unit, weather permitting. Dogs are allowed on the trails. The camping and tent areas also allow dogs. There is a dog walk area at the campground. There are no electric or water hookups at the campground. 2 dogs may be allowed.

Blue Knob State Park
124 Park Road
Imler, PA
814-276-3576 (888-727-2757)
Popular for wildlife viewing through all seasons and for its feel of wilderness, this 6,100+ acre park is the 2nd highest place in the state and offers great views in addition to a wealth of recreational activities. Dogs are allowed for an additional $2 per pet per stay when camping, and no charge for day use. They must be well behaved, under their owner's control, on no more than a 6 foot leash or crated, and cleaned up after at all times. Dogs must be licensed with proof of vaccinations. Aggressive dogs are not allowed. Dogs may not be left unattended outside at any time and if in a vehicle-for very short times. Dogs must stay on selected pet routes/trails and areas. They are not allowed in swim areas or in park buildings. The campsites have tables, fire rings, water, playground equipment, modern restrooms, showers, laundry tubs, and a dump station. This RV park is closed during the off-season. The camping and tent areas also allow dogs. There is a dog walk area at the campground. There are no water hookups at the campgrounds. 2 dogs may be allowed.

Pymatuning State Park
2660 Williamsfield Road
Jamestown, PA
724-932-3141 (888-PA-PARKS (727-2757))
This is the state's largest park at 21,122 acres; it has the largest lake, unique protected natural areas, environmental interpretive programs, miles of hiking trails, and a wide range of land and water recreation. The camp area has modern restrooms with showers, a playground, amphitheater, a dump station, camp store, and more. There

are some breed restrictions. This RV park is closed during the off-season. The camping and tent areas also allow dogs. There is a dog walk area at the campground. There are no water hookups at the campgrounds. 2 dogs may be allowed.

Jonestown/I-81,78 KOA
145 Old Route 22
Jonestown, PA
717-865-2526 (800-562-1501)
koa.com
Dogs of all sizes are allowed, but there can only be 1 large dog or 2 small dogs per site. There are no additional pet fees. Dogs may not be left unattended, and they must be leashed and cleaned up after. There are some breed restrictions. This RV park is closed during the off-season. The camping and tent areas also allow dogs. There is a dog walk area at the campground.

Wolf's Camping Resort
308 Timberwolf Run
Knox, PA
814-797-1103
wolfscampingresort.com
Dogs of all sizes are allowed. There are no additional pet fees. Dogs must be quiet, well behaved, not left unattended, and leashed and cleaned up after. There is limited winter camping. The camping and tent areas also allow dogs. There is a dog walk area at the campground. Multiple dogs may be allowed.

Blue Rocks Family Campground
341 Sousley Road
Lenhartsville, PA
610-756-6366
bluerockscampground.com
Dogs of all sizes are allowed. There are no additional pet fees. Dogs must have current shot records and be quiet and well behaved. Dogs must be leashed and cleaned up after. This RV park is closed during the off-season. The camping and tent areas also allow dogs. There is a dog walk area at the campground. Multiple dogs may be allowed.

Robin Hill Camping Resort
149 Robin Hill Road
Lenhartsville, PA
610-756-6117
robinhillrvresort.com
Dogs of all sizes are allowed. There are no additional pet fees. Dogs must be well behaved, not left unattended, and be leashed and cleaned up after. This RV park is closed during the off-season. The

camping and tent areas also allow dogs. There is a dog walk area at the campground. Multiple dogs may be allowed.

Pinch Pond Family Campground
2649 Camp Road
Manheim, PA
717-665-7120
gretnaoaks.com
Dogs of all sizes are allowed. There are no additional pet fees. Dogs must be leashed and cleaned up after. This RV park is closed during the off-season. The camping and tent areas also allow dogs. There is a dog walk area at the campground. Multiple dogs may be allowed.

Tri-State RV Park
200 Shay Lane
Matamoras, PA
800-562-2663
tsrvpark.com
Dogs of all sizes are allowed. There are no additional pet fees. Dogs must have current shot records, be leashed, and cleaned up after. There is a dog walk area at the campground.

Erie KOA
6645 West Road
McKean, PA
814-476-7706 (800-562-7610)
eriekoa.com
Dogs of all sizes are allowed. There are no additional pet fees. Dogs may not be left unattended, must be leashed, and cleaned up after. This RV park is closed during the off-season. The camping and tent areas also allow dogs. There is a dog walk area at the campground. Dogs are allowed in the camping cabins. Multiple dogs may be allowed.

Brookdale Family Campground
25164 H 27
Meadville, PA
814-789-3251
brookdalecampground.com
Dogs of all sizes are allowed. There are no additional pet fees. Dogs must be quiet, be leashed at all times, and be cleaned up after. Dogs may not be tied up outside alone. They can be left in the camper or RV if they are well behaved and have cool air. This RV park is closed during the off-season. The camping and tent areas also allow dogs. There is a dog walk area at the campground. Multiple dogs may be allowed.

Mercer/Grove City KOA
1337 Butler Pike

Mercer, PA
724-748-3160 (800-562-2802)
mercerkoa.com
Dogs of all sizes are allowed. There are no additional pet fees. Dogs must be well behaved, leashed, and cleaned up after. This RV park is closed during the off-season. The camping and tent areas also allow dogs. There is a dog walk area at the campground. Dogs are allowed in the camping cabins. Multiple dogs may be allowed.

Hidden Valley Campgrounds
162 Hidden Valley Lane
Mifflinburg, PA
570-966-1330
hiddenvalleycamping.com
Dogs of all sizes are allowed. There are no additional pet fees. Dogs must be quiet, well behaved, leashed, and cleaned up after. This RV park is closed during the off-season. The camping and tent areas also allow dogs. There is a dog walk area at the campground. Multiple dogs may be allowed.

Jelllystone Park
839 Mill Run Road
Mill Run, PA
724-455-2929 (800-HEY-YOGI (439-9644))
jellystonemillrun.com
Dogs of all sizes are allowed. There is a $2 per night per pet additional fee. Dogs must be leashed and cleaned up after. Dogs are not allowed in the rentals. The camping and tent areas also allow dogs. There is a dog walk area at the campground. Multiple dogs may be allowed.

Jellystone Park
670 Hidden Paradise Road
Milton, PA
570-524-4561 (800-445-6660)
slcreek.com/
A family-style fun resort, this fun campground offers creek-side sites, a swimming and wading pool, general store, café, theme weekends, a game room, gaming fields/courts, hiking trails, sports and fishing rod rentals, free Wi-Fi, a laundry, and much more. Dogs are allowed for no additional fee in the campground; there is a $25 one time fee per pet for the cabins. Only 2 dogs are allowed per cabin; there may be more than 2 dogs per site in the RV/tent area. Dogs may not be left unattended, they must be on no more than a 6 foot leash, and cleaned up after at all times. There are some breed restrictions. This RV

park is closed during the off-season. The camping and tent areas also allow dogs. There is a dog walk area at the campground. Dogs are allowed in the camping cabins.

Rose Point Campground
314 Rose Point Road
New Castle, PA
724-924-2415 (800-459-1561)
rosepointpark.com/
Some of the amenities at this full service campground included a 4-star recreation program, landscaped grounds, several play/gaming areas, free Wi-Fi, a camp store, and miles of hiking trails. Well behaved dogs of all sizes are allowed for no additional pet fee. Dogs must be under owner's control, leashed, and cleaned up after at all times. There are some breed restrictions. The camping and tent areas also allow dogs. There is a dog walk area at the campground.

Nittany Mountain Campground
2751 Miller's Bottom Road
New Columbia, PA
570-568-5541
fun-camping.com
One dog of any size is allowed in the rentals. Dogs of all sizes are allowed in the camping and RV area. There is a $1 per night per pet additional fee. Dogs must be leashed and cleaned up after. This RV park is closed during the off-season. The camping and tent areas also allow dogs. There is a dog walk area at the campground. Dogs are allowed in the camping cabins.

Williamsport South / Nittany Mtn. KOA
2751 Millers Bottom Road
New Columbia, PA
570-568-5541 (800-562-4208)
koa.com/where/pa/38182/
A petting zoo, an 18 hole mini-golf, an indoor play gym, theme weekends, ice cream socials, free Wi-Fi, a large swimming pool, playing fields/courts, a snack bar, and lots more can be enjoyed at this camp area. Dogs are allowed for no additional fee. Only 1 dog is allowed per cabin; there may be more than 2 dogs per site in the RV/tent area. Dogs must have proof of current vaccinations; they may not be left unattended, and they must be on no more than a 6 foot leash and cleaned up after at all times. There are some breed

restrictions. The camping and tent areas also allow dogs. There is a dog walk area at the campground. Dogs are allowed in the camping cabins.

Spring Gulch
475 Lynch Road
New Holland, PA
866-864-8524
rvonthego.com
Dogs of all sizes are allowed. There are no additional pet fees. Dogs must be well behaved, leashed, and cleaned up after. Dogs are not allowed in the rentals This RV park is closed during the off-season. The camping and tent areas also allow dogs. There is a dog walk area at the campground. 2 dogs may be allowed.

Allentown KOA
6750 KOA Drive
New Tripoli, PA
610-298-2160 (800-562-2138)
koa.com
Dogs of all sizes are allowed. There are no additional pet fees. Dogs must be leashed and cleaned up after. There are some breed restrictions. This RV park is closed during the off-season. The camping and tent areas also allow dogs. There is a dog walk area at the campground. Multiple dogs may be allowed.

Yogi-on-the-River
213 Yogi Blvd
Northumberland, PA
570-473-8021 (800-243-1056)
riverandfun.com
Dogs of all sizes are allowed. There are no additional pet fees. Dogs may not be left unattended, must be leashed, and cleaned up after. Dogs are allowed to go to the river, but you may not access the river across others' sites. This RV park is closed during the off-season. The camping and tent areas also allow dogs. There is a dog walk area at the campground. 2 dogs may be allowed.

Oil Creek State Park
305 State Park Road
Oil City, PA
814-676-5915
This park is home to the world's first commercial oil well, and there are trails that wind throughout. There is no tent or RV camping, and there are no cabins. They have trail shelters available. Dogs of all sizes are allowed. There is a $2 per night per pet additional fee. Dogs must be

leashed and cleaned up after. Dogs are allowed on the trails and at the day use areas. There is a dog walk area at the campground. There are no electric or water hookups at the campground. 2 dogs may be allowed.

Prince Gallitzin State Park
966 Marina Road
Patton, PA
814-674-1000
Dogs of all sizes are allowed. There is a $2 per night per pet additional fee. Pets are to be walked in designated walking areas of the campground and on designated pet walkways when accessing other areas of the park from the campground. Dogs must be leashed, under physical control at all times, and pet waste must be disposed of quickly and properly. Pet food must remain inside the camping unit, and dogs must have a current rabies certificate and shot records, be quiet and well behaved. Dogs are allowed on the trails and day use areas, but they are not allowed in the swim areas or in any of the buildings. Dogs can be at the boat launch area and on the trails. Dogs may not be left unattended except for very short periods; then they must be left inside your unit, weather permitting. This campground is closed during the off-season. The camping and tent areas also allow dogs. There is a dog walk area at the campground. There are no water hookups at the campground. 2 dogs may be allowed.

Black Moshannon State Park
4216 Beaver Road
Philipsburg, PA
814-342-5960 (888-727-2757)
Rich in environmental education and recreation, this park covers almost 4,000 acres with a 250 acre spring fed lake, plus there are a network of boardwalks and trails for exploring this unique, natural park. Dogs are allowed for an additional $2 per pet per stay when camping, and no charge for day use. They must be well behaved, under their owner's control, on no more than a 6 foot leash or crated, and cleaned up after at all times. Dogs must be licensed with proof of vaccinations. Aggressive dogs are not allowed. Dogs may not be left unattended outside at any time and if in a vehicle for very short times. Dogs must stay on selected pet routes/trails and areas. They are not allowed in swim areas or in park

buildings. The campsites have tables, fire rings, modern restrooms, showers, laundry tubs, and a dump station. This RV park is closed during the off-season. The camping and tent areas also allow dogs. There is a dog walk area at the campground. There are no water hookups at the campgrounds. 2 dogs may be allowed.

Pine Grove KOA
1445 Suedburg Road
Pine Grove, PA
717-865-4602 (800-562-5471)
twingrovecampground.koa.com
Dogs of all sizes are allowed. There are no additional pet fees. Dogs must be quiet, leashed, and cleaned up after. There are some breed restrictions. The camping and tent areas also allow dogs. There is a dog walk area at the campground. Dogs are allowed in the camping cabins. Multiple dogs may be allowed.

Bear Run Campground
184 Badger Hill Road
Portersville, PA
888-737-2605
bearruncampground.com
Dogs of all sizes are allowed. There are no additional pet fees. Dogs must be leashed and cleaned up after. Dogs are not allowed in the buildings or rentals. There are some breed restrictions. This RV park is closed during the off-season. The camping and tent areas also allow dogs. There is a dog walk area at the campground. 2 dogs may be allowed.

Jellystone Park
340 Blackburn Road
Quarryville, PA
717-786-3458
jellystonepa.com
Dogs of all sizes are allowed. There are no additional pet fees. Dogs must be quiet and well behaved. Dogs may not be left unattended, must be leashed, and cleaned up after. This RV park is closed during the off-season. The camping and tent areas also allow dogs. There is a dog walk area at the campground. 2 dogs may be allowed.

Madison/Pittsburgh SE KOA
764 Waltz Mill Road
Ruffs Dale, PA
724-722-4444 (800-562-4034)
pittsburghkoa.com
Dogs of all sizes are allowed. There are no additional pet fees. Dogs must be leashed and cleaned up

after. There are some breed restrictions. This RV park is closed during the off-season. The camping and tent areas also allow dogs. There is a dog walk area at the campground. Dogs are allowed in the camping cabins. Multiple dogs may be allowed.

Shawnee Sleepy Hollow Campground
147 Sleepy Hollow Road
Schellsburg, PA
814-733-4380
bedfordcounty.net/camping/sleepy
Dogs up to about 65 pounds are allowed. There is a $1 per night per pet additional fee. Dogs must be quiet, well behaved, leashed and cleaned up after. There are some breed restrictions. This RV park is closed during the off-season. The camping and tent areas also allow dogs. There is a dog walk area at the campground. Multiple dogs may be allowed.

Shawnee State Park
132 State Park Road
Schellsburg, PA
814-733-4218
dcnr.state.pa.us/stateparks
Dogs of all sizes are allowed. There is a $2 per night per pet additional fee. Pets are to be walked in designated walking areas of the campground and on designated pet walkways when accessing other areas of the park from the campground. Dogs must be leashed and under physical control at all times, and pet waste must be disposed of quickly and properly. Pet food must remain inside the camping unit, and dogs must have current rabies certificate and shot records, be quiet and well behaved. Dogs are allowed on the trails and day use areas, but they are not allowed on any sand areas, at the beach shoreline, or in any of the buildings. Dogs may not be left unattended except for very short periods; then they must be left inside your unit, weather permitting. There are some breed restrictions. This campground is closed during the off-season. The camping and tent areas also allow dogs. There is a dog walk area at the campground. There are no water hookups at the campground. 2 dogs may be allowed.

Appalachian Campsites
60 Motel Drive
Shartlesville, PA
610-488-6319
appalachianrvresort.com

Dogs of all sizes are allowed. There are no additional pet fees. Dogs must be leashed and cleaned up after. The camping and tent areas also allow dogs. There is a dog walk area at the campground. 2 dogs may be allowed.

Cooper's Lake Campground
205 Currie Road
Slippery Rock, PA
724-368-8710
cooperslake.com
Friendly dogs of all sizes are allowed. There are no additional pet fees. Dogs must be quiet, not left unattended, leashed and cleaned up after. The camp closes for the month of August every year. This RV park is closed during the off-season. The camping and tent areas also allow dogs. There is a dog walk area at the campground. Multiple dogs may be allowed.

Kooser State Park
934 Glades Pike
Somerset, PA
814-445-7725
Dogs of all sizes are allowed. There is a $2 per night per pet additional fee. Pets are to be walked in designated walking areas of the campground and on designated pet walkways when accessing other areas of the park from the campground. Dogs must be leashed, under physical control at all times, and cleaned up after. Pet food must remain inside the camping unit, and dogs must have current shot records and a rabies certificate, be quiet, and well behaved. Dogs are allowed on the trails and day use areas, but they are not allowed on the beach, in any swim areas, or in any of the buildings. Dogs may not be left unattended except for very short periods; then they must be left inside your unit, weather permitting. Dogs are allowed on the trails. The camping and tent areas also allow dogs. There is a dog walk area at the campground. There are no water hookups at the campground. 2 dogs may be allowed.

Tobyhanna State Park
On H 423
Tobyhanna, PA
570-894-8336 (888-PA-PARKS 727-2757)
Dogs of all sizes are allowed. There is a $2 per night per pet additional fee. Pets are to be walked in designated walking areas of the campground and on designated pet walkways when accessing other

areas of the park from the campground. Dogs must be leashed, under physical control at all times, and cleaned up after. Pet food must remain inside the camping unit, and dogs must have current shot records and a rabies certificate, be quiet, and well behaved. Dogs are allowed on the trails and day use areas, but they are not allowed on the beach, in any swim areas, or in any of the buildings. Dogs may not be left unattended except for very short periods; then they must be left inside your unit, weather permitting. Dogs are allowed on the trails. This campground is closed during the off-season. The camping and tent areas also allow dogs. There is a dog walk area at the campground. There are no electric or water hookups at the campground. 2 dogs may be allowed.

Jellystone Park
30 Campground Road
Tunkhannock, PA
570-836-4122 (800-558-2954 (Enter Park # 184))
northeastpacamping.com/
This beautiful, family fun park is nestled along Tunkhannock Creek and offers daily planned activities, theme weekends, a swimming pool, game room, playground, Wi-Fi, a camp store, laundry, and a lot more. Dogs are allowed for no additional fee. Dogs must be quiet, leashed, cleaned up after, and they may not be left alone outside for more than a ½ hour. There are some breed restrictions. This RV park is closed during the off-season. The camping and tent areas also allow dogs. There is a dog walk area at the campground. Multiple dogs may be allowed.

Colonial Woods Family Camping Resort
545 Lonely Cottage Drive
Upper Black Eddy, PA
610-847-5808
colonialwoods.com
Dogs of all sizes are allowed. There are no additional pet fees. Dogs must be quiet, well behaved, leashed, and cleaned up after. This RV park is closed during the off-season. The camping and tent areas also allow dogs. There is a dog walk area at the campground. Multiple dogs may be allowed.

Allegheny National Forest
222 Liberty Street
Warren, PA

814-723-5150
fs.fed.us/r9/forests/allegheny/
This park is located in northwestern Pennsylvania and covers over 24,000 acres. Dogs of all sizes are allowed. There are no additional pet fees. Dogs may not be left unattended, and they must have a current rabies certificate and shot records. Dogs must be quiet during quiet hours, be leashed, and cleaned up after. Dogs are allowed on the trails, but not on the beach or in the buildings. This campground is closed during the off-season. The camping and tent areas also allow dogs. There is a dog walk area at the campground. There are no water hookups at the campground. Multiple dogs may be allowed.

Washington KOA
7 KOA Road
Washington, PA
724-225-7590 (800-562-0254)
koa.com
Dogs of all sizes are allowed. There are no additional pet fees. In the cabins there can only be one large dog or two small dogs. There are a couple of more dogs allowed on tent and RV sites. Dogs must be leashed and cleaned up after. The camping and tent areas also allow dogs. There is a dog walk area at the campground. Dogs are allowed in the camping cabins.

Keen Lake Camping and Cottage Resort
155 Keen Lake Road
Waymart, PA
570-488-5522
keenlake.com
Dogs of all sizes are allowed, and there are no additional pet fees for RV or tent sites. There is a $50 one time additional pet fee for a cottage rental plus a $250 refundable pet deposit. Dogs must be quiet, may not be left unattended, and must be leashed and cleaned up after. This RV park is closed during the off-season. The camping and tent areas also allow dogs. There is a dog walk area at the campground. Dogs are allowed in the camping cabins. 2 dogs may be allowed.

Hickory Run State Park
H 534
White Haven, PA
570-443-0400 (888-PA-PARKS (727-2757))
Three natural areas, more than 40 miles of scenic, blazed hiking trails rich in history, miles of trout streams, and a National Natural Landmark-the

Boulder Field, are on site, and there are a variety of year round land and water recreational and educational opportunities available. Dogs of all sizes are allowed for an additional $2 per pet per stay. Dogs must be well behaved, under their owner's control, leashed or crated, and cleaned up after at all times (exceptions during hunting season). Dogs must be licensed and have proof vaccinations. Aggressive dogs are not allowed. Dogs may not be left unattended outside at any time and may only be left alone in a vehicle for VERY short periods. Dogs must stay on selected pet routes/trails and areas; they may not be in designated swim areas or in park buildings. The camp area offers forested or open sites with modern restrooms, a dump station, and a general store. This RV park is closed during the off-season. The camping and tent areas also allow dogs. There is a dog walk area at the campground. There are no water hookups at the campgrounds. 2 dogs may be allowed.

Frances Slocum State Park
565 Mount Olivet Road
Wyoming, PA
570-696-3525 (888-PA-PARKS (727-2757))
Offering a good variety of land and water recreation, this 1,000+ acre park has a beautiful horseshoe shaped 165 acre lake, and 9 miles of blazed trails, including an interpretive trail that starts at the environmental center. Dogs of all sizes are allowed for no additional fee. Dogs must be well behaved, under their owner's control, leashed or crated, and cleaned up after at all times (exceptions during hunting season). Dogs must be licensed and have proof vaccinations. Aggressive dogs are not allowed. Dogs may not be left unattended outside at any time and may only be left alone in a vehicle for very short periods. Dogs must stay on selected pet routes/trails and areas; they may not be in designated swim areas or in park buildings. Reservations are highly recommended as pet camp sites are limited. The camp area has 100 sites available, each with a picnic table and fire ring, and modern restrooms, showers, potable water, and a dump station are close by. This RV park is closed during the off-season. The camping and tent areas also allow dogs. There is a dog walk area at the campground. There are no water hookups at the campgrounds. 2 dogs may be allowed.

Rhode Island

Burlingame State Campground
Route 1
Charlestown, RI
401-322-7337
riparks.com/burlgmcamp.htm
Featuring 3,100 acres of rocky woodland, an almost 600 acre lake, extensive picnic facilities, and a swimming beach with a bathhouse have made this a popular recreational destination. Dogs are allowed for no additional fee; they must have a valid license tag, and owners must carry proof of current rabies inoculation. Dogs must be quiet, well behaved, leashed (6 foot), and properly cleaned up after at all times. They may not be left unattended; with exception for hunting season or dog trials at which time dogs may be left alone in a vehicle. Dogs are not allowed at bathing beaches, or to be washed in any natural body of water. Dogs must be registered with the state prior to camping (not needed for day use), and the form can be obtained at http://www.riparks.com/pdfs/Pet%20Certification%20Form.pdf. Dogs are not allowed at the Burlingame picnic area from April 1st through September 30th. The camp area offers several hundred sites on a first come first served basis. There is a camp store, restrooms with showers as well as porta-potties, and dumping stations. This RV park is closed during the off-season. The camping and tent areas also allow dogs. There is a dog walk area at the campground. There are no electric or water hookups at the campgrounds. 2 dogs may be allowed.

George Washington Management Area
2185 Putnam Park
Chepachet, RI
401-568-2248
riparks.com
Dogs of all sizes are allowed. There are no additional pet fees. Dogs may not be left unattended, they must have current rabies certificate and shot records, be leashed, and cleaned up after. Dogs are allowed on the trails, but not on the beach. This campground is closed during the off-season. The camping and tent areas also allow dogs. There is a dog walk area at the campground.

There are no electric or water hookups at the campground. Multiple dogs may be allowed.

Ginny-B Campground
7 Harrington Road
Foster, RI
401-397-9477
ginny-b.com
Dogs of all sizes are allowed. There are no additional pet fees. Dogs must be well behaved, leashed, and cleaned up after. The camping and tent areas also allow dogs. Multiple dogs may be allowed.

Bowdish Lake
40 Safari Road
Glocester, RI
401-568-8890
bowdishlake.com
Dogs of all sizes are allowed, but some breeds are not. There is a $10 per night per pet additional fee. Dogs must be well behaved, leashed, and cleaned up after. The camping and tent areas also allow dogs. There is a dog walk area at the campground. Multiple dogs may be allowed.

George Washington Memorial Camping Area
Putnam Pike
Glocester, RI
401-568-2013
riparks.com/georgewashcamp.htm
There are a variety of plant, bird, and wildlife habitats to explore here, as well as historic sites, many trails with varying difficulties, and various land and water recreation. Dogs are allowed for no additional fee; they must have a valid license tag, and owners must carry proof of current rabies inoculation. Dogs must be quiet, well behaved, leashed (6 foot), and properly cleaned up after at all times. They may not be left unattended; with exception for hunting season or dog trials at which time dogs may be left alone in a vehicle. Dogs are not allowed at bathing beaches, or to be washed in any natural body of water. Dogs must be registered with the state prior to camping (not needed for day use), and the form can be obtained at http://www.riparks.com/pdfs/Pet%20Certification%20Form.pdf. Campsites are available on a first come, first served basis, drinking water is available, there are gaming areas, waterfront sites, and they have either outhouses or pit toilets. This RV park is closed during the off-season. The camping and tent areas also allow dogs. There is a dog walk area at the campground. There are

no electric or water hookups at the campgrounds. 2 dogs may be allowed.

Whispering Pines
41 Sawmill Road
Hope Valley, RI
401-539-7011
whisperingpinescamping.com
Well behaved dogs of all sizes are allowed. There are no additional pet fees. No aggressive dogs are allowed, and they must be kept leashed and cleaned up after. There are some breed restrictions. Multiple dogs may be allowed.

Holiday Acres Camping Resort
591 Snakehill Road
N Scituate, RI
401-934-0780
holidayacrescampground.com
Dogs of all sizes are allowed, however some breeds are not. There are no additional pet fees. Dogs must be well behaved and they are not allowed on other sites or the beach. They must be leashed and cleaned up after. The camping and tent areas also allow dogs. There is a dog walk area at the campground. 2 dogs may be allowed.

Fishermen's State Park and Campground
1011 Point Judith Road
Narragansett, RI
401-789-8374
riparks.com/fisherma.htm
With landscaped grounds and tree-lined paths, this 90 acre park can feel more like a seaside village, and they offer a good variety of land and water recreational opportunities. Dogs are allowed for no additional fee; they must have a valid license tag, and owners must carry proof of current rabies inoculation. Dogs must be quiet, well behaved, leashed (6 foot), and properly cleaned up after at all times. They may not be left unattended; with exception for hunting season or dog trials at which time dogs may be left alone in a vehicle. Dogs are not allowed at bathing beaches, or to be washed in any natural body of water. Dogs must be registered with the state prior to camping (not needed for day use), and the form can be obtained at http://www.riparks.com/pdfs/Pet%20Certification%20Form.pdf. The camp area offers picnic tables, a playground, restrooms, coin operated showers, and a dump station. This RV park is closed during the off-season. The camping and tent areas also allow dogs. There is

a dog walk area at the campground. 2 dogs may be allowed.

Wordon Pond Family Campground
416 A Worden Pond Road
Wakefield, RI
401-789-9113
wordenpondcampground.com/
Dogs of all sizes are allowed. There are no additional pet fees. Dogs must be leashed and cleaned up after. This RV park is closed during the off-season. The camping and tent areas also allow dogs. There is a dog walk area at the campground. 2 dogs may be allowed.

Wawaloam Campground
510 Gardner Road
West Kingston, RI
401-294-3039
wawaloam.com
Dogs of all sizes are allowed. There is a $3 per night per pet additional fee. Dogs must be leashed and cleaned up after. The camping and tent areas also allow dogs. There is a dog walk area at the campground. 2 dogs may be allowed.

South Carolina

Anderson/Lake Hartwell KOA
200 Wham Road
Anderson, SC
864-287-3161 (800-562-5804)
koa.com
Dogs of all sizes are allowed. There are no additional pet fees. Dogs may not be left unattended, and they must be quiet, well behaved, leashed, and cleaned up after. The camping and tent areas also allow dogs. There is a dog walk area at the campground. Dogs are allowed in the camping cabins. Multiple dogs may be allowed.

Kings Mountain State Park
1277 Park Road
Blacksburg, SC
803-222-3209 (866-345-PARK (7275))
Rich in American history, this picturesque park offers self guided tours of a living history farm in addition to various land and water recreation. Dogs of all sizes are allowed at no additional fee. Dogs may not be left unattended unless they will be quiet and well behaved, and they must be on no more than a 6 foot leash, and cleaned up after. Dogs are allowed on the trails. The

camping and tent areas also allow dogs. There is a dog walk area at the campground. Multiple dogs may be allowed.

Barnwell State Park
223 State Park Road
Blackville, SC
803-284-2212 (866-345-PARK (7275))
Although popular for its great fishing and recreation center, this 307 acre park also features a 1½ mile interpretive trail with signage on many of the plants and trees. Dogs are allowed throughout the park, on the beach, and at campground; they are not allowed in the cabin areas. Dogs must be on no more than a 6 foot leash and cleaned up after. The campground has about 25 sites with restrooms, hot showers, and a dump station on site. The camping and tent areas also allow dogs. There is a dog walk area at the campground. Multiple dogs may be allowed.

Calhoun Falls State Park
46 Maintenance Shop Road
Calhoun Falls, SC
864-447-8269 (866-345-PARK (7275))
This park, located on one of the states most popular fishing lakes, also provides a scenic trail, nature study opportunities, and a variety of recreation. Dogs of all sizes are allowed at no additional fee. Dogs may not be left unattended, and they must be on no more than a 6 foot leash, and be cleaned up after in camp areas. Dogs are not allowed in buildings or on the beach. Dogs are allowed on the trails. The camping and tent areas also allow dogs. There is a dog walk area at the campground. Multiple dogs may be allowed.

James Island County Park Campground
871 Riverland Drive
Charleston, SC
843-795-7275
ccprc.com
Dogs of all sizes are allowed. There are no additional pet fees. Dogs may not be left unattended outside, and may only be left inside an RV if there is temperature control. Dogs must be quiet during quiet hours, leashed, and cleaned up after. There is an a fenced in Dog Park where dogs may run off lead. The camping and tent areas also allow dogs. There is a dog walk area at the campground. Multiple dogs may be allowed.

Oak Plantation Campground
3540 Savannah H
Charleston, SC
843-766-5936
oakplantationcampground.com
Dogs of all sizes are allowed. There are no additional pet fees. Dogs may not be left unattended outside, they must be leashed at all times, and cleaned up after. There is a large fenced in dog run where dogs may run off lead. There is a dog walk area at the campground. 2 dogs may be allowed.

Francis Marion and Sumter National Forests
4931 Broad River Road
Columbia, SC
803-561-4000
fs.fed.us/r8/fms/
Four ranger districts oversee more than 600,000 acres of forest lands rich with diverse ecosystems that support a large variety habitats and wildlife, cultural history, and recreational opportunities. There is also an environmental education center with numerous activities and programs, a 36 mile trail that goes from the mountains to the sea, and many other sites of interest. Dogs are allowed throughout the forest and campground areas; they must be leashed and under their owner's control at all times. There are a variety of camp sites in numerous settings each with their own special features. Campsites may have all or some of the following: flush or vault toilets, restrooms, showers, tables, grills, lantern holders, drinking water, and a dump station. The camping and tent areas also allow dogs. There is a dog walk area at the campground. There are no electric or water hookups at the campgrounds. Multiple dogs may be allowed.

Sesquicentennial State Park
9564 Two Notch Road
Columbia, SC
803-788-2706
A major recreation destination, this scenic 1,419 acre park offers a long list of amenities, activities, a 30 acre lake, interpretive nature programs, and much more. This park is also home to a 2 acre, double sectioned, off-leash dog park. Permits are required; they are available at the park office by the year or by the day. Dogs must be there for their photo, and proof of license, spayed/neutered, rabies, parvo and kennel cough are required. Dogs must be sociable, under their owner's control at all times, and be on no

more than a 6 foot leash when not in designated off-lead areas. The camp area offers picnic tables, a playground, playing fields/courts, showers, restrooms, and a dump station. The camping and tent areas also allow dogs. There is a dog walk area at the campground. There are special amenities given to dogs at this campground. Multiple dogs may be allowed.

Big Cypress Lake RV Park
6531 Browns Way Shortcut Road
Conway, SC
843-397-1800
bigcypressfishing.com
Dogs of all sizes are allowed. There are no additional pet fees. Dogs must be quiet, well behaved, leashed, and cleaned up after. The camping and tent areas also allow dogs. There is a dog walk area at the campground. Multiple dogs may be allowed.

Little Pee Dee State Park
1298 State Park Road
Dillon, SC
843-774-8872 (866-345-PARK (7275))
The serene setting of this 835 acre park has made it a popular relaxation, fishing, and nature viewing area. Dogs are allowed throughout the park, on the beach, and at campground; they are not allowed in park buildings. Dogs must be on no more than a 6 foot leash and cleaned up after. There are about 50 sites in the campground with restrooms, hot showers, and a dump station on site. The camping and tent areas also allow dogs. There is a dog walk area at the campground. Multiple dogs may be allowed.

South of the Border Campgrounds
H 301/501
Dillon, SC
843-774-2411 (800-845-6011)
This South-of-the-Border themed stop offers lodging, campgrounds, shopping, dining, entertainment, and more. Dogs are allowed throughout the grounds, in the inn and at the campgrounds for no additional pet fee; they are not allowed in most of the park buildings or in food service areas. Dogs must be leashed and under owner's control/care at all times. The camping and tent areas also allow dogs. There is a dog walk area at the campground. Multiple dogs may be allowed.

Edisto Beach State Park
8377 State Cabin Road
Edisto Island, SC
843-671-2810
In addition to its popularity for its palmed beach and great shelling, this 1,255 acre oceanfront park is also home to an environmental education center, well-developed handicapped-friendly trails and facilities, a dense maritime forest, and an extensive salt march. Dogs are allowed throughout the park, on the beach, and at campground; they are not allowed in the cabin areas. Dogs must be on no more than a 6 foot leash and cleaned up after. The camp area offers 113 sites with a day use area, fire rings, picnic tables, showers, restrooms, a playground, store, concessionaires, a laundry, and a dump station. The camping and tent areas also allow dogs. There is a dog walk area at the campground. Multiple dogs may be allowed.

Lake Hartwell State Rec Area
19138 A H 11S
Fair Play, SC
864-972-3352 (866-345-PARK (7275))
Sports enthusiasts, campers, and nature lovers all like the easy access to this park with 14 miles of Lake Hartwell shoreline. Dogs of all sizes are allowed at no additional fee. Dogs may not be left unattended outside, and may only be left inside if they will be quiet, well behaved, and comfortable. Dogs must be on no more than a 6 foot leash, and be cleaned up after. Dogs are allowed on the trails. The camping and tent areas also allow dogs. There is a dog walk area at the campground. Multiple dogs may be allowed.

Florence KOA
1115 E Campground Road
Florence, SC
843-665-7007 (800-562-7807)
koa.com
Dogs of all sizes are allowed. There are no additional pet fees. Dogs may not be left unattended, even at the dog pen area. Dogs must be leashed and cleaned up after. The camping and tent areas also allow dogs. There is a dog walk area at the campground. Dogs are allowed in the camping cabins. Multiple dogs may be allowed.

Hilton Head Island Motor Coach Resort
133 L Street
Hilton Head Island, SC

800-722-2365
hiltonheadmotorcoachresort.com
Dogs of all sizes are allowed. There
are no additional pet fees. Dogs
must be leashed at all times and
cleaned up after. This is an RV only,
Class A resort. There is a dog walk
area at the campground. Multiple
dogs may be allowed.

Lake Aire RV Park Campground
4375 H 162
Hollywood, SC
843-571-1271
lakeairerv.com
Dogs of all sizes are allowed. There
are no additional pet fees. Dogs may
not be left unattended, and may only
be left in the RV if there is
temperature control. Dogs must be
well behaved, friendly, leashed, and
cleaned up after. There is a dog walk
area at the campground. Multiple
dogs may be allowed.

Hunting Island State Park
2555 Sea Island Parkway
Hunting Island, SC
843-838-2011 (866-345-PARK
(7275))
The state's most popular recreation
destination, there is an abundance of
wildlife, plenty of water and land fun,
a maritime forest, tidal creeks, a
saltwater lagoon, an historic publicly
accessible lighthouse, and one of the
longest public beaches in the low
country can be found at this 5,000
acre semi-tropical barrier island park.
Dogs are allowed throughout the
park, on the beach, and at
campground; they are not allowed in
the cabin areas. Dogs must be on no
more than a 6 foot leash and cleaned
up after. The camp area offers a day
use area, fire rings, picnic tables,
showers, restrooms, a playground,
store, concessionaires, a laundry,
and a dump station. The camping
and tent areas also allow dogs.
There is a dog walk area at the
campground. Multiple dogs may be
allowed.

Charleston KOA
9494 H 78
Ladson, SC
843-797-1045 (800-562-5812)
koa.com
Dogs of all sizes are allowed. There
are no additional pet fees. Dogs may
not be left unattended, and they must
be leashed and cleaned up after.
The camping and tent areas also
allow dogs. There is a dog walk area
at the campground. Dogs are
allowed in the camping cabins.

Andrew Jackson State Park
196 Andrew Jackson Park Road
Lancaster, SC
803-285-3344 (866-345-PARK
(7275))
Historic, as it is the only park
dedicated to a US president, and
popular for the blending of its
history to the present with a
museum of President Jackson's life
here, art/community activities, and a
living history museum. There are
also annual festivals, a fishing lake,
picnic areas, a campground, and
plenty of hiking trails at this 360
acre site. Dogs are allowed in most
of the outdoor areas; they must be
on a leash no longer than 6 feet and
under their owner's control at all
times. The campground can
accommodate RVs up to 30 feet,
and there are restrooms, hot
showers, and a dump station on
site. The camping and tent areas
also allow dogs. There is a dog
walk area at the campground.
Multiple dogs may be allowed.

Barnyard RV Park
201 Oak Drive
Lexington, SC
803-957-1238
barnyardrvpark.com
Dogs of all sizes are allowed. There
are no additional pet fees. Dogs
must be leashed and cleaned up
after. There is a dog walk area at
the campground. Multiple dogs may
be allowed.

Willow Tree Resort
520 Southern Sights Drive
Longs, SC
866-207-2267
willowtreerv.com
Dogs of all sizes are allowed. There
are no additional pet fees. Dogs
may not be left unattended outside,
and they must be leashed and
cleaned up after. The camping and
tent areas also allow dogs. There is
a dog walk area at the campground.
Multiple dogs may be allowed.

Francis Marion National Forest
1015 Pinckney
McClellanville, SC
843-887-3257 (877-444-6777)
fs.fed.us/r8/fms/
This forest's diverse ecosystems
support a large variety of plants,
fish, mammals, bird species, and
recreation. Dogs of all sizes are
allowed at no additional fee. Dogs
may not be left unattended, and
they must be leashed and cleaned
up after. On the trails, dogs must be
under verbal or physical restraint at

all times; keep in mind they are multi-
use trails and use a leash when
populated. The camping and tent
areas also allow dogs. There is a
dog walk area at the campground.
There are no water hookups at the
campground. Multiple dogs may be
allowed.

Baker Creek State Park
863 Baker Creek Road
McCormick, SC
864-443-2457 (866-345-PARK
(7275))
Although popular for all the common
land and water recreational activities,
this 1305 acre park also has a 10
mile mountain bike skill trail. Dogs
are allowed throughout the park, on
the beach, and at campground; they
are not allowed in the cabin areas.
Dogs must be on no more than a 6
foot leash and cleaned up after.
There are two 50 site lakeshore
camp areas with picnic tables, hot
showers, restrooms, and a dump
station. The camping and tent areas
also allow dogs. There is a dog walk
area at the campground. Multiple
dogs may be allowed.

Mt Pleasant/Charleston KOA
3157 H 17
Mount Pleasant, SC
843-849-5177 (800-562-5769)
koa.com
Dogs of all sizes are allowed. There
are no additional pet fees. Dogs may
not be left unattended outside, and
they must be leashed and cleaned
up after. The camping and tent areas
also allow dogs. There is a dog walk
area at the campground. Dogs are
allowed in the camping cabins.
Multiple dogs may be allowed.

Oconee State Park
624 State Park Road
Mountain Rest, SC
864-638-5353 (866-345-PARK
(7275))
Developed by the CCC in the 1930's,
this 1165 acre park has since been a
popular recreation destination
offering a wide variety of water and
land recreation, and an 80 mile
wilderness hike. Dogs are allowed
throughout the park, on the beach,
and at campground; they are not
allowed in the cabin areas. Dogs
must be on no more than a 6 foot
leash and cleaned up after. The
camp area offers more than 150
sites with picnic tables,
restrooms/hot showers, laundry
facilities, and a dump station. The
camping and tent areas also allow
dogs. There is a dog walk area at the

campground. Multiple dogs may be allowed.

Huntington Beach State Park
16148 Ocean H
Murrells Inlet, SC
843-237-4440 (866-345-PARK (7275))
In addition to a number of recreational pursuits, this 2,500 acre park also offers an environmental center with ongoing programs, an abundance of wildlife, a beautiful Moorish-style home owned by the benefactors of the park, an interpretive trail, and several boardwalks through a freshwater lagoon and the salt marshes. Dogs are allowed throughout the park, on the beach, and at campground; they are not allowed in the cabin areas or in park buildings. Dogs must be kept on no more than a 6 foot leash and cleaned up after at all times. The camp area offers a wonder sea breeze in addition to the normal amenities; restrooms, showers, a camp store, and a dump station. The camping and tent areas also allow dogs. There is a dog walk area at the campground. Multiple dogs may be allowed.

Apache Family Campground
9700 Kings Road
Myrtle Beach, SC
843-449-7323
apachefamilycampground.com
Dogs of all sizes are allowed. There are no additional pet fees. Dogs must be leashed and cleaned up after. There are some breed restrictions. The camping and tent areas also allow dogs. There is a dog walk area at the campground. Multiple dogs may be allowed.

Myrtle Beach KOA
613 5th Avenue S
Myrtle Beach, SC
843-448-3421 (800-562-7790)
koa.com
Dogs of all sizes are allowed. There are no additional pet fees. Dogs must be quiet, well behaved, leashed, and cleaned up after. There are some breed restrictions. The camping and tent areas also allow dogs. There is a dog walk area at the campground. Multiple dogs may be allowed.

Myrtle Beach State Park
4401 South Kings H
Myrtle Beach, SC
843-238-5325 (866-345-PARK (7275))
A major recreation area, this park

also offers a nature center with ongoing programs, a wooded oceanfront camp area, and it is home to one of the states last stands of accessible maritime forest. Dogs are allowed throughout the park and at campground; they are not allowed in the cabin areas or in park buildings. Dogs are not allowed on the beach between the hours of 8 Am to 5 PM from May 15th to September 15th, (effective on all public beaches in Horry County). Dogs must be well behaved, kept on no more than a 6 foot leash, and cleaned up after at all times. There are well over 300 camp sites, and restrooms, hot showers, a laundry, camp store, and dump station are nearby. The camping and tent areas also allow dogs. There is a dog walk area at the campground. Multiple dogs may be allowed.

Myrtle Beach Travel Park
10108 Kings Road
Myrtle Beach, SC
843-449-3714
myrtlebeachtravelpark.com
Dogs of all sizes are allowed. There are no additional pet fees. Dogs must be quiet, well behaved, leashed, and cleaned up after. The camping and tent areas also allow dogs. There is a dog walk area at the campground. Multiple dogs may be allowed.

Pirateland Family Campground
5401 S Kings Road
Myrtle Beach, SC
843-238-5155
pirateland.com
Dogs of all sizes are allowed. There are no additional pet fees. Dogs may not be left unattended at any time, and they must be on no more than a 6 foot leash, and be cleaned up after. There are some breed restrictions. The camping and tent areas also allow dogs. There is a dog walk area at the campground. Multiple dogs may be allowed.

Lake Greenwood State Rec Area
302 State Park Road
Ninety-Six, SC
864-543-3535 (866-345-PARK (7275))
This 914-acre park covers five peninsulas on beautiful Lake Greenwood offering ample fishing, hiking, lake shore camping, and an interactive educational center. Dogs of all sizes are allowed at no additional fee. Dogs may not be left unattended unless for a shore time,

and only if they will be quiet and well behaved. Dogs must be leashed at all times, and cleaned up after. Dogs are not allowed in any of the buildings, but they are allowed on the trails. The camping and tent areas also allow dogs. There is a dog walk area at the campground. Multiple dogs may be allowed.

Table Rock State Park
158 E Ellison Lane
Pickens, SC
864-878-9813 (866-345-PARK (7275))
Popular since its construction by the CCC in the 1930s for its recreational activities, lakes, and natural beauty, this almost 3100 acre park is now listed on the National Register of Historic Places, and it is home to an extensive trail system that takes hikers through a variety of sites/habitations. Dogs are allowed throughout the park, on the beach, and at campground; they are not allowed in the cabin areas. Dogs must be on no more than a 6 foot leash and cleaned up after. There are 2 camping areas with more than 90 sites available; they provide restrooms, hot showers, a laundry, and a dump station. The camping and tent areas also allow dogs. There is a dog walk area at the campground. Multiple dogs may be allowed.

Hamilton Branch State Rec Area
111 Campground Road
Plum Branch, SC
864-333-2223 (866-345-PARK (7275))
This 731 acre park takes up almost an entire peninsula, allowing for ample fishing, hiking, and lakeside camping. Dogs of all sizes are allowed at no additional fee. Dogs must be on no more than a 6 foot leash and be cleaned up after. Dogs are allowed on the trails. The camping and tent areas also allow dogs. There is a dog walk area at the campground. Multiple dogs may be allowed.

Dreher Island State Recreation Area
3677 State Park Road
Prosperity, SC
803-364-4152 (866-345-PARK (7525))
Although a popular hiking and fishing destination, there are a lot of activities to enjoy at this lakeshore 348 acre recreational park; the park is actually 3 islands linked to shore. Dogs are allowed throughout the park and campground; they are not

allowed in the villas or the villa areas. Dogs must be on no more than a 6 foot leash and cleaned up after. There are 2 lakeside camps offering easy access and great views of the lake, more than 100 sites, picnic tables, hot showers, and restrooms. The camping and tent areas also allow dogs. There is a dog walk area at the campground. Multiple dogs may be allowed.

Santee State Park
251 State Park Road
Santee, SC
803-854-2408 (866-345-PARK (7275))
A popular recreational destination, this 2,500 acre park offers an array of activities and 2 lakes that cover over 170,000 acres for lots of great fishing. Dogs are allowed throughout the park, on the beach, and at campground; they are not allowed in the cabin areas. Dogs must be on no more than a 6 foot leash and cleaned up after. There are more than 150 sites in the camp area with restrooms, hot showers, a laundry, and a dump station on site. The camping and tent areas also allow dogs. There is a dog walk area at the campground. Multiple dogs may be allowed.

Scuffletown USA
603 Scuffletown Road
Simpsonville, SC
864-967-2276
scuffletownusa.com
Dogs of all sizes are allowed. There are no additional pet fees. Dogs must be leashed and cleaned up after. The camping and tent areas also allow dogs. There is a dog walk area at the campground. Multiple dogs may be allowed.

River Bottom Farms
357 Cedar Creek Road
Swansea, SC
803-568-4182
riverbottomfarms.com
Dogs of all sizes are allowed. There are no additional pet fees. Dogs must be well behaved, leashed, and cleaned up after. There are some breed restrictions. The camping and tent areas also allow dogs. There is a dog walk area at the campground. Dogs are allowed in the camping cabins. Multiple dogs may be allowed.

Lake Hartwell Camping and Cabins
400 Ponderosa Point
Townville, SC
888-427-8935

lakehartwell.com
Dogs of all sizes are allowed, and there are no additional pet fees for tent or RV sites. There is a $25 one time pet fee for the cabins. Dogs must be leashed and cleaned up after. There are some breed restrictions. The camping and tent areas also allow dogs. There is a dog walk area at the campground. Multiple dogs may be allowed.

Crooked Creek RV Park
777 Arvee lane
West Union, SC
864-882-5040
crookedcreekrvpark.com
Dogs of all sizes are allowed. There are no additional pet fees. Dogs are not allowed in the buildings or the pool area, and they must be leashed and cleaned up after. The camping and tent areas also allow dogs. There is a dog walk area at the campground. Multiple dogs may be allowed.

Sumter National Forest
H 66
Whitmeyer, SC
803-276-4810 (877-444-6777)
fs.fed.us/r8/fms/
This forest' diverse ecosystems support a large variety of plants, fish, mammals, bird species, and recreation. Dogs of all sizes are allowed at no additional fee. Dogs may not be left unattended, and they must be leashed and cleaned up after. On the trails, dogs must be under verbal or physical restraint at all times; keep in mind they are multi-use trails and use a leash when populated. The camping and tent areas also allow dogs. There is a dog walk area at the campground. There are no electric or water hookups at the campground. Multiple dogs may be allowed.

Lake Wateree State Rec Area
881 State Park Road
Winnsboro, SC
803-482-6401 (866-345-PARK (7275))
This 238 acre park along a more than a 13,000 acre lake provides premier fishing, lake shore camping, hiking, and a variety of recreational pursuits. Dogs of all sizes are allowed at no additional fee. Dogs may not be left unattended at any time, and they must be on no more than a 6 foot leash, and be cleaned up after. Dogs are not allowed in the swim areas or in buildings. Dogs are allowed on the trails. The camping

and tent areas also allow dogs. There is a dog walk area at the campground. Multiple dogs may be allowed.

Point South KOA
14 Campground Road
Yemassee, SC
843-726-5733 (800-562-2948)
pointsouthkoa.com
Dogs of all sizes are allowed. There are no additional pet fees. Dogs may not be left unattended, and they must be leashed and cleaned up after. There are some breed restrictions. The camping and tent areas also allow dogs. There is a dog walk area at the campground. Dogs are allowed in the camping cabins. Multiple dogs may be allowed.

South Dakota

Big Sioux Recreation Area
410 Park Street
Brandon, SD
605-582-7243 (800-710-CAMP (2267))
This riverside park holds historical significance, plus they have a number of fun amenities to offer- including a 14 point archery range, an archery trail, a 9-hole disc golf course, and a canoe launch ramp. Dogs are allowed for no additional fee. They must be on no more than a 10 foot leash and be cleaned up after at all times. Dogs are not allowed on designated swimming beaches or in any park buildings. The campground has 50 sites, picnic tables, grills, flush toilets, showers, potable water, and a dump station. The camping and tent areas also allow dogs. There is a dog walk area at the campground. There are no water hookups at the campgrounds. Multiple dogs may be allowed.

Yogi Bear Jellystone Park
26014 478th Avenue
Brandon, SD
605-332-2233 (800-638-9043)
jellystonesiouxfalls..com
Dogs of all sizes are allowed. There are no additional pet fees. Dogs must be leashed and cleaned up after. Pets allowed in cabins with a security deposit or a credit card on file. This RV park is closed during the off-season. The camping and tent areas also allow dogs. There is a dog walk area at the campground. Dogs are allowed in the camping

cabins. Multiple dogs may be allowed.

Oakwood Lakes State Park
46109 202nd Street
Brookings, SD
605-627-5441 (800-710-CAMP (2267))
Born from ancient glaciers, this park is rich in natural and cultural history and offers historical sites, an archeology display, an almost 3,000 acre lake, and a variety of land and water recreation. Dogs of all sizes are allowed at no additional fee. Dogs may not be left unattended unless they will be quiet and well behaved. Dogs must be leashed and cleaned up after. Dogs are not allowed on beaches or in buildings. Dogs are allowed on the trails. The camping and tent areas also allow dogs. There is a dog walk area at the campground. Multiple dogs may be allowed.

Newton Hills State Park
28767 482nd Avenue/H 135
Canton, SD
605-987-2263 (800-710-CAMP (2267))
Born of glacial activity, this park has some unique geological features, and native artifacts have been found dating back as far as 300 BC. In addition to a number of recreational and educational opportunities, the park is host to many folk music concerts through the year. Dogs are allowed for no additional fee. They must be on no more than a 10 foot leash and be cleaned up after at all times. Dogs are not allowed on designated swimming beaches or in any park buildings. The campground offers shady, grassy sites, picnic tables, fire pits, restrooms, showers, potable water, a playground, and a dump station. The camping and tent areas also allow dogs. There is a dog walk area at the campground. There are no water hookups at the campgrounds. Multiple dogs may be allowed.

Big Pine Campground
12084 Big Pine Road
Custer, SD
800-235-3981
bigpinecampground.com
Dogs of all sizes are allowed. There are no additional pet fees. Dogs must be leashed and cleaned up after. There are some breed restrictions. The camping and tent areas also allow dogs. There is a dog walk area at the campground. Multiple dogs may be allowed.

Black Hills National Forest
25041 N H 16
Custer, SD
605-673-9200 (800-710-2267)
fs.fed.us/r2/blackhills/
This 1.2 million acre forest, at altitudes up to 7,242 feet, offers 1,300 miles of streams, over 13,000 acres of wilderness, 2 scenic byways and over 450 miles of trails. Dogs of all sizes are allowed at no additional fee. Dogs may not be left unattended, and they must be leashed in the camp ares, and cleaned up after. Dogs may be off lead in the forest only if they are under strict voice command and will not chase wildlife. The camping and tent areas also allow dogs. There is a dog walk area at the campground. There are no electric or water hookups at the campground. Multiple dogs may be allowed.

Crazy Horse Kampground
1116 N 5th Street
Custer, SD
605-673-2565
rushmorecabins.com
Dogs of all sizes are allowed. There are no additional pet fees. Dogs may not be left unattended, they must be well behaved, leashed, and cleaned up after. This RV park is closed during the off-season. The camping and tent areas also allow dogs. There is a dog walk area at the campground. Dogs are allowed in the camping cabins. Multiple dogs may be allowed.

Custer State Park
13329 H 16A
Custer, SD
605-255-4515 (800-710-CAMP (2267))
Steeped in natural and cultural history, this park of 71,000 acres of spectacular terrain offers living history demonstrations, guided nature walks, gold-panning excursions, one of the largest bison herds in the world and a variety of recreational pursuits. Dogs of all sizes are allowed at no additional fee. Dogs may not be left unattended, and they must be leashed and cleaned up after in camp areas. Dogs are allowed on the trails, and they may be off lead then only if they are under strict voice command. Dogs are not allowed on beaches or in buildings. The camping and tent areas also allow dogs. There is a dog walk area at the campground. There are no electric or water hookups at the

campground. Multiple dogs may be allowed.

Fort WeLikit Family Campground
24992 Sylvan Lake Road/H 89
Custer, SD
605-673-3600 (888-946-2267)
fortwelikit.com/
Nestled among the tall evergreens in the Black Hills, this family campground offers 100 sites, modern restrooms, showers, laundry facilities, a playground, free Wi-Fi, and a dump station. There is also a mobile RV repairman on site. Dogs are allowed for no additional fee; they must be leashed and cleaned up after-at all times. The camping and tent areas also allow dogs. There is a dog walk area at the campground. Dogs are allowed in the camping cabins. Multiple dogs may be allowed.

KOA Campground
U.S. Highway 16
Custer, SD
605-673-4304
koa.com/where/sd/41107/
This KOA campground is located in the Black Hills. They have tent sites, RV campsites and pet-friendly Kamping Kabins. Amenities include a heated pool, croquet, a playground, snack bar, modem dataport, maximum pull-thru length of 60 feet and 50 amp service available. Well-behaved leashed dogs are allowed and there is a dog walk area on the premises. Please remember to clean up after your pet. The campground is open from April 15 to October 1. They are located 3 miles west of the town of Custer on Highway 1 towards Jewel Cave and New Castle, Wyoming. Mt. Rushmore is about a 30 minute drive from the campground, possibly more if there is traffic.

The Flintstones Bedrock City Campground
US Highways 16 and 385
Custer, SD
605-673-4079
flintstonesbedrockcity.com/
Enjoy a camping or RV stay at this Flintstone's themed campground. The camp sites are located in an open meadow hilltop location. This full service campground offers tent camping and RV camping. Amenities include full hookups, showers, laundry facility, store, heating swimming pool and arcade. Also on site is the Flintstone's theme park which offers a miniature train ride around the park, several

playgrounds, a Flintmobile car ride, gift shop, and a drive-in restaurant which has Brontoburgers, Chickasaurus and more. They are open from mid May until the beginning of September. Well-behaved leashed dogs are welcome, but are not allowed inside any buildings, including the camping cabins. Pets are allowed in the theme park including on the miniature train ride and at the outdoor dining seats at the drive-in restaurant. Please remember to clean up after your pet.

The Roost Resort
12462 H 16 A
Custer, SD
605-673-2326
blackhills.com/roost
Dogs of all sizes are allowed at no additional fee for tent or RV sites. For the cabins, there is a $5 per night per pet additional fee for a small dog, and a $10 per night per pet additional fee for medium to large dogs. Dogs may not be left unattended, and they must be quiet, well behaved, leashed, and cleaned up after. The camping and tent areas also allow dogs. There is a dog walk area at the campground. Dogs are allowed in the camping cabins. Multiple dogs may be allowed.

Deadwood KOA
1 mile W of Deadwood on H 14A
Deadwood, SD
605-578-3830 (800-562-0846)
koa.com/where/sd/41108.htm
Dogs of all sizes are allowed. There are no additional pet fees. Dogs may not be left unattended in the cabins or outside. Dogs must be leashed and cleaned up after. This RV park is closed during the off-season. The camping and tent areas also allow dogs. There is a dog walk area at the campground. Dogs are allowed in the camping cabins. Multiple dogs may be allowed.

Griffen Park
222 E Dakota Street
Fort Pierre, SD
605-773-7407
This park offers a variety of recreational pursuits, trails, and year round activities. Dogs of all sizes are allowed at no additional fee. Dogs must be quiet, leashed and cleaned up after. Dogs are not allowed on the beach. Dogs are allowed on the trials. The camping and tent areas also allow dogs. There is a dog walk area at the campground. Multiple dogs may be allowed.

Oahe Downstream Rec Area
20439 Marina Loop Road
Fort Pierre, SD
605-223-7722 (800-710-CAMP (2267))
This park is located on the south side of the dam that was built by the Corp, creating one of the largest constructed reservoirs in the US, and offers a wide range of activities and recreation. Dogs of all sizes are allowed at no additional fee. Dogs may not be left unattended, and they must be on no more than a 10 foot leash, and cleaned up after in camp areas. Dogs may be off lead in the off season if they are well behaved and under strict voice command. Dogs are not allowed on the swim beach or in buildings. Dogs are allowed on the trails. This campground is closed during the off-season. The camping and tent areas also allow dogs. There is a dog walk area at the campground. There are no water hookups at the campground. Multiple dogs may be allowed.

Palisades State Park
25495 485th Avenue
Garretson, SD
605-594-3824 (800-710-CAMP (2267))
Historic sites, 1.2 billion year old quartzite spires, vertical cliffs (popular with climbers), scenic overlooks, and a variety of recreation can all be enjoyed at this lush riverside park. Dogs are allowed for no additional fee. They must be on no more than a 10 foot leash and be cleaned up after at all times. Dogs are not allowed on designated swimming beaches or in any park buildings. The campground offers 35 sites, picnic tables, showers, potable water, a playground, amphitheater, and a dump station. The camping and tent areas also allow dogs. There is a dog walk area at the campground. There are no water hookups at the campgrounds. Multiple dogs may be allowed.

Crooked Creek Resort
24184 S H 385/16
Hill City, SD
800-252-8486
crookedcreeksd.com
Dogs of all sizes are allowed. There are no additional pet fees. Dogs may not be left unattended, and they must be leashed and cleaned up after. This RV park is closed during the off-season. The camping

and tent areas also allow dogs. There is a dog walk area at the campground. Dogs are allowed in the camping cabins. 2 dogs may be allowed.

Horsethief Campground
24391 H 87
Hill City, SD
605-574-2668
horsethief.com
Dogs of all sizes are allowed. There are no additional pet fees. Dogs may not be left unattended, and they must be leashed and cleaned up after. This RV park is closed during the off-season. The camping and tent areas also allow dogs. Multiple dogs may be allowed.

KOA Campground and Resort
12620 Highway 244
Hill City, SD
605-574-2525
koa.com/where/sd/41125/
This KOA Campground is located at an elevation of 5,400 feet and is just 5 miles from Mt. Rushmore. The campground is adjacent to the Peter Norbeck Wildlife Preserve and the Black Elk Wilderness Area and minutes to Custer State Park. They have almost 500 tent sites and RV campsites, and 55 Kamping Kabins with one or two bedroom options. Amenities include 2 outdoor pools, 3 hot tubs, sauna, waterslide, mini-golf, volleyball court, basketball court, fishing pond, hayrides, evening movies, paddle boats, bike rentals, restaurant, laundry facilities, comfort stations and dump stations. Well-behaved leashed dogs are allowed in the campground, and in the cabins, some of which have bathrooms. Please remember to clean up after your pet.

Rafter J Bar Ranch
12325 Rafter J Road
Hill City, SD
605-574-2527
rafterj.com
Dogs of all sizes are allowed. There are no additional pet fees. Dogs may not be left unattended, they must be quiet, leashed, and cleaned up after. This RV park is closed during the off-season. The camping and tent areas also allow dogs. There is a dog walk area at the campground. Multiple dogs may be allowed.

Angostura Recreation Area
13157 N Angostura Road
Hot Springs, SD
605-745-6996 (800-710-CAMP (2267))

236

Home to one of the largest reservoirs in the western part of the state offering 36 miles of shoreline, it is quite popular for all types of water activities. The park has concessionaires, and regular educational and interpretive programs through the summer. Dogs are allowed for no additional fee. They must be on no more than a 10 foot leash and be cleaned up after at all times. Dogs are not allowed on designated swimming beaches or in any park buildings. There are 4 campgrounds-each with their own special features, that offer a total of 168 sites. There are modern restrooms, showers, picnic tables, grills, playgrounds, and dump stations. The camping and tent areas also allow dogs. There is a dog walk area at the campground. There are no water hookups at the campgrounds. Multiple dogs may be allowed.

Elk Mountain Campground/Wind Cave National ParkHot
26611 H 385 (Visitor Ctr)
Hot Springs, SD
605-745-4600
This campground is located in the Wind Cave National Park which is home to the 4th longest cave in the world and above ground-home to 28,295 acres of rich prairie and wildlife. Dogs are allowed in the park and in the campground for no additional fee; they must be leashed and under their owner's control. Campsites are first come first served and running water and flush toilets are available during the warmer months, and in off season only pit toilets are available. The camping and tent areas also allow dogs. There is a dog walk area at the campground. There are no electric or water hookups at the campgrounds. Multiple dogs may be allowed.

Hot Springs KOA
HCR 52, Box 112-C
Hot Springs, SD
605-745-6449 (800-562-0803)
koa.com
Dogs of all sizes are allowed, and there are no additional pet fees for tent or RV sites. There is a $3 per night additional fee for pets in the cabins. Dogs must be quiet, well behaved, leashed and cleaned up after. This RV park is closed during the off-season. The camping and tent areas also allow dogs. There is a dog walk area at the campground. Dogs are allowed in the camping cabins. Multiple dogs may be

allowed.

Badland National Park
25216 Ben Reifel Place
Interior, SD
605-433-5361
nps.gov/badl/
This park of 244,000 acres of sharply eroded buttes, pinnacles, spires, and home to the largest protected mixed grass prairie in the US, offers interpretive programs, an active paleontological dig site, and a variety of recreational pursuits. Dogs of all sizes are allowed at no additional fee. Dogs may not be left unattended at any time-including in automobiles, and they must be leashed and cleaned up after. Dogs are not allowed on the trails or grass, and are to remain on asphalt areas. The camping and tent areas also allow dogs. There is a dog walk area at the campground. There are no electric or water hookups at the campground. Multiple dogs may be allowed.

Badlands/White River KOA
20720 H 44
Interior, SD
605-433-5337 (800-562-3897)
koa.com
Dogs of all sizes are allowed. There are no additional pet fees. Dogs may not be left unattended unless they will be quiet. Dogs must be leashed and cleaned up after. They have a Pet Park where your dog can be off leash. This RV park is closed during the off-season. The camping and tent areas also allow dogs. There is a dog walk area at the campground. There are special amenities given to dogs at this campground. Multiple dogs may be allowed.

Kennebec KOA
311 S H 273
Kennebec, SD
605-869-2300 (800-562-6361)
koa.com
Dogs of all sizes are allowed. There are no additional pet fees. Dogs must be leashed and cleaned up after. A pet waiver must be signed if the dog(s) are any of the known aggressive breeds. This RV park is closed during the off-season. The camping and tent areas also allow dogs. There is a dog walk area at the campground. Dogs are allowed in the camping cabins. Multiple dogs may be allowed.

Fort Sisseton State Park
11907 434th Avenue

Lake City, SD
605-448-5474 (800-710-CAMP (2267))
Rich in military and cultural history, this park is listed as a National Historic Landmark and it details fort life on the western frontier. In addition to a number of recreational and educational opportunities, there are annual reenactments and special events. Dogs are allowed for no additional fee. They must be on no more than a 10 foot leash and be cleaned up after at all times. Dogs are not allowed on designated swimming beaches or in any park buildings. The campground has 17 sites, restrooms, showers, and potable water. The camping and tent areas also allow dogs. There is a dog walk area at the campground. There are no water hookups at the campgrounds. Multiple dogs may be allowed.

Lake Herman State Park
23409 State Park Drive
Madison, SD
605-256-5003 (800-710-CAMP (2267))
Evidence points to this beautiful peninsula area being a popular camping area for hundreds of years. Hiking trails will take visitors through lush green environments, grassy prairies, wetlands, and by historic sites. Dogs are allowed for no additional fee. They must be on no more than a 10 foot leash and be cleaned up after at all times. Dogs are not allowed on designated swimming beaches or in any park buildings. The campground has 70 RV sites-including an accessible site, 2 tent sites, picnic tables, fire rings, restrooms, showers, potable water, and a dump station. The camping and tent areas also allow dogs. There is a dog walk area at the campground. There are no water hookups at the campgrounds. Multiple dogs may be allowed.

Belvidere East KOA
24201 H 63
Midland, SD
605-344-2247 (800-562-2134)
koa.com
Dogs of all sizes are allowed. There are no additional pet fees. Dogs must be leashed and cleaned up after. There is a fenced in pet playground where dogs may be off leash. This RV park is closed during the off-season. The camping and tent areas also allow dogs. There is a dog walk area at the campground. Multiple dogs may be allowed.

Dakota Campground
1800 Spruce
Mitchell, SD
605-996-9432
Dogs of all sizes are allowed. There are no additional pet fees. Dogs may not be left unattended, they must be quiet, leashed, and cleaned up after. This RV park is closed during the off-season. The camping and tent areas also allow dogs. There is a dog walk area at the campground. Multiple dogs may be allowed.

Mitchell KOA
41244 H 38
Mitchell, SD
605-996-1131 (800-562-1236)
koa.com
Dogs of all sizes are allowed. There are no additional pet fees. Dogs must be quiet, well behaved, leashed, and cleaned up after. This RV park is closed during the off-season. The camping and tent areas also allow dogs. There is a dog walk area at the campground. Dogs are allowed in the camping cabins. Multiple dogs may be allowed.

Rondees Campground
911 East K
Mitchell, SD
605-996-0769
rondeescampground.com
Dogs of all sizes are allowed. There are no additional pet fees. Dogs may not be left unattended outside, and they must be quiet, well behaved, leashed, and cleaned up after. This RV park is closed during the off-season. The camping and tent areas also allow dogs. There is a dog walk area at the campground. Multiple dogs may be allowed.

Indian Creek Rec Area
12905 288th Avenue
Mobridge, SD
605-845-7112 (800-710-CAMP (2267))
Beautiful river views from the rolling hills of this park make this a popular destination. In addition to its historical interest, the park offers a marina, a hiking trail, and a variety of recreational pursuits. Dogs of all sizes are allowed at no additional fee. Dogs may not be left unattended, and they must be on no more than a 6 foot leash, and cleaned up after. The camping and tent areas also allow dogs. There is a dog walk area at the campground. There are no water hookups at the campground. Multiple dogs may be allowed.

Sioux City KOA
601 Streeter Drive
North Sioux City, SD
605-232-4519 (800-562-5439)
koa.com
Dogs of all sizes are allowed. There are no additional pet fees. Dogs must be well behaved, leashed, and cleaned up after. This RV park is closed during the off-season. The camping and tent areas also allow dogs. There is a dog walk area at the campground. Dogs are allowed in the camping cabins. Multiple dogs may be allowed.

Oasis Campground
1003 H 16
Oacoma, SD
605-734-6959
alsoasis.com
Dogs of all sizes are allowed. There are no additional pet fees. Dogs may be off lead if they are friendly and well behaved, but they must be cleaned up after at all times. This RV park is closed during the off-season. The camping and tent areas also allow dogs. There is a dog walk area at the campground. Multiple dogs may be allowed.

Elk Creek Lodge and Resort
8220 Elk Creek Road
Piedmont, SD
605-787-4884 (800-846-2267)
Located on 150 acres of rolling hills next to an amazing petrified forest, this campground offers flat, open sites, showers, a laundry, store, swimming pool, hot tub, dump station, and more. Dogs are allowed for no additional fee in the campground and in the cabins. They must be leashed and cleaned up after at all times. Dogs must be crated when left alone in the cabin, and they are not allowed in the rental RV units, the lodge, buildings, or in food service areas. The camping and tent areas also allow dogs. There is a dog walk area at the campground. Dogs are allowed in the camping cabins. Multiple dogs may be allowed.

Farm Island Rec Area
1301 Farm Island Road
Pierre, SD
605-773-2885 (800-710-2267)
Naturalist, recreationalists, and sports enthusiasts can all find their niche at this rec area. In addition to a wide range of land and water recreation, the park has a nature observation blind and an island nature area with 8 miles of

pathways. The campgrounds have picnic tables, grills, showers, a playground, and a dump station. Dogs are allowed for no additional fee. Dogs must be leashed and cleaned up after, and they are not allowed in buildings, on the beach, in the water, or at the playground. The camping and tent areas also allow dogs. There is a dog walk area at the campground. There are no water hookups at the campgrounds. Multiple dogs may be allowed.

Berry Patch Campground
1860 E North Street
Rapid City, SD
800-658-4566
Dogs of all sizes are allowed. There are no additional pet fees. Dogs may not be left unattended outside, and must be leashed and cleaned up after. The camping and tent areas also allow dogs. There is a dog walk area at the campground. Multiple dogs may be allowed.

Happy Holiday Resort
8990 H 16S
Rapid City, SD
605-342-7365
happyholidayrvresort.com
Dogs of all sizes are allowed. There is a $1 one time additional fee per pet. Dogs may not be left unattended outside, and they must be leashed and cleaned up after. The camping and tent areas also allow dogs. There is a dog walk area at the campground. Multiple dogs may be allowed.

KOA Campground
P.O. Box 2592
Rapid City, SD
605-348-2111
koa.com/where/sd/41102/
This KOA campground is off of I-90 in Rapid City and is located about an hour from the area's popular attractions. They have tent sites, RV campsites and pet-friendly Kamping Kabins. Well-behaved leashed dogs are allowed in the campground and in the cabins. Please remember to clean up after your pet. Amenities include a swimming pool, hot tub/sauna, snack bar, modem dataport, cable TV, maximum pull-thru length of 60 feet and 50 amp service available. The campground is open from April 15 to October 15. Upon arrival, they usually have a grab bag with treats for pets. There are some breed restrictions.

Rushmore Shadows
23645 Clubhouse Drive

Rapid City, SD
800-231-0425
rushmoreshadows.com
Dogs of all sizes are allowed. There are no additional pet fees. Dogs may not be left unattended, and must be leashed and cleaned up after. This RV park is closed during the off-season. The camping and tent areas also allow dogs. There is a dog walk area at the campground. Multiple dogs may be allowed.

Camp America
25495 H 81
Salem, SD
605-425-9085
campsalemsd.com/
Dogs of all sizes are allowed. There are no additional pet fees. Dogs must be leashed at all times, and cleaned up after. This RV park is closed during the off-season. The camping and tent areas also allow dogs. There is a dog walk area at the campground. Multiple dogs may be allowed.

Sioux Falls KOA
1401 E Robur Drive
Sioux Falls, SD
605-332-9987 (800-562-9865)
koa.com
Dogs of all sizes are allowed. There are no additional pet fees. Dogs must be well behaved, leashed, and cleaned up after. This RV park is closed during the off-season. The camping and tent areas also allow dogs. There is a dog walk area at the campground. Dogs are allowed in the camping cabins. Multiple dogs may be allowed.

Spearfish KOA
41 H 14
Spearfish, SD
605-642-4633 (800-562-0805)
koa.com
Dogs of all sizes are allowed. There are no additional pet fees. Dogs may not be left unattended at any time, and they must be leashed and cleaned up after. There are some breed restrictions. This RV park is closed during the off-season. The camping and tent areas also allow dogs. There is a dog walk area at the campground. Multiple dogs may be allowed.

Bear Butte State Park
PO Box 688; E Hwy 79
Sturgis, SD
605-347-5240 (800-710-2267)
Rich in geology, history, and culture, this park features interpretive programs, an education center, a

variety of trails, and various recreational pursuits. Dogs of all sizes are allowed at no additional fee. Dogs may not be left unattended at any time; they must be on no more than a 10 foot leash, and be cleaned up after. Dogs are allowed on all the trails except the Summit Trail. Dogs are not allowed in park buildings. The camping and tent areas also allow dogs. There is a dog walk area at the campground. There are no electric or water hookups at the campground. Multiple dogs may be allowed.

Elkview Campground
13014 Pleasant Valley Road
Sturgis, SD
877-478-5162
elkviewcampground.com
Dogs of all sizes are allowed. There are no additional pet fees. Dogs may not be left unattended unless they will be quiet and well behaved. Dogs must be leashed and cleaned up after. This RV park is closed during the off-season. The camping and tent areas also allow dogs. There is a dog walk area at the campground. Multiple dogs may be allowed.

Red Barn RV Park
47003 272nd Street
Tea, SD
605-368-2268
Dogs of all sizes are allowed. There are no additional pet fees. Dogs may not be left unattended, and must be leashed and cleaned up after. This RV park is closed during the off-season. There is a dog walk area at the campground. Multiple dogs may be allowed.

Arrow Campground
PO Box 366
Wall, SD
605-279-2112 (800-888-1361)
blackhillsbadlands.com/arrow
Dogs of all sizes are allowed. There are no additional pet fees. Dogs may not be left unattended outside, and they must be leashed and cleaned up after. Dogs are not allowed at the playground. The camping and tent areas also allow dogs. There is a dog walk area at the campground. Multiple dogs may be allowed.

Sleepy Hollow Campground
116 4th Avenue W
Wall, SD
605-279-2100
Dogs of all sizes are allowed. There are no additional pet fees. Dogs

must be leashed and cleaned up after. Dogs are not allowed in buildings or on the lawn by the office. This RV park is closed during the off-season. The camping and tent areas also allow dogs. There is a dog walk area at the campground. Multiple dogs may be allowed.

Chief White Crane Rec Area
43349 Hwy 52
Yankton, SD
605-668-2985 (800-710-2267)
This park is rich in history, but their main feature is being a winter home for the American Eagle, and motor vehicles are not allowed in the park from November 1st through March 31 due to nesting. Dogs of all sizes are allowed at no additional fee. Dogs may not be left unattended, and they must be leashed and cleaned up after. Dogs are not allowed in public swim areas or in buildings. Dogs are allowed on the trails. This campground is closed during the off-season. The camping and tent areas also allow dogs. There is a dog walk area at the campground. Multiple dogs may be allowed.

Lewis and Clark Recreation Area
43349 H 52
Yankton, SD
605-668-2985 (800-710-CAMP (2267))
One of the state's most popular parks, this resort offers a wide variety of recreational activities and amenities. Dogs are allowed for no additional fee. They must be on no more than a 10 foot leash and be cleaned up after at all times. Dogs are not allowed on designated swimming beaches or in any park buildings. The campground has 374 sites, picnic tables, fire pits, modern bath houses, potable water, and a dump station. This RV park is closed during the off-season. The camping and tent areas also allow dogs. There is a dog walk area at the campground. There are no water hookups at the campgrounds. Multiple dogs may be allowed.

Tennessee

Cherokee National Forest/Ocoee / Hiwassee Ranger District
3171 Highway 64
Benton, TN
423-476-9700 (877-444-6777)

fs.fed.us/r8/cherokee/
The state's largest public use land with 640,000 forested acres also sits in one of the most diverse environments in the world. In addition to a wide range of recreational and educational pursuits, this working forest also provides a wide variety of community resources. Dogs are allowed throughout the forest; they are not allowed in buildings, swimming areas, beaches, or where posted. Dogs must be on no more than a 6 foot leash (except during legal hunting), caged, or in a vehicle and under their owner's control at all times. There are 30 developed campgrounds and several primitive camping areas available with all, some, or none of the following: running water, restrooms, showers, picnic tables, fire rings, and grills. The campsites are first come first served except for 3 of the developed campgrounds that require reservations. The camping and tent areas also allow dogs. There is a dog walk area at the campground. There are no water hookups at the campgrounds. Multiple dogs may be allowed.

Bristol/Kingsport KOA
425 Rocky Branch Road
Blountville, TN
423-323-7790 (800-562-7640)
koa.com
Dogs of all sizes are allowed. There are no additional pet fees. Dogs may not be tied up or left unattended outside, and they must be leashed and cleaned up after. There is a fenced in dog run area, and a Kennel Day Kare on site for $10 per day per pet. The camping and tent areas also allow dogs. There is a dog walk area at the campground. There are special amenities given to dogs at this campground. Multiple dogs may be allowed.

Paris Landing State Park
16055 H 79 N
Buchanan, TN
731-641-4465 (800-250-8614)
This 841 acre park along the shores of the Tennessee River offers a variety of land and water recreation. Dogs of all sizes are allowed at no additional fee for camping. There is an additional fee of $10 per night per pet for the lodge and for the 1 pet friendly cabin. Dogs may not be left unattended, and they must be leashed and cleaned up after. Dogs are allowed on the trails. The camping and tent areas also allow dogs. There is a dog walk area at the

campground. Dogs are allowed in the camping cabins. Multiple dogs may be allowed.

Montgomery Bell State Park
1020 Jackson Hill Road
Burns, TN
615-797-9052 (800-250-8613)
This park of over 3,700 acres offers a variety of naturalist interpretive programs in addition to various land and water recreation. Dogs of all sizes are allowed at no additional fee for the camping area. There is a $10 per night per pet additional fee for the 1 pet friendly cabin and the lodge. Dogs must be leashed at all times and cleaned up after. Dogs are not allowed in the lake or in park buildings; they are allowed on the trails. The camping and tent areas also allow dogs. There is a dog walk area at the campground. Dogs are allowed in the camping cabins. Multiple dogs may be allowed.

Cove Lake State Park
110 Cove Lake Lane
Caryville, TN
423-566-9701
This mountain valley park on 673 acres offers a variety of land and water activities and recreational pursuits. Dogs of all sizes are allowed at no additional fee. Dogs may not be left unattended, and they must be leashed and cleaned up after. Dogs are not allowed in buildings. Dogs are allowed on the trails. The camping and tent areas also allow dogs. There is a dog walk area at the campground. Multiple dogs may be allowed.

Royal Blue RV Resort
305 Luther Seiber Road
Caryville, TN
423-566-4847
royalblueresort.com
Dogs of all sizes are allowed. There are no additional pet fees. Dogs must be quiet, leashed, and cleaned up after. The camping and tent areas also allow dogs. There is a dog walk area at the campground. Multiple dogs may be allowed.

Raccoon Mountain Caverns/RV Park and Campground
319 W Hills Road
Chattanooga, TN
423-821-9403 (800-823-CAMP (2267))
raccoonmountain.com/
The caves here currently have over 5½ miles of mapped passageways and are considered one of the top

10 cave sites in the country. This park is close to numerous other attractions in the area and there is a go-kart track also on site. Although dogs are not allowed in the caves or the gift shop, they are allowed throughout the park, on the trails, and in the camp area. Dogs must be well behaved, leashed, and under their owner's control at all times. In addition to providing some great views of Raccoon and Lookout Mountains, the camp area offers picnic tables, grills, a playground, store, pool, restrooms, and a dump station. There are some breed restrictions. The camping and tent areas also allow dogs. There is a dog walk area at the campground. Multiple dogs may be allowed.

Clarksville RV Park and Campground
1270 Tyler Road
Clarksville, TN
931-648-8638
clarksvillervpark.com
Dogs of all sizes are allowed. There are no additional pet fees. Dogs may not be left unattended outside, must be leashed, and cleaned up after. The camping and tent areas also allow dogs. There is a dog walk area at the campground. Multiple dogs may be allowed.

Texas T Campground
2499 Lynnville H
Cornersville, TN
931-293-2500
texastcampground.com
Dogs of all sizes are allowed. There are no additional pet fees. Dogs must be leashed and cleaned up after. The camping and tent areas also allow dogs. There is a dog walk area at the campground. Multiple dogs may be allowed.

Ballyhoo Campground
256 Werthwyle Drive
Crossville, TN
931-484-0860
ballyhoocampground.com
Dogs of all sizes are allowed, up to three, and there are no additional pet fees for tent or RV sites. There is a $5 one time additional pet fee for the cabins, and only one dog is allowed. Dogs must be well behaved, leashed, and cleaned up after. There are some breed restrictions. The camping and tent areas also allow dogs. There is a dog walk area at the campground. Dogs are allowed in the camping cabins.

Cumberland Mountain State Park
24 Office Dirve

Crossville, TN
931-484-6138 (800-250-8618)
This 1,720-acre park is said to be the largest timbered plateau in America, and offers interpretive programs, scenic trails, and a variety of land and water recreation. Dogs are allowed at no additional fee for tent or RV sites. There is an additional $5 per night per pet fee for the cabins. Dogs must be leashed and cleaned up after. Dogs are allowed on the trails. The camping and tent areas also allow dogs. There is a dog walk area at the campground. Dogs are allowed in the camping cabins. Multiple dogs may be allowed.

Roam and Roost RV Campground
255 Fairview Drive
Crossville, TN
931-707-1414
Dogs of all sizes are allowed. There are no additional pet fees. Dogs must be well behaved, leashed, and cleaned up after. There are some breed restrictions. This RV park is closed during the off-season. There is a dog walk area at the campground. 2 dogs may be allowed.

Arrow Creek Campground
4721 E Parkway
Gatlinburg, TN
865-430-7433
arrowcreekcamp.com
Dogs of all sizes and numbers are allowed for tent and RV sites. Only 2 dogs are allowed in the cabins. There are no additional pet fees. Dogs may not be left unattended, must be quiet, leashed, and cleaned up after. This RV park is closed during the off-season. The camping and tent areas also allow dogs. There is a dog walk area at the campground. Dogs are allowed in the camping cabins.

Great Smoky Jellystone
4946 Hooper H
Gatlinburg, TN
423-487-5534 (800-210-2119)
greatsmokyjellystone.com
Dogs up to 75 pounds are allowed. There are no additional pet fees. Dogs must be well behaved, not left unattended, be leashed, and cleaned up after. There are some breed restrictions. This RV park is closed during the off-season There is a dog walk area at the campground. 2 dogs may be allowed.

Great Smoky Mountain National Park
107 Park Headquarters Road
Gatlinburg, TN

865-436-1200 (877-444-6777)
nps.gov/grsm/
A hiker's, naturalist's, and recreationalist's paradise; this popular park features over 800 miles of trails, a world renowned abundance of flora and fauna, and numerous recreational and educational opportunities. Dogs are allowed along roadways, picnic areas, waterways, on 2 of the trails, and the camp area. Dogs must be leashed and under their owner's control at all times. Front-country camping provides camping near your vehicle and provides picnic tables, grills, fire rings, restrooms, water, and flush toilets. Backpacker camping is also available. The camping and tent areas also allow dogs. There is a dog walk area at the campground. There are no electric or water hookups at the campgrounds. Multiple dogs may be allowed.

Smoky Bear Campground
4857 E Parkway
Gatlinburg, TN
865-436-8372
smokybearcampground.com
Dogs of all sizes are allowed at the tent and RV sites. Small dogs only are allowed in the rentals or cabins. There are no additional pet fees. Dogs may not be left unattended except for very short periods. Dogs must be leashed and cleaned up after. This RV park is closed during the off-season. The camping and tent areas also allow dogs. There is a dog walk area at the campground. Dogs are allowed in the camping cabins. Multiple dogs may be allowed.

Twin Creek RV Resort
E Parkway
Gatlinburg, TN
865-436-7081
twincreekrvresort.com/
Dogs of all sizes are allowed. There are no additional pet fees. Canvas or Pop-up trailers are not allowed with pets. Dogs may not be left unattended, and dog pens are not allowed. Dogs must be leashed and cleaned up after. There are some breed restrictions. There is a dog walk area at the campground. 2 dogs may be allowed.

Harrison Bay State Park
8411 Harrison Bay Road
Harrison, TN
423-344-2272
This scenic wooded park of 1,200 acres with 40 miles of shoreline

holds historical interest and provides a variety of land and water activities. Dogs of all sizes are allowed at no additional fee. Dogs may not be left unattended for long periods, and they must be leashed and cleaned up after. Dogs are not allowed in public swim areas or in buildings. Dogs are allowed on the trails. The camping and tent areas also allow dogs. There is a dog walk area at the campground. Multiple dogs may be allowed.

Chickasaw State Rustic Park
20 Cabin Lane
Henderson, TN
731-989-5141 (800-458-1752)
This scenic park has over 1,280 acres for recreation, and a variety of trails as well as land and water activities. Dogs of all sizes are allowed at no additional fee for the tent and RV sites. There is a $10 per night per pet additional fee for the cabins. Dogs may not be left unattended for very long or left out at night. Dogs must be leashed and be cleaned up after. Dogs are allowed on the trails. The camping and tent areas also allow dogs. There is a dog walk area at the campground. Dogs are allowed in the camping cabins. Multiple dogs may be allowed.

Standing Stone State Park
1674 Standing Stone Park H (H 52)
Hilham, TN
931-823-6347 (800-713-5157)
This scenic 1100 acre park hosts a variety of activities and recreational pursuits. Dogs of all sizes are allowed at no additional fee for the camping area. There is a $10 additional pet fee for the first night, and $5 per night per pet thereafter, for the 1 pet friendly cabin. Dogs may not be left unattended, and they must be leashed at all times, and cleaned up after. Dogs are allowed on the trails. The camping and tent areas also allow dogs. There is a dog walk area at the campground. Dogs are allowed in the camping cabins.

Meriwether Lewis Park
389.9 Natchez Trace Parkway
Hohenwald, TN
931-796-2675
nps.gov/natr/
Known for the site where Meriwether Lewis of Lewis and Clark fame (and then governor of the Upper Louisiana Territory) died of a gunshot wound; this beautiful memorial site offers a variety of recreation, a pioneer

cemetery, exhibits, trails, and more. Dogs are allowed in the park and at the campground. Dogs may not be left unattended at any time; they must have proof of vaccinations, be quiet, kept leashed or crated, and under their owner's immediate control at all times. Dogs are not allowed in buildings. Campsites are free and first come first served; there are 32 sites and potable water is available. The camping and tent areas also allow dogs. There is a dog walk area at the campground. There are no electric or water hookups at the campgrounds. Multiple dogs may be allowed.

Buffalo/I-40/Exit 143 KOA
473 Barren Hollow Road
Hurricane Mills, TN
931-296-1306 (800-562-0832)
koa.com
Dogs of all sizes are allowed, but there can only be up to 2 large or three small dogs per site. There are no additional pet fees. Dogs may not be left unattended, and they must be quiet, well behaved, leashed, and cleaned up after. There are some breed restrictions. The camping and tent areas also allow dogs. There is a dog walk area at the campground. Dogs are allowed in the camping cabins.

Loretta Lynn's Ranch
44 Hurricane Mills
Hurricane Mills, TN
931-296-7700
lorettalynn.com
Dogs of all sizes are allowed. There are no additional pet fees. Dogs are not allowed on tours or in the buildings. Dogs must be in at night, leashed, and cleaned up after. The camping and tent areas also allow dogs. There is a dog walk area at the campground. Multiple dogs may be allowed.

Pickett State Park
4605 Pickett Park H/H 154
Jamestown, TN
931-879-5821 (877-260-0010)
A beautiful park rich with botanical and geological features have made this a popular recreational as well as educational destination. Dogs are allowed in the campground for no additional fee; there is an additional fee of $10 per night per pet (up to two dogs) for the cabins. Dogs may not be left unattended at any time; they must have proof of vaccinations, be quiet, kept leashed or crated, and under their owner's immediate control at all times. Courtesy litter

bags are provided. They are not allowed in buildings, food service or designated swim areas, or where otherwise posted. The campground offers 40 first come first served sites with picnic tables, grills, restrooms, hot showers, and a dump station. Some backpacking sites are also available. The camping and tent areas also allow dogs. There is a dog walk area at the campground. Dogs are allowed in the camping cabins. Multiple dogs may be allowed.

Indian Mountain State Park
143 State Park Circle
Jellico, TN
423-784-7958
This beautiful 200 acre park provides nature study in addition to a variety of land and water recreation. Dogs of all sizes are allowed at no additional fee. Dogs may not be left unattended, and they must be leashed and cleaned up after. Dogs are allowed on the trails. The camping and tent areas also allow dogs. There is a dog walk area at the campground. Multiple dogs may be allowed.

Warriors Path State Park
490 Hemlock Road
Kingsport, TN
423-239-8531
This park got it's name from being an ancient war and trading path of the Cherokees, and now this scenic area provides a variety of land and water activities and recreation. Dogs of all sizes are allowed at no additional fee. Dogs may not be left unattended for very long and then only if they will be quiet and very well behaved. Dogs must be leashed and cleaned up after. Dogs are not allowed on the beach or in the buildings. Dogs are allowed on the trails. The camping and tent areas also allow dogs. There is a dog walk area at the campground. Multiple dogs may be allowed.

Southlake RV Park
3730 Maryville Pike
Knoxville, TN
865-573-1837
southlakervpark.com
Dogs of all sizes are allowed. There are no additional pet fees. Dogs may not be left unattended outside, must be leashed, and cleaned up after. The camping and tent areas also allow dogs. There is a dog walk area at the campground. Multiple dogs may be allowed.

Knoxville East KOA
241 KOA Way
Kodak, TN
865-933-6393 (800-562-8693)
koa.com
Dogs of all sizes are allowed. There are no additional pet fees. Dogs must be quiet, well behaved, leashed, and cleaned up after. This RV park is closed during the off-season. The camping and tent areas also allow dogs. There is a dog walk area at the campground. Multiple dogs may be allowed.

David Crockett State Park
1400 W Gaines Street
Lawrenceburg, TN
931-762-9408
This historically rich park offers a museum, interpretive programs, and a variety of land and water activities and recreation. Dogs of all sizes are allowed at no additional fee. Dogs may not be left unattended, and they must have current rabies and shot records. Dogs must be leashed at all times and cleaned up after. Dogs are not allowed in buildings, but they are allowed on the trails. The camping and tent areas also allow dogs. There is a dog walk area at the campground. Multiple dogs may be allowed.

Cedars of Lebanon State Park
328 Cedar Forest Road
Lebanon, TN
615-443-2769 (800-713-5180)
Because of the unique ecosystems of this park, 19 rare and endangered species of plants grow profusely only at this spot on Earth. In addition to nature study and programs, there are a variety of land and water recreational activities. Dogs of all sizes are allowed at no additional fee for the camp area, but there is a $5 per night per pet additional fee for the 1 pet friendly cabin. Dogs may not be left unattended for very long, and they must be quiet, well behaved, leashed and cleaned up after. Dogs are not allowed in buildings, but they are allowed on the trails. The camping and tent areas also allow dogs. There is a dog walk area at the campground. Dogs are allowed in the camping cabins. Multiple dogs may be allowed.

Countryside RV Resort
2100 Safari Camp Road
Lebanon, TN
615-449-5527
countrysideresort.com
Dogs of all sizes are allowed. There are no additional pet fees. Dogs

must be leashed and cleaned up after. The camping and tent areas also allow dogs. There is a dog walk area at the campground. Multiple dogs may be allowed.

Manchester KOA
586 Campground Road
Manchester, TN
931-728-9777 (800-562-7785)
koa.com
Dogs of all sizes are allowed. There are no additional pet fees. There is a pet waiver to sign for cabin rentals. Dogs may not be left unattended outside, and they must be quiet, leashed, and cleaned up after. There is a field nearby where dogs may run off lead if they are well behaved, and under voice control. The camping and tent areas also allow dogs. There is a dog walk area at the campground. Dogs are allowed in the camping cabins. Multiple dogs may be allowed.

Old Stone Fort State Archaeological Park
732 Stone Fort Drive
Manchester, TN
931-723-5073
Much more than a just major recreation area, this 876 acre park is home to a sacred 50 acre 2,000+ years old Native American ceremonial mound. The museum offers a number of fun and entertaining educational programs that details its history. Dogs are allowed for no additional fee. They must be kept leashed, picked after, and they are not allowed in buildings. There are 51 first come, first served wooded campsites with picnic tables, grills, and a seasonal dump station. Modern restrooms and showers are on site. The camping and tent areas also allow dogs. There is a dog walk area at the campground. Multiple dogs may be allowed.

Chattanooga North/Cleveland KOA
648 Pleasant Grove Road
McDonald, TN
423-472-8928 (800-562-9039)
koa.com
Two dogs of any size are allowed at the tent or RV sites. There can only be one dog up to 20 pounds in the cabins. There is a pet policy to sign at check in and there are no additional pet fees. Dogs may not be left unattended outside, and they must be leashed and cleaned up after. The camping and tent areas also allow dogs. There is a dog walk area at the campground. Dogs are allowed in the camping cabins.

Memphis Graceland RV Park and Campground
3691 Elvis Presley Blvd
Memphis, TN
901-396-7125
memphisgracelandrvpark.com
Dogs of all sizes are allowed. There are no additional pet fees. Dogs must be leashed and cleaned up after. The camping and tent areas also allow dogs. There is a dog walk area at the campground. Multiple dogs may be allowed.

T. O. Fuller State Park
1500 W Mitchell Road
Memphis, TN
901-543-7581
This park of over 1100 acres is within the city limits of Memphis, is mostly forested, and offers an Olympic sized swimming pool, an 18 hole golf course, and acres of grassy fields. Dogs of all sizes are allowed at no additional fee. Dogs may not be left unattended, and they must be leashed and cleaned up after. Dogs are not allowed on the golf course, but they are allowed on the trails. The camping and tent areas also allow dogs. There is a dog walk area at the campground. Multiple dogs may be allowed.

Cumberland Gap National Historical Park
H 25E
Middlesboro, KY
606-248-2817
nps.gov/cuga
From scenic vistas, lush forests, and cooling waterfalls above ground to the awe-inspiring chamber caverns below, this beautiful park is sure to please. It also features more than 70 miles of trails and an overlook that overlooks 3 states. Dogs are allowed in the campground for no additional fee. Dogs may not be left unattended at any time; they must have proof of vaccinations, be quiet, kept leashed or crated, and under their owner's immediate control at all times. They are not allowed in buildings, designated swim areas, or where otherwise posted. The campground offers 160 shady sites on a first-come, first-served basis, and offer comfort stations, showers, and potable water. (This camp area is closed for repairs from June 2nd to June 30th 2008.) The camping and tent areas also allow dogs. There is a dog walk area at the campground. There are no water hookups at the

campgrounds. Multiple dogs may be allowed.

Meeman-Shelby Forest State Park
910 Riddick Road
Millington, TN
901-876-5215 (800-471-5293)
A museum and interactive nature center are offered here in addition to providing a variety of recreation areas, woodlands, trails, and wildlife habitats. Dogs of all sizes are allowed at no additional fee for the camping areas. There is a $10 per night per pet fee for the first night, and $5 per night per pet fee for each night thereafter for the 1 pet friendly cabin. Dogs must be leashed at all times. Dogs are allowed on the trails. The camping and tent areas also allow dogs. There is a dog walk area at the campground. Dogs are allowed in the camping cabins. Multiple dogs may be allowed.

Panther Creek State Park
2010 Panther Creek Road
Morristown, TN
423-587-7046
This park, of over 1,400 acres located on the shores of the Cherokee Reservoir, provides 13 scenic hiking and biking trails (of which 5 are hiking only), and a variety of land and water recreation. Dogs of all sizes are allowed at no additional fee. Dogs may not be left unattended, and they must be leashed. They request dogs do their business off trails, or they must be cleaned up after. The camping and tent areas also allow dogs. There is a dog walk area at the campground. Multiple dogs may be allowed.

Jellystone Park
2572 Music Valley Drive
Nashville, TN
615-889-4225 (800-547-4480)
nashvillejellystone.com
Dogs of all sizes are allowed. There are no additional pet fees. Dogs may not be left unattended, must be leashed, and cleaned up after. They are also not allowed to be tied up outside unless an adult is present. There are some breed restrictions. The camping and tent areas also allow dogs. There is a dog walk area at the campground. Multiple dogs may be allowed.

Two Rivers Campground
2616 Music Valley Drive
Nashville, TN
615-883-8559
tworiverscampground.com
Dogs of all sizes are allowed. There

are no additional pet fees. Dogs may not be left unattended, must be well behaved, leashed, and cleaned up after. The camping and tent areas also allow dogs. There is a dog walk area at the campground. Multiple dogs may be allowed.

Riveredge RV Park
4220 Huskey Street
Pigeon Forge, TN
865-453-5813
stayriveredge.com
Dogs of all sizes are allowed. There are no additional pet fees. Dogs must in your RV and not left outside alone when gone. Dogs must be leashed and cleaned up after. There is a dog walk area at the campground. Multiple dogs may be allowed.

Fall Creek Falls State Park
2009 Village Camp Road
Pikeville, TN
423-881-5298 (800-250-8610)
This 20,000+ acre resort park has one of the tallest waterfalls in eastern America, plus there are 34 miles of trails, an 18-hole golf course, and a restaurant that has a daily southern style buffet. Dogs are allowed in the campground for no additional fee; there is an additional fee of $10 (+ tax) per night per pet for the cabin(s). Dogs may not be left unattended at any time; they must have proof of vaccinations, be quiet, kept leashed or crated, and under their owner's immediate control at all times (courtesy litter bags are provided). They are not allowed in buildings, food service or designated swim areas, or where posted. The campground offers 228 sites in three different area; all have tables, grills, and modern bathhouses. The camping and tent areas also allow dogs. There is a dog walk area at the campground. Dogs are allowed in the camping cabins. 2 dogs may be allowed.

Chattanooga South/Lookout Mtn KOA
199 KOA Blvd
Ringgold, TN
706-937-4166 (800-562-4167)
koa.com
Dogs of all sizes are allowed, and there are no additional pet fees for tent or RV sites. There is a $10 per night additional pet fee for the cabins. There can be up to 3 dogs at the tent or RV sites and up to 2 dogs at the cabins. Dogs may not be placed in outdoor pens, and may not be left unattended outside. Dogs

must be leashed and cleaned up after. There are some breed restrictions. The camping and tent areas also allow dogs. There is a dog walk area at the campground. Dogs are allowed in the camping cabins.

Roan Mountain State Park
1015 H 143
Roan Mountain, TN
423-772-0190 (877-260-0010)
This 2,006 acre forested park features a diverse area for a variety of recreational and educational opportunities. Dogs are allowed in the campground for no additional fee; there is an additional fee of $10 (+ tax) per night per pet (up to 2 dogs) for the cabins. Dogs may not be left unattended at any time; they must have proof of vaccinations, be quiet, kept leashed or crated, and under their owner's immediate control at all times. They are not allowed in buildings, food service or designated swim areas, or where otherwise posted. The campground offers 107 sites with picnic tables, grills, restrooms, hot showers, and a dump station. Self-contained camping only is allowed from mid-November until April 1st. The camping and tent areas also allow dogs. There is a dog walk area at the campground. Dogs are allowed in the camping cabins. Multiple dogs may be allowed.

Rock Island State Park
82 Beach Road
Rock Island, TN
931-686-2471
The Great Falls of the Caney Fork River add to the scenic beauty of this park that provides a variety of special programs, activities, and recreation. Dogs of all sizes are allowed at no additional fee. Dogs may not be left unattended outside, and they must be leashed and cleaned up after. Dogs are allowed on the trails. The camping and tent areas also allow dogs. There is a dog walk area at the campground. Multiple dogs may be allowed.

River Plantation RV Park
1004 Parkway
Sevierville, TN
865-429-5267
riverplantationrv.com
Dogs of all sizes are allowed. There are no additional pet fees. Dogs must be leashed and cleaned up after. There is a dog walk area at the campground. Multiple dogs may be allowed.

Edgar Evins State Park
1630 Edgar Evins Park Road
Silver Point, TN
931-858-2446 (800-250-8619)
This park of over 6,000 acres is along the shores of one of the most beautiful reservoirs in Tennessee and provides miles of hiking trails, opportunities for nature study, and a variety of land and water recreation. Dogs of all sizes are allowed at no additional fee for the camping area. There is a $10 per night per pet additional fee for the cabins, and dogs must be 30 pounds or under. The cabins are closed for one month in off season. Dogs may not be left unattended, and they must be leashed and cleaned up after. Dogs are allowed on the trails. The camping and tent areas also allow dogs. There is a dog walk area at the campground. Dogs are allowed in the camping cabins.

Reelfoot Lake State Park
3120 H 213
Tiptonville, TN
731-253-7756 (800-250-8617)
Nestled among the trees, this lakeside park features a number of recreational pursuits, a nature trail, boat launch pad, fish cleaning area, and seasonal interpretive programs. Dogs are allowed in the campground for no additional fee. Dogs may not be left unattended at any time; they must have proof of vaccinations, be quiet, kept leashed or crated, and under their owner's immediate control at all times (courtesy litter bags are provided). They are not allowed in buildings, food service or designated swim areas, or where posted. There are 2 campgrounds in the park available first come, first served with picnic tables, grills, 2 modern bathhouses with a washer/dryer, and a dump station. The camping and tent areas also allow dogs. There is a dog walk area at the campground. 2 dogs may be allowed.

Townsend / Great Smokies KOA
8533 H 73
Townsend, TN
865-448-2241 (800-562-3428)
koa.com/where/tn/42175/
In a forested setting, this riverside park offers beauty and relaxation in addition to a full line of activities and amenities. They offer free cable TV and Wi-Fi, a store and gas station, an ice cream/fudge shop, an arcade, tube and bike rentals, and an outdoor movie cinema. Dogs are

allowed for no additional fee. Dogs may not be left unattended outside, and they may only be left alone inside if they will be quiet. Dogs must be on no more than a 6 foot leash and cleaned up after at all times. Dogs are not allowed near the cabins or lodge. There are some breed restrictions. The camping and tent areas also allow dogs. There is a dog walk area at the campground. Dogs are allowed in the camping cabins. Multiple dogs may be allowed.

Tremont Hills Campground
118 Stables Drive
Townsend, TN
865-448-6363
tremontcamp.com
Dogs of all sizes are allowed. There are no additional pet fees. Dogs may not be left unattended, and must be leashed and cleaned up after. The camping and tent areas also allow dogs. There is a dog walk area at the campground. Multiple dogs may be allowed.

Tom Sawyer's Mississippi River RV Park
1286 S 8th Street
West Memphis, AR
870-735-9770
Dogs of all sizes are allowed. There are no additional pet fees. Dogs must be quiet, well behaved, leashed, and cleaned up after. Dogs are also welcome to swim at the river. The camping and tent areas also allow dogs. There is a dog walk area at the campground. Multiple dogs may be allowed.

Tims Ford State Park
570 Tims Ford Drive
Winchester, TN
931-962-1183 (800-471-5295)
Known as one of the best bass fishing areas in the south, this park also holds archaeological interest, and is host to a variety of recreation. Dogs of all sizes are allowed at no additional fee for the camping area. There is a $10 per night per pet additional fee for the cabins. Dogs may not be left unattended, and they must be leashed and cleaned up after. Dogs are not allowed in buildings. The camping and tent areas also allow dogs. There is a dog walk area at the campground. Dogs are allowed in the camping cabins. Multiple dogs may be allowed.

Texas

Abilene KOA
4851 W Stamford Street
Abilene, TX
915-672-3681 (800-562-3651)
texaskoa.com
Dogs of all sizes are allowed. There are no additional pet fees. Dogs must be leashed and cleaned up after. Dogs may be left unattended for short periods, and only if they will be quiet and well behaved. There is a fenced dog run for off lead. There are some breed restrictions. The camping and tent areas also allow dogs. There is a dog walk area at the campground. Dogs are allowed in the camping cabins. Multiple dogs may be allowed.

Elephant Mountain Wildlife Management Area
109 S Cockrell/H 118
Alpine, TX
432-837-3251 (800-792-1112)
This 23,147 acre wildlife area offers some great hiking areas and the unusual feature of Elephant Mountain-a monolith rising over 6,000 feet above sea level with more than 2,000 acres on its flat top. (The top of the mountain is closed to the public.) Dogs are allowed throughout the park and in the camp area; they are not allowed in buildings. Dogs may not be left unattended at any time, they must be on no more than a 6 foot leash, and under their owner's control at all times. Camping is permitted in designated primitive camp areas only; fire rings are provided. A "Limited Use Permit" is required for campers over the age of 17 and can be obtained wherever hunting licenses are sold. It is suggested that visitors bring drinking water. The camping and tent areas also allow dogs. There is a dog walk area at the campground. There are no electric or water hookups at the campgrounds. Multiple dogs may be allowed.

Lost Alaskan RV Park
2401 N H 118
Alpine, TX
800-837-3604
lostalaskan.com
Dogs of all sizes are allowed. There are no additional pet fees. Dogs must be leashed and cleaned up after. There is a fenced "Paw Paw Park" on site for off lead. There is a dog walk area at the campground. There are special amenities given to dogs at this campground. Multiple dogs may be allowed.

Stillwell Store and RV Park
Farm Road 2627 (HC 65 - Box 430)
Alpine, TX
432-376-2244
stillwellstore.com/
This desert ranch camp area shares an interesting history, amazing rock hunting, lots of hiking areas, and 65 sites with fire rings, modern restrooms, showers, and an old-fashioned general store. Dogs are allowed wherever your car can go and in the campground for no additional fee; they are not allowed on trails in Big Bend National Park, on the river, off the roads, or where otherwise noted. Dogs must be on no more than a 6 foot leash and be cleaned up after all times. Dogs may not be left unattended outside at any time or in a vehicle if it could possibly create a danger to the animal. Pet owners must take extra precaution due to natural predators and extreme heat conditions. The camping and tent areas also allow dogs. There is a dog walk area at the campground. 2 dogs may be allowed.

Amarillo KOA
1100 Folsom Road
Amarillo, TX
806-335-1762 (800-562-3431)
koa.com

Dev Dog = Ok
Called 9/8

Dogs of all sizes are allowed, and there are no additional pet fees for tent or RV sites. There is a $5 per night per pet additional fee for the cabins. Dogs must be leashed and cleaned up after. There are some breed restrictions. The camping and tent areas also allow dogs. There is a dog walk area at the campground. Dogs are allowed in the camping cabins. Multiple dogs may be allowed.

Amarillo Ranch
1414 Sunrise
Amarillo, TX
806-373-4962 (866-244-7447)
amarillorvranch.com
Dogs of all sizes are allowed. There are no additional pet fees. Dogs may not be left unattended outside, and they may only be left inside if there is climate control. Dogs must be leashed and cleaned up after. There is a dog walk area at the campground. Multiple dogs may be allowed.

Fort Amarillo RV Resort
10101 Amarillo Blvd
Amarillo, TX
806-331-1700 (866-431-7866)
fortrvparks.com
Dogs of all sizes are allowed. There are no additional pet fees. Dogs must be leashed and cleaned up after. There is a dog run for off lead. Dogs are not allowed in the courtyard or at the putting green. There is a dog walk area at the campground. Multiple dogs may be allowed.

Treetops RV Village
1901 W Arbrook
Arlington, TX
817-467-7943
treetopsvillage.com
Dogs of all sizes are allowed, but there can only be 2 large dogs or 3 if they are very small. There are no additional pet fees. Dogs may not be left unattended outside, and may not be left inside RV unless the conditions are safe and comfortable. Dogs must be leashed and cleaned up after. There are some breed restrictions. There is a dog walk area at the campground.

Atlanta State Park
927 Park Road 42
Atlanta, TX
903-796-6476 (800-792-1112)
With 1,475 acres and 170 miles of shoreline, this park has plenty of hiking and nature trails, and is home to a variety of plants, birds, and wildlife. Dogs of all sizes are allowed at no additional fee. Dogs may not be left unattended, they must have current rabies and shot records, be on no more than a 6 foot leash, and be cleaned up after. Dogs are not allowed in public swim areas. The camping and tent areas also allow dogs. There is a dog walk area at the campground. Multiple dogs may be allowed.

Austin Lone Star RV Resort
7009 S IH 35
Austin, TX
512-444-6322
austinlonestar.com
Dogs of all sizes are allowed. There are no additional pet fees. Dogs may not be left unattended outside, and they must be leashed and cleaned up after. There are some breed restrictions. The camping and tent areas also allow dogs. There is a dog walk area at the campground. Multiple dogs may be allowed.

Oak Forest RV Park
8207 Canoga Avenue

Austin, TX
800-478-7275
oakforest-rvpark.com
Dogs of all sizes are allowed. There are no additional pet fees. Dogs may not be left unattended, and they must be leashed and cleaned up after. There is a fenced dog run for off lead. There are some breed restrictions. There is a dog walk area at the campground. Multiple dogs may be allowed.

Pioneer Rivers Resort
1203 Maple
Bandera, TX
830-796-3751
pioneerriverresort.com
Dogs of all sizes are allowed. There are no additional pet fees. Dogs must be leashed and cleaned up after. There are some breed restrictions. The camping and tent areas also allow dogs. There is a dog walk area at the campground. Multiple dogs may be allowed.

Bastrop State Park
3005 H 21
Bastrop, TX
512-321-2101 (800-792-1112)
This 5,962 acre park has been providing recreational opportunities since 1937. There is also a beautiful 12 mile scenic drive starting on Park Road 1C that travels between Bastrop and Buescher State Parks and takes visitors through the famous Lost Pines forest area. Dogs are allowed throughout the park and the campground for no additional fee; they are not allowed in buildings, designated swim areas, or in food service areas. Dogs may not be left unattended at any time; they must have proof of vaccinations, be well mannered, on no more than a 6 foot leash, and under their owner's immediate control at all times. The camp area offers restrooms, showers, picnic tables, grills, a seasonal swimming pool with 2 wading pools, gaming areas, a Texas camp store, and a dump station. The camping and tent areas also allow dogs. There is a dog walk area at the campground. Multiple dogs may be allowed.

Houston East/Baytown KOA
11810 I-10E
Baytown, TX
281-383-3618 (800-562-3418)
koa.com
Dogs of all sizes are allowed. There are no additional pet fees. Dogs must be leashed and cleaned up after. The camping and tent areas

also allow dogs. There is a dog walk area at the campground. Multiple dogs may be allowed.

Belton/Temple/Killeen KOA
2901 S I 35
Belton, TX
254-939-1961 (800-562-1902)
koa.com
Dogs of all sizes are allowed. There are no additional pet fees. Dogs may not be left unattended outside, and they must be on no more than a 6 foot leash, and cleaned up after. The camping and tent areas also allow dogs. There is a dog walk area at the campground. Dogs are allowed in the camping cabins. Multiple dogs may be allowed.

Big Bend National Park
Rio Grande Village Drive
Big Bend National Park, TX
432-477-2251 (877-444-6777)
nps.gov/bibe
Offering 3 distinct regions to explore, waterways, mountain, and desert, this National Park offers much in recreation and educational opportunities. There are more than 112 miles of paved roads in the park and over 150 miles of unpaved roads. Dogs are allowed wherever your car can go; they are not allowed on trails, on the river, off the roads, or where otherwise noted. Pets are also allowed at backcountry roadside campsites. Dogs must be on no more than a 6 foot leash and be cleaned up after all times. Dogs may not be left unattended outside at any time or in a vehicle if it could possibly create a danger to the animal. Pet owners must take extra precaution due to natural predators and extreme heat conditions. Camping is varied and a permit for backcountry camping is required at least 24 hours in advance. Other camp areas may have all or some of the following: picnic tables, pit or flush toilets, showers, laundry, camp store, concessionaires, or a dump station. The camping and tent areas also allow dogs. There is a dog walk area at the campground. Multiple dogs may be allowed.

Blanco State Park
101 Park Road 23
Blanco, TX
830-833-4333 (800-792-1112)
This park offers land and water recreation year round. Dogs of all sizes are allowed at no additional fee. Dogs may not be left unattended, they must have current rabies and shot records, be on no

more than a 6 foot leash, and be cleaned up after. Dogs are not allowed in buildings or at the river. Dogs are allowed on the trails. The camping and tent areas also allow dogs. There is a dog walk area at the campground. Multiple dogs may be allowed.

Houston West/Brookshire KOA
35303 Cooper Road
Brookshire, TX
281-375-5678 (800-562-5417)
koa.com
Dogs of all sizes are allowed. There are no additional pet fees. Dogs may not be left unattended, and they must be leashed and cleaned up after. The camping and tent areas also allow dogs. There is a dog walk area at the campground. Multiple dogs may be allowed.

Breeze Lake RV Campground
1710 N Vermillion
Brownsville, TX
956-831-4427 (877-296-3329)
breezelakervcampground.com
Dogs of all sizes are allowed. There are no additional pet fees. Dogs may not be left unattended outside, and they must be on no more than a 6 foot leash, and be cleaned up after. There is a dog walk area at the campground. Multiple dogs may be allowed.

Paul's RV Park
1129 N Minnesota Avenue
Brownsville, TX
800-352-5010
paulsrvpark.com
Dogs of all sizes are allowed. There are no additional pet fees. Dogs may not be left unattended outside, and they must be leashed and cleaned up after. The owner is known to carry dog biscuits around so he can have treats all his four legged guests. There are some breed restrictions. The camping and tent areas also allow dogs. There is a dog walk area at the campground. Multiple dogs may be allowed.

Lake Brownwood State Park
200 State H Park Road 15
Brownwood, TX
325-784-5223 (800-792-1112)
Lake Brownwood State Park offers over 500 acres, a reservoir, 2 1/2 miles of trails, a half mile nature trail and a variety of year round recreation. Dogs of all sizes are allowed at no additional fee. Dogs may not be left unattended, they must have current rabies and shot records, be on no more than a 6 foot

leash, and be cleaned up after. Dogs are not allowed in the buildings or shelters. Dogs are allowed on the trails. The camping and tent areas also allow dogs. There is a dog walk area at the campground. Multiple dogs may be allowed.

Primrose Lane
2929 Stevens Drive
Bryan, TX
979-778-0119
primrose-lane.org
Dogs of all sizes are allowed. There are no additional pet fees. Dogs must be leashed and cleaned up after. The camping and tent areas also allow dogs. There is a dog walk area at the campground. Multiple dogs may be allowed.

RV Ranch
2301 S I 35W
Burleson, TX
888-855-9091
rvranch.com
Dogs of all sizes are allowed. There are no additional pet fees. Dogs may not be left unattended outside, and they must be quiet, leashed, and cleaned up after. There are some breed restrictions. There is a dog walk area at the campground. Multiple dogs may be allowed.

Inks Lake State Park
3630 Park Road 4W
Burnet, TX
512-793-2223 (800-792-1112)
Inks Lake, surrounded by granite hills, is one of the lakes located in the Highland Lakes chain of 7 lake. Inks Lake State Park offers a variety of land and water recreation. Dogs of all sizes are allowed at no additional fee. Dogs may not be left unattended, they must have current rabies and shot records, be leashed at all times, and be cleaned up after. Dogs are not allowed in public swim areas or buildings. Dogs are allowed on the trails, and there is a designated dog swim area. The camping and tent areas also allow dogs. There is a dog walk area at the campground. Multiple dogs may be allowed.

Possum Kingdom State Park
3901 Park Road 35
Caddo, TX
940-549-1803 (800-792-1112)
This park of over 1500 acres is adjacent to Possum Kingdom Lake that has over 20,000 acres of water. There are a variety of land and water recreational activities. The

park is open for day use during the winter season. Dogs of all sizes are allowed at no additional fee. Dogs may not be left unattended, they must have current rabies and shot records, be on no more than a 6 foot leash, and be cleaned up after. Dogs are not allowed in public swim areas or any buildings. Dogs are allowed on the trails. This campground is closed during the off-season. The camping and tent areas also allow dogs. There is a dog walk area at the campground. Multiple dogs may be allowed.

Choke Canyon State Park
Park Road 8
Calliham, TX
361-786-3868 (800-792-1112)
The habitats at this park provide some of the best areas for birds and bird watchers, and there is a wildlife educational center, a mile long bird trail, and 2 miles of hiking trails. Dogs of all sizes are allowed at no additional fee. Dogs may not be left unattended, they must have current rabies and shot records, be leashed, and cleaned up after. Dogs are not allowed in public swim areas or buildings. Dogs are allowed on the trails. The camping and tent areas also allow dogs. There is a dog walk area at the campground. Multiple dogs may be allowed.

Palo Duro Canyon State Park
11450 Park Road 5
Canyon, TX
806-488-2227
palodurocanyon.com/
Considered to have the 2nd largest canyon in the United States, this 26,275 acre park has some of the most spectacular scenery in the state, thousands of years of cultural and natural history, a variety of recreational and educational opportunities, and much more. Dogs are allowed throughout the park and the campground for no additional fee; they are not allowed in buildings, at the theater from June to mid-August, or in food service areas. Dogs may not be left unattended at any time; they must be quiet, on no more than a 6 foot leash and under owner's immediate control and care at all times. Dogs are not allowed in designated swim areas or in the beach/land area adjacent to the swim area. The camp areas have all or some of the following: picnic tables, a fire ring, restrooms, showers, and potable water. The camping and tent areas also allow dogs. There is a dog walk area at the

campground. Multiple dogs may be allowed.

Jellystone Park
12915 Hwy 306
Canyon Lake, TX
830-964-3731 (877-964-3731)
jellystonehillcountry.com/
A family-style fun resort, this lakeside campground offers a tournament size beach volleyball court, a playground, an indoor heated pool with spa, a large outdoor pool, themed weekends, daily activities, 28 wooded acres to explore, pedal cart rentals, and much more. Dogs are allowed for no additional fee in the campground; there is an additional fee of $20 per night per pet for the lodge. Only 2 dogs are allowed in the 1 pet friendly room in the lodge; there may be more than 2 dogs per site in the RV/tent area. Dogs must be on no more than a 6 foot leash, and cleaned up after at all times. There are some breed restrictions. The camping and tent areas also allow dogs. There is a dog walk area at the campground.

Cedar Hill State Park
1570 W FM 1382
Cedar Hill, TX
972-291-3900 (800-792-1112)
Cedar Hill State Park is an urban nature preserve of over 1,800 acres located on a 7500 acre reservoir. It is home to the Penn Farm Agricultural History Center. Well behaved dogs of all sizes are allowed at no additional fee. Dogs may not be left unattended, they must have current rabies and shot records, be on no more than a 6 foot leash, and be cleaned up after. Dogs are not allowed in buildings or in public swim areas, but they are allowed on trails. The camping and tent areas also allow dogs. There is a dog walk area at the campground. Multiple dogs may be allowed.

Seminole Canyon State Park & Historic Site
Box 820/ H 90 W
Comstock, TX
432-292-4464 (800-792-1112)
This park is over 2000 acres and provides a historical study of ancient peoples and pictograph sites. There are nature and interpretive attractions, and land and water recreation. No hiking is allowed in the canyon area without a guide. Dogs of all sizes are allowed at no additional fee. Dogs may not be left unattended, they must have current rabies and shot records, be on no

more than a 6 foot leash at all times, and be cleaned up after. Dogs are not allowed in buildings or on guided tours. Dogs are allowed on hiking trails. The camping and tent areas also allow dogs. There is a dog walk area at the campground. Multiple dogs may be allowed.

Garner State Park
234 RR 1050
Concan, TX
830-232-6132 (800-792-1112)
High mesas, deep canyons, an abundance of plant and animal life, and a variety of recreation greet visitors to this park. Dogs of all sizes are allowed at no additional fee. Dogs may not be left unattended, they must have current rabies and shot records, be on no more than a 6 foot leash, and be cleaned up after. Dogs are not allowed in public swim areas or buildings. Dogs are allowed on the trails. The camping and tent areas also allow dogs. There is a dog walk area at the campground. Multiple dogs may be allowed.

Cooper Lake State Park/South Suphur Unit
1664 Farm Road 1529
Cooper, TX
903-395-3100 (800-792-1112)
The South Sulphur Unit of Cooper Lake is over 2,000 acres of land and water recreation, with sandy beaches, an outdoor amphitheater, and miles of trails. Due to budget cuts this park is only open for day use and/or camping on Friday, Saturday, and Sunday. Dogs of all sizes are allowed at no additional fee. Dogs may not be left unattended, they must have current rabies and shot records, be on no more than a 6 foot leash, and be cleaned up after. Dogs are not allowed in public swim areas or buildings. Dogs are allowed on the trails. The camping and tent areas also allow dogs. There is a dog walk area at the campground. Multiple dogs may be allowed.

Padre Island National Seashore
Park Road
Corpus Christi, TX
361-949-8068
nps.gov/pais/
The longest undeveloped barrier island left in the world, this 130,434 acre natural area is also unique in that it is one of the most significant nesting beaches in the country for the endangered Kemp's Ridley sea turtles. Dogs are allowed

throughout the park and the campground for no additional fee; they are not allowed in buildings, on the deck of the visitor center or in the swim area by the visitor center. Dogs may not be left unattended at any time; they must be quiet, on no more than a 6 foot leash and under their owner's immediate control at all times. Dogs are allowed on the beach. Fifty campsites are available on a first come, first served basis. There is a gray water dump station and potable water at the entrance to the campground. A camping permit is required and can be obtained from patrolling rangers, the campground host, the entrance station, or at the Malaquite Visitor Center. The camping and tent areas also allow dogs. There is a dog walk area at the campground. There are no electric or water hookups at the campgrounds. Multiple dogs may be allowed.

Daingerfield State Park
455 Park Road 17
Daingerfield, TX
903-645-2921 (800-792-1112)
With over 550 land acres and an 80 acre lake, there are plenty of recreational pursuits at this park. Dogs of all sizes are allowed at no additional fee. Dogs may not be left unattended, they must have current rabies and shot records, be on no more than a 6 foot leash, and be cleaned up after. Dogs are not allowed in public swim areas or buildings. Dogs are allowed on the trails. The camping and tent areas also allow dogs. There is a dog walk area at the campground. Multiple dogs may be allowed.

Caddo-LBJ National Grasslands
1400 H 81/287
Decatur, TX
940-627-5475
With Caddo at almost 18,000 acres with 3 lakes, and the LBJ Grasslands at over 20,000 acres, this forest provides a wide variety of habitats, trails, nature study, and land and water recreation. Dogs of all sizes are allowed at no additional fee. Dogs may not be left unattended, and they must be on no more than a 6 foot leash, unless being used for hunting during a designated hunting season where the uses of dogs are legal. Dogs are allowed everywhere unless otherwise posted. The camping and tent areas also allow dogs. There is a dog walk area at the campground. There are no electric or water hookups at the campground. Multiple dogs may be allowed.

Amistad National Rec Area
H 90
Del Rio, TX
830-775-7491
nps.gov/amis/
Located along the Rio Grande the park is known for the pre-historic Native American rock art that is more than 4,000 years old. This site is also home to the country's third largest collection of pre-historic artifacts. Dogs are allowed on the grounds and in the camp area; they must be leashed and cleaned up after at all times. Dogs are not allowed in park buildings. Campsites are first come first served, and there are about 70 sites with some or all of the following: potable water, covered picnic tables, and grills. The camping and tent areas also allow dogs. There is a dog walk area at the campground. There are no electric or water hookups at the campgrounds. Multiple dogs may be allowed.

Eisenhower State Park
50 Park Road 20
Denison, TX
903-465-1956 (800-792-1112)
A variety of nature sites, land and water recreation, interpretive programs, and trails greet visitor's here. Dogs of all sizes are allowed at no additional fee. Dogs may not be left unattended, they must have current rabies and shot records, be on no more than a 6 foot leash, and be cleaned up after. Dogs are not allowed in public swim areas or buildings. Dogs are allowed on the trails. The camping and tent areas also allow dogs. There is a dog walk area at the campground. Multiple dogs may be allowed.

Lake Texoma Recreation Area
351 Corp Road
Denisons, TX
903-465-4990
laketexoma.com/
This recreational destination is located on an 89,000 acre lake shared by Texas and Oklahoma and is quite popular for fishing and water sports. Dogs are allowed throughout the park and in the campground for no additional fee. Dogs must be quiet, well behaved, and be on no more than a 10 foot leash or crated. Owners must show proof of current inoculations-including rabies. Dogs may not be left unattended in any was as to cause harm, and they are not allowed in park buildings, designated swim beaches, or where noted. Dogs must be picked up after

at all times. There are several camp areas in a variety of settings and they may have all or some of the following: picnic tables, grills, modern restrooms, and showers. Primitive camping requires a permit. The camping and tent areas also allow dogs. There is a dog walk area at the campground. Multiple dogs may be allowed.

Green Caye RV Park
2401 Owens Drive
Dickinson, TX
280-337-0289
greencayervpark.com
Dogs of all sizes are allowed. There are no additional pet fees. Dogs must be leashed and cleaned up after. There is a dog walk area at the campground. Multiple dogs may be allowed.

Lake Texana State Park
46 Park Road 1
Edna, TX
361-782-5718 (800-792-1112)
This 575 acre park with an 11,000 acre lake offers a wide variety of recreational and educational activities. Dogs are allowed throughout the park and the campground for no additional fee; they are not allowed in buildings, designated swim areas, or in food service areas. Dogs may not be left unattended at any time; they must have proof of vaccinations, be well mannered, on no more than a 6 foot leash, and under their owner's immediate control at all times. The camp area has comfort stations, picnic tables, grills, potable water, a playground, a Texas Park Store, and a dump station. The camping and tent areas also allow dogs. There is a dog walk area at the campground. Multiple dogs may be allowed.

El Paso Roadrunner RV Park
1212 LaFayette
El Paso, TX
915-598-4469
Dogs of all sizes are allowed. There are no additional pet fees. Dogs must be quiet, leashed, and cleaned up after. There is a dog walk area at the campground. Multiple dogs may be allowed.

Franklin Mountains State Park
1331 McKelligon Canyon Road
El Paso, TX
915-566-6441 (800-792-1112)
Although located within the city limits, this 24,247 acre park is the largest urban park in America and it

offers thousands of years of cultural and natural history, a number of outdoor recreation, public tours and more. This park is also home to a gondola that travels up the mountain to Ranger Peak to 5,632 feet; only dogs that can be carried are allowed on the gondola. Dogs are allowed throughout the park; they must be leashed and under their owner's control and care at all times. There are a limited number of tent and RV sites so reservations are recommended; there is no water or electricity available, and ground fires are not permitted. The camping and tent areas also allow dogs. There is a dog walk area at the campground. There are no electric or water hookups at the campgrounds. Multiple dogs may be allowed.

Sampson RV Park
11300 Gateway Blvd
El Paso, TX
915-859-8383
Dogs of all sizes are allowed. There are no additional pet fees. Dogs may not be left unattended outside, and they must be leashed and cleaned up after. There is a dog walk area at the campground. Multiple dogs may be allowed.

Leisure Camp & RV Park
1 River Lane
Fentress, TX
512-488-2563
leisurecamp.net
Dogs of all sizes are allowed. There are no additional pet fees. Dogs must be leashed and cleaned up after. There is a fenced pet park area. Dogs are not allowed in public swim areas. The camping and tent areas also allow dogs. There is a dog walk area at the campground. Multiple dogs may be allowed.

Davis Mountains State Park
Canyon Drive/H 118
Fort Davis, TX
432-375-2370 (800-792-1112)
Located in the most extensive mountain range in the state, there are a variety of habitats and environments to explore as a result of significant differences in altitudes in the park. Dogs are allowed throughout the park and in the camp area; they are not allowed in buildings or at public swim areas. Dogs may not be left unattended at any time, they must be on no more than a 6 foot leash, and under their owner's control at all times. Campsites are varied and may have some or all of the following; picnic

tables, fire rings, grills, TV connections, restrooms, showers, and a playground. The camping and tent areas also allow dogs. There is a dog walk area at the campground. Multiple dogs may be allowed.

Fort Davis Motor Inn & Campground
I Mile N of Fort Davis on H 17N
Fort Davis, TX
800-803-2847
Dogs of all sizes are allowed. There are no additional pet fees. Dogs may not be left unattended, and they must be leashed and cleaned up after. There is also an inn on site that allows dogs for a $10 per night per pet additional fee in a smoking room only. There is a dog walk area at the campground. 2 dogs may be allowed.

Enchanted Rock State Natural Area
16710 Ranch Road 965
Fredericksburg, TX
830-685-3636 (800-792-1112)
There are more than 1,600 recreational acres at this site that has evidence of habitation for at least 11,000 years. It is on the National Register of Historic Places for the massive pink granite exfoliation dome that rises 425 feet above ground and is one of the largest batholiths in America. Dogs are allowed throughout the park and the campground for no additional fee; they are not allowed in buildings, swim areas, or in food service areas. Dogs may not be left unattended at any time; they must be quiet, on no more than a 6 foot leash and under their owner's immediate control at all times. There is primitive camping only in a variety of settings and they may have all or some of the following: modern restrooms, composting toilets, showers, picnic sites with tables and grills, an interpretive center, or a Texas State Park store. The camping and tent areas also allow dogs. There is a dog walk area at the campground. There are no electric or water hookups at the campgrounds. Multiple dogs may be allowed.

Fredericksburg KOA
5681 H 290E
Fredericksburg, TX
830-997-4796 (800-562-0796)
koa.com
Dogs of all sizes are allowed, but there can only be 2 dogs per site unless they are under 10 pounds, then there can be up to 3. There are no additional pet fees. Dogs must be leashed, cleaned up after, and inside

at night. There are some breed restrictions. The camping and tent areas also allow dogs. There is a dog walk area at the campground.

Oakwood RV Resort
#78 FM 2093
Fredericksburg, TX
830-997-9817
oakwoodrvresort.com
Dogs of all sizes are allowed. There are no additional pet fees. Dogs may not be left unattended, and they must be quiet, leashed, and cleaned up after. The camping and tent areas also allow dogs. There is a dog walk area at the campground.

Lake Meridith National Rec Area
419 E. Broadway/H 136 (park headquarters)
Fritch, TX
806-857-3151
nps.gov/lamr/
Dramatic scenic contrasts of high mountain plains, 200 foot canyons, and a 10,000 acre reservoir add to the enjoyment of this popular recreational park. There are several entrances to the rec area around the lake. Dogs are allowed throughout the park; they are not allowed on boat rentals or at the fish house. Dogs must be leashed and under their owner's control and care at all times. Campsites are varied and in several locations; they may have some or all of the following: flush or vault toilets, picnic tables, shade shelters, grills, running water, a boat ramp, and dump stations. The camping and tent areas also allow dogs. There is a dog walk area at the campground. There are no electric or water hookups at the campgrounds. Multiple dogs may be allowed.

Dellanera RV Park
10901 San Louis Pass Road
Galveston, TX
409-797-5102 (888-425-4753)
dellanerarvpark.com
Dogs of all sizes are allowed. There are no additional pet fees. Dogs may not be left unattended outside, they must be in at night, and leashed and cleaned up after. There is a dog walk area at the campground. Multiple dogs may be allowed.

Fort Travis Seashore Park
900 H 87
Galveston, TX
409-934-8100
crystalbeach.com/travis.htm
In addition to a variety of

recreational and educational activities, this 60 acre park has a long military and natural history to explore. Dogs are allowed in the park for day use and camping for no additional fee; they must be kept leashed and cleaned up after at all times. Dogs are allowed on the beach. There is tent and cabana camping and picnic areas with cooking facilities available. There are also large grassy areas for sports/games, and a well furnished playground. The camping and tent areas also allow dogs. There is a dog walk area at the campground. There are no electric or water hookups at the campgrounds. Multiple dogs may be allowed.

Galveston Island State Park
14901 FM 3005
Galveston, TX
409-737-1222 (800-792-1112)
This recreational island park offers a variety of land and water activities. Dogs of all sizes are allowed at no additional fee. Dogs may not be left unattended, they must have current rabies and shot records, be on no more than a 6 foot leash at all times, and be cleaned up after. Dogs are not allowed in public swim areas or buildings. Dogs are allowed on the trails. The camping and tent areas also allow dogs. There is a dog walk area at the campground. Multiple dogs may be allowed.

Dinosaur Valley State Park
1629 Park Road 59
Glen Rose, TX
254-897-4588
Home to some of the best preserved dinosaur tracks in the world representing an age about 113 million years ago, this 1,500+ acre park delights visitors with 2 fiberglass dinosaurs (70 and 45 feet tall) and offers an interpretive center plus a number of outdoor recreational opportunities. The tracks are in the riverbed, so a call ahead for river conditions is a good idea. Dogs are allowed in the park and campground; they must be well behaved, on no more than a 6 foot leash, and picked up after at all times. The camp area offers fire rings and grills, picnic tables, restrooms, showers, and a dump station; an amphitheater and park store are close by. Primitive campers can get water at the trail head-there are no restrooms. The camping and tent areas also allow dogs. There is a dog walk area at the campground. Multiple dogs may be allowed.

Goliad State Park
108 Park Road 6
Goliad, TX
361-645-3405 (800-792-1112)
This amazing blend of 3 ecological zones along the San Antonio River offers visitors a large variety of flora, fauna, recreational and educational opportunities, and a long cultural history. Dogs are allowed throughout the park and the campground for no additional fee; they are not allowed in buildings, swim areas, the compound, or the mission. Dogs may not be left unattended at any time; they must be well mannered, on no more than a 6 foot leash and under their owner's immediate control at all times. The camp area offers picnic tables, grills, restrooms, showers, a playground, and a dump station. The camping and tent areas also allow dogs. Multiple dogs may be allowed.

Palmetto State Park
78 Park Road 11 S
Gonzales, TX
830-672-3266 (800-792-1112)
Due to the unusual botanical features of this area, there is a great diversity of flora and fauna at this 270+ acre park named for the tropical Dwarf Palmetto plant that grows here. It is also located on the Great Texas Coastal Birding Trail with more than 240 bird species viewed. Dogs are allowed throughout the park and the campground for no additional fee; they are not allowed in buildings, designated swim areas, or in food service areas. Dogs may not be left unattended at any time; they must have proof of vaccinations, be well mannered, on no more than a 6 foot leash, and under their owner's immediate control at all times. The camp area offers restrooms with baby changing stations, showers, picnic tables, playgrounds, a Texas Park Store, 3 miles of interpretive trails, and a dump station. The camping and tent areas also allow dogs. There is a dog walk area at the campground. Multiple dogs may be allowed.

Ole Towne Cotton Gin RV Park
230 Market Street
Goodlett, TX
940-674-2477
oletownecottonginrvpark.com
Dogs of all sizes are allowed, and there are no additional pet fees for tent or RV sites. There is a $35 one time pet fee for the cabins. Dogs may not be left unattended, and they must be leashed and cleaned up

after. The camping and tent areas also allow dogs. There is a dog walk area at the campground. Dogs are allowed in the camping cabins. Multiple dogs may be allowed.

Paradise On the Brazos
7600 H 16 S
Graham, TX
940-549-8478 (866-549-7682)
Campsites are located along the Brazos River and Filabuster Creek and offer picnic tables, stone fire rings, and portable restrooms. In addition to being close to several other sites of interest, there are a number of recreational opportunities at this 1000+ acre ranch. Dogs are allowed throughout the ranch, in the lodge, and in the camp area for no additional pet fee. Dogs must be under their owner's control at all times. The camping and tent areas also allow dogs. There is a dog walk area at the campground. Multiple dogs may be allowed.

Trader's Village
2602 Mayfield Road
Grand Prairie, TX
972-647-8205
tradersvillage.com
Dogs of all sizes are allowed. There are no additional pet fees. Dogs may not be left unattended outside, and they must be leashed and cleaned up after. The camping and tent areas also allow dogs. There is a dog walk area at the campground. 2 dogs may be allowed.

Sabine National Forest
201 S Palm
Hemphill, TX
409-787-2791 (866-235-1750)
This ecologically diverse forest provides archeological, historic, and prehistoric sites to explore in addition to offering a variety of trails, and land and water recreation. Dogs of all sizes are allowed at no additional fee. Dogs may not be left unattended; they must be cleaned up after in camp areas, and be on no more than a 6 foot leash unless being used for hunting during a designated hunting season where the uses of dogs are legal. Dogs are allowed everywhere in the park unless posted. The camping and tent areas also allow dogs. There is a dog walk area at the campground. There are no water hookups at the campground. Multiple dogs may be allowed.

All Star RV Resort
10650 SW Plaza Court

Houston, TX
713-981-6814
allstar-rv.com
Dogs of all sizes are allowed. There are no additional pet fees. Dogs must be leashed and cleaned up after. There is a dog walk area at the campground. Multiple dogs may be allowed.

Houston Central KOA
1620 Peachleaf
Houston, TX
281-442-3700 (800-562-2132)
koa.com
Dogs of all sizes are allowed. There are no additional pet fees. Dogs may not be left unattended outside, and they must be leashed and cleaned up after. There is only 1 pet friendly cabin. There are some breed restrictions. The camping and tent areas also allow dogs. There is a dog walk area at the campground. Multiple dogs may be allowed.

Houston Leisure RV Resort
1601 S Main Street
Houston, TX
281-426-3576
houstonleisurervresort.com
Dogs of all sizes are allowed. There are no additional pet fees. Dogs may not be left unattended outside, and they must be leashed and cleaned up after. The camping and tent areas also allow dogs. There is a dog walk area at the campground. Multiple dogs may be allowed.

Lake Houston Park
22031 Baptist Encampment Road
Houston, TX
713-845-1000
There are almost 5,000 acres of lush forest, beautiful trails, waterways, and a variety of land and water recreation available at this park that is also a real favorite among naturists. Dogs are allowed throughout the park and camp areas. Dogs must be leashed and cleaned up after at all times. There are 3 camp areas with 8 campsites each; they are walk in, tent only campsites, available on a first come first served basis. The sites have picnic tables, fire rings, tent pads, and lantern hooks, with restrooms, water, and showers nearby. The camping and tent areas also allow dogs. There is a dog walk area at the campground. There are no electric or water hookups at the campgrounds. Multiple dogs may be allowed.

Trader's Village
7979 N Eldridge Road

Houston, TX
281-890-5500
tradersvillage.com
Dogs of all sizes are allowed. There are no additional pet fees. Dogs may not be left unattended, and they must be leashed and cleaned up after. There is a dog walk area at the campground. Multiple dogs may be allowed.

Huntsville State Park
Park Road 40 W
Huntsville, TX
936-295-5644 (800-792-1112)
From some fairly rough beginnings, this 2083+ acre park with a 210 acre "stocked" lake now offers visitors plenty of hiking trails to explore its natural beauty and a variety of land and water recreation. Dogs are allowed throughout the park and in the camp area; they are not allowed in buildings or at public swim areas. Dogs may not be left unattended at any time, they must be on no more than a 6 foot leash, and under their owner's control at all times. Camp areas may have all or some of the following: a shade shelter, picnic table, fire ring, lantern post, restrooms, showers, a playground, fishing pier, or dump station. The camping and tent areas also allow dogs. There is a dog walk area at the campground. Multiple dogs may be allowed.

Fort Richardson State Park
228 State Park Road 61
Jacksboro, TX
940-567-3506 (800-792-1112)
This was one of the most northern of the Federal Forts built after the Civil War, and there are still 7 restored original buildings and 2 replicas of the officers and enlisted mens barracks. This 454+ acre site is also home to the Lost Creek Reservoir State Trailway-a beautiful 10 mile multi-use trail. Dogs are allowed throughout the park and in the camp area; they are not allowed in buildings, shelters, or at public swim areas. Dogs may not be left unattended at any time. They must be leashed and under their owner's control at all times. The camp area offers picnic tables, grills, restrooms, showers, playing courts and fields, a store, and a dump station. The camping and tent areas also allow dogs. There is a dog walk area at the campground. Multiple dogs may be allowed.

Pedernales Falls State Park
2585 Park Road 6026

Johnson City, TX
830-868-7304 (800-792-1112)
Pedernales Falls draws visitors from all over to it's scenic overlook. The park also offers more than 150 species of birds, abundant plant and animal life and a variety of recreation. They close only for a couple of weeks each January. Dogs of all sizes are allowed at no additional fee. Dogs may not be left unattended, they must have current rabies and shot records, be on no more than a 6 foot leash, and be cleaned up after. Dogs are not allowed in public swim areas or buildings. Dogs are not allowed in the river anywhere. Dogs are allowed on the trails. The camping and tent areas also allow dogs. There is a dog walk area at the campground. Multiple dogs may be allowed.

Junction KOA
2145 Main Street
Junction, TX
325-446-3138 (800-562-7506)
junctionkoa.com
Dogs of all sizes are allowed. There are no additional pet fees. Dogs may not be left unattended, and they must be on no more than a 6 foot leash, and be cleaned up after. Dogs are not allowed on the playground, at the pool, or at the bathrooms. There are some breed restrictions. The camping and tent areas also allow dogs. There is a dog walk area at the campground. Multiple dogs may be allowed.

Caddo Lake State Park
245 Park Road 2
Karnack, TX
903-679-3351
The namesake of this park is actually a shallow 26,810 acre cypress swamp lake teeming with a variety of flora and fauna. Walking the boardwalks in the swamp and fishing are favorites here - there are over 70 species of fish. Dogs are allowed throughout the park and in the camp area; they are not allowed in buildings or at public swim areas. Dogs may not be left unattended at any time and they must be on no more than a 6 foot leash. The camp area offers picnic tables, grills, fire rings, restrooms, showers, a playground, and dump station. The camping and tent areas also allow dogs. There is a dog walk area at the campground. Multiple dogs may be allowed.

Marina Bay RV Resort

925 FM 2094
Kemeh, TX
281-334-9944
marinabayrvresort.com
Dogs of all sizes are allowed. There are no additional pet fees. Dogs must be leashed, cleaned up after, and walked in designated areas. There is a dog walk area at the campground. 2 dogs may be allowed.

Davy Crockett National Forest
18551 H 7 East
Kennard, TX
936-655-2299 (877-444-6777)
In addition to numerous recreational and educational opportunities, this 160,000 acre forest features spectacular scenery, an interpretive forest trail, and very diverse ecosystems that support a large variety of flora and fauna. Dogs are allowed throughout the forest and in the camp areas; they are not allowed on the beach or at swimming areas. Dogs must be leashed at all times and under their owner's control. The lakeside camp area offers 76 sites, restrooms, showers, a fishing pier, a swimming beach, amphitheater, concessionaires, and a wildlife viewing area. The camping and tent areas also allow dogs. There is a dog walk area at the campground. There are no water hookups at the campgrounds. Multiple dogs may be allowed.

Kerrville KOA
2950 Goat Creek Road
Kerrville, TX
830-895-1665 (800-562-1665)
koa.com
Dogs of all sizes are allowed. There are no additional pet fees. Dogs may not be left unattended outside, and they must be leashed and cleaned up after. The camping and tent areas also allow dogs. There is a dog walk area at the campground. Dogs are allowed in the camping cabins. Multiple dogs may be allowed.

Big Thicket National Preserve
6044 H 420
Kountze, TX
409-951-6725
nps.gov/bith/
Born of glacial activity, the wonderfully diverse flora and fauna here was "carried" from all over to this region creating a very unique environment. They also have a state-of-the-art interactive discovery center sharing the secrets of the Big Thicket. Dogs are allowed for no additional fee; they must be leashed

and under their owner's control at all times. Only backcountry camping is available and a Backcountry Use Permit is required. They can be obtained at the Headquarter office or at the Visitor Center. The camping and tent areas also allow dogs. There is a dog walk area at the campground. There are no electric or water hookups at the campgrounds. Multiple dogs may be allowed.

Kenwood RV Resort
1201 N Main #1
La Feria, TX
856-797-1851
suncommunities.com
Dogs of all sizes are allowed, but there can only be 1 large dog or 2 small dogs per site. There are no additional pet fees. Dogs may not be left unattended outside, and no outdoor kennels are allowed. Dogs must be leashed and cleaned up after. This is a 55 years or older park. There is a dog walk area at the campground.

Space Center RV Resort
301 Gulf Freeway S
League City, TX
888-846-3478
spacecenterrv.com
Dogs of all sizes are allowed. There are no additional pet fees. Dogs may not be left unattended outside, and they must be leashed and cleaned up after. There is a dog walk area at the campground. 2 dogs may be allowed.

Buffalo Springs Lake
9999 High Meadow Road
Lubbock, TX
806-747-3353
buffalospringslake.net/
This park is not only a major land and water recreational destination; it is also the site of many yearly festivals and major events. Dogs are allowed throughout the park and campground for no additional fee; they must have current tags and proof of inoculations. Dogs must be leashed and under their owner's control and care at all times. The campsites offer lots of shade trees, Wi-Fi, picnic tables, and paved or grassy sites, and a playground, golf course, restrooms, and dump stations are nearby. The camping and tent areas also allow dogs. There is a dog walk area at the campground. Multiple dogs may be allowed.

Lubbock KOA
5502 County Road 6300

Lubbock, TX
806-762-8653 (800-562-8643)
koa.com
Dogs of all sizes are allowed. There are no additional pet fees. Dogs may not be left unattended outside, and they must be leashed and cleaned up after. The camping and tent areas also allow dogs. There is a dog walk area at the campground. Dogs are allowed in the camping cabins. Multiple dogs may be allowed.

Lubbock RV Park
4811 N I 27
Lubbock, TX
806-747-2366
Dogs of all sizes are allowed. There are no additional pet fees. Dogs must be leashed and cleaned up after. There is a dog walk area at the campground. Multiple dogs may be allowed.

Village Creek State Park
8854 Park Road 74
Lumberton, TX
409-755-7322 (800-792-1112)
This heavily forested 1,090 acre park is popular for canoeing through the forest swamps, nature viewing, and for a number of other recreational activities. Dogs are allowed throughout the park and in the camp area; they are not allowed in buildings or at public swim areas. Dogs may not be left unattended at any time, they must be on no more than a 6 foot leash, and under their owner's control at all times. Campsites offer picnic tables, fire rings, lantern posts, restrooms, showers, a playground, and a dump station. The camping and tent areas also allow dogs. There is a dog walk area at the campground. Multiple dogs may be allowed.

Lake Corpus Christi State Park
23194 Park Road 25
Mathis, TX
361-547-2635 (800-792-1112)
This 14,111+ acre major recreation destination has a 21,000 acre lake and it offers a wide variety of fun pursuits, educational and naturalist activities. Dogs are allowed throughout the park and the campground for no additional fee; they are not allowed in buildings or food service areas. Dogs may not be left unattended at any time; they must be quiet, on no more than a 6 foot leash and under their owner's immediate control at all times. Dogs are not allowed in designated swim areas or within the beach and land

area adjacent to the swim area. The camp area offers restrooms, showers, picnic sites, grills, fishing piers, fish cleaning shelters, boat launches, and a dump station. The camping and tent areas also allow dogs. There is a dog walk area at the campground. Multiple dogs may be allowed.

Lake Corpus Christi/Mathis KOA
101 C ounty Road 371
Mathis, TX
361-547-5201 (800-562-8601)
koa.com
Dogs of all sizes are allowed. There are no additional pet fees. Dogs must be well behaved, leashed, and cleaned up after. The camping and tent areas also allow dogs. There is a dog walk area at the campground. Dogs are allowed in the camping cabins.

Meridian State Park
173 Park Road 7
Meridian, TX
254-435-2536 (800-792-1112)
A hiking trail circles this park's 72-acre lake, creating a haven for fishing enthusiasts and nature lovers alike. Dogs of all sizes are allowed at no additional fee. Dogs may not be left unattended, they must have current rabies and shot records, be on no more than a 6 foot leash, and be cleaned up after. Dogs are not allowed in public swim areas or buildings. Dogs are allowed on the trails. The camping and tent areas also allow dogs. There is a dog walk area at the campground. Multiple dogs may be allowed.

Fort Parker State Park
194 Park Road 28
Mexia, TX
254-562-5751 (800-792-1112)
This park of over 1,400 acres, with a 700 acre lake, offers a variety of naturescapes and land and water recreation. Dogs of all sizes are allowed at no additional fee. Dogs may not be left unattended, they must have current rabies and shot records, be on no more than a 6 foot leash, and be cleaned up after. Dogs are not allowed in public swim areas or buildings. Dogs are allowed on the trails. The camping and tent areas also allow dogs. There is a dog walk area at the campground. Multiple dogs may be allowed.

Hillbilly Haven Campground
10885 I-20W
Millsap, TX
817-341-4009

hillbillyhavencg.com
Dogs of all sizes are allowed. There are no additional pet fees. Dogs may not be left unattended, and they must be quiet, leashed, and cleaned up after. The camping and tent areas also allow dogs. There is a dog walk area at the campground. Multiple dogs may be allowed.

Lake Mineral Wells State Park and Trailway
100 Park Road 71
Mineral Wells, TX
940-328-1171 (800-792-1112)
This park of over 2000 acres, with a 210 acre lake, offers a variety of naturescapes, land and water recreation, and has a 20 mile trailway that connects to other trails. Dogs of all sizes are allowed at no additional fee. Dogs may not be left unattended, they must have current rabies and shot records, be on no more than a 6 foot leash, and be cleaned up after. Dogs are not allowed on the beaches or in buildings. Dogs are allowed on the trails. The camping and tent areas also allow dogs. There is a dog walk area at the campground. Multiple dogs may be allowed.

Bentsen Palm Village RV Park
2500 S Benson Pond Drive
Mission, TX
956-585-5568 (877-BIRDPARK (247-3727))
bentsenpalmvillage.com
Dogs of all sizes are allowed. There are no additional pet fees. Dogs may not be left unattended outside, and they must be quiet, leashed, and cleaned up after. Pets must be walked in assigned areas. This is a 50 years old or older resort. There is a dog walk area at the campground. Multiple dogs may be allowed.

Bentson-Rio Grande Valley State Park
2800 Bentson Palm Drive
Mission, TX
956-585-1107 (800-792-1112)
This parks is known for the variety of birds that live here. Vehicles are not allowed inside this park, and they do have a tram to transport visitors inside or they can walk in. Dogs are allowed at no additional fee, but they are not allowed on the trams. Dogs may not be left unattended, they must have current rabies and shot records, be on no more than a 6 foot leash, and be cleaned up after. Dogs are not allowed in buildings. Dogs are allowed on the trails. The camping and tent areas also allow

dogs. There is a dog walk area at the campground. There are no electric or water hookups at the campground. Multiple dogs may be allowed.

Monahans Sandhills State Park
Park Road 41
Monahans, TX
432-943-2092 (800-792-1112)
Although popular for camping, hiking, equestrian activities, and the Texas Camel Treks, the main attraction here are the more than 3,840 acres of sand dunes. Sand toboggans and disks are available for rent at the park headquarters. Dogs are allowed throughout the park and at the campground for no additional fee. Dogs must be leashed and cleaned up after. The campground offers shade shelters, restrooms, showers, and a dump station. The camping and tent areas also allow dogs. There is a dog walk area at the campground. Multiple dogs may be allowed.

Mt Pleasant KOA
2322 Greenhill Road
Mount Pleasant, TX
903-572-5005 (800-562-5409)
mpkoa.com
Dogs of all sizes are allowed. There are no additional pet fees. Dogs must be leashed and cleaned up after. Dogs may not be left unattended, but they may be outside alone as long as there is an adult in the RV. There are some breed restrictions. The camping and tent areas also allow dogs. There is a dog walk area at the campground. Dogs are allowed in the camping cabins. Multiple dogs may be allowed.

Brazos Bend State Park
21901 FM 762/Crab River Road
Needville, TX
979-553-5101 (800-792-1112)
This lush park is home to the George Observatory, more than 270 species of birds, and a variety of land and water recreation. Dogs of all sizes are allowed at no additional fee. Dogs may not be left unattended, they must have current rabies and shot records, be on no more than a 6 foot leash, and be cleaned up after. Dogs are not allowed in public swim areas or buildings. Dogs are not allowed to drink out of or be by the water anywhere. Dogs are allowed on the trails. The camping and tent areas also allow dogs. There is a dog walk area at the campground.

Multiple dogs may be allowed.

Sam Houston National Forest
FM 1375 W
New Waverly, TX
936-344-6205 (877-444-6777)
One of only 4 in the state, this 163,037 acre national forest supports a large variety of wildlife and offers numerous recreational and educational opportunities. In addition to several points of interest, this forest is also home to the blazed 128 mile Lone Star Hiking Trail. Dogs are allowed throughout the forest and in the camp areas; they are not allowed on the beach or at swimming areas. Dogs must be leashed at all times and under their owner's control. There are a variety of camping experiences to be enjoyed from primitive to modern, and the camp areas may have some or all of the following: picnic tables, grills, lamp posts, restrooms, hot showers, or concessionaires. The camping and tent areas also allow dogs. There is a dog walk area at the campground. Multiple dogs may be allowed.

Artesian Springs Resort
Rt 1 Box 670-12 H 26/26
Newton, TX
409-379-8826
artesianspringsresort.com
Dogs of all sizes are allowed, and there are no additional pet fees for tent or RV sites. There is a $25 pet fee for the cabins, $15 of which, is refundable, and only 2 dogs up to 25 pounds each is allowed. Dogs may not be left unattended, and they must be leashed and cleaned up after. There are some breed restrictions. This RV park is closed during the off-season. The camping and tent areas also allow dogs. There is a dog walk area at the campground. Dogs are allowed in the camping cabins.

Midessa Oil Patch RV Park
4220 S County Road 1290
Odessa, TX
432-563-2368
Dogs of all sizes are allowed. There are no additional pet fees. Dogs may not be left unattended outside, and they must be leashed and cleaned up after. There is a fenced pet run for off lead. The camping and tent areas also allow dogs. There is a dog walk area at the campground. Multiple dogs may be allowed.

Serendipity Bay Resort
1001 Main Street
Palacios, TX
361-972-5454

serendipityresort.com
Dogs of all sizes are allowed. There are no additional pet fees. Dogs may not be left unattended, and they must be leashed and cleaned up after. There are 2 fishing piers in the park. There are some breed restrictions. There is a dog walk area at the campground. Multiple dogs may be allowed.

Island RV Resort
Avenue G & 6th Street
Port Aransas, TX
361-749-5600
islandrvresort.com
Dogs of all sizes are allowed. There are no additional pet fees. Dogs may not be left outside unattended, and they must be leashed and cleaned up after at all times. There is a walking path of a couple of miles across the street from the RV park, and dogs are also allowed to walk along the beach. There are some breed restrictions. The camping and tent areas also allow dogs. There is a dog walk area at the campground. 2 dogs may be allowed.

Mustang Island State Park
17047 H 361
Port Aransas, TX
361-749-5246 (800-792-1112)
This 3,954 acre coastal barrier island park offers about 5 miles of beach and a distinctive and complex ecosystem. This is also a premier viewing area for spring and fall bird migrations. Dogs are allowed for no additional fee; they are not allowed in designated swim areas or within the beach/land area adjacent to the swim area. Dogs may not be left unattended at any time; they must be kept leashed-even when in the water, and under their owner's immediate control at all times. The camp areas are varied and may have all or some of the following: picnic areas, restrooms, showers, shade shelters, portable toilets, rinsing showers, and/or bulk water supply. The camping and tent areas also allow dogs. There is a dog walk area at the campground. Multiple dogs may be allowed.

Pioneer Beach Resort
120 Gulfwinds Drive
Port Aransas, TX
888-480-3246
pioneerresorts.com
Dogs of all sizes are allowed. There are no additional pet fees. Dogs must be leashed and cleaned up after. There are some breed restrictions. There is a dog walk area

at the campground. 2 dogs may be allowed.

Sea Breeze RV Park
1026 Sea Breeze Lane
Portland, TX
361-643-0744
seabreezerv.com
Dogs of all sizes are allowed. There are no additional pet fees. Dogs may not be left unattended outside, nor inside unless weather permits. Dogs must be leashed and cleaned up after. There are some breed restrictions. There is a dog walk area at the campground. 2 dogs may be allowed.

Big Bend Ranch State Park
The River Road (H 170)
Presidio, TX
432-424-3327 (877-444-6777)
Almost 300,000 acres of Chihuahuan Desert wilderness with a vast variety of plant and animal life await visitors here. This park is mostly for primitive camping. Dogs are allowed at no additional fee. Dogs may not be left unattended, and they must be leased and cleaned up after. Dogs are not allowed in public swim areas or in buildings. Dogs are allowed on the trails, but they are not allowed on the guided river trips. The camping and tent areas also allow dogs. There is a dog walk area at the campground. There are no electric or water hookups at the campground. Multiple dogs may be allowed.

Copper Breaks State Park
777 Park Road 62
Quanah, TX
940-839-4331 (800-792-1112)
This year round park offers 2 lakes, 10 miles of trails, summer educational and interpretive programs, a wide variety of plant and wildlife, and a natural history museum (open Friday through Sunday). Dogs of all sizes are allowed at no additional fee. Dogs may not be left unattended, they must have current rabies and shot records, be on no more than a 6 foot leash, and be cleaned up after. Well behaved dogs are allowed in the museum when they are not real busy. Dogs are allowed on the trails. They will allow only fully self-contained RVs to stay in off season. This campground is closed during the off-season. The camping and tent areas also allow dogs. There is a dog walk area at the campground. Multiple dogs may be allowed.

Caprock Canyons State Park
850 Caprock Canyons Park Road
Quitaque, TX
806-455-1492 (800-792-1112)
There are numerous recreational opportunities here with almost 90 miles of multi-use trails, an auto tour, a 120 surface acre lake, and more. However, as a result of its rich natural, cultural, and prehistoric history, there are educational opportunities as well. Dogs are allowed throughout the park and in the camp area; they are not allowed in buildings or at public swim areas. Dogs may not be left unattended at any time, they must be on no more than a 6 foot leash, and under their owner's control at all times. Camp areas are varied and may have all or some of the following: a shade shelter, picnic table, fire ring, lantern post, restrooms, showers, a playground, fishing pier, or dump station. The camping and tent areas also allow dogs. There is a dog walk area at the campground. Multiple dogs may be allowed.

Rusk KOA
745 H 343 E
Rusk, TX
903-683-6641 (800-562-4143)
koa.com/where/tx/43233/
There are a variety of fun activities in the park and in the surrounding area for visitors to enjoy here. The park offers free Wi-Fi, a large seasonal saltwater swimming pool, a club room, and bicycle rentals. Quiet, well behaved dogs are allowed for no additional fee. Only 2 dogs are allowed per cabin; there may be more than 2 dogs per site in the RV/tent area. Dogs may not be left unattended outside, and they may only be left alone inside if they will be quiet. Dogs must be on no more than a 6 foot leash and cleaned up after at all times. There are some breed restrictions. The camping and tent areas also allow dogs. There is a dog walk area at the campground. Dogs are allowed in the camping cabins.

Guadalupe Mountains National Park
H 62/180
Salt Flat, TX
915-828-3251
nps.gov/gumo/
There is an unusual and complex collection of flora and fauna at this park. At 5,000+ feet above the desert floor is home to one of the world's best examples of fossilized reef. Dogs are allowed wherever your car

can go and in the campground for no additional fee. They are also allowed on the trail between the campground and the visitor center and on the Pinery Trail at the visitor center. Dogs must be on no more than a 6 foot leash and be cleaned up after all times. Dogs may not be left unattended at any time. Pet owners must take extra precaution due to natural predators and extreme heat conditions. The camp area offers a total of 39 RV and tent sites with potable water, restrooms, a utility sink, picnic tables, and a drink machine. The camping and tent areas also allow dogs. There is a dog walk area at the campground. There are no electric or water hookups at the campgrounds. Multiple dogs may be allowed.

San Angelo KOA
6699 Knickerbocker Road
San Angelo, TX
325-949-3242 (800-562-7519)
koa.com
Dogs of all sizes are allowed. There are no additional pet fees. Dogs may not be left unattended outside, and they must be leashed and cleaned up after. Dogs may not be at the pool or in the buildings. There is a fenced area where dogs may be left for short periods. There are some breed restrictions. The camping and tent areas also allow dogs. There is a dog walk area at the campground. Dogs are allowed in the camping cabins. Multiple dogs may be allowed.

San Angelo State Park
3900-2 Mercedes
San Angelo, TX
325-949-4757 (800-792-1112)
Activities are year round at this park that covers four ecological zones, and it offers a variety of tours, trails, plants, animals, birds, and recreation. Dogs of all sizes are allowed at no additional fee. Dogs may not be left unattended, they must have current rabies and shot records, be on no more than a 6 foot leash, and be cleaned up after. Dogs are not allowed in public swim areas or buildings. Dogs are allowed on the trails. The camping and tent areas also allow dogs. There is a dog walk area at the campground. Multiple dogs may be allowed.

Admiralty RV Resort
1485 N Ellison Drive
San Antonio, TX
800-999-7872
admiraltyrvresort.com

Dogs of all sizes are allowed. There are no additional pet fees. Dogs must be leashed and cleaned up after. There is a dog walk area at the campground. Multiple dogs may be allowed.

Blazing Star RV Resort
1120 W H 1604N
San Antonio, TX
210-680-7827
blazingstarrv.com
Dogs of all sizes are allowed. There are no additional pet fees. Dogs may not be left unattended outside, and they may be left inside only if they are quiet and comfortable. Dogs must be leashed and cleaned up after. There are some breed restrictions. The camping and tent areas also allow dogs. There is a dog walk area at the campground. 2 dogs may be allowed.

San Antonio KOA
602 Gembler Road
San Antonio, TX
210-224-9296 (800-562-7783)
koa.com
Dogs of all sizes are allowed. There are no additional pet fees. Dogs may not be left unattended outside, and they must be quiet, leashed, and cleaned up after. There are some breed restrictions. The camping and tent areas also allow dogs. There is a dog walk area at the campground. 2 dogs may be allowed.

Traveler's World RV Resort
2617 Roosevelt Avenue
San Antonio, TX
210-532-8310
travelersworldrv.com
Dogs of all sizes are allowed. There are no additional pet fees. Dogs may not be left unattended outside, and they must be leashed and cleaned up after. There is a dog walk area at the campground. Multiple dogs may be allowed.

Stone Creek RV Park
18905 IH 35N
Schertz, TX
830-609-7759
Dogs of all sizes are allowed. There are no additional pet fees. Dogs may not be left unattended outside, and they must be leashed and cleaned up after. There are some breed restrictions. The camping and tent areas also allow dogs. There is a dog walk area at the campground. Multiple dogs may be allowed.

Natchez Trace RV Park

189 County Road 506
Shannon, TX
662-767-8609
Dogs of all sizes are allowed. There are no additional pet fees. Dogs must be quiet, well behaved, leashed, and cleaned up after. There is a dog walk area at the campground. Multiple dogs may be allowed.

Buescher State Park
100 Park Road 1E
Smithville, TX
512-237-2241 (800-792-1112)
There are over a 1,000 acres with a small lake at this park that provides a variety of recreational and nature pursuits. Well behaved dogs of all sizes are allowed at no additional fee. Dogs may not be left unattended, they must have current rabies and shot records, be on no more than a 6 foot leash, and be cleaned up after. Dogs are not allowed in public swim areas or buildings. Dogs are allowed on the trail. The camping and tent areas also allow dogs. There is a dog walk area at the campground. Multiple dogs may be allowed.

Wagon Wheel Guest Ranch
5996 County Road 2128
Snyder, TX
325-573-2348 (800-792-1112)
This guest ranch offers a country music venue and a variety of recreational pursuits. Dogs of all sizes are allowed at no additional fee. Dogs may not be left unattended, they must have current rabies and shot records, be on no more than a 6 foot leash, and be cleaned up after. Dogs are not allowed in buildings. Dogs are allowed on the trails. The camping and tent areas also allow dogs. There is a dog walk area at the campground. Multiple dogs may be allowed.

Lake Somerville State Park and Trailway (AKA-Birch Creek SP)
14222 Park Road 57
Somerville, TX
979-535-7763 (800-792-1112)
A multitude of land and water recreational opportunities await visitors at this park. Dogs of all sizes are allowed at no additional fee. Dogs may not be left unattended, they must have current rabies and shot records, be on no more than a 6 foot leash, and be cleaned up after. Dogs are not allowed in public swim areas or buildings. Dogs are allowed on the trails. The camping and tent

areas also allow dogs. There is a dog walk area at the campground. Multiple dogs may be allowed.

Caverns of Sonora
Private Road 4468
Sonora, TX
325-387-3105
cavernsofsonora.com/
In addition to the incredible sites this constantly growing natural cave provides, visitors can also go gemstone panning, hike the nature trail, camp, or explore this working ranch. Dogs are allowed on the grounds and in the camp area; they are not allowed in the cave. However, free locked kennels are provided for guests with pets who are taking the cave tour. Dogs must be leashed and under their owner's control at all times. The camp area offers 48 sites, restrooms, and showers. The camping and tent areas also allow dogs. There is a dog walk area at the campground. 2 dogs may be allowed.

Isla Blanc Park
33174 State Park Road 100
South Padre Island, TX
956-761-5493
co.cameron.tx.us/park/blanca.htm
In addition to more than a mile of sandy white beaches, a fishing jetty, playgrounds, picnic areas, and a marina, this recreational/RV Mecca also has several eateries, nightclubs, a waterpark, retail shops, and more. Dogs are allowed throughout the park; they must be on leash at all times-including on the beaches, and owners must be visibly carrying some kind of pet clean-up supplies. Pooper scoopers are available at the office if needed. Dogs must be well behaved and they are not allowed in park buildings. The campground offers almost 600 RV sites and a myriad of tent sites with the proximity of restrooms, showers, gaming areas, a laundry, and a dump station. The camping and tent areas also allow dogs. There is a dog walk area at the campground. Multiple dogs may be allowed.

Guadalupe River State Park
3350 Park Road 31
Spring Branch, TX
830-438-2656 (800-792-1112)
Bisected by the beautiful cypress tree lined Guadalupe River, this park offers a variety of recreational and educational activities. Dogs are allowed throughout the park and the campground for no additional fee; they are not allowed in buildings or in

food service areas. Dogs may not be left unattended at any time; they must be quiet, on no more than a 6 foot leash and under their owner's immediate control at all times. Dogs are not allowed in designated swim areas or within the beach and land area adjacent to the swim area. Campsites offer a variety of settings and may have all or some of the following: restrooms, showers, potable water, a dump station, or a Texas park store. The camping and tent areas also allow dogs. There is a dog walk area at the campground. Multiple dogs may be allowed.

Study Butte RV Park
On H 118
Study Butte, TX
432-371-2468
Well behaved dogs of all sizes are allowed at no additional fee. Dogs may not be left unattended, and they must be leashed and cleaned up after. The camping and tent areas also allow dogs. There is a dog walk area at the campground. Multiple dogs may be allowed.

Terlingua Oasis RV Park
At H 118 & H 170
Study Butte, TX
432-371-2218 (800-848-2363)
Dogs of all sizes are allowed at no additional fee for tent or RV sites. Dogs may not be left unattended, and they must be leashed and cleaned up after. There is a motel on site that also allows dogs in smoking rooms only at $5 per night per pet. Dogs are allowed on the trails inside the campground. The camping and tent areas also allow dogs. There is a dog walk area at the campground. Multiple dogs may be allowed.

Big Bend Motor Inn & RV Campground
100 Main Street
Terlingua, TX
800-848-2363
Dogs of all sizes are allowed, but there can only be one large dog or two small dogs per site. There are no additional pet fees. Dogs may not be left unattended, and they must be leashed and cleaned up after. There is a motel on site that also allows dogs at $5 per night per pet additional fee in a smoking room only. There is a dog walk area at the campground.

Big Bend RV Park
Terlingua Creek Bridge
Terlingua, TX

432-371-2250 (877-444-6777)
Dogs are allowed at no additional fee. Dogs may not be left unattended, and they must be leashed and cleaned up after. Dogs are not allowed in public swim areas or in buildings. Dogs are allowed on the trails. This park also has a restaurant where your pet may join you on the patio. The camping and tent areas also allow dogs. There is a dog walk area at the campground. Multiple dogs may be allowed.

Texarkana KOA
500 W 53rd Street
Texarkana, TX
903-792-5521 (888-562-5697)
texarkanarvpark.com
Dogs of all sizes are allowed, and there are no additional pet fees for tent or RV sites. There is a $10 one time additional pet fee for the cabins. Dogs must be leashed and cleaned up after. The camping and tent areas also allow dogs. There is a dog walk area at the campground. Dogs are allowed in the camping cabins. Multiple dogs may be allowed.

Cowtown RV Park
7000 I-20
Toledo, TX
817-441-7878
cowtownrv.com
Dogs of all sizes are allowed. There are no additional pet fees. Dogs may not be left unattended outside, and they must be leashed and cleaned up after. They also have 2 fenced in dog run areas. There are some breed restrictions. The camping and tent areas also allow dogs. There is a dog walk area at the campground. Multiple dogs may be allowed.

Balmorhea State Park
9207 H 17S
Toyahvale, TX
432-375-2370 (800-792-1112)
In the late 1930s this park gained star status when the CCC constructed the 1 3/4 acre sized, 25 foot deep artesian spring fed pool that swimmers also share with other aquatic life, delighting swimmers and scuba divers alike. Another popular draw is the underwater viewing station at Cienega. Dogs are allowed throughout the park and in the camp area; they are not allowed in buildings, the motel, or the pool. Dogs may not be left unattended at any time, they must be on no more than a 6 foot leash, and under their owner's control at all times. Campsites are varied and may have some or all of the following; shade

shelters, picnic tables, fire rings, cable TV hookups, restrooms, and showers. The camping and tent areas also allow dogs. There is a dog walk area at the campground. Multiple dogs may be allowed.

Abilene State Park
150 Park Road 32
Tuscola, TX
325-572-3204
Once a favored spot of Native Americans, this area now provides a number of educational and recreational opportunities. There are seasonal concessionaires and swimming pool, gaming areas, and plenty of places to hike. Dogs are allowed throughout the park and in the camp area; they are not allowed in buildings or at public swim areas. Dogs may not be left unattended at any time and they must be on no more than a 6 foot leash. The camp area offers picnic tables, grills, restrooms, showers, a playground, and dump stations. The camping and tent areas also allow dogs. There is a dog walk area at the campground. Multiple dogs may be allowed.

Ray Roberts Lake State Park
100 PW 4153/Johnson Branck
Valley View, TX
940-637-2294 (800-792-1112)
This state park consists of 2 units: The second unit is Isle du Bois, located at 100 PW 4137, Pilot Point, TX, 76258,(940-686-2148). There is a variety of land and water recreation offered in both areas, and they also have an interpretive and educational program. Dogs of all sizes are allowed at no additional fee. Dogs may not be left unattended, they must have current rabies and shot records, be on no more than a 6 foot leash, and be cleaned up after. Dogs are not allowed on the beaches or in buildings. Dogs are allowed on the trails. The camping and tent areas also allow dogs. There is a dog walk area at the campground. Multiple dogs may be allowed.

Van Horn KOA
10 Kamper's Lane
Van Horn, TX
432-283-2728 (800-562-0798)
vanhorntexaskoa.com
Dogs of all sizes are allowed. There are no additional pet fees. Dogs may not be left unattended outside, and they must be leashed and cleaned up after. The camping and tent areas also allow dogs. There is a dog walk area at the campground. Dogs are allowed in the camping cabins.

Multiple dogs may be allowed.

Lost Maples State Natural Area
37221 H 187
Vanderpool, TX
830-966-3413
With over 2,000 acres on the Sabinal River, this park offers a variety of nature and archaeological study, in addition to land and water recreation. Dogs of all sizes are allowed at no additional fee. Dogs may not be left unattended, and they must be on no more than a 6 foot leash, and be cleaned up after. Dogs are not allowed in public swim areas or buildings. Dogs are allowed on the trails. The campgrounds are closed for a couple of weeks each year in January for hunting. The camping and tent areas also allow dogs. There is a dog walk area at the campground. Multiple dogs may be allowed.

Waco North KOA
24132 N I 35
Waco, TX
254-826-3869 (800-562-4199)
koa.com
Dogs of all sizes are allowed. There are no additional pet fees. Dogs may not be left unattended outside, and they must be leashed and cleaned up after. The camping and tent areas also allow dogs. There is a dog walk area at the campground. Multiple dogs may be allowed.

I 35 RV Park
1513 N I 35
Waco, TX
254-829-0698
i35rvpark.com
Dogs of all sizes are allowed. There are no additional pet fees. Dogs must be leashed and cleaned up after. There are some breed restrictions. There is a dog walk area at the campground. 2 dogs may be allowed.

Jellystone Park
34843 Betka Road
Waller, TX
979-826-4111
lonestarcamping.com
Dogs of all sizes are allowed. There are no additional pet fees. Dogs must be quiet, well behaved, may not be left unattended, and must be leashed and cleaned up after. Dogs must be quiet and may not be tied up outside alone. The camping and tent areas also allow dogs. There is a dog walk area at the campground. 2 dogs may be allowed.

Lake Whitney State Park
Box 1175; (on FM-1244)
Whitney, TX
254-694-3793 (800-792-1112)
This park of more than 1200 acres runs along the east shore of Lake Whitney and offers a variety of nature study and land and water recreation. Dogs of all sizes are allowed at no additional fee. Dogs may not be left unattended, and they must be on no more than a 6 foot leash, and be cleaned up after. Dogs are not allowed in the swim or day use areas, but they are allowed on the trails. The camping and tent areas also allow dogs. There is a dog walk area at the campground. Multiple dogs may be allowed.

Lake Arrowhead State Park
229 Park Road 63
Wichita Falls, TX
940-528-2661 (800-792-1112)
In addition to a wide range of land and water activities at this 524 acre park with a 16,000+ acre lake, the park also offers interpretive/educational programs, a group dining hall, lighted fishing piers and annual events. They are home to a Black-tailed Prairie Dog Town. Dogs are allowed throughout the park and the campground for no additional fee; they must have proof of current shots and be licensed. Dogs may not be left unattended at any time; they must be quiet, on no more than a 6 foot leash and under owner's immediate control and care at all times. Dogs are not allowed in designated swim areas, buildings, or in food service areas. The campsites have picnic tables and a fire ring, and may have all or some of the following: restrooms with or without showers, picnic tables, and dump station. The camping and tent areas also allow dogs. There is a dog walk area at the campground. Multiple dogs may be allowed.

Wichita Falls RV Park
2944 Seymour H
Wichita Falls, TX
940-723-1532
Dogs of all sizes are allowed. There are no additional pet fees. Dogs may not be left unattended outside, and they must be leashed and cleaned up after. There is a dog walk area at the campground. Multiple dogs may be allowed.

Angelina National Forest
111 Walnut Ridge Road
Zavalla, TX

936-897-1068
One of only 4 in the state, this 153,179 acre national forest sits in the upper gulf coastal plain along the shores of an 114,500 acre lake. This is a working forest and in addition to providing diverse ecosystems to support a large variety of flora and fauna, there are historic sites and numerous recreation and educational activities. Dogs are allowed throughout the forest and in the camp areas; they are not allowed on the beach or at swimming areas. Dogs must be leashed at all times and under their owner's control. Camp areas offer level sites, picnic tables, campfire rings, potable water, toilets, and great views of the reservoir. The camping and tent areas also allow dogs. There is a dog walk area at the campground. There are no electric or water hookups at the campgrounds. Multiple dogs may be allowed.

Utah

Beaver KOA
1428 Manderfield Road
Beaver, UT
435-438-2924 (800-562-2912)
koa.com
Dogs of all sizes are allowed. There are no additional pet fees. Dogs must be leashed and cleaned up after. This RV park is closed during the off-season. The camping and tent areas also allow dogs. There is a dog walk area at the campground. Dogs are allowed in the camping cabins. Multiple dogs may be allowed.

Goosenecks State Park
660 West 400 North/End of H 316
Blanding, UT
435-678-2238 (800-322-3770)
This park shares 300 million years of geologic history with its visitors from an observation shelter located at 1000 feet over the San Juan River. From here you can see the path of the river's erosion. Dogs are allowed at no additional fee. Dogs may be off lead if there is voice control. The camping and tent areas also allow dogs. There is a dog walk area at the campground. There are no electric or water hookups at the campground. Multiple dogs may be allowed.

Cadillac Ranch
640 E Main
Bluff, UT
800-538-6195
Dogs of all sizes are allowed. There are no additional pet fees. Dogs must be leashed and cleaned up after. The camping and tent areas also allow dogs. There is a dog walk area at the campground. Multiple dogs may be allowed.

Ruby's Inn Campground and RV Park
1280 S H 63
Bryce Canyon, UT
435-834-5301 (866-866-6616)
brycecanyoncampgrounds.com/
This scenic camp area is a great place to stay when visiting the Bryce Canyon National Park; it is AAA approved, offer over 200 shaded campsites, and large pull-thru sites to accommodate modern RV's. Some of the amenities include showers, clean restrooms, a large Laundromat, heated pool, a post office, dump station, 2 stores, and various recreational activities. The campground is located near Ruby's Inn, and they ask that you check in there at the front desk for camp sites. Dogs of all sizes are allowed for no additional fee. Dogs must be quiet, well behaved, leashed and cleaned up after at all times. They are not allowed to be left unattended outside the RV, and they may not be left inside tents alone. Dogs are not allowed in Bryce Canyon, on the rim or on trails. Dogs are allowed throughout the campgrounds, and on the connecting ATV trails. This RV park is closed during the off-season. The camping and tent areas also allow dogs. There is a dog walk area at the campground.

Cannonville/Bryce Valley KOA
H 12 at Red Rocks Road
Cannonville, UT
435-679-8988 (888-562-4710)
brycecanyonkoa.com
Dogs of all sizes are allowed. There are no additional pet fees. Dogs must be well behaved, leashed, and cleaned up after. This RV park is closed during the off-season. The camping and tent areas also allow dogs. There is a dog walk area at the campground. Dogs are allowed in the camping cabins. Multiple dogs may be allowed.

Kodachrome Basin State Park
P. O. Box 238/Kodachrome Drive
Cannonville, UT
435-679-8562 (800-322-3770)
Multi-colored and red tinged rock formations against incredible blue skies give rise to this park's name. It boasts the world's only collection of 'sand pipes'; oddly shaped sandstone pillers that rise from 6 to 170 feet from the ground. There are several short trails in the park that lead to very scenic views, a visitor's center, a camping supply store, and guided tours. Dogs are allowed at no additional fee. They must be on no more than a 6 foot leash, they are not allowed in park buildings, but they can be around the park and on the trails. Dogs may not be left unattended, and they must be cleaned up after. Located in a natural amphitheater among desert vegetation, this well maintained campground offers a pavilion area with picnic tables, fire pit, barbecue grills, fresh spring water, modern restrooms, showers, dump station, and firewood. They are open year round, but water is shut off in winter. Campers do not have to pay an additional day use fee for the park. The camping and tent areas also allow dogs. There is a dog walk area at the campground. There are no electric or water hookups at the campgrounds. Multiple dogs may be allowed.

Broken Bow RV Park
495 W Main Street
Escalante (Cannonville), UT
435-826-4959
brokenbowrvpark.com
This campground in the red rock country has 28 pull-thru sites, full hookups and more. Pets are allowed in your campsites. The campground is located 1 hour from Bryce and 1 1/2 hours to Capital Reef National Park.

Cedar City KOA
1121 N Main
Cedar City, UT
435-586-9872 (800-562-9873)
cedarcitycampgrounds.com
There can be up to 3 dogs of any size for the tent or RV sites, and there are no additional pet fees. There is a $5 per night per pet additional fee for the cabins, and only up to 2 dogs are allowed. Dogs may not be left unattended, and they must be leashed and cleaned up after. There are some breed

restrictions. The camping and tent areas also allow dogs. There is a dog walk area at the campground. Dogs are allowed in the camping cabins.

Dixie National Forest
1789 N Wedgewood Lane
Cedar City, UT
435-865-3700
fs.fed.us/dxnf
This is the largest National Forest in Utah and dogs of all sizes are allowed. There are no additional pet fees. Dogs may not be left unattended, and they must be leashed and cleaned up after. Dogs are allowed on all the trails, but they are not allowed on the beaches or in the water. This campground is closed during the off-season. The camping and tent areas also allow dogs. There is a dog walk area at the campground. Multiple dogs are allowed.

Hovenweep
Campground/Hovenweep National Monument
On H 10 (McElmo Route)
Cortez, UT
970-562-4282 (800-322-3770)
nps.gov/hove/
This park is the safeguard for six prehistoric, Puebloan-era villages, and offers a variety of historical, geological, and scenic sites. Dogs are allowed at no additional fee. Dogs may not be left unattended outside, and they must be leashed and cleaned up after. Dogs are allowed on the trails, and they must stay on the trails. The camping and tent areas also allow dogs. There is a dog walk area at the campground. There are no electric or water hookups at the campground. Multiple dogs may be allowed.

Escalante State Park
710 N Reservoir Road
Escalante, UT
435-826-4466 (800-322-3770)
This park, along the Wide Hollow Reservoir, has a couple of popular trails; The Petrified Forest Trail which winds through lava flows and petrified wood, and for more of a challenge there is the Sleeping Rainbows trail. Dogs are allowed at no additional fee. Dogs may not be left unattended, and they must be leashed and cleaned up after. Dogs are allowed on the trails. The camping and tent areas also allow dogs. There is a dog walk area at the campground. There are no electric or water hookups at the campground.

Multiple dogs may be allowed.

Lagoon RV Park and Campground
375 N Lagoon Drive
Farmington, UT
801-451-8000 (800-748-5246)
lagoonpark.com/camping.php
This RV park and campground offers such amenities as a general store, laundry, restrooms with showers, a sandwich shop, a gourmet ice cream parlor, and a bicycle/walking trail around a large lagoon. Reservations are recommended, and they usually start taking them about mid-February. This park also sits along side the Lagoon Amusement Park and Pioneer Village, a world class amusement park of over 100 acres with dozens of rides and attractions, and dogs are allowed in some of the areas there. Dogs of all sizes are allowed for no additional fee for camping or the park. Dogs may not be left unattended at the campsite, and they must be leashed and cleaned up after at all times. This RV park is closed during the off-season. The camping and tent areas also allow dogs. There is a dog walk area at the campground. 2 dogs may be allowed.

Sunset Campground
Farmington Canyon
Farmington City, UT
877-444-6777
This campground is located at an elevation of 6,400 feet in the Wasatch-Cache National Forest, east of Farmington City and north of Salt Lake City. There are 16 camp sites with tables, fire circles and grills. Campground amenities include toilets and drinking water but no trash cans or RV hookups. The maximum vehicle length allowed is 28 feet. Sites are paved with pull-thru capabilities. Some of the sites are shaded and wheelchair accessible. Dogs must be leashed at the campgrounds and on the 1/2 mile Sunset Trail. Please clean up after your pets. All camp sites are first come, first serve and no reservations are accepted. The campground is open from June through October. To get there from Salt Lake City, head north on Interstate 15 and take the Farmington Exit. At the stop sign, turn right. Go to 100 East Street and turn left (heading north). Take this road 5.3 miles up the canyon (Farmington Canyon) to the campground.

Fillmore KOA
900 S 410 W
Fillmore, UT
435-743-4420 (800-562-1516)
koa.com
Dogs of all sizes are allowed, and there can be up to 3 dogs at the tent and RV sites. Two small dogs only are allowed at the cabins, and they must stay off the beds. There are no additional pet fees. Dogs are not allowed at the playground or the pool, and they must be leashed and cleaned up after. There are some breed restrictions. This RV park is closed during the off-season. The camping and tent areas also allow dogs. There is a dog walk area at the campground. Dogs are allowed in the camping cabins.

Bear Lake State Park
Box 184/ Off H 30
Garden City, UT
435-946-3343 (800-322-3770)
This beautiful lake park is located high in the Rocky Mountains and is open year round. Dogs are allowed at no additional fee. Dogs may not be left unattended, and they must be leashed and cleaned up after. Dogs may be off lead when out of the camp areas if there is voice control. Dogs are allowed on the trails unless otherwise marked. This campground is closed during the off-season. The camping and tent areas also allow dogs. There is a dog walk area at the campground. Multiple dogs may be allowed.

Bear Lake/Garden City KOA
485 N Bear Lake Blvd
Garden City, UT
435-946-3454 (800-562-3442)
koa.com
Dogs of all sizes are allowed. There are no additional pet fees. Dogs may not be left unattended, and they must be leashed and cleaned up after. There is an off leash dog run area. The tent and RV sites are seasonal, and the cabins stay open all year. There are some breed restrictions. The camping and tent areas also allow dogs. There is a dog walk area at the campground. Dogs are allowed in the camping cabins. Multiple dogs may be allowed.

Glendale KOA
11 Koa Street
Glendale, UT
435-648-2490 (800-562-8635)
koa.com
Dogs of all sizes are allowed. There are no additional pet fees. Dogs must be leashed and cleaned up

after. There is a fenced in dog run for off lead. This RV park is closed during the off-season. The camping and tent areas also allow dogs. There is a dog walk area at the campground. Multiple dogs may be allowed.

Goblin Valley State Park
P.O. Box 637
Green River, UT
435-564-3633 (800 322-3770)
A vast unearthly landscape greets visitors with thousands of intricately eroded sandstone creations, that someone obviously thought looked like goblins. The movie Galaxy Quest was filmed here because of this unusual scenery. There are plenty of places to hike to and through, a visitor observation shelter, visitor's center, and picnicking. They are open daily year round. Dogs are allowed at no additional fee. They must be on no more than a 6 foot leash, and they are not allowed in park buildings. Dogs may not be left unattended, and they must be cleaned up after. Camping is allowed in designated areas only, and they offer modern restrooms, showers, covered tables, drinking water, and a dump station. The camping and tent areas also allow dogs. There is a dog walk area at the campground. There are no electric or water hookups at the campgrounds. Multiple dogs may be allowed.

Green River KOA
235 S 1780 E
Green River, UT
435-564-8195 (800-562-5734)
koa.com/where/ut/44154/
In addition to being close to fine dining and local sites of interest, this park offers a camp store, laundry facilities, free Wi-Fi, a large seasonal pool, gaming areas, and a playground. Dogs are allowed for no additional fee. Dogs may not be left unattended, and they must be on no more than a 6 foot leash and cleaned up after at all times. There are some breed restrictions. There is a dog walk area at the campground. Multiple dogs may be allowed.

Green River State Park
125 Fairway Avenue
Green River, UT
435-564-3633 (800-322-3770)
This park has it's own recreational activities and a golf course, but is is also a central point to access other recreational areas and trails. Dogs are allowed at no additional fee. Dogs may not be left unattended,

and they must be leashed and cleaned up after. Dogs are allowed on the trails. This campground is closed during the off-season. The camping and tent areas also allow dogs. There is a dog walk area at the campground. There are no electric or water hookups at the campground. Multiple dogs may be allowed.

United Campground of Green River
910 E Main Street
Green River, UT
435-564-8195
Dogs of all sizes are allowed. There are no additional pet fees. Dogs must be leashed and cleaned up after. The camping and tent areas also allow dogs. There is a dog walk area at the campground. Multiple dogs may be allowed.

Goblin Valley State Park
P.O. Box 637/Hanksville Road
Hanksville, UT
435-564-3633 (800-322-3770)
Goblin Valley is so named as a result of the unusual rock formations and the scenery of the park. Dogs are allowed at no additional fee. Dogs may not be left unattended, and they must be leashed and cleaned up after. Dogs are allowed on the trails. The camping and tent areas also allow dogs. There is a dog walk area at the campground. There are no electric or water hookups at the campground. Multiple dogs may be allowed.

Huntington State Park
P.O. Box 1343/ On H 10
Huntington, UT
435-687-2491 (800-322-3770)
The beautiful reservoir here is surrounded by sandstone cliffs, and a variety of recreation is available. Dogs are allowed at no additional fee. Dogs may not be left unattended, and they must be leashed and cleaned up after. Dogs are allowed on the trails. The camping and tent areas also allow dogs. There is a dog walk area at the campground. There are no electric or water hookups at the campground. Multiple dogs may be allowed.

Snowbasin: A Sun Valley Resort
3925 E. Snowbasin Road
Huntsville, UT
801-620-1000 (888-437-5488)
snowbasin.com/index_s.asp
Located in the spectacular Wasatch-Cache National Forest,

Snowbasin's 2,959 vertical feet truly offer terrain to suit everyone's needs. There are 17 designated trails of varying degrees of difficulty, and a variety of recreational pursuits. Amenities include two eateries, a summer concert series and other planned activities, some picnic tables along the trails, a new Disc Golf course, and they offer a trail map to show you the ideal rest, viewing, and picnic areas. Dog of all sizes are allowed for no additional fee. They are not allowed up on the mountain or on the ski runs in the winter, or in park buildings. They are allowed at the plaza, on several of the all season trails, and at the Nordic area. There are some unpopulated areas where dogs may be off lead if they are under firm voice control. Dogs must be leashed and cleaned up after on the trails and at the resort. There is a dog walk area at the campground. Multiple dogs may be allowed.

Brentwood RV Resort
15N 3700W
Hurricane, UT
800-447-2239
zionsgaterv.com
One dog of any size is allowed. There are no additional pet fees. Dogs must be leashed and cleaned up after. There is a dog walk area at the campground.

Quail Creek State Park
H 318 M.P. #2
Hurricane, UT
435-879-2378 (800-322-3770)
This park provides a variety of year round recreation, and the man-made reservoir here is known for the warmth of its water in the summer. Dogs are allowed at no additional fee. Dogs must be on no more than a 6 foot leash and be cleaned up after. Dogs are not allowed on the beach between the grass areas. The camping and tent areas also allow dogs. There is a dog walk area at the campground. There are no electric or water hookups at the campground. Multiple dogs may be allowed.

Snow Canyon State Park
1002 Snow Canyon Drive
Ivins, UT
435-628-2255
This park ranges from 3,100 to almost 5,000 feet altitude, and covers about 7,100 acres. Rarely snowed in, they are open year round, and some of the features offered are 16 miles of hiking trails, technical rock climbing, wildlife viewing,

camping, and plenty of photo ops of this visually striking area. Dogs of all sizes are allowed at no additional fee. They must be on no more than a 6 foot leash, and they are not allowed in park buildings. Dogs may not be left unattended outside an RV or tent, or inside a tent, and they must be cleaned up after quickly. Dogs are allowed around the campground, and on the Whiptail Trail and the West Canyon Rim Trail only. The campground offers 33 sites, modern restrooms, showers, drinking water, picnicking, and a dump station. Campers do not have to pay an additional day use fee for the park. The camping and tent areas also allow dogs. There is a dog walk area at the campground. Multiple dogs may be allowed.

Coral Pink Sand Dunes State Park
2500 Sand Dunes Road
Kanab, UT
435-648-2800
A phenomenon known as the Venturi Affect helped to created these 10,000 to 15,000 year old dunes, and the beautiful contrasting colors of this park really showcase its unique geological features. The park, at an elevation of almost 6,000 feet, is open daily year round, and they offer hiking and interpretive trails, off-roading, picnicking, and a visitor's center. There is also an interesting and diverse population of insects and other desert wildlife. Dogs are allowed for no additional fee, and they are allowed throughout the park and on all the trails. Dogs may not be left unattended, and they must be on no more than a 6 foot leash and cleaned up after at all times. Camping is allowed only in designated campsites. Some of the amenities include modern restrooms, showers, tables, drinking water, and a dump station. Campers do not have to pay an additional day use fee for the park. The camping and tent areas also allow dogs. There is a dog walk area at the campground. There are no electric or water hookups at the campgrounds. Multiple dogs may be allowed.

Kanab RV Corral
483 S 100 E
Kanab, UT
435-644-5330
kanabrvcorral.com
Dogs of all sizes are allowed. There are no additional pet fees. Dogs may not be left unattended, and they must be leashed and cleaned up after. There is a dog walk area at the

campground. Multiple dogs may be allowed.

Cherry Hill RV Resort
1325 S Main
Kaysville, UT
801-451-5379
cherryhill.com
Dogs of all sizes are allowed. There are no additional pet fees. Dogs must be well behaved, leashed, and cleaned up after. Dogs may only be left alone if they will be quiet and comfortable. The camping and tent areas also allow dogs. There is a dog walk area at the campground. Multiple dogs may be allowed.

Bullfrog Resort and Marina Campground
On H 276
Lake Powell, UT
435-684-7000 (800-322-3770)
lakepowell.com/campgrounds.php
Every Summer this park has interpretive programs about the ancestral Puebloans who lived here, and about the geology and wildlife of the area, but there are also activities year round. There is a car ferry that travels across the lake and dogs are allowed on the 30 minute ride. For ferry crossing times call (435)684-3000. Dogs are also allowed in the rentals, on the trails (unless otherwise marked), and on rented boats. Dogs must be leashed and cleaned up after. Dogs are not allowed at the ruins. The camping and tent areas also allow dogs. There is a dog walk area at the campground. Multiple dogs may be allowed.

Village Center at Halls Crossing Marina
End of H 276
Lake Powell, UT
435-684-7000 (800-322-3770)
lakepowell.com/campgrounds.php
Every Summer this park has interpretive programs about the ancestral Puebloans who lived here, and about the geology and wildlife of the area, but there are activities year round. There is a car ferry that travels across the lake and dogs are allowed on the 30 minute ride. For ferry crossing times call (435)684-3000. Dogs are also allowed in the rentals, on the trails (unless otherwise marked), and on the rented houseboats. Dogs must be leashed and cleaned up after. Dogs are not allowed at the ruins. The camping and tent areas also allow dogs. There is a dog walk area at the campground. Multiple

dogs may be allowed.

Red Cliffs Recreation Area
4.5 miles from Leeds on I-15
Leeds, UT
435-688-3246
This recreational site has 10 campsites among the bright colored canyon walls of the area. Dogs are allowed at no additional fee, and they must be leashed and cleaned up after. Information and maps can be gotten from the BLM office at 345 E. Riverside Drive, St. George, Utah. The camping and tent areas also allow dogs. There is a dog walk area at the campground. There are no electric or water hookups at the campground. Multiple dogs may be allowed.

Flaming Gorge National Recreation Area, Ashley Nat'l Forest
P.O. Box 279/ H 191
Manila, UT
435-784-3445
The Flaming Gorge area is a diverse land of scenic beauty, and is administered by the Ashley National Forest. Against a backdrop of brilliant red cliffs runs the 91 mile reservoir offering over 300 miles of shoreline, boat ramps, full service marinas and lodges, and a wide variety of land and water recreation. The 'Gorge', although an aquatic paradise, it is most famous for its fishing. There is a host of land recreational pursuits as well with plenty of trails to walk with your pet. The trails wind through meadows, tree-covered slopes, mountain peaks above timberline, and the five-mile Canyon Rim Trail is accessible from three areas. Day use permits and annual passes are available at the visitor's center. Dogs of all sizes are allowed for no additional fee. Dogs must be on a leash in campgrounds, picnic areas, and trailheads at all times. Dogs are not allowed in park buildings, they must be under their owner's control, and cleaned up after. Your dog is welcome to camp with you at the campgrounds; amenities include picnic tables, drinking water, fire rings, grills, water, and toilets. Campers do not have to pay an additional day use fee for the park. This RV park is closed during the off-season. The camping and tent areas also allow dogs. There is a dog walk area at the campground. Multiple dogs may be allowed.

Flaming Gorge/Manila KOA
H 43 & 3rd W
Manila, UT

435-784-3184 (800-562-3254)
koa.com
Dogs of all sizes are allowed. There is a $10 cash only refundable pet deposit. Dogs must be leashed and cleaned up after. This RV park is closed during the off-season. The camping and tent areas also allow dogs. There is a dog walk area at the campground. Dogs are allowed in the camping cabins. Multiple dogs may be allowed.

Wasatch Mountain State Park
Box 10/1281 Warm Springs Drive
Midway, UT
435-654-1791
This nearly 22,000 acre preserve sits at 6,000 feet, is one of Utah's newest golf destination with two 18 hole championship courses, and offers many year round recreational pursuits; with activities varying by the season. They hosted the 2002 Olympic Winter Games at Soldier Hollow, and the venue remains open to the public featuring a variety of activities and events. There are also a couple of historic sites to explore, and campfire and junior ranger programs. The Wasatch Park Café is located in the Mountain Clubhouse, and there is a snack bar and full-service catering too. Dogs are allowed at no additional fee. They must be on a maximum 6 foot leash, and they are not allowed in park buildings or on the golf courses. They are allowed on the trails. Dogs must be well behaved, and cleaned up after at all times. The park has 139 camping/picnicking areas, modern restrooms, hot showers, and your pet is welcome. There is even a pond where small children can go fishing. Campers do not have to pay an additional day use fee for the park. The phone number directly to the campgrounds is 435-654-3961. The camping and tent areas also allow dogs. There is a dog walk area at the campground. Multiple dogs may be allowed.

Arch View Resort
10 miles N of Moab on H 191
Moab, UT
435-259-7854
archviewresort.com
Dogs of all sizes are allowed. There are no additional pet fees. Dogs must be quiet, well behaved, leashed, and cleaned up after. This RV park is closed during the off-season. The camping and tent areas also allow dogs. There is a dog walk area at the campground. Dogs are allowed in the camping cabins.

Multiple dogs may be allowed.

Canyonlands Campground
555 S Main Street
Moab, UT
800-522-6848
canyonlandsrv.com
Dogs of all sizes are allowed. There are no additional pet fees. Dogs may not be left unattended, and they must be quiet, leashed, and cleaned up after. The camping and tent areas also allow dogs. There is a dog walk area at the campground. Multiple dogs may be allowed.

Dead Horse Point State Park
P. O. Box 609/ H 131
Moab, UT
435-259-2614
Dead Horse Point, towering 2,000 feet above the Colorado River, offers breathtaking views of the canyon country and the pinnacles and buttes of Canyon Lands National Park. The park, at an elevation of almost 6,000 feet, is open year round, and they offer hiking and interpretive trails, picnicking, and a visitor's center. Dogs are allowed at no additional fee. They must be on no more than a 6 foot leash, and they are not allowed in park buildings. Dogs may not be left unattended, and they must be cleaned up after. Dogs are allowed throughout the park and on the trails. The campground offers a modern restroom, drinking water, tables, and a dump station. There is limited water here as it must be trucked in, so they ask that you fill your water tanks before arriving. Campers do not have to pay an additional day use fee for the park. The camping and tent areas also allow dogs. There is a dog walk area at the campground. There are no water hookups at the campgrounds. Multiple dogs may be allowed.

Moab KOA
3225 S H 191
Moab, UT
435-259-6682 (800-562-0372)
koa.com
Dogs of all sizes and numbers are allowed, and there is a $5 one time fee for tent or RV sites. Dogs may not be left unattended outside, or inside an RV unless there is air conditioning. There is a $5 one time fee for the cabins also, only 2 dogs are allowed, and they must be crated if left. Dogs must be quiet, leashed, and cleaned up after. There are some breed restrictions.

This RV park is closed during the off-season. The camping and tent areas also allow dogs. There is a dog walk area at the campground. Dogs are allowed in the camping cabins.

Squaw Flat
Campground/Canyonlands National Park
End of H 211
Moab, UT
435-259-4711 (Needles) (800-322-3770)
nps.gov/cany/
This park provides a colorful landscape of sedimentary sandstone created by the erosion of the Colorado River and it's tributaries. Dogs are allowed on the main roads and in the campground. Dogs are not allowed on the trails, in the back country, or on the 4-wheel drive trails. Dogs must be leashed and cleaned up after. The closest services and gas are about 50 miles away in Monticello. The camping and tent areas also allow dogs. There is a dog walk area at the campground. There are no electric or water hookups at the campground. Multiple dogs may be allowed.

Gouldings RV Park
1000 Main Street
Monument Valley, UT
435-727-3235
Both tent sites and full hookup RV sites are offered at this campground. Rates are from $16 to $26 per site per night. The rates are for two people. There is a $3 per site extra fee per additional person. Well-behaved leashed pets are welcome. Campground amenities includes a view of Monument Valley, heated indoor pool, laundry, hot showers, grocery store, playground and cable TV. The campground is located north of the Arizona and Utah border, adjacent to the Navajo Tribal Park in Monument Valley. They are open year round with limited service from November 1 to March 14. There is a dog walk area at the campground. Multiple dogs may be allowed.

East Canyon State Park
5535 South Highway 66
Morgan, UT
801-829-6866 (877-UTPARKS (887-2757))
Rich in pioneer history, this oasis sits in a mountainous desert at 5,700 feet, and offers a variety of trails, land and water recreation/activities, food service, wildlife viewing, and historic sites. The Donner/Reed party, the Mormons, the Overland

Stage, and the Pony Express all utilized the East Canyon. Now there is boating and year round fun, fishing, camping, and it provides a great get away for travelers. A day-use permit covers your own watercraft launches, and annual passes are available at the visitor's center. Dogs are not allowed on the boat rentals. Dogs of all sizes are allowed at no additional fee, and may be walked anywhere in the park, but they are not allowed on the private property/trails that boundary the park. They must be on a maximum 6 foot leash, and they are not allowed in park buildings. Dogs must be well behaved, and cleaned up after at all times. The camp area offers modern restrooms, hot showers, picnic sites, and your pet is welcome. The camping and tent areas also allow dogs. There is a dog walk area at the campground. Multiple dogs may be allowed.

Panguitch KOA
555 Main Street
Panguitch, UT
435-676-2225 (800-562-1625)
koa.com
Dogs of all sizes are allowed. There are no additional pet fees. Dogs must be leashed and cleaned up after. This RV park is closed during the off-season. The camping and tent areas also allow dogs. There is a dog walk area at the campground. Multiple dogs may be allowed.

Paradise RV Park
2153 N H 89
Panguitch, UT
435-676-8348
Dogs of all sizes are allowed at the tent and RV sites. Only small, lightly furred dogs are allowed at the cabins. There are no additional pet fees. Dogs may not be left unattended, and they must be leashed and cleaned up after. This RV park is closed during the off-season. The camping and tent areas also allow dogs. There is a dog walk area at the campground. Dogs are allowed in the camping cabins.

Red Canyon RV Park
3279 Scenic Highway 12
Panguitch, UT
435-676-2690
This campground sits at 7,400 feet altitude in a Ponderosa Pine setting, and is surround by striking Pink Limestone formations. Sites are available on a first-come, first-served basis, and there are a variety of extensive trail systems for multi-use,

many scenic overlooks, and a visitor's center. Some of the amenities include drinking water, a modern restroom and showers, gaming courts, fire rings and grills, paved sidewalks, free cable TV, and a dump station. Dogs of all sizes are allowed for no additional fee. Dogs must be well behaved, leashed, and cleaned up after at all times. Dogs are allowed throughout the park and on the trails by the park. They are not allowed in park buildings, or on the trails leading into the Bryce Canyon National Park. This RV park is closed during the off-season. The camping and tent areas also allow dogs. There is a dog walk area at the campground. There are no electric or water hookups at the campgrounds. Multiple dogs may be allowed.

Red Canyon Park
P. O. Box 80/H 12
Panguitch, UT
435-676-9300
The beautiful Red Canyon Park can serve as a dog-friendly substitute to see the rock formations that make Bryce Canyon famous. Dogs are not allowed on any trails at Bryce Canyon but are allowed on leash throughout Red Canyon Park. The park sits at a 7,400 foot altitude in a Ponderosa Pine setting surrounded by striking red and pink Limestone formations that rival those of the National Park. There are a variety of extensive trail systems for multi-use, many scenic overlooks (one allows visitors to see 3 different states), and a visitor's center. Dogs of all sizes are allowed for no additional fee. Dogs must be well behaved, leashed, and cleaned up after at all times. Dogs are allowed throughout the park and on the trails by the park. They are not allowed in park buildings, or on the trails leading into the nearby Bryce Canyon National Park. Camp sites are available on a first-come, first-served basis. Some of the amenities include drinking water, modern restroom and showers, gaming courts, fire rings and grills, paved sidewalks, free cable TV, and a dump station. This RV park is closed during the off-season. The camping and tent areas also allow dogs. There is a dog walk area at the campground. Multiple dogs may be allowed.

Red Canyon RV Park
3279 H 12
Panguitch, UT

435-676-2690
redcanyon.net/rc_rvpark
Dogs of all sizes are allowed. There are no additional pet fees. Dogs must be leashed and cleaned up after. This RV park is closed during the off-season. The camping and tent areas also allow dogs. There is a dog walk area at the campground. 2 dogs may be allowed.

Park City RV Resort
2200 Rasmussen Road
Park City, UT
435-649-2535
parkcityrvresort.com
This resort offers a convenient location with dramatic mountain views, concrete pads or acres of grassy sites, and a creek with a bridge. Some of the amenities include showers, fire pits, a club house, game room, a climbing wall, summer concerts, and a variety of other land and water recreation. Dogs of all sizes are allowed at no additional fee. There is a pet policy to sign at check-in. Dogs are allowed in most of the park and on the trails; they are not allowed in any building, in the horseshoe pit area, or the grass areas on the upper level. Your dog must go with you if you leave the campground. Dogs must be on a leash at all times, and cleaned up after immediately. There is also a fenced in dog run on site. There are some breed restrictions. The camping and tent areas also allow dogs. There is a dog walk area at the campground. Multiple dogs may be allowed.

Rockport State Park
9040 North Highway 302
Peoa, UT
435-336-2241 (877-UTPARKS (887-2757))
This state park offers a wide variety of land and water recreation year round, miles of hiking trails, and opportunities for nature study. The park is located at an elevation of 6,000 feet, covers 770 acres with the reservoir at over a thousand water acres, and is home to many wildlife species. The Rockport Sports and Recreation offers boat rentals, and a general store and grill. Dogs ride free and are allowed to join you on one of the watercraft rentals. The pontoon boats appear to be their favorite because of the nice flat bottom. Day use hours are from 6 am until they close the gates at 11 pm, daily. A day-use permit covers your own watercraft launches, and annual passes are available at the visitor's

center. Dogs are allowed at no additional fee. They must be on a maximum 6 foot leash, and they are not allowed in park buildings. Dogs must be well behaved, and cleaned up after at all times. Camping is allowed in any one of 5 developed and primitive campgrounds and your pet is welcome. Services for the campground close for the winter, but if no services are needed, they will allow for RV camping. Campers do not have to pay an additional day use fee for the park. The camping and tent areas also allow dogs. There is a dog walk area at the campground. Multiple dogs may be allowed.

Brigham City/Perry South KOA
1040 W 3600 S
Perry, UT
435-723-5503 (800-562-0903)
koa.com
Dogs of all sizes are allowed. There are no additional pet fees. Dogs must be leashed and cleaned up after. There are some breed restrictions. This RV park is closed during the off-season. The camping and tent areas also allow dogs. There is a dog walk area at the campground. Multiple dogs may be allowed.

Manti-La Sal National Forest
599 W. Price River Dr.
Price, UT
435-636-3500
fs.fed.us/r4/mantilasal/
This forest of more than 1.4 million acres, with elevations from 5,000 feet to over 12,000 feet, provides a variety of landscapes and year round recreational opportunities. Dogs are allowed at no additional fee. Dogs may not be left unattended, and they must be leashed and cleaned up after when in camp areas. Dogs may be off lead in the forest if there is voice control. Dogs are allowed on the trails. This campground is closed during the off-season. The camping and tent areas also allow dogs. There are no electric or water hookups at the campground. Multiple dogs may be allowed.

Lakeside RV Campground
4000 W Center Street
Provo, UT
801-373-5267
lakesidervcampground.com
Dogs of all sizes are allowed. There are no additional pet fees. Dogs may not be left unattended at any time, and they must be quiet, leashed, and cleaned up after. Dogs are not allowed in the store, at the pool, or at

the playground. The camping and tent areas also allow dogs. There is a dog walk area at the campground. Multiple dogs may be allowed.

Provo KOA
320N 2050 W
Provo, UT
801-375-2994 (800-562-1894)
koa.com
Dogs of all sizes are allowed. There are no additional pet fees. Dogs may not be left unattended at the cabins, and they must be leashed and cleaned up after. The camping and tent areas also allow dogs. There is a dog walk area at the campground. Dogs are allowed in the camping cabins. Multiple dogs may be allowed.

Uinta National Forest
88 W 100 N
Provo, UT
801-377-5780 (877-444-6777)
fs.fed.us/r4/uinta
Dogs of all sizes are allowed. There are no additional pet fees. Dogs may not be left unattended, and they must be quiet, well behaved, leashed, and cleaned up after. This campground is closed during the off-season. The camping and tent areas also allow dogs. There is a dog walk area at the campground. There are no water hookups at the campground. Multiple dogs may be allowed.

Utah Lake State Park
4400 West Center Street
Provo, UT
801-375-0733
This park sits at an altitude of 4,500 feet, is Utah's largest freshwater lake at 96,600 acres, offers several species of fish, and a good variety of land and water recreation. Some of the amenities include a full service marina, food service, and a visitor's center. Dogs are allowed at no additional fee. They must be on no more than a 6 foot leash, and they are not allowed in park buildings. They are allowed on the trails and the beach. Dogs may not be left unattended, and they must be cleaned up after quickly. There are 71 sites for camping, and some of the amenities are modern restrooms, showers, drinking water, fishing area for the disabled, and a dump station. Campers do not have to pay an additional day use fee for the park. This RV park is closed during the off-season. The camping and tent areas also allow dogs. There is a dog walk area at the

campground. Multiple dogs may be allowed.

Fishlake National Forest
115 East 900 North
Richfield, UT
435-896-9233 (877-444-6777)
fs.fed.us/r4/fishlake
Dogs of all sizes are allowed. There are no additional pet fees. Dogs may not be left unattended, and they must be leashed and cleaned up after. Dogs are allowed on the trails. This campground is closed during the off-season. The camping and tent areas also allow dogs. There is a dog walk area at the campground. Multiple dogs may be allowed.

Richfield KOA
600 W 600 S
Richfield, UT
435-896-6674 (888-562-4703)
koa.com
Dogs up to about 75 pounds are allowed. There are no additional pet fees. Dogs may not be left unattended, and they must be quiet, leashed, and cleaned up after. There are some breed restrictions. This RV park is closed during the off-season. The camping and tent areas also allow dogs. There is a dog walk area at the campground. 2 dogs may be allowed.

Salt Lake City KOA
1400 W North Temple
Salt Lake City, UT
801-355-1214 (800-562-9510)
koa.com/where/ut/44143/
Dogs of all sizes are allowed. There are no additional pet fees. Dogs may not be left unattended, and they must be quiet, well behaved, leashed, and cleaned up after. The camping and tent areas also allow dogs. There is a dog walk area at the campground. Multiple dogs may be allowed.

Wasatch -Cache National Forest
3285 East 3800 S
Salt Lake City, UT
801-466-6411 (800-322-3770)
fs.fed.us/r4/wcnf/
There are ample recreational opportunities in this forest of over a million acres comprised of high desert and alpine landscapes with 6 ranger districts. Dogs are allowed at no additional fee. Dogs may not be left unattended, and they must be leashed and cleaned up after. Dogs are allowed on the trails, but they are not allowed in any watershed areas. The camping and tent areas also allow dogs. There is a dog walk area at the campground. There are no

water hookups at the campground. Multiple dogs may be allowed.

Quail Run RV Park
9230 S State Street
Sandy, UT
801-255-9300
quailrunrvpark.com
Dogs of all sizes are allowed. There are no additional pet fees. Dogs must be quiet, well behaved, leashed, and cleaned up after. Dogs may not be left unattended, or chained to the lamp posts or trees. Multiple dogs may be allowed.

Fremont Indian State Park
3820 W Clear Creek Canyon Road
Sevier, UT
435-527-4631
Historical, recreational, scenic, and geologically popular can all describe this park. You can pick up a trail guide at the visitor's center that will guide you to rock art panels, geological wonders, dramatic viewpoints, bubble caves, and a favorite trail takes you to an amazing canyon overlook area. There is an ATV trail system that runs through the park, but the hiking trails are for non-motorized use only. There is also a visitor's center and a museum of the Indian village uncovered here. Dogs are allowed at no additional fee. They must be on a maximum 6 foot leash at all times, and they are not allowed in park buildings. Dogs are allowed on all the trails and at the overlook areas. Dogs must be well behaved, and cleaned up after at all times. The Castle Rock Campground is the only place you can camp in the park, and it offers a scenic setting complete with a creek, flush toilets, and your pet is welcome. Campers do not have to pay an additional day use fee for the park. The camping and tent areas also allow dogs. There is a dog walk area at the campground. There are no electric or water hookups at the campgrounds. Multiple dogs may be allowed.

Zion Canyon Campground & Resort
479 Zion Park Blvd
Springdale, UT
435-772-3237
zioncamp.com
Dogs of all sizes are allowed. There are no additional pet fees. Dogs may not be left inside a tent or outside on any site unattended, and they may be left in an RV only if there is air conditioning. Dogs must be quiet, well behaved, leashed, and cleaned up after. There are some breed

restrictions. The camping and tent areas also allow dogs. There is a dog walk area at the campground. 2 dogs may be allowed.

Snow Canyon State Park
1002 Snow Canyon Drive (H 18)
St George, UT
435-628-2255 (800-322-3770)
Sand dunes, quiet beauty, and many trails bring visitors to this park. Dogs are allowed at no additional fee. Dogs may not be left unattended, and they must be leashed and cleaned up after. Dogs are allowed on the Whiptail Trail and the West Canyon Trail only. The camping and tent areas also allow dogs. There is a dog walk area at the campground. Multiple dogs may be allowed.

Templeview RV Resort
975 S Main
St George, UT
800-381-0321
templeviewrv.com
Dogs of all sizes are allowed. There are no additional pet fees unless the stay is monthly; then there is a $5 additional pet fee. Dogs must be leashed and cleaned up after. The camping and tent areas also allow dogs. There is a dog walk area at the campground. 2 dogs may be allowed.

Palisade State Park
2200 Palisade Road
Sterling, UT
435-835-7275 (800-322-3770)
The Palisade Reservoir of 70 acres provides many water sports. There is a golf course, driving range, several trails, and Six-Mile Canyon for the off-roaders. Dogs are allowed at no additional fee. Dogs may not be left unattended, and they must be leashed and cleaned up after. Dogs are allowed on the trails. The camping and tent areas also allow dogs. There is a dog walk area at the campground. Multiple dogs may be allowed.

Antelope Island State Park
4528 West 1700 South
Syracuse, UT
801-773-2941
This park is easily accessed over a 7-mile paved causeway, or by boat and an abundance of flora and fauna, a bison herd, and numerous migrating birds are some of the things that await you. The visitor center offers information on the island's unique biology, geology and history, and some of the amenities

include white sandy beaches, a sailboat marina, nearly 40 miles of hiking and multi-use trails, wildlife viewing, picnicking, and, because of the distance from the city and its lights, stargazing. Hours vary throughout the year. Dogs of all sizes are allowed at no additional fee. Dogs are not allowed on the beach, park buildings, or on Prairie Creek Trail; other trails are okay. Dogs must be on no more than a 6 foot leash and cleaned up after at all times. Camping is allowed in designated areas only, and they offer modern restrooms, showers, a food service area, and drinking water. Campers do not have to pay an additional day use fee for the park. The camping and tent areas also allow dogs. There is a dog walk area at the campground. There are no electric or water hookups at the campgrounds. Multiple dogs may be allowed.

Ashley National Forest
355 N Vernal Avenue
Vernal, UT
435-789-1181 (877-444-6777)
fs.fed.us/r4/ashley/
Dogs of all sizes are allowed. There are no additional pet fees. Dogs may not be left unattended, and they must be leashed and cleaned up after. This campground is closed during the off-season. The camping and tent areas also allow dogs. There is a dog walk area at the campground. Multiple dogs may be allowed.

Red Fleet State Park
8750 North Highway 191
Vernal, UT
435-789-4432 (877-UTPARKS (877-2757))
Red Fleet is almost 2,000 acres with a reservoir of 750 water acres, and sits in what is known as 'the heart of Dinosaurland' at an elevation of 5,500 feet. Tracks believed to be more than 200 million years old can be reached by hiking a rather strenuous 1.25 mile trail of several up and down sections. There is a variety of land and water recreation, hiking trails, wildlife viewing, and camping and/or picnicking. Day use permits cover personal watercraft launches, and annual passes are available at the visitor's center. Park hours are shortened for the winter. Dogs are allowed throughout the park, on the trails, and on the beach. Dogs must be on a maximum 6 foot leash, and they are not allowed in park buildings. Dogs must be well behaved, and cleaned up after at all

times. The campground overlooks a sandstone and desert landscape, and they offer modern restrooms, picnic sites, and drinking water. Campers do not have to pay an additional day use fee for the park. The camping and tent areas also allow dogs. There is a dog walk area at the campground. There are no electric or water hookups at the campgrounds. Multiple dogs may be allowed.

Vernal/Dinosaurland KOA
930 N Vernal Avenue
Vernal, UT
435-789-2148
koa.com/where/ut/44152/
Dogs of all sizes are allowed. There are no additional pet fees. Dogs may not be left unattended at any time, and they must be quiet, leashed, and cleaned up after. Only 2 dogs at a time are allowed in the cabins, and up to 3 dogs at the tent or RV sites. There are some breed restrictions. This RV park is closed during the off-season. The camping and tent areas also allow dogs. There is a dog walk area at the campground. Dogs are allowed in the camping cabins.

Zion River Resort
730 E H 9
Virgin, UT
800-838-8594
zionriverresort.com
Dogs of all sizes are allowed. There are no additional pet fees. Dogs must be leashed and cleaned up after. There is a fenced in area where dogs may run off lead. There is a dog walk area at the campground. 2 dogs may be allowed.

Willard Bay State Park
900 West 650 North #A/ On H 315
Willard, UT
435-734-9494 (800-322-3770)
Willard Bay has 2 marinas open to the public, and is a freshwater reservoir providing fresh water for farming as well as recreation. Dogs are allowed at no additional fee. Dogs may not be left unattended, and they must be leashed and cleaned up after. Dogs are allowed on the trails. The camping and tent areas also allow dogs. There is a dog walk area at the campground. Multiple dogs may be allowed.

Vermont

Alburg RV Resort
1 Blue Rock Road
Alburg, VT
802-796-3733
Dogs of all sizes are allowed. There are no additional pet fees. Dogs are not allowed at the pool or lake, must be leashed at all times, and cleaned up after. This RV park is closed during the off-season. There is a dog walk area at the campground. Multiple dogs may be allowed.

Camping on the Battenkill
Route 7A-Camping on the Battenkill
Arlington, VT
802-375-6663
Dogs of all sizes are allowed. There are no additional pet fees. Dogs must have a current rabies certificate, be on leash and cleaned up after. This RV park is closed during the off-season. There is a dog walk area at the campground. Multiple dogs may be allowed.

Wilgus State Park
On H 5
Ascutney, VT
802-674-5422 (888-409-7579)
vtstateparks.com
Dogs of all sizes are allowed. There are no additional pet fees. Dogs may not be left unattended, and they must be leashed and cleaned up after. Dogs are not allowed on the beach, the picnic areas, the day use area, and they must have proof of rabies shots. This campground is closed during the off-season. The camping and tent areas also allow dogs. There is a dog walk area at the campground. Multiple dogs may be allowed.

Greenwood Lodge and Campsites
311 Greenwood Drive
Bennington, VT
802-442-2547
campvermont.com/greenwood
Dogs of all sizes are allowed. There are no additional pet fees. Dogs must have their shot records and they may not be left unattended. Dogs must be quiet, leashed and cleaned up after. They are allowed to swim at the lake and be off lead at that time if the owner has voice control, but they may not swim in any of the ponds. This RV park is closed during the off-season. The camping and tent areas also allow

dogs. There is a dog walk area at the campground. 2 dogs may be allowed.

Woodford State Park
142 State Park Road
Bennington, VT
802-447-7169 (888-409-7579)
You'll get great views here; the state's highest park at 2,400 feet sits amid plush vegetation, trees, and bodies of water with 398 recreational acres and plenty of hiking trails. Dogs of all sizes are allowed for no additional pet fee, and they must be declared at the time of reservation. All dogs must have proof of rabies inoculation, be on no more than a 10 foot leash or crated, and cleaned up after at all times. Dogs must be quiet, well behaved, and never left unattended. Dogs are not allowed at beaches, picnic areas, or playgrounds; they are allowed on the trails and camping areas. The camp area offers 103 sites (including 20 lean-tos), flush toilets, hot showers ($), and a dump station. This RV park is closed during the off-season. The camping and tent areas also allow dogs. There is a dog walk area at the campground. There are no electric or water hookups at the campgrounds. Multiple dogs may be allowed.

Smoke Rise Campground
2111 Grove Street
Brandon, VT
802-247-6984
Dogs of all sizes are allowed. There are no additional pet fees. Dogs may not be left unattended, must be leashed, and cleaned up after. This RV park is closed during the off-season. The camping and tent areas also allow dogs. There is a dog walk area at the campground. Multiple dogs may be allowed.

Fort Dummer State Park
517 Old Guilford Road
Brattleboro, VT
802-254-2610 (888-409-7579)
In addition to offering a rich cultural history, this forested park offers 217 acres for recreational use. Dogs of all sizes are allowed for no additional pet fee, and they must be declared at the time of reservation. All dogs must have proof of rabies inoculation, be on no more than a 10 foot leash or crated, and cleaned up after at all times. Dogs must be quiet, well behaved, and never left unattended. Dogs are not allowed in picnic areas or playgrounds; they are allowed on the trails and camping areas. The

camp area has 51 sites and 10 lean-tos, restrooms, hot showers ($), a large open grassy field, and a dump station. This RV park is closed during the off-season. The camping and tent areas also allow dogs. There is a dog walk area at the campground. There are no electric or water hookups at the campgrounds. Multiple dogs may be allowed.

Canton Place Campground
2419 East Road
Cavendish, VT
802-226-7767
Dogs of all sizes are allowed. There are no additional pet fees. Dogs must be leashed and cleaned up after. This RV park is closed during the off-season. The camping and tent areas also allow dogs. There is a dog walk area at the campground. Multiple dogs may be allowed.

Mount Philo State Park
5425 Mt Philo Road
Charlotte, VT
802-425-2390 (888-409-7579)
vtstateparks.com/htm/philo.cfm
This scenic park offers some great hiking areas and is the state's oldest state park. Because of the steep road, trailers are not recommended. Dogs of all sizes are allowed for no additional pet fee, and they must be declared at the time of reservation. All dogs must have proof of rabies inoculation, be on no more than a 10 foot leash or crated, and cleaned up after at all times. Dogs must be quiet, well behaved, and never left unattended. Dogs are not allowed in picnic areas or playgrounds; they are allowed on the trails and camping areas. The camp area has a total of 10 sites (including 3 lean-tos) with great views of the lake and valley, flush toilets, and showers ($). This RV park is closed during the off-season. The camping and tent areas also allow dogs. There is a dog walk area at the campground. There are no electric or water hookups at the campgrounds. Multiple dogs may be allowed.

Lone Pine Campsites
52 Sunset View Road
Colchester, VT
802-878-5447
lonepinecampsites.com
One dog of any size is allowed. There are no additional pet fees. Dogs may not be left unattended, must be leashed, and cleaned up after. There are some breed restrictions. This RV park is closed during the off-season. The camping

and tent areas also allow dogs. There is a dog walk area at the campground.

Sugar Ridge RV Village
24 Old Stage Coach Road
Danville, VT
802-684-2550
sugarridgervpark.com
Dogs of all sizes are allowed. There are no additional pet fees. Dogs must current rabies certificate, and be leashed and cleaned up after. Dogs are not allowed in the rentals. This RV park is closed during the off-season. There is a dog walk area at the campground. Multiple dogs may be allowed.

Dorset RV Park
1567 H 30
Dorset, VT
802-867-5754
dorsetrv.com
Dogs of all sizes are allowed. There are no additional pet fees. Dogs may not be left unattended, must be leashed, and cleaned up after. This RV park is closed during the off-season. The camping and tent areas also allow dogs. There is a dog walk area at the campground. Multiple dogs may be allowed.

Emerald Lakes State Park
75 Emerald Lake Lane
East Dorset, VT
802-254-2610
vtstateparks.com
Dogs of all sizes are allowed. There are no additional pet fees. Dogs may not be left unattended at any time, they must be on no more than a 10 foot leash, and be cleaned up after. Dogs are not allowed in any day use areas, including parking lots, picnic areas, playgrounds, beaches, or buildings. Dogs must be at least 6 months old and have a current rabies certificate and shot records. Dogs on leash are allowed on the trails. The camping and tent areas also allow dogs. There is a dog walk area at the campground. There are no electric or water hookups at the campground. Multiple dogs may be allowed.

KOA Brattleboro N
1238 US Route 5
East Dummerston, VT
802-254-5908 (800-562-5909)
koa.com
Dogs of all sizes are allowed. There are no additional pet fees. Dogs must be leashed and cleaned up after. This RV park is closed during the off-season. The camping and

tent areas also allow dogs. There is a dog walk area at the campground. 2 dogs may be allowed.

Rest N Nest Campground
300 Latham
East Thetford, VT
802-785-2997
restnnest.com
Dogs of all sizes are allowed. There are no additional pet fees. Dogs may not be left unattended, must be leashed, and cleaned up after. This RV park is closed during the off-season. The camping and tent areas also allow dogs. There is a dog walk area at the campground. Multiple dogs may be allowed.

Lake Carmi State Park
460 Marsh Farm Rd
Enosburg Falls, VT
802-933-8383
vtstateparks.com
Dogs of all sizes are allowed. There are no additional pet fees. Dogs may not be left unattended at any time, they must be on no more than a 10 foot leash, and be cleaned up after. Dogs are not allowed in any day use areas, including parking lots, picnic areas, beach and swim areas, playgrounds, or buildings. Dogs must be at least 6 months old and have a current rabies certificate and shot records. Dogs on lead are allowed on the trails. The camping and tent areas also allow dogs. There is a dog walk area at the campground. Dogs are allowed in the camping cabins. There are no electric or water hookups at the campground. Multiple dogs may be allowed.

Bomoseen State Park
22 Cedar Mountain Rd,
Fair Haven, VT
802-265-4242
vtstateparks.com
Dogs of all sizes are allowed. There are no additional pet fees. Dogs may not be left unattended at any time, they must be on no more than a 10 foot leash, and be cleaned up after. Dogs are not allowed in any day use areas, including parking lots, picnic areas, beach and swim areas, playgrounds, or buildings. Dogs must be at least 6 months old and have a current rabies certificate and shot records. Dogs on leash are allowed on the trails. The camping and tent areas also allow dogs. There is a dog walk area at the campground. There are no electric or water hookups at the campground. Multiple dogs may be allowed.

Grand Isle State Park
36 East Shore South
Grand Isle, VT
802-372-4300 (888-409-7579)
Located on the largest island on the lake, this 226 acre park is a commemorative to the early settlers who lived here that served in the American Revolution, and offers a variety of land and water recreation. Dogs of all sizes are allowed for no additional pet fee, and they must be declared at the time of reservation. All dogs must have proof of rabies inoculation, be on no more than a 10 foot leash or crated, and cleaned up after at all times. Dogs must be quiet, well behaved, and never left unattended. Dogs are not allowed at the cabins, beaches, picnic areas, or playgrounds; they are allowed on the trails and camping areas. This is the state's 2nd largest state campground, and they have running water, hot showers, a dump station, gaming areas, and sites large enough to take self-contained RVs. This RV park is closed during the off-season. The camping and tent areas also allow dogs. There is a dog walk area at the campground. There are no electric or water hookups at the campgrounds. Multiple dogs may be allowed.

Big Deer State Park
303 Boulder Beach Road
Groton, VT
802-372-4300
vtstateparks.com
Dogs of all sizes are allowed. There are no additional pet fees. Dogs may not be left unattended, and they must be on no more than a 10 foot leash, and be cleaned up after. Dogs are not allowed at the swim beach, however dogs are allowed to swim at the beach by the boat docks. Dogs must have current rabies shot records. There are a series of trails nearby, and dogs on lead are allowed. This campground is closed during the off-season. The camping and tent areas also allow dogs. There is a dog walk area at the campground. There are no electric or water hookups at the campground. Multiple dogs may be allowed.

Stillwatere State Park
44 Stillwater Road
Groton, VT
802-584-3822
vtstateparks.com
Dogs of all sizes are allowed. There are no additional pet fees. Dogs may not be left unattended, they must be on no more than a 10 foot leash, and

be cleaned up after. Dogs are not allowed at the swim beach, however dogs are allowed to swim at the beach by the boat docks. Dogs must have current rabies shot records. There are a series of trails nearby, and dogs on lead are allowed. This campground is closed during the off-season. The camping and tent areas also allow dogs. There is a dog walk area at the campground. There are no electric or water hookups at the campground. Multiple dogs may be allowed.

Lake Bomoseen Campground
18 Campground Drive
Hubbardton, VT
802-273-2061
lakebomoseen.com
Dogs of all sizes are allowed. There is a $1 per night per pet additional fee. Dogs may not be left unattended, must be leashed, and cleaned up after. Dogs must have shot records. There are some breed restrictions. This RV park is closed during the off-season. The camping and tent areas also allow dogs. There is a dog walk area at the campground. Multiple dogs may be allowed.

Brighton State Park
102 State Park Road
Island Pond, VT
802-723-4360
vtstateparks.com
Dogs of all sizes are allowed. There are no additional pet fees. Dogs may not be left unattended at any time, and they must be quiet, well behaved, leashed and cleaned up after. Dogs are not allowed on the beach, the trails, the day use areas, or the buildings. Dogs must have up to date rabies shot records and a current license. This campground is closed during the off-season. The camping and tent areas also allow dogs. There is a dog walk area at the campground. There are no electric or water hookups at the campground. Multiple dogs may be allowed.

Jamaica State Park
285 Salmon Hole Lane
Jamaica, VT
802-874-4600
vtstateparks.com
Dogs of all sizes are allowed. There are no additional pet fees. Dogs may not be left unattended at any time, they must be on no more than a 10 foot leash, and be cleaned up after. Dogs are not allowed in any

day use areas, including parking lots, picnic areas, beach and swim areas, playgrounds, or buildings. Dogs must be at least 6 months old and have a current rabies certificate and shot records. Dogs on leash are allowed on all the trails, except the children's nature trail. The camping and tent areas also allow dogs. There is a dog walk area at the campground. There are no electric or water hookups at the campground. Multiple dogs may be allowed.

Elmore State Park
856 H 12
Lake Elmore, VT
802-888-2982
vtstateparks.com
Dogs of all sizes are allowed. There are no additional pet fees. Dogs may not be left unattended, and they must be leashed and cleaned up after. Dogs are not allowed on the beach, the picnic areas, or in day use areas. Dogs on lead are allowed on the trails. Dogs must have current rabies shot records. This campground is closed during the off-season. The camping and tent areas also allow dogs. There is a dog walk area at the campground. There are no electric or water hookups at the campground. Multiple dogs may be allowed.

New Discovery State Park
4239 H 232
Marshfield, VT
802-426-3042
vtstateparks.com
Dogs of all sizes are allowed. There are no additional pet fees. Dogs may not be left unattended at any time, they must be on no more than a 10 foot leash, and be cleaned up after. Dogs are not allowed in any day use areas, including parking lots, picnic areas, playgrounds, or buildings. Dogs must be at least 6 months old and have a current rabies certificate and shot records. Dogs on leash are allowed on the trails. The camping and tent areas also allow dogs. There is a dog walk area at the campground. There are no electric or water hookups at the campground. Multiple dogs may be allowed.

Homestead Campgrounds
864 Ethan Allen H
Milton, VT
802-524-2356
homesteadcampgrounds.net
Dogs of all sizes are allowed. There are no additional pet fees. Dogs must be well behaved, be on a leash, and cleaned up after. This RV park is closed during the off-season. The

camping and tent areas also allow dogs. There is a dog walk area at the campground. Multiple dogs may be allowed.

Green Valley Campground
1368 H 2
Montpelier, VT
802-223-6217
greenvalleyrvpark.com
Dogs of all sizes are allowed. There are no additional pet fees. Dogs may not be left unattended, must be leashed, and cleaned up after. This RV park is closed during the off-season. The camping and tent areas also allow dogs. There is a dog walk area at the campground. Multiple dogs may be allowed.

North Hero State Park
3803 Lakeview Drive
North Hero, VT
802-372-8727
vtstateparks.com
Dogs of all sizes are allowed. There are no additional pet fees. Dogs may not be left unattended at any time, they must be on no more than a 10 foot leash, and be cleaned up after. Dogs are not allowed in any day use areas, including parking lots, picnic areas, pools, beaches, playgrounds, or buildings. Dogs must be at least 6 months old and have a current rabies certificate and shot records. Dogs on leash are allowed on the trails. The camping and tent areas also allow dogs. There is a dog walk area at the campground. There are no electric or water hookups at the campground. Multiple dogs may be allowed.

Crown Point Camping
131 Bishop Camp Road
Perkinsville, VT
802-263-5555
crownpointcamping.com
Dogs of all sizes are allowed. There are no additional pet fees. Dogs must be well behaved and leashed and cleaned up after. The camping and tent areas also allow dogs. There is a dog walk area at the campground. Multiple dogs may be allowed.

Coolidge State Park
855 Coolidge State Park Road
Plymouth, VT
802-672-3612
vtstateparks.com
Dogs of all sizes are allowed. There are no additional pet fees. Dogs may not be left unattended, and they must be leashed and cleaned up after. Dogs must have current rabies shot records. Dog on lead are allowed on

the trails. This campground is closed during the off-season. The camping and tent areas also allow dogs. There is a dog walk area at the campground. There are no electric or water hookups at the campground. Multiple dogs may be allowed.

Lake St Catherine State Park
3034 H 30S
Poultney, VT
802-287-9158
vtstateparks.com
Dogs of all sizes are allowed. There are no additional pet fees. Dogs may not be left unattended at any time, they must be on no more than a 10 foot leash, and be cleaned up after. Dogs are not allowed in any day use areas, including parking lots, picnic areas, pools, beaches, playgrounds, or buildings. Dogs must be quiet during quiet hours. Dogs must be at least 6 months old and have a current rabies certificate and shot records. Dogs on leash are allowed on the trails. The camping and tent areas also allow dogs. There is a dog walk area at the campground. There are no electric or water hookups at the campground. Multiple dogs may be allowed.

Lake Champagne Campground
53 Lake Champagne Drive
Randolph Center, VT
802-728-5293
lakechampagne.com
Dogs of all sizes are allowed. There are no additional pet fees. Dogs must be leashed and cleaned up after; they are not allowed on the beach or the picnic areas. This RV park is closed during the off-season. The camping and tent areas also allow dogs. There is a dog walk area at the campground. Multiple dogs may be allowed.

Green Mountain National Forest
On H 7N
Rutland, VT
802-747-6700
vtstateparks.com
Dogs of all sizes are allowed. There are no additional pet fees. Dogs may not be left unattended, and they must be well behaved, leashed, and cleaned up after. Dogs are not allowed in the picnic or pond areas. Dogs on lead are allowed on all the trails. There are 7 campgrounds in this national forest, 2 remain open all year. The camping and tent areas also allow dogs. There is a dog walk area at

the campground. There are no electric or water hookups at the campground. Multiple dogs may be allowed.

Lake Dunmore
1457 Lake Dunmore Road
Salisbury, VT
802-352-4501
kampersville.com
Dogs of all sizes are allowed. There are no additional pet fees. Dogs must have current shot records, be well behaved, and be leashed and cleaned up after. This RV park is closed during the off-season. The camping and tent areas also allow dogs. There is a dog walk area at the campground. 2 dogs may be allowed.

Shelburne Camping Area
4385 Shelburne Road
Shelburne, VT
802-985-2540
shelburnecamping.com
Dogs of all sizes are allowed. There are no additional pet fees. Dogs may not be left unattended, must be leashed at all times, and cleaned up after. The camping and tent areas also allow dogs. There is a dog walk area at the campground. Multiple dogs may be allowed.

Apple Island Resort
71 H 2W
South Hero, VT
802-372-3800
appleislandresort.com/
Some of the perks at this 188 acre resort are their marina, a 9-hole executive golf course, lots of special events, many planned fun activities, and a full service campground with all the extras including a heated pool and hot tub. Dogs of all sizes are allowed for no additional pet fee; however, they must be current on tags and shots. Dogs must be well behaved, leashed, cleaned up after at all times, and may never be left unattended. Dogs are allowed throughout the park, on the trails, and they are also allowed on watercraft rentals. This RV park is closed during the off-season. The camping and tent areas also allow dogs. There is a dog walk area at the campground.

Burton Island State Park
Burton Island
St Albans, VT
802-524-6353 (800-449-2580)
vtstateparks.com/htm/burton.cfm
This 253 acre island park is accessible only by boat; ferry service

is available from Kill Kare State Park. No RVs can get to the island and only tent camping is available. There is a 100 slip full-service marina, boat moorings, a nature center/museum, and plenty of hiking trails. Dogs of all sizes are allowed for no additional pet fee, and they must be declared at the time of reservation. All dogs must have proof of rabies inoculation, be on no more than a 10 foot leash or crated, and cleaned up after at all times. Dogs must be quiet, well behaved, and never left unattended. Dogs are not allowed at the pool, beaches, picnic areas, or playgrounds; they are allowed on the trails and camping area. The camp area offers 17 tent sites, 26 lean-to sites, picnic areas, restrooms with hot showers, a park store, and food service. This campground is closed during the off-season. The camping and tent areas also allow dogs. There is a dog walk area at the campground. There are no electric or water hookups at the campgrounds. Multiple dogs may be allowed.

Moose River Campground
2870 Portland Street
St Johnsbury, VT
802-748-4334
mooserivercampground.com
Dogs of all sizes are allowed. There are no additional pet fees. Dogs must be quiet and may not be left unattended. Dogs must be leashed and cleaned up after. Pets are not allowed in any of the rentals. This RV park is closed during the off-season. The camping and tent areas also allow dogs. There is a dog walk area at the campground. Multiple dogs may be allowed.

Smugglers Notch State Park
6443 Mountain Road/H 108
Stowe, VT
802-253-4014 (888-409-7579)
This corridor park provides easy access for some great picnicking along this scenic byway, and it is also a trailhead for some of the state's most popular hiking trails. Dogs of all sizes are allowed for no additional pet fee, and they must be declared at the time of reservation. All dogs must have proof of rabies inoculation, be on no more than a 10 foot leash or crated, and cleaned up after at all times. Dogs must be quiet, well behaved, and never left unattended. Dogs are not allowed in picnic areas or playgrounds; they are allowed on the trails and camping areas. The campground offers great views, water, hot showers,

restrooms, and a dump station. This RV park is closed during the off-season. The camping and tent areas also allow dogs. There is a dog walk area at the campground. There are no electric or water hookups at the campgrounds. Multiple dogs may be allowed.

Thetford Hill State Park
622 Academy Road
Thetford Center, VT
802-785-2266
vtstateparks.com
Dogs of all sizes are allowed. There are no additional pet fees. Dogs may not be left unattended at any time, they must be on no more than a 10 foot leash, and be cleaned up after. Dogs are not allowed in any day use areas, including parking lots, picnic areas, beach and swim areas, playgrounds, or buildings. Dogs must be at least 6 months old and have a current rabies certificate and shot records. Dogs on leash are allowed on the trails. The camping and tent areas also allow dogs. There is a dog walk area at the campground. There are no electric or water hookups at the campground. Multiple dogs may be allowed.

Bald Mountain Campground
1760 State Forest Road
Townshend, VT
802-365-7510
Dogs of all sizes are allowed. There are no additional pet fees. Dogs may not be left unattended, and must be leashed and cleaned up after. This RV park is closed during the off-season. The camping and tent areas also allow dogs. There is a dog walk area at the campground. Multiple dogs may be allowed.

Townshend State Park
2755 State Forest Road
Townshend, VT
802-365-7500 (888-409-7579)
This park is located at the foot of the mountain on a bend in the river with a 1,100 foot, vertical, geologically interesting trail that leads to the top of the mountain and panoramic views. Dogs of all sizes are allowed for no additional pet fee, and they must be declared at the time of reservation. All dogs must have proof of rabies inoculation, be on no more than a 10 foot leash or crated, and cleaned up after at all times. Dogs must be quiet, well behaved, and never left unattended. Dogs are not allowed on beaches, at picnic areas, or

playgrounds; they are allowed on the trails and camping areas. The wooded camp area has 30 sites and 4 lean-tos, restrooms, and showers ($). This RV park is closed during the off-season. The camping and tent areas also allow dogs. There is a dog walk area at the campground. There are no electric or water hookups at the campgrounds. Multiple dogs may be allowed.

Button Bay State Park
5 Button Bay State Park Road
Vergennes, VT
802-475-2377 (888-409-7579)
Sitting high on the bluff, this 253 acre treed park features large grassy fields overlooking the lake, picnic areas, a playground, and plenty of land and water recreation. Dogs of all sizes are allowed for no additional pet fee, and they must be declared at the time of reservation. All dogs must have proof of rabies inoculation, be on no more than a 10 foot leash or crated, and cleaned up after at all times. Dogs must be quiet, well behaved, and never left unattended. Dogs are not allowed at the pool, beaches, picnic areas, or playgrounds; they are allowed on the trails and camping areas. The camp area offers 73 sites and 13 lean-tos, flush toilets, showers, and a dump station. This RV park is closed during the off-season. The camping and tent areas also allow dogs. There is a dog walk area at the campground. There are no electric or water hookups at the campgrounds. Multiple dogs may be allowed.

Pine Valley RV Resort
3700 Woodstock Road
White River Junction, VT
802-296-6711
pinevalleyrv.com
Dogs of all sizes are allowed. There are no additional pet fees. Dogs must be well behaved, not left unattended, and must be leashed and cleaned up after. There are some breed restrictions. This RV park is closed during the off-season. There is a dog walk area at the campground. Multiple dogs may be allowed.

Quechee / Pine Valley KOA
3700 Woodstock Road
White River Junction, VT
802-296-6711 (800-562-1621)
koa.com/where/vt/45122/
A pond with canoe and pedal boat rentals, free Wi-Fi, a laundry facilities, cable TV, a camp store, a seasonal pool, and more can

be enjoyed at this campground. They are also close to a number of attractions in the area. Dogs are allowed for no additional fee. Dogs may not be left unattended outside, and they may only be left alone inside if they will be quiet. Dogs must be on no more than a 6 foot leash and cleaned up after at all times. There are some breed restrictions. The camping and tent areas also allow dogs. There is a dog walk area at the campground. Multiple dogs may be allowed.

Quechee Gorge State Park
764 Dewey Mills Road
White River Junction, VT
802-295-2990
vtstateparks.com
Dogs of all sizes are allowed. There are no additional pet fees. Dogs may not be left unattended at any time, they must be on no more than a 10 foot leash, and be cleaned up after. Dogs are not allowed in any day use areas, including parking lots, picnic areas, beach and swim areas, playgrounds, or buildings. Dogs must be at least 6 months old and have a current rabies certificate and shot records. Dogs on leash are allowed on the trails. The camping and tent areas also allow dogs. There is a dog walk area at the campground. There are no electric or water hookups at the campground. Multiple dogs may be allowed.

Limehurst Lake Campground
4104 H 14
Williamstown, VT
802-433-6662
limehurstlake.com
Dogs of all sizes are allowed. There are no additional pet fees. Dogs must be quiet, well behaved, and leashed and cleaned up after. There are some breed restrictions. This RV park is closed during the off-season. The camping and tent areas also allow dogs. There is a dog walk area at the campground. Dogs are allowed in the camping cabins. Multiple dogs may be allowed.

Molly Stark State Park
705 Route 9 East
Wilmington, VT
802-464-5460 (888-409-7579)
This park offers wide open lawn areas, woods, picnic areas, amazing fall foliage, and a hiking trail that leads to an old fire tower and some fantastic views. Dogs of all sizes are allowed for no additional pet fee, and they must be declared at the time of reservation. All dogs must have proof

of rabies inoculation, be on no more than a 10 foot leash or crated, and cleaned up after at all times. Dogs must be quiet, well behaved, and never left unattended. Dogs are not allowed at the picnic areas or playgrounds; they are allowed on the trails and camping areas. The camping loops have 23 sites and 11 lean-tos, restrooms, showers, and a playground. This RV park is closed during the off-season. The camping and tent areas also allow dogs. There is a dog walk area at the campground. There are no electric or water hookups at the campgrounds. Multiple dogs may be allowed.

Ascutney State Park
1826 Back Mountain Road
Windsor, VT
802-674-2060
vtstateparks.com
Dogs of all sizes are allowed. There are no additional pet fees. Dogs may not be left unattended at any time, they must be on no more than a 10 foot leash, and be cleaned up after. Dogs are not allowed in any day use areas, including parking lots, picnic areas, beach and swim areas, playgrounds, or buildings. Dogs must be at least 6 months old and have a current rabies certificate and shot records. Dogs on leash are allowed on the trails. The camping and tent areas also allow dogs. There is a dog walk area at the campground. There are no electric or water hookups at the campground. Multiple dogs may be allowed.

Virginia

Holiday Lake State Park
Rt 2, Box 622; State Park Road 692
Appomattox, VA
434-248-6308 (800-933-PARK (7275))
A paradise for the outdoor enthusiast, this park offers a variety of land and water activities, and recreational pursuits. Dogs of all sizes are allowed for $3 per night per dog. Dogs must be leashed and cleaned up after. Dogs may be left tethered on site if they will be quiet, well behaved, are shaded, and have food and water. Dogs are allowed on the trails, but they are not allowed in the lake. The camping and tent areas also allow dogs.

There is a dog walk area at the campground. Multiple dogs may be allowed.

Peaks of Otter Lodge and Campground
Mile Post 86 Blue Ridge Parkway
Bedford, VA
540-586-7321
blueridgeparkway.org/
Although dogs are not allowed at the lodge here, they are allowed at the campground for no additional fee. A 24 acre lake with a 1-mile loop trail, a visitor center, amphitheater, and gift shop are some of the features here. Campsites are on a first come first served basis, and provide drinking water, restrooms, and a dump station. There are several hiking trails, including the Sharp Top Trail which marked the most northern land of the Cherokee Nation. Dogs are allowed throughout the park and on the trails. Dogs must be well behaved, under owner's control, on no more than a 6 foot leash, and cleaned up after at all times. This RV park is closed during the off-season. The camping and tent areas also allow dogs. There is a dog walk area at the campground. There are no electric or water hookups at the campgrounds. Multiple dogs may be allowed.

Otter Creek Campground
Blue Ridge Parkway M.P. 60.8
Big Island, VA
434-299 5941
blueridgeparkway.org/
There are 45 tent and 24 RV sites available on a first come first served basis with many by the river, and campfire circles, drinking water, restrooms, dump stations, concessionaires, and interpretive services are available here. Four beautiful trails can be accessed, one being the James River Canal Trail leading to the restored 1845-51 canal locks that went from Richmond to Buchanan, Virginia. Dogs are allowed throughout the park and on the trails for no additional pet fee. Dogs must be well behaved, under owner's control, on no more than a 6 foot leash, and cleaned up after at all times. This RV park is closed during the off-season. The camping and tent areas also allow dogs. There is a dog walk area at the campground. There are no electric or water hookups at the campgrounds.

Breaks Interstate Park
769 H 80
Breaks, VA

276-865-4413
This year round 4,600 acre park has often been called the "Little Grand Canyon", and in addition to panoramic views, there is a wide variety of land and water activities. Dogs are allowed at no additional fee for camping; there is a $7 per night per pet additional fee for the lodge. Dogs may not be left unattended in rooms, but they may be tethered in the camp area if they will be well behaved, quiet, and checked in on. Dogs are allowed on the trails. This campground is closed during the off-season. The camping and tent areas also allow dogs. There is a dog walk area at the campground. Dogs are allowed in the camping cabins. Multiple dogs may be allowed.

Harrisonburg/New Market
12480 Mountain Valley Road
Broadway, VA
540-896-8929 (800-562-5406)
koa.com
Up to 2 dogs are allowed per RV or tent site, at no additional fee. There is a $20 per stay fee for one dog only in the cabins. Dogs may not be left unattended, must be leashed, and cleaned up after. The camping and tent areas also allow dogs. There is a dog walk area at the campground. Dogs are allowed in the camping cabins.

Bull Run Regional Park
7700 Bull Run Drive
Centreville, VA
703-631-0550
nvrpa.org/bullruncamp.html
This scenic park offers year round recreation, and is close to Washington DC, and other area attractions. Dogs of all sizes are allowed at no additional fee. Dogs may not be left unattended, and they must be leashed and cleaned up after. Dogs are not allowed in the pool area, but they are allowed on the trails. The camping and tent areas also allow dogs. There is a dog walk area at the campground. There are no water hookups at the campground. Multiple dogs may be allowed.

Charlottesville KOA
3825 Red Hill Lane
Charlottesville, VA
434-296-9881 (800-562-1743)
charlottesvillekoa.com
Dogs of all sizes are allowed. There are no additional pet fees. Dogs must be leashed and cleaned up after. This RV park is closed during the off-season. The camping and

tent areas also allow dogs. There is a dog walk area at the campground. Multiple dogs may be allowed.

Pocohontas State Park
10301 State Park Road
Chesterfield, VA
804-796-4255 (800-933-PARK (7275))
Popular, educational, multi-functional, and recreational, all describe this year round park. Dogs of all sizes are allowed for an additional $3 per night per pet. Dogs may not be left unattended outside or in a tent, and they must be leashed and cleaned up after. Dogs are not allowed in food areas or at the pool. Dogs are allowed on the trails. This campground is closed during the off-season. The camping and tent areas also allow dogs. There is a dog walk area at the campground. Multiple dogs may be allowed.

Occoneechee State Park
1192 Occoneechee Park Road
Clarksville, VA
434-374-2210 (800-933-PARK (7275))
This historical park is located on Virginia's largest lake and offers a variety of land and water recreation, however, swimming is not allowed. Dogs of all sizes are allowed at $3 per dog per day for the camp area. Dogs may not be left unattended unless very well behaved, and they must have current rabies and shot records. Dogs must be on no more than a 6 foot leash, and be cleaned up after. This campground is closed during the off-season. The camping and tent areas also allow dogs. There is a dog walk area at the campground. Multiple dogs may be allowed.

Douthat State Park
Rt 1, Box 212
Clifton Forge, VA
540-862-8100 (800-933-PARK (7275))
This park, a Nationally Registered Historic District, offers interpretive programs, more than 40 miles of hiking trails, and a variety of land and water events and recreation. Dogs of all sizes are allowed for $3 per night per pet for the camp area, and at $5 per night per pet for the cabins. Dogs may not be left unattended, and they must be leashed and cleaned up after. Dogs are not allowed at the lodge or on the beach, but they are allowed on the trails. This campground is

closed during the off-season. The camping and tent areas also allow dogs. There is a dog walk area at the campground. Dogs are allowed in the camping cabins. Multiple dogs may be allowed.

Misty Mountain Campground
56 Misty Mountain Road
Crozet, VA
888-647-8900
mistycamp.com/
This scenic 50 acre park has a creek that runs through the property, and they offer secluded treed sites, a pond for some fishing, several playground/game areas, a general store, recreation room, live music and dances, and special events throughout the year. Dogs of all sizes are allowed for an additional pet fee of $2 per night per pet. Dogs must be well behaved, leashed or crated, and cleaned up after at all times. There are some breed restrictions. The camping and tent areas also allow dogs. There is a dog walk area at the campground. Multiple dogs may be allowed.

Bear Creek State Park
929 Oak Hill Road
Cumberland, VA
804-492-4410 (800-933-PARK (7275))
This park of 326 acres has a lake of 40 acres, and offers fishing, hiking, nature study, and a variety of land and water recreation. Dogs of all sizes are allowed for an additional fee of $3 per night per pet. Dogs may not be left unattended, and they must be on no more than a 6 foot leash, and be cleaned up after. Dogs are not allowed on the beach or in the water. Dogs are allowed on the trails. This campground is closed during the off-season. The camping and tent areas also allow dogs. There is a dog walk area at the campground. Multiple dogs may be allowed.

Bluecat on the New Camping
2800 Wysor H (100)
Draper, VA
276-766-3729
bluecatonthenew.com/
This campground of over 4 acres with 1,200 feet of riverfront has tipis for rent or one of 6 campsites for tent camping only. Dogs of all sizes are allowed in the tipis and in the camp area for no additional fee. Dogs must be under owner's control, leashed, and cleaned up after at all times. This RV park is closed during the off-season. The camping and tent areas also allow dogs. There is a dog walk

area at the campground. There are no electric or water hookups at the campgrounds. Multiple dogs may be allowed.

Natural Tunnel State Park
Rt 3, Box 250
Duffield, VA
276-940-2674 (800-933-PARK (7275))
This park offers a visitor center, an amphitheater, interpretive programs, a wide variety of recreational pursuits, and more, but its amazing natural tunnel is the real attraction. Dogs of all sizes are allowed for an additional fee of $3 per night per pet. Dogs may not be left unattended, they must be leashed at all times, and cleaned up after. Dogs are allowed on the trails. This campground is closed during the off-season. The camping and tent areas also allow dogs. There is a dog walk area at the campground. Multiple dogs may be allowed.

Jellystone Park
2940 Sussex Drive
Emporia, VA
434-634-3115
campingbear.com
Dogs of all sizes are allowed. There are no additional pet fees. Dogs must be well behaved, may not be left unattended, and be leashed and cleaned up after. Dogs are not allowed in the buildings or at the playground. The camping and tent areas also allow dogs. There is a dog walk area at the campground. Multiple dogs may be allowed.

Fancy Gap KOA
47 Fox Trail Loop
Fancy Gap, VA
276-728-7776 (800-562-1876)
koa.com/where/va/46183/
In addition to a lush green setting, some of their amenities include free Wi-Fi, free fishing, paddle boats, a club house with a large 52 inch TV, and a seasonal swimming pool. Dogs are allowed for no additional fee. Dogs may not be left unattended outside, and they may only be left alone inside if they will be quiet. Dogs must be on no more than a 6 foot leash and cleaned up after at all times. There are some breed restrictions. This RV park is closed during the off-season. The camping and tent areas also allow dogs. There is a dog walk area at the campground. Multiple dogs may be allowed.

New River Trail State Park

176 Orphanage Drive
Foster Falls, VA
276-699-6778 (800-933-PARK (7275))
This 57 mile long, converted "Rails to Trails" state park parallels 39 miles of one of the world's oldest rivers, passes through 2 tunnels, crosses about 30 smaller bridges and trestles, and offers access to many other recreational activities along the way. Dogs are allowed in the day use areas of the park for no additional fee; there is an additional fee of $3 per night per pet for camping. Dogs must be leashed and cleaned up after at all times. There are 5 campgrounds with various site options, fire rings, a lantern post, picnic table, non-flush toilets, and drinking water. The camping and tent areas also allow dogs. There is a dog walk area at the campground. There are no electric or water hookups at the campgrounds. 2 dogs may be allowed.

Fredericksburg/Washington DC S KOA
7400 Brookside Lane
Fredericksburg, VA
540-898-7252 (800-562-1889)
fredericksburgkoa.com
Dogs of all sizes are allowed. There are no additional pet fees, for tent or RV sites. There is a $5 per night per pet additional fee for cabins. Dogs must be quiet, well behaved, leashed, and cleaned up after. The camping and tent areas also allow dogs. There is a dog walk area at the campground. Dogs are allowed in the camping cabins. 2 dogs may be allowed.

James River State Park
Rt 1, Box 787
Gladstone, VA
434-933-4355 (800-933-PARK (7275))
A fairly new park offers 20 miles of multiple use trails, three fishing ponds, and various activities and recreation. Dogs of all sizes are allowed for an additional $3 per night per pet for camping, and for $5 per night per pet for cabins. Cabins are available year round. Dogs may not be left unattended, and they must be leashed in camp areas, and cleaned up after. Dogs are allowed on the trails. The camping and tent areas also allow dogs. There is a dog walk area at the campground. Dogs are allowed in the camping cabins. There are no electric or water hookups at the

campground. Multiple dogs may be allowed.

Twin Lakes State Park
788 Twin Lakes Road
Green Bay, VA
434-392-3435 (800-933-PARKS (7275))
This secluded park also provides a conference center in addition to a variety of lakefront activities, recreation, and interpretive programs. Dogs of all sizes are allowed for an additional $3 per night per pet for camping, and for $5 per night per pet for cabins. Cabins are available year round. Dogs may not be left unattended, and they must be leashed and cleaned up after. Dogs are not allowed on the beach or in the lake, but they are allowed on the trails. This campground is closed during the off-season. The camping and tent areas also allow dogs. There is a dog walk area at the campground. Dogs are allowed in the camping cabins. Multiple dogs may be allowed.

Smith Mountain State Park
1235 State Park Road
Huddleston, VA
540-297-6066 (800-933-PARK (7275))
Hardwood and pine forests, secluded coves and picturesque vistas are the backdrop for a variety of trails, land,water activities, and recreation at this year round park. Dogs of all sizes are allowed for an additional $3 per night per pet for camping, and for $5 per night per pet for cabins. Cabins are available year round. Dogs may not be tied to trees, and they must be leashed and cleaned up after. Dogs may only be left unattended if they will be quiet and well behaved in owners' absence. Dogs are allowed on the trails. This campground is closed during the off-season. The camping and tent areas also allow dogs. There is a dog walk area at the campground. Dogs are allowed in the camping cabins. Multiple dogs may be allowed.

Belle Isle State Park
Lancaster, VA
804-462-5030 (800-933-PARK (7275))
This 733 acre park also has 7 miles of waterfront footage on the north shore of the Rappahannock with Deep and Mulberry creeks along its boarder creating a variety of diverse wetland areas and wildlife. Dogs of all sizes are allowed for an additional fee of $3 per night per pet. Dogs

must be kept on a leash no longer than 6 feet when outside and they must be brought in at night. Campsites have fire rings, grills, a picnic table, lantern hanger, modern restroom with showers, a laundry, a free boat launch for overnight guests, a camp store, and dump station. This RV park is closed during the off-season. The camping and tent areas also allow dogs. There is a dog walk area at the campground. Multiple dogs may be allowed.

Pohick Bay Park
6501 Pohick Bay Drive
Lorton, VA
703-352-5900
This water oriented 1,000 acre park has one of only 3 access points to the Potomac River in northern Virginia, and many other features make this a popular recreation area also, with a "treehouse" playground area, mini-golf, an outdoor freeform pool, plenty of bird and wildlife, and hiking trails. Dogs are allowed throughout the park and the campground for no additional fee. Dogs may not be left unattended in the campground, and they must be under their owner's control, leashed, and cleaned up after at all times. Campsites have grills, fire rings, picnic tables, and a camp store, restrooms, hot showers, a laundry, and a dump station are close by. The camping and tent areas also allow dogs. There is a dog walk area at the campground. Multiple dogs may be allowed.

Big Meadows Campground
Skyline Drive, Milepost 51.2
Luray, VA
540-999-3500 (877-444-6777)
nps.gov/shen/
Although secluded, this camp area is close to major amenities and popular trails, and offer wide sweeping meadows (many times with wildlife), and 3 nearby waterfalls. There are restrooms, hot showers, a laundry, water, and a dump station as well. Dogs of all sizes are allowed for no additional fee. Dogs must be under owner's control, on no more than a 6 foot leash or securely crated, and cleaned up after at all times. Dogs are not to be left unattended. Dogs are not allowed on about 14 miles of the trails; please ask the attendant at the gate for a list of the trails. Dogs are not allowed in buildings. This RV park is closed during the off-season. The camping and tent areas also allow dogs. There is a dog walk area at the campground. There are no

electric or water hookups at the campgrounds. Multiple dogs may be allowed.

Jellystone Park
2250 H 211E
Luray, VA
540-743-4002 (800-420-6679)
campluray.com
Dogs of all sizes are allowed. There are no additional pet fees. Dogs must be well behaved, leashed, and cleaned up after. Dogs are not allowed to be left staked outside your unit. They may be left inside your RV if they will be quiet. This RV park is closed during the off-season. The camping and tent areas also allow dogs. There is a dog walk area at the campground. Dogs are not allowed in the camping cabins. Multiple dogs may be allowed.

Lewis Mountain Campground
Skyline Drive, Milepost 57.5
Luray, VA
540-743-3500
nps.gov/shen/
This is the smallest campground in the park and offers a quiet rustic setting. The 32 sites are on a first-come first-served basis, and flush toilets, coin showers, a laundry, and a camp store are on site. Since the Appalachian Trail runs through this campground, hikers pitching a tent for the night are a common sight. Dogs of all sizes are allowed for no additional fee. Dogs must be under owner's control, on no more than a 6 foot leash or securely crated, and cleaned up after at all times. Dogs are not to be left unattended. Dogs are not allowed on about 14 miles of the trails; please ask the attendant at the gate for a list of the trails. Dogs are not allowed in buildings. This RV park is closed during the off-season. The camping and tent areas also allow dogs. There is a dog walk area at the campground. There are no electric or water hookups at the campgrounds. Multiple dogs may be allowed.

Loft Mountain, Shenandoah National Park
Skyline Blvd, Milepost 79.5
Luray, VA
540-999-3500 (877-444-6777)
nps.gov/shen/
This is the parks largest and southern-most camp area, and sitting atop a mountain at 3,400 feet it offers great panoramic views. There are 219 fairly secluded sites

available on a first come first served basis and by reservation, and the camp area provides restrooms, showers, a laundry, picnic tables, fire grates, amphitheater, a camp store, dump station, and close by is a restaurant and gas station. Dogs of all sizes are allowed for no additional fee. Dogs must be under owner's control, on no more than a 6 foot leash or securely crated, and cleaned up after at all times. Dogs are not to be left unattended. Dogs are not allowed on about 14 miles of the trails; please ask the attendant at the gate for a list of the trails. Dogs are not allowed in buildings. This RV park is closed during the off-season. The camping and tent areas also allow dogs. There is a dog walk area at the campground. There are no electric or water hookups at the campgrounds. Multiple dogs may be allowed.

Mathews Arm Campground
Skyline Drive, Milepost 22.1
Luray, VA
540-999-3500 (877-444-6777)
nps.gov/shen/
This is the closest camp area entering from the north, and it offers a nature trail, a hiking trail to the tallest waterfall in the park, and a seasonal wayside with a cafeteria, camp store, snack bar, and gift shop. There is also potable water and a dump station. Dogs of all sizes are allowed for no additional fee. Dogs must be under owner's control, on no more than a 6 foot leash or securely crated, and cleaned up after at all times. Dogs are not to be left unattended outside, or for more than an hour inside an RV. Dogs are not allowed on about 14 miles of the trails; please ask the attendant at the gate for a list of the trails. Dogs are not allowed in buildings. This RV park is closed during the off-season. The camping and tent areas also allow dogs. There is a dog walk area at the campground. There are no electric or water hookups at the campgrounds. Multiple dogs may be allowed.

Hungry Mother State Park
2854 Park Blvd
Marion, VA
276-781-7400 (800-933-PARK (7275))
This park is rich in folklore and history, and offers interpretive programs, a variety of land and water activities, and recreation. Dogs of all sizes are allowed for an additional $3 per night per pet for camping, and for

$5 per night per pet for cabins. Cabins are available year round. Dogs may not be left unattended, and they must be leashed and cleaned up after. Dogs are not allowed on the beaches or in buildings, but they are allowed on the trails. This campground is closed during the off-season. The camping and tent areas also allow dogs. There is a dog walk area at the campground. Dogs are allowed in the camping cabins. Multiple dogs may be allowed.

Mount Rogers National Rec Area
3714 H 16
Marion, VA
540-265-5100 (877-444-6777)
fs.fed.us/r8/gwj/mr/
Home to a vast variety of plant, bird, and wildlife, this diverse recreation area offers plenty of land and water recreation, including over 400 miles of designated trails, scenic drives, wilderness and wildlife areas, and more. Dogs are allowed throughout the park and at the camp areas. Dogs must be leashed and cleaned up after, and they are not allowed in swimming areas or park buildings. There are 7 campgrounds with varying amenities and environments. This RV park is closed during the off-season. The camping and tent areas also allow dogs. There is a dog walk area at the campground. Multiple dogs may be allowed.

Rocky Knob Campground
Blue Ridge Parkway, Milepost 167-169
Meadows of Dan, VA
540-745-9662
blueridgeparkway.org/
This camp area with 100+ sites offers a campfire circle that can accommodate up to 150 campers, picnic areas, restrooms, Mabry Mill's eatery and gift shop, and one of the hikes here takes visitors to Rockcastle Gorge, a 124 acre wooded gorge displaying 2 waterfalls. Dogs are allowed throughout the park and on the trails. Dogs must be well behaved, under owner's control, on no more than a 6 foot leash, and cleaned up after at all times. This RV park is closed during the off-season. The camping and tent areas also allow dogs. There is a dog walk area at the campground. There are no electric or water hookups at the campgrounds. Multiple dogs may be allowed.

Westmoreland State Park
1650 State Park Road

Montross, VA
804-493-8821 (800-933-PARK (7275))
At almost 1,300 acres, this park features about a mile and a half of Potomac riverfront with great views, seasonal historical and ecological programs, and self-guided interpretive, nature trails. Dogs of all sizes are allowed for an additional fee of $3 per night per pet for the campground and $5 per night per pet for camping cabins; there is no fee for day use. Dogs must be kept on a leash no longer than 6 feet when outside and they must be brought in at night. Camp areas have fire rings, grills, a camp store, a boat launch for overnight guests, restrooms with showers, laundry facilities at campground A, and concessionaires. This RV park is closed during the off-season. The camping and tent areas also allow dogs. There is a dog walk area at the campground. Dogs are allowed in the camping cabins. Multiple dogs may be allowed.

Grayson Highlands State Park
829 Grayson Highlands Lane
Mouth of Wilson, VA
276-579-7092 (800-933-PARK (7275))
Nestled away in the Jefferson National Forest, this 4,800+ acre state park offers stunning views, 9 hiking trails, nature/history programs, event venues, festivals, workshops, and much more. Dogs are allowed throughout the park and in the campground for an additional fee of $3 per night per pet; there is no charge for day use only. Dogs must be well behaved, leashed, and cleaned up after. Dogs are not allowed in any buildings. Camp areas have mostly wooded sites, fire rings/grills, restrooms, and showers. This RV park is closed during the off-season. The camping and tent areas also allow dogs. There is a dog walk area at the campground. 2 dogs may be allowed.

Natural Bridge/Lexington KOA
214 Killdeer Lane
Natural Bridge, VA
540-291-2770 (800-562-8514)
naturalbridgekoa.com
Dogs of all sizes are allowed, and there can be more than two dogs. There are no additional pet fees for tent or RV sites. There is a $5 per stay per pet additional fee for cabins, and there can be 2 dogs. Dogs must be well behaved,

leashed, and cleaned up after. The camping and tent areas also allow dogs. There is a dog walk area at the campground. Dogs are allowed in the camping cabins.

Yogi Bear at Natural Bridge
16 Recreation Lane
Natural Bridge Station, VA
540-291-2727 (800-258-9532)
campnbr.com/index2.html
This scenic park, located along the James River, offers a variety of land and water activities and recreational pursuits. Dogs of all sizes are allowed at no additional fee. Dogs may not be left unattended, and they must be leashed and cleaned up after. Dogs are not allowed on the beach, the game area, food areas, or in buildings. Dogs are allowed on the trails. This campground is closed during the off-season. The camping and tent areas also allow dogs. There is a dog walk area at the campground. Dogs are allowed in the camping cabins. 2 dogs may be allowed.

Petersburg KOA
2809 Cortland Road
Petersburg, VA
804-732-8345 (800-562-8545)
koa.com
Dogs of all sizes are allowed. There are no additional pet fees. Dogs must be quiet, leashed, and cleaned up after. The camping and tent areas also allow dogs. There is a dog walk area at the campground. Dogs are allowed in the camping cabins. Multiple dogs may be allowed.

Chesapeake Bay Camp Resort
382 Campground Road
Reedville, VA
804-453-3430
A popular recreation destination, this 20 acre park sits out on the point where the Potomac meets the Chesapeake Bay offering great views plus a good variety of land and water activities. A KOA for many years, there are a number of amenities and extras here such as a crabbing pier and a marina. Dogs of all sizes are allowed, and there is no fee for one medium or large, or 2 small dogs per site in the camp area. There is a $7 per night per pet fee for the cabins, and "doggy visitors" are not allowed at any cabin unless they are registered there. Dogs must be leashed and cleaned up after at all times. Dogs are not allowed in the buildings or in the pool area. This RV park is closed during the off-season. The camping and tent areas also

allow dogs. There is a dog walk area at the campground. Dogs are allowed in the camping cabins.

Lake Fairfax Park
1400 Lake Fairfax Drive
Reston, VA
703-471-5415
This park of 476 acres, with an 18 acre lake, offers fishing, hiking, nature study, and a variety of land and water recreation. Dogs of all sizes are allowed at no additional fee. Dogs may not be left unattended outside, and they must be leashed and cleaned up after. Dogs are not allowed on the athletic fields, but they are allowed on the trails. The camping and tent areas also allow dogs. There is a dog walk area at the campground. There are no water hookups at the campground. Multiple dogs may be allowed.

George Washington and Jefferson National Forests
5162 Valleypointe Parkway/S area Forest HQ
Roanoke, VA
540-265-5100 (877-444-6777)
fs.fed.us/r8/gwj/index.shtml
A headquarters plus 8 ranger districts take care of the almost 1.8 million acres of this forest that spreads over 3 states, making it one of the largest public land areas in the eastern US. There are a wide variety of landscapes and habitats providing for innumerable bird, plant, and wildlife, year round activities and recreational pursuits, and many educational opportunities as well. Dogs are allowed throughout the forest, in the campgrounds, and on the trails. Dogs must be leashed and cleaned up after in developed recreational sites, and they are not allowed in swimming areas. Developed and primitive camping is available at several different locations throughout the forest. Reservations are suggested for favored areas. Most of the developed sites offer tables, grills, drinking water, toilet facilities, and are closer to recreational areas. Primitive camping requires campers to "Leave No Trace" and offers no services. This RV park is closed during the off-season. The camping and tent areas also allow dogs. There is a dog walk area at the campground. There are no water hookups at the campgrounds. Multiple dogs may be allowed.

Staunton River State Park
1170 Staunton Trail

Scottsburg, VA
434-572-4623 (800-933-PARK (7275))
This year round park covers almost 1,600 acres, is home to the largest lake in Virginia, offers interpretive programs, and a variety of land and water recreation. Dogs of all sizes are allowed for an additional $3 per night per pet for camping, and for $5 per night per pet for cabins. Cabins are available year round. Dogs may not be left unattended outside or in a tent, and they must be leashed and cleaned up after. Dogs are not allowed in the pool area, but they are allowed on the trails. This campground is closed during the off-season. The camping and tent areas also allow dogs. There is a dog walk area at the campground. Dogs are allowed in the camping cabins. Multiple dogs may be allowed.

Fairy Stone State Park
967 Fairystone Lake Drive
Stuart, VA
276-930-2424 (800-933-PARK (7275))
Rich in folklore, this park of 4,868 acres with a 168 acre lake provides a variety of land and water recreation, but the Fairy Stones (naturally formed crosses in small rocks) are the real attraction in this park. Dogs of all sizes are allowed for an additional $3 per night per pet for camping, and for $5 per night per pet for cabins. Cabins are available year round. Dogs must be leashed and cleaned up after in camp areas. Dogs are not allowed on the beach, in the water, or at the conference center. Dogs are allowed on the trails. This campground is closed during the off-season. The camping and tent areas also allow dogs. There is a dog walk area at the campground. Dogs are allowed in the camping cabins. Multiple dogs may be allowed.

Chippokes Plantation
695 Chippokes Park Road
Surry, VA
757-294-3625 (800-933-PARK (7275))
As one of the oldest working farms in the US, Chippokes is a living historical exhibit, and among the cultivated gardens and woodlands, all the traditional recreation is offered. Dogs of all sizes are allowed for an additional $3 per night per pet. Dogs may not be left unattended, and they must be on no

more than a 6 foot leash, and be cleaned up after. Dogs are not allowed in the buildings, but they are allowed on the trails unless otherwise marked. This campground is closed during the off-season. The camping and tent areas also allow dogs. There is a dog walk area at the campground. Multiple dogs may be allowed.

Prince William Forest Park
18100 Park Headquarters Road
Triangle, VA
703-221-7181 (800-933-PARK (7275))
nps.gov/prwi/
With over 19,000 acres, this park offers a variety of nature study, and land and water recreation. Dogs of all sizes are allowed at no additional fee. Dogs may not be left unattended, and they must be on no more than a 6 foot leash, and be cleaned up after. Dogs are not allowed in the Chopawamsic backcountry, Turkey Run Ridge Group Campground, or in the buildings. Dogs are allowed on the trails. The camping and tent areas also allow dogs. There is a dog walk area at the campground. There are no electric or water hookups at the campground. Multiple dogs may be allowed.

Staunton/Verona KOA
296 Riner Lane
Verona, VA
540-248-2746 (800-562-9949)
koa.com
Dogs of all sizes are allowed, and there are no additional pet fees for tent or RV sites. There is a $10 per night per pet additional fee for cabins. Dogs must be leashed and cleaned up after. This RV park is closed during the off-season. The camping and tent areas also allow dogs. There is a dog walk area at the campground. Dogs are allowed in the camping cabins. Multiple dogs may be allowed.

Roanoke Mountain Campground
Blue Ridge Parkway M.P. 120.4
Vinton, VA
540-745-9660
blueridgeparkway.org/
This camp area offers easy access to Explore Park, an 1,100 acre living history museum depicting life from the first settlers to the present with several special events throughout the year, and the Roanoke River giving a variety of land and water recreational opportunities. There is hiking along the river, the ridge,

through mountains, and up the Roanoke Mountain Summit Trail. Dogs are allowed throughout the park and on the trails. Dogs must be well behaved, under owner's control, on no more than a 6 foot leash, and cleaned up after at all times. This RV park is closed during the off-season. The camping and tent areas also allow dogs. There is a dog walk area at the campground. There are no electric or water hookups at the campgrounds. Multiple dogs may be allowed.

False Cape State Park
4001 Sandpiper Road
Virginia Beach, VA
757-426-3657 (800-933-PARK (7275))
As one of the last undeveloped spaces along the east coast, this park offers a true "back to nature" experience with constant efforts to protect the very diverse environment and its inhabitants, an active education center, history programs, special events, and more. There is no vehicular access, and boat, foot, bike, beach transporter, or tram allow the only accesses and services vary depending on the season. Dogs are allowed in the park; they are not allowed through/in the refuge, except during October. Pets can be brought in by boat or the beach trail only from November 1st to March 31st, and from April to September they can only come to the park by boat. Dogs must be under their owner's control, leashed, and cleaned up after at all times. There are 12 primitive campsites available with drinking water and pit toilets nearby. Reservations are required (no exceptions) and can be made on the same day or in advance. This is a carry in/carry out camp area. The camping and tent areas also allow dogs. There is a dog walk area at the campground. There are no electric or water hookups at the campgrounds. 2 dogs may be allowed.

First Landing State Park
2500 Shore DriveH 60
Virginia Beach, VA
757-412-2320 (800-933-PARK (2725))
This 2,888 acre historic park has over a mile of beach, 9 walking trails covering almost 19 miles, interpretive programs, an authentic Indian village, and a variety of land and water recreational opportunities. Dogs of all sizes are allowed for no additional fee for day use, and $3 per night per pet for overnight campers.

They are allowed throughout the park and on the beach here (not so at other park beaches). Dogs must be under their owner's control, on no more than a 6 foot leash, and cleaned up after at all times. Owners must carry proof of rabies vaccination as it is a requirement for dogs in Virginia Beach. The camp sites each have a picnic table and fire grill, and there are restrooms, hot showers, and laundry facilities close by. The camping and tent areas also allow dogs. There is a dog walk area at the campground. 2 dogs may be allowed.

Holiday Trav-L-Park
1075 General Booth Blvd
Virginia Beach, VA
757-425-0249 (866-849-8860)
htpvabeach.com/
A major recreation destination, this campground has almost 1000 sites, 3 camp stores and dump stations, modern restrooms and laundry facilities, Wi-Fi, playing fields/courts, 6 playgrounds, mini-golf, and a fenced dog park. Seasonally, the park offers 4 large pools, 1 kiddie pool, a rec room, nightly music, themed weekends, outdoor movies, a café, and special events and activities. Quiet, well mannered dogs are allowed for no additional fee. They may not be left unattended outside, and they must be leashed and cleaned up after at all times. Dogs are not allowed in buildings, pool areas, or in cabin vicinities. There are some breed restrictions. The camping and tent areas also allow dogs. There is a dog walk area at the campground. 2 dogs may be allowed.

Virginia Beach KOA
1240 General Booth Blvd
Virginia Beach, VA
757-428-1444 (800-562-4150)
koa.com/where/va/46109/
In addition to having a great location to numerous sites of interest, this park offers Wi-Fi, ice cream socials, planned activities, mini-golf, a seasonal swimming pool, bike rentals, and a fenced Kamp K9 off leash interactive dog park. Dogs are allowed for no additional fee. Dogs may not be left unattended, and they must be on no more than a 6 foot leash and cleaned up after at all times. There are some breed restrictions. The camping and tent areas also allow dogs. There is a dog walk area at the campground. There are special amenities given to dogs at this

campground. Multiple dogs may be allowed.

Pottery Campground
Lightfoot Road/H 646
Williamsburg, VA
757-565-2101 (800-892-0320)
Only minutes from Williamsburg Pottery where purchases can earn free camping nights, this 550 site campground offers wooded sites, comfort stations, a playground, and a large swimming pool. Dogs of all sizes are allowed for no additional fee. Dogs must be well behaved, leashed, and cleaned up after at all times. The camping and tent areas also allow dogs. There is a dog walk area at the campground. Multiple dogs may be allowed.

Williamsburg KOA
5210 Newman Road
Williamsburg, VA
757-565-2907 (800-562-1733)
williamsburgkoa.com
Dogs of all sizes are allowed. There are no additional pet fees. Dogs must be leashed and cleaned up after. This RV park is closed during the off-season. The camping and tent areas also allow dogs. There is a dog walk area at the campground. Multiple dogs may be allowed.

Williamsburg/Colonial KOA
4000 Newman Road
Williamsburg, VA
757-565-2734 (800-562-7609)
koa.com
Dogs of all sizes are allowed. There are no additional pet fees. Dogs must be leashed and cleaned up after. This RV park is closed during the off-season. The camping and tent areas also allow dogs. There is a dog walk area at the campground. Multiple dogs may be allowed.

Whtheville KOA
231 KOA Road
Wytheville, VA
276-228-2601 (800-562-3380)
wythevillekoa.com
Dogs of all sizes are allowed. There are no additional pet fees. Dogs must be leashed and cleaned up after. There are some breed restrictions. The camping and tent areas also allow dogs. There is a dog walk area at the campground. Dogs are allowed in the camping cabins. Multiple dogs may be allowed.

Washington

Fidalgo Bay Resort
4701 Fidalgo Bay Road
Anacortes, WA
360-293-5353
fidalgobay.com
Dogs of all sizes are allowed. There are no additional pet fees. Dogs may not be left unattended, and they must be quiet, well behaved, leashed at all times, and cleaned up after. Dogs may not be kenneled outside. This is an RV only park. There is a dog walk area at the campground. 2 dogs may be allowed.

Pioneer Trails RV Resort
7337 Miller Road
Anacortes, WA
360-293-5355
pioneertrails.com
Dogs of all sizes are allowed. There is a $2 per night per pet additional fee. Dogs must be leashed and cleaned up after. Dogs are not allowed in the covered wagons. There are some breed restrictions. There is a dog walk area at the campground. 2 dogs may be allowed.

Fields Spring State Park
992 Park Road
Anatone, WA
509-256-3332
This state park has a variety of year round land and water recreational activities. Dogs of all sizes are allowed at no additional fee. Dogs may not be left unattended, and they must be leashed and cleaned up after. Dogs are allowed on the trails, but they are not allowed at any public swim areas. The camping and tent areas also allow dogs. There is a dog walk area at the campground. There are no electric or water hookups at the campground. Multiple dogs may be allowed.

Mount Rainier National Park
Tahoma Woods Star Route (H706)
Ashford, WA
360-569-2211
nps.gov/mora/
This park is home to Mount Rainier, an active volcano encrusted by ice, and at 14,411 feet it towers 8,000 feet above the surrounding Cascades peaks and creates it own weather. There is a variety of land and water recreation. Dogs are allowed at no additional fee. Dogs

must be leashed and cleaned up after. Dogs are not allowed in any of the buildings, or on any of the trails except for the Pacific Coast Trail. Dogs must otherwise stay on the roads and parking lots of the camp areas. This campground is closed during the off-season. The camping and tent areas also allow dogs. There is a dog walk area at the campground. There are no electric or water hookups at the campground. Multiple dogs may be allowed.

Flaming Geyser State Park
23700 SE Flaming Geyser Road
Auburn, WA
253-931-3930
This 475 acre day-use park, located only 8 miles from Seattle's waterfront, offers lots of activities, and land and water recreation. There are large open lawns, over 200 picnic sites with tables, multi-use trails, and a self-guided ADA accessible Salmon Interpretive Trail, but it's main features are its' two geysers and other bubbling springs. Dogs of all sizes are allowed. Dogs must be on no more than an 8 foot leash and be cleaned up after at all times. The park has provided clean-up stations throughout the park. Pets are not permitted on designated swimming beaches. There is a dog walk area at the campground. Multiple dogs may be allowed.

Jellystone Park
11354 County H X
Bagley, WA
608-996-2201 (800-999-6557)
jellystonebagley.com
Dogs of all sizes are allowed. There are no additional pet fees. Dogs must be leashed and cleaned up after. This RV park is closed during the off-season. The camping and tent areas also allow dogs. There is a dog walk area at the campground. Multiple dogs may be allowed.

Wyalusing State Park
13081 State Park lane
Bagley, WA
608-996-2261 (888-WIPARKS (947-2757))
This park holds historical significance as one of Wisconsin's oldest parks. It has over 24 miles of trails, including a canoe trail, water and land recreation, an interpretive center, and more. Dogs are allowed at no additional fee. Dogs may not be left unattended, and they must be leashed and cleaned up after.

Dogs are not allowed in the picnic areas, in buildings, on cross-country ski trails once there is snow, or on the Sugar Maple Nature trail. Dogs are allowed on the hiking trails, and they may be off lead when out of the camp area if there is voice control. The camping and tent areas also allow dogs. There is a dog walk area at the campground. There are no water hookups at the campground. Multiple dogs may be allowed.

Fay Bainbridge State Park
15446 Sunrise Drive NE
Bainbridge Island, WA
206-842-3931 (888-226-7688)
This 17 acre marine camping park, with 1,420 feet of saltwater shoreline, offers excellent scenery and a host of water and land recreation. Dogs of all sizes are allowed at no additional fee. Dogs may not be left unattended, and they must be leashed and cleaned up after. Dogs are not allowed in park buildings, however they are allowed on the trails. The camping and tent areas also allow dogs. There is a dog walk area at the campground. Multiple dogs may be allowed.

Bay Center/Willapa Bay KOA
457 Bay Center Road
Bay Center, WA
360-875-6344 (800-562-7810)
koa.com/where/wa/47121.html
Dogs of all sizes are allowed. There are no additional pet fees. Dogs may not be left unattended outside, must be quiet, leashed, and cleaned up after. Dogs are met at the door with doggy treats. Dogs are not allowed on the playground, at the cabins, or in the buildings. There are some breed restrictions. This RV park is closed during the off-season. The camping and tent areas also allow dogs. There is a dog walk area at the campground. There are special amenities given to dogs at this campground. Multiple dogs may be allowed.

Bellingham RV Park
3939 Bennett Drive
Bellingham, WA
360-752-1224
bellinghamrvpark.com
Dogs of all sizes are allowed. There are no additional pet fees. Dogs must be leashed and cleaned up after. There are some breed restrictions. The camping and tent areas also allow dogs. There is a dog walk area at the campground. Multiple dogs may be allowed.

Larrabee State Park
245 Chuckanut Drive
Bellingham, WA
360-676-2093
This year round recreational park features 8,100 feet of saltwater shoreline, 2 freshwater lakes, and many miles of trails to explore. The I-5 route is suggested for larger RVs. Dogs of all sizes are allowed at no additional fee. Dogs may not be left unattended, and they must be leashed and cleaned up after. Dogs are allowed on the trails, but not in any buildings. The camping and tent areas also allow dogs. There is a dog walk area at the campground. Multiple dogs may be allowed.

Birch Bay State Park
5105 Helwig
Blaine, WA
360-371-2800 (888-226-7688)
Year around recreation is offered at this park. There are 194 acres with over 8,200 feet of saltwater shoreline, a rich archeological history, miles of trails, and a variety of land and water activities. Dogs of all sizes are allowed at no additional fee. Dogs may not be left unattended at any time, they must be on no more than a 6 foot leash, and be cleaned up after. Dogs are allowed on the trails, but they are not allowed on the beach. The camping and tent areas also allow dogs. There is a dog walk area at the campground. Multiple dogs may be allowed.

Lake Pleasant RV Park
24025 Bothell Everett H SE
Bothell, WA
425-487-1785
Dogs of all sizes are allowed. There are no additional pet fees. Dogs must be leashed and cleaned up after. There are some breed restrictions. There is a dog walk area at the campground. 2 dogs may be allowed.

Illahee State Park
3540 Bahia Vista
Bremerton, WA
360-478-6460 (888-CAMP OUT (226-7688))
This park is a marine camping park with almost 1800 feet of saltwater frontage. There is only 1 site that has hook-ups. Dogs of all sizes are allowed. There are no additional pet fees. Dogs may not be left unattended, and they must be leashed and cleaned up after. Dogs are allowed on the trails, but not in any buildings. The camping and tent areas also allow dogs. There is a

dog walk area at the campground. There are no electric or water hookups at the campground. Multiple dogs may be allowed.

Burlington/Anacortes KOA
6397 N Green Road
Burlington, WA
360-724-5511 (800-562-9145)
koa.com
Dogs of all sizes are allowed. There are no additional pet fees. Dogs must be well behaved, quiet, be on no more than a 6 foot leash, and be cleaned up after. Dogs may not be left unattended at any time and can not be on the beds in the cabins. The camping and tent areas also allow dogs. There is a dog walk area at the campground. Dogs are allowed in the camping cabins. Multiple dogs may be allowed.

Seaquest State Park
Spirit Lake H
Castle Rock, WA
206-274-8633 (888-226-7688)
There are 475 acres at this year round recreational park with 8 miles of hiking trails, over a mile of lake shoreline, and a variety of activities. Dogs of all sizes are allowed at no additional fee. Dogs may not be left unattended at any time, they must be on no more than a 6 foot leash, and be cleaned up after. Dogs are allowed on the trails. The camping and tent areas also allow dogs. There is a dog walk area at the campground.

Scotts RV Park
118 h 12
Chehalis, WA
360-262-9220
Dogs of all sizes are allowed. There are no additional pet fees. Dogs may not be left unattended, must be leashed, and cleaned up after. The camping and tent areas also allow dogs. There is a dog walk area at the campground. Dogs are allowed in the camping cabins. 2 dogs may be allowed.

Klinks Williams Lake Resort
18617 Williams Lake Road
Cheney, WA
509-235-2391
klinksresort.com
Dogs of all sizes are allowed. There are no additional pet fees. Dogs must be friendly, well behaved, leashed, and cleaned up after. Dogs are not allowed at the beach. There are some breed restrictions. This RV park is closed during the off-season. The camping and tent

areas also allow dogs. There is a dog walk area at the campground. 2 dogs may be allowed.

Granite Lake RV Resort
306 Granite Lake Drive
Clarkston, WA
509-751-1635
granitelakervresort.com
Dogs of all sizes are allowed. There is no fee for one dog. If you have a 2nd dog there is an additional fee of $1 per day. Dogs may not be left unattended, and if needed, there is a dog sitter on site. Dogs may walk along the river, and they must be leashed and cleaned up after. There are some breed restrictions. There is a dog walk area at the campground. 2 dogs may be allowed.

Colville National Forest
765 Main (Forest Supervisor's Office)
Colville, WA
509-684-7000
fs.fed.us/r6/colville/
Dogs of all sizes are allowed. There are no additional pet fees. Dogs may not be left unattended, and they must be leashed and cleaned up after. There are some beaches that dogs are allowed on, but they are not allowed at any of the public swim areas. Dogs are allowed on the trails unless otherwise marked. This campground is closed during the off-season. The camping and tent areas also allow dogs. There is a dog walk area at the campground. There are no electric or water hookups at the campground. Multiple dogs may be allowed.

Concrete/Grandy Creek KOA
7370 Russell Road
Concrete, WA
360-826-3554 (888-562-4236)
koa.com
Dogs of all sizes are allowed. There are no additional pet fees. Dogs may not be left unattended at any time, must be leashed, and cleaned up after. There are some breed restrictions. This RV park is closed during the off-season. The camping and tent areas also allow dogs. There is a dog walk area at the campground. Dogs are allowed in the camping cabins. Multiple dogs may be allowed.

Lone Fir Motel and RV Resort
16806 Lewis River Road
Cougar, WA
360-238-5210
lonefirresort.com
Dogs of all sizes and numbers are allowed, and there are no additional

pet fees for the tent and RV sites. There is a $10 per night per pet additional fee for the motel and only 2 dogs are allowed per room. Dogs must be quiet, well behaved, leashed, and cleaned up after. The camping and tent areas also allow dogs. There is a dog walk area at the campground. Dogs are allowed in the camping cabins. Multiple dogs may be allowed.

Sun Lakes Park Resort
34228 Park Lake Road NE
Coulee City, WA
509-632-5291
sunlakesparkresort.com
Dogs of all sizes are allowed. There is a $7 per night per pet additional fee for the cabins, tent or RV sites. Dogs may not be left unattended, are not allowed at the swim beach, and must be leashed and cleaned up after. There is an area where the dogs are also allowed to go swim. This RV park is closed during the off-season. The camping and tent areas also allow dogs. There is a dog walk area at the campground. Dogs are allowed in the camping cabins. Multiple dogs may be allowed.

Sun Lakes-Dry Falls State Park
34875 Park Lake Road NE
Coulee City, WA
509-632-5538 (888-CAMPOUT (226-7688))
This park is full of beautiful natural formations, but its real attraction is the gigantic dried-up waterfall now standing as a dry cliff 400 feet high and 3.5 miles long; once 10 times larger than Niagara Falls. The park has a visitor's center by the falls, and some of the park amenities include 15 miles of hiking trails, interpretive activities, 2 boat ramps, 9 lakes, a park store, a 9 hole golf course, and a miniature golf course. Dogs of all sizes are allowed for no additional fee. Dogs must be under physical control at all times, leashed, and cleaned up after. Dogs are not allowed in park buildings or on designated swimming beaches. The campground offers about 200 campsites, fire pits, restrooms, showers, a dump station, and laundry facilities. The camping and tent areas also allow dogs. There is a dog walk area at the campground. There are no electric or water hookups at the campgrounds. Multiple dogs may be allowed.

Lake Roosevelt National Recreation area
Spring Canyon Road

Coulee Dam, WA
509-633-9441
nps.gov/laro
This year round recreational area has 28 campgrounds around the lake, miles of trails, and a variety of fun activities. Dogs of all sizes are allowed at no additional fee. Dogs may not be left unattended, and they must be leashed and cleaned up after. Dogs are allowed on the trails, but not in any day use or public swim areas. The camping and tent areas also allow dogs. There is a dog walk area at the campground. There are no electric or water hookups at the campground. Multiple dogs may be allowed.

Fort Ebey State Park
400 Hill Valley Drive
Coupeville, WA
360-678-4636 (888-226-7688)
Popular, historical, educational, recreational, and pre-historic, all describe this scenic park that offer interpretive programs and several miles of trails. Dogs of all sizes are allowed at no additional fee. Dogs may not be left unattended, and they must be leashed and cleaned up after. Dogs are allowed on the trails. The camping and tent areas also allow dogs. There is a dog walk area at the campground. Multiple dogs may be allowed.

Coulee Playland Resort
401 Coulee Blvd E (H 155)
Electric City, WA
509-633-2671
couleeplayland.com
Dogs of all sizes are allowed. There are no additional pet fees. Dogs may not be left unattended outside, and they must be leashed and cleaned up after. This RV park is closed during the off-season. The camping and tent areas also allow dogs. There is a dog walk area at the campground. Multiple dogs may be allowed.

Steamboat Rock State Park
Banks Lake
Electric City, WA
509-633-1304 (888-CAMPOUT (226-7688))
This park with more than 3,500 acres along Banks Lake is an oasis in desert surroundings, and a variety of activities and recreation are offered. Dogs of all sizes are allowed at no additional fee. Dogs may not be left unattended, and they must be leashed and cleaned up after. Dogs are not allowed in

public swim areas or in buildings. Dogs are allowed on the trails. The camping and tent areas also allow dogs. There is a dog walk area at the campground. Multiple dogs may be allowed.

Ellensburg KOA
32 Thorp H S
Ellensburg, WA
509-925-9319 (800-562-7616)
koa.com
Dogs of all sizes are allowed. There are no additional pet fees. Dogs may not be left unattended, must be leashed, and cleaned up after. Dogs are allowed at the river, but the river is very swift. The camping and tent areas also allow dogs. There is a dog walk area at the campground. Multiple dogs may be allowed.

Oasis RV Park and Golf
2541 Basin Street SW
Ephrata, WA
509-754-5102
Dogs of all sizes are allowed. There are no additional pet fees. Dogs may not be left unattended, must be well behaved, leashed, and cleaned up after. This RV park is closed during the off-season. There is a dog walk area at the campground. Multiple dogs may be allowed.

Lakeside Park
12321 H 99S
Everett, WA
425-347-2970
Dogs of all sizes are allowed. There are no additional pet fees. Dogs may not be left unattended at any time, must be leashed, and cleaned up after. The camping and tent areas also allow dogs. There is a dog walk area at the campground. 2 dogs may be allowed.

Maple Grove RV Resort
12417 H 99
Everett, WA
425-423-9608
maplegroverv.com
Dogs of all sizes are allowed. There are no additional pet fees. Dogs may not be tied up outside alone, and they must be leashed and cleaned up after. There is a dog walk area at the campground. 2 dogs may be allowed.

Dash Point State Park
5700 SW Dash Point Road
Federal Way, WA
253-661-4955 (888-CAMP OUT (226-7688))
This park has 11 miles of trails and 3,301 feet of saltwater shoreline on

Puget Sound. Dogs of all sizes are allowed. There are no additional pet fees. Dogs may not be left unattended, they must be on no more than an 8 foot leash, and be cleaned up after. Dogs are allowed on the trails and beach but not in buildings. This campground is closed during the off-season. The camping and tent areas also allow dogs. There is a dog walk area at the campground. Multiple dogs may be allowed.

The Cedars RV Resort
6335 Portal Way
Ferndale, WA
360-384-2622
holidaytrailsresorts.com
Dogs of all sizes are allowed. There is a $2 per night per pet additional fee. Dogs must be leashed and cleaned up after, and they are not allowed at the playground or in the buildings. The camping and tent areas also allow dogs. There is a dog walk area at the campground. Multiple dogs may be allowed.

Lakedale Resort
4313 Roche Harbor Road
Friday Harbor, WA
360-378-2350
lakedale.com
Dogs of all sizes are allowed. There is a $2 per night per pet additional fee for tent or RV sites. There is a $20 per night per pet additional fee for the lodge, however, depending on size and number, the fee for the lodge is flexible. Dogs may not be left unattended, and they must be quiet, well behaved, leashed, and cleaned up after. A ferry from Anacortes off I 5, or other ferries in the area will transport your pet on the car deck only. The camping and tent areas also allow dogs. There is a dog walk area at the campground. Dogs are allowed in the camping cabins. Multiple dogs may be allowed.

San Juan Island National Historical Park
4668 Cattle Point Road-Visitor Center
Friday Harbor, WA
360-378-2240
nps.gov/sajh/
This scenic park commemorates the peaceful resolution of the 19th century boundary dispute between the US and Great Britain. It has become a popular educational, historical, and recreational destination offering many features and activities-even whale watching.

Dogs are allowed throughout the park and on the trails. Dogs must be well behaved, leashed, and cleaned up after. There is a dog walk area at the campground. 2 dogs may be allowed.

Gig Harbor RV Resort
9515 Burnham Drive NW
Gig Harbor, WA
253-858-8138
Dogs of all sizes are allowed. There are no additional pet fees. Dogs may not be left outside alone, must be leashed at all times, and cleaned up after. The camping and tent areas also allow dogs. There is a dog walk area at the campground. Multiple dogs may be allowed.

Wallace Falls State Park
14503 Wallace Lake Road
Gold Bar, WA
360-793-0420
Because of the outstanding scenery in this 678 acre park and the overlooks at Wallace Falls (265 feet), it is a favorite of hikers. There are numerous other waterfalls, a rock climbing wall, hiking trails, an interpretive trail, picnic tables, 3 back country lakes, and a river that offer a wide variety of recreational pursuits. Dogs of all sizes are allowed for no additional fee. Dogs must be under physical control at all times, leashed, and cleaned up after. Pets are not permitted in park buildings or at designated swimming beaches. Tent camping is available at 7 beautiful, private walk-in sites on a first come first serve basis. Sites have picnic tables, campfire rings, drinking water, and a restroom. The camping and tent areas also allow dogs. There is a dog walk area at the campground. There are no electric or water hookups at the campgrounds. Multiple dogs may be allowed.

Ilwaco/Long Beach KOA
1509 H 101
Ilwaco, WA
360-642-3292 (800-562-3258)
koa.com
Dogs of all sizes are allowed. There are no additional pet fees. Dogs must be leashed and cleaned up after. There is an off leash fenced in area for dogs also. There are some breed restrictions. This RV park is closed during the off-season. The camping and tent areas also allow dogs. There is a dog walk area at the campground. 2 dogs may be allowed.

Issaquah Highlands
10610 Renton Issaquah Road
Issaquah, WA
425-392-2351
Dogs of all sizes are allowed. There are no additional pet fees. Dogs must be leashed and cleaned up after. The camping and tent areas also allow dogs. There is a dog walk area at the campground. 2 dogs may be allowed.

Seattle/Tacoma KOA
5801 S 212th Street
Kent, WA
253-872-8652 (800-562-1892)
seattlekoa.com
Dogs of all sizes are allowed. There are no additional pet fees. Dogs must have current shot records, be leashed, and cleaned up after. Dogs may be left in your RV if they will be quiet and comfortable. There are some breed restrictions. The camping and tent areas also allow dogs. There is a dog walk area at the campground. Multiple dogs may be allowed.

Lonesome Creek RV Park
490 Ocean Drive
LaPush, WA
360-374-4338
Dogs of all sizes are allowed. There are no additional pet fees. Dogs must be leashed and cleaned up after. The camping and tent areas also allow dogs. There is a dog walk area at the campground.

Lake Wenatchee State Park
21588A H 207
Leavenworth, WA
509-662-0420 (888-CAMPOUT (226-7688))
This 489 acre park along a glacier fed lake offers an amphitheater, interpretive programs, nature study, a variety of trails, and various land and water activities and recreation. Dogs of all sizes are allowed at no additional fee. Dogs may not be left unattended, and they must be leashed and cleaned up after. Dogs are not allowed in buildings, but they are allowed on the trails. The camping and tent areas also allow dogs. There is a dog walk area at the campground. Multiple dogs may be allowed.

Leavenworth/Wenatchee KOA
11401 Riverbend Drive
Leavenworth, WA
509-548-7709 (800-562-5709)
pinevillagekoa.com
Dogs of all sizes are allowed. There

are no additional pet fees. Dogs must be leashed and cleaned up after. Dogs may be left unattended if they are quiet and well behaved. There are some breed restrictions. This RV park is closed during the off-season. The camping and tent areas also allow dogs. There is a dog walk area at the campground. Multiple dogs may be allowed.

Andersen's RV Park on the Ocean
1400 138th Street (H 103)
Long Beach, WA
800-645-6795
andersensrv.com/
Dogs of all sizes are allowed. There are no additional pet fees. Dogs may not be left unattended unless they will be very quiet and well behaved. Dogs must be leashed and cleaned up after. Dogs may be off lead along the beach only if they will respond to voice command. This is an RV only park. There is a dog walk area at the campground. Multiple dogs may be allowed.

Spencer Spit State Park
521A Baker View Road
Lopez Island, WA
360-468-2251 (888-CAMPOUT (226-7688))
There is a 45 minute ferry ride from Anacordes to this park, and dogs must remain on the car deck during the crossing. This is a marine and camping park along the Strait of Juan de Fuca, and beachcoming and nature study are favorites here. Pets must be on a leash and under physical control at all times. Dogs are not permitted on designated swimming beaches. Dogs are allowed on the trails. The camping and tent areas also allow dogs. There is a dog walk area at the campground. There are no electric or water hookups at the campground. 2 dogs may be allowed.

Lynden/Bellingham KOA
8717 Line Road
Lynden, WA
360-354-4772 (800-562-4779)
koa.com
Dogs of all sizes are allowed. There are no additional pet fees. Dogs must be well behaved, leashed, and cleaned up after. The camping and tent areas also allow dogs. There is a dog walk area at the campground. Multiple dogs may be allowed.

Twin Cedars RV Park
17826 H 99N
Lynnwood, WA
425-742-5540

Dogs of all sizes are allowed. There are no additional pet fees. Dogs may not be left unattended, must be leashed, and cleaned up after. Dogs may be off leash at the dog run if they are well behaved. There is a dog walk area at the campground. Multiple dogs may be allowed.

Mount Spokane State Park
26107 N Mount Spokane Park Drive
Mead, WA
509-238-4258
This camping park of almost 14,000 acres, reaches an elevation of over 5,880 feet, and at times you can see great views of Washington, Idaho, and Montana. They offer interpretive activities, a variety of recreational pursuits, and over 100 miles of multi-use trails for spring/summer/fall that becomes cross-country ski trails in winter. Dogs are allowed on hiking trails except in winter. Dogs must be under physical control at all times, leashed, and cleaned up after. The campground is on a first come first served basis, and has 12 standard campsites with water and a flush restroom. This RV park is closed during the off-season. The camping and tent areas also allow dogs. There is a dog walk area at the campground. There are no electric or water hookups at the campgrounds. Multiple dogs may be allowed.

Crawford State Park
Boundary Road
Metaline Falls, WA
509-446-4065
This state park is a 49 acre, forested day-use park featuring a tourable cave-the 3rd largest limestone cavern in the state. There is a restroom, one kitchen shelter (without electricity), and 2 sheltered and 11 unsheltered picnic tables available on a first come first served basis. This park closes in September and reopens in April. Dogs of all sizes are welcome at the park, but they may not go into the cave. Dogs must be leashed and cleaned up after at all times. There is a dog walk area at the campground. Multiple dogs may be allowed.

Lake Sylvia State Park
1812 Lake Sylvia Road
Montesano, WA
360-249-3621 (888-CAMPOUT (226-7688))
This 233-acre camping park with

15,000 feet of freshwater shoreline is rich with logging lore and history. It offers 5 miles of hiking trails, and a variety of land and water recreation. Dogs of all sizes are allowed at no additional fee. Dogs may not be left unattended, and they must be quiet, well behaved, be on no more than an 8 foot leash, and be cleaned up after. Dogs are not allowed in public swim areas, buildings, or in the Environmental Learning Center area. This campground is closed during the off-season. The camping and tent areas also allow dogs. There is a dog walk area at the campground. There are no electric or water hookups at the campground. Multiple dogs may be allowed.

Mt. Baker-Snoqualmie National Forest
21905 64th Avenue W
Mountlake Terrace, WA
425-775-9702 (800-627-0062)
fs.fed.us/r6/mbs/
Snoqualmie National Forest extends more than 140 miles along the west side of the Cascade Mountains and offers a wide variety of recreational activities year round. Dogs of all sizes are allowed at no additional fee. Dogs may not be left unattended, and they must be leashed and cleaned up after. Dogs are allowed on the trails, but not in public swim areas. This campground is closed during the off-season. The camping and tent areas also allow dogs. There is a dog walk area at the campground. There are no electric or water hookups at the campground. Multiple dogs may be allowed.

Riverside State Park
Charles Road
Nine Mile Falls, WA
509-465-5064 (888-CAMPOUT (226-7688))
This 10,000-acre park along the Spokane Rivers offers interpretive centers, 55 miles of scenic hiking trails, opportunities for nature study, and a variety of land and water recreation. Dogs of all sizes are allowed at no additional fee. Dogs may not be left unattended, and they must be leashed at all times, and cleaned up after. Dogs are not allowed in the natural heritage area or in the Spokane River. Dogs are allowed on the trails. The camping and tent areas also allow dogs. There is a dog walk area at the campground. Multiple dogs may be allowed.

Fort Flager State Park

10541 Flagler Road
Nordland, WA
360-385-1259 (888-CAMPOUT (226-7688))
This historic, 784-acre marine park, sits atop a high bluff overlooking the Puget Sound, and offers a museum, interpretive programs, several miles of trails, and land and water activities. Dogs are allowed at no addtional fee. Dogs may not be left unattended, and they must be leashed and cleaned up after. Dogs are not allowed in any of the buildings, but they are allowed on the trails. The camping and tent areas also allow dogs. There is a dog walk area at the campground. Multiple dogs may be allowed.

Deception Pass State Park
41227 State Route 20
Oak Harbor, WA
360-675-2417 (888-CAMPOUT (226-7688))
Rich in natural and cultural history, this 4,134 acre marine and camping park is home to a large variety of plant/animal/bird life, and offers ample land and water recreational opportunities. Some of the amenities/features include salt and freshwater shorelines, 3 lakes, 2 amphitheaters, 6 fire circles, interpretive activities/signage, a museum, hiking trails plus a 1.2 mile ADA hiking trail, and breath-taking viewing areas. Dogs of all sizes are allowed for no additional fee. Dogs must be under physical control, leashed, and cleaned up after at all times. Dogs are not allowed on designated swimming beaches. Camping is available year round, although some sites may be closed for winter. Amenities include picnic tables (some sheltered), over 200 camp sites, restrooms, showers, and dump stations. The camping and tent areas also allow dogs. There is a dog walk area at the campground. Multiple dogs may be allowed.

North Whidbey RV Park
565 W Coronet Bay Road
Oak Harbor, WA
360-675-9597
northwhidbeyrvpark.com
Dogs of all sizes are allowed. There are no additional pet fees. Dogs may not be left unattended, or tied up outside alone. Dogs must be leashed and cleaned up after. There is a dog walk area at the campground. Multiple dogs may be allowed.

Ocean Park Resort
25904 R Street

Ocean Park, WA
360-665-4585
opresort.com
Dogs of all sizes and numbers are allowed, and there are no additional pet fees. There is a $7 per night per pet additional fee for the motel, and only 2 dogs are allowed per room. Dogs must be leashed and cleaned up after. There are some breed restrictions. The camping and tent areas also allow dogs. There is a dog walk area at the campground. Multiple dogs may be allowed.

Okanogan National Forest
1240 South Second Avenue
Okanogan, WA
509-826-3275
fs.fed.us/r6/oka/
This forest of a million and a half acres has a variety of water and land recreation year round. Dogs are allowed at no additional fee. Dogs may not be left unattended, and they must be leashed and cleaned up after. Dogs are not allowed in the back country, and on many of the trails. Dogs must remain on paved areas or on marked trails. This campground is closed during the off-season. The camping and tent areas also allow dogs. There is a dog walk area at the campground. There are no electric or water hookups at the campground. Multiple dogs may be allowed.

Olympic National Forest
1835 Black Lk Blvd SW
Olympia, WA
360-956-23300
fs.fed.us/r6/olympic/
This park is a unique geographic province in that it contains 5 different major landscapes, and is home to an astounding diversity of plants, animals, and recreational pursuits. The campground at Round Creek is the only camp area that stays open year round. Dogs of all sizes are allowed at no additional fee. Dogs may not be left unattended, and they must be leashed and cleaned up after. Dogs are allowed on the trails. The camping and tent areas also allow dogs. There is a dog walk area at the campground. Dogs are allowed in the camping cabins. There are no electric or water hookups at the campground. Multiple dogs may be allowed.

Spokane KOA
N 3025 Barker Road
Otis Orchards, WA

509-924-4722 (800-562-3309)
koa.com
Dogs of all sizes are allowed. There are no additional pet fees. Dogs may not be left unattended, can be on no more than a 6 foot leash, and must be cleaned up after. There are some breed restrictions. The camping and tent areas also allow dogs. There is a dog walk area at the campground. Dogs are allowed in the camping cabins. Multiple dogs may be allowed.

Pacific Beach State Park
On H 109
Pacific Beach, WA
360-276-4297 (888-CAMPOUT (226-7688))
This 10 acre camping park, with 2,300 feet of ocean shoreline, offers a variety of land and water recreation. Dogs of all sizes are allowed at no additional fee. Dogs may not be left unattended, and they must be quiet, well behaved, be on no more than an 8 foot leash, and be cleaned up after. Dogs are not allowed in public swim areas or buildings. Dogs are allowed on the trails. This campground is closed during the off-season. The camping and tent areas also allow dogs. There is a dog walk area at the campground. Multiple dogs may be allowed.

Sandy Heights RV Park
8801 St Thomas Drive
Pasco, WA
877-894-1357
Dogs of all sizes are allowed. There are no additional pet fees. Dogs must be leashed and cleaned up after. There are some breed restrictions. There is a dog walk area at the campground. 2 dogs may be allowed.

Mountain View RV Park
1375 SE 3rd Street
Pendleton, WA
866-302-3311
nwfamilyrvresorts.com
Dogs of all sizes are allowed. There are no additional pet fees. Dogs must be leashed and cleaned up after. There are some breed restrictions. The camping and tent areas also allow dogs. There is a dog walk area at the campground. 2 dogs may be allowed.

Log Cabin Resort
3183E Beach Road
Port Angeles, WA
360-928-3325
logcabinresort.net/home.htm

This resort style park offers spectacular scenery, a variety of accommodations as well as recreational pursuits. Dogs of all sizes are allowed at no additional fee for RV sites, however there is a $10 (plus tax)per night per pet additional fee for the rustic cabins. Dogs may not be left unattended, and they must be leashed and cleaned up after. Dogs are not allowed on the trails in the Olympic National Forest area. There is a dog walk area at the campground. Dogs are allowed in the camping cabins. Multiple dogs may be allowed.

Olympia National Park
600 East Park Avenue
Port Angeles, WA
360-452-4501
nps.gov/olym/
From rainforest to glacier capped mountains, this forest's diverse and impressive eco-system is home to 8 plants and 15 animals that are not found anywhere else on earth. It also provides an abundant variety of year round recreational pursuits. Dogs of all sizes are allowed at no additional fee. Dogs may not be left unattended, and they must be leashed and cleaned up after. Dogs are allowed in the camp areas and the parking lot at Hurricane Ridge; dogs are not allowed on the trails. The camping and tent areas also allow dogs. There is a dog walk area at the campground. There are no electric or water hookups at the campground. Multiple dogs may be allowed.

Port Angeles/Swquim KOA
80 O'Brien Road
Port Angeles, WA
360-457-5916 (800-562-7558)
portangeleskoa.com
Dogs of all sizes are allowed. There are no additional pet fees. Dogs may not be left unattended, must be on no more than a 6 foot leash, and cleaned up after. There are some breed restrictions. This RV park is closed during the off-season. The camping and tent areas also allow dogs. There is a dog walk area at the campground. 2 dogs may be allowed.

Point Hudson Resort Marina and RV Park
103 Hudson
Port Townsend, WA
360-385-2828
portofpt.com
Dogs of all sizes are allowed. There are no additional pet fees. Dogs

must be leashed and cleaned up after. Dogs are allowed to go to the beach, and if you bring them in the office they usually have doggy treats on hand. There is a dog walk area at the campground. There are special amenities given to dogs at this campground. Multiple dogs may be allowed.

Eagle Tree RV Park
16280 H 305
Poulsbo, WA
360-598-5988
eagletreerv.com
Dogs of all sizes are allowed. There are no additional pet fees. Dogs may not be tied up outside alone, must be leashed, and cleaned up after. There are some breed restrictions. There is a dog walk area at the campground. Multiple dogs may be allowed.

Wine Country RV Park
330 Merlot Drive
Prosser, WA
800-726-4969
winecountryrvpark.com
Dogs of all sizes are allowed. There are no additional pet fees. Dogs must be quiet, well behaved, leashed, and cleaned up after. No stakes are allowed put in the ground to tie your pet to. Dogs are allowed to run in the field across the street unleashed as long as there is control by the owner. The camping and tent areas also allow dogs. There is a dog walk area at the campground. Multiple dogs may be allowed.

Horn Rapids RV Resort
2640 Kings Gate Way
Richland, WA
509-375-9913
hornrapidsrvresort.com
Dogs of all sizes are allowed. There are no additional pet fees. Dogs must be leashed and cleaned up after. There is a dog run and a dog bathing area on site. There is a dog walk area at the campground. Multiple dogs may be allowed.

Outback RV Park
19100 Huntington
Rochester, WA
360-273-0585
outbackrvpark.com
Dogs of all sizes are allowed. There are no additional pet fees. Dogs may not be left unattended at any time, or tied up outside alone. Dogs must be leashed and cleaned up after. There is a dog walk area at the campground. 2 dogs may be

allowed.

Blake Island State Park
P.O. Box 42650
Seattle, WA
360-731-8330
A highlight of this 475 acre marine-camping park, reachable only by tour or private boat, is its 5 mile sandy shoreline offering outstanding views of the Olympic Mountains, volcanoes, and the Seattle skyline. In addition to offering a rich history, features/amenities include interpretive trails and activities, miles of hiking trails, a host of land and water recreation, and an impressive variety of plant, animal, and marine life. The park is also home to Tillicum Village where you can enjoy a Northwest Indian dining and cultural experience. Dogs of all sizes are allowed for no additional fee around the park and the village (except for the longhouse). Dogs must be leashed at all times, and cleaned up after. They are not allowed on designated swimming beaches. Camping is on a first come first served basis. There are barbecue grills located in the day use area. They offer a dump station, restrooms (one ADA), and a shower area. There are specific camp sites on the west end of the island for canoers and kayakers, as well as some additional primitive sites. The camping and tent areas also allow dogs. There is a dog walk area at the campground. There are no electric or water hookups at the campgrounds. 2 dogs may be allowed.

Blue Sky RV Park
9002 302nd Avenue SE
Seattle, WA
425-222-7910
blueskypreston.com
Dogs of all sizes are allowed. There are no additional pet fees. Dogs may not be left tied up outside alone, and must be leashed and cleaned up after. There is a dog walk area at the campground. Multiple dogs may be allowed.

North Cascades National Park
810 State Route 20
Sedro-Wooley, WA
360-856-5700
nps.gov/noca/
Know as the North American Alps, the North Cascades National Park is home to an astounding diversity of plants and animals, and provides a variety of recreational pursuits. Dogs of all sizes are allowed at no additional fee. Dogs may not be left

unattended, and they must be leashed and cleaned up after. Dogs are allowed at the Ross Lake National Recreation area, and on close-in trails. Dogs are not allowed in the back country. This campground is closed during the off-season. The camping and tent areas also allow dogs. There is a dog walk area at the campground. There are no electric or water hookups at the campground. Multiple dogs may be allowed.

Rainbows End RV Park
261831 H 101
Sequim, WA
360-683-3863
rainbowsendrvpark.com
Dogs of all sizes are allowed. There are no additional pet fees. Dogs may not be left unattended, must be leashed, and cleaned up after. There is, however, a large fenced in doggy play yard where they can run off leash. The camping and tent areas also allow dogs. There is a dog walk area at the campground. 2 dogs may be allowed.

Beacon Rock State Park
34841 State Route 14
Skamania, WA
509-427-8265
Beacon Rock is actually the core of an ancient volcano, and the mile-long trail to its summit gives the viewer a stunning panoramic view of the Columbia River Gorge. With over 4,600 acres, more than 20 miles of multi-use trails, and 9,500 feet of freshwater shoreline, there is an abundance of plant and wildlife, and land and water recreation. Dogs of all sizes are allowed for no additional fee. Dogs must be under physical control at all times, leashed, and cleaned up after. Dogs are not allowed on designated swimming beaches. The park's main campground is seasonal, but there are 2 campsites near the moorage area available year round on a first come first served basis. The camp, being an older camp, is more suited to tent camping rather than RV, and there are only a limited number of sites that will accommodate rigs over 20 feet. There is a restroom and showers. This RV park is closed during the off-season. The camping and tent areas also allow dogs. There is a dog walk area at the campground. There are no electric or water hookups at the campgrounds. Multiple dogs may be allowed.

Alderwood RV Resort

14007 N Newport H
Spokane, WA
509-467-5320
alderwoodrv.com
Dogs of all sizes are allowed. There are no additional pet fees. Dogs may not be left outside alone, and outside pens for pets are not allowed. Dogs must be leashed and cleaned up after. The camping and tent areas also allow dogs. There is a dog walk area at the campground. Multiple dogs may be allowed.

Trailer Inns RV Park
6021 E 4th
Spokane Valley, WA
509-535-1811
trailerinnsrv.com
Dogs of all sizes are allowed. There are no additional pet fees for up to 2 dogs, and there is no deposit unless you stay by the month. If there are more than 2 dogs, the fee is $3 per night per pet. Dogs may not be left unattended, must be leashed, and cleaned up after. There is a dog walk area at the campground. Multiple dogs may be allowed.

Wenberg State Park
15430 E Lake Goodwin Road
Stanwood, WA
360-652-7417 (888-CAMPOUT (226-7688))
This 46 acre camping park, with 1,140 feet of freshwater shoreline, offers great fishing and a variety of land and water recreation. Dogs of all sizes are allowed at no additional fee. Dogs may not be left unattended, and they must be leashed at all times, and cleaned up after. Dogs are not allowed in public swim areas or in buildings. The camping and tent areas also allow dogs. There is a dog walk area at the campground. Multiple dogs may be allowed.

Yakama Nation RV Resort
280 Buster Road
Toppenish, WA
509-865-2000
yakamanation.com
Dogs of all sizes are allowed. There are no additional pet fees. Dogs must be leashed and cleaned up after. In addition to tent and RV sites, they have teepee sites, and dogs are allowed there also. There are some breed restrictions. The camping and tent areas also allow dogs. There is a dog walk area at the campground. Multiple dogs may be allowed.

Gifford Pinchot National Forest

10600 N.E. 51st Circle
Vancouver, WA
360-891-5000
fs.fed.us/gpnf/
There are 67 campgrounds in this forest, and it is also home to the Mount St. Helens National Volcanic Monument. Dogs are not allowed out of the car at the monument. Dogs of all sizes are allowed, and there are no additional pet fees. Dogs may not be left unattended, and they must be quiet, leashed, and cleaned up after. Dogs must be walked in designated areas. This campground is closed during the off-season. The camping and tent areas also allow dogs. There is a dog walk area at the campground. There are no electric or water hookups at the campground. Multiple dogs may be allowed.

Vancouver RV Park
7603 NE 13th Avenue
Vancouver, WA
360-695-1158
vancouverrvparks.com
Dogs of all sizes are allowed. There are no additional pet fees. Dogs may not be left unattended or tied up alone outside. Dogs must be quiet, well behaved, leashed, and cleaned up after. There are some breed restrictions. The camping and tent areas also allow dogs. There is a dog walk area at the campground. 2 dogs may be allowed.

Iron Horse State Park
P. O. Box 1203
Vantage, WA
509-856-2700
This linear park of over 1,600 acres celebrates its railroading history, spans several geological zones, protects several ecosystems and their inhabitants, and provides a variety of recreational pursuits. It is also home to Snoqualmie Pass Tunnel (seasonal) that is almost 2 miles long-bring your flashlight, and the Iron Horse Trail that is over 100 miles long following along the route of the railroad. Dogs are allowed for no additional fee. Pets must be on a leash, under physical control at all times, and cleaned up after (even on trails). Dogs are not allowed on any designated swimming beaches. Camping is allowed on a first come first served basis, and there are four primitive campgrounds along the trail, each with 3 to 4 sites, a picnic table and a vault toilet. There is also camping available by the trail near the U. S. Forest Service at Tinkham, Denny Creek, Lake Kachess, and Crystal Springs. The camping and

tent areas also allow dogs. There is a dog walk area at the campground. There are no electric or water hookups at the campgrounds. Multiple dogs may be allowed.

Fairway RV Resort
50 W George Street (entrance Burns St)
Walla Walla, WA
509-525-8282
fairwayrvresort.com
Dogs of all sizes are allowed. There are no additional pet fees for 2 dogs. If there are more than 2 dogs, then the fee is $1 per night per pet additional. Dogs may not be left unattended or staked outside alone, they must be leashed, and cleaned up after. The camping and tent areas also allow dogs. There is a dog walk area at the campground. Multiple dogs may be allowed.

Rock Island State Park
Rt. 1, Box 118A
Washington Island, WA
920-847-2235 (888-936-7463)
Bequeathed to the state by a wealthy inventor who lived here from 1910 to 1945, this 912 acre island has several stone buildings that he built, including his home, a boat house, and water tower. No vehicles-not even bicycles, are allowed on the island, and it is accessed only by boat or ferry (dogs are allowed on the ferry). There are house exhibits, seasonal naturalist programs, and several miles of hiking trails. Dogs are allowed for no additional fee; they must be leashed and under their owner's control at all times. Forty campsites are available for reservations; picnic tables, fire rings, and pit toilets are on site. Drinking water and firewood are available near the dock and boathouse. This RV park is closed during the off-season. The camping and tent areas also allow dogs. There are no electric or water hookups at the campgrounds. 2 dogs may be allowed.

Wenatchee National Forest
215 Melody Lane (forest HQ)
Wenatchee, WA
509-664-9200
fs.fed.us/r6/wenatchee/
This forest is divided into 6 ranger districts and covers 2.2 million acres with a variety of trails totaling about 2,500 miles. Dogs of all sizes are allowed at no additional fee. Dogs may not be left unattended, and they must be leashed and cleaned up after in camp areas. Dogs are

allowed on the trails, but they are not allowed in public swim areas or any buildings. The camping and tent areas also allow dogs. There is a dog walk area at the campground. There are no electric or water hookups at the campground. Multiple dogs may be allowed.

Totem RV Park
2421 N Nyhus
Westport, WA
360-268-0025 (888-TOTEMRV (868-3678))
totemrv.com
Dogs of all sizes are allowed. There are no additional pet fees. Dogs may not be left unattended, and they must be quiet, well behaved, leashed, and cleaned up after. If you would like to view this area from their tower, the site is westportcam.com. The camping and tent areas also allow dogs. There is a dog walk area at the campground. Multiple dogs may be allowed.

Bridge RV Park & Campground
65271 H 14
White Salmon, WA
509-493-1111
bridgerv.com/
Dogs of all sizes are allowed. There is a $1 per night per pet additional fee. Dogs may not be left unattended, and they must be quiet, well behaved, leashed, and cleaned up after. The camping and tent areas also allow dogs. There is a dog walk area at the campground. Multiple dogs may be allowed.

Winthrop/N Cascades National Park KOA
1114 H 20
Winthrop, WA
509-996-2258 (800-562-2158)
methownet.com/koa
Dogs of all sizes are allowed. There are no additional pet fees. Dogs must be leashed and cleaned up after. Dogs may be left unattended if they are quiet and well behaved, and you can also tie your pet by the office. This RV park is closed during the off-season. The camping and tent areas also allow dogs. There is a dog walk area at the campground. Dogs are allowed in the camping cabins. Multiple dogs may be allowed.

Columbia Riverfront RV Park
1881 Pike Road
Woodland, WA
360-225-8051
columbiariverfrontrvpark.com

Dogs of all sizes are allowed. There are no additional pet fees for up to 2 pets. If there are more than 3 dogs, then the fee is an additional $1 per night per pet. Dogs must be leashed and cleaned up after, and they are allowed at the beach. There are some breed restrictions. There is a dog walk area at the campground. 2 dogs may be allowed.

Trailer Inns RV Park
1610 N 1st Street
Yakima, WA
509-452-9561
trailerinns.com
Dogs of all sizes are allowed. There are no additional pet fees. Dogs may not be left unattended, or tied up outside alone. Dogs must be leashed and cleaned up after. The camping and tent areas also allow dogs. There is a dog walk area at the campground. Multiple dogs may be allowed.

Yakima KOA
1500 Keys Road
Yakima, WA
509-248-5882 (800-562-5773)
koa@html.com
Dogs of all sizes are allowed. There are no additional pet fees. Dogs must be well behaved, leashed, and cleaned up after. There are some breed restrictions. The camping and tent areas also allow dogs. There is a dog walk area at the campground. Dogs are allowed in the camping cabins. 2 dogs may be allowed.

West Virginia

Beech Fork State Park
5601 Long Branch Road
Barboursville, WV
304-528-5794 (800-CALL WVA (225-5982))
beechforksp.com/
Offering an abundance of flora and fauna, this 3,144 acre lakeside park also offers a variety of land and water recreation. Healthy dogs are allowed in camp areas for no charge and the cabins/cottages for a $50 refundable deposit, plus $40 for the first night and $5 for each additional night per pet. A credit card must be on file, and there is a pet agreement to sign at check in. Pets may not be left unattended outside, they must be securely crated when left alone in the cabins or cottages, they are not allowed to be tied/chained on the

porch or yard, and their food may not be kept outside. Dogs must have certified proof of inoculations from a veterinarian, be on no more than a 10 foot leash, and picked up after. The campground offers 275 sites in various settings and each site has a picnic table and grill, with restrooms, showers, a laundry, and playground nearby. The camping and tent areas also allow dogs. There is a dog walk area at the campground. Dogs are allowed in the camping cabins. 2 dogs may be allowed.

Big Bear Lake Campground
Hazelton Big Bear Lake Road
Bruceton Mills, WV
304-379-4382
bigbearwv.com
Dogs of all sizes are allowed. There are no additional pet fees. Dogs may not be left unattended, and they must be leashed and cleaned up after. This RV park is closed during the off-season. The camping and tent areas also allow dogs. There is a dog walk area at the campground. Dogs are allowed in the camping cabins. There are no water hookups at the campgrounds. Multiple dogs may be allowed.

Audra State Park
Rt. 4 Box 564
Buckhannon, WV
304-457-1162 (800-CALL WVA)
audrastatepark.com/
A highlight of this wooded park along the Middle Fork River is the stunning view from the boardwalk that follows along the cave's overhanging ledge. Healthy dogs are allowed for no additional pet fee. Dogs must be restrained on no more than a 10 foot leash, be picked up after, and have certified proof of inoculations from a veterinarian. Open from mid-April to mid-October on a first come, first served basis, this camp area offers 2 modern bathhouses, a laundry, playground, and a dump station. The sites each have a picnic table and grill. This RV park is closed during the off-season. The camping and tent areas also allow dogs. There is a dog walk area at the campground. There are no electric or water hookups at the campgrounds. 2 dogs may be allowed.

Greenbrier State Forest
HC 30 Box 154/Harts Run Road
Caldwell, WV
304-536-1944 (800-CALL WVA (225-5982))
greenbriersf.com/
Amid more than 5,100 acres of

forested mountain sits this major family recreation destination that offers gaming courts/fields, shooting ranges, picnicking areas, a pool, and a variety of special events. Healthy dogs are allowed in camp areas for no charge and the cabins/cottages for a $50 refundable deposit, plus $40 for the first night and $5 for each additional night per pet. A credit card must be on file, and there is a pet agreement to sign at check in. Pets may not be left unattended outside, they must be securely crated when left alone in the cabins or cottages, they are not allowed to be tied/chained on the porch or yard, and their food may not be kept outside. Dogs must have certified proof of inoculations from a veterinarian, be on no more than a 10 foot leash, and picked up after. The 16 site campground offers restrooms with hot showers, drinking water, and each site has a table and stone fireplace grill. This RV park is closed during the off-season. The camping and tent areas also allow dogs. There is a dog walk area at the campground. Dogs are allowed in the camping cabins. There are no water hookups at the campgrounds. 2 dogs may be allowed.

Camp Creek State Park
2390 Camp Creek Road
Camp Creek, WV
304-425-9481 (800-CALLWVA (225-5982))
campcreekstatepark.com/
This scenic mountain park offers a variety of trails, land and water recreation, and it is also adjacent to the Camp Creek State Forest. Dogs of all sizes are allowed at no additional fee. Dogs may not be left unattended, and they must be leashed and cleaned up after. Dogs are allowed on the trails. This campground is closed during the off-season. The camping and tent areas also allow dogs. There is a dog walk area at the campground. There are no water hookups at the campground. Multiple dogs may be allowed.

Kanawha State Forest
Rt. 2 Box 285
Charleston, WV
304-558-3500 (800-CALL WVA (225-5982))
kanawhastateforest.com/
Featuring diverse habitats with an abundance of bird and wildlife, this lush 9,300 acre forest provides a number of recreational pursuits,

great hiking trails, and a variety of special events during the season. Dogs are allowed throughout the park and in the camp area for no additional fee. Dogs must be leashed and under their owner's control at all times. The campground offers 46 sites, each with picnic tables and fireplaces, and bathhouses, a laundry facility, and a dump station are nearby. There is also a children's playground, and firewood and ice is available on site. This RV park is closed during the off-season. The camping and tent areas also allow dogs. There is a dog walk area at the campground. Multiple dogs may be allowed.

Babcock State Park
HC 35, Box 150
Clifftop, WV
304-438-3004 (800-CALL WVA (225-5982))
babcocksp.com/
Offering over 4,000 scenic, diverse acres with an abundance of land and water recreation, this park also has a recreated working Grist Mill where visitors may purchase milled products. Healthy dogs are allowed in camp areas for no charge, and the cabins/cottages for a $50 refundable deposit, plus $40 for the first night and $5 for each additional night per pet. A credit card must be on file, and there is a pet agreement to sign at check in. Pets must be securely crated when left alone in the cabins or cottages, they are not allowed to be tied/chained on the porch or yard, and their food may not be kept outside. Dogs must have certified proof of inoculations from a veterinarian, be on no more than a 10 foot leash, and picked up after. The 52 site campground is open from mid-April to mid-October and offer picnic tables, grills, restrooms, showers, a laundry, drinking water, and 2 dump stations. This RV park is closed during the off-season. The camping and tent areas also allow dogs. There is a dog walk area at the campground. Dogs are allowed in the camping cabins. There are no water hookups at the campgrounds. 2 dogs may be allowed.

Blackwater Falls State Park
Blackwater Falls Road
Davis, WV
304-259-5216 (800-CALL WVA (225-5982))
blackwaterfalls.com/
Named for the amber colored waters and the beautiful falls (a popular photography site), this park also

offers a wide variety of land and water recreation, and many special fun events throughout the season. Healthy dogs are allowed in camp areas for no charge and the cabins/cottages for a $50 refundable deposit, plus $40 for the first night and $5 for each additional night per pet. A credit card must be on file, and there is a pet agreement to sign at check in. Pets may not be left unattended outside, they must be securely crated when left alone in the cabins or cottages, they are not allowed to be tied/chained on the porch or yard, and their food may not be kept outside. Dogs must have certified proof of inoculations from a veterinarian, be on no more than a 10 foot leash, and picked up after. The 65 unit camp area has modern restrooms, showers, a laundry, and a dump station. This RV park is closed during the off-season. The camping and tent areas also allow dogs. There is a dog walk area at the campground. Dogs are allowed in the camping cabins. 2 dogs may be allowed.

Canaan Valley Resort
HC70, Box 330
Davis, WV
304-866-4121 (800-622-4121)
canaanresort.com/
Surrounded by a million acres of forest at 3,300 feet, this scenic resort offers all the year round recreational opportunities, plus numerous special events, and casual or fine dining. Healthy dogs are allowed in camp areas for no charge and the cabins/cottages for a $50 refundable deposit, plus $40 for the first night and $5 for each additional night per pet. A credit card must be on file, and there is a pet agreement to sign at check in. Pets may not be left unattended outside, they must be securely crated when left alone in the cabins or cottages, they are not allowed to be tied/chained on the porch or yard, and their food may not be kept outside. Dogs must have certified proof of inoculations from a veterinarian, be on no more than a 10 foot leash, and picked up after. The camp area has 34 paved, wooded sites with restrooms, showers, and a laundry, plus a playground and gaming; a dump station is nearby. The camping and tent areas also allow dogs. There is a dog walk area at the campground. Dogs are allowed in the camping cabins. 2 dogs may be allowed.

Cabwaylingo State Forest

Rt. 1 Box 85/H 41
Dunlow, WV
304-385-4255 (800-CALL WVA (225-5982))
cabwaylingo.com/
Developed by the CCC, this 8,123 acre state forest offers visitors outstanding scenery full of wildlife, plenty of hiking trails, picnic areas, a fire tower, and a wide range of recreation. Healthy dogs are allowed in camp areas for no charge and the cabins/cottages for a $50 refundable deposit, plus $40 for the first night and $5 for each additional night per pet. A credit card must be on file, and there is a pet agreement to sign at check in. Pets may not be left unattended outside, they must be securely crated when left alone in the cabins or cottages, they are not allowed to be tied/chained on the porch or yard, and their food may not be kept outside. Dogs must have certified proof of inoculations from a veterinarian, be on no more than a 10 foot leash, and picked up after. There are 2 campsite areas: 1 modern and 1 rustic. All sites have tables, fireplaces, firewood, and drinking water; restrooms and showers are nearby. This RV park is closed during the off-season. The camping and tent areas also allow dogs. There is a dog walk area at the campground. Dogs are allowed in the camping cabins. 2 dogs may be allowed.

Seneca State Forest
Rt. 1 Box 140/H 28
Dunmore, WV
304-799-6213 (800-CALL WVA (225-5982))
senecastateforest.com/
As the state's oldest forest with 11,684 acres, there is an abundance of land and water recreation available. Healthy dogs are allowed in camp areas for no charge and the cabins/cottages for a $50 refundable deposit, plus $40 for the first night and $5 for each additional night per pet. A credit card must be on file, and there is a pet agreement to sign at check in. Pets may not be left unattended outside, they must be securely crated when left alone in the cabins or cottages, they are not allowed to be tied/chained on the porch or yard, and their food may not be kept outside. Dogs must have certified proof of inoculations from a veterinarian, be on no more than a 10 foot leash, and picked up after. The rustic camp area offers large,

secluded sites on a first come, first served basis with picnic tables, fireplaces, drinking water, and vault toilets. Firewood, showers, and a laundry are available for a small fee. This RV park is closed during the off-season. The camping and tent areas also allow dogs. There is a dog walk area at the campground. Dogs are allowed in the camping cabins. There are no electric or water hookups at the campgrounds. 2 dogs may be allowed.

Jellystone Park
Route 33 E Faulkner Road
Elkins, WV
304-637-8898 (866-988-5267)
jellystonewestvirginia.com
Dogs of all sizes are allowed. There are no additional pet fees. Dogs must be quiet, leashed, and cleaned up after. This RV park is closed during the off-season. The camping and tent areas also allow dogs. There is a dog walk area at the campground. Dogs are allowed in the camping cabins. 2 dogs may be allowed.

Monongahela National Forest
200 Sycamore Street
Elkins, WV
304-636-1800 (800-CALLWVA (225-5982))
fs.fed.us/r9/mnf/index.shtml
This forest has 6 ranger districts, almost a million acres, and diverse ecosystems that support a large variety of plants, animals, and recreation. Dogs are allowed at no additional fee. Dogs may not be left unattended, and they must be leashed and cleaned up after in the camp areas. Dogs are allowed on the trails. The camping and tent areas also allow dogs. There is a dog walk area at the campground. There are no water hookups at the campground. Multiple dogs may be allowed.

Revelle's River Resort
9 Faulkner Road
Elkins, WV
877-988-2267
revelles.com
Dogs of all sizes are allowed, and there are no additional pet fees for tent or RV sites. There is a $5 per night per pet additional fee plus a cash security deposit of $50 for the regular cabins, and the same daily fee plus a $100 deposit for the upscale cabins. Dogs must be leashed and cleaned up after. The camping and tent areas also allow dogs. There is a dog walk area at the

campground. Dogs are allowed in the camping cabins. 2 dogs may be allowed.

Moncove Lake State Park
HC 83, Box 73A
Gap Mills, WV
304-772-3450 (800-CALLWVA (225-5982))
moncovelakestatepark.com/
This park of 250 acres has an adjoining 500 acre wildlife management area and a 144 acre lake in addition to a variety of land and water recreational pursuits. Dogs of all sizes are allowed at no additional fee. Dogs may not be left unattended, and they must be quiet, well behaved, leashed and cleaned up after. This campground is closed during the off-season. The camping and tent areas also allow dogs. There is a dog walk area at the campground. There are no water hookups at the campground. Multiple dogs may be allowed.

New River Gorge National River
104 Main Street
Glen Jean, WV
304-465-0508
nps.gov/neri/
In addition to a number of recreational activities, this dramatically scenic and diverse 70,000 acre park offers a rich natural cultural history as well as educational opportunities. Also, once a year the New River Gorge Bridge is opened for parachute BASE jumpers, and Amtrak is available at 3 stops in the park. Dogs are allowed for no additional fee; they must be leashed and under their owner's control at all times. There are 4 primitive, riverside camp areas with limited restroom facilities and no drinking water. They are Stone Cliff Beach off H 25 near Thurmond; Army Camp off H 41 near Prince; Grandview Sandbar on Glade Creek Road, and Glade Creek at the end of Glade Creek Road. The camping and tent areas also allow dogs. There is a dog walk area at the campground. There are no electric or water hookups at the campgrounds. Multiple dogs may be allowed.

The Gauley River National Recreation Area
H 129/ P. O. Box 246
Glen Jean, WV
304-465-0508
nps.gov/gari/
Although home to one of the most adventurous white water rafting corridors in the east, this recreation area offers hiking trails, scenic gorges, a variety of natural habitats, and historic sites. Dogs are allowed for no additional pet fees. Dogs must be under their owner's control at all times. Primitive camping is allowed at the Summersville Dam tail-waters area. The camping and tent areas also allow dogs. There is a dog walk area at the campground. There are no electric or water hookups at the campgrounds. Multiple dogs may be allowed.

Cedar Creek State Park
2947 Cedar Creek Road
Glenville, WV
304-462-7158 (800-CALLWVA (225-5982))
cedarcreeksp.com/
This park offers 2,483 lush acres of rolling hills, wide valleys, and a variety of recreational pursuits. Dogs of all sizes are allowed at no additional fee. Dogs may not be left unattended, and they must be quiet, well behaved, leashed and cleaned up after. Dogs are not allowed in buildings or at the pool, but they are allowed on the trails. This campground is closed during the off-season. The camping and tent areas also allow dogs. There is a dog walk area at the campground. Multiple dogs may be allowed.

Tygart Lake State Park
Rt. 1 Box 260
Grafton, WV
304-265-6144 (800-CALL WVA (225-5982))
tygartlake.com/
Located among rolling hills next to a 10 mile long, 1,750 acre lake, this park has plenty of land and water recreation plus they offer free guided nature programs, and special events/performers through the summer. Healthy dogs are allowed in camp areas for no charge and the cabins/cottages for a $50 refundable deposit, plus $40 for the first night and $5 for each additional night per pet. A credit card must be on file, and there is a pet agreement to sign at check in. Pets may not be left unattended outside, they must be securely crated when left alone in the cabins or cottages, they are not allowed to be tied/chained on the porch or yard, and their food may not be kept outside. Dogs must have certified proof of inoculations from a veterinarian, be on no more than a 10 foot leash, and picked up after. The camp area offers a total of 40 sites, each with a fire ring and picnic table. There is also drinking water, restrooms with showers on site, and ice and firewood for sale. This RV park is closed during the off-season. The camping and tent areas also allow dogs. There is a dog walk area at the campground. Dogs are allowed in the camping cabins. There are no water hookups at the campgrounds. 2 dogs may be allowed.

Holly River State Park
680 State Park Road
Hacker Valley, WV
304-493-6353 (800-CALL WVA (225-5982))
hollyriver.com/
Nestled in a narrow valley bordered by dense forest, lies this scenic, secluded 8,101 acre park that offers a number of recreation and activities. Healthy dogs are allowed in camp areas for no charge and the cabins/cottages for a $50 refundable deposit, plus $40 for the first night and $5 for each additional night per pet. A credit card must be on file, and there is a pet agreement to sign at check in. Pets may not be left unattended outside, they must be securely crated when left alone in the cabins or cottages, they are not allowed to be tied/chained on the porch or yard, and their food may not be kept outside. Dogs must have certified proof of inoculations from a veterinarian, be on no more than a 10 foot leash, and picked up after. They are also allowed at the outer tables of their seasonal restaurant. There are 88 camps sites with picnic tables and grills at each site, and restrooms, hot showers, a laundry, and a dump station are nearby. Firewood is also available for a small fee. This RV park is closed during the off-season. The camping and tent areas also allow dogs. There is a dog walk area at the campground. Dogs are allowed in the camping cabins. There are no water hookups at the campgrounds. 2 dogs may be allowed.

Harpers Ferry/Washington DC NW KOA
343 Campground Road
Harpers Ferry, WV
304-535-6895 (800-562-9497)
harpersferrykoa.com
Dogs of all sizes are allowed. There is a $3 per pet per stay additional fee. Dogs must be leashed and cleaned up after. There are some breed restrictions. The camping and tent areas also allow dogs. There is a dog walk area at the campground. Dogs are allowed in the camping

cabins. Multiple dogs may be allowed.

Bluestone State Park
HC 78 Box 3/H 20
Hinton, WV
304-466-2805 (800-CALL WVA (225-5982))
bluestonesp.com/
Offering historical as well as recreational interests, this 2,100 forested, mountain park sits adjacent to the states 3rd largest body of water. Healthy dogs are allowed in camp areas for no charge and the cabins/cottages for a $50 refundable deposit, plus $40 for the first night and $5 for each additional night per pet. A credit card must be on file, and there is a pet agreement to sign at check in. Pets may not be left unattended outside, they must be securely crated when left alone in the cabins or cottages, they are not allowed to be tied/chained on the porch or yard, and their food may not be kept outside. Dogs must have certified proof of inoculations from a veterinarian, be on no more than a 10 foot leash, and picked up after. Campsites consist of 32 sites with central restrooms, showers, and a dump station; a 44 rustic site camp area with restrooms and cold showers, and a 39 site area that is accessible only by boat. This RV park is closed during the off-season. The camping and tent areas also allow dogs. There is a dog walk area at the campground. Dogs are allowed in the camping cabins. There are no water hookups at the campgrounds. 2 dogs may be allowed.

Kumbrabow State Forest
Kumbrabow Forest Road/H 219
Huttonsville, WV
304-335-2219 (800-CALL WVA (225-5982))
kumbrabow.com/
There is an emphasis on outdoor recreation and entertainment at this 9,474 multi-colored, thriving forest (the state's tallest); they offer seasonal Story Tellers and a variety of live shows. Healthy dogs are allowed in camp areas for no charge and the cabins/cottages for a $50 refundable deposit, plus $40 for the first night and $5 for each additional night per pet. A credit card must be on file, and there is a pet agreement to sign at check in. Pets may not be left unattended outside, they must be securely crated when left alone in the cabins or cottages, they are not allowed to be tied/chained on the

porch or yard, and their food may not be kept outside. Dogs must have certified proof of inoculations from a veterinarian, be on no more than a 10 foot leash, and picked up after. Along a stream where flowers bloom in abundance, there are 13 campsites with picnic tables, fireplaces, drinking water, and pit toilets. Showers, a laundry, firewood and ice are available at the forest headquarters. This RV park is closed during the off-season. The camping and tent areas also allow dogs. Dogs are allowed in the camping cabins. There are no electric or water hookups at the campgrounds. 2 dogs may be allowed.

Bluestone Wildlife Management Area
HC 65/91 Indian Mills Road
Indian Mills, WV
304-466-3398 (800-CALL WVA (225-5982))
bluestonewma.com/
With well over 17,000 acres adjacent to the state's 2nd largest lake, this park offers a wide variety of outdoor recreational pursuits. Healthy dogs are allowed for no additional fee. A credit card must be on file, and there is a pet agreement to sign at check in. Pets may not be left unattended outside, and their food may not be kept outside. Dogs must have certified proof of inoculations from a veterinarian, be on no more than a 10 foot leash, and picked up after. There are more than 330 primitive campsites available in a variety of settings. The camping and tent areas also allow dogs. There is a dog walk area at the campground. There are no electric or water hookups at the campgrounds. Multiple dogs may be allowed.

Chief Logan State Park
General Delivery
Logan, WV
304-792-7125 (800-CALLWVA (225-5982))
chiefloganstatepark.com/
This 4,000 acre park offers a modern restaurant, an outdoor amphitheater, a wildlife center, miles of trails, and a variety of recreational pursuits. Dogs of all sizes are allowed at no additional fee. Dogs must be well behaved, leashed, and cleaned up after. Dogs are not allowed at the wildlife exhibit or at the pool, but they are allowed on the trails. This campground is closed during the

off-season. The camping and tent areas also allow dogs. There is a dog walk area at the campground. Multiple dogs may be allowed.

Watoga State Park
HC 82, Box 252
Marlinton, WV
304-799-4087 (800-CALL WVA (225-5982))
watoga.com/
There are over 10,000 recreational acres at this mountain park that also provides a park commissary, restaurant (no outside seating for pets), naturalist programs, a seasonal pool, and gaming fields/courts. Healthy dogs are allowed in camp areas for no charge and the cabins/cottages for a $50 refundable deposit, plus $40 for the first night and $5 for each additional night per pet. A credit card must be on file, and there is a pet agreement to sign at check in. Pets may not be left unattended outside, they must be securely crated when left alone in the cabins or cottages, they are not allowed to be tied/chained on the porch or yard, and their food may not be kept outside. Dogs must have certified proof of inoculations from a veterinarian, be on no more than a 10 foot leash, and picked up after. Two separate campgrounds offer a total of 88 sites; each site has tables and grills, and bathhouses, restrooms, a laundry, and dishwashing stations are nearby. This RV park is closed during the off-season. The camping and tent areas also allow dogs. There is a dog walk area at the campground. Dogs are allowed in the camping cabins. There are no water hookups at the campgrounds. 2 dogs may be allowed.

Fox Fire Resort
Route 2, Box 655
Milton, WV
304-743-5622
foxfirewv.com/
Dogs of all sizes are allowed. There are no additional pet fees. Dogs must be leashed and cleaned up after. This RV park is closed during the off-season. There are some breed restrictions. 2 dogs may be allowed.

Huntington / Fox Fire KOA
290 Fox Fire Road
Milton, WV
304-743-5622 (800-562-0898)
koa.com/where/wv/48118/
There is a nice swim lake with a sandy beach at this 110 site

campground; plus they offer mostly grassy and shady sites, free Wi-Fi, and 2 stocked catch and release fishing ponds. Dogs are allowed for no additional fee. Dogs may not be left unattended outside, and they may only be left alone inside if they will be quiet. Dogs must be on no more than a 6 foot leash and cleaned up after at all times. There are some breed restrictions. The camping and tent areas also allow dogs. There is a dog walk area at the campground. Multiple dogs may be allowed.

Twin Falls Resort State Park
Route 97, Box 667
Mullens, WV
304-294-4000 (800-CALL WVA (225-5982))
twinfallsresort.com/
This mountain recreation getaway offers 12 hiking trails, an amphitheater, an 18-hole golf course, an 1830's living history farm, and much more. Healthy dogs are allowed in camp areas for no charge and the cabins/cottages for a $50 refundable deposit, plus $40 for the first night and $5 for each additional night per pet. A credit card must be on file, and there is a pet agreement to sign at check in. Pets may not be left unattended outside, they must be securely crated when left alone in the cabins or cottages, they are not allowed to be tied/chained on the porch or yard, and their food may not be kept outside. Dogs must have certified proof of inoculations from a veterinarian, be on no more than a 10 foot leash, and picked up after. The campground has 50 sites-25 can be reserved, and there is a small convenience store, a laundry, 2 bathhouses, picnic tables and grills, and a dump station. The camping and tent areas also allow dogs. There is a dog walk area at the campground. Dogs are allowed in the camping cabins. There are no water hookups at the campgrounds. 2 dogs may be allowed.

Pipestem Resort State Park
H 20 N/
Pipestem, WV
304-466-1800 (800-CALL WVA (225-5982))
pipestemresort.com/
Two golf courses, a Nature Center, an eatery, recreation center with a pool, an amphitheater, a 3600 foot aerial tramway, and 20 different hiking trails are just some of the amenities found at this popular park. Healthy dogs are allowed in camp areas for no charge and the

cabins/cottages for a $50 refundable deposit, plus $40 for the first night and $5 for each additional night per pet. A credit card must be on file, and there is a pet agreement to sign at check in. Pets may not be left unattended outside, they must be securely crated when left alone in the cabins or cottages, they are not allowed to be tied/chained on the porch or yard, and their food may not be kept outside. Dogs must have certified proof of inoculations from a veterinarian, be on no more than a 10 foot leash, and picked up after. Dogs are allowed on the aerial tram. The campground offers 82 sites with a heated bathroom, a camp store, laundry, a playground, and other gaming areas. The camping and tent areas also allow dogs. There is a dog walk area at the campground. Dogs are allowed in the camping cabins. 2 dogs may be allowed.

Stonewall Resort
940 Resort Drive
Roanoke, WV
304-269-7400 (888-278-8150)
stonewallresort.com/
In addition to the numerous amenities at this full service 2,000 acre lake resort with 82 miles of shoreline, they also provide a 374-slip marina, a golf course, driving range, fitness facilities, pools, and much more. Although dogs are not allowed at the resort, they are allowed in the campground for no additional pet fee. Campers are welcome to use the amenities at the resort. Dogs must be leashed and cleaned up after at all times. The campsites are located lakeside and offer tables, fire pits, a playground, mooring posts, and comfort stations. The camping and tent areas also allow dogs. There is a dog walk area at the campground. 2 dogs may be allowed.

Plum Orchard Lake Wildlife Management Area
Plum Orchard Lake Road
Scarbro, WV
304-469-9905 (800-CALL WVA (225-5982))
plumorchardlakewma.com/
There are 3,201 recreational acres at this forested park with a 202 acre, 6 ½ mile shoreline lake that's quite popular for fishing. Healthy dogs are allowed for no additional fee. A credit card must be on file, and there is a pet agreement to sign at check in. Pets may not be left unattended outside, and their food

must be kept inside. Dogs must have certified proof of inoculations from a veterinarian, be on no more than a 10 foot leash, and picked up after. The park has 21 primitive sites at Beech Bottom, and 17 primitive sites above the dam, each with a tent pad, picnic table, and grill. Restrooms and drinking water is nearby. The camping and tent areas also allow dogs. There is a dog walk area at the campground. There are no electric or water hookups at the campgrounds. Multiple dogs may be allowed.

Yokum's Vacationland
HC 59, Box 3
Seneca Rocks, WV
800-772-8343
yokums.com
Dogs of all sizes are allowed, and there are no additional pet fees for tent or RV sites. There is a $10 per night per pet additional fee for the motel. Dogs must be leashed and cleaned up after. The camping and tent areas also allow dogs. There is a dog walk area at the campground. Dogs are allowed in the camping cabins. Multiple dogs may be allowed.

Milleson's Walnut Grove Campground
28/5 Milleson's Road
Springfield, WV
304-822-5284
millesonscampground.com
Dogs of all sizes are allowed at no additional fee. Dogs may not be left unattended outside, and they must have current rabies and shot records. Dogs must be leashed and cleaned up after. There are some breed restrictions. This RV park is closed during the off-season. The camping and tent areas also allow dogs. There is a dog walk area at the campground. Multiple dogs may be allowed.

Lake Stephens Park
1400 Lake Stephens Road/H 3
Surveyor, WV
304-256-1747
lakestephenswv.com/
There is a wide variety of activities and recreation at this 2,300 acre county park that also has a 300 acre clear mountain lake. Dogs are allowed for no additional pet fees; they must be on no more than a 10 foot leash, and cleaned up after at all times. The campground has 100 RV and 28 tent sites with an additional overflow area. The sites have picnic tables, and restrooms and showers are located at the campground

store/office. Also in the camp area is a laundry, recreation area, and gaming courts. This RV park is closed during the off-season. The camping and tent areas also allow dogs. There is a dog walk area at the campground. Multiple dogs may be allowed.

Wheelings Dallas Pike Campground
Road 1, Box 231
Triadelphia, WV
304-547-0940
dallaspikecampgrounds.com
Dogs of all sizes are allowed. There are no additional pet fees. Dogs must be leashed and cleaned up after. There are some breed restrictions. The camping and tent areas also allow dogs. There is a dog walk area at the campground. Multiple dogs may be allowed.

Berwind Lake Wildlife Management Area
Rt. 16 Box 38
Warriormine, WV
304-875-2577 (800-CALL WVA (225-5982))
berwindlake.com/
One of the largest wildlife management areas in the state with 18,000 mountainous acres, it also has hiking trails, an overlook, a 20 acre lake with a foot trail around it, and an accessible fishing pier. Healthy dogs are allowed for no additional fee. A credit card must be on file, and there is a pet agreement to sign at check in. Pets may not be left unattended outside, and their food must be kept inside. Dogs must have certified proof of inoculations from a veterinarian, be on no more than a 10 foot leash, and picked up after. There are 8 campsites, each with a picnic table, lantern post, and grill. The camping and tent areas also allow dogs. There is a dog walk area at the campground. Multiple dogs may be allowed.

Wisconsin

Hixton/Alma Center KOA
N9657 H 95
Alma Center, WI
715-964-2508 (800-562-2680)
hixtonkoa.com
Dogs of all sizes are allowed, however, if they are large dogs, there are only 2 dogs allowed per site. There are no additional pet fees. Dogs must be quiet and well

behaved. Dogs may not be left unattended, must be leashed, and cleaned up after. There is a large fenced-in area for dogs to run off leash. This RV park is closed during the off-season. The camping and tent areas also allow dogs. There is a dog walk area at the campground. There are special amenities given to dogs at this campground.

Jellystone Park
11354 H X
Bagley, WI
608-996-2201 (800-999-6557)
jellystonebagley.com/
Specializing in family-style entertainment, this fun campground offers daily planned activities, theme weekends, a heated pool, game room, and gaming fields/courts. Plus there is regular viewing of Yogi Bear cartoons, 2 playgrounds, mini-golf, a large jumping pillow, an adult lounge, a store, and a lot more. Dogs are allowed for no additional fee; they must be quiet, leashed, and cleaned up after at all times. Dogs are not allowed in park buildings. This RV park is closed during the off-season. The camping and tent areas also allow dogs. There is a dog walk area at the campground. Multiple dogs may be allowed.

Wyalusing State Park
13081 State Park Lane
Bagley, WI
608-996-2261 (888-WI PARKS (947-2757))
One of the states oldest parks, there are historical sites, 2,628 scenic acres of forests, bluffs, wetlands, waterfalls, miles of trails, and more, plus a number of educational opportunities. Dogs are allowed with current license and rabies vaccinations. They may not be left unattended at campsites/cars, and they must be quiet, on no more than an 8 foot leash, and picked up after at all times. Dogs are not allowed in buildings, picnic or swim areas, marked nature trails, beaches, playgrounds, or on the cross country ski trails in winter. There are 109 regular campsites offering picnic tables, fire rings, potable water, showers, pit/flush toilets, a dump station, and a park concession stand. The camping and tent areas also allow dogs. There is a dog walk area at the campground. There are no water hookups at the campgrounds. Multiple dogs may be allowed.

Baraboo Hill Campground
E 10545 Terrytown Road
Baraboo, WI
800-226-7242
baraboohillscampground.com
Dogs of all sizes are allowed. There are no additional pet fees. Dogs may not be left unattended, must be leashed, and cleaned up after. This RV park is closed during the off-season. The camping and tent areas also allow dogs. There is a dog walk area at the campground. Multiple dogs may be allowed.

Devil's Lake State Park
S5975 Park Rd.
Baraboo, WI
608-356-8301 (888-WI PARKS (947-2757))
Historical sites, a 360 acre spring fed lake, scenic trails-including a section of the Ice Age National Scenic Trail, a full-time naturalist, amazing rock formations, and abundant recreation have made this 10,000 acre park a popular destination. Dogs are allowed with current license and rabies vaccinations. They may not be left unattended at campsites/cars, and they must be quiet, on no more than an 8 foot leash, and picked up after at all times. Dogs are not allowed in buildings, picnic or swim areas, marked nature trails, beaches, playgrounds, or on the cross country ski trails in winter. The camp areas offer open/grassy, or wooded sites, picnic tables, fire rings, restrooms, showers, a camp store, and a dump/fill station. The camping and tent areas also allow dogs. There is a dog walk area at the campground. There are no water hookups at the campgrounds. Multiple dogs may be allowed.

Mirror Lake State Park
E10320 Fern Dell Road
Baraboo, WI
608-254-2333 (888-WIPARKS (947-2757))
This park and lake offers a variety of recreational pursuits year round. Dogs of all sizes are allowed. There are no additional pet fees. Dogs may not be left unattended at any time, they must be on no more than an 8 foot leash at all times, be cleaned up after, and be in your unit at night. Dogs must have a current rabies certificate and shot records. Dogs are not allowed at the picnic area, in buildings, at the beach, and not on the nature trail. Dogs are allowed on the hiking trails. The camping and tent areas also allow dogs. There is

a dog walk area at the campground. There are no electric or water hookups at the campground. Multiple dogs may be allowed.

Natural Bridge State Park
S5975 Park Road
Baraboo, WI
608-356-8301 (888-WIPARKS (947-2757))
A natural arch of sandstone with a rock shelter used by people over 11,000 years ago is a point of interest at this park. Dogs of all sizes are allowed at no additional fee. Dogs may not be left unattended at any time, they must be on no more than an 8 foot leash, be cleaned up after, and be in your unit at night. Dogs must have a current rabies certificate and shot records. Dogs are not allowed at the picnic area, in buildings, at the beach, playgrounds, and not on the nature trails. Dogs are not allowed at the Natural Bridge or on the main trail to it. Dogs are allowed on the hiking trails. The camping and tent areas also allow dogs. There is a dog walk area at the campground. There are no water hookups at the campground. Multiple dogs may be allowed.

Rocky Arbor State Park
E10320 Fern Dell Road
Baraboo, WI
608-339-6881 (888-WIPARKS (947-2757))
This park is only open from Memorial to Labor Day, and their off season phone number is 608-254-2333. Dogs of all sizes are allowed at no additional fee. Dogs may not be left unattended, they must be on no more than an 8 foot leash, be cleaned up after, and be in your unit at night. Dogs must have a current rabies certificate and shot records. Dogs are not allowed at the picnic area, in buildings, and not on the nature trails. Dogs are allowed on the hiking trails. This campground is closed during the off-season. The camping and tent areas also allow dogs. There is a dog walk area at the campground. There are no water hookups at the campground. Multiple dogs may be allowed.

Apostle Islands National Lakeshore
415 Washington Avenue
Bayview, WI
715-779-3397
nps.gov/apis/
In addition to the spectacular beauty of this area, its numerous recreational opportunities, and rich cultural history, this group of 21 islands (and 12 miles of mainland) also offers a unique bio-diversity to explore. Dogs are allowed for no additional fee. Dogs may not be left unattended at any time, and they must be leashed, cleaned up after, and kept under owner's immediate control. There are primitive campsites available with advance reservations and permits are required. Permits must be picked up in person at the lakeshore's headquarters visitor center located at 415 Washington Avenue in Bayfield, Wisconsin. This RV park is closed during the off-season. The camping and tent areas also allow dogs. There is a dog walk area at the campground. There are no electric or water hookups at the campgrounds. 2 dogs may be allowed.

Pineland Camping Park
916 H 13
Big Flats, WI
608-564-7818
pinelandcamping.com
Dogs of all sizes are allowed. There are no additional pet fees. Dogs must be leashed and cleaned up after. There are some breed restrictions. This RV park is closed during the off-season. The camping and tent areas also allow dogs. There is a dog walk area at the campground. Multiple dogs may be allowed.

Black River State Forest
10325 H 12 E
Black River Falls, WI
715-284-4103 (800-404-4008)
This recreational park has a variety of activities year round. There are many scenic and geological sites along its many trails and glacial remnants. Dogs of all sizes are allowed. There are no additional pet fees. Dogs may not be left unattended at any time, they must be on no more than an 8 foot leash, be cleaned up after, and they must be in your unit at night. Dogs must have a current rabies certificate and shot records. Dogs are not allowed at the picnic area, in buildings, at the beach, and not on the nature trails. Dogs are allowed on the hiking trails, and they are allowed to go in the water as long as it is not near a swim area. The camping and tent areas also allow dogs. There is a dog walk area at the campground. There are no water hookups at the campground. Multiple dogs may be allowed.

Blue Mound State Park
4350 Mounds Park Road
Blue Mounds, WI
608-437-5711 (888-WI PARKS (947-2757))
Lush grounds, spectacular views/scenery, observation towers, miles of hiking trails, and numerous recreational activities have made this 1,153 acre park a popular destination. Dogs are allowed with current license and rabies vaccinations. They may not be left unattended at campsites/cars, and they must be quiet, on no more than an 8 foot leash, and picked up after at all times. Dogs are not allowed in buildings, picnic or swim areas, marked nature trails, beaches/pools, playgrounds, or on the cross country ski trails in winter. The camp area offers 77 wooded sites with picnic tables and fire rings; a modern restroom with showers, water fountains, and a dump station are located nearby. The camping and tent areas also allow dogs. There is a dog walk area at the campground. There are no water hookups at the campgrounds. Multiple dogs may be allowed.

Northern-Highland American Legion State Forest
4125 County H M
Boulder Junction, WI
715-385-2727 (888-WIPARKS (947-2757))
This forest has many recreational activities with more than 225,000 acres of lakes and forest. Dogs of all sizes are allowed at no additional fee. Dogs may not be left unattended, they must be on no more than an 8 foot leash, be cleaned up after, and be in your unit at night. Dogs are not allowed on the nature trails, but they are allowed on the hiking trails. The camping and tent areas also allow dogs. There is a dog walk area at the campground. There are no electric or water hookups at the campground. Multiple dogs may be allowed.

Jellystone Park
8425 H 38
Caledonia, WI
262-835-2526
jellystone-caledonia.com
Dogs of all sizes are allowed. There are no additional pet fees. Dogs must be quiet, well behaved, leashed, and cleaned up after. This RV park is closed during the off-season. The camping and tent areas also allow dogs. There is a dog walk area at the campground. Multiple

dogs may be allowed.

Mill Bluff State Park
15819 Funnel Rd.
Camp Douglas, WI
608-427-6692 (888-WIPARKS (947-2757))
The unusual, tall bluffs rising abruptly from the flat plains create a variety of picturesque rock formations at this park which is one of nine units of the Ice Age National Scientific Reserve. Dogs are allowed off lead in the forest if they are under voice control and will not chase other animals. Dogs must be on lead and cleaned up after in the camping areas. Dogs are allowed on the trails, but not in the swim areas. The camping and tent areas also allow dogs. There is a dog walk area at the campground. There are no electric or water hookups at the campground. Multiple dogs may be allowed.

Hoeft's Resort
W9070 Crooked Lake Drive
Cascade, WI
262-626-2221
wisvacations.com/hoeftsresort/
One dog of any size is allowed. There are no additional pet fees. Dogs are not allowed at the cabins or at the beach. Dogs must be leashed and cleaned up after. This RV park is closed during the off-season. The camping and tent areas also allow dogs. There is a dog walk area at the campground.

Nelson Dewey State Park
12190 County Road V V
Cassville, WI
608-725-5374 (888-WIPARKS (947-2757))
This park is along the Mississippi River and was the home to Wisconsin's first governor. There is also a reconstructed 1890 village on site. Dogs may not be left unattended, and they must be leashed and cleaned up after. Dogs are not allowed in the picnic areas, the buildings, or the nature trail. Dogs are allowed on the hiking trails. The camping and tent areas also allow dogs. There is a dog walk area at the campground. There are no water hookups at the campground. Multiple dogs may be allowed.

Lake Wissota State Park
18127 H O
Chippewa Falls, WI
715-382-4574 (888-WDNRINFo 888-936-7463)
There are over a 1000 recreational acres at this park, but the real

attraction is the 6,300 acre lake popular for fishing and swimming with its 285 foot beach. They also have a scenic lakeside trail that winds through the marshlands, forests, and prairie fields. Dogs are allowed for no additional fee; they must have ID and current rabies vaccinations. They may not be left unattended at campsites or in cars, and they must be quiet, on no more than an 8 foot leash, and picked up after at all times. Dogs are not allowed in buildings, picnic areas or on the grass at the picnic sites, marked nature trails, beaches, or playgrounds. The campground has secluded sites, picnic tables, fire rings, and restrooms. This RV park is closed during the off-season. The camping and tent areas also allow dogs. There is a dog walk area at the campground. There are no water hookups at the campgrounds. Multiple dogs may be allowed.

Brunet Island State Park
23125 255th Street
Cornell, WI
715-239-6888
Dogs of all sizes are allowed. There are no additional pet fees. Dogs may not be left unattended, and they must be leashed and cleaned up after. Dogs are not allowed on the beach, in the picnic areas, any of the buildings, or on the one 3/4 mile guided Jean Burnet Trail. There are many other trails where dogs are allowed. There is also a pet run area where they have set up a mini picnic area with tables. The camping and tent areas also allow dogs. There is a dog walk area at the campground. There are no water hookups at the campground. Multiple dogs may be allowed.

Apple Creek Family Campground
3831 County Road U
De Pere, WI
920-532-0132
applecreekcampground.com
Dogs of all sizes are allowed. There are no additional pet fees. Dogs must be well behaved, leashed, and cleaned up after. Dogs may be left for short times in your unit if they will be quiet. There are some breed restrictions. This RV park is closed during the off-season. The camping and tent areas also allow dogs. There is a dog walk area at the campground. 2 dogs may be allowed.

Madison KOA
4859 CTH-V

DeForest, WI
608-846-4528 (800-562-5784)
koa.com
Dogs of all sizes are allowed. There are no additional pet fees. Dogs may not be left unattended, must be leashed, and cleaned up after. Dogs are not allowed at the playground or in the rentals. This RV park is closed during the off-season. The camping and tent areas also allow dogs. There is a dog walk area at the campground. Multiple dogs may be allowed.

Lapham Peak Unit, Kettle Moraine State Forest
W 329 N 846 County Road C
Delafield, WI
262-646-3025 (888-947-2757)
Along the Ice Age Trail in this park there is a campsite that must be backpacked into. The southern unit of this park has tent and RV camping. Lapham Peak has over 21 miles of hiking trails, more than 17 miles of cross country ski trails, and a lookout tower at the highest point in Waukesha County. Dogs are allowed at no additional fee. Dogs may not be left unattended, and they must be leashed and cleaned up after. Dogs are allowed on the trails, but they are not allowed in the picnic areas, or on ski trails after snow. The camping and tent areas also allow dogs. There is a dog walk area at the campground. There are no electric or water hookups at the campground. Multiple dogs may be allowed.

Governor Dodge State Park
4175 H 23
Dodgeville, WI
608-935-2315
Dogs of all sizes are allowed. There are no additional pet fees. Dogs may not be left unattended, they must be on no more than an 8 foot leash, and be cleaned up after. Dogs are not allowed on the beach, and at certain picnic areas. There is a separate picnic area where dogs are allowed. Dogs are allowed on lead throughout the park. The camping and tent areas also allow dogs. There is a dog walk area at the campground. There are no water hookups at the campground. Multiple dogs may be allowed.

Kettle Moraine State Forest-Northern Unit
N1765 H G
Dundee, WI
262-626-2116
Dogs of all sizes are allowed. There are no additional pet fees. Dogs may

not be left unattended, and they must be well behaved, leashed, and cleaned up after. Dogs are not allowed on certain smaller nature trails, but there are several trails they can be on. This information is available at the Forest Headquarters in the park. This forest has 2 campgrounds. The camping and tent areas also allow dogs. There is a dog walk area at the campground. There are no water hookups at the campground. Multiple dogs may be allowed.

Kettle Moraine State Forest-Southern Unit
S91 W39091 Highway 59
Eagle, WI
262-594-6200 (888-947-2757)
Dogs of all sizes are allowed. There are no additional pet fees. Dogs may not be left unattended at any time, they must be on no more than an 8 foot leash at all times, be cleaned up after, and be in your unit at night. Dogs must have a current rabies certificate and shot records. Dogs are not allowed at the picnic area, in buildings, at the beach, and not on the nature trails. Dogs are allowed on the hiking trails. The camping and tent areas also allow dogs. There is a dog walk area at the campground. There are no water hookups at the campground. Multiple dogs may be allowed.

Newport State Park
475 H NP
Ellison Bay, WI
920-854-2500
This is the states only designated wilderness park and it features over 2,370 acres with 11 miles of Lake Michigan shoreline, 38 miles of year around trails, wetlands, and interpretive/naturalist programs. Dogs are allowed for no additional fee; they must have ID and current rabies vaccinations. They may not be left unattended at campsites or in cars, and they must be quiet, on no more than an 8 foot leash, and picked up after at all times. Dogs are not allowed in buildings, picnic or swim areas, marked nature trails, beaches, playgrounds, or on the cross country ski trails in winter. Tent camping only is available here; 13 can be reserved, and for the hardy-there is winter backpack camping available. The camping and tent areas also allow dogs. There is a dog walk area at the campground. There are no electric or water hookups at the campgrounds. Multiple dogs may be allowed.

Peninsula State Park
9462 Shore Road
Fish Creek, WI
920-868-3258
Educational as well as recreational opportunities can be pursued at this 3,776 acre park. There is an 18-hole golf course, an historic lighthouse, great views and hiking, seasonal musical theater in the park, a sandy swim beach, and more. Dogs are allowed for no additional fee; they must have ID and current rabies vaccinations. They may not be left unattended at campsites or in cars, and they must be quiet, on no more than an 8 foot leash, and picked up after at all times. Dogs are not allowed in buildings, picnic or swim areas, marked nature trails, beaches, playgrounds, or on the cross country ski trails in winter. Dogs are allowed at areas of undeveloped shoreline. The camp areas offer 468 sites and they may have all or some of the following; picnic tables, fire rings, pit or vault toilets, a camp store, or potable water. Showers, flush toilets, and the dump station are seasonal. The camping and tent areas also allow dogs. There is a dog walk area at the campground. There are no water hookups at the campgrounds. Multiple dogs may be allowed.

Fond Du Luc KOA
5099 H B
Fond Du Lac, WI
920-477-2300 (800-562-3912)
koa.com
Dogs of all sizes are allowed, and there are no additional pet fees for tent or RV sites. There is a $5 one time additional pet fee for cabin rentals. Dogs must be well behaved, leashed, and cleaned up after. This RV park is closed during the off-season. The camping and tent areas also allow dogs. There is a dog walk area at the campground. Dogs are allowed in the camping cabins. Multiple dogs may be allowed.

Jellystone Park
N 551 Wishing Well Drive
Fort Atkinson, WI
920-568-4100 (877-BEARFUN (232-7386))
bearsatfort.com
Dogs of all sizes are allowed. There are no additional pet fees. Dogs may not be left unattended, must be quiet, leashed, and cleaned up after. There are some breed

restrictions. This RV park is closed during the off-season. The camping and tent areas also allow dogs. There is a dog walk area at the campground. Multiple dogs may be allowed.

Merrick State Park
S2965 H 35
Fountain City, WI
608-687-4936 (888-WIPARKS (947-2757))
You can dock your boat at your campsite at this park. Dogs are allowed at no additional fee. Dogs may not be left unattended, they must be on no more than an 8 foot leash, be cleaned up after, and be in your unit at night. Dogs must have a current rabies certificate and shot records. With the exception of one marked picnic area, dogs are not allowed in picnic areas, in buildings, at the beach, or on the nature trails. Dogs are allowed on the hiking trails. The camping and tent areas also allow dogs. There is a dog walk area at the campground. There are no water hookups at the campground. Multiple dogs may be allowed.

Yogi Bear's Jellystone Park
E6506 H 110
Fremont, WI
920-446-3420 (800-258-3315)
fremontjellystone.com
Dogs of all sizes are allowed. There are no additional pet fees. Dogs must be quiet, well behaved, leashed, and cleaned up after. This RV park is closed during the off-season. The camping and tent areas also allow dogs. There is a dog walk area at the campground. Multiple dogs may be allowed.

Roche-A-Cri State Park
1767 H 13
Friendship, WI
608-339-6881 (888-WIPARKS (947-2757))
A 303 step wooden stairway takes you to the top of the 300-foot high rock outcropping called the Roche-A-Cri Mound offering panoramic views of the park. Dogs are allowed in camping areas, on roads, and in other areas of the park not developed for public use. Dogs are not allowed on the stairway. Dogs may not be left unattended, they must be quiet, on no more than an 8 foot leash, and be cleaned up after. Dogs are not allowed on the beach, the picnic areas, playgrounds, on cross-country ski trails or nature trails. Dogs are allowed on the hiking trails. The off season phone number

is 608-565-2789. The camping and tent areas also allow dogs. There is a dog walk area at the campground. There are no water hookups at the campground. Multiple dogs may be allowed.

Westward Ho Camp Resort
N5456 Division Road
Glenbeulah, WI
920-526-3407
westwardhocampresort.com
Dogs of all sizes are allowed. There are no additional pet fees. Dogs may not be left unattended, must be leashed, and cleaned up after. This RV park is closed during the off-season. The camping and tent areas also allow dogs. There is a dog walk area at the campground. Multiple dogs may be allowed.

Governor Knowles State Forest
(Box 367) H 70 @ St Croix River & entrances in WI & MN
Grantsburg, WI
715-463-2898
Dogs of all sizes are allowed. There are no additional pet fees. Dogs may not be left unattended at any time, they must be on no more than an 8 foot leash and be cleaned up after. Dogs are allowed on all the trails, except the ski trail in the winter. Dogs on lead are allowed throughout the forest, at the picnic area, and at the Wayside just before entering the park. This campground is closed during the off-season. The camping and tent areas also allow dogs. There is a dog walk area at the campground. There are no electric or water hookups at the campground. Multiple dogs may be allowed.

Pike Lake Unit - Kettle Moraine State Forest
3544 Kettle Moraine Road
Hartford, WI
262-670-3400 (888-WIPARKS (947-2757))
This park is located in the middle of the Kettle Moraine. The year round park is known for it's glacial landscapes. There are many trails here. Dogs are allowed at no additional fee. Dogs may not be left unattended, and they must be leashed and cleaned up after. Dogs are not allowed on the beach, the picnic areas, the self-guided nature trails, or the groomed ski trails. Dogs are allowed on the hiking trails. This campground is closed during the off-season. The camping and tent areas also allow dogs. There is a dog walk area at the campground. There are no water hookups at the

campground. Multiple dogs may be allowed.

Hayward KOA
11544 N H 63
Hayward, WI
715-634-2331 (800-562-7631)
koa.com
Dogs of all sizes are allowed. There are no additional pet fees. Dogs must be leashed and cleaned up after. Dogs may be left alone if they will be quiet and well behaved. Dogs must be crated when left unattended in the cabins. There are some breed restrictions. This RV park is closed during the off-season. The camping and tent areas also allow dogs. There is a dog walk area at the campground. Dogs are allowed in the camping cabins. Multiple dogs may be allowed.

Willow River State Park
1034 County H A
Hudson, WI
715-386-5931 (888-WIPARKS (947-2757))
There is year round recreation at this park of almost 3,000 acres. There are trails of varying difficulty, a nature center, and scenic overlooks. Dogs of all sizes are allowed at no additional fee. Dogs may not be left unattended, they must be on no more than a 6 foot leash, and be cleaned up after. Dogs are not allowed in the picnic areas, in buildings, at the beach, on ski trails, or on the nature trails. Dogs are allowed on the hiking trails. The camping and tent areas also allow dogs. There is a dog walk area at the campground. There are no water hookups at the campground. Multiple dogs may be allowed.

Richard Bong State Recreation Area
26313 Burlington Road
Kansasville, WI
262-878-5600 (888-WIPARKS (947-2757))
This recreational park has numerous activities year round. Dogs are allowed at no additional fee. Dogs may not be left unattended, and they must be leashed and cleaned up after. Dogs are not allowed on the beach, the picnic shelters, in buildings, or the self-guided nature trails. Dogs are allowed on the hiking trails. The camping and tent areas also allow dogs. There is a dog walk area at the campground. There are no

water hookups at the campground. Multiple dogs may be allowed.

Lake Dubay Shores Campground
1713 Dubay Drive
Knowlton, WI
715-457-2484
Dogs of all sizes are allowed. There is a $1 per night per pet additional fee. Dogs must be leashed and cleaned up after. They may be left in your RV if they will be quiet. This RV park is closed during the off-season. The camping and tent areas also allow dogs. There is a dog walk area at the campground. Multiple dogs may be allowed.

Goose Island Campground
H 35
La Crosse, WI
608-788-7018
Set in the woods along the Mississippi River, this campground has some great fishing, scenic areas, and a number of special events throughout the season. The camp area offers shady sites, picnic tables, fire rings, bathhouses, concessionaires, a playground, dump stations, and a boat ramp. Dogs are allowed for no additional fee; they are not allowed in swim areas or in buildings. Dogs must be leashed and under their owner's control. This RV park is closed during the off-season. The camping and tent areas also allow dogs. There is a dog walk area at the campground. Multiple dogs may be allowed.

Yogi Bear's Waterpark Camp Resort
S 1915 Ishnala Road
Lake Delton, WI
608-254-2568 (800-462-9644)
dellsjellystone.com
Dogs of all sizes are allowed. There are no additional pet fees. Dogs must be quiet, well behaved, leashed, and cleaned up after. This RV park is closed during the off-season. The camping and tent areas also allow dogs. There is a dog walk area at the campground. Multiple dogs may be allowed.

Big Foot Beach State Park
1550 S. Lake Shore Drive
Lake Geneva, WI
262-248-2528 (888-947-2757)
This park offers hiking and nature trails. Dogs of all sizes are allowed. There are no additional pet fees. Dogs may not be left unattended, and they must be leashed and cleaned up after. Dogs are not allowed on the beach or at the picnic

areas. The camping and tent areas also allow dogs. There is a dog walk area at the campground. There are no water hookups at the campground. Multiple dogs may be allowed.

Crystal Lake Campground
N550 Gannon Road
Lodi, WI
608-592-5607
Dogs of all sizes are allowed. If there is only one dog there is no fee. If there are more than one the fee is $5 per night per dog. Dogs may not be left unattended, must be leashed, and cleaned up after. Dogs may swim from the pier, but they may not be in the swim zone or on the beach. This RV park is closed during the off-season. The camping and tent areas also allow dogs. There is a dog walk area at the campground. Multiple dogs may be allowed.

Copper Falls State Park
Copper Falls Road
Mellen, WI
715-274-5125
Dogs of all sizes are allowed. There are no additional pet fees. Dogs may not be left unattended, and they must be quiet, well behaved, leashed and cleaned up after. Dogs are not allowed on the beach, in the picnic areas, the main hiking trail, or in any of the buildings. There is a specified walking trail for dogs. There are two campgrounds in the park, and the pet rules apply at both. The camping and tent areas also allow dogs. There is a dog walk area at the campground. There are no water hookups at the campground. Multiple dogs may be allowed.

Turtle Flambeau Scenic Water Area
3291 State House Circle
Mercer, WI
715-332-5271
This park has 60 campsites and is accessible by boat only from seven public boat landings and from private resorts. It provides for a variety of plants, fish, mammals, bird species, and recreational opportunities. Dogs are allowed at no additional fee. Dogs may not be left unattended, and they must be leashed at all times and cleaned up after. Dogs are allowed on the trails. This campground is closed during the off-season. The camping and tent areas also allow dogs. There is a dog walk area at the campground. There are no water hookups at the campground. Multiple dogs may be allowed.

Council Grounds State Park
N 1895 Council Grounds Drive
Merrill, WI
715-536-8773
Dogs of all sizes are allowed. There are no additional pet fees. Dogs may not be left unattended, they must be on no more than an 8 foot leash, and be cleaned up after. Dogs are not allowed on the beach or picnic areas. Dogs are allowed on the trails. This campground is closed during the off-season. The camping and tent areas also allow dogs. There is a dog walk area at the campground. There are no water hookups at the campground. Multiple dogs may be allowed.

Hidden Valley RV Resort
872 E State Road 59
Milton, WI
608-868-4141
hiddenvalleyrvresort.com
Dogs of all sizes are allowed. There are no additional pet fees. Dogs may be left in RV if the inside is cool but they may not be left unattended for long periods. Dogs are not allowed in the play areas, and must be leashed and cleaned up after. This RV park is closed during the off-season. The camping and tent areas also allow dogs. There is a dog walk area at the campground. Multiple dogs may be allowed.

Wisconsin State Fair RV Park
601 S 76th Street
Milwaukee, WI
414-266-7035
wistatefair.com
Dogs of all sizes are allowed. There are no additional pet fees. Dogs must be well behaved, quiet, leashed, and cleaned up after. Dogs may be left in your RV if they will be quiet and it is cool. There is a dog walk area at the campground. Multiple dogs may be allowed.

Wilderness Campground
N1499 H 22
Montello, WI
608-297-2002
wildernesscampground.com
One dog of any size is allowed. There are no additional pet fees. Dogs may not be left unattended, must be leashed, and cleaned up after. This RV park is closed during the off-season. The camping and tent areas also allow dogs. There is a dog walk area at the campground.

Country View Campground

S110 W26400 Craig Avenue
Mukwonago, WI
262-662-3654
countryviewcamp.com/
Open or wooded campsites, a heated swimming pool, game room, playground, a sand volleyball court, a gaming field, and designated special activities can all be enjoyed by visitors here. They also offer modern restrooms, showers, a laundry, store, picnic tables, fire rings, and a dump station. Dogs are allowed for no additional fee. Dogs must be quiet, well mannered, leashed, and under owner's control at all times. This RV park is closed during the off-season. The camping and tent areas also allow dogs. There is a dog walk area at the campground. Dogs are allowed in the camping cabins. Multiple dogs may be allowed.

Buckhorn State Park
W8450 Buckhorn Avenue
Necedah, WI
608-565-2789
Dogs of all sizes are allowed. There are no additional pet fees. Dogs may not be left unattended, and they must be leashed at all times, and be cleaned up after. Dogs are not allowed in the picnic areas, at the shelters, or in any of the buildings. Dogs are also not allowed on the 303 step stairway that is next to the park. There is electric provided at the handicap site only. The camping and tent areas also allow dogs. There is a dog walk area at the campground. There are no electric or water hookups at the campground. Multiple dogs may be allowed.

New Glarus Woods State Park
W5446 County Trunk H NN
New Glarus, WI
608-527-2335 (888-WIPARKS 9947-2757))
Restoration programs, interpretive programs, an active Amphitheater, hiking, recreation, and more makes this a pretty busy park. Dogs are allowed at no additional fee. Dogs may not be left unattended, they must be on no more than an 8 foot leash, be cleaned up after, and be in at night. Dogs must have a current rabies certificate and shot records. Dogs are not allowed in the picnic area, at the playground, in buildings, at the beach, or on nature trails. Dogs are allowed on the hiking trails. The camping and tent areas also allow dogs. There is a dog walk area at the campground. There are no water hookups at the campground. Multiple dogs may be allowed.

Oakdale KOA
200 J Street
Oakdale, WI
608-372-5622 (800-562-1737)
koa.com
Dogs of all sizes are allowed. There are no additional pet fees. Dogs must be leashed and cleaned up after. There are some breed restrictions. This RV park is closed during the off-season. The camping and tent areas also allow dogs. There is a dog walk area at the campground. Multiple dogs may be allowed.

Wildcat Mountain State Park
E13660 State Highway 33, PO Box 99
Ontario, WI
608-337-4775 (888-WIPARKS (947-2757))
This park of more than 3,600 acres offers more than 25 miles of hiking trails, an interpretive nature trail, a variety of other trails, and a nature center. Dogs are allowed at no additional fee. Dogs may not be left unattended, and they must be leashed and cleaned up after except when in the woods. Dogs are allowed on the trails. The camping and tent areas also allow dogs. There is a dog walk area at the campground. There are no electric or water hookups at the campground. Multiple dogs may be allowed.

Chequamegon-Nicolet National Forest
1170 4th Avenue South (Forest HQ)
Park Falls, WI
715-362-1300
fs.fed.us/r9/cnnf/
This national forest offers a million and a half acres of spectacular scenery, 5 wilderness areas, hundreds of miles of trails, and diverse ecosystems that support a large variety of flora, fauna, recreation, and educational opportunities. Dogs of all sizes are allowed at no additional fee. Dogs may not be left unattended, and they must be leashed and cleaned up after. There are several campsites from developed to primitive to backpack camping; some areas offer comfort stations, potable water, and visitor centers. This RV park is closed during the off-season. The camping and tent areas also allow dogs. There is a dog walk area at the campground. There are no electric or water hookups at the campgrounds. Multiple dogs may be allowed.

Chequamegon/Nicolet National Forest
68 S Stevens Street -Nicolet Division
Rhinelander, WI
715-362-2461
fs.fed.us/r9/cnnf/
This forest provides a variety of camping areas and trails, and the diverse ecosystems here support a large variety of plants, fish, mammals, and bird species. Dogs are allowed at no additional fee. Dogs may not be left unattended, and they must be leashed and cleaned up after in the camp areas. Dogs are allowed on the trails unless otherwise marked. The camping and tent areas also allow dogs. There is a dog walk area at the campground. There are no electric or water hookups at the campground. Multiple dogs may be allowed.

Rice Lake/Spooner KOA
1876 29 3/4 Avenue
Rice Lake, WI
715-234-2360 (800-562-3460)
koa.com
Dogs of all sizes are allowed, and there are no additional pet fees for tent or RV sites. There is a $5 per night per pet additional pet fee for cabin rentals. Dogs may not be left alone except in your own RV, and only if they will be quiet and well behaved. Dogs must be leashed and cleaned up after. This RV park is closed during the off-season. The camping and tent areas also allow dogs. There is a dog walk area at the campground. Dogs are allowed in the camping cabins. Multiple dogs may be allowed.

Frontier Campground & RV Park
11296 W H 2
Saxon, WI
715-893-2461
Dogs of all sizes are allowed. There are no additional pet fees. Dogs must be well behaved, quiet, leashed, and cleaned up after. The camping and tent areas also allow dogs. There is a dog walk area at the campground. Multiple dogs may be allowed.

Kohler-Andrae State Park
1020 Beach Park Lane
Sheboygan, WI
920-451-4080
Dogs of all sizes are allowed. There are no additional pet fees. Dogs may not be left unattended, they must be leashed at all times, and be cleaned up after. There is a

separate picnic area for those with dogs, and dogs are not allowed in the buildings. There is a pet area map in the office that shows what trails and areas that are pet friendly. The camping and tent areas also allow dogs. There is a dog walk area at the campground. There are no water hookups at the campground. Multiple dogs may be allowed.

High Cliff State Park
N7630 State Park Rd.
Sherwood, WI
920-989-1106
This 1,187 acre park offers scenic natural areas, significant archaeological sites, and plenty of land and marine recreation, but one of its main attractions is the 12 foot statue Winnebago Indian Chief Red Bird. Vehicle admission stickers (required) can be obtained at the park office or self registration stations. Dogs are allowed with current license and rabies vaccinations. They may not be left unattended at campsites/cars, and they must be quiet, on no more than an 8 foot leash, and picked up after at all times. Dogs are not allowed in buildings, picnic or swim areas, marked nature trails, beaches, playgrounds, or on the cross country ski trails in winter. There are 8 group sites and 112 regular campsites; they offer picnic tables, fire rings, potable water, restrooms, and a playground. The camping and tent areas also allow dogs. There is a dog walk area at the campground. There are no water hookups at the campgrounds. Multiple dogs may be allowed.

Lower Wisconsin State Riverway/Tower Hill State Park
5808 County Road C
Spring Green, WI
608-588-2116 (888-947-2757)
This park has a vast variety of archaeological, scenic, and historical sites to explore. Dogs are allowed at no additional fee. Dogs may not be left unattended, and they must be leashed and cleaned up after. Dogs are allowed on the trails. This campground is closed during the off-season. The camping and tent areas also allow dogs. There is a dog walk area at the campground. There are no electric or water hookups at the campground. Multiple dogs may be allowed.

Tower Hill State Park
5808 H C
Spring Green, WI

609-588-2116 (888-WDNRINFo 888-936-7463)
Great bluff trails, panoramic views, numerous recreational opportunities, and more can be enjoyed at this historical site-once the site for lead shot making in the 1800s. Dogs are allowed for no additional fee; they must have ID and current rabies vaccinations. They may not be left unattended at campsites or in cars, and they must be quiet, on no more than an 8 foot leash, and picked up after at all times. Dogs are not allowed in buildings, picnic areas, marked nature trails, beaches, playgrounds, the observation tower, or on the cross country ski trails in winter. The campground offers first come first served sites, restroom, and potable water. This RV park is closed during the off-season. The camping and tent areas also allow dogs. There is a dog walk area at the campground. There are no water hookups at the campgrounds. Multiple dogs may be allowed.

Interstate State Park
H 35
St Croix Falls, WI
715-483-3747 (888-WI PARKS (947-2757))
This is the state's oldest state park, and visitors will find a variety of recreational and educational opportunities here. Vehicle admission stickers (required) can be obtained at the park office or self registration stations. Dogs are allowed with current license and rabies vaccinations. They may not be left unattended at campsites/cars, and they must be quiet, on no more than an 8 foot leash, and picked up after at all times. Dogs are not allowed in buildings, picnic or swim areas, marked nature trails, beaches, playgrounds, or on the cross country ski trails in winter. There is a special picnic area where pets are allowed. There are two campgrounds offering 85 campsites with picnic tables, grills, modern restrooms, showers, potable water, pit/vault toilets, showers, a playground, camp store, and a dump station. The camping and tent areas also allow dogs. There is a dog walk area at the campground. There are no water hookups at the campgrounds. Multiple dogs may be allowed.

Lake Kegonsa State Park
2405 Door Creek Road
Stoughton, WI
608-873-9695
With a 3,209 acre lake and 342

acres on land, there are plenty of recreational choices at this park. They offer a wetland boardwalk, almost a mile of shoreline, over 5 miles of trails, and a fishing pier. Dogs are allowed for no additional fee; they must have ID and current rabies vaccinations. Dogs may not be left unattended at campsites or in cars, and they must be quiet, on no more than an 8 foot leash, and picked up after at all times. Dogs are not allowed in buildings, picnic or swim areas, the White Oak Nature Trail, or on the cross country ski trails in winter. They do have a designated pet swim area. The campground provides 80 sites, picnic tables, fire rings, gaming areas, playgrounds, and seasonal showers, flush toilets, and dump station. This RV park is closed during the off-season. The camping and tent areas also allow dogs. There is a dog walk area at the campground. There are no water hookups at the campgrounds.

Jellystone Park
3677 May Road
Sturgeon Bay, WI
920-743-9001
doorcountyjellystone.com
Dogs of all sizes are allowed. There are no additional pet fees. Dogs must be leashed and cleaned up after. This RV park is closed during the off-season. The camping and tent areas also allow dogs. There is a dog walk area at the campground. Multiple dogs may be allowed.

Potawatomi State Park
3740 H PD
Sturgeon Bay, WI
920-746-2890
Nestled along the shore of Sturgeon Bay, this 1,225 acre park offers a number of land and marine recreation. Dogs are allowed for no additional fee; they must have ID and current rabies vaccinations. Dogs may not be left unattended at campsites or in cars, and they must be quiet, on no more than an 8 foot leash, and picked up after at all times. Dogs are not allowed in buildings, picnic or swim areas, marked nature trails, beaches, or playgrounds. The camp area offers a total of 123 sites, a camp store, potable water, vault toilets, and an amphitheater. The camping and tent areas also allow dogs. There is a dog walk area at the campground. There are no water hookups at the campgrounds. Multiple dogs may be allowed.

Pattison State Park
6294 S H 35
Superior, WI
715-399-3111 (888-WI PARKS (947-2757))
Home to the states highest waterfalls (the US' 4th east of the Rockies), this 1,436 acre park also offers educational and recreational activities, a lake with nice sandy beaches, 9 miles of hiking trails, and much more. Dogs are allowed with current license and rabies vaccinations. They may not be left unattended at campsites/cars, and they must be quiet, on no more than an 8 foot leash, and picked up after at all times. Dogs are not allowed in buildings, picnic or swim areas, marked nature trails, beaches, playgrounds, or on the cross country ski trails in winter. Dogs are allowed at the Big or Little Falls picnic areas. There are 3 backpack and 59 campsites available here with picnic tables, fire rings, potable water, seasonal flush toilets and showers, and a dump station The camping and tent areas also allow dogs. There is a dog walk area at the campground. There are no water hookups at the campgrounds. Multiple dogs may be allowed.

Perrot State Park
W26247 Sullivan Road
Trempealeau, WI
608-534-6409 (888-WIPARKS (947-2757))
This park has access to the Great River State Trail and year round recreation. Dogs of all sizes are allowed at no additional fee. Dogs may not be left unattended, they must be on no more than an 8 foot leash, be cleaned up after, and be in your unit at night. Dogs must have a current rabies certificate and shot records. Dogs are not allowed at the picnic area, in buildings, and not on the nature trails. Dogs are allowed on the hiking trails. The camping and tent areas also allow dogs. There is a dog walk area at the campground. There are no water hookups at the campground. Multiple dogs may be allowed.

Point Beach State Forest
9400 County H O
Two Rivers, WI
920-794-7480 (888-WIPARKS (947-2757))
There are high sand dunes, woods, and more than five miles of undeveloped Lake Michigan shoreline to explore within walking

distance of each site. Dogs are allowed at no additional fee. Dogs may not be left unattended, and they must be quiet, leashed and cleaned up after. Dogs are not allowed on the beach, in buildings, north of the lighthouse, on the Swales Nature Trail, or the groomed ski trails. Dogs may be off lead if hunting or swimming, and they are allowed on hiking trails, and south of the lighthouse on the beach. The camping and tent areas also allow dogs. There is a dog walk area at the campground. There are no water hookups at the campground. Multiple dogs may be allowed.

Jellystone Park
1500 Jellystone Park Drive
Warrens, WI
608-378-4303 (888-386-9644)
jellystonewarrens.com
Dogs of all sizes are allowed. There are no additional pet fees. Dogs may not be left unattended, must be well behaved, be leashed, and cleaned up after. Dogs are not allowed in the buildings, the water park, the fishing lake, or the beach and pool areas. The camping and tent areas also allow dogs. There is a dog walk area at the campground. 2 dogs may be allowed.

Hartman Creek State Park
N2480 Hartman Creek Road
Waupaca, WI
715-258-2372 (888-947-2757)
This park offers a variety of trails, a sandy beach swimming area, and 7 lakes (no gas motors) for recreation. Dogs of all sizes are allowed. There are no additional pet fees. Dogs may not be left unattended at any time, they must be on no more than an 8 foot leash, be cleaned up after, and be in your unit at night. Dogs must have a current rabies certificate and shot records. Dogs are not allowed at the picnic area, in the buildings, or at the beach. Dogs are allowed on the hiking trails, but not on the equestrian trails. Generator use is prohibited. The camping and tent areas also allow dogs. There is a dog walk area at the campground. There are no water hookups at the campground. Multiple dogs may be allowed.

Rib Mountain State Park
4200 Park Road
Wausau, WI
715-842-2522
This 1,480 acre park is home to one of the oldest geological formations on earth. Visitors will also enjoy

outstanding scenery and views from the 60 foot lookout tower with 2 observation decks, several miles of hiking trails, and seasonal naturalist programs. Dogs are allowed with current license and rabies vaccinations. They may not be left unattended at campsites/cars, and they must be quiet, on no more than an 8 foot leash, and picked up after at all times. Dogs are not allowed in buildings, picnic or swim areas, playgrounds, or on the cross country ski trails in winter. There are 30 campsites available first-come, first-served and offer picnic tables, fire rings, playgrounds, and concessionaires. This RV park is closed during the off-season. The camping and tent areas also allow dogs. There is a dog walk area at the campground. There are no water hookups at the campgrounds. Multiple dogs may be allowed.

Menominee River Natural Resources Area
Verhayen Lane
Wausaukee, WI
715-856-9160 (888-WIPARKS (947-2757))
Campers at this park will need to hike in or canoe to camp sites, as it is mostly limited to foot traffic. Dogs may be off lead if they are under voice control and will not chase other animals. Dogs are restricted to a lead during nesting times, which is usually from mid-April through June. Dogs may not be left unattended at any time. This campground is closed during the off-season. The camping and tent areas also allow dogs. There is a dog walk area at the campground. There are no electric or water hookups at the campground. Multiple dogs may be allowed.

Neshonoc Lakeside Camp Resort
N4668 H 16
West Salem, WI
608-786-1792
neshonoclakeside.com/
Dogs of all sizes are allowed. There are no additional pet fees. Dogs must be leashed and cleaned up after. There are some breed restrictions. This RV park is closed during the off-season. The camping and tent areas also allow dogs. There is a dog walk area at the campground. 2 dogs may be allowed.

Veterans Memorial Campground
N 4668 H 16
West Salem, WI

608-786-4011
Located along the La Crosse River, this well maintained campground offers a family-oriented ambiance with several special events throughout the season. The camp area has first come, first served sites, picnic tables, fire rings, showers, a camp store, playing fields, a playground, dump stations, and a canoe landing. Dogs are allowed for no additional fee; they are not allowed in swim areas or in buildings. Dogs must be leashed and under their owner's control. This RV park is closed during the off-season. The camping and tent areas also allow dogs. There is a dog walk area at the campground. Multiple dogs may be allowed.

Flambeau River State Forest
W1613 CR W
Winter, WI
715-332-5271
Dogs of all sizes are allowed. There are no additional pet fees. Dogs may not be left unattended, they must be quiet, be on no more than an 8 foot leash, and be cleaned up after. Dogs are allowed on the trails, but not in public use or picnic areas. The camping and tent areas also allow dogs. There is a dog walk area at the campground. There are no electric or water hookups at the campground. Multiple dogs may be allowed.

Arrowhead Resort Campground
W1530 Arrowhead Road
Wisconsin Dells, WI
608-254-7244
rvinthesun.com/arrowhead
Dogs of all sizes are allowed. There are no additional pet fees. Dogs are not allowed in the rentals, they may not be left unattended, and must be leashed and cleaned up after. This RV park is closed during the off-season. The camping and tent areas also allow dogs. There is a dog walk area at the campground. 2 dogs may be allowed.

Wisconsin Dells KOA
S 235 Stand Rock Road
Wisconsin Dells, WI
608-254-4177 (800-562-4178)
wisdellskoa.com
Dogs of all sizes are allowed. There are no additional pet fees. Dogs may not be left unattended at any time. They must be leashed, and cleaned up after. There are some breed restrictions. This RV park is closed during the off-season. The camping and tent areas also allow dogs. There is a dog walk area at the

campground. Multiple dogs may be allowed.

Willow Flowage Scenic Waters Area
Cedar Falls Road
Woodruff, WI
715-356-5211 (888-WIPARKS (947-2757))
This wilderness area has more than 106 islands and covers more than 17,000 acres. Dogs are allowed at no additional fee. Dogs may not be left unattended, and they must be leashed and cleaned up after. Dogs are not allowed on the public beach swimming areas, the picnic areas, or nature trails. Dogs are allowed on the hiking trails, and they may be off lead when out of the camp areas if there is voice control. This campground is closed during the off-season. The camping and tent areas also allow dogs. There is a dog walk area at the campground. There are no electric or water hookups at the campground. Multiple dogs may be allowed.

Wyoming

Buffalo KOA
87 H 16E
Buffalo, WY
307-684-5423 (800-562-5403)
koa.com
Dogs of all sizes are allowed, and there are no additional pet fees for tent or RV sites. There is a $5 per night per pet additional fee for the cabins. Dogs must be leashed and cleaned up after. Dogs may not be left unattended outside or in the cabins. This RV park is closed during the off-season. The camping and tent areas also allow dogs. There is a dog walk area at the campground. Dogs are allowed in the camping cabins. Multiple dogs may be allowed.

Deer Park RV Park
Box 568, On H 16E
Buffalo, WY
307-684-5722 (800-222-9960)
deerparkrv.com
Dogs of all sizes are allowed. There are no additional pet fees. Dogs must be quiet, well behaved, leashed, and cleaned up after. Dogs may not be left unattended. This RV park is closed during the off-season. There is a dog walk area at the campground. Multiple dogs may be allowed.

Indian Campground
660 E Hart Street
Buffalo, WY
307-684-9601
indiancampground.com
Dogs of all sizes are allowed, however there can only be up to 3 dogs at tent and RV sites, and up to 2 dogs at the cabins. There are no additional pet fees. Dogs may not be left unattended, and they must be leashed and cleaned up after. This RV park is closed during the off-season. The camping and tent areas also allow dogs. There is a dog walk area at the campground. Dogs are allowed in the camping cabins.

Casper KOA
1101 Prairie Lane
Casper, WY
307-577-1664 (888-562-4704)
koa.com
Dogs of all sizes are allowed. There are no additional pet fees. Dogs must be leashed and cleaned up after. This RV park is closed during the off-season. The camping and tent areas also allow dogs. There is a dog walk area at the campground. Dogs are allowed in the camping cabins. Multiple dogs may be allowed.

Fort Casper Campground
4205 Fort Caspar Road
Casper, WY
888-243-7709
fortcaspar.org
Dogs of all sizes are allowed. There are no additional pet fees. Dogs may not be left unattended for very long at a time, nor placed in outdoor kennels, or tied up outside alone. Dogs must be well behaved, leashed, and cleaned up after. There are some breed restrictions. This RV park is closed during the off-season. The camping and tent areas also allow dogs. There is a dog walk area at the campground. 2 dogs may be allowed.

Cheyenne KOA
8800 Archer Frontage Road
Cheyenne, WY
307-638-8840 (800-562-1507)
cheyennekoa.com
Dogs of all sizes are allowed. There are no additional pet fees. Dogs must be quiet, well behaved, leashed, and cleaned up after. The camping and tent areas also allow dogs. There is a dog walk area at the campground. Dogs are allowed in the camping cabins. Multiple

dogs may be allowed.

Curt Gowdy State Park
1319 Hynds Lodge Road
Cheyenne, WY
307-632-7946 (877-WYOPARK (996-7275)
wyoparks.state.wy.us/CGslide.htm
This park has two lakes, an amphitheater, and many hiking trails. Well behaved dogs of all sizes are allowed. There are no additional pet fees. Dogs may not be left unattended, they must be on no more than a 10 foot leash, and be cleaned up after. Dogs are not allowed on public beaches or in buildings. The camping and tent areas also allow dogs. There is a dog walk area at the campground. There are no electric or water hookups at the campground. Multiple dogs may be allowed.

Terry Bison Ranch
51 I 25 Service Road E
Cheyenne, WY
307-634-4171
terrybisonranch.com
Dogs of all sizes are allowed. There are no additional pet fees. Dogs must be leashed and cleaned up after. The camping and tent areas also allow dogs. There is a dog walk area at the campground. Multiple dogs may be allowed.

Buffalo Bill State Park
47 Lakeside Road
Cody, WY
307-587-9227 (877-996-7275)
The Absaroka Mountains gives a stately feel to this park that also offers a variety of land and marine recreation. Dogs are allowed; they must be on no more than a 10 foot leash, or in a vehicle, and picked up after at all times. They are not allowed in food/store areas, public buildings, or on designated beaches, and they may not be left unattended for more than 1 hour. There are two developed campgrounds with almost 200 sites: they all have picnic tables and grills; potable water and restrooms are nearby. This RV park is closed during the off-season. The camping and tent areas also allow dogs. There is a dog walk area at the campground. There are no electric or water hookups at the campgrounds. Multiple dogs may be allowed.

Cody KOA
5561 Greybull H
Cody, WY
307-587-2369 (800-562-8507)
codykoa.com

Dogs of all sizes are allowed. There are no additional pet fees. Dogs must be leashed and cleaned up after. There are some breed restrictions. This RV park is closed during the off-season. The camping and tent areas also allow dogs. There is a dog walk area at the campground. Dogs are allowed in the camping cabins. Multiple dogs may be allowed.

Ponderosa Campground
1815 8th Street
Cody, WY
307-587-9203
codyponderosa.com
Dogs of all sizes are allowed. There are no additional pet fees. Dogs must be leashed and cleaned up after. Dogs may not be left unattended at the cabins or outside. This RV park is closed during the off-season. The camping and tent areas also allow dogs. There is a dog walk area at the campground. Dogs are allowed in the camping cabins. Multiple dogs may be allowed.

Shoshone National Forest
203 A Yellowstone Avenue
Cody, WY
307-527-6241
fs.fed.us/r2/shoshone/
This park has 2.4 million acres of recreational land, and it is also the first National Forest in the United States. Dogs of all sizes are allowed. There are no additional pet fees. Dogs must be leashed and cleaned up after, and they are allowed on the trails. Dogs may be off lead in the forest if they are under voice control. The camping and tent areas also allow dogs. There is a dog walk area at the campground. There are no water hookups at the campground. Multiple dogs may be allowed.

Yellowstone Valley Inn
3324 Yellowstone Park H
Cody, WY
307-587-3961 (877-587-3961 (outside WY only))
yellowstonevalleyinn.com/
Set in a beautiful valley, surrounded by mountains, this stopover offers a number of amenities such as an outdoor heated pool, an indoor hot tub, a playground and accessible showers and restrooms. There is also a restaurant and lounge, laundry facilities, and a dump station on site. Dogs are not allowed in the lodge, but they are allowed in the cabins for an additional fee of $15 per night per pet and in the campground for no additional fee. Dogs may not be left

unattended anywhere; they must be leashed, and under their owner's control at all times. This RV park is closed during the off-season. The camping and tent areas also allow dogs. There is a dog walk area at the campground. Dogs are allowed in the camping cabins. Multiple dogs may be allowed.

Devil's Tower National Monument
P O Box 10
Devils Tower, WY
307-467-5283
nps.gov/deto
Rising 1,267 feet above the river below and surrounded by woods and grasslands, the Devils Tower was the nation's first National monument. It is also considered a sacred site by more than 20 native tribes. Although dogs are not allowed on the trails or near the monument, they are allowed in the camp area, the parking lot, and along roadways. Dogs must be leashed and under their owner's control at all times. Dogs may not be left unattended or left in a vehicle at any time, and they may not be tied to any objects. Primitive camping is available on a first come, first served basis. This RV park is closed during the off-season. The camping and tent areas also allow dogs. There is a dog walk area at the campground. There are no electric or water hookups at the campgrounds. Multiple dogs may be allowed.

Devils Tower KOA
60 H 110
Devils Tower, WY
307-467-5395 (800-562-5785)
koa.com
Dogs of all sizes are allowed. There are no additional pet fees. Dogs must be leashed and cleaned up after. This RV park is closed during the off-season. The camping and tent areas also allow dogs. There is a dog walk area at the campground. Dogs are allowed in the camping cabins. Multiple dogs may be allowed.

Douglas KOA
168 H 91
Douglas, WY
307-358-2164 (800-562-2469)
koa.com
Dogs of all sizes are allowed. There are no additional pet fees. Dogs must be leashed and cleaned up after. There is a fenced in dog run where dogs are allowed to run off lead. This RV park is closed during

the off-season. The camping and tent areas also allow dogs. There is a dog walk area at the campground. Multiple dogs may be allowed.

Lazy Acres Campground and Motel
110 Fields Avenue
Encampment, WY
307-327-5968
lazyacreswyo.com/
Nestled among the trees, this riverside park offers a number of amenities including cable TV, a laundry, picnic tables, grills, and modern bathhouses. Two dogs are allowed in the campground and one dog in the motel for no additional fee; they must be leashed and under their owner's control at all times. This RV park is closed during the off-season. The camping and tent areas also allow dogs. There is a dog walk area at the campground. 2 dogs may be allowed.

Fort Bridger RV Camp
64 Groshon Rd
Fort Bridger, WY
307-782-3150
users.bvea.net/fbrv/
A well kept-up camp area; there are grassy level lots that can handle even the big rigs. The park sits close to many local recreational pursuits, and they offer Wi-Fi, picnic tables, restrooms, showers, laundry facilities, and cable TV. Dogs are allowed for no additional fee. They must be leashed and cleaned up after. This RV park is closed during the off-season. The camping and tent areas also allow dogs. There is a dog walk area at the campground. 2 dogs may be allowed.

High Plains Campground
1500 S Garner Lake Road
Gillette, WY
307-687-7339
Dogs of all sizes are allowed. There are no additional pet fees. Dogs may not be left unattended outside, and they must be leashed at all times and cleaned up after. Dogs must be friendly and well behaved. The camping and tent areas also allow dogs. There is a dog walk area at the campground. Multiple dogs may be allowed.

Glendo State Park
397 Glendo Park Road
Glendo, WY
307-735-4433
This is one of the state's most popular boating parks with its deep blue waters and a number of fish-catch records. Dogs are allowed;

they must be on no more than a 10 foot leash, or in a vehicle, and picked up after at all times. They are not allowed in food/store areas, public buildings, or on designated beaches, and they may not be left unattended for more than 1 hour. Dogs are allowed on the watercraft rentals available at Hall's Glendo Marina. Campground amenities include potable water, picnic tables, grills, and comfort stations. The camping and tent areas also allow dogs. There is a dog walk area at the campground. There are no electric or water hookups at the campgrounds. Multiple dogs may be allowed.

Hall's Glendo Marina and RV Park
383 Glendo Park Road
Glendo, WY
307-735-4216
hallsglendomarina.com/
In addition to a full service marina with a store, café, bar, and much more, this RV area offers sites to fit even the big rigs and most have a lake view. Dogs are allowed for no additional fee in the RV park and on the watercraft rentals. Dogs must be well behaved, leashed, and under their owner's control at all times. This RV park is closed during the off-season. The camping and tent areas also allow dogs. There is a dog walk area at the campground. Multiple dogs may be allowed.

Grand Teton Park RV Resort
Box 92, 6 miles E of Moran
Grand Teton, WY
307-733-1980 (800-563-6469)
yellowstonerv.com
Dogs of all sizes are allowed. There are no additional pet fees. Dogs must be leashed at all times and cleaned up after. The camping and tent areas also allow dogs. There is a dog walk area at the campground. Multiple dogs may be allowed.

Campgrounds in Grand Teton
Various
Grand Teton National Park, WY
800-628-9988
nps.gov/grte/pphtml/camping.html
Dogs on leash are allowed in campgrounds thoughout Grand Teton National Park. Pets may not be left unattended and must be cleaned up after.

Colter Bay Campground
Colter Bay
Grand Teton National Park, WY
800-628-9988
nps.gov/grte/pphtml/camping.html
This RV Park is located in Grand

Teton National Park. It is the only RV Park in the park with electric hookups and the only one that will handle campers over 30 feet in length. Dogs on leash are allowed in the RV park.

Lizard Creek Campground
North End of Park
Grand Teton National Park, WY
800-672-6012
nps.gov/grte/pphtml/camping.html
This RV Park and campground is located at the north end of Grand Teton National Park. This RV park has no electric hookups but does have water and dumping. RVs less than 30 feet in length are allowed. The campground is open seasonally from about June to September. Dogs on leash are allowed in the campground. No reservations are accepted, it is first come first serve.

Signal Mountain
16 Miles north of Jenny Lake
Grand Teton National Park, WY
800-672-6012
nps.gov/grte/pphtml/camping.html
This RV Park and campground is located at the north end of Grand Teton National Park. This RV park has no electric hookups but does have water and dumping. RVs less than 30 feet in length are allowed. The campground is open seasonally from about May to October. Dogs on leash are allowed in the campground. No reservations are accepted, it is first come first serve.

Buckboard Marina
H 530/Flaming Gorge Lake (HCR 65, Box 100)
Green River, WY
307-875-6927
In addition to the RV park, this site offers a full service marina, a fully stocked store, moorage, and boat rentals. Dogs are allowed on the rentals for no additional fee unless there is extreme cleaning needed. There are 40 campsites, restrooms, and accessible showers available. Dogs must be leashed and cleaned up after. This RV park is closed during the off-season. There is a dog walk area at the campground. 2 dogs may be allowed.

Greybull KOA
333 N 2nd Street
Greybull, WY
307-765-2555 (800-562-7508)
koa.com
Dogs of all sizes are allowed. There

are no additional pet fees. Dogs must be leashed and cleaned up after. There are some breed restrictions. This RV park is closed during the off-season. The camping and tent areas also allow dogs. There is a dog walk area at the campground. Dogs are allowed in the camping cabins. Multiple dogs may be allowed.

Guernsey State Park
On H 317
Guernsey, WY
307-836-2334 (877-WYO-PARK (996-7275))
wyoparks.state.wy.us/GUslide.htm
This is a recreational park and lake, however there are 2 times a year when they drain the lake. So check ahead if you want water sports. Dogs of all sizes are allowed. There are no additional pet fees. Dogs may not be left unattended, and they must be leashed and cleaned up after. Dogs are allowed on the trails, but some of the beaches are restricted. This campground is closed during the off-season. The camping and tent areas also allow dogs. There is a dog walk area at the campground. Multiple dogs may be allowed.

Hawk Springs Recreation Area
3 miles south of Hawk Springs off H 85
Guernsey, WY
307-836-2334 (877-WYOPARK (996-7275))
wyoparks.state.wy.us/HWslide.htm
Dogs of all sizes are allowed. There are no additional pet fees. Dogs must be leashed and cleaned up after. The camping and tent areas also allow dogs. There is a dog walk area at the campground. There are no electric or water hookups at the campground. Multiple dogs may be allowed.

Bridger-Teton National Forest
340 Cash Street
Jackson, WY
307-739-5500
fs.fed.us/btnf
This park covers 3.4 million acres, and it is first come first serve for camping. Dogs of all sizes are allowed. There are no additional pet fees. Although it is not advised, dogs may be off lead in the forest if you have voice control. Dogs must be cleaned up after at all times, and they must be on leash in the camp areas. The camping and tent areas also allow dogs. There is a dog walk area at the campground. There are no electric or water hookups at the

campground. 2 dogs may be allowed.

Curtis Canyon Campground
Flat Creek Road
Jackson, WY
307-739-5400 (307-739-5400)
Located in the Jackson Ranger District of the Bridger-Teton National Forest, this campsite sits at 6,600 feet elevation, and offers great scenery, plenty of nearby recreation, potable water, and restrooms. Dogs are allowed; they must all be on leash in campgrounds, picnic areas, and trailheads at all times. They may not be left unattended. This RV park is closed during the off-season. The camping and tent areas also allow dogs. There is a dog walk area at the campground. There are no electric or water hookups at the campgrounds. Multiple dogs may be allowed.

Jackson South/Hoback Junction KOA
9705 S H 89
Jackson, WY
307-733-7078 (800-562-1878)
koa.com
Dogs of all sizes are allowed. There are no additional pet fees. Dogs may not be left unattended, and must be quiet, leashed, and cleaned up after. There are some breed restrictions. This RV park is closed during the off-season. The camping and tent areas also allow dogs. There is a dog walk area at the campground. Dogs are allowed in the camping cabins. Multiple dogs may be allowed.

Virginian RV Resort
750 W Broadway
Jackson, WY
307-733-7189
virginianlodge.com
Dogs of all sizes are allowed. There are no additional pet fees. Dogs must be leashed and cleaned up after. This RV park is closed during the off-season. There is a dog walk area at the campground. Multiple dogs may be allowed.

Sinks Canyon State Park
3079 Sinks Canyon Road
Lander, WY
307-332-6333
wyoparks.state.wy.us/SCslide.htm
Throughout the summer experts on the Sinks Canyon area present weekly programs in it's botany, history, geology, and wildlife. Dogs are allowed everywhere in the park and on the trails. Dogs may not be left unattended, and they must be leashed and cleaned up after. There

are no additional pet fees. This campground is closed during the off-season. The camping and tent areas also allow dogs. There is a dog walk area at the campground. There are no electric or water hookups at the campground. Multiple dogs may be allowed.

Sleeping Bear Ranch and RV Resort
715 E Main Street (H 287)
Lander, WY
307-332-5159
Dogs of all sizes are allowed. There are no additional pet fees. Dogs must be well behaved, leashed, and cleaned up after. The camping and tent areas also allow dogs. There is a dog walk area at the campground. Multiple dogs may be allowed.

Laramie KOA
1271 W Baker Street
Laramie, WY
307-742-6553 (800-562-4153)
koa.com
Dogs of all sizes and numbers are allowed. There are no additional pet fees. There are only 2 dogs allowed at the cabins. Dogs must be leashed and cleaned up after. There are some breed restrictions. The camping and tent areas also allow dogs. There is a dog walk area at the campground. Dogs are allowed in the camping cabins.

Medicine Bow-Routt National Forests and Thunder Basin National Grassland
2468 Jackson Street
Laramie, WY
307-745-2300
fs.fed.us/r2/mbr/
This working national forest offers 2,883,943 acres of spectacular scenery, hundreds of miles of trails, and diverse ecosystems that support a large variety of flora, fauna, and recreation. This is also a topographically diverse area with elevations from 5,500 to 12,940 feet with 10 wilderness areas, 8 mountain lakes, and 8 ranger districts. Dogs of all sizes are allowed at no additional fee. Dogs may not be left unattended, and they must be leashed and cleaned up after. There are several developed and primitive camping choices here and they may have some or all of the following: picnic tables, fire pits, potable water, and pit toilets. This RV park is closed during the off-season. The camping and tent areas also allow dogs. There is a dog walk area at the

campground. There are no electric or water hookups at the campgrounds. Multiple dogs may be allowed.

Vedauwoo Recreation Area
Verdauwoo Glen Road
Laramie, WY
307-745-2300
vedauwoo.org/
This 8,000 foot altitude park is famous-and popular for its "awesome rock climbing". The towering rocky crags overlook high mountain meadows and offer visitors some fantastic views. Dogs must be in a vehicle or on no more than a 10 foot leash in the campground and public areas, and under strict voice control when off lead in other areas of the park. They are not allowed in food/store areas, public buildings, or on designated beaches, and they may not be left unattended for more than 1 hour. Free dispersed camping is available (except where expressly prohibited) within a maximum of 200 feet from the road. The campground offers 28 first-come, first-served sites, picnic tables, grills, potable water, fire rings, and vault toilets. This RV park is closed during the off-season. The camping and tent areas also allow dogs. There is a dog walk area at the campground. There are no electric or water hookups at the campgrounds. Multiple dogs may be allowed.

Lyman KOA
1531N H 413
Lyman, WY
307-786-2188 (800-562-2762)
koa.com
Dogs of all sizes are allowed. There are no additional pet fees. Dogs must be leashed at all times and must be cleaned up after. This RV park is closed during the off-season. The camping and tent areas also allow dogs. There is a dog walk area at the campground. Multiple dogs may be allowed.

Keyhole State Park
353 McKean Road
Moorcroft, WY
307-756-3596 (877 WYO-PARK (996-7275))
wyoparks.state.wy.us/KEslide.htm
This recreational park has 9 campgrounds, all overlooking the lake, and touts more than 200 species of birds. Dogs of all sizes are allowed. There are no additional pet fees. Dogs are allowed on the trails, but they are not allowed in the stores, public eating areas, the swim beach, or any buildings. The

camping and tent areas also allow dogs. There is a dog walk area at the campground. There are no electric or water hookups at the campground. Multiple dogs may be allowed.

Flagg Ranch Resort
Box 187, 2 miles S of Yellowstonw
Moran, WY
800-443-2311
flaggranch.com
Dogs of all sizes are allowed, and there are no additional pet fees for tent or RV sites. There is a $10 per night per pet additional fee for the cabins. Dogs must be leashed and cleaned up after. This RV park is closed during the off-season. The camping and tent areas also allow dogs. There is a dog walk area at the campground. Dogs are allowed in the camping cabins. Multiple dogs may be allowed.

Grand Teton Park RV Resort
P.O. Box 92 - Highway 26/287
Moran, WY
307-733-1980 (800-563-6469)
yellowstonerv.com/camp_rv.htm
This campground is only 32 miles from Yellowstone National Park, and just outside the entrance to the Grand Teton National Park. Amenities include great views of the Grand Teton Mountains, planned activities, Wi-Fi, a laundry, store, fishing tackle and license, a recreation room, a heated pool, and a hot tub, just to name a few. Dogs of all sizes are allowed for no additional fees. Dogs are not allowed in buildings, and they may not be left unattended. Dogs must be quiet, well behaved, leashed, and cleaned up after. The camping and tent areas also allow dogs. There is a dog walk area at the campground. Multiple dogs may be allowed.

Pine Bluffs RV Park
10 Paint Brush Road
Pine Bluffs, WY
800-294-4968
Dogs of all sizes are allowed. There are no additional pet fees. Dogs must be leashed and cleaned up after. The camping and tent areas also allow dogs. There is a dog walk area at the campground. Multiple dogs may be allowed.

Conner Battlefield State Historic Site
Off H 67
Ranchester, WY
307-684-7629
Once the site of a major conflict between the Arapahoe and American troops from Fort Laramie, this natural

scenic area along the Tongue River now offers a memorial and a recreation site. Dogs are allowed; they must be on no more than a 10 foot leash, or in a vehicle, and picked up after at all times. They are not allowed in food/store areas, public buildings, or on designated beaches, and they may not be left unattended for more than 1 hour. The camp area has 20 first-come, first-served shady sites with picnic tables, grills, restrooms, a playground, and horseshoe pits. This RV park is closed during the off-season. The camping and tent areas also allow dogs. There is a dog walk area at the campground. There are no electric or water hookups at the campgrounds. Multiple dogs may be allowed.

RV World Campground
3101 Wagon Circle Road
Rawlins, WY
307-328-1091 (877-328-1091)
rvworldcampground.com/
Much more than an RV park, this high mountain desert camp area offers a large, enclosed swimming pool, Wi-Fi, mini-golf, modern restrooms with showers, cable TV, a playhouse for kids, a store/gift shop, a laundry, dump station, and a lot more; even a doggy run. Dogs are allowed for no additional fee; they must be leashed and under their owner's control at all times. There is a dog walk area at the campground. Multiple dogs may be allowed.

Rawlins KOA
205 E H 71
Rawlins, WY
307-328-2021 (800-562-7559)
koa.com
Dogs of all sizes are allowed. There are no additional pet fees. Dogs may not be left unattended, and must be leashed, and cleaned up after. There are some breed restrictions. This RV park is closed during the off-season. The camping and tent areas also allow dogs. There is a dog walk area at the campground. Dogs are allowed in the camping cabins. Multiple dogs may be allowed.

Western Hills Campground
2500 Wagon Circle Road
Rawlins, WY
888-568-3040
westernhillscampground.com
Dogs of all sizes are allowed. There are no additional pet fees. Dogs are not allowed to be tied to bumpers,

poles, picnic tables, or any campground equipment. Dogs must be leashed and cleaned up after. There is a fenced in play area where dogs may be off lead. Dogs must be well behaved and not left unattended at any time. The camping and tent areas also allow dogs. There is a dog walk area at the campground. Multiple dogs may be allowed.

Wind River RV Park
1618 E Park Avenue
Riverton, WY
800-528-3913
windriverrvpark.com/index2.html
Dogs of all sizes are allowed. There are no additional pet fees. Dogs must be quiet, well behaved, leashed, and cleaned up after. This is an RV mostly park. They can make exception and place a tent on the lawn, but they water the lawns automatically everyday. There is a dog walk area at the campground. Multiple dogs may be allowed.

Rock Springs KOA
86 Foothill Blvd
Rock Springs, WY
307-362-3063 (800-562-8699)
rockspringskoa.com
Dogs of all sizes are allowed. There are no additional pet fees. Dogs may not be tied up outside unattended. Dogs must be leashed and cleaned up after. There are some breed restrictions. This RV park is closed during the off-season. The camping and tent areas also allow dogs. There is a dog walk area at the campground. Dogs are allowed in the camping cabins. Multiple dogs may be allowed.

Bighorn National Forest
2013 Eastside 2nd Street/H 16
Sheridan, WY
307-674-2600
fs.fed.us/r2/bighorn/
Visitors can experience a diversity of landscapes here. There are over 1,500 miles of trails, 32 campgrounds, hundreds of miles of streams, and an abundance of flora, fauna, recreation, and educational opportunities. Dogs are allowed in the forest; they must be leashed in all public and some wilderness areas. They should not be off lead in other areas unless well trained because of wildlife. Dogs must be under their owner's control at all times. The three ranger districts all have numerous developed and primitive camping areas available, and most have toilet and potable water access. This RV park is closed

during the off-season. The camping and tent areas also allow dogs. There is a dog walk area at the campground. There are no electric or water hookups at the campgrounds. Multiple dogs may be allowed.

Sheridan/Big Horn Mountains KOA
63 Decker Road
Sheridan, WY
307-674-8766 (800-562-7621)
koa.com
Dogs of all sizes are allowed. There are no additional pet fees. Well trained dogs may be off lead. Dogs must be cleaned up after. This RV park is closed during the off-season. The camping and tent areas also allow dogs. There is a dog walk area at the campground. Dogs are allowed in the camping cabins. Multiple dogs may be allowed.

Boysen State Park
15 Ash, Boysen Route
Shoshoni, WY
307-876-2796
wyoparks.state.wy.us/BOslide.htm
Dogs of all sizes are allowed. There are no additional pet fees. Dogs may not be left unattended, and they must be leashed and cleaned up after. Dogs are allowed on the trails, but not at the swim beaches. The camping and tent areas also allow dogs. There is a dog walk area at the campground. There are no electric or water hookups at the campground. Multiple dogs may be allowed.

Teton Village/Jackson West KOA
2780 Moose Wilson Road
Teton Village, WY
307-733-5354 (800-652-9043)
koa.com
Dogs of all sizes are allowed. There are no additional pet fees. Dogs may not be left unattended, and they must be leashed and cleaned up after. There are some breed restrictions. This RV park is closed during the off-season. The camping and tent areas also allow dogs. There is a dog walk area at the campground. Dogs are allowed in the camping cabins. Multiple dogs may be allowed.

Eagle RV Park
204 H 20S
Thermopolis, WY
888-865-5707
eaglervpark.com
Dogs of all sizes are allowed. There are no additional pet fees. Dogs must be quiet, leashed, and cleaned up after. This RV park is closed during the off-season. The camping and tent areas also allow dogs.

There is a dog walk area at the campground. Dogs are allowed in the camping cabins. Multiple dogs may be allowed.

Fountain of Youth
250 H 20N
Thermopolis, WY
307-864-3265
Dogs of all sizes are allowed. There are no additional pet fees. Dogs are not allowed by the pool, and they must be leashed and cleaned up after. This RV park is closed during the off-season. The camping and tent areas also allow dogs. There is a dog walk area at the campground. Multiple dogs may be allowed.

Yellowstone Park/West Entrance KOA
3305 Targhee Pass H
West Yellowstone, WY
406-646-7606 (800-562-7591)
yellowstonekoa.com
Dogs of all sizes are allowed. There are no additional pet fees. Dogs may not be left unattended in the cabins, and they must be leashed and cleaned up after. There are some breed restrictions. This RV park is closed during the off-season. The camping and tent areas also allow dogs. There is a dog walk area at the campground. Dogs are allowed in the camping cabins. Multiple dogs may be allowed.

Campsites in Yellowstone National Park
Throughout
Yellowstone National Park, WY
307-344-7311
All Yellowstone campgrounds allow pets. Pets must be leashed at all times. Pets may not be left unattended, may not bark continuously, and must be cleaned up after. Pets are not allowed on park trails and must not be more than 100 feet from a roadway or parking area outside of the campground.

Fishing Bridge RV Park
Lake Yellowstone
Yellowstone National Park, WY
307-344-7311
travelyellowstone.com
This RV Park is located in the middle of Yellowstone National Park on the north side of Lake Yellowstone. It is open seasonally from May through October. Dogs are required to be on leash at all times.

307

Canada

Alberta

Tweedsmuir South Provincial Park
40 kilometers west of Anahim Lake
Anahim Lake, AB
250-397-2523
Of special note, they suggest caution and to call ahead to check road conditions on Highway 20 as it has up to an 18% grade in places. This park provides spectacular scenery, a rich cultural history, and diverse ecosystems that support a large variety of plants, animals, and recreation. Dogs of all sizes are allowed at no additional fee. Dogs may not be left unattended, and they must be leashed and cleaned up after. Dogs are allowed on the trails on leash. This campground is closed during the off-season. The camping and tent areas also allow dogs. There is a dog walk area at the campground. There are no electric or water hookups at the campground. Multiple dogs may be allowed.

Whispering Spruce Campground
Range Road 10, 262195
Balzac, AB
403-226-0097
whisperingspruce.com
Dogs of all sizes are allowed. There is a pet policy to sign at check in and there are no additional pet fees. Dogs must be quiet, well behaved, may not be left unattended, and must be leashed and cleaned up after. Dogs are not allowed in the picnic or playground areas. This RV park is closed during the off-season. There is a dog walk area at the campground. Multiple dogs may be allowed.

Banff National Park of Canada
224 Banff Avenue
Banff, AB
403-762-1550 (888-773-8888)
Nestled in the Canadian Rocky Mountains, this park is home to a national historic site, and offers interpretive programs/events, opportunities for nature study, and a wide range of land, water, and ice recreation. Dogs of all sizes are allowed at no additional fee. Dogs may not be left unattended at any time, and they must be inside your unit at night. Dogs must be leashed and cleaned up after. The camping

and tent areas also allow dogs. There is a dog walk area at the campground.

Pioneer Campground
H 43
Beaverlodge, AB
780-354-2201
This camp area offers easy access, restrooms with showers, a dump station, and impressive views of the Rocky Mountains. They are open from May to September, weather permitting. Dogs are allowed for no additional fee; they must be leashed and cleaned up after. This RV park is closed during the off-season. The camping and tent areas also allow dogs. There is a dog walk area at the campground. Multiple dogs may be allowed.

Dinosaur Provincial Park
Prairie Road 30
Brooks, AB
403-378-3700
Dogs of all sizes are allowed. There are no additional pet fees. Dogs must be leashed and cleaned up after. The camping and tent areas also allow dogs. There is a dog walk area at the campground. Multiple dogs may be allowed.

Calaway Park
245033 Range Road 33
Calgary, AB
403-240-3822
calawaypark.com/aboutrv.html
Offering more "fun" activities than most camps, this park sits only a short walk from one of the country's largest outdoor family amusement park offering a wide variety of activities, rides, games, food, and stores. Dogs are allowed for no additional pet fee. Dogs may not be left unattended, and they must be quiet, leashed, and cleaned up after at all times. There is a secured, day kennel at the Calaway Amusement Park where they will watch visitors' canine companions for a small fee of $3 per pet per day. They ask owners bring food and a comfort item. This RV park is closed during the off-season. The camping and tent areas also allow dogs. There is a dog walk area at the campground. 2 dogs may be allowed.

Hinton/Jasper KOA
4720 Vegas Road NW
Calgary, AB
403-288-8351 (888-562-4714)
koa.com/where/ab/51124/htm
Dogs of all sizes are allowed, and there are no additional pet fees for

the tent or RV sites. There is a $10 per night per pet additional fee for the cabins. Dogs must be leashed and cleaned up after. There are some breed restrictions. This RV park is closed during the off-season. The camping and tent areas also allow dogs. There is a dog walk area at the campground. Dogs are allowed in the camping cabins. 2 dogs may be allowed.

Pine Creek RV Campground
On McCloud Trail
Calgary, AB
403-256-3002
Dogs of all sizes are allowed. There are no additional pet fees. Dogs must be well behaved, leashed, and cleaned up after. There is an off-lead fenced in area for the dogs to run. This RV park is closed during the off-season. There is a dog walk area at the campground. 2 dogs may be allowed.

Symon's Valley RV Park
260011 Symon's Valley Road NW
Calgary, AB
403-274-4574
symonsvalleyranch.com
Dogs of all sizes are allowed. There are no additional pet fees. Dogs must be leashed and cleaned up after. There is a dog walk area at the campground. 2 dogs may be allowed.

Spring Creek Mountain Village
502 3rd Avenue
Canmore, AB
403-678-5111
restwelltrailerpark.com
Dogs of all sizes are allowed. There is a $2 per night per dog additional fee. Dogs must be leashed and cleaned up after. There is a dog walk area at the campground. Multiple dogs may be allowed.

Dinosaur Trail RV Resort
North Dinosaur Trail/H 838
Drumheller, AB
403-823-9333
Located in a lush rural setting yet still close to a number of attractions, this riverside camp area offers numerous land and water recreational opportunities, a convenience store, laundry, playground, a dump station, and more. They are open from May 1st to September 30th. Dogs of all sizes are allowed for an additional fee of $2 per night per pet. Dogs must be leashed and cleaned up after at all times. This RV park is closed during the off-season. The camping and tent areas also allow

dogs. There is a dog walk area at the campground. Multiple dogs may be allowed.

Glowing Embers RV Park
26309 Acheson
Edmonton, AB
877-785-7275
glowingembersrvpark.com
Dogs of all sizes are allowed. There are no additional pet fees. Dogs must be leashed and cleaned up after. The camping and tent areas also allow dogs. There is a dog walk area at the campground. Multiple dogs may be allowed.

Whitemud Creek Gold and RV Park
3428 156th Street SW
Edmonton, AB
780-988-6800
whitemudcreek.com
Dogs of all sizes are allowed. There are no additional pet fees. Dogs must be leashed and cleaned up after. There is a dog walk area at the campground. 2 dogs may be allowed.

East of Eden Campground and RV Park
162 Range Road
Edson, AB
780-723-2287
Dogs of all sizes are allowed. There are no additional pet fees. Dogs must be quiet, well behaved, leashed, and cleaned up after. Dogs may not be left unattended outside, and may not be tied to any of the trees. There may be a minimal pet fee per night. This RV park is closed during the off-season. There is a dog walk area at the campground. 2 dogs may be allowed.

Buffalo Plains
H 785 T
Fort Macleod, AB
403-553-2592
buffaloplains.com/
This camp area offers grassy and treed large sites, and provides modern restrooms, hot showers, a laundry, picnic areas, a playground, and Wi-Fi is available for a small fee. Their season runs from May 1st to October 15th, weather permitting. Dogs of all sizes are allowed for no additional fee. Dogs must be leashed and cleaned up after at all times. This RV park is closed during the off-season. The camping and tent areas also allow dogs. There is a dog walk area at the campground. Multiple dogs may be allowed.

Elk Island National Park of Canada

Site 4, RR #1
Fort Saskatchewan, AB
780-922-5790 (888-773-8888)
This striking park is home to some of the most endangered habitats in Canada, to herds of free roaming bison, moose, elk, and deer. With 250 species of birds it is also a bird watcher's paradise. The park offers a variety of year round recreational pursuits. Dogs of all sizes are allowed at no additional fee. Dogs may not be left unattended, and they must be leashed and cleaned up after. Pets and pet food must be brought in at night. Dogs are allowed on the trails on lead. This campground is closed during the off-season. The camping and tent areas also allow dogs. There is a dog walk area at the campground. Multiple dogs may be allowed.

Camp Tamarack R.V. Park
H 40
Grand Prairie, AB
780-532-9998 (877-532-9998)
camptamarackrv.com/contact.html
This camp area is open from April to October (weather permitting) and offers a store, laundry, restrooms with showers, an RV wash, picnic tables, fire pits, rec hall, dump station, Wi-Fi, and more. Dogs of all sizes are allowed for no additional fee. Dogs must be leashed and cleaned up after at all times. This RV park is closed during the off-season. The camping and tent areas also allow dogs. There is a dog walk area at the campground. 2 dogs may be allowed.

Country Roads RV Park
RR 2
Grand Prairie, AB
866-532-6323
countryroadsrvpark.com/
This park offers a variety of activities, attractions like a seasonal corn field maze, recreation-on site and locally, venues for special occasions, extra large sites, and a wide range of amenities including an indoor RV wash. Dogs of all sizes are allowed for no additional fee. They are not allowed to be tied to park property or in the buildings, and they may not be left unattended at any time. Dogs must be leashed and cleaned up after at all times. There is a designated pet walk area just across the bridge, and a fine will be imposed if pets are not cleaned up after. The camping and tent areas also allow dogs. There is a dog walk area at the campground. Multiple dogs may be allowed.

Granview Recreation Park
602 Dufferin Street
Granum, AB
403-687-3830 (888-788-2222)
This scenic family camp area offers a 2-acre lake, gaming areas, modern facilities, and great views of the Rocky Mountains. Their season runs from early May to mid-October, weather permitting. Dogs of all sizes are allowed for no additional fee. Dogs must be leashed and cleaned up after at all times. This RV park is closed during the off-season. The camping and tent areas also allow dogs. There is a dog walk area at the campground.

Best Canadian Motor Inn and RV Park
386 Smith Street
Hinton, AB
780-865-5099
Dogs of all sizes and numbers are allowed, and there are no additional pet fees for RV sites. There is a $25 per night per pet additional fee for up to 2 dog at the motel, and pets are allowed in the smoking rooms only. Dogs must be quiet, well behaved, leashed, and cleaned up after. Dogs may not be left unattended at any time. There is a dog walk area at the campground.

Jasper National Park
500 Connaught Drive
Jasper, AB
780-852-6176 (877-737-3783 (877-RESERVE))
As Canada's largest and most northerly national park with more than 600 miles of trails, there is also a long rich cultural and natural history to explore in addition to spectacular landscapes that support a large variety of animal, bird, and plant life. It is also 1 of the 4 national parks that make up the Rocky Mountain World Heritage Site. Dogs are allowed throughout the park, on the tram, and in the camp areas for no additional fee. They suggest visitors with pets to stop by the visitor center to get a trail map brochure because there are several trails where dogs are not allowed due to the wildlife. Dogs may not be left unattended outside at any time, and their food has to be brought in at night. Dogs must be under their owner's control, leashed, and cleaned up after. There are 10 campgrounds with a total of 1,172 sites offering varied services. Restrooms, showers, and dump stations are available in many

locations. There is only 1 winter campground, located at Wapiti. The camping and tent areas also allow dogs. There is a dog walk area at the campground. There are no water hookups at the campgrounds. Multiple dogs may be allowed.

Sir Winston Churchill Provincial Park
End of H 36N
Lac Lac La Biche, AB
780-623-4144
Located on an island accessible by a 2.5 km causeway, this park is host to more than 200 bird species. It offers various trails including a boardwalk trail that goes through a 300-year-old boreal forest and a variety of land and water recreation. Dogs of all sizes are allowed at no additional fee. Dogs may not be left unattended, and they must be quiet, well behaved, leashed and cleaned up after. Dogs are not allowed on the beach or in buildings, however, they are allowed on the trails on leash. This campground is closed during the off-season. The camping and tent areas also allow dogs. There is a dog walk area at the campground. Multiple dogs may be allowed.

Bridgeview RV Resort
1501 2nd Avenue W
Lethbridge, AB
403-381-2357
This river-side resort offers year round land and water recreation and a long list of amenities. Dogs of all sizes are allowed for an additional fee of $2 per night per pet. Dogs may not be left unattended, and they must be leashed and cleaned up after. The camping and tent areas also allow dogs. There is a dog walk area at the campground. Multiple dogs may be allowed.

Henderson Lake Campground
3419 Parkside Drive S
Lethbridge, AB
403-328-5452
hendersoncampground.com/
This family campground is only a short walk from town and several attractions and recreational opportunities, plus there is a store, laundry, dump station, and modern restrooms on site. Dogs of all sizes are allowed for an additional fee of $2 per night per pet. Dogs must be leashed and cleaned up after at all times. The camping and tent areas also allow dogs. There is a dog walk area at the campground. 2 dogs may be allowed.

Wild Rose Trailer Park

28B Camp Drive SW
Medicine Hat, AB
403-526-2248
Dogs of all sizes are allowed. There are no additional pet fees. Dogs may not be left unattended, must be leashed, and cleaned up after. There is a dog walk area at the campground. Multiple dogs may be allowed.

Writing on Stone Provincial Park
H 4/P. O. Box 297
Milk River, AB
403-647-2364
Home to North America's largest collection of native petroglyphs and pictographs with thousands of figures at more than 50 sites, this 4400 acre park also holds one of the biggest protected prairie areas of all the parks. Dogs of all sizes are allowed for no additional fee. They are not allowed on the guided tours or on swim beaches. Dogs must be kept leashed and cleaned up after. The camp area offers 64 sites with fire-pits, firewood, tables, flush toilets, showers, dump stations, and a playground. The camping and tent areas also allow dogs. There is a dog walk area at the campground. There are no water hookups at the campgrounds. Multiple dogs may be allowed.

Kinbrook Island Provincial Park
H 535
Newell County No 4, AB
403-362-2962
There are lots of shade trees, an interpretive trail along a large marsh area with an abundance of flora and fauna, and an observation tower with a spotting scope at this park. They also provide picnic tables, fire pits, a fish cleaning station, dump station, a playground, pit/vault toilets, showers, potable water, and a boat launch and pier. Dogs are allowed for no additional fee; they must be leashed and cleaned up after. Dogs are allowed off leash in the water at the boat pier and at the end of Loop F. This RV park is closed during the off-season. The camping and tent areas also allow dogs. There is a dog walk area at the campground. There are no water hookups at the campgrounds. Multiple dogs may be allowed.

Fintry Provincial Park and Protected Area
Fintry Delta Road
Okanagan Lake, AB
250-260-3590 (800-689-9025)
With two dramatically different

topographical areas, this park has a variety of habitats, trails, historical features, a spectacular triple waterfall, and various land and water recreation to offer. Dogs of all sizes are allowed at no additional fee. Dogs may not be left unattended, and they must be quiet, well behaved, leashed at all times, and cleaned up after. Dogs are not allowed on the swim beach, but they are allowed on the trails on leash. This campground is closed during the off-season. The camping and tent areas also allow dogs. There is a dog walk area at the campground. There are no electric or water hookups at the campground. Multiple dogs may be allowed.

Green Acres
Box 66
Pine Lake, AB
403-886-4833
campingreenacres.com
Dogs of all sizes are allowed. There are no additional pet fees. Dogs must be leashed and cleaned up after. This RV park is closed during the off-season. There is a dog walk area at the campground. Multiple dogs may be allowed.

Lions Campground
4759 Riverside Drive
Red Deer, AB
403-342-8183
Open from the 1st of May through the end of September (weather permitting), this riverside camp area offers 126 sites, restrooms with showers, a laundry, playground, a dump station, and a variety of land and water recreation. Dogs of al sizes are allowed for no additional fee. Dogs must be leashed and cleaned up after at all times. This RV park is closed during the off-season. The camping and tent areas also allow dogs. There is a dog walk area at the campground. Multiple dogs may be allowed.

Westerner Campground
4847-D 19th Street
Red Deer, AB
403-352-8801
westernercampground.com/
This neat and scenic campground offers modern facilities and sits central to a number of local activities and recreation. Dogs of all sizes are allowed for no additional fee. Dogs must be quiet, leashed, and cleaned up after at all times. The camping and tent areas also allow dogs. There is a dog walk area at the campground. Multiple dogs may be

allowed.

Lessard Lake Campground
Range Road 51
Sangudo, AB
780-785-4125
This lakeside camp area offers about 50 campsites, modern washroom facilities, fire pits, picnic tables, a large playground, beach, boat launch, a restaurant, and more. They are open from May 15th to September 30th. Dogs of all sizes are allowed for no additional fee. Dogs must be leashed and cleaned up after at all times. This RV park is closed during the off-season. The camping and tent areas also allow dogs. There is a dog walk area at the campground. Multiple dogs may be allowed.

Half Moon Lake Resort
21524 Township Road 520
Sherwood Park, AB
780-922-3045
halfmoonlakeresort.com/
This popular recreation destination offers a variety of activities, sports, special events, gaming areas, and all the amenities for a fun family get-a-way at this lakeside resort. They are open from May 1st to mid-October, weather permitting. Dogs of all sizes are allowed for no additional fee. There is one large dog or 2 small dogs allowed per site. Dogs may not be left unattended outside at any time, and they must be leashed and cleaned up after. They are not allowed on the beach or in the water at the beach area. This RV park is closed during the off-season. The camping and tent areas also allow dogs. There is a dog walk area at the campground.

Spring Lake Resort
499 Lakeside Drive
Spring Lake, AB
780-963-3993
springlakeresort.com/
Being nestled among trees and green grass alongside a spring-fed lake are only some of the popular sites at this park that also offers a variety of land and water recreation and gaming areas, a 9 acre island, a large, private sandy beach, scenic trails, a store, modern facilities, and more. Their season runs from May 1st to September 30th, depending on weather. Dogs of all sizes are allowed for no additional fee. Dogs must be leashed and cleaned up after at all times, and they are not allowed on the beach. There is a dog walk area at the campground.

Multiple dogs may be allowed.

Carson Pegasus Provincial Park
P.O. Box 9002
Sylvan Lake, AB
780-778-2664
A park of mixed wood forests and home to a wide variety of plant, bird, marine, and wildlife as well as being one of the province's most popular trout fishing areas, they also have many scenic hiking trails to explore. Dogs of all sizes are allowed for no additional fee. Dogs must be leashed and cleaned up after at all times, and they are not allowed on the beach. The campground offers 181 treed, private sites, modern restrooms and showers, a laundry, an amphitheater hosting a variety of activities, concessionaires, and a modern playground. The camping and tent areas also allow dogs. There is a dog walk area at the campground. There are no water hookups at the campgrounds. Multiple dogs may be allowed.

Nisga'a Memorial Lava Bed Provincial Park
Kalum Lake Drive N
Terrace, AB
250-638-8490
These parks were combined to protect and interpret the natural features and native culture of the area. It also affords visitors the unique opportunity to explore a volcanic landscape. They offer guided tours, special events, and various trails and recreation. Dogs of all sizes are allowed at no additional fee. Dogs may not be left unattended, and they must be leashed and cleaned up after. Dogs are not allowed on the guided tour trail to the volcano, however, they are allowed on the other trails on leash. This campground is closed during the off-season. The camping and tent areas also allow dogs. There is a dog walk area at the campground. There are no electric or water hookups at the campground. Multiple dogs may be allowed.

Sherks RV Park
38th Avenue/ P. O. Box Box 765
Valleyview, AB
780-524-4949
This camp area is open from May 1st to September 30 (weather permitting) and offers a laundry, restrooms with showers, nature trails, picnic tables, rec hall, playground, and more. Dogs of all

sizes are allowed for no additional fee. Dogs must be leashed and cleaned up after at all times. This RV park is closed during the off-season. The camping and tent areas also allow dogs. There is a dog walk area at the campground. Multiple dogs may be allowed.

Vermilion Campground
5301 48th Street
Vermilion, AB
780-853-4372
Dogs of all sizes are allowed. There are no additional pet fees. Dogs must be leashed and cleaned up after. This RV park is closed during the off-season. The camping and tent areas also allow dogs. There is a dog walk area at the campground. Multiple dogs may be allowed.

Waterton Lakes National Park
H 6 (P. O. Box 200)
Waterton Park, AB
403-859-2224
In addition to spectacular scenery, numerous and diverse ecological regions/resources, and being a crucial north-south wildlife corridor, this park is also designated as an International Peace Park and listed as a World Heritage site. Dogs of all sizes are allowed throughout the park for no additional fee. Dogs may not be left unattended outside at any time, and they must be leashed and cleaned up after. Four campgrounds are available with selections from landscaped lawns to forest settings. Depending on the area, flush toilets, hot showers, storage containers, kitchen shelters, fire rings, and a dump station are available. The camping and tent areas also allow dogs. There is a dog walk area at the campground. Multiple dogs may be allowed.

Sagitawah RV Park
43 Whitecourt Avenue
Whitecourt, AB
780-778-3734
Located by the Athabasca River, this scenic park offers a variety of recreational opportunities and a number of amenities including modern washroom facilities, a laundry, playground, store, concessionaires, fire pits with free firewood, and a hot tub. They are open from April 1st to December 1st. Dogs of all sizes are allowed for no additional fee. Dogs must be leashed and cleaned up after at all times. This RV park is closed during the off-season. The camping and tent areas also allow dogs. There is a dog walk

area at the campground. Multiple dogs may be allowed.

British Columbia

Canyon Alpine RV Park and Campground
50490 H 1
Boston Bar, BC
604-867-9734
This campground allows dogs of all sizes for no additional pet fee. Dogs must be leashed and cleaned up after at all times. This RV park is closed during the off-season. The camping and tent areas also allow dogs. There is a dog walk area at the campground. Multiple dogs may be allowed.

Burnaby Cariboo RV Park
8765 Cariboo Place
Burnaby, BC
604-420-1722
bcrvpark.com
One dog of any size is allowed. There are no additional pet fees. Dogs may not be left unattended nor left tied up outside alone. Dogs must be leashed and cleaned up after. This RV park is closed during the off-season. The camping and tent areas also allow dogs. There is a dog walk area at the campground.

Beaver Point Resort
16272 H 35
Burns Lake, BC
250-695-6519
bcnorth.ca/beaverpoint
Dogs of all sizes are allowed. There are no additional pet fees. Dogs must be leashed at all times and cleaned up after. Well behaved and quiet dogs may be left unattended at your site. This RV park is closed during the off-season. The camping and tent areas also allow dogs. There is a dog walk area at the campground. Multiple dogs may be allowed.

Burns Lake KOA
4 miles E of Burns Lake on H 16
Burns Lake, BC
250-692-3105 (800-562-0905)
koa.com
Dogs of all sizes are allowed. There are no additional pet fees. Dogs may not be left unattended, must be leashed, and cleaned up after. This RV park is closed during the off-season. The camping and tent areas also allow dogs. There is a dog walk

area at the campground. Dogs are allowed in the camping cabins. Multiple dogs may be allowed.

Brookside Campsite
1621 E Trans Canada H
Cache Creek, BC
250-457-6633
brooksidecampsite.com
Dogs of all sizes are allowed. There are no additional pet fees. Dogs may not be left unattended, must be leashed, and cleaned up after. This RV park is closed during the off-season. The camping and tent areas also allow dogs. There is a dog walk area at the campground. Multiple dogs may be allowed.

Evergreen Fishing Resort
1820 Loon Lake Road
Cache Creek, BC
250-459-2372
evergreenfishingresort.ca/
Being one of the last naturally stocked lakes in B.C. with great fishing because of its deep, narrow channel has helped make this a popular fishing resort. Dogs of all sizes are allowed in the campground area for no additional fee. Dogs must be well behaved, leashed, and cleaned up after at all times. The camping and tent areas also allow dogs. There is a dog walk area at the campground. Multiple dogs may be allowed.

Historic Hat Creek Ranch
Junction of Highway 97 and 99, 11 km north of Cache Creek
Cache Creek, BC
250-457-9722 (800-782-0922)
hatcreekranch.com/
Rich in natural and cultural history, this park has much to share in addition to camping. Dogs of all sizes are allowed in the camp area for no additional fee, and reservations are recommended. Dogs must be attended to, leashed, cleaned up after at all times, and they are not allowed at the historic sites. The campground is open from May 1st to mid-October. This RV park is closed during the off-season. The camping and tent areas also allow dogs. There is a dog walk area at the campground. There are no water hookups at the campgrounds. 2 dogs may be allowed.

Elk Falls Provincial Park Quinsam Campground
H 28
Campbell River, BC
250-248-9460 (800-689-9025)

This park has been called "The Salmon Capitol of the World", but also offers an extensive network of forest trails, a waterfall, and a variety of land and water recreation. Dogs of all sizes are allowed at no additional fee. Dogs may not be left unattended, and they must be quiet, well behaved, leashed and cleaned up after. Dogs are allowed on the trails on leash. The camping and tent areas also allow dogs. There is a dog walk area at the campground. There are no electric or water hookups at the campground. Multiple dogs may be allowed.

Ripple Rock RV Park
15011 Browns Bay Road
Campbell River, BC
250-287-7108
brownsbagresort.com
Dogs of all sizes are allowed. There are no additional pet fees. Dogs must be leashed and cleaned up after. This RV park is closed during the off-season. The camping and tent areas also allow dogs. There is a dog walk area at the campground. Multiple dogs may be allowed.

Salmon Point
2176 Salmon Point Road
Campbell River, BC
250-923-6605
salmonpoint.com
Dogs of all sizes are allowed. There is a $1 per night per pet additional fee for small dogs, and a $2 per night per pet additional fee for medium to large dogs. Dogs must be leashed and cleaned up after. The camping and tent areas also allow dogs. There is a dog walk area at the campground. Dogs are allowed in the camping cabins. Multiple dogs may be allowed.

Caron Creek RV Park
7537 H 97S
Chetwynd, BC
250-788-2522
This full service park offers 40 sites, a laundry, modern restrooms, and showers. Dogs of all sizes are allowed for no additional fee. Dogs must be leashed and cleaned up after at all times. This RV park is closed during the off-season. The camping and tent areas also allow dogs. There is a dog walk area at the campground. Multiple dogs may be allowed.

Westwind RV Park
4401 53rd Avenue
Chetwynd, BC
250-788-2190

karo-ent.com/westwind.htm
This is the area's most complete full service RV park with large pull-thru sites, modern restrooms and showers, a laundry, hiking trails, gaming areas, and more. Dogs of all sizes are allowed for no additional fee. Dogs must be well behaved leashed, and cleaned up after. This RV park is closed during the off-season. The camping and tent areas also allow dogs. There is a dog walk area at the campground. Multiple dogs may be allowed.

Cottonwood Meadows RV Country Club
44280 Luckakuck Way
Chilliwack, BC
604-824-7275
cottonwoodrvpark.com/
This modern 117 site RV park offers guests a clubhouse, a Jacuzzi, secured facilities, and a good central location to many other activities and interesting sites. Dogs of all sizes are allowed for no additional fee. Dogs must be well behaved, leashed, and cleaned up after at all times. There are some breed restrictions. The camping and tent areas also allow dogs. There is a dog walk area at the campground. Multiple dogs may be allowed.

Vedder River Campground
5215 Giesbrecht Road
Chilliwack, BC
604-823-6012
Open from May 1st until October 31st, this riverfront camp area offers modern and wilderness sites, a variety of land and water recreation, and various special events throughout the season. Dogs of all sizes are allowed for an additional $3 per night per pet. Dogs must be kept leashed (even on site) and cleaned up after. Dogs are not allowed at the playground or swim beaches, but they are allowed to go in the river. This RV park is closed during the off-season. The camping and tent areas also allow dogs. There is a dog walk area at the campground. 2 dogs may be allowed.

Cascade Cove RV Park
1120 River Road
Christina Lake, BC
250-447-9510
christinalakeaccomodations.com
One dog of any size is allowed. There are no additional pet fees. Dogs may not be left unattended, must be leashed, and cleaned up after. There are some breed restrictions. This RV park is closed

during the off-season. The camping and tent areas also allow dogs. There is a dog walk area at the campground.

Clearwater/Well Gray KOA
373 Clearwater Valley Road
Clearwater, BC
250-674-3909 (800-562-3239)
clearwaterbckoa.com
Dogs of all sizes are allowed, and there are no additional pet fees for tent or RV sites. There is a $5 per night per pet additional fee for the motel. Dogs must be leashed and cleaned up after. This RV park is closed during the off-season. The camping and tent areas also allow dogs. There is a dog walk area at the campground. 2 dogs may be allowed.

Clinton Pines
1204 Cariboo Ave Box 759
Clinton, BC
250-459-0030
This scenic camp area offers shady level sites, clean washrooms, hot showers, internet access, a laundry, and plenty of places to walk since town is in walking distance and there are also nature trails to explore. Dogs of all sizes are allowed for no additional fee. Dogs must be well behaved, leashed, and cleaned up after at all times. The camping and tent areas also allow dogs. There is a dog walk area at the campground. Multiple dogs may be allowed.

Coal River Lodge and RV Park
Mile 533 Alaska Hwy
Coal River, BC
250-776-7306
coalriverlodge.com/
This well-kept, full service park can also provide fuel, minor repairs, food and specialty treats, and souvenirs. Dogs of all sizes are allowed for no additional fee for the camp area, and they are not allowed in the lodge or near any of the buildings. Dogs must be under owner's control, leashed, and cleaned up after at all times. There is a large open grassy area across from the park they call "pooch-park" where guests may take their pets for a romp. They are open from May through September. This RV park is closed during the off-season. The camping and tent areas also allow dogs. There is a dog walk area at the campground. Multiple dogs may be allowed.

Osborne Bay Resort

1450 Charlette Street
Crofton, BC
250-246-4787
osbornebayresort.com
Friendly dogs of all sizes are allowed, and there are no additional pet fees for tent or RV sites. Up to two very well behaved dogs are allowed in the cottages, and there is no extra fee unless it is an extra large, or heavy shedding dog. Dogs may not be left unattended in cottages, and they must be leashed and cleaned up after. The camping and tent areas also allow dogs. There is a dog walk area at the campground. Dogs are allowed in the camping cabins.

Sunnyside Campground
3405 Columbia Valley H
Cultus Lake, BC
604-858-5253
cultuslake.bc.ca/sunnyside/
This beautiful lakeside, 65 acre campground offers modern facilities, a boat launch, numerous family activities, and it sits within walking distance to several other recreational opportunities. They are open from April 1st until September 30th. Dogs of all sizes are allowed for an additional $3 per night per pet. Dogs must be kept leashed (even on site) and cleaned up after. Dogs are not allowed at the playgrounds, beaches, wharves, cabins, or in the lake. There are some off-leash areas in the park available; ask at the gatehouse for directions. This RV park is closed during the off-season. The camping and tent areas also allow dogs. There is a dog walk area at the campground. 2 dogs may be allowed.

Alahart RV Park
1725 Alaska Avenue/H 49E
Dawson Creek, BC
250-782-4702
pris.bc.ca/alahart/
Located in mile "0" city of the Alaska Highway, this full service park has large grassy lawns, easy pull-thru sites, and is a good place to rest and supply up for northbound adventures; there is also a restaurant on site. Dogs of all sizes are allowed for no additional fee. Dogs must be leashed and cleaned up after at all times. The camping and tent areas also allow dogs. There is a dog walk area at the campground. Multiple dogs may be allowed.

Mile Zero Park and Campground
1901 Alaska Avenue
Dawson Creek, BC

250-782-2590
Dogs of all sizes are allowed. There are no additional pet fees. Dogs may not be left unattended, must be leashed, and cleaned up after. This RV park is closed during the off-season. The camping and tent areas also allow dogs. There is a dog walk area at the campground. Multiple dogs may be allowed.

Northern Lights RV Park
9636 Friesen Sub-division
Dawson Creek, BC
250-782-9433 (888-414-9433)
nlrv.com/
This camp area has the distinction of being at Mile 0 of the Alaskan Highway, and they offer guests a number of amenities including free Wi-Fi, but nature presents the best amenity via the Northern Lights display. Dogs of all sizes are allowed for no additional fee. Dogs must be leashed and cleaned up after at all times. The camping and tent areas also allow dogs. There is a dog walk area at the campground. Multiple dogs may be allowed.

Tubby's RV Park
1913 96th Avenue
Dawson Creek, BC
250-782-2584
karo-ent.com/dawson.htm
Open all year, this full service RV park has 97 easy pull-thru sites, picnic tables, modern restrooms with free hot showers, a car and RV wash area, and a dump site. Dogs of all sizes are allowed for no additional fee. Dogs must be leashed and cleaned up after at all times. The camping and tent areas also allow dogs. There is a dog walk area at the campground. Multiple dogs may be allowed.

Dease Lake RV Park
M.P. 488 H 37
Dease Lake, BC
250-771-4666
Dogs of all sizes are allowed. There are no additional pet fees. Dogs must be leashed and cleaned up after. This RV park is closed during the off-season. There is a dog walk area at the campground. Multiple dogs may be allowed.

Fairmont Hot Springs Resort
5225 Fairmont Hot Springs
Fairmont, BC
800-663-4979/ask for RV
fairmonthotsprings.com
Dogs of all sizes are allowed. There are no additional pet fees. Dogs must be quiet, leashed, and cleaned

up after. This RV park is closed during the off-season. The camping and tent areas also allow dogs. There is a dog walk area at the campground. Multiple dogs may be allowed.

Yoho National Park of Canada
P. O. Box 99/H 1
Field, BC
250-343-6783 (888-773-8888)
This visually impressive park is home to a wide variety of habitats, spectacular waterfalls, towering rock walls, and a unique ecology. It offers more than 400 km of trails, interpretive signs and exhibits and various recreation. Dogs of all sizes are allowed at no additional fee. Dogs may not be left unattended, and they must be leashed and cleaned up after. Dogs are allowed on the trails on leash. This campground is closed during the off-season. The camping and tent areas also allow dogs. There is a dog walk area at the campground. There are no electric or water hookups at the campground. Multiple dogs may be allowed.

Fort Nelson Truck Stop and RV Park
Mile 293 Alaska Hwy
Fort Nelson, BC
250-774-7270
This full service RV camp area offers numerous amenities including a restaurant, fuels, a store, and more. Dogs of all sizes are allowed for no additional fee. Dogs must be leashed and cleaned up after at all times. This RV park is closed during the off-season. The camping and tent areas also allow dogs. There is a dog walk area at the campground. Multiple dogs may be allowed.

Westend RV Campground
5651 Alaska Hwy
Fort Nelson, BC
250-774-2340
karo-ent.com/westend.htm
This full service camp area has all the amenities plus a new "old west" restaurant and saloon on site. Dogs must be well behaved, leashed, and cleaned up after. The camping and tent areas also allow dogs. There is a dog walk area at the campground. Multiple dogs may be allowed.

Ross H. Maclean Rotary RV Park
13016 Lakeshore Drive
Fort St John, BC
250-785-1700
charlielake-rotaryrvpark.com
There is wireless Internet available

at the RV park. Dogs of all sizes are allowed. There are no additional pet fees. Dogs must be friendly, well behaved, leashed, and cleaned up after. Dogs can be walked by the lake. There are some breed restrictions. This RV park is closed during the off-season. The camping and tent areas also allow dogs. There is a dog walk area at the campground. Multiple dogs may be allowed.

Harrison Springs Camping and RV Park
740 Hot Springs Road
Harrison, BC
604-796-8900
harrisonsprings.com
Dogs of all sizes are allowed, but only small dogs, 10 pounds or under, are allowed in the cabins. There are no additional pet fees. Dogs must be quiet, friendly, may not be left alone, must be leashed at all times, and cleaned up after. This RV park is closed during the off-season. The camping and tent areas also allow dogs. There is a dog walk area at the campground. Dogs are allowed in the camping cabins. Multiple dogs may be allowed.

Hope Valley Campground
62280 Flood Hope Road
Hope, BC
604-869-9857
hopevalleyresort.com/
Dogs of all sizes are allowed. There are no additional pet fees. Dogs may not be left unattended, must be leashed, and cleaned up after. This RV park is closed during the off-season. The camping and tent areas also allow dogs. There is a dog walk area at the campground. Multiple dogs may be allowed.

Othello Tunnels Campground and RV Park
67851 Othello Road
Hope, BC
604-869-9448 (877-869-0543)
othellotunnels.com/
This year-around campground offers a long list of amenities, land and water recreation, close proximity to various other interesting sites/activities, and some great scenic hiking areas including a piece of the Kettle Valley Rail Trail that follows along the river. Friendly dogs of all sizes are allowed for no additional fee. Dogs must be well behaved, leashed, and cleaned up after. The camping and tent areas also allow dogs. There is a dog walk area at the campground. Multiple

dogs may be allowed.

Wild Rose Campground
62030 Flood Hope Road
Hope, BC
604-867-9734 (800-463-7999)
wildrosecamp.com/
Nestled in a park like setting with lots of trees and spacious grassy areas, this campground is open April 1st to September 30th; they offer numerous amenities, and close proximity to a number of other activities and sites of interest. Dogs of all sizes are allowed for no additional fee. Dogs must be friendly, well behaved, leashed, and cleaned up after at all times. There are some breed restrictions. This RV park is closed during the off-season. The camping and tent areas also allow dogs. There is a dog walk area at the campground. Multiple dogs may be allowed.

Houston Motor Inn RV Park
2940 H 16W
Houston, BC
250-845-7112 (800-994-8333)
This full hook-up RV park has a restaurant and coffee shop, and a 56 room inn on site that allows dogs for an additional $10 per night per pet. Coin showers and laundry are available. Dogs must be leashed and cleaned up after. There is a dog walk area at the campground. Multiple dogs may be allowed.

Shady Rest
3960 Drive-in Road
Houston, BC
250-845-2314
Open from about the beginning of May to the end of September weather permitting, this camp area offers grass and shaded sites, pull-thrus, a laundry, and modern washroom facilities. Dogs of all sizes are allowed for no additional fee. Dogs must be leashed and cleaned up after. This RV park is closed during the off-season. The camping and tent areas also allow dogs. There is a dog walk area at the campground. Multiple dogs may be allowed.

Lynx Creek RV Park
H 29E
Hudsons Hope, BC
250-783-5333
lynxcreekrvpark.com/
This camp area sits aside a wide creek in a small green valley flanked by trees, making it a great getaway with a variety of land and water recreational opportunities. Dogs of all

sizes are allowed for no additional fee. Dogs must be well behaved leashed, and cleaned up after. The camping and tent areas also allow dogs. There is a dog walk area at the campground. Multiple dogs may be allowed.

Tatogga Lake Resort
At about M.P. 390 on H 37 (Box 5995)
Iskut, BC
250-234-3526
karo-ent.com/tatogga.htm
Dogs of all sizes are allowed at the tent and RV site, but only one dog is allowed in the cabins. There are no additional pet fees. Dogs may be off leash if well behaved. This RV park is closed during the off-season. The camping and tent areas also allow dogs. There is a dog walk area at the campground. Dogs are allowed in the camping cabins.

Jade City RV Park
At about Mile Post 603/604 on H 37
Jade City, BC
250-239-3022
jadecitybccanada.com
Dogs of all sizes are allowed. There are no additional pet fees. Dogs must be leashed and cleaned up after while in the campground, but there is a big field close by where they can run off leash. This RV park is closed during the off-season. There is a dog walk area at the campground. Multiple dogs may be allowed.

Cassiar RV Park
1535 Barcalow Road
Kitwanga, BC
250-849-5799
cassiarrv.ca
Dogs of all sizes are allowed. There are no additional pet fees. Dogs must be leashed and cleaned up after. This RV park is closed during the off-season. There is a dog walk area at the campground. Multiple dogs may be allowed.

Fir Crest Resort
Fir Crest Road
Lac La Hache, BC
250-396-7337
fircrestresort.com/
Terraced sites allow all to have a waterfront or lake view at this park, and in addition to the beauty of its natural setting, they offer fire pits, picnic tables, modern restrooms, a laundry, store, café, and more. Dogs of all sizes are allowed in the campground for $1 per night per

pet; there is a $5 per night per pet additional fee for the cabins. Dogs must be leashed and cleaned up after at all times, especially since there is also a dog sled team on site. Guests may even learn to drive a sled team here. This RV park is closed during the off-season. The camping and tent areas also allow dogs. There is a dog walk area at the campground. Dogs are allowed in the camping cabins. 2 dogs may be allowed.

E. C. Manning Provincial Park
7500 H 3
Manning Park, BC
250-840-8822 (800-689-9025)
This park has 5 of BC's 14 biogeoclimatic zones creating very diverse landscapes, flora, fauna, land and water recreational opportunities, and numerous trails for exploring. This resort also provides several amenities including a recreation center, fitness center, and several annual events. Dogs of all sizes are allowed in the park and in the campground for no additional fee. There is an additional fee of $25 per pet per 3 day stay for the cabins with a pet waiver to sign, and 2 dogs are allowed. Dogs must be well behaved, leashed, and cleaned up after at all times. Four campgrounds are open for summer usually from April to November depending on camp area, and 2 are open through winter for self-contained units. There are also 10 wilderness camp areas. Most areas provide pit/flush toilets, tap water, fire wood, and Lightning Lake has an amphitheater. The camping and tent areas also allow dogs. There is a dog walk area at the campground. Dogs are allowed in the camping cabins. There are no electric or water hookups at the campgrounds.

Bamberton Provincial Park
Mill Bay Road
Mill Bay, BC
250-474-1336 (800-689-9025)
This park features a warm water bay, a long sandy beach, and a variety of recreational areas, woodlands, trails, and wildlife habitats. Dogs of all sizes are allowed at no additional fee. Dogs may not be left unattended except for short periods and then only if they will be quiet and well behaved. Dogs must be leashed and cleaned up after. Dogs are not allowed on the beach, however, they can be on the trails on lead. The camping and tent areas also allow dogs. There is a dog walk area at the

campground. There are no electric or water hookups at the campground. Multiple dogs may be allowed.

J and H Wilderness Resort and RV Park
M.P. 463 Alaska Hwy
Muncho Lake, BC
250-776-3453
bcfroa.bc.ca/member/121/J-/
Dogs of all sizes are allowed. There are no additional pet fees. Dogs may not be left unattended, must be leashed, and cleaned up after. This RV park is closed during the off-season. The camping and tent areas also allow dogs. There is a dog walk area at the campground. Multiple dogs may be allowed.

Northern Rockies Lodge
M.P. 462 Alaska Hwy
Muncho Lake, BC
250-776-3481
northernrockieslodge.com
Dogs of all sizes are allowed, and there are no additional pet fees for tent or RV sites. There is a $10 per night per pet additional fee for the lodge. Dogs may not be left unattended, must be leashed, and cleaned up after. The camping and tent areas also allow dogs. There is a dog walk area at the campground. 2 dogs may be allowed.

Oliver/Gallagher Lake KOA
RR2 Site 41, Comp 8
Oliver, BC
250-498-3358 (800-562-9017)
gallagherlake.com
Dogs of all sizes are allowed. There are no additional pet fees. Dogs must be quiet, well behaved, leashed, and cleaned up after. Dogs are not allowed on the beach sites. This RV park is closed during the off-season. The camping and tent areas also allow dogs. There is a dog walk area at the campground. Multiple dogs may be allowed.

Nk'Mip Resort
8000 45th Street
Osoyoos, BC
250-495-7279
campingosoyoos.com
Dogs of all sizes are allowed. There is a $4 per night per pet additional fee. Dogs may not be left unattended in the Yurts and may only be left in RVs if weather permits, or if the units have air conditioning. Dogs must be leashed and cleaned up after. There is a dog walk area at the campground. 2 dogs may be allowed.

Parks Sands Beach Resort
105 E Island H
Parksville, BC
250-248-3171 (877-873-1600)
parksands.com/
Dogs of all sizes are allowed. There are no additional pet fees. Dogs may not be left unattended, and they must be leashed at all times, and cleaned up after. Dogs are not allowed on the beach at any time between March 1st and April 30th. This park is located on Vancouver Island and is accessible by ferry. Most of the ferry companies will allow dogs on the auto deck only. The camping and tent areas also allow dogs. There is a dog walk area at the campground. Multiple dogs may be allowed.

Surfside RV Resort
200 N Corfield Street
Parksville, BC
866-642-2001
surside.bc.ca
Dogs of all sizes are allowed. There are no additional pet fees. Dogs must be well behaved, may not be left unattended, must be leashed, and cleaned up after. There is a dog walk area at the campground. 2 dogs may be allowed.

Beatton Provincial Park
244 Road
Peace River, BC
250-964-2243 (800-689-9025)
This year round recreational destination offers a 312 hectare park along the shores of Charlie Lake. Dogs are allowed in the park and camp area; they are not allowed in park buildings, beach areas, or in the backcountry. Dogs must be leashed and cleaned up after at all times. There are 37 vehicle accessible campsites; 11 are reservable. Pit toilets and potable water are available, and there are gaming areas, an adventure playground, and a large grassy area in the day use area. This RV park is closed during the off-season. There is a dog walk area at the campground. There are no electric or water hookups at the campgrounds. Multiple dogs may be allowed.

Pink Mountain
Mile 143 Alaska Hwy
Pink Mountain, BC
250-772-5133
karo-ent.com/akhwybc.htm
This full service camp area has a gas station and a store in addition to a variety of other amenities. Dogs

of all sizes are allowed for no additional fee. Dogs must be leashed and cleaned up after at all times, and they may not be in the store area because of a resident German Shepherd. They suggest making reservation well in advance as at times they fill up with migrant workers. The camping and tent areas also allow dogs. There is a dog walk area at the campground. 2 dogs may be allowed.

Kinnikinnick Campground
Skinna Drive
Port Edward, BC
250-628-9449 (866-628-9449)
kinnikcamp.com/home.htm
This beautiful camp area is only a 2 or 3 minute walk to town, its close to various recreational activities, has modern amenities, and sites are uniquely designed for privacy on level sites with each having a picnic table and fire ring. They are open from mid-May to mid-September. Dogs of all sizes are allowed for no additional fee. Dogs must be leashed and cleaned up after at all times; they are not allowed in buildings. This RV park is closed during the off-season. The camping and tent areas also allow dogs. There is a dog walk area at the campground. Multiple dogs may be allowed.

Bee Lazee RV Park and Campground
15910 H 97 S
Prince George, BC
250-963-7263 (866-963-7263)
beelazee.ca/
This landscaped and treed camp area offers a variety of recreational opportunities, a laundry, modern restrooms with no pay showers, a store, and a heated pool. Dogs of all sizes are allowed with advance reservations for no additional fee. Dogs must be leashed and cleaned up after. Their season runs from May 1st to September 30th. This RV park is closed during the off-season. The camping and tent areas also allow dogs. There is a dog walk area at the campground. Multiple dogs may be allowed.

Blue Spruce RV Park and Campground
4433 Kimball Road
Prince George, BC
250-964-7272
This beautifully treed camp area has 30 acres of wilderness to explore, miles of trails, a beaver pond, a playground, and close to shopping and a variety of other activities. Dogs

are welcome for no additional fee. Dogs must be well behaved, leashed, and cleaned up after. Their season runs from April 1st to October 31st. This RV park is closed during the off-season. The camping and tent areas also allow dogs. There is a dog walk area at the campground. Multiple dogs may be allowed.

Hartway RV Park
7729 S Kelly Road
Prince George, BC
250-962-8848
Dogs of all sizes are allowed. There are no additional pet fees. Dogs may not be left unattended at any time, must be leashed, and cleaned up after. This RV park is closed during the off-season. The camping and tent areas also allow dogs. There is a dog walk area at the campground. Multiple dogs may be allowed.

Sintich Trailer Park
7817 H 97
Prince George, BC
250-963-9862
sintichpark.bc.ca
Dogs of all sizes are allowed. There are no additional pet fees. Dogs must be leashed and cleaned up after. This RV park is closed during the off-season. The camping and tent areas also allow dogs. There is a dog walk area at the campground. Multiple dogs may be allowed.

Stone Creek RV Park and Campground
31605 H 97 S
Prince George, BC
250-330-4321
Nestled along Fraser River and Stone Creek in a natural setting, has made this a popular getaway for fishing, hiking, relaxing, and nature observation. Dogs are welcome for no additional fee. Dogs must be well behaved, leashed, and cleaned up after. Their season runs from May to October. This RV park is closed during the off-season. The camping and tent areas also allow dogs. There is a dog walk area at the campground. There are no water hookups at the campgrounds. Multiple dogs may be allowed.

Park Avenue Campground
1750 Park Avenue/Yellowhead H/H 16
Prince Rupert, BC
250-627-1000 (877-624-5861)
princerupertrv.com/Home.html
This lush, green camp area is the city's only RV campground, and

there are plenty of amenities and wildlife to enjoy. Reservations are highly recommended during the summer. Dogs of all sizes are allowed for no additional fee. Dogs must be quiet, well behaved, leashed, and cleaned up after at all times. The camping and tent areas also allow dogs. There is a dog walk area at the campground. There are no water hookups at the campgrounds. Multiple dogs may be allowed.

Gwaii Haanas National Park Reserve & Haida Heritage Site
P. O. Box 37
Queen Charlotte, BC
250-559-8818
Comprised of some 138 islands that stretch 90 kilometers from north to south, the rugged beauty and rich ecology of this park will allow visitors to have a complete wilderness experience. On islands where you may camp, you may only camp on the beaches. It is recommended that visitors not bring their pets with them into Gwaii Haanas, but if you do, when onshore, your pet must be kept on a leash at all times with an adult. They encourage you not to bring your pet ashore at any of the Watchmen sites. Hotspring Island is closed to pets. You must also register for an orientation prior to being allowed to this park. Only one dog is allowed per campsite. There is a dog walk area at the campground. There are no electric or water hookups at the campground.

Lazy Daze
714 Ritchie Road
Quesnel, BC
250-992-6700
This resort offers accommodations and recreational activities year round. Dogs of all sizes are allowed for no additional fee in the camp area as long as they do not have to clean up after your pet, then there may be a fee of $5 per pet. Dogs must be well mannered, leashed, and cleaned up after at all times. The camping and tent areas also allow dogs. There is a dog walk area at the campground. Multiple dogs may be allowed.

Kootenay National Park of Canada
P. O. Box 220/ Kootenay Parkway
Radium Hot Springs, BC
250-347-9615 (877-737-3783.)
This park offers a diversity of naturescapes, elevations, climates,

ecology, and recreation to its visitors. Dogs of all sizes are allowed at no additional fee. Dogs may not be left unattended, and they must be leashed and cleaned up after. Pets and pet food must be brought inside at night. Dogs are allowed on the trails on lead. This campground is closed during the off-season. The camping and tent areas also allow dogs. There is a dog walk area at the campground. Multiple dogs may be allowed.

Canyon Hot Springs Resort
35 KM E of Revelstoke on H 1
Revelstoke, BC
250-837-2420
canyonhotsprings.com
One dog of any size is allowed. There are no additional pet fees. Dogs may not be left unattended, must be leashed, and cleaned up after. This RV park is closed during the off-season. The camping and tent areas also allow dogs. There is a dog walk area at the campground.

Glacier National Park of Canada
P.O. Box 350
Revelstoke, BC
250-837-7500 (888-773-8888)
Born from ancient glaciers and rich in natural history, this park protects unique old growth forests and critical habitats for threatened and endangered wildlife. Home to the Rogers Pass National Historic Site, the park offers interpretive programs as well as a variety of recreational pursuits. Dogs of all sizes are allowed at no additional fee. Dogs may not be left unattended, and they must be leashed and cleaned up after. Pets and pet food must be brought inside at night. Dogs are not allowed at Balu Pass, but they are allowed on the trails on lead. This campground is closed during the off-season. The camping and tent areas also allow dogs. There is a dog walk area at the campground. There are no electric or water hookups at the campground. Multiple dogs may be allowed.

Lamplighter Campground
1760 Nixon
Revelstoke, BC
250-837-3385
seerevelstoke.com
Dogs of all sizes are allowed. There are no additional pet fees. Dogs may not be left unattended, must be leashed, and cleaned up after. This RV park is closed during the off-season. The camping and tent areas also allow dogs. There is a dog walk

area at the campground. Multiple dogs may be allowed.

Revelstoke KOA
2411 KOA Road
Revelstoke, BC
250-837-2085 (800-562-3905)
revelstokekoa.com
Dogs of all sizes are allowed. There are no additional pet fees. Dogs must be leashed and cleaned up after. This RV park is closed during the off-season. The camping and tent areas also allow dogs. There is a dog walk area at the campground. 2 dogs may be allowed.

Williamson's Lake Campground
1816 Williamson Lake Road
Revelstoke, BC
250-837-5512
williamsonlakecampground.com
Dogs of all sizes are allowed. There are no additional pet fees. Dogs may not be left unattended, must be leashed, quiet, and cleaned up after. Dogs are not allowed on the beach nor at the cabins. They do have one teepee on site where dogs are welcome. This RV park is closed during the off-season. The camping and tent areas also allow dogs. There is a dog walk area at the campground. Multiple dogs may be allowed.

Camperland
53730 Bridal Falls Road
Rosedale, BC
604-794-7361
This park offers a wide variety of activities and recreation in addition to a central location to many other popular family attractions. This is also a "members" park, and during the summer months only members are allowed on the weekends. During the spring and fall, weekends are available to non-members, and reservations are recommended at all times. The park is open from April 1st to October 31st. Dogs of all sizes are allowed for an additional $2 per night per pet. Dogs may not be left unattended, and they must be well behaved, leashed, and cleaned up after. The camping and tent areas also allow dogs. There is a dog walk area at the campground. 2 dogs may be allowed.

Shuswap Lake Provincial Park
Squilax Road
Scotch Creek, BC
250-955-0861 (800-689-9025)
This very popular park offers a variety of habitats, scenic views, numerous trails, and various

recreational pursuits. Dogs of all sizes are allowed at no additional fee. Dogs may not be left unattended, and they must be leashed and cleaned up after. Dogs may be off lead when in your camp only if they are under voice control, and will not leave the perimeter of your site. Dogs are not allowed in beach areas, beach trails, park buildings, or day-use areas, however, a stretch of beach is available adjacent to the boat launch where visitors may swim with their dogs. Dogs are allowed on the trails on leash. This campground is closed during the off-season. The camping and tent areas also allow dogs. There is a dog walk area at the campground. There are no electric or water hookups at the campground. Multiple dogs may be allowed.

Sicamous KOA
3250 Oxboro Road
Sicamous, BC
250-836-2507 (800-562-0797)
koa.com
Dogs of all sizes are allowed, and there are no additional pet fees for tent or RV sites. There is a $5 per night per pet additional fee for cabins. Dogs may not be left unattended, must be leashed, and cleaned up after. This RV park is closed during the off-season. The camping and tent areas also allow dogs. There is a dog walk area at the campground. Dogs are allowed in the camping cabins. Multiple dogs may be allowed.

Gulf Islands
2220 Harbour Road
Sidney, BC
250-654-4000 (888-773-8888)
Spread 35 km over 15 islands, this first national park reserve of the 21st century, was initiated to protect the ecological integrity of the area, and to provide an educational experience of the culture and of the coastal island landscape. The islands are reached by ferry and other watercraft. BC Ferry will transport pets, but they must remain on vehicle decks for the duration of the voyage. This campground is closed during the off-season. The camping and tent areas also allow dogs. There is a dog walk area at the campground. There are no electric or water hookups at the campground. Multiple dogs may be allowed.

Bear River RV Park

2200 Davis Street
Stewart, BC
250-636-9205
stewartbc.com/rvpark
Dogs of all sizes are allowed. There are no additional pet fees. Dogs must be quiet, may not be left unattended, must be leashed, and cleaned up after. This RV park is closed during the off-season. There is a dog walk area at the campground. Multiple dogs may be allowed.

Okanagan Lake Provincial Park
On H 97, 11 km N of Summerland
Summerland, BC
250-494-6500 (800-689-9025)
This park offers panoramic views, interpretive programs, sandy beaches, self-guided trails, and a variety of land and water recreation. Dogs of all sizes are allowed at no additional fee. Dogs may not be left unattended, and they must be leashed and cleaned up after. Dogs are not allowed in buildings, on beaches, or in the back country. This campground is closed during the off-season. The camping and tent areas also allow dogs. There is a dog walk area at the campground. There are no electric or water hookups at the campground.

Dogwood Campground and RV Park
15151 112th Avenue
Surrey, BC
604-583-5585
dogwoodcampgrounds.com
Dogs of all sizes are allowed. There are no additional pet fees. Dogs must be leashed and cleaned up after. There are some breed restrictions. The camping and tent areas also allow dogs. There is a dog walk area at the campground. 2 dogs may be allowed.

Hazelmere RV Park
18843 8th Avenue
Surrey, BC
877-501-5007
hazelmere.ca
Dogs of all sizes and numbers are allowed, however there can only be two dogs at a time in the cabins. There are no additional pet fees. Dogs must be quiet, well behaved, leashed and cleaned up after. Dogs are not to be left unattended in the cabins at any time. The camping and tent areas also allow dogs. There is a dog walk area at the campground. Dogs are allowed in the camping cabins.

Lakelse Lake Provincial Park

P. O. Box 1124
Terrace, BC
250-638-8490 (800-689-9025)
Surrounded by mountains, this scenic park offers a variety of habitats, trails, ecosystems, and land and water recreation. Dogs of all sizes are allowed at no additional fee. Dogs may not be left unattended, and they must be leashed and cleaned up after. Dogs are not allowed on the beach or in buildings; they are allowed on the trails on leash. This campground is closed during the off-season. The camping and tent areas also allow dogs. There is a dog walk area at the campground. There are no electric or water hookups at the campground. Multiple dogs may be allowed.

Skihist Provincial Park
Trans Canada H 1
Thompson-Nicola, BC
250-455-2708
Open from the end of April to September 30th, this popular 33 hectares camp site along the Thompson River offers a variety of land and water recreational opportunities, spectacular views of Thompson Canyon, and scenic trails-including some of the old Cariboo Wagon Road. Dogs of all sizes are allowed in the park on a leash no longer than 2 meters and they must be cleaned up after at all times. Dogs are not allowed on the beaches or in day use areas. Camp sites are on a first come, first served basis and can accommodate up to large camping unites. Four of the 58 sites are walk-in sites for tents only. This RV park is closed during the off-season. The camping and tent areas also allow dogs. There is a dog walk area at the campground. There are no electric or water hookups at the campgrounds. Multiple dogs may be allowed.

Poplars Campground and Cafe
Mile 426 Alaska Hwy
Toad River, BC
250-232-5465
karo-ent.com/muncho.htm
This well-kept, full service park can also provide fuel, minor repairs, food and fresh baked goods, and souvenirs. Dogs of all sizes are allowed for no additional fee for the camp area, and they are not allowed in the cabins. Dogs must be under owner's control, leashed, and cleaned up after at all times. Dogs may sit at the outer tables of the café. This RV park is closed during the off-season. The camping and tent areas also allow dogs. There is

a dog walk area at the campground. Multiple dogs may be allowed.

Toad River RV Camp and Lodge
Mile 422 Alaska Hwy
Toad River, BC
250-232-5401
karo-ent.com/toadriv.htm
A lot can be accomplished at this stop with an RV park (and motel) that accepts pets, a restaurant and bakery, showers, laundry facilities, a dump station, fuels, and a 6,000+ hat collection adorning the lodge. Dogs are allowed in the motel for $5 per night per pet, and there is no additional fee in the camp area. Dogs are also allowed at the outer tables of the restaurant-weather permitting. Dogs must be well mannered, under owner's control, leashed, and cleaned up after at all times. The camping and tent areas also allow dogs. There is a dog walk area at the campground. Multiple dogs may be allowed.

Mussel Beach Campground
Gravel Road, Section 54 off Port Albion Road
Tofino, BC
250-537-2081
musselbeachcampground.com/
Dogs of all sizes are allowed. There are no additional pet fees. Dogs may not be left unattended outside, and they must be leashed and cleaned up after. Dogs may be off lead only if they respond to voice control. This park is on Vancouver Island, is accessible by ferry, and dogs are allowed on most of them on the auto deck only. The camping and tent areas also allow dogs. There is a dog walk area at the campground. There are no electric or water hookups at the campgrounds. Multiple dogs may be allowed.

Pacific Rim National Park Reserve of Canada
2185 Ocean Terrace Road
Ucluelet, BC
250-726-7721 (888-773-8888)
This park has an abundance of natural and cultural treasures, is home to the rare ecosystem of a lush coastal temperate rainforest, and offers a wide variety of trails, long beaches and various recreational pursuits. Dogs of all sizes are allowed at no additional fee. Dogs may not be left unattended, and they must be leashed and cleaned up after. Dogs are not allowed in buildings. Dogs are allowed on the trails on lead.

This campground is closed during the off-season. The camping and tent areas also allow dogs. There is a dog walk area at the campground. There are no electric or water hookups at the campground. Multiple dogs may be allowed.

Fort Victoria RV Park
340 Island H
Victoria, BC
250-479-8112
fortvictoria.ca
Dogs of all sizes are allowed. There are no additional pet fees. Dogs may not be left unattended, must be leashed, and cleaned up after. There is a dog walk area at the campground. 2 dogs may be allowed.

Victoria West KOA
230 Trans-Canada H 1
Victoria, BC
250-478-3332 (800-562-1732)
koa.com/where/bc/52130/
Dogs of all sizes are allowed. There are no additional pet fees. Dogs must be friendly, leashed, and cleaned up after. Dogs may be off leash on the dog walk if they are under voice control. This RV park is closed during the off-season. The camping and tent areas also allow dogs. There is a dog walk area at the campground. Dogs are allowed in the camping cabins. Multiple dogs may be allowed.

Weir's Beach RV Resort
5191 William Head Road
Victoria, BC
250-478-3323
weirsbeachrvresort.bc.ca
Dogs of all sizes are allowed. There are no additional pet fees. Dogs must be leashed when in the park and cleaned up after. Dogs can be off leash at the river. There is a dog walk area at the campground. Multiple dogs may be allowed.

Westbay Oceanfront RV Park
453 Head Street
Victoria, BC
250-385-1831
westbay.bc.ca
Dogs of all sizes are allowed. There are no additional pet fees. Dogs must be leashed and cleaned up after. There are some breed restrictions. The camping and tent areas also allow dogs. There is a dog walk area at the campground. 2 dogs may be allowed.

Riverside RV Resort and Campground

8018 Mons Road
Whistler, BC
604-905-5533
whistlercamping.com/home.html
In addition to being a premium #1 skiing and golfing destination, this park is also a recreational destination in its own right with outdoor and indoor gaming areas, trails, a putting green, and plenty of modern amenities for a comfortable stay. Dogs of all sizes are allowed in the campground area for an additional $3 (+tax) per night per pet. There is a $23.20 per night fee for 1 pet per cabin (shedding dogs not allowed in cabin). Dogs may not be left unattended at any time, and they must be under owner's control, leashed, and cleaned up after at all times. Dogs are not allowed on the beach, in the playground areas, or in buildings. The camping and tent areas also allow dogs. There is a dog walk area at the campground. Dogs are allowed in the camping cabins.

Big Bar Lake Provincial Park
181 1st Avenue
Williams Lake, BC
250-398-4414
Popular for fishing, there is also an abundance of other recreational opportunities here, and a 3.5 mile self-guided Otter Marsh Interpretive Trail. Dogs are allowed in the park and campground areas; they are not allowed in day use, beach areas, or in the back country. There is no additional pet fee for the campground. Dogs must be leashed and cleaned up after at all times. All campsites are on a first-come, first-served basis and provide campfire rings and pit toilets, with an adventure playground is close by. This RV park is closed during the off-season. The camping and tent areas also allow dogs. There is a dog walk area at the campground. There are no electric or water hookups at the campgrounds. 2 dogs may be allowed.

Springhouse Trails Ranch
3067 Dog Creek Road
Williams Lake, BC
250-392-4780
springhousetrails.com/
Open from May to September, this family resort offers a variety of "all ages" recreation, a playground with a trampoline, outdoor barbecues, a dining and dancing area, showers, laundry facilities, and more. Dogs of all sizes are allowed in the campground for no additional fee

only if the owner is responsible in cleaning up after their pet. There is a $10 per night per pet fee for pets in cabins. Dogs must be leashed and cleaned up after in all areas at all times. This RV park is closed during the off-season. The camping and tent areas also allow dogs. There is a dog walk area at the campground. Dogs are allowed in the camping cabins. 2 dogs may be allowed.

Williams Lake Stampede
850 McKinsey Avenue
Williams Lake, BC
250-369-6718 (In BC: 800-71-RODEO)
For more than 80 years during the first long weekend in July and still going strong, this park is home to the Annual Williams Lake Stampede Rodeo. Dogs are allowed for no additional fee. Dogs must be leashed and cleaned up after at all times. There is a dog walk area at the campground. Multiple dogs may be allowed.

Manitoba

Curran Park Campground
Box 6, 305 RR 3
Brandon, MB
204-571-0750
curranpark.com
Dogs of all sizes are allowed. There are no additional pet fees. Dogs must be leashed and cleaned up after. This RV park is closed during the off-season. The camping and tent areas also allow dogs. There is a dog walk area at the campground. Multiple dogs may be allowed.

Meadowlark Campground
1629 Middleton
Brandon, MB
204-728-7205
meadowlarkcampground.ca
Dogs of all sizes are allowed. There are no additional pet fees. Dogs must be quiet, leashed, and cleaned up after. This RV park is closed during the off-season. The camping and tent areas also allow dogs. There is a dog walk area at the campground. Multiple dogs may be allowed.

Rainbow Beach Campground
17 km E of Dauphin on H 20
Dauphin, MB
204-638-9493

Dogs of all sizes are allowed. There are no additional pet fees. Dogs must be leashed and cleaned up after, and they may not be on the beach. This RV park is closed during the off-season. The camping and tent areas also allow dogs. There is a dog walk area at the campground. Multiple dogs may be allowed.

Whiteshell Provincial Park
H 1 and H 44
Falcon Lake, MB
888-482-CAMP (2267)
whiteshell.mb.ca/index.html
In addition to providing nature-oriented activities, outstanding scenery, and some of the best hiking trails in the province, this park is also home to the deepest lake in the province. Dogs are allowed for no additional fee; they must be leashed and cleaned up after at all times. They must be quiet, well behaved, and they are not allowed on the beaches or in the water. The campground offers modern restrooms, showers, potable water, a playground, and a dump station. This RV park is closed during the off-season. The camping and tent areas also allow dogs. There is a dog walk area at the campground. Multiple dogs may be allowed.

Whitemouth River RV Park and Campground
On Government Jet Road
Hadashville, MB
204-392-7110
One dog of any size is allowed. There are no additional pet fees. Dogs must be leashed and cleaned up after. This RV park is closed during the off-season. The camping and tent areas also allow dogs. There is a dog walk area at the campground.

Minnedosa Campground
Beach Road/H 262
Minnedosa, MB
204-867-3450
minnedosa.com/campground.php
Playing fields/courts, washroom/showers, a boat dock, mini-golf, playground, concessionaires, and a dump station are all available at this campground. Dogs are allowed for no additional fee; they must be leashed and under their owner's control at all times. Dogs are allowed on the beach. This RV park is closed during the off-season. The camping and tent areas also allow dogs. There is a dog walk area at the campground. Multiple dogs may be allowed.

Lion's Riverbend Campground
450 Broadway Avenue
Neepawa, MB
204-476-7676
Lion's Riverbend Campground
More than 75 sites are available at this camp area. They offer restrooms, showers, potable water, and a dump station, plus there is a swimming pool right beside the park. Quiet, well behaved dogs are allowed for no additional fee; they must be leashed and under their owner's control at all times. This RV park is closed during the off-season. The camping and tent areas also allow dogs. There is a dog walk area at the campground. Multiple dogs may be allowed.

Miller's Camping Resort
6 miles E of Portage on H 1
Portage la Prairie, MB
204-857-4255
Dogs of all sizes are allowed. There are no additional pet fees. Dogs must be quiet, leashed, and cleaned up after. This RV park is closed during the off-season. The camping and tent areas also allow dogs. There is a dog walk area at the campground. Multiple dogs may be allowed.

Portage Campground
8 miles E of Portage on H 1
Portage la Prairie, MB
204-267-2191
Dogs of all sizes are allowed. There are no additional pet fees. Dogs must be quiet, leashed, and cleaned up after. This RV park is closed during the off-season. The camping and tent areas also allow dogs. There is a dog walk area at the campground. 2 dogs may be allowed.

Rock Garden Campground
Provincial Road #302
Richer, MB
204-422-5441 (866-422-5441)
rockgarden.ca/
A family friendly campground, they have playing fields/courts, an arcade, playground, a solar heated pool, mini golf, and Wi-Fi. They also offer a grocery story, a canteen, snack bar, modern restrooms, hot showers, laundry facilities, and a dump station. Dogs are allowed for no additional fee; they must be leashed and cleaned up after at all times. Dogs are not allowed in the pool area. This RV park is closed during the off-season. The camping and tent areas also allow dogs. There is a dog walk

area at the campground. Multiple dogs may be allowed.

Asessippi Provincial Park
H 482
Russell, MB
204-564-2473 (888-4U2-CAMP (482-2267))
Rich in natural, historic, and cultural history, this park is located at the south end of the Lake of the Prairies. In addition to numerous water activities, they have self-guided interpretive trails, a playground, swim beach, modern restrooms, and showers. Dogs are allowed for no additional pet fee; they must be leashed and cleaned up after at all times. This RV park is closed during the off-season. The camping and tent areas also allow dogs. There is a dog walk area at the campground. Multiple dogs may be allowed.

Wikiwak Campground
55 S Cove
Shediac, MB
506-532-6713
sn2000.nb.ca/comp/wikiwak
Dogs of all sizes are allowed. There are no additional pet fees. Dogs must be quiet, well behaved, leashed and cleaned up after. Dogs may not be left unattended. This RV park is closed during the off-season. The camping and tent areas also allow dogs. There is a dog walk area at the campground. Multiple dogs may be allowed.

Debonair Campground
P. O. Box 68
St Malo, MB
204-347-5543 (866-DEB-CAMP (866-332-2267))
debonaircampground.com
Dogs of all sizes are allowed. There are no additional pet fees. Dogs may not be left unattended outside, and may be left inside only if they will be quiet and well behaved. Dogs must be leashed and cleaned up after. This RV park is closed during the off-season. The camping and tent areas also allow dogs. There is a dog walk area at the campground. Multiple dogs may be allowed.

Duck Mountain Provincial Park
P. O. Box 640
Swan River, MB
204-734-3429 (888-4U2-CAMP (482-2267))
This park of forested hills and river valleys offers a variety of trails and abundant year round recreation.

Dogs of all sizes are allowed at no additional fee. Dogs may not be left unattended, and they must be leashed and cleaned up after. Dogs are allowed on the trails on leash. This campground is closed during the off-season. The camping and tent areas also allow dogs. There is a dog walk area at the campground. There are no water hookups at the campground. Multiple dogs may be allowed.

Virden's Lion's Campground
Corner &th and H 257
Virden, MB
204-748-6393
Dogs of all sizes are allowed. There are no additional pet fees. Dogs must be leashed and cleaned up after. This RV park is closed during the off-season. The camping and tent areas also allow dogs. There is a dog walk area at the campground. Multiple dogs may be allowed.

Riding Mountain National Park of Canada
On H 10
Wasagaming, MB
204-848-7275 (888-773-8888)
This park is an island mountain reserve that is home to a wide range of plant and animal life. It also offers panoramic views, numerous hiking trails, a lookout tower, and various recreational pursuits. Dogs of all sizes are allowed at no additional fee. Dogs may not be left unattended, and they must be leashed at all times, and cleaned up after. Dogs are not allowed on the beach. Dogs are allowed on the trails on lead. This campground is closed during the off-season. The camping and tent areas also allow dogs. There is a dog walk area at the campground. Multiple dogs may be allowed.

Whiteshell Provincial Park
P. O. Box 119
West Hawk Lake, MB
204-349-2245 (888-4U2-CAMP (482-2267))
You will find rock alignments (petroforms) throughout this park that was created by natives over 8000 years ago. The park also offers interpretive programs, guided trails and is home to some of the province's nicest hiking trails. Dogs of all sizes are allowed at no additional fee. Dogs may not be left unattended, and they must be leashed and cleaned up after. Dogs are not allowed on the beach, however, they are allowed on trails

on leash. This campground is closed during the off-season. The camping and tent areas also allow dogs. There is a dog walk area at the campground. Multiple dogs may be allowed.

Bird's Hill Provincial Park
On Lagimodiere/H 59
Winnipeg, MB
888-482-2267
Dogs of all sizes are allowed. There are no additional pet fees. Dogs must be leashed and cleaned up for, and they are not allowed on the beach. This RV park is closed during the off-season. The camping and tent areas also allow dogs. There is a dog walk area at the campground. Multiple dogs may be allowed.

Northgate Trailer Park
2695 Main
Winnipeg, MB
204-339-6631
Dogs of all sizes are allowed. There are no additional pet fees. Dogs must be leashed and cleaned up after. This RV park is closed during the off-season. The camping and tent areas also allow dogs. There is a dog walk area at the campground. Multiple dogs may be allowed.

Traveller's RV Resort
56001 Murdock Road
Winnipeg, MB
204-256-2186
travellersresort.com
Dogs of all sizes are allowed. There are no additional pet fees. Dogs must be leashed and cleaned up after. This RV park is closed during the off-season. The camping and tent areas also allow dogs. There is a dog walk area at the campground. Multiple dogs may be allowed.

New Brunswick

Fundy National Park of Canada
P.O.Box 1001
Alma, NB
506-887-6000 (888-773-8888)
This forest protects some of the last remaining wilderness in the area, and an interesting feature here are the tidal fluctuations in the Bay of Fundy, which are the highest in the world. They offer year round recreation and interpretive programs during the summer. Dogs of all sizes are allowed at no additional fee. Dogs may not be left unattended,

and they must be leashed and cleaned up after. Pets and pet food must be brought in at night. Dogs are allowed on the trails on lead. This campground is closed during the off-season. The camping and tent areas also allow dogs. There is a dog walk area at the campground. Multiple dogs may be allowed.

Camping Colibri
913 C Boul Acadian/H 11
Bertrand, NB
506-727-2222
In addition to the campground, this park is a major recreational destination with numerous activities, pools, water slides, special events, and theme days. They also offer Wi-Fi, a convenience store, an eatery, showers, laundry facilities, a playground, gaming areas, and more. Dogs are allowed for no additional fee; they must be leashed and under their owner's control at all times. Dogs are not allowed in rental units. There are some breed restrictions. This RV park is closed during the off-season. The camping and tent areas also allow dogs. There is a dog walk area at the campground. 2 dogs may be allowed.

Sandy Beach Tent and Trailer Park
380 Bas-cap-pele
Cap Pele, NB
506-577-2218
plagesandybeach.ca
Dogs of all sizes are allowed. There are no additional pet fees. Dogs may not be left unattended, must be leashed, and cleaned up after. This RV park is closed during the off-season. The camping and tent areas also allow dogs. There is a dog walk area at the campground. Multiple dogs may be allowed.

Hardings Point Campground
71 Hardings Point Landing
Carter's Point, NB
506-763-2517
Visitors arrive at this beautiful waterside camp area by the free 5 minute Westfield Ferry (dogs allowed) that operates 24/7 and can give passage to any size RV. In addition to lush green grounds, there are nature trails, a heated pool, an eatery/ice cream shop, a full roster of activities, and it is a great spot for fishing and bird watching. Dogs are allowed for no additional fee; they must be leashed and under their owner's control at all times. This RV park is closed during the off-season. The camping

and tent areas also allow dogs. There is a dog walk area at the campground. Multiple dogs may be allowed.

Camping St Basile
14411 Road 144
Edmundston, NB
506-263-1183
campingstbasile.com
Dogs of all sizes are allowed. There are no additional pet fees. Dogs must be leashed and cleaned up after. This RV park is closed during the off-season. The camping and tent areas also allow dogs. There is a dog walk area at the campground. Multiple dogs may be allowed.

Hartt Island RV Resort
2475 Woodstock Road
Fredericton, NB
866-462-9400
harttisland.com
Dogs of all sizes are allowed. There are no additional pet fees. Dogs must be leashed and cleaned up after. This RV park is closed during the off-season. The camping and tent areas also allow dogs. There is a dog walk area at the campground. Multiple dogs may be allowed.

Camping Plage Gagnon Beach
30 Ch Plage Gagnon Beach
Grand Barachois, NB
506-577-2519 (800-658-2828)
Located at the confluence of 3 maritime provinces gives visitors a central point to explore several other sites of interest. In addition to great ocean views and a private sandy beach, this camp area offers more than 250 sites, a large rec hall and playground, a grocery store, planned activities, free Wi-Fi, a laundry, and dump station. Dogs are allowed for no additional fee; they must be kept leashed and cleaned up after at all times. Dogs are allowed on the beach; they are not allowed in buildings. This RV park is closed during the off-season. The camping and tent areas also allow dogs. There is a dog walk area at the campground. Multiple dogs may be allowed.

Ponderosa Pines Camping
4325 H 114
Hopewell Cape, NB
800-822-8800
ponderosapines.ca
Dogs of all sizes are allowed. There are no additional pet fees. Dogs must be leashed and cleaned up after. This RV park is closed during the off-season. The camping and

tent areas also allow dogs. There is a dog walk area at the campground. Multiple dogs may be allowed.

Kouchibouguac National Park of Canada
186, Route 117
Kouchibouguac National Park, NB
506-876-2443 (877-773-8888)
This wilderness park offers spectacular scenery and diverse ecosystems that support a large variety of plants, fish, mammals, bird species. It also offers 60 km of trails and year round recreation. Dogs of all sizes are allowed at no additional fee. Dogs may not be left unattended, and they must be quiet, well behaved, leashed and cleaned up after. Dogs are not allowed on the beach. Dogs are allowed on the trails on lead. The camping and tent areas also allow dogs. There is a dog walk area at the campground. There are no water hookups at the campground. Multiple dogs may be allowed.

Cosy Cabins Campground
2335 H 165
Lower Woodstock, NB
506-328-3344 (888-923-9009)
cosycabins.ca/campground.htm
This campground offers waterfront sites and modern restrooms. Cabin rentals are also available. Dogs are allowed for no additional fee; they must be leashed and cleaned up after at all times. This RV park is closed during the off-season. The camping and tent areas also allow dogs. There is a dog walk area at the campground. Dogs are allowed in the camping cabins. There are no water hookups at the campgrounds. 2 dogs may be allowed.

Camper's City RV Park
138 Queens Way Drive
Moncton, NB
877-512-7868
camperscity.ca
Dogs of all sizes are allowed. There are no additional pet fees. Dogs must be leashed and cleaned up after. This RV park is closed during the off-season. The camping and tent areas also allow dogs. There is a dog walk area at the campground. Dogs are allowed in the camping cabins. Multiple dogs may be allowed.

Stonehurst Trailer Park
47915 Homestead Road
Moncton, NB
506-852-4162
sn2000.nb.ca/comp/stonehurst

Dogs of all sizes are allowed. There are no additional pet fees. Dogs must be leashed and cleaned up after. This RV park is closed during the off-season. The camping and tent areas also allow dogs. There is a dog walk area at the campground. Multiple dogs may be allowed.

Oak Bay Campground
742 H 1
Oak Bay, NB
506-466-4999
oakbaycampground.ca/
Located only 5 miles from the American boarder, this camp area sits central to a number of interesting sites, dining, shopping, and recreational opportunities. Dogs must be kept on a leash no longer than 8 feet, cleaned up after, and they may not be left unattended at any time. Animal control will be called for any dogs left alone on the property. Dogs must be kept inside at night, and they are not allowed at all on Sand Beach. This RV park is closed during the off-season. The camping and tent areas also allow dogs. There is a dog walk area at the campground. There are no water hookups at the campgrounds. 2 dogs may be allowed.

Camping Panoramic
14 Road Albert
Saint Jacques, NB
506-739-6544
Dogs of all sizes are allowed. There are no additional pet fees. Dogs must be leashed and cleaned up after. This RV park is closed during the off-season. The camping and tent areas also allow dogs. There is a dog walk area at the campground. Multiple dogs may be allowed.

Rockwood Park
142 Lakeside Drive S
Saint John, NB
506-652-4050
Dogs of all sizes are allowed. There are no additional pet fees. Dogs must be leashed and cleaned up after. This RV park is closed during the off-season. The camping and tent areas also allow dogs. There is a dog walk area at the campground. Multiple dogs may be allowed.

National Daigles Park
10787 H 134
Saint Louis-de-Kent, NB
877-324-4531
campingdaigle.com
Dogs of all sizes are allowed. There are no additional pet fees. Dogs may not be left unattended, must be

leashed, and cleaned up after. This RV park is closed during the off-season. The camping and tent areas also allow dogs. There is a dog walk area at the campground. 2 dogs may be allowed.

Ocean Surf Travel Park
73 Chemin Belliveau Beach Road
Shediac, NB
506-532-5480 (888-532-5480)
oceansurf.ca/campground.php
In addition to providing a full roster of special events and planned activities, this camp area offers live music every Saturday night, Wi-Fi, showers, laundry facilities, a small convenience store, dump stations, and a beach only a short walk away. Dogs are allowed for no additional fee; they must be leashed and cleaned up after at all times. This RV park is closed during the off-season. There is a dog walk area at the campground. Multiple dogs may be allowed.

Wishing Star Campground
218 Main Street
Shediac, NB
506-532-6786
wishingstar.ca/
Only a short walk to the popular Parlee Beach, this campground offers some beautiful scenery, pull-thru sites, picnic tables, fire rings, flush toilets, showers, a recreation center, playground, cable TV, laundry facilities, and a dump station. Dogs are allowed for no additional fee; they must be leashed and cleaned up after at all times. This RV park is closed during the off-season. The camping and tent areas also allow dogs. There is a dog walk area at the campground. Multiple dogs may be allowed.

Camping Janine du Have
48 ch. Chiasson Savoy Landing
Shippagan, NB
506-336-8884
This campground offers waterfront sites, picnic tables, restrooms, and a central location to a number of local attractions and activities. Dogs are allowed for no additional fee; they must be leashed and cleaned up after at all times. This RV park is closed during the off-season. The camping and tent areas also allow dogs. There is a dog walk area at the campground. There are no water hookups at the campgrounds. Multiple dogs may be allowed.

Century Farm Family Campground
670 Ocean Wave Drive

St Martins, NB
866-394-4400
Dogs of all sizes and numbers are allowed, but only 2 dogs are allowed per cabin, and they are not to be on the furniture. There are no additional pet fees. Dogs may not be left unattended, must be well behaved, leashed, and cleaned up after. This RV park is closed during the off-season. The camping and tent areas also allow dogs. There is a dog walk area at the campground. Dogs are allowed in the camping cabins. Multiple dogs may be allowed.

Jellystone Park at Kozy Acres
174 Hemlock Street
Woodstock, NB
506-328-6287 (888-222-YOGI (9644))
nbcanada.com/yogi.html
Dogs of all sizes are allowed. There are no additional pet fees. Dogs must be leashed and cleaned up after. This RV park is closed during the off-season. The camping and tent areas also allow dogs. There is a dog walk area at the campground. Multiple dogs may be allowed.

Newfoundland

Arnold's Cove RV Park
5 km E of Arnold's Cove on H 1
Arnold's Cove, NF
709-685-6767
puttnpullcamp.com
Dogs of all sizes are allowed. There are no additional pet fees. Dogs must be leashed and cleaned up after. This RV park is closed during the off-season. The camping and tent areas also allow dogs. There is a dog walk area at the campground.

JT Cheesman Provincial Park
H 1
Channel Port Aux Basques, NF
709-695-7222
This park is conveniently located within 15 minutes of the ferry; which is the first and last stop on the island. Hiking the natural areas and the beach are popular pastimes here. Dogs are allowed for no additional fee; they must be leashed and under their owner's control at all times. The campground has 102 sites, pit toilets, potable water, and a playground. This RV park is closed during the off-season. The camping and tent areas also allow dogs. There is a dog walk area at the campground. There are

no electric or water hookups at the campgrounds. Multiple dogs may be allowed.

Grand Codroy RV Camping Park
On Doyle Station Road
Doyles, NF
877-955-2520
Dogs of all sizes are allowed. There are no additional pet fees. Dogs must be leashed and cleaned up after. This RV park is closed during the off-season. The camping and tent areas also allow dogs. There is a dog walk area at the campground. Multiple dogs may be allowed.

Eastport Peninsula Sunshine Park
On the Road to the Beaches-H 310
Eastport, NF
709-677-2438
eastport.ca/sunshinepark/
Dogs of all sizes are allowed. There are no additional pet fees. Dogs must be leashed and cleaned up after. This RV park is closed during the off-season. The camping and tent areas also allow dogs. There is a dog walk area at the campground. Dogs are allowed in the camping cabins. Multiple dogs may be allowed.

Hidden Hilltop Family Campground
2600 H 4
Glenholme, NF
902-662-3391 (866-662-3391)
hiddenhilltop.com/
This family oriented campground offers 148 sites, a full roster of special events and planned activities, theme weekends, summer acoustic jam sessions on Thursday nights, and a daily children's program. They also have a pool with a slide, gaming fields/courts, a playground, an arcade, a laundry, and a camp store. Quiet dogs are allowed for no additional fee; they must be leashed and cleaned up after at all times. This RV park is closed during the off-season. The camping and tent areas also allow dogs. There is a dog walk area at the campground. Multiple dogs may be allowed.

Terra Nova National Park of Canada
Trans Canada #1
Glovertown, NF
709-533-2801 (888-773-8888)
Trails wind from bogs, ponds, and rolling forested hills to the rugged cliffs and inlets of the coastal region, offering a variety of habitats and recreational opportunities. Dogs of all sizes are allowed at no

additional fee. Dogs may not be left unattended, and they must be leashed and cleaned up after. Dogs are not allowed on the beach. Dogs are allowed on the trails on lead. The camping and tent areas also allow dogs. There is a dog walk area at the campground. Multiple dogs may be allowed.

Golden Arm Trailer Park
12 miles from H 1 on H 80
Green's Harbour, NF
709-582-3600
One dog of any size is allowed. There are no additional pet fees. Dogs must be leashed and cleaned up after. Long hair/shedding type dogs are not allowed in the cabins, and they must stay off the furniture. This RV park is closed during the off-season. The camping and tent areas also allow dogs. There is a dog walk area at the campground. Dogs are allowed in the camping cabins.

Blow Me Down Provincial Park
H 450
Lark Harbour, NF
709-681-2430 (800-563-6353)
Nestled in the woods, this peninsula park sits on the Bay of Islands and is known for its winds, scenic beauty, and recreational opportunities. Dogs are allowed for no additional fee; they must be leashed and cleaned up after at all times. The campground offers a comfort station, pit toilets, a playground, laundry facilities, showers, potable water, and a dump station. This RV park is closed during the off-season. The camping and tent areas also allow dogs. There is a dog walk area at the campground. There are no electric or water hookups at the campgrounds. Multiple dogs may be allowed.

Lomand River Lodge
10 km from H 430 on H 431
Lomand River, NF
877-456-6663
lomand-river-lodge.com
Dogs of all sizes are allowed. There are no additional pet fees. Dogs may not be left unattended, especially at the cabins. Dogs must be leashed and cleaned up after. This RV park is closed during the off-season. The camping and tent areas also allow dogs. There is a dog walk area at the campground. Dogs are allowed in the camping cabins. Multiple dogs may be allowed.

Cochrane Pond Family Campground
Box 283
Manuels/Conception Bay South, NF

709-747-5519
This family oriented campground offers 100 sites, a laundry, showers, flush toilets, a playground, a canteen, and a dump station. Although open year around, access depends on weather. Dogs are allowed for no additional fee; they must be leashed and cleaned up after at all times. The camping and tent areas also allow dogs. There is a dog walk area at the campground. There are no water hookups at the campgrounds. Multiple dogs may be allowed.

Gros Morne National Park of Canada
P.O. Box 130
Rocky Harbour, NF
709-458-2417 (888-773-8888)
Designated as a UNESCO World Heritage Site, this park, rich in natural beauty, offers unique geological features, an in depth Discovery Center, a wide variety of plant, marine, and animal life, and a multitude of recreational activities. Dogs of all sizes are allowed at no additional fee. Dogs may not be left unattended, and they must be leashed and cleaned up after. Pets and pet food must be brought inside at night. Dogs are allowed on the trails on lead unless otherwise marked. This campground is closed during the off-season. The camping and tent areas also allow dogs. There is a dog walk area at the campground. There are no electric or water hookups at the campground. Multiple dogs may be allowed.

Kona Beach Trailer Park
On H 1 80 80 km W of Grand Falls
South Brook, NF
709-657-2400
Dogs of all sizes are allowed. There are no additional pet fees. Dogs must be leashed and cleaned up after. This RV park is closed during the off-season. The camping and tent areas also allow dogs. There is a dog walk area at the campground. Multiple dogs may be allowed.

Triple Falls RV Park
H 430/Viking Trail
St Anthony, NF
709-454-2599
Large sites, shade trees, mini golf, a recreation hall, convenience store, playground, flush toilets, hot showers, a swimming beach, and a dump station are just some of the amenities here. They also have a licensed Salmon River within the park. Dogs are allowed for no additional fee; they must be leashed

and under their owner's control at all times. This RV park is closed during the off-season. The camping and tent areas also allow dogs. There is a dog walk area at the campground. Multiple dogs may be allowed.

Pippy RV Park
34 Nagles Place
St Johns, NF
709-737-3669
pippypark.com
Dogs of all sizes are allowed. There are no additional pet fees. Dogs must be quiet, well behaved, leashed, and cleaned up after. This RV park is closed during the off-season. The camping and tent areas also allow dogs. There is a dog walk area at the campground. Multiple dogs may be allowed.

Northwest Terr.

Nahanni National Park Reserve of Canada
P. O. Box 348
Fort Simpson, NT
867-695-3151
The raw nature and breathtaking scenery of this park will give the adventurous visitor a true wilderness experience. The park is accessible only by aircraft. It provides tent camping only and there are no concessions at this park. Dogs are allowed at no additional fee. Dogs may not be left unattended at any time, and they must be leashed at all times. Dogs are not allowed on river trips or tours. There are no developed trails or roads in or to the park. Only one dog is allowed per campsite. The camping and tent areas also allow dogs. There is a dog walk area at the campground. There are no electric or water hookups at the campground.

Wood Buffalo National Park of Canada
149 McDoogle Road
Fort Smith, NT
867-872-7900 (888-773-8888)
This park is a UNESCO World Heritage Site, it is Canada's largest national park and has been recognized as a critical habitat for migratory birds. The park offers a variety of interesting trails and various recreational pursuits. Dogs of all sizes are allowed at no

additional fee. Dogs may not be left unattended, and they must be leashed and cleaned up after. Dogs are allowed on the trails on leash. The camping and tent areas also allow dogs. There is a dog walk area at the campground. There are no electric or water hookups at the campground. Multiple dogs may be allowed.

Auyuittuq National Park of Canada
P. O. Box 353
Pangnirtung, NT
867-473-2500 (888-773-8888)
This park lies at the Arctic Circle and is still vibrant with ongoing glacial activity. It is accessible by air only; being a 5 hour trip from the closest departure area. You will find everything from steep-walled ocean fjords, to jagged mountain peaks, and deep valleys. The are no services available at all. Dogs must be leashed and with you at all times. This campground is closed during the off-season. There are no electric or water hookups at the campground.

Aulavik National Park of Canada
Box 29
Sachs Harbour, NT
867-690-3904
Rich in pre-historic history, this arctic park is an isolated wilderness area with a variety of landscapes from seacoasts, river valleys and polar deserts to the buttes and badlands. It is only accessible by air. There are no services at all or developed trails. Dogs are allowed if they can make the flight, and must be kept with owners at all times. This campground is closed during the off-season. There are no electric or water hookups at the campground.

Prelude Lake Provincial Park
H 4/Ingram Trail
Yellowknife, NT
867-873-7184
This primitive camp area offers potable water, picnic tables, and fire rings or camp stove. Dogs are allowed; they must be on no more than a 6 foot leash and under their owner's control at all times. This RV park is closed during the off-season. The camping and tent areas also allow dogs. There is a dog walk area at the campground. There are no electric or water hookups at the campgrounds. Multiple dogs may be allowed.

Reid Lake Provincial Park
H 4/Ingram Trail

Yellowknife, NT
867-873-7184
This wilderness park sits 38 miles east of Yellowknife and is a popular area for canoeing. There are 28 sites, potable water, picnic tables, and fire rings or camp stove. Dogs are allowed; they must be on no more than a 6 foot leash and under their owner's control at all times. This RV park is closed during the off-season. The camping and tent areas also allow dogs. There is a dog walk area at the campground. There are no water hookups at the campgrounds. Multiple dogs may be allowed.

Nova Scotia

Camper's Haven Campground
9700 H 3
Arcadia/Yarmouth, NS
902-742-4848
Quiet, well mannered dogs are allowed at this campground for no additional fee. Dogs are to be current on vaccinations and license, kept leashed, and they must be cleaned up after at all times. Campers may not have guests with pets on site, and dogs must be inside at night. This RV park is closed during the off-season. The camping and tent areas also allow dogs. There is a dog walk area at the campground. 2 dogs may be allowed.

Adventures East Campground
9585 Trans Canada Hwy 105
Baddeck, NS
902-295-2417
adventureseast.ca
There are 75 wooded or shaded campsites. Many of the sites have full hookups. Dogs are not allowed in the cottages. The campground is open from May 30 to October 19 annually. Up to two dogs may be allowed.

Plantation Campground and RV Park
210 W Steadmon Road
Barwick, NS
888-363-8882
plantationcampground.ca
Dogs of all sizes are allowed at the tent and RV sites, but there can only be up to 2 small dogs (under 15 pounds) in the cabins. There are no additional pet fees. Dogs must be leashed and cleaned up after. This RV park is closed during the off-season. The camping and tent areas

also allow dogs. There is a dog walk area at the campground. Dogs are allowed in the camping cabins.

Baddeck Cabot Trail Campground
9584 H 105
Cape Breton, NS
902-295-2288 (866 404 4199)
In addition to pull thru sites for rigs up to 85 feet, this campground offers a grocery/gift store, an eatery-The Captain's Shanty, a heated swimming pool, playground, free Wi-Fi, heated washrooms, and laundry facilities. Dogs are allowed for no additional fee; they must be leashed and cleaned up after at all times. This RV park is closed during the off-season. The camping and tent areas also allow dogs. There is a dog walk area at the campground. Multiple dogs may be allowed.

Cape Breton Highlands National Park of Canada
16648 Cabot Trail
Cheticamp, NS
902-224-2306 (888-773-8888)
Rich in natural and cultural heritage with a human heritage dating back to the ice age, this park provides spectacular scenery, abundant wildlife, and a variety of recreational pursuits. Dogs of all sizes are allowed at no additional fee. Dogs may not be left unattended unless they will be quiet and well behaved. Dogs must be leashed and cleaned up after. Dogs are allowed on the trails, unless otherwise marked, and they are not allowed on the Skyline Trial. The camping and tent areas also allow dogs. There is a dog walk area at the campground. Multiple dogs may be allowed.

Sand Point Beach Campground
412 Wharf Road
Five Islands, NS
902-254-2755
sandpointcampground.com
Dogs of all sizes are allowed. There are no additional pet fees. Dogs must be leashed and cleaned up after. This RV park is closed during the off-season. The camping and tent areas also allow dogs. There is a dog walk area at the campground. Multiple dogs may be allowed.

Wayside RV Park
10295 H 333/Peggys Cove Road
Glen Margaret, NS
902-823-2271
waysidecampground.com/

Some of the amenities at this ocean inlet park include free Wi-Fi, laundry facilities, hot showers, flush toilets, and a dump station. Dogs are allowed for no additional fee; they must be leashed and cleaned up after at all times. This RV park is closed during the off-season. The camping and tent areas also allow dogs. There is a dog walk area at the campground. Multiple dogs may be allowed.

Elm River Park
Glenholme Loop
Glenholme, NS
902-662-3162 (888-356-4356)
There are 112 sites available at this riverside campground. They offer open and wooded sites, showers, a convenience store, a swimming pool, and laundry facilities. Dogs are allowed for no additional fee; they must be leashed and cleaned up after at all times. This RV park is closed during the off-season. The camping and tent areas also allow dogs. There is a dog walk area at the campground. Multiple dogs may be allowed.

Dunromin Campground
4618 H 1
Granville Ferry, NS
902-532-2808 (800-565-0000)
dunromincampsite.com/
This waterfront campground offers more than 2000 feet of shoreline, modern restrooms with showers, a rec hall, a large playground, store, swimming pool, free Wi-Fi, laundry facilities, and a café offering gourmet meals. They also offer watercraft rentals/instruction and fresh or saltwater fishing. Dogs are allowed for no additional fee. Only 2 dogs are allowed per cabin; there may be more than 2 dogs per site in the RV/tent area. Dogs may not be left unattended, and they must be quiet, leashed, and cleaned up after at all times. Dogs are not allowed at the outer tables of the café. This RV park is closed during the off-season. The camping and tent areas also allow dogs. There is a dog walk area at the campground. Dogs are allowed in the camping cabins.

Woodhaven RV Park
1757 Hammonds Pines Road
Halifax, NS
902-835-2271
woodhavenrvpark.com
Dogs of all sizes are allowed. There are no additional pet fees. Dogs may not be left unattended, must be

leashed, and cleaned up after. This RV park is closed during the off-season. The camping and tent areas also allow dogs. There is a dog walk area at the campground. Multiple dogs may be allowed.

Scotia Pine Campground
1911 H 2
Hilden, NS
902-893-3666 (877-893-3666)
scotiapine.ca/
This well maintained family campground offers open and wooded sites, Wi-Fi, cable TV, a swimming pool, sauna, playground, walking trails, and laundry facilities. Dogs are allowed for no additional fee. Dogs must be quiet, well mannered, leashed, and cleaned up after. This RV park is closed during the off-season. The camping and tent areas also allow dogs. There is a dog walk area at the campground. Multiple dogs may be allowed.

Hubbards Beach Campground
226 Shore Club Road
Hubbards, NS
902-857-9460
hubbardsbeach.com
Dogs of all sizes are allowed. There are no additional pet fees. Dogs must be well behaved, leashed and cleaned up after, and may not be on the beach. This RV park is closed during the off-season. The camping and tent areas also allow dogs. There is a dog walk area at the campground. Multiple dogs may be allowed.

Plage St Pierre Beach and Campground
635 Cheticamp Island Road
Inverness County, NS
902-224-2112 (800-565-0000)
A highlight of this family oriented camp area is the long, wonderful stretch of open beach frontage. They also offer 144 wooded or open sites, a canteen, playground, rec room, mini-golf, laundry facilities, pure well-water, picnic tables, fire pits, and more. Dogs are allowed for no additional fee in the campground; there is an additional one time pet fee of $20 per unit for the rental trailers. Dogs must be leashed and cleaned up after at all times. Dogs are allowed on the beach. This RV park is closed during the off-season. The camping and tent areas also allow dogs. There is a dog walk area at the campground. Dogs are allowed in the camping cabins. Multiple dogs may be allowed.

Jellystone Park
43 Boo Boo Blvd
Kingston, NS
888-225-7773
jellystonens.com
Dogs of all sizes are allowed. There are no additional pet fees. Dogs must be leashed and cleaned up after. This RV park is closed during the off-season. The camping and tent areas also allow dogs. There is a dog walk area at the campground. Multiple dogs may be allowed.

Arm of Gold Campground
Corner of Church Street and H 105
Little Bras d'or, NS
866-736-6516
armofgoldcamp.com
Dogs of all sizes are allowed. There are no additional pet fees. Dogs must be leashed and cleaned up after. This RV park is closed during the off-season. The camping and tent areas also allow dogs. There is a dog walk area at the campground. Multiple dogs may be allowed.

Seal Island/North Sydney KOA
3779 New Harris Road
New Harris, NS
902-674-2145 (800-562-7452)
sealisle.com
Dogs of all sizes are allowed. There are no additional pet fees. Dogs may not be left outside unattended, must be leashed, and cleaned up after. This RV park is closed during the off-season. The camping and tent areas also allow dogs. There is a dog walk area at the campground. Dogs are allowed in the camping cabins. Multiple dogs may be allowed.

River Ryan Campground
5779 Union H
New Waterford, NS
902-862-8367
Dogs of all sizes are allowed. There are no additional pet fees. Dogs may not be left unattended, must be leashed, and cleaned up after. This RV park is closed during the off-season. The camping and tent areas also allow dogs. There is a dog walk area at the campground. Multiple dogs may be allowed.

Harbour Light Campground
2881 Tree Brooks
Pictou, NS
902-485-5733
harbourlightcampground.com
Dogs of all sizes are allowed. There are no additional pet fees. Dogs must be leashed and cleaned up after, and they are not allowed on

the beach. This RV park is closed during the off-season. The camping and tent areas also allow dogs. There is a dog walk area at the campground. Multiple dogs may be allowed.

Hide-Away Campground
401 Shore Road
S Harbour, NS
902-383-2116
Dogs of all sizes are allowed. There are no additional pet fees. Dogs must be leashed and cleaned up after. Dogs are allowed at the beach, and only 1 dog is allowed in the cabins. This RV park is closed during the off-season. The camping and tent areas also allow dogs. There is a dog walk area at the campground. Multiple dogs may be allowed.

Seafoam Campground
3493 River John
Seafoam, NS
902-351-3122
Dogs of all sizes are allowed. There are no additional pet fees. Dogs must be leashed and cleaned up after, and they are allowed to go to the beach area. This RV park is closed during the off-season. The camping and tent areas also allow dogs. There is a dog walk area at the campground. Multiple dogs may be allowed.

Scotia Pine Campground
On Route 2
Truro, NS
877-893-3666
scotiapine.ca
Dogs of all sizes are allowed. There are no additional pet fees. Dogs may not be left unattended, must be leashed, and cleaned up after. This RV park is closed during the off-season. The camping and tent areas also allow dogs. There is a dog walk area at the campground. Dogs are allowed in the camping cabins. Multiple dogs may be allowed.

Halifax West KOA
3070 H 1
Upper Sackville, NS
902-865-4342 (888-562-4705)
koa.com
Dogs of all sizes are allowed. There are no additional pet fees. Dogs must be quiet, well behaved, leashed, and cleaned up after. Dogs may not be left unattended. This RV park is closed during the off-season. The camping and tent areas also allow dogs. There is a dog walk area at the campground. Dogs are allowed in the camping cabins.

Multiple dogs may be allowed.

Lake Breeze Campground and Cottages
H 1
Yarmouth, NS
902- 649-2332
This family campground sits nestled among the trees on the shores of Darling Lake. The sites have picnic tables, fire rings, and there is a dump station available. Dogs are allowed for no additional fee; they must be leashed and cleaned up after at all times. This RV park is closed during the off-season. The camping and tent areas also allow dogs. There is a dog walk area at the campground. Multiple dogs may be allowed.

Ontario

Jellystone Park
4610 County Road 18
Amherstburg, ON
519-736-3201
campybear.com
Dogs of all sizes are allowed. There are no additional pet fees. Dogs must be leashed and cleaned up after. This RV park is closed during the off-season. The camping and tent areas also allow dogs. There is a dog walk area at the campground. Multiple dogs may be allowed.

Barrie KOA
3138 Penetanguishene Road
Barrie, ON
705-726-6128 (800-562-7397)
barriekoa.com
Dogs of all sizes are allowed. There are no additional pet fees. Dogs may not be left unattended, must be on no more than a 6 foot leash, and cleaned up after. There are some breed restrictions. This RV park is closed during the off-season. The camping and tent areas also allow dogs. There is a dog walk area at the campground. Dogs are allowed in the camping cabins. Multiple dogs may be allowed.

Chippawa Easy Living Camping and RV Park
RR 1, 835 Chippawa Road
Barry's Bay, ON
613-267-8507 (800-267-8507)
chippawaresort.com
Dogs of all sizes are allowed. There are no additional pet fees. Dogs must be leashed and cleaned up after. There are some breed

restrictions. This RV park is closed during the off-season. The camping and tent areas also allow dogs. There is a dog walk area at the campground. 2 dogs may be allowed.

United Empire Loyalist Heritage Centre & Park
54 Adolphustown Park Road
Bath, ON
613-342-9646
uel.ca/Camping.html
A site for camping since colonial times, this scenic 72 acre park also has an on site museum dedicated to preserving the Loyalist Heritage. In addition numerous recreational activities, there are historic reenactments and musical events on site. Dogs are allowed for no additional pet fee; they must be leashed and cleaned up after at all times. This RV park is closed during the off-season. The camping and tent areas also allow dogs. There is a dog walk area at the campground. Multiple dogs may be allowed.

Yogi Bear's Jellystone Park
3666 Simcoe Road 88
Bradford, ON
905-775-1377
jellystonetoronto.com
Dogs of all sizes are allowed. There are no additional pet fees. Dogs must be well behaved, leashed and cleaned up after. Pit bull breeds are not allowed. This RV park is closed during the off-season. The camping and tent areas also allow dogs. There is a dog walk area at the campground. Multiple dogs may be allowed.

Indian Line Campground
7625 Finch Avenue W
Brampton, ON
905-678-1233
trcacamping.ca
Dogs of all sizes are allowed. There are no additional pet fees. Dogs may not be left unattended, must be leashed, and cleaned up after. This RV park is closed during the off-season. The camping and tent areas also allow dogs. There is a dog walk area at the campground. There are some breed restrictions. Multiple dogs may be allowed.

Brighton/401 KOA
15043 Telephone Road
Brighton, ON
613-475-2186 (800-562-0906)
koa.com/where/on/55205/
Dogs of all sizes are allowed. There are no additional pet fees. Dogs

must be leashed and cleaned up after. There are some breed restrictions. This RV park is closed during the off-season. The camping and tent areas also allow dogs. There is a dog walk area at the campground. Dogs are allowed in the camping cabins. Multiple dogs may be allowed.

Happy Green acres Tent and Trailer park
RR 3
Brockville, ON
613-342-9646
This camp area offers picnic tables, fire rings, modern restrooms, hot showers, laundry facilities, a pool, rec room, and a dump station. Dogs are allowed for no additional pet fee; they must be leashed and cleaned up after at all times, and they may not be left unattended. If owners have good voice control with their pets, they may have them off lead in the large field adjacent to the campground. This RV park is closed during the off-season. The camping and tent areas also allow dogs. There is a dog walk area at the campground. Multiple dogs may be allowed.

Valens Conservation Area
1691 Regional Park Road 97
Cambridge, ON
905-525-2183
Dogs of all sizes are allowed. There are no additional pet fees. Dogs must be leashed and cleaned up after. Dogs are not allowed at the sand beach, but they are allowed at the doggy beach. There are some breed restrictions. The camping and tent areas also allow dogs. There is a dog walk area at the campground. Multiple dogs may be allowed.

Toronto West KOA
9301 Second Line Nassagaweya,
RR 1
Campbellville, ON
905-845-2495 (800-562-1523)
torontowestkoa.on.ca/
Dogs of all sizes are allowed. There are no additional pet fees. Dogs must be well behaved, may not be left unattended, and must be leashed and cleaned up after. No visitor pets are allowed. They offer a complimentary dog sitting service for up to 2 dogs and they also greet your dog with pet treats at the door. There are some breed restrictions. This RV park is closed during the off-season. The camping and tent areas also allow dogs. There is a dog walk area at the campground. There are

special amenities given to dogs at this campground. Multiple dogs may be allowed.

Cardinal KOA
609 Pittston Road
Cardinal, ON
613-657-4536 (800-562-3643)
koa.com/where/on/55124/
Dogs of all sizes are allowed. There are no additional pet fees. Dogs may not be left unattended, must be leashed, and cleaned up after. There are some breed restrictions. This RV park is closed during the off-season. The camping and tent areas also allow dogs. There is a dog walk area at the campground. Dogs are allowed in the camping cabins. Multiple dogs may be allowed.

Quinte's Isle Campark
237 Salmon Point Road
Cherry Valley, ON
613-476-6310
qicampark.com
Dogs of all sizes are allowed. There are no additional pet fees. Dogs must be leashed and cleaned up after. The camping and tent areas also allow dogs. There is a dog walk area at the campground. Multiple dogs may be allowed.

Toronto North/Cookstown KOA
139 Reive Blvd
Cookstown, ON
705-458-2267 (800-562-2691)
torontonorthkoa.com
Dogs of all sizes are allowed. There are no additional pet fees. Dogs must be well behaved, may not be left unattended, and must be leashed and cleaned up after. There are some breed restrictions. This RV park is closed during the off-season. The camping and tent areas also allow dogs. There is a dog walk area at the campground. Multiple dogs may be allowed.

Carolinian Forest Campground
9589 Ipperwash Road
Forest, ON
519-243-2258
ipperwash.on.ca
One dog of any size is allowed. There are no additional pet fees. Dogs may not be left unattended, must be quiet and well behaved, and leashed and cleaned up after. Dogs are allowed at the beach. There are some breed restrictions. This RV park is closed during the off-season. The camping and tent areas also allow dogs. There is a dog walk area at the campground.

Coboury East Campground
253 Benlock Road
Grafton, ON
905-349-2594
ceccamp.ca/
A family park with a variety of planned activities, they also provide large pull-thru sites, a swimming pool, playground, creekside tenting, a rec room, convenience store, laundry facilities, hot showers, and gaming fields/courts. Dogs are allowed for no additional pet fee; they must be leashed and cleaned up after at all times. This RV park is closed during the off-season. The camping and tent areas also allow dogs. There is a dog walk area at the campground. 2 dogs may be allowed.

Gravenhurst/Muskoka KOA
1083 Reay Road E
Gravenhurst, ON
705-687-2333 (800-562-9883)
koa.com/where/on/55102/
Dogs of all sizes are allowed. There are no additional pet fees. Dogs may not be left unattended, must be leashed, and cleaned up after. There are some breed restrictions. This RV park is closed during the off-season. The camping and tent areas also allow dogs. There is a dog walk area at the campground. Multiple dogs may be allowed.

Heidi's Campground and RV Superstore
3982 Hwy 11 S RR 2
Hawkestone, ON
705-487-3311 (888-322-3614)
heidisrv.com/campground1.htm
Lush greenery and shade trees greet visitors at this campground. They also offer an RV store, an indoor heated pool and whirlpool, gaming courts/fields, a rec room, planned activities, a grocery store, laundry facilities, and a playground. Dogs are allowed for no additional pet fee; they must be leashed and cleaned up after at all times. This RV park is closed during the off-season. The camping and tent areas also allow dogs. There is a dog walk area at the campground. Multiple dogs may be allowed.

Pukaskwa National Park of Canada
P. O. Box 212/h 627
Heron Bay, ON
807-229-0801 (888-773-8888)
Rich in ancient and modern history, this beautiful park is the only wilderness national park in Ontario, and offers a variety of habitats, wildlife, trails, and recreation. Dogs

of all sizes are allowed at no additional fee. Dogs may not be left unattended, and they must be quiet, leashed, and cleaned up after. Dogs are not allowed in the back country, but they are allowed on the day trails on lead. The camping and tent areas also allow dogs. There is a dog walk area at the campground. There are no water hookups at the campground. Multiple dogs may be allowed.

Our Ponderosa Family Campground
9338 W Ipperwash Road
Ipperwash Beach, ON
888-786-2267
ourponderosa.com
Dogs of all sizes are allowed. There are no additional pet fees. Dogs must be leashed at all times and cleaned up after. This RV park is closed during the off-season. The camping and tent areas also allow dogs. There is a dog walk area at the campground. Multiple dogs may be allowed.

Grenville Park
2323 County Road 2 RR3
Johnstown, ON
613-925-2000
grenvillepark.com
Dogs of all sizes are allowed. There are no additional pet fees. Dogs must be leashed and cleaned up after. Dogs may not be on the furniture or beds in the cabin. This RV park is closed during the off-season. The camping and tent areas also allow dogs. There is a dog walk area at the campground. Dogs are allowed in the camping cabins. Multiple dogs may be allowed.

Rene Brunelle Provincial Park
Provincinial Park Road
Kapuskasing, ON
705-367-2692
Dogs of all sizes are allowed. There are no additional pet fees. Dogs must be leashed and cleaned up after, and they are not allowed on the beach. This RV park is closed during the off-season. The camping and tent areas also allow dogs. There is a dog walk area at the campground. Multiple dogs may be allowed.

Anicinabe Park
955 Golf Course Road
Kenora, ON
807-467-2700 (877-318-CAMP (2267))
Located in a beautiful treed setting, this waterside park offer 83 sites, a large sandy beach, a convenience store, showers, laundry facilities, a

playground, barbecue pits, and 2 boat launch areas. Dogs are allowed for no additional pet fee; they must be leashed and cleaned up after at all times. This RV park is closed during the off-season. The camping and tent areas also allow dogs. There is a dog walk area at the campground. Multiple dogs may be allowed.

Aintree Trailer Park
2435 Huron Consession 12 Road
Kincardine, ON
519-396-8533
aintreepark.com
Dogs of all sizes are allowed. There are no additional pet fees. Dogs may not be left unattended, must be quiet, leashed, and cleaned up after. Dogs are allowed at the beach. This RV park is closed during the off-season. The camping and tent areas also allow dogs. There is a dog walk area at the campground. Multiple dogs may be allowed.

1000 Islands/Kingston KOA
2039 Cordukes Road
Kingston, ON
613-546-6140
koa.com
Friendly dogs of all sizes are allowed. There are no additional pet fees. Dogs may not be left unattended, must be leashed, and cleaned up after. There are some breed restrictions. This RV park is closed during the off-season. The camping and tent areas also allow dogs. There is a dog walk area at the campground. Dogs are allowed in the camping cabins. Multiple dogs may be allowed.

Lake Ontario Park
1000 King Street W
Kingston, ON
613-542-6574
Dogs of all sizes are allowed. There are no additional pet fees. Dogs must be leashed and cleaned up after. This RV park is closed during the off-season. The camping and tent areas also allow dogs. There is a dog walk area at the campground. Multiple dogs may be allowed.

Rideau Acres
1014 Cunningham Road
Kingston, ON
613-546-2711
rideauacres.com
Dogs of all sizes are allowed. There are no additional pet fees. Dogs must be leashed and cleaned up after, and may not be on the beach. This RV park is closed during the off-

season. The camping and tent areas also allow dogs. There is a dog walk area at the campground. Multiple dogs may be allowed.

Bingeman's Campground
425 Bingeman's Drive
Kitchener, ON
519-744-1002
bingemans.com
Dogs of all sizes are allowed. There are no additional pet fees. Dogs may not be left unattended, must be quiet, well behaved, leashed at all times and cleaned up after. There are some breed restrictions. This RV park is closed during the off-season. The camping and tent areas also allow dogs. There is a dog walk area at the campground. Multiple dogs may be allowed.

1000 Islands Camping Resort
382 1000 Islands Parkway
Lans Downe, ON
613-659-3058
Dogs of all sizes are allowed. There are no additional pet fees. Dogs must be leashed and cleaned up after. There are some breed restrictions. This RV park is closed during the off-season. The camping and tent areas also allow dogs. There is a dog walk area at the campground.

1000 Islands/Ivy Lea KOA
514 1000 Islands Parkway
Lansdowne, ON
613-659-2817 (800-562-2471)
1000islandskoa.com
Dogs of all sizes are allowed. There are no additional pet fees. Dogs must be quiet, well behaved, leashed, and cleaned up after. There are some breed restrictions. This RV park is closed during the off-season. The camping and tent areas also allow dogs. There is a dog walk area at the campground. Dogs are allowed in the camping cabins. Multiple dogs may be allowed.

London/401 KOA
136 Cromarty Drive
London, ON
519-644-0222 (800-562-7398)
koa.com/where/on/55210/
Dogs of all sizes are allowed. There are no additional pet fees. Dogs must be leashed and cleaned up after. There are some breed restrictions. This RV park is closed during the off-season. The camping and tent areas also allow dogs. There is a dog walk area at the campground. 2 dogs may be

allowed.

All Star Resort
1 Major Lake Road
Madawaska, ON
613-637-5592
allstarresort.com/
Dogs of all sizes are allowed, and there are no additional pet fees for tent or RV sites, which are seasonal. There is a $10 per night per pet additional fee for the cabins, and the cabins are available year around. Dogs must be leashed and cleaned up after. This RV park is closed during the off-season. The camping and tent areas also allow dogs. There is a dog walk area at the campground. Dogs are allowed in the camping cabins. 2 dogs may be allowed.

1000 Islands/Mallorytown KOA
1477 County Road 2
Mallorytown, ON
613-923-5339 (800-562-9725)
1000islandscamping.com
Dogs of all sizes are allowed. There are no additional pet fees. Dogs may not be left unattended, must be leashed, and cleaned up after. Dogs must be crated in the cabins when left, and at night. There are some breed restrictions. This RV park is closed during the off-season. The camping and tent areas also allow dogs. There is a dog walk area at the campground. Dogs are allowed in the camping cabins. Multiple dogs may be allowed.

St. Lawrence Islands National Park of Canada
2 County Road 5, RR3
Mallorytown, ON
613-923-5261 (888-773-8888)
A very lush and complex park of more than 20 islands and about 90 islets, it is accessible only by watercraft. There is a 100 acre compound at the mainland headquarters which offers a nature trial and exhibits. Dogs of all sizes are allowed at no additional fee. Dogs must be leashed at all times and be cleaned up after. The park does not make any arrangements for water transport. This campground is closed during the off-season. Only one dog is allowed per campsite. The camping and tent areas also allow dogs. There is a dog walk area at the campground. There are no electric or water hookups at the campground.

Marmora KOA
178 KOA Campground Road

Marmora, ON
613-472-2233 (800-562-9156)
marmorakoa.com/
Dogs of all sizes are allowed. There are no additional pet fees. Dogs may not be left unattended, must be leashed, and cleaned up after. There are some breed restrictions. This RV park is closed during the off-season. The camping and tent areas also allow dogs. There is a dog walk area at the campground. Dogs are allowed in the camping cabins. Multiple dogs may be allowed.

Wildwood Golf and RV Resort
11112 11 Consession
McGregor, ON
519-726-6176
golfwindsorweb.com
Dogs of all sizes are allowed. There are no additional pet fees. Dogs must be leashed and cleaned up after. There are some breed restrictions. This RV park is closed during the off-season. There is a dog walk area at the campground. Multiple dogs may be allowed.

Georgian Bay Island National Park of Canada
P. O. Box 9
Midland, ON
705-526-9804, ext. 235 (888-773-8888)
This park, accessible by boat and only for tent camping, offers spectacular landscapes, diverse habitats, the rugged beauty of the Canadian Shield, an incredible variety of plants and animals, and a variety of year round recreation. Dogs of all sizes are allowed at no additional fee. Dogs may not be left unattended, and they must be leashed and cleaned up after. Pets and pet food must be brought in at night. Dogs are allowed on the trails on lead. This campground is closed during the off-season. The camping and tent areas also allow dogs. There is a dog walk area at the campground. There are no electric or water hookups at the campground. Multiple dogs may be allowed.

Smith's Camp
736 King Street
Midland, ON
705-526-4339
smithscamp.ca
Dogs of all sizes are allowed. There are no additional pet fees. Dogs must be quiet, have up to date shot records, be leashed at all times, and cleaned up after. Dogs are not allowed on the beach. There are some breed restrictions. This RV

park is closed during the off-season. The camping and tent areas also allow dogs. There is a dog walk area at the campground. 2 dogs may be allowed.

Milton Heights Campground
8690 Tremaine Road
Milton, ON
905-878-6781
miltonhgtscampgrd.com
Dogs of all sizes are allowed. There are no additional pet fees. Dogs may not be left unattended, must be leashed, and cleaned up after. There are some breed restrictions. The camping and tent areas also allow dogs. There is a dog walk area at the campground. Multiple dogs may be allowed.

Campark Resort
9387 Lundy's Lane
Niagara Falls, ON
877-226-7275
campark.com
Dogs of all sizes are allowed. There are no additional pet fees. Dogs may not be left outside unattended or be at the pool area. Dogs must be leashed and cleaned up after. This RV park is closed during the off-season. The camping and tent areas also allow dogs. There is a dog walk area at the campground. Due to Ontario law Pit Bulls and similar dogs are not allowed. Multiple dogs may be allowed.

Jellystone Park
8676 Oakwood Drive
Niagara Falls, ON
905-354-1432
jellystoneniagara.ca
One dog of any size is allowed. There are no additional pet fees. Dogs are not allowed in rentals or tents. Dogs may not be left unattended, must be leashed, and cleaned up after. Due to Ontario law Pit Bulls and similar dogs are not allowed. This RV park is closed during the off-season. There is a dog walk area at the campground.

King Waldorf's Tent and Trailer Park
9015 Stanley S Avenue
Niagara Falls, ON
905-295-8191
marinelandcanada.com
Dogs of all sizes are allowed. There are no additional pet fees. Dogs may not be left unattended, must be leashed, and cleaned up after. This RV park is closed during the off-season. The camping and tent areas also allow dogs. There is a

dog walk area at the campground. Due to Ontario law Pit Bulls and similar dogs are not allowed. Multiple dogs may be allowed.

Niagara Falls KOA
8625 Lundy's Lane
Niagara Falls, ON
905-356-2267 (800-562-6478)
niagarakoa.com
Dogs of all sizes are allowed. There are no additional pet fees. Dogs must be well behaved, may not be left unattended, and must be leashed and cleaned up after. Dogs are not allowed in the rentals or the buildings. There are some breed restrictions. This RV park is closed during the off-season. The camping and tent areas also allow dogs. There is a dog walk area at the campground. 2 dogs may be allowed.

Scott's Tent and Trailer Park
8845 Lundy's Lane
Niagara Falls, ON
905-356-6988 (800-649-9497)
scottstrailerpark.com/
This popular park has been offering recreational fun for over 30 years. They have large shaded sites, a big heated pool and baby pool, a rec room, playground, gaming fields/courts, laundry facilities, showers, and a grocery store. Dogs are allowed for no additional fee; they must be leashed and cleaned up after at all times, and they may not be left unattended. This RV park is closed during the off-season. The camping and tent areas also allow dogs. There is a dog walk area at the campground. Multiple dogs may be allowed.

Champlain Tent and Trailer Park
1202 Premier Road
North Bay, ON
705-474-4669
champlaintent&trailerpark.com
Dogs of all sizes are allowed. There are no additional pet fees. Dogs must be quiet, well behaved, leashed, and cleaned up after. This RV park is closed during the off-season. The camping and tent areas also allow dogs. There is a dog walk area at the campground. Multiple dogs may be allowed.

Poplar Grove Tourist Camp
6154 Bank Street
Ottawa, ON
613-821-2973
myvacationguide.com
Dogs of all sizes are allowed. There are no additional pet fees. Dogs

must be quiet, leashed, and cleaned up after. There are some breed restrictions. This RV park is closed during the off-season. The camping and tent areas also allow dogs. There is a dog walk area at the campground. 2 dogs may be allowed.

Rec-Land
1566 Canaan Road
Ottawa, ON
613-833-2974
rec-land.com
Dogs of all sizes are allowed. There are no additional pet fees. Dogs must be leashed and cleaned up after. There are some breed restrictions. This RV park is closed during the off-season. The camping and tent areas also allow dogs. Multiple dogs may be allowed.

Owen Sound KOA
RR6 28th Avenue E
Owen Sound, ON
519-371-1331 (800-562-8675)
koa.com/where/on/55245/
One dog of any size is allowed. There are no additional pet fees. Dogs must be quiet and well behaved. Dogs may not be left unattended, must be leashed, and cleaned up after. There are some breed restrictions. This RV park is closed during the off-season. The camping and tent areas also allow dogs. There is a dog walk area at the campground.

Leisure Time Park
8431 H 9
Palgrave, ON
905-880-4921
leisuretime.ca
Dogs of all sizes are allowed. There are no additional pet fees. Dogs may not be left unattended, must be quiet, well behaved, leashed and cleaned up after. There are some breed restrictions. This RV park is closed during the off-season. The camping and tent areas also allow dogs. There is a dog walk area at the campground. Multiple dogs may be allowed.

Parry Sound KOA
276 Rankin Lake Road
Parry Sound, ON
705-378-2721 (800-562-2681)
koa.com/where/on/55225/index.htm
Dogs of all sizes are allowed. There are no additional pet fees. Dogs must be quiet, may not be left unattended, and must be leashed and cleaned up after. There are some breed restrictions. This RV

park is closed during the off-season. The camping and tent areas also allow dogs. There is a dog walk area at the campground. Dogs are allowed in the camping cabins. Multiple dogs may be allowed.

Trailside Park
105 Blue Lake Road RR#2
Parry Sound, ON
705-378-2844 (800 951-3303)
trailsidepark.com/mainpage.htm
There are 300 gorgeous acres at this park that has 3 lakes, 200 camp sites, flush toilets, showers, a rec hall, convenience store, playground, laundry facilities, game areas, and a dump station. Dogs are allowed for no additional pet fee; they must be leashed and cleaned up after at all times. Dogs are not allowed on the swimming beach; they are allowed in the water from other areas. They are also not allowed in buildings, including no blow-drying dogs hair in the women's washroom. This RV park is closed during the off-season. The camping and tent areas also allow dogs. There is a dog walk area at the campground. Multiple dogs may be allowed.

The Dunes Campground
9910 Northville Cresent
Phedford, ON
519-243-2500
dunesoakridge.com
Dogs of all sizes are allowed. There are no additional pet fees. Dogs must be leashed at all times and cleaned up after. There are some breed restrictions. This RV park is closed during the off-season. The camping and tent areas also allow dogs. There is a dog walk area at the campground. 2 dogs may be allowed.

Grenville park
2323 H 2
Prescott, ON
613-925-2000
grenvillepark.com/
Located along the St Lawrence River, this scenic campgrounds offers175 sites, adult and children's planned activities, a playground, rec hall, concessionaires, showers, a convenience store, gaming fields/courts, movies, and much more. Dogs are allowed for no additional pet fee; they must be leashed and cleaned up after at all times. This RV park is closed during the off-season. The camping and tent areas also allow dogs. There is

a dog walk area at the campground. Dogs are allowed in the camping cabins. Multiple dogs may be allowed.

Renfrew KOA
2826 Johnston Road
Renfrew, ON
613-432-6280 (800-562-3980)
koa.com/where/on/55235/
Dogs of all sizes are allowed. There are no additional pet fees. Dogs must be leashed and cleaned up after. There are some breed restrictions. This RV park is closed during the off-season. The camping and tent areas also allow dogs. There is a dog walk area at the campground. Multiple dogs may be allowed.

Cedar Grove Camp
6845 H 534
Restoule, ON
705-729-2030
cedargrovecamp.com/
Dogs of all sizes are allowed, and there may be up to 3 dogs in the tent or RV areas, but only 2 dogs are allowed per cabin. There are no additional pet fees. Dogs may not be left unattended unless they will be quiet and well behaved, and they must be leashed and cleaned up after. This RV park is closed during the off-season. The camping and tent areas also allow dogs. There is a dog walk area at the campground. Dogs are allowed in the camping cabins. There are no water hookups at the campgrounds.

Leisure Lake Campgroud
510 County Road 31
Ruthven, ON
519-326-1255
leisurelakecamp.com
Dogs of all sizes are allowed. There are no additional pet fees. Dogs must be quiet, well behaved, leashed, and cleaned up after. This RV park is closed during the off-season. The camping and tent areas also allow dogs. There is a dog walk area at the campground. Multiple dogs may be allowed.

Sauble Beach Resort Camp
877 County Road 8
Sauble Beach, ON
519-422-1101
saubleresortcamp.com
Dogs of all sizes are allowed. There are no additional pet fees. Dogs may not be left unattended, must be leashed, and cleaned up after. There are some breed restrictions. This RV park is closed during the off-season.

The camping and tent areas also allow dogs. There is a dog walk area at the campground. Multiple dogs may be allowed.

Woodland Park Family Campground
47 Sauble Falls Parkway
Sauble Beach, ON
519-422-1161
woodlandpark.on.ca
Dogs of all sizes are allowed. There is no fee for one dog. If there are two dogs, then the fee is $2 per night per dog. Dogs are not allowed on the beach, and must be leashed and cleaned up after. There are some breed restrictions. This RV park is closed during the off-season. The camping and tent areas also allow dogs. There is a dog walk area at the campground. 2 dogs may be allowed.

Sault Ste Marie KOA
501 5th Line
Sault Ste. Marie, ON
705-759-2344 (800-562-0847)
koa.com
Dogs of all sizes are allowed. There are no additional pet fees. Dogs must be leashed and cleaned up after. They may be left for only short periods and only if they will be quiet and well behaved. There are some breed restrictions. This RV park is closed during the off-season. The camping and tent areas also allow dogs. There is a dog walk area at the campground. Dogs are allowed in the camping cabins. Multiple dogs may be allowed.

Batman's Trailer Park
11408 H 6
Sheguiandah, ON
705-368-2180 (877-368-2180)
batmanscamping.com
Dogs of all sizes are allowed. There are no additional pet fees. Dogs may not be left unattended, must be quiet, leashed at all times, and cleaned up after. This RV park is closed during the off-season. The camping and tent areas also allow dogs. There is a dog walk area at the campground. Multiple dogs may be allowed.

Spragge KOA
4696 H 17
Spragge, ON
705-849-2210 (800-562-3416)
koa.com
Dogs of all sizes are allowed, but they want to know ahead of time if you have large dogs so they can provide a space to accommodate. There are no additional pet fees. Dogs must be quiet and well

behaved. Dogs may not be left unattended, must be leashed, and cleaned up after. Your dog can run off leash at the river if there is voice control and no one is around. There are some breed restrictions. This RV park is closed during the off-season. The camping and tent areas also allow dogs. There is a dog walk area at the campground. Dogs are allowed in the camping cabins. Multiple dogs may be allowed.

River View Campground
22164 Valley View Road
Thorndale, ON
866-447-7197
riverviewcampground.ca
Dogs of all sizes are allowed. There are no additional pet fees. Dogs must be leashed and cleaned up after. This RV park is closed during the off-season. The camping and tent areas also allow dogs. There is a dog walk area at the campground. Multiple dogs may be allowed.

Thunder Bay KOA
162 Spruce River Road
Thunder Bay, ON
807-683-6221 (800-562-4162)
koa.com
Dogs of all sizes are allowed. There are no additional pet fees. Dogs must be leashed and cleaned up after. Some breeds are not allowed. This RV park is closed during the off-season. The camping and tent areas also allow dogs. There is a dog walk area at the campground. Dogs are allowed in the camping cabins. Multiple dogs may be allowed.

Bruce Peninsula National Park of Canada
P.O. Box 189
Tobermory, ON
519-596-2263 (888-773-8888)
This park, sitting in the heart of a World Biosphere Reserve, is home to the largest remaining chunk of natural habitat in Southern Ontario. The park offers thousand year old cedar trees and an array of habitats from clear lakes to dense forests and rare alvars. Dogs of all sizes are allowed at no additional fee. Dogs may not be left unattended, and they must be leashed at all times and cleaned up after. Dogs are allowed on the trails on lead. This campground is closed during the off-season. The camping and tent areas also allow dogs. There is a dog walk area at the campground. There are no water hookups at the

campground. Multiple dogs may be allowed.

Glen Rouge Campground
7450 Kingston Road
Toronto, ON
416-338-2267
Dogs of all sizes are allowed. There are no additional pet fees. Dogs may not be left unattended, must be leashed, and cleaned up after. This RV park is closed during the off-season. The camping and tent areas also allow dogs. There is a dog walk area at the campground. There are some breed restrictions. Multiple dogs may be allowed.

N.E.T. Camping Resort
2325 Regional Park Road 24
Vineland, ON
905-892-3737 (866-490-4745)
netcampingresort.com/
In addition to offering a good central location to many other sites of interest and activities, this park offers 2 large pools, a splash pad for children, special events, theme days, and a recreation/banquet center. Dogs are allowed for no additional fee; they must be leashed and cleaned up after at all times, and they may not be left unattended on campsites. Dogs must be well mannered, licensed, and be current on all shots. This RV park is closed during the off-season. The camping and tent areas also allow dogs. There is a dog walk area at the campground. 2 dogs may be allowed.

Roth Park Family Campground
Burford Lake Road
Wiarton, ON
519-534-0145
visitontario.com/roth_park.htm
Dogs of all sizes are allowed. There are no additional pet fees. Dogs may not be left unattended unless they will be quiet and well behaved, and they must be leashed and cleaned up after. This RV park is closed during the off-season. The camping and tent areas also allow dogs. There is a dog walk area at the campground. Dogs are allowed in the camping cabins. Multiple dogs may be allowed.

Prince Edward Island

Sun-N-Shade Campground
PO Box 2193/ H 1A
Borden-Carleton, PE
902-855-3492
sun-n-shade.com/
There are over 90 campsites, laundry facilities, a small store, and gaming areas, but the real highlight of this campground are the free live musical entertainment 6 days a week from locals and even some of the campers that join in and play too. Dogs are allowed for no additional fee; they must be leashed and cleaned up after. Dogs are not allowed in buildings or by the cabins. This RV park is closed during the off-season. The camping and tent areas also allow dogs. There is a dog walk area at the campground. Multiple dogs may be allowed.

Cavendish KOA
198 Forest Hill Lane
Cavendish, PE
902-963-2079 (800-562-1879)
koa.com
Dogs of all sizes are allowed. There are no additional pet fees. Dogs may not be left unattended, must be leashed, and cleaned up after. Dogs must be well behaved and friendly. A dog sitter is sometimes available. There are some breed restrictions. This RV park is closed during the off-season. The camping and tent areas also allow dogs. There is a dog walk area at the campground. Dogs are allowed in the camping cabins. Multiple dogs may be allowed.

Pine Hills RV Park
1531 Brackley Point Road
Charlottetown, PE
902-672-2081 (877-226-2267)
pinehillsrvpark.com/
Located on 41 acres in a beautiful green setting, this RV park offers more than 200 sites, Wi-Fi, a camp store, laundry facilities, a pool, planned activities, and a dump station. Dogs are allowed for no additional fee; they must be leashed and cleaned up after. This RV park is closed during the off-season. The camping and tent areas also allow dogs. There is a dog walk area at the campground. Multiple dogs may be allowed.

Prince Edward Island National Park of Canada
2 Palmers Lane
Charlottetown, PE
902-672-6350 (800-414-6765)
Dogs of all sizes are allowed at no additional fee. Dogs may not be left unattended, and they must be

leashed and cleaned up after. Dogs are not allowed on the beaches from mid-April to the end of October. Dogs are allowed on the trails on lead. This campground is closed during the off-season. The camping and tent areas also allow dogs. There is a dog walk area at the campground. Multiple dogs may be allowed.

Twin Shores
702 Lower Darnley Road
Kensington, PE
902-836-4142 (877-PEI-CAMP (734-2257)
twinshores.com/
An internet café, a snack bar, laundry facilities, a camp store, playing fields/courts, a playground, movie room, and more are offered at this oceanside campsite. Dogs are allowed for no additional fee; they must be leashed and cleaned up after. Dogs are not allowed in buildings. This RV park is closed during the off-season. The camping and tent areas also allow dogs. There is a dog walk area at the campground. Multiple dogs may be allowed.

Quebec

Camping Carrousel
1699 Shephard Street
Bromont, PQ
450-534-2404
campingcarrousel.com
Dogs of all sizes are allowed. There are no additional pet fees. Dogs are not allowed at the pool or the beach, and they must be leashed and cleaned up after. This RV park is closed during the off-season. The camping and tent areas also allow dogs. There is a dog walk area at the campground. Multiple dogs may be allowed.

Camping Parc Bromont
24 La Fontaine
Bromont, PQ
450-534-2712
campingbromont.com
Dogs of all sizes are allowed. There are no additional pet fees. Dogs must be quiet, well behaved, leashed, and cleaned up after. This RV park is closed during the off-season. The camping and tent areas also allow dogs. There is a dog walk area at the campground. 2 dogs may be allowed.

Camping Cabano
71 Road 185
Cabano, PQ
418-854-9133
campingcabanodell.net
Dogs of all sizes are allowed. There are no additional pet fees. Dogs must be leashed and cleaned up after. The camping and tent areas also allow dogs. There is a dog walk area at the campground. 2 dogs may be allowed.

Camping de Compton
24 Chemin De La Station
Compton, PQ
800-563-5277
Dogs of all sizes are allowed. There are no additional pet fees. Dogs must be leashed and cleaned up after. This RV park is closed during the off-season. The camping and tent areas also allow dogs. There is a dog walk area at the campground. Multiple dogs may be allowed.

Montreal West KOA
171 H 338
Coteau du Lac, PQ
450-763-5625 (800-562-9395)
koa.com
Dogs of all sizes are allowed. There are no additional pet fees. Dogs must be quiet, well behaved, leashed, and cleaned up after. This RV park is closed during the off-season. The camping and tent areas also allow dogs. There is a dog walk area at the campground. Multiple dogs may be allowed.

Camping La Detente
1580 Fontaine Bleau
Drummondville, PQ
819-478-0651
Dogs of all sizes are allowed. There are no additional pet fees. Dogs must be leashed and cleaned up after. This RV park is closed during the off-season. The camping and tent areas also allow dogs. There is a dog walk area at the campground. Multiple dogs may be allowed.

Forillon National Park of Canada
122 Gaspe Boulevard
Gaspe, PQ
418-368-5505 (888-773-8888)
Home to the Grande-Grave National Heritage Site and located on the Gaspé Peninsula, this park features spectacular scenery, a long rich cultural history, marine and wildlife viewing, and a variety of year round recreation. Dogs of all sizes are allowed at no additional fee. Dogs

may not be left unattended outside, and they must be leashed and cleaned up after. Pets and pet food must be brought inside at night. Dogs are allowed on the trails on lead. This campground is closed during the off-season. The camping and tent areas also allow dogs. There is a dog walk area at the campground. Multiple dogs may be allowed.

Camping Pionnier
184 Road 105
Gracefield, PQ
819-463-4163
Dogs of all sizes are allowed. There are no additional pet fees. Dogs must be leashed and cleaned up after. This RV park is closed during the off-season. Only one dog is allowed per campsite. The camping and tent areas also allow dogs. There is a dog walk area at the campground.

Camping Lac LaFontaine
110 Boul
Grand Heron, PQ
450-431-7373
laclafontaine.ca
Dogs of all sizes are allowed. There is a $3 per stay per pet additional fee. Dogs must be leashed and cleaned up after. This RV park is closed during the off-season. The camping and tent areas also allow dogs. There is a dog walk area at the campground. 2 dogs may be allowed.

Camping Plage Fortier
1400 Lucen Francoes
L'ange-Gardien, PQ
888-226-7387
campingplagefortier.ca
Dogs of all sizes are allowed. There are no additional pet fees. Dogs may not be left unattended, must be leashed, and cleaned up after. This RV park is closed during the off-season. The camping and tent areas also allow dogs. There is a dog walk area at the campground. Multiple dogs may be allowed.

La Tuque Campground
15 Road 155N
La Tuque, PQ
819-523-4561
Dogs of all sizes are allowed, however there can only be up to 2 dogs any size or up to 3 small dogs per site. There are no additional pet fees. Dogs must be leashed and cleaned up after. This RV park is closed during the off-season. The camping and tent areas also allow

dogs. There is a dog walk area at the campground.

Tarmigan Campground
907 Ch. Poisson Blanc
Norte Dame du Laus, PQ
819-767-2559
tarmigan.com
Dogs of all sizes are allowed for an additional $3.50 per night per pet for the tent or RV area, and an additional fee of $5 per night per pet for the cottages. Dogs may not be left unattended, and they must be leashed and cleaned up after. There is an area where the dog may run off lead, but only if they are well behaved, under voice control, and will not chase, as there are several other animals residing at this park. This RV park is closed during the off-season. The camping and tent areas also allow dogs. There is a dog walk area at the campground. Dogs are allowed in the camping cabins. Multiple dogs may be allowed.

Camping Aeroport
2050 Aeroport
Quebec City, PQ
800-294-1574
campingaeroport.com
Dogs of all sizes are allowed. There are no additional pet fees. Dogs must be quiet, well behaved, leashed, and cleaned up after. This RV park is closed during the off-season. The camping and tent areas also allow dogs. There is a dog walk area at the campground. Multiple dogs may be allowed.

Camping Parc Beaumont
432 Fleuve
Quebec City, PQ
418-837-3787
Dogs of all sizes are allowed. There are no additional pet fees. Dogs must be leashed and cleaned up after. This RV park is closed during the off-season. The camping and tent areas also allow dogs. There is a dog walk area at the campground. 2 dogs may be allowed.

Motel and Camping de l'Anse
1105 St. Hermaine Blvd
Rimouski, PQ
418-721-0322
Dogs of all sizes are allowed. There are no additional pet fees. Dogs must be quiet, well behaved, leashed, and cleaned up after. This RV park is closed during the off-season. The camping and tent areas also allow dogs. There is a dog walk area at the campground. 2

dogs may be allowed.

Camping Du Quai
70 Ancrage
Riviere-du-loup, PQ
418-860-3111
Dogs of all sizes are allowed. There are no additional pet fees. Dogs must be leashed and cleaned up after. This RV park is closed during the off-season. The camping and tent areas also allow dogs. There is a dog walk area at the campground. 2 dogs may be allowed.

Camping Alouette
3449 L'Industrie
Saint-Mathieu-de-beloeil, PQ
450-464-1661
campingalouette.com
Dogs of all sizes are allowed. There is a $1 per night per pet additional fee. Dogs must be leashed and cleaned up after. This RV park is closed during the off-season. The camping and tent areas also allow dogs. There is a dog walk area at the campground. Multiple dogs may be allowed.

La Mauricie National Park of Canada
702 5th Street, Box 160, Stn. Bureau-chef
Shawinigan, PQ
819-538-3232 (877-737-3783)
This park offers spectacular scenery, diverse ecosystems, a five day hiking trail through the Laurentian forest, an interpretation center, a nature observatory, and a variety of recreation. Dogs of all sizes are allowed at no additional fee. Dogs may not be left unattended at any time, and they must be leashed and cleaned up after. Dogs are strictly forbidden in the forest, in watercraft, on beaches, on hiking trails, and in all public buildings. In camp areas, dogs and their food must be brought inside at night. The camping and tent areas also allow dogs. There is a dog walk area at the campground. There are no water hookups at the campground. Multiple dogs may be allowed.

Quebec City KOA
684 Chemin Olivier Street
St Nicolas, PQ
418-831-1813 (800-562-3644)
koa.com
Dogs of all sizes are allowed, but they want to know ahead of time how many pets there are so they can place accordingly. There are no additional pet fees. Dogs must be well behaved, leashed, and cleaned up after. There is one pet friendly

cabin available, and they offer a complimentary dog walking service. There are some breed restrictions. This RV park is closed during the off-season. The camping and tent areas also allow dogs. There is a dog walk area at the campground. Dogs are allowed in the camping cabins. Multiple dogs may be allowed.

Montreal South KOA
130 Monette Blvd
St Philippe de Laprairie, PQ
450-659-8626 (800-562-8636)
koamontreal.com
Dogs of all sizes are allowed, and there are no additional pet fees for tent or RV sites. There is only one dog allowed in the cabins and there is a $20 refundable deposit. Dogs may not be left unattended outside, they must be leashed, and cleaned up after. This RV park is closed during the off-season. The camping and tent areas also allow dogs. There is a dog walk area at the campground. Dogs are allowed in the camping cabins.

Saskatchewan

Assiniboia Regional Park
Off Center Street
Assiniboia, SK
306-642-5620
Dogs of all sizes are allowed. There are no additional pet fees. Dogs must be cleaned up after. They may be off leash if well behaved and under control of owner. This RV park is closed during the off-season. The camping and tent areas also allow dogs. There is a dog walk area at the campground. Multiple dogs may be allowed.

Eiling Kramer Campground
15th Street E and Central Avenue
Battleford, SK
306-937-6212
Located adjacent to the Fort Battleford National Historic site, this camp area offers 74 sites, picnic tables, showers, a playground, and a dump station. Dogs are allowed for no additional fee; they must be leashed and cleaned up after at all times. This RV park is closed during the off-season. The camping and tent areas also allow dogs. There is a dog walk area at the campground. Multiple dogs may be allowed.

Silver Dollar RV Park and

Campground
Corner of H 1 and H 19
Chaplin, SK
306-395-2332
Dogs of all sizes are allowed. There are no additional pet fees. This RV park is closed during the off-season. The camping and tent areas also allow dogs. There is a dog walk area at the campground. Multiple dogs may be allowed.

Craven World Campground
Russ Hill Road
Craven, SK
306-731-3336
cravenworld.com/contact.htm
Dogs of all sizes are allowed. There are no additional pet fees. Dogs may not be left unattended outside, and they must be leashed and cleaned up after. This RV park is closed during the off-season. The camping and tent areas also allow dogs. There is a dog walk area at the campground. Multiple dogs may be allowed.

Meadow Lake Provincial Park
H 4
Dorintosh, SK
306-236-7680
tpcs.gov.sk.ca/MeadowLake
Set amid a lush forest, this popular park has more than 20 lakes, several rivers/streams, an abundance of bird, marine, and wildlife, hiking trails, and a variety of recreational opportunities. Quiet, well behaved dogs are allowed; they must be on no more than a 6 foot leash and under their owner's control at all times. Dogs are not allowed on the beach. There are several camp areas; they may have all or some of the following; picnic tables, fire rings, modern restrooms, hot showers, and concessionaires. This RV park is closed during the off-season. The camping and tent areas also allow dogs. There is a dog walk area at the campground. Multiple dogs may be allowed.

Grenfell Regional Park
709 Lake Street
Grenfell, SK
306-697-3055
There is plenty to do at this park with mini and 9-hole golf courses, gaming fields/courts, a pool, playground, and planned recreation and children's activities. Dogs are allowed for no additional fee; they must be leashed and cleaned up after at all times. They are not allowed at the pool or on the golf courses. The campground offers

picnic tables, wood barbecue/fire pit, modern restrooms, showers, and a dump station. This RV park is closed during the off-season. The camping and tent areas also allow dogs. There is a dog walk area at the campground. Multiple dogs may be allowed.

Indian Head KOA
1100 McKay Street
Indian Head, SK
306-695-3635 (800-562-2608)
koa.com
Dogs of all sizes are allowed. There is a $2 per night per pet additional fee. Dogs must be leashed and cleaned up after. This RV park is closed during the off-season. The camping and tent areas also allow dogs. There is a dog walk area at the campground. Dogs are allowed in the camping cabins. Multiple dogs may be allowed.

Lac La Ronge Provincial Park
La Ronge Avenue
La Ronge, SK
306-425-4234
tpcs.gov.sk.ca/LacLaRonge
Rich in majestic beauty, cultural and natural history, this park offers numerous recreational opportunities, an abundance of bird and wildlife, and the beautiful Northern Lights at night. Dogs are allowed for no additional fee; they must be on no more than a 6 foot leash and under their owner's control at all times. There are 3 camp areas in the park offering sites from rustic to convenient and may have some or all of the following; restrooms, showers, picnic tables, and fire rings or a camp stove. Potable water is available. This RV park is closed during the off-season. The camping and tent areas also allow dogs. There is a dog walk area at the campground. There are no water hookups at the campgrounds. Multiple dogs may be allowed.

Moose Horn Lodge and Campground
Mile 62 Hanson Lake Road
Little Bear Lake, SK
306-426-2700
moosehorn@sympatico.ca
Dogs of all sizes are allowed. There are no additional pet fees. Dogs must be quiet, well behaved, leashed, and cleaned up after. This RV park is closed during the off-season. The camping and tent areas also allow dogs. There is a dog walk area at the campground. Dogs are allowed in the camping cabins. Multiple dogs may be allowed.

Weaver Park Campground
On H 16 at Bar Colony Museum
Lloydminster, SK
306-825-3726
lloydminster.ca/weaverpk.html
Dogs of all sizes are allowed. There are no additional pet fees. Dogs must be leashed and cleaned up after. This RV park is closed during the off-season. The camping and tent areas also allow dogs. There is a dog walk area at the campground. Multiple dogs may be allowed.

Eagle Valley Park Campground
H 1
Maple Creek, SK
306-662-2788
eagle.sasktelwebhosting.com/
Located in a serene wooded setting along the creek, this camp area is a popular bird viewing area, is rich with wildlife, and they offer Wi-Fi and cable TV. Dogs are allowed for no additional fee; they must be leashed and cleaned up after at all times. This RV park is closed during the off-season. The camping and tent areas also allow dogs. There is a dog walk area at the campground. Multiple dogs may be allowed.

Lion's Regional Park
On H 4 at H 55
Meadow Lake, SK
306-236-4447
Dogs of all sizes are allowed. There are no additional pet fees. Dogs must be leashed and cleaned up after. Dogs may be tied up outside, only if they are very friendly. This RV park is closed during the off-season. The camping and tent areas also allow dogs. There is a dog walk area at the campground. Multiple dogs may be allowed.

Besant Trans-Canada Campground
25 miles W of Moose Jaw on H 1
Moose Jaw, SK
306-756-2700
besantpark.com
Dogs of all sizes are allowed. There are no additional pet fees. Dogs must be leashed and cleaned up after. Dogs can be at the creek but not the beach. This RV park is closed during the off-season. The camping and tent areas also allow dogs. There is a dog walk area at the campground. Multiple dogs may be allowed.

Prairie Oasis Campground and Motel
955 Thatcher
Moose Jaw, SK
306-693-8888

prairie-oasis.com
Dogs of all sizes are allowed. There are no additional pet fees. Dogs must be quiet, leashed, and cleaned up after. There is also a motel on site that accepts dogs at no extra fee. This RV park is closed during the off-season. The camping and tent areas also allow dogs. There is a dog walk area at the campground. 2 dogs may be allowed.

River Park Campground
300 River Drive
Moose Jaw, SK
306-692-5474
Dogs of all sizes are allowed. There are no additional pet fees. Dogs may not be left unattended, must be leashed, and cleaned up after. This RV park is closed during the off-season. The camping and tent areas also allow dogs. There is a dog walk area at the campground. Multiple dogs may be allowed.

Fieldstone Campground
Box 1524
Moosomin, SK
306-435-2677 (800-511-2677)
fieldstonecampground.com
Dogs of all sizes are allowed, and up to 3 small dogs or up to 2 average size dogs are allowed per site. There are no additional pet fees. Dogs must be leashed and cleaned up after. This RV park is closed during the off-season. The camping and tent areas also allow dogs. There is a dog walk area at the campground.

David Laird Campground
Box 1383
North Battleford, SK
306-445-3552
Dogs of all sizes are allowed. There are no additional pet fees. Dogs must be leashed and cleaned up after. This RV park is closed during the off-season. The camping and tent areas also allow dogs. There is a dog walk area at the campground. Multiple dogs may be allowed.

Country View Motel and RV Park
4 km S on H 2S
Prince Albert, SK
306-764-2374
Dogs of all sizes and numbers are allowed on tent and RV sites, and there are no additional pet fees. Only 2 dogs are allowed per room (smoking only) at the motel, which is open all year, and also for no additional fee. Dogs must be well behaved, not left unattended, and

leashed and cleaned up after. This RV park is closed during the off-season. The camping and tent areas also allow dogs. There is a dog walk area at the campground.

Prince Albert Exhibition RV Park
6th and 10th Street E
Prince Albert, SK
306-764-1611
Dogs of all sizes are allowed. There are no additional pet fees. Dogs must be quiet, well behaved, leashed, and cleaned up after. This RV park is closed during the off-season. The camping and tent areas also allow dogs. There is a dog walk area at the campground. Multiple dogs may be allowed.

Buffalo Lookout Campground
2 miles E of Regina on H 1
Regina, SK
306-525-1448
Dogs of all sizes are allowed. There are no additional pet fees. Dogs must be leashed and cleaned up after. This RV park is closed during the off-season. The camping and tent areas also allow dogs. There is a dog walk area at the campground. Multiple dogs may be allowed.

Kings Acres Campground
I km E of Regina on H 1, N service road
Regina, SK
306-522-1619
kingsacrescampground.com
Dogs of all sizes are allowed. There are no additional pet fees. Dogs may not be left unattended, must be leashed, and cleaned up after. This RV park is closed during the off-season. The camping and tent areas also allow dogs. There is a dog walk area at the campground. Multiple dogs may be allowed.

Sherwood Forest Country Club
RR 2 Box 16
Regina, SK
306-545-0330
sherwoodforest.com
Dogs of all sizes are allowed. There are no additional pet fees. Dogs must be leashed and cleaned up after. This RV park is closed during the off-season. The camping and tent areas also allow dogs. There is a dog walk area at the campground. Multiple dogs may be allowed.

Gordon Howe Campground
Avenue P South
Saskatoon, SK
306-975-3328
Dogs of all sizes are allowed. There

are no additional pet fees. Dogs may not be left unattended, must be quiet, leashed, and cleaned up after. This RV park is closed during the off-season. The camping and tent areas also allow dogs. There is a dog walk area at the campground. Multiple dogs may be allowed.

Saskatoon 16 West RV Park
Corner of 71st Street and H 16
Saskatoon, SK
306-931-8905
saskatoonrvpark.com
Dogs of all sizes are allowed. There are no additional pet fees. Dogs must be leashed and cleaned up after. This RV park is closed during the off-season. There is a dog walk area at the campground. Multiple dogs may be allowed.

Ponderosa Campground
On H 1 a quarter mile E of
Swift Current, SK
306-773-5000
campponderosa@shaw.ca
Dogs of all sizes are allowed. There are no additional pet fees. Dogs must be quiet, well behaved, leashed, and cleaned up after. This RV park is closed during the off-season. The camping and tent areas also allow dogs. There is a dog walk area at the campground. Multiple dogs may be allowed.

Trail Campground
701 11th Avenue NW
Swift Current, SK
306-773-8088
Dogs of all sizes are allowed. There are no additional pet fees. Dogs may not be left unattended, must be leashed, and cleaned up after. This RV park is closed during the off-season. The camping and tent areas also allow dogs. There is a dog walk area at the campground. Multiple dogs may be allowed.

Grasslands National Park of Canada
P. O. Box 150
Val Marie, SK
306-298-2257 (888-773-8888)
This is the first national park in Canada to preserve a portion of the vast mixed prairie grasslands. It offers guided hikes, interpretive trails, bird watching, and a variety of other recreational pursuits. Dogs of all sizes are allowed at no additional fee. Dogs may not be left unattended, and they must be leashed and cleaned up after. Pets and pet food must be brought inside at night. Dogs are allowed on the trails on lead, unless otherwise

marked. The camping and tent areas also allow dogs. There is a dog walk area at the campground. There are no electric or water hookups at the campground. Multiple dogs may be allowed.

Prince Albert National Park of Canada
P. O. Box 100
Waskesiu Lake, SK
306-663-4522 (888-773-8888)
This park is full of natural and cultural wonders. It is the only fully protected white pelican nesting colony in Canada and also features a free-range herd of bison, special events, interpretive programs, and a variety of recreational pursuits. Dogs of all sizes are allowed at no additional fee. Dogs may not be left unattended at any time, and they must be leashed and cleaned up after. Dogs are allowed on the trails on lead unless otherwise marked. This campground is closed during the off-season. The camping and tent areas also allow dogs. There is a dog walk area at the campground. Multiple dogs may be allowed.

Yorkton City Campground
On H 16 W of Yorkton
Yorkton, SK
306-786-1757
Dogs of all sizes are allowed. There are no additional pet fees. Dogs must be leashed and cleaned up after. This RV park is closed during the off-season. The camping and tent areas also allow dogs. There is a dog walk area at the campground. Multiple dogs may be allowed.

Yukon

1202 RV Park and Motor Inn
Mile 1202 Alaska H
Beaver Creek, YU
867-862-7600 (800-661-0540)
karo-ent.com/ahytwest.htm
This RV area offers pull-thru sites, showers, laundry facilities, a restaurant and bakery, lounge, gift shop, fuel services, and a motel that also accepts pets. Dogs are allowed in the RV camp area and at the motel for no additional fee. Two dogs are allowed at the motel and there is no set limit on dogs in one's RV. Dogs must be leashed and cleaned up after at all times. The camping and tent areas also allow dogs. There is a dog walk area at

the campground. There are no water hookups at the campgrounds.

Westmark RV Park
M.P. 1202 Alaska Hwy
Beaver Creek, YU
867-862-7501
westmarkhotels.com
Dogs of all sizes are allowed, and there are no additional pet fees for tent or RV sites. There is a $15 per night per dog additional fee for the hotel, and only two dogs are allowed with two adults; 1 dog if there is a family. Dogs must be quiet, leashed, and cleaned up after. Dogs can also walk along the creek. This RV park is closed during the off-season. The camping and tent areas also allow dogs. There is a dog walk area at the campground.

Montana Services and RV Park
105 S Klondike H/H 2
Carcross, YU
867-821-3708
This camp area is home to the oldest store in the Yukon, and there is a restaurant on site as well as a museum. Dogs are allowed for no additional fee. Dogs must be leashed and cleaned up after, and they are not allowed in buildings. There is a dog walk area at the campground. There are no water hookups at the campgrounds. Multiple dogs may be allowed.

Spirit Lake Wilderness Resort
M.M. 72.1 S Klondike H
Carcross, YU
866-739-8566
spiritlakeyukon.com
Dogs of all sizes are allowed for tent or RV sites, and there are no additional pet fees. There is a $5 per night per pet additional fee for the Motel. Dogs must be well behaved, only 2 maximum are allowed, and dogs are not allowed on the beds. Dogs may not be left unattended at any time, must be leashed, and cleaned up after. This RV park is closed during the off-season. The camping and tent areas also allow dogs. There is a dog walk area at the campground.

Hotel Carmacks RV Park
Free Gold Road
Carmacks, YU
867-863-5221
Dogs of all sizes are allowed. There are no additional pet fees. Dogs must be leashed and cleaned up after. There is a motel on site that has one pet friendly room, also for no additional pet fee. This RV park is

closed during the off-season. There is a dog walk area at the campground. 2 dogs may be allowed.

Bonanza Gold RV Park
715.2 N Klondike H
Dawson City, YU
888-993-6789
bonanzagold.ca
Dogs of all sizes are allowed, and there are no additional pet fees for tent or RV sites. There is a $20 one time fee per pet for the Motel. Dogs must be leashed and cleaned up after. This RV park is closed during the off-season. The camping and tent areas also allow dogs. There is a dog walk area at the campground.

Gold Rush Campground
Between 4th & 5th Streets on York Street
Dawson City, YU
867-993-5247
goldrushcampground.com
Dogs of all sizes are allowed. There are no additional pet fees. Dogs may not be tied up outside unattended, must be leashed, and cleaned up after. This RV park is closed during the off-season. The camping and tent areas also allow dogs. There is a dog walk area at the campground. Multiple dogs may be allowed.

Guggieville RV Park
M.M. 712 Bonanza Gold Road
Dawson City, YU
867-993-5008
yukoninfo.com/guggieville/
Dogs of all sizes are allowed. There are no additional pet fees. Dogs must be leashed and cleaned up after. There are some breed restrictions. This RV park is closed during the off-season. There is a dog walk area at the campground. Multiple dogs may be allowed.

Cottonwood Park Campground
Km 717 Alaska H
Destruction Bay, YU
867-841-4066
yukonweb.com/tourism/cottonwood/
This lakeside wilderness resort is a popular recreational destination with a wide variety of activities available, and they also offer un-metered hot showers, a laundry, and a small convenience store. Dogs of all sizes are allowed for no additional fee. Dogs must be on no more than a 6 foot leash (or crated), and cleaned up after at all times. This RV park is closed during the off-season. The camping and tent areas also allow dogs. There is a dog walk area at the

campground. There are no water hookups at the campgrounds. Multiple dogs may be allowed.

Destruction Bay Lodge
M.M. 1083 Alaska Hwy
Destruction Bay, YU
867-841-5332
Dogs of all sizes are allowed. There are no additional pet fees for either the camp/RV sites or the Lodge. Dogs must be well behaved and cleaned up after. They can be off leash as long as they show no aggressive behavior, and are under voice control. This RV park is closed during the off-season. The camping and tent areas also allow dogs. There is a dog walk area at the campground. Multiple dogs may be allowed.

Eagle Plains Hotel and Campground
On the Dempster H
Eagle Plains, YU
867-993-2453
Dogs of all sizes are allowed. There are no additional pet fees. Dogs must be well behaved, quiet, and cleaned up after. They may be off lead if they are under voice control. The camping and tent areas also allow dogs. There is a dog walk area at the campground. Multiple dogs may be allowed.

Haines Junction
1016 Alaska H
Haines Junction, YU
867-634-2505
This campground offers 25 spacious pull-thrus, a sanidump, store, gas and diesel, a dump station, a 3 mile hiking trail, and more. They are open May to the end of September, weather permitting. Dogs of all sizes are allowed for no additional fee in the camp area. Dogs must be leashed and cleaned up after. This RV park is closed during the off-season. The camping and tent areas also allow dogs. There is a dog walk area at the campground. There are no water hookups at the campgrounds. Multiple dogs may be allowed.

Kluane National Park and Reserve of Canada
P. O. Box 5495/ 117 Logan Street
Haines Junction, YU
867-634-7250
Home to lush valleys, immense icefields, and high mountains, this park is a nationally significant example of Canada's North Coast Mountains natural and cultural

heritage. There are a variety of land and water recreational pursuits within the park. Dogs of all sizes are allowed at no additional fee. Dogs may not be left unattended, and they must be leashed and cleaned up after. Pets and pet food must be inside at night. Dogs are allowed on the trails on lead. This campground is closed during the off-season. The camping and tent areas also allow dogs. There is a dog walk area at the campground. There are no electric or water hookups at the campground. Multiple dogs may be allowed.

Kluane RV Campground
Km 1635.9 Alaska H
Haines Junction, YU
867-634-2709
This campground offers travelers hot showers, laundry facilities, a car wash, gift shop, gas station, and more. Dogs of all sizes are allowed for no additional fee. Dogs must be quiet, well behaved, leashed, and cleaned up after at all times. There is a special dog walk area where they ask visitors to take their pets to do their business. This RV park is closed during the off-season. The camping and tent areas also allow dogs. There is a dog walk area at the campground. Multiple dogs may be allowed.

Otter Falls Cutoff
1546 Alaska H
Haines Junction, YU
867-634-2812
otterfallscutoff.com/
This rest stop has a convenience store, laundry facilities, showers, a wildlife museum, gas and diesel, a motel, and a 2 mile nature trail. They are open May through September, weather permitting. Dogs of all sizes are allowed for no additional fee in the camp area; they are not allowed in the motel or the museum. Dogs must be leashed and cleaned up after. This RV park is closed during the off-season. The camping and tent areas also allow dogs. There is a dog walk area at the campground. 2 dogs may be allowed.

Iron Creek Lodge & RV
596 Alaska Hwy
Iron Creek, YU
867-536-2266
Dogs of all sizes and numbers are allowed, and there are no additional pet fees for tent or RV sites. There is a $5 per night per pet additional fee for the lodge, and only 2 dogs are allowed. No extra large dogs are allowed at the lodge, and there is

only one pet friendly room. The camping and tent areas also allow dogs. There is a dog walk area at the campground.

Johnson's Crossing
KM 1347 Alaska H
Johnson's Crossing, YU
867-390-2607 (867-390-2607)
This stop along the Alaska Highway offers travelers an eatery, gas station, store, and a full service campground with modern restrooms, showers, and laundry facilities. Dogs of all sizes are allowed for no additional fee in the camp area; they are not allowed in the motel. Dogs must be leashed and cleaned up after. The camping and tent areas also allow dogs. There is a dog walk area at the campground. Multiple dogs may be allowed.

Keno City RV Park
On Main Street behind Museum
Keno City, YU
867-995-2792
Dogs of all sizes are allowed. There are no additional pet fees. Dogs must be well behaved, leashed, and cleaned up after. This RV park is closed during the off-season. The camping and tent areas also allow dogs. There is a dog walk area at the campground. Multiple dogs may be allowed.

Kluane Wilderness Village
Campground
1118 Alasaka H
Kluane Wilderness Village, YU
867-841-4141
Dogs of all sizes are allowed, and there are no additional pet fees for the tent or RV sites. There is a $5 per night per pet additional fee for the motel. Up to 3 dogs can be on tent or RV sites and up to 2 dogs at the motel. Dogs must be friendly, well behaved, leashed, and cleaned up after. The camping and tent areas also allow dogs. There is a dog walk area at the campground.

Bedrock Motel and RV Park
Lot 99 Silvertrail H
Mayo, YU
867-996-2290
bedrockmotel.yk.ca
Dogs of all sizes are allowed. There are no additional pet fees. Dogs may not be left unattended at any time, must be leashed, and cleaned up after. The RV park is seasonal, but the motel is open year around. This RV park is closed during the off-season. The camping and tent areas also allow dogs. There is a dog walk

area at the campground. 2 dogs may be allowed.

Dawson Peaks Resort
Km 1232 Alaska H
Teslin, YU
867-390-2244 (866-402-2244)
Nestled among the trees, this lakeside resort offers camping, a motel, a restaurant well known for it's prize winning rhubarb pie, a gift shop with locally crafted items, watercraft rentals, charters, tours, great scenery, and more. Dogs are allowed for no additional fee at the motel, in the cabins, campground, and on watercraft rentals. Dogs are also allowed at the outside tables of the restaurant. There is only 1 dog allowed in the motel and they must be well groomed and may not be left alone in the room. Two dogs are allowed in the camp areas. Dogs must be well behaved, leashed, and cleaned up after at all times. The resort is open from the 20th of May to September 1st. This RV park is closed during the off-season. The camping and tent areas also allow dogs. There is a dog walk area at the campground. Dogs are allowed in the camping cabins. There are no water hookups at the campgrounds.

Baby Nugget RV Park
1003 Alaska H
Watson Lake, YU
867-536-2307 (888-536-2307)
nuggetcity.com/
This one-stop-does-it-all offers travelers modern facilities, a restaurant and bakery, a licensed mechanic on site, an RV wash, a gift shop, Wi-Fi, and every fall-an amazing light show from the Northern Lights. Dogs of all sizes are allowed for no additional fee; there may be an additional fee for pets in cabins. Dogs must be leashed and cleaned up after. The camping and tent areas also allow dogs. There is a dog walk area at the campground. Dogs are allowed in the camping cabins. Multiple dogs may be allowed.

Campground Services Campground
18 Adela Trail
Watson Lake, YU
867-536-7448
Dogs of all sizes are allowed. There are no additional pet fees. Dogs must be leashed and cleaned up after. This RV park is closed during the off-season. The camping and tent areas also allow dogs. There is a dog walk area at the campground. Multiple dogs may be allowed.

Downtown RV Park
Mile 635 Alaska H
Watson Lake, YU
867-536-2646
Nestled along the shores of Wye Lake at the center of town, this camp area gives easy access to numerous services and attractions, and they also provide an in-house restaurant, long, easy pull-thrus and a free RV wash for guests. Weather permitting; they're open from May to about the first week in October. Dogs of all sizes are allowed for no additional fee. Dogs must be leashed and cleaned up after at all times. This RV park is closed during the off-season. The camping and tent areas also allow dogs. There is a dog walk area at the campground. Multiple dogs may be allowed.

Racheria RV Park
M.M. 710 Alaska Hwy (70 miles past Watson Lake)
Watson Lake, YU
867-851-6456
Dogs of all sizes are allowed, and there are no additional pet fees for the tent or RV sites. There is a $10 per night per pet additional fee for the lodge. Dogs may not be left unattended, must be leashed, and cleaned up after. This RV park is closed during the off-season. The camping and tent areas also allow dogs. There is a dog walk area at the campground. Multiple dogs may be allowed.

Tetlin National Wildlife Refuge
Mile 1229 Alaska H
Watson Lake, YU
907-883-5312
tetlin.fws.gov/
This 730,000 acre refuge is home to an abundance of fish, wildlife, resident and migratory birds, and a diversity of habitats offering a variety of educational and recreational opportunities. Dogs are allowed for no additional fee; they must be leashed and cleaned up after. There are 2 free primitive camp areas; Dead Man Lake campground is at mile 1242, and Lakeview campground is at mile 1266. The camping and tent areas also allow dogs. There is a dog walk area at the campground. There are no electric or water hookups at the campgrounds. Multiple dogs may be allowed.

Caribou RV Park
Km 1403 Alaska H
Whitehorse, YU
867-668-2961

caribou-rv-park.com/
Spacious, treed sites, modern restrooms and showers, a laundry, car wash, great drinking water, hiking trails, and more are offered to guests at this rest stop. Weather permitting; they are open from the end of May to September or October. Dogs are allowed for no additional fee; they must be leashed and cleaned up after. This RV park is closed during the off-season. The camping and tent areas also allow dogs. There is a dog walk area at the campground. There are no water hookups at the campgrounds. Multiple dogs may be allowed.

Hi Country RV Park
91374 Alaska H
Whitehorse, YU
867-667-7445
hicountryrvyukon.com/
Open from mid-May to mid-September, this camp area offers a wide range of services including free Wi-Fi, Internet access, a gift shop, wildlife display, a convenience store, and more. Dogs of all sizes are allowed for no additional fee. Dogs must be leashed and cleaned up after. This RV park is closed during the off-season. The camping and tent areas also allow dogs. There is a dog walk area at the campground. Multiple dogs may be allowed.

Pioneer Park
91091 Alaska H (Km 1414.7)
Whitehorse, YU
867-668-5944
pioneer-rv-park.com/
Whether it's a short stay on the way through or a base for exploring the area, this camp area offers a number of amenities, including a store, repair shop, a high pressure RV/car wash, and a special pet wash area. The park is open from mid-May to September 30th. Dogs of all sizes are allowed for no additional fee. Dogs must be leashed and cleaned up after. This RV park is closed during the off-season. The camping and tent areas also allow dogs. There is a dog walk area at the campground. There are no water hookups at the campgrounds. Multiple dogs may be allowed.

Chapter 2

Day Use Park Guide

United States

Alabama

Horseshoe Bend National Military Park
11288 Horseshoe Bend Road
Daviston, AL
256-234-7111
nps.gov/hobe/index.htm
Dogs must be on leash and must be cleaned up after in this National park. They are not allowed in any buildings. The park features hiking, auto touring, fishing, boating, and historical sites. It is open all year 9am-4:30pm except Christmas.

Little River Canyon National Preserve
2141 Gault Avenue North
Fort Payne, AL
256-845-9605
nps.gov/liri/index.htm
Dogs must be on leash and must be cleaned up after in this park. They are not allowed in any buildings. Located in Lookout Mountain and part of Appalachian Plateau landscapes. It is open year round. The park features auto touring, fishing, hiking, boating, camping, swimming, and more.

Leeds Historical Park
1159 Montevallo Road/Hwy 119
Leeds, AL
205-699-6131
Developed through the efforts of the community, this park commemorates the city's 3 Medal of Honor recipients. Leashed dogs are welcome.

Medal of Honor Park at Cottage Hill Park
1711 Hillcrest Rd
Mobile, AL
251-208-1601
This city park is named in honor of PFC John D. New U.S.M.C. The park offers playing fields/courts, a playground, picnic areas, restrooms, and a walking path. Leashed dogs are allowed on sited.

Alaska Listings

Delany Park Strip
300 West 9th Avenue

Anchorage, AK
907-456-5774
muni.org/parks/index.cfm
A park of many uses through the years, this "strip" park is now a popular park for bringing together the ethnically and economically diverse neighborhoods of the area with a variety of social and gaming spaces, and it is also home to a number of major events and festivals throughout the year. Dogs are allowed; they must be legally licensed, have a current rabies vaccination, and be under their owner's control, leashed, and cleaned up after at all times.

Earthquake Park
4306 W Northern Lights Blvd
Anchorage, AK
907-343-4355
muni.org/parks/parksntrails.cfm
This park was hit with a 9.2 earthquake in March of 1964, and years later it was developed for park use with reader boards and monuments of the event. Dogs are allowed; they must be legally licensed, have a current rabies vaccination, and be under their owner's control, leashed, and cleaned up after at all times.

Hillside Park
Abbot Road
Anchorage, AK
907-343-4355
muni.org/parks/index.cfm
Dogs are allowed at this park; they must be legally licensed, have a current rabies vaccination, and be under their owner's control, leashed, and cleaned up after at all times.

Wrangell-St Elias National Park and Preserve
PO Box 439
Copper Center, AK
907-822-5234
nps.gov/wrst/index.htm
Dogs on leash are allowed in the park. They are not allowed in buildings. The park features camping, hiking, auto touring, and more.

Denali National Park and Preserve
PO Box 9
Denali Park, AK
907-683-2294
nps.gov/dena/index.htm
Dogs must be on leash and must be cleaned up after in Denali National Park. Dogs are only allowed on the paved roads and dirt roads. One place to walk is on the road to Savage after mile 15, which is a dirt

road and only the park buses are allowed. Access is by car depending on weather. Dogs on leash are allowed in the Denali National Park campgrounds, but they may not be left unattended in the campgrounds. The park features auto touring, camping, and scenery.

Birch Hill Cross Country Ski Center
101 Wilderness Drive
Fairbanks, AK
907-457-4488
Although this recreation area is off limits to dogs during the winter season, there are several months of the year when they are allowed. Dogs are allowed throughout the grounds, on the hiking trails, and at the disc golf course. Dogs must be under their owner's control, leashed, and cleaned up after at all times; they are not allowed in any of the buildings.

Gates of the Arctic National Park and Preserve
201 First Avenue
Fairbanks, AK
907-692-5494
nps.gov/gaar/index.htm
Dogs must be on leash and must be cleaned up after in the park. The park is accessed by plane, foot and car depending on weather. Dogs are allowed in the backcountry of the park but there are no man-made trails. It is a wilderness park. The nearest places to stay when visiting the park is the town of Bettles Field or Wiseman. There are no campgrounds in the park and there are no facilities in the park.

Yukon-Charley Rivers National Preserve
201First Avenue
Fairbanks, AK
907-547-2233
nps.gov/yuch/index.htm
Dogs on leash are allowed. The park is accessed by plane and some roads for cars. The park features camping, boating, hiking, fishing, and more.

Glacier Bay National Park
1 Park Road
Gustavus, AK
907-697-2230
nps.gov/glba
This national park offers coastal beaches and high mountains. The way to arrive at this park is by plane, boat, or ferry, usually from Juneau. The Glacier Bay Visitor Center is open daily from May 27 to September 11, from noon to 8:45

p.m. Dogs are not allowed to be off the road more than 100 feet, and they are not allowed on any of the trails into the back country. They are also not allowed on the Barlett Trail or on the Forest Loop Trail, or in any of the camp buildings. The Visitor Information Station for boaters and campers, is open May through June from 8 to 5 p.m.; June, July, and August from 7 to 9 p.m., and September 8 to 5 p.m. Dogs are allowed at no additional fee, and they can be in the developed Barlett Cove area, or on any of the marked trails. Dogs may not be left unattended at any time, and they must be leashed at all times, and cleaned up after.

Mendenhall Wetlands State Game Refuge
Egan Drive
Juneau, AK
907-465-4267
These wetlands, created by the melding of land and sea, create habitats for a wide variety of marine, bird, and wildlife as well as allowing for recreational, educational, and scientific opportunities. There are several entrances to the refuge; miles 3 and 6 of Egan Drive, just west of the airport at the end of Radcliffe Road, mile 8.5 on the North Douglas H, and several public access sites along the shoreline in Juneau City and Borough. Dogs are allowed; they must be leashed, or under strict voice control, and cleaned up after at all times.

Point Bridget State Park
400 Willoughby Avenue, Suite 500
Juneau, AK
907-465-4563
In addition to a variety of habitats with marine, bird, and wildlife, this 2,850 acre park is also home to salmon spawning streams, hiking trails-including a planked trail that goes through a rainforest musket, and a variety of year round recreational opportunities. Dogs of all sizes are allowed throughout the park. They must be under their owner's control, leashed, and cleaned up after.

Alagnak Wild River
PO Box 7
King Salmon, AK
907-246-3305
nps.gov/alag/index.htm
Dogs on leash are allowed in the park. The park is accessed only by power boat or plane. It features camping, boating, fishing, hiking, swimming, and whitewater rafting.

Aniakchak National Monument and Preserve
PO Box 7
King Salmon, AK
907-246-3305
nps.gov/ania/index.htm
Dogs must be on leash and must be cleaned up after. The park is accessed only by boat or plane. It features camping, fishing, boating, whitewater rafting and more.

Katmai National Park and Preserve
PO Box 7
King Salmon, AK
907-246-3305
nps.gov/katm/index.htm
Dogs on leash are allowed only in developed areas. They are not allowed in the Brooks camping area. The park is accessed by plane or dogsled only.

Cape Krusenstern National Monument
PO Box 1029
Kotzebue, AK
907-442-3890
nps.gov/cakr/index.htm
Dogs must be on leash and must be cleaned up after in park. The park is accessed by boat, plane, snowmobile or foot only. It features hiking, fishing, and boating.

Kobuk Valley National Park
PO Box 1029
Kotzebue, AK
907-442-3760
nps.gov/kova/index.htm
Dogs on leash are allowed in the park. The park is accessed by plane, foot, or dogsled only.

Noatak National Preserve
PO Box 1029
Kotzebue, AK
907-442-3760
nps.gov/noat/index.htm
Dogs on leash are allowed. Accessed by plane, foot, dogsled, or watercraft only. The park features camping, boating, hiking, fishing, and more.

Western Arctic National Parklands
PO Box 1029
Kotzebue, AK
907-442-3760
nps.gov/nwak/index.htm
Pets are allowed. There is not an official pet policy. The park is accessed by plane and dogsledding.

Bering Land Bridge National

Preserve
PO Box 220
Nome, AK
907-443-2522
nps.gov/bela/index.htm
Dogs must be on leash and must be cleaned up after. The park is accessed by boat, plane, or dog sled only. The park features camping, boating, hiking, fishing, and more.

Lake Clark National Park and Preserve
1 Park Place
Port Alsworth, AK
907-781-2218
nps.gov/lacl/index.htm
Dogs on leash are allowed in the park area. The park is accessed by plane or dogsled only. The park features boating, camping, fishing, hiking, and more.

Kenai Fjords National Park
PO Box 1727
Seward, AK
907-224-2132
nps.gov/klgo/index.htm
Dogs on leash are only allowed in the parking lot area and along roads. They are not allowed in buildings, on trails, or in the back country.

Sitka National Historical Park
103 Monastery Street
Sitka, AK
907-747-0110
nps.gov/sitk/
Located in a 113 acre temperate rain forest setting, this park is all that remains as a testament to the last major conflict between Native Alaskans and Europeans, and is the state's oldest federally designated park. Dogs are allowed around the grounds and on the trails; they are not allowed in buildings. Dogs must be leashed and cleaned up after at all times.

Klondike Gold Rush National Historical Park
PO Box 517
Skagway, AK
907-983-2921
nps.gov/klgo/index.htm
Dogs on leash are allowed in the park. They are not allowed in buildings. The park features camping, hiking, boating, and more.

Aleutian World War II National Historic Area
400 Salmon Way
Unalaska, AK
907-581-9944
nps.gov/aleu/index.htm
Dogs must be on leash and must be

cleaned up after. You must have a land use permit. The park features war structures, forts, hiking, boating, and more.

Kincaid Park
9401 W. Raspberry Road
Wasilla, AK
907-343-6397
muni.org/parks/parksntrails.cfm
Located on 1,400 green acres, there are plenty of places to explore with a variety of recreational activities, and there is also a large center on site for special events. Dogs are allowed; they must be legally licensed, have a current rabies vaccination, and be under their owner's control, leashed, and cleaned up after at all times.

Arizona

Cabeza Prieta Wildlife Refuge
1611 N 2nd Avenue
Ajo, AZ
520-387-6483
Most of this 1,000-square-mile refuge is designated wilderness where temperatures may top 100 degrees for more than 100 days at a time. Although a water challenged area, there are as many as 420 plant species and more than 300 kinds of wildlife. This park offers a free lecture series from November to March, interpretive trails, hunting, opportunities for wildlife observation, and primitive camping. Before entering the refuge, you must obtain a free, valid Refuge Entry Permit and sign a Military Hold Harmless Agreement There are no facilities for gasoline, sanitation, or potable water. They suggest you bring two gallons of water per day, per person, plus water for your pet. A large part of the refuge falls within the air space of a Military training base, and there may be closures of the park during training exercises. Normally, the park is open from Monday through Friday, and closed weekends. Well behaved, friendly dogs of all sizes are allowed. Dogs are allowed throughout the park. They may not be left unattended, and they must be leashed at all times and cleaned up after.

Organ Pipe Cactus National Monument
10 Organ Pipe Drive
Ajo, AZ
520-387-6849

nps.gov/orpi/index.htm
Dogs on leash are allowed in the campground, paved roadways, and the Palo Verde Trail. Dogs are not allowed on any other trails.

Lost Dutchman State Park
6109 N Apache Trail
Apache Junction, AZ
480-982-4485
Named after the fabled lost gold mine, this desert park, at 2000 feet, is located at the base of the Superstition Mountains, a place of mystery and legend since early times. The park offers a variety of hiking trails of varying difficulty, nature trails, visitors' center, picnic facilities with restrooms, and special programs throughout the year. Well behaved dogs of all sizes are allowed. Dogs must be leashed at all times and cleaned up after. Dogs may not be left unattended in the park or in automobiles. Dogs are allowed throughout the park and on the trails, but not in public buildings. There is also a 70 unit campground (no hook-ups) with a dump station and showers that allow pets for no additional fee.

Fort Verde State Historical Park
125 Holloman Street
Camp Verde, AZ
928-567-3275
This historic Park was a primary army base, and is the best preserved example of an Indian Wars era fort in Arizona. Rich in cultural and American history, they offer living history presentations, special craft and building projects, historic house museums furnished in 1880s period, picnic tables, restrooms, and RV parking. They are ADA accessible, and open 8:00 a.m. - 5:00 p.m. every day. The park is closed on Christmas Day. Dogs of all sizes are allowed. Dogs may not be left unattended anywhere in the park or in automobiles. Dogs must be leashed and cleaned up after. They are allowed throughout the park except in buildings.

Montezuma Castle National Monument
2800 Montezuma Castle H
Camp Verde, AZ
928-567-3322
nps.gov/moca/
This park is home to one of the best preserved cliff dwellings in North America. The 20 room, 5 story cliff dwelling sits high above a creek in a limestone recess, and served as a "high-rise apartment building" for

Sinagua Indians over 600 years ago. Exhibits along the self-guiding trail describe the cultural and natural history of the site and a diorama/audio program shows the interior view of the cliff dwellings. Dogs must be on no more than a six foot leash at all times and cleaned up after. Dogs may not be left unattended in the park or in automobiles. They are open every day of the year, including Christmas day. Winter hours: 8 AM to 5 PM; Summer hours (May 30th through Labor Day): 8 AM to 6 PM MST.

Tuzigoot National Monument
PO Box 219
Camp Verde, AZ
928-634-5564
nps.gov/tuzi/index.htm
Dogs must be on leash and must be cleaned up after in the park and on trails.

Canyon de Chelly National Monument
PO Box 588
Chinle, AZ
928-674-5500
nps.gov/cach/index.htm
Dogs on leash are allowed in campsites, roads that lead up to overlooks and parking lot. Dogs are not allowed in canyons or trails.

Sunset Crater Volcano National Monument
6400 N Hwy 89
Flagstaff, AZ
928-526-1157
nps.gov/sucr/index.htm
Dogs on leash are allowed in the park areas. Dogs are not allowed on the trails. You may not leave pets in vehicles in the park.

Walnut Canyon National Monument
6400 N Hwy 89
Flagstaff, AZ
928-526-1157
nps.gov/waca/index.htm
Dogs on leash are allowed on paved roads and picnic areas only. Dogs are not allowed in buildings or on park trails.

Wupatki National Monument
6400 N Hwy 89
Flagstaff, AZ
928-526-1157
nps.gov/wupa/index.htm
Dogs on leash are allowed in the parking areas and picnic areas. Dogs are not allowed in the buildings or on the park trails.

Pipe Spring National Monument
406 North Pipe Spring Road
Fredonia, AZ
928-643-7105
nps.gov/pisp/index.htm
Dogs on leash are allowed on the picnic grounds and paved areas. Dogs are not allowed in the fort, unpaved trails, or garden.

Coronado National Memorial
4101 E Montezuma Canyon Road
Hereford, AZ
520-366-5515
nps.gov/coro/
A memorial park dedicated to its explorer, Coronado. There is auto touring, picnicking, hiking, bird watching, and a museum. Dogs are not allowed in buildings, in caves, or on most all the trails. They are allowed on all paved roads, and on the Crest Trail the 5.3 miles one way to Miller Peak (elevations: 6575 feet to 9456 feet at Miller Peak) and into the National Forest. The trailhead is across the road at the northeast end of the Montezuma Pass parking area. The trail climbs for 2 miles to the northwestern boundary of the Memorial, where it enters the Coronado National Forest. There it continues along the crest of the Huachuca Mountains to the turnoff for Miller Peak, the highest peak in the Huachucas. Dogs must be kept leashed at all times, and cleaned up after. Dogs may not be left unattended anywhere in the park or in automobiles.

Cattail Cove State Park
P. O. Box 1990
Lake Havasu City, AZ
928-855-1223
This 2,000 acre park offer a beach, boat ramp, an amphitheater, and a variety of year round land and water recreation. Day use is from sunrise to 10 pm. Dogs must be leashed at all times, and cleaned up after. Dogs may not be left unattended at any time. There is also a campground here where pets are allowed for no additional fee.

Rainbow Bridge National Monument
PO Box 1507
Page, AZ
928-608-6404
nps.gov/rabr/index.htm
Pets are not allowed on the short hike and boat to the monument. Permission must be granted by the tribe to hike the 17 mile trail to the site.

Bill Williams River National Wildlife

Refuge
60911 Hwy 95
Parker, AZ
928-667-4144
This 6,105-acre refuge has a rich natural and cultural history. Dogs of all sizes are allowed for no additional fee. Dogs must be kept leashed at all times, and cleaned up after. Dogs are allowed throughout the park on the trails or just along side the trails. Dogs may not be left unattended at any time.

Buckskin Mountain State Park
5476 Hwy 95
Parker, AZ
928-667-3231
This scenic park sits along an 18-mile stretch of the Colorado River between Parker Dam and Headgate Dam. They have different activities throughout the year. There are ranger led hikes, weekly speakers, ice cream socials, boating safety classes, and campfire programs. They also offer basketball and volleyball courts, a playground, clothing boutique, restaurant, camp store, arcade, and a gas dock. Dogs of all sizes are allowed for no additional fee. They may not be left unattended at any time, and they must be leashed at all times, and cleaned up after. Dogs are not allowed in the cabaña area or on the beach from the day use area to the cabañas. At the River Island area, dogs are allowed in the water, but must be kept on right side of boat ramp. Well behaved dogs on lead are allowed on the variety of trails and throughout the rest of the park. There is also tent and RV camping at this park, and pets are allowed for no additional fee.

North Mountain Area
7th Street
Phoenix, AZ
602-262-6862
phoenix.gov/PARKS/hikenort.html
North Mountain is over 2,100 feet and offers panoramic views of Phoenix. There are a variety of trails rated easy to difficult. The trailheads for two of the easy to moderate trails are located at the north end of Mountain View Park at 7th Avenue and Cheryl Drive. The North Mountain National Trail is rated moderate to difficult hiking and the trailhead is located at the Maricopa picnic area of 7th Street (not 7th Avenue). Parking is available. Pets must be leashed and please clean up after them.

Papago Park
Van Buren Street and Galvin Parkway
Phoenix, AZ
602-256-3220
This park of 1,200 acres has easy trails and a natural landscape in addition to a variety of recreational pursuits. There is an archery range, an exercise course of 1.7 miles, over 7 acres of fishing lagoons, a ranger station that is near the Hole In The Rock, a softball complex, an orienteering course, picnic facilities, and unusual rock formations that took millions of years to form. The park is open from 6 am to 10 pm daily. Dogs are allowed for no additional fee. Dogs must be leashed at all times and it is important that you clean up after your pet. They are allowed throughout the park on all the trails.

Piestewa Peak/Dreamy Draw Area
Squaw Peak Drive
Phoenix, AZ
602-262-6862
phoenix.gov/PARKS/hikesqua.html
Piestewa Peak (formally Squaw Peak) is 2,608 feet high and is one of the best known peaks in Phoenix. The summit trail does not allow dogs or horses, all other trails in the park allow leashed dogs. To take your dog up most of the summit for the views you can use the 3 3/4 mile Freedom Trail which is a more gradual slope than the Summit Trail. There are several other easy trails as well as difficult ones on which you may take your dog. Some of the trails begin off Squaw Peak Drive. Parking is available. Pets must be leashed and please clean up after them.

Reach 11 Recreation Area
Cave Creek Road
Phoenix, AZ
602-262-6862
phoenix.gov/PRL/r11.html
This 1,500 acre park is about 7 miles long and less than 1/2 mile wide. The park runs along the north side of the Central Arizona Project canal. There are about 18 miles of multi-use trails to enjoy. In general the trails are flat and easy. The trails run the length of the recreation area from Cave Creek Road east to Scottsdale Road. Access points include Cave Creek Road, Tatum Blvd., Scottsdale Road and 56th Street. Pets must be leashed and please clean up after them.

South Mountain Park/Preserve
10919 South Central Avenue

346

Phoenix, AZ
602-495-0222
phoenix.gov/PARKS/hikesoth.html
This park of mostly undeveloped desert has many hiking trails that wind through a variety of habitats and picturesque geographic formations. The diverse ecosystems support a large variety of plants, animals, bird species, and recreation. There is also an educational center and museum at the visitor's center. The park is open daily from 5:30 am to 11pm. Dogs of all sizes are allowed for no additional fee. Dogs may not be left unattended at any time. It is also very important that dogs are on lead and under owners' control at all times, and cleaned up after.

Picacho Peak State Park
P. O. Box 275
Picacho, AZ
520-466-3183
This park has a rich natural and cultural history, and was once used as a landmark by early explorers. The park offers picnic areas, ramadas, restrooms, a variety of trails with varying difficulty and interests, historical markers, playground, and the Civil War Re-enactment of 3 different battles. The park is open from 8:00 a.m. to 10:00 p.m. Dogs of all sizes are allowed. Dogs must be leashed and cleaned up after, and they may not be left unattended at any time. Dogs are allowed on the trails, but not in any park buildings. They also have a campground (some sites with electric) with grills and a dumpstation.

Tonto National Monument
HC 02 Box 4602
Roosevelt, AZ
928-467-2241
nps.gov/tont/index.htm
Dogs on leash are allowed in the park and the Lower Cliff Dwelling Trail. Dogs are not allowed on the Upper Cliff Dwelling Trail.

Slide Rock State Park
6871 N Hwy 89A
Sedona, AZ
928-282-3034
This day use park was put on the National Register of Historic Places in 1991. In addition to sharing a rich natural and cultural history, this park provides swimming, picnicking, birdwatching, fishing (no glass bait jars please), a nature trail and access to other trails, a volleyball court, and special events and programs. Dogs of all sizes are allowed at no additional fee. Dogs are not allowed at the creek, in the water or at the swim beaches. The dogs are allowed to go as far as the top of the stairs that lead to some of these areas. They are allowed on the trails on lead. Dogs may not be left unattended at any time, including being left in automobiles. Dogs must be on leash and under control at all times, and be cleaned up after.

Boyce Thompson Arboretum State Park
223 Hwy 60
Superior, AZ
520-689-2811
This 323 acre park is Arizona's oldest and largest botanical garden. They feature the plants of the desert, a streamside forest, panoramic views, various natural habitats and wildlife, a desert lake, specialty gardens, and more. They also offer an interpretive center, a demonstration garden, visitor center, guided tours, picnic grounds with tables, gift shop, and restrooms. Well behaved dogs of all sizes are allowed for no additional fee. They must be kept on a short lead, under their owner's control at all times, and cleaned up after. Dogs are not allowed anywhere in the water or in the gift shop. They are allowed throughout the rest of the park, and may even join their owners on the guided tours. The park is open daily from 8:00 a.m. to 5:00 p.m (October 1 - April 30). Summer hours are from 6:00 a.m. to 3:00 p.m. (May 1 - September 30).

Navajo National Monument
HC 71 Box 3
Tonalea, AZ
928-672-2700
nps.gov/nava/index.htm
Dogs must be on leash and must be cleaned up after in campsites, picnic, and parking areas. Dogs are not allowed on the trails.

Rillito River Trail
La Cholla Blvd
Tucson, AZ
520-877-6000
This popular paved trail stretches for miles, offering plenty of opportunity for your pooch to stretch his or her legs. Just be careful to go early in the morning or early evening if it is a hot day, as the paved path and the adjacent desert sand can become too hot for paws.

A popular section of the trail is located between La Cholla Blvd. and Campbell Avenue, along the Rillito River. There is parking and restrooms available near La Cholla Boulevard.

Saguaro National Park
3693 South Old Spanish Trail
Tucson, AZ
520-733-5100
nps.gov/sagu/index.htm
Dogs must be on leash and must be cleaned up after on roadways and picnic areas. They are not allowed on any trails or buildings.

Chiricahua National Monument
13063 E Bonita Canyon Rd
Willcox, AZ
520-824-3560
nps.gov/chir/index.htm
Dogs on leash are allowed in campsites and on paved roads. Dogs are not allowed on hiking trails in the park.

Kaibab National Forest
800 South 6th Street
Williams, AZ
928-635-8200
fs.fed.us/r3/kai/
Dogs on leash are allowed on many trails throughout this national forest. Hiking trails range greatly in difficulty, from easy to very difficult. A couple of the more popular trails are the Keyhole Sink Trail and the Bill Williams Mountain Trail. The Keyhole Sink Trails is an easy trail that is 2 miles round trip. Walk through a ponderosa pine forest until you reach a box canyon. At the canyon, you will find petroglyphs (prehistoric sketches on the rock), that are about 1,000 years old. The message suggests that the area was an important hunting ground. To get there from Williams, take I-40 east to the Pitman Valley Exit (#171). Turn left and cross over the Interstate. Proceed east on Historic Route 66 for about 2 miles to the Oak Hill Snowplay Area. The trail begins on the north side of the road. Park in the lot provided. The Bill Williams Mountain Trail is rated moderate and is about 4 miles long. The trailhead starts at 7,000 feet. To get there, go west from downtown Williams on Bill Williams Avenue about one mile; turn left at Clover Hill and proceed along the frontage road to the turnoff for Williams Ranger District office. Follow the signs to the trailhead.

Homolovi Ruins State Park
HCR 63 Box, State Route 87N

Winslow, AZ
928-289-4106
This park now serves as a research center recording the late migration period of the Hopi from the 1200's to the late 1300's. Park facilities include a visitor center and museum, various trails, and pullouts that provide opportunities to observe wildlife over the 4,000 acres at an elevation of 4,900 feet. Dogs are allowed to go on all the trails, the ruins, the park grounds, and the visitor's center. Dogs must be leashed or crated at all times, and they may not be left unattended in the park or automobiles. There is camping available with hook-ups, several covered picnic tables, showers, and a dump station.

Sanguinetti House Museum & Garden
240 S Madison
Yuma, AZ
928-782-1841
yumalibrary.org/ahs/index.htm
Purchased in 1890 by a pioneer merchant, this home is now a museum of the history of the era, and the beautiful Italian-style gardens and aviaries that were started back then are still maintained today. They are open from Tuesday through Saturday. Dogs are allowed to walk through the gardens with their owners, and there is no additional fee for them. Dogs must be on leash at all times, and cleaned up after. Dogs are not allowed in the museum or any of the park buildings.

Arkansas

Hot Springs National Park
369 Central Avenue
Hot Springs, AR
501-624-2701
nps.gov/hosp
There are 47 hot springs here, and this reserve was established in 1832 to protect them. That makes this park our oldest national park. The park is open daily from 9:00 a.m. to 5:00 p.m., except in the summer from May 28 to August 12, when they stay open until 6:00 p.m. Dogs are allowed at no additional fee at the park and in the campground, which does not have hookups. Dogs may not be left unattended, they must be leashed, and cleaned up after. Dogs are allowed throughout the park, trails and in the camp area.

Mammoth Spring State Park
17 Hwy 63N
Mammoth Spring, AR
870-625-7364
Home to the state's largest natural spring with a flow of 9 million gallons of water an hour, this park also shares the area's history with an authentic early 1900's train station and the remains of a mill and hydroelectric plant. There are picnic areas, a trail, game field, and a playground on site. Dogs are allowed throughout the park; they are not allowed in buildings. Dogs must be leashed and cleaned up after.

Parkin Archeological State Park
60 Hwy 184
Parkin, AR
870-755-2500
This park offers a number of recreational and educational opportunities at this significant historical site that shows evidence of occupation since 1000 to 1500 AD. Also on site are picnic areas, a playground, an interpretive exhibit area, and gift shop. Dogs are allowed throughout the park; they are not permitted in buildings. Dogs may not be left alone at any time and must be leashed and under their owner's immediate control.

Hobbs State Park-Conservation Area
21392 East Hwy 12
Rogers, AR
479-789-2380
A nature lover's and hiker's paradise, this 12,000+ acre park sits along the southern end of a 28,370 acre lake and offers a wide range of recreational as well as educational activities. Dogs are allowed throughout the park; they must be leashed and under their owner's control and care at all times.

Pinnacle Mountain State Park
11901 Pinnacle Valley Road
Roland, AR
501-868-5806
Dedicated to environmental education and preservation, this park also offers abundant land and water recreation, a variety of habitats and inhabitants, scenic hiking trails, interpretive programs and trails, picnic sites with comfort stations, an arboretum, and more. Dogs are allowed throughout the park; they must be leashed and under their owner's control and care

at all times.

White River National Wildlife Refuge
57 S CC Camp Road
St Charles, AR
870-282-8200
stateparks.com/white_river.html
This refuge was finally procured for the protection of migratory birds in 1935 and over half of the state's birds can be found here. There are also more than 300 lakes and ponds and a bottomland hardwood forest. Dogs are allowed throughout the park; they must be leashed at all times and stay on the trails.

California

Peter Strauss Ranch
Mulholland Highway
Agoura Hills, CA
805-370-2301
nps.gov/samo/maps/peter.htm
The Peter Strauss Trail is an easy .6 mile round trip trail which traverses through chaparral and oak trees. Dogs are allowed on the trail but must be leashed and people need to clean up after their pets. From the Ventura Freeway/101, take the Kanan exit and head south for 2.8 miles to Troutdale Rd. Turn left onto Troutdale Rd and then left on Mulholland Highway. This park is part of the Santa Monica Recreation Area.

Rocky Oaks Park
Mulholland Highway
Agoura Hills, CA
805-370-2301
This park offers an open grassland area with oak groves and small rock outcroppings. There are four trails ranging from 100 yards to just over one mile and are rated easy to moderate. Dogs are allowed on the trails but must be leashed and people need to clean up after their pets. To get there take the Ventura Freeway/101 to Kanan Road. Head south on Kanan and then turn right on Mulholland Highway. Then make a right into the parking lot. This park is part of the Santa Monica Recreation Area.

Vasquez Rocks Natural Area Park
10700 W Escandido Canyon Road
Agua Dulce, CA
661-268-0840
This high desert, 745 acre park offers unique towering rock

formations, "Birds of Prey" presentations that begin each October, Star Group parties, and various recreational opportunities. The park features a history trail tour of the Tatavian Indians and Spanish settlers, a seasonal stream, and hiking trails. Dogs are allowed throughout the park and on the trails. Dogs must be on leash and please clean up after them.

Modoc National Forest
800 West 12th Street
Alturas, CA
530-233-5811
fs.fed.us/r5/modoc/
This national forest covers over 1.9 million acres of land which ranges in elevation from 4,300 to 9,934 feet. Please see our listings in this region for dog-friendly hikes and/or campgrounds.

Santa Ana River Path
E. La Palma Ave.
Anaheim, CA

This path stretches for about 20 miles each way. The trail parallels the Santa Ana River. In most spots, there are two sets of trails, one for bikes and one for horses. Dogs are allowed on either trail (paved and dirt). Parking is available at the Yorba Regional Park which is located on E. La Palma Avenue between the Imperial Hwy (Hwy 90) and S. Weir Canyon Rd. There is a minimal fee for parking.

Yorba Regional Park
E. La Palma Ave.
Anaheim, CA
714-970-1460
This regional park has 175 acres with several streams and four lakes. There are also over 400 picnic tables and over 200 barbecue stoves. If you want an longer walk or jog, the park is adjacent to the twenty mile long Santa Ana River Bike Path and Trail. The park is located on E. La Palma Avenue between the Imperial Hwy (Hwy 90) and S. Weir Canyon Rd. There is a minimal fee for parking.

Utica Park
Hwy 49
Angels Camp, CA
209-736-2187
Utica Park was built in 1954 on the site of the Utica Mine after the ground had been leveled and shafts filled to the 60 foot level. Today it is a great park for having a picnic or watching the kids have fun in the large playground area. The historic

Lightner Mine at this park operated from 1896-1915. It produced over $6 million dollars in ore. The mine was filled, but you will still see some of the equipment that was used above ground. The park is located off Hwy 49, just north of downtown Angels Camp.

Forest of Nisene Marks
Aptos Creek Road
Aptos, CA
831-763-7062
Dogs on leash are allowed in part of this park. They are allowed on a beautiful wooded trail that parallels the gravel Aptos Creek Road (on the left or west side of the road only). A good starting point is at the park entrance booth. Park after paying the minimal day use fee and then join the trail next to the parking lot. On this trail, head into the park (north). Dogs are allowed on the dirt trail up to the Steel Bridge (about 1 mile each way). You can continue on Aptos Creek Rd to the Porter Family Picnic Area, but dogs need to stay on the road (cars also allowed). The dirt trail up to the bridge is usually the best hiking trail that allows dogs and it includes several trails that divert towards the creek. Here your pup can enjoy playing in the water. To get there from Hwy 17, exit Hwy 1 south towards Watsonville. Drive through Santa Cruz and Capitola on Hwy 1 and then exit at the Seacliff Beach/Aptos exit. Turn left onto State Park Drive. Then turn right on Soquel Avenue. After going under the train bridge, you'll soon turn left onto Aptos Creek Rd. It's a small street, so be careful not to miss it. Drive up this road until you reach the park entrance booth.

Angeles National Forest
701 N Santa Anita Ave
Arcadia, CA
626-574-1613
fs.fed.us/r5/angeles/
This national forest covers over 650,000 acres and is known as the backyard playground to the metropolitan area of Los Angeles. Elevations range from 1,200 to 10,064 feet. Please see our listings in this region for dog-friendly hikes and/or campgrounds.

Arcata Community Forest
11th and 14th Streets
Arcata, CA
707-822-3619
arcatacityhall.org/forest.html
Leashed dogs are allowed on this

600+ acre park which offers 18 trails. The trails range from 1/10 of a mile to almost 2 miles long. The park is located on the east side of the City of Arcata, accessible from Redwood Park located at the east ends of 11th and 14th Streets; on the southern side from Fickle Hill Road, which begins at the east end of 11th and 7th Streets at Bayside Road; and from the east end of California Street which connects with L.K. Wood Blvd. north of Humboldt State University.

Calaveras Big Trees State Park
Highway 4
Arnold, CA
209-795-2334
Just three species of redwood trees remain; the dawn redwood in central China; the coast redwood along the coast of northern California and southern Oregon; and the Sierra redwoods which grow at Calaveras Big Trees State Park and other widely scattered groves along the western slope of the Sierra Nevada. These redwood trees have evolved from the Mesozoic Era, the time when dinosaurs roamed the Earth. Dogs are not allowed on the trails, but are allowed on the dirt fire roads. There are miles of fire roads at this park. They are used by hikers, bicyclists and equestrians. Dogs must be on leash. The state park is about a 35 minute drive from Angel's Camp on Highway 4.

Crab Creek Trail
off Green Valley Road
Arrowbear, CA
909-337-2444
This 2.5 mile moderate rated trail is located in the San Bernardino National Forest. On the trail, you may have to cross Deep Creek. Do not attempt to cross the creek when the water is high as it is too dangerous. Pets are allowed but must be on a 6 foot or less leash. Please clean up after them. The trailhead is located at Forest Road 3N34, west of the Crab Flats Campground. To get there take 330 north and go through Running Springs and Arrowbear to Green Valley Road. Turn left and go about 4 miles to the Crab Flats Campground sign at Forestry (dirt road). Turn left and go about 4.5 miles.

Crabflats Trail
off Green Valley Road
Arrowbear, CA
909-337-2444
This 1.3 mile long moderate rated trail is located in the San Bernardino

National Forest. The trail descends and joins up with the Pacific Crest Trail west of the Holocomb Crossing Trail Camp. Pets are allowed but must be on a 6 foot or less leash. Please clean up after them. The trailhead is located at Forest Road 3N34, west of the Crab Flats Campground. To get there take 330 north and go through Running Springs and Arrowbear to Green Valley Road. Turn left and go about 4 miles to the Crab Flats Campground sign at Forestry (dirt road). Turn left and go about 4.5 miles.

Pacific Coast National Scenic Trail
off Green Valley Road
Arrowbear, CA
909-337-2444
The 40 mile one way moderate rated trail is located in the San Bernardino National Forest. Pets are allowed but must be on a 6 foot or less leash. Please clean up after them. One entry point to this trail is at Forest Road 3N16, which is near the Crab Flats Campground. To get there take 330 north and go through Running Springs and Arrowbear to Green Valley Road. Turn left and go about 4 miles to the Crab Flats Campground sign at Forestry (dirt road). Turn left and go about 4.5 miles.

Lake Lopez Recreation Area
6820 Lopez Drive
Arroyo Grande, CA
805-781-5930
This lake has 22 miles of shoreline and is a popular place for fishing, camping, boating, sailing, water skiing, canoeing, birdwatching and hiking. There are miles of hiking trails, ranging from easy to strenuous. The marina allows dogs on their boat rentals for an extra $10 fee. Dogs must be leashed at all times and people need to clean up after their pets.

Heilmann Regional Park
Cortez Avenue
Atascadero, CA
805-781-5930
This park offers hiking trails, tennis courts and a disc golf course. The Blue Oak trail is 1.3 miles and is an easy multi-use trail. The Jim Green trail is 1.7 miles multi-use trail that is rated moderate. Dogs must be leashed at all times and people need to clean up after their pets.

Auburn State Recreation Area
Highway 49 or Auburn-Foresthill Rd.
Auburn, CA
530-885-4527
Dogs on leash are allowed everywhere except at Lake Clementine. Located in the heart of the gold country, this recreation area covers over 35,000 acres along 40 miles of the North and Middle Forks of the American River. Major recreational uses include hiking, swimming, boating, fishing, camping, mountain biking, gold panning and off-highway motorcycle riding. One of the more popular trails is the Western States National Recreation Trail. It hosts the Tevis Cup Endurance Ride and Western States100 Endurance Run each summer. The park is located south of Interstate 80, stretching from Auburn to Colfax. The main access is from Auburn, either on Highway 49 or the Auburn-Foresthill Road.

Mohave National Preserve
72157 Baker Road
Baker, CA
760-255-8800
nps.gov/moja/
Located in the heart of the Mohave Desert, this 1.6 million acre park offers rose-colored sand dunes, volcanic cinder cones and Joshua tree forests. The park offers hundreds of miles of dirt roads to explore the land in your own 4 wheel drive vehicle. There are many hiking opportunities including the Teutonia Peak Hike. This trail lets you explore a dense Joshua tree forest on the way to a peak on Cima Dome. The 4 mile roundtrip trail is located 10.5 miles south of I-15 on Cima Road. Dogs are allowed on trails and in the campgrounds. They must be leashed except dogs that are being used for hunting. Please clean up after your pet. For more park details and information, including maps, visit the Baker Desert Information Center in Baker. They are open all year from 9am to 5pm.

Beach Park
Oak Street and Rosedale Hwy
Bakersfield, CA

This city park is a good park to take your dog while in Bakersfield. The Kern River Parkway paved exercise trail passes through here and there are picnic tables and open areas. Dogs must be on leash in the park and on the Kern River Parkway trail.

Hart Park
Harrell Highway

Bakersfield, CA
661-868-7000
co.kern.ca.us/parks/hart.htm
Hart Park is 8 miles northeast of Bakersfield on Alfred Harrell Highway. It is on 370 acres along the Kern River. There are hiking trails and fishing. Pets are allowed but must always be on leash.

Kern River County Park
Lake Ming Road
Bakersfield, CA
661-868-7000
This park consists of over 1,000 acres and includes a river, a lake, campgrounds and picnic areas. Hills surround the lake, and the Greenhorn Mountains stretch along the eastern horizon. Please note that Kern River currents are very strong at times and can be extremely dangerous. Do not leave children or dogs unattended at the river. The park is located about10 miles northeast of Bakersfield, off the Alfred Harrell Highway on the Lake Ming Road exit. Dogs must be on leash.

Kern River Parkway
Oak Street and Rosedale Hwy
Bakersfield, CA

The Kern River Parkway trail is a paved biking, walking and running trail along the Kern River. It can be entered at many points, including Beach Park at the address listed here. The trail is about 12 miles long. Dogs on leash are permitted.

The Bluffs - Panorama Park
Panorama Drive
Bakersfield, CA

This walking and jogging trail overlooks the oil wells in the valley below. It stretches a number of miles from Bakersfield along Panorama Drive towards Lake Ming and Hart Park. There is also an exercise trail. Dogs on leash are permitted.

Mojave National Preserve
2701 Barstow Road
Barstow, CA
760-252-6100
nps.gov/moja/index.htm
Dogs on leash are allowed in the park. This park features nearby camping, auto touring, hiking, climbing, and more.

The Way of the Mono Trail
off Road 222
Bass Lake, CA
559-877-2218

350

fs.fed.us/r5/sierra/
On this .5 mile trail you can see authentic Mono Indian grinding holes, plus you will get some great views of Bass Lake. The trail is located next to Bass Lake in the Sierra National Forest. Stop at the Yosemite/Sierra Visitors Bureau at 41969 Highway 41 in Oakhurst for the trail location. The office is open 7 days a week from 8:30am to 5pm.

Yellow Creek Trail
Highway 70
Belden, CA
530-283-0555
This trail is located in the Plumas National Forest and is an easy one way 1.4 mile trail. This day hike ends in a box canyon. Dogs on leash or off-leash but under direct voice control are allowed. Please clean up after your pets. The trailhead is location about 25 miles west of Quincy on Highway 70. It is to the right of the Ely Stamp Mill rest area, across from Belden.

Benicia State Recreation Area
Interstate 780
Benicia, CA
707-648-1911
This park covers 720 acres of marsh, grassy hillsides and rocky beaches along the narrowest portion of the Carquinez Strait. Dogs on leash are allowed. Cyclists, runners, walkers and roller skaters enjoy the park's 2 miles of road and bike paths. Picnicking, bird watching and fishing are also attractions. The recreation area is 1.5 miles west of the outskirts of Benicia on I-780. Cars can enter the park through a toll gate.

Tilden Regional Park
Grizzly Peak Blvd.
Berkeley, CA
510-562-PARK
ebparks.org/parks/tilden.htm
This regional park has over 2,000 acres including Lake Anza. Dogs must be on leash in the parking areas, picnic areas, lawns and developed areas. Your dog can run off-leash in other areas and trails, just make sure they are under voice control and you must carry a leash. Your dog should be under voice control around bicyclists and equestrians - this has been the biggest area of conflict for unleashed dogs. At Lake Anza, dogs are not allowed at swimming pools or swim beaches. But you should be able to find a non-swim beach where your dog can play and swim in the water. The park can be reached via Canon

Drive, Shasta Road, or South Park Drive, all off Grizzly Peak Boulevard in Berkeley.

Bald Mountain Trail
Road #57
Berry Creek, CA
530-534-6500
This trail is located in the Plumas National Forest and is a short one way .5 mile hike through the forest to impressive rock formations. The elevation ranges from 3100 feet to 3270 feet. Big Bald Rock provides great views of Oroville Lake and the Sacramento Valley. The trail is usually open for hiking from February to December, weather permitting. Dogs on leash or off-leash but under direct voice control are allowed. Please clean up after your pets. To get there from Oroville, take Highway 162 east. Drive for about 17-18 miles and turn right onto Bald Rock Road. Drive for about 5.8 on the gravel road. Then turn left at the Big Bald Rock turn-off and go .1 miles.

Roxbury Park
471 S. Roxbury Dr.
Beverly Hills, CA
310-285-2537
This city park offers gently rolling green hills and shady areas. The park has large children's playgrounds, tennis courts and other sports courts. Dogs are allowed but must be on a 6 foot or less leash and people are required to clean up after their pets.

Alpine Pedal Path
Hwy 38
Big Bear Lake, CA
This path is mostly paved and is about a 4-5 mile round trip. Throughout most of the path, there are various access points to the lake and various beaches. The beginning of the path is located off of the Stanfield Cutoff (bridge over Big Bear Lake, close to the village). For easier access, (going away from the village), take the Stanfield Cutoff to the other side of the lake and turn left onto Hwy 38. In about 1/4 - 1/2 mile, parking will be on the left.

Cougar Crest Trail
Highway 38
Big Bear Lake, CA
909-866-3437
Within the San Bernardino National Forest this trail is well known to visitors and residents alike. Leashed dogs are allowed

throughout the San Bernardino Forest Trails in Big Bear. The trailhead is located on Highway 38 west of Big Bear. There is parking at the trailhead. The trail heads two miles up and connects to the Pacific Crest Trail on which you can extend your hike significantly should you desire. The trail offers spectacular views of the lake valley. The Cougar Crest Trail is strenuous and please bring enough water for dogs and people.

Grout Bay Trail
Hwy 38
Big Bear Lake, CA
909-866-3437
This hiking trail is about 3-5 miles each way and is rated easy to moderate. To get there from the village, head west on Hwy 18. Take Hwy 38 to the right, towards the northwest corner of the lake. The trail begins by the Grout Bay Picnic Area.

Pine Knot Trail
Tulip Lane
Big Bear Lake, CA
909-866-3437
This hiking trail is about 3 miles each way and is rated moderate to difficult. To get there from the village, head west on Hwy 18 and turn left onto Tulip Lane. The trail begins by the Alpine Glen Picnic Area. Remember, to park here, you'll need a Forest Day Pass. Check with your hotel or some of the stores in the village for info on where to purchase this pass.

Woodland Trail / Nature Walk
Hwy 38
Big Bear Lake, CA
909-866-3437
This is a nature trail with about 20 informational stops. Pick up one of the maps and follow the self-guided 1.5 mile nature walk. This is rated as an easy loop. To get there, (going away from the village), take the Stanfield Cutoff to the other side of the lake and turn left onto Hwy 38. In about 1/2 mile, parking will be on the right.

Big Pine Canyon Trails
Glacier Lodge Road
Big Pine, CA
760-873-2500
fs.fed.us/r5/inyo
These trails start and an elevation of 7,800 feet and go up to 12,400 feet. There are about 15 miles of trails. The trails lead into the dog-friendly John Muir Wilderness. One of the closest lakes, Willow Lake, is a 4

mile hike from the trailhead. At the campgrounds pets must be on a 6 foot or less leash. While hiking on the trails, pets must be on leash or under voice command at all times. Dogs are also allowed in the lake. Please clean up after your pets. This trail is located in the Inyo National Forest. To get there from Highway 395, exit in Big Pine and go 11 miles west on Glacier Lodge Road.

John Muir Wilderness Trails
Glacier Lodge Road
Big Pine, CA
760-873-2500
fs.fed.us/r5/inyo
The wilderness trails are located in the Inyo National Forest and can be accessed from many points, including the Big Pine Canyon Trails near Big Pine. See our listing for Big Pine Creek Canyon Trail. From these trailheads, there are about 9 miles of hiking trails and several campgrounds. To get there from Highway 395, exit in Big Pine and go 11 miles west on Glacier Lodge Road.

Los Padres National Forest
Big Sur Station #1
Big Sur, CA
831-385-5434
r5.fs.fed.us/lospadres/
While dogs are not allowed in the state park in Big Sur, they are welcome in the adjacent Los Padres National Forest. Dogs should be on leash. One of the most popular trails is the Pine Ridge Trail. This trail is miles long and goes through the Los Padres National Forest to the dog-friendly Ventana Wilderness. To get there, take Highway 1 south, about 25-30 miles south of Carmel. Park at the Big Sur Station for a minimal fee. From the Big Sur Station in Big Sur, you can head out onto the Pine Ridge Trail. The Los Padres National Forest actually stretches over 200 miles from the Carmel Valley all the way down to Los Angeles County. For maps and more information about the trails, contact the Monterey Ranger District at 831-385-5434 or at the Forest Headquarters in Goleta at 805-968-6640.

Hilton Lakes Trail
Rock Creek Canyon Rd.
Bishop, CA
760-873-2500
fs.fed.us/r5/inyo
This trail is located in the Inyo National Forest. It starts at an elevation of 9,600 feet and goes up to 10,720 feet over 5.25 miles. From

the trailhead you can hike to several lakes. At the campgrounds pets must be on a 6 foot or less leash. While hiking on the trails, pets must be on leash or under voice command at all times. Please clean up after your pets. To get there from Highway 395, exit at Tom's Place. Go up Rock Creek Canyon Road. The trail starts before the Rock Creek Pack Station on the road to Mosquito Flat.

Inyo National Forest
351 Pacu Lane, Suite 200
Bishop, CA
760-873-2400
fs.fed.us/r5/inyo/
This national forest covers thousands of acres of land ranging in elevations up to 14,246 feet in the White Mountain Range which is located near Mt. Whitney. Please see our listings in the Sierra Nevada region for dog-friendly hikes and/or campgrounds.

Little Lakes Trail
Rock Creek Canyon Rd.
Bishop, CA
760-873-2500
fs.fed.us/r5/inyo
This trail is located in the Inyo National Forest. It starts at an elevation of 10,300 feet and the first 1.5 miles of the trail goes up to 10,440 to Heart Lake. From there you can go several more miles up to elevations around 11,000 feet. At the campgrounds pets must be on a 6 foot or less leash. While hiking on the trails, pets must be on leash or under voice command at all times. Please clean up after your pets. To get there from Highway 395, exit at Tom's Place. Go up Rock Creek Canyon Road to the end, about 10 miles to the Mosquito Flat parking.

Plumas-Eureka State Park
Johnsonville Road
Blairsden, CA
530-836-2380
Dogs are allowed on one trail which is called the Grass Lake Trail. This 3.8 mile trail climbs steadily to the Pacific Crest Trail passing several lakes. Pets must be on leash and please clean up after them. The trailhead is at the Jamison Mine. To get there take Johnsonville Road (County Road A14) off Highway 89 in Graeagle. Go about 4.5 miles to the unimproved Jamison Mine Road. There should be a sign on the left for the Jamison Mine/Grass Lake Trail. Continue another 1.5 miles to the parking area.

Westside Regional Park
2400 Westshore Road
Bodega Bay, CA
707-565-2041
Located on Bodega Bay, this park is a popular spot for fishing. Dogs are allowed but must be on a 6 foot or less leash and proof of a rabies vaccination is required. To get there from Highway 1, take Eastshore Road.

Anza-Borrego Desert State Park
Highway 78
Borrego Springs, CA
760-767-5311
Dogs are not allowed on any trails. They are allowed in day use areas and on over 500 miles of dirt roads. The roads can be used by cars but there is usually not too much traffic. Pets must be leashed and please clean up after them. The park is located about a 2 hour drive from San Diego, Riverside and Palm Springs off Highways S22 and 78.

Lake San Antonio
2610 San Antonio Road
Bradley, CA
805-472-2311
lakesanantonio.net/
This park offers a variety of activities including boating, swimming, fishing and miles of hiking trails. Dogs are allowed on the trails and in the water. This park also offers dog-friendly campgrounds. Pets need to be leashed and please clean up after them. There is a $6 day use fee per vehicle.

Lakeshore Trail
off La Porte Road
Brownsville, CA
This trail is located in the Plumas National Forest and is an easy but long 13.5 mile hike around the Little Grass Valley Reservoir. The trail is at a 5,100 foot elevation and is heavily used by hikers. In some areas the trail becomes a walk along the beach. Dogs on leash are allowed on the trail and in the water. The trail is usually open for hiking from early June to early September, weather permitting. Please clean up after your pets. To get there from Oroville, take Highway 162 east. Drive for about 7 miles and then turn right onto Forbestown Road (Challenge Cut-Off). Drive 16.6 miles and then turn left on La Porte Road. Go 27.4 miles and then make a right at Road #57 (South Fork Rec Area).

Gold Lake Trail

Forest Road 24N29X
Bucks Lake, CA
530-283-0555
This trail is located in the Plumas
National Forest and is an easy one
way 1.5 mile trail. This trail provides
access to the Bucks Lake
Wilderness and the Pacific Crest
Trail. At Bucks Lake swimming and
fishing are popular activities. Dogs
on leash or off-leash but under direct
voice control are allowed. Dogs are
allowed on the trails and in the water.
Please clean up after your pets. To
get there from Quincy, go west 9.2
miles on Bucks Lake Road. Turn
right on a gravel road, 24N29X
(Silver Lake sign). Go 6.4 miles to
the lake and the Silver Lake
Campground. The trail begins at the
campground.

Ahmanson Ranch Park
26135 Mureau Road
Calabasas, CA
818-878-4225
smmc.ca.gov/
This park is part of the Santa Monica
Mountains Conservancy and allows
leashed dogs on the trails. Please
clean up after your pets. No hunting
is allowed in the park. In the past,
some movies have been filmed at
this ranch, including Gone With The
Wind. The easiest access to the
trails is at the north end of Las
Virgenes Road. In early 2004 there
are plans to having a parking area at
the end of Victory Blvd. in Woodland
Hills.

Los Gatos Creek Park
Dell Avenue
Campbell, CA
408-356-2729
This 80 acre park has a small lake, a
couple of ponds, picnic benches,
barbecues and restroom facilities.
The Campbell-Los Gatos Creek Trail
runs through the park which goes to
the Los Gatos Vasona Park and
downtown Los Gatos. Leashed dogs
are welcome at this park and on the
Creek Trail.

Los Gatos Creek Trail
various-see comments
Campbell, CA
408-356-2729
The Los Gatos Creek Trail is about 7
miles long each way. Most of it is
paved until you enter the path at
downtown Los Gatos heading
towards the Lexington Reservoir
County Park. You can gain access to
the trail at numerous points. Some of
the popular starting sites are at the
Campbell Park in Campbell

(Campbell Ave & Gilman Ave), Los
Gatos Park in Campbell (Dell Ave &
Hacienda Ave), Vasona Lake Park
in Los Gatos (Blossom Hill Rd
between Highway 17 & University
Ave), and downtown Los Gatos
(Main Street & Maple Ln-near Hwy
17).

Rebel Ridge Trail
Marysville Road
Camptonville, CA
530-288-3231
This 1.6 mile moderate rated trail is
open all year. Pets must be either
leashed or off-leash but under direct
voice control. Please clean up after
your pets. It is located in the Tahoe
National Forest, on Marysville
Road, .6 miles west of Highway 49.

Garland Ranch Regional Park
Carmel Valley Rd.
Carmel Valley, CA
831-659-4488
mprpd.org/parks/garland.html
This 4,500 acre regional park offers
about 5 to 6 miles of dirt single-
track and fire road trails. The trail
offers a variety of landscapes, with
elevations ranging from 200 to 2000
feet. If you are looking for some
exercise in addition to the beaches,
this is the spot. Dogs must be on a
7 foot or less leash. They can also
be under direct voice control which
is defined by park management as
you having close visual contact of
your dog, not letting them run far
ahead or behind you, and having a
dog that listens to your commands.
Dogs are not allowed to bother any
wildlife, other people or other dogs.
People who violate this regulation
may be citied and lose access
priviledges. Please also clean up
after your pet. The park is located
8.6 miles east of Highway 1 on
Carmel Valley Road.

Bidwell Park
Highway 99
Chico, CA
530-895-4972
This park exceeds 3,600 acres,
making it the third largest municipal
park in the United States. The park
is comprised of three major
sections: Lower Park, Middle Park
and Upper Park. Lower Park has
children's playgrounds, natural
swimming areas, and vehicle-free
roads for runners, cyclists,
rollerbladers and walkers. Middle
Park features ball-playing fields,
picnic areas, the "World of Trees"
walk, which is accessible to the
physically challenged, and the

park's environmental and
informational headquarters. Upper
Park remains relatively untouched
with majestic canyons overlooking
Big Chico Creek, which contains
some of the most spectacular
swimming areas in Northern
California. Dogs on leash are
allowed. Please clean up after them.

Red Hills Area Hiking
Red Hills Road
Chinese Camp, CA
916-985-4474
ca.blm.gov/folsom/redhills.html
This 7,000 acres of public land has
just over 17 miles of trails with
various loops. Elevations vary
between 750 and 1,750 feet. This is
a popular area for hunting, hiking,
horseback riding and wildflower
viewing. Leashed dogs are welcome.
Please clean up after your dog.
There are no park fees. The land is
located near Highways 49 and 120.
From Sonora, take Highway 49 south
15 miles to Chinese Camp. Then
drive south on Red Hills Road for .5
miles.

Rusch Community Park and Gardens
Antelope Road & Auburn Blvd
Citrus Heights, CA

This is a nice city park with
walkways, bridges and views plus a
botanical garden to explore. The
botanical garden is accessed from
Antelope Rd and Rosswood. Dogs
must be on leash at all times.

Sierra National Forest
1600 Tollhouse Road
Clovis, CA
559-297-0706
r5.fs.fed.us/sierra/
The dog-friendly Sierra National
Forest, just south of Yosemite,
consists of 1.3 million acres. Your
leashed dog is allowed in this forest
and on over 1,000 miles of trails.
Just make sure you stay within the
Sierra National Forest and do not
accidentally cross over to the
bordering National Parks which don't
allow dogs on hiking trails. The
Sierra National Forest trails offer
gentle meadows, pristine lakes and
streams, and rugged passes in the
forest's five wilderness areas. A
Wilderness Visitor Permit is required
if you plan on hiking into one of the
five wilderness areas. In the Sierra
National Forest, one of the more
popular trails is the Lewis Creek
National Recreation Trail. This 3.7
mile hike makes a great day hike as
it offers scenic views of waterfalls

like the Corlieu and Red Rock Falls. The trail gains 880 feet in elevation from south to north. There are three trailheads along the Lewis Creek Trail. From Oakhurst, take Highway 41 north towards Yosemite National Park. The southernmost trailhead, located 7 miles from Oakhurst, is about 0.5 mile off the highway along the Cedar Valley Road. The middle trailhead is about 3 miles further along Highway 41, at a large turnout just beyond the snow chain station. The northernmost trailhead is just off Highway 41 along the Sugar Pine Road, 500 feet past the bridge on the south side of the road.

Stevens Trail
North Canyon Way
Colfax, CA
916-985-4474
This 4.5 mile trail is a popular year-round hiking, mountain biking and horseback riding trail which follows the northwestern slope of the North Fork of the American River. The trail offers a gentle slope that is suitable for novice hikers. Along the trail you can enjoy great views of the river, pass by several mine shafts, and see the China Wall built by Chinese laborers during the Gold Rush era in the 1850s. Please stay away from the mines because they are extremely dangerous and unstable. In April and May there should be a nice wildflower display. Leashed dogs are welcome. Please clean up after your dog. To get there from Sacramento, head east on Highway 80 towards Colfax. Take the North Canyon Way exit. Take this road past the Colfax cemetery to the trailhead. On weekends and in high use season, parking may be very limited.

Dave Moore Nature Area
Highway 49
Coloma, CA
916-985-4474
ca.blm.gov/folsom/dmna.html
This nature area features a one mile loop and about half of the trail is wheelchair, walker and stroller accessible. It starts at the parking lot and goes down to the South Fork of the American River and back, passing through several types of habitat. Located in the heart of the historic Gold Rush area, the trail is lined with remnants from about 150 years ago when Chinese laborers channeled the creek water by hand with a pick and shovel to find gold. Leashed dogs are welcome. Please clean up after your dog. To get there

from Sacramento, take Highway 50 east towards Placerville. In Shingle Springs, take the Ponderosa Road exit and go over the freeway bridge to the stop sign (located just north of Highway 50). Turn right onto North Shingles Road and go 3 miles. Turn left at the Y in the road onto Lotus Road. Continue for 5 miles heading north. At Highway 49 turn left and cross the bridge at the river. Continue for about 1 mile along Highway 49. Turn left at the cobblestone wall. There are no park fees, but donations are accepted.

Colusa National Wildlife Refuge
Hwy 20 at Ohair Road
Colusa, CA
530-934-2801
This 4,507 acre refuge consists mostly of seasonal wetlands, uplands, restored/maintained habitats for migratory birds and endangered species, and the preservation/maintenance of as much of the indigenous flora and fauna as possible. The area is popular for wildlife viewing, nature photography, hiking, and hunting. There is a 3 mile graveled auto tour that wanders through freshwater wetlands, a 1 mile Discovery Trail walk along dense riparian marshes, and it is home to more than 200,000 ducks and 50,000 geese every winter. Dogs are allowed and they may go just about anywhere their human companions can go. Dogs must be kept under control, leashed, and cleaned up after at all times.

Bayshore Bikeway
Silver Strand Blvd.
Coronado, CA
If you are in Coronado and really want to stretch your legs, you can go for a run or walk on the Bayshore Bikeway. The path is about 6 miles long each way. It starts by the Glorietta Bay Park and continues south along Silver Strand Blvd. There's not too much shade along this path, so your pup might not want to go on a hot day. Dogs need to be leashed.

Centennial & Tidelands Parks
Orange Ave and First St.
Coronado, CA
We have combined these two parks because there is a scenic 1/2 - 1 mile path between them. Both of these parks provide nice photo opportunities of downtown San Diego and the San Diego Bay. Dogs must be leashed.

Talbert Nature Preserve
Victoria Street
Costa Mesa, CA
949-923-2250
ocparks.com/Talbert/
This 180 acre park offers hiking trails. Dogs on a 6 foot or less leash are allowed and please clean up after them.

Redwood National and State Parks
1111 Second Street
Crescent City, CA
707-464-6101
nps.gov/redw/
The National and State Parks do not allow dogs on any trails but some of the beaches and campgrounds welcome dogs. Pets are allowed on Crescent Beach, Gold Bluffs Beach and the Freshwater Spit Lagoon. The campgrounds that allow pets include Jedediah Smith Redwoods State Park campground, Prairie Creek Redwoods State Park campground and Gold Bluffs Beach campground. One way to see a number of redwood groves with dogs is to take the Newton B. Drury Scenic Bypass off of Highway 101. You may see large elk grazing near the parking lots as you drive through the park. Dogs are also allowed to walk along some gravel roads. Two roads that can be walked along with dog include Cal Barrel Road (3 miles long) and Howland Hill Rd (6 miles long). These roads will usually not be too crowded with cars except at the busiest times. Old growth Redwood groves line these gravel roads. Pets must be leashed and attended at all times and please clean up after them.

Fremont Older Preserve
Prospect Road
Cupertino, CA
650-691-1200
openspace.org/OLDER.html
This preserve offers excellent views of the Santa Clara Valley. There are about 9 miles of trails. Dogs must be leashed. One of the popular hikes starts at Prospect Road, goes to Hunter's Point and then continues to Seven Springs Loop. On a hot day, you may want to bring some water with you. Here are directions to the park: From Hwy 280, take DeAnza Blvd south towards Saratoga. After crossing Hwy 85, you will soon come to Prospect Road. Turn right onto Prospect. Go about 1.5 miles on Prospect. Before Prospect Road ends, turn left onto a one lane road (should be signs to Fremont Older).

There is parking for approximately 15 cars.

Community Park
1405 F Street
Davis, CA
Dogs on leash are permitted in this and most parks in Davis. The park is 28 acres in size.

Cuyamaca Ranch State Park
12551 Highway 79
Descanso, CA
760-765-0755
cuyamaca.statepark.org
Leashed dogs are allowed on the paved Cuyamaca Peak Fire Road and the Los Caballos/Stonewall Mine Road trails. Bicycles and horseback riders are also allowed on these trails. Dogs are not allowed on any other trails in the park. The Cuyamaca Peak Fire Road is approximately 3.5 miles and goes all the way to the top of the park. The Cuyamaca Peak Fire Road begins at Hwy 79 about 1/4 mi south of the Paso Picacho Campground (the road is also accessible from the campground).

North Yuba Trail
Highway 49
Downieville, CA
530-288-3231
This 7.5 mile moderate rated trail is located in the Tahoe National Forest. Pets must be either leashed or off-leash but under direct voice control. Please clean up after your pets. The trail is located on Highway 49, 7.5 miles west of Downieville at the Rocky Rest Campground.

El Segundo Recreation Park
Grande Ave at Eucalyptus Dr
El Segundo, CA
This park allows dogs during all hours that the park is open, but they must be on leash at all times. Please clean up after your dogs, so the city continues to allow their presence. This park is bounded by the following streets: North by E. Pine St, South by Grande Ave, West by Eucalyptus Dr. and East by Penn St. Thanks to one of our readers for recommending this park.

Beilenson Park Lake Balboa
6300 Balboa Blvd
Encino, CA
818-756-9743
This park consists of large grass fields, sports fields and a nice lake. There is an approximate 1 mile walk around the lake perimeter. You and your leashed pup are welcome to explore this 70+ acre park. To get there, take the Balboa Blvd exit from Hwy 101. Head north on Balboa.

San Vicente Mountain Park
17500 Mulholland Drive
Encino, CA
310-589-3200
This 10.2 acre park is a historical military site, complete with a radar tower that features 360 degree spectacular views, making it a great place for sunsets. There are self-guided interpretive displays, restrooms, drinking water, picnic tables, and a large network of multi-use trails. The park is located about a 10 minute walk along a dirt road from the parking area. Dogs are allowed at this park; they must be leashed, under their owner's immediate control, and cleaned up after at all times.

San Pasqual Battlefield State Historical Park
15808 San Pasqual Valley Road
Escondido, CA
760-737-2201
This historic park honors the soldiers who fought here and stands as a reminder of the passions that can drive countries to bloodshed, and not as a monument to the Mexican-American war. There are interpretive exhibits/programs, nature and hiking trails, picnic areas, restrooms, and a visitor center. The park is only open on Saturday and Sunday, but during the week you can park on the street and walk into the park. Dogs of all sizes are allowed. Dogs must be on no more than a 6 foot leash, and leashed and cleaned up after at all times. Dogs are allowed throughout the park and on the trails.

Fort Humboldt State Historic Park
3431 Fort Avenue
Eureka, CA
707-445-6567
This old military post was established in 1853 to assist in resolving conflicts between Native Americans and settlers who were searching for gold. Dogs are not allowed inside any buildings but they can walk through the outdoor exhibits and view historic logging equipment. There is also a grassy bluff area where you can walk your dog. Pets must be on leash and please clean up after them. The park is located south of Eureka off Highway 101. Go east on Highland Avenue for one block.

Six Rivers National Forest
1330 Bayshore Way
Eureka, CA
707-442-1721
fs.fed.us/r5/sixrivers/
This national forest covers almost 1 million acres of land which ranges in elevation from sea level to almost 7,000 feet. Please see our listings in this region for dog-friendly hikes and/or campgrounds.

Deer Park
Porteous Avenue
Fairfax, CA
415-499-6387
Leashed dogs are allowed at this park including the nature trails. The 54 acre park is located in a wooded setting.

Hanna Flat Trail
Rim of the World Drive
Fawnskin, CA
909-337-2444
This 9 mile round trip moderate rated trail is located in the San Bernardino National Forest. Pets on leash are allowed and please clean up after them. This trail is closed every year from November 1 to April 1 due to the bald eagle wintering habitat. To get there take Highway 18 to Big Bear Lake Dam. Go straight, do not cross over the dam. Highway 18 becomes Highway 38. Go the Fawnskin Fire Station and turn left onto the Rim of the World Drive. Go about 2.5 miles on a dirt road to the campsite and trailhead.

Henry Cowell State Park
Highway 9
Felton, CA
831-335-4598
Dogs are allowed in the picnic area, the campground, and on Pipeline Road, Graham Hill Trail, and Meadow Trail. They are not allowed on any other trails or interior roads. Dogs must be leashed. The park is near Felton on Highway 9 in the Santa Cruz Mountains. Traveling from San Jose to the main entrance: Take Highway 17 towards Santa Cruz. After you go over the mountains, turn right on Mt. Hermon Road. Follow Mt. Hermon road until it ends at Graham Hill Road. Turn right, and go to the next stop light (Highway 9). Turn left on Highway 9 and go through downtown Felton. The park entrance will be a half mile down on your left. You can park outside and walk a half mile into the park, or you can drive in and pay a

fee.

Folsom Lake State Recreation Area
various (see comments)
Folsom, CA
916-988-0205
This popular lake and recreation area is located in the Sierra Foothills. The Folsom Lake State Rec Area is approximately 18,000 acres, of which, 45% is land. Leashed dogs are allowed almost everywhere in this park except on the main beaches (there will be signs posted). But there are many other non-main beaches all around Folsom Lake where your dog is welcome. There are about 80 miles of dog-friendly trails in this park. This park is also adjacent to the American River Parkway, a 32 mile paved and dirt path, which stretches from Folsom Lake to downtown Sacramento. Folsom Lake has various entry points and can be reached via Hwy 80 or Hwy 50. It is located about 25 miles east of Sacramento. From Hwy 80, exit Douglas Blvd in Roseville and head east. From Hwy 50, exit Folsom Blvd. and head north. There is a minimal day use fee.

Big Trees Loop
Mosquito Ridge Road
Foresthill, CA
530-367-2224
This .5 mile easy trail is located in the Tahoe National Forest and is a popular interpretive trail. The trail is accessible when the road is open, generally from late May to early November. Pets on leash are allowed and please clean up after them. To get there from Foresthill, take Mosquito Ridge Road 24 miles to Road 16.

French Meadows Reservoir
Mosquito Ridge Road
Foresthill, CA
530-367-2224
Activities at this reservoir include fishing, boating, swimming, picnicking, hiking, and viewing scenery. Dogs are allowed in the water. Pets must be either leashed or off-leash but under direct voice control. Please clean up after your pets. The reservoir is located in the Tahoe National Forest, 36 miles east of Foresthill on Mosquito Ridge Road.

Little Bald Mountain Trail
Foresthill Divide Road
Foresthill, CA
530-367-2224
This trail is located in the Tahoe

National Forest and is a 3.39 mile moderate rated trail. The trail is open from May to November, weather permitting. Pets must be either leashed or off-leash but under direct voice control. Please clean up after your pets. To get there, go 28 miles from Foresthill on Foresthill Divide Road to Robinson Flat and park in the day use area.

Sugar Pine Trail
Foresthill Divide Road
Foresthill, CA
530-367-2224
This popular 3.5 mile easy trail goes around Sugar Pine Reservoir. Dogs are allowed on the trail and in the water on non-designated swim beaches. Pets must be either leashed or off-leash but under direct voice control. Please clean up after your pets. The primary season for this trail is usually from May to October. This trail is located in the Tahoe National Forest. To get there from Foresthill, go 18 miles northeast on Foresthill Divide Road.

Kelsey Trail
Scott River Road
Fort Jones, CA
530-468-5351
The historic Kelsey Trail offers excellent opportunities for scenic day hikes or longer trips into the Marble Mountain Wilderness. The trail is located in the Klamath National Forest and begins at the Bridge Flat Campground. The campground is located on the Scott River approximately 17 miles from Fort Jones towards the town of Scott Bar, at a 2,000 foot elevation. Dogs should be on leash.

Coyote Hills Regional Park
Patterson Ranch Rd.
Fremont, CA
510-562-PARK
ebparks.org/parks/coyote.htm
This regional park has Ohlone Indian shellmound sites with fascinating archaeological resources. This Indian site can be viewed from the Chochenyo Trail. For a longer hike, try the 3.5 mile long BayView bike trail. There are many other numerous trails that wind through the park which offer scenic vistas of the San Francisco Bay. Dogs must be on leash. They are not allowed in the seasonal wetlands, marshes, or the Visitor Center lawn area. But there are plenty of dog-friendly trails around to satisfy you and your pup. Coyote Hills is at the west end of Patterson

Ranch Road/ Commerce Drive in Fremont. From I-880, take Highway 84 west, exit at Paseo Padre Parkway and drive north. Turn left on Patterson Ranch Road (parking fee).

Sunol Regional Wilderness
Geary Rd.
Fremont, CA
510-562-PARK
ebparks.org/parks/sunol.htm
This park is home to the Ohlone Wilderness Trail and Little Yosemite. The Wilderness Trail is at least 7 miles long in each direction. It spans the length of the park and connects up to the Mission Peak Regional Preserve. Hikers who cross into the San Francisco Water Department lands that connect Mission Peak Regional Preserve, Sunol, Ohlone Regional Wilderness and Del Valle Regional Park must carry an Ohlone Wilderness Trail map/permit. Little Yosemite is a scenic gorge on the Alameda Creek. It is open to the public through a lease agreement with the San Francisco Water Department, who owns the property. The Canyon View Trail is about 1.5 miles each way and leads into Little Yosemite. There are approximately 6-7 other popular trails ranging from 1.2 miles to over 7 miles. Dogs must be on leash in the parking areas, picnic areas, lawns and developed areas. Your dog can run off-leash on most of the trails, just make sure they are under voice control and you must carry a leash. Check with the ranger as to which trails require your dog to be leashed. To get there from the Fremont area, drive north on I-680 and exit at Calaveras Road. Turn right on Calaveras and proceed to Geary Road, which leads directly into the park.

Kearny Park
7160 W. Kearney Blvd
Fresno, CA
559-441-0862
This park consists of over 220 green acres with a variety of trees and plants. The park features several playgrounds, picnic tables, soccer fields, and the Kearny Mansion Museum. The Kearney Mansion was the home of M. Theo Kearney. It was constructed in the early 1900s. Kearny was a key Fresno land developer and agricultural leader. He was known as the "Raisin King of California" and formed the California Raisin Growers' Association. When he passed away in 1906, he donated his entire 5000 acre estate to the University of California. Thus 220

acres were developed into Kearny Park. Dogs on leash are allowed at the park, but not in the museum. The park is located about 7 miles west of Fresno off Kearny Road.

Roeding Park
W. Olive Avenue
Fresno, CA
559-498-1551
This large city park has public tennis courts, an exercise course, barbecue and picnic areas, and playgrounds. Leashed dogs are allowed. There is a minimal fee for parking. The park entrance is on W. Olive Avenue by Hwy 99.

Woodward Park
E. Audubon Drive
Fresno, CA
Leashed dogs are allowed at this regional park. There are over 280 acres for you and your pup to explore. This park has some small hills, lakes and streams. There is also a fenced off-leash area in the park. It is located on the north side of Fresno, near Hwy 41. Take Hwy 41, exit N. Friant Rd to the right. Turn left onto Audubon and the park will be on the right.

Benbow Lake State Recreation Area
1600 Highway 101
Garberville, CA
707-923-3238
Leashed dogs are allowed. The park consists of about 1,200 acres with campsites and a large day-use picnic area. Hiking, picnicking and camping are popular summer time activities, while salmon and steelhead fishing are popular in the winter.

Myrtle Creek Trail
Highway 199
Gasquet, CA
707-442-1721
This trail is located in the Smith River National Recreation Area and is part of the Six Rivers National Forest. The trail is an easy 1 mile interpretive hiking path. The elevations range from 250 to 500 feet. From this trail you can also access the Smith River. Pets on leash are allowed and please clean up after them. The trail is located 8 miles west of Gasquet at Milepost 7.0. Park on the south (river) side of the highway. Use caution when crossing Highway 199 to reach the trailhead.

Jack London State Historic Park
2400 London Ranch Road
Glen Ellen, CA
707-938-5216

This park is a memorial to the famous writer and adventurer Jack London. He lived here from 1905 until his death in 1916. Dogs on leash are allowed around the ranch and historic buildings, but not inside. Pets are also allowed on the Wolf House Trail which is a 1.2 mile round trip trail. Please clean up after your pet. The park is located about 20 minutes north of Sonoma.

Sonoma Valley Regional Park
13630 Sonoma Highway
Glen Ellen, CA
707-565-2041
This 162 acre park offers both paved and dirt trails which are used for hiking, bicycling and horseback riding. Dogs are allowed but must be on a 6 foot or less leash. The Elizabeth Anne Perrone Dog Park is also located within this park and allows dogs to run leash-free within the one acre. There is a $3 parking fee.

Lake Tahoe State Park/Spooner Lake
Hwy 28
Glenbrook, NV
775-831-0494
state.nv.us/stparks/lt.htm
This hiking trail is known as the world famous "Flume Trail". This is one of the most beautiful places in the world to mountain bike. But as a hiker, you'll hardly notice the bicyclists because this trail is so long and a good portion of the path consists of race wide fire trails. It starts at Spooner Lake and the entire loop of the Flume Trail is about 25 miles which can satisfy even the most avid hiker. For a shorter hike, try the trail that loops around Spooner Lake. For a longer 10-12 mile out and back hike, start at Spooner Lake and hike up to Marlette Lake. Although there is a rise in elevation, it's not a rock climbing path as most of this is a fire road trail. Even if you are used to hiking 10 miles, don't forget about the altitude which will make you tired quicker. Also, do not forget to bring enough water and food. To get to the start of the trail, from South Lake Tahoe, take Hwy 50 towards Nevada (north). Then turn left onto Hwy 28. Follow the signs to the Lake Tahoe State Park and Spooner Lake. Parking for Spooner Lake is on the right. There is a parking fee of approx. $5-7. This includes an extra fee for the pup - but well worth it. From South Lake Tahoe, it's about a 25-30 minute

drive to Spooner Lake. Dogs must be leashed in the park.

Deukemjian Wilderness Park
5142 Dunsmore Avenue
Glendale, CA
818-548-2000
Sitting on 700 acres of chaparral-covered slopes at the northernmost part of the city, this park has a variety of multi-use trails available for first time and experienced hikers, a year round stream, and great views. Dogs are allowed throughout the park and on the trails. Dogs must be under their owner's immediate control, leashed, and cleaned up after at all times.

Grassy Lake Trail
County Road 519
Graeagle, CA
530-836-2575
This trail is located in the Plumas National Forest and is an easy one way .8 mile trail. This trail starts at an elevation of 6,320 feet and goes past Grassy Lake. It then crosses Gray Eagle Creek to join with the Long Lake Trail. If you continue on this trail, you can hike another 3 miles one way on a moderate rated trail. Long Lake Trail gradually climbs to Long Lake. Dogs on leash or off-leash but under direct voice control are allowed. Dogs are allowed on the trails and in the water. Please clean up after your pets. The trailhead is located in the Lakes Basin Campground. The campground is located 9 miles southwest of Graeagle on County Road 519.

O'Melveny Park
Orozco Street
Granada Hills, CA

This 600+ acre park has a nice variety of single track and fire road hiking trails. The park is popular with bird watchers, mountain bikers, hikers and leashed dogs. The best way to get there is from Hwy 118. Take the Balboa Blvd. exit and head north. Go about 1.5 to 2 miles and turn left onto Orozco. Take this road to the park.

Garin and Dry Creek Regional Parks
Garin Ave
Hayward, CA
ebparks.org/parks/garin.htm
There are over 3,000 acres of land between these two parks. Combined, these parks have over 20 miles of unpaved trails. You'll also find several creeks that run through the parks. To get there from Mission

Blvd, take Garin Rd to the park entrance. There is a minimal fee for parking.

Huntington Central Park
Golden West Street
Huntington Beach, CA
949-960-8847
This city park is over 350 acres with six miles of trails. There are expansive lawns, lots of trees and two lakes. Huntington Lake is by Inlet Drive between Golden West and Edwards Streets and next to Alice's Breakfast in the Park Restaurant. Talbert Lake is off Golden West near Slater Ave and Gothard St. The Huntington Dog Park is located within this park.

Humber Park
Fern Valley Road
Idyllwild, CA
909-659-2117
The Devil's Slide Trail begins at this park. It is rated as a moderately difficult trail. The trail goes for about 6 miles and there is about a 3,000 foot elevation gain. Day passes are required. To get there, take Highway 243 to North Circle Drive. Turn right onto South Circle Drive, and then left to Fern Valley Road. Follow the signs to Humber Park.

Idyllwild Park Nature Center
Highway 243
Idyllwild, CA
909-659-3850
idyllwildnaturecenter.net/
This park offers 5 1/2 miles of hiking trails. Most of the trails are rated as easy, with the exception of one steep trail. Dogs are allowed, but need to be leashed. Your dog will also need to have a current rabies identification tag. The day use fees are $2 per person, $2 per dog and $1 per child. The park is located on Highway 243, about one mile northwest of Idyllwild.

Tijuana River National Estuarine Research Reserve
301 Caspian Way
Imperial Beach, CA
619-575-3613
This research center works to monitor, improve, and educate about the estuaries and watersheds. The visitor center provides maps for trails and picnic areas where dogs are allowed. Dogs are allowed for no additional fee, they must be under their owner's control at all times, and be leashed and cleaned up after. Dogs are not allowed on the beach.

Manzanar National Historic Site

P.O. Box 426
Independence, CA
760-878-2932
nps.gov/manz/
This site was one of ten camps where Japanese and Japanese American citizens were interned during World War II. It is located at the base of the Sierra Nevada mountains and has been identified as the best preserved camp. Dogs are allowed at the site, on the self-guided walking tour which takes about 1-2 hours, and on the 3.2 mile self-guided auto tour. A tour description and map is available at the camp entrance. Pets must be on leash and please clean up after them. The park is open all year and there is no parking fee. It is located off Highway 395, 12 miles north of Lone Pine and 5 miles south of Independence.

Lake Cahuilla Recreation Area
Avenue 58
Indio, CA
760-564-4712
Come here to sit by the lake, walk around it or on one of the many trails at this 710 acre park. There are also 50 campsites at the park. The park is located in Indio, 4 miles southeast of La Quinta. To get there, take Interstate 10 to Washington St., south on Washington 3 miles to Highway 111, east on 111, 2 miles to Jefferson Street, south on Jefferson, 3 miles to Avenue 54, east on Avenue 54 one mile to Madison Street, south on Madison 2 miles to Avenue 58, west on Avenue 58 one mile to the park. There is a day use fee. Dogs must be leashed.

Santa Fe Dam Recreation Area
15501 E. Arrow Highway
Irwindale, CA
626-334-1065
This 836 acre park has a 70 acre lake which popular for sailing and fishing. The lake is stocked with bass, trout and catfish. Other park amenities include picnic areas and hiking and biking trails. Dogs are allowed on the hiking trails, but not in the lake. Pets must be leashed and people need to clean up after their pet.

W.F. Detert Park
Hwy 49
Jackson, CA
This is a small but nice city park that allows leashed dogs. It has some picnic tables and a children's

playground. It is located on Hwy 49, between the Jackson Gold Lodge and historic downtown Jackson.

Trail of a Hundred Giants
off Mountain Road 50
Johnsondale, CA
559-539-2607
This trail is located in the Giant National Sequoia Monument which is part of the Sequoia National Forest. The universally accessible trail meanders through over 125 giant sequoias in the Long Meadow Grove. The estimated age of the trees here are estimated between 500 and 1,500 years old. Pets must be leashed and attended at all times. Please clean up after your pet. The trail is located about 45 miles northwest of Kernville. From Kernville, take State Mountain Road 99 north to Johnsondale. Go west on 50 to the Western Divide Highway turnoff. Go 2 miles to the Redwood Meadow Campground. The trail is located across the road from the campground.

June Lake Area of Inyo National Forest
Highway 158 (June Lake Loop)
June Lake, CA
760-647-3044
This popular resort area is known for skiing in winter (both downhill and cross-country) and hiking and enjoying the four lakes along the June Lake Loop in the summer. These lakes are June Lake, Gulf Lake, Sliver Lake, and Grant Lake. There are a number of marinas at the lakes which may allow your dog on some of their boat rentals. This entire area is within the Inyo National Forest, which allows dogs throughout the forest on leash. Dogs are not supposed to swim in any of the lakes but they are allowed on leash up to them and on boats in the lakes. There are many hiking trails in the area, however, if you are planning a long hike make sure that you keep your dog out of land in Yosemite National Park, where dogs are not allowed. They need to stay in the National Forest.

Clear Lake State Park
Soda Bay Road
Kelseyville, CA
707-279-4293
While dogs are not allowed on the trails or the swimming beaches at this park, they are allowed in the campgrounds and in the water at non-designated swim areas. One of the non-designated swim beaches is

located between campgrounds 57 and 58. Pets must be on leash and please clean up after them. The park is located is 3.5 miles northeast of Kelseyville.

San Lorenzo Regional Park
1160 Broadway
King City, CA
831-385-5964
This park is located in the foothills of the Santa Lucia Mountains and along the Salinas River. Amenities include a walking trail along the river, picnic areas, playgrounds, volleyball courts, softball areas and camping. Dogs are allowed but must be leashed. Please clean up after your pets.

North Tahoe Regional Park
National Avenue
Kings Beach, CA
In the summer this park is used for hiking and during the winter, it's used by cross-country skiers. There are about 3-4 miles of wooded trails at this park. Want to go for a longer hike? There is a National Forest that borders up to this regional park and dogs are allowed on those trails as well. To get there, take Hwy 28 by Kings Beach to Gun Club Road (north). Turn left on Donner Road and then right on National Avenue. There is a large parking lot at the end. Dogs must be on a leash in the park.

Meiss Lake Trail
Highway 88
Kirkwood, CA
530-622-5061
This 4 mile moderate rated trail is used by both hikers and equestrians. Bicycling is prohibited. Take the Pacific Crest Trail one mile to the ridge, which offers great views and a wildflower display around mid-summer. Hike another three miles to Meiss Lake. The trailhead is located on the north side of Highway 88, immediately west of the Carson Pass Information Center. There is a parking fee. Pets must be leashed and please clean up after them.

Indian Rock Trail
Highway 173
Lake Arrowhead, CA
909-337-2444
This .5 mile easy walk is located in the San Bernardino National Forest. The trail takes you to large stone slabs that were used by the Serrano Indians to grind acorns into flour. Pets on leash are allowed and please clean up after them. To get there take Highway 173 north to the

Rock Camp Station.

North Shore National Recreation Trail
Torrey Road
Lake Arrowhead, CA
909-337-2444
This 1.7 mile moderate rated trail is located in the San Bernardino National Forest. The trail descends to Little Bear Creek and then goes to Forest Road 2N26Y. Pets on leash are allowed and please clean up after them. To get there from the Lake Arrowhead Marina, go east on Torrey Road. At the first left, take the dirt road to Forest Road 2N25 to the trailhead.

Lake Isabella
Highways 155 and 178
Lake Isabella, CA
661-868-7000
co.kern.ca.us/parks/isabella.htm
This lake is set at an elevation of over 2,500 feet and with a surface area of 11,200 acres it is Kern County's largest body of year round water. The lake is a popular spot for fishing and boating. Dogs are allowed at the lake and in the lake but must be on leash. Please clean up after your pets. There are nearby dog-friendly Sequoia National Forest trails within driving distance, including the Trail of a Hundred Giants. See our listing for this trail or call the Greenhorn Rangers District at 760-379-5646 for details.

Lake Perris State Recreation Area
off Cajalco Expressway
Lakeview, CA
909-657-0676
While dogs are not allowed in the lake or within 100 feet of the water, they are allowed on miles of trails including the bike trail that loops around the lake. Pets must be leashed and please clean up after them. Pets are also allowed in the campgrounds. The park is located 11 miles south of Riverside via Highway 60 or Interstate 215.

Hansen Dam
11770 Foothill Blvd.
Lakeview Terrace, CA
818-756-8190
This 1,437-acre basin has lots of hills and grassy meadows. There are several large picnic areas and firepits, and a children's play area. There wasn't much water in the lake but your leashed pup will have lots of land to roam. To get there, take Hwy 210 and exit Foothill Blvd south. The park will be on your left.

Fort Tejon State Historical Park
Interstate 5
Lebec, CA
661-248-6692
Fort Tejon State Historical Park is a nice stop on the Grapevine about 77 miles north of LA. Dogs on leash can roam the grounds, the historical cabins and the small museum.

Standish-Hickey State Recreation Area
69350 Highway 101
Leggett, CA
707-925-6482
While dogs are not allowed on the trails, they are allowed on a few fire roads. The fire roads are not passable during the winter because of the river, but are fine during the summer months. The fire roads are located near the campground and near the main swimming hole. Dogs are also allowed in the water. Pets must be on leash and please clean up after them. The park is located 1.5 miles north of Leggett on Highway 101.

Blue Lake National Recreation Trail
Forest Service Road 64
Likely, CA
530-233-5811
This 1.5 mile one way trail is located at Blue Lake, in the Modoc National Forest, at an elevation of 6,000 feet. At least 90 percent of the trail is shaded by white fir and massive ponderosa pine trees. The trailhead begins at the Blue Lake Campground and ends at the boat ramp. Dogs on leash are allowed at the campgrounds, on the trail and in the water. Please clean up after your pets. The trail is located is 16 miles from the small town of Likely. From Highway 395 go east on Forest Service Road 64. At about 10 miles you will come to a road junction. Stay on Forest Service Road 64 for the remaining 6 miles.

Clear Lake Trail
Mill Creek Rd.
Likely, CA
530-233-5811
This trail is located in the Modoc National Forest at an elevation of 5,700 feet. At .5 miles into the trail, you will reach Mills Creek Falls. Beyond that the trail serves as a major entry way to the trails of the South Warner Wilderness. Dogs on leash are allowed on the trail and in the water. Please clean up after your pets. To get there from the town of Likely, go 9 miles east on Co. Rd.

#64. Then go northeast on West Warner Road for 2.5 miles. Go east on Mill Creek access road for 2 more miles. The trailhead is located in the Mill Creek Falls Campground.

Bethany Reservoir State Recreation Area
off Grant Line Road
Livermore, CA
209-874-2056
This park offers activities like fishing and windsurfing. There is also a bike trail that follows the California Aqueduct. Leashed dogs are allowed on the trails. The person we spoke at the park office believes that dogs are also allowed in the lake. Please clean up after your pets. The recreation area is northeast of Livermore, 7 miles off Interstate 580 at the Grant Line Road exit.

Del Valle Regional Park
Del Valle Road
Livermore, CA
510-562-PARK
ebparks.org/parks/delval.htm
This park is over 3,997 acres of land and it includes a five mile long lake. The park is in a valley surrounded by oak-covered hills. Miles of trails surround the lake. If you would rather view the scenery from the water, you and your dog can rent a patio boat at the Marina Boat Rentals (see Attractions). Dogs must be on leash in the parking areas, picnic areas, lawns and developed areas. Your dog can run off-leash in other areas and on trails, just make sure they are under voice control and you must carry a leash. Your dog should be under voice control around bicyclists and equestrians - this has been the biggest area of conflict for unleashed dogs. Dogs are not allowed at swimming pools or swim beaches. But with a 5 mile long lake, you should be able to find a non-swim beach where your dog can play in the water. To get there from Hwy 580 heading east, exit S. Vasco Road. Turn right onto Vasco and head south. When Vasco ends, turn right onto Tesla Rd. Then turn left onto Mines Rd. Turn right onto Del Valle Road. Follow Del Valle Rd to the park entrance.

Ohlone Regional Wilderness
Del Valle Rd
Livermore, CA
510-562-PARK
ebparks.org/parks/ohlone.htm
This park's centerpiece is the 3,817-foot Rose Peak, just 32 feet lower than Mount Diablo. Surrounding

Rose Peak are 9,156 acres of grassy ridges, flowered in season. Wildlife found at this park includes golden eagles, mountain lions, and tule elk. The wilderness trail through this park is 28 miles of mountain and canyon terrain in southern Alameda County. Your dog is allowed to run off-leash, as long as he or she is under voice control. There are several entrances to this park and the trail, including the Del Valle Regional Park (off Del Valle Rd) and the Sunol Regional Wilderness (off Geary Rd).

Sycamore Grove Park
Wetmore Road
Livermore, CA
510-373-5700
This park has over 360 acres and provides walking paths, jogging paths and picnic areas. There are many kinds of wildlife here such as deer, fox, bobcat, hawks and more. Dogs must be on leash. To get there from Hwy 580 heading east, take the First Street exit. Turn right and follow First Street until it turns into Holmes Ave. Then turn left onto Wetmore Road. The park entrance is on the right. There is a minimal fee for parking.

La Purisima Mission State Historic Park
2295 Purisima Road
Lompoc, CA
805-733-3713
This mission was founded in 1787 and is one of the most completely resorted Spanish missions in California. While dogs are not allowed in the buildings, they are allowed on the grounds and on miles of trails. Pets must be on a 6 foot or less leash and please clean up after them. The park is located about 2 miles northeast of Lompoc.

Mt. Whitney Trail
Whitney Portal Road
Lone Pine, CA
760-876-6200
fs.fed.us/r5/inyo
Dogs are allowed on the first eight miles of the main Mt. Whitney Trail in the Inyo National Forest, but not on the last three miles of the trail leading to the summit which is located in Sequoia/Kings Canyon National Park. Dogs must be leashed on this trail and please clean up after them. The national forest advises that people should be aware of the high elevation affect on dogs. There is no shade or cover available and the heat of the sun at

higher elevations can be intense for pets. The trail is located 13 miles west of Lone Pine on Whitney Portal Road.

Sugar Pine Railroad Grade Trail
Fraser Flat Road
Long Barn, CA
209-586-3234
This 3 mile easy rated trail parallels the South Fork of the Stanislaus River and overlays the historic Sugar Pine Railroad System. Pets on leash are allowed and please clean up after them. This trail is located in the Stanislaus National Forest. One access point to this trail is the Fraser Flat Campground. To get there, drive 3 miles north of Highway 108 at Spring Gap turnoff (Fraser Flat Road).

Elysian Park
929 Academy Road
Los Angeles, CA
805-584-4400
At 600 acres, this is the 2nd largest city park in Los Angeles, and much of the landscape of natural chaparral is crisscrossed with hiking trails. There are barbecue pits, a small man-made lake, restrooms, and a children's play area at the central picnic area.

Griffith Park
Los Feliz Blvd.
Los Angeles, CA
This park has the Griffith Observatory, the famous Hollywood sign and plenty of hiking trails. The Mt. Hollywood Trail is about a 6 mile round trip and can get very hot in the summer season, so head out early or later in the evening during those hot days. There is also a more shaded trail that begins by the Bird Sanctuary. Be careful not to go into the Sanctuary because dogs are not allowed there. Instead go to the trail to the left of the Sanctuary entrance. That trail should go around the perimeter of the Bird Sanctuary. For more trail info, pick up a map at one of the Ranger stations (main Ranger's station is at Crystal Springs/Griffith Park Drive near Los Feliz Blvd). To get to there, take Hwy 5 to the Los Feliz Blvd exit and head west. Turn right on Hillhurst or Vermont Ave (they merge later). The trail by the Bird Sanctuary will be on the right, past the Greek Theater. To get to the Mt. Hollywood Trail, continue until you come to the Griffith Observatory. Park here and the trail is across the parking lot from the Observatory (near the outdoor cafe).

Please note that no one is allowed to actually hike to the famous Hollywood sign - it is very well guarded. But from some of the trails in this park, you can get a long distance view of the sign. Dogs must be leashed in the park.

Los Gatos Creek Reservoir Trail
University Avenue
Los Gatos, CA
408-356-2729
This is a popular hike with about 5-7 miles of trails. There is a nice combination of fire roads and single track trails with streams. A loop trail begins at University Ave (by Hwy 17). The fire road trail parallels Hwy 17 for a while until you reach the Lexington Reservoir. Across the street from the parking lot (the one w/the portable restrooms) by the Reservoir, the trail continues. You'll hike uphill to the top and then back towards the bottom where you started. There are several forks in the trail. Always stay to the left and you'll be back where you started.

Vasona Lake Park
Blossom Hill Rd
Los Gatos, CA
408-356-2729
Your dog is welcome at this 151 acre park. This is a very popular park during the summer because of the nice lake, green landscape, walking trails and picnic tables. There are six miles of paved trails that wind through the park. The paved trails join the Los Gatos Creek Park to the south and the Los Gatos Creek Trail to the north. In the summer, there is usually a hot dog stand by the chilen's playground. Your pup can also get his or her paws wet in the lake. The easiest spot is near the playground. The park is located on Blossom Hill Road between University Ave and Hwy 17 (no Hwy exit here). From southbound Hwy 17, take the Saratoga-Los Gatos (Hwy 9) exit and head east/right. At University Avenue, turn right. Turn right again at Blossom Hill and the park will be on the left. There is a fee for parking.

Ruth Lake Recreation Area
Lower Mad River Rd, south of Hwy 36
Mad River, CA
800-500-0285
Dogs on leash are allowed on the trails and in the lake. RV and camp sites are available with reservations.

Circle X Ranch
Yerba Buena Road

Malibu, CA
805-370-2301
There are both easy and strenuous trails at this park. The Backbone Trail is a strenuous 3 mile round trip hike which starts at an elevatio of 2,050 feet. This trail offers views on the Conejo and San Fernando Valleys and the Pacific Coast. This trail continues to Point Mugu State Park but dogs are not allowed on those trails. The Grotto Trail is a 3.5 mile round trip trail rated moderate to strenuous. The trail is all downhill from the starting point which means you will be hiking uphill when you return. The Canyon View Trail is almost 2 miles and is rated easy to moderate. There are many access points to this trail, but one is located .3 miles east of the Ranger Station on Yerba Buena Road. Dogs are allowed but must be leashed and people need to clean up after their pets. To get there go about 5.4 miles north on Yerba Buena Road from Highway 1. This park is part of the Santa Monica Recreation Area.

Escondido Canyon Park
Winding Way
Malibu, CA
805-370-2301
smmc.ca.gov/escontral.html
The Escondido Falls trail is a little over 4 miles long. The trailhead is reached by a one mile walk up the road from the parking lot. The trail will cross the creek several times before opening up to grassland. You will see the waterfall about one mile from the trailhead. Hiking, horseback riding, and mountain bicycling are popular activities at the park. Dogs on a 6 foot or less leash are allowed and people need to clean up after their pets. The park is located in Malibu, about one mile from the Pacific Coast Highway on Winding Way. This park is part of the Santa Monica Recreation Area.

Santa Clarita Woodlands Park
5750 Ramiraz Canyon Road
Malibu, CA
310-589-3200
A very important park with concern to the wildlife habitat corridor that it provides, it also supplies 4000 acres of recreational land. Some of the features/amenities include globally unique combinations of tree species, lush greenery and spring wildflowers, abundant bird and wildlife, year round streams, a nature center, hiking and multi-use trails, and picnic areas. Dogs are

allowed throughout the park and on the trails. Dogs must be under their owner's immediate control, leashed, and cleaned up after at all times.

Solstice Canyon Park
Corral Canyon Road
Malibu, CA
805-370-2301
nps.gov/samo/maps/solstice.htm
This park is a wooded, narrow coastal canyon which offers five trails, ranging from easy to moderate hikes. One of the trails is called the Solstice Canyon Trail. This is an easy 2.1 mile round trip walk which passes by the Keller House which is believed to be the oldest existing stone building in Malibu. Dogs are allowed on the trails but must be leashed and people need to clean up after their pets. To get there from the Pacific Coast Highway 1, go through Malibu and turn inland onto Corral Canyon Road. In about .25 miles the entrance will be on your left at a hairpin curve in the road. This park is part of the Santa Monica Recreation Area.

Ansel Adams Wilderness
off Highway 203
Mammoth Lakes, CA
760-934-2289
fs.fed.us/r5/inyo
The wilderness can be accessed at many points, including the John Muir Trail. See our listing for this trail under the city of Mammoth Lakes. There are miles of on or off-leash hiking opportunities.

Devil's Postpile National Monument
Minaret Rd.
Mammoth Lakes, CA
760-934-2289
nps.gov/depo
During the summer only, take a bus ride/shuttle to the Devil's Postpile National Monument with your pup. The shuttle is the only way to drive to this National Monument unless you have a camping permit or have a vehicle with 11 people or more. The shuttle begins at the Mammoth Mountain Inn off Hwy 203 and takes you and your dog on a scenic ride along the San Joaquin River to the National Monument. The travel time is about 45 minutes to Reds Meadow (past the Monument), but there are 10 stops along the way to get out and stretch or hike. Once at the Monument, there is a short 1/2 mile walk. The Monument is a series of basalt columns, 40 to 60 feet high, that resembles a giant pipe organ. It was made by hot lava that cooled

and cracked 900,000 years ago. The John Muir Trail crosses the monument, so for a longer hike, join up with nearby trails that are in the dog-friendly Inyo National Forest. Dogs should be on a leash.

John Muir Trail
off Highway 203
Mammoth Lakes, CA
760-934-2289
fs.fed.us/r5/inyo
This trail crosses the dog-friendly Devil's Postpile National Monument. The John Muir Trail offers miles of hiking trails. Dogs must be on leash at the monument but can be off leash under direct voice control in the Inyo National Forest and Ansel Adams Wilderness. The trailhead is located near the ranger's station at the monument. To get there, you can drive directly to the monument and trailhead ONLY if you have a camping permit or a vehicle with 11 people or more. All day visitors must ride a shuttle bus from the Mammoth Mountain Ski Area at the end of Highway 203. Well-behaved leashed dogs are allowed on the bus. From Highway 395, drive 10 miles west on Highway 203 to Minaret Summit. Then drive 7 miles on a paved, narrow mountain road. Or take the shuttle bus at the end of Highway 203. The bus ride takes about 45 minutes to the monument with several stops along the way.

Lake George
Lake George Rd.
Mammoth Lakes, CA
At Lake George, you can find the trailheads for the Crystal Lake and Mammoth Crest trails. You'll be hiking among the beautiful pine trees and snow covered peaks. The trails start at the north side of Lake George. The hike to Crystal Lake is about a 3 mile round trip. If you want a longer hike, you'll have the option on your way to Crystal Lake. The Mammoth Crest trail is the trail that branches to the right. The Mammoth trail is about a 6 mile round trip and it's a more strenuous trail. To get there from the intersection of Main Street and Hwy 203, take Lake Mary Road to the left. Go past Twin Lakes. You'll see a road that goes off to the left (Lake Mary Loop Rd.). Go past this road, you'll want the other end of the loop. When you come to another road that also says Lake Mary Loop Rd, turn left. Then turn right onto Lake George Rd. Follow this road almost to the end and you should see signs for the Crystal Lake Trail.

Dogs should be leashed.

Lake Mary
Lake Mary Loop Rd.
Mammoth Lakes, CA
Here's another lake and hiking trail to enjoy up in the high country. Lake Mary is known as one of the best fishing spots in the Eastern Sierra, regularly producing trophy size trout. After your water dog is done playing in the lake, head to the southeast side of the lake to go for a hike on the Emerald Lake Trail. The trail starts at the Cold Water trailhead next to the Cold Water campgrounds. Take the trail to the right towards Emerald Lake and Sky Meadows. The trail to Emerald Lake is about 1 1/2 miles round trip (out and back). If you continue on to Sky Meadows, then your hike is about 4 miles round trip. To get there from the intersection of Main Street and Hwy 203, take Lake Mary Road to the left. Pass Twin Lakes and then you'll come to Lake Mary. Turn left onto Lake Mary Loop Road and the trailhead is located on the southeast side of the lake. Dogs should be on a leash.

Mammoth Mountain
Minaret Rd.
Mammoth Lakes, CA
760-934-2571 (800-MAMMOTH)
mammothmountain.com/
You can hike with your dog on "The" Mammoth Mountain in three ways. One way is to take the Gondola ride with your pup (summer only) up to the top of the mountain and then hike down. The second is to hike up the mountain from the parking lot by the Mammoth Mountain Inn and the Gondola. The third option is to start on the backside of the mountain and hike up and then of course down. For the third option, you can start at Twin Lakes (off Lake Mary Rd). The Dragon's Back Trail is on the west side of the lakes (by the campgrounds). Dogs must be leashed.

Shady Rest Park and Trail
Sawmill Cutoff Rd.
Mammoth Lakes, CA
760-934-8983
This park serves as a multi-use recreation park. During the winter it's popular with cross country skiers - yes dogs are allowed. In the summer, you can go for a hike on the 5-6 miles of single track and fire road trails. It's also used by 4x4 off

road vehicles too, so just be aware. To get there from the Mammoth Visitor's Center, take Hwy 203 towards town. The first street on your right will be Sawmill Cutoff Road. Turn right and Shady Rest Park is at the end of the road. There are restrooms at this park which can come in handy for the humans before starting out on the trails. Dogs must be leashed.

Tamarack Cross Country Ski Center
Lake Mary Road
Mammoth Lakes, CA
760- 934-2442
tamaracklodge.com/xcountry/
During the summer and fall (until first snowfall), dogs are allowed at Tamarack. They offer watercraft rentals, fishing, easy to strenuous hiking trails, an eatery, a lodge that allows dogs, and great scenery. Dogs are welcome on the deck of the restaurant. Dogs must be under their owner's control at all times, and be leashed and cleaned up after.

John Muir National Historic Site
4202 Alhambra Avenue
Martinez, CA
925-228-8860
nps.gov/jomu/
While dogs are not allowed in any buildings or on the nature trails, they are allowed on the adjacent Mt. Wanda fire road trail. Hike up to the top and back with your pooch. Pets must be leashed and rangers actively patrol the area and will issue citations to anyone who has their dog off leash. To get to the trail, park at the historic site or at the Park and Ride lot on Franklin Canyon and Alhambra. Please clean up after your pet.

McGee Creek Trailhead
McGee Creek Road
McGee Creek, CA
760-873-2500
fs.fed.us/r5/inyo
This trail is rated moderate to strenuous. It is located in the Inyo National Forest. From the trailhead you can hike to several lakes including Steelhead Lake. Pets must either be leashed or off-leash but under direct voice control. Please clean up after your pets. To get there from Highway 395, take the first exit after Crowley Lake. Go 4 miles heading south on McGee Creek Road to the trailhead.

Mendocino Headlands State Park
off Hesser Drive
Mendocino, CA

This trail (1-2 miles each way) is located next to the village of Mendocino and it follows the Mendocino peninsula and coastline on bluffs above the beach. The trail is part of the Mendocino Headlands State Park. To get there, take Hwy 1, exit Main Street/Jackson toward the coastline. When Main Street ends, turn right onto Hesser Drive. Go 4 blocks and turn left to continue on Hesser Drive. There are many trailheads or starting points along Hesser Drive, but in the summer, watch out for foxtails.

Mill Valley-Sausalito Path
Almonte Blvd.
Mill Valley, CA
This multi-purpose path is used by walkers, runners, bicyclists and equestrians. Dogs on leash are allowed. The path is located in the Bothin Marsh Open Space Preserve.

Mount Tamalpais State Park
801 Panoramic Highway
Mill Valley, CA
415-388-2070
While dogs are not allowed on most of the trails, they are allowed on the Old Stage Road. This path is about . 5 to .75 miles and leads to the Marin Municipal Water District Land which allows dogs on their trails. Dogs must be leashed on both the state park and the water district lands. Please clean up after your pets. To get there, take Highway 101 north of San Francisco's Golden Gate Bridge. Then take Highway 1 to the Stinson Beach exit and follow the signs up the mountain.

Muir Woods National Monument
Highway 1/Muir Woods Exit
Mill Valley, CA
415-388-2595
nps.gov/muwo/index.htm
Dogs must be on leash and must be cleaned up after on the Muir Beach coastal trail. Dogs are not allowed in the woods.

Dixon Landing Park
Milmont Drive
Milpitas, CA
Dixon Landing Park is a relatively small park, but has much to offer. There are numerous picnic tables, a children's playground, tennis courts and a basketball court. You can grab food to go at one of the restaurants near Dixon Landing Rd and Milmont Drive, then bring it back to enjoy at the picnic tables. This park is a few blocks away (heading west) from the Levee Path. To get there from Hwy

880 heading north, exit Dixon Landing Rd. At the light, turn left then make a right onto Dixon Landing Rd. Turn right onto Milmont Dr/California Circle. The park will be on the right.

Ed Levin County Park
3100 Calveras Blvd.
Milpitas, CA
408-262-6980
parkhere.org
Dogs are allowed on the Bay Area Ridge Trail from Sandy Wool Lake to Mission Peak. They are not allowed on any other trails in the park. Dogs must be leashed, except when in the off-leash dog park.

Holy Jim Historic Trail
Trabuco Canyon Road
Mission Viejo, CA
909-736-1811
This trail is part of the Cleveland National Forest. It is about a 4.5 mile hike on a combination of fire roads and single track trails. You can see a small waterfall on this trail which is best viewed in early spring. This trail is used by both hikers and mountain bikers. Pets on leash are allowed and please clean up after them. To get there from Highway 5, exit El Toro Road and head north (away from the coast). Take Live Oak Canyon Road to the right, then turn left onto Trabuco Canyon Road.

El Estero Park
Camino El Estero & Fremont St
Monterey, CA
831-646-3860
This is a city park with a lake, trails around the lake, a children's play area and many places to walk your dog. It's located on the east side of town.

Jacks Peak County Park
25020 Jacks Peak Park Road
Monterey, CA
831-755-4895
This wooded park offers great views of the Monterey Bay area. You and your dog can enjoy almost 8.5 miles of hiking trails which wind through forests to ridge top vistas. Park amenities include picnic areas and restrooms. There is a $2 vehicle entrance fee during the week and a $3 fee on weekends and holidays. Dogs need to be leashed and please clean up after them.

Anderson Lake/Park
Cochrane Rd.
Morgan Hill, CA

408-779-3634
The 2,365 acre Anderson Lake/Park also features the Coyote Creek Parkway's multiple use trails. Dogs on a 6 foot leash are allowed. Anderson Lake and the picnic areas along the Coyote Creek are located off of Cochrane Road in Morgan Hill, east of Highway 101.

Havasu National Wildlife Refuge
Box 3009 (Mojave County Road 227)
Needles, CA
760-326-3853
This refuge is one of more than 500 managed by the Fish and Wildlife Service, and is dedicated to conserving our wildlife heritage. Various habitats provide for a wide variety of plant, bird, and animal species. The refuge office hours are 8am-4pm Monday through Friday, and they suggest you come in there first for brochures and any updates on the area. Dogs of all sizes are allowed. Dogs must be kept on lead at all times and cleaned up after. Dogs are allowed throughout the park, but may not chase or disturb the wildlife in any way.

Salmon Lakes Trail
Road 38
Nevada City, CA
530-265-4531
This 2 mile easy rated trail is located in the Tahoe National Park. It used by hikers, mountain bikers and equestrians. Pets must be leashed in the campground and please clean up after them. To get there from I-80 at Yuba Gap, go south for .3 miles and turn right toward Lodgepole Campground. After 1.1 miles, turn right on Road 19 (unpaved). After 2 miles turn left on Road 38. The trailhead is 2 miles ahead and .5 miles past Huysink Lake.

South Yuba Trail
North Bloomfield Road
Nevada City, CA
916-985-4474
This 12 mile trail is popular with hikers, runners, mountain bikers and horseback riders. The trail offers pine tree covered canyons, gentle slopes and open meadows. Along the trail you will see historic flumes and waterworks. Leashed dogs are welcome. Please clean up after your dog. The South Yuba River Recreation Area is located about 10 miles northeast of Nevada City. From Nevada City, take Highway 49 north to North Bloomfield Road. Drive 10 miles to the South Yuba Recreation Area. From the one lane bridge at

Edwards Crossing, go about 1.5 miles on a dirt/gravel road to the campground and trailhead. Trailers and motorhomes should take Highway 49 and then turn right at the junction of Tyler Foote Road. At the intersection of Grizzly Hill Road turn right and proceed to North Bloomfield Road.

Tahoe National Forest
631 Coyote Street
Nevada City, CA
530-265-4531
fs.fed.us/r5/tahoe/
This national forest includes the Lake Tahoe Basin Management Area. Elevations range from 1,500 feet up to 9,400 feet. Please see our listings in the Gold Country and Sierra Nevada region for dog-friendly hikes and/or campgrounds.

Caliente Mountain Access Trail
Highway 166
New Cuyama, CA
661-391-6000
This trail is popular with hikers and mountain bikers. It is also used by hunters who take the trail to get access to adjacent public lands. This open space has a nice display of wildflowers in the Spring. The trailhead is located about 14 miles west of New Cuyama. The trail starts on the north side of the highway after crossing a bridge over the Cuyama River. Dogs are allowed on the trail.

Placerita Canyon Nature Center
19152 Placerita Canyon Road
Newhall, CA
661-259-7721
This 350 acre nature park is one of the first places where gold was discovered in California. An early frontier cabin called Walker's Cabin is located at this park. Hiking trails are accessible for wheelchairs and strollers. The paved trail is about .3 miles. Dogs must be on leash and please clean up after them.

William S. Hart Regional Park
24151 N. San Fernando Road
Newhall, CA
661-259-0855
This 265 acre ranch was donated to the public by William S. Hart, also known as "Two Gun Bill". He was a popular cowboy actor during the silent film era. The park includes a western art museum and barnyard animals including wild buffalo. Dogs are allowed at the park and on trails, but not inside any buildings. Pets must be leashed and please clean up after them.

Upper Newport Bay Regional Park
University Dr & Irvine Ave
Newport Beach, CA
949-640-1751
This regional park borders the Newport Back Bay and consists of approximately 140 acres of open space. This coastal wetland is renowned as one of the finest bird watching sites in North America. During winter migration, there can be tens of thousands of birds at one time. It is also home to six rare or endangered bird species. The park has a 2-3 mile one-way paved path that is used by walkers, joggers and bicyclists. Additional dirt trails run along the hills. You can park at a variety of points along the road, but many people park at Irvine Ave and University Dr. Dogs must be leashed in the park.

Gibson Ranch Park
Elverta Rd West of Watt Ave
North Highlands, CA
916-875-6961
gibson-ranch.com/Gib_Five.htm
This park allows dogs on leash. There are a lot of dirt walking or jogging trails which must be shared with horses as this is predominantly an equestrian park. There is a lake in the center with picnic areas and fishing available.

Lake Casitas Rec Area
11311 Santa Ana Road
Oak View, CA
805-649-2233
Lake Casitas was created as a drinking water reservoir by the creation of the Casitas Dam. It is well known as one of the top bass fishing lakes in America. Hiking, camping and boating are available in the Recreation Area. Dogs must be on a six foot leash at all times. They must be under control and are not allowed within 50 feet of the lake or streams or inside the Water Adventure area. Dogs are allowed in boats on the lake including the rental boats. There is an $8.00 automobile fee to enter the Rec Area and a $1.50 pet fee per pet per day to use the Rec Area. There is camping in the Rec Area for RVs with lots priced from $19 to $50 per night. Full hookups are available.

Shadow of the Giants Trail
off Sky Ranch Road
Oakhurst, CA
559-297-0706
fs.fed.us/r5/sierra/
This one mile each way self-guided

trail is located in the Nelder Grove Giant Sequoia Preservation Area. Along the trail you will see some of the best giant sequoia trees in the state. Pets on leash are allowed and please clean up after them. The trail is located in the Nelder Grove Giant Sequoia Preservation Area. To get there from Oakhurst, go about 5 miles north on Highway 41. Turn right (east) onto Sky Ranch Road. Along Sky Ranch Road you will find Nelder Grove.

Lake Merritt
Lakeside Drive
Oakland, CA
lakemerritt.com/
This park and lake is in the center of Oakland. Dogs are not allowed inside the park or lake. However, if you keep your dog leashed, you can walk the perimeter (furthest outside) sidewalk. You'll want to remember this rule, since a $270 ticket could be imposed if you venture into the park. It has a nice approximately 3 mile perimeter path that winds around the lake. It is a popular walking, jogging and biking path. To get there from Hwy 880 heading north, take the Oak Street exit towards Lakeside Drive. Turn right onto Oak Street. Oak Street becomes Lakeside Drive. There is ample parking.

Cozy Dell Trail
Highway 33
Ojai, CA
This trail offers great panoramic views of the Ojai Valley. It is about a 4 mile round trip trail and can take a couple of hours to walk. It is rated an easy to moderate trail. The trail might be a little overgrown during certain times of the year. To get there, take Highway 33 north and go about 3.3 miles north of Ojai. The trail begins near the Friends Ranch Packing House. Park on the left side of the highway. Dogs need to be leashed.

Libbey Park
Ojai Ave at Signal Street
Ojai, CA
805-646-5581
This city park that is home to many events is located in the heart of picturesque Ojai. Dogs must be on leash at all times. The park boasts a music ampitheatre, playground and a well-cut grass area. There are clean up bags for dogs located in the park.

Ojai Valley Trail
Hwy 33 at Casitas Vista Rd
Ojai, CA
805-654-3951

This 9.5 mile trail has a paved pedestrian path and a wood-chip bridle path. Dogs are allowed but must always be on leash. The trail parallels Highway 33 from Foster Park, just outside Ventura to Fox Street, in Ojai.

Bolinas Ridge Trail
Drake Blvd
Olema, CA
Dogs on leash may accompany you on the Bolinas Ridge Trail. The trailhead is about 1 mile from the Pt Reyes National Seashore Visitor Center in Olema. Dogs are not allowed on trails in Pt Reyes (see Point Reyes National Seashore) so this is the closest trail available. The trailhead is one mile up Drake Blvd from Olema on the right. Parking is at the side of the road.

Squaw Valley USA
1960 Squaw Valley Rd
Olympic Valley, CA
530-583-6985 (888 SNOW 3-2-1)
squaw.com
In the summer (non-snow season) you and your pup can hike on the trails at this ski resort. Both of you will feel very welcome at Squaw. You can take your dog into the lobby to purchase the tickets for the dog-friendly Cable Car ride and/or snacks. As for the trails, there are many miles of hiking trails. One of the main hikes is from High Camp to the main parking lot or visa versa. It's the trail designed for night skiing (follow the light posts). During the summer, Squaw Valley has several dog-friendly events like the Star Gazing and Full Moon Hikes where dogs are welcome. Dogs must be leashed at all times.

Cucamonga-Guasti Park
800 N. Archibald Ave.
Ontario, CA
909-945-4321
This regional park allows leashed dogs. There is a nice path that winds along the lake which is a popular fishing spot. There is a minimal day use fee.

Pacific Crest Trail-Owens Peak Segment
Highway 178
Onyx, CA
661-391-6000
The Owens Peak Segment of the Pacific Crest Trail is managed by the Bureau of Land Management. This section begins at Walker Pass in Kern County and goes 41 miles north to the Sequoia National Forest at Rockhouse Basin. Elevations on this portion range from 5,245 feet at Walker Pass to 7,900 feet on Bear Mountain. The trail offers great views of the surrounding mountains and valleys. Dogs are allowed on the Owen's Peak Segment of the Pacific Crest Trail. Trail conditions can change due to fires, storms and landslides. To confirm current conditions, contact the Bakersfield BLM Office at 661-391-6000. There are many trailheads, but one of the more popular staging areas is at Walker Pass. From Ridgecrest go 27 miles west on Highway 178 to Walker Pass.

Irvine Regional Park
1 Irvine Park Rd
Orange, CA
714-633-8074
Located in the foothills, this is California's oldest regional park. With over 470 acres, this park has a variety of Oak and Sycamore groves, streams, a pond, a paved trail, picnic tables and barbecues. There are also several historical sites and plaques located throughout the park. Maps are available from the park ranger at the main entrance. Because this park is also a wilderness area with mountain lions, park rules state that minors must be under adult supervision at all times. Dogs must be leashed. There is a minimal parking fee.

Peters Canyon Regional Park
Canyon View Ave
Orange, CA
714-973-6611
This park has over 350 acres of coastal sage scrub, woodlands, a freshwater marsh, and a 55 acre reservoir. They have a variety of dirt paths and trails (approx. 2-3 miles) which are frequented by hikers, mountain bikers, equestrians and of course, leashed dogs. All trails are closed for three days following rainfall. To get there from Hwy 5 or Hwy 405, take the Jamboree Road exit north. Then turn left at Canyon View Ave. Proceed 1/4 mile to the park entrance and parking lot. Maps should be available at a stand near the parking lot.

Orangevale Community Park
Oak Ave & Filbert Ave
Orangevale, CA
916-988-4373
Dogs must be on leash at this city park.

Orchard Park
Geranium Place
Oxnard, CA
This small city park has tennis courts and a nice playground for kids. It is located on the corner of Geranium Place and Camelot Way. Dogs must be on leash.

Temescal Gateway Park
15601 Sunset Blvd.
Pacific Palisades, CA
310-454-1395
smmc.ca.gov/temtrail.html
There are several trails at this park. Dogs are allowed but must be on a 6 foot or less leash and people need to clean up after their pets. The Sunset Trail is almost a half mile trail that begins at the lower parking lot by Sunset Blvd. It parallels Temescal Creek. Dogs are not allowed in the attached Temescal State Park. The park is located at the intersection of Temescal Canyon Road and Sunset Blvd. This park is part of the Santa Monica Recreation Area.

Pacifica State Beach
Highway 1
Pacifica, CA
650-738-7381
This wide crescent shaped beach is located off Highway 1 in downtown Pacifica. Dogs on leash are allowed and please clean up after them.

Magnesia Park
Palm Desert Comm. Park
Palm Desert, CA
760-347-3484
Enjoy walking through this shaded park or having lunch at one of the many picnic tables. It's located in the city of Palm Desert at Magnesia Falls Drive and Portola Avenue. Dogs must be leashed.

Lykken Trail
Ramon Road
Palm Springs, CA
When you begin this hike, there is a choice of two trails (one is pretty steep) which eventually join together up the mountain. The hike is a total of 6 miles round trip and includes a 1,000 foot elevation gain. This trail provides excellent views. It is located at the west end of Ramon Road. Dogs must be leashed. There are many rattlesnakes in the area.

Palo Alto Baylands Preserve
San Antonio Road
Palo Alto, CA
650-329-2506
The Palo Alto Baylands Preserve is a

365

flat mostly unpaved 5 mile loop trail. Leashed dogs are allowed, unless posted in special bird nesting areas. There are several entrance points. One of the main starting points is from Hwy 101 heading north, exit San Antonio Road and turn right. San Antonio Road will bring you directly into the start of the Preserve. Please note that there is an adjacent park on the right which is a City of Mountain View park that does not allow dogs. However, no need to worry, the dog-friendly Palo Alto side has plenty of trails for you and your pooch to walk or run.

Stanford University
Palm Drive
Palo Alto, CA
408-225-0225
Stanford University has miles of tree covered sidewalks and paths that wind through the campus. There is also a park at the end of Palm Drive which is a small but popular hang out for locals and their leashed dogs on warm days . To get there from downtown Palo Alto, take University Ave west toward the hills. University Ave turns into Palm Drive. There are tree lined walking paths along this street. The park is at the end of Palm. Ample parking is available.

Observatory National Recreational Trail
Observatory Campground
Palomar Mountain, CA
760-788-0250
This trail is located in the dog-friendly Cleveland National Forest. The 2. 2 mile trail offers a pleasant hike to the Palomar Observatory site. It meanders through pine and oak woodlands and offers some great views of the Mendenhall and French Valleys. There is a 200 foot elevation gain, with a starting elevation of 4800 feet. Dogs are allowed on leash. From San Diego, drive north on I-15 to Highway 76 (Oceanside-Pala exit) Head east on Hwy 76 to S6 and drive north toward Palomar Mountain. Follow S6 to Observatory Campground. Trailhead parking is near the amphitheater inside the campground (follow the signs). The trailhead is adjacent to the amphitheater. Vehicles must display a Forest Adventure Pass. The pass can be purchased from local vendors and from the Forest Service Offices. Call (760) 788-0250 for a list of forest offices.

Brookside Park
360 N Arroyo Blvd
Pasadena, CA
626-744-4386
A 61.1 acre park, and the city's largest fully maintained park, is located just south of the Rose Bowl Stadium, and offers a variety of recreational opportunities. Some of the park's features/amenities include lighted gaming fields, picnic areas-most with barbecue pits, drinking fountains, playground areas, and restrooms. Dogs of all sizes are allowed. They must be well mannered, and leashed and cleaned up after at all times.

Eaton Canyon Nature Center
1750 N Altadena Drive
Pasadena, CA
626-398-5420
ecnca.org/
This 190 acre day-use park is considered to be a zoological, botanical, and geological wonderland, and there are also a variety of recreational opportunities available. Some of the features/amenities include a nature center/gift shop, hiking trails, and restrooms. Dogs of all sizes are allowed for no additional fee. Dogs must be under their owner's control at all times, and be leashed and cleaned up after.

Hahamongna Watershed
Oak Grove Drive
Pasadena, CA
The Hahamongna Watershed Park (formerly Oak Grove Park) allows leashed dogs on the trails and on the world's first disc golf course. During the summer months, there can be rattlesnakes here, so make sure your dog stays leashed. You'll also want to keep your pup away from the ground squirrels. Some squirrels in this mountain range have been known to carry rabies. Aside from being a very popular disc golf course, this park is also very popular with bird watchers. To get there from Hwy 210, take the Berkshire Ave. exit and head east. Turn left onto Oak Grove Drive and the park will be on the right. To get to one of the trails, follow the signs to the disc golf course. After going downhill, turn right and the trail begins.

Lake Nacimiento
Lake Nacimiento Drive
Paso Robles, CA
805-238-3256
nacimientoresort.com/dayuse.htm
There are approximately 170 miles

of tree lined shoreline at this lake. This is a popular lake for boating and fishing. It is the only lake in California that is stocked with White Bass fish. There is also a good population of largemouth and smallmouth bass. The lake offers over 400 campsites and RV sites have both full or partial hook ups. Dogs are allowed around and in the lake. They must be on leash and attended at all times. There is a $5 per day charge for dogs. The lake is located west of Hwy 101, seventeen miles north of Paso Robles. Take the 24th Street (G-14 West) exit in Paso Robles and proceed west on G-14 to the lake.

Devil's Punchbowl Nature Center
28000 Devil's Punchbowl Road
Pearblossom, CA
661-944-2743
This 1,310 acre nature park offers unusual rock formations and is just one mile away from the famous San Andreas fault. The park elevation starts at 4,200 feet and climbs up to 6,500 feet. There are miles of trails rated easy to strenuous. The visitor center is open daily from 9am to 4pm. There is no charge for parking. Dogs must be on leash and please clean up after them.

Harford Springs Reserve
Gavilan Road
Perris, CA
909-684-7032
This 325 acre park offer hiking and equestrian trails. The park is located about 7 miles west of Perris, 2 miles south of Cajalco Road on Gavilan Road. Dogs must be leashed and please clean up after them.

Butano State Park
Highway 1
Pescadero, CA
650-879-2040
This 2,200 acre park is located in a secluded redwood-filled canyon. While dogs are not allowed on the trails, they are allowed in the campground and on miles of fire roads. Mountain biking is also allowed on the fire roads. Pets must be on a 6 foot or less leash. Please clean up after them. The park is located on the San Mateo Coast off Highway 1. To get there go 4.5 miles southeast of Pescadero via Pescadero and Cloverdale Roads.

Big Laguna Trail
Sunrise Highway
Pine Valley, CA
619-445-6235
fs.fed.us/r5/cleveland

This 6.7 mile easy rated trail is located in the Cleveland National Forest. The trail elevation changes from 5,400 to 5,960 feet. It is a popular trail for hiking, horseback riding and mountain biking. The trail is open year round except during winter storms. Pets on leash are allowed and please clean up after them. To reach the upper end, take Sunrise Highway from I-8 (near Pine Valley) and drive north 13.5 miles to just past the second cattle guard on the highway. Vehicles should park on either side of the highway on the paved turnouts. The access to the Big Laguna trail is via the Nobel Canyon trail that departs the western turnout and is marked by a small sign. Follow the Nobel Canyon trail about 100 yards to reach the Big Laguna trail junction. The other end of the Big Laguna trail makes a junction with the Pacific Crest Trail about .25 miles northeast of the Laguna Station (the Forest Service fire station).

El Dorado Trail
Mosquito Rd.
Placerville, CA
This part of the El Dorado Trail is a nice paved path that is popular with runners and walkers. Leashed dogs are allowed. The trail was originally 2 miles each way for a total of 4 miles, but the trail has been expanded a few extra miles. Most of the path is wide enough that there is a dirt trail paralleling the paved trail. It is located near historic downtown Placerville. To get there from Hwy 50 heading east, exit Broadway and turn right. When Broadway ends, turn right onto Mosquito Rd and go back under the freeway. At the second street, turn left. If you go too far, you'll end up going back onto Hwy 50. The trail will be on the right. Park along the street.

Eldorado National Forest
100 Forni Road
Placerville, CA
530-622-5061
fs.fed.us/r5/eldorado/
This national forest covers over 590,000 acres of land which ranges in elevation from 1,000 feet in the foothills to more than 10,000 feet along the Sierras. Please see the listings in our Sierra Nevada region for dog-friendly hikes and/or campgrounds.

Gold Bug Park
2635 Gold Bug Lane
Placerville, CA

530-642-5207
goldbugpark.org
Gold Bug Park is a 60 acre park that was once the home of many gold mines. Your leashed dog is allowed at the picnic areas and on the trails, but is not allowed into the mine.

Shadow Cliffs
Stanley Blvd.
Pleasanton, CA
510-562-PARK
ebparks.org/parks/shadow.htm
Special thanks to one of our readers for the info on this great dog-friendly park. This 296-acre park includes an 80-acre lake. Dogs must be on leash in the parking areas, picnic areas, lawns and developed areas. Your dog can run off-leash in other areas and trails, just make sure they are under voice control and you must carry a leash. Your dog should be under voice control around bicyclists and equestrians - this has been the biggest area of conflict for unleashed dogs. Dogs are not allowed at swimming pools or swim beaches. But you should be able to find a non-swim beach where your dog can play and swim in the water. To get there, from I-580 take the Santa Rita Road south, turn left onto Valley Ave, then left onto Stanley Blvd. Turn right off Stanley into the park. There is a minimal entrance fee.

Cedar Park Trail
Sly Park Road
Pollock Pines, CA
530-644-2349
This easy paved trail, set amongst pine and conifer trees, has two small paved loops which total 1.2 miles in length. The elevation ranges from about 3,640 to 3,700 feet. Pets must be leashed and please clean up after them. The trail is located in the Eldorado National Forest. From Highway 50 in Pollock Pines, take Sly Park Road south (away from the Safeway). Drive about 6 miles to the parking area and trailhead on the left side of the road. There is ample parking.

Sly Park/Jenkinson Lake
4771 Sly Park Road
Pollock Pines, CA
530-644-2545
This beautiful wooded recreation area is at an elevation of 3500 feet. There is an 8 mile loop trail that circles Jenkinson Lake. It is a popular park for hiking, horseback

riding, fishing and camping. Leashed dogs are allowed on the trails and in the campgrounds. The west side of the park (next to the campgrounds) offers wide fire road trails, while the east side has single track trails. Be sure to check your pup for ticks after walking here. The park is open from sunrise to sunset. It is located about 30 minutes from Placerville. To get there from Hwy 50, take the Sly Park Rd exit and turn right. Drive about 5-10 minutes and the park will be on the left.

Ganesha Park
McKinley Ave
Pomona, CA
It is not a large park, but is a nice place to walk with your dog. The park also has several playground and picnic areas. Dogs must be leashed.

Windy Hill Preserve
Hwys 84 and 35
Portola Valley, CA
650-691-1200
openspace.org/WINDY.html
At this park there are views of the Santa Clara Valley, San Francisco and the ocean. This preserve features grassy meadows and redwood, fir, and oak trees. Leashed dogs are allowed on designated trails. Directions: From Hwy 280, take Hwy 84 west (La Honda Rd). Go about 2.3 miles to Hwy 35 (Skyline Blvd). The main parking is at the intersection of Hwys 84 and 35. Another starting option is to park at the Portola Valley Town Hall and begin there.

Milk Ranch Loop
Potter Valley, CA
530-934-3316
This trail is 9.5 miles long and is rated moderate. Located in the Mendocino National Forest at an elevation of 5,200 feet, this trail is one of the most popular loops on Snow Mountain. The route offers dense red fir forests, meadows and a barren peak. The Milk Ranch meadow is private property, but the landowner allows horse and foot travelers to pass through on the trail. They just request that no camps be set up within the posted portion of the meadow. Pets are allowed on the trail. They must be leashed in the campground, but are allowed off-leash under voice control on the trail. Please clean up after your pets. The loop can be started at the Summit Springs Trailhead. To get there from Ukiah, take Highway 101 North then take Highway 20 East towards Upper

Lake/Williams. Go about 5 miles and turn left onto Potter Valley Road towards Potter Valley. Turn right on Forest Service Road M8 towards Lake Pillsbury. The road towards the lake is not paved. The trail starts near the lake at the Summit Springs Trailhead. Dogs are also allowed at the lake but should be leashed.

Chambers Creek Trail
Highway 70
Pulga, CA
530-283-0555
This trail is located in the Plumas National Forest and is a moderate one way 4.2 mile trail. There are some great waterfalls at the bridge. It takes about 2 to 3 hours to reach the bridge and a total of 6 hours to the top of the trail. Dogs on leash or off-leash but under direct voice control are allowed. Please clean up after your pets. The trailhead is location about 40 miles west of Quincy on Highway 70, or about 40 miles from Oroville.

Plumas National Forest
159 Lawrence Street
Quincy, CA
530-283-2050
fs.fed.us/r5/plumas/
This national forest covers over 1.1 million acres of land which ranges in elevation from around 2,000 to over 7,000 feet. Please see our listings in this region for dog-friendly hikes and/or campgrounds.

Red Bluff Recreation Area
825 North Humboldt Avenue
Red Bluff, CA
530-934-3316
The popular Red Bluff Recreation Area is part of the Mendocino National Forest. The recreation area includes the Lake Red Bluff Trail (1.5 mi.), which is accessible and paved. The trail travels along the Sacramento River and through a wildlife viewing area. Popular activities at the lake include boating, water skiing, swimming, camping and fishing. The facilities include accessible restrooms with showers, a boat ramp and campground. Dogs are allowed including on the trails and in the water but pets should be leashed. The park is located just east of the city of Red Bluff in the Sacramento Valley. If you are heading North on I-5, take the Highway 36 East exit towards Central Red Bluff/Chico. Continue of Antelope Blvd for less than 1/2 mile and turn right on Sale Lane. The park is open year round unless there

is flooding or high winds.

Samuel Ayer/Dog Island Park
1360 Main Street
Red Bluff, CA
530-527-2605
This day-use park offers multi-use trails, fishing on the Sacramento River, a large group barbecue area, horseshoe pits, picnic areas with fire pits, and restrooms. Dogs of all sizes are allowed; they must be leashed and cleaned up after at all times.

Sacramento River Trail
North Market Street
Redding, CA
530-224-6100
This trail attracts people of all ages, from the walkers and joggers to bicyclists and fisherman looking for an ideal angling spot. The complete trail, round-trip, is approximately 6 miles and can easily be walked in a couple of hours. It is located along the Sacramento River from the North Market Street bridge to Keswick Dam. There are also several access points to the paved trail in Caldwell Park.

Shasta Lake
Redding, CA
530-365-7500
Dogs on leash are allowed on the trails and in the lake. There are miles of trails near this beautiful lake. The easiest trail to reach from Interstate 5 is the Bailey Cove Trail. For a map of all trails, stop at the Visitors Center and Ranger's Station located just south of the lake on Interstate 5 at the Wonderland Blvd exit in Mountain Gate. The Visitor's Center is about 8 miles north of Redding.

Shasta-Trinity National Forest
3644 Avtech Pkwy
Redding, CA
530-226-2500
fs.fed.us/r5/shastatrinity/
This national forest covers over 2 million acres of land which ranges in elevation from 1,000 to 14,162 feet. Please see our listings in this region for dog-friendly hikes and/or campgrounds.

Turtle Bay Exploration Park
840 Auditorium Drive
Redding, CA
800-TURTLEBAY (887-8532)
turtlebay.org/
This amazing exploration park is 300 acres of educational and entertaining activities with a focus

on relationships between humans and nature through the telling of the region and its peoples. It is home to the translucent Sundial Bridge, a free-standing, technical marvel spanning the Sacramento River that connects the north and south campuses of the park. There is also a historical railroad exhibit, an arboretum that extends over 200 acres, a series of climate display gardens, a medicinal garden, children's garden, a variety of several other gardens, and much more. Dogs are allowed throughout most of the park, in the gardens, the bridge, and on the hiking trails. They are not allowed at Paul Bunyan's Forest Camp or in the museum. Dogs must be leashed and cleaned up after at all times. There are doggy clean-up supplies on site.

Prospect Park
Cajon Street
Redlands, CA
909-798-7572
Prospect Park is a 11.4 acre natural park with trails and picnic facilities. Dogs on leash are allowed.

Pulgas Ridge Open Space Preserve
Edmonds Road
Redwood City, CA
650-691-1200
openspace.org/PULGAS.html
This park has about 293 acres and some great trails. There are are about 3 miles of trails that will provide moderate to strenuous exercise. Leashed dogs are allowed on the trails. The park offers some nice shade on warm days. To get there from Interstate 280, take the Edgewood Road exit. Travel 0.75 miles northeast on Edgewood Road toward San Carlos and Redwood City. Turn left (north) on Crestview Drive, and then immediately turn left on Edmonds Road. Limited roadside parking is available along Crestview Drive and Edmonds Road.

Wildcat Canyon Regional Park
5755 McBride
Richmond, CA
510-562-PARK (7275)
ebparks.org/parks/wildcat.htm
Rich in natural and cultural history, this park of over 2,400 acres supports an assortment of plant and animal life, and offers a variety of land and water recreational pursuits, and interpretive programs. There are picnic areas, restrooms, and lots of trails to walk. Dogs of all sizes are allowed throughout the park except where noted. Dogs must be on no

more than a 6 foot leash, and be cleaned up after at all times. Dogs are not allowed in any swim areas, park buildings, or the Tilden's Nature Area.

Box Springs Mountain Reserve
Pigeon Pass Road
Riverside, CA
909-684-7032
This 1,155 acre park offers hiking and equestrian trails. The park is located 5 miles east of Riverside off Highway 60 and Pigeon Pass Road. Dogs must be leashed and please clean up after them.

Hidden Valley Wildlife
Arlington Avenue
Riverside, CA
909-785-6362
Dogs on leash are allowed at this wildlife reserve. It is a popular spot for birdwatching and walking. There is a minimal fee for day use. This reserve is part of the Santa Ana River Regional Park. To get there from the 91 Fwy, go east to the city of Riverside. Exit on La Sierra Ave. and turn left (north). La Sierra dead-ends into Arlington. Bear left at the signal. Drive past the hills until you come to the sign that says "Hidden Valley." Take the first dirt road to the right.

Mount Rubidoux Park
Mt. Rubidoux Drive
Riverside, CA
This park is the highest point in downtown Riverside. It is a popular hiking trail which offers a spectacular 360 degree view of Riverside. Dogs on leash are allowed on the trails. To get there from downtown Riverside, take Mission Inn Avenue northeast (towards the Santa Ana River). Turn left (west) onto Redwood Street. Continue straight to stay on Redwood (otherwise you will go onto University Ave). Turn right on 9th Street and follow it to the park.

Rancho Jurupa Park
Crestmore Road
Riverside, CA
909-684-7032
This 350 acre park is part of the Santa Ana Regional Park and has more than 10 miles of hiking and equestrian trails. There are also horseshoe pits and picnic areas. To get there from downtown Riverside, take Mission Inn Ave northwest (towards the Santa Ana River). Go over the river and turn left at Crestmore Road. Follow this road to the park entrance. There is a minimal

fee for parking and for dogs. Dogs must be leashed.

Ice House Bike Trail
Ice House Road
Riverton, CA
530-644-2349
This 3.1 mile dirt trail winds along the ridge tops and shaded slopes, through old and new forest growths. The trail, located in the Eldorado National Forest at about 5,400 feet, is rated easy and offers great views of the Ice House Reservoir. Both hikers and mountain bikers use this trail. Dogs should be on leash and are allowed on the trail and in the water. To get there from Placerville, take Highway 50 east for 21 miles to Ice House Road turnoff. Turn left and go 11 miles north to the campground turnoff. Then go one mile to the campgrounds. The trail can be accessed from any of the Ice House Reservoir campgrounds or at the intersection of Road 12N06 and Ice House Road which is located about 200 yards north of the turnoff to Big Hill Lookout.

Union Valley Bike Trail
Ice House Road
Riverton, CA
530-644-2349
This 4.8 mile two-lane paved trail is located in the Eldorado National Forest. Elevations range from 4,860 to 5,160 feet. The trail connects all the campgrounds on the east side of Union Valley Reservoir, from Jones Fork to Wench Creek Campgrounds. Parking is available at the campgrounds except for Lone Rock and Azalea Cove. Views and interpretive signs complement this high country trail. Dogs should be on leash and are allowed on the trail and in the water. To get there from Placerville, take Highway 50 east and go 21 miles to Riverton. Turn left on Ice House Road. Go about 19 miles north to the reservoir.

Crane Creek Regional Park
5000 Pressley Road
Rohnert Park, CA
707-565-2041
sonoma-county.org/parks
Located just east of Sonoma State University, this 128 acre foothills park offers hiking and bicycling trails. There are picnic tables and restrooms at the trailhead. Dogs must be kept on a 6 foot or less leash. There is a $3 per car parking fee.

Maidu Park
Rocky Ridge Rd & Maidu Dr
Roseville, CA
916-774-5969
Dogs must be on leash in this new 152 acre park in Roseville.

Schabarum Regional Park
17250 E. Colima Road
Rowland Heights, CA
626-854-5560
This 640 acre wilderness park offers open space, picturesque canyons and rolling hills. Popular activities at the park including hiking, biking and horseback riding. Park amenities include an 18 station fitness trail, picnic areas, equestrian center, playgrounds and sports fields. There is a parking fee on weekends, holidays and during special events. Dogs are allowed at the park and on the hiking trails. Pets must be leashed and people need to clean up after their pet.

American River Parkway
various (see comments)
Sacramento, CA
916-875-6672
The American River Parkway is a very popular recreation trail for locals and visitors. There are over 32 miles of paved and dirt paths that stretch from Folsom Lake in the Sierra Foothills to Old Sacramento in downtown Sacramento. It is enjoyed by hikers, wildlife viewers, boaters, equestrians and bicyclists. And of course, by dogs. Dogs must be on leash. There are various starting points, like the Folsom Lake State Recreation Area in Folsom or just north of downtown Sacramento. To start just north of downtown, take Hwy 5 north of downtown and exit Richards Blvd. Turn left onto Richards Blvd. Then turn right on Jibboom Street. Take Jibboom St to the parking lot.

William Land Park
4000 S Land Park Drive
Sacramento, CA
916-808-5200
With just over 166 developed acres, this park offers a variety of recreational opportunities and amenities, some of which include family and group picnic areas, gaming courts, playing fields, an adventure play area, an amphitheater, rock garden, and a jogging path. They are also home to the Sacramento Zoo, Fairytale town, Funderland, and a golf course. Dogs are allowed throughout the park unless otherwise noted. They must

be leashed and cleaned up after at all times.

Toro County Park
501 Monterey-Salinas Highway 68
Salinas, CA
831-755-4895
This 4,756 acre park offers over 20 miles of hiking, biking and horseback riding trails. Other park amenities include playgrounds, picnic sites, volleyball courts and an equestrian staging area. There is a $3 vehicle entrance fee during the week and a $5 fee on weekends and holidays. This park is located 6 miles from downtown Salinas and 13 miles from the Monterey Peninsula. Dogs need to be leashed and please clean up after them.

San Bernardino National Forest
1824 S. Commercenter Circle
San Bernardino, CA
909-382-2600
fs.fed.us/r5/sanbernardino/
This national forest covers over 600,000 acres of land which ranges in elevation from 2,000 to 11,502 feet. Please see our listings in this region for dog-friendly hikes and/or campgrounds.

Balboa Park
El Prado St
San Diego, CA
619-235-1121
balboapark.org
Balboa Park is a 1200 acre urban cultural park located just east of downtown. Dogs must be leashed and under control of the owner at all times, including on the trails and in the canyons. The park is known for its brilliant displays of seasonal flowers, an award-winning rose garden, shady groves of trees, and meandering paths. Many of Balboa Park's museums are magnificent Spanish Colonial Revival buildings, originally constructed for the 1915-1916 Panama-California Exposition. If you are interested in the architecture, you and your pup can take an outdoor walking tour around the various buildings. Work up an appetite after walking around? There is a concession stand called In the Park. It has many outdoor seats and is located at the corner of Village Place and Old Globe Way. For a map of the park, stop by the Visitors Center on El Prado St near Hwy 163. There is also an unfenced dog run on the west side of the park by El Prado and Balboa Drive.

Cabrillo National Monument

1800 Cabrillo Memorial Drive
San Diego, CA
619-557-5450
nps.gov/cabr
This day-use park is rich in cultural and natural resources, and because of its location, it features a rather biologically diverse ecosystem creating habitats for a vast variety of plant, bird, marine life, and wildlife. The park rests on 160 acres at the southern-most tip of a peninsula, and is open every day of the year. Dogs are allowed here on leash, and they must be cleaned up after. Dogs are allowed in the dirt lot parking area at the lower end of the park, and on the trails to the tide pools only. The best time for viewing the tide pools is in the winter. Dogs are not allowed on any other trails, at the main parking lot where the visitor center is, or the lighthouse.

Cleveland National Forest
10845 Rancho Bernardo Rd., Suite 200
San Diego, CA
858-673-6180
fs.fed.us/r5/cleveland/
This national forest covers 460,000 acres and offers 356 miles of trails. Please see our listings in this region for dog-friendly hikes and/or campgrounds.

Embarcadero Marina Park North and South
Foot of Kettner (N) or Marina Park Way (S), Port of San Diego
San Diego, CA
619-686-6225
This small but popular public park is split in half by the entrance from San Diego Bay into Embarcadero Marina, and is bordered by Seaport Village and the San Diego Convention Center. Set between two peninsulas, there is great scenery, ample parking, a fishing pier, multi-use paths, exercise stations, gaming courts, gazebos, and a concessionaire. Dogs are welcome; they must be well behaved, leashed and cleaned up after at all times.

Harbor Island
2036 Harbor Island Drive
San Diego, CA
619-686-6200
This day use park is located near the west end of the island and offers visitors spectacular panoramic views of the bay and its activities. There is a shoreline path for hikers as well as a route for

bikers. Dogs are allowed at the picnic area and on the trails. Dogs must be under their owner's control, and leashed and cleaned up after at all times.

Mission Bay Park
Mission Bay Drive
San Diego, CA
619-221-8900
Leashed dogs are allowed in this park from 6pm to 9am. There are over 20 miles of beaches that make up this park (including Fiesta Island). If you come during the above mentioned hours, there is also a nice path that meanders through the grass and trees.

Mission Trails Regional Park
1 Father Junipero Serra Trail
San Diego, CA
619-668-3275
mtrp.org/
This 6,000 acre regional park has a nice variety of trails ranging from an easy 1 mile loop to a strenuous 5 mile hike with elevation gains of up to 1150 feet. Dogs are allowed, but must be leashed at all times. Don't forget to bring enough water since it can get pretty warm here year-round. The park is located off Mission Gorge Rd at the corners of Father Junipero Serra Trail and Echo Dell Rd. It is located about 8-9 northeast of downtown San Diego. Maps are available at the Visitor and Interpretive Center on Father Junipero Serra Trail.

Park at the Park (Petco Park)
Ninth Avenue at J Street
San Diego, CA
This 2.7 acre grassy park offers a panoramic view of Petco Park, the San Diego Padres baseball stadium. It is located beyond the outfield fences. The park is dog-friendly most of the time, except during baseball games when an admission fee of $5 is charged and dogs are not permitted. They are allowed to attend one Padres game each year at Petco Park's "Dog Days of Summer" event. Please clean up after your dog.

Presidio Park
Jackson St
San Diego, CA
619-235-1100
This is a nice park for your pup to stretch his or her legs before or after you visit Old Town State Historic Park which is located about 2-3 blocks away. Dogs must be leashed in the park.

Sunset Cliffs Park
Sunset Cliffs Boulevard
San Diego, CA
619-235-1100
This park was named for its spectacular sunset vistas and it covers 68 acres of bluffs and walking paths that tower above the Pacific Ocean. Sunset Cliffs Boulevard is also popular for the coastal scenic drive that begins at Adair Street and runs south to Ladera Street. In winter, from high on the bluffs you can see migrating whales. The day use is an overview area and there are only portable restrooms available. Dogs are allowed here and on the bluff trails; they must be under their owner's control at all times, leashed, and cleaned up after.

Tecolote Canyon Natural Park
Tecolote Road
San Diego, CA
619-581-9952
This is a very nice natural park with over 6 miles (12 round trip) of walking, running or mountain biking trails. There are nine entry points into the park, but we recommend you start at the Visitors and Nature Center where you can pick up a trail map from the ranger. If you start at the Nature Center, most of the trail (first five miles) is relatively flat. It gets steeper in the last mile and there could be some creek crossings. From the Nature Center, follow the path which will take you past a golf course. At the end of the golf course, you'll need to take Snead Ave which will join up with the rest of the path. There might be a few more street crossings, but the majority of the walk is on the dirt trail. With the all the natural surroundings it seems like it is far from the city, but it's located only 6-7 miles from downtown. To get there, take Tecolote Road until it ends. Dogs must be on leash in the park.

Frank Bonelli Park
120 Via Verde Road
San Dimas, CA
909-599-8411
This 1,980 acre park has a 250 acre lake for swimming, water skiing, wind surfing, sailing and fishing. The lake is stocked with trout, bluegill, catfish, and largemouth bass. Park amenities include hiking trails, playgrounds and food stands. There is a parking fee on weekends, holidays and during special events. Dogs are allowed at the park and on the hiking trails, but not in the water or at the beach area. Pets must be leashed and people

need to clean up after their pet.

San Dimas Canyon Nature Center
1628 N. Sycamore Canyon Road
San Dimas, CA
909-599-7512
This 1,000 plus acre park offers a variety of nature trails. There is a minimal parking fee. Dogs are allowed on the trails, but must be leashed. Please clean up after your dog.

Angeles National Forest
Little Tujunga Canyon Rd.
San Fernando, CA
626-574-1613
This forest is over 690,000 acres and covers one-fourth of the land in Los Angeles County. We have selected a couple of trails near San Fernando Valley ranging from 2.5 to 3 miles. Dogs are allowed on leash or leash free but under voice control. Both of the trails are single-track, foot trails. The first trail is called Gold Creek Trail. It is about 2.5 miles long. The second trail is called Oaks Springs Trail and it is about 3 miles long. To get there from Hwy 215, take the Foothill Blvd. exit and head north towards the mountains. Turn left onto Little Tujunga Canyon Rd. You will see the Little Tujunga Forest Station on the left. After you pass the station, continue on Little Tujunga Canyon Rd. Go about 1-1.5 miles and then turn right onto Gold Creek Rd. Go about 1 mile and on the right you will see the trailhead for Oak Springs Trail. If you continue to the end of Gold Creek Rd, you will see the trailhead for Gold Creek Trail. There should be parking along the road.

Alta Plaza Park
Clay Street
San Francisco, CA
This park is bordered by Jackson, Clay, Steiner and Scott streets. It is across from the tennis courts. The first Sunday of every month is Pug Day at this park. It's a casual meeting of pug owners which takes place at the north end of park, usually between 3:30 - 5:00, weather permitting. At the gathering, there can be 20-50 pugs. Dogs need to be on leash but residents are trying to make it a legal off-leash area.

Candlestick Point State Recreation Area
Next to Monster Park
San Francisco, CA

415-671-0145
This park offers views of the San Francisco Bay. Amenities include hiking trails, picnic areas, fishing, a fitness course for seniors, and special cultural and educational programs planned throughout the year. Dogs are allowed at the park and on the trails. Pets must be on a 6 foot or less leash, with the exception of the leash free areas. The off-leash areas are the big dirt lots near Monster Park where sports fans park on game days. The off-leash areas are not available on game days. Please clean up after your pet. The park is located next to Monster Park. Take the Monster Park exit from Highway 101.

Crissy Field Park
Mason Street
San Francisco, CA
415-561-4700
crissyfield.org/
This 100 acre shoreline park is part of the Golden Gate National Recreation Area. Enjoy scenic views of the Golden Gate Bridge while you walk or jog along the paved paths. Off leash areas include the beaches along the waterline and the large, grassy landing field, with the exception of the West beach nearest to Fort Point where they must be leashed. They must be under firm voice control when not on lead. Dogs must be leashed when not in the off lead areas, and they must be cleaned up after at all times. Dogs are not allowed in the fenced restoration zones or the lagoon area. The park is located north of Mason Street and southeast of the Golden Gate Bridge.

Golden Gate National Recreation Area
San Francisco, CA
415-556-0560
nps.gov/goga/
This dog-friendly Recreation Area spans 76,500 acres of land and water. It starts at the coastline south of San Francisco, goes into San Francisco and then north of the Golden Gate Bridge. Many of the San Francisco beaches and parks are part of this Rec Area including Baker Beach, Fort Funston and Ocean Beach. One of the trails is located south of Baker Beach. From Lincoln Avenue, turn onto Bowley Street and head towards the ocean. There is a parking lot next to the beach. Dogs must be on leash.

Presidio of San Francisco

Hwy 1/Park Presidio Blvd.
San Francisco, CA
415-561-4323
nps.gov/prsf/
This land was an Army base and is now a dog-friendly national park (borders up to the Golden Gate Recreation Area.) The park has over 500 historic buildings and miles of nice hiking trails. Leashes may or may not be required as this issue is going back and forth in the courts currently. It's located south of the Golden Gate Bridge. From the Bridge and Hwy101, take Hwy 1 south. It will turn into Park Presidio Blvd. You can also enter the park from Arguello Blvd.

Almaden Quicksilver
McAbee Ave.
San Jose, CA
408-268-8220
parkhere.org/prkpages/aq.htm
This park encompasses over 3900 acres. Dogs are allowed on a 6 foot leash. During early spring the park offers a wildflower display. Remnants of the mining era also offer a look at the mining operations of the 1800's. The park may be accessed from three areas. The McAbee entrance at the north end of the park can be accessed off McAbee Road. This entrance is accessible to pedestrians and equestrians only. Turn south off Camden Avenue and follow McAbee Road until it ends (.6 miles). Only street parking is available. The Mockingbird Hill entrance is accessed off Mockingbird Hill Lane. This entrance is accessible to pedestrians and equestrians only. From Highway 85, take the Almaden Expressway exit south 4.5 miles to Almaden Road. Proceed .5 miles on Almaden Road to Mockingbird Hill Lane, turn right and continue .4 miles to the parking entrance is accessible to all users, including bicyclists. From Almaden Expressway, proceed 3 miles along Almaden Road through the town of New Almaden to the unpaved staging area on the right.

Coyote Creek Parkway
various-see comments
San Jose, CA
408-225-0225
The Coyote Creek Trail is approximately 13 miles each way. The north end is paved and popular with bicyclders, rollerbladers and hikers. The sound end (south of Metcalf Rd) has an equestrian dirt trail that parallels the paved trail. Leashed dogs are allowed on both the paved and dirt trails. You can

gain access to the trail at numerous points. The south trail access has parking off Burnett Ave. From Hwy 101 South, exit Cochrane Rd. Turn right on Cochrane. Then turn right on Monterey Hwy (Hwy 82). Right on Burnett Ave and the parking will be at the end of Burnett. The north trail access has parking at Hellyer Park. From Hwy 101, exit Hellyer Ave and head west. Continue straight, pay at the booth and then park. There is also parking at Silver Creek Valley Blvd for north trail access. Take Hwy 101 and exit Silver Creek Valley Blvd. Head east (toward the hills). Parking will be on the right.

Guadalupe River Park & Gardens
715 Spring Street
San Jose, CA
408-298-7657
grpg.org/
The river park is a 3-mile section of land that runs along the banks of the Guadalupe River in the heart of downtown, and adjacent to the park are the gardens, together providing 150 acres open to the public. The Heritage Rose Garden has over 3,700 varieties of roses, and has been further developed to include 2.6 miles of trails, over 15,000 trees, 9,000 shrubs, and 60,000 groundcover plants, and is also beneficial in providing the town with 100 year flood protection. Dogs of all sizes are welcome. Dogs must be on lead at all times, cleaned up after, and all must stay on the paths.

Santa Teresa County Park
San Vicente Avenue
San Jose, CA
408-268-3883
parkhere.org/prkpages/santat.htm
Dogs are allowed on a 6 foot leash. This diverse 1,688 acre park, located ten miles south of downtown San Jose, is rich in history and offers spectacular views from its trails located above the Almaden and Santa Clara Valleys. The secluded upland valleys of the park provide a quiet place for exploring the natural environment minutes away from the surrounding developed areas. From San Jose, follow Almaden Expressway until it ends. Turn right onto Harry Road, then turn left onto McKean Road. Travel approximately 1.3 miles to Fortini Road. Turn left onto Fortini Road toward the Santa Teresa Hills. At the end of Fortini Road, turn left onto San Vicente Avenue.

A ten car parking area is located on the right about 500 feet from Fortini Road.

Civic Center Lagoon Park
Civic Center Drive
San Rafael, CA
415-499-6387
This 20 acre park has an 11 acre lagoon which is used for fishing and non-motorized boating. The park also has picnic areas and a children's playground. Leashed dogs are allowed.

John F. McInnis Park
Smith Ranch Road
San Rafael, CA
415-499-6387
This 440 acre parks offers nature trails, sports fields, and a golf course. Dogs are allowed not allowed on the golf course. Pets are allowed off leash but must be under immediate verbal control at all times. Owners must also carry a leash and pick up after their pets.

Samuel P. Taylor State Park
Sir Francis Drake Blvd.
San Rafael, CA
While dogs are not allowed on the hiking trails, they are allowed on the bike trail that runs about six miles through the park. The path is nearly level and follows the Northwest Pacific Railroad right-of-way. The trail is both paved and dirt and it starts near the park entrance. Dogs are also allowed in the developed areas like the campgrounds. Pets must be leashed and please clean up after your pet. The park is located north of San Francisco, 15 miles west of San Rafael on Sir Francis Drake Blvd.

Manning Park
Manning Park
San Ysidro, CA
805-969-0201
The park is open 8 am to Sunset. Dogs on leash are allowed throughout the city park.

Centennial Regional Park
3000 W Edinger Avenue
Santa Ana, CA
714-571-4200
This large, day-use park features a 10 acre lake stocked with fish and an historic trail that follows the original path of the Santa Ana River. There are picnic areas, restrooms, and several multi-use trails. Dogs are allowed throughout the park and on the trails. Dogs must be well behaved, leashed, and cleaned up

after at all times.

Beach Walkway
Cabrillo Blvd.
Santa Barbara, CA
We couldn't find the official name of
this paved path (it might be part of
Chase Palm Park), so we are
labeling it the "Beach Walkway". This
path parallels the beach. While dogs
are not allowed on this beach, they
can walk along the paved path which
has grass and lots of palm trees.
There are also many public
restrooms along the path. The path
is about 1.5 miles long each way.

Chase Palm Park
323 E. Cabrillo Boulevard
Santa Barbara, CA
805-564-5433
This beautiful waterfront city park
opened in May 1998. It is about a
mile long and has many sections
including a carousel, plaza, pavilion,
shipwreck playground, the wilds,
fountain gateway and casa las
palmas. It is on Cabrillo Blvd.
between Garden Street and Calle
Cesar Chavez Street.

Plaza Del Mar
129 Castillo Street
Santa Barbara, CA
This city park is about 4 blocks long
and is close to several hotels and
restaurants. The park is home to the
Old Spanish Days Carriage Museum.
While dogs are not allowed inside
the museum, you can see many of
the carriages from the outside.

Shoreline Park
1200 Shoreline Drive
Santa Barbara, CA
This 1/2 mile paved path winds along
the headlands and provides scenic
overlooks of Santa Barbara and the
ocean. It is located northwest of
Leadbetter Beach and Santa
Barbara City College.

Lighthouse Field
West Cliff Drive
Santa Cruz, CA
831-429-3777
Leashes are required at all times
now at Lighthouse Field. It used to
have off-leash hours but this was
discontinued. This field is not fenced
and there are several busy streets
nearby, so if your dog runs off-leash,
make sure he or she is very well
trained. It is located on West Cliff
Drive, just north of the Lighthouse,
and south of Columbia Street. It is
also across from the West
Lighthouse Beach. To get there,

head south on Hwy 17. Take the
Hwy 1 North exit, heading towards
Half Moon Bay and Hwy 9. Merge
onto Mission Street (Hwy 1). Turn
left onto Swift Street. Then turn left
on West Cliff Drive. Limited parking
will be on the right or on other sides
of the field.

West Cliff Drive Walkway
West Cliff Drive
Santa Cruz, CA
831-429-3777
This is a popular paved walking
path that follows the beautiful Santa
Cruz coastline. It is about 2 miles
long each way and is frequented by
walkers, runners, bicyclists and of
course, dogs. It is located on West
Cliff Drive, north of the Santa Cruz
Beach Boardwalk and south of
Natural Bridges State Beach. While
dogs are not allowed on either the
Boardwalk or the State Beach,
there is a dog beach along this path
called West Lighthouse Beach.
There are several areas where you
can park near the path. The easiest
is by the north end of the path:
Heading south on Hwy 17, take the
Hwy 1 North exit towards Half Moon
Bay and Hwy 9. Merge onto Mission
Street (Hwy 1). Turn left onto Swift
Street. Then turn right on West Cliff
Drive. Turn right onto Swanton Blvd.
Parking is available on Swanton
Blvd. If you prefer to park closer to
the Boardwalk, follow these
directions: From Hwy 17 heading
south, take the Hwy 1 North exit
towards Half Moon Bay and Hwy 9.
Merge onto Chestnut Street. Turn
left onto Laurel Street, then right
onto Center Street. Make a slight
left onto Washington Street and
Washington will become Pacific
Avenue. Then turn right onto Beach
Street. There is limited metered
parked available near the Municipal
Wharf.

Santa Margarita Lake Regional
Park
off Pozo Road
Santa Margarita, CA
805-781-5930
This lake is popular for fishing,
boating and hiking. Swimming is not
allowed at the lake because it is a
reservoir which is used for city
drinking water. There is a seasonal
swimming pool at the park. Hiking
can be enjoyed at this park which
offers miles of trails, ranging from
easy to strenuous. Dogs must be
leashed at all times and people
need to clean up after their pets.

Hood Mountain Regional Park
3000 Los Alamos Road
Santa Rosa, CA
707-565-2041
This 1,450 acre wilderness park
offers bicycling, equestrian and
rugged hiking trails for experienced
hikers in good physical condition.
Dogs are allowed at this park, but
must be on a 6 foot or less leash.
Access to the park is on Los Alamos
Road which is a very narrow and
winding road. There is a $3 per car
parking fee.

Spring Lake Regional Park
391 Violetti Drive
Santa Rosa, CA
707-785-2377
This 320 acre park with a 72 acre
lake offers miles of easy walking
trails and a campground. Dogs are
allowed but must be on a 6 foot or
less leash and proof of a rabies
vaccination is required.

Santa Ynez Recreation Area
Paradise Road
Santa Ynez, CA
805-967-3481
Dogs on leash are allowed on the
nature trails and hikes. There are
miles of trails at this park. Other
activities include swimming and
fishing. This recreation area is
actually part of the Los Padres
National Forest. From Highway l0l at
west end of Santa Barbara, turn
north on Highway l54 (San Marcos
Pass Road) for about10- l2 miles,
then go east on Paradise Road to
the Santa Ynez Recreation Area.

Joe Rodota Trail
Petaluma Avenue
Sebastopol, CA
707-565-2041
This is a 2.8 mile paved trail that
runs parallel to an abandoned
railway line. There are agricultural
ranches and farms along the trail.
Dogs are allowed, but must be on a
6 foot or less leash. Parking is
available in the town of Sebastopol,
at the trailhead located off of
Petaluma Avenue.

Ragle Ranch Regional Park
500 Ragle Road
Sebastopol, CA
707-565-2041
This 157 acre park offers walking
trails, sports courts, picnic areas and
a children's playground. Dogs are
allowed, but must be on a 6 foot or
less leash. There is a $3 per car
parking fee.

Hirz Bay Trail
Gilman Road
Shasta Lake, CA
530-275-1587
This 1.6 mile easy rated trail is located in the Shasta-Trinity National Forest. The trail follows the shoreline and crosses several cool, shady creeks. It also provides scenic vistas of the lake. The trailhead is located at Hirz Bay Campground which is 10 miles from Interstate 5 on Gilman Road. Dogs are allowed in the lake, but not at the designated swimming beaches. Pets must be leashed and please clean up after them.

Van Nuys/Sherman Oaks Park
14201 Huston St
Sherman Oaks, CA
818-783-5121
This park has an approximate 1.5 mile walking and jogging path that winds through and around the sports fields. There are also many picnic tables near the Recreation Center. To get there from Hwy 101, take the Van Nuys exit and head north.

Corriganville Park
7001 Smith Road
Simi Valley, CA
805-584-4400
Once owned by a cowboy actor and used as a western setting for hundreds of movies and TV shows in the 1940's and 50's, this 190 acre day use park now offers visitors several recreational activities, hiking trails, picnic areas, park benches, restrooms, and drinking fountains. Dogs are allowed throughout the park and on the trails. Dogs must be under their owner's immediate control, leashed, and cleaned up after at all times.

Hans Christian Andersen Park
Atterdag Road
Solvang, CA
You and your leashed pup can enjoy a 1.3 mile round trip hike along meadows lined with majestic oak trees. This park's 50 acres also has picnic facilities, a playground for kids and tennis courts. It is open daily from 8 a.m. to dusk. The park is located within walking distance of the village. It on Atterdag Road, just 3 blocks north of Mission Drive and the village of Solvang.

Nojoqui Falls Park
Alisal Road
Solvang, CA
Nojoqui Falls is a 160+ foot waterfall which towers over the park grounds. It is best viewed after a rainy period.

You and your leashed pup can view the waterfall by embarking on an easy 10 minute hike through a wooded canyon. This park also has a sports playing field, playgrounds for kids, and a picnic area. The park is open every day from dawn to dusk. It is located on Alisal Road, just 7 miles south of Solvang on a country road.

Solvang Park
Mission Drive
Solvang, CA
This small city park is located in the middle of the Solvang village. It is a nice spot to rest after walking around town. It is located on Mission Drive at the corner of First Street.

Maxwell Farms Regional Park
100 Verano Avenue
Sonoma, CA
707-565-2041
This 85 acre park offers meadow nature trails on 40 acres, multi-use fields for soccer and softball, a children's playground and picnic areas. Dogs are allowed but must be on a 6 foot or less leash. There is a $3 parking fee.

Stanislaus National Forest
19777 Greenley Road
Sonora, CA
209-532-3671
fs.fed.us/r5/stanislaus/
This national forest covers almost 900,000 acres of land which ranges in elevation from 1,200 to over 10,000 feet. Please see our listings in the Sierra Nevada region for dog-friendly hikes and campgrounds.

Whittier Narrows Nature Center
1000 N. Durfee Ave.
South El Monte, CA
626-575-5523
This park has over 200 acres of natural woodland and includes four lakes which offer a winter sanctuary for migrating waterfowl. Dogs are allowed on the trails, but not in the water. Pets must be leashed and please clean up after them.

Whittier Narrows Recreation Area
823 Lexinton-Gallatin Road
South El Monte, CA
310-589-3200
This 1,400 acre day use park offers a wide variety of land and water recreational opportunities, in addition to hosting carnivals, festivals, and dog shows. Some of the features/amenities include fishing lakes, comfort stations,

gaming courts/fields, playgrounds, picnicking areas, and hiking and multi-use trails. Dogs are allowed throughout the park and on the trails. Dogs must be under their owner's immediate control, leashed, and cleaned up after at all times.

Cove East
Venice Drive East
South Lake Tahoe, CA
This short but nice path is located near the boat rentals and Tahoe Keys Resort. It's approximately 1-2 miles and will give your pup a chance to take care of business before hopping on board your rental boat. To get there from Hwy 89 north, take Hwy 50 east. Turn left onto Tahoe Keys Blvd and then right at Venice Drive East. Dogs must be leashed.

Desolation Wilderness
Fall Leaf Lake Road
South Lake Tahoe, CA
530-644-2349
fs.fed.us/r5/eldorado/
This wilderness area is located in the Eldorado National Forest and has many access points. One of the trailheads is located at Fallen Leaf Lake. See our Fallen Leaf Lake listing in South Lake Tahoe for more details. Dogs need to be leashed and please clean up after them.

Eagle Falls
Hwy 89
South Lake Tahoe, CA
This beautiful moderate to strenuous hiking trail in the Desolation Wilderness starts at Hwy 89 and goes up to Eagle Lake. This trail is pretty popular because it's about a 1 mile hike from the road to the lake. If you want a longer hike, you can go another 4-5 miles where there are 3 other lakes. Dogs must be leashed. To get there from the intersection of Hwys 50 and 89, take Hwy 89 north and go approximately 8 miles. The Eagle Falls Picnic Area and parking are on the left. Day and Camping Wilderness Permits are required. Go here early because it is extremely popular and parking spots fill up fast. There is a minimal fee for parking. Dogs must be on leash on the trail.

Echo Lakes Trail
off Johnson Pass Road
South Lake Tahoe, CA
See a variety of alpine lakes on this moderate rated trail. Take Highway 50 to Echo Summit and turn onto Johnson Pass Road. Stay left and the road will lead you to the parking area by Lower Echo Lake. For a

short hike, go to the far end of Upper Echo Lake. A longer hike leads you to one of the many lakes further down the trail. Day hikers, pick up your permit at the self serve area just to the left of the Echo Lake Chalet. Dogs should always be on leash.

Fallen Leaf Lake
Fallen Leaf Lake Rd off Hwy 89
South Lake Tahoe, CA
There are some nice walking trails on the north shore of Fallen Leaf Lake and the surrounding areas. To get there from the intersection of Hwys 89 and 50, take Hwy 89 north approximately 2.5 to 3 miles to Fallen Leaf Lake Rd. Turn left and in about 1/2 mile there will be parking on the right. The Fallen Leaf Lake Trail begins here. For a longer hike, there are two other options. For the first option, instead of taking the trailhead on the right, take the trail on the left side of Fallen Leaf Lake Rd. This trail is also known as the Tahoe Mountain Bike Trail. Option number two is to take Fallen Leaf Lake Rd further to the south side of Fallen Leaf Lake. Park at the Glen Alpine trailhead which offers about 3-4 miles of trails (parking is across from Lily Lake). There is also a trail here that heads off to the Desolation Wilderness which has miles and miles of trails. Dogs should be leashed.

Biz-Johnson Trail
2950 Riverside Drive
Susanville, CA
530-257-0456
This 25 mile trail follows the old Fernley and Lassen Branch Line of the Southern Pacific Railroad. It begins in Susanville at 4,200 feet and climbs 1,300 feet to a high point of 5,500 feet. Following the Susan River, the trail crosses over the river many times and passes through a former railroad tunnel. During the winter the trail's upper segment, located west of Highway 36, is used for cross-country skiing. Dogs on leash are allowed. Please clean up after your dog. To check on current trail conditions, call the Eagle Lake BLM Field Office at 530-257-0456. To get there from Alturas, take Highway 36 to Susanville. Follow Main Street to the stop light at the bottom of the hill by historic Uptown Susanville. Turn left on Weatherlow Street which becomes Richmond Road. Follow Richmond Road .5 miles across Susan River to Susanville Railroad Depot Trailhead and Visitor Center.

Lassen National Forest
Highways 44 and 89
Susanville, CA
530-257-4188
fs.fed.us/r5/lassen
Within this forest you can explore a lava tube, watch prong-horn antelope, drive four-wheel trails into high granite country or discover spring wildflowers on foot. Dogs are allowed on leash. If you want to check out a lava tube take a self-guided tour of the Subway Cave. Be sure to bring a flashlight, as there are no other sources of light underground. Subway Cave is located near the town of Old Station, 1/4 mile north of the junction of Highway 44 & 89 across from Cave Campground. The temperature inside the cave remains a cool 46 degrees F. year around. The cave is open late May through October and closed during the winter months. Or try a hike instead. Try the Spattercone Trail which explores the volcanic landscape and how life adapts to it. Three of the four kinds of volcanoes in the world can be seen along the Spattercone Trail. The trailhead and parking area are located at the Sanitary Dump Station across the highway form Hat Creek Campground on Highway 89 in Old Station. The trail has a round-trip distance of 1.5 miles. This trail is not shaded, so during the summer, try an early morning or late afternoon walk. For information about other miles of trails throughout this beautiful forest, stop by any National Forest Offices in Susanville including the Eagle Lake Ranger District Office located at 477-050 Eagle Lake Road in Susanville.

Truckee River Bike Path
Hwy 89
Tahoe City, CA
This paved path starts at Tahoe City and heads towards Squaw Valley, paralleling Highway 89. It's about 5 miles each way with spots for your water dog to take a dip in the Truckee River (just be careful of any quick moving currents.) To get there, the path starts near the intersection of Hwys 89 and 28 in Tahoe City. You can also join the path 1/2 - 1 mile out of town by heading north on Hwy 89 and then there are 1 or 2 parking areas on the left side which are adjacent to the path. Dogs must be on leash.

Tehachapi Mountain Park

Highway 58
Tehachapi, CA
661-868-7000
co.kern.ca.us/parks/tehachap.htm
This 5,000 acre park offers views of the Tehachapi Mountains, the dividing line between the San Joaquin Valley and the Los Angeles Basin. The Nuooah Nature Trail is an interesting interpretative 1/4 mile trail. The park is located between Bakersfield and Mojave. It is 8 miles southwest of the town of Tehachapi and is on the southern side of Hwy. 58. Dogs must be on leash.

Duck Pond
Rancho California and Ynez Rd
Temecula, CA
909-836-3285
Dogs on leash are allowed in the park. Owners must pick up after their dog.

Lake Skinner Recreation Area
Rancho California Road
Temecula, CA
909-926-1541
This 6,040 acre park features a lake, hiking trails, equestrian trails and camping. Dogs are allowed on the trails and in the campgrounds, but not in the lake or within 50 feet of the lake. Dogs must be on a 6 foot or less leash and please clean up after them. To get there, take Highway 15 to Rancho California Road and go north 10 miles. There is a minimal fee for day use of the park.

Sam Hicks Park
Old Town Temecula
Temecula, CA
909-836-3285
Dogs are allowed on leash. Owners must pick up after their pets.

Santa Monica Mountains National Recreation Area
401 West Hillcrest Drive
Thousand Oaks, CA
805-370-2301
nps.gov/samo/index.htm
Dogs on leash are allowed in the park. They must stay on trails, roads and campgrounds. They are not allowed in any buildings or undeveloped areas. This park features fishing, hiking, camping, swimming, and more.

Wildwood Regional Park
Ave. De Los Arboles
Thousand Oaks, CA

This park has hiking trails that run along a beautiful hill and streams (the streams have water at certain times of the year). It makes for a great morning hike in the summer. Leashed dogs are allowed on the trails. There are also picnic tables at the park. During the winter (rainy season), the trails are subject to flash flooding. To get there from the 101 freeway, take the Lynn Road exit and head north. Turn left onto Avenida de los Arboles. Go until you reach Wildwood School. Park there and take the trail to the left of the parking lot. It will take you to a large wooden "Fort". Go past or through the fort to the trails. Thanks to one of our readers for recommending this park.

Sequoia and Kings Canyon National Park
47050 General Highway
Three Rivers, CA
559-565-3341
nps.gov/seki/
This national park does not really have much to see or do if you bring your pooch, except for driving through a giant redwood forest in your car and staying overnight at the campgrounds. However, located to the west and south of this national park is the dog-friendly Giant National Sequoia Monument. There you will be able to find dog-friendly hiking, sightseeing and camping. Pets must be leashed and attended at all times. Please clean up after your pet.

O'Neill Regional Park
30892 Trabuco Canyon Road
Trabuco Canyon, CA
949-923-2260
ocparks.com/oneillpark/
This heavily wooded park offers hiking trails. Dogs on a 6 foot or less leash are allowed and please clean up after them.

Trinity Lakeshore Trail
Highway 3
Trinity Center, CA
530-623-2121
This easy to moderate hike follows the western shore of Trinity Lake. The four mile trail runs from Clark Springs Campground to a private resort. There are a few short, steep stretches along the route. The trail offers shade and goes through an old-growth forest. Please stay on the trail when walking through private facilities. The majority of this trail is in the Shasta-Trinity National Forest. The trailhead at the Clark Springs Campground which is located 18 miles north of Weaverville off Highway 3. Pets should be leashed

and please clean up after them.

Commemorative Overland Emigrant Trail
Alder Creek Road
Truckee, CA
530-587-3558
This 15 mile moderate rated trail is located in the Tahoe National Forest. While the trail is open from May to November, it is most heavily used in the spring. The trail is popular with both hikers and mountain bikers. Pets must be either leashed or off-leash but under direct voice control. To get there from Interstate 80, take the Highway 89 North exit and go 2.3 miles to Alder Creek Road. Turn left and go 3 miles. The trail starts on the south side of the road.

Donner Memorial State Park
Highway 80
Truckee, CA
530-582-7892
While dogs are not allowed at the China Cove Beach Area and the nature trail behind the museum, they are allowed on the rest of the trails at this park. Dogs are also allowed in the lake. Pets must be on leash at all times and please clean up after them. The park has campgrounds but they are undergoing renovation from 2003 to 2004. It is located off Highway 80 in Truckee.

Glacier Meadow Loop Trail
Castle Peak
Truckee, CA
530-587-3558
This .5 mile easy loop trail is located in the Tahoe National Forest and is used for hiking only. It is a very popular trail from June to October. Pets must be either leashed or off-leash but under direct voice control. To get there from I-80, exit Castle Peak, on the south side of I-80, turn left. The trailhead is on the east side of the parking lot.

Sand Ridge Lake Trail
Castle Peak
Truckee, CA
530-587-3558
This 6 miles one way moderate rated trail is located in the Tahoe National Forest. From June to October, it is heavily used for hiking and horseback riding. Pets must be either leashed or off-leash but under direct voice control. To get there from I-80, exit Castle Peak, on the south side of I-80, turn left. The

trailhead is on the east side of the parking lot.

Summit Lake Trail
Castle Peak
Truckee, CA
530-587-3558
This 2 mile easy rate trail is located in the Tahoe National Forest and is popular for hiking, mountain biking and horseback riding. The trail is most frequently used from June to October. Pets must be either leashed or off-leash but under direct voice control. To get there from Interstate 80, exit Castle Peak, on the south side of I-80, turn left. The trailhead is on the east side of the parking lot.

Lava Beds National Monument
1 Indian Well
Tulelake, CA
530-667-2282
nps.gov/labe/
This national park does not really have much to see or do if you bring your pooch, except for staying overnight at the Indian Well Campground. However, the dog-friendly Modoc National Forest surrounds the national park. At the national forest you will be able to find dog-friendly hiking, sightseeing and camping. See our Modoc National Forest listing in this region for more details. Pets must be leashed and attended at all times. Please clean up after your pet.

Joshua Tree National Park
74485 National Park Drive
Twentynine Palms, CA
760-367-5500
nps.gov/jotr
Dogs are not allowed on the trails, cannot be left unattended, and must be on leash. However, they are allowed on dirt and paved roads including the Geology Tour Road. This is actually a driving tour, but you'll be able to see the park's most fascinating landscapes from this road. It is an 18 mile tour with 16 stops. The park recommends taking about 2 hours for the round trip. At stop #9, about 5 miles out, there is room to turnaround if you do not want to complete the whole tour.

Bryan Meadows Trail
Bryan Road
Twin Bridges, CA
530-644-2545
This 4 mile moderate rated trail passes through stands of lodgepole pine and mountain hemlock. From the parking area, hike one mile up Sayles Canyon Trail along the creek

to the junction of Bryan Meadows Trail. The trail continues east for about three miles. The elevation ranges from about 7,200 to 8,400 feet. Pets must be leashed and please clean up after them. This trail is located in the Eldorado National Forest. From Highway 50 go about 48 miles east of Placerville. Turn onto the Sierra-At-Tahoe Road and go 2 miles. Turn right onto Bryan Road (17E13). Go another 2.5 miles to the parking area where the trailhead is located.

Pyramid Creek Loop Trail
Highway 50
Twin Bridges, CA
530-644-2545
This 1.7 mile Eldorado National Forest trail is rated moderate to strenuous. The elevation ranges from 6,120 to 6,400 feet. At the trailhead, begin your hike by heading east and then north up to Pyramid Creek. Turn right (east) at the sign and follow the trail along the creek. The trail offers great views of the American River Canyon, Lover's Leap, Horsetail Falls and other geological interests. Follow the trail north, then loop back south on the old trail bed down to the granite slabs and return to Highway 50. Pets must be leashed and please clean up after them. The trailhead is located on the north side of Highway 50 at Twin Bridges, about .5 miles east of Strawberry.

Cache Creek Recreation Area
2550 N State Street/Ukiah Field Office
Ukiah, CA
707-468-4000
blm.gov/ca/ukiah/cachecreek.html
Rich in natural and cultural history, this day-use primitive recreation area has no developed camp areas or facilities and is located along Highways 20 and 16. It is maintained and managed for wildlife habitat, rare plants, the protection of archaeological resources, and to provide primitive recreational opportunities including offering multi-use trails, wildlife viewing, river running, hunting, and fishing. Dogs of all sizes are allowed for no additional fee. Dogs must be under their owner's control at all times. They may be off lead if they are under voice command. Please clean up after your pet, especially on the trails.

Mendocino National Forest
10025 Elk Mountain Road

Upper Lake, CA
707-275-2361
This forest consists of one million acres of mountains and canyons and offers a variety of recreational opportunities like camping, hiking, backpacking, boating, fishing, hunting, nature study, photography, and off highway vehicle travel. Elevations in the forest range from 750 feet to 8092 feet with an average elevation of about 4000 feet. For a map of hiking trails, please visit the Visitor Center at 10025 Elk Mountain Road in the town of Upper Lake.

Sunset Nature Trail Loop
County Road 301/Forest Road M1
Upper Lake, CA
530-934-3316
This self-guided interpretive trail is an easy .5 mile one way hike. Elevation begins at 1,800 feet and has a 100 foot climb. The trail is located in the Mendocino National Forest, adjacent to a campground. Pets on leash are allowed. Please clean up after your pets. To get there from Upper Lake, take County Road 301 north for 31 miles. The trail begins at the Sunset Campground.

Channel Islands National Park
1901 Spinnaker Drive
Ventura, CA
805-658-5730
nps.gov/chis/index.htm
Pets are not allowed on the islands.

Grant Park
Brakey Road
Ventura, CA
The park has a few hiking trails and the Padre Serra Cross. There are some great views of the Ventura Harbor from this park. It is located about 1/2 mile north of Hwy 101, near California Street. Dogs must be on leash.

Ojai Valley Trail
Hwy 33 at Casitas Vista Rd
Ventura, CA
805-654-3951
This 9.5 mile trail has a paved pedestrian path and a wood-chip bridle path. Dogs are allowed but must always be on leash. The trail parallels Highway 33 from Foster Park, just outside Ventura to Fox Street, in Ojai.

Ventura River Trail
Old Town Ventura to Foster Park
Ventura, CA
805-658-4740

This 6.5 mile paved trail heads from Old Town Ventura near Main Street and Hwy 33 along the Ventura River to Foster Park where it hooks up with the Ojai Valley Trail which continues to Ojai nearly 10 miles away. Dogs on leash may share the trail with joggers, bicycles and others.

Sunset Park
Monte Verde and Liserdra
Visalia, CA
559-713-4300
Thanks to one of our readers who writes "It is a well kept park with plenty of friendly people and dogs."

San Miguel Park Off-leash hours
Los Cerros Avenue at San Carlos Drive
Walnut Creek, CA
925-943-5899x232
San Miguel Park is a 4 acre city park with a playground, sports and walking trails. Dogs are allowed to be off-leash and under voice control in the park until 9 am. After 9 am dogs must be on-leash. From Ygnacio Valley Rd turn south onto San Carlos Drive and turn right onto Los Cerros Ave to the park.

Barker Spur Trail
Forest Road 9S07
Warner Springs, CA
760-788-0250
This 3.4 mile moderate rated trail is located in the Cleveland National Forest. The trail elevation changes from 4,000 to 5,100 feet. It is open from early spring through late fall. Pets on leash are allowed and please clean up after them. To get there, take Highway 79 south toward Warner Springs. At about 2 miles southeast of Sunshine Summit take Forest Road 9S07 west. In about 7 miles the trailhead sign will be found on the left side of the road. Parking is in the wide area along the road. (Vehicles must display a Forest Adventure Pass.)

Mount Madonna
Watsonville, CA
408-842-2341
This 3,219 acre park is dominated by a redwood forest. The park offers redwood and oak forests as well as meadows. Visitors may choose from 118 drive-in and walk-in first-come, first-served campsites spread throughout four campgrounds. Each site comes equipped with a barbecue pit, food locker and picnic table. Showers (for a small fee) are also available, as well as 17 partial hook-up RV sites. Hikers have access to

an extensive 20 mile trail system. Park visitors may learn about areas where Ohlone Indians hunted and harvested. A one mile self-guided nature trail winds around the ruins of cattle baron Henry Miller's summer home. White fallow deer, descendants of a pair donated by William Randolph Hearst in 1932, can be viewed in an enclosed pen. The park is located on Highway 152 (Hecker Pass Highway), ten miles west of Gilroy.

Royal Oaks Park
537 Maher Road
Watsonville, CA
831-755-4895
This 122 acre park offers miles of hiking trails, a playground, picnic areas, basketball, volleyball and tennis courts. There is a $3 vehicle entrance fee during the week and a $5 fee on weekends and holidays. Dogs need to be leashed and please clean up after them.

Humboldt Redwoods State Park
Avenue of the Giants
Weott, CA
707-946-2409
This park is located along the scenic Avenue of the Giants. While dogs are not allowed on the trails, they are allowed in the campgrounds and on miles of fire roads and access roads. These paths are used mainly for mountain biking, but dogs are allowed too. There are both steep and gently sloping fire roads. Some of the fire roads are located next to the Albee Creek Campground. Pets on leash are allowed and please clean up after them. The park is located along the Avenue of the Giants, about 45 miles south of Eureka and 20 miles north of Garberville.

Whiskeytown National Recreation Area
P.O. Box 188
Whiskeytown, CA
530-246-1225
nps.gov/whis/
The main highlight of this park is Whiskeytown Lake. Popular activities include swimming, sailing, water-skiing, scuba diving and fishing. The land surrounding the lake offers ample opportunities for hiking, mountain biking and horseback riding. Dogs are allowed on the trails, in the campgrounds and in the water at non-swim beaches which are beaches without sand. Pets are not allowed on the sandy swimming beaches or inside any buildings.

Dogs must be leashed and attended at all times. Please clean up after your pet. This recreation area is located on Highway 299 near Highway 5.

Chemise Mountain Trail
Chemise Mountain Road
Whitehorn, CA
707-825-2300
This trail is about 1.5 miles long and involves an 800 foot climb. At the top of the trail you will see vistas of the coastline and inland mountain ranges. This trail is popular with hikers and mountain bikers. Pets are required to be leashed in the campgrounds. On the trails there is no leash requirement but your dog needs to be under direct voice control. There is a $1 day use fee. To get there, take Highway 101 to Redway. Go west on Briceland/Shelter Cove Road for 22 miles and then head south on Chemise Mountain Road for just over 1.5 miles. Trailhead parking is available at the Wailaki or Nadelos Campgrounds. Travel time from Highway 101 is about 55 minutes.

Sacramento National Wildlife Refuge
752 County Road 99W
Willows, CA
530-934-2801
This day use park is one of the state's premier waterfowl refuges with hundreds of thousands of geese and ducks making their winter home here, and numerous other birds and mammals making it their home year round. The habitat consists of almost 11,000 acres of seasonal marsh lands, permanent ponds, and uplands. There are interpretive kiosks, a six mile auto tour, a two mile walking trail, and benches and restrooms outside the visitor center. Dogs of all sizes are allowed throughout the park and on the trails. Dogs must be under their owner's control at all times, and be leashed and cleaned up after.

Foothill Regional Park
1351 Arata Lane
Windsor, CA
707-565-2041
Hiking, bicycling, horseback riding and fishing are popular activities at this 211 acre park. Dogs must be kept on a 6 foot or less leash. No swimming, wading or boating is allowed on the lakes. There is a $3 per car parking fee.

Badger Pass Ski Area

P.O. Box 578/Badger Pass Road
Yosemite National Park, CA
209-372-1220
yosemitepark.com/BadgerPass.aspx
This popular family-friendly ski area offers great scenery, and a variety of activities, festivals, and friendly competitions throughout the season. Although dogs are not allowed on the ski slopes in winter, they are allowed to go anywhere a car can go-being paved roads and developed areas. Dogs must be under their owner's control at all times, and be leashed and cleaned up after.

Klamath National Forest
1312 Fairlane Road
Yreka, CA
530-842-6131
r5.fs.fed.us/klamath
This forest has over 1,700,000 acres of land throughout Siskiyou County in California and Jackson County in Oregon. Dogs should be on leash. Hiking from East Fork Campground provides access to the lakes in the Caribou Basin, Rush Creek, and Little South Fork drainages. The campground is located 27 miles southwest of Callahan next to the East and the South Forks of the Salmon River, at a 2,600 foot elevation. From the Bridge Flat Campground, the historic Kelsey Trail offers excellent opportunities for scenic day hikes or longer trips into the Marble Mountain Wilderness. The campground is located on the Scott River approximately 17 miles from Fort Jones, at a 2,000 foot elevation. For more details, call or visit the Salmon River Ranger District, 11263 N. Highway 3,Fort Jones, (530) 468-5351. The Klamath National Forest offers miles of other hiking trails. For maps and more information on trails throughout this forest, please contact the forest office in Yreka.

Colorado

Cherry Creek State Park
4201 South Parker Road
Aurora, CO
303-699-3860
parks.state.co.us/cherry_creek
Dogs on a 6 foot or less leash are allowed, except on wetland trails, and swim beaches. But there are plenty of dog-friendly hiking trails in this park. There is also an off-leash area in this park, located near Parker

and Orchard Roads. For details of which hiking trails allow dogs, please visit one of the Entrance Stations at the park.

Mountain City Historic Park
Gregory Street
Black Hawk, CO
303-582-2525
Black Hawk is known for having many casinos and a large variety of seasonal attractions. Against a backdrop of being a distinct old west gold mining town with restored old buildings, an active historical society museum, and several historic mining sites, there is a city block park they consider a prime attraction. It is a stroll back in time that offers a glimpse of the intermingling of Victorian and Gothic architectural styles, and the park features other sites/statues, like the mama bear and her 3 cubs. This day use park is free of charge and is open daily. Dogs of all sizes are allowed throughout the park. Dogs must be leashed at all times, and they request that you bring supplies to clean up after your pet.

Boulder Creek Path
9th street and Parallels Arapahoe Avenue
Boulder, CO
303-413-7200
ci.boulder.co.us
This multi-use nature and exercise trail runs about 16 miles through the city and into the adjacent mountains with no street crossings. Some of the attractions along the way include a sculpture garden, fishing ponds, cottonwood groves, a restored steam locomotive, city parks, a playground, and the state university. Dogs are allowed on the trail if they are leashed and you clean up after your pet. There are trash receptacles along the way, but you will need to bring your own clean up supplies.

Boulder Reservoir
5100 N 51st Street
Boulder, CO
303-441-3456
This reservoir offers a great scenic view to enjoy with your hiking. Dogs are allowed on the North Shore only, and the trails on that side. You can access this area from 51st Street, past the main gate to the trailhead, and then walk to the shore from there. Dogs are not allowed at any swim beach, food areas, or on boat rentals. Dogs must be leashed and cleaned up after.

Chautauqua Park
900 Baseline Road
Boulder, CO
303-442-3282
chautauqua.com/
Situated on 26 gorgeous acres, this historic landmark park on the National Register, features buildings that date back to its beginnings, beautiful gardens, and now provides a retreat experience in the heart of Bolder. Run and preserved by the Colorado Chautauqua Association, their goal is to help build their community through social, cultural, educational, and recreational opportunities. Dogs of all sizes are allowed throughout the park and on the trails. They must be on leash except in off lead areas, and for your dog to be legally off lead, an off-leash tag must be purchased. Dogs are not allowed in park buildings or on the upper section of the McClintock Trail, and they must be cleaned up after at all times.

University of Colorado-Boulder
914 Broadway St
Boulder, CO
303-492-1411
colorado.edu/
Your pet may walk with you through this beautiful campus, but they must be well behaved, leashed, and cleaned up after at all times. Please bring your own clean up supplies. Dogs are not allowed in any of the buildings or in food service areas.

Garden of the Gods Park
1805 N 30th Street
Colorado Springs, CO
719-634-6666
gardenofgods.com
Dogs on leash are allowed in the park. You must cleanup after your dog at all times. There is a section between Gateway Road and 30th Street that is fenced in for off-leash dogs. They are also allowed to sit at the outside tables of the cafe in the park.

Red Rock Canyon Open Space
31st Street at Highway 24
Colorado Springs, CO
719-385-2489
redrockcanyonopenspace.org
The Red Rock Canyon Open Space is a beautiful series of canyons and hills in the east slope of the Rockies. In 2003 the City of Colorado Springs purchased nearly 800 acres for the purpose of providing trails, hiking, cycling, equestrian activities and trails for

people with dogs. Dogs on leash are allowed throughout the picturesque trails. There are over 10 miles of trails in the open space. However, there are two dog loops on which dogs are allowed to be off-leash if they are under voice control. These trails total about 5/8 mile in length and are located just south of the main entrance to the park.

Seven Falls
2850 S Cheyenne Rd
Colorado Springs, CO
719-632-0765
sevenfalls.com
Dogs on leash are allowed in the park. The park is open all year round and features a waterfall with hiking trails and picnic areas. There are 200 plus steps up to the viewing station at the waterfall or you and your dog can tell the elevator. There is a fee for people but dogs are free. You must cleanup after your pets. The park is located about 15 minutes from downtown Colorado Springs and is at a very high altitude in the Rockies.

Hovenweep National Monument
McElmo Route
Cortez, CO
970-562-4282
nps.gov/hove/index.htm
Dogs must be on leash and must be cleaned up after in the park area. The park features hiking, camping, and sightseeing. The monument protects six Puebloan-era villages spread over a twenty-mile expanse of mesa tops and canyons along the Utah-Colorado border.

Bible Park
Yale Avenue
Denver, CO
303-964-2580
This is a 70 acre park and about half of it is developed with sports fields, picnic areas and restrooms. The park has many walking trails and it is bordered by the High Line Canal Trail and the Cherry Creek Trail. The park is located at Yale Avenue and Pontiac Street. Dogs must be leashed.

City Park
17th Avenue
Denver, CO
303-964-2580
This park is Denver's largest city park. It covers over 300 acres and offers tennis courts, fountains, flower gardens, sports fields, a lake and more. The park is located just east of downtown on 17th Avenue and York

Street. Pets must be on a leash.

Washington Park
Franklin Drive and Exposition Blvd
Denver, CO
303-698-4962
This park, known as Denver's premium park with over 155 acres, two lakes, formal flower gardens (one being a replica of the President Washington's garden at Mt Vernon), a historic bathhouse and gazebo, attracts all ages. A great trail system, including a 2.5 scenic loop, big open lawns, beautiful scenery, gaming courts, and planned venues also make this a great mini-get-a-way. Dogs of all sizes are allowed as long as they are on a leash. Dog are allowed throughout the park and on the trails, but they must be cleaned up after; please carry supplies.

Animas River Trail
32nd Avenue (at East 2nd Ave)
Durango, CO
The Animas River Trail is a 5 mile paved trail that runs along the river and through Durango. It is a popular trail with walkers, runners, in-line skaters and of course, dogs. If your pooch wants to cool off along the way, he or she can take a dip in the refreshing river. The north end of the trail is located at 32nd Avenue and East 2nd Avenue. Dogs must be leashed on the trail.

Eldorado Canyon State Park
9 Kneale Road, Box B
Eldorado Springs, CO
303-494-3943
Famous for its geological history with rocks calculated to be over 1.5 billion years old this park has plenty to do. Some of the features/activities include technical rock climbing, picnicking by running streams, hiking trails for all abilities, fishing, biking, sightseeing, wildlife viewing, and a visitor's center. Dogs of all sizes are allowed throughout the park and on the trails. Dogs must be leashed at all times and be cleaned up after.

Arapaho-Roosevelt National Forest
240 West Prospect Rd
Fort Collins, CO
970-498-1100
There are numerous trails in this national forest that allow dogs. Some of the trails are located off Highway 34 or Highway 36, near Estes Park. The following are examples of three trails. The North Fork Trail is over 4 miles long and is rated easy. To get there from Loveland take Highway 34

west to Drake, turn right onto County Road #43 and travel approximately 6 miles. Turn right onto Dunraven Glade Road (there will be a Forest Service access sign) and travel to the end of the road. The Lions Gulch Trail/Homestead Meadows Trail is almost 3 miles long and is rated moderate. The trailhead is located on Highway 36, seven miles east of Estes Park, or twelve miles west of Lyons. The Round Mountain Trail is about 4.5 miles long and is rated moderate to difficult. Take Highway 34 west of Loveland for approximately 12 miles. The traillhead is on the south side of the highway, across from the Viestenz-Smith Mountain Park.

Castlewood Canyon State Park
2989 S Hwy 83
Franktown, CO
303-688-5242
Located in the famous Black Forest, this day-use park offers unique sightseeing and recreational opportunities. Explore ancient ruins, a century old dam, or a variety of hiking trails that wind into the deepest regions of the canyon. There are plenty of chances for nature study, bird watching, photography, technical rock climbing, and picnicking. Amenities include rest rooms, a scenic overlook, an amphitheater, a concrete surface trail, and a Visitor's Center. Dogs are welcome throughout the park and on the trails. Dogs must be leashed and cleaned up after at all times.

Colorado National Monument
Fruita, CO
970-858-3617
nps.gov/colm/index.htm
Dogs on leash are allowed in campgrounds and paved areas only. Dogs are not allowed on any hiking trails or backcountry.

The Colorado Trail
710 10th Street, #210
Golden, CO
303-384-3729
coloradotrail.org/
This is Colorado's premier long distance trail at almost 500 miles stretching from Denver to Durango. Spectacular scenery greets the traveler all the way to where the trail tops out at 13,334 feet. There are 6 wilderness areas, 8 mountain ranges, abundant wildlife, lakes, creeks, and many diverse

ecosystems. Dogs are allowed in all areas along the trail with the exception of the first 7 miles from the Denver side. Both points of access into this area (Waterton Canyon and Roxborough State) prohibit dogs. You may begin the trail with your dog at the S Platte River Bridge Trailhead. The Guidebook also mentions another route from the Indian Creek Campground onto the Indian Creek Equestrian Trail. Dogs must be on leash through the wilderness areas, under owners control at all times, and cleaned up after on the trail and any camp areas.

Black Canyon of the Gunnison National Park
102 Elk Creek
Gunnison, CO
970-641-2337
nps.gov/blca/index.htm
This unique canyon in the Rockies is narrow and deep. Dogs may view the Canyon with you from the Rim Rock Trail. Dogs on leash are allowed on roads, campgrounds, overlooks, the Rim Rock trail, Cedar Point Nature trail, and North Rim Chasm View Nature trail. They are not allowed on other hiking trails, inner canyon routes, or in the wilderness area within the park. Dogs on leash are permitted throughout the Curecanti National Recreation Area nearby.

Curecanti National Recreation Area
102 Elk Creek
Gunnison, CO
970-641-2337
nps.gov/cure/index.htm
Dogs on leash are allowed in all of the park areas. The park features auto touring, boating, camping, fishing, hiking, swimming, and more.

Echo Lake Park
Hwy 103
Idaho Springs, CO
303-697-4545
Echo Lake Park is a 617-acre park west of Denver along the Mount Evans Scenic Byway, the highest paved road in North America. Being nestled in a glacially formed hanging valley at over 10,000 feet, it also offers spectacular views. Park amenities include a stone shelter, picnic tables, and barbecue grills. Dogs of all sizes are allowed. They must be kept leashed at all times and cleaned up after.

Daniels Park
1315 Welch Street
Lakewood, CO

303-987-7800
This 1000+ acre park is home to a Bison preserve and natural area where they can be viewed in their high-plains habitat. Some of the amenities include a picnic shelter with 8 tables, 2 barbecue grills, horseshoe pits, tennis courts, gaming courts/fields, and restrooms. Dogs must be kept leashed at all times and cleaned up after.

Mesa Verde National Park
PO Box 8
Mesa Verde, CO
970-529-4465
nps.gov/meve/index.htm
Dogs on leash are allowed in the campgrounds and parking lots only. Dogs are not allowed on hiking trails or archaeological sites. Pets cannot be left alone or in vehicles.

Great Sand Dunes National Park and Preserve
11999 Highway 150
Mosca, CO
719-378-6300
nps.gov/grsa/index.htm
The dunes of Great Sand Dunes National Park rise over 750 feet high. Dogs are allowed throughout the park and must be on leash. You must clean up after your dog and dogs may not be left unattended in the park. Leashed dogs are also welcome in the campgrounds. The park features auto touring, camping fishing, hiking, and more.

Fish Creek Falls
Fish Creek Falls Road
Steamboat Springs, CO
970-879-1870
fs.fed.us/r2/mbr/
Although located in the Routt National Forest, it is only a short distance to this worthy sight. You will find a short, semi-steep trail leading to the bottom of a stunning 283 foot waterfall, or take the short walk to a scenic overlook, ramped for those with disabilities. There are picnic areas and a variety of other trails along the way-some of them more challenging. Dogs are allowed for no additional fee at this day-use park, and they are allowed on the trails. If your dog responds firmly to voice control they do not have to be on leash.

Telluride Town Park
500 E Colorado Avenue
Telluride, CO
970-728-2173
Town Park in Telluride is a 36 acre landscaped public park and festival grounds tucked away in a dramatic box canyon surrounded by 12 and 13 thousand foot mountain peaks. Some of the features here include a community built play ground (Imagination Station), a kids fishing pond, gaming courts, multi-purpose ball fields, a pool, camping (refer to our listing for Town Park Campground), a concert area, picnic areas with barbecues, and a core area for special activities/events. In winter they feature a sledding hill, an ice rink pavilion, and groomed cross country ski trails. Dogs of all sizes are allowed throughout the park and on the trails in the summer. They are not allowed at the event center during festivals or other planned events. Dogs must be leashed at all times, and cleaned up after.

Connecticut

Talcott Mountain State Park
Hwy 185
Bloomfield, CT
860-424-3200
Built as a summer retreat in 1914, there are some great scenic walking trails here, including part of the Metacomet Trail and the 1¼ mile hike to the Tower where a 1,000 promontory offers outstanding views of over 12,000 square miles. Dogs are permitted for no additional pet fees. Dogs are allowed at the picnic areas and on the hiking trails; they are not allowed in park buildings. Dogs must be under their owner's control at all times, and be leashed and cleaned up after.

Devil's Hopyard State Park
366 Hopyard Road
East Haddam, CT
860-873-8566
Born through glacial activity, this park has many interesting geological features, scenic hiking trails, viewing vistas, and the Chapman Falls which has more than a 60 foot drop over a series of rocky steps. Dogs are permitted for no additional pet fees. Dogs are allowed at the picnic areas and on the hiking trails; they are not allowed in the campground, in park buildings, or in swimming areas. Dogs must be owner's control at all times, and be leashed and cleaned up after.

Gillette Castle State Park
67 River Road
East Haddam, CT
860-526-2336
The focal point of this 184 acre park located along the Connecticut River is the 24 room medieval fortress, but the grounds are as interesting with stone-arch bridges, a vegetable cellar, a RR station, ponds, and a variety of trails that run through tunnels, over trestles, and along a 3 mile stretch of a former railroad. Dogs are permitted for no additional pet fees. Dogs are allowed at the picnic areas and on the hiking trails; they are not allowed in park buildings, or on decks, terraces or walkways leading to the castle. Dogs must be under their owner's control at all times, and be leashed and cleaned up after.

Sherwood Island State Park
Sherwood Island Connector Road
Green Farms, CT
203-226-6983
Covering 235 acres with miles of waterfront, this scenic park offers several picnic sites, a variety of recreation, concessionaires, and an observation platform for viewing marsh life. Dogs are not allowed at this park from April 15th through September 30th. From October 1st through April 14th dogs are allowed on leash only. Dogs are not allowed on the beach at any time, in park buildings, swimming areas, or park campgrounds. Dogs must be under their owner's control and cleaned up after at all times.

Bluff Point State Park
Depot Road
Groton, CT
860-444-7591
This is the last remaining significant piece of undeveloped land along the state's coast, and because of being designated a Coastal Reserve, access to the bluff is only allowed by foot or non-motorized vehicles to this unique and beautiful area. Dogs are permitted for no additional pet fee. Dogs are allowed throughout the park. Dogs must be under their owner's control at all times, and be leashed and cleaned up after.

Fort Griswold Battlefield State Park
57 Fort Street
Groton, CT
860-444-7591
This seasonal monument park is an historic Revolutionary War site where the infamous Benedict Arnold led a 1781 massacre. Dogs are permitted

throughout the park; they must be leashed and cleaned up after at all times.

Sleeping Giant State Park
200 Mount Carmel Avenue
Hamden, CT
203-789-7498
Offering scenic vistas from a stone observation tower, nature trails, stream fishing (a designated trout stocked park), and some great hiking trails, this park is also known for the 2 miles of the mountaintop that resemble a large "sleeping giant". Dogs are permitted for no additional pet fees. Dogs are allowed at the picnic areas and on the hiking trails; they are not allowed in park buildings. Dogs must be under their owner's control at all times, and be leashed and cleaned up after.

Kent Falls State Park
462 Kent Cornwall Road
Kent, CT
860-927-3238
Lush greenery, scenic hiking trails and picnic areas, and falls that take a series of drops and cascades 250 feet down on its way to the Housatonic River, are some of the features of this park. This park is a member of the Impressionist Art Trail with reproductions of art painted in the 19th century exhibited at this park and at other host sites. Dogs are permitted for no additional pet fees. Dogs are allowed at the picnic areas and on the hiking trails; they are not allowed in park buildings or in swimming areas. Dogs must be under their owner's control at all times, and be leashed and cleaned up after.

Topsmead State Forest
Buell Road
Litchfield, CT
860-567-5694
Originally a summer estate, this beautiful 1925 English Tudor home and landscaped grounds have been kept much as they were upon the owner's passing upon her request. They offer free seasonal guided tours, and guests may informally picnic on the grounds or residence lawns (no fires/grills), or walk the numerous trails and a 7/10 mile interpretive walk. Dogs are permitted for no additional pet fees. Dogs are allowed on the grounds and on the hiking trails; they are not allowed in park buildings. Dogs must be under their owner's control at all times, and be leashed and cleaned up after.

Silver Sands State Park
Silver Sands Parkway
Milford, CT
203-735-4311
This park has an island that holds a mystery; in 1699 did Captain Kidd really bury his treasure on the island that is reached from the park by a sand/gravel bar that is exposed at high tide? Dogs are permitted for no additional pet fees, and they are allowed throughout the park except on the beach. Dogs must be under their owner's control at all times, and be leashed and cleaned up after.

New Haven Green
Temple Street
New Haven, CT
203-946-8019
newhavenparks.org
Sitting serenely amid a hub of activity, this park is bordered by College, Chapel, Church and Elm streets in the heart of the city, and is the site of numerous concerts, events, and community gatherings. This park was originally the town square and created in 1638. Well mannered dogs are allowed. Dogs must be on leash and cleaned up after at all times.

Fort Trumbull State Park
90 Walbach Street
New London, CT
860-444-7591
This area along Thames River, that has been an active military site since early colonial days, now shares its rich history and unusual fort with visitors, and informative markers and displays are throughout the park. Dogs are permitted around the park for no additional pet fees; they are not allowed in park buildings (including the fort) or on the fishing pier. Dogs must be under their owner's control at all times, and be leashed and cleaned up after.

Haystack Mountain State Park
Hwy 272
Norfolk, CT
860-482-1817
Lush greenery, scenic (sometimes tree canopied) hiking trails, an overlook, picnic areas, and a 34 foot stone tower at the top of the summit offers views from the Long Island Sound to the peaks of New York. Dogs are permitted for no additional pet fees. Dogs are allowed at the picnic areas and on the hiking trails. Dogs must be under their owner's control at all

times, and be leashed and cleaned up after.

Mashamoquet Brook State Park
147 Wolf Den Drive
Pomfret Center, CT
860-928-6121
Actually 3 parks, each rich in folklore, and natural and cultural history, combined to what is now a 900 acre park with miles of hiking trails and a variety of recreational opportunities. Dogs are permitted for no additional pet fees. Dogs are allowed at the picnic areas and on the hiking trails; they are not allowed in the campground, on the beach, or at the picnic shelter. Dogs must be under their owner's control at all times, and be leashed and cleaned up after.

Quinebaug and Shetucket Rivers Valley National Heritage Center
107 Providence Street
Putnam, CT
860-963-7226
nps.gov/qush/index.htm
Dogs must be on leash and must be cleaned up after on most of trails around the river areas. You must follow local and state park rules and pet policies. The park features auto touring, hiking and boating.

Housatonic Meadows
Hwy 7
Sharon, CT
860-672-6772
Located along the scenic Housatonic River in a nature's paradise setting, this park has a variety of land and water recreation opportunities. Dogs are permitted for no additional pet fees. Dogs are allowed at the picnic areas and on the hiking trails; they are not allowed in the campground, in park buildings, or in swimming areas. Dogs must be under their owner's control at all times, and be leashed and cleaned up after.

Southford Falls State Park
175 Quaker Farms Road
Southbury, CT
203-264-5169
Born of glacial activity, this park features a lot of exposed geology with ever changing scenery, waterfalls, a fire tower that gives some nice views of the valley below, year round recreation, and is a designated Trout Park. Dogs are permitted for no additional pet fee. Dogs are allowed at the picnic areas and on hiking trails; they are not allowed in park buildings or in swimming areas. Dogs must be under their owner's control at all

times, and be leashed and cleaned up after.

Burr Pond State Park
Mountain Road
Torrington, CT
860-482-1817
This historic park shows evidence of its colonial beginnings, the businesses that evolved from the convergence of the several mountain streams, and it has the distinction of being the place where evaporated milk was born. Dogs are permitted for no additional pet fee in the picnic areas and on the miles of hiking trails; they are not allowed on the beach. Dogs must be under their owner's control at all times, and be leashed and cleaned up after.

Metacomet-Monadnock Trail
Rising Corner Road (beginning)
West Suffield, CT
617-523-0655
amcberkshire.org/mm-trail
This long distance, maintained hiking footpath covers almost 114 miles from the Metacomet Trail at the Connecticut state line to Mt. Monadnock in NH., and passes through some of the most beautiful landscapes in the state. It is maintained by the Appalachian Mountain Club. The trails are marked, but they suggest buying a trail guidebook (can be ordered from website) to use in addition to the excerpts of information on the web. Dogs are allowed on this trail. They must be under their owner's control at all times, leashed, and cleaned up after.

Weir Farm National Historic Site
735 Nod Hill Road
Wilton, CT
203-834-1896
nps.gov/wefa/index.htm
Dogs must be on leash and must be cleaned up after in the park. Dogs are not allowed in buildings. The park features hiking, nature walks, and more.

D.C.

Chesapeake Bay Gateways Network
National Park
410 Severn Avenue Ste 109
Annapolis, MD
888-BAYWAYS
nps.gov/cbpo/index.htm
Dogs must be on leash and must be

cleaned up after in most of the park areas. The park is located in Washinton D.C., Maryland, New York, Pennsylvania, Virginia, and West Virginia. You must follow all local and state park rules pertaining to pets. The park features in most states camping, auto touring, hiking, swimming, fishing, boating, and more.

C & O Canal Towpath
M Street
Washington, DC
301-739-4200
fred.net/kathy/canal.html
The 184 mile towpath extends all the way from Georgetown, in Washington, DC to Cumberland, MD. It is a dirt trail and can be accessed at many points along the way. Dogs must be leashed on the towpath.

Capital Crescent Trail
Water Street, NW
Washington, DC
This paved bike trail starts in Georgetown and heads to the Maryland Suburbs. Dogs must be leashed on the trail.

National Arboretum
3501 New York Ave NE
Washington, DC
202-245-2726
ars-grin.gov/na/
The National Arboretum allows dogs on leash. There are miles of walking trails here through the many beautiful gardens.

Rock Creek Park
Washington, DC
202-426-6828
nps.gov/rocr/
Rock Creek Park is a large city park run by the National Park Service. Dogs on leash are allowed in the park. There is a paved trail and lots of picnic areas, trails and activities. The park extends from near downtown Washington to Maryland.

Delaware

Assawoman Wildlife Area
Mulberry Landing Road
Bayard, DE
302-539-3160
Divided in 3 sections, and managed for migrating, wintering, and resident bird and plant/wildlife, this unique and interesting park offers

an auto tour marked by wooden stakes along the road with a corresponding brochure to guide you along. The trail can also be hiked, and be sure to check ahead during times of inclement weather in case of road closures. Entrance is free for both pets and their owners. Dogs must be licensed, under their owner's control at all times, and cleaned up after.

Fenwick Island State Park
Hwy 1
Bethany Beach, DE
302-539-1055 (May/October)
Open daily from 8 am to sunset year round, this 344 acre park is a 3 mile long barrier island with plenty of surf and turf recreational opportunities. Concessionaires and modern conveniences are available. Dogs are allowed throughout the park and on the surf fishing beaches; they are not allowed on swim beaches. Dogs must be well behaved, leashed, and cleaned up after at all times.

Silver Lake Park
Washington Street and Kings H
Dover, DE
302-736-7050
This 183 acre park offers open spaces, forested areas, picnic areas, an exercise court, playing courts/fields, various trails, and much more. Dogs are allowed throughout the park and on the trails. Dogs must be under their owner's control, leashed, and cleaned up after at all times.

Prime Hook National Wildlife Refuge
11978 Turkle Pond Road
Milton, DE
302-684-8419
fws.gov/northeast/primehook/
This 10,000 acre refuge has quite a diverse ecology with one of the largest freshwater impoundments on the East Coast, and offers a home or a migration area for a wide variety of bird and wildlife. Dogs are allowed throughout the park on the trails. Dogs must be under their owner's control, leashed, and cleaned up after at all times.

Bellevue State Park
800 Carr Road
Wilmington, DE
302-761-6963
destateparks.com/bvsp/bvsp.htm
This 328 acre park offers a bevy of features and activities such as a Summer Concert Series, a 1+ mile fitness track, a catch and release fishing pond, paved and unpaved

trails, gaming courts/fields, an arts center, and much more. Dogs are allowed throughout the park and on the trails. Dogs must be under their owner's control, leashed, and cleaned up after at all times.

Tubman-Garrett Riverfront Park
End of Market Street
Wilmington, DE
302-425-4890
This 2.4 amphitheater style park offers scenic repose sitting along the river at the edge of the city and it is also a popular area for holding special events. Dogs are welcome throughout the park. They must be under their owner's control at all times, leashed, and cleaned up after.

Florida

Wekiwa Springs State Park
Wekiwa Springs Road at SR-434
Apopka, FL
407-884-2008
Dogs are allowed in the park but are not allowed in the springs. Dogs must be leashed in the park.

South County Regional Park
11200 Park Access Rd
Boca Raton, FL
561-966-6600
Dogs must be leashed in the park.

Falling Waters State Park
1130 State Park Rd
Chipley, FL
850-638-6130
floridastateparks.org
Dogs on leash are allowed in this park. This park is open 8am-sundown all year round. Dogs are allowed everywhere but on the public beaches and in the bathhouses. The park features a waterfall, butterfly garden, lake, picnic areas, and camping for a fee.

Barnacle State Historic Site
3485 Main Highway
Coconut Grove, FL
305-448-9445
Dogs are allowed in the outdoor areas of the park. Dogs must be leashed in the park.

Crystal River Archaeological State Park
3400 N. Museum Point
Crystal River, FL
352-795-3817
This park is open from 8 a.m. until sundown, 365 days a year. Visitor center/museum hours are 9:00 a.m. to 5:00 p.m. daily. Designated a National Historic Landmark, this 61-acre, pre-Columbian, Native American site has six burial mounds, temple/platform mounds, a plaza area, and the site contains domestic refuse and ancient household artifacts, indicative of long-term human occupation. The park also sits on the edge of an expansive coastal marsh for saltwater and freshwater fishing, and it is part of the Great Florida Birding Trail. Dogs of all sizes are allowed at no additional fee. Dogs must be on a 6 foot leash or a retractable leash, and they must be cleaned up. Dogs on lead are allowed on the trails.

Crystal River Preserve State Park
3266 Sailboat Avenue
Crystal River, FL
352-563-0450
A place of exceptional natural beauty, this park is especially cherished by nature lovers and photographers. You can hike or bicycle along nine miles of trails or enjoy the two-and-a-half mile interpretive trail. They have very active interpretive/education programs, and they will continue to expand this in addition to adding new exhibits to the visitors' center. Dogs of all sizes are allowed at no additional fee. Dogs must be on no more than a 6 foot leash at all times, and cleaned up after. Dogs are allowed on the trails, but they are not allowed anywhere by the water due to alligators.

Tree Tops Park
3900 S.W. 100th Ave
Davie, FL
954-370-3750
co.broward.fl.us/pri02100.htm
Dogs must be leashed in the park.

Quiet Waters Park
401 S. Powerline Rd
Deerfield Beach, FL
954-360-1315
co.broward.fl.us/pri01800.htm
Dogs must be leashed in the park.

Rainbow Springs State Park
19158 Southwest 81st Place Rd
Dunnellon, FL
352-465-8555
floridastateparks.org
Dogs on leash are allowed in this park. They are not allowed in the public beach areas or bathhouses. The park is open 8am-sundown all year round. There is a fee for this park which features picnic tables, boating, tubing, and more.

Bike Trail - Fort Lauderdale
along A1A near the beach
Fort Lauderdale, FL
This trail follows A1A through the Fort Lauderdale beach area. Dogs must be leashed on the trail.

Hugh Taylor Birch State Park
3109 East Sunrise Boulevard
Fort Lauderdale, FL
954-564-4521
Dogs must be leashed in this park near the ocean. Dogs are not allowed on any of the beaches nearby except for the Canine Beach.

Snyder Park
3299 SW 4th Avenue
Fort Lauderdale, FL
954-828-4585
Offering 93 oasis-like acres, this park offers nature trails, 2 spring-fed lakes, gaming fields/courts/rentals, and an off leash area that can accommodate large and small pets in separate 1 acre lots. Dogs must be sociable, current on all vaccinations and license, and under their owner's control at all times. Dogs must be leashed when not in designated off-lead areas. Although there is no additional fee for the off leash doggy area, there is a fee for Snyder Park; annual passes are available at 954-828-DOGS (3647).

Buckingham Community Park and Barkingham Dog Park
9800 Buckingham Road
Fort Myers, FL
239-338-3288
leeparks.org/
In addition to the community park providing a long list of recreational opportunities, this was the county's first off lead dog area. The off lead area has park benches, watering holes, a doggie shower, agility equipment, a separate small dog area, a disposal station, and shaded areas. Dogs are allowed throughout the rest of the park on leash unless otherwise noted; they are not allowed in the ponds. Dogs may not be left alone at any time, and they must be well behaved, under their owner's control at all times, licensed, vaccinated, and cleaned up after.

Gulf Islands National Seashore
1801 Gulf Breeze Parkway
Gulf Breeze, FL
850-934-2600
nps.gov/guis/index.htm

Dogs must be on leash and must be cleaned up after in the camping and trail areas. Dogs are not allowed on beaches or in buildings. This park features hiking, camping, 19th Century forts, and more. Located in Florida and Mississippi.

Flatwoods Wilderness Park
Morris Bridge Road
Hillsborough, FL
There are a number of hiking trails here. Dogs are allowed on leash.

Biscayne National Park
9700 SW 328 Street
Homestead, FL
305-230-7275
nps.gov/bisc/index.htm
Biscayne National Park displays the coral reefs that thrive in the Miami area. Dogs are allowed in the developed areas of Elliott Key and Convoy Point on the mainland. They must be leashed and attended at all times and are not allowed in the buildings or swimming area. Pets are not allowed at all on the islands of Boca Chita Key or Adams Key or even in boats docked at the islands. Dogs may camp with you at Elliott Key.

Everglades National Park
40001 State Road 9336
Homestead, FL
305-242-7700
nps.gov/ever/index.htm
Dogs on leash are allowed in the parking lot and campgrounds of Everglades National park. They are not allowed on trails or wilderness areas. It is open year round this is the only subtropical preserve in North America. In the campgrounds and anywhere throughout this region where pets are allowed, pay close attention to them as alligators and snakes are always a danger. For more freedom to hike with your pet, try the Big Cypress National Preserve nearby.

Katheryn Abby Hanna Park
500 Wonderwood Dr
Jacksonville, FL
904-249-4700
coj.net
Dogs are allowed in this park for camping, hiking, picnics and on the dog friendly beach.

Timucuan Ecological and Historic Preserve
12713 Fort Caroline Rd
Jacksonville, FL
904-641-7155
nps.gov/timu/index.htm

Dogs on leash are allowed in this Historic Preserve. It is open year round 9 am-5 pm. The preverve features hiking, fishing, and more.

Bill Baggs State Park
1200 S. Crandon Blvd
Key Biscayne, FL
305-361-5811
Dogs are allowed on leash. This park has trails and a lighthouse (to view from outside). Dogs are not allowed on the beach near the lighthouse.

Dry Tortugas National Park
PO Box 6208
Key West, FL
305-242-7700
nps.gov/drto/index.htm
This set of Islands is 70 miles west of Key West in the Gulf of Mexico. Dogs must be on leash and must be cleaned up after on this island. Dogs are not allowed on the ferry but they can come over by private boat or charter from Key West. The park features picnicking, camping, fishing, swimming and more. It is open year round.

Fort Zachary Taylor State Park
Truman Annex
Key West, FL
305-292-6713
A National Historic Landmark, this oceanside park offers a long rich cultural and military history in addition to a wide array of recreational and educational activities. Dogs are allowed in all the common areas of the park; they are not allowed on the beach, playgrounds, buildings, or concession areas. Dogs must be well behaved, on no more than a 6 foot leash, and under their owner's control at all times.

John Prince Park
2700 6th Ave. S
Lake Worth, FL
Dogs must be leashed in the park.

Lummas Park
Ocean Drive
Miami Beach, FL
This park borders the ocean in the Art Deco district of Miami Beach. Dogs must be leashed in the park.

Milton Canoe Adventures
8974 Tomahawk Landing Road
Milton, FL
850-623-6197
adventuresunlimited.com/
Whether you take two hours or

many days, you can experience canoeing here with your dog. The spring fed rivers flow at an average depth of two feet over a soft, sandy bottom. Your pet and you can enjoy a canoe trip together for an additional $10 for the dog. Dogs must be kept leashed at all times, and cleaned up after. They are open year round.

Oleta River State Park
3400 N.E. 163rd Street
North Miami, FL
This park has hiking, jogging, and waterfront on the Biscayne Bay. Dogs are allowed on leash.

Easterlin Park
1000 N.W. 38th St
Oakland Park, FL
954-938-0610
co.broward.fl.us/pri01300.htm
Dogs must be leashed in the park.

Big Cypress National Preserve
33100 Tamiami Trail East
Ochopee, FL
239-695-1201
nps.gov/bicy/index.htm
Dogs must be on leash and must be cleaned up after in this National preserve. It is open year round 9am-4:30pm except Christmas. The park features auto touring, camping, hiking, boating, and more. The park does not recommend taking pets near lakes or areas where wildlife are present for their safety in this Alligator preservation.

Cady Way Trail
Bennett Rd and Corrine Dr.
Orlando, FL
407-836-6200
parks.onetgov.net/6Cadyway.htm
There is a 3.5 mile paved bike and hiking trail which links Winter Park and Orlando. Dogs on leash are allowed.

Lake Eola Park
Rosalind and Washington St
Orlando, FL
407-246-2827
This is a downtown urban park with a 1 mile jogging trail, grassy areas and a lake. The park has outdoor entertainment periodically. Dogs are allowed on leash.

Lake Trail
Sunset Ave and Bradley
Palm Beach, FL
This is a 3 1/2 mile paved trail along the intercoastal waterway. Dogs must be leashed on the trail.

Lake Jessup Park
South end of Sanford Ave
Sanford, FL
This is a small park for walking or picnicing. Dogs must be leashed in this park.

Lower Wekiva River State Preserve
S.R. 46
Sanford, FL
407-884-2008
Dogs are allowed on the trails but are not allowed in the camping areas. Dogs must be leashed in this park.

JN Darling National Wildlife Refuge
1 Wildlife Drive
Sanibel, FL
239-472-1100
fws.gov/dingdarling/
Enjoy a 4 1/2 mile nature and wildlife scenic tour by car, as well as the other recreational activities offered here. This park is known for it's migratory bird population. If you stop to look or take pictures, park on the right and stay on the pavement. The refuge is closed Friday, and open Saturday through Thursday from 7:30 am to sunset. Dogs are allowed at no additional fee, and they must be leashed and cleaned up after.

Castillo de San Marcos National Monument
A1A, near historic downtown
St Augustine, FL
904-829-6506, ext 234
nps.gov/casa/
This park is situated on 25 acres along the waterfront. The historic fort was built from 1672 to 1695 and it served primarily as the Spanish Empire post which guarded St. Augustine. Its secondary purpose was to protect the sea route for Spanish treasure ships. Even though this fort served many different nations, it was never taken by force. The United States purchased the fort from the Spanish in 1821 and in 1924 the fort was declared a national monument. Pets are welcome on the park grounds, but need to be on a 6 foot or less leash. Pets are not allowed inside the fort. The park is located between the waterfront and downtown, off Castillo Drive near Fort Alley.

North Shore Park
North Shore Dr and 13th Ave
St Petersburg, FL
Dogs must be leashed in the park.

Lake Park
17302 N. Dale Mabry
Tampa, FL
813-264-3806
Here your leashed dog will have to share the trails with horses and people. The park is 600 acres. There is an off-leash area in the park.

Upper Tampa Bay County Park
8001 Double Branch Road
Tampa, FL
813-855-1765
Dogs must be leashed in the park.

Edward Ball State Park
550 Wakulla Park Drive
Wakulla Springs, FL
850-224-5950
Listed on the Natural Register of Historic Places and designated as a National Natural Landmark, this park is home of one of the largest and deepest freshwater springs in the world, and is host to an abundance of wildlife, including alligators, turtles, deer, and birds. They provide daily guided riverboat tours, various interpretive programs, swimming, picnicking, and a nature trail. Dogs of all sizes are allowed at no additional fee. Dogs are not allowed in buildings, boats, the beach, or any waterfront area due to alligators. Dogs must be leashed at all times, and cleaned up after. They are open year round from 8 am to sunset.

Georgia

Chattahoochee River National Recreation Area
1978 Island Ford Parkway
Atlanta, GA
770-399-8070
nps.gov/chat
Dogs are allowed, but must be kept on a leash and under control at all times. Please clean up after your pooch. There are many separate areas or units that make up this park. One of the more popular trails starts near the Park Headquarters at the Island Fort Unit. The Cochran Fitness Trail follows the Chattahoochee River and is a great place to walk or run. For a map and more details, call or visit the Park Headquarters at the Island Ford Unit at 1978 Island Ford Parkway. Take Highway 400/19 and exit Northridge Road. The park is

located about 15 minutes north of downtown Atlanta.

Grant Park
840 Cherokee Ave., SE
Atlanta, GA
404-875-7275
This park has over 125 acres and miles of scenic trails. While dogs are not allowed in the Zoo or in the Atlanta Cyclorama, they can walk with you around this park. Dogs must be leashed and pet owners must clean up after their dogs.

Piedmont Park
400 Park Drive Northeast
Atlanta, GA
404-875-7275
Located in Midtown is the popular Piedmont Park, which consists of 185 acres. The park offers many paths for walking or running. Dogs must be leashed, except for the designated off-leash area located north of the Park Drive bridge. Dog owners are required to clean up after their dogs. Dogs are not allowed in the lake, in the botanical gardens, on the tennis courts, ball fields or playgrounds. Of special interest to dog lovers, is the Atlanta Symphony Orchestra's Annual Bark in the Park event. The event usually takes place in August and is held in Piedmont Park. To get to the park, take I-85/75 north and take exit 101 (10th Street). Go straight to the first light, then turn right on 10th Street. Turn left at Piedmont and the park entrance will be on the right.

Seminole State Park
7870 State Park Dr
Donalsonville, GA
229- 861--3137
gastateparks.org
Dogs on leash are allowed in this state park. They are allowed in some of the cabins for an additional fee of $40 per pet (limit 2 dogs). They are also allowed in the campgrounds. This park features canoeing, hiking, swimming, fishing, boating, and more.

Suwanee Canal Recreation Area
Route 2, Box 3325
Folkston, GA
912-496-7156
okefenokeeadventures.com/
Visitors can experience a bit of what swamp living was like at the turn of the century at this uniquely landscaped region; there are knowledgeable docents, original buildings, an 8 mile auto/walking tour, educational programs, café, gift

shop, and visitor center. Dogs are allowed on the grounds; they are not allowed on the boat rentals. Dogs must be leashed and cleaned up after at all times. Dogs must be kept away from water's edge/walkways because of alligators.

Tugaloo Park
1763 Tugaloo State Park Rd
Lavonia, GA
706- 356--4362
gastateparks.org
Dogs on leash are allowed in this state park. They are allowed in some of the cabins for a fee of $40 per pet (limit 2 dogs). They are also allowed in the campgrounds. This park features canoeing, saltwater fishing, hiking, picnic areas, swimming, and more.

Providence Canyon State Park
Route 1, Box 158/On Hwy 39C
Lumpkin, GA
229-838-6202
In addition to a several events throughout the year and a number of recreational activities, the strikingly beautiful colors of their "little Grand Canyon"-only upstaged by its display of wildflowers and greenery, is the real popularity at this 1,003 acre park. Dogs are allowed throughout the park on no more than a 6 foot leash and cleaned up after at all times.

Ocmulgee National Monument
1207 Emery Highway
Macon, GA
478-752-8257
nps.gov/ocmu
Dedicated to preserving, protecting, and educating visitors and future generations of the significance of this unique memorial, they have preserved more than its 12,000 years of diverse history and culture. Dogs are allowed throughout the grounds; they must be leashed and under their owner's control at all times.

Cumberland Island National Seashore
P. O. Box 806
St Marys, GA
912-882-4336 ext. 254
nps.gov/cuis/
The 50+ miles of hiking trails on this beautiful forested island takes visitors through a variety of natural habitats abundant with marine/bird/wildlife, historic areas, open fields, and by various waterways and beaches. Dogs are allowed on the island; however, they are not allowed in campgrounds or

on the ferry to the island. Dogs are not allowed in buildings or swimming areas; they must be on no more than a 6 foot leash at all times; they may not be left unattended at any time, and they must be cleaned up after.

Hawaii

Haleakala National Park
It is located off Hana Highway
Hawaii, HI
808-572-4400
nps.gov/hale
Dogs are not allowed on the trails or in any wilderness area. They are allowed in the campgrounds. There are no water or bathroom facilities at this park, so be sure to bring enough for you and your pet.

Hawaii Volcanoes National Park
MM 31.5 Hwy 11
Hawaii National Park, HI
808-985-6000
nps.gov/havo
This park covers the top of earth's most massive volcano the Mauna Loa at almost 14,000 feet. The park is open 7 days a week year round. Dogs are allowed at no additional fee, but they may only be on paved roads, the developed areas, and the campgrounds. They are not allowed on any of the trails or off the roads. Dogs may not be left unattended at any time, and they must be leashed and cleaned up after.

Idaho

City of Rocks National Reserve
PO Box 169
Almo, ID
208-824-5519
nps.gov/ciro/index.htm
Dogs must be on leash and must be cleaned up after on all trails and park grounds. The park features auto touring, picnicking, camping, and hiking.

Julia Davis Park
700 S Capital Blvd
Boise, ID
208-384-4228
This park of 86 acres has become known as the "cultural, historical, and artistic gateway to the heart of

the city". The park offers museums, a discovery center, zoo, an outdoor sculpture garden, a band shell, playground, gaming courts, lagoon and river walking areas, and an amazing Rose Garden-given it's accreditation in 1992. Dogs of all sizes are allowed on the grounds and trails of the park. They are not allowed in the zoo or buildings. Dogs must be well mannered, and leashed and cleaned up after at all times; please bring your own supplies.

Ridge to Rivers Trail System
Various Locations
Boise, ID
208-514-3756
The Ridge to Rivers Trail System of Boise consists of over 85 miles of trails around the Boise foothills. Many of these trails allow dogs off-leash provided that the dog is under voice control and remains within 30 feet of its owner. Please check signs for off-leash areas. You must clean up after your dog and the number one complaint heard from users of the trails is the failure of pet owners to clean up after their dogs.

The Boise Foothills
Various Locations
Boise, ID
208-384-4240
cityofboise.org/parks/foothills/
The city of Boise is surrounded by foothills consist of many trails and park areas. There are many areas of these parks that allow dogs. Some areas allow dogs off-leash and others allow dogs on-leash only. In off-leash areas dogs must be under voice control and within 30 feet of their owners. Please clean up after your dog as there are many complaints about people who don't clean up after their pets. One section of the foothills is the Ridge to Rivers section which has over 85 miles of trails. Ridge to Rivers is a collaborative effort between Boise and the county and federal authorities.

Weiser River Trail
3494 Rush Creek Road
Cambridge, ID
208-414-0452
weiserrivertrail.org/
This is Idaho's longest rail trail at 84 miles and it travels through rolling hills, roadless canyons, into the Payette National Forest. The trail offers a wide variety of wildlife and ever changing scenery along this multi-use trail. Dogs are allowed on this trail and they may be off lead in

non-populated areas if they are under good voice control. Please clean up after your pet on the trail or in populated areas.

Hagerman Fossil Beds National Monument
221 North State Street
Hagerman, ID
208-837-4793
nps.gov/hafo/index.htm
Dogs must be on leash and must be cleaned up after in park. Dogs are not allowed in any buildings. The park features auto touring, hiking, fishing, boating, and more. The park contains the largest concentration of Hagerman Horse fosssils in North America.

Minidoka Internment National Monument
PO Box 570
Hagerman, ID
208-837-4793
nps.gov/miin/index.htm
Dogs must be on leash and must be cleaned up after at the park. There are no facilties at the site but you are able to see the structures and monument of the Japanese American internment camp during WWII.

Nez Perce National Historical Park
39063 US Highway 95
Spalding, ID
208-843-2261
nps.gov/nepe/index.htm
Dogs on leash are allowed in this historical park. They are not allowed in any buildings. Located in Idaho, Montana, Oregon, and Washington. The park features camping, auto touring, fishing, hiking, swimming, and more.

Centennial Waterfront Park
4185 North 2874 East at Blue Lakes Blvd
Twin Falls, ID
208-734-9491
This seasonal, day use park offers a variety of water and land recreation, picnic shelters, hiking trails, interpretive exhibits, and great scenic views. Dogs of all sizes are allowed for no additional fee. Dogs must be under their owner's control, and leashed and cleaned up after at all times.

Shoshone Falls Park
Road 3300 East
Twin Falls, ID
208-736-2265
The falls at this park drop 212 feet and are higher than Niagara Falls.

They are considered one of the most spectacular natural beauties on the Snake River. There is a variety of land and water recreation, and some of the amenities include large shaded grass areas, picnicking, playgrounds, hiking trails, restrooms, a concession stand, boat ramp, and a scenic overlook. Dogs of all sizes are allowed for no additional fee. Dogs must be under their owner's control, and leashed and cleaned up after at all times.

Twin Falls Park
3500 East
Twin Falls, ID
208-773-3974
This day-use park features 10 wooded acres and lawns providing excellent picnicking and sightseeing opportunities. Some of the features include a boat ramp and dock, interpretive exhibits, various land and water recreation, and picnic shelters. Dogs of all sizes are allowed for no additional fee. Dogs must be under their owner's control, and leashed and cleaned up after at all times.

Illinois

Aurora West Forest Preserve
40W244 Hankes Road
Aurora, IL
630-232-5980
Mature woodlands and diverse native shrubs make up most of this park, and with the trails and all the places to sniff out, it is a great place for off-lead dog training. Dogs are welcome throughout the park, and they may be off lead if they are under good voice control. Dogs must be leashed when in other parts of the park and cleaned up after at all times.

Batavia Riverwalk
Houston Street at Island Avenue
Batavia, IL
630-879-5235
bataviaparks.org/park27.htm
Features of this popular 12 acre, peninsula, riverwalk park include a boardwalk, an outdoor ice rink, a wildflower sanctuary, picnic areas, a playground, historical markers, and more. Dogs are allowed throughout the park; they must be leashed and cleaned up after.

Iroquois State Wildlife Area
R.R. #1, 2803 E. 3300 N. Rd.
Beaverville, IL
815-435-2218
Home to the largest single region of rare native savanna in the state, this 2,480 acre wildlife area has a variety of year round trails through several habitats and landscapes. An archery range and dog training/hunting area are also on site. Dogs of all sizes are allowed throughout the park; they must be leashed (except in training area) and cleaned up after.

Cache River State Natural Area
930 Sunflower Lane
Belknap, IL
618-634-9678
Glacial floodwaters helped to develop the wetlands, swamps, and ancient forests of this 14,314 natural area and in addition to being a bird lover's paradise, there are a number of trails to explore-including boardwalks and a canoe trail through forested swamps, and an educational wetlands center. Dogs are allowed throughout the park; they must be on leash except during hunting season and cleaned up after.

Grant Park
Congress and Columbus
Chicago, IL
312-742-7648
Dogs on leash are allowed in this famous park in downtown known as Chicago's Front Lawn. The famous Buckingham Fountain is located in this park. The park offers some nice views of Lake Michigan. The Lakefront Trail is near this park. There is now a Chicago DFA (Dog Friendly Area) in the park. Dogs are allowed throughout the rest of the park on leash except for a few areas. Dogs are not allowed on Northerly Island, Millennium Park and at the Agora statutes at Roosevelt & Michigan. Dogs must be cleaned up after in the park. There are very stiff fines for violations of leash laws and clean up laws in the park.

The Lakefront Trail
Lake Shore Drive
Chicago, IL
312-742-7529
chicagoparkdistrict.com/
This popular trail offers 18 miles of paved paths alongside Lake Michigan. Walkers, joggers, rollerbladers, bicyclists, and of course dogs, frequent this path. One of the starting points is at Lake Shore Drive and Wacker Drive, where the Riverwalk Gateway is located.

Effective August 2003, dogs are allowed on part of the beach near Montrose. Dogs can run leash-free on the beach but must be leashed from the parking lot to the beach.

River Action Trail
822 East River Drive
Davenport, IA
563-322-2969
Taking in both sides of the Mississippi River, the 65 mile river trail takes visitors by parks, overlooks, trails, by numerous attractions with many recreational opportunities, and through more than a dozen communities in both Illinois and in Iowa. Dogs are allowed on the trail; they must be leashed and cleaned up after at all times.

Galena River Bike Trail
Park Avenue
Galena, IL
815-777-1050
cityofgalena.org/recreation.cfm
This publically owned linear park offers 3½ miles of a year round multi-use trail. Since land on each side of the trail is private, they ask that visitors stay on the trail and to rest at designated "rest areas" only. Dogs must be under their owner's control, leashed, and cleaned up after at all times.

Grant Park
Park Avenue
Galena, IL
815-777-1050
cityofgalena.org/recreation.cfm
Although only 3.5 acres, this park offers gaming areas, a playground, gazebo, pavilion with tables, historic features, and a walk bridge that crosses the Galena River to downtown. Dogs are allowed throughout the park; they must be under their owner's control, leashed, and cleaned up after at all times. The park provides doggy sanitation stations.

Linmar Gardens
504 S Prospect Street
Galena, IL
815-777-1177
galena.org/index/G5button/50
In addition to a number of events during the year, this 3.5 acre private garden has a mine replica, ruins of one of the first African-American churches in the state, and various water features. Dogs are allowed throughout the park; they must be leashed and cleaned up after. The park is open from about the end of May to the end of September.

Billie Limacher Bicentennial Park
201 West Jefferson (Hwy 52) at Bluff Street
Joliet, IL
815-724-3760
bicentennialpark.org/
Realizing the importance of preserving riverfront towns, the city renovated the entire area (the city's first street) with landscaping, memory plaques, an outdoor bandshell, a stage, and gathering areas. Dogs are allowed throughout the park; they must be under their owner's control, leashed, and cleaned up after at all times.

Derwen Mawr Nature Preserve
Deerpath and Golf Lane
Lake Forest, IL
847-234-3880
Dedicated to the preservation, conservation, and education of the community's natural heritage, this preserve is 1 of Open Lands 5 dog friendly preserves in the area, and with many of its areas being restored to its original prairie and wetlands, this scenic 26 acre preserve has been thriving with bird and wildlife. Dog owners must register with the preserve (272 E Deerpath, Suite 318, Lake Forest IL 60045) as members of Open Lands with dog walking privileges and receive a current dog-walking decal. Dogs must be leashed when in view of other people or animals, and they must be cleaned up after at all times. Only 3 dogs are permitted to be walked by one individual at a time, and all dogs must be licensed, healthy, and be current on all distemper, parvo, and rabies shots. Dogs must be well mannered, under their owner's control, and remain on the trails at all times. Dogs are not allowed in the wetlands or streams.

Everett Farm Nature Preserve
James Court
Lake Forest, IL
847-234-3880
Once an abandoned tree nursery from the 50's, this 35 acre scenic preserve is considered one Open Land's most successful efforts with reclaimed areas creating multiple mini-habitats, and the nursery left an unusual variety of trees behind not common to the area. Dedicated to the preservation, conservation, and education of the community's natural heritage, this preserve is 1 of Open Lands 5 dog friendly parks in the area. Dog owners must

register with the preserve (272 E Deerpath, Suite 318, Lake Forest IL 60045) as members of Open Lands with dog walking privileges and receive a current dog-walking decal. Dogs must be leashed when in view of other people or animals, and they must be cleaned up after at all times. Only 3 dogs are permitted to be walked by one individual at a time, and all dogs must be licensed, healthy, and be current on all distemper, parvo, and rabies shots. Dogs must be well mannered, under their owner's control, and remain on the trails at all times. Dogs are not allowed in the wetlands or streams.

Skokie River Nature Preserve
Laurel Avenue
Lake Forest, IL
847-234-3880
Dedicated to the preservation, conservation, and education of the community's natural heritage, this preserve is 1 of Open Lands 5 dog friendly parks in the area. Dog owners must register with the preserve (272 E Deerpath, Suite 318, Lake Forest IL 60045) as members of Open Lands with dog walking privileges and receive a current dog-walking decal. Dogs must be leashed when in view of other people or animals, and they must be cleaned up after at all times. Only 3 dogs are permitted to be walked by one individual at a time, and all dogs must be licensed, healthy, and be current on all distemper, parvo, and rabies shots. Dogs must be well mannered, under their owner's control, and remain on the trails at all times. Dogs are not allowed in the wetlands or streams.

West Skokie Nature Preserve
Westleigh Road
Lake Forest, IL
847-234-3880
Dedicated to the preservation, conservation, and education of the community's natural heritage, this preserve is 1 of Open Lands 5 dog friendly preserves in the area, and the area is rich in native grasses and flowers, and at the south end is a lovely secluded wetland with a boardwalk and teaching platform. Dog owners must register with the preserve (272 E Deerpath, Suite 318, Lake Forest IL 60045) as members of Open Lands with dog walking privileges and receive a current dog-walking decal. Dogs must be leashed in view of other people or animals, and they must be cleaned up after at all times.

Only 3 dogs are permitted to be walked by one individual at a time, and all dogs must be licensed, healthy, and be current on all distemper, parvo, and rabies shots. Dogs must be well mannered, under their owner's control, and remain on the trails at all times. Dogs are not allowed in the wetlands or streams.

Lisle Station Park
1825 Short Street
Lisle, IL
630-968-0499
Considered the centerpiece for numerous special events and for sports, this community park also offers an amphitheatre, a community center, nature hiking trails, several gaming fields/courts, fishing ponds, an outdoor skating rink, concessionaires, and more. Dogs are allowed throughout the park and on the trails; they are not allowed in buildings. Dogs must be under their owner's control, leashed, and cleaned up after at all times.

Crab Orchard National Wildlife Refuge
8588 Hwy 148
Marion, IL
618-997-3344
fws.gov/midwest/CrabOrchard/
With an emphasis on wildlife conservation, agriculture, and industry, this 43,890 acre refuge also offers 3 man-made lakes, a large variety of habitats and wildlife, and a wide range of recreational pursuits. All visitors must obtain a pass at the visitor center for all vehicles and boats entering the refuge. Dogs are allowed in the refuge; they must be leashed and cleaned up after at all times.

Allerton Park and Retreat Center
515 Old Timber Road
Monticello, IL
217-762-2721
Whether for pleasure, a special occasion, or for educational exploration, this estate is considered one of the 7 wonders of the state with 1,500 acres of impeccable scenery that includes natural areas, formal gardens with unique sculptures gathered from around the world, a 100+ year old Georgian mansion, ongoing special events, and a visitor center/gift shop. Dogs are welcome; they must be under their owner's control, on no more than a 6 foot leash, and cleaned up after at all times.

Valentin Park

Cemetary Road
Monticello, IL
217-762-2583
This county forest preserve park offers self-guided nature trails, a bird watching area, picnic tables and grills, and is a favored spot for quiet relaxation. Dogs are allowed on leash; they must be under their owner's control and cleaned up after at all times.

Goose Lake Prairie State Natural Area
5010 N Jugtown Road
Morris, IL
815.942.2899
At 2,537 acres, this natural area is the largest remainder of tall grass prairie in the state with miles of hiking trails including a trail over a floating bridge that allow visitors great plant, bird, and wildlife viewing. There are also marshlands, picnic areas, and the Cragg Cabin-a testament to the pioneer spirit. Dogs are allowed throughout the park and on the trails; they must be leashed and cleaned up after at all times. Dogs are not allowed in hunting areas.

Riverwalk
Jackson Avenue
Naperville, IL
630-871-2857
In addition to being one of the most beautiful walking areas in the city with covered bridges, lush foliage, fountains, and historic reminders, this area is also a popular community gathering arena with numerous activities monthly throughout the year. Dogs are allowed throughout the Riverwalk area, and they must be under their owner's control, leashed, and cleaned up after at all times. Dogs are not allowed in buildings.

Scoville Park
156 N Oak Park Avenue
Oak Park, IL
708-524-7800
oprf.com/oppd/ScovillePark/
Rich in cultural heritage, this park now offers visitors a number of activities, leisure spaces, and sites of interest such as the bronze War Memorial at its center and the Horse Show Fountain; there are also gaming courts and a playground. Dogs are allowed throughout the park. Dogs must be leashed and cleaned up after at all times.

Castle Rock State Park

1365 W Castle Road
Oregon, IL
815-732-7329
Home to one of the states largest significant natural areas, this almost 2,000 acre park has a 710 acre restricted section dedicated to its study, preservation, and interpretation. There are also some wonderful trails and boardwalks through this park; primitive camping is allowed and accessible only by canoe. Dogs are allowed throughout the park; they must be leashed and cleaned up after at all times.

Buffalo Rock State Park
1300 North 27th Road/Hwy 34
Ottawa, IL
815-433-2220
Interesting to look at from afar or close up, the unique "earth art" here is a tribute to ancient burial grounds and depicts a water strider, catfish, frog, snake, and a turtle. A nature lover's delight, there are almost 300 acres to explore plus a couple of resident buffalos. Although mostly a day use area, primitive camping is allowed but there no amenities. Dogs are allowed throughout the park; they must be leashed and cleaned up after at all times.

Tower Park
1203 E Kingman Avenue
Peoria Heights, IL
309-682-8732
villageofpeoriaheights.org/
Open from about the 1st of April through October; weather permitting, this unique one-of-a-kind 200 foot observation tower has glass elevators for great scenes on the way up, and the top deck gives visitors spectacular views of the river valley and beyond. There is also a children's playground, an open air water fountain, and a sculpture of Abraham Lincoln in the park below. The Tower is closed on Mondays. Dogs are welcome throughout the park and they may also go up in the tower. Dogs must be under their owner's control, leashed, and cleaned up after at all times.

Pomona Natural Bridge
Hwy 127
Pomona, IL
Dogs on leash are allowed at this park. Tables for picnics, bathroom facilities, and a hiking trail are a part of this natural bridge site. The bridge is 25 feet high and 6-9 feet wide and sits above a natural creek. It is located 3 miles west on Hwy 127 from Pomona.

Black Hawk State Historic Site
1510 46th Avenue/Hwy 5
Rock Island, IL
309-788-0177
blackhawkpark.org/
Offering a museum, an early amusement park, a nature center, and a long Native American history, this 208 acre river-side park is home to a colonial burial ground, numerous birds and wildlife, and various special events throughout the year. Dogs are allowed throughout the park; they must be leashed and cleaned up after at all times.

Illinois and Michigan Canal State Trail
Brandon Road
Rockdale, IL
815-942-9501
Currently 61 miles long connecting Rockdale and LaSalle/Peru, this multi-use canal trail passes many historic and natural sites along the way. Dogs are allowed on the trail; they must be leashed and cleaned up after at all times.

Fox River Bluff and West Forest Preserve
N 2nd St/Hwy 31
St Charles, IL
630-232-5980
This beautiful, natural river's edge park was a gift to the Forest Preserve District with only one condition-that no structures would ever be built on the property. Dogs are welcome throughout the park, and there is a 50 acre section where dogs under good voice control may be off lead. They must be leashed when in other parts of the park and cleaned up after at all times.

Tekakwitha Woods Forest Preserve
35WO76 Villa Marie Road
St Charles, IL
630-232-5980
Named in honor of an Indian maiden, this 65 acre forested park also has an educational environmental center. Dogs are allowed throughout the preserve; they are not allowed in buildings. Dogs must be leashed and cleaned up after at all times.

Meadowbrook Park
Windsor Road and Race Street
Urbana, IL
217-384-4062
This beautifully landscaped park has 80 acres of recreated Tallgrass prairie, an ornamental tree grove, a variety of garden settings, a farmstead, sculptures, the largest

play structure in the district, and various walking trails to explore it all. Dogs are allowed throughout the park, but they are not allowed in the woods or in park buildings. Dogs must be well behaved, leashed, and cleaned up after at all times.

Tunnel Hill State Trail Park
Hwy 146 E
Vienna, IL
618-658-2168
From farm lands to forests, bluffs, and lush wetlands, this 45 mile park trail stretches from Harrisburg to Karnak and passes many sites of interest along the way including a 543 foot long tunnel, 23 trestles, and abundant wildlife. Dogs are allowed on the trail; they must be leashed and cleaned up after at all times.

Danada Forest Preserve and Equestrian Center
3 S 580 Naperville Road
Wheaton, IL
630-933-7200
In addition to being dedicated to holistic equestrian care and training, this 783 acre forest preserve offers miles of scenic hiking trails, recreational and educational opportunities, historic sites, a model farm exhibit, and more. Dogs are allowed on the grounds, but they must not be a disturbance to wildlife. Dogs must be well behaved, under their owner's control, leashed, and cleaned up after at all times.

Lincoln Marsh Natural Area
Harrison and Pierce Roads
Wheaton, IL
630-871-2810
A wildlife haven and recreational refuge, this 130 acre park is a complex mix of woods, prairie, and marsh with trails/boardwalks, great views from the Prairie Path, and an abundant variety of birdlife. Dogs are allowed throughout the park, and doggy sanitary stations are provided along the trails. Dogs must be leashed and cleaned up after at all times.

Midewin National Tallgrass Prairie
30239 S Hwy 53
Wilmington, IL
815-423-6370
fs.fed.us/mntp/
Even though much of the park is not yet available for public use while the Army continues contamination clean-up, there are still more than 6,400 acres with 20 miles of multi-

use trails to explore, and 2 entrances to the park are located at the Hoff Road and Iron Bridge Trailheads. Dogs are allowed throughout the park; they must be on no more than an 8 foot leash and picked up after.

Indiana

Bonneyville Mill County Park
53373 County Road 131
Bristol, IN
574-535-6458
elkhartcountyparks.org
There are 223 scenic natural acres at this recreational park with a nice fishing river and miles of woodland trails. Dogs are allowed throughout the park; they must be on no more than a 6 foot leash and under their owner's control at all times. Pets are not allowed in buildings.

Falls of the Ohio State Park
201 West Riverside Drive
Clarksville, IN
812-280-9970
fallsoftheohio.org/
This park is home to 220 acres of naturally exposed 386 million year old fossil beds. A wonderful interpretive center offers numerous programs and special events regarding the fossils. Dogs are allowed on the grounds and trails; they are not allowed in buildings. Dogs must be on no more than a 6 foot leash and under their owner's control at all times.

Krider Gardens
Bristol Street
Middlebury, IN
574-825-1499
Considered the crown jewel of the city's park system, this garden was originally designed for the 1933/34 World's Fair and it has been recreated at this site. There is a mill house with a water wheel, lily ponds, fountains, a Dutch windmill, waterfalls, picnic areas, and historical signage throughout. Dogs are allowed in the park; they must be leashed and under their owner's control.

Bluhm County Park
3855 S. 1100 W
Westville, IN
219-325-8315
Bluhm County Park is 96 acres of spring wildflowers, upland forest, wetlands, a pond, and a prairie. This

park is well known for its wildflower viewing and the east property is dedicated to nature trails only to protect the natural beauty. The west side is designated multiple use with hiking trails, mountain biking, horseback riding, cross country skiing in the winter, and is host to a large waterfowl population. There are also paved trails, picnic areas, a playground, restrooms, and a great off-leash dog exercise area. This fully fenced-in 2 acre "Bark Park" features many events for the dog to enjoy and exercise, like the tire jump, a window jump, dog walk, a rover jump over area, a doggie crawl, tables, hills, drinking fountains, benches, and, of course, Fire Hydrants. Registration and a daily or annual permit are required for each dog present in this area, and owners must present them upon request. Daily fees are paid on site and Annual fees can be paid at Red Mill County Park, 0185 South Holmesville Road in LaPorte, or the LaPorte County Small Animal Shelter, 2855 West State Road 2 in LaPorte. The cost is $1 per dog per day for residents, or $2 per dog per day for out of county residents. The park is open from dawn to dusk. Dogs must be leashed when out of the off leash area, and cleaned up after at all times.

Iowa

Vander Veer Botanical Park
215 W. Central Park Avenue
Davenport, IA
563-326-7818
For only being a 33 acre park there is a lot to see, including an amazing collection of trees, themed gardens, native and non-native flora, and it was one of the first gardens registered as an American Hosta Society National Display Garden. The park also has a wonderful "Grand Allee" walkway leading to a popular Stone Fountain of dancing and lighted waters, a children's playground, and a catch-and-release stocked lagoon. Dogs are allowed throughout the park; they are not allowed in buildings. Dogs must be leashed and under their owner's control at all times.

Gray's Lake Park
Fluer Drive and George Flagg
Parkway (Valley Road)

Des Moines, IA
515-237-4533
In addition to being a popular meeting place, this city park offers multi-use trails, a number of land and water recreational opportunities, and a colorfully lit ¼ mile pedestrian bridge. Dogs must be kept leashed and cleaned up after at all times. Pet waste stations can be found at the beach, the Overlook Terrace parking lots, and every ½ mile on the trail.

Big Creek State Park
8794 NW 125th Avenue
Polk City, IA
515-984-6473
The highlight of this 3,550 acre park is the 866 acre stocked lake that provides a variety of recreational options. They also have a sports field, several boat ramps, and a 26 mile multi-use trail that takes visitors from the beach area all the way to Des Moines. Dogs are allowed for no additional fees; they must be on no more than a 6 foot leash and picked up after at all times.

Sunset Park
Marion Avenue
Washington, IA
319-653-3272
Located just a few blocks from the downtown area, this lush park features large grassy places, lots of shade trees, playgrounds in separate areas of the park, ornate bridges, and a historic 1840 log cabin. Dogs are welcome; they must be leashed and under their owner's control at all times. Dogs are not allowed at the cabin.

Kansas

Tallgrass Prairie National Preserve
2480 Hwy 177
Strong City, KS
620-273-8494
nps.gov/tapr/
In addition to detailing the rich natural and cultural aspects of this 10,894 acre preserve, its main focus is the protection and continuation of the tallgrass prairie ecosystem. Dogs are allowed on the 2 front country trails only; they are the Interpretive Bottomland Trail with overlooks, and the Southwind Nature Trail that allows visitors close-up views of prairie

ecosystems. Dogs must remain leashed and under their owner's control at all times.

Gage Park
635 SW Gage Blvd
Topeka, KS
785-368-3838
Once a family farm, this site has grown to a 160 acre park with numerous recreational facilities, and includes an Aquatic Center, gardens, an historic carousel, plus they are also home to the city zoo and the Helen Hocker Theater. Dogs are allowed throughout the park, except at the zoo or in buildings. Dogs must be leashed and under their owner's control at all times.

Kentucky

Falls of the Ohio State Park
201 W Riverside Drive
Clarksville, IN
812-280-9970
fallsoftheohio.org/
This park is home to 386 million year old fossil beds that represent some of the biggest naturally exposed Devonian fossil beds anywhere. In addition to a great interpretive center there are also a number of recreational activities to enjoy. Leashed dogs are allowed throughout the park; they are not allowed in buildings.

Old Fort Harrod State Park
100 S College Street
Harrodsburg, KY
859-734-3314
This reconstructed fort offers visitors a trip to colonial times with costumed docents, pioneer craftspeople at work, special events, and a museum. Dogs are allowed throughout the grounds; they are not allowed in the museum. Dogs must be leashed and under their owner's control at all times.

Cumberland Gap National Historic Park
US 25E South
Middlesboro, KY
606-248-2817
nps.gov/cuga/index.htm
Dogs on 6 ft leash are allowed in the park. The park features auto touring, camping, caving, hiking, and picnicking.

Louisiana

Handy Break National Wildlife Refuge
Cooper Lake Road
Bastrop, LA
318-726-4222
In addition to providing a protective habitat for migratory and resident birds and wildlife, the bayous, cypress swamps, and bottom and upland forests, there are many recreational and educational opportunities available. A wildlife observation tower overlooks the wetlands. Leashed dogs are allowed on the grounds; they are not allowed in buildings.

Cypremort Point State Park
306 Beach Lane
Cypremort Point, LA
337-867-4510
This park is home to a ½ mile section of beach on the Gulf of Mexico, and in addition to being a popular site for nature enthusiasts; there are a good variety of recreational opportunities to pursue. Dogs are allowed throughout the park. Dogs are not allowed in public swim areas, buildings, in the cabins, or on the walkways to the cabins. Dogs must be on no more than a 6 foot leash and under their owner's control at all times.

D'Arbonne National Wildlife Refuge
11372 Highway 143
Farmerville, LA
318-726-4222
fws.gov/darbonne/
In addition to providing a protective habitat for a multiplicity of migratory and resident bird and wildlife, there are also recreational and educational opportunities available and a wildlife observation tower overlooking the wetlands. Leashed dogs are allowed on the grounds; they are not allowed in buildings.

Black Bayou Lake National Wildlife Refuge
480 Richland Place
Monroe, LA
318-387-1114
There are 4,200 scenic acres of wetlands, bottomland hardwoods, restored agricultural fields, a lake, recreational and educational opportunities, and more at this refuge. Leashed dogs are allowed on the grounds; they are not allowed in

any of the buildings.

New Orleans City Park
1 Palm Drive
New Orleans, LA
504-482-4888
neworleanscitypark.com
Dogs on leash are allowed in the park. Dogs are allowed on walking paths, lake area, and the picnic area.

Maine

Portland Head Light Park
1000 Shore Road
Cape Elizabeth, ME
207-799-266
portlandheadlight.com/home.html
This park offers 90 acres, spectacular ocean views, picnic facilities, recreation areas, historic structures, plenty of hiking trails, and a lighthouse complex. Dogs are allowed throughout the park; they are not allowed in buildings. Dogs must be under their owner's control, leashed, and cleaned up after at all times.

Two Lights State Park
7 Tower Drive
Cape Elizabeth, ME
207-799-5871
Rocky coastlines, powerful rolling surf, outstanding panoramic Casco Bay and ocean views, and great hiking and picnicking areas have made this 40 acre park a popular destination. Dogs are allowed throughout the park and on the trails; they are not allowed on the beaches. Dogs must be well behaved, on no more than a 4 foot leash, cleaned up after at all times, and never be left unattended.

Mackworth Island
Andrews Avenue
Falmouth, ME
207-624-6076
An area rich in cultural and ghostly lore, this small island is a sanctuary for birds, animals and people with a hundred acres to explore and a 1.25 mile walking trail that takes visitors around the entire island for some great views of harbor activity and bird and marine life. There is also a private walled area to commemorate the 19 Irish Setters who were the "lifelong friends and companions" of the Governor who donated this island. Dogs are

welcome here, and they must be leashed and cleaned up after at all times.

Wolfe's Neck Woods State Park
426 Wolfe's Neck Road
Freeport, ME
207-865-4465
Varied ecosystems and wildlife give visitors a real "back to nature" feel even though this 233 acre park is only a few minutes from a busy city, and they provide interpretive signage, picnic tables and grills, bathrooms, and 5 miles of wooded and shoreline trails. Dogs are allowed throughout the park and on the trails; they are not allowed on the beach. Dogs must be well behaved, on no more than a 4 foot leash, cleaned up after at all times, and never be left unattended.

Quoddy Head State Park
973 N Lubec Road
Lubec, ME
207-733-0911
Located on the easternmost point of land in the US, this 532 acre diversely landscaped and inhabited park offers 5 different trails showcasing the varying features of the park. Dogs are allowed; they must be under their owner's control, leashed, and cleaned up after at all times.

Roosevelt Campobello International Park
PO Box 97
Lubec, ME
506-752-2922
nps.gov/roca/index.htm
Dogs must be on leash and must be cleaned up after in park. They ar not allowed in any buildings. Vistor center is open all year 9am-5pm. The park features auto touring, camping, hiking, nature walks, and more. This 2800 acre park is a joint memorial by Canada and the US as a symbol of the close relationship between the two countries.

Grafton Notch State Park
1941 Bear River Road
Newry, ME
207-824-2912
A day use park for all seasons with a variety of recreational pursuits, there are 3000 lush acres to explore here, and picnic grills and tables available. Dogs are allowed for no additional pet fee. Dogs must be on no more than a 4 foot leash, cleaned up after at all times, and never be left unattended. Dogs are allowed throughout the park and on the trails;

they are not allowed on the beaches.

Rachel Carson National Wildlife
Refuge
321 Port Road
Wells, ME
207-646-9226
fws.gov/northeast/rachelcarson/
This park was established in 1966 for
the protection of important salt
marshes and migratory bird
estuaries, and there are great
opportunities for bird and wildlife
viewing/photography, picnicking,
hiking, and they offer special events
throughout the year. Dogs are
allowed on site and on the Carson
Trail. Dogs must be under their
owner's control, leashed, and
cleaned up after at all times.

Maryland

Back Creek Nature Center
Edgewood Road
Annapolis, MD
410-263-1183
In addition to being developed as an
environmental educational resource
area with several important eco-
related projects completed or in
progress, there are scenic trails,
nature areas, a fishing pier, picnic
areas, and restrooms. Dogs must be
well mannered, under their owner's
control, leashed, and cleaned up
after at all times.

BWI Bike Trail
Dorsey Road
BWI Airport, MD
This trail is a nice paved trail at the
airport, near a number of the dog-
friendly hotels.

Cromwell Valley Park
2175 Cromwell Bridge Rd
Baltimore, MD
410-887-2503
Dogs on leash are welcome.

Cylburn Arboretum
4915 Greenspring Ave
Baltimore, MD
410-396-0180
Well behaved dogs on leash are
welcome at this over 20 acre nature
preserve and city park.

Druid Hill Park
Druid Park Lake Drive
Baltimore, MD
Druid Hill Park is a large city park in

the center of Baltimore. Dogs on
leash are allowed in the park.

Federal Hill
Key Hwy and Light St
Baltimore, MD
baltimoremd.com/federalhill/
This nice park with a nice view of
the Inner Harbor is also easy
walking distance from the Inner
Harbor. Most of the park is up on a
hill overlooking downtown. Dogs on
leash are welcome.

Fort McHenry
2400 E Fort Avenue
Baltimore, MD
410-962-4290
nps.gov/fomc/
Rich in colonial history, this star-
shaped 18th century fort was the
birthplace of the country's National
Anthem. Dogs are allowed around
the outer (landscaped) grounds,
down by the river, and at the picnic
areas; they are not allowed inside
gated areas. Dogs must be leashed
and cleaned up after at all times.

Gwynns Fall Trail and Park
Franklintown Rd and Holly Ave
Baltimore, MD
This is a city park with a paved bike
trail. Dogs on leash are welcome.

Robert E Lee Park
Falls Road and Lake Ave
Baltimore, MD
Dogs must be on leash at all times
in the park.

Oregon Ridge Park
Beaver Dam Road
Cockeysville, MD
410-887-1818
Dogs on leash are allowed. This is
a very large park with lots of trails.

C and O Canal Historical Park
Cumberland Visitor Center/13
Canal Street
Cumberland, MD
301-739-4200
nps.gov/choh/
Dedicating to preserving and
educating the public about the canal
era and America's transportation
history, several visitor centers can
be found along this 184½ mile long
canal trail as well as various
recreation opportunities. The trail
goes from Georgetown in the
District of Columbia to Cumberland,
Maryland, and the park is also
home to the 3,118 foot Paw Paw
Tunnel that took more than 6 million
bricks and 12 years to build. Dogs

are allowed throughout the park and
on the canal trail. Dogs must be
under their owner's control, leashed,
and cleaned up after at all times.

Fort Howard Park
North Point Blvd
Edgemere, MD
410-887-7529
Dogs must be leashed in this park.

North Point State Park
Old North Point Rd
Edgemere, MD
410-592-2897
Dogs must be leashed in this park.

Baltimore & Annapolis Bike Trail
Glen Burnie, MD
This is a 13 mile paved trail from
Baltimore to Annapolis. Leashed
dogs are allowed.

Glen Echo Park
7300 MacArthur Blvd
Glen Echo, MD
301-492-6229
nps.gov/glec
Some of the highlights at this park
include a carousel, a Spanish
ballroom, weekend "night" programs,
and year-around events and
educational activities. Dogs are
allowed throughout the grounds and
at the events. Dogs must be friendly
to both people and other animals,
under their owner's control, leashed,
and cleaned up after at all times.

Greenbelt Park
6565 Greenbelt Rd
Greenbelt, MD
301-344-3944
nps.gov/gree/
Dogs must be leashed in this park.

Frank Hutchins Memorial Park
Congress Street at the Susquehanna
River
Havre de Grace, MD
410-939-6724
This 2-acre waterfront park is located
on the bank of the Susquehanna
River with a nice pier for fishing.
Dogs are allowed in the park and on
the pier. Dogs must be under their
owner's control, leashed, and
cleaned up after at all times.

Gunpowder Falls State Park
Hereford, MD
410-592-2897
This is a huge park with over 100
miles of trails. It follows the
Gunpowder Falls River and extends
as far as Pennsylvania. Dogs on
leash are allowed.

Rocks State Park
3318 Rocks Chrome Hill Road
Jarrettsville, MD
410-557-7994
Dense with forest and large boulders, this 855 acre park sits above Deer Creek popular for fishing and tubing, and there are also many secluded areas along the creek and hiking trails that connect different areas of the park. Dogs of all sizes are allowed throughout the park for no additional fee; they must be leashed and cleaned up after at all times. Dogs are not allowed in picnic or historic areas or at the cabins.

Chesapeake and Ohio Canal National Historical Park
11710 MacArthur Blvd, Great Falls Tavern Visitor Center
Potomac, MD
301-767-3714
nps.gov/choh
Dedicating to preserving and educating the public about the canal era and America's transportation history, several visitor centers can be found along this 184 mile long canal trail. Dogs are allowed throughout the park and on the canal trail. Dogs must be under their owner's control, leashed, and cleaned up after at all times.

Eastern Neck National Wildlife Refuge
1730 Eastern Neck Road
Rock Hall, MD
410-639-7056
fws.gov/northeast/easternneck/
Observation towers, boardwalks, and various trails allow visitors to truly explore and enjoy this wildlife refuge. They suggest visitors pick up a map at the entrance. Dogs are allowed throughout the park and on the trails. Dogs must be under their owner's control, leashed, and cleaned up after at all times.

Jefferson Patterson Park and Museum
10515 Mackall Road
St Leonard, MD
410-586-8500
jefpat.org/
This state history and archaeology museum is dedicated to educating and preserving the history and cultures of the past 12,000 years of the Chesapeake Bay region. Dogs are allowed throughout the park, along the riverfront, and on the trails; they are not allowed in the museum or other park buildings. Dogs must be well behaved, leashed, and

cleaned up after at all times.

Hampton Historical Site
535 Hampton Lane
Towson, MD
410-823-1309
nps.gov/hamp/
Dogs on leash are allowed in the outdoor areas. There is an admission fee to the park, which is an 1800's plantation.

Wheaton Regional Park
2000 Shorefield Rd
Wheaton, MD
our-kids.com/wheaton.htm
An excellent park for kids and dogs. There are a number of annual dog events here and trails to jog or walk on. Dogs must be leashed in the park except within the fenced off-leash dog area.

Massachusetts

Mount Holyoke Range State Park
Hwy 116
Amherst, MA
413-586-0350
This day use park of over 3000 acres provides several diverse habitats for a variety of wildlife, and there are more than 30 miles of multi-use marked trails for year round activities. Dogs are allowed for no additional fee. Dogs must be under their owner's control, leashed, and cleaned up after at all times.

Arnold Arboretum
125 Arborway
Boston, MA
617-524-1718
arboretum.harvard.edu/
Dogs must be on leash and must be cleaned up after at all times. The arboretum has a collection of trees, shrubs, and vines on 265 acres.

Back Bay Fens
The Fenway and Park Drive
Boston, MA
Leashed dogs are allowed at this Back Bay park.

Boston Common Park
Beacon Street/Hwy 2
Boston, MA
617-635-4505
At 350 years old, this is the country's oldest park and it boasts an interesting cultural and natural history. The Freedom Trail Visitor

Center is on site, and the park is a hub for the Emerald Necklace system that links several parks and areas of the city. The 50 acre park is also home to many large, public events, a children's play area, a public garden, several memorials, the Frog Pond (skating in winter and a spray pool for summer), and the entrance to the oldest subway in America is here as well. Dogs are welcome here, on the trails, and may be present during public events. Dogs must be well behaved, be on no more than an 8 foot leash, and be cleaned up after. Dogs are not allowed in the community garden. There are off-leash hours in certain areas of the park in the early mornings and evenings.

Boston Harbor Islands
408 Atlantic Avenue Ste 228
Boston, MA
617-223-8666
nps.gov/boha/
Dogs must be on leash and must be cleaned up after on the ferry ride. Dogs are only allowed on the more developed islands of Deer and Nut. They are not allowed on other islands in the park. The park is accessed only by ferry or private boat.

Boston National Historical Park
Charleston Navy Yard
Boston, MA
617-242-5642
nps.gov/bost/
Dogs must be on leash and must be cleaned up after in the park. They are not allowed in any buildings. The park features the revolutionary generation of Bostonians who blazed a trail from colonialism to independence.

Fort Independence
William J. Day Blvd
Boston, MA
This park and a historical fort can be viewed by your dog.

Sudbury, Assabet, and Concord Wild and Scenic Rivers
15 State Street
Boston, MA
617-223-525
nps.gov/suas/
Dogs must be on leash and must be cleaned up after in most park areas. You must follow local and state park rules. The park features camping, hiking, fishing, boating, and more.

Nickerson State Park
Route 6A

Brewster, MA
508-896-3491
state.ma.us/dem/parks/nick.htm
This state park has 1900 acres of land and miles of trails. Dogs are allowed on the hiking trails, and paved trails. Dogs are not allowed in the pond or on public beaches. However, you can take your dog to an uncrowded beach, where there are not many other people. Dogs must be leashed and you must have proof of your dog's rabies vaccination. Your dog is also welcome at the campgrounds, but they ask that your dog never be left unattended.

Frederick Law Olmsted National Historic Site
99 Warren Street
Brookline, MA
617-566-1689
nps.gov/frla/
Dogs must be on leash and must be cleaned up after on the property. They are not allowed in buildings. The park features nature walks at Frederick Law Olmsted's former home, who is recognized as the founder of American landscape architecture and the nation's foremost parkmaker.

Larz Anderson Park
Goddard St and Newton St
Brookline, MA
Dogs are allowed on-leash only.

Fresh Pond Reservation
Fresh Pond Parkway
Cambridge, MA
617-349-4800
Dogs are allowed off-leash in this park. They need to be under direct voice control and need to be cleaned up after. The park is located in Northwest Cambridge and is bounded by Fresh Pond Parkway, Blanchard Avenue, Concord Avenue, Grove Street and Huron Avenue.

Whitney and Thayer Woods Park
Rte 3A
Cohasset, MA
617-821-2977
e-guide.com/venues/v0006214.htm
Dogs on leash are allowed.

Cape Cod Rail Trail
Dennis - Wellfleet, MA
508 896-3491
A former railroad right-of-way, this 22 mile rail trail offers visitors a paved surface with few hills, scenic viewing areas, occasional restrooms, good markings, and year round recreation. You will find several free parking

areas along the trail. Due to some construction on the trail, please check ahead for closed areas. Dogs are welcome; they must be under their owner's control, leashed, and cleaned up after at all times.

Belle Isle Reservation
Bennington Street
East Boston, MA
617-727-5350
Dogs must be leashed in the park.

Frank Newhall Look Memorial Park
300 N Main Street
Florence, MA
413-584-5457
lookpark.org/
Gifted to the city by Mrs. Fannie B. Look, this 150 acre park features a variety of activities, attractions, recreation, a picnic store, and a visitor center. Dogs are allowed for no additional fee. Dogs must be under their owner's control, leashed, and cleaned up after at all times. Dogs are allowed on the walking path and throughout the park; they are not allowed on the rides or at the zoo.

Callahan State Park
Millwood Street
Framingham, MA
508-653-9641
state.ma.us/dem/parks/call.htm
Dogs are allowed on leash or in some areas, off-leash but under strict voice control. This 820 acre day use park offers 7 miles of hiking and walking trails, and a pond where dogs can swim. The park is located west of Boston. Take Route 9 to Edgell Road in Framingham, turn left on Belknap and then right onto Millwood St.

Poets Seat Tower
Mountain Road and Maple Street
Greenfield, MA
413-773-5463
Views from the historic tower area are wide and reaching across Greenfield and its green, fertile valley to the mountains on the other side. In addition to the incredible views, there are miles of woodland trails, wildlife, and bird/eagle viewing. Dogs are welcome for no additional fees. Dogs must be leashed and cleaned up after.

J.A. Skinner State Park
Hwy 47
Hadley, MA
413-586-0350
Scenic views, year round hiking trails, 20 picnic sites with grills, a

historical site, various habitats and wildlife, and a variety of recreational opportunities are all to be found at this 390 acre park. Dogs must be under their owner's control, be on no more than a 10 foot leash, cleaned up after, and have proof of current rabies inoculation.

Wompatuck State Park
Union St
Hingham, MA
781-749-7160
Dogs on leash are allowed this park.

World's End Park
Martin's Lane
Hingham, MA
781-821-2977
Dogs are allowed on leash. There is a $4 fee per person to enter. This park offers over 240 acres and about 5 miles of shoreline.

Dinosaur Footprints Park
Hwy 5
Holyoke, MA
413-684-0148
This small, narrow park by the railroad tracks is home to 134 of some of our biggest land animals that frequented the area 190 million years ago, and were uncovered during the construction of Route 5. Crossing the tracks for river access is not allowed here. Dogs are allowed for no additional fee. Dogs must be under their owner's control, leashed, and cleaned up after at all times.

Ashuwillticook Rail Trail
Lanesborough, Cheshire, Adams, MA
413-442-8928
This former RR now provides a 10 foot wide, 11+ mile, accessible, easy recreation path from the Berkshire Mall off Hwy 8 in Lanesborough to the center of Adams, and offers some beautiful scenery following along the river and wetlands. Picnic areas, parking, and restrooms are available along the way. Dogs are allowed with current proof of rabies inoculation. Dogs must be on no more than a 10 foot leash and be cleaned up after.

Lexington Battle Green
Massachusetts Ave and Bedford St
Lexington, MA
Dogs on leash are allowed in the park.

Minuteman Commuter Bikeway
Massachusetts Ave and Waltham

Lexington, MA
This 10 mile trail extends from Arlington, thru Lexington, and to Bedford. Dogs must be leashed in this park.

Lowell National Historical Park
67 Kirk Street
Lowell, MA
978-970-5000
nps.gov/lowe/
Dogs must be on leash and must be cleaned up after in the park area. They are not allowed in any buildings. The park shows the history of America's Industrial Revolution in Lowell, Massachusetts.

Lynn Woods Reservation
Great Woods Road
Lynn, MA
781-593-7773
lynndpw.com/woods/lynnwood.htm
Dogs must be leashed in this park.

Manuel F. Correllus State Forest
Barnes Road
Marthas Vineyard, MA
508-693-2540
Originally set aside as a Heath Hen Reserve in the early 1900's, this park covers 5,100+ acres in the heart of Martha's Vineyard, and is now the focal point of one of the largest environmental restorations projects in the continental US. Dogs are allowed throughout the park and on the trails. Dogs must be under their owner's control, be on no more than a 10 foot leash, cleaned up after, and have proof of current rabies inoculation.

Blue Hills Reservation
1904 Canton Ave
Milton, MA
617-698-1802
Leashed dogs are allowed in this park which offers over 125 of trails.

New Bedford Whaling National Historical Park
33 William Street
New Bedford, MA
508-996-4095
nps.gov/nebe/
Dogs must be on leash and must be cleaned up after in the park area. They are not allowed in any buildings. It is open daily 9am-5pm. The park commemorates the heritage of the world's preeminent whaling port during the 19th century.

Natural Bridge State Park
Mc Cauley Road
North Adams, MA

413-663-6392
This 48 acre seasonal park offers many unique geological features, an old marble quarry, a short walkway through a chasm, walking trails, picnic areas, and scenic overlooks. Dogs are allowed throughout the park and on the trails. Dogs must be under their owner's control at all times, be on no more than a 10 foot leash, cleaned up after, and have proof of current rabies inoculation.

Tufts University School of Veterinary Medicine
200 Westboro Rd/Hwy 30
North Grafton, MA
508-839-5302
The campus of this veterinary school is located among rolling hills with several great walking trails, and although private property, they welcome hikers with their canine companions. If you are eastbound on Highway 30, there is a parking area off to the left as you are just passing the university. Dogs may be off lead only if they are friendly and well behaved with people as well as other animals, and they respond to voice control. Please clean up after your pet when on the trails and you will need to bring your own supplies.

Norwottuck Rail Trail
Damon Road
Northampton, MA
413 586-8706 ext. 12
Because of the path's level landscape, this 8.5 mile walking path is an easy, safe passage for all ages and abilities. There is parking at both ends of the trail, and restrooms are available at the Elwell parking area. Dogs are welcome to walk this path also. They must be under their owner's control, leashed, and cleaned up after at all times.

Tully Mountain Wildlife Management Area and Trail
Tully Road
Orange, MA
508-835-3607
northquabbinwoods.org/entries/44
A very diverse area with at least 13 habitat types from a variety of forests, rich wetlands, to open slabs of bedrock, this 1200 acre wildlife area supports numerous species, and offers a 22 mile trail that winds through several sections of the park. Dogs are allowed for no additional fee. Dogs may only be off lead if they are under good voice control, and they will not chase

wildlife. Dogs must be leashed in public areas, and cleaned up after at all times.

Pilgrim Memorial State Park
Water Street
Plymouth, MA
508 866-2580
Although the smallest park in the state, it draws a large number here to see where the passengers of the Mayflower first disembarked on this continent and turned an unassuming glacial bolder that sat on the shore into a famous symbol for the pioneering spirit. Dogs must be under their owner's control at all times, be on no more than a 10 foot leash, cleaned up after, and have proof of current rabies inoculation.

Wachusett Mountain State Reservation
345 Mountain Road
Princeton, MA
978 464-2987
This day-use park offers 3000 acres of year round recreational opportunities, a historic site, 17+miles of trails, a visitor center, an interesting bog area, and a variety of habitats and wildlife. Dogs must be on no more than a 10 foot leash, be cleaned up after, and have proof of current rabies inoculation.

Halibut Point State Park
Gott Avenue
Rockport, MA
978-546-2997
Rich in cultural and natural history, this day-use coastal park offers sweeping views, trails and tide pools, meadows of wildflowers, a visitor center in an historic 60 foot tall building that gives views up to the coast of Maine, and summer interpretive programs. Dogs must be under their owner's control, be on no more than a 10 foot leash, cleaned up after, and have proof of current rabies inoculation.

Essex National Heritage Area
140 Washington Street
Salem, MA
978-740-0444
nps.gov/esse/
Dogs must be on leash and must be cleaned up after in most of the park areas. You must follow local and state park rules and pet policies for trails and camping. The area starts 10 miles north of Boston and extends for 40 miles along the scenic coast of Massachusetts. It features auto touring, boating, camping, hiking, swimming, and more.

Salem Common
Washington Square
Salem, MA
Leashed dogs are allowed. This park
is the second largest municipal park
in the United States and offers over
30 miles of trails.

Salem Maritime National Historic Site
174 Derby Street
Salem, MA
978-740-1650
nps.gov/sama/
Dogs must be on leash and must be
cleaned up after in the park and
walking areas. Dogs are not allowed
in any buildings. It is open daily 9am-
5pm. The park features walking
tours, fishing, boating, and more.
This is the first National Historic site
in the National Park System, was
established to preserve and interpret
the maritime history of New England
and the US.

Winter Island Maritime Park
50 Winter Island Road
Salem, MA
978-745-9430
Dogs on leash are allowed
throughout the park except that dogs
are not permitted at all on the
beaches.

Forest Park
Sumner Avenue and Main Greeting
Road
Springfield, MA
413-787-6440
This city park features plenty of
gaming and picnic areas, a pool,
spray structure and water fountain,
and accessible restrooms. Dogs are
welcome and they must be under
their owner's control at all times,
leashed, and cleaned up after.

Springfield Armory National Historic
Site
One Armory Square Ste 2
Springfield, MA
413-734-8551
nps.gov/spar/
Dogs must be on leash and must be
cleaned up after on the grounds.
Dogs are not allowed in any
buildings. This is the first National
Armory that began manufacturing
muskets in 1794. Within decades
Springfield Armory had perfected
pioneering manufacturing methods
that were critical to American
industrialization.

Cape Cod National Seashore

99 Marconi Station Site Road
Wellfleet, MA
508-349-3785
The Seashore is a forty-mile long
stretch of pristine sandy beach.
Dogs of all sizes are allowed. There
are no additional pet fees, but they
request that guests pick up a pet
brochure at the visitor's center when
they arrive. Dogs may not be left
unattended, and they must be
leashed and cleaned up after. Dogs
are not allowed on the self guided
nature trails, at the fresh water
ponds, nor in the the picket fenced
areas. Parking lots are open 6 A.M.
to midnight, daily, year-round. The
Salt Pond Visitor Center is open
from 9 A.M. to 4:30 P.M. daily, year-
round, with extended hours during
the summer months. The Province
Lands Visitor Center is open from 9
A.M. to 5 P.M. daily, early-May
through late-October.

Cape Cod Rail Trail
off Route 6
Wellfleet, MA
508-896-3491
state.ma.us/dem/parks/ccrt.htm
This paved trail extends 25 miles
through the towns of Dennis,
Harwich, Brewster, Orleans,
Eastham and Wellfleet. The paved
trail is for bicycles, and there is a
wide unpaved shoulder for walkers,
runners, and horseback riders.
Dogs on leash are allowed. There
are multiple parking areas along the
trail. One is located off Route 6 at
LeCount Hollow Road in Wellfleet.
Another is located in Nickerson
State Park, off Route 6A.

Cedar Tree Neck Sanctuary/Bruce
Irons Trail
Obed Dagget Road
West Tisbury, MA
508-693-5207
This is one of the areas managed
by the Sheriff's Meadow Foundation
who are dedicated to educating
about and preserving the natural
character of all the natural habitats
and wildlife here on Martha's
Vineyard. Dogs are welcome to
walk this area; they must be
leashed and cleaned up after at all
times. Dogs, nor their owners, are
allowed on the dunes.

Michigan

Battle Creek Linear Park

Off Roosevelt or River Road
Battle Creek, MI
269-966-3431
This linear park runs more than 17
miles passing many historical,
cultural, and sites of interest along
the way with mile-posting and 50
educational signs describing plants,
animals, or particular interests of the
area. There are several entrances,
including easy access and parking
from the Riverview Park or Bailey
Park. Dogs are allowed on the trail;
they must be under their owner's
control, leashed, and cleaned up
after at all times.

Bay City Riverwalk
Veterans Memorial Park
Bay City, MI
989-893-1222
In addition to beautiful, changing
scenery, this riverwalk will also give
visitors a glimpse into the city's
amazing maritime history. Dogs are
allowed on the trail; they must be
under their owner's control, leashed,
and cleaned up after at all times.

Lower Huron Metropark
Haggerty Rd and Huron River Dr.
Belleville, MI
800-477-3182
metroparks.com/lowerhuron.html
Dogs must be leashed in the park.

Nipissing Dune Trails
I-94, exit 16
Bridgman, MI
800-548-2555 (800-548-2555)
cookinfo.com/trails.htm
American Electric Power sponsors
this guided nature tour near the Cook
Nuclear Plant which generates and
transmits 2.1 million kilowatts of
electricity to thousands of
consumers. Carved through the
Cook Center's coastal dunes, forest
and wetland are three miles of
Nipissing Dune Trails. Educational
signs mark the three trails, giving
hikers full-color photographs and
descriptions of the wildlife and
geology they may see along the
paths. Open sunrise to sundown all
four seasons - it is an invigorating
hike through Michigan's wilderness.
You and your leashed dog are
welcome to take the guided or self-
guided tour. Pooches are not allowed
inside the buildings, but that's no
problem because the tours are
outside. Due to recent Federal
security restrictions near the nuclear
plant trails may be closed to the
public. Call ahead if you plan on
going to the site.

Sanilac Petroglyphs Historic State Park
8251 Germania Road
Cass City, MI
989-856-4411
This park has the states only know Native American rock carvings, and their viewing is by request; however there are 240 scenic acres to hike and explore as well. Dogs are allowed throughout the park and on the trails. Dogs may not be left unattended at any time, and they must be on no more than a 6 foot leash and cleaned up after at all times.

Waterloo Rec Area
16345 McClure Rd
Chelsea, MI
734-475-8307
Dogs on leash are allowed throughout this large 20,000 acre Michigan park about 30 minutes from Ann Arbor. Dogs are not allowed in any of the buildings. This park offers a number of trails around a lake region and cross country skiing in the winter on ungroomed trails. One place to pick up a number of trails is at the Gerald E. Eddy Discovery Center at 17030 Bush Road. From I-94 take Pierce Road north to Bush Road. Turn west on Bush Road. There is also rv and tent camping in the park.

River Rouge Park
Lower Rouge Parkway
Dearborn, MI
Dogs must be leashed in the park.

Presque Isle State Park
301 Peninsula Drive
Erie, MI
814-833-7424
Although a favorite spot for visitors, the many inhabitants, and migratory birds, this park is also an important education center dedicated to the preservation and continuing research of this unique peninsula. In addition to the interactive exhibits, there is a 75 foot observation tower. Dogs are allowed on the grounds and on the trails, and they are only allowed on the beaches after swim season is over and the lifeguards are gone. Dogs must be leashed and cleaned up after at all times.

Genesee Recreation Area
5045 E Stanley Rd
Flint, MI
810-736-7220

This 4,540 acre recreation area sits along the shores of Mott Lake and includes Richfield Park and a wide variety of land and water activities. Dogs are allowed throughout the park except the beaches and park buildings. Dogs must be under their owner's control, leashed, and cleaned up after at all times.

Lake Erie Metropark
Jefferson Ave and Lower Huron Dr.
Gibraltar, MI
734-379-5020
metroparks.com/lakeerie.html
Leashed dogs are allowed at this Detroit area park. The park offers views of Lake Erie.

Nub's Nob Ski Area Summer Use
500 Nub's Nob Road
Harbor Springs, MI
231-526-2131
nubsnob.com/directions.html
This world class mountain ski area is a beautiful area for spring, summer, and fall hiking. Dogs are allowed on the trails until snowfall. Dogs must be leashed and cleaned up after.

Negwegon State Park
248 State Park Road
Harrisville, MI
989-724-5126
Mostly popular for hunting, hiking, and metal detecting, this undeveloped area is a mixture of forest, lowlands, meadows and sandy beaches. Artesian well water and vault toilets are on site. Dogs of all sizes are allowed throughout the park except on the swim beach; there is a nice beach cove on the far northern end where dogs may go. Dogs must be on no more than a 6 foot leash and be cleaned up after.

Lake Lansing Park North
6260 E Lake Drive
Haslett, MI
517-676-2233
Dogs are allowed at this park in the ballfield and picnic areas of the north section only. Dogs must be under their owner's control at all times.

Isle Royale National Park
800 East Lakeshore Drive
Houghton, MI
906) 482-0984
nps.gov/isro
No dogs are allowed within the park.

Cascades Falls Park (Sparks Foundation County Park)
1401 S Brown Street
Jackson, MI
517-788-4320
In addition to a wide range of recreational activities available at this 457 acre park, the main attraction is the dramatic man-made Cascade Falls; 6 fountains stagger to 64 feet tall and cascade down 16 falls (11 are illuminated). They put on an amazing light show up and down the levels in time to musical accompaniment. There are also 126 steps up each side that visitors can walk for a better view. Dogs are allowed throughout the park on walking paths with the exception of inside the fall gates or up the steps. Dogs must be under their owner's control, leashed, and cleaned up after at all times.

Kal-Haven Trail
10th Street at the Red Caboose
Kalamazoo, MI
269-674-8011
This Rails to Trails linear park is a 34.5 mile long multi-use trail that connects Kalamazoo to the shores of Lake Michigan passing several historical, cultural, recreational, and other sites of interest along the way. There is a $3 fee for day use or a $15 annual fee (April to April), and entrances are available at trailheads located at 10th Street 2 miles North of West Main; the depot in Bloomingdale, the DNR lot in Grand Junction, or in South Haven at Wells Street and Bailey Avenue. Dogs are allowed on the trail; they must be under their owner's control, leashed, and cleaned up after at all times.

Bald Mountain Rec Area
1330 E Greenshield Road
Lake Orion, MI
248-693-6767
This day use park offers a variety of recreational opportunities, and they are open year round from 8 am to sunset. Dogs are allowed at no additional fee. Dogs may not be left unattended, and they must be leashed and cleaned up after. Dogs are allowed on the trails.

Adado Riverfront Park and River Trail System
501 N Grand Avenue
Lansing, MI
517-483-4277
This festival-designed park offers plenty of roaming room plus an 8 mile pathway that winds past historic and other sites of interest, lush

parks, the Grand and Red Cedar Rivers, and for about a 2 mile walk visitors can cover a million scale miles per footstep as they explore a journey through the solar system. Dogs are allowed at the park and on the trail; they are not allowed off the 8 mile trail in certain marked areas. Potter Park is one of the places where dogs may walk through but not stop. Dogs must be under their owner's control, leashed, and cleaned up after at all times.

City of Lansing River Trail
300 N Grand Avenue
Lansing, MI
517-483-4277
This 8 mile pathway winds past historic and other sites of interest, lush parks, the Grand and Red Cedar Rivers, and for about a 2 mile walk visitors can cover a million scale miles per footstep as they explore a journey through the solar system. Dogs are allowed at the park and on the trail; they are not allowed off the trail in certain marked areas. Potter Park is one of the places where dogs may walk through but not stop. Dogs must be under their owner's control, on no more than a 6 foot leash, and cleaned up after at all times.

Woldumar Nature Center
5739 Old Lansing Road
Lansing, MI
517-322-0030
woldumar.org/
Home to one of the areas most diverse ecosystems, this 150 acre riverside park provides environmental education in addition to 150 acres of woods and prairie to explore. Dogs are allowed throughout the park and on the trails; they must be leashed and cleaned up after at all times.

Mackinac Island and Fort Mackinac Historic Park
Accessible by ferry
Mackinac Island, MI
231-436-5563
The majority of Mackinac Island is managed by the Michigan State Park service. There are hiking trails throughout the island, many of which are within walking distance from the hotels. Swimming is also popular on the island. The shoreline usually has a rocky shore bottom so you might want to wear some shoes or sandals when wading in the water. The water on the east side of the island is shallow and good for children. The south side has stronger currents. There are no lifeguards along the

water. If you have children and need a playground, there is one in the center of the island at Great Turtle Park and one at the Mackinac Island Public School located west of downtown and across the boardwalk. Dogs are allowed on the hiking trails and in the water but need to be leashed at all times and cleaned up after. Please note that at the Fort there are often cannons being fired and throughout the island, rifles being fired for historical demonstration purposes. If your pooch does not like loud noises, you might want to stay away from those areas and be sure to hold on tight to your dog's leash.

Pere Marquette Rail Trail
Off Saginaw Road
Midland, MI
989-631-9244
lmb.org/pmrt/
Covering a distance of about 30 miles from Midland to the outskirts of Clare, this linear park provides numerous educational and recreational opportunities along the way as it passes through a variety of habitats and historical areas, over unique bridges, and through populated areas. Dogs are welcome on the trail; they must be under their owner's control, leashed, and cleaned up after at all times.

Willow and Oakwoods Metropark
New Boston, MI
734-697-9181
Leashed dogs are allowed in the parks.

Kensington Metropark
I-96 and Kensington
New Hudson, MI
248-685-1561
metroparks.com/kensington.html
Leashed dogs are allowed in the park.

Maybury State Park
20145 Beck Road
Northville, MI
248-349-8390
Dogs on leash are allowed throughout this Michigan State Park about 30 minutes from Ann Arbor. This 1,000 acre park offers a number of trails and cross country skiing in the winter on ungroomed trails. The park is located at Eight Mile Road at Beck Rd about five miles west of I-275.

Pinckney Recreation Area
8555 Silver Hill Road

Pinckney, MI
734-426-4913
Dogs on leash are allowed throughout this Michigan park about 25 minutes from Ann Arbor. This large 11,000 acre park offers a number of trails from the Pinckney-Silver Lake Trail (2 miles) to the Pinckney - Waterloo Trail (35 miles). During the winter months cross country skiing is available. There is camping at Bruin Lake Campground within the park. To get to the park from Ann Arbor take 23 North to exit 49 (N. Territorial Rd). Go west 11 miles and turn right on Dexter-Townhall Rd or Hadley Rd depending on where in the park you are headed.

Palmer Park and Boardwalk
2829 Armour Street
Port Huron, MI
810-984-9751
This 7.8 acre wooded park offers a wide variety of land and water recreational opportunities, including a skating rink in winter and a year round staffed recreation center. Dogs are allowed at the park and on all the trails; they are not allowed in buildings. Dogs must be under their owner's control, leashed, and cleaned up after at all times.

Pine Haven Rec Area
Maynard Road
Sanford, MI
989-832-6874
Offering some of the most diverse terrain in the state, this 325 acre park was originally built for cross-country skiing so all the trails are posted as to their difficulty. Dogs are allowed throughout the park where they may safely go. Dogs may not be left unattended at any time, and they must be on no more than a 6 foot leash and cleaned up after at all times. Dogs are not allowed in park buildings or on designated swimming or wading beaches.

Seney National Wildlife Refuge
1674 Refuge Entrance Road
Seney, MI
906-586-9851
Visitors can hike or take an auto tour of this 95,212 acre refuge that is home to many diverse habitats, an abundance of birds, marine, and wildlife, as well as being an important migratory stopover. Dogs are allowed on the trails; they must be leashed and cleaned up after at all times.

Grand Mere State Park
Thorton Drive

Stevensville, MI
269-426-4013
In addition to an undeveloped natural area with 3 lakes, this day use park has a mile of shoreline and an impressive display of sand dunes. Dogs are allowed throughout the park, including the beach. Dogs may not be left unattended at any time, and they must be on no more than a 6 foot leash, and cleaned up after at all times.

Peninsula Point Lighthouse
County Road 513
Stonington, MI
906-786-4062
The forty foot tower lighthouse and the keeper's dwelling were commissioned in 1864 and the historic light was extinguished in 1936; it is now preserved for the people-providing a beautiful setting for walks and picnicking. Dogs are allowed on the grounds; they are not allowed in buildings. Dogs must be leashed and cleaned up after.

Hidden Lake Gardens
6214 W Monroe Road/Hwy 50
Tipton, MI
517-431-2060
hiddenlakegardens.msu.edu/
This park is an extension of the Michigan State University, and in addition to educational programs/exhibits, visitors can travel paths through the woods, by the lake, the arboretum, green open fields, a bonsai courtyard, a vibrant demonstration garden, and a beautiful hillside garden. Dogs of all sizes are allowed throughout the park on the pathways. Dogs must be under their owner's control, leashed, and cleaned up after at all times.

Independence Lake County Park
3200 Jennings Road
Whitmore Lake, MI
734-449-4437
A major year round recreation destination, this park offers numerous activities and recreational opportunities; hiking trails through a variety of diverse habitats, interpretive programs, and more. Dogs are welcome at the park; they must be well behaved, leashed, and cleaned up after.

Rolling Hills County Park
7660 Stony Creek Road
Ypsilanti, MI
734-484-9676
A major year round recreation destination, this 363 acre park offers numerous activities and recreational

opportunities including a seasonal water park, almost 2 miles of paved trails, 3 miles of nature trails, an 18 hole disc golf course, a handicapped accessible fishing pier, gaming fields/courts, concessionaires, and more. Dogs are welcome at the park on designated paved trails only; they must be well behaved, leashed, and cleaned up after. The park has provided doggy clean-up stations.

Minnesota

Hyland Lake Park Reserve
10145 Bush Lake Road
Bloomington, MN
763-694-7687
A nature lover's delight, this 1,000+ acre reserve offers a nature center, a wildlife feeding and viewing station, concessionaires, a large creative playground, picnic areas, a fishing pier, woodlands, a breathtaking prairie, several waterways, and a 3.7 mile dog trail with 3 more miles to open soon. Dogs must be kept on no more than a 6 foot leash, be cleaned up after, and they must be under their owner's control at all times. The visitor center offers dog trail maps as there are some places that dogs are not allowed to go.

Minnesota Valley National Wildlife Refuge
3815 American Blvd E
Bloomington, MN
952-854-5900
fws.gov/midwest/MinnesotaValley/
Dedicated to restoring, protecting and offering environmental education, this refuge covers some 34 miles, 14,000 acres, and 8 separate sections along the Minnesota River; each offer their own special wildlife habitats, recreation, and activities. Dogs are allowed throughout the refuge except where indicated. Dogs must be leashed and cleaned up after at all times.

Duluth Lakewalk
27th Avenue East to Bayfront Festival Park
Duluth, MN
218-730-4300
This scenic path along the shores of Lake Superior offers 4½ miles of paved walkways to enjoy, many sites along the way, and the

activities of a working port. Dogs are allowed on the path; they must be on no more than a 6 foot leash and cleaned up after at all times. The animal disposal law is strictly enforced, and the city provides "mutt mitts" all along the way.

Grand Portage State Park
9393 E Hwy 61
Grand Portage, MN
218-475-2360
Spring and early summer are great times to view the 120 foot falls - the highest in the state, and the wonderful array of wildflowers. There is an accessible half mile trail and boardwalk that takes visitors to a falls overlook area. Dogs are allowed throughout the park; they must be kept on no more than a 6 foot leash and cleaned up after. Dogs may not be left unattended at any time.

Voyageurs National Park
3131 Hwy 53S
International Falls, MN
218-283-9821
nps.gov/voya
Voyageurs is a water based park located on the northern edge of Minnesota, and has some of the oldest exposed rock formations in the world. The park can also be accessed on Highway 11 from the west. There is camping, but a boat is required to access the trailheads to get there. There is another camping area just outside of the park as well. Dogs are allowed in developed areas of the park, outside visitor centers, at boat ramps, picnic areas, at tent camping areas, houseboats, and day use sites on the four main lakes. There are no additional pet fees. Dogs may not be left unattended at any time, they must be on no more than a 6 foot leash, and be cleaned up after. Pets are not allowed on park trails or in the backcountry.

Lake Elmo Park Reserve
1515 Keats Avenue N
Lake Elmo, MN
651-430-8370
There are over 2,100 acres of a variety of landscapes full of wildlife here; 20% of this reserve offers an abundance of land and water recreation with the other 80 percent of the park being returned to its natural state. Dogs are allowed on the trails and parking lot; they are not allowed in the campground or on the ski trails in winter. They do have a winter trail for dogs. They are also not allowed in picnic or beach areas. Dogs must be leashed and cleaned

up after at all times. Owners must be on foot only with their pets-no bikes or skates.

Grand Rounds National Scenic Byway
2117 West River Road (Parks & Recreation)
Minneapolis, MN
612-230-6400
This 50+ mile trail is a great way to experience all this cosmopolitan city has to offer. Along the way visitors will pass historic sites and homes, major shopping areas, stunning river scenery with falls, a stone arc bridge and dam, various geological wonders of the Mississippi River, an abundance of recreational and entertainment opportunities, gardens, parks, an interpretive center and a lot more. There are several entrances to the byway around the city. Dogs are allowed on the trail; they must be leashed and under their owner's control and care at all times.

Mill Ruins Park
500 W River Parkway
Minneapolis, MN
612-230-6400
There are 2 large playgrounds, picnic tables, and lots of green areas at this riverside park. Dogs are allowed at most areas in the park; they are not allowed at the archeological dig or in buildings. Dogs must be leashed and under their owner's control and care at all times.

Minnehaha Park
48th Street and Minnehaha Ave S
Minneapolis, MN
612-230-6400
A 53 foot waterfall, woodlands, wild flowers, statuary, scenic river overlooks, and a real natural beauty are just some of the reasons that this is one of the city's most popular parks. There is also an abundance of recreation, summer concerts, concessionaires, and an off leash dog park at the southern end of the park. Dogs are allowed throughout the park; they must be on no more than a 6 foot leash when not in the off lead area and be picked up after at all times.

Como Park
1325 Aida Place
St Paul, MN
651-266-6400
stpaul.gov/depts/parks/
Covering more than 347 acres, this active recreational park offers a number of educational opportunities

as well as featuring a tot lot playground, picnic areas, gaming fields and courts, a golf course, pool, and more. Dogs are allowed throughout the park; they must be licensed, on no more than a 6 foot leash, and under their owner's control and care at all times. Dogs are not allowed in Como Zoo, the conservatory, pool, or in the visitor center.

Fort Snelling State Park
101 Snelling Lake
St Paul, MN
612-725-2389
As well as offering a wide variety of land and water recreational opportunities, this almost 3000 acre park also offers interpretive programs and exhibits, naturalist programs year round, an abundance of wildlife and trails that link to Minnehaha Park and the Minnesota Valley National Wildlife Refuge. Dogs are allowed throughout the park; they are not allowed in buildings or on the public swim beach. Dogs must be leashed and under their owner's control and care at all times.

Hidden Falls Park
1309 Mississippi River Blvd S
St Paul, MN
651-266-6400
Selected as a city park in 1887, it gained popularity in the late 1930s when it got an overhaul. Work in the 1960s further developed the primitive, picnic, boating, and the waterfalls areas. There is also a beautiful paved 6.7 mile trail in the park. Dogs are allowed throughout the park; they must be licensed, on no more than a 6 foot leash, and under their owner's control and care at all times.

Indian Mounds Regional Park
Earl Street and Mounds Blvd
St Paul, MN
651-266-6400
Established in the late 1800s, this is the region's oldest park and it is home to ancient Native American burial mounds; only 6 remain of the 37 that once set along the bluffs. There are paved trails to the bluffs giving spectacular views of the city's skyline and the Mississippi River. Dogs are allowed throughout the park; they must be licensed, on no more than a 6 foot leash, and under their owner's control and care at all times.

Mississippi National River Rec Area

120 W Kellogg Blvd (Visitor Center and HQ)
St Paul, MN
651-290-4160
nps.gov/miss
Rich with a long natural and cultural history, this urban treasure offers a multitude of recreation and educational opportunities along its many miles covering 11 regional parks, more than 20 major sites of interest, and a dozen informative visitor centers. Dogs are allowed throughout the byways, parks, and at many of the sites of interest; they are not allowed in any buildings. Dogs may not be left unattended at any time, and they must be well behaved, leashed, and under their owner's control and care at all times.

Sherburne National Wildlife Refuge
17076 293rd Avenue/Hwy 9
Zimmerman, MN
763-389-3323
fws.gov/midwest/sherburne/
As a transitional zone from tall-grass prairie to forest, this 30,700 acre refuge has a diverse biological environment that supports a wide variety of birds, marines, and wildlife. There are oak savannas, 23 restored wetlands, and continuous ongoing restoration. Dogs are allowed on the trails and the 7.3 mile auto tour. They must be leashed and under their owner's control at all times.

Mississippi

Natchez National Historical Park
1 Melrose Montebello Parkway
Natchez, MS
601-446-5790
nps.gov/natc/
Sitting on 80 acres, this estate features beautifully manicured grounds and gardens, and gives a great example of an antebellum estate. Dogs are allowed on the grounds; they are not allowed in buildings. Dogs must be leashed and under their owner's control at all times.

Natchez Trace Parkway
2680 Natchez Trace Parkway
Tupelo, MS
800-305-7417
nps.gov/natr/index.htm
Dogs on leash are allowed on most of the trail areas. They are not allowed in buildings. You must follow the rules and pet policies of camping

and park sites along the way. This is the 444 mile trail connecting the Mississippi River to central Tennessee used between 1745 to 1820 by Choctaw, Chickasaw and others. The trail is located in Mississippi and Tennessee.

Vicksburg National Military Park
3201 Clay Street
Vicksburg, MS
601-636-0583
nps.gov/vick/index.htm
Dogs must be on leash and must be cleaned up after in this Civil War battlesite. Dogs are not allowed in any buildings. The park features auto touring, hiking, and more.

Missouri

Arrow Rock State Historic Site
P.O Box 1
Arrow Rock, MO
660-837-3330
mostateparks.com/arrowrock.htm
Dogs on leash are allowed in the park. Clean up stations are provided. This is a historic town with walking tours, camping, fishing, hiking, and picnicking. Pets are not allowed in the buildings, but can go on tours.

Elephant Rocks State Park
Hwy 21
Belleview, MO
573-546-3454
The features of this park were born of volcanic activity and left amazing red granite boulders lined up "circus elephant" style. There is a Braille Trail, an overlook, 30 picnic sites, and a playground. Dogs are allowed throughout the park; they are not allowed in buildings. Dogs must be on no more than a 10 foot leash and under their owner's control.

Ha Ha Tonka State Park
1491 Hwy D
Camdenton, MO
573-346-2986
mostateparks.com/hahatonka.htm
There are many natural geological wonders to explore at this park. There are 15 miles of trails (some accessible), castle ruins, caves, scenic overlooks, a large natural bridge, and the park is also home to the state's 12th largest spring. Leashed dogs are allowed throughout the park.

Cape Rock Park

N Cape Rock Drive
Cape Girardeau, MO
573-335-5421
This 21+ acre park gives visitors a scenic natural area with stunning views of the Mississippi River. Dogs are allowed throughout the park. Dogs must be leashed and under their owner's control at all times.

Precious Moments Park
4105 Chapel Road
Carthage, MO
800-445-2220
The amazing chapel here is done in the Precious Moments genre - Sistine Chapel style and it is also home to the largest Precious Moments store in the world. The meticulously manicured park offers dozens of spectacular gardens, lush greenery, tranquil pathways, and more. Dogs are allowed on the grounds; they are not allowed in buildings. Dogs must be leashed and under their owner's control at all times.

Roaring River State Park
Route 4 Box 4100
Cassville, MO
417-847-2539
Dogs on leash are allowed in the park. Clean up stations are provided. This state park features camping, swimming, hiking, fishing, and picnicking.

Rock Bridge Memorial Park
5901 S Hwy 163
Columbia, MO
573-449-7402
mostateparks.com/rockbridge.htm
Walk the Devil's Icebox Boardwalk to pass both under and over the rock bridge, explore a cave, an underground spring, or the miles of trails, and more at this scenic day use park. Dogs of all sizes are allowed at no additional fee. Dogs may not be left unattended, and they must be on no more than a 10 foot leash at all times, and cleaned up after. Dogs are not allowed in the caves or in buildings, but they are allowed on the trails. The park is open year round from dawn to dusk.

Route 66 State Park
97 North Outer Rd
Eureka, MO
636-938-7198
mostateparks/route66.htm
Dogs on leash are allowed in the park. Clean up stations are provided. This state park features camping, hiking, fishing, and

picnicking.

Riverview Park
2000 Harrison Hill
Hannibal, MO
573-221-0154
There are 465 beautiful natural acres at this recreational park. There are memorials, picnicking areas, a playground, nature trails, and restrooms on site. Dogs are welcome in the park; they must be leashed and under their owner's control.

Mastodon State Historical Park
1050 Museum Drive
Imperial, MO
636-464-2976
mostateparks.com/mastodon.htm
This park is an important archaeological and paleontological site; they have a museum that displays a full-size replica of a mastodon skeleton, and they offer educational programs and a variety of trails. Dogs of all sizes are allowed at no additional fee. Dogs may not be left unattended, and they must be leashed and cleaned up after. Dogs are not allowed in buildings, but they are allowed on the trails. From December through February, the museum is open Monday, Thursday through Saturday from 11 a.m. to 4 p.m., Sunday from 12 p.m. to 4 p.m. and is closed Tuesday and Wednesday. The remainder of the year, the museum is open Monday through Saturday from 9 a.m. to 4:30 p.m. and Sunday from 12 p.m. to 4:30 p.m. The museum is closed on New Year's Day, Easter, Thanksgiving and Christmas.

Trail of Tears State Park
429 Moccasin Springs
Jackson, MO
573-334-1711
Dogs on leash are allowed in the park. Clean up stations are provided. This state park features camping, bicycling, swimming, hiking, fishing, and picnicking. Pets are not allowed on public beaches but can swim in designated areas. Located along the Mississippi River and part of the Cherokee Trail of Tears.

Loose Park
Wornall Rd and 51st Street
Kansas City, MO
816-784-5300
Dogs on leash are allowed in the park. This park features a lake, walking paths, Civil War Sites, picnicking, and a Rose Garden. Cleanup is a must at all times.

Mill Creek Park
47th Street and Broadway
Kansas City, MO
816-513-7500
Dogs on leash are allowed in the park. Cleanup is a must at all times.

Swope Park
Swope Parkway and Meyer Blvd
Kansas City, MO
816-513-7500
kcmo.org/parks.nsf/web/swope
The city's largest and very first park, it is home to a number of attractions like the zoo, a theater, golf course, nature center, pool, playing fields/courts, and numerous picnicking areas. Dogs are allowed throughout the park; they must be leashed and under their owner's control at all times. They are not allowed in the zoo.

Theis Park
Oak St and 47th St
Kansas City, MO
816-513-7500
Dogs on leash are allowed in the park. The park features walking paths and open areas for picnicking and playing.

Thousand Hills State Park
20431 State Hwy 157
Kirksville, MO
660-665-6995
Dogs on leash are allowed in the park. Clean up stations are provided. This state park features camping, bicycling, swimming, hiking, fishing, canoeing, and picnicking.

Sam A Baker State Park
Patterson, MO
573-856-4411
mostateparks.com/baker.htm
Dogs on leash are allowed in the park. Clean up stations are provided. This state park features camping, hiking, fishing, canoeing, swimming, and picnicking. This is a very family (pets included) oriented state park.

Fort Davidson State Historic Site
118 E Maple/Hwy 22
Pilot Knob, MO
573-546-3454
mostateparks.com/ftdavidson.htm
The peaceful setting of this park belies the fact that it was once the site of the state's fiercest and largest battle. There is an interpretive center, picnic areas, and a playground. Dogs are allowed on the grounds; they are not allowed in buildings. Dogs must be on no more than a 10 foot leash and under their owner's control.

Pomme de Terre State Park
HC77 Box 890
Pittsburg, MO
417-852-4291
Dogs on leash are allowed in the park. Clean up stations are provided. This state park features camping, bicycling, swimming, hiking, fishing, and picnicking.

Krug Park and Pool
3500 St. Joseph Avenue/Hwy 59
St Joseph, MO
816-271-5500
This well-kept park offers a variety of beautiful settings, historic sites, various picnic areas, shaded pathways, an urban trail system and many other sites of interest. Dogs are allowed for no additional fee; they must be leashed and under their owner's control at all times.

Carondelet Park
5600 Clayton Rd
St Louis, MO
stlouis.missouri.org
Dogs on leash are allowed in this park. There are cleanup stations provided for your pets. The park features two lakes, picnic areas, barbecue grills, playgrounds and more.

Tower Grove Park
4256 Magnolia Ave
St Louis, MO
314-771-2679
Dogs on leash are allowed in this park. The park features picnic areas, trails, sculptures, and more. This is the location of the 1904 World's Fair in St Louis.

Grand Gulf State Park
Hwy W
Thayer, MO
417-264-7600
mostateparks.com/grandgulf.htm
Known as the state's "Little Grand Canyon" there are numerous natural wonders to explore at this 322 acre park. There is a natural bridge formed from a collapsed cave, outdoor informational exhibits, and miles of trails and boardwalks to explore this scenic area. Dogs are allowed throughout the park; they must be on no more than a 10 leash and under their owner's control at all times. Dogs are not allowed in buildings.

Weston Bend State Park
16600 Hwy 45 North
Weston Bend, MO

816-640-5443
mostateparks.com/westonbend.htm
Dogs on leash are allowed in the park. Clean up stations are provided. This state park features camping, hiking, fishing, and picnicking. It is located near Kansas City and would make a good day trip.

Dr Edmund A Babler Memorial State Park
800 Guy Park Drive
Wildwood, MO
636-458-3813
mostateparks.com/babler.htm
Dogs on leash are allowed in the park. Clean up stations are provided. This state park features camping, hiking, fishing, and picnicking.

Montana

Greycliff Prairie Dog Town State Park
At Greycliff Exit
Billings, MT
406-247-2940
This historic 98 acre site is home to the Blacktailed Prairie Dog, and interpretive signage offers their fascinating story and tells of their importance to the prairie ecosystem. Dogs are allowed throughout the park; they must be firmly leashed and under their owner's control at all times.

Pictograph Cave
5 miles S on County Road from I 90
Billings, MT
406-247-2955
Evidence here indicates habitation from generations of prehistoric peoples. Listed as a National Historic Landmark, this 93 acre site was also the state's first professional archaeological study/excavation area. Dogs are allowed throughout the park and where the pictographs are; they must be leashed and under their owner's control at all times.

Rosebud Battlefield State Park
3 miles W on County Road from Hwy 314
Decker, MT
406-234-0900
In addition to prehistoric sites and a homestead ranch, this 3,000 acre prairie park also offers the history of the significant battle waged between General Crook (supported by Crow and Shoshone) and the Sioux and Cheyenne. It set the stage for the

victory against Lt. Col. Custer 8 days later. Dogs are allowed throughout the park; they must be leashed and under their owner's control at all times.

Travelers' Rest State Park
5755 Hwy 12W
Lolo, MT
406-273-4253
This historic "crossroads" area has been offering connections among peoples and repose for travelers for numerous generations, and was twice a camp site for the Lewis and Clark expedition. Dogs are allowed in the day use area and parking lot only; they are not allowed on the trails. Dogs must be leashed and picked up after at all times.

Pirogue Island State Park
On County Road 2 miles S from Kinsey Road
Miles City, MT
406-234-0900
This 210 acre island park is one of 51 managed sites on the Yellowstone River and it can be accessed either by float or by foot when the water is low, and is an excellent area for bird and wildlife viewing. Dogs are allowed throughout the park; they must be leashed and under their owner's control at all times.

Granite Ghost Town State Park
3201 Spurgin Road (mailing address)
Missoula, MT
406-542-5500
Touted as the richest silver mine in the world, this 1 acre parcel at 6,549 feet once yielded $40,000,000-and that was in the late 1800s. Now only remnants of this active village remain. Vehicles with a high clearance are recommended; RVs are not advised. Dogs are allowed throughout the park; they must be leashed and under their owner's control at all times.

Chief Plenty Coups State Park
1 Edgar Road
Pryor, MT
406-252-1289
Once the home of the last chief of the Crow-Chief Plenty Coups; this park preserves and shares this historic site and the stories that go with it. Dogs are allowed throughout the park; they must be leashed and under their owner's control at all times.

Glacier National Park
PO Box 128

West Glacier, MT
406-888-7800
nps.gov/glac/index.htm
Dogs must be on leash and must be cleaned up after in the park area. Dogs are not allowed on the hiking trails. They are allowed in the camping, picnic areas and along roadways and parking lots.

Big Hole National Battlefield
PO Box 237
Wisdom, MT
406-689-3155
nps.gov/biho/index.htm
Dogs must be on leash and must be cleaned up after around the visitor center area. Dogs are not allowed on the hiking trails or in buildings.

Nebraska

Scotts Bluff National Monument
190276 Old Oregon Trail/Hwy 92W
Gering, NE
308-436-9700
nps.gov/scbl/
This 3,000 acre park is home to some of the state's most interesting geological features; the bluff rises 800 feet over the prairie and there are great views from the top. This site has been a natural landmark for various peoples since ancient times. Dogs are allowed in the park and on the trails; they must be leashed and under their owner's control at all times. They caution to keep pets close because of snakes.

Platte River State Park
14421 346th Street
Louisville, NE
402-234-2217
In addition to being a major recreation destination, this scenic 418 acre park has planned park activities, special events/programs, 10 miles of hiking trails, and much more. Dogs are allowed for no additional fee. They must be well behaved, on no more than a 6 foot leash, crated, or otherwise restricted at all times, and cleaned up after. Dogs are not allowed in food service areas, public buildings, or on designated swimming beaches.

Cody Park
1400 N Jeffers/Hwy 83
North Platte, NE
308-535-6700
Named after Buffalo Bill Cody, this

park features a life-size bronze statue of its namesake and a long list of fun activities. There are live animals like deer, ducks, and llamas to feed, a large fishing pond and swimming pool, 3 playgrounds, playing courts/fields, concessionaires, a railroad museum, amusement rides, and more. Dogs are allowed at the park; they must be leashed and cleaned up after at all times. Dogs are not allowed in the amusement or pool areas.

Niobrara National Scenic River
146 S Hall Street (Ranger Station)
Valentine, NE
402-376-1901
nps.gov/niob/
This river park offers 76 miles on the longest river in the state, and is a favorite among river floaters. An unusual mix of land and climate create quite a bio-diverse area to explore as well. There are several access points to the river off Highway 12. Dogs are allowed; they must be on no more than a 6 foot leash, crated, or otherwise restricted at all times, and cleaned up after. Dogs are not allowed in food service areas, public buildings, or on designated swimming beaches.

Nevada

Great Basin National Park
100 Great Basin
Baker, NV
775-234-7331
nps.gov/grba
The Great Basin Park rises to over 13,000 feet and hosts the Lehman Caves and an abundant variety of wildlife, plants, and waterways. They are open year round for tent and RV camping with no hook ups. There is no additional fee for dogs, but they may not be left unattended, they must be on no more than a 6 foot leash, and be cleaned up after. Dogs are not allowed on any of the trails.

Spring Mountain Ranch State Park
P. O. Box 124
Blue Diamond, NV
702-875-4141
parks.nv.gov/smr.htm
This luxury retreat offers a long and colorful history with such owners as Howard Hughes and Vera Krupp. In addition the park offers great scenery, a visitor's center, picnicking, historic sites, living history programs,

guided tours, opportunities for nature study, and various trails. Dogs of all sizes are allowed at no additional fee. Dogs may not be left unattended, and they must be leashed and cleaned up after.

Lake Mead National Recreation Area
Lakeshore Rd/166
Boulder City, NV
702-293-8907
nps.gov/lame/
This recreation area covers 1.5 million acres. The west side of the park is about 25 miles from downtown Las Vegas. We didn't see any designated trails, but leashed dogs are allowed on many of the trails and at the lake. To get there from Las Vegas, take Hwy 146 east to Lakeshore Rd./166. Lakeshore Rd. is the scenic drive along Lake Mead.

Kershaw-Ryan State Park
P. O. Box 985/300 Kershaw Canyon Drive
Caliente, NV
775-726-3564
parks.nv.gov/kr.htm
This high mountain desert day park offers a spring-fed pond, scenic rugged landscapes, a picnic area, restrooms, trails, and various outdoor recreation. Dogs of all sizes are allowed at no additional fee. Dogs may not be left unattended, and they must be leashed and cleaned up after. Dogs are allowed on the trails. Hours may vary between the seasons, however winter hours are daily from 8 am to 4:30 pm, and summer hours are daily from 7 am to 8 pm.

Toiyabe National Forest
Hwy 395
Carson City, NV
There are several dog-friendly hiking trails on the national forest land in Carson City. These are desert-like trails, so only go with your dog when the weather is cooler. If it's hot, the sand may burn your pup's paws. Visit the Carson Ranger Station for maps and trail information about the Toiyable National Forest. The station is located on Hwy 395, near S. Stewart Street. Dogs should be leashed.

Washoe Lake State Park
4855 East Lake Blvd.
Carson City, NV
775-687-4319
This park is frequently used for bird watching, hiking, horseback riding, picnicking, windsurfing, water skiing,

jet skiing, fishing and during certain times of the year, hunting. There are many trails at this park for hikers, mountain bikers, and equestrians. Pets must be leashed at all times, except at the Wetlands during hunting season. The park is located off U.S. 395, 10 miles north of Carson City and 15 miles south of Reno.

Walker Lake, c/o Fallon Region Headquarters
16799 Lahontan Dam
Fallon, NV
775-867-3001
parks.nv.gov/walk.htm
This rec area is on one of the last remnants of an ancient inland sea that covered the area about 10,000 years ago. There is a boat launch, shade ramadas, tables and grills along a sandy beach. Recreation includes fishing, boating, swimming and picnicking. Dogs of all sizes are allowed at no additional fee. Dogs may not be left unattended, and they must be leashed and cleaned up after.

Desert Breeze County Park
8425 W. Spring Mtn. Road
Las Vegas, NV
This county park has picnic tables, sports fields, a bike/walking path and a dog park. It is located approximately 5 miles east of downtown Las Vegas and the Strip. From Flamingo Road/589 in downtown, head west and pass Hwy 15. Turn right on Durango Drive. Then turn right onto Spring Mountain Road and the park will be on the corner. Dogs must be leashed, except for in the dog park.

Floyd Lamb State Park
9200 Tule Springs Road
Las Vegas, NV
702-486-5413
parks.nv.gov/fl.htm
This park offers tree-shaded groves alongside four small fishing lakes, allowing for nature study, and some of the amenities include picnic areas with tables and grills, restrooms, group areas, a walking/bicycle path that winds through the park, and historic sites. Dogs of all sizes are allowed at no additional fee. Dogs may not be left unattended, and they must be leashed at all times, and cleaned up after. Times vary through the seasons, but the winter hours are from 7 am to 5 pm, and in June and July they are open from 7 am to 8 pm.

Lorenzi Park
3333 W. Washington Ave.
Las Vegas, NV
702-229-6297
This park is about a mile west of downtown Las Vegas. Leashed dogs are allowed. Lorenzi Park features tennis courts, playgrounds, picnic tables and a five acre lake.

Red Rock Canyon National Area
Charleston Blvd/159
Las Vegas, NV
702-363-1921
nv.blm.gov/redrockcanyon
Located just 20-25 minutes west of downtown Las Vegas is the beautiful Red Rock Canyon National Conservation Area. This preserve has over 60,000 acres and includes unique geological formations. There is a popular 13 mile one-way scenic loop road that winds around the park, providing sightseeing, vistas and overlooks. Many of the hiking trails begin off this road. Leashed dogs are allowed on most of the trails. Some of the trails they are not allowed on are more like rock climbing expeditions than hiking trails. There are a variety of hiking trails ranging from easy to difficult. The visitor center is open daily and should have trail maps. On the trails, be aware of extreme heat or cold. Also watch out for flash floods, especially near creeks and streams. According to the BLM (Bureau of Land Management), violent downpours can cause flash flooding in areas untouched by rain. Do not cross low places when water is running through a stream. The park entrance fee is $5 per vehicle and $5 per dog. To get there from downtown Las Vegas, take Charleston Blvd./159 and head west.

Spring Mountain National Recreation Area
Echo Road
Mount Charleston, NV
702-515-5400
This 316,000 acre park, part of the Toiyabe National Forest, is located about 35 miles northwest of Las Vegas. Mt. Charleston is located in this dog-friendly park and has many hiking trails. Temperatures here can average 25 to 30 degrees cooler than in Las Vegas. The Mary Jane Falls trail, located on Mt. Charleston, is one of the more popular trails. The trail passes a seasonal waterfall and several small caves. The trail is about 2.4 miles and starts at about 7840 foot elevation. To reach the trailhead, take State Route 157,

travel 2 miles west of the ranger station to Echo Road. After traveling .35 mile, take the left fork off Echo Road and continue up until the road ends. Dogs must be on leash.

Valley of Fire State Park
off Interstate 15, exit 75
Overton, NV
702-397-2088
state.nv.us/stparks/vf.htm
This park derives its name from red sandstone formations, formed from great shifting sand dunes during the age of dinosaurs, 150 million years ago. Ancient trees are represented throughout the park by areas of petrified wood. There is also a 3,000 year-old Indian petroglyph. Popular activities include camping, hiking, picnicking and photography. Sites of special interest are the Atlatl Rock, the Arch Rock, the Beehives, Elephant Rock, Seven Sisters, and more. There are many intriguing hikes available. Please inquire at the visitor center for suggestions on day hikes of varying length and terrain. The visitor's center is open daily, 8:30am to 4:30pm. The park is open all year. Pets are welcome, but they must be kept on a leash of not more than six feet in length. They are not allowed in the visitor center. The park is located six miles from Lake Mead and 55 miles northeast of Las Vegas via Interstate 15 and on exit 75.

Donnelly Park
Mayberry Drive
Reno, NV
This is a small, but nice park to walk around with your dog. It is across the street from Scraps Dog Bakery and Walden's Coffee. Dogs must be leashed.

Rancho San Rafael Park
1595 N. Sierra Street
Reno, NV
775-828-6642
washoecountyparks.com/
Dogs are allowed in the undeveloped areas of this park. Dogs must be leashed with one exception. Dogs may be off-leash only at certain times at the multi-use pasture area. If there are special events or activities on the multi-use area then dogs are not allowed at all on the field. This includes when the hay is being cut and harvested. Portions of the field may be muddy when the pasture is being irrigated. Leashed dogs are allowed on a hiking and walking path which crosses over McCarren Blvd. It

is a dirt trail which narrows to a single track trail once you cross over McCarren Blvd. Just be careful when crossing over McCarren because the speed limit on the road is about 45-50mph. To get there from Hwy 80, exit Keystone Ave. Head north on Keystone. Turn right onto Coleman Drive. Take Coleman until it almost ends and turn right into the park. Park near the Coleman intersection and the trailhead will be nearby.

Pyramid Lake
Hwy 445
Sutcliffe, NV
775-574-1000
Pyramid Lake is located in an Indian reservation, but visitors to the lake are welcomed guests of the Pyramid Lake Tribe of the Paiute Indians. Your leashed dog is also welcome. The lake is a beautiful contrast to the desert sandstone mountains which surround it. It is about 15 miles long by 11 miles wide, and among interesting rock formations. Pyramid Lake is Nevada's largest natural lake. It is popular for fishing and photography. The north end of the lake is off-limits to visitors because it is a sacred area to the Paiutes. There is a beach area near the ranger's station in Sutcliffe. Be careful when wading into the water, as there are some ledges which drop off into deeper water. Also, do not wade in the water at the south end of the lake because the dirt acts like quick sand. The lake is about 35-40 minutes north of Reno, off Hwy 445.

New Hampshire

Rockingham Recreation Trail
Windham Depot Road
Derry, NH
603-271-3254
This 18 mile multi-use, easy to moderate trail (with a few sandy spots) is the state's longest rail trail taking visitors through several small towns, past wooded areas, fields, wetlands, and ponds, and connects Derry to Fremont in Rockingham County. Dogs are welcome on this path. They must be under their owner's control, leashed, and cleaned up after at all times.

Rhododendron State Park
Hwy 119W

Fitzwilliam, NH
603-532-8862 (Monadnock St Pk)
There is a trail a little over a half mile long that encircles the 16 acre, fragrant, pink blossomed Rhododendron flower grove, a focal point of this 2,723 acre scenic park, and another trail that winds through forest and wildflowers. Dogs of all sizes are allowed at this park for no additional fee. Dogs must be well behaved, leashed, cleaned up after, and owners are responsible for them at all times. Dogs may not be left unattended at any time.

Cardigan State Park
Cardigan Mountain Road
Orange, NH
603-823-7722, ext. 757
This day use park covers over 5,600 acres and is a favorite among hikers. A mountain road and trails lead to its 3,121 foot summit and a fire tower where visitors can get a 360 degree panoramic view of neighboring states, plus there are plenty of interesting sites along the way. Dogs of all sizes are allowed at this park for no additional fee. Dogs must be well behaved, leashed, cleaned up after, and owners are responsible for them at all times. Dogs may not be left unattended at any time.

Miller State Park
Hwy 101E
Peterborough, NH
603-924-3672
The state's oldest state park, it is a popular scenic driving/hiking area with great places for picnicking, and an operational fire tower at the top of the mountain offers outstanding views. Dogs of all sizes are allowed at this park for no additional fee. Dogs must be well behaved, leashed, cleaned up after, and owners are responsible for them at all times. Dogs may not be left unattended at any time.

Urban Forestry Center
45 Elwyn Road
Portsmouth, NH
603-431-6774
In the mist of a bustling city, this 182 acre wilderness preserve has much to offer year round; in addition to its marshes, creeks, woodlands, fields, herb garden, and bird observation areas, there are exhibits and educational programs offered at the Forestry Center campus. The real treat here for hikers are the excellent array of easy terrain trails brimming with lush greenery, and self-guided trails like the tree identification trail

and the plant/wildlife woodlands trail. Dogs are allowed on leash, and please clean up after your pet.

Rollins State Park
Kearsarge Mountain Road
Warner, NH
603-456-3808
There is a scenic auto road from the park entrance that travels 3½ miles through the woodlands to a parking and picnic area in a natural wooded glen setting near the top, and from there visitors can take the ½ mile trail to the summit for some more great views. This park is seasonal. Dogs are allowed at this park. Dogs must be well behaved, leashed, cleaned up after, and owners are responsible for them at all times. Dogs may not be left unattended at any time.

New Jersey

Palisades Interstate Park
Palisades Interstate Parkway
Alpine, NJ
201-768-1360
njpalisades.org/
Designated a National Historic Landmark, this park features more than 30 miles of hiking trails with great views of the Palisades, the Hudson River, and the New York skyline along the way, a scenic riverside drive, riverfront picnic areas, historic sites, and more. Dogs are welcome to explore the park and all the trails. Dogs must be under their owner's control, leashed, and cleaned up after at all times. Dogs are not allowed in the Greenbrook Sanctuary.

Kittatinny Valley State Park
PO Box 621
Andover, NJ
973-786-6445
Dogs on leash are allowed in the state park. They are not allowed in the campground areas. The park features hiking, fishing, picnicking, boating, and more.

Historic Gardner's Basin
800 New Hampshire Avenue
Atlantic City, NJ
609-348-2880
oceanlifecenter.com/hours.html
This is an 8 acre sea-oriented park where visitors can view working fishermen, shop the local artists "cabins", picnic, or just hike around with your pet. Dogs are allowed; they

must be well mannered, under their owner's control, leashed, and cleaned up after at all times. Dogs are not allowed in the restaurants or in the aquarium.

Henry Hudson
Aberdeen to Atlantic Highlands
Atlantic Highlands, NJ
732-787-3033
Dogs on a six foot leash are allowed on this fifteen mile paved trail along an old railroad right of way. The trail may be extended in the future to Freehold Borough.

Barnegat Lighthouse State Park
PO Box 167
Barnegat Light, NJ
609-494-2016
Dogs on leash are allowed in the park grounds. The park features fishing, picnicking, trails, and lighthouse.

Double Trouble State Park
PO Box 175
Bayville, NJ
732-341-6662
Dogs on leash are allowed on the state park grounds. The park features fishing, hiking trails, Cedar swamps, cranberry, bogs, picnicking, and more. This an old cranberry farm with a historical village for touring.

Fairview Farm Wildlife Preserve
2121 Larger Cross Road
Bedminster, NJ
908-234-1852
urwa.org/land/bedminster.html
A bit unusual for a "park" as there are no picnic tables, trash cans, or play areas, this park is about preserving, educating, protecting, and providing a quality nature experience for all the wildlife inhabitants who call it home (even for a short migrating time) and its visitors. Dogs are welcome here; they must be leashed and cleaned up after at all times. Dogs are allowed throughout the park and on the trails, they are not allowed in the ponds.

Stokes State Forest
1 Coursen Road
Branchville, NJ
973-948-3820
Dogs on a 6 ft leash are allowed in the state park. They are not allowed in the campground areas. Features hiking, swimming, fishing, boating, and more. Located in Sunrise Mountain along the Appalachian Trail.

Bridgeton City Park
Mayor Aitken Drive
Bridgeton, NJ
609-455-3230 ext. 280
This city park provides 1100 recreational acres for a wide range of land and water activities, and they are also home to historic sites, an amphitheater, and a zoo. Well behaved dogs are welcome throughout the park and on the trails; they are not allowed at the zoo or on the ball fields. Dogs must be under their owner's control, leashed, and cleaned up after at all times.

Dr. Ulysses S. Wiggins Waterfront Park
Between the Delaware River and Mickle Blvd
Camden, NJ
856-795-7275
This park was developed for recreational boating, but the beauty of the area also makes it a nice walking and relaxing area. Dogs are allowed throughout the park and on the walkways. Dogs must be leashed at all times on land and on the boats, and they must be cleaned up after at all times.

Cape May Point State Park
PO Box 107
Cape May Point, NJ
609-884-2159
Dogs on leash are allowed on the state park grounds. They are only allowed on the beach after September 15th due to bird nesting. The park features picnicking, trails, lighthouse, and WWII bunkers located on the beach.

Spruce Run Recreation Area
68 Van Syckel's Road
Clinton, NJ
908-782-8572
Home to the 3rd largest reservoir in the state, this year round park offers a wide variety of land and water recreation. Dogs are allowed for no additional fee. Dogs must be under their owner's control at all times, be on no more than a 6 foot leash, and cleaned up after. Dogs are allowed throughout the park and on the trails; they are not allowed in the campgrounds or on the beach.

Dorbrook Recreation Area
209 Route 537
Colts Neck, NJ
732-542-1642
Dogs on a six foot leash are allowed on the trails at this 535 acre park. There are 2 1/2 miles of paved trails

in the park.

Turkey Swamp Park
200 Georgia Road
Freehold Twp, NJ
732-462-7286
There are 4 miles of trails and rowboat rentals available on the 17 acre lake. Dogs on a six foot leash are allowed on the trails and in the rowboats.

Voorhees State Park
251 County Road Route 513
Glen Gardner, NJ
908-638-6969
Dogs on leash are allowed in the state park for day use only. They are not allowed in the campground area. The park features hiking, fishing, picnicking, and more. This park was once a Civilian Conservation Corps used to help young men get back to work during the Depression. It was in use between 1933-1941 after being established by President Franklin Roosevelt.

Allamuchy Mountain State Park
800 Willow Grove St
Hackettstown, NJ
908-852-3790
Dogs on leash are allowed in the state park. They are not allowed in the camping area. The park features hiking, fishing, picnicking, boating, and more. Also featured is the Waterloo Village, a 400 year old Lenape Indian Village that later became a port for the Morris Canal.

Wharton State Park
4110 Nesco Rd
Hammonton, NJ
609-561-0024
Dogs on leash are allowed in the park grounds, except for the campground. The park features hiking, picnicking, and Batsto Village, which is an historical village.

Wawayanda State Park
885 Warwick Tunpike
Hewitt, NJ
973-853-4462
Covering more than 34,000 acres, this park features a natural 2,167 acre swamp area, more than 60 miles of well marked trails (including a piece of the Appalachian Trail), a beautiful lake surrounded by forested hills, and a variety of land and water recreation. Dogs of all sizes are allowed at this park for no additional fee. Dogs must be well behaved, leashed, cleaned up after, and owners are responsible for them at all times. Dogs may not be left

unattended at any time.

Gateway National Rec Area/Sandy Hook Unit
128 S Hartshorne Drive
Highlands, NJ
732-872-5970
nps.gov/gate/faq-sandy-hook.htm
This park has a long history as a defense lookout point for America, its home to the country's oldest operating lighthouse, and it is a year round recreational destination. Dogs are allowed on the ocean beaches except during the Piping Plover nesting season from March 15 through September 15. Dogs are not allowed at any time in the Jamaica Bay Wildlife Refuge area. There is a dog beach area on the bay side of the park. Dogs must be under their owner's control, leashed, and cleaned up after at all times.

Elysian Park
10th and Hudson Street
Hoboken, NJ
201-420-229
This neighborhood park has a long cultural history and is known for being the place that hosted the first officially recorded, organized baseball game on June 19, 1846. There are gaming courts/fields, lots of shade, and a fenced in dog run area. Well behaved dogs are allowed throughout the park on leash and they must be cleaned up after at all times; the exception being when they are in the fenced dog run area.

Hoboken Riverfront Walkway
Waterfront in Hoboken
Hoboken, NJ
Dogs on leash are permitted on the Waterfront Walkway along the Hudson River. Dogs are not permitted on the grass areas or other interior walkways. Dogs are not permitted in the Shipyard Park.

Holmdel Park
44 Longstreet Road
Holmdel, NJ
732-946-3758
monmouthcountyparks.com
One of the county's most popular and beautiful parks for nature enjoyment and a variety of recreation, this 564 acre park offers 10 miles of trails, a playground, gaming courts, and on 9 acres they have re-created a living history farm. Well behaved dogs are welcome throughout the park and

on the trails; they are not allowed in any of the buildings or at the farm. Dogs must be under their owner's control, leashed, and cleaned up after at all times.

Jenny Jump State Park
330 State Park Road
Hope, NJ
908-459-4366
This recreation destination offers a variety of activities, panoramic views and green rolling hills, a shaded picnic area with tables and grills, hiking trails, and is it home to the Greenwood Observatory. Dogs are allowed; they must be under their owner's control, leashed, and cleaned up after at all times. Dogs are allowed throughout the park and on the trails; they are not allowed at the observatory.

Manasquan Reservoir
311 Windeler Road
Howell, NJ
732-919-0996
Dogs on a six foot leash are allowed on the five mile perimeter trail that circles the Manasquan Reservoir. They are also allowed to accompany you in a rowboat on the water. Rowboats may be rented at the park.

Libery State Park
Morris Pesin Drive
Jersey City, NJ
201-915-3440
libertystatepark.org/
Once the heart of an extensive transportation network for industry, this area served an even bigger role as the passage point for thousands and thousands of immigrants in the 19th and early 20th century, and now it provides over 300 developed acres for public recreation less than 2,000 feet from the Statue of Liberty. Dogs are allowed throughout the park, on the trails, and at the picnic areas. Dogs must be leashed and cleaned up after at all times.

Silas Condict County Park
William Lewis Arthur Drive
Kennelon Boroughs, NJ
973-326-7600
Featuring 1,000 acres of activities and recreation for every age, this year round park also offers event and private meeting space. Dogs of all sizes are allowed. They must be under their owner's control, leashed, and cleaned up after.

Round Valley Rec Area
1220 Lebanon-Stanton Road
Lebanon, NJ

908-236-6355
There is a good variety of water recreation with a 2,000+ acre reservoir at this 3,684 acre park in addition to some great hiking trails, and scenic picnic areas with tables, grills, restrooms, and playgrounds. Dogs are allowed throughout the park and on the trails. Dogs must be leashed and cleaned up after at all times. Dogs are not allowed in the campground or on the beach. There are places where they may go in the water, but they must still be on lead.

Huber Woods Park
25 Brown's Dock Road
Locust, NJ
732-872-2670
Dogs on a six foot leash are allowed on the approximately seven miles of trails. Also enjoy the views of the Navesink River flowing by.

Hacklebarney State Park
119 Hacklebarney Rd
Long Valley, NJ
908-638-6969
A long stone staircase brings visitors into this 978 acre glacial valley with gorges carved from the Black River, steep ravines covered in hard-wood forests, rare plants and animals, miles of trails, and a variety of land and water recreation. Dogs are allowed throughout the park and on the trails. Dogs must be leashed and cleaned up after at all times.

Monmouth Battlefield State Park
347 Freehold-Englishtown Rd
Manalapan, NJ
732-462-9616
Dogs on leash are allowed in the state park. The park features picnicking, hiking, and a reenactment held every June. This is the historical site of the Battle of Monmouth during the American Revolution.

Cheesequake State Park
300 Gordon Road
Matawan, NJ
732-566-2161
This is a unique park as it sits between 2 different ecosystems of saltwater and freshwater marches, Pine Barrens and hardwood forest, and there are 5 blazed trails of varying difficulty to explore the unusual geology of the area. Well behaved dogs are welcome throughout the park and on the trails; they are not allowed in any of the buildings, at the campground, or on the swimming beach. Dogs must be under their owner's control, leashed, and cleaned up after at all times.

Hartshorne Woods Park
Navesink Avenue
Middletown, NJ
732-872-0336
Dogs on a six foot leash are allowed on the trails at this 741 acre park with 15 miles of dirt trails and 3 miles of roads closed to vehicles. The park is used by hikers, bicycles and equestrians.

Tatum Park
251 Red Hill Road
Middletown, NJ
732-671-6050
Dogs on a six foot leash are allowed on the four miles of trails.

Morristown National Historical Park
Tempe Wick Road
Morristown, NJ
973-539-2016
nps.gov/morr
There are over 27 miles of foot and horse trails, the beginning of a 2 mile auto loop tour, and a visitor center at the Jockey Hollow area of this park that marks the winter-quarters for the Continental Army during a rather harsh weather period. Dogs are allowed on the grounds and on the trails. Dogs must be on no more than a 6 foot leash and cleaned up after at all times.

Watchung Reservation/Trailside Nature & Science Center
452 New Providence Road
Mountainside, NJ
908-789-3670
ucnj.org/trailside/index.html
Rich in folk-lore and cultural history, this 1,900+ acre park is popular for the many hiking and riding trails; and there is a playground, picnic areas, stables, a trailside nature center, and a visitor center as well. It is suggested that a trail map is picked up at the science center, adjacent to the parking lot, prior to hiking in any unfamiliar area as there may be trail closures in effect at different times. Dogs are allowed throughout the park and on the trails. They are not allowed in any park buildings. Dogs must be under their owner's control, leashed, and cleaned up after at all times.

Bass River State Forest
762 Stage Rd
New Green, NJ
609-296-1114
Dogs on leash are allowed in the state park. They are not allowed in the campground area or public

beaches. The park features hiking, fishing, picnicking, boating, and more.

Penn State Forest
PO Box 118
New Gretna, NJ
609-296-1114
Dogs on leash are allowed in the state park. They are not allowed in the campground area. The park features hiking, fishing, canoeing, and picnicking.

Batona Trail
Hwy 72
New Lisbon, NJ
609-561-3262
Located in the Brendan T. Byrne State Forest, this 50 mile hiking trail winds over 50 miles through the New Jersey Pinelands, and it is also used for cross-country skiing and snow shoeing in the winter months. Dogs are allowed on the trail throughout the year. Dogs must be under their owner's control, leashed, and cleaned up after at all times.

Brendan T Byrne State Forest
PO Box 215
New Lisbon, NJ
609-726-1191
Dogs on leash are allowed in the state park. They are not allowed in the campground area. The park features hiking, fishing, picnicking, and more. The park also includes the deserted Whitesbog Village and some cranberry farms.

Pinelands Natural Area
15 Springfield Road
New Lisbon, NJ
609-894-7300
nj.gov/pinelands/reserve/
This 1.1 million acre ecologically important region is the largest open space area on the Mid-Atlantic seaboard, is home to some of the purest water available, is part of the US Biosphere Reserve of Man and the Biosphere Program, and it also holds the distinction of being the country's first National Reserve area. Dogs are allowed throughout the park and on the trails; they are not allowed in wildlife sensitive areas or in park buildings.

Rancocas
PO Box 215
New Lisbon, NJ
609-726-1191
Dogs on leash are allowed in the state park. They are not allowed in the campground areas. The park features hiking, picnicking, and a

replica of the Powhatan Indian Village of the 1600s.

Branch Brook Park
Park Avenue and Lake Street
Newark, NJ
973-263-3500
America's oldest county park (on the Registers of Historic Places) is a major recreation destination with one of the largest recreational open green spaces to be found in the county, a large lake, playgrounds, gaming fields/courts, a four mile scenic drive, trails and pedestrian bridges, 2,000 cherry trees that bloom every April, and more, plus there are various special events and festivals held here throughout the year. Dogs are allowed throughout the park and on the trails; they are not allowed in buildings. Dogs must be well mannered, leashed, and cleaned up after.

New Jersey Coastal Heritage Trail Route National Park
389 Fortescue Road
Newport, NJ
856-447-0103
nps.gov/neje/index.htm
Dogs must be on leash and must be cleaned up after on most trails and stops on the route. You must follow local and state parks rules and pet policies along the route. Mainly auto touring, but also features hiking, boating, swimming, and more.

Corson's Inlet State Park
Ocean Drive and Bay Avenue
Ocean City, NJ
609-861-2404
This 350 acre oceanfront park is home to a rich diversity of natural habitats and wildlife, exceptional scenery, hiking trails, and it is also a popular area for saltwater fishing and crabbing. Dogs are allowed throughout the park with the exception they are not allowed on the beach from April 1st through to September 15th. Dogs must be under their owner's control, leashed, and cleaned up after at all times.

Edwin B. Forsythe National Wildlife Refuge
800 Great Creek Road
Oceanville, NJ
609-652-1665
fws.gov/northeast/forsythe/
This 46,000 acre refuge is open 7 days a week with a few exceptions for wildlife management, so they suggest calling ahead or checking the website. There is excellent wildlife viewing at the Brigantine

Division of the park where there are also accessible facilities, the start of several walking trails, and an 8 mile auto tour. Dogs are allowed for no additional fee. Dogs must be kept on a short lead, be under their owner's control at all times, leashed, and cleaned up after. Dogs are not allowed at the Holgate's dune area.

Great Falls of the Passaic River
McBride Avenue
Paterson, NJ
973-279-9587
This 89 acre National Historic Site Park boasts a long, rich cultural and industrial history, trails, and a 77+ foot waterfall. Well behaved dogs are welcome. Dogs must be under their owner's control, leashed, and cleaned up after at all times. Dogs are not allowed in buildings.

Fort Mott State Park
454 Fort Mott Road
Pennsville, NJ
856-935-3218
Once used as a coastal defense system, this park now features interpretive signs with in-depth descriptions throughout the fort, and there are nice places along the Delaware River for walking and picnicking. Dogs are allowed throughout the park and on the trails. They are not allowed in any buildings. Dogs must be well mannered, leashed, and cleaned up after at all times.

Parvin State Park
701 Almond Road
Pittsgrove, NJ
856-358-8616
Dogs on leash are allowed in the state park. They are not allowed in the campground area or beach. The park features canoeing, picnicking, hiking, swimming, fishing, and more. The park also has history of American Indians, Civilian Conservation Corps in 1933-1941, summer camp for children of displaced Japanese Americans in 1943, POW camp for German prisoners in 1944, and temporary housing for the Kalmychs of Eastern Europe in 1952.

Shakespeare Garden/Cedar Brook Park
Pemberton and Park Avenues
Plainfield, NJ
908-753-3000
This county park is home to a 1920's garden containing a bust of Shakespeare along with plants that

were cited in his works. Dogs are allowed throughout the park and on the trails. Dogs must be leashed and cleaned up after at all times.

Hasenclever Iron Trail
1304 Sloatsburg Road, c/o Ringwood State Park
Ringwood, NJ
973-962-7031
From deep woodlands to rocky vistas, this trail that connects Ringwood and Skylands State Parks and offers hikers blazed trails. Dogs are allowed on the trail. They must be on no more than a 6 foot leash and cleaned up after at all times.

Long Pond Ironworks State Park
1304 Sloatsburg Rd
Ringwood, NJ
973-962-7031
Dogs on leash are allowed in the state park. The park features hiking, fishing, and boating. It is the historical site of Long Pond Ironworks of 1766 ironwork building and a reconstructed waterwheel. There is no swimming for people but pets can wade in the water while leashed.

Ramapo Mountain State Forest
1304 Sloatsburg Rd
Ringwood, NJ
973-962-7031
Dogs on leash are allowed in the state park. The park features hiking, fishing, and canoeing. People are not allowed to swim but pets are allowed to wade in the water while on leash.

Ringwood State Park
1304 Sloatsburg Road
Ringwood, NJ
973-962-7031
Home to such attractions as a 74 acre lake, 2 mansions, 96 acres of gardens, and numerous blazed trails, this 4000+ acre park also provides a wide variety of year round land and water recreation. Dogs are allowed throughout the park and on the trails; they are not allowed in any of the buildings or in public swim areas. They must be under their owner's control, leashed, and cleaned up after at all times.

High Point State Park
1480 Hwy 23
Sussex, NJ
973-875-4800
There are more than 15,000 scenic acres at this park that offers numerous trails (including a piece of the Appalachian Trail), panoramic views of 3 states from its high point,

a spring-fed lake, year round interpretive and educational programs, and much more. Dogs of all sizes are allowed at this park for no additional fee. Dogs must be well behaved, leashed, cleaned up after, and owners are responsible for them at all times. Dogs may not be left unattended at any time. Dogs are not allowed in the campground area.

Swartswood State Park
PO Box 123
Swartswood, NJ
973-383-5230
Dogs on leash are allowed in the state park. They are not allowed in the campground areas. The park features hiking, fishing, picnicking, boating, and swimming. This was the first established state park in NJ.

Washington Crossing State Park
355 Washington Crossing-Pennington Road
Titusville, NJ
609-737-0623
This was the historic site where General George Washington and his army landed after crossing the Delaware, and the park is now home to a wide variety of plant, animal, and birdlife, with year round recreation, and more than 15 miles of trails for exploring. Well behaved dogs are welcome throughout the park and on the trails; they are not allowed in any of the buildings or in the campground. However, you will be able to see a good portion of the park from outside. Dogs must be under their owner's control, be on no more than a 6 foot leash, and cleaned up after at all times.

New Jersey State House
West State Street
Trenton, NJ
609-633-2709
Home to the State Assembly and other state offices, this beautiful building and landscaped area is open to the public and your well mannered dog is welcome to join you on the grounds. Dogs are not allowed inside the building. Dogs must be under their owner's control, leashed, and cleaned up after at all times.

Clayton Park
Emley's Hill Road
Upper Freehold, NJ
609-259-5794
Dogs on a six foot leash are allowed on the trails at this 421 acre park. The park is used by hikers, bicycles and equestrians.

Assunpink Wildlife Management Area
Monmouth County
Upper Freehold Township, NJ
609-259-2132
This 6,000+ acre park has a 225 acre lake making for a variety of land and water recreation, and especially popular for fishing and hiking. Dogs are allowed throughout the park on leash from September 1st through April 31st, and from May 1st through August 31 they are allowed in the dog training area only. They may be off lead in the training area if they are under good voice control. Dogs must be cleaned up after at all times.

Shark River Park
1101 Schoolhouse Road
Wall, NJ
732-922-4080
Dogs on a six foot leash are allowed on the trails at this 588 acre park. The park is used by hikers, bicycles and equestrians.

New Mexico

Petroglyph National Monument
6001 Unser Blvd NW
Albuquerque, NM
505-899-0205
nps.gov/petr/
This historical park is open daily from 8 am to 5 pm, and is home to an impressive display of petroglyphs. Dogs of all sizes are allowed at no additional fee. Dogs may not be left unattended, and they must be leashed and cleaned up after. Dogs are not allowed in buildings or in the Boca Negra Canyon. Dogs are allowed on the trails unless otherwise marked.

Rio Grande Nature Center State Park
2901 Candelaria Road NW
Albuquerque, NM
505-344-7240
This park offers a trail system allowing for wildlife viewing and nature study, hands-on activities at their Nature Center, and a glass walled library complete with the sounds of the outside wildlife. Dogs of all sizes are allowed at no additional fee. Dogs may not be left unattended, and they must be leashed and cleaned up after. Dogs are not allowed in the buildings or

on the Nature Trail. Dogs are allowed on the bike trail. The gates open daily at 8 am; the nature center at 10 am, and they close at 5 pm.

Aztec Ruins National Monument
84 County Road 2900
Aztec, NM
505-334-6174
nps.gov/azru/index.htm
Dogs on leash are allowed in picnic areas and parking lot areas. Dogs are not allowed on trails.

Capulin Volcano National Monument
Po Box 40
Capulin, NM
505-278-2201
nps.gov/cavo/index.htm
Dogs on leash are allowed only on paved areas of the park and roads. Dogs are not allowed on unpaved park trails.

Carlsbad Canyon National Park
727 Carlsbad Canyon Hwy 62/180
Carlsbad, NM
505-785-2232
nps.gov/cave/
This national park was established to preserve the Carlsbad Caverns, and over 100 other caves housed within a fossil reef. It is also home to America's deepest and 4th longest limestone cave. Dogs are not allowed at the park, except in the parking lot and at the kennel that is on site, and they must be on leash and cleaned up after.

Eagle Nest Lake State Park
P. O. Box 185
Eagle Nest, NM
505-377-1594
This day-use park of 2,485 acres is situated at an altitude of 8,300 feet and is home to a 2,400 acre lake that is surrounded by 2 of the state's tallest peaks. There is an abundance of wildlife, great fishing, and a variety of land and water recreational opportunities. Some of the amenities include boat ramps, restrooms, and picnic areas. Dogs of all sizes are allowed throughout the park and on the trails. Dogs must be under owners control at all times, and they must be leashed and cleaned up after.

El Malpais National Monument
123 E Roosevelt Avenue
Grants, NM
505-783-4774
nps.gov/elma/index.htm
Dogs on leash are allowed on the trails. They prefer you not take pets on lava trails unless they are wearing

dog boots as it will hurt their feet. Dogs are not allowed in caves or backcountry for safety reasons. The park features auto touring, hiking, and camping with a permit.

Bandelier National Monument
15 Entrance Road
Los Alamos, NM
505-672-3861
nps.gov/band/index.htm
Dogs on leash are allowed in camping and picnic areas. Dogs are not allowed on trails.

Pecos National Historic Park
P. O. Box 418
Pecos, NM
505-757-6414
nps.gov/peco
This day-use park safeguards and preserves more than 12,000 years of cultural and geographical history of the ancient Pueblo of Pecos, the mission ruins and trails of the area, the Forked Lighting Ranch, and the site of the Civil War Battle of Glorieta Pass. Some of the amenities here include a 1-1/4 mile hiking trail, picnic areas, restrooms, and a museum. Dogs are allowed at the park for no additional fee. Dogs are allowed on the trails and around the park, but not in park buildings. Dogs must be leashed, and please clean up after your pet.

Sandia Peak Ski Area/Summer Use
Tramway Blvd
Sandia Park, NM
505-242-9052
sandiapeak.com/
The park's parking lot is over 10,000 feet with trails reaching an elevation of over 12,000 feet. The park is open year round, but their ski season is usually mid-December through mid-March with the exception of a couple of 2 week closures for maintenance. They have a full service base community, an extensive biking/hiking system, sand pit volleyball, picnic areas, eateries, and more. Dogs are allowed on the mountain all year, but they are not allowed on the ski trails during the ski season or on the tram or chair lift at any time. Pets may join you at the outdoor dining tables, picnic areas, and on many of the trails. Dogs must be well behaved, leashed and cleaned up after at all times.

Ski Santa Fe
Hwy 475 (Artist Road/Hyde Park Road)
Santa Fe, NM
505-982-4429

skisantafe.com/
This park is nestled high in the beautiful Sangre de Cristo Mountains, reaches to a 12,075 foot summit, and their season here is usually from Thanksgiving to Easter. In the off-season months, dogs are allowed on the mountain and the numerous trails. There are restrooms available, but no other services are available in the off-season. Dogs must be under their owner's control at all times, leashed, and cleaned up after on the trails. Dogs are not allowed in the ski park during the ski season.

State Capitol Grounds
491 Old Santa Fe Trail
Santa Fe, NM
505-986-4589
legis.state.nm.us
The New Mexico capitol building is the only round capitol building in the U.S., and it was made to resemble a Zia Pueblo sun sign, which is also the state symbol. Surrounding the building are 6 ½ acres of lush gardens with more than 100 varieties of flowering plants, nut and fruit trees, sequoias, and shrubs. Dogs are welcome to explore the area with you. Dogs must be leashed and cleaned up after at all times.

Gila Cliff Dwellings National Monument
HC 68 Box 100
Silver City, NM
505-536-9461
nps.gov/gicl/index.htm
Dogs must be on leash and must be cleaned up after in park. Dogs are not allowed on trails leading to the caves but you may take them on other trails. They offer a free on-site kennel if you want to hike to caves. The park features camping, fishing, hiking, and more.

New York

Albany Riverfront Park at the Corning Preserve
25 Quackenbush Square
Albany, NY
518-434-2032
This riverfront preserve park offers a boat launch, a bike trail, an amphitheater, visitor center, comfort stations, and beautiful places to walk. The park is also connected to the city and all it has to offer via the

Hudson River Way Pedestrian Bridge. Dogs are allowed throughout the park and there is no fee. This park is host to several events through the year and dogs are not allowed at the park during events. Dogs must be under their owner's control, leashed, and cleaned up after at all times.

Hudson Highlands State Park
Hwy 9D
Beacon, NY
Consisting of nearly 6,000 acres of undeveloped preserve, this day-use park is a perfect place for a number of outdoor activities, and the extensive trails system goes from easy to challenging with some outstanding views. Dogs are allowed throughout the park on no more than a 10 foot lead and they must be cleaned up after. They suggest not bringing dogs on a hot day, and to always bring extra water for them when hiking upland.

Bear Mountain State Park
7 Lakes Drive
Bear Mountain, NY
845-786-2701
Dogs of all sizes are allowed at no additional fee. Dogs must be on no more than a 6 foot leash and be cleaned up after. Dogs are not allowed in the zoo, in any of the buildings, or at the picnic areas. The park is open from dawn to dusk year round.

Kershaw Park-Canandaigua Lake
Lakeshore Dr
Canandaigua, NY
585-396-5080
Dogs on leash are allowed in this park. The only restriction is that they are not allowed on the beach. There are walking paths, a boat launch area, picnic areas, and a snack bar. It is open seven days a week from 6am-11pm.

Vischer Ferry Nature Preserve
Riverview Rd.
Clifton Park, NY
The nature preserve, popular with local dog walkers, follows the Mohawk River and the Erie Canal for a number of miles. You will see a number of historical sites such as locks on the canal and other various historical markers. The area is also a wetland habitat for birds and plants. Dogs must be on leash at all times and must be cleaned up after. Take Cresent Road (Hwy 92) west from I-87 2.5 miles and turn left onto Van Vranken Rd. Turn right at Riverview

Rd and the preserve will be on your left.

Ice Caves of the Shawangunks
400 Sams Point Road
Cragsmoor, NY
518-272-0195
Born of glacial activity, this park features an unusual landscape with miles of hiking trails and impressive geological features, but the ice caves (some rare) are the exciting draw here. A few of the caves may not be pet friendly, so they suggest using some caution, bring an electric torch light, and dress warm. Dogs are allowed throughout the park and on the trails. Dogs must be under their owner's care at all times, be leashed, and cleaned up after.

Flushing Meadows Corona Park
Grand Central Parkway
Flushing, NY
718-760-6565
One of New York City's flagship parks, this 1,255 acre major recreational destination also holds environmental and historical importance. The park is home to Shea Stadium, a tennis center, the New York Hall of Science, the Queens Museum of Art, a wildlife center, Meadow Lake, children's playgrounds, and much more. There are several entrance points depending on the activity. Dogs are allowed throughout the park; they are not allowed in buildings or at the playgrounds. Dogs must be well behaved, under their owner's control, leashed, and cleaned up after at all times.

Mohonk Preserve Nature
3197 Hwy 44/55
Gardiner, NY
845-255-0919
mohonkpreserve.org/
Open year round, this mountain refuge provides over 6,500 acres of forests, fields, lakes, ponds, streams, and cliffs, have more than 100 miles of multi-use trails, and it is also one of the best premier rock climbing/scrambling areas in the Northeast. Dogs of all sizes are allowed for no additional fee from spring through fall; they are not allowed in the park in the winter or after snowfall. Dogs must be kept close to owners, preferably on a 4 foot to a 6 foot leash, depending on the dog due to snakes in the area. Dogs are not allowed on the Mountain House property; maps are available at the visitor center. Please clean up after your pet on the trails

and common areas.

Finger Lakes National Forest
5218 Hwy 414
Hector, NY
607-546-4470
Dogs are allowed on the trails. Dogs must be on a leash.

West Hills County Park
Sweet Hollow Rd
Huntington, NY
631-854-4423
This is an over 700 acre park with nature trails and hiking including the Whitman Trail to the 400 foot Jayne's Hill which is Long Island's highest point. There is also a horseback riding facility and bridle paths in the park. Dogs must be on leash in the park outside of the small off-leash enclosed dog run in the park.

Eleanor Roosevelt National Historic Site
4097 Albany Post Road
Hyde Park, NY
845-229-9115
nps.gov/elro/index.htm
Dogs must be on leash and must be cleaned up after on the grounds and trails. Dogs are not allowed in any buildings. This is the only National Historic Site dedicated to a First Lady.

Minnewaska State Park Preserve
5281 Hwy 44/55
Kerhonkson, NY
845-255-0752
Covering about 16,000 square miles with almost 60 miles of hiking and biking trails and carriage roads, this beautiful park also features several waterfalls, 2 lakes, and a variety of recreational pursuits. Dogs of all sizes are allowed for no additional fee. Dogs must be on no more than a 6 foot leash at all times, and they are not allowed in park buildings, the summer camp area, on ski trails in the winter, or the picnic or swimming areas. Dogs must be cleaned up after in common areas and on the trails.

Earl W. Bydges Artpark
450 S 4th Street
Louiston, NY
716-754-9000
artpark.net
This park was created for the the education, entertainment, and interative enjoyment of the arts. Dogs are allowed on leash, and they must be cleaned up after.

Montauk Point Lighthouse and Museum
2000 Montauk H
Montauk, NY
631-668-2544
montauklighthouse.com/home.htm
This lighthouse is the oldest one in the state, and only the 4th oldest active lighthouse in the U.S. and the beauty of the area leads to a number of special events taking place here. Although dogs are not allowed in the lighthouse or in the museum, they are allowed for day use, on the beach, and the area offers a number of areas to hike and explore. Dogs must be leashed, cleaned up after, and under their owner's control at all times.

Battery Park
State Street
New York, NY
ci.nyc.ny.us/html/dpr/
From this 23 acre city park, you can view the Statue of Liberty and Ellis Island in the distance. There are numerous picnic tables and several sidewalk vendors in the park. This park also contains several sculptures and the Clinton Castle Monument, a sandstone fort built in 1811. Your leashed dog is allowed in the park, but much of the grass area is fenced off.

Canine Court
Henry Hudson Parkway
New York, NY
ci.nyc.ny.us/html/dpr/
In April of 1998, New York City's first public dog playground (agility course) opened in Van Cortlandt Park. Canine Court was also the first public dog agility course/playground in the country. Canines now have a fenced-in play area that totals 14,000 square feet - one half as a dog run and the other half as a dog agility course. The agility equipment consists of several chutes or tunnels for pooches to run through, a teeter-totter and a pair of hurdles. Canine Court was made possible by $3,000 from the Friends of Van Cortlandt Park and $1,000 from the City Parks Foundation (CPF). The NYC event called PawsWalk, held every April/May helped to fund some of the equipment, fencing and benches. The doggie playground is located in Van Cortlandt Park in the Bronx. From the Henry Hudson Parkway, follow signs to Van Cortlandt Park. Canine Court is located across the Parkway from the horse barn/stable.

It is located between a running track/soccer field area and the Parkway. You cannot really see it from the road, so you will need to park and then walk along the running path, towards the Parkway.

Central Park
Central Park W & Fifth Ave.
New York, NY
centralpark.org/
Central Park, located the heart of Manhattan, is the world's most famous park. This 843 acre park is so nice and refreshing that you'll find it hard to believe it is in the middle of the country's largest city. When we visited Central Park, it seemed very clean and safe, however there are two rules of thumb to follow. Only walk in the park during daylight hours and stay on the main paths. It is best to go on main paths where other people are walking. The park is 6 miles long and has an inner path which is a 4 mile loop. Also inside the park is a popular running track which is a 1.58 mile loop (between 86th and 96th Streets). When inside the park, be sure to stop by the Shakespeare Garden - leashed pooches are welcome on the paths. And don't miss Balto - a bronze sculpture of Balto, the sled dog. Balto is located between the Shakespeare Garden and Fifth Street (around 67th Street). If 66th Street were to go through the Park, the statue of Balto would be on 66th Street. Another popular area for dog fanatics is "Dog Hill". On a nice day, you will find dogs of all shapes, sizes and breeds socializing here. It is located near Central Park West and 79th Street (north of 79th Street.) Sections of Central Park now have off-leash hours. Be sure to follow the signs for the correct areas and hours for off-leash activity.

Manhattan Sites National Park Service
26 Wall Street
New York, NY
212-825-6888
nps.gov/masi/index.htm
Dogs must be on leash and must be cleaned up after on the pathways in this city park on Wall Street. There are six separate sites representing the 1600's to the present.

Riverside Park
Riverside Drive
New York, NY
ci.nyc.ny.us/html/dpr/
This waterfront park has a path which stretches for 4 miles alongside the Hudson River. Your leashed pooch is welcome.

Sampson State Park
6096 Route 96A
Romulus, NY
315-585-6392
nysparks.state.ny.us
Dogs on a 6 foot leash are allowed in this park. You must carry proof of your dog's rabies vaccination at all times. Dogs are not allowed in the bathing areas. This state park features electric hookups and dry camping, a playground, swimming, hiking, fishing, and more. It is open year round.

Congress Park
Broadway and Congress
Saratoga Springs, NY
518-587-3550
This beautiful city park has natural mineral water springs, large grassy lawns, flowers throughout, ponds, and historic statues. Well behaved dogs are welcome here. They must be on leash and cleaned up after at all times.

Sarasota Springs State Park
19 Roosevelt Drive
Saratoga Springs, NY
518-584-2535
saratogaspastatepark.org/
In addition to eateries, theater, mineral baths, automobile and dance museums, golf courses, picnic areas with comfort stations, and more, this year round recreation and entertainment destination offers a wide variety of year round, multi-use trails. Well behaved dogs on leash are allowed for no additional fee, and they must have current proof of rabies inoculation. Dogs must be under their owner's control at all times and be cleaned up after. Dogs are allowed throughout the park and on the trails; they are not allowed in any of the buildings, food, or swim areas.

Dean's Cove
2678 Lower Lake Rd
Seneca Falls, NY
315-568-5163
nysparks.state.ny.us
Dean's Cove is open year round. Dogs on leash are allowed in this park. Fishing, boating, hiking, picnic tables and more are available to keep you occupied. Dogs are not allowed on the public beaches but may be able to find other non-public areas to wade into the lake.

Women's Rights National Hist. Park
136 Fall Street
Seneca Falls, NY
315-568-2991
nps.gov/wori/index.htm
Dogs must be on leash and must be cleaned up after on grounds. Dogs are not allowed in any buildings.

Gateway National Recreation Area
210 New York Avenue
Staten Island, NY
718-354-4606
nps.gov/gate/index.htm
Dogs must be on leash and must be cleaned up after in the park. The park features auto touring, boating, fishing, and more. You must follow any local or state park rules and pet policies.

Saratoga National Historical Park
648 Hwy 32
Stillwater, NY
518-664-9821
nps.gov/sara
Home to a crucial American Victory, there are 3 main historical sites at this 3400 acre scenic park; 1st and largest being the battlefield, 2nd is the Schuyler House, and 3rd is the Saratoga Monument. Dogs are welcome for no additional fees. Dogs must be attended to, leashed, and cleaned up after at all times. Dogs are allowed throughout the park and on the trails; they are not allowed in any of the buildings.

Erie Canalway National Heritage Corridor
PO Box 219
Waterford, NY
518-237-8643
nps.gov/erie/index.htm
Dogs must be on leash and must be cleaned up after in most of the park area. You must follow local and state park rules for pets. Some auto touring is involved with stops for fishing, hiking, boating, and more.

North Carolina

Nantahala National Forest
various
Asheville, NC
828-257-4200
cs.unca.edu/nfsnc/
The forest offers miles of dog-friendly hiking trails. It is located about 2 hours from the Great Smoky Mountains National Park.

Pisgah National Forest
various
Asheville, NC
828-257-4200
cs.unca.edu/nfsnc/
The forest offers miles of dog-friendly hiking trails. It is located about 2 hours from the Great Smoky Mountains National Park.

Fort Macon State Park
2300 E Fort Macon Road/Hwy 58
Atlantic Beach, NC
252-726-3775
This historic site is located on a barrier island peninsula, which creates a lively coastal ecosystem and plenty of recreational activities, plus it shares a rich colonial history with a Civil War fort and regularly held educational and interpretive programs. Dogs are allowed on the grounds and trails; they are not allowed in the fort or park buildings. Dogs must be under their owner's control, on no more than a 6 foot leash, and cleaned up after at all times.

Moses H. Cone Memorial Park
MM 295 Blue Ridge Parkway
Blowing Rock, NC
828-271 4779
Located in the Grandfather Mountain corridor, this scenic 3,600 acre park's centerpiece is the turn-of-the-century Cone Manor-now a visitor and craft center. There are picnic areas, numerous trails, and waterways. Dogs are allowed on the grounds; they are not allowed in buildings. Dogs must be leashed and under their owner's control at all times.

Carolina Beach Lake Park
400 S Lake Park Blvd/Hwy 421
Carolina Beach, NC
910-458-7416
Once listed in the Guinness Book of World Records as the closest freshwater lake to salt water, this park offers a range of water and land recreation, a sheltered picnic area, playground, restrooms, and gazebos. Leashed dogs are allowed in the park year round and on the beach from November 1st to February 28th. Pet owners must carry clean-up supplies and pick-up after their pets at all times.

Freeman Park Recreation Area
1204 N Lake Park BlvdHwy 421
Carolina Beach, NC
910-458-4716
This popular park offers a wide range of land and sea recreation, bird,

marine, and wildlife, and scenic sand dunes blended against sea grasses and sea. Permits for the park are available at the entrance and several other places in town. Dogs are allowed at the park; from April 1st to September 30th dogs must be on leash, and from October 1st to March 31st dogs may be off lead only if they are under good voice control. Dogs must be under their owner's control and cleaned up after at all times.

Hemlock Bluffs Nature Preserve
2616 Kildaire Farm Road
Cary, NC
919-387-5980
Popular for the excellent bird and wildlife viewing, this park also features about 3 miles of wooded hiking trails and scenic observation platforms, plus it is home to the Stevens Nature Center where they have an outdoor educational shelter, a native wildflower garden, and a hands-on educational exhibit hall. Dogs are allowed throughout the preserve on the trails only. Dogs must be leashed and picked up after, and they are not allowed in buildings.

Whitewater Falls
Off Hwy 281
Cashiers, NC
828-257-4200
At 411 feet, this is the highest waterfall east of the Rocky Mountains, and its lush environment gives way to an abundance of flora and fauna and some great sightseeing trails and lookouts. Restrooms and picnic tables are on site. Dogs are allowed, but they must be kept leashed and picked up after at all times. This falls continue into South Carolina and there is another 400 foot waterfall.

Freedom Park
1900 East Boulevard
Charlotte, NC
704-336-2884
parkandrec.com
This is a popular park complete with athletic fields, tennis and basketball courts, playgrounds, a 7 acre lake, picnic shelters, concessions, and paved trails. Pets must be leashed and under your control at all times. From this park, you can begin the Lower Little Sugar Creek Trail (1.3 mile trail).

Lower Little Sugar Creek Trail
1900 East Boulevard
Charlotte, NC

704-336-3854
parkandrec.com
Take your pooch out for some exercise on this 1.3 mile paved trail. Pets must be leashed and under your control at all times. Use the parking lot at Freedom Park and begin your walk.

Mallard and Clark's Creek Greenway
9801 Mallard Creek Road
Charlotte, NC
704-336-8866
parkandrec.com
Go for a walk or jog with your dog on this 3.6 mile paved trail. Pets must be leashed and under your control at all times. Parking is available at the Mallard Creek Elementary School, off Mallard Creek Road.

McAlpine Creek Greenway
8711 Monroe Road
Charlotte, NC
704-568-4044
parkandrec.com
You can go for a nice long walk with your dog at this trail system which offers over 8 miles of paved and gravel trails. Pets must be leashed and under your control at all times. There are many starting points, but you can park at either the McAlpine Creek Park (has a 5K championship cross country course) located at 8711 Monroe Road or the James Boyce Park located at 300 Boyce Road.

Upper Little Sugar Creek Trail
2100 North Davidson Street
Charlotte, NC
704-336-3367
parkandrec.com
Go for a walk on this 1.1 mile trail which joins Cordelia Park and Alexander Park. Pets must be leashed and under your control at all times. You can begin your walk at the parking lot in Cordelia Park.

Chimney Rock Park
Hwy 64/74A
Chimney Rock, NC
800-277-9611
chimneyrockpark.com/
This park offers the best of the mountains in one place, from unique geological formations to sweeping views. Enjoy spectacular 75-mile plus views from the top of the Skyline Trail (Exclamation Point) or Inspiration Point, explore a 404-foot waterfall from the top or bottom, check out a variety of interesting trails, or try the 185 stair walk that threads between a narrow passage, and is called the "eye of the needle".

You'll also find a variety of special events, a nature center, a native plant nursery, guided tours, and much more. Dogs are allowed throughout the park and on the stairs, but they are not allowed on the elevator or in the Skylight Cafe. Dogs must be well behaved, on leash, and cleaned up after at all times.

Tanglewood Park
4061 Clemmons Road
Clemmons, NC
336-778-6300
forsyth.cc/tanglewood/
A year round recreation destination, this park features gardens, gaming areas, green pastures, wooded areas, and waterways. Dogs are allowed on leash, and they must be picked up after.

The Duck Trail
Hwy 12
Duck, NC
252-255-1234
townofduck.com/ducktrail.htm
This scenic paved walk is a great place for walking pets. Dogs must be licensed, have current rabies tags, be under their owner's control, leashed, and cleaned up after at all times.

Duke University Forest
W Main Street/Hwy 70
Durham, NC
919-613-8013
env.duke.edu/forest/
Dedicated to the management, resources, ecological and environmental sciences, the 7,000+ acre Duke University Forest is unequaled by any other university as an outdoor forest laboratory, and there are a number of recreational pursuits allowed here as well. There are six sections to the forest with 45 separate entrances. Dogs are allowed in the forest and on all the trails; they must be well behaved, under their owner's control, leashed, and cleaned up after at all times.

Sarah P. Duke Gardens
426 Anderson Street
Durham, NC
919-684-3698
hr.duke.edu/dukegardens/
Recognized as one of the country's premier public gardens, this 55 acre site, located on Duke's University West campus, is world renowned for its design, diversity, quality, and for its stunning and inspiring beauty. Dogs are allowed on campus and in the garden; they must be well

behaved, under their owner's control, leashed, and cleaned up after at all times.

Guilford Courthouse National Military Park
2332 New Garden Road
Greensboro, NC
336-288-1776
nps.gov/guco/
As well as having a comprehensive visitor center/book store regarding the events of the significant battle that was fought here and other Revolutionary War actions, they also feature almost 30 honorary monuments throughout the park and a walking trail. Visitors must be sure to have cars parked outside the gates before 5 PM when they lock them for the night. Dogs must be leashed and under their owner's care at all times.

Tannenbaum Historic Park
2200 New Garden Road
Greensboro, NC
336-545-5315
This park preserves and educates the public of the historic significance of this area during America's colonial times as well as being a venue for various events throughout the year. Dogs are welcome, but they must be leashed and cleaned up after.

Cape Lookout National Seashore
Harkers Island Road
Harkers Island, NC
252-728-2250
nps.gov/calo
Accessible by boat or ferry only, this park consists of 56 miles of beaches covering 4 barrier islands, and dogs are allowed on the beaches here. They must be leashed and cleaned up after at all times. They suggest bringing fresh water for pets as there is little shade on the island and dogs are not allowed in buildings. Dogs may not be left alone at any time.

Holmes Educational State Forest
1299 Crab Creek Road
Hendersonville, NC
828-692-0100
ncesf.org/HESF/home.htm
Scenic views, brilliant seasonal flora, and well marked trails with displays and exhibits, offer visitors an educational experience as well as a recreational one. Leashed dogs are allowed.

Fort Fisher State Historic Park
1610 Fort Fisher Blvd S/Hwy 421

Kure Beach, NC
910-458-5538
Rich in colonial history, this park affords visitors educational as well as recreational avenues with exhibits, interpretive programs, and special events. Dogs are allowed throughout the park; they are not allowed in buildings or on the beach. Dogs must be on no more than a 6 foot leash and cleaned up after at all times.

Jockey's Ridge State Park
Carolista Drive/Milepost 12 of Hwy 158 Bypass
Nags Head, NC
252-441-7132
jockeysridgestatepark.com/
Home to the tallest natural sand dunes in the Eastern US, this park also has a 384 foot long boardwalk ending in a stunning view of the ridge from the overlook, a wide range of land, water, and airborne activities, a visitor center, museum, and picnicking areas. Dogs of all sizes are allowed on the grounds and trails; they are not allowed in the buildings. Dogs must be under their owner's control, on no more than a 6 foot leash, and cleaned up after at all times.

Ocracoke Island
P. O. Box 456
Ocracoke, NC
252-928-6711
ocracoke-nc.com/
Walking maps are available at the Association for exploring this beautiful island. Dogs are allowed throughout the area and on the beaches; they must be leashed and cleaned up after at all times.

McMullen Creek Greenway
Pineville-Matthews Road
Pineville, NC
704-643-3405
parkandrec.com
Enjoy a stroll with your pooch on this 1.5 mile paved and gravel trail. Pets must be leashed and under your control at all times. The parking lot as well as a picnic area is located off Pineville-Matthews Road (across from the McMullen Creek Marketplace.)

Mordecai Historic Park
One Mimosa Street
Raleigh, NC
919-857-4364
This historic park allows visitors to experience a glimpse of colonial village life with the structures, gardens, special events, and guided tours. Dogs of all sizes are allowed

throughout the park; they are not allowed in any of the buildings or on the trolley. Dogs must be leashed and cleaned up after at all times.

Pullen Park
520 Ashe Avenue
Raleigh, NC
919-831-6468
This beautiful 63 acre park has the distinction of having a TV Land tribute statue of Opie and Andy Taylor honoring the Andy Griffith Show, as well as a number of attractions, gaming fields, playgrounds, and picnic areas. Dogs are allowed throughout the park unless otherwise noted; they are not allowed in buildings, on the train, or on the carousel. Dogs may not be left alone at any time, and they must be under their owner's control, leashed and cleaned up after at all times.

Mattamuskeet National Wildlife Refuge
2 Mattamuskeet Road
Swan Quarter, NC
252-926-4021
Covering some 50,000 acres of woodlands, marshes, and water and home to a shallow 18 mile long/7 mile wide lake, this refuge is home to over 800 species of birds and wildlife and is known for being a place of quiet, serene beauty. Dogs are welcome on the trails of the refuge; they are not allowed to disturb wildlife in any way. Dogs must be under their owner's control, leashed, and cleaned up after at all times.

Brunswick Town State Historic Site
8884 St Phillips Road SE
Winnabow, NC
910-371-6613
Displays inside the visitor center and on the grounds, monuments, self-guided trails with signage, living history 18th century colonial and 19th century Civil War events, and more tell of the rich colonial and military history of this historic area. Dogs are allowed throughout the park and on the trails; they are not allowed in buildings. Dogs must be leashed and cleaned up after at all times.

Bethabara Park
2147 Bethabara Road
Winston-Salem, NC
336-924-2580
bethabarapark.org/maphome.htm
Dedicated to obtaining, preserving, and educating visitors about the historic culture of this Moravian 1753

religious center and trading outpost, this 175 acre wildlife preserve (a National Historic Landmark) offers a living history program complete with a reconstructed village, a visitor center, and nature trails.

North Dakota

Double Ditch State Rec Area
Hwy 1804
Bismarck, ND
701-667-6340
Located along the Missouri River, this 116 acre day use area offers wayside exhibits, hiking trails, and a variety of land and water recreation. It is located across from the Double Ditch Indian Village-one of the most significant of the Mandan Villages along the Missouri River. Dogs are allowed on site and at the village; they must be leashed and under their owner's control at all times.

Theodore Roosevelt National Park
On I 94 at Exits 25 or 27 (South Unit)
Medora, ND
701-623-4466
nps.gov/thro
This Park is located in the North Dakota Badlands. It is named after the 26th president, Theodore Roosevelt. He was a great conservationist, who, out of concern for the future of our lands, established the National Forest Service in 1906. The park is open all year although some roads close at times due to snow. The campgrounds are also open all year (no hookups). Dogs are allowed in the park and the campgrounds at no additional fee, but dogs may not be left unattended at any time, and they are not allowed in any of the buildings, or on any of the trails. However, there are trails just outside the park where dogs are allowed. One of the trails is the Maahdaahhey Trail.

Knife River Indian Villages National Historical Site
564 County Road 37
Stanton, ND
701-745-3300
nps.gov/knri/
Registered as a National Historic Site, this park recreates the living history of the lives of the Northern Plains Indians, and they offer self-guided walking tours, 11 miles of

hiking trails, and a variety of plant and animal life. Dogs of all sizes are allowed at no additional fee. Dogs may not be left unattended, and they must be on no more than a 6 foot leash, and cleaned up after. Dogs are not allowed in any of the buildings. The park is open year round from dawn to sunset.

Ohio

Akron City Parks
various locations
Akron, OH
330-375-2810
ci.akron.oh.us
In general, dogs are allowed at Akron City Parks. Pets must be leashed and cleaned up after.

Firestone Metro Park
2620 Harrington Road
Akron, OH
330-867-5511
Activities at this park include hiking, fishing, cross country skiing and sledding. The park has three easy rated trails ranging in length from .8 to 1.6 miles. Pets are allowed at the park and on the trails but need to be leashed and cleaned up after. Pets are not allowed in picnic areas. To get there from I-277 and U.S. Route 224 exit at South Main Street. Take S. Main Street south one mile to Warner Road and go east. There is a park entrance on the left or continue about .5 miles to Harrington Road. Turn left on Harrington Rd. to the park entrances on the left.

Hampton Hills Metro Park
2925 Akron-Peninsula Road
Akron, OH
330-867-5511
Activities at this park include hiking, soccer, softball and nature observation. The park has two trails including the steep 3.2 mile Adam Run Trail and the steep 1.6 mile Spring Hollow Trail. Pets are allowed at the park and on the trails but need to be leashed and cleaned up after. Pets are not allowed in picnic areas. To get there from Route 8 north, exit Steel Corners Road. Go left (west) on Steel Corners Road about 5 miles to Akron-Peninsula Road. Turn left (south) on Akron-Peninsula Road and go .25 miles to the park entrance on the left.

Portage Lakes State Park

5031 Manchester Road
Akron, OH
330-644-2220
Dogs are allowed at this park including on the 5 miles of hiking trails and in the campgrounds but not in the lake water. Pets must be leashed, cleaned up after and are not allowed inside any buildings. This park permits hunting in certain areas.

Sand Run Metro Park
1350-1750 Sand Run Parkway
Akron, OH
330-867-5511
Activities at this park include hiking, jogging, soccer, ice skating, sledding and cross country skiing. The park has 5 trails including an easy rated section of the statewide Buckeye Trail, the steep 1.8 mile Dogwood Trail and the easy rated 4.7 mile Parkway Jogging Trail. Pets are allowed at the park and on the trails but need to be leashed and cleaned up after. Pets are not allowed in picnic areas. To get there, take Interstate 77 and exit at Miller Road. Turn east onto Miller Road and follow it until it ends into Sand Run Parkway and turn right. After you cross Revere Road, you will enter the park. The parkway is about 3 miles long with various parking areas and trailheads.

Towpath Trail
1337 Merriman Road
Akron, OH
330-867-5511
This 8 mile trail is popular for hiking, biking and jogging. This path travels along part of the original Ohio and Erie Canal Towpath. There are many trail entrances. One of them is at the Big Bend trailhead. To get there from I-77, exit at Miller Road. Turn east onto Miller Road and follow it until it ends. Then turn right on Sand Run Parkway. After you cross Revere Road you will be in Sand Run Metro Park. Follow the parkway until it ends at Merriman Road. Turn right onto Merriman Road and go about .25 miles. Go past Treaty Line Road on the right and turn left at the park entrance.

Withrow Nature Preserve
Old Five Mile Road
Anderson Township, OH
513-521-PARK
hamiltoncountyparks.org
This 269 acre park offers a moderate rated 2 mile nature trail. Pets are allowed but must be on a 6 foot or less leash, under control, and picked up after. Pooper scooper dispensers

are located at each trailhead and are available from the Park District Rangers. To get to the park, take I-275 and head south on Five Mile Road. Go left at the stop sign to Old Five Mile Road to the park entrance on the left.

Woodland Mound Park
Nordyke Road
Anderson Township, OH
513-521-PARK
hamiltoncountyparks.org
This 984 acre park has several nature trails which are rated moderate and range from about .5 to 1 mile in length. Pets are allowed but must be on a 6 foot or less leash, under control, and picked up after. Pooper scooper dispensers are located at each trailhead and are available from the Park District Rangers. To get to the park, take I-275 and head west on Route 125 (Beechmont Avenue). Then turn left on Nordyke Road to the park entrance on the right. The park is also accessible via U.S. 52. Turn left on Eight Mile Road, and right on Old Kellogg to the park entrance on the left.

Pymatuning State Park
6260 Pymatuning Lake Road
Andover, OH
440-293-6030
Popular activities at this park include camping, fishing, boating and swimming. About one-fourth of the reservoir is located in Ohio and the other three-fourths is in Pennsylvania. While dogs are not allowed in the lake water, they are allowed at the rest of the park including the 2 miles of hiking trails and in the campgrounds. Pets must be leashed, cleaned up after and are not allowed inside any buildings. This park permits hunting in certain areas.

Hockhocking Adena Bikeway
throughout Adena County
Athens, OH
800-878-9767
This 17 mile paved recreation path runs throughout Athens County. The path is located on the old Hocking Valley Railroad bed and offers a scenic connection between the cities of Athens and Nelsonville. Points of interest along the bikeway include rock outcroppings, high cliffs, views of the Hocking River, displays of wildflowers, as well as birds and other wildlife. The path starts on the east side of Athens and winds around the Ohio

University campus and along the Hocking River. It goes through a historic coal company town and a part of Wayne National Forest. The path ends at Robbins Crossing which is a 19th century living village on the Hocking College campus. Pets on leash are allowed and need to be cleaned up after.

Strouds Run State Park
11661 State Park Road
Athens, OH
740-592-2302
This park offers wooded hills and a scenic lake. Dogs are allowed at this park including on the 15 miles of hiking trails, in the water and in the campgrounds. Pets must be leashed, cleaned up after and are not allowed inside any buildings. This park permits hunting in certain areas.

Paint Creek State Park
14265 US Route 50
Bainbridge, OH
937-365-1401
This park features hiking trails and a large lake for fishing, boating and swimming. There is also a pioneer farm on the west side of the lake which includes a log house, collection of log buildings, livestock, garden and fields all which represent a typical farm in the early 1800s. Dogs are allowed at this park including on the 3 miles of hiking trails, in the water and at the campgrounds. Pets must be leashed, cleaned up after and are not allowed inside any buildings. This park permits hunting in certain areas.

Pike Lake State Park
1847 Pike Lake Road
Bainbridge, OH
740-493-2212
This park is located in the scenic wooded hills of southern Ohio. Dogs are allowed at the park including on the 6 miles of strenuous and easy hiking trails and in the campgrounds, but not in the water. Pets must be leashed, cleaned up after and are not allowed inside any buildings. Hunting is permitted in the adjacent state forest.

O'Neil Woods Metro Park
2550 Martin Road
Bath Township, OH
330-867-5511
Activities at this park include hiking and nature observation. The park has two trails including a steep part of the statewide Buckeye Trail and the moderate rated 1.8 mile Deer Run Trail. Pets are allowed at the

park and on the trails but need to be leashed and cleaned up after. Pets are not allowed in picnic areas. The park is located off Martin Road, south of Ira Road and west of Riverview Road in Bath Township.

Huntington Reservation Metropark
various entrances
Bay Village, OH
216-351-6300
This park is located on the shores of Lake Erie. The Porter Creek Trail is a 1 mile trail which goes along Porter Creek Drive from Lake Road in Bay Village to Wolf Road, and from Porter Creek Drive east, past the Wolf Picnic Area connecting to the city of Bay Village's bike trail. Dogs are allowed on a 8 foot or less leash and need to be a cleaned up after.

Bedford Reservation Metropark
various entrances
Bedford, OH
216-351-6300
This park is located in Bedford, Bedford Heights, Oakwood, Valley View and Walton Hills. The park offers miles of trails, picnic areas, and a gorge which has been declared as a National Natural Landmark. One of the trails is an all purpose trail called Gorge Parkway Trail. It is a 5 to 6 mile trail which goes from Alexander Road in Walton Hills along Overlook Lane, Gorge Parkway and Egbert Lane to Union Street in Bedford. It connects with South Chagrin Reservation via Hawthorn Parkway. Dogs are allowed on a 8 foot or less leash and need to be cleaned up after.

Barkcamp State Park
65330 Barkamp Road
Belmont, OH
740-484-4064
Woodlands, open meadows and a scenic lake are all features of this secluded 1000 acre park. Dogs are allowed at this park including on the 4 miles of hiking trails and in the campgrounds. While pets are not allowed at the designated swim beach, they can take a dip in the water outside of the sandy swim beach area. Pets must be leashed, cleaned up after and are not allowed inside any buildings. This park permits hunting in certain areas.

Mill Stream Run Reservation
Metropark
various entrances
Berea, OH
216-351-6300
Artifacts that have been found at this

park indicate that Native American tribes frequented the area over 8,000 years ago. Today the park offesr many trails and picnic areas. The Valley Parkway Trail is an 8.5 mile trail from Bagley Road to West 130th Street with a loop around the Bonnie Park Picnic Area. Park entrances are off Routes 42 and 82, Albion, Handle, Lee, Prospect, Eastland, Edgerton, and Bagley roads, South Rocky River Drive and W. 130th Street. Dogs are allowed on a 8 foot or less leash and need to be cleaned up after.

Secor Metropark
10000 W. Central Avenue
Berkey, OH
419-829-2761
metroparkstoledo.com/
This park has more than 400 acres of woodland, meadow and taillgrass praire land. Trails at the park range from .5 miles to over 3 miles. The trailhead begins at the Nature Discover Center. Dogs must be on leash and please clean up after them. The park is located on West Central Avenue, six miles west of US 23/1-475.

Muskingum River State Park
7924 Cutler Lake Road
Blue Rock, OH
740-674-4794
This river parkway has 10 hand-operated locks with dams and is now recognized as one of America' great engineering accomplishments. The river is popular for boaters with unlimited horsepower motors, house boats, pontoon boats, canoes and rowboats. Fishing with a license is permitted from boats and at each of the lock sites but not at the lock walls. Dogs are allowed at this park including on the one mile hiking trail and in the campgrounds. Pets must be leashed, cleaned up after and are not allowed inside any buildings. This park does not allow hunting.

Brecksville Reservation Metropark
various entrances
Brecksville, OH
216-351-6300
This park has seven distinct gorges were there are many unusual and endangered plants. The park offers miles of trails including a section of the Buckeye Trail. The Valley Parkway Trail is a 4 mile all purpose trail. This trail runs along Valley Parkway from Brecksville Road to Chippewa Creek Drive and from

Route 82 to Riverview Road. Park entrances are off routes 82 and 21, and Riverview and Parkview roads. Dogs are allowed on a 8 foot or less leash and need to be cleaned up after.

Cuyahoga Valley National Park
Canal Road
Brecksville, OH
216-524-1497
nps.gov/cuva/
This national park consists of 33,000 acres along the banks of the Cuyahoga River. Scenery and terrain varies from a rolling floodplain to steep valley walls, ravines and lush upland forests. Popular activities at this park include hiking, bicycling, birdwatching and picnicking. Dogs are allowed at the park including the hiking trails. Pets must be leashed and cleaned up after. Pets are not allowed inside any buildings. The park is open daily and can be accessed by many different highways, including I-77, I-271, I-80/Ohio Turnpike, and State Route 8. To get to Canal Visitor Center, exit I-77 at Rockside Road. Go approximately 1 mile east to Canal Road and turn right. The visitor center is about 1.5 miles on the right. To get to Happy Days Visitor Center, take State Route 8 to west State Route 303. The visitor center is about 1 mile on the left. There is no park entrance fee.

Wolf Run State Park
16170 Wolf Run Road
Caldwell, OH
740-732-5035
Dogs are allowed at this park including on the hiking trails and in the campgrounds, but not in the water. There are 4.5 miles of trails at the park. A 3 mile section of the Buckeye Trail passes along the west side of the lake, a 1/2 mile loop trail starts at the nature center, and a 1.5 mile Lakeview Trail skirts the lake. Pets must be leashed, cleaned up after and are not allowed inside any buildings. This park permits hunting in certain areas.

Slate Run Park and Historical Farm
1375 State Route 674 North
Canal Winchester, OH
614-891-0700
metroparks.net/slaterun.htm
While dogs are not allowed at the historical farm, they are allowed on the designated Pet Trail at this park, which is at least 1 mile long. Pets must be on leash, under control and cleaned up after. To get there from I-

420

270, take U.S. 33 east toward Lancaster to the Canal Winchester/S.R. 674 exit. Turn right onto Gender Rd./S.R. 674 and go about 2 miles until it dead ends into Lithopolis Road. Turn left and go about 1/2 mile to S.R. 674. Turn right and go about 4 miles to the entrance on the right.

Great Seal State Park
635 Rocky Road
Chillicothe, OH
740-663-2125
This state park offers challenging trails that take hikers to scenic vistas to view distant ridgetops and the Scioto Valley. The park allows hunting in designated areas. Dogs are allowed at this park including on the 5 miles of hiking trails, at the picnic areas and in the campgrounds. Pets must be leashed and cleaned up after. Pets are not allowed inside any buildings. To get there from Columbus, take U.S. 23 South through Circleville 17 miles to the Delano Exit. Follow the signs to the park. The park is located 3 miles east off of U.S. 23.

Cincinnati City Parks
various locations
Cincinnati, OH
513-352-4080
cincinnati-oh.gov/parks/
In general, dogs on leash are allowed in Cleveland City Parks, but not inside buildings. Please remember to clean up after your pets.

Ohio State Nature Preserves
various locations
Cincinnati, OH
614-265-6561
ohiodnr.com
While dogs are allowed in Ohio State Parks, they are not allowed in Ohio State Nature Preserves. Please check our other parks listings for dog-friendly places to hike, picnic or just to enjoy nature.

A.W. Marion State Park
7317 Warner-Huffer Road
Circleville, OH
740-869-3124
This park offers boating, fishing and hiking. The Hargus Lake Trail offers a 5 mile scenic trail that provides access to the entire lake shoreline. There is also a shorter one mile nature trail. Dogs are allowed at this park including on the hiking trails and in the campgrounds. Pets must be leashed, cleaned up after and are not allowed inside any buildings. This

park permits hunting in certain areas.

Cleveland City Parks
various locations
Cleveland, OH
216-664-2485
In general, dogs on leash are allowed in Cleveland City Parks, but not inside buildings. Please remember to clean up after your pets.

Cleveland Lakefront State Park
8701 Lakeshore Blvd. NE
Cleveland, OH
216-881-8141
While this park offers many sandy beaches, pets are not allowed on any beach area within the park. Dogs are allowed at the rest of the park including on the walking and bicycling trails. The nine mile Cleveland Lakefront Bike Trail follows the Lake Erie shoreline along Lakeshore Boulevard from East 9th Street to East 185th Street. Pets must be leashed, cleaned up after and are not allowed inside any buildings.

Ohio State Nature Preserves
various locations
Cleveland, OH
614-265-6561
ohiodnr.com
While dogs are allowed in Ohio State Parks, they are not allowed in Ohio State Nature Preserves. Please check our other parks listings for dog-friendly places to hike, picnic or just to enjoy nature.

Farbach-Werner Nature Preserve
Poole Road
Colerain Township, OH
513-521-PARK
hamiltoncountyparks.org
This 23 acre park offers an easy .6 mile paved nature trail. Pets are allowed but must be on a 6 foot or less leash, under control, and picked up after. Pooper scooper dispensers are located at each trailhead and are available from the Park District Rangers. The park is located one mile south of Northgate Mall. Take Colerain Avenue to Poole Road to the entrance on the left.

Hueston Woods State Park
6301 Park Office Road
College Corner, OH
513-523-6347
This parks offers almost 3,000 acres for hiking, fishing, boating, camping and hunting. There are

over ten miles of hiking trails at the park. Dogs are allowed at this park including on the hiking trails and in the campgrounds. They are not allowed inside any buildings including the lodge, on swimming beaches or in the nature preserve (200 acres of old-growth forest). Pets must be leashed and cleaned up after. To get there from Cincinnati, take Route 27 North to Oxford. In the center of Oxford, turn right onto 732 North and take it to the park entrance.

Blendon Woods Metro Park
4265 East Dublin-Granville Rd.
Columbus, OH
614-891-0700
metroparks.net/blendon.htm
This park is listed as one of Ohio's 80 Watchable Wildlife sites and is popular with bird-watchers. Pets are allowed at the park but not on the trails except for the designated 1.2 mile Pet Trail called the Goldenrod Trail. Pets must be on leash, under control and cleaned up after. To get there from I-270, take the State Route 161/New Albany exit east to the Little Turtle exit and turn right. Go to Old S.R. 161/Cherry Bottom Rd. and turn right. The park entrance is 1/2 mile on the left.

Columbus City Parks
various addresses
Columbus, OH
614-645-3300
columbusrecparks.com/
Dogs are allowed in Columbus city parks but not inside buildings. Dogs must be on a 6 foot or less leash and clean up after your pet. As of May 2004 there were no designated off-leash areas, but some of the city parks might be considered for off-leash areas. These parks include Whetstone, Big Walnut, Big Run and Berliner parks as well as an unspecified downtown location.

Ohio State Nature Preserves
various locations
Columbus, OH
614-265-6561
ohiodnr.com
While dogs are allowed in Ohio State Parks, they are not allowed in Ohio State Nature Preserves. Please check our other parks listings for dog-friendly places to hike, picnic or just to enjoy nature.

Mosquito Lake State Park
1439 State Route 305
Cortland, OH
330-637-2856

This park offers one of the largest lakes in Ohio. Popular activities include boating, fishing, hiking and camping. Dogs are allowed at this park including on the hiking trails and in the campgrounds. While dogs cannot go on the designated swim beach, they can go into the water outside of the swim beach area. Pets must be leashed, cleaned up after and are not allowed inside any buildings. This park permits hunting in certain areas.

Miami Whitewater Forest
various entrances
Crosby, OH
513-521-PARK
hamiltoncountyparks.org
This 4,279 acre park has many nature and paved trails which range from easy to moderate and about .5 to over 7 miles in length. Pets are allowed but must be on a 6 foot or less leash, under control, and picked up after. Pooper scooper dispensers are located at each trailhead and are available from the Park District Rangers. Campgrounds are located at this park. To get to the park, take I-74 to Dry Fork Road exit, turn right on Dry Fork Road, turn right on West Road to the park entrance. The park is also accessible from Route 128 to Mt. Hope Road.

Gorge Metro Park
1160-1270 Front Street
Cuyahoga Falls, OH
330-867-5511
Activities at this park include hiking, fishing, ice skating and nature observation. The park has several trails including the easy rated 1.8 mile Glens Trail, the steep 1.8 mile Gorge Trail and the moderate rated 3.2 mile High Bridge Trail. Pets are allowed at the park and on the trails but need to be leashed and cleaned up after. Pets are not allowed in picnic areas. To get there, take Route 8 north to Cuyahoga Falls and exit Broad Blvd. Turn left on Broad Blvd and go to Front Street. Turn left on Front Street and go south about one mile. The park entrance will be on the right, before crossing the Cuyahoga River bridge. If you are going to the High Bridge Trail, continue and cross over the Cuyahoga River bridge and turn right into the parking lot.

Independence Dam State Park
27722 State Route 424
Defiance, OH
419-237-1503
This park is situated along the banks

of the Maumee River. The river is popular for boating, water-skiing, fishing and canoeing. Dogs are allowed at this park and on the 6 to 7 miles of hiking trails including a 3 mile forested trail that was once the towpath of the Miami and Erie Canal. Pets must be leashed and cleaned up after. Pets are not allowed inside any buildings. This park does not allow hunting.

Alum Creek State Park
3615 S. Old State Road
Delaware, OH
740-548-4631
This 4,600 acre park features a large reservoir and rolling fields and woodlands. Dogs are allowed at this park including on the 9.5 miles of hiking trails and in the campgrounds but not in the water or on the beach. Pets must be on a 6 foot or less leash, cleaned up after and are not allowed inside any buildings. The park permits hunting in certain areas.

Delaware State Park
5202 US 23 North
Delaware, OH
740-369-2761
This park features a reservoir, woodlands and meadows. Dogs are allowed at this park including on the 7 miles of hiking trails and in the campgrounds. While they are not allowed at the swim beach, dogs can go into the water outside the buoy area. Pets must be leashed, cleaned up after and are not allowed inside any buildings. This park permits hunting in certain areas. To get there from Columbus, go north on US 23. Go 5 miles north of the city of Delaware and the park entrance is on the east side of the road at the traffic light.

Goodyear Heights Metro Park
2077 Newton Street
East Akron, OH
330-867-5511
Activities at this park include hiking, fishing, ice skating, cross country skiing and sledding. The park has three easy rated trails ranging in length from 1.4 to 2 miles. Pets are allowed at the park and on the trails but need to be leashed and cleaned up after. Pets are not allowed in picnic areas. To get there, take I-76 east and exit Gilchrist Road. Turn left and go to State Route 91/Darrow Road. Go right on Darrow Road about .5 miles to Newton Street. Turn left on Newton Street and go .25 miles to the park

entrance on the right.

Beaver Creek State Park
12021 Echo Dell Road
East Liverpool, OH
330-385-3091
Located in the foothills of the Appalachian Mountains, this is one of the most scenic parks in Ohio. Dogs are allowed at the park including on the 16 miles of hiking trails and in the campgrounds. Pets must be leashed, cleaned up after and are not allowed inside any buildings. This park permits hunting in certain areas.

Euclid Creek Reservation Metropark
various entrances
Euclid, OH
216-351-6300
This park features Euclid Creek, wooded hillsides and rare rock chestnut oak trees. The Euclid Creek Trail is a 2.5 mile all purpose trail. It goes from the Highland Picnic Area in Euclid to Green Road in South Euclid. Park entrances are off of Highland and Green roads. Dogs are allowed on a 8 foot or less leash and need to be cleaned up after.

Harrison Lake State Park
26246 Harrison Lake Road
Fayette, OH
419-237-2593
This state park offers scenic woodlands located in a rich agricultural region. The lake here is popular for swimming, fishing, canoeing and camping. This park does not allow hunting. Dogs are allowed at this park including on the four miles of hiking trails around the lake, in the picnic areas, and in the campgrounds. Dogs cannot go onto the designated swimming beaches, but are allowed in the lake at non-designated swim areas. Pets must be leashed and cleaned up after. Pets are not allowed inside any buildings. To get there from Toledo, take U.S. 20 West through Fayette to County Road 27. Turn left and drive 2 miles to the park.

Battelle-Darby Creek Metro Park
1775 Darby Creek Dr.
Galloway, OH
614-891-0700
metroparks.net/batelle.htm
This park has two creeks, Big and Little Darby Creeks, which are called one of the 12 "Last Great Places" in the Western Hemisphere by the Nature Conservancy. Both rivers are also designated State and National Scenic Rivers. The rivers are home to

several species of fish and freshwater mussels, some of which are listed as endangered or threatened. While much of the land in this area has been converted to farmland, the park management has been able to restore several praires within the park. Pets are allowed at the park but not on the trails except for the designated 1.6 mile Pet Trail. Pets must be on leash, under control and cleaned up after. To get to the Pet Trail, go to the parking lot on the east side of Georgesville-Wrightsville Road. It is adjacent to a praire site.

Garfield Park Reservation Metropark
various entrances
Garfield Heights, OH
216-351-6300
This park features green space for wildlife, trails and picnic areas. The Garfield Park Trail is a 2.4 mile trail that goes from Broadway Avenue to Turney Road. The park entrances are off Broadway Avenue and Turney Road. Dogs are allowed on a 8 foot or less leash and need to be cleaned up after.

Geneva State Park
4499 Padanarum Road
Geneva, OH
440-466-8400
Dogs are allowed at this park including on the 3 miles of hiking trails and in the campgrounds. While dogs are cannot go on the swim beach, they can go in the water outside of the designated swim beach. Pets must be leashed, cleaned up after and are not allowed inside any buildings. This park allows hunting in certain areas. To get there from Cleveland, take Interstate 90 east to Route 534 north. The park entrance is six miles north on Route 534, on the left.

Burr Oak State Park
10220 Burr Oak Lodge Road
Glouster, OH
740-767-3570
This park offers 28 miles of hiking trails including a section of the Buckeye Trail and a loop trail which goes around the lakeshore. The trails offer scenic vistas and unique outcroppings. Dogs are allowed at this park including on the hiking trails and in the campgrounds. While pets are not allowed on the designated swim beach, there is a certain pet area on the beach where they can take a dip in the water. Pets must be leashed, cleaned up after and are not allowed inside any buildings. This park permits hunting in certain areas.

Providence Metropark
US 24 at SR 578
Grand Rapids, OH
419-832-6004
metroparkstoledo.com/
This park offers a 1.5 mile trail and the Towpath Trail which was left from the original Miami and Erie Canal. The trail connects Providence Metropark with Bend View and Farnsworth Metroparks. Dogs must be on leash and please clean up after them. The park also has canal boat rides and mill demonstrations, but dogs are not allowed at either attraction. The park entrance is located on U.S. 24 at State Route 578 across from Grand Rapids.

Towpath Trail
US 24 at SR 578
Grand Rapids, OH
419-832-6004
metroparkstoledo.com/
Three metroparks, Farnsworth, Bend View and Providence Metroparks are connected by this 8 mile Towpath Trail which runs along the Maumee River. From Farnsworth to Bend View Overlook is a 2.2 mile trail. From Bend View Overlook to Providence is a 6.1 mile trail. From Farnsowrth to Indianola Sheltherhouse is a .5 mile trail. From Indianola Shelterhouse Trailhead to Roche de Bout is a .6 mile trail. Dogs must be on leash and please clean up after them. The Providence Metropark entrance is located on U.S. 24 at State Route 578 across from Grand Rapids.

Three Creeks Metro Park
3860 Bixby Road
Groveport, OH
614-891-0700
metroparks.net/3creeks.htm
Dogs are allowed at the park but not on the trails except for the designated Pet Trail which is at least 1 mile long. Pets must be on leash, under control and cleaned up after. To get there from I-270, take S.R. 33 east to the S. Hamilton Rd. exit. Turn right and go about 1 mile to Bixby Rd. and turn right. The park entrance is about 1 mile on the right.

Quail Hollow State Park
13480 Congress Lake Avenue
Hartville, OH
330-877-1528
This 700 acre park offers rolling meadows, marshes, pines and woods. Dogs are allowed at the

park including on the 19 miles of hiking trails. Pets must be leashed, cleaned up after and are not allowed inside any buildings. This park does not permit hunting.

Prairie Oaks Metro Park
2009 Amity Road
Hilliard, OH
http://www.metroparks.net/prairieoaks.htm
614-891-0700
This park features some of the oldest and largest burr oak and sycamore trees in Ohio, dating back to before European settlement of the area. Dogs are allowed at the park but not on the trails except for the designated Pet Trail called the Sycamore Plains Trail. Pets must be on leash, under control and cleaned up after. This nature trail is located at 2009 Amity Road, about 1 mile north of Roberts Road. To get to the trailhead from I-270, take I-70 west to Plain City-Georgesville Rd./S.R. 142 exit and go south for about .5 miles. Turn left on High Free Pike. Go about 1.2 miles to Roberts Rd. and turn left. Go about 1 mile on Roberts. Rd. to Amity Rd. and turn left. The entrance is on the left.

Rocky Fork State Park
9800 North Shore Drive
Hillsboro, OH
937-393-4284
Dogs are allowed at this park including on the 2 miles of hiking trails and in the campgrounds, but not in the water. Pets must be leashed, cleaned up after and are not allowed inside any buildings. This park permits hunting in certain areas.

Hinckley Reservation Metropark
various entrances
Hinckley Township, OH
216-351-6300
Features of this park include the 90-acre Hinckley Lake and Whipp's Ledges with elevations rising 350 Hinckley Lake which were formed over 250 million years ago. The Hinckley Lake Trail is a 3 mile loop trail around Hinckley Lake, along West Drive, State Road, East Drive, and Bellus Road in Hinckley Township. Park entrances are located off Bellus and State roads. Dogs are allowed on a 8 foot or less leash and need to be cleaned up after.

Kelleys Island State Park
Division Street
Kelleys Island, OH
419-746-2546

Beaches, campgrounds and six miles of hiking trails which lead to scenic vistas are offered at this 676 acre park. Dogs are allowed on the hiking trails and in the campgrounds. While pets are not allowed at the small 100 foot swimming beach, they are welcome to join you at the "long beach" but you will need to keep them away from other beachgoers. Pets must be leashed and cleaned up after and are not permitted inside any buildings. Limited hunting is allowed in designated areas of the park. To get there you will need to take a ferry to the island. Kelleys Island Ferry Boat Line operates year round, weather permitting, and offers passenger and limited vehicle service from Marblehead, Ohio to the island. Leashed pets are welcome on the ferry. Once on Kelleys Island, go west on E. Lakeshore Drive and turn right on Division Street. The park is at the end of Division Street on the right.

Lake Milton State Park
16801 Mahoning Avenue
Lake Milton, OH
330-654-4989
The reservoir at this park is popular for boating, swimming and fishing. Dogs are allowed at the park including on the almost 2 miles of hiking trails and in the campgrounds. While dogs cannot go on the designated swim beach, they can go into the water by the park office or by the lighthouse. Pets must be leashed, cleaned up after and are not allowed inside any buildings. This park permits hunting in certain areas.

Indian Lake State Park
12774 State Route 235 N
Lakeview, OH
937-843-2717
This lake is popular for boating and fishing. Dogs are allowed at this park including on the 7 miles of hiking trails and in the campgrounds. While they cannot go on the sand beach, dogs can go into the water at a designated spot. From the main beach, head north along the sidewalk which will make a sharp left turn to the water. From that point on dogs can take a dip in the water. Pets must be leashed, cleaned up after and are not allowed inside any buildings. This park permits hunting in certain areas. To get there from Columbus, take U.S. 33 towards Marysville. The park is about an hour and 15 minutes northwest on U.S. 33.

Rocky River Reservation Metropark
various entrances
Lakewood, OH
216-351-6300
This park features the Rocky River and massive cliffs that rise above the willows, sycamores and cottonwoods. There are many trails in the park that wind through the valley's deep floodplain forests, meadows and wildflowers. The Valley Parkway Trail is a 13 mile trail which goes from the Scenic Park Picnic Area off the Detroit Road entrance in Lakewood, south along Valley Parkway to Bagley Road in Bereau, connecting with Mill Stream Run Reservation Metropark. Park entrances are off of Detroit Road, Riverside Drive, Wooster and Mastick roads, Brookway Lane, Cedar Point, Old Lorain, Spafford, Barrett and Bagley roads, and Shepard Lane. Dogs are allowed on a 8 foot or less leash and need to be cleaned up after.

Highbanks Metro Park
9466 Columbus Pike (US Rt 23 N)
Lewis Center, OH
614-891-0700
metroparks.net/highbanks.htm
This park's name comes from the 100 foot high shale bluffs that tower over the Olentangy State Scenic River. Pets are allowed at the park but not on the trails except for the designated 3.5 mile Pet Trail which is an unimproved trail. Pets must be on leash, under control and cleaned up after. This trail is closed when skiing conditions exist. To get there from I-270, take U.S. 23 north about 3 miles. The park entrance is on the left, just before Powell Rd.

Hocking Hills State Park
19852 State Route 664 South
Logan, OH
740-385-6842
This state park offers a great natural setting with towering cliffs, caves, waterfalls and deep hemlock-shaded gorges. Dogs are allowed at this park including on the 26 miles of hiking trails, at the picnic areas, in the caves like Old Man's Cave, and in the campgrounds. This park does not allow hunting. Pets must be leashed and cleaned up after. Pets are not allowed inside any buildings or at the nearby nature preserve. To get there from Columbus, take U.S. 33 East through Lancaster to Logan and exit onto State Route 664 South.

Lake Logan State Park
30443 Lake Logan Road
Logan, OH
740-385-6842
This park features one of the best fishing lakes in Ohio. Dogs are allowed at the park on the 4 miles of hiking trails including a section of the Buckeye Trail and in the campgrounds. While dogs cannot go onto the designated swim beach, they can go into the water outside of the swim beach area. Pets must be leashed, cleaned up after and are not allowed inside any buildings. This park does not allow hunting.

Ohio State Nature Preserves
various locations
Logan, OH
614-265-6561
ohiodnr.com
While dogs are allowed in Ohio State Parks, they are not allowed the Ohio State Nature Preserves. Please check our other parks listings for dog-friendly places to hike, picnic or just to enjoy nature.

Salt Fork State Park
14755 Cadiz Road
Lore City, OH
740-439-3521
This is Ohio's largest state park and offers forested hills, open meadows, valleys and numerous streams. Dogs are allowed at the park including on the 14 miles of hiking trails and in the campgrounds. While dogs cannot go on the designated swim beach, they can go into the water at the boat launching ramps. However, please use caution to make sure that your dog does not get too close to the boats. Pets must be leashed, cleaned up after and are not allowed inside any buildings. This park permits hunting in certain areas.

Mohican State Park
3116 State Route 3
Loudonville, OH
419-994-5125
This park offers more than 13 miles of hiking including trails that lead to waterfalls, views of the lake and a scenic wooden bridge. Dogs are allowed at the park including on the hiking trails and in the campgrounds. Pets must be leashed, cleaned up after and are not allowed inside any buildings. This park does not allow hunting.

Malabar Farm State Park
4050 Bromfield Road
Lucas, OH
419-892-2784

This farm reflects the agricultural tradition of Ohio. It also focuses on Louis Bromfield's life and philosophies. Bromfield was a Pulitzer Prize winner and the designer of the farm house located at the park. Dogs are allowed at this park including on the 12 miles of field and forest hiking trails and in the campgrounds. Pets must be leashed, cleaned up after and are not allowed inside any buildings. This park does not permit hunting.

Ohio State Nature Preserves
various locations
Marblehead, OH
614-265-6561
ohiodnr.com
While dogs are allowed in Ohio State Parks, they are not allowed in Ohio State Nature Preserves. Please check our other parks listings for dog-friendly places to hike, picnic or just to enjoy nature.

Side Cut Metropark
River Road
Maumee, OH
419-893-2789
metroparkstoledo.com
This park has trails as well as a monument for the 1794 Battle of Fallen Timbers. Trails at this park range from .5 miles to over 4 miles in length. Dogs on leash are allowed and please clean up after them. This park is located along River Road between Jerome and Wayne Roads.

North Chagrin Reservation Metropark
various entrances
Mayfield Village, OH
216-351-6300
This park offers trails and picnic areas. The Buttermilk Falls Parkway Trail is a 4 mile trail that goes from Chardon Road in Willoughby Hills, south along Buttermilk Falls Parkway in Mayfield Village's trails and two spurs west to SOM Center Road. Park entrances are off of SOM Center (Route 91), Chagrin River and Chardon roads. Dogs are allowed on a 8 foot or less leash and need to be cleaned up after.

Lake Hope State Park
27331 State Route 278
McArthur, OH
This 2,900 acre park offers hiking trails, swimming, fishing, boating, camping and picnicking. Dogs are allowed at this park including on the 17 mile of hiking trails and in the campgrounds. While dogs are not allowed on the designated swim

beach, they can go on leash into the water outside of the swim beach area. Pets must be leashed, cleaned up after and are not allowed inside any buildings. Hunting is permitted in the adjacent state forest.

Mary Jane Thurston State Park
1-466 State Route 65
McClure, OH
419-832-7662
This park is situated along the Maumee River and is popular for camping, boating, fishing and hunting. Dogs are allowed at the park including the campgrounds and the hiking trails. There is about a one mile section of the Bukeye Trail that passes through the park. Pets must be leashed and cleaned up after. Pets are not allowed inside any buildings.

James A Garfield Nat.Historic Site
8095 Mentor Avenue
Mentor, OH
440-255-8722
nps.gov/jaga/
James A. Garfield became the 20th President of the United States in 1881. In 1876, before his presidency, Garfield purchased a farmhouse which he renovated and expanded. Today the farmhouse is a National Historic Site. Dogs are not allowed inside the buildings at this park, but you can walk your pooch on almost 8 acres and view the many historic sites from the outside. Pets must be on leash and please clean up after your dog.

Mitchell Memorial Forest
Zion Road
Miami Township, OH
513-521-PARK
hamiltoncountyparks.org
This 1,336 acre park offers a moderate rated 1.3 mile nature trail. Pets are allowed but must be on a 6 foot or less leash, under control, and picked up after. Pooper scooper dispensers are located at each trailhead and are available from the Park District Rangers. To get to the park, take I-74 to Cleves exit, right on Route 128 to Miamitown, right on Harrison Avenue, right on East River Rd., left on Gum Rum Road, right on Buffalo Ridge Road, and left on Zion Road to the park entrance on the right.

Shawnee Lookout Park
Miamiview Road
Miami Township, OH
513-521-PARK

hamiltoncountyparks.org
This 1,156 acre park has several nature trails which are rated moderate and range in length from 1.3 to 2 miles. Pets are allowed but must be on a 6 foot or less leash, under control, and picked up after. Pooper scooper dispensers are located at each trailhead and are available from the Park District Rangers. To get to the park, take I-275 to Kilby Road exit, right on Kilby Road, right onto U.S. 50, and left onto Lawrenceberg Road. Then cross the bridge, go right on Miamiview Road to the entrance on the left (about 1.5 miles).

Buckeye Lake State Park
2905 Liebs Island Road
Millersport, OH
740-467-2690
Constructed as a canal feeder lake in 1826, Buckeye Lake is Ohio's oldest state park. It is a popular vacation spot and offers activities such as swimmer, skiing, boating and fishing. Dogs are allowed at this park including in the water. Pets must be leashed, cleaned up after and are not allowed inside any buildings. This park permits hunting in certain areas.

Mount Gilead State Park
4119 State Route 95
Mount Gilead, OH
419-946-1961
Hiking, camping and fishing are popular activities at this 200 acre park. Dogs are allowed at the park including on the 6 miles of hiking trails and in the campgrounds. Trail access is from the park office, campground and Route 42 entrance. Pets must be leashed, cleaned up after and are not allowed inside any buildings. This park does not allow hunting.

Deer Creek State Park
20635 Waterloo Road
Mount Sterling, OH
740-869-3124
Located in the heart of Ohio's agricultural country, this park offers nine miles of hiking trails that go through meadows and scattered woodlands, boating, swimming, fishing, hunting and camping. Dogs are allowed at this park including on the hiking trails, in the campgrounds and in a designated portion of the lake. While dogs cannot go on the designated swimming beach they are allowed in the pet swim area. People are not allowed in the water at the pet area. Pets must be leashed (except when in the water), cleaned

up after and are not allowed inside any buildings or the golf course. To get the the pet swim area, take Route 207 to Picnic Area/Road 9. Go down the road towards the lake and there should be signs.

Madison Lake State Park
20635 Waterloo Road
Mount Sterling, OH
740-869-3124
This 180 acre park features a 106 acre lake which is popular for boating, fishing and swimming. There is a short one half mile hiking trail that goes through woodlands and along the shoreline. Dogs are allowed at this park including on the hiking trail and in a designated portion of the lake. While dogs cannot go on the swimming beach they are allowed in the pet swim area which is located before the swimming beach (there should be signs). People are not allowed in the water at the pet swim area. Pets must be leashed (except when in the water), cleaned up after and are not allowed inside any buildings. This park allows hunting in certain areas.

Metro Parks Bike and Hike Trail
various locations
Munroe Falls, OH
330-867-5511
This 32 mile long trail follows an old railroad trail. It was one of the first rail to trail conversions in the country. Hiking, biking, jogging and skiing are all popular activities along this path. Pets are allowed but need to be leashed and cleaned up after. Pets are not allowed in picnic areas. The trail goes from Hudson Drive in Stow and heads north to Route 8 in Boston Heights. About half of the trail parallels Route 8. In Munroe Falls, the path follows the Cuyahoga River and there you might see Great Blue Herons, Canada Geese, ducks and frogs. The park system has toilets along the path at Springdale, Route 91, Boston Mills Road, Stow Silver Springs Park and Route 303. To get to the trail, there are many starting points including off N. Main Street, State Route 91, just north of the Cuyahoga River in Munroe Falls and off Boston Mills Road, one mile west of Olde Eight Road in Boston Heights.

Munroe Falls Metro Park
521 S. River Road
Munroe Falls, OH
330-867-5511
Activities at this park include hiking, fishing, nature observation, cross country skiing and sledding. The park has an easy rated 2.2 mile trail called the Indian Spring Trail. Pets are allowed at the park and on the trail but need to be leashed and cleaned up after. Pets are not allowed in picnic areas. From north of Cuyahoga Falls, take Route 8 to Graham Road and then turn left. Go to State Route 91 (Darrow Road) and turn right. Cross over the Cuyahoga River, cross some railroad tracks and pass Munroe Falls Avenue. After passing Munroe Falls Ave., go about .25 miles to South River Road. Turn left on South River Road and go about 1 mile to the park entrance which will be on the right.

Dillon State Park
5265 Dillon Hills Drive
Nashport, OH
740-453-4377
This park offers 8 miles of hiking trails including the Ruffed Grouse Nature Trail (3/4 mile) and the Licking Bent Trail (6 miles) which skirts the lakeshore. Dogs are allowed at the park including on the hiking trails and in the campgrounds, but not in the water or inside any buildings. Pets must be leashed and cleaned up after. This park permits hunting in certain areas.

Nelson Kennedy Ledges State Park
State Route 282
Nelson Township, OH
440-564-2279
This small but scenic 167 acre park offers rugged cliffs and unique rock formations. There are 3 miles of hiking trails including paths to formations like Devil's Icebox, Indian Pass and Old Maid's Kitchen. Dogs are allowed at this park including on the hiking trails and in the picnic area. Pets must be leashed and cleaned up after. This park does not permit mountain biking or hunting. The park is located northwest of Warren, on State Route 282, between U.S. 422 and State Route 305.

Punderson State Park
11755 Kinsman Road
Newbury, OH
440-564-2279
Dogs are allowed at this park including on the 14 miles of hiking trails and in the campgrounds. While dogs cannot go on the designated sand swim beach, they can swim outside of the swim beach area. Pets must be leashed,

cleaned up after and are not allowed inside any buildings or on the golf course. This park does not allow hunting.

Silver Creek Metro Park
5199 Medina Line Road
Norton, OH
330-867-5511
Activities at this park include hiking, fishing, boating and horseback riding. The park has several easy rated trails ranging in length from 1.2 to 2 miles. Pets are allowed at the park and on the trails but need to be leashed and cleaned up after. Pets are not allowed in picnic areas. To get there, take I-76/U.S. Route 224 west to State Route 21 and go south. Take State Route 21 south about 3 miles to State Route 585. Take State Route 585 south and immediately exit at Hametown Road. Turn left on Hametown Road and go .5 miles to the park entrance on the left.

Maumee Bay State Park
1400 State Park Road
Oregon, OH
419-836-7758
Dogs are allowed at this park including on the 10 miles of hiking trails and in the campgrounds. While dogs are not allowed at any beaches, either on the Lake Erie shore or at the park's inland lake, dogs are permitted to take a dip in the water at the end of the inland lake which is on the south side of the road. Pets must be leashed even when in the water, cleaned up after and are not allowed inside any buildings. This park permits hunting in certain areas.

Pearson Metropark
State Route 2
Oregon, OH
419-691-3997
metroparkstoledo.com/
One of the last remaining stands of the Great Black Swamp is located at this park. Amenities at the park include a large playground, ball fields, tennis courts, pedalboats and a fishing pond. Trails at this park range in length from about 1 mile to 3 miles, with about a total of about 20 miles in trails. The trailhead begins at the Packer-Hammersmith Center. Dogs must be on leash and please clean up after them. The park is located on Lallendorf Road at State Route 2.

Deep Lock Quarry Metro Park
5779 Riverview Road
Peninsula, OH

330-867-5511
Activities at this park include hiking, fishing and nature observation. The park has several trails including an easy rated part of the statewide Buckeye Trail, the moderate rated 13 mile Cuyahoga Trail and the easy rated 1.2 mile Quarry Trail. Pets are allowed at the park and on the trails but need to be leashed and cleaned up after. Pets are not allowed in picnic areas. The park is located off Riverview Road, .75 miles south of State Route 303 in Peninsula.

Stonelick State Park
2895 Lake Drive
Pleasant Plain, OH
513-625-7544
Dogs are allowed at this park including on the 5 miles of hiking and mountain biking trails and in the campgrounds. Dogs are not allowed in the water. Pets must be leashed, cleaned up after and are not allowed inside any buildings. This park permits hunting in certain areas.

Catawba Island State Park
4049 East Moores Dock Rd.
Port Clinton, OH
419-797-4530
This day use park offers a small beach, launch ramps, fishing pier and picnic areas. Swimming is permitted but there are no lifeguards. Dogs are welcome at the beach but need to be leashed when not in the water. The park is off of State Route 53.

East Harbor State Park
Route 269
Port Clinton, OH
419-734-4424
Located on the shores of Lake Erie, this park is popular for boating, fishing, swimming and camping. Dogs are allowed at the park including on the 7 miles of hiking trails and in the campgrounds. While they are not allowed on any sandy beach, dogs can take a dip in the pond which is located off the exit road, next to the shelter road. Pets must be leashed, cleaned up after and are not allowed inside any buildings. This park does not allow hunting. To get there from Cleveland, take State Route 2 West to State Route 269 North. The park is located on State Route 269. To get there from Port Clinton, go east on Route 163 to Route 269 north.

Shawnee State Park
4404 State Route 125
Portsmouth, OH

740-858-6652
This park is located in the Appalachian foothills near the banks of the Ohio River and is surrounded by state forest. Dogs are allowed at this park including on the miles of hiking trails in the state forest and in the campgrounds. While dogs are not permitted on the designated swim beach, they can go into the water outside of the swim beach area. Pets must be leashed, cleaned up after and are not allowed inside any buildings. The adjacent state forest permits hunting.

Perry's Victory & International Peace Memorial
93 Delaware Ave
Put-in-Bay, OH
419-285-2184
nps.gov/pevi/
This island memorial was built between 1912 and 1915 to commemorate the American naval triumphs by Commodore Perry in 1812 and 1813. It also commemorates the Rush-Bagot Agreement between the United States and Canada that resulted in peaceful relations between the two countries. While dogs are not allowed in the monument, they are welcome to accompany you around the grounds. Pets must be leashed and cleaned up after. To visit this memorial you will need to take a ferry or airplane. Dogs are allowed on the Miller Boat Line ferry which transports both passengers and vehicles to the island. To get there from the east, take the Ohio Turnpike to US 250. Take US 250 north to State Route 2 west. Take State Route 2 to 53 N/Catawba Island exit to the Miller Boat Line. Once on the island there are many ways to get around including a shuttle bus or golf cart rentals, both of which allow leashed dogs. The park is open daily from the end of April to mid-October.

West Branch State Park
5708 Esworthy Road
Ravenna, OH
330-296-3239
This park is popular with boaters, fishermen, swimmers, hikers and campers. Dogs are allowed at the park including on the 40 miles of hiking trails and in the campgrounds, but not in the water. Pets must be leashed, cleaned up after and are not allowed inside any buildings. This park permits hunting in certain areas.

Forked Run State Park
63300 State Route 124
Reedsville, OH
740-378-6206
Located in the heart of Appalachia, this park offers forested hills and a lake. Dogs are allowed at the park including on the 4 miles of hiking trails and in the campgrounds. Dogs cannot go onto the swim beach but they can go into the water at the boat dock. Just be sure to watch out for the boats. Pets must be leashed, cleaned up after and are not allowed inside any buildings. This park permits hunting in certain areas.

Furnance Run Metro Park
3100 Brush Road
Richfield, OH
330-867-5511
Activities at this park include hiking, nature observation, cross country skiing, sledding and ice skating. The park has four easy-rated trails that are about one mile long each. One trail is called the H.S. Wagner Daffodil Trail which is where thousands of daffodil bulbs have been planted. Pets are allowed on the trail but need to be leashed and cleaned up after. Pets are not allowed in picnic areas. The Daffodil trail is located at 3100 Brush Road, east of Brecksville Road in Richfield.

Sharon Woods Park
Lebanon Road
Sharonville, OH
513-521-PARK
hamiltoncountyparks.org
This 755 acre park has several nature and paved trails which range from easy to moderate and about 1 to over 2.5 miles in length. Pets are allowed but must be on a 6 foot or less leash, under control, and picked up after. Pooper scooper dispensers are located at each trailhead and are available from the Park District Rangers. To get to the park, take I-275 to the Sharonville (Route 42) exit. Then head south on Route 42/Lebanon Road to the park entrance on the left.

South Chagrin Reservation Metropark
various entrances
Solon, OH
216-351-6300
This park's forest contains hemlock, white oak, red oak, shagbark hickory trees, and beech and sugar maples. There are several trails at the park including the Hawthorn Parkway Trail. This trail is 3.5 miles in length.

427

It runs along Hawthorn Parkway from the Harper Ridge Picnic Area, just north of Solon Road in Solon to the Squaw Rock Picnic Area, continuing north to Chagrin River Road with a loop back along Sulphur Springs Drive to Hawthorn Parkway. Park entrances are located off Miles, Chagrin River, SOM Center (Route 91), Cannon, Harper, and Richmond roads. Dogs are allowed on a 8 foot or less leash and need to be cleaned up after.

South Bass Island State Park
Catawba Avenue
South Bass Island, OH
419-285-2112
This 32 acre park is popular for fishing, boating and swimming. However, dogs are not allowed on the beach. They are welcome to walk around with you in the rest of the park and stay overnight at the campground. There are not really any hiking trails here. Pets must be leashed and cleaned up after. Pets are not allowed inside any buildings. This park does not allow hunting. To get there you will need to take a ferry to South Bass Island. Miller Boat Line departs from Catawba and Jet Express departs from Port Clinton. Both ferries go to the island and both allow leashed dogs. Jet Express requires that dogs stay on the outside deck. While both ferries offer passenger transportation, Miller Boat Line also offers limited vehicle service. Once on the island, you can either drive your own car or rent a dog-friendly golf cart. From the village, take Catawba Avenue until you reach the park.

Buck Creek State Park
1901 Buck Creek Lane
Springfield, OH
937-322-5284
The park is located in an agricultural area and offers about 2,000 acres of land and 2,000 acres of water. Dogs are allowed at this park including on the over 7.5 miles of hiking trails, at the beach, at the picnic areas and in the campgrounds. Pets must be leashed, cleaned up after and are not allowed inside any buildings. This park allows hunting in designated areas. To get there from Columbus, take Interstate 70 west to exit #62. Take Route 40 west 3 miles to the first traffic light, then turn right on North Bird Road to Buck Creek Lake. The park is about 48 miles from Columbus. To get there from Columbus, take Interstate 70 west to exit #62 to Route 40 west. Go 3

miles to the first traffic light and turn right on North Bird Road to Buck Creek Lane.

Winton Woods
Winton Road
Springfield Township, OH
513-521-PARK
hamiltoncountyparks.org
This 2,465 acre park has several nature and paved trails which range from easy to moderate and .7 to 1.7 miles in length. Pets are allowed but must be on a 6 foot or less leash, under control, and picked up after. Pooper scooper dispensers are located at each trailhead and are available from the Park District Rangers. Campgrounds are located at this park. To get to the park, take I-275 to the Winton Road-Forest Park exit, and head south on Winton Road to the park entrances on left and right. The park is also accessible via the Ronald Reagan-Cross County Highway. Take the Winton Road exit, and head north on Winton Road to the park entrances on the left and right.

Grand Lake Saint Marys State Park
834 Edgewater Drive
St Marys, OH
419-394-3611
Once the largest man-made reservoir in the world, this lake is popular for swimming, boating, fishing, camping and hunting in certain areas. While dogs are not permitted on any designated swimming beaches, they can go into the water outside of the buoyed areas. Dogs are also welcome at the campgrounds. Pets must be leashed, cleaned up after and are not allowed inside any buildings. To get there from Columbus, head west on Route 33 to St. Marys (33 becomes 29 at St. Marys). Stay on the four lane road to Route 364, then go south to 703. Take 730/364 East to the park entrance.

Lake Loramie State Park
834 Edgewater Drive
St Marys, OH
419-394-3611
This park has one of the original canal feeder lakes and it offers many recreational activities including swimming, boating, fishing and hiking. There are over eight miles of trails including a portion that follows the Miami-Erie Canal and a trail that is part of the Buckeye Trail. Dogs are welcome at the park including the trails and campground. While dogs are not

permitted on the swimming beaches, they can go into the water outside of the designated swim areas. Pets must be leashed, cleaned up after and are not allowed inside any buildings.

Tinker's Creek State Park
10303 Aurora Hudson Road
Streetsboro, OH
440-564-2279
Hiking and fishing are popular activities at this park. Dogs are allowed at the park including on the 3.5 miles of hiking trails. Pets must be leashed, cleaned up after and are not allowed inside any buildings. This park does not allow hunting.

Big Creek Reservation Metropark
various entrances
Strongsville, OH
216-351-6300
The highlight of this park is Lake Isaac which is classified as a "glacial pothole" created thousands of years ago and today is a waterfowl refuge, especially for migrant waterfowl. There are several trails at the park including the Big Creek Trail. This trail is 7.5 miles long and goes from Brookpark Road, following Big Creek Parkway, South to Whitney Road and connecting with Mill Stream Run Reservation via Valley Parkway in Strongsville. Park entrances are off Brookpark, Eastland, Snow and Stumph roads, West 130th Street, East Bagley, Fowles and Whitney Roads, and Valley Parkway. Dogs are allowed on a 8 foot or less leash and need to be cleaned up after.

Oak Openings Preserve Metropark
State Route 2
Swanton, OH
419-826-6463
metroparkstoledo.com/
Trails at this park range in length from .5 miles to 17 miles. The trailhead begins at the Buehner Center at the Mallard Lake area. Part of the Wabash Cannonball Trail runs through the park. Accessible paths are graded and lead to public facilities and along the west side of Mallard Lake. Children 14 and under can fish in Mallard Lake and adults with fishing licenses can fish in Evergreen Lake. Dogs on leash are allowed and please clean up after them. This park is located two miles west of Toledo Express Airport off State Route 2.

Ohio State Nature Preserves
various locations
Toledo, OH

614-265-6561
ohiodnr.com
While dogs are allowed in Ohio State Parks, they are not allowed in the Ohio State Nature Preserves. Please check our other parks listings for dog-friendly places to hike, picnic or just to enjoy nature.

Swan Creek Preserve Metropark
Airport Highway or Glendale Ave.
Toledo, OH
419-382-4664
metroparkstoledo.com/
This park offers great views of the floodplain and in the spring offers a show of wildflowers.

Toledo City Parks
various addresses
Toledo, OH
419-936-2875
In general, dogs are allowed on leash at Toledo city parks but not inside buildings. Please clean up after your pets.

University/Parks Trail
various addresses
Toledo, OH
419-535-3050
metroparkstoledo.com/
This 6.3 mile paved trail is used for walking, jogging, bicycling and rollerblading. The trail runs between King Road in Sylvania and the University of Toledo. This trail also has connector trails to Wildwood Preserve Metropark, Ottawa Park and Franklin Park Mall. Dogs must be on leash and please clean up after them. To get to the trail, park at one of the following places: Tam-O-Shanter, McCord Road, Wildwood Preserve, Ottawa Market, Ottawa Hills Municipal Building, the University of Toledo Southwest Academic Center or Ottawa Park.

Wildwood Preserve Metropark
W. Central Avenue
Toledo, OH
419-535-3050
metroparkstoledo.com/
One of the best tallgrass prairies in Ohio is preserved at this park. Trails in the park range from about .5 miles to over 2 miles in length. There is also a connector trail which leads to the University/Parks Trail. The trailhead begins at the Metz Visitor Center. The park is located on West Central Avenue, between Corey and Reynolds.

Sycamore State Park
4675 N. Diamond Mill Road
Trotwood, OH

513-523-6347
This 2,384 acre park is located amidst farmland and offers meadows, woodlots and still waters. Hiking, picnicking, fishing and horseback riding are popular activities at the park. There are about eight miles of hiking trails including the three mile shady Ghost Hedge Nature Trail and the one and a half mile meadow Beech Ridge Trail. This park allows hunting on about 1,500 acres. Dogs are allowed at the park including on the hiking trails. Pets must be leashed, cleaned up after and are not allowed inside any buildings.

Van Buren State Park
12259 Township Rd. 218
Van Buren, OH
419-832-7662
Fishing, boating, picnicking and hiking are all popular activities at this park. Dogs are allowed at the park including the campgrounds and on the six miles of multi-use trails used for hiking, horseback riding and mountain biking. The trails range from gentle terrain in the scenic woodlands to steep ravines. Pets must be leashed and cleaned up after. Pets are not allowed inside any buildings. This park permits fishing and hunting. The park is located in the agricultural plains of northwest Ohio.

Farnsworth and Bend View
Metroparks
8505 US 24
Waterville, OH
419-878-7641
metroparkstoledo.com
This park is a long narrow belt of parkland that slopes gently from 30 foot bluffs to the banks of the Maumee River. An 8 mile towpath trail runs through these parks. There is a 2.2 mile trail from Farnsworth to Bend View Overlook. Dogs on leash are allowed and please clean up after them.

Caesar Creek State Park
8570 East S.R. 73
Waynesville, OH
513-897-3055
This 3,700 acre park features clear blue waters, woodlands, meadows and steep ravines. Boating, hiking, fishing, hunting (in certain areas) and camping are all popular activities at the park. There are over forty miles of hiking trails many of which offer scenic views. The park also has a pioneer village with

fifteen historic buildings depicting life in the early 1800s. And for children, there are playgrounds located in day use areas and campgrounds. Dogs are allowed at this park including on the hiking trails and in the campgrounds. While dogs are not permitted on the swimming beaches, they can go into the water outside of the designated swim areas. Pets must be leashed, cleaned up after and are not allowed inside any buildings. To get there from Cincinnati, take Interstate 71 north to Route 73. Turn left onto Route 73. Go about 6 miles and the park entrance will be on the right.

Little Miami State Park
8570 East State Route 73
Waynesville, OH
513-897-3055
This state park offers a popular fifty mile long paved bicycle trail that was once a railroad right-of-way. The park averages sixty-six feet in width over a distance of about fifty miles. Canoeing on the Little Miami River is another popular activity at the park. Dogs are allowed at this park including on the trail. Pets must be on a six foot or shorter leash, cleaned up after and are not allowed inside any buildings. This park does not allow hunting. There are many access points to the trail including the following staging areas. The Corwin Staging Area is located in the heart of Corwin, Ohio. Access is available off of Route 73 or Route 42. The Morrow Staging Area is in the middle of Morrow, Ohio. Access is off of Route 22/3 or Route 123. The Loveland Staging Area is in the middle of downtown Loveland, Ohio next to the municipal building. Access is off of Route 48 or Interstate 275. The Morrow and Loveland staging areas offer picnic areas and restrooms.

Findley State Park
25381 State Route 58
Wellington, OH
440-647-4490
This heavily wooded state park offers scenic hiking trails and swimming. Dogs are allowed at the park including on 10 miles of hiking trails and in the campgrounds. While they cannot go onto the swim beach, dogs can go into the water at the shoreline outside of the swim beach area. Pets must be leashed, cleaned up after and are not allowed inside any buildings. This park permits hunting in certain areas. To get there from Cleveland, take Interstate 480

west to Route 10 west and continue to Route 20 west. Then go to Route 58 south and go ten miles. The park is 2.5 miles south of Wellington on the east side of the road.

Adams Lake State Park
14633 State Route 41
West Union, OH
740-858-6652
Located in Ohio's Bluegrass region, this 49 acre park offers boating, fishing, picnicking and trails. Dogs are allowed at this park including in the water and on the accessible 3/4 mile walking path. Pets must be leashed, cleaned up after and are not allowed inside any buildings. This park does not allow hunting.

Inniswood Metro Gardens
940 South Hempstead Road
Westerville, OH
614-891-0700
metroparks.net/inniswood.htm
While dogs are not allowed at the gardens, they are allowed on the designated Pet Trail called the Chipmunk Chatter Trail. The trail is located near the North Street entrance, off Sunbury Road. Pets must be on leash, under control and cleaned up after. To get to the park from I-270, take the S.R. 3/Westerville Rd. exit south to Dempsey Rd. and turn left. Go about 1 mile to Hempstead Rd. and turn left. The park entrance is about 1/2 mile on the right.

Cowan Lake State Park
1750 Osborn Road
Wilmington, OH
937-382-1096
Dogs are allowed at this park including on the 4 miles of hiking trails and in the campgrounds. Dogs are not allowed in the water. Pets must be leashed, cleaned up after and are not allowed inside any buildings. This park permits hunting in certain areas.

Glenwood Gardens
10405 Springfield Pike
Woodland, OH
513-521-PARK
hamiltoncountyparks.org
This 335 acre park offers a couple of trails including the Garden Loop, a 1.1 mile paved easy trail and the Wetland Loop, a 1.7 mile nature. Pets are allowed but must be on a 6 foot or less leash, under control, and picked up after. Pooper scooper dispensers are located at each trailhead and are available from the Park District Rangers. The park is

located on Route 4 at the intersection of Glendale-Milford Road.

John Bryan State Park
3790 State Route 370
Yellow Springs, OH
937-767-1274
This is the most scenic state park in western Ohio, according to the Ohio State Parks division. The park features a limestone gorge cut by the Little Miami River and a portion of the gorge is designated as a national natural landmark. Over nine miles of hiking and mountain biking trails follow the river gorge and meander through woodlands. This park also offers picnicking and camping. Dogs are allowed at the park including on the hiking trails and in the campgrounds. Pets must be leashed, cleaned up after and are not allowed inside any buildings. This park allows fishing and bow hunting in certain areas.

Oregon

Lewis and Clark National Historical Park
92343 Fort Clatsop Rd
Astoria, OR
503-861-2471
nps.gov/lewi/index.htm
Dogs must be on leash and must be cleaned up after in the park grounds. They are not allowed in visitor center or in the rooms in the fort. The park features hiking, nature walks and more.

Bullards Beach State Park
Hwy 101, 2 miles North of Bandon
Bandon, OR
541-347-2209
oregonstateparks.org/park_71.php
This scenic park sits at the mouth of the Coquille River on Oregon's south coast, and features a historic lighthouse that is located at the end of the beach access road. During the summer months they offer evening history, nature and entertainment programs in the park's amphitheater. Park amenities also include a variety of trails, 4.5 miles of beach, historic sites and displays, a boat launch, ADA restrooms, interpretive signage, and various land and water recreation. The park is open daily from 7 a.m. to sunset. Dogs of all sizes are allowed for no additional fee. Dogs

may not be left unattended at any time, and they must be on no more than a 6 foot leash, and cleaned up after. Dogs are allowed on all the trails and throughout the park. There is camping at this park with full RV hook-ups, and dogs are allowed at tent or RV sites, but not at the yurts.

Bridal Veil Falls State Park
M.P. 28 on the Columbia River Scenic H
Bridal Veil, OR
800-551-6949
Located in a large timber stand, this park offers nice grassy areas, picnic tables, and restrooms, all within easy walking distance from the parking area. One trail is an upper walking/interpretive trail that takes visitors around the precipice of the cliffs of the Gorge. Sign boards along the way point out distinctive native wild plants that grow abundantly in the area. The lower trail takes visitors downhill to the base of the 120 foot Bridal Veil Falls and is about a mile round trip. They say it is dangerous to walk along the bridge over the Historic Highway to view the falls, and to PLEASE view the falls from the trail. The falls can be fully appreciated from the deck of a viewing platform. Dogs of all sizes are allowed. Dogs must be leashed at all times and cleaned up after. They are allowed throughout the park and on the trails.

Azalea Park
Chetcho River Road
Brookings, OR
541-469-2021
A labor of love by volunteers brought this beautiful park and it's long rich history to life again. They filled the garden with year-round plants with more than 400 rhododendrons, bulbs, annuals, shrubs, and ornamental trees. Now it is a place for rest and relaxation, picnics, weddings, birthday parties, reunions, civic affairs, and concerts (including the American Music Festival Free Summer Concert Series). Well behaved dogs are allowed. They must be on a lead, under the owners' control at all times, and cleaned up after. They do not provide clean up bags.

Oregon Caves National Monument
19000 Caves Highway
Cave Junction, OR
541-592-2100
nps.gov/orca/index.htm
Dogs must be on leash and must be cleaned up after on all trails. They

are not allowed in any caves.

Cape Arago State Park
End of Cape Arago H
Coos Bay, OR
800-551-6949
oregonstateparks.org/park_94.php
Cape Arago sits on a scenic
headland jetting out into the ocean,
making it a premium place for
watching ships, marine mammals,
birds, terrestrial wildlife, and the off-
shore colonies of seals and sea lions
at Shell Island. The trail is closed
March 1- June 30 to protect seal
pups. There is a network of hiking
trails that connect Cape Arago with
nearby Sunset Bay and Shore Acres
State Parks. These trails give the
hiker opportunities to experience the
coastal forests, seasonal wildflowers,
and the spectacular ocean vistas of
the area. There is a fully enclosed
observation building that has
interpretive panels describing the
history of the Simpson estate along
the way. From points along the trail
you can see views of Gregory Point
and the Cape Arago lighthouse. The
park is open year round from 8 a.m.
until sunset. Dogs on lead at all
times are allowed, and pets must be
cleaned up after. Dogs may not be
left unattended at any time. There is
a campground here that offers a
variety of activities and recreation.

Shore Acres State Park
Coos Bay Road
Coos Bay, OR
541-888-3732
oregonstateparks.org/park_97.php
Perched on rugged sandstone cliffs
high above the ocean, Shore Acres
is a combination of beautiful natural
and constructed features. There is a
garden here that has flowers from all
over the world. Although pets are not
allowed in the garden, they are
allowed throughout the day use
areas and trails, and may be left in
your auto (weather permitting) while
you tour the gardens. There is a
network of hiking trails that connect
Sunset Bay with nearby Shore Acres
and Cape Arago State Parks. These
trails give the hiker opportunities to
experience the pristine coastal
forests, seasonal wildflowers, and
the spectacular ocean views. There
is a fully enclosed observation
building that has interpretive panels
describing the history of the Simpson
estate along the way. From points
along the trail you can see views of
Gregory Point and the Cape Arago
lighthouse. The park is open year
round from 8 a.m. until sunset.

Crater Lake National Park
PO Box 7
Crater Lake, OR
541-594-3100
nps.gov/crla/index.htm
Dogs must be on leash and must be
cleaned up after in park. Dogs must
remain in the developed portions of
the park and are not allowed on the
dirt trails or in the backcountry.
They are allowed on the roads and
the sidewalks. There is a road and
sidewalk surrounding Crater Lake
so you and your dog may view the
lake and walk quite a ways around
it. Dogs are not allowed in any
buildings. Dogs are allowed in the
campgrounds on leash in the park.

Cove Palisades State Park
7300 SW Jordan Road
Culver, OR
541-546-3412
oregonstateparks.org/park_32.php
This popular year round
recreational park features a myriad
of land and water recreational
opportunities, a store, restaurant,
marina and rental services, a variety
of planned activities and
celebrations, and nearly 10 miles of
hiking trails that give access to
areas rich in wildlife and splendid
scenery. This park also has a
designated off-leash area for your
pet at the Deschutes campground.
A leash no longer than 6 feet is
required elsewhere in the park.
Dogs of all sizes are allowed, but
they must be cleaned up after and
under owners' control at all times.
For those wanting to camp, there is
a full service campground at this
park.

John Day Fossil Beds National
Monument
32651 Highway 19
Kimberly, OR
541-987-2333
nps.gov/joda/index.htm
Dogs must be on leash and must be
cleaned up after. Dogs are only
allowed in the developed areas and
a few designated trails.

Hart Mountain National Antelope
Refuge
P.O. Box 111, 18 South G Street
(Fish and Wildlife Complex)
Lakeview, OR
541-947-3315
This 278,000-acre refuge has one
of the west's most expansive wildlife
habitats free of domestic livestock.
Originally this park was set aside in
the 1930s for the conservation of

pronghorn antelope, and now acts
for protection and restoration of
native ecosystems for the public's
enjoyment and education. There is
also a wide variety of land and water
recreation available. Potable water,
compressed air, and restrooms are
available at the refuge headquarters.
Dogs of all sizes are allowed. Dogs
may not be left unattended, and all
pets must be leashed. Dogs used for
hunting during the waterfowl or
upland bird hunts, are permitted to
be unleashed as long as they remain
under strict voice control. Dogs are
allowed on the trails (trails not
maintained). There is primitive
camping here, but none of them
have any RV hook-ups, drinking
water, firewood, or fire rings.

Yaquina Head Outstanding Natural
Area
750 Lighthouse Drive
Newport, OR
541-574-3100
Home to the tallest lighthouse in
Oregon, this day-use park also offers
an interpretive center, and the
headlands provide visitors with one
of the most accessible wildlife and
ocean viewing locations on the
Pacific Coast. The lighthouse is
undergoing restoration, and may not
be available to the public for a time
to come; the grounds are open all
year from sunrise to sunset. Dogs of
all sizes are allowed. They must be
on no more than a 6 foot leash,
cleaned up after, and friendly. Dogs
are allowed on the trails and down to
the beach, but they are not allowed
in the bird nesting areas or where
otherwise posted.

Forest Park
NW 29th Ave & Upshur St to
Newberry Rd
Portland, OR
503-823-7529
This city park is the largest city park
in the US at almost 5,000 acres. A
forested park, it has a massive tree
canopy with substantial undergrowth,
allowing the park to serve as a
natural air purifier, water collector,
and erosion controller. Some of the
amenities include a natural area,
guided tours, hiking/biking/equestrian
trails, a vista point, and more than
112 bird and 62 mammal species.
Dogs of all sizes are allowed
throughout the park. Dogs must be
friendly, well behaved, leashed and
cleaned up after at all times, and
displaying tags showing proof of
current license and rabies
vaccination. Dogs must be under

their owner's control at all times.

Portland Rose Gardens
various locations
Portland, OR
503-823-7529
There are three main rose gardens in Portland. The Internation Rose Test Garden in Washington Park is one of the world's most famous rose gardens. It is a popular tourist site with great views and more than 8,000 roses. Ladd's Addition Rose Garden, located at SE 16th and Harrison, displays over 3,000 roses. The Peninsula Park Rose Garden, located at N. Ainsworth between Kerby and Albina, offers more than 8,800 fragrant roses. Dogs may accompany you to all of the rose gardens, but pets must be leashed and you are required to clean up after your dog.

Powell Butte Nature Park
SE 162nd Avenue and Powell Blvd
Portland, OR
503-823-7529
This 592 acre park is an extinct volcano and is Portland's second largest park. There are over 9 miles of hiking trails which are popular with mountain bicyclists, horseback riders, and hikers. Dogs must be leashed and people must clean up after their dogs.

Tom McCall Waterfront Park
Naito Parkway
Portland, OR
503-823-7529
This waterfront park follows the Willamette River, between SW Clay and NW Glisan. The park offers walking and bicycling trails. Dogs are allowed but must be leashed and people need to clean up after their pets.

Washington Park
SW Park Place
Portland, OR
503-823-7529
This 129 acre park offers hiking trails and a popular rose garden. Dogs must be leashed and people must clean up after their dogs.

Malheur National Wildlife Refuge
3691 Sodhouse Lane
Princeton, OR
541-493-2612
This park consists of more than 185,000 acres of prime wildlife habitat, and is famous for its diversity and spectacular concentrations of wildlife. This park also protects 120,000 acres of a vast complex of

wetlands. Birdwatchers and wildlife enthusiasts can enjoy the more than 320 species of birds, 58 species of mammals, 10 species of native fish, and a number of reptiles on the refuge. Dogs of all sizes are allowed. Dogs must be leashed at all times and properly cleaned up after. Dogs must remain in the car on the Central Patrol Road (a scenic drive road). They are allowed throughout the park and on the trails. The refuge and museum are open daily from dawn to dusk. The office and visitor center are open Monday through Thursday, 7:00 a.m. to 4:30 p.m., and Friday from 7:00 a.m. to 3:30 p.m. With the help of volunteers, the visitor center is open most weekends during spring and summer. They are closed on the weekends in winter.

Jewel Meadows Wildlife Area
79878 Hwy 202
Seaside, OR
503-755-2264
The reserve is for all the wildlife and birds here and it provides a winter habitat and supplemental feeding area for the Roosevelt elk, which are most visible from November through April. The largest viewing area is at the headquarters, and they offer parking for eighty vehicles and an RV lane, a central interpretive kiosk, a large lawn area, picnic tables, brochures, and flush toilets (the only toilets in the park). There are four elk viewing areas in the reserve along Hwy 202. Dogs are may journey this reserve with their owners, and they are allowed to go on the short trails to the viewing areas. Dogs must be on leash at all times, be well behaved, and quiet so as not to disturb the wildlife.

Mt Hood National Forest
65000 E Hwy 26 (Visitors' Center)
Welches, OR
888-622-4822
mthood.info/usdafs/index.html
With more than a million acres, and 189,200 acres of designated wilderness, this forests' diverse ecosystems support a large variety of plants, fish, mammals, bird species, and recreation. Dogs of all sizes are allowed for no additional fee. Dogs are allowed throughout the forest, except at the Timberline Lodge, park buildings, or public swim areas. Dogs are allowed on some of the cross country ski trails. Dogs may not be left unattended at any time, and they must be leashed

and cleaned up after. There are also several campground areas and a beautiful scenic drive to the top of Mt Hood.

Pennsylvania

Locust Lake State Park
Burma Road/Hwy 1006
Barnesville`, PA
570-467-2404
A mountain lake surrounded by beautiful forests with plenty of recreation, easy to difficult hiking trails, and a lot more are all offered at this 1,089 acre park. Dogs are allowed at the park for day use from mid-October to the beginning of April only. They are not allowed when the campground is open from early April to mid-October. Dogs must be well behaved, under their owner's control, on no more than a 6 foot leash or crated, and cleaned up after at all times. Dogs must be licensed with proof of vaccinations. Aggressive dogs are not allowed. Dogs may not be left unattended outside at any time and if in a vehicle-for very short times. Dogs must stay on selected pet routes/trails and areas; they may not be in designated swim areas, park buildings, or in the campground area.

Upper Delaware Scenic and Recreational River National Park
274 River Road
Beach Lake, PA
570-685-4871
nps.gov/upde/index.htm
Dogs must be on leash and must be cleaned up after in most of the national park areas. You must follow state and local park rules. The park features auto touring, camping, boating, fishing, and more.

Ricketts Glen State Park
695 State Route 487
Benton, PA
570-477-5675
The main attraction at this 13,000+ acre park is the Glens Natural Area, a registered National Natural Landmark, where visitors will find 21 waterfalls along its Falls Trail. Dogs must be well behaved, under their owner's control, leashed or crated, and cleaned up after at all times (exceptions during hunting season). Dogs must be licensed and have proof of all vaccinations. Aggressive dogs are not allowed. Dogs may not

be left unattended outside at any time and may only be left alone in a vehicle for VERY short periods. Dogs must stay on selected pet routes/trails and areas; they may not be in designated swim areas or in park buildings.

Bushkill Falls
P.O. Box 151
Bushkill, PA
888-628-7454
visitbushkillfalls.com
This park features a series of 8 waterfalls and natural beauty. Dogs on leash are allowed in the park. Dogs are allowed on most of the trails throughout the park. Dogs are not allowed in the buildings and must be cleaned up after.

Delaware National Scenic River Park
HQ River Rd off Rt 209
Bushkill, PA
570-588-2452
nps.gov/dela/index.htm
Dogs on leash are allowed in most park areas. They are not allowed at Smithfield Beach and McDade Trail during certain seasons. Call the park for more details. Dogs are not allowed in any of the campsites in New Jersey.

Keen Lake
Route 6
Carbondale, PA
570-488-6161
keenlake.com
Dogs on leash are allowed in the park and camping areas. They are not allowed in the pool, buildings, or public beaches. The park features boating, swimming, picnicking and camping. Located in Poconos Mountains.

Cherry Springs State Park
4639 Cherry Springs Road
Coudersport, PA
814-435-5010
This park offers a variety of events (mostly stargazing), year round environmental interpretive programs, and the Susquehanna Trail passes nearby for miles of hiking. Dogs are allowed at the park for day use. Dogs must be well behaved, under their owner's control, on no more than a 6 foot leash or crated, and cleaned up after at all times. Dogs must be licensed with proof of vaccinations. Aggressive dogs are not allowed. Dogs may not be left unattended outside at any time and in a vehicle for very short times. Dogs must stay on selected pet routes/trails and areas; they may not be in park

buildings, or in the campground area.

Susquehannock State Forest
Hwy 6
Coudersport, PA
814-274-3600
This state forest is home to numerous diverse ecosystems that support a large variety of plants, fish, mammals, bird species, and year round recreation. There are several multi-use trails; the main trail is an 85 mile loop through some magnificent scenery, especially in the fall, and there are also 16 vistas points for greater viewing. Primitive camping is allowed. Dogs must be under their owner's control, leashed, and cleaned up after at all times.

Buchanan's Birthplace State Park
Hwy 16
Cove Gap, PA
717-485-3948
Birthplace to one of our most renowned Presidents, this park shares the history of his and his youngest daughter's very important contributions to the country, and offers a variety of recreational pursuits and an environmental education program as well. Dogs are allowed; they must be well behaved, on no more than a 6 foot leash or crated, and cleaned up after at all times. Dogs must be licensed with proof of vaccinations. Aggressive dogs are not allowed. Dogs may not be left unattended outside at any time and if in a vehicle-for very short times. Dogs must stay on selected pet routes/trails and areas. They are not allowed in swim areas or in park buildings.

Delaware Water Gap National Recreation Area
In the Gap Road
Delaware Water Gap, PA
570-426-2435
nps.gov/dewa
Visitors can enjoy a variety of recreational pursuits here, walk the trails that have been used for hundreds of years, or enjoy all the benefits the Middle Delaware River has to offer. Dogs of all sizes are allowed at this park for no additional fee. Dogs must be well behaved, leashed, cleaned up after, and owners are responsible for them at all times. Dogs may not be left unattended at any time. Dogs are allowed on the trails unless otherwise marked, and they are not

allowed on beaches.

Peace Valley Park
Peace Valley Park Creek Road
Doylestown, PA
215-345-1097
Dogs on leash are allowed in the park and lake. The park features hiking, fishing, camping, and more.

Mountain Vista Campground
50 Taylor Dr
East Stroudsburg, PA
570-223-0111
mtnvistacampground.com
Dogs on leash are allowed in the park and camping areas. The park features camping, hiking, swimming, and more.

Delaware and Lehigh National Heritage Corridor
1 South Third Street 8th Floor
Easton, PA
610-923-3548
nps.gov/dele/index.htm
Dogs must be on leash and must be cleaned up after in most of the corridor. You must follow local and state park rules and pet policies. The corridor features auto touring, boating, hiking, and more.

Pool Wildlife Sanctuary, Wildlands Conservancy
3701 Orchid Place
Emmaus, PA
610-965-4397
This 72 acre wildlife area sits alongside Little Lehigh Creek, and in addition to the beautifully kept grounds, there are a variety of informative and interactive exhibits to explore. Dogs are allowed on the grounds, but they are not allowed on the nature trails or in buildings. Dogs must be under their owner's control, leashed, and cleaned up after at all times.

Presque Isle
301 Peninsula Drive
Erie, PA
814-833-7424
This 3,200 acre sandy peninsula park on Lake Erie allows for the states only "seashore", and in addition to its historical significance, it is a geological and biological diverse area with many endangered species. There is an educational center on site with interactive exhibits and a 75 foot observation tower. Dogs must be well behaved, under their owner's control, be on no more than a 6 foot leash or crated, and cleaned up after at all times. Dogs must be licensed and have

proof of all vaccinations. Aggressive dogs are not allowed. Dogs may not be left unattended outside at any time and may only be left alone in a vehicle for VERY short times. Dogs must stay on selected pet routes/trails and areas; they may not be in designated swim areas or in park buildings.

Evansburg State Park
US Route 422
Evansburg, PA
Pets must be leashed. This park is over 1000 acres.

Fort Necessity National Battlefield
One Washington Parkway
Farmington, PA
724-329-5512
nps.gov/fone/index.htm
Dogs must be on leash and must be cleaned up after in the site. It is open daily 9am-5pm. This is the site of the opening battle of the French and Indian War that began a seven year struggle between Great Britian and France for control of North America. The site features hiking and picnicking.

World's End State Park
Hwy 154
Forks, PA
570-924-3287
Nestled in a narrow valley with a swift moving stream, this park offers incredible scenery (especially the fall foliage), interpretive programs, and over 20 miles of moderate to difficult trails. Dogs are allowed at the park for day use. Dogs must be well behaved, under their owner's control, on no more than a 6 foot leash or crated, and cleaned up after at all times. Dogs must be licensed with proof of vaccinations. Aggressive dogs are not allowed. Dogs may not be left unattended outside at any time and in a vehicle for very short times. Dogs must stay on selected pet routes/trails and areas; they may not be in designated swim areas, park buildings, or in the campground area.

Fort Washington State Park
Bethlehem Pike
Fort Washington, PA
Dogs must be leashed. This park offers over 3.5 miles of hiking trails.

Allegheny Portage Railroad National Historic Site
110 Federal Park Road
Gallitzin, PA
814-886-6150
nps.gov/alpo/index.htm

Dogs must be on leash and must be cleaned up after on the grounds. Dogs are not allowed in buildings. The site features hiking, museum, picnicking and more. The Allegheny Portage Railroad was the first railroad constructed over the Allegheny Mountains.

Stony Valley Railroad Grade Trail
2001 Elmerton Avenue
Harrisburg, PA
717-787-9612
This former RR corridor now offers 22 miles of multi-use trail and is quite popular because of its location and beauty. Well mannered dogs are allowed on the trail. Dogs must be under their owner's control, leashed, and cleaned up after at all times.

Canoe Creek State Park
William Penn H
Hollidaysburg, PA
814-695-6807
This 958 acre day use area has a 155 acre lake allowing for a variety of land and water recreational opportunities. Dogs are allowed; they must be well behaved, on no more than a 6 foot leash or crated, and cleaned up after at all times. Dogs must be licensed with proof of vaccinations. Aggressive dogs are not allowed. Dogs may not be left unattended outside at any time and if in a vehicle-for very short times. Dogs must stay on selected pet routes/trails and areas. They are not allowed in swim or campground areas, or in park buildings.

Hyner Run State Park
86 Hyner Park Road
Hyner, PA
570-923-6000
Nestled in a small valley amid steep mountains, this park offers a cozy getaway for picnicking, hiking (they are the eastern trailhead for the 50-mile Donut Hole Trail system), and a variety of other recreation. Dogs are allowed; they must be well behaved, under their owner's control, on no more than a 6 foot leash or crated, and cleaned up after at all times. Dogs must be licensed with proof of vaccinations. Aggressive dogs are not allowed. Dogs may not be left unattended outside at any time and if in a vehicle-for very short times. Dogs must stay on selected pet routes/trails and areas. They are not allowed in swim or campground areas, or in park buildings.

Hyner View State Park
Hyner Mountain Rd
Hyner, PA
570-923-6000
The central attraction at this state park is the overlook wall giving visitors breathtaking views of the Susquehanna River and the nearby mountains. It is also a favorite spot for hang gliding. Dogs are allowed; they must be well behaved, under their owner's control, on no more than a 6 foot leash or crated, and cleaned up after at all times. Dogs must be licensed with proof of vaccinations. Aggressive dogs are not allowed. Dogs may not be left unattended outside at any time and if in a vehicle-for very short times. Dogs must stay on selected pet routes/trails and areas.

Lehigh Gorge State Park
Lehigh Gorge Drive
Jim Thorpe, PA
570-443-0400
This 4,548 acre park follows about 30 miles along the Lehigh River with some 26 miles of abandoned railroad grade creating a number of year round land and water recreational opportunities, and some great sightseeing areas. Dogs must be well behaved, under their owner's control, leashed or crated, and cleaned up after at all times (exceptions during hunting season). Dogs must be licensed and have proof of all vaccinations. Aggressive dogs are not allowed. Dogs may not be left unattended outside at any time and may only be left alone in a vehicle for VERY short periods. Dogs are not allowed in designated swim areas or in park buildings.

Loyalsock Trail
Hwy 87
Loyalsockville, PA
570-745-3375
lycoming.org/alpine/Index.htm
Lush forest, spectacular views, waterfalls, unique rock formations, and miles of blazed trails to explore it all, are offered on this almost 60 mile linear trail. It begins in Wyoming County, PA and ends on Meade Road 2 miles from Hwy 220 near Laporte. Dogs are allowed on the trail, and they may be off lead if they are under very good voice control, although caution is needed for dogs off lead as the area has porcupines. Dogs must be under their owner's control and cleaned up after, especially on the trail.

Driftstone on the Delaware

2731 River Rd
Mount Bethel, PA
888-355-6859
driftstone.com
Dogs on leash are allowed in the park and camping areas. The park features swimming, hiking, boating, camping, and more.

New Hope Towpath
3620 Windy Rd
New Hope, PA
This towpath dirt walking trail begins in the center of New Hope. There are a number of dog-friendly restaurants in New Hope.

Ohiopyle State Park
171 Dinner Bell Road
Ohiopyle, PA
724-329-8591
Offering over 19,000 recreational acres, this park's several trails take visitors by waterfalls, unique geological formations, overlook platforms offering stunning views, and there are more than 14 miles of the Youghiogheny River Gorge running through the heart of the park. Dogs are allowed at the park for day use for no additional fee. Dogs must be quiet, well behaved, under their owner's control, leashed or crated, and cleaned up after at all times. Dogs must be licensed and have proof of all vaccinations. Aggressive dogs are not allowed. Dogs may not be left unattended outside at any time and may only be left alone in a vehicle for VERY short times. Dogs must stay on selected pet routes/trails and areas; they may not be in designated swim areas or in park buildings, and pet food may not be left outside.

Oil Creek State Park
305 State Park Road
Oil City, PA
814-676-5915
Historical interpretive displays/programs, including full-scale building tableaus (movie-set style) depicting the eras of Oil Creek, an excursion train that takes visitors on a 26 mile guided tour of the area, and more are offered at this park. Dogs are allowed throughout the park and on the train for no additional fee (guests with pets must sign a pet waiver for the train rides). Dogs must be on no more than a 6 foot leash or crated, and cleaned up after at all times, and licensed with proof of vaccinations. Aggressive dogs are not allowed. Dogs may not be left unattended outside at any time and if in a vehicle-for very short

times. Dogs must stay on selected pet routes/trails and areas. They are not allowed in swim areas or in park buildings.

Ben Franklin Parkway
Ben Franklin Pkwy and 19th St.
Philadelphia, PA
Ben Franklin Parkway is a large avenue surrounded by Grass and Trees. It is scenic and a good area to walk a dog in downtown Philadelphia.

Deshler-Morris House National Park
5442 Germantown Avenue
Philadelphia, PA
215-596-1748
nps.gov/demo/index.htm
Dogs must be on leash and must be cleaned up after in the park. Dogs are not allowed in the house.

Fairmount Park
4231 N. Concourse Dr
Philadelphia, PA
215-685-0000
This address is the Park commission headquarters, in the park. The park is very big and stretches from the Center of Philadelphia to the northwest. Leashed dogs are allowed.

Manuyunk Towpath and Canal
Main Street
Philadelphia, PA
This is a two mile path in the Manayunk area of Philadelphia. There are a lot of dog-friendly eating places in the area, also.

Pennypack Park
Algon Ave and Bustleton Ave
Philadelphia, PA
balford.com/fopp/
Leashed dogs are allowed at this large 1600 acre city park.

Rittenhouse Square Park
Walnut St and 18th St
Philadelphia, PA
Located in downtown Philadelphia, this park is a gathering spot for people who wish to sit and rest on a bench or on the lawn. Leashed dogs are allowed.

Washington Square Park
Walnut St and 6th St
Philadelphia, PA
Leashed dogs are allowed at this city park.

Hartwood County Park and Amphitheater
215 Saxonburg Blvd

Pittsburgh, PA
412-767-9200
This 629 acre park allows dogs on leash in most of the park and off-leash in an unfenced specified off-leash dog exercise area. Off special interest in the park is the outdoor amphitheater and its Summer Concert Series and other musical events. Your leashed dog is allowed to accompany you to listen to the concerts. There is an off-leash area in the park behind the amphitheater

Highland Park
The Hill Road
Pittsburgh, PA
412-682-7275
This park is home to the Pittsburgh Zoo and the PPG Aquarium, but other popular features include a hilltop walking trail that overlooks a large reservoir and the city's only long-course swimming pool. Dogs are allowed throughout the park with exception to playgrounds and gaming courts. Dogs must be under their owner's control, leashed, and cleaned up after at all times in all areas of the park.

Point State Park
101 Commonwealth Place
Pittsburgh, PA
412-471-0235
A majestic 150 foot tall water fountain, a paved river promenade, dramatic city views, 23 commemorative historic markers, trails that connect the area to several points in the city, and more are offered at this 36 acre park that sits at the tip of the city's "Golden Triangle". Dogs are allowed throughout the grounds; they must be leashed and cleaned up after.

Schenley Park
3898 Boulevard of the Allies
Pittsburgh, PA
412-682-7275
pittsburghparks.org/_76.php
This beautifully landscaped 456 acre park offers reprieve amongst a bustling university and business district with a long list of recreational opportunities, special events/programs, a pool, easy to difficult hiking trails, and a Plaza area. The Plaza, a public green space, offers food, restrooms, lawns and gardens, and free Wi-Fi. Dogs are allowed throughout the park with exception to playgrounds and gaming courts. Dogs are allowed at the Plaza on paved areas only, and they must be under their owner's control, leashed, and cleaned up

after at all times in all areas of the park.

The Duquesne Incline
1220 Grandview Avenue
Pittsburgh, PA
412-381-1665
incline.pghfree.net/
The Duquesne Incline is actually a working museum with 2 original 1877 cable cars that connects the upper and lower levels of the city, and not only does this tram save miles and gives outstanding views of the city, but your pooch can ride too. There is free parking at the bottom, but not at the top. Dogs must be well behaved, under their owner's control, leashed, and cleaned up after at all times.

McConnells Mill State Park
McConnells Mills Road
Portersville, PA
724-368-8091
Rich in environmental and geological education and recreation, this 2,546 acre glacially carved park features an 1800's gristmill, a steep scenic gorge, waterfalls, and river rafting/hiking trails of varying difficulty. Dogs are allowed throughout the park. Dogs may not be left unattended at any time, and they must be leashed and cleaned up after at all times.

Nockamixon State Park
1542 Mountain View Drive
Quakertown, PA
215-529-7300
This 5,283 acre state park has a 1,450 acre lake for a wide variety of land and water recreational opportunities. Dogs are allowed throughout the park and on the trails; they are not allowed at the cabins or in the pool area. Dogs must be well behaved, leashed, and cleaned up after at all times.

Archbald Pothole State Park
Scranton Carbondale H/Hwy 6
Scranton, PA
570-945-3239
Named for a glacially created geological feature that formed about 15,000 years, this 150 acre park offers a variety of educational and recreational opportunities. Dogs of all sizes are allowed for no additional fee. Dogs must be under their owner's control, leashed, and cleaned up after at all times.

Sewickley Heights Park
Fern Hollow Rd
Sewickley Heights, PA
This park west of Pittsburgh has

about 12 miles of trails. Dogs under voice control are allowed off leash throughout the park. There are streams, hills and meadows in the park.

Flight 93 National Memorial Park
109 West Main Street Ste 104
Somerset, PA
814-443-4557
nps.gov/flni/index.htm
Dogs on leash are allowed roadside to view the memorial for the passengers and crew of flight 93 that gave their lives on 9/11.

Johnstown Flood National Memorial
733 Lake Road
South Fork, PA
814-495-4643
nps.gov/jofl/index.htm
Dogs must be on leash and must be cleaned up after on the grounds. Dogs are not allowed in buildings. Hiking and picnicking areas are avabilable. The Johnstown Flood Museum and site is the story of a wealthy resort, the destruction of a working class city, and an inspiring relief effort. Occurring in 1889, over 2000 people died and more were injured when the dam gave thru, making it one of the worst disasters in our Nation's history.

Colton Point State Park
Forest Road
Wellsboro, PA
570-724-3061
This park offers several areas with stunning views of the 800 foot deep, glacially carved canyon (the Grand Canyon of PA.), educational and recreational activities, and miles of hiking trails, including the Turkey Path Trail featuring a 70 foot waterfall about a ½ mile down the trail. Dogs are allowed at the park for day use for no additional fee. Dogs must be well behaved, under their owner's control, on no more than a 6 foot leash or crated, and cleaned up after at all times. Dogs must be licensed with proof of vaccinations. Aggressive dogs are not allowed. Dogs may not be left unattended outside at any time and in a vehicle for very short times. Dogs must stay on selected pet routes/trails and areas; they may not be in designated swim areas, park buildings, or in the campground area.

Leonard Harrison State Park
4797 Hwy 660
Wellsboro, PA
570-724-3061

This 585 acre park offers a variety of educational programs, recreational opportunities, trails (medium to difficult), and an overlook at the visitor center that offers stunning views. Dogs are allowed at the park for day use for no additional fee. Dogs must be well behaved, under their owner's control, on no more than a 6 foot leash or crated, and cleaned up after at all times. Dogs must be licensed and have proof of all vaccinations. Aggressive dogs are not allowed. Dogs may not be left unattended outside at any time and may only be left alone in a vehicle for very short times. Dogs must stay on selected pet routes/trails and areas; they may not be in designated swim areas, in park buildings, or in the campground area.

Heritage Rail Trail County Park
Pershing Avenue
York, PA
717-840-7440
This Rail Trail covers 176 acres over 21 miles, starts in York behind the county Colonial Courthouse and runs to the Maryland state line sharing great scenery, historic sites, a tunnel, and 2 train stations along the way. Dogs are allowed on the trail. They must be leashed, under their owner's control at all times, and kept off the tracks as the railway is operational. Pets must be cleaned up after.

Rhode Island

Beavertail State Park
Beavertail Road
Jamestown, RI
401-884-2010
riparks.com/beaverta1.htm
Displaying some of the most beautiful New England coastline, this park can be enjoyed by car to the 4 overlooks or by foot through various hiking trails. Dogs are allowed for no additional fee; they must have a valid license tag, and owners must carry proof of current rabies inoculation. Dogs must be quiet, well behaved, leashed (6 foot), and properly cleaned up after at all times. They may not be left unattended; with exception for hunting season or dog trials at which time dogs may be left alone in a vehicle. Dogs are not allowed at bathing beaches, or to be washed in any natural body of water.

Fort Wetherill State Park

Fort Wetherill Road
Jamestown, RI
401-423-1771
riparks.com/fortweth.htm
This 61 acre day-use park sits on 100 foot high cliffs offering fantastic views of Newport Harbor and the East Passage of Narragansett Bay in addition to a number of recreational activities. Dogs are allowed; they must be leashed and under their owner's control at all times.

Snake Den State Park
2321 Hartford Avenue
Johnston, RI
401-222-2632
riparks.com/snakeden.htm
This 1000 acre park features self-guided walking trails through floral and forested areas. There is a small parking lot on Brown Avenue, and they are open year round from sunrise to sunset. There are no facilities of any kind. Dogs are allowed on the grounds and the trails; they are not allowed in the working farm area. Dogs must be under their owner's control at all times, and leashed and cleaned up after.

The Aquidneck Land Trust's
Sakonnet Greenway Trail
East Main Road/Hwy 38
Middletown, RI
401-849-2799
ailt.org/trails_sakonnet.html
Being developed in stages, this pathway will eventually provide a 7 mile uninterrupted trail through the Sakonnet Greenway taking in The Glen in Portsmouth past the Newport and Orchard Golf Courses to the recreational complex on Wyatt Road in Middletown. From East Main Road/Hwy 138, the trail can be accessed at Linden Road, or turn onto Mitchell's Lane from E Main Road, Wyatt Road, or Third Beach Road. Dogs must be leashed and under their their owner's control at all times.

Brenton Point State Park
Ocean Drive
Newport, RI
401-849-4562
riparks.com/BRENTON.HTM
This park is located on the grounds of a grand old estate that offer gardens, scenic hiking trails, about 20 picnic tables on a first come first served basis, and outstanding views of where the ocean meets the rocky headlands here. Dogs (2) of all sizes are allowed for no additional fee; they must have a valid license tag,

and owners must carry proof of current rabies inoculation. Dogs must be quiet, well behaved, leashed (6 foot), and properly cleaned up after at all times. They may not be left unattended at any time; with exception for hunting season or dog trials at which time dogs may be left alone in a vehicle. Dogs are not allowed at bathing beaches, and they may not be washed in any natural body of water.

Fort Adams State Park
Harrison Avenue
Newport, RI
401-847-2400
riparks.com/fortadams.htm
In addition to sitting prominently on Newport Harbor with spectacular panoramic views and year round recreation, this historic park is also host to various festivals and concerts. Dogs are allowed for no additional fee; they must have a valid license tag, and owners must carry proof of current rabies inoculation. Dogs must be quiet, well behaved, leashed (6 foot), and properly cleaned up after at all times. They may not be left unattended; with exception for hunting season or dog trials at which time dogs may be left alone in a vehicle. Dogs are not allowed at bathing beaches, or to be washed in any natural body of water.

Roger Williams Park
1000 Elmwood Avenue
Providence, RI
401-785-3510
Nationally declared as one of America's premier historic urban parks, it is multi-recreational/educational and offers the public more than just a "Jewel" of a park with miles of trails, grassy or shady picnic areas, and various year round events. Dogs of all sizes are allowed in the park; they are not allowed in the zoo. Dogs must be under their owner's control, leashed, and cleaned up after at all times.

Watch Hill Lighthouse
14 Lighthouse Road
Watch Hill, RI
401-596-7761
lighthouse.cc/watchhill/
Although the lighthouse is not open to the public, it is a nice 15 minute walk from town to this scenic area, and in addition to the lighthouse there is an 1856 keeper's house, a

1909 fog signal building, garage, and oil house. There is no parking close to the lighthouse. Your pooch is welcome here but they must be leashed and cleaned up after at all times.

South Carolina

Landsford Canal State Park
2051 Park Drive
Catawba, SC
803-789-5800
Rich in natural, cultural, and colonial history, this riverside park still has an intact mill site, locks, and a home from the early 1800's plus interpretive signage, and favorite pastimes here include wildlife viewing, hiking, fishing, and in late May and early June-to watch the spectacular blooms of the white spider lily flowers. Dogs are allowed throughout the park; they must be on no more than a 6 foot leash and under their owner's control at all times.

Audubon Swamp Garden
3550 Ashley River Road/Hwy 61
Charleston, SC
843-571-1266
Boardwalks, bridges, boats, and dikes take visitors through this unique inner world where there is a tremendous diversity of plant, animal, and bird life living among the black swamp waters, forests, and floating islands. Dogs are allowed throughout the park; they must be leashed and under their owner's control at all times.

Charles Towne Landing State Historic Site
1500 Old Town Road
Charleston, SC
843-852-4200
This park reopened in the Fall of 2006 with a few new interesting features such as a re-built replica of an 18th-century trading ship (The Adventure), a new visitors center--complete with a museum and archaeology lab, an interpretive trail, and an Animal Forest. Dogs of all sizes are allowed at no additional fee. Dogs may not be left unattended, and they must be on no more than a 6 foot leash at all times, and be cleaned up after. Pets are not allowed in buildings, the Animal Forest, and on the Adventure, however, they are allowed in most

other outdoor areas while on lead. The park is open daily from 8:30 am to 5 pm.

Hampton Park
corner of Rutledge and Grove
Charleston, SC
charlestoncity.info
This park has a fenced dog run for your pet. Dogs must be on leash when not in the dog run.

James Island County Park
871 Riverland Drive
Charleston, SC
843-795-7275
ccprc.com
James Island County Park is a 643 acre nature-oriented park for family and group use, with many additional activities and facilities. There is tidal creek fishing, peddle boat and kayak rentals, paved trails for walking, biking, skating, a children's Funyard playground, a Spray Play Fountain area (seasonal), a picnic center, and an Off-Leash pet area. Dogs must be leashed when entering and exiting the Dog Park and at all times when outside of the designated off-leash area, and dogs must be current on rabies vaccinations and wear current tags.

Waterfront Park
corner of Vedue Range and Concord
Charleston, SC
843-724-7321
This park is used to a lot of dog traffic. They have doggy fountains and provide clean up bags. Dogs must be on leash.

White Point Gardens
On Murray Street at the end of E Bay Street
Charleston, SC
843-724-7327
The park is open daily from dawn to dusk. Dogs on leash are allowed.

Congaree National Park
48 Old Bluff Road
Columbia, SC
803-776-4396
nps.gov/cosw
This 22,200-acre park protects the largest contiguous tract of old-growth bottomland hardwood forest still in the US. The park's floodplain forest has one of the highest canopies and some of the tallest trees in the eastern US. Enjoy hiking, primitive camping, birdwatching, picnicking, canoeing, kayaking, Ranger guided interpretive walks, canoe tours, nature study, and environmental

education programs. Open all year; Monday to Thursday from 8:30 am to 5 pm, and Friday to Sunday from 8 am to 7 pm. To walk the trails after hours park outside the gate. Well behaved dogs on leash are allowed on the trails and the outside guided tours, but they are not allowed on the Boardwalk or in the buildings.

Finlay Park
930 Laurel Street
Columbia, SC
803-545-3100
A beautiful green oasis in the mist of the city, this 18 acre park offers daily recreation and repose, and it is also host to several special events and festivals throughout the year. Dogs are allowed throughout the park; they must be leashed and under their owner's control at all times.

Saluda Shoals Park
5605 Bush River Road
Columbia, SC
803-731-5208
icrc.net
Located along the banks of the Saluda River, this 300 acre regional park offers many amenities such as paved and unpaved trails for hiking, biking and horseback riding, a river observation deck, accommodations for canoeing and kayaking as well as a boat launch, picnic areas and shelters, a fish cleaning station and more. The park is open daily from dawn to dusk. Dogs on leash are allowed at the park but not in the canoes. There is also an off-leash area in the park.

Towpath Trail and Park
Laurel at Huger Street
Columbia, SC
803-545-3100
In addition to being the location of the world's first electrically operated textile mill and home to the state's oldest, and still operating, hydroelectric plant, this 167 acre park offers an amphitheater, and a great liner walking trail that follows along the canal and Congaree River. Dogs are allowed throughout the park; they must be leashed and under their owner's control at all times.

Rivers Bridge State Historic Site
325 State Park Road
Ehrhardt, SC
803-267-3675
Listed on the National Register of Historic Places, this 390 acre

memorial park provides special programs and guided tours about this area's significance during the Civil War, and they feature a ¾ mile self-guided Battlefield Interpretive Trail. Dogs are allowed throughout the park; they must be on no more than a 6 foot leash and under their owner's control at all times.

Hampton Plantation State Historic Site
1950 Rutledge Road
McClellanville, SC
843-546-9361
Listed as a National Historic Landmark, this park offers interpretive programs, tours, a 2 mile nature trail, fishing, and a 19th century plantation. Dogs of all sizes are allowed at no additional fee. Dogs may not be left unattended at any time, and they must be on no more than a 6 foot leash, and be cleaned up after. Dogs are not allowed in the villas, buildings, or on tours. Dogs must be quiet and well behaved, and they are allowed to walk the trails. From Memorial to Labor Day the park grounds are open daily from 9am-6pm. The remainder of the year, the park is open Th-M 9am-6pm. From Memorial Day to Labor Day, the mansion is open from 11 a.m. to 4 p.m. The remainder of the year, hours are Thursday through Monday, 1 to 4 p.m.

Old Santee Canal Park
900 Stony Landing Road
Moncks Corner, SC
843-899-5200
oldsanteecanalpark.org
In addition to the natural beauty of this 195 acre park, it shares a long cultural, military, and natural history, an 1843 plantation home, many scenic trails and waterways, boardwalks (4 miles), trails, several monthly events, and a museum/heritage center featuring over 12,000 years of the area's past. Dogs are allowed throughout the park and on the boardwalks; they must be leashed and under their owner's control at all times. Dogs are not allowed in buildings.

Charles Pincheny National Historic Site
1254 Long Point Road
Mount Pleasant, SC
843-881-5516
nps.gov/chpi
The historic site was established to show Charles Pinckney's plantation named Snee Farm, his role in the

development of the United States Constitution and the transition of the United States from a group of colonies to a young nation. Dogs on leash are allowed on the grounds but not in the house. They are open all year from 9:00 a.m. to 5:00 p.m.

Palmetto Island County Park
444 Needle Rush Parkway
Mount Pleasant, SC
843-884-0832
ccprc.com
Palmetto Islands County Park is a nature-oriented, 943 acre park designed for family and group use. It is built in a tropical setting, with bikepaths, boardwalks and picnic sites located throughout the park. There are fishing and crabbing docks, an observation Tower with play area, a nature island, seasonal waterpark, and more, Dogs on leash are allowed at this park, but not in the buildings or on the playgrounds.

Ninety Six National Historic Site
1103 Hwy 248
Ninety-Six, SC
864-543-4968
nps.gov/nisi/
Being the home of 2 Revolutionary War battles, the beautiful woods and countryside at this park belie the battles that occurred here; however, the cultural and colonial history is preserved through exhibits, special events, interpretive trails, and reenactments. Dogs are allowed throughout the park; they are not allowed in buildings. Dogs must be leashed and under their owner's control at all times.

Woods Bay State Natural Area
11020 Woods Bay Road
Olanta, SC
843-659-4445
Registered as a Heritage Trust Site, and complete with a nature center and boardwalk, the unique geology here creates diverse ecosystems that support a large variety of plants, fish, mammals, bird species, and recreation. Dogs of all sizes are allowed at no additional fee. Dogs may not be left unattended at any time, they must be on no more than a 6 foot leash, and be cleaned up after. Dogs are not allowed in buildings, but they are allowed on the trails. The park is open daily from 9 am to 6 pm.

Pendleton Village Green
125 E Queen Street
Pendleton, SC
864-646-3782

Located in one of the largest historic districts in America (50+ pre-1850 buildings) and listed on the National Register of Historic Places, the Village Green is home to the landmark Pendleton Farmers Society Hall from whose beginnings brought about the Clemson University, a hall with a very large collection of the area's history and genealogy, and an active business district of eateries and various shops. Dogs are allowed throughout the town; they are not allowed in buildings (unless invited). Dogs must be leashed and under their owner's control at all times.

Oconee Station State Historic Site
500 Oconee Station Road
Walhalla, SC
864-638-0079
In addition to its historic significance as a military outpost in the late 1700's, then as a trading post in the early 1800's (still 2 buildings on site), this 210 acre park offers a fishing pond and a 1½ mile nature trail that leads into a National forest and ends at a beautiful 60 foot waterfall. Dogs are allowed throughout the park; they must be on no more than a 6 foot leash and under their owner's control at all times.

South Dakota

Custer State Park
Highway 16A
Custer, SD
605-255-4515
This 71,000 acre state park is located in the Black Hills. Popular activities at the park include hiking, mountain biking, fishing and more. Many of the hiking trails range in level of difficulty and most of them are between .5 and 3 miles. You can also drive the 18 mile Wildlife Loop Road and look for buffalo (they have a herd of 1,500 bison that freely roam the park), pronghorn antelope, mountain goats, deer, bighorn sheep, elk, wild turkeys and some burros.There is a park entrance fee year round. Pets must be on a 10 foot or less leash when in public use areas and campgrounds. When outside of these areas, pets need to be under immediate control and more than 200 feet from other park guests and pets. Pets are not allowed inside

park buildings or within the posted area at zoned swimming beaches. Remember to clean up after your pet.

Black Hills National Forest
Highway 244
Hill City, SD
605-673-9200
fs.fed.us/r2/blackhills/
This national forest covers 1.2 million acres of land and 450 miles of hiking trails. Some of these trails are located along the Scenic Byway, Highway 244, between Hill City and Mt. Rushmore. It is a nice place to stop and get some exercise before heading over to Mt. Rushmore, since the National Park does not allow dogs on any of its trails. Dogs are welcome on the national forest trails but must be leashed or under strict voice control. Also check your dog for ticks after a hike, especially if he or she was in some tall grass or bushes.

Wind Cave National Park
26611 Hwy 385
Hot Springs, SD
605-745-4600
nps.gov/wica
This park is home to one of the world's longest and most complex caves. The park is open year round from 8 to 5 pm during summer hours and until 4:30 pm winter hours. Dogs are allowed at the park and at the campground (no hookups) for no additional fee, but basically they can only go where your car can go. The campground is open year round except when it snows and they have to close the roads to the camping areas. Dogs are not allowed on the trails, they may not be left unattended, they must be leashed at all times, and cleaned up after.

Badlands National Park
25216 Ben Reifel Rd
Interior, SD
605-433-5361
nps.gov/badl/
This park covers 160 square acres, has America's largest mixed grass prairies, and is home to the Badlands National Monument. Highway 240 is the Badlands Loop Scenic Byway and is 31 1/2 miles long with 14 lookouts. Dogs are not allowed on any of the trails in the park. They are allowed only at the campground or the parking lots. The contact station for the Cedar Pass Campground is on Highway 240, and this campground has an amphitheater. The other campground, White River,

has a visitor's center on Highway 27. The campgrounds are open year round, and there are no hook-ups at either camp. Dogs of all sizes are allowed in the campgrounds. There are no additional fees. Dogs may not be left unattended outside, and only inside if it creates no danger to the pet. Dog must be leashed and cleaned up after.

Mobridge City Park
North Main Street
Mobridge, SD
605-845-2387
This beautiful green park is home to a number of stones that the Indian peoples used as prayer or initiation stones. Dogs are allowed; they must be leashed and under their owner's control at all times.

Dinosaur Park
940 Skyline Drive
Rapid City, SD
605-394-4175
This unique city park is listed on the official National Register of Historic Places. There are a handful of life-sized dinosaurs joined by a paved and hilly walkway. Along with each statue you will find plaques that give details about each dinosaur and its relevance to South Dakota. Leashed dogs are welcome in the park and on the self-guided walking tour, but not in the gift shop. Remember to clean up after your dog.

Memorial Park
Rapid City, SD
605-394-4175
This large downtown city park has much to offer. Paved trails meander through the park and take you to a wonderfully scented rose garden. A piece of history is also located in this park. Two sections of the Berlin Wall are located here and serve as a memorial to the Cold War. The wall is located southwest of the Rushmore Plaza Civic Center. Other park amenities include picnic tables and restrooms. The park is located next to the Holiday Inn at 404 North Fifth Street. Leashed dogs are welcome at the park and you will need to clean up after your pet.

Arrowhead Park
1600 Riverbluff Road
Sioux Falls, SD
605-367-7060
This city park has a nice waterside walking path and picnic areas. Dogs are allowed throughout the park; they must be leashed and under their owner's control at all times.

Falls Park
309 E Falls Park Drive
Sioux Falls, SD
605-367-7430
This park is the birthplace of Sioux Falls. The city was named for the series of waterfalls in the park. Dogs on leash are allowed in the park which offers a nice view of the falls and some paved trails and grass.

Sherman Park
W 12th Street and S Kiwanis Avenue
Sioux Falls, SD
605-367-8222
This city park offers a lot of green and some great picnic and hiking areas; it is open from 5 a.m. to 10 p.m. Dogs are allowed; they must be leashed and under their owner's control at all times.

Tennessee

Red Clay State Historic Park
1140 Red Clay Park
Cleveland, TN
423-478-0339
Offering a rich natural and cultural history, this 263 acre day use park features a 1.7 mile loop trail from behind the amphitheater at the picnic area to an overlook tower. It is also host to a natural spring that has been used since ancient times. Dogs are allowed throughout the park. They must be leashed and under their owner's control at all times.

Sycamore Shoals State Historic Park
1651 W Elk Avenue/Hwy 91/321
Elizabethton, TN
423-543-5808
Rich in natural and cultural history, this site was the first permanent American settlement beyond the first 13 colonies and where the first majority-rule system was implemented. Dogs are allowed throughout the park; they must be on no more than a 6 foot leash and under their owner's control at all times. Dogs may pnly enter buildings if they can be carried.

Shelby Farms
500 Pine Lake Drive
Memphis, TN
901-382-0235

Shelby Farms is the one of the largest urban parks in the United States. At approximately 4500 acres it is five times larger than New York City's Central Park. Park visitors will enjoy walking, fishing, mountain biking, horseback riding, even inline skating, and a lot more. The Lucius E. Burch Jr. State Natural Area is about 700 acres of wetlands and hardwood forest, and is located in the southern portion of Shelby Farms. The park is open daily from sunrise to sunset. Shelby Farms Visitors Center, located on the north side of Patriot Lake, is open daily and staffed Monday through Friday from 8:00 am to 4:30 pm. Dogs must be well behaved, not disturb the wildlife, and be leashed except where allowed to be off lead. Dogs must be cleaned up after.

Meeman-Shelby Forest State Park
910 Riddick Road
Millington, TN
901-876-5215
Bordering the Mississippi River, two-thirds of this 13,467-acre park are forests of large oak, cypress and tupelo. The park also contains two lakes, many miles of hiking trails, and the Meeman Museum and Nature Center. Dogs must be crated, caged, on a leash, or otherwise under physical restrictive control at all times. Pets are prohibited in park inns or cabins (except where rooms and/or cabins have been designated for pets), lodges, public eating places, food stores, the buildings, on designated swimming beaches, and pools at all times. Dogs must be cleaned up after throughout the park.

Bell Meade Plantation
5025 Harding Rd
Nashville, TN
615-356-0501
Pets on leash are allowed on the grounds of the plantation, but not in the buildings.

Centennial Park and Parthenon Reproduction
2500 West End Avenue
Nashville, TN
615-862-8431
nashville.gov/parthenon/
In addition to the numerous recreational pursuits at this premier urban park, visitors can also enjoy Wi-Fi, the off-lead dog park, or the highlight of the park - a full scale reproduction of ancient Greece's Parthenon complete with a 42 foot statue of the goddess Athena. This structure now serves as the city's art

museum. Dogs are allowed throughout the grounds; they are not allowed in buildings or at the pool. Dogs must be leashed and under their owner's control at all times.

Grand Ole Opry Park
2804 Opryland Dr
Nashville, TN
This is a city park surrounding the world-famous concert hall. Leashed dogs are allowed.

J. Percy Priest Lake Park
I-40 and Stewards Ferry Pike
Nashville, TN
There are miles of trails next to this lake. The park is only 15-20 minutes from downtown. Leashed dogs are not allowed in the day use areas but are allowed on the trails.

Percy Warner Park
7311 Highway 100
Nashville, TN
Dogs are allowed on leash. There are many trails in this large park.

Riverfront Park
1st Ave and Broadway
Nashville, TN
Dogs on leash are allowed in this downtown park. There is also a fort, Fort Nashborough to view here. This is where the CityWalk walking tour of downtown starts.

Shelby Park
2021 Fatherland St
Nashville, TN
615-862-8474
Dogs are allowed on leash in the park.

Big South Fork National River and Recreation Area
4564 Leatherwood Rd
Oneida, TN
423-286-7275
nps.gov/biso/index.htm
Dogs must be on leash and cleaned up after. The park is located in Kentucky and Tennessee at the fork of the Cumberland River. it features camping, whitewater rafting, kayaking, canoeing, hiking, fishing, and more.

Patriot Park
Light #7, Parkway
Pigeon Forge, TN
This is a nice city park with a Jogging and Walking trail. Dogs on leash are welcome.

Pinson Mounds State Archaeological Park

460 Ozier Road/Hwy 197
Pinson, TN
731-988-5614
Rich in pre-historic culture, this park is home to ancient ceremonial mounds and related earthworks. Interpretive programs are offered, plus they have a nature trail, a boardwalk leading to an overlook of the river, picnic areas with grills, and miles of hiking trails. Dogs are allowed in the park; they are not allowed in the museum. Dogs must be leashed and under their owner's control at all times.

Shiloh National Military Park
1055 Pittsburg Landing Rd
Shiloh, TN
731-689-5696
Dogs must be on leash and must be cleaned up after. The park features auto touring, hiking, and picnicking. It is open all year 8am-5pm except Christmas. Shiloh Battlesite was preserved in 1894 for being the first major Civil War battlesite.

Obed Wild and Scenic River
208 North Maiden St
Wartburg, TN
423-346-6294
nps.gov/obed/index.htm
Dogs must be on leash and must be cleaned up after in the National park. Dogs are allowed on leash throughout the park. The park is located in the Cumberland Plateau of Tennessee with over 45 miles of creeks and rivers. It features hiking, fishing, whitewater boating, camping, swimming in most areas. It is open all year round.

Texas

Barton Creek Greenbelt Preserve
3755 B Capital of Texas Hwy
Austin, TX
512-472-1267
This popular greenbelt follows a creek and offers about 7 miles of walking, hiking and mountain biking trails. There are also several popular swimming holes along the creek. Dogs are allowed, but must be on a leash. Some of the more popular access points to the trails are Zilker Metropolitan Park, and Loop 360 (south of MoPac/Loop 1).

Town Lake
2100 Barton Springs Road
Austin, TX

512-974-6700
This is a popular walking and swimming spot for people and dogs. Dogs must be on a 6 foot or less leash. The park offers 10 miles of walking, hiking and bicycling trails. There are many beaches located along the lake. From March through early November at dusk, you can also watch the bats fly out from under the popular Congress Avenue Bridge at this park. Playgrounds, picnic tables, and restrooms are available at Town Lake. There are many access points to this park, including Zilker Metropolitan Park at 2100 Barton Springs Road. To get there from I-35, take the Riverside exit. Go west on Riverside towards downtown. After you pass Congress Avenue, turn left onto Barton Springs. Go about 2 miles to the park. The entrance will be on the left.

Zilker Metropolitan Park
2100 Barton Springs Road
Austin, TX
512-974-6700
ci.austin.tx.us/zilker/
This is one of Austin's most popular parks. There are about 350 acres and 1.5 miles of trails to enjoy. Leashed dogs are allowed, but not in buildings or areas like the theatre, nature center or the Umlauf sculpture garden. Dogs are welcome at the Zilker Botanical Gardens. A playground, picnic tables, and restrooms are also available at this park. To get there from I-35, take the Riverside exit. Go west on Riverside towards downtown. After you pass Congress Avenue, turn left onto Barton Springs. Go about 2 miles to the park. The entrance will be on the left.

Aransas National Wildlife Refuge
1 Wildlife Circle
Austwell, TX
361-286-3559
This 59,000 acre refuge has the distinction of being a winter host to the last of the migrating whooping cranes, 390 bird species, and home to a wide variety of flora and fauna. Dogs are allowed in the refuge; they are not allowed in buildings, by the edge of the water, or where otherwise noted. Dogs must be short leashed and under owner's care at all times. Small dogs must be picked up and carried when walking by the alligator ponds and larger dogs should be under complete control.

Big Bend National Park
P.O. Box 129

Big Bend National Park, TX
432-477-2251
nps.gov/bibe/
This park is at the big bend of the Rio Grande, and there are 2 entrances; in the North on Highway 118, and in the West on Highway 385. Dogs are not allowed anywhere in the back country, on any of the trails, at the river, or off any of the roads. There are 3 campgrounds, and an RV park. The RV park is the only camp area with full hookups. It is concession operated, sites are on a first come/ first served basis, and full hookup capability is required. Dogs may not be left unattended at any time, they must be leashed or crated at all times, and be cleaned up after.

Bachman Lake Park
Bachman Drive
Dallas, TX
214-670-1923
This park offers a 3 mile path around a lake. The trail is popular with walkers and joggers. The park is located northwest of downtown Dallas, near the Dallas Love Field Airport. Dogs on leash are allowed and you must pick up after your pet. There are heavy fines for dogs off leash and for folks who do not clean up after their pets.

Dallas Nature Center
7171 Mountain Creek Parkway
Dallas, TX
972-296-1955
dallasnaturecenter.org/
Dogs are allowed on leash at this 600 acre park that offers 10 miles of hiking trails. The hikes are rated from very easy meadow trails to difficult steep hikes. The park is located on Mountain Creek Pkwy, about 2 1/2 miles south of Interstate 20.

White Rock Lake Park
8300 E. Lawther Drive
Dallas, TX
214-670-8895
Enjoy a 9 plus mile hiking and bicycling trail at this city lake park. Bring your lunch and enjoy it at one of the many scenic picnic areas. Dogs on leash are allowed and you must pick up after your pet. There are heavy fines for dogs off leash and for folks who do not clean up after their pets.

Asczarate Lake City Park
6900 Delta Drive
El Paso, TX
915-722-3941
In addition to being home to one of only a few Olympic sized competition pools in the county, this 448 acre lakefront park also features picnic areas with grills, easy walking trails, playing fields and courts, playgrounds, a golf course, and many other recreational opportunities. Dogs are allowed throughout the park; they are not allowed at the pool. Dogs must be leashed, well behaved, and cleaned up after at all times.

Farmer's Branch Historical Park
2540 Farmer's Branch Lane
Farmers Branch, TX
972-406-0184
This park was opened in 1986 express the heritage of Farmers Branch, which was founded in 1841. There are a number of historical buildings are 22 acres. Dogs on leash are allowed, and they must be cleaned up after. Dogs are not allowed in the buildings.

Fort Worth Nature Center and Refuge
9601 Fossil Ridge Road
Fort Worth, TX
817-237-1111
fwnaturecenter.org/
Dedicated to the preservation, protection, and education of these complex wetlands and wilderness areas, this center offers a variety of interpretive educational programs and over 20 miles of hiking trails through various habitats rich with wildlife. Dogs are allowed throughout the park and the buildings; they must be leashed and under their owner's control and care at all times.

Hermann Park
Fannin
Houston, TX
713-845-1000
hermannpark.org/
Features at this park include a relecting pool and a 2 mile jogging trail. Picnic tables and restrooms are available. The park is located south of downtown Houston, bordered by South Main, Hermann Drive, Almeda, Brays Bayou and the Texas Medical Center. Dogs on leash are allowed.

Memorial Park
Memorial Drive
Houston, TX
713-845-1000
Leashed dogs are allowed at this park. At over 1,400 acres, this is the largest urban park in Texas. There is a 3 mile popular jogging course. The park is located on Memorial Drive, near the I-610 Loop.

Sam Houston Park
1000 Bagby
Houston, TX
713-845-1000
This 19 acre park is located in downtown Houston. Leashed dogs are allowed outside, but not in the historic houses. The park is located off I-45 and Allen Parkway.

Tranquillity Park
400 Rusk Street
Houston, TX
713-845-1000
Dogs are allowed at this park featuring the Apollo Space Program. Dogs must be on leash and be cleaned up after, and they are not allowed in any of the buildings. The park is normally open from sunrise to sunset, and on some occasions they are open until 11 pm.

Sylvan Beach Park
Sylvan Beach Drive
La Porte, TX
281-471-5020
laportetexas.net/sylvan.htm
Sitting on Galveston Bay, this large and popular city park offers a ¼ mile lighted fishing pier, a huge playground, picnic areas with tables and grills, a gazebo, a rentable pavilion, a train depot, and a Centennial statue. Dogs are allowed throughout the park and on the beach; they are not allowed in the pavilion or in park buildings.

MacKenzie Park
301 Interstate 27
Lubbock, TX
806-775-2687
A major one-stop recreation destination, this large park offers athletic facilities, disc golf, two 18 hole golf courses, an amusement park, playground, an amphitheater, picnic areas, concessionaires, seasonal and special events and festivals, a Prairie Dog Town and a lot more. Dogs are allowed throughout the park; they are not allowed in buildings. Dogs must be leashed and under their owner's control and care at all times.

Guadalupe Mountains National Park
Hwy 62/180
Pine Springs, TX
915-828-3251
nps.gov/gumo
This parks hosts an extensive Permisan Limestone fossil reef. The park is open year-round; visitor

center hours are from 8:00 a.m. to 4:30 p.m., and a bit longer in summer. Dogs on lead are allowed to go to the Sitting Bull Falls and the Last Chance Canyon. Dogs are not allowed on any of the other trails, but they are allowed on the trails in the neighboring Lincoln National Forest. This forest is very rugged, and pets must be watched very closely that they do not step on the plant called Letchigia Cactus. It may even go through tires and must be removed only by surgical means. Dogs are allowed at no additional fee at either of the campgrounds, and the campsites do not have hookups. Dogs may not be left unattended, they must be leashed, and cleaned up after. This park can also be accessed from the New Mexico side on Highway 137.

Aransas National Wildlife Refuge
FM 2040
Rockport, TX
361-286-3559
This 70,000 plus acre refuge is home to cranes, alligators, deer and other wildlife. Dogs must be on leash and are only allowed on certain trails that do not have alligators. Check with park rangers upon arrival to get details about which trails allow pets. To get there from Rockport, take Highway 35 north about 20 miles. Turn right on FM 774 and go about 9 miles to FM 2040. Turn right and follow FM 2040 for 7 miles to the refuge entrance.

Sea Rim State Park
19335 Hwy 87
Sabine Pass, TX
409-971-2559
This 4,141+ acre park is so named for the marsh grasses that grow right into the surf creating a unique environment for a variety of wetland species. The park is currently undergoing hurricane repairs and they should be opening in May 2008 for day use, but they suggest calling ahead to be sure. Camping may not be available at this park for a while. Dogs are allowed and they must be leashed and under their owner's control at all times.

River Walk
Downtown
San Angelo, TX
325-657-4279
Watched over by the bigger-than-life mermaid sculpture holding the Concho Pearl found only in local waters, this recreation area offers a visitor center, a 4 mile hiking trail, a

9-hole golf course, beautiful gardens and more. Dogs are allowed throughout the area; they must be leashed and under their owner's control at all times.

Brackenridge Park
3910 N. St. Marys Street
San Antonio, TX
210-207-3000
There are walking and bicycling paths throughout this 343 acre urban park. Dogs on leash are allowed, and owners must clean up after their pets. The park is located near downtown San Antonio.

Braunig Park
17500 Donop Road
San Antonio, TX
210-207-3000
The lake located in this park is a popular fishing and boating spot. Swimming is not permitted in the lake. Picnic tables, restrooms, and concession stands are available. There is a minimal day use fee. Dogs on leash are allowed, and owners must clean up after their pets. The park is located southeast of downtown, off Highway 37 and Exit 130.

Calaveras Park
12991 Bernhardt Road
San Antonio, TX
210-207-3000
This 140 plus acre park offers picnic tables, restrooms, and concession stands. Dogs on leash are allowed, and owners must clean up after their pets. The park is located southeast of downtown, off Loop 1604.

Eisenhower Park
19399 Northwest Military Drive
San Antonio, TX
210-207-3000
This 320 acre park offers 5 miles of hiking and running trails. Picnic areas and restrooms are available. Dogs on leash are allowed, and owners must clean up after their pets. The park is located south of Camp Bullis.

McAllister Park
Jones-Maltsberger Rd
San Antonio, TX
210-207-3000
There are over 6 miles of hiking and biking trails at this 800 plus acre park. Dogs on leash are allowed, and owners must clean up after their pets. The park is adjacent to the San Antonio International Airport.

Lyndon B. Johnson State Park and Historic Site
199 State Park Road 52
Stonewall, TX
830-644-2252
In addition to the historical detailing of the life of President Johnson and life as it was in the early 1900's, this park also features buffalo, deer, and longhorn herds, a seasonal pool, nature trails, historic structures and many recreational areas. Dogs are allowed throughout the park; they are not allowed in buildings or in the living history farm. Dogs may not be left unattended at any time; they must be well mannered, on no more than a 6 foot leash and under their owner's immediate control at all times.

Cooper Lake State Park/Doctors Creek Unit
1664 Farm Rd. 1529 South
Sulphur Springs, TX
903-395-3100
This day use park of over 700 acres offers a variety of land and water recreational activities. Dogs of all sizes are allowed at no additional fee. Dogs may not be left unattended, they must have current rabies shot records, be on no more than a 6 foot leash, and be cleaned up after. Dogs are not allowed in public swim areas or buildings. Dogs are allowed on the trails.

Challenger Seven Memorial Park
3501 W NASA Blvd
Webster, TX
713-440-1587
Dogs are allowed at this memorial park. Dogs must be leashed and cleaned up after, and they are not allowed in any of the buildings. The park is open from 7 am to 9 pm during the summer and from 7 am to 7 pm in the winter.

River Bend Nature Center
2200 3rd Street
Wichita Falls, TX
940-767-2661
riverbendnaturecenter.org/
There are a variety of interpretive/educational programs at this nature center that offers more than 15 miles of trails, a variety of habitats, flora, and fauna, a 6,700 square foot pavilion for all kinds of gatherings and a butterfly and nature conservatory. Dogs are allowed on the trails and around the grounds; they are not allowed in the conservatory. Dogs must be leashed and under their owner's control and

care at all times.

Utah

Timpanogos Cave National Monument
RR 3 Box 200
American Fork, UT
801-756-5238
nps.gov/tica/index.htm
Pets on leash are allowed on the Canyon Nature trail. Dogs are not allowed on the cave trail. There is an on-site kennel with water provided for free if you decide to go on the cave trail.

Bryce Canyon National Park
PO Box 640201/ On Hwy 63
Bryce, UT
435-834-5322
nps.gov/brca/
This park is famous for it's unique geology, creating vast and unusual limestone formations throughout the region. Dogs are not allowed on any of the trails, the shuttle, the viewpoints, or the visitor's center. The park is open 24 hours a day year round. There are 2 campgrounds; Loop A, the north campground, is open all year, and the Sunset campground is only open for the season. There are no hookups at either campground. Dogs can walk along the road in the campground. There are no additional fees for the dogs. Dogs may not be left unattended, they must be leashed at all times, and cleaned up after.

Cedar Breaks National Monument
2390 West Highway 56 Ste #11
Cedar City, UT
435-586-9451
nps.gov/cebr/index.htm
Dogs must be on leash and must be cleaned up after on paved areas and in campgrounds. Dogs are not allowed on hiking trails or the backcountry.

Natural Bridges National Monument
HC 60 Box 1
Lake Powell, UT
435-692-1234
nps.gov/nabr.index.htm
Dogs must be on leash and must be cleaned up after in campgrounds and paved areas. Dogs are not allowed on hiking trails or in the backcountry.

Arches National Park
PO Box 907

Moab, UT
435-719-2299
nps.gov/arch/index.htm
Pets on leash with cleanup are allowed in the campsites and paved areas of the parks. Dogs are not allowed on any trails or backcountry. They are allowed unattended if well-behaved in the Devil's Garden campground.

Canyonlands National Park
2282 SW Resource Blvd
Moab, UT
435-719-2313
nps.gov/cany/index.htm
Pets on leash are allowed in developed areas, such as campgrounds, paved roads, and the Potash/Shafer Canyon road between Moab and the Island in the Sky. They are not allowed on hiking trails or in the backcountry.

Monument Valley Navajo Tribal Park
P. O. Box 360289
Monument Valley, UT
435-727-5870
Rich in natural and cultural history, this great valley is home to sandstone masterpieces towering to 1,000 feet and surrounded by miles of mesas and buttes, shrubs, trees, and windblown sand. There is a scenic drive through this park; the hours for summer-(May-Sept) 6:00am - 8:30pm, and Winter-(Oct - Apr) 8:00am - 4:30pm. In summer, the visitor center features the Haskenneini Restaurant, which specializes in both native Navajo and American cuisines, and film/snack/souvenir shop. There are year-round restroom facilities. Dogs of all sizes are allowed for no additional fee. Dogs must be leashed at all times, cleaned up after, and under their owner's control. Dogs are allowed throughout the park; they are not allowed in buildings.

Big Water Trail
Mill Creek Canyon Road
Salt Lake City, UT
801-466-6411
This Wasatch-Cache National Forest trail is located in Mill Creek Canyon. It is a 3 mile trail, rated easy, and takes about 2 hours one way. The trail starts at an elevation of 7600 feet and climbs 1240 feet up to an elevation of 8840 feet. The trail leads up to Dog Lake, which is a popular destination. Please note that while dogs are allowed on the trail, they are not allowed in Big

Cottonwood Canyon which is just past Dog Lake. These rules are strictly enforced by many Salt Lake City agencies including the Sheriff's Office. On the trail, dogs must be leashed on EVEN numbered calendar days. On ODD numbered days, dogs are permitted off-leash on the trail. Dogs still need to be leashed at all times in developed sites which include parking lots, trailheads, picnic sites, campgrounds and cabins. This is also a popular trail for mountain biking but no biking is permitted on ODD numbered days. Please remember to pick up after your dog. The trail is located southeast of downtown Salt Lake City. Take I-80 east heading out of Salt Lake City. Take Highway 215 south and exit at Mill Creek Canyon Road (3800 South Wasatch Blvd). Head east towards the mountains. Drive about 9.1 miles up the canyon to the parking lot. Please note that the upper parking lots can fill up quickly on the weekends.

Ensign Peak Trail
Ensign Vista Drive
Salt Lake City, UT
801-972-7800
Located just a short drive from downtown, this .5 mile trail offers panoramic views of the valley and the lake. It also offers some historical value. This peak was used by Indians, pioneers and explorers. Brigham Young, along with eight other pioneers, climbed to this summit on July 26, 1847, two days after the Mormon pioneers arrived in the Salt Lake Valley. They used this peak to view their surroundings. The trail leads up to a stone monument located at the peak. The elevation gain is about 400 feet. Dogs must be on a leash. To get there, drive north on East Capitol Blvd. and go past the State Capitol Building. Continue for about 8 blocks and then turn left on Ensign Vista Drive.

Liberty Park
589 East 1300 South
Salt Lake City, UT
801-972-7800
This large popular city park offers walking paths, several nice playgrounds, picnic areas, tennis courts and a children's amusement park with a carousel, miniature car and plane rides and more. The park also has a variety of events during the summer. Dogs are allowed at the park, including at many of the events. There will be signs posted where dogs are not allowed, like a

444

few children's water areas. Pets must be leashed and please clean up after them.

Memory Grove Park
300 N. Canyon Road/130 East
Salt Lake City, UT
801-972-7800
This park features a replica of the Liberty Bell as well as memorials to Utah's veterans. A bridge connects Memory Grove to City Creek Park which features a stone-lined stream. Dogs on leash are allowed at the park. Please clean up after your pet.

Millcreek Canyon
East End of 3800 S.
Salt Lake City, UT
801-236-3400
fs.fed.us/r4/wcnf/faq/
In the Millcreek Canyon area of the Wasatch-Cache National Forest dogs are allowed off-leash on odd numbered days. They must be leashed on even numbered days. There are many trails to take which are mostly quite strenuous. The Salt Lake Overlook Trail, for example, climbs 1,250 feet in 1.75 miles. Once there you will get a nice view of the city to the west. To get to Millcreek Canyon exit I-215 at 3300 or 3900 South. Go to 3800 S. and head east to the canyon.

Salt Lake State Marina
13312 W Hwy 202
Salt Lake City, UT
801-250-1898
This well-developed marina with water, electricity, and a pumpout station, is located on the South shore of the Great Salt Lake in the Great Salt Lake State Park. Some of the amenities include modern restrooms, drinking water, wildlife viewing, beautiful scenery, picnicking, and a variety of year round land and water recreation. Dogs of all sizes are allowed to explore the area with their owners. They are allowed all along the waterfront, picnic areas, and the beach. Dogs must be friendly, and leashed and cleaned up after at all times.

Sugarhouse Park
1300 East 2100 South
Salt Lake City, UT
801-467-1721
Sugar House Park, a favorite recreation place, is one of the city's largest and most beautiful parks. Some of the attractions include a trail that outlines the park's outer edge, paved trails, a creek that runs through the park to a duck pond on

the west end, pavilions for barbecues, playgrounds, sport fields/courts, hills (perfect for sledding in winter),and acres of grass. There are also several events held here each year such as the 4th of July fireworks, and the Strut Your Mutt fundraiser (for homeless pets) usually held in May. The park is open daily from 8 am to 10 pm. Dogs of all sizes are welcome throughout the park, but they must be leashed and cleaned up after at all times.

Sunset Trail
100 East Street
Salt Lake City, UT
This Wasatch-Cache National Forest trail has been rated as a hike that is suitable for families with children. It is .5 miles one way, rated easy, and takes about 20 minutes one way. The trail starts at an elevation of 6400 feet and goes down to the falls at an elevation of 6120 feet. The waterfalls are the main attraction on this trail. The trail also provides views of Farmington Canyon. No bicycles, motorized vehicles or skiing is allowed on this trail. Dogs are allowed but must be leashed. Please remember to clean up after your pets. To get there from Salt Lake City, go north on I-15 and take the Farmington exit. At the stop sign turn right/east and go to 100 East Street and turn left/north. Follow the road into Farmington Canyon and go 5.3 miles up the canyon to Sunset Campground.

This is the Place State Park
2601 Sunnyside Avenue
Salt Lake City, UT
801-582-1847
thisistheplace.org/
This is the Place" Heritage Park marks the end of the 1,300 mile journey of the first Mormon settlers into the Salt Lake Valley in 1847, and is home to the Old Deseret Village (seasonal), a living history museum/town depicting life of that era. The monument, erected in 1947 and sitting just south of the village, is over 60 feet tall, 86 feet long, and acknowledges the early Spanish explorers and missionaries, the trappers, the Donner-Reed party, and the Mormon pioneers. The park is open year round from dawn to dusk for day use. There is picnicking, a visitor's center and museum (hours vary), a Mormon handicraft store, modern rest rooms, drinking water, and hiking trails nearby. Dogs of all

sizes are allowed at the monument and around the park; they are not allowed in the Old Deseret Village. Dogs must be leashed and cleaned up after at all times.

Capitol Reef National Park
HC 70 Box 15
Torrey, UT
435-425-3791
nps.gov/care/index.htm
Dogs on leash are allowed in campsites and on paved road areas. Dogs are not allowed on hiking trails or in the backcountry.

Virgin Islands (US)

Virgin Islands National Park
1300 Cruz Bay Creek
St John, VI
340-776-6201
nps.gov/viis
The Virgin Islands National Park is one of breathtaking beauty offering white sandy beaches, tropical forests, and coral reefs. The visitor center is open daily from 8 to 4:30pm. Park areas are open 24 hours a day year-round. Dogs are allowed in the park and on the trails. They are not allowed at the campground, or at Trunk Bay. Dogs must be leashed, cleaned up after, and under owners control at all times.

Vermont

Burlington Bike Path
Lake Champlain Shoreline
Burlington, VT
802-864-0123
enjoyburlington.com/bikepath.cfm
Dogs on leash are allowed to accompany you as you walk or jog this 7.6 mile bike path on the shore of beautiful Lake Champlain. It stretches from Oakledge Park in the south to the Winooski River in the north. Please clean up after your dog.

Killington Ski Resort
Killington Road
Killington, VT
802-422-6200
killington.com/
Although dogs are not allowed on the mountain during the winter months,

this scenic park has plenty to see and do the rest of the year with some great hiking trails and a variety of recreational opportunities. Dogs are allowed on the trails and throughout the park. Dogs must be under their owner's control, leashed, and cleaned up after.

Hazen's Notch
Hazen's Notch Road/Hwy 58
(Welcome Center)
Montgomery Center, VT
802-326-4799
hazensnotch.org/Hiking.htm
More than 15 miles of trails winding through a variety of wildlife habitats, fields of wildflowers, ponds, and wooded areas are maintained by the Hazen Notch Association for public use in summer and fall. Trails are closed to all hikers during winter and spring mud season from December 15th to May 19th. Trail information can be obtained at the Bear Paw Pond and High Ponds Farm parking areas, or at the Welcome Center (partially staffed in summer/fall) where maps and nature brochures are available outside if no one is on site. Dogs must be under their owner's control; kept on a short leash at all times (no retractables), and be cleaned up after.

Green Mountain National Forest
Hwy 7N
Rutland, VT
802-747-6700
Located in southwestern and west-central Vermont and covering almost 400,000 acres, this "recovered" forest now offers abundant habitats for all forms of wildlife and a wide variety of recreational opportunities. Dogs are allowed throughout the park, campground, and on the trails; they are not allowed in picnic or pond areas. Dogs may not be left unattended, and they must be well behaved, leashed, and cleaned up after at all times.

Missisquoi National Wildlife Refuge
29 Tabor Road
Swanton, VT
802-868-4781
Over 6,500 acres of quiet waters, wetlands, open meadows, and forest draw thousands of migratory birds here in addition to providing habitat for a wide variety of resident and other wildlife. Dogs are allowed on site. They must be under their owner's control, leashed, and cleaned up after at all times.

Marsh-Billings-Rockefeller National

Historical Park
54 Elm Street/Hwy 12
Woodstock, VT
802-457-3368
okemo.com/okemosummer/
Miles and miles of scenic trails and carriage roads crisscross through one of the oldest sustainable managed woodlands in the US at this park. When you need a rest, try a bench at the 14 acre pond near the top of the mountain summit that offers great views of the valley below. Dogs are welcome throughout the park; they are not allowed on the formal grounds or the mansion tour. Dogs must be under their owner's control, leashed, and cleaned up after at all times.

Virginia

Virginia Creeper Trail
P.O. Box 2382
Abingdon, VA
vacreepertrail.org/
This multi-use trail covers about 34 miles through some of the state's most breathtaking mountain scenery from Abingdon through Damascus to the N. Carolina state line traversing 47 trestles, passing 3 seasonal visitor centers, historic sites, several small communities, and more. They also feature special events including a Dog Sled event. Dogs are allowed on the trail, and they must be kept on no more than a 6 foot leash and cleaned up after at all times. Primitive camping is allowed off trail on non-private property away from waterways.

Holmes Run Park
Holmes Run Pkwy and S Jordon St
Alexandria, VA
This park has a bike trail, creek, and picnic areas. Dogs are allowed on leash. There is also an off leash dog park at the Duke St intersection with the park.

Huntley Meadows Park
3701 Lockheed Blvd
Alexandria, VA
703-768-2525
users.erols.com/huntleymeadows/
Dogs on leash are allowed in most of the park. However, they are not allowed on the wooden boardwalk.

Mount Vernon Trail
George Washington Parkway

Alexandria, VA
703-285-2601
This bike trail is very scenic and connects Mt Vernon with Washington. Dogs on leash are allowed.

Gravelly Point Park
George Washington Pkwy
Arlington, VA
You and your dog can watch the airline traffic at National Airport. It can get noisy. You need to access the park from the northbound direction on the George Washington Parkway. Dogs must be leashed in this park.

Theodore Roosevelt Island Park and Memorial
George Washington Parkway
Arlington, VA
703-289-2500
nps.gov/this/
Theodore Roosevelt Island park has nice dirt trails and an impressive memorial to Theodore Roosevelt. Your dog will probably like this memorial the most in Washington as it has many acres of trails and nature. Dogs may accompany you on leash in the park. Parking is on the George Washington Parkway on the north-bound side and you walk to the island over a bridge.

Washington and Old Dominion Trail
21293 Smiths Switch Road (office)
Ashburn, VA
703-729-0596
wodfriends.org/
A Regional Park and designated a National Recreation Trail, this is one of the skinniest parks at about 100 feet across, but it is also one of the longest with a 45 mile long multi-use trail. There are several historic sites and many points of interest along the way, and the website lists a number of points of entry. Dogs are allowed throughout the park; they must be under their owner's control, leashed, and cleaned up after at all times.

Virginia Tech Campus
Southgate Drive and Duckpond Drive
Blacksburg, VA
540-231-6000
vt.edu/
This beautifully landscaped 2,600 acre campus was founded in 1872 and has bloomed into a comprehensive, innovated research university with the states largest full-time student population, and it has more than 100 buildings, an airport, and more. Dogs are allowed on the

grounds but not in any of the buildings. Dogs must be well behaved, under their owner's control, leashed, and cleaned up after at all times.

Pen Park
Pen Park Road
Charlottesville, VA
434-970-3589
At 280 acres, it is the city's largest park and it provides a myriad of recreational facilities and gaming/play areas for all ages, including a physical fitness course, a mile and a half nature trail along the river, and an 18-hole golf course. Dogs are allowed throughout the park and on the trials. Dogs must be well mannered, under their owner's control, leashed, and cleaned up after at all times. The park usually has a stock of plastic bags available at the start of the Fitness Trail.

Rivanna River Greenbelt Trail
end of Chesapeake Street
Charlottesville, VA
434-970-3333
This beautifully treed and paved pedestrian trail encircles the city, marks off the ¼ mile, offers fishing spots along the way, and common wildlife sightings. Dogs are allowed off leash on designated portions of the Rivanna Trail on Tuesdays, Wednesdays, and Thursdays only. At all other times dogs must be leashed. Dogs must be under their owner's control and cleaned up after at all times.

Dismal Swam Canal Trail
Dominion Blvd and Hwy 17
Chesapeake, VA
757-382-6411
Running 8½ miles along the Dismal Swam Canal on the eastern side of the refuge, this former highway multi-use trail features some of the most significant historical and ecological habits in the US, and offers plenty of land and water recreation along the way. Dogs are welcome; they must be well behaved, leashed at all times, and cleaned up after.

Grandview Nature Preserve
22 Lincoln Street
Hampton, VA
757-850-5134
A beautiful nature trail leads to a 2½ mile long sandy beach at this 500 acre preserve, and it is a great place for bird and wildlife viewing. Dogs are allowed throughout the park and on the beach from September 16th through May 14th; they are not

allowed during the summer on any Hampton public beach. Dogs must be leashed and cleaned up after at all times.

Sandy Bottom Nature Park and Off Leash Dog Park
1255 Big Bethel Road
Hampton, VA
757-825-4657
hampton.gov/sandybottom/
This 456 acre environmental education and wildlife management facility offers a variety of programs, events, activities, recreational opportunities, and an off leash dog park. The dog park requires pre-registration which can be obtained at the front office for a fee of $10. Dogs must be licensed and have proof of current vaccinations and rabies shots. Dogs are allowed throughout the park; they are not allowed in buildings. Dogs must be leashed (except in designated areas) and cleaned up after at all times.

Caledon Natural Area
11617 Caledon Road/Hwy 218
King George, VA
540-663-3861
This natural area allots visitors the rare opportunity to learn about and view bald eagles, and there are 5 scenic hiking trails through mature forests that are open year round. One of the trails (Boyd's Hole Trail) is only open from October 1st to March 1st. Dogs of all sizes are allowed. Dogs must be under their owner's control, on no more than a 6 foot leash, and cleaned up after.

Ball's Bluff Regional Park
17500 Balls Bluff Road NE
Leesburg, VA
703-737-7800
leesburgva.gov/about/BallsBluff/
Home to one of the smallest national cemeteries with only 25 headstones, this historic 168 acre wooded park saw the largest Civil War battle of the county, and offers trails, interpretive exhibits, scenic views of the Potomac River, and day use areas. Dogs are welcome throughout the park and on the trails. Dogs must be leashed and cleaned up after.

Morven Park
17263 S Planter Lane
Leesburg, VA
703-777-2414
morvenpark.org/
Reenactments, living history programs, the Winmill Carriage

Collection, formal gardens and grounds, an equestrian center, numerous special events throughout the year, and a mansion are some of the highlights of this multi-recreational 1,200 acre park. (An extensive restoration project may limit access to some areas.) Dogs of all sizes are allowed throughout the park, at the picnic areas, and on the trails; they are not allowed in any of the buildings or on any of the tours. Dogs must be under their owner's control, leashed, and cleaned up after at all times. They ask that visitors, and their pets, stay in designated areas only.

Shenandoah National Park
3655 U.S. Highway 211 East
Luray, VA
540-999-3500
nps.gov/shen/
Shenandoah National Park is one of the most dog-friendly National Parks, with dogs allowed on most of the trails. Covering 300 mostly forested square miles of the Blue Ridge Mountains the park provides many diverse habitats for thousands of birds and wildlife. The park also provides a wide range of recreational opportunities. There are more than 500 miles of trails, including 101 miles of the Appalachian Trail, summer and fall festivals/reenactments, a rich cultural history to share, interpretive programs, and breathtaking natural beauty. There are several highlights along the 105 mile long, 35 MPH, Skyline Drive (the only public road through the park), such as 75 scenic overlooks and Mary's Rock Tunnel at milepost 32. The 610 foot-long tunnel was considered an engineering feet in 1932; just note that the clearance for the tunnel is 12'8". Dogs of all sizes are allowed for no additional fee. Dogs must be under their owner's control, on no more than a 6 foot leash or securely crated, cleaned up after at all times, and are not to be left unattended. Dogs are not allowed in buildings or on about 14 miles of the trails; please ask the attendant at the gate for a list of the trails.

Brown's Island
N 7th and Tredegar Streets
Richmond, VA
804-788-6466
brownsisland.com/
When not being used for concerts and special events, this island park offers a variety of outdoor recreational activities. Dogs are

allowed throughout the island, except during events. Dogs must be leashed and cleaned up after at all times.

Explore Park
Milepost 115 Blue Ridge Parkway
Roanoke, VA
540-427-1800
explorepark.org/
This major land and water recreation destination is an 1,100 acre park on the Blue Ridge Parkway astride the Roanoke River that also features an outdoor living history museum, a film center, special event venues, miles of trails, historic areas, and stunning views of its beautiful diversity. Dogs are welcome throughout the park with the exception of the Historic Park area or in buildings. For visitors with pets who would like to visit the historic areas, there are free locked kennels; just pick up keys and a water bowl at the admissions office. Dogs must be leashed and cleaned up after at all times.

Wolf Trap National Park for the Performing Arts
1551 Trap Road
Vienna, VA
703-255-1800
nps.gov/wotr/
This park is the first national park for the performing arts, and it offers a wealth of natural and cultural resources, interpretive programs, and "Theater in the Woods". The park is open daily from dawn to dusk, however there are some exceptions; during park festivals and Filene Center performances. Dogs are allowed throughout the park, except they are not allowed in the concert area during performances. Dogs of all sizes are allowed at no additional fee. Dogs may not be left unattended, and they must be leashed and cleaned up after.

Back Bay National Wildlife Refuge
4005 Sandpiper Road
Virginia Beach, VA
757-721-2412
fws.gov/backbay/
Located on a barrier island, this 9000 acre park is home to a vast number of bird and wildlife, migrating birds, and habitats. They also offer various educational opportunities. Dogs are not allowed here in the summer at all; they are allowed from November 1st to March 31st in areas open to the public only. Dogs must be leashed, or under strict voice control when not crowded, and cleaned up after at all times.

Quarterpath Park
Quarterpath Road and Rt 60 East
Williamsburg, VA
757-220-6170
This is a small city park with a ballfield and playground. Dogs on leash are allowed. Please clean up after your dog.

Waller Mill Park
Airport Road
Williamsburg, VA
757-220-6178
This park has a number of trails and hiking areas. It is a little out of town.

Washington

Mount Rainer National Park
Tahoma Woods State Route
Ashford, WA
360-569-2211
nps.gov/mora/index.htm
Dogs must be on leash where they are allowed. Dogs are only allowed on roads, parking lots, and campgrounds. They are not allowed on trails, snow, in buildings, or any wilderness areas. There is a small portion of Pacific Crest Trail near the park's eastern boundary that allows pets on leash.

Maritime Heritage Park
West Holly Street
Bellingham, WA
360-676-6985
This park of over 11 acres offers a lush green setting, open play areas, picnic facilities, a playground, fishing area, a fish hatchery, and an amphitheater. They are open year round, and to get there drive west on Holly Street from downtown Bellingham and the park will be on your right. Dogs of all sizes are allowed throughout the park, but they are not allowed in any of the buildings. Dogs must be leashed and cleaned up after at all times.

Peace Arch State Park
P. O. Box 87
Blaine, WA
360-332-8221
This gorgeous, 20 acre day-use park features lush lawns, expansive gardens (they plant more than 20,000 flowers annually), outstanding views of the ocean and the surrounding area, and an impressive Peace Arch that stands astride the boundary of the United States and Canada. The arch

commemorates treaties and agreements that arose from the War of 1812. Some of the amenities include picnic areas, interpretive programs/signs, recreational programs, horticultural displays, and peace concerts. Dogs of all sizes are allowed throughout the park, but not in buildings or planted areas. Dogs must be leashed and cleaned up after at all times-please bring supplies.

McNary National Wildlife Refuge
311 Lake Road
Burbank, WA
509-547-4942
nwr.mcnary.wa.us/
This refuge of over 15,000 acres provides a wide variety of habitats for a priceless diversity of fish, wildlife, birds, and plants. It extends along the east bank of the Columbia River from the junction of the Snake River to the mouth of the Walla Walla River then downstream into Oregon. Dogs of all sizes are welcome. Dogs must be under their owner's control and leashed at all times, and please bring supplies to clean up after your pet. The exception to dogs being off lead is when they are assisting waterfowl hunters in retrieving downed birds during hunting season. Dogs, nor people, are allowed at Sanctuary Pond or off the roads or trails at any time.

Cheney Turnbull National Wildlife Refuge
26010 S Smith Road
Cheney, WA
509-235-4723
Home to one of the most unique ecosystems in the world, this refuge provides a variety of habitats to a large animal and birdlife population. Some of the features here include a 5-mile auto tour, interpretive signage, environmental education sites, plenty of multi-use trails, and about 2,300 acres for public use. Dogs of all sizes are allowed for no additional fee. They must be kept on the trails and in public use areas. Dogs must be leashed and cleaned up after at all times.

Lake Roosevelt National Recreation Area
1008 Crest Drive
Coulee Dam, WA
509-738-6266
nps.gov/laro/index.htm
Dogs must be on leash and must be cleaned up after. The park features boating, auto touring, camping, fishing, hiking, and more.

Ebey's Landing National Historic Reserve
162 Cemetery Road
Coupeville, WA
360-678-6084
nps.gov/ebla/index.htm
Dogs on a 6 ft leash are allowed at this reserve. There are two off leash areas that you will need a map from the visitor's center to find. The park features camping, auto touring, boating, fishing, hiking, and more.

Luther Burbank Park
2040 84th Avenue SE
Mercer Island, WA
206-205-7532
This 77 acre park offers great views of Lake Washington and is popular for boating and fishing. There are almost 3 miles of walking paths. Dogs on leash are allowed. There is also a special off-leash area for dogs located at the north end of the park. To get there from I-5, take I-90 East to Mercer Island and take the Island Crest Way exit (#7). At the top of the ramp, turn right on SE 26th Street. At the stop sign turn left on 84th Avenue SE and drive straight to the park after another stop sign at SE 24th Street.

North Cascades National Park
State Route 20
Newhalem, WA
360-856-5700
nps.gov/noca
Dogs are allowed on one of the hiking trails, the Pacific Crest Trail. This scenic hiking trail runs through the park and is rated moderate to difficult. The trail is located off Highway 20, about one mile east of Rainy Pass. At the Bridge Creek Trailhead, park on the north side of the highway and then hike north (uphill) or south (downhill). A Northwest Forest Pass is required to park at the trailhead. The cost is about $5 and can be purchased at the Visitor's Center in Newhalem. For a larger variety of trails, including a less strenuous hike, dogs are also allowed on trails at the adjacent Ross Lake National Recreation Area and the Lake Chelan National Recreation Area. Both recreation areas are managed by the national park.

Olympic National Forest
1835 Black Lake Blvd. SW
Olympia, WA
360-956-2402
fs.fed.us/r6/olympic/
Leashed dogs are allowed on the national forest trails. Of particular interest is the Mt. Mueller Trail which offers great views of the Strait of Juan de Fuca and the mountains. Maps for this 13 mile loop trail and other trails can be picked up for free at a Forest Ranger Station including the one located at 551 Forks Avenue South, Forks, Washington.

Columbia National Wildlife Refuge
735 E Main Street 24
Othello, WA
509-488-2668
fws.gov/columbiarefuge/
This refuge of about 30,000 acres is located within the Columbia Basin of central Washington, and provides a variety of diverse environments that supply critical habitats for numerous species. To tour the refuge drive NW from Othello on McManamon Road, then turn North on Morgan Lake Road (the major north/south public road that takes you through the center of the refuge). There are maps available at the Main Street office, and at almost every parking area inside the refuge. Dogs are welcome, but they must be under their owner's control and leashed at all times. Please bring supplies to clean up after your pet.

Howe Farm Historic Park and Off-Leash Dog Area
Long Lake Rd at Sedgwick Rd
Port Orchard, WA
360-337-5350
visitkitsap.com/kitsap.asp
Howe Farm County Park is a Historic Farm with Walking Trails. Dogs are allowed on leash at outside areas of the park. In addition, there is a 5.5 acre off-leash area. This area is not fenced and dogs should be under voice control and well-behaved. To get to Howe Farm take Hwy 16 to Sedgwick. Head east on Sedgwick for three miles to Long Lake Road. Turn left on Long Lake Rd to the park.

Marymoor Park and Off-Leash Area
6046 West Lake Sammamish Pkwy NE
Redmond, WA
206-296-8687
This park offers 640 acres of land for recreational activities. Some special areas in the park include a velodrome (for bicyclist training and racing), a climbing rock, a model airplane flying field, and the historic Willowmoor Farm. Dogs on leash are allowed at the park. There is also a 40 acre off-leash dog exercise area where dogs can run free while under voice control. To get there from I-5 or I-405, take State Route 520 east to the West Lake Sammamish Pkwy exit. At the bottom of the ramp, go right (south) on W. Lake Sammamish Parkway NE. The park entrance is the next left at the traffic light.

Point Defiance Park
5400 N Pearl Street
Ruston, WA
253-305-1016
Spectacular views, saltwater beaches, and a natural forest are only a few of the features at this 702 acre park. Other features include a zoo and aquarium, gardens, hiking trails, a living history museum of the first fort here (Fort Nisqually), special events and educational programs, a marina, a family picnic area, and playground area, and more. Dogs are allowed at this park for no additional fee. They must be leashed and cleaned up after at all times. Dogs are allowed throughout the park with the exception of the zoo area.

Discovery Park
3801 W. Government Way
Seattle, WA
206-386-4236
Discovery Park is located northwest of downtown Seattle. It has over 500 acres and is the city's largest park. It offers views of both the Olympic and Cascade mountain ranges. Dogs on leash are allowed on about 7 miles of trails except for beaches, ponds, wetlands and the Wolf Tree Nature Trail.

Sand Point Magnuson Park
7400 Sand Point Way NE
Seattle, WA
206-684-4075
The park is northeast of Seattle and is located across the lake from the city of Kirkland. This park has about 350 acres and is Seattle's second largest park. You will find over four miles of walking trails along Lake Washington, through grassy fields, trees and brush. Dogs are not allowed in the water at Lake Washington, except at the off-leash area.

Lake Chelan National Recreation Area
810 State Route 20
Sedro-Woolley, WA
360-856-5700
nps.gov/lach/index.htm

449

Dogs must be on leash and must be cleaned up after in this National Recreation Area. They are not allowed on the Picture Lake Boardwalk, Table Mountain Trail or the National Park Proper. They are allowed on the rest of the trails and the Stehekin Shuttle bus tours. Features camping, boating, fishing, and hiking. Accessed only by ferry or floatplane.

Ross Lake National Recreation Area
810 State Route 20
Sedro-Woolley, WA
360-856-5700
nps.gov/rola/index.htm
Dogs on leash are allowed in the park area and lake. The park features boating, camping, fishing, hiking, and more. It sits in the North Cascade Mountains.

Riverfront Park
507 N Howard
Spokane, WA
509-625-6600
spokaneriverfrontpark.com/
Once the site of the 1974 World's Fair, this 110 acre, lush, urban park in downtown Spokane offers an array of recreational pursuits, special events, food, and entertainment on a backdrop of the scenic Spokane Falls. They are also home to a 1909 Looff Carrousel and a seasonal outdoor skating rink. Dogs are allowed throughout the park with the exception of special events and some holidays. Dogs must be well behaved, leashed, and please bring supplies to clean up after your pet.

West Virginia

Fitzpatrick Park
896 Fitzpatrick Road/Hwy 20
Beckley, WV
304-934-5323
This 12 acre park offers a fishing pond, playground, picnic shelter, and 4 ball fields. Dogs on leash are allowed.

Berkeley Springs State Park
#2 S Washington Street
Berkeley Springs, WV
304-258-2711
Berkeley Springs State Park
This park has drawn visitors since pre-colonial times for the warm spring mineral waters believed to have curative powers. Dogs are allowed on the grounds, but they are

not allowed in the back of the park where the mineral spas are. Dogs must be leashed and under their owner's control at all times.

Cacapon Resort State Park
818 Cacapon Lodge Drive
Berkeley Springs, WV
304-258-1022 (800-CALL WVA (225-5982))
cacaponresort.com/
There is a wide number of land and water recreation options, nature education programs, 20 miles of hiking trails, and much more are available at this 6,000 acre mountain resort. Healthy dogs are allowed in cabins/cottages for a $50 refundable deposit, plus $40 for the first night and $5 for each additional night per pet. A credit card must be on file, and there is a pet agreement to sign at check in. Pets may not be left unattended outside, they must be securely crated when left alone in the cabins or cottages, they are not allowed to be tied/chained on the porch or yard, and their food may not be kept outside. Dogs must have certified proof of inoculations from a veterinarian, be on no more than a 10 foot leash, and picked up after. 2 dogs may be allowed.

Cass Scenic Railroad State Park
Snowshoe-Cass-Greenback Road
Cass, WV
304-456-4300 (800-CALL WVA (225-5982))
cassrailroad.com/
The highlight of this park is the early 1900's stream-driving locomotives that take visitors for a ride back in time, the recreated logging camp, and the restored railroad town of Cass. Dogs are not allowed on the train, but an attendant will walk/water/feed pets that have kennels. Healthy dogs are for a $50 refundable deposit, plus $40 for the first night and $5 for each additional night per pet. A credit card must be on file, and there is a pet agreement to sign at check in. Pets may not be left unattended outside, they must be securely crated when left alone in the cabins or cottages, they are not allowed to be tied/chained on the porch or yard, and their food may not be kept outside. Dogs must have certified proof of inoculations from a veterinarian, be on no more than a 10 foot leash, and picked up after. There are a limited number of cabins that are pet friendly, and no RV/tent camping. 2 dogs may be allowed.

Cato Park
Edgewood Drive
Charleston, WV
304-348-6860
This is the city's largest municipal park and it offers such features as an Olympic-sized pool, scenic picnic areas, a par 3 golf course and pro shop, picnic areas, and gaming fields/courts. Dogs are allowed at the park; they are not allowed on the golf course. Dogs must be leashed and under their owner's control at all times

Coonskin Park
2000 Coonskin Drive
Charleston, WV
304-341-8000
This popular city park offers a variety of land and water recreational opportunities, a home team Soccer field, an amphitheater, fishing lake, swimming pool, putt-putt golf, an 18-hole golf course, picnic areas, and nature trails. Dogs are allowed at the park. They are not allowed on the golf course, Soccer field, or swim areas. Dogs must be leashed and under their owner's control at all times.

Canaan Valley State Park
32 Canaan Valley
Davis, WV
304-866-4121
canaanresort.com
This state park is home to the Canaan Valley Resort. The park offers 18 miles of hiking and mountain biking trails with adjacent Monongahela National Forest trails. During the winter the resort rents cross-country skis and snowshoes. Pets are allowed on the trails and on the ski trails but need to be on a 10 foot or less leash at all times. The resort also allows leashed pets in their RV park and campground.

Bluestone National Scenic River
P. O. Box 246
Glen Jean, WV
304-465-0508
nps.gov/blue/
Unspoiled natural landscapes, a variety of habitats and wildlife, a warm water fishing spot, and the beautiful 10½ mile Turnpike Trail all combine to make this a popular relaxing or recreational destination. Dogs are allowed throughout the park and on the trails on leash.

Potomac Heritage National Scenic Trail
PO Box B
Harpers Ferry, WV

202-619-7222
nps.gov/pohe/index.htm
Dogs must be on leash and must be cleaned up after on the trail sites and park areas. You must follow all rules of the state parks. The park features in most areas camping, boating, hiking, swimming, and more. The trail is a partnership to develop and sustain a system of trails for recreation, transportation, health, and education between the mouth of the Potomac River and the Allegheny Highlands.

Wisconsin

Dave's Falls County Park
Hwy 141
Amberg, WI
800-236-6681
Located in the states most waterfall populated county, this 66 acre park offers upper and lower waterfalls, other topographical sites of interest, a bridge over a boisterous river, and a variety of recreational activities. Dogs are allowed; they must be leashed and under their owner's control at all times.

Harrington Beach State Park
531 Hwy D
Belgium, WI
262-285-3015
This is a day use park that is open year round from 6 am to 11 pm. Dogs of all sizes are allowed. There are no additional pet fees. Dogs may not be left unattended, and they must be leashed at all times and cleaned up after. Dogs are not allowed at the north beach or on the nature trails. Dogs are allowed at the south beach and the Scenic Picnic area.

Governor Thompson State Park
N10008 Paust Lane
Crivitz, WI
715-757-3979
This day use park is open year round from 6 am to 11 pm. Dogs of all sizes are allowed. There are no additional pet fees. Dogs may not be left unattended, and they must be on no more than an 8 foot leash, and be cleaned up after. Dogs are not allowed in any swim areas, on the beach, in the water except by the pier, at the observation tower, the picnic areas, or the playground. Dogs are allowed on all the trails except for the marked nature trails.

Peshtigo River State Forest
N10008 Paust Lane
Crivitz, WI
715-757-3965
This forest has over 9000 acres of rustic forest along some 70 miles of the Peshtigo River. There is ample hiking, canoeing, boating, fishing, hunting, and more at this day use only park. Dogs do not have to be on lead as long as there is voice control, although they suggest dogs be on lead by the boat launches. Dogs may not be left unattended, and they are not allowed on the ski trails once there is snow.

Whitnall Park
5879 S 92 Street
Franklin, WI
414-425-8550
This is a nice green park if just looking for an easy scenic walk with the pooch. Dogs must be leashed and cleaned up after at all times. They are allowed on the roads and hiking trail only; they are not allowed in picnic areas, the playground, gardens, golf course, or the nature center.

Loew Lake Unit, Kettle Moraine State Forest
3544 Kettle Moraine Road
Hartford, WI
262-670-3400
This is a rustic, undeveloped park, and motor vehicles are not allowed inside. Parking is along Emerald Drive. There is hunting, hiking, horseback riding, and the Ice Age National Scenic Trial goes through the forest on the west side of the Oconomowoc River. Dogs are allowed, and they must be on leash when on the trails. They may be off lead for hunting or when off the trails.

Aztalan State Park
N 6200 Hwy Q
Lake Mills, WI
920-648-8774
There are educational as well as recreational opportunities at this park as it is home to one of the state's most significant archaeological areas with sites dating back to 1000-1300 AD. Dogs are allowed at the park in the day use areas only; they are not allowed near the burial grounds. Dogs must be leashed and under their owner's control at all times.

North Country National Scenic Trail
700 Rayovac Drive Ste 100
Madison, WI

608-441-5610
nps.gov/noco/index.htm
Dogs must be on leash and must be cleaned up after on most of the trail. You must follow all state and local park rules and pet policies. The trail links scenic, natural, historic, and cultural areas in seven northern states. Approximately four thousand miles, the trail includes a variety of hikes from easy walking to challenging treks.

Fisher Creek State Recreation Area
4319 Expo Drive
Manitowoc, WI
920-683-4185
dnr.state.wi.us/org/land/parks/
This 123 acre area has nearly a mile of Lake Michigan shoreline, scenic wooded bluffs, grasslands and wetlands. Dogs of all sizes are allowed. There are no additional pet fees. Dogs may not be left unattended at any time, and they must be leashed and cleaned up after.

George W. Mead Wildlife Area
S2148 Hwy S
Milladore, WI
715-457-6771
meadwildlife.org/
This is the place for the outdoor enthusiast featuring almost 30,000 acres of grass and wetlands and forests. More than 265 species of birds have been noted, and there is hiking, biking, hunting, boating, and wildlife viewing opportunities. This area is also used for dog training, trials, and events. Dogs must be leashed except when participating in training exercises, and cleaned up after.

Havenwoods State Forest
6141 N Hopkins
Milwaukee, WI
414-527-0232
dnr.state.wi.us/org/land/parks/
Havenwoods is an island of nature within the city of Milwaukee. Environmental education programs and walking trails are available for various types of groups. Dogs of all sizes are allowed. There are no additional pet fees. Dogs may not be left unattended at any time, and they must be leashed and cleaned up after. Dogs are not allowed at the picnic area and on some of the trails. There is a display board with a map in the parking area that shows which trails are off limits. The park is open daily from 6 am to 8 pm.

Pere Marquette Park

451

900 N Plankington Avenue
Milwaukee, WI
414-276-6696
Among the most urban of the county parks, this park offers a variety of additional amenities, such as free seasonal concerts every Wednesday, Movies under the Stars in August, various river events and activities, and much more. Dogs are allowed in the park; they must be well mannered, leashed, and under their owner's control at all times.

Tiffany Bottoms Wildlife Area
Hwy 25
Nelson, WI
608-266-2621
This natural area features a good example of lower and upper floodplain forests, and they are also host to some rather rare and uncommon birds. Dogs are allowed in the park; they must be on no more than an 8 foot leash, current on license and shots, and under their owner's control at all times. During hunting season, trained hunting dogs may be off lead.

Kinnickinnic State Park
W 11983 820th Avenue
River Falls, WI
715-425-1129
This day-use recreational park offers several miles of trails and a scenic overlook. They are open from 8:30 am to 11 pm in the summer, and from 8:30 am to 5:30 pm in the winter. Dogs are allowed at no additional fee. Dogs may not be left unattended, they must be on no more than an 8 foot leash, and be cleaned up after. Dogs are not allowed in the picnic or swim areas, but they are allowed on the trails.

Straight Lake State Park
(Box 703) 12 miles NE of St. Croix Falls
St Croix Falls, WI
715-483-3747
This natural, undeveloped 2,780 acre day use park is open only to foot traffic until it is further developed. The park is open from 6 am to 11 pm daily. Dogs are allowed at no additional fee. Dogs may not be left unattended, must be on no more than an 8 foot leash, and be cleaned up after. Dogs are allowed on all the trails, and they request extra care be taken during hunting season.

Whitefish Dunes State Park
3275 County Hwy WD (Clark Lake Road)
Sturgeon Bay, WI
920-823-2400
Beautiful, easy strolls along the lake, year around interpretive programs, boardwalks over wetlands, scenic trails, historic sites, and more have made this the state's most visited day use park. This 865 acre day use park was established to protect the fragile dune environment located here. It has the highest and best preserved dunes in Wisconsin. The park is open from 8 am to 8 pm year round. Visitors nor pets are allowed on the dunes, and all must stay on the flat sandy areas. Dogs are allowed; they must be on no more than an 8 foot leash except during certain times in winter. They must be well behaved, and they are not allowed to be left unattended or tied up. Dogs are not allowed in buildings, picnic or swim areas, marked nature trails, beaches, or playgrounds. They do have a designated pet swim area. Pets are restricted to the area of the beach south of the third beach access; to reach this area, walk your leashed animal from the parking area down the red trail and then onto the beach. Dogs are allowed on the beach from November 1st to April 1st only.

Governor Nelson State Park
5140 County Hwy. M
Waunakee, WI
608-831-3005
This is a day use park that is open year round from dawn to dusk. Dogs of all sizes are allowed. There are no additional pet fees. Dogs may not be left unattended, and they must be leashed and cleaned up after. Dogs are not allowed in any swim areas, on the beach, or in the water except by the pier. The trails and areas where pets are not allowed are marked.

Lizard Mound County Park
S Indian Lore Road
West Bend, WI
262-335-4445
A self-guided anthropological trail will take visitors on about a mile walk through some of the best preserved Effigy Mounds in the state. The site is listed on the National Register of Historic Places. Dogs are allowed on no more than

a 6 foot leash and under their owner's control at all times.

Wyoming

Casper City Parks
1801 E 4th
Casper, WY
307-235-8403
casperwy.gov
This city has more than 40 developed parks for visitors and locals to enjoy. Dogs are allowed at all the city parks; they must be leashed and picked up after at all times. Dogs are not allowed in buildings or on swimming beaches.

Shoshone National Forest
808 Meadow Lane
Cody, WY
307-527-6241
There are numerous dog-friendly trails in the forest, many of which are located between the town of Cody and Yellowstone National Park. One of the trails is the Eagle Creek Trail, which is about 16 miles long, at an elevation of 6700 to 9900 feet with a hiking difficulty of moderate. This trail is located off Highways 14 and 16, between Cody and Yellowstone.

Devils Tower National Monument
PO Box 10
Devils Tower, WY
307-467-5283
nps.gov/deto/index.htm
Dogs must be on leash and must be cleaned up after in park areas and camp sites. Dogs are not allowed on the trails to Devil's Tower.

Bear River State Park
601 Bear River Drive
Evanston, WY
307-789-6547
Live herds of buffalo and elk, 300 natural acres for exploring and recreation, year around trails, and all set along the Bear River have made this a popular day excursion. Dogs are allowed in the park and on the trails; they are not allowed near the fenced herd areas. Dogs must be leashed, picked up after, and under owner's control at all times.

Edness K Wilkins State Park
87000 E Hwy 25/26
Evansville, WY
307-577-5150
Serene and natural best describe this park along the N Platte River. In addition to nice shady areas from large old cottonwood trees, the park also features a popular accessible fishing pier, a 2.8 mile hard-surface walking path, an abundance of wildlife, a playground, picnic areas, and a launch area for small watercraft. Dogs are allowed; they must be on no more than a 10 foot leash and picked up after at all times. They are not allowed on designated swim beaches.

Fort Laramie National Historic Site
965 Gray Rocks Road
Fort Laramie, WY
307-837-2221
nps.gov/fola/index.htm
Dogs must be on leash and must be cleaned up after in the historic site. Dogs are not allowed in the fort. It is open daily 8am-dusk. The site features fishing, hiking, and site touring.

Bridger-Teton National Forest
various
Jackson, WY
307-739-5500
fs.fed.us/btnf/teton/hiking.html
This national forest offers over 1200 miles of trails for you and your pooch to enjoy. You can take a short hike or take a week-long backpacking trip. There are many trails near Jackson and Buffalo. Here are two trails located near Jackson. The first is Cache Creek Trail which is about 6 miles long and follows the creek. It is a popular trail and offers good views of the town and surrounding area. You might spot wildlife like moose, deer, elk and more during the summertime. This hike has a gentle grade which makes it a good trail for the entire family. To get there from the town square, travel east on Broadway to Redmond Street. Follow Redmond to Cache Creek Drive then follow Cache Creek Drive to parking lot. Another trail is the Black Canyon Overlook/Pass Ridge Trail. This trail is rated moderate and is about 2 miles long. The trail follows the ridge and travels through meadows and forest, with views of Jackson Hole and the surrounding mountains. To get there from Jackson, follow Highway 22 West to the summit of Teton Pass. Park at the top of Teton Pass on the left. The trailhead is well

marked on the south side of the road at the parking area.

Fossil Butte National Monument
PO Box 592
Kemmerer, WY
307-877-4455
nps.gov/fobu/index.htm
Pets on leash are allowed at this site. The site features auto touring, hiking, and site-seeing of the a 50-million year old lake bed in one of the richest fossil localities in the world.

Sinks Canyon State Park
3079 Sinks Canyon Road
Lander, WY
332-6333
wyoparks.state.wy.us/SCslide.htm
Experts on the Sinks Canyon area present weekly programs on it's botany, history, geology, and wildlife. Dogs are allowed everywhere in the park and on the trails. There is also a camping area where dogs are allowed at no additional charge. The Visitor's Center phone number is 307-332-3077. The park is open from 6 am to 10 pm from Memorial Day weekend through the Labor Day weekend.

Bighorn Canyon National Recreation Area
20 Highway 14A East
Lovell, WY
406-666-2412
nps.gov/bica/index.htm
Dogs must be on leash and must be cleaned up after in the recreation area. The park features auto touring, boating, camping, fishing, hiking, swimming, and more.

John D Rockefeller Jr Memorial Parkway National Park
PO Box 170
Moose, WY
307-739-3300
nps.gov/jodr/index.htm
Pets on leash with cleanup are allowed on roads, road shoulders, campgrounds, and picnic areas. Dogs are not allowed on hiking trails or in the park backcountry.

Hot Springs State Park
538 N Park Street/Hwy 20/789
Thermopolis, WY
307-864-2176
Free therapeutic mineral baths, amazing mineral "flow-rock features, a bison herd that visitors can watch being fed in the winter, a suspension bridge over the Bighorn River, glorious summer gardens,

accessible trails, and more have made this a popular recreation and relaxation destination. Dogs are allowed; they must be leashed and under their owner's control at all times. Dogs are not allowed in buildings.

Canada

Alberta

Calgary Pathways and Bikeways
800 Macleod Trail SE
Calgary, AB
403-215-1570
This city is home to the most extensive urban pathways in North America crossing almost 900 kms, 67 bridges, passing more than 750 signs, and most of the pathways connect to parks and numerous activity areas. Most of the paths are even cleared in winter for year round enjoyment; the pathway hotline is 403-268-2300. Pathway maps can be obtained at the above address or at any Calgary Co-op location for $2. Dogs are allowed on the pathways. They must stay to the right, and be leashed (unless in off-lead area) and cleaned up after. Dogs must be under their owner's control at all times, and cycling or in-line skating with a leashed dog is prohibited.

Fish Creek Provincial Park
Acadia Dr at Canyon Meadows Drive
Calgary, AB
403-268-2489
Fish Creek Provincial Park has more than 50 miles of trails some paved and some unpaved. It is home to a variety of wildlife such as deer and coyotes. Dogs on leash are allowed in most of the park. The park follows Fish Creek and the Bow River and snakes through the city.

Nose Hill Park
5620 14 St NW
Calgary, AB
403-268-2489
Nose Hill Park, located in north west Calgary, is 11 square kilometers in size. It is the largest municipal park in Canada. The park is mostly grassland. You can hike up on the hills to see the city below you. There are many types of birds and animals in the park. Dogs are allowed throughout the park but must be on-leash at all times and you must clean up after your dog.

Dawson Bridge/Highlands Hiking Trail
110 Ave NW and 50 St
Edmonton, AB
780-496-1475
The trail along the North Saskatchawan River is partially on-leash and partially off-leash.It snakes through Edmonton along the river. Please observe the signs regarding where your dog can be off-leash. Dogs must be licensed and you must carry a leash with you even in the off-leash area. For detailed rules please see the Edmonton city website.

Mill Creek Ravine Walking Trail
68 Ave at 93 St
Edmonton, AB
780-496-1475
The walking trail through the Mill Creek Ravine allows dogs off-leash from 68 Ave and 93 St to the Mill Creek Bridge at 82 Ave. North of 82 Ave dogs must be leashed. Then between 44 Ave and 34 Ave dogs may again be off-leash. Dogs must be licensed and you must carry a leash with you even in the off-leash area. For detailed rules please see the Edmonton city website.

Patricia Ravine Hiking Trail
Patricia Drive
Edmonton, AB
780-496-1475
This is a gravel hiking trail. Dogs are allowed to be off-leash on most of this trail. The trail goes from Whitemud Drive to the river. The total distance is just about one mile. Dogs must be licensed and you must carry a leash with you even in the off-leash area. For detailed rules please see the Edmonton city website.

British Columbia

Burnaby Lake Regional Park
Sprott Street
Burnaby, BC
604-294-7450
Dogs on leash are allowed at this park and on the trails. This park is popular for birdwatching. Be on the lookout for bald eagles, great blue herons, or even green-backed herons. Along the shoreline you might see beavers, ducks and turtles. For some good exercise, try one of the trails that circles the lake.

Burnaby Mountain Park
Centennial Way
Burnaby, BC
604-294-7450
Dogs on leash are allowed at this park and on the trails. The park offers mountain, water and city views from the top of Burnaby Mountain. You might even see some deer or bald eagles. To get there, take Lougheed Highway and turn north on Gaglardi Way to Centennial Way.

Central Park
Boundary Road
Burnaby, BC
604-294-7450
Dogs on leash are allowed at this park and on the trails. This park is an urban forest with douglas fir, western hemlock, poplar and maple trees. To get there, take the Trans Canada Highway to Boundary Road. Go south to get to the park.

Confederation Park
Willingdon Avenue
Burnaby, BC
604-294-7450
Dogs on leash are allowed at this park and on the trails. There is an off-leash area located north of Penzance Drive, roughly between Willingdon and Gamma Avenues. To get to the park, take Hastings Road and then go North on Willingdon Avenue.

Great Blue Heron Nature Reserve
5200 Sumas Prairie Road
Chilliwack, BC
604-823-6603
chilliwackblueheron.com/
This 325 acre reserve is located in the un-dyked floodplain of the Vedder River, and is home to more than 200 Great Blue Heron nests in addition to a variety of vegetation and wildlife. Dogs are not allowed throughout the entire reserve; they are allowed on the main center trail that leads to the river. Dogs must be under their owner's control, leashed, and cleaned up after at all times.

Colony Farm Regional Park
Colony Farm Road
Coquitlam, BC
604-224-5739
gvrd.bc.ca/parks/ColonyFarm.htm
This park offers large open fields with wildflowers. It is a good birdwatching spot to find hawks and herons. Dogs on leash are allowed on the trails, except for beaches or where posted. To get there, take the Trans Canada Highway (Highway 1) east. Take the Cape Horn Interchange to Highway 7 (Lougheed), then turn right onto Colony Farm Road.

454

Coquihalla Canyon Provincial Park &
Othello Tunnels
Othello Rd
Fraser Valley, BC
604-476-9069
The highlights of this 135 hectare
park are the Coquihalla Gorge, the
Kettle Valley Railway grade built over
3 mountain ranges (rails to trails),
and the tunnels that were made to
pass through them. Visitors can
enjoy the breathtaking views from
April 1st to October 31st. It is
suggested that visitors bring water
and a flashlight, as the light can be
dim in the tunnels and water is not
available. Dogs are allowed on the
hiking trials, and they must be
leashed and cleaned up after at all
times. Dogs are not allowed in the
back country due to wildlife issues.

Capilano River Regional Park
Capilano Park Road
North Vancouver, BC
604-224-5739
This park offers lush forest trails and
is also home to the Capilano Fish
Hatchery. Dogs on leash are allowed
on the trails, except for beaches or
where posted. The park is located in
North Vancouver, next to the
Cleveland Dam.

Mount Revelstoke National Park of
Canada
Meadows-in-the-Sky Parkway
Revelstoke, BC
250-837-7500
This park has unique ecological and
geological features, and it is home to
2 popular trails, the ancient Giant
Cedars hiking trail, and birders are
drawn to the jungle-like wetland of
the Skunk Cabbage trail. The
parkway is open and staffed from
7:00 a.m. until 10:00 p.m., from mid-
June to the August long weekend. In
August, the parkway hours of
operation are 7:00 a.m. until 8:30
p.m. In May and early June, and in
September and early October, the
parkway hours of operation are 9:00
a.m. until 5:00 p.m. Dogs of all sizes
are allowed at no additional fee.
Dogs must be leashed at all times
and cleaned up after. Dogs are
allowed on the trails.

Francis/King Regional Park
Munn Road
Saanich, BC
250-478-3344
crd.bc.ca/parks/francis_king.htm
There are many hiking trails in this
park. One of the trails is the Elsi King
Trail. This interpretive trail is
accessible and also good for families

with young children. Dogs must be
leashed in all high use areas
including the Elsi King Trail. Dogs
may be allowed off-leash in other
areas as long as they are under
voice control. The park is located
about 30 minutes from Victoria.
Take the Trans-Canada Highway
from Victoria and then take the
Helmcken Road exit. Turn left onto
Burnside Road West and then turn
right on Prospect Lake Road. Keep
left on Munns Road and it will lead
to the park entrance on the right.

East Sooke Regional Park
East Sooke Road
Sooke, BC
250-478-3344
crd.bc.ca/parks/east_sooke.htm
This park offers miles of trails
through forests and along the
rugged coastline. Enjoy views of the
Olympic Mountains and the Strait of
Juan de Fuca. The trails are rated
easy to challenging. Dogs are
welcome at the park and on the
trails, but not on the beaches during
the summer. The park district
recommends that you keep your
pets on leash in all high use areas
and that pets need to be under your
control at all times. The park is
located about one hour from
Victoria. To get there, take the
Trans Canada Highway from
Victoria and take the Colwood exit.
Follow Old Island Highway which
turns into Sooke Road. Turn left
onto Gillespie Road and then turn
right onto East Sooke Road.

Charleson Park Off-Leash Area
6th Avenue
Vancouver, BC
604-257-8400
city.vancouver.bc.ca/parks/4.htm
Dogs are allowed off-leash year-
round in the Grass Bowl from 6am
to 10pm. At the Waterfall Pond,
dogs are allowed off-leash before
10am and after 7pm from June
through September. During the rest
of the year, there are no restricted
off-leash hours at the Waterfall
Pond.

Pacific Spirit Regional Park
Southwest Marine Drive
Vancouver, BC
604-224-5739
This is a popular park for jogging
and running. The park offers over
30 miles or 54 kilometers of trails.
Dogs on leash are allowed on the
trails, except for beaches or where
posted. There is also an off-leash
area in this park which will be

posted with signs.

Queen Elizabeth Park
Cambie Boulevard
Vancouver, BC
604-257-8400
city.vancouver.bc.ca/parks/3.htm
This 130 acre (52 hectare) park has
about 6 million visitors per year. The
popular Quarry Gardens is located at
the top of the hill in the park. This
land used to be an actual quarry
before it became a city park. Dogs
are allowed in the park and on the
walkways and trails, except where
posted. Dogs must be on leash. The
park is located off Cambie Boulevard
and is surrounded by the following
streets: Cambie Blvd., Kersland Dr.,
37th Ave., Midlothian Ave., and 27th
Ave.

Stanley Park
Georgia Street
Vancouver, BC
604-257-8400
This park is the largest city park in
Canada and the third largest urban
park in North America. It attracts
about 8 million people per year. The
park has 1,000 forested acres and
offers miles of trails, including a 6.2
mile paved trail around the perimeter.
On the north side of the park, you will
get a view of Lion's Gate Bridge. This
bridge connects Vancouver and
North Vancouver and is similar in
size to the San Francisco Golden
Gate Bridge. Dogs are allowed in the
park, except on beaches or where
posted. Your dog is welcome to walk
or jog with you on the trails. Stanley
Park is located just north of
downtown Vancouver. To get there,
take Georgia Street towards North
Vancouver. Dogs must be leashed.

Beacon Hill Park
Douglas Street
Victoria, BC
250-385-5711
Views from oceanside bluffs and
wildflowers on slopes can both be
enjoyed at this park. The interior of
the park features manicured
flowerbeds and bridges over
streams. Dogs on leash are allowed.
Dogs can be off-leash at the gravel
beach located along Dallas Road,
between Douglas and Cook Street.

Manitoba

Lower Fort Garry National Historic

Site of Canada
5925 Hwy 9
St Andrews, MB
888-773-8888
The oldest intact fur trading post in North America, this stone fort is also noted for being the site where the 1st Treaty was signed between the local natives and England. Costumed docents and re-enactments add to the flavor of the mid-1800's experience. Dogs are allowed throughout the grounds; they are not allowed in buildings unless they can be carried. Dogs must be leashed and under their owner's control at all times.

Ontario

Point Pelee National Park of Canada
407 Monarch Lane, RR 1
Leamington, ON
519-322-2365
This tiny green oasis lies at the most southern point of the Canadian mainland, and it has become known world wide for bird and autumn monarch butterfly migrations. They offer a wide range of habitats, a rich human history, and various recreational pursuits. The hours for the park vary through the seasons. Dogs of all sizes are allowed at no additional fee. Dogs may not be left unattended, and they must be leashed at all times, and cleaned up after. Dogs are not allowed in the group camp. Dogs are allowed on the trails on lead.

Bluffer's Park
Brimley Road South
Toronto, ON
416-397-8186
Leashed dogs are allowed in the park and on the beach. This 473 acre park is located east of the Toronto Harbour and The Beaches neighborhood. The park offers a beach and scenic overlooks from the bluffs. It is located at Brimley Road South and Kingston Road.

Dog Beach - Kew Gardens
2075 Queen Street
Toronto, ON
Located in The Beaches neighborhood, dogs are allowed to run leash-free on this section of the beach. Dogs can run leashless 24 hours a day. The dog beach area is located at the foot of Kew, on Beach,

between snow fence and Lake.

High Park
1873 Bloor Street West
Toronto, ON
416-397-8186
Leashed dogs are allowed in this park. The park covers almost 400 acres and offers many nature hiking trails and a picnic area. High Park is located west of the Toronto Harbour.

Kortright Centre
9550 Pine Valley Drive
Woodbridge, ON
416-661-6600
kortright.org/
Dogs on leash are allowed, but must be cleaned up after and are not allowed in the Visitor's Center. This 800 acres of green space offers about 10 miles of nature trails, a river valley, marshes, meadows, forests, and more. The park also focuses on promoting green energy. It is located about 10 minutes north of Toronto. To get there, take Highway 400 north to Major Mackenzie Drive. Follow Major Mackenzie Drive about 2 km west to Pine Valley Drive. Follow Pine Valley Drive south 1 km to Kortright.

Prince Edward Island

Buffalo Land Provincial Park
Commercial Road/Hwy 4
Montague, PE
902-652-8950
Located at Milltown Cross, this day use park features a boardwalk leading to a deck with a display kiosk that details information about the buffalo herd and white tailed deer. It overlooks a 100 acre enclosed area where the buffalo herd can be observed. They also provide picnic areas. Leashed dogs are allowed on site.

Quebec

Sentier de la Presqu'île (Trail)
2001 Jean-Pierre
Le Gardeur, PQ
450-585-0121

Only 30 minutes from Montreal is this family-oriented trail that has a network of four, well marked hiking trails that wander through forest and country field settings. There are picnic tables, ponds, and in spring, maple sugar shacks, to be found along the way. Dogs are welcome here, and if they are well behaved and respond to voice command, they can even be off lead. Dogs must be cleaned up after at all times.

Lafontaine Park
Sherbrook at Papineau
Montreal, PQ
514-872-9800
This 100 acre park in the Plateau Mont-Royal area offers two ponds, interesting landscaping and fountains and waterfalls. Dogs on leash are allowed. Dogs must be cleaned up after at all times.

McGill University Campus
859 rue Sherbrooke Ouest
Montreal, PQ
514-398-4455
mcgill.ca
The McGill University Campus has a lot of open areas. Well-behaved, leashed dogs are allowed in the outside areas of the campus.

Mont-Royal Park
1260, Chemin Remembrance
Montreal, PQ
514-843-8240
lemontroyal.qc.ca/en_index2.html
Functioning both as an environmentally educational park and a great get-a-way spot, there is a wide variety of activities, special events, year round water and land recreational opportunities, guided tours, and more to enjoy at this beautiful day use park. Some of the features/amenities include the historical Smith House (a testament to the area's past), rental equipment, look-out points, multi-use trails, a bird feeding route, picnic sites, a playground, a café and a snackbar, and restrooms. Access to the park is free; parking is $2.50 per hour to a total cost of $6 for the day. Dogs are allowed for no additional fee. Dogs must be under their owner's control, leashed, and cleaned up after at all times.

Parc Jean-Drapeau
Ile Notre-Dame
Montreal, PQ
514-872-6120
parcjeandrapeau.com
This island park sits on the islands of Ile Ste-Helene and Ile Notre-Dame in

the St Lawrence River. There are green areas, flower gardens, and the Old Fort. Dogs on leash are allowed at the outside areas of the park. They are not allowed on the beaches.

Artillery Park Heritage Site
2 D'Auteuil Street
Quebec, PQ
418-648-4205 (888-773-8888)
This park is located at the site of four historical buildings that were used to defend the city in the 17th century. Dogs on leash are allowed in the park but they are not allowed in the buildings or the museums.

Battlefield Park
835 Wilfrid-Laurier Avenue
Quebec, PQ
418-648-3506
Battlefield Park consists of 270 acres on the heights overlooking the St Lawrence River. The Plains of Abraham within the park was the location of a battle between the English and French on September 13, 1759. Throughout the park there are a number of monuments to generals from the past and a collection of ordinances from famous battles. Dogs on leash are allowed in the park. They must be cleaned up after and are not allowed in buildings.

Cartier - Brebeuf National Historic Site
175 l'Espinay Street
Quebec, PQ
418-648-4038 (888-773-8888)
This historical site commemorates the travels and the arrival in Quebec of Jacques Cartier. Located on the north shore of the Saint-Charles River, the park has parkland, monuments and an exhibit on the voyages of Jacques Cartier, the Jesuits and the native Indians. Dogs on leash are allowed. There may be water bowls for thisty pups. Please clean up after your dog.

Domaine Maizerets
2000, boulevard Montmorency
Quebec, PQ
418-641-6335
sracquebec.ca/maizerets.html
This historic site has fabulous landscaped gardens and a historic chateau. The chateau contains an exhibition on the history of the site. Well-behaved, leashed dogs are allowed in the outdoor areas. They are not allowed in any buildings. A bicycle and foot path sets out from the location. The area is used for

cross-country skiing in the winter.

Dufferin Terrace
at Chateau Frontenac
Quebec, PQ
This terraced park, built in 1838, provides an excellent view of the city and the St Lawrence River, Ile Orleans, the Old-Port and the Chateau Frontenac. Dogs on leash may accompany you in the park but not inside buildings.

Saint-Louis Forts and Chateaux National Historic Site
2 D'Auteuil Street
Quebec, PQ
418-648-7016 (888-773-8888)
The site is the location of the Saint-Louis forts and the chateaux that served as the governor's residence. Dogs on leash are allowed in the outdoor areas. They must be cleaned up after and are not allowed in buildings.

Saskatchewan

Wascana Centre
2900 Wascana Drive
Regina, SK
306-522-3661
wascana.sk.ca/
The Centre is one of the North America's largest urban parks with some 2,300 acres right in the city, and in addition to being dedicated to providing recreation, education, environmental conservation, and cultural arts opportunities, the Centre also offers 6 separate parks (each with their own special beauty and ambiance) and 4 unique self-guided walking tours. Dogs are allowed throughout the parks; they must be well behaved, leashed, and cleaned up after at all times.

Cranberry Flats Conservation Area
Hwy 219
Saskatoon, SK
306-665-6887
A self guided nature trail, an accessible interpretive trail, beaches and an abundance of bird and wildlife can all be found at this sand-based conservation area. Leashed dogs are allowed on site.

Meewasin Valley Trail
402 Third Avenue S (Interpretive Centre)
Saskatoon, SK
306-665-6888

meewasin.com/facilities/trail/
Traversing through the city along and in (by canoe) the river, this popular scenic trail takes visitors by 6 parks, 3 lookout points, beaches, historical sites/homes, an island sanctuary, a reserve, various habitats, significant natural areas, and more. The trail is accessible from Hwy 16/Circle Drive at either College Drive (Hwy 5) or at the 8th Street East exit. Leashed dogs are allowed on the trail; they must be under their owner's control at all times.

Chapter 3

Dog-Friendly Beach Guide

United States

California

Rio Del Mar Beach
Rio Del Mar
Aptos, CA
831-685-6500
Dogs on leash are allowed at this beach which offers a wide strip of sand. From Highway 1, take the Rio Del Mar exit.

Mad River Beach County Park
Mad River Road
Arcata, CA
707-445-7651
Enjoy walking or jogging for several miles on this beach. Dogs on leash are allowed. The park is located about 4-5 miles north of Arcata. To get there, take Highway 101 and exit Giuntoli Lane. Then go north onto Heindon Rd. Turn left onto Miller Rd. Turn right on Mad River Road and follow it to the park.

Avila Beach
off Avila Beach Drive
Avila Beach, CA
805-595-5400
This beach is about a 1/2 mile long. Dogs are not allowed between 10am and 5pm and must be leashed.

Olde Port Beach
off Avila Beach Drive
Avila Beach, CA
805-595-5400
This beach is about a 1/4 mile long. Dogs are not allowed between 10am and 5pm and must be leashed.

Big Bear Lake Beaches
Hwy 38
Big Bear Lake, CA
There are various beaches along the lake on Hwy 38. You can get to any of the beaches via the Alpine Pedal Path. To get there, (going away from the village), take the Stanfield Cutoff to the other side of the lake and turn left onto Hwy 38. In about 1/4 - 1/2 mile, parking will be on the left.

Pfieffer Beach
Sycamore Road
Big Sur, CA
805-968-6640
Dogs on leash are allowed at this day use beach which is located in the Los Padres National Forest. The beach is located in Big Sur, south of the Big Sur Ranger Station. From

Big Sur, start heading south on Highway 1 and look carefully for Sycamore Road. Take Sycamore Road just over 2 miles to the beach. There is a $5 entrance fee per car.

Doran Regional Park
201 Doran Beach Road
Bodega Bay, CA
707-875-3540
This park offers 2 miles of sandy beach. It is a popular place to picnic, walk, surf, fish and fly kites. Dogs are allowed but must be on a 6 foot or less leash and proof of a rabies vaccination is required. There is a minimal parking fee. The park is located south of Bodega Bay.

Agate Beach
Elm Road
Bolinas, CA
415-499-6387
During low tide, this 6 acre park provides access to almost 2 miles of shoreline. Leashed dogs are allowed.

Cardiff State Beach
Old Highway 101
Cardiff, CA
760-753-5091
This is a gently sloping sandy beach with warm water. Popular activities include swimming, surfing and beachcombing. Dogs on leash are allowed and please clean up after your pets. The beach is located on Old Highway 101, one mile south of Cardiff.

Carmel City Beach
Ocean Avenue
Carmel, CA
831-624-9423
This beach is within walking distance (about 7 blocks) from the quaint village of Carmel. There are a couple of hotels and several restaurants that are within walking distance of the beach. Your pooch is allowed to run off-leash as long as he or she is under voice control. To get there, take the Ocean Avenue exit from Hwy 1 and follow Ocean Ave to the end.

Carmel River State Beach
Carmelo Street
Carmel, CA
831-624-9423
This beach is just south of Carmel. It has approximately a mile of beach and leashes are required. It's located on Carmelo Street.

Garrapata State Park

Highway 1
Carmel, CA
831-649-2836
There are two miles of beach front at this park. Dogs are allowed but must be on a 6 foot or less leash and people need to clean up after their pets. The beach is on Highway 1, about 6 1/2 miles south of Rio Road in Carmel. It is about 18 miles north of Big Sur.

Caspar Beach
14441 Point Cabrillo Drive
Caspar, CA
707-937-5804
Dogs on leash are allowed at this sandy beach across from the Caspar Beach RV Park. The beach is located about 4 miles north of Mendocino. Please clean up after your dog.

Cayucos State Beach
Cayucos Drive
Cayucos, CA
805-781-5200
This state beach allows leashed dogs. The beach is located in the small town of Cayucos. To get to the beach from Hwy 1, exit Cayucos Drive and head west. There is a parking lot and parking along the street.

Cloverdale River Park
31820 McCray Road
Cloverdale, CA
707-565-2041
This park is located along the Russian River and offers seasonal fishing and river access for kayaks and canoes. There are no lifeguards at the beach area. Dogs are allowed, but must be on a 6 foot or less leash. They can wade into the water, but cannot really swim because pets must remain on leash. There is a $3 per car parking fee.

Corona Del Mar State Beach
Iris Street and Ocean Blvd.
Corona Del Mar, CA
949-644-3151
This is a popular beach for swimming, surfing and diving. The sandy beach is about a half mile long. Dogs are allowed on this beach during certain hours. They are allowed before 9am and after 5pm, year round. Pets must be on a 6 foot or less leash. Tickets will be issued if your dog is off leash.

Coronado Dog Beach
100 Ocean Blvd
Coronado, CA
619-522-7342

Coronado's Dog Beach is at the north end of Ocean Blvd. Just north of the famous Hotel del Coronado (unfortunately dogs are not allowed at the hotel)the area that is designated off leash is marked by signs. The off-leash beach is open 24 hours. Dogs must be supervised and cleaned up after. Dogs must be leashed outside of the off-leash area and fines are very steep for any violations. There are also fines for not cleaning up after your dog at the dog beach. Food and Pet Treats are not allowed at the beach.

Beachfront Park
Front Street
Crescent City, CA
707-464-9507
Dogs are allowed at park and the beach, but must be leashed. Please clean up after your pets. To get there, take Highway 101 to Front Street. Follow Front Street to the park.

Crescent Beach
Enderts Beach Road
Crescent City, CA
707-464-6101
nps.gov/redw/home.html
While dogs are not allowed on any trails in Redwood National Park, they are allowed on a couple of beaches, including Crescent Beach. Enjoy beachcombing or bird watching at this beach. Pets are also allowed at road accessible picnic areas and campgrounds. Dogs must be on a 6 foot or less leash and people need to pick up after their pets. The beach is located off Highway 101, about 3 to 4 miles south of Crescent City. Exit Enderts Beach Road and head south.

Davenport Beach
Hwy 1
Davenport, CA
831-462-8333
This beautiful beach is surrounded by high bluffs and cliff trails. Leashes are required. To get to the beach from Santa Cruz, head north on Hwy 1 for about 10 miles.

Del Mar Beach
Seventeenth Street
Del Mar, CA
858-755-1556
Dogs are allowed on the beach as follows. South of 17th Street, dogs are allowed on a 6 foot leash year-round. Between 17th Street and 29th Street, dogs are allowed on a 6 foot leash from October through May (from June through September, dogs

are not allowed at all). Between 29th Street and northern city limits, dogs are allowed without a leash, but must be under voice control from October through May (from June through September, dogs must be on a 6 foot leash). Owners must clean up after their dogs.

Rivermouth Beach
Highway 101
Del Mar, CA
This beach allows voice controlled dogs to run leash free from September 15 through June 15 (no specified hours). Leashes are required during mid-summer tourist season from mid June to mid Sept. Fans of this beach are trying to convince the Del Mar City council to extend the leash-free period to year round. The beach is located on Highway 101 just south of Border Avenue at the north end of the City of Del Mar. Thanks to one of our readers for recommending this beach.

MacKerricher State Park
Highway 1
Fort Bragg, CA
707-964-9112
Dogs are allowed on the beach, but not on any park trails. Pets must be leashed and people need to clean up after their pets. Picnic areas, restrooms and campsites (including an ADA restroom and campsites), are available at this park. The park is located three miles north of Fort Bragg on Highway 1, near the town of Cleone.

Noyo Beach Off-Leash Dog Beach
North Harbor Drive
Fort Bragg, CA
Hwy
frankhartzell.com/MCDOG
The dog beach is located at the north side of where the Noyo River enters the Pacific Ocean. To get to the dog beach, turn EAST (away from the ocean) on N. Harbor Drive from Highway 1. N. Harbor will go down to the river and circle under Highway 1 to the beach. The beach was organized by MCDOG (Mendocino Coast Dog Owners Group) which is now working on an off-leash dog park for the Mendocino area.

Goleta Beach County Park
5990 Sandspit Road
Goleta, CA
805-568-2460
Leashed dogs are allowed at this county beach. The beach and park

are about 1/2 mile long. There are picnic tables and a children's playground at the park. It's located near the Santa Barbara Municipal Airport in Goleta, just north of Santa Barbara. To get there, take Hwy 101 to Hwy 217 and head west. Before you reach UC Santa Barbara, there will be an exit for Goleta Beach.

Kirk Creek Beach and Trailhead
Highway 1
Gorda, CA
831-385-5434
Both the Kirk Creek Beach and hiking trails allow dogs. Pets must be leashed. You can park next to the Kirk Creek Campground and either hike down to the beach or start hiking at the Kirk Creek Trailhead which leads to the Vicente Flat Trail where you can hike for miles with your dog. The beach and trailhead is part of the Los Padres National Forest and is located about 25 miles south of Big Sur.

Sand Dollar Beach
Highway 1
Gorda, CA
805-434-1996
Walk down a path to one of the longest sandy beaches on the Big Sur Coast. This national forest managed beach is popular for surfing, fishing and walking. Dogs must be on leash and people need to clean up after their pets. There is a minimal day use fee. The dog-friendly Plaskett Creek Campground is within walking distance. This beach is part of the Los Padres National Forest and is located about 5 miles south of the Kirk Creek and about 30 miles south of Big Sur.

Willow Creek Beach
Highway 1
Gorda, CA
831-385-5434
Dogs on leash are allowed at this day use beach and picnic area. The beach is part of the Los Padres National Forest and is located about 35 miles south of Big Sur.

Gualala Point Regional Park Beach
42401 Coast Highway 1
Gualala, CA
707-565-2041
This county park offers sandy beaches, hiking trails, campsites, picnic tables and restrooms. Dogs are allowed on the beach, on the trails, and in the campground, but they must be on a 6 foot or less leash. People also need to clean up after their pets. There is a $3 day

use fee.

Blufftop Coastal Park
Poplar Street
Half Moon Bay, CA
650-726-8297
Leashed dogs are allowed at this beach. The beach is located on the west end of Poplar Street, off Highway 1.

Montara State Beach
Highway 1
Half Moon Bay, CA
650-726-8819
Dogs on leash are allowed at this beach. Please clean up after your pets. The beach is located 8 miles north of Half Moon Bay on Highway 1. There are two beach access points. The first access point is across from Second Street, immediately south of the Outrigger Restaurant. The second access point is about a 1/2 mile north on the ocean side of Highway 1. Both access points have steep paths down to the beach.

Surfer's Beach
Highway 1
Half Moon Bay, CA
650-726-8297
Dogs on leash are allowed on the beach. It is located at Highway 1 and Coronado Street.

Healdsburg Memorial Beach
13839 Old Redwood Highway
Healdsburg, CA
707-565-2041
This man-made swimming beach is located on the Russian River. Dogs are allowed at this park, but must be on a 6 foot or less leash. They can wade into the water, but cannot really swim because pets must remain on leash. People are urged to swim only when lifeguards are present, which is usually between Memorial Day and Labor Day. The beach area also offers picnic tables and a restroom. There is a $3 to $4 parking fee per day, depending on the season.

Huntington Dog Beach
Pacific Coast Hwy (Hwy 1)
Huntington Beach, CA
714-841-8644Hwy
dogbeach.org
This beautiful beach is about a mile long and allows dogs from 5 am to 10 pm. Dogs must be under control but may be off leash and owners must pick up after them. Dogs are only allowed on the beach between Golden West Street and Seapoint

Ave. Please adhere to these rules as there are only a couple of dog-friendly beaches left in the entire Los Angeles area. The beach is located off the Pacific Coast Hwy (Hwy 1) at Golden West Street. Please remember to pick up after your dog... the city wanted to prohibit dogs in 1997 because of the dog waste left on the beach. But thanks to The Preservation Society of Huntington Dog Beach (http://www.dogbeach.org), it continues to be dog-friendly. City ordinances require owners to pick up after their dogs. It is suggested that you bring plenty of quarters in order to feed the parking meters near the beach.

Imperial Beach
Seacoast Drive at Imperial Beach Blvd
Imperial Beach, CA
619-424-3151
Dogs on leash are allowed on the portions of the beach that are north of Palm Avenue and south of Imperial Beach Blvd. They are not allowed on the beach between Palm Avenue and Imperial Beach Blvd.

Stillwater Cove Regional Park
22455 Highway 1
Jenner, CA
707-565-2041
This 210 acre park includes a small beach, campground, picnic tables, and restrooms. The park offers a great view of the Pacific Ocean from Stillwater Cove. Dogs are allowed on the beach, and in the campground, but they must be on a 6 foot or less leash. People also need to clean up after their pets. There is a $3 day use fee. The park is located off Highway 1, about 16 miles north of Jenner.

Coon Street Beach
Coon Street
Kings Beach, CA
Located at the end of Coon Street, on the east side of Kings Beach is a small but popular dog beach. There are also picnic tables, barbecues and restrooms at this beach.

La Jolla Shores Beach
Camino Del Oro
La Jolla, CA
619-221-8900
Leashed dogs are allowed on this beach and the adjacent Kellogg Park from 6pm to 9am. The beach is about 1/2 mile long. To get there, take Hwy 5 to the La Jolla Village Drive exit heading west. Turn left

onto Torrey Pines Rd. Then turn right onto La Jolla Shores Drive. Go 4-5 blocks and turn left onto Vallecitos. Go straight until you reach the beach and Kellogg Park.

Point La Jolla Beaches
Coast Blvd.
La Jolla, CA
619-221-8900
Leashed dogs are allowed on this beach and the walkway (paved and dirt trails) from 6pm to 9am. The beaches and walkway are at least a 1/2 mile long and might continue further. To get there, exit La Jolla Village Drive West from Hwy 5. Turn left onto Torrey Pines Rd. Turn right on Prospect and then park or turn right onto Coast Blvd. Parking is limited around the village area.

Main Beach
Pacific Hwy (Hwy 1)
Laguna Beach, CA
949-497-3311
Dogs are allowed on this beach between 6pm and 8am, June 1 to September 16. The rest of the year, they are allowed on the beach from dawn until dusk. Dogs must be on a leash at all times.

Long Beach Dog Beach Zone
between Roycroft and Argonne Avenues
Long Beach, CA
562-570-3100
hautedogs.org/
This 3 acre off-leash unfenced dog beach is the only off-leash dog beach in Los Angeles County. It is open daily from 6am until 8pm. It opened on August 1, 2003. The "zone" is 235 yards along the water and 60 yards deep. There is a fresh water fountain called the "Fountain of Woof" which is located near the restrooms at the end of Granada Avenue, near the Dog Zone. Only one dog is allowed per adult and dog owners are entirely responsible for their dog's actions. The beach is located between Roycroft and Argonne avenues in Belmont Shore, Long Beach. It is a few blocks east of the Belmont Pier and Olympic pool. From Ocean Blvd, enter at Bennett Avenue for the beachfront metered parking lot. The cost is 25 cents for each 15 minutes from 8am until 6pm daily. Parking is free after 5pm in the beachfront lot at the end of Granada Avenue. You can check with the website http://www.hautedogs.org for updates and additional rules about the Long Beach Dog Beach Zone.

Leo Carrillo State Beach
Hwy 1
Malibu, CA
818-880-0350
This beach is one of the very few dog-friendly beaches in the Los Angeles area. In a press release dated November 27, 2002, the California State Parks clarified the rules for dogs at Leo Carrillo State Beach. We thank the State Parks for this clear announcement of the regulations. Dogs are allowed on a maximum 6 foot leash when accompanied by a person capable of controlling the dog on all beach WEST (up coast) of lifeguard tower 3 at Leo Carrillo State Park, Staircase Beach, County Line Beach, and all Beaches within Point Mugu State Park. Dogs are NOT allowed EAST of lifeguard tower 3 at Leo Carrillo State Beach at any time. And please note that dogs are not allowed in the tide pools at Leo Carrillo. There should be signs posted. A small general store is located on the mountain side of the freeway. Here you can grab some snacks and other items. The park is located on Hwy 1, approximately 30 miles northwest of Santa Monica. We ask that all dog people closely obey these regulations so that the beach continues to be dog-friendly.

Manresa State Beach
San Andreas Road
Manresa, CA
831-761-1795
Surfing and surf fishing are both popular activities at this beach. Dogs are allowed on the beach, but must be leashed. To get there from Aptos, head south on Highway 1. Take San Andreas Road southwest for several miles until you reach Manresa. Upon reaching the coast, you will find the first beach access point.

Clam Beach County Park
Highway 101
McKinleyville, CA
707-445-7651
This beach is popular for fishing, swimming, picnicking and beachcombing. Of course, there are also plenty of clams. Dogs on leash are allowed on the beach and at the campgrounds. There are no day use fees. The park is located off Highway 101, about eight miles north of Arcata.

Big River Beach
N. Big River Road
Mendocino, CA

707-937-5804
This small beach is located just south of downtown Mendocino. There are two ways to get there. One way is to head south of town on Hwy 1 and turn left on N. Big River Rd. The beach will be on the right. The second way is to take Hwy 1 and exit Main Street/Jackson heading towards the coastline. In about 1/4-1/2 mile there will be a Chevron Gas Station and a historic church on the left. Park and then walk behind the church to the trailhead. Follow the trail, bearing left when appropriate, and there will be a wooden staircase that goes down to Big River Beach. Dogs must be on leash.

Van Damme State Beach
Highway 1
Mendocino, CA
This small beach is located in the town of Little River which is approximately 2 miles south of Mendocino. It is part of Van Damme State Park which is located across Highway 1. Most California State Parks, including this one, do not allow dogs on the hiking trails. Fortunately this one allows dogs on the beach. There is no parking fee at the beach and dogs must be on leash.

Monterey Recreation Trail
various (see description)
Monterey, CA
monterey.org/rec/rectrl96.html
Take a walk on the Monterey Recreation Trail and experience the beautiful scenery that makes Monterey so famous. This paved trail extends for miles, starting at Fisherman's Wharf and ending in the city of Pacific Grove. Dogs must be leashed. Along the path there are a few small beaches that allow dogs such as the one south of Fisherman's Wharf and another beach behind Ghirardelli Ice Cream on Cannery Row. Along the path you'll find a few more outdoor places to eat near Cannery Row and by the Monterey Bay Aquarium. Look at the Restaurants section for more info.

Monterey State Beach
various (see comments)
Monterey, CA
831-649-2836
Take your water loving and beach loving dog to this awesome beach in Monterey. There are various starting points, but it basically stretches from Hwy 1 and the Del

Rey Oaks Exit down to Fisherman's Wharf. Various beaches make up this 2 mile (each way) stretch of beach, but leashed dogs are allowed on all of them . If you want to extend your walk, you can continue on the paved Monterey Recreation Trail which goes all the way to Pacific Grove. There are a few smaller dog-friendly beaches along the paved trail.

Muir Beach
Hwy 1
Muir Beach, CA
Dogs on leash are allowed on Muir Beach with you. Please clean up after your dog on the beach. To get to Muir Beach from Hwy 101 take Hwy 1 North from the north side of the Golden Gate Bridge.

Newport and Balboa Beaches
Balboa Blvd.
Newport Beach, CA
949-644-3211
There are several smaller beaches which run along Balboa Blvd. Dogs are only allowed before 9am and after 5pm, year round. Pets must be on a 6 foot or less leash and people are required to clean up after their pets. Tickets will be issued if your dog is off leash. The beaches are located along Balboa Blvd and ample parking is located near the Balboa and Newport Piers.

Dog Beach
Point Loma Blvd.
Ocean Beach, CA
619-221-8900
Dogs are allowed to run off leash at this beach anytime during the day. This is a very popular dog beach which attracts lots and lots of dogs on warm days. To get there, take Hwy 8 West until it ends and then it becomes Sunset Cliffs Blvd. Then make a right turn onto Point Loma Blvd and follow the signs to Ocean Beach's Dog Beach.

Ocean Beach
Point Loma Blvd.
Ocean Beach, CA
619-221-8900
Leashed dogs are allowed on this beach from 6pm to 9am. The beach is about 1/2 mile long. To get there, take Hwy 8 West until it ends and then it becomes Sunset Cliffs Blvd. Then make a right turn onto Point Loma Blvd and follow the signs to Ocean Beach Park. A separate beach called Dog Beach is at the north end of this beach which allows dogs to run off-leash.

Dog-Friendly Beaches - California - Please call ahead to confirm an establishment is still dog-friendly.

Oceano Dunes State Vehicular
Recreation Area
Highway 1
Oceano, CA
805-473-7220
This 3,600 acre off road area offers 5
1/2 miles of beach which is open for
vehicle use. Pets on leash are
allowed too. Swimming, surfing,
horseback riding and bird watching
are all popular activities at the beach.
The park is located three miles south
of Pismo Beach off Highway 1.

Point Reyes National Seashore
Olema, CA
415-464-5100
nps.gov/pore/
Leashed dogs (on a 6 foot or less
leash) are allowed on four beaches.
The dog-friendly beaches are the
Limantour Beach, Kehoe Beach,
North Beach and South Beach. Dogs
are not allowed on the hiking trails.
However, they are allowed on some
hiking trails that are adjacent to Point
Reyes. For a map of dog-friendly
hiking trails, please stop by the
Visitor Center. Point Reyes is located
about an hour north of San
Francisco. From Highway 101, exit at
Sir Francis Drake Highway, and
continue west on Sir Francis Drake
to Olema. To find the Visitor Center,
turn right in Olema onto Route 1 and
then make a left onto Bear Valley
Road. The Visitor Center will be on
the left.

Freshwater Lagoon Beach -
Redwood National Park
Highway 101 south end of Redwood
National Park
Orick, CA
707-464-6101
nps.gov/redw/home.html
Dogs are allowed on the ocean
beaches around Freshwater Lagoon,
but not on any trails within Redwood
National Park. Picnic tables are
available at the beach. Pets are also
allowed at road accessible picnic
areas and campgrounds. Dogs must
be on a 6 foot or less leash and
people need to pick up after their
pets. The beach is located off
Highway 101 behind the Redwood
Information Center at the south end
of the Redwood National Park. The
parking area for the beach is about 2
miles south of Orick. Some portions
of this beach are rather rocky but
there are also sandy portions as well.

Gold Bluffs Beach - Redwood NP
Davison Road
Orick, CA

707-464-6101
nps.gov/redw/home.html
Dogs are allowed on this beach, but
not on any trails within this park.
Picnic tables and campgrounds are
available at the beach. Pets are
also allowed at road accessible
picnic areas and campgrounds.
Dogs must be on a 6 foot or less
leash and people need to pick up
after their pets. The beach is
located off Highway 101. Take
Highway 101 heading north. Pass
Orick and drive about 3-4 miles,
then exit Davison Rd. Head towards
the coast on an unpaved road
(trailers are not allowed on the
unpaved road).

Hollywood Beach
various addresses
Oxnard, CA
This beach is located on the west
side of the Channel Islands Harbor.
The beach is 4 miles southwest of
Oxnard. Dogs must be on leash and
owners must clean up after their
pets. Dogs are allowed on
Hollywood Beach before 9 am and
after 5 pm.

Oxnard Shores Beach
Harbor Blvd.
Oxnard, CA
This beach stretches for miles. If
you enter at 5th Street and go
north, there are no houses and very
few people. Dogs must be on leash
and owners must clean up after
their pets. Thanks to one of our
readers for recommending this
beach.

Silverstrand Beach
various addresses
Oxnard, CA
This beach is located between the
Channel Islands Harbor and the
U.S. Naval Construction Battalion
Center. Dogs are now only allowed
on the beach after 5 pm and before
8 am. The beach is 4 miles
southwest of Oxnard. Dogs must be
on leash and owners must clean up
after their pets.

Asilomar State Beach
Along Sunset Drive
Pacific Grove, CA
831-372-4076
Dogs are permitted on leash on the
beach and the scenic walking trails.
If you walk south along the beach
and go across the stream that leads
into the ocean, you can take your
dog off-leash, but he or she must be
under strict voice control and within
your sight at all times.

Esplanade Beach
Esplanade
Pacifica, CA
650-738-7381
This beach offers an off-leash area
for dogs. To get to the beach, take
the stairs at the end of Esplanade.
Esplanade is just north of Manor
Drive, off Highway 1.

Lake Nacimiento Resort Day Use
Area
10625 Nacimiento Lake Drive
Paso Robles, CA
805-238-3256
nacimientoresort.com/
In addition to the campgrounds and
RV area, this resort also offers day
use of the lake. Dogs can swim in
the water, but be very careful of
boats, as this is a popular lake for
water-skiing. Day use fees vary by
season and location, but in general
rates are about $5 to $8 per person.
Senior discounts are available. Dogs
are an extra $5 per day. Proof of
your dog's rabies vaccination is
required.

Bean Hollow State Beach
Highway 1
Pescadero, CA
650-879-2170
This is a very rocky beach with not
much sand. Dogs are allowed but
must be on a 6 foot or less leash.
Please clean up after your pets. The
beach is located 3 miles south of
Pescadero on Highway 1.

Pismo State Beach
Grand Ave.
Pismo Beach, CA
805-489-2684
Leashed dogs are allowed on this
state beach. This beach is popular
for walking, sunbathing, swimming
and the annual winter migration of
millions of monarch butterflies (the
park has the largest over-wintering
colony of monarch butterflies in the
U.S.). To get there from Hwy 101,
exit 4th Street and head south. In
about a mile, turn right onto Grand
Ave. You can park along the road.

Sonoma Coast State Beach
Highway 1
Salmon Creek, CA
707-875-3483
Dogs on leash are allowed at some
of the beaches in this state park.
Dogs are allowed at Shell Beach,
Portuguese Beach and Schoolhouse
Beach. They are not allowed at Goat
Rock or Salmon Creek Beach due to
the protected seals and snowy

463

plovers. Please clean up after your pets. While dogs are allowed on some of the beaches and campgrounds, they are not allowed on any hiking trails at this park.

Samoa Dunes Recreation Area
New Navy Base Road
Samoa, CA
707-825-2300
ca.blm.gov/caso/wf-samoadun.html
The Bureau of Land Management oversees this 300 acre sand dune park. It is a popular spot for off-highway vehicles which can use about 140 of the park's acres. Dogs are allowed on leash or off-leash but under voice control. Even if your dog runs off-leash, the park service requests that you still bring a leash just in case. To get there, take Highway 255 and turn south on New Navy Base Road. Go about four miles to the parking area.

Fiesta Island
Fiesta Island Road
San Diego, CA
619-221-8900
On this island, dogs are allowed to run off-leash anywhere outside the fenced areas, anytime during the day. It is mostly sand which is perfect for those beach loving hounds. You might, however, want to stay on the north end of the island. The south end was used as the city's sludge area (mud and sediment, and possibly smelly) processing facility. The island is often used to launch jet-skis and motorboats. There is a one-way road that goes around the island and there are no fences, so please make sure your dog stays away from the road. About half way around the island, there is a completely fenced area on the beach. Please note that the fully enclosed area is not a dog park. The city of San Diego informed us that is supposed to be locked and is not intended to be used as a dog park even though there may occasionally be dogs running in this off-limits area.

Mission Beach & Promenade
Mission Blvd.
San Diego, CA
619-221-8900
Leashed dogs are allowed on this beach and promenade walkway from 6pm to 9am. It is about 3 miles long and located west of Mission Bay Park.

Baker Beach
Lincoln Blvd and Bowley St/Golden

Gate Nat'l Rec Area
San Francisco, CA
415-561-4700
nps.gov/prsf/places/bakerbch.htm
This dog-friendly beach in the Golden Gate National Recreation Area has a great view of the Golden Gate Bridge. Dogs are permitted off leash under voice control on Baker Beach North of Lobos Creek; they must be leashed South of Lobos Creek. The beach is located approx. 1.5 to 2 miles south of the Golden Gate Bridge. From Lincoln Avenue, turn onto Bowley Street and head towards the ocean. There is a parking lot next to the beach. This is a clothing optional beach, so there may be the occasional sunbather.

Fort Funston/Burton Beach
Skyline Blvd./Hwy 35
San Francisco, CA
nps.gov/goga/
This is a very popular dog-friendly park and beach. In the past, dogs have been allowed off-leash. However, currently all dogs must be on leash. Fort Funston is part of the Golden Gate National Recreation Area. There are trails that run through the dunes & ice plant from the parking lot above with good access to the beach below. It overlooks the southern end of Ocean Beach, with a large parking area accessible from Skyline Boulevard. There is also a water faucet and trough at the parking lot for thirsty pups. It's located off Skyline Blvd. (also known Hwy 35) by John Muir Drive. It is south of Ocean Beach. Thanks to one of our readers for this info. Expect to see lots and lots of dogs having a great time. But not to worry, there is plenty of room for everyone.

Lands End Off Leash Dog Area
El Camino Del Mar
San Francisco, CA
415-561-4700
Owned and operated by the Golden Gate National Recreation Area, Lands End is everything west of and including the Coast Trail, and is an extraordinary combination of parkland, natural areas, and dramatic coastal cliffs. It offers great hiking, ocean and city views, a museum, the ruins of the Sutro Baths, and includes the Sutro Heights Park (dogs must be on lead in this area). This area can be accessed at Merrie Way for the cliffside paths, and at this entrance or the large lot at the end of El

Camino Del Mar off Point Lobos for the Coast Trail and beaches. Dogs must be on leash on the Coast Trail, under firm voice control when in off leash areas, and they must be cleaned up after.

Ocean Beach
Great Hwy
San Francisco, CA
415-556-8642
You'll get a chance to stretch your legs at this beach which has about 4 miles of sand. The beach runs parallel to the Great Highway (north of Fort Funston). There are several access points including Sloat Blvd., Fulton Street or Lincoln Way. This beach has a mix of off-leash and leash required areas. Thanks to the San Francisco Dog Owners Group (SFDOG) for providing the following information: Dogs must be on leash on Ocean Beach between Sloat Blvd and Stairwell #21 (roughly at Fulton). North of Fulton to the Cliff House and South of Sloat for several miles are still okay for off-leash dogs, however parts of these areas may be impassible at high tide. The Golden Gate National Rec Area (GGNRA) strictly enforces the on-leash area between Sloat and Fulton. They usually give no warning tickets ($50 fine). As with all other leash required areas, we encourage dog owners to comply with the rules.

Coastal Access
off Hearst Drive
San Simeon, CA
There is parking just north of the Best Western Hotel, next to the "Coastal Access" sign. Dogs must be on leash.

Arroyo Burro Beach County Park
2981 Cliff Drive
Santa Barbara, CA
805-967-1300
Leashed dogs are allowed at this county beach and park. The beach is about 1/2 mile long and it is adjacent to a palm-lined grassy area with picnic tables. To get to the beach from Hwy 101, exit Las Positas Rd/Hwy 225. Head south (towards the ocean). When the street ends, turn right onto Cliff Drive. The beach will be on the left.

Arroyo Burro Off-Leash Beach
Cliff Drive
Santa Barbara, CA
While dogs are not allowed off-leash at the Arroyo Burro Beach County Park (both the beach and grass

area), they are allowed to run leash free on the adjacent beach. The dog beach starts east of the slough at Arroyo Burro and stretches almost to the stairs at Mesa Lane. To get to the off-leash area, walk your leashed dog from the parking lot to the beach, turn left and cross the slough. At this point you can remove your dog's leash.

Rincon Park and Beach
Bates Road
Santa Barbara, CA
This beach is at Rincon Point which has some of the best surfing waves in the world. In the winter, it is very popular with surfers. In the summer, it is a popular swimming beach. Year-round, leashed dogs are welcome. The beach is about 1/2-1 mile long. Next to the parking lot there are picnic tables, phones and restrooms. The beach is in Santa Barbara County, about 15-20 minutes south of Santa Barbara. To get there from Santa Barbara, take Hwy 101 south and go past Carpinteria. Take the Bates Rd exit towards the ocean. When the road ends, turn right into the Rincon Park and Beach parking lot.

East Cliff Coast Access Points
East Cliff Drive
Santa Cruz, CA
831-454-7900
There are many small dog-friendly beaches and coastal access points that stretch along East Cliff Drive between 12th Avenue and 41st Avenue. This is not one long beach because the water comes up to cliffs in certain areas and breaks it up into many smaller beaches. Dogs are allowed on leash. Parking is on city streets along East Cliff or the numbered avenues. To get there from Hwy 17 south, take the Hwy 1 exit south towards Watsonville. Take the exit towards Soquel Drive. Turn left onto Soquel Avenue. Turn right onto 17th Avenue. Continue straight until you reach East Cliff Drive. From here, you can head north or south on East Cliff Drive and park anywhere between 12th and 41st street to access the beaches.

Its Beach
West Cliff Drive
Santa Cruz, CA
831-429-3777
This is not a large beach, but it is big enough for your water loving dog to take a dip in the water and get lots of sand between his or her paws. Dogs must be on leash at all times. The

beach is located on West Cliff Drive, just north of the Lighthouse, and south of Columbia Street.

Mitchell's Cove Beach
West Cliff Drive at Almar
Santa Cruz, CA
831-420-5270
Dogs are allowed off-leash on Mitchell's Cove Beach between sunrise and 10 am and from 4 pm to sunset. They must be on-leash during other hours. The beach is along West Cliff Drive between Woodward and Almar. While off-leash dogs must be under voice control.

Seabright Beach
Seabright Ave
Santa Cruz, CA
831-429-2850
This beach is located south of the Santa Cruz Beach Boardwalk and north of the Santa Cruz Harbor. Dogs are allowed on leash. Fire rings are available for beach bonfires. It is open from sunrise to sunset. To get there from Hwy 17 south, exit Ocean Street on the left towards the beaches. Merge onto Ocean Street. Turn left onto East Cliff Drive and stay straight to go onto Murray Street. Then turn right onto Seabright Ave. Seabright Ave will take you to the beach (near the corner of East Cliff Drive and Seabright).

Twin Lakes State Beach
East Cliff Drive
Santa Cruz, CA
831-429-2850
This beach is one of the area's warmest beaches, due to its location at the entrance of Schwann Lagoon. Dogs are allowed on leash. The beach is located just south of the Santa Cruz Harbor where Aldo's Restaurant is located. Fire rings for beach bonfires, outdoor showers and restrooms are available. It is open from sunrise to sunset. To get there from Hwy 17 south, exit Ocean Street on the left towards the beaches. Merge onto Ocean Street. Turn left onto East Cliff Drive and stay straight to go onto Murray Street. Murray Street becomes Eaton Street. Turn right onto 7th Avenue.

Sea Ranch Coastal Access Trails
Highway 1
Sea Ranch, CA
707-785-2377
Walk along coastal headlands or the beach in Sea Ranch. There are

six trailhead parking areas which are located along Highway 1, south of the Sonoma Mendocino County Line. Access points include Black Point, Bluff Top Trail, Pebble Beach, Stengal Beach, Shell Beach and Walk on Beach. Dogs must be on a 6 foot or less leash. There is a $3 per car parking fee. RVs and vehicles with trailers are not allowed to use the parking areas.

Kiva Beach
Hwy 89
South Lake Tahoe, CA
530-573-2600
This small but lovely beach is a perfect place for your pup to take a dip in Lake Tahoe. Dogs must be on leash. To get there from the intersection of Hwys 89 and 50, take Hwy 89 north approx 2-3 miles to the entrance on your right. Follow the road and towards the end, bear left to the parking lot. Then follow the path to the beach.

Upton Beach
Highway 1
Stinson Beach, CA
415-499-6387
Dogs not allowed on the National Park section of Stinson Beach but are allowed at Upton Beach which is under Marin County's jurisdiction. This beach is located north of the National Park. Dogs are permitted without leash but under direct and immediate control.

Pebble Beach/Dog Beach
Hwy 89
Tahoe City, CA
This beach is not officially called "pebble beach" but it is an accurate description. No sand at this beach, but your water-loving dog won't mind. The water is crisp and clear and perfect for a little swimming. It's not a large area, but it is very popular with many dogs. There is also a paved bike trail that is parallel to the beach. There was no official name posted for this beach, but it's located about 1-2 miles south of Tahoe City on Hwy 89. From Tahoe City, the beach and parking will be on your left. Dogs should be on leash on the beach.

Trinidad State Beach
Highway 101
Trinidad, CA
707-677-3570
Dogs are unofficially allowed at College Cove beach, as long as they are leashed and under control. The residents in this area are trying keep this beach dog-friendly, but the rules

can change at any time. Please call ahead to verify.

Harbor Cove Beach
West end of Spinnaker Drive
Ventura, CA
805-652-4550
This beach is considered the safest swimming area in Ventura because of the protection of the cove. Dogs of all sizes are allowed at this beach as well as on the 6 miles of Ventura City Beaches and on the long wooden pier, but they are not allowed on any of the beaches south of the Ventura Pier or on any of the State beaches. Dogs must be leashed and cleaned up after at all times.

Promenade Park
Figueroa Street at the Promenade
Ventura, CA
805-652-4550
This park is a one acre oceanfront park on the site of an old Indian village near Seaside Park. Dogs of all sizes are allowed at this beach as well as on the 6 miles of Ventura City Beaches and on the long wooden pier, but they are not allowed on any of the beaches south of the Ventura Pier or on any of the State beaches. Dogs must be leashed and cleaned up after at all times.

Surfer's Point at Seaside Park
Figueroa Street at the Promenade
Ventura, CA
800-483-6215
This park is one of the area's most popular surfing and windsurfing beaches, and it offers showers, picnic facilities and restrooms, and is connected with the Ventura Pier by a scenic landscaped Promenade walkway and the Omer Rains Bike Trail. Dogs are allowed on the 6 miles of Ventura City Beaches and on the long wooden pier, but they are not allowed on any of the beaches south of the Ventura Pier or on any of the State beaches. Dogs must be leashed and cleaned up after at all times.

Westport-Union Landing State Beach
Highway 1
Westport, CA
707-937-5804
This park offers about 2 miles of sandy beach. Dogs must be on a 6 foot or less leash at all times and people need to clean up after their pets. Picnic tables, restrooms (including an ADA restroom) and campsites are available at this park. Dogs are also allowed at the

campsites, but not on any park trails. The park is located off Highway 1, about 2 miles north of Westport or 19 miles north of Fort Bragg.

North Beach at Zephyr Cove Resort
460 Highway 50
Zephyr Cove, NV
775-588-6644
Dogs are not allowed at the main beach at the Zephyr Cove Resort. They are allowed on leash, however, at the north beach at the resort. There is a $5.00 parking fee for day use. When you enter Zephyr Cover Resort head to the right (North) to the last parking area and walk the few hundred feet to the beach. The North Beach is located just into the National Forest. There usually are cleanup bags on the walkway to the beach but bring your own in case they run out. This is a nice beach that is used by a lot of people in the summer. The cabins at Zephyr Cove Resort also allow dogs.

Colorado

Union Reservoir Dog Beach
County Line Rd at E 9th Ave
Longmont, CO
303-651-8447
This is an unfenced off-leash area where dogs may swim in the Union Reservoir. Dogs may only be off-leash in the designated area and must be leashed when in the rest of the rec area. Dogs are not allowed on beaches outside of the dog beach. To get to Union Reservoir Rec Area from I-25 take Ute Hwy west to E County Line Rd and turn left (south). Turn left onto Highway 26 into the park in just over one mile.

Connecticut

Town of Fairfield Beaches
off Highway 1
Fairfield, CT
203-256-3010
Dogs are only allowed on the town beaches during the off-season. Pets are not allowed on the beaches from April 1 through October 1. Dogs must be on leash and people

need to clean up after their pets.

Delaware

Bethany Beach
off Route 1
Bethany Beach, DE
302-539-8011
townofbethanybeach.com/FAQ.shtml
From May 15 to September 30, pets are not allowed on the beach or boardwalk at any time. But during the off-season, dogs are allowed but need to be leashed and cleaned up after.

Dewey Beach
Coastal Highway/Route 1
Dewey Beach, DE
302-227-1110
Dogs are allowed on the beach year-round only with a special license and with certain hour restrictions during the summer season. A special license is required for your dog to go on the beach. You do not have to be a resident of Dewey Beach to get the license. You can obtain one from the Town of Dewey Beach during regular business hours at 105 Rodney Avenue in Dewey Beach. The cost is $5 per dog and is good for the lifetime of your dog. During the summer, from May 15 to September 15, dogs are only allowed before 9:30am and after 5:30pm. During the off-season there are no hourly restrictions. Year-round, dogs can be off-leash but need to be under your control at all times and cleaned up after.

Fenwick Island Beach
off Route 1
Fenwick Island, DE
302-539-2000
fenwickisland.org
From May 1 to September 30, dogs are not allowed on the beach at any time. The rest of the year, pets are allowed on the beach but must be leashed and cleaned up after. The beach is located of Route 1, south of Dewey Beach.

Cape Henlopen State Park
42 Cape Henlopen Drive
Lewes, DE
302-645-8983
destateparks.com/chsp/chsp.htm
This park draws thousands of visitors who enjoy sunbathing and ocean swimming. Dogs on a 6 foot or less leash are allowed on the beach, with

some exceptions. Dogs are not allowed on the two swimming beaches during the summer, but they are allowed on surfing and fishing beaches, bike paths and some of the trails. Pets are not allowed on the fishing pier. During the off-season, dogs are allowed on any of the beaches, but still need to be leashed. People are required to clean up after their pets. The park is located one mile east of Lewes, 1/2 mile past the Cape May-Lewes Ferry Terminal.

Delaware Seashore State Park
Inlet 850
Rehoboth Beach, DE
302-227-2800
destateparks.com/dssp/dssp.asp
This park offers six miles of ocean and bay shoreline. Dogs on a 6 foot or less leash are allowed on the beach, with a couple of exceptions. Dogs are not allowed at the lifeguarded swimming areas. However, there are plenty of non-guarded beaches where people with dogs can walk or sunbathe. During the off-season, dogs are allowed on any of the beaches, but still need to be leashed. People are required to clean up after their pets. The park is located south of Dewey Beach, along Route 1.

Rehoboth Beach
off Route 1
Rehoboth Beach, DE
302-227-6181
cityofrehoboth.com/
From April 1 to October 31, pets are not allowed on the beach or boardwalk at any time. However, during the off-season, dogs are allowed but need to be leashed and cleaned up after. The beach is located off Route 1, north of Dewey Beach.

South Bethany Beach
off Route 1
South Bethany, DE
302-539-3653
southbethany.org/
From May 15 to October 15, dogs are not allowed on the beach at any time. The rest of the year, during the off-season, dogs are allowed on the beach. Pets must be leashed and cleaned up after. The beach is located of Route 1, south of Dewey Beach.

Florida

De Soto National Memorial Beach Area
PO Box 15390
Bradenton, FL
941-792-0458
nps.gov/deso/index.htm
Dogs must be on leash and must be cleaned up after in this park. Leashed dogs are allowed in the beach area, which is past a hut following a shell path.

Cape San Blas Barrier Dunes
Cape San Blas, FL
This is one of the nicer pet-friendly beaches in Florida. Leashed dogs are allowed year round on the beach which has a number of stations with clean up bags. Please clean up after your dog.

Carrabelle Beach
Carrabelle Beach Rd
Carrabelle, FL
850-697-2585
Dogs are allowed on this beach, but the following rules apply. Dogs must be on leash when near sunbathers. In areas where there are no sunbathers, dogs can be off-leash, but must be under direct voice control. Picnic areas and restrooms are available. The beach is located 1.5 miles west of town.

Dog Island Park
Dog Island, FL
850-697-2585
This island is a small remote island that is accessible only by boat, ferry or airplane. Dogs are allowed on the beach, but must be on leash. There are some areas of Dog Island that are within a nature conservancy and dogs are not allowed in these areas. Dog owners will be fined in the nature conservancy. This island is south of Carrabelle.

Veteran's Memorial Park
Highway 1
Duck Key, FL
305-872-2411
Dogs on leash are allowed at this park and on the beach. People need to clean up after their pets. The park is located near mile marker 40, off Highway 1.

Honeymoon Island State Park
1 Causeway Blvd.

Dunedin, FL
727-469-5942
Dogs on a 6 foot or less leash are allowed on part of the beach. Please ask the rangers for details when you arrive at the park. The park is located at the extreme west end of SR 586, north of Dunedin.

Fernandina City Beach
14th St at the Atlantic Ocean
Fernandina Beach, FL
904-277-7305
The Fernandina City Beaches allow dogs on leash. The beach is about 2 miles long. Please make sure that you pick up after your dog.

Flagler Beach
A1A
Flagler Beach, FL
386-517-2000
Dogs are allowed north of 10th Street and south of 10th Street. They are not allowed on or near the pier at 10th Street. Dogs must be on leash and people need to clean up after their dogs.

Canine Beach
East End of Sunrise Blvd
Fort Lauderdale, FL
954-761-5346
There is a 100 yard stretch of beach which dogs can use. Dogs must be on leash when they are not in the water. The beach is open to dogs only on Friday, Saturday and Sundays. In winter, the hours are 3 pm - 7 pm and the summer hours are 5 pm - 9 pm. A permit is required to use the Canine Beach. There are annual permits available for $25 for residents of the city or $40 for non-residents or you can get a one weekend permit for $5.65. Permits can be purchased at Parks and Recreation Department, 1350 W. Broward Boulevard. Call (954) 761-5346 for permit information.

Dog Swim at Snyder Park
3299 SW 4th Avenue
Fort Lauderdale, FL
954-828-4343
There is a $1 park admission fee for entering the park for the doggy swim area; it is available on Saturdays and Sundays from 10AM to 5PM (closed Christmas/New Years). Dogs must be sociable, current on all vaccinations and license, and under their owner's control at all times. Dogs must be leashed when not in designated off-lead areas.

Dog Beach
Estero Blvd/H 865

Fort Myers Beach, FL
239-461-7400
Located just north of the New Pass Bridge, this barrier island beach offers a perfect off-leash area for beach-lov'in pups.This beach is actually in Bonita Beach on the city line with Fort Myers Beach. Dogs are allowed in designated areas only, and they must be licensed, immunized, and non-aggressive to people, other pets, or wildlife. Dogs may not be left unattended at any time, and they must be under their owner's control at all times; clean-up stations are provided. Two healthy dogs are allowed per person over 15 years old. Dogs on Fort Myers Beach must be leashed at all times.

Fort Myers Dog Beach
3410 Palm Beach Blvd
Fort Myers Beach, FL
239-461-7400
Dogs are allowed off leash on this section of the beach. Cleanup stations are provided. Must have a copy of health records with you at all times. The beach is run by Lees County Parks and Recreation.

Lee County Off-Leash Dog Beach Park
Route 865
Fort Myers Beach, FL
Dogs are allowed off-leash at this beach. Please clean up after your dog and stay within the dog park boundaries. Dog Beach is located south of Ft. Myers Beach and north of Bonita Beach on Route 865. Parking is available near New Pass Bridge.

Fort Pierce Inlet State Park
905 Shorewinds Drive
Fort Pierce, FL
772-468-3985
Dogs are not allowed on the ocean beach, but they are allowed on the cove beach. Pets must be leashed and people need to clean up after their pets. The park is located four miles east of Ft. Pierce, via North Causeway.

Hollywood Dog Beach
North Broadwalk at Pershing St
Hollywood, FL
dboh.org
This dog beach with limited hours was approved and opened in 2008. The beach is located between Pershing Street and Custer Street along N. Broadwalk and one block from A1A. Dogs are allowed on the beach only on Fridays, Saturdays and Sundays. Please do not bring a

dog to the beach on any other day. In addition during the Summer dogs are allowed on the beach only from 5 pm to 9 pm and in the Winter months they are allowed from 3 pm to 7 pm. Summer months begin when Daylight Savings time begins in March and end when Eastern Standard time is resumed in the fall. The permission to use the beach will be reviewed every six months or so so it is very important that all dog owners clean up and follow the hours and other rules of the beach. For more information see the website at http://www.dboh.org. The beach is sponsored and maintained by the "Dog Beach of Hollywood" organization.

Anne's Beach
Highway 1
Islamorada, FL
Dog on leash are allowed at this beach. Please clean up after your dog. The beach is located around mile markers 72 to 74. There should be a sign.

Dogwood Park Lake Bow Wow
7407 Salisbury Rd South
Jacksonville, FL
904-296-3636
jaxdogs.com
This dog park is great for any size canine. It has 25 fenced acres in a 42 acre park. Dogs can be off leash in any part of the park. The park offers picnic tables, a pond for small dogs, a pond for large dogs (Lake Bow Wow), shower for dogs, warm water for dog baths, tennis balls and toys for play, a playground with games for your dogs, trails to walk on, and bag stations for cleanup. Locals can become members for the year for about $24.00 per month or out-of-town visitors can pay about $11 for a one time visit.

Huguenot Memorial Park
10980 Hecksher Drive
Jacksonville, FL
904-251-3335
Dogs are allowed in the park and on the beach. Dogs must be leashed and people need to clean up after their dogs. The park is located off A1A.

Katheryn Abby Hanna Park Beach
500 Wonderland Dr
Jacksonville, FL
904-249-4700
coj.net
Dogs are allowed in this park for camping, hiking, picnics and on the dog friendly beach.

Jupiter Beach
A1A at Xanadu Road
Jupiter, FL
This is a wide, nice, white sandy beach that stretches 2 miles along the Atlantic Coast. It is one of the nicer beaches that allow dogs in South Florida. Please follow the dog rules requiring leashes and cleaning up after your dog.

Hobe Sound National Wildlife Refuge
North Beach Road
Jupiter Island, FL
772-546-6141
hobesound.fws.gov/
This refuge has sea turtle nesting areas and endangered species like the scrub jay and gopher tortoise. Dogs on leash are allowed at the beach. The leash law is enforced and people need to clean up after their pets. The park headquarters is located 2 miles south of SR 708 (Bridge Road) on U.S. 1. The beach is located 1.5 miles north of Bridge Road on North Beach Road.

Dog Beach
Vernon Ave and Waddell Ave
Key West, FL
This tiny stretch of beach is the only beach we found in Key West that a dog can go to.

Rickenbacker Causeway Beach
Rickenbacker Causeway
Miami, FL
This beach extends the length of the Rickenbacker Causeway from Downtown Miami to Key Biscayne. Dogs are allowed on the entire stretch. There are two types of beach, a Tree lined Dirt beach and a standard type of sandy beach further towards Key Biscayne. Dogs should be leashed on the beach.

Delnor-Wiggins Pass State Park
11100 Gulfshore Drive
Naples, FL
239-597-6196
Dogs are not allowed on the beaches in this park, but they can take dip in the water at the boat and canoe launch only. Dogs must be on leash. Please clean up after your dog. This park is located six miles west of Exit 17 on I-75.

Smyrna Dunes Park
Highway 1
New Smyrna Beach, FL
386-424-2935
Dogs are not allowed on the ocean beach, but are allowed almost

everywhere else, including on the inlet beach and river. Bottlenosed dolphins are typically seen in the inlet as well as the ocean. Dogs must be leashed and people need to clean up after their pets. The park is located on the north end of New Smyrna Beach.

Bayview Dog Beach
In Bayou Texar off E Lloyd Street
Pensacola, FL
850-436-5511
This water park for dogs offers pets beach and water fun, and there are benches, picnic tables, trash cans, pooper scooper stations, and a washing station on site. Dogs must be sociable, current on all vaccinations, licensed, and under their owner's control at all times. Dogs must be leashed when not in designated off-lead areas.

Lighthouse Point Park
A1A
Ponce Inlet, FL
386-239-7873
You might see some dolphins along the shoreline at this park. The park is also frequented by people watching a space shuttle launch out of Cape Canaveral. If you go during a shuttle launch, be sure to hold on tight to your pooch, as the shuttles can become very, very noisy and loud. Dogs on leash are allowed at the park and on the beach. Please clean up after your dog. This park is located at the southern point of Ponce Inlet.

Algiers Beach
Algiers Lane
Sanibel, FL
239-472-6477
This beach is located in Gulfside City Park. Dogs on leash are allowed and people need to clean up after their pets. Picnic tables and restrooms are available. There is an hourly parking fee. This beach is located about mid-way on the island. From the Sanibel causeway, turn right onto Periwinkle Way. Turn left onto Casa Ybel Rd and then left on Algiers Lane.

Bowman's Beach
Bowman Beach Road
Sanibel, FL
239-472-6477
Walk over a bridge to get to the beach. Dogs on leash are allowed and people need to clean up after their pets. Picnic tables are available. This beach is located on the west side of the island, near Captiva. From the Sanibel causeway, turn

right on Periwinkle Way. Turn right on Palm Ridge Rd and then continue on Sanibel-Captiva Road. Turn left onto Bowman's Beach Rd.

Lighthouse Park Beach
Periwinkle Way
Sanibel, FL
239-472-6477
This park offers a long thin stretch of beach. Dogs on leash are allowed and people need to clean up after their pets. Picnic tables are available. This park is located on the east end of the island. From Causeway Road, turn onto Periwinkle Way.

Tarpon Bay Road Beach
Tarpon Bay Road
Sanibel, FL
239-472-6477
Take a short walk from the parking lot to the beach. Dogs on leash are allowed and people need to clean up after their pets. Picnic tables and restrooms are available. There is an hourly parking fee. This beach is located mid-way on the island. From the Sanibel causeway, turn right onto Periwinkle Way. Then turn left onto Tarpon Bay Road.

Fort Matanzas National Monument
8635 A1A South
St Augustine, FL
904-471-0116
nps.gov/foma/index.htm
Dogs on 6 ft leash are allowed in this National monument. Dogs are allowed in the park, on the beach, and on the trails. They are not allowed in the visitor center, boats, or fort.

St Augustine Lighthouse and Museum
81 Lighthouse Avenue
St Augustine, FL
904-829-0745
Dogs on leash are allowed on the grounds of the lighthouse and beach area. There are some tables for picnics or bring a blanket. There is a fee to enter the lighthouse grounds.

St Augustine Beach
Most Beaches
St Augustine Beach, FL
904-209-0655
The St. Augustine Beach allows leashed dogs. Owners must clean up after their pets. This policy extends to most of the beaches in St John's County but other rules will apply to beaches in State Parks, many of which don't allow dogs.

Public Access Beaches
Gulf Beach Drive
St George Island, FL
St. George Island beaches have been consistently ranked as one of the top 10 beaches in America. One third of the island is Florida state park land which does not allow dogs. But the rest of the island offers Franklin County public beaches, which do allow dogs on a 6 foot leash or off-leash and under direct voice control.

St George Island Beaches
St George Island, FL
850-927-2111
Dogs on leash are allowed on the beaches of St George Island. However, they are not allowed on the beaches, trails, or boardwalks in St. George State Park. Dog Owners can be fined in the state park.

Gandy Bridge Causeway
Gandy Bridge east end
St Petersburg, FL
This stretch of beach allows dogs to run and go swimming. We even saw a horse here. Dogs should be leashed on the beach.

Pinellas Causeway Beach
Pinellas Bayway
St Petersburg, FL
This stretch of beach is open to humans and dogs. Dogs should be on leash on the beach.

Davis Island Dog Park
Severn Ave and Martinique Ave
Tampa, FL
davisislanddogs.com
This dog beach is fenced and offers a large parking area and even a doggie shower. To get there go towards Davis Island and head for the Peter Knight Airport. Loop around until you reach the water (the airport should be on the left). Thanks to one of our readers for the updated information.

Georgia

Jekyll Island Beaches and Trails
off SR 520
Jekyll Island, GA
877-453-5955
These beaches look like a Carribean island setting. It is hard to believe that you just drove here over a causeway. Dogs on leash are

welcome year round on the beach and the paved and dirt trails. There are about 10 miles of beaches and 20 miles of inland paved and dirt trails. It is recommended that your pooch stay on the paved trails instead of the dirt trails during the warm summer months because there are too many ticks along the dirt trails. On warmer days you might choose a beach walk rather than the inland trails anyway because of the cooler ocean breezes.

St. Simons Island Beaches
off U.S. 17
St Simons Island, GA
912-554-7566
Dogs are allowed, but only during certain hours in the summer. From Memorial Day through Labor Day, dogs are allowed on the beach before 9:30am and after 4pm. During the rest of the year, dogs are allowed anytime during park hours. Dogs must be on leash and people need to clean up after their pets.

Hawaii

Oahu Dog-Friendly Beaches
(Leashes required)
Various
Honolulu, HI
808-946-2187
According to the Hawaiian Humane Society website in November, 2006 the following beaches on Oahu allow dogs on leash. Please check with them at:
http://www.hawaiianhumane.org/prog rams/dogparks/dogbeaches.html for updates. The beaches that allow well-behaved, leashed dogs are:
Aukai Beach, Jauula
Gray's Beach (Halekulani Beach), Waikiki
Haleaha Beach, Punaluu
Hanakailio Beach, Kahuku
Kaalawai Beach, Diamond Head
Kahala Beach, Kahala
Kahuku Golf Course Beach, Kahuka
Kailua Beach, Kahuku
Kaipapau Beach, Hauula
Kakela Beach, Hauula
Kaloko Beach,Kokohead
Kaluahole Beach, Diamond Head
Kanenelu Beach, Kaaawa
Kapaeloa Beach, North Shore
Kawela Bay Beach, North Shore
Kealia Beach, Mokuleia
,Kualoa Sugar Mill Beach,Kualoa
Kuilima Cove Beach, Kahuku
Laie Beach, Laie

Lanikai Beach, Kailua
Laniloa Beach, Laie
Mahakea Beach, Laie
Makao Beach, Hauula
Makua Beach, Makua
Manner's Beach, Kahe
Mokuleia Army Beach, Mokuleia
Moluleia Beach, Mokuleia
Niu Beach, Niu Valley
Oneawa Beach, Kailua
Outrigger Canoe Club Beach, Waikiki
Pahipahialua Beach, North Shore
Paiko Beach,Kuliouou
Punaluu Beach, Punaluu
Puuiki Beach, Mokuleia
Royal-Moana Beach, Waikiki
Turtle Bay Beach, North Shore.

Illinois

Montrose Harbor Dog Beach
Lake Shore Drive
Chicago, IL
312-742-7529
Dogs are allowed on part of the beach near Montrose. Dogs can run leash-free on the beach. Please note that people who violate the leash law by not having their dog on a leash between the parking lot and the beach are being fined with $75 tickets, so be sure to bring your dog's leash. Beginning in September, 2005 all dogs that use the dog parks are required to have an annual permit. The permits currently cost $5 per dog. You will have to visit an approved location to get a permit. Proof of certain vaccinations are also required.

Evanston Dog Beach
Church Street
Evanston, IL
847-866-2900
Dogs are not allowed on this beach unless you first purchase a token from the city of Evanston. The cost per dog for one season is $88 for non-residents of Evanston and $44 for residents. Prices are subject to change. To purchase a token, you must have proof of your dog's current rabies vaccination and a current dog license. Dog beach is a large strip of sand located just north of the Church Street launch facility, where Church Street meets the lake. Beach hours are 7am to 8pm, May through October, weather permitting. Dog beach tokens can be purchased at the Dempster Street Beach Office from 10am to

5pm weekends only in May and after memorial day the office is open seven days a week. Tokens can also be purchased at the City Collectors Office in the Civic Center at 2100 Ridge Avenue, 8:30am to 5pm, Monday through Friday. Dog beach rules and regulations are available at the Dempster Street Beach Office.

Indiana

Indiana Dunes National Lakeshore
off Highway I-94
Porter, IN
219-926-7561x225
nps.gov/indu/
Dogs are not allowed on all of the beaches, but are allowed on two beaches which are located at the far east side of the park. One of the beaches is near Mt. Baldy and the other is near Central Avenue. Check with the visitor center when you arrive for exact locations. Pets are also allowed on some of the trails, campground and picnic area but must be leashed and cleaned up after. The park is located on Lake Michigan. To get there, take Highway 94 east and take Exit 26 Chesterton/49 North and head north.

Louisiana

Cameron Parish Beaches
433 Marshall Street (Chamber of Commerce)
Cameron, LA
337-775-5222
user.camtel.net/cameron/public/
Located in the southwestern part of the state bordering Texas, this parish offers over 25 miles of beaches on the Gulf of Mexico to be enjoyed by people and pooches. Dogs must be kept leashed and picked up after at all times.

Grand Isle State Park
Admiral Craik Drive
Grand Isle, LA
985-797-2559
lastateparks.com/
Dogs on leash are allowed at the beaches, except for some designated swimming areas. This park offers many recreational opportunities like fishing, crabbing, sunbathing, nature watching and

camping. Leashed pets are also allowed at the campsites. The park is located on the east end of Grand Isle, off Highway 1 on Admiral Craik Drive. It is about 2 hours outside of New Orleans.

Maine

Hadley Point Beach
Highway 3
Bar Harbor, ME
Dogs are allowed on the beach, but must be leashed. The beach is located about 10 minutes northwest of downtown Bar Harbor, near Eden.

Kennebunk Beaches
Beach Avenue
Kennebunk, ME
Dogs are allowed with certain restrictions. During the summertime, from about Memorial Day weekend through Labor Day weekend, leashed dogs are only allowed on the beach before 8am and after 6pm. During the rest of the year, dogs are allowed on the beach during park hours. There are a string of beaches, including Kennebunk, Gooch's and Mother's, that make up a nice stretch of wide sandy beaches. People need to clean up after their pets. The beaches are located on Beach Avenue, off Routes 9 and 35.

Goose Rocks Beach
Dyke Street
Kennebunkport, ME
Leashed dogs are allowed, with certain restrictions. From June 15 through September 15, dogs are only allowed on the beach before 8am and after 6pm. During the rest of the year, dogs are allowed on the beach during park hours. People need to clean up after their pets. The beach is located about 3 miles east of Cape Porpoise. From Route 9, exit onto Dyke Street.

Old Orchard Beach City Beach
Old Orchard Beach, ME
207-934-0860
Leashed dogs are allowed on this beach at all hours from the day after Labor Day to the day before Memorial Day. Dogs are not allowed on the beach from Memorial Day through Labor Day except before 8 am and after 4 pm. People need to make sure they pick up their dog's waste with a plastic bag and throw it away in a trash can.

East End Beach
Cutter Street
Portland, ME
207-874-8793
Dogs are only allowed on this beach from the day after Labor Day to the day before Memorial Day. Dogs are not allowed on the beach from Memorial Day through Labor Day. During the months that dogs are allowed, they can be off-leash but need to be under direct voice control. People need to make sure they pick up their dog's waste with a plastic bag and throw it away in a trash can.

Old Orchard
Cutter Street
Portland, ME
207-874-8793
Dogs are only allowed on this beach from the day after Labor Day to the day before Memorial Day. Dogs are not allowed on the beach from Memorial Day through Labor Day. During the months that dogs are allowed, they can be off-leash but need to be under direct voice control. People need to make sure they pick up their dog's waste with a plastic bag and throw it away in a trash can.

Willard Beach
South Portland, ME
207-767-7601
At Willard Beach there are restrooms, lifeguards, and parking for 75 cars. Dogs are only allowed on the beach from 6:00 a.m. to 9:00 a.m. year round. Dogs must be kept away from bird eggs and out of the dunes. There are dog bag stations at many entrances to the mile long beach. Dogs must be cleaned up after at all times. Dogs must be leashed at all times or off-leash and under excellent voice control within a limited distance of the owner.

Wells Beach
Route 1
Wells, ME
207-646-2451
Leashed dogs are allowed, with certain restrictions. During the summer, from June 16 through September 15, dogs are only allowed on the beach before 8am and after 6pm. The rest of the year, dogs are allowed on the beach during all park hours. There are seven miles of sandy beaches in Wells. People are required to clean up after their pets.

Long Sands Beach
Route 1A
York, ME
207-363-4422
Leashed dogs are allowed, with certain restrictions. During the summertime, from about Memorial Day weekend through Labor Day weekend, dogs are only allowed on the beach before 8am and after 6pm. During the off-season, dogs are allowed during all park hours. This beach offers a 1.5 mile sandy beach. Metered parking and private lots are available. The beach and bathhouse are also handicap accessible. People are required to clean up after their pets.

Short Sands Beach
Route 1A
York, ME
207-363-4422
Leashed dogs are allowed, with certain restrictions. During the summertime, from about Memorial Day weekend through Labor Day weekend, dogs are only allowed on the beach before 8am and after 6pm. During the off-season, dogs are allowed during all park hours. At the beach, there is a large parking area and a playground. People are required to clean up after their pets.

York Harbor Beach
Route 1A
York, ME
207-363-4422
Leashed dogs are allowed, with certain restrictions. During the summertime, from about Memorial Day weekend through Labor Day weekend, dogs are only allowed on the beach before 8am and after 6pm. During the off-season, dogs are allowed during all park hours. This park offers a sandy beach nestled against a rocky shoreline. There is limited parking. People are required to clean up after their pets.

Maryland

Quiet Waters Park Dog Beach
600 Quiet Waters Park Road
Annapolis, MD
410-222-1777
friendsofquietwaterspark.org
This park is located on Chesapeake Bay, not on the ocean. Dogs are welcome to run off-leash at this dog beach and dog park. The dog park is closed every Tuesday. Leashed dogs

are also allowed at Quiet Waters Park. The park offers over 6 miles of scenic paved trails, and a large multi-level children's playground. People need to clean up after their pets. To get there, take Route 665 until it ends and merges with Forrest Drive. Take Forrest Drive for 2 miles and then turn right onto Hillsmere Drive. The park entrance is about 100 yards on the right. The dog beach is located to the left of the South River overlook. Park in Lot N.

Assateague Island National Seashore
Route 611
Assateague Island, MD
410-641-1441
nps.gov/asis/
Dogs on leash are allowed on beaches, except for any lifeguarded swimming beaches (will be marked off with flags). There are plenty of beaches to enjoy at this park that are not lifeguarded swimming beaches. Dogs are not allowed on trails in the park. The park is located eight miles south of Ocean City, at the end of Route 611.

Elm's Beach Park
Bay Forest Road
Hermanville, MD
301-475-4572
The park is located on Chesapeake Bay, not on the ocean. Enjoy great views of the bay or swim at the beach. Dogs on leash are allowed at the beach. People need to clean up after their pets. Take Route 235 to Bay Forest Road and then go 3 miles. The park will be on the left.

Ocean City Beaches
Route 528
Ocean City, MD
1-800-OC-OCEAN
Dogs are only allowed during certain times of the year on this city beach. Pets are not allowed on the beach or boardwalk at any time from May 1 through September 30. The rest of the year, dogs are allowed on the beach and boardwalk, but must be on leash and people must clean up after them.

Downs Park Dog Beach
8311 John Downs Loop
Pasadena, MD
410-222-6230
This dog beach is located on Chesapeake Bay, not on the ocean. People are not permitted to go swimming, but dogs can run off-leash at this beach. The dog beach is closed every Tuesday. Dogs on

leash are also allowed in Downs Park. People need to clean up after their pets. Take Route 100 until it merges with Moutain Road (Rt. 177 East). Follow Mt. Road for about 3.5 miles and the park entrance will be on your right. The dog beach is located in the northeast corner of the park.

Massachusetts

Barnstable Town Beaches
off Route 6A
Barnstable, MA
508-790-6345
Dogs are allowed only during the off-season, from September 15 to May 15. Dogs must be on leash or under voice control. People need to clean up after their pets. The town of Barnstable oversees Hyannis beaches and the following beaches: Craigville, Kalmus, and Sandy Neck. Before you go, always verify the seasonal dates and times when dogs are allowed on the beach.

Carson Beach
I-93 and William Day Blvd
Boston, MA
617-727-5114
Dogs are only allowed on the beach during the off-season. Pets are not allowed from Memorial Day weekend through Labor Day weekend. Dogs must be leashed and people are required to clean up after their pets.

Chatham Town Beaches
off Route 28
Chatham, MA
508-945-5100
Dogs are allowed only during the off-season, from mid September to end the end of May. Dogs must be leashed and people need to clean up after their pets. The town of Chatham oversees the following beaches: Hardings, Light, and Ridgevale. Before you go, always verify the seasonal dates and times when dogs are allowed on the beach.

Dennis Town Beaches
Route 6A
Dennis, MA
508-394-8300
Dogs are allowed only during the off-season, from after Labor Day up to Memorial Day. There is one exception. Dogs are allowed year-

round on the four wheel drive area of Chapin Beach. Dogs must be leashed on all town beaches, and people need to clean up after their pets. The town of Dennis oversees the following beaches: Chapin, Mayflower, Howes Street and Sea Street. Before you go, always verify the seasonal dates and times when dogs are allowed on the beach.

Joseph Sylvia State Beach
Beach Road
Edgartown, MA
508-696-3840
Dogs are allowed during the summer, only before 9am and after 5pm. You will need to keep your dog away from any bird nesting areas, which should have signs posted. During the off-season, from mid-September to mid-April, dogs are allowed all day. This beach is about 2 miles long. Dogs must be leashed and people need to clean up after their pets. Before you go, always verify the seasonal dates and times when dogs are allowed on the beach.

Norton Point Beach
end of Katama Road
Edgartown, MA
508-696-3840
Dogs are allowed during the summer, only before 9am and after 5pm. You will need to keep your dog away from any bird nesting areas, which should have signs posted. During the off-season, from mid-September to mid-April, dogs are allowed all day. This beach is about 2.5 miles long. Dogs must be leashed and people need to clean up after their pets. Before you go, always verify the seasonal dates and times when dogs are allowed on the beach.

South Beach State Park
Katama Road
Edgartown, MA
508-693-0085
Dogs are allowed during the summer, only after 5pm. During the off-season, from mid-September to mid-April, dogs are allowed all day. This 3 mile beach is located on the South Shore. Dogs must be leashed and people need to clean up after their pets. Before you go, always verify the seasonal dates and times when dogs are allowed on the beach.

Falmouth Town Beaches
off Route 28
Falmouth, MA
508-457-2567
Dogs are not allowed during the

summer from May 1 through October 1. During the off-season, dogs are allowed all day. Dogs must be leashed and people need to clean up after their pets. The town of Falmouth oversees the following beaches: Menauhant, Surf Drive, and Old Silver. Before you go, always verify the seasonal dates and times when dogs are allowed on the beach.

Harwich Town Beach
off Route 28
Harwich, MA
508-430-7514
Dogs are allowed only during the off-season, from October to mid-May. Dogs must be on leash or under voice control. People need to clean up after their pets. The town of Harwich oversees Red River Beach. Before you go, always verify the seasonal dates and times when dogs are allowed on the beach.

Singing Beach
Beach Street
Manchester, MA
978-526-2040
Dogs under excellent voice control are allowed off-leash from October 1 through May 1 on the pristine Singing Beach. Dogs are not allowed on the beach during the other months. From Manchester, take Beach Street to the water. Parking can be difficult in this area.

Nantucket Island Beaches
various locations
Nantucket, MA
508-228-1700
Dogs are allowed during the summer on beaches with lifeguards only before 9am and after 5pm. On beaches that have no lifeguards, or during the winter months, dogs are allowed all day on the beach. Dogs must always be leashed. Before you go, always verify the seasonal dates and times when dogs are allowed on the beach.

Eastville Point Beach
At bridge near Vineyard Haven
Oak Bluffs, MA
508-696-3840
Dogs are allowed during the summer, only before 9am and after 5pm. You will need to keep your dog away from any bird nesting areas, which should have signs posted. During the off-season, from mid-September to mid-April, dogs are allowed all day. Dogs must be leashed and people need to clean up after their pets. Before you go,

always verify the seasonal dates and times when dogs are allowed on the beach.

Orleans Town Beaches
off Route 28
Orleans, MA
508-240-3775
Dogs are allowed only during the off-season, from after Columbus Day to the Friday before Memorial Day. Dogs are allowed off leash, but must be under voice control. People need to clean up after their pets. The town of Orleans oversees Nauset and Skaket beaches. Before you go, always verify the seasonal dates and times when dogs are allowed on the beach.

Plymouth City Beach
Route 3A
Plymouth, MA
508-747-1620
The beach in Plymouth allows dogs year round on the beach and in the water. Dogs must be leashed and cleaned up after.

Provincetown Town Beaches
off Route 6
Provincetown, MA
508-487-7000
Dogs on leash are allowed year-round. During the summer, from 6am to 9am, dogs are allowed off-leash. Before you go, always verify the seasonal dates and times when dogs are allowed on the beach.

Sandwich Town Beaches
off Route 6A
Sandwich, MA
508-888-4361
Dogs are allowed only during the off-season, from October through March. Dogs must be leashed and people need to clean up after their pets. The town of Sandwich oversees the following beaches: East Sandwich and Town Neck. Before you go, always verify the seasonal dates and times when dogs are allowed on the beach.

Truro Town Beaches
off Route 6
Truro, MA
508-487-2702
Dogs are allowed during the summer, only before 9am and after 6pm. This policy is in effect from about the third weekend in June through Labor Day. During the off-season, dogs are allowed all day. Dogs must be leashed and people need to clean up after their pets. The town of Truro oversees the

following beaches: Ballston, Corn Hill, Fisher, Great Hollow, Head of the Meadow, Longnook and Ryder. Before you go, always verify the seasonal dates and times when dogs are allowed on the beach.

Cape Cod National Seashore
Route 6
Wellfleet, MA
508-349-3785
nps.gov/caco
The park offers a 40 mile stretch of pristine sandy beaches. Dogs on leash are allowed year-round on all of the seashore beaches, except for seasonally posted nesting or lifeguarded beaches. Leashed pets are also allowed on fire roads, and the Head of the Meadow bicycle trail in Truro. Check with the visitor center or rangers for details about fire road locations. To get there from Boston, take Route 3 south to the Sagamore Bridge. Take Route 6 east towards Eastham.

Wellfleet Town Beaches
off Route 6
Wellfleet, MA
508-349-9818
Dogs are allowed during the summer, only before 9am and after 6pm. During the off-season, from after Labor Day to the end of June, dogs are allowed all day. Dogs must be leashed and people need to clean up after their pets. The town of Wellfleet oversees the following beaches: Marconi, Cahoon Hollow, and White Crest. Before you go, always verify the seasonal dates and times when dogs are allowed on the beach.

Sandy Neck Beach
425 Sandy Neck Road
West Barnstable, MA
508-362-8300
In addition to being a haven for endangered bird and wildlife, this 6 mile long coastal barrier beach also shares a unique ecology and rich cultural history. There is an off-road beach, a public beach and miles of trails here. Dogs are allowed on the trails and on the Off-Road beach area anytime (but stay on water side) throughout the year, but they are not allowed on the public beach from May 15 to September 15. Dogs are not allowed in the primitive camp area. Visitors and their pets must remain on designated trails, off the dunes, and off the few areas of private property. Please consult trail maps. Dogs must be leashed and cleaned up after at all times.

Michigan

Young State Park Beach
C56 off 131
Boyne City, MI
231-582-7523
While dogs are not allowed on the beach, they can go into the water past the boat launch. There is a sandy and rocky area that leads to the water. Pets must be leashed and attended at all times and cleaned up after.

Burt Lake State Park Beach
Old 27 Highway
Burt Lake, MI
231-238-9392
This is not a Great Lakes beach, but is conveniently located off of I-75. While dogs are not allowed on the swimming beach, there is a special designated spot where dogs can go into the water. It is near campsite lot number 42, off Road 1, at the west end of the park. The road leads to the beach and dog run. Pets must be on a 6 foot or less leash and attended at all times.

Aloha State Park Beach
off I-75
Cheboygan, MI
231-625-2522
This is not a Great Lakes beach, but is conveniently located off of I-75. The park has a special pet swimming area which is located by the playground. Pets need to be leashed and cleaned up after. The park is located 7 miles south of Cheboygan and 25 miles from the Mackinac Bridge.

Sleeping Bear Dunes National Lakeshore Beaches
off M-72
Empire, MI
231-326-5134
nps.gov/slbe/
While pets are not allowed in certain areas of the park like the islands, Dune Climb, backcountry campsites, or inside buildings, they are allowed on some trails, campgrounds and on the following beaches. Pets are welcome on the the south side of the beach at Esch Road (south of Empire), on the south side of Peterson Beach and on Empire Beach. Dogs must be leashed at all times and cleaned up after. To get there from Traverse City, take M-72

west to Empire.

Wilderness State Park Beach
Wilderness Park Drive
Mackinaw City, MI
231-436-5381
Dogs are not allowed at the beach but they can swim in the water on the other side of the boat launch. Pets must be a on a 6 foot or less leash and cleaned up after. The park is located 11 miles west of Mackinaw City.

Pier Cove Beach
Lakeshore Drive
Saugatuck, MI
269-857-1701
Visitors may bring their pooches here to explore the beach. Dogs must be under their owner's control, leashed, and cleaned up after at all times.

Grand Mere State Park Beach
Thornton Drive
Stevensville, MI
269-426-4013
Dogs on leash are allowed at the beach and on the hiking trails. The one mile beach is located along the shoreline of Lake Michigan. Remember to clean up after your pet. To get there, take I-94 south of St. Joseph and take Exit 22. Go west .25 miles to Thornton Drive and head south on Thornton for .5 miles.

Mississippi

Hancock County Beaches
Beach Blvd.
Bay St Louis, MS
228-463-9222
Dogs on leash are allowed on Hancock County beaches. People need to clean up after their pets. The county beaches are located along the coast, between the cities of Waveland and Bay St. Louis.

Montana

Canine Beach at Bozeman Ponds
700 - 550 N. Fowler Lane
Bozeman, MT
406-582-3200
bozeman.net/parks/parks.aspx
The Canine Beach is an off-leash

dog beach on the west side of the Bozeman Pond. The park is open from 8 am to 10 pm daily. Pets must be picked up after at the beach and leashed outside of the leash-free area.

New Jersey

Barnegat Lighthouse State Park Beaches
At Broadway and the Bay
Barnegat Light, NJ
609-494-2016
Although dogs are not allowed in the lighthouse or on the beaches from April 15th to August 15, and never on the trails here, they are allowed in the park and picnic areas which provide visitors with great views of the ocean and waterway activities. Dogs are allowed on the park beaches from August 16 through April 14 each year. Dogs are welcome for no additional fee. Dogs must be under their owner's control, leashed, and cleaned up after at all times.

Higbee Beach Wildlife Management Area
County Road 641
Cape May, NJ
609-628-2103
This park offers a 1 1/2 mile stretch of beach. The beach is managed specifically to provide habitat for migratory wildlife. Dogs on leash and under control are allowed at the beach from September through April. To get there, take SR 109 west to US9. Turn left onto US9 and go to the first traffic light. Turn left onto County Road 162 (Seashore Rd.). Then turn right onto Country Road 641 (New England Rd.). Take CR641 for 2 miles to the end and the beach access parking area. Parking areas near the beach may be closed during the summer. The park is open daily from dawn to dusk.

Cape May Point State Park
Lighthouse Avenue
Cape May Point, NJ
609-884-2159
Dogs are only allowed on the beach during the off-season. Pets are not allowed from April 15 through September 15. Pets must be on a 6 foot or less leash and people need to clean up after their pets. The park is located off the southern end of the Garden State Parkway. Go over the Cape May Bridge to Lafayette Street.

At the intersection, go right onto Route 606 (Sunset Blvd.), then turn left onto Lighthouse Ave.

Fisherman's Cove Conservation Area
391 Third Avenue
Manasquan, NJ
732-922-4080
This is a 52 acre tract on the Manasquan Inlet. It is used for fishing, walking on the beach and sunbathing. Dogs must be on-leash everywhere in the park. To get to the beach take exit 98 from the Garden State Parkway and head south on Rt 34 which becomes Rt 35. Turn right on Higgins Avenue, then left onto Union Avenue (Rt 71), right on Fisk Avenue and right onto 3rd Ave.

Island Beach State Park
off Route 35
Seaside Park, NJ
732-793-0506
One of the states last significant remnants of a barrier island ecosystem, it is home to diverse wildlife and maritime plant life, and with a variety of land and water activities and 8 interesting trails. During the winter months, dogs are allowed on all of the beaches, but must be on a 6 foot or less leash. People are required to clean up after their pets. To get to the park, take Route 37 east. Then take Route 35 south to the park entrance. Dogs are not allowed on the lifeguarded swimming beaches during the summer. Dogs are not allowed on the Spizzle Creek Bird Blind Trail at any time of year.

New York

New York City Beaches and Boardwalks
Various
Brooklyn, NY
212-NEW-YORK
From October 1 through April 30 each year, leashed dogs are allowed on the sand and the boardwalk at certain beaches. Currently, these beaches are Rockaway Beach, Coney Island, Brighton Beach, Manhattan Beach, Midland Beach and South Beach. Dogs are not allowed on the sand at any New York City beaches between May 1 and September 30. Leashed dogs are allowed year-round on the boardwalks and promenade at Coney Island, Brighton, Midland,

South and Manhattan Beaches. Please check the website at http://www.nycgovparks.org for updated information and changes.

Camp Hero State Park
50 South Fairview Avenue
Montauk, NY
631-668-3781
nysparks.com/maps/
The park boasts some of the best surf fishing spots in the world. Dogs on a 6 foot or less leash are allowed on the beach year-round, but not in the picnic areas. To get to the park, take Route 27 (Sunrise Highway) east to the end. The park is about 130 miles from New York City.

Hither Hills State Park
50 South Fairview Avenue
Montauk, NY
631-668-2554
nysparks.com/maps/
This park offers visitors a sandy ocean beach. Dogs are allowed with certain restrictions. During the off-season, dogs are allowed on the beach. During the summer, dogs are not allowed on the beach, except for the undeveloped area on the other side of the freeway. Dogs must be on a 6 foot or less leash and people need to clean up after their pets. Dogs are not allowed in buildings or on walkways and they are not allowed in the camping, bathing and picnic areas.

Montauk Point State Park
50 South Fairview Avenue
Montauk, NY
631-668-3781
nysparks.com/maps/
This park is located on the eastern tip of Long Island. Dogs are allowed on the beach, but not near the food area. Dogs must be on a 6 foot or less leash and people need to clean up after their pets. Dogs are not allowed in buildings or on walkways and they are not allowed in the camping, bathing and picnic areas. Please note that dogs are not allowed in the adjacent Montauk Downs State Park. The park is located 132 miles from Manhattan, off Sunrise Highway (Route 27).

New York City Beaches and Boardwalks
Various
New York, NY
212-NEW-YORK
From October 1 through April 30 each year, leashed dogs are allowed on the sand and the boardwalk at certain beaches.

These beaches are Rockaway Beach, Coney Island, Brighton Beach, Manhattan Beach, Midland Beach and South Beach. Dogs are not allowed on the sand at any New York City beaches between May 1 and September 30. Leashed dogs are allowed year-round on the boardwalks and promenade at Coney Island, Brighton, Midland, South and Manhattan Beaches. Please check the website at http://www.nycgovparks.org for updated information and changes.

Prospect Park Dog Beach
Prospect Park - Brooklyn
New York, NY
212-NEW-YORK
This man made, concrete beach was designed for our canine friends. It is located in Prospect Park, off 9th Street on the path leading down from the Tennis House. Dogs may only be off-leash before 9 am and after 9 pm in the summer and after 5 pm in the winter. People are not permitted to swim in the dog pool. There is a fence to keep the dogs in so you don't have to chase them across the pond.

North Carolina

Fort Macon State Park
Highway 58
Atlantic Beach, NC
252-726-3775
This park offers beach access. Dogs on a 6 foot leash or less are allowed on the beach, but not inside the Civil War fort located in the park. People need to clean up after their pets. The park is located on the eastern end of Bogue Banks, south of Morehead City.

Corolla Beaches
Ocean Trail
Corolla, NC
252-232-0719
outerbanks.com/
Dogs are allowed on the beaches in and around the Corolla area year round; they must be leashed and cleaned up after at all times.

Duck Beach
H 12
Duck, NC
252-255-1234
townofduck.com/
Dogs are welcome to romp on the beach here, and they may be off

leash if they are under good voice control. Dogs must be licensed, have current rabies tags, be under their owner's control, and cleaned up after at all times. Dogs must be on no more than a 10 foot leash when off the beach.

Kill Devil Hills Beaches
N Virginia Dare Trail
Kill Devil Hills, NC
252-449-5300
kdhnc.com/
From May 15th to September 15th dogs are not allowed on the beaches between 9 AM and 6 PM. When dogs are allowed on the beach, they must be licensed, have current rabies tags, be under their owner's control, on no more than a 10 foot leash, and cleaned up after at all times.

Kitty Hawk Beaches
Virginai Dare Trail/H 12
Kitty Hawk, NC
252-261-3552
townofkittyhawk.org/
Between 10 am and 6 pm from the Friday before Memorial Day until the day after Labor Day, dogs may be on the beach on a maximum 6 foot leash; for all other times they may be on a retractable leash up to 12 feet. Well trained dogs may be off-lead from Labor Day to the Friday before Memorial Day if they are under strict voice control and never more than 30 feet from the owner. Resident dogs must display a county registration tag plus a valid rabies tags, and non-resident dogs must have a valid rabies tag. Dogs must be under their owner's control and cleaned up after at all times.

Ft. Fisher State Recreation Area
Highway 421
Kure Beach, NC
910-458-5798
Enjoy miles of beachcombing, sunbathing or hunting for shells at this beach. Dogs on leash are allowed everywhere on the beach, except for swimming areas that have lifeguards on duty. People need to clean up after their pets. The park is located on the southern tip of Pleasure Island, near Wilmington.

Cape Hatteras National Seashore
Highway 12
Manteo, NC
252-473-2111
nps.gov/caha/
This park offers long stretches of pristine beach. Dogs on a 6 foot or less leash are allowed year-round,

except on any designated swimming beaches. Most of the beaches are non-designated swim beaches. People are required to clean up after their pets.

Nags Head Beaches
N Vriginia Dare Trail/H 12
Nags Head, NC
252-441-5508
townofnagshead.net/
The beaches here consist mostly of open spaces and low-density building. Dogs are allowed on the beaches year round; they must be licensed, have current rabies tags, be under their owner's control, on no more than a 10 foot leash, and cleaned up after at all times.

Oak Island Beaches
Beach Drive
Oak Island, NC
910-278-5011
oakislandnc.com/
Dogs are allowed on city beaches year round, but from mid November to about the 1st of April dogs may be off lead if they are under strict voice control. Dogs must be under their owner's control, leashed April to November, and cleaned up after at all times.

Southern Shores Beaches
H 12
Southern Shores, NC
252-261-2394
From May 15th to September 15th dogs are not allowed on the beaches. Dogs must be licensed, have current rabies tags, be under their owner's control, on no more than a 10 foot leash, and cleaned up after at all times. A parking permit is required for parking in town and can be obtained at the Town Hall, 5375 N. Virginia Dare Trail.

Topsail Beach
Ocean Blvd
Topsail Beach, NC
910-328-5841
topsailbeach.org/
There are about 20 public assesses to the beaches in this town. From May 15th to September 30th dogs must be leashed when on the beach; otherwise dogs may be off lead if they are under strict adult voice control. Dogs must be cleaned up after at all times and always be leashed when not on the beach.

Ohio

Geneva State Park
4499 Padanarum Road
Geneva, OH
440-466-8400
While dogs are cannot go on the swim beach, they can go in the water outside of the designated swim beach. Pets must be leashed and cleaned up after. To get there from Cleveland, take Interstate 90 east to Route 534 north. The park entrance is six miles north on Route 534, on the left.

Kelleys Island State Park Beach
Division Street
Kelleys Island, OH
419-746-2546
While pets are not allowed at the small 100 foot swimming beach, they are welcome to join you at the "long beach" but you will need to keep them away from other beachgoers. Pets must be leashed and cleaned up after. To get there you will need to take a ferry to the island. Kelleys Island Ferry Boat Line operates year round, weather permitting, and offers passenger and limited vehicle service from Marblehead, Ohio to the island. Leashed pets are welcome on the ferry. Once on Kelleys Island, go west on E. Lakeshore Drive and turn right on Division Street. The park is at the end of Division Street on the right.

Maumee Bay State Park Beach
1400 State Park Road
Oregon, OH
419-836-7758
While dogs are not allowed at any beaches at this park, either on the Lake Erie shore or at the park's inland lake, dogs are permitted to take a dip in the water at the end of the inland lake which is on the south side of the road. Pets must be leashed even when in the water, and cleaned up after.

Catawba Island State Park Beach
4049 East Moores Dock Rd.
Port Clinton, OH
419-797-4530
Swimming is permitted on this small beach but there are no lifeguards. Dogs are welcome at the beach but need to be leashed when not in the water. The park is off of State Route 53.

East Harbor State Park Beach
Route 269
Port Clinton, OH
419-734-4424
While dogs are not allowed on any sandy beach at this park, they can take a dip in the pond which is located off the exit road, next to the shelter road. Pets must be leashed and cleaned up after. To get there from Cleveland, take State Route 2 West to State Route 269 North. The park is located on State Route 269. To get there from Port Clinton, go east on Route 163 to Route 269 north.

Oregon

Bullards Beach State Park
Highway 101
Bandon, OR
541-347-2209
oregonstateparks.org/park_71.php
Enjoy a walk along the beach at this park. Picnic tables, restrooms, hiking and campgrounds are available at the park. There is a minimal day use fees. Leashed dogs are allowed on the beach. Dogs are also allowed on hiking trails and campgrounds. They must be on a six foot or less leash at all times and people are required to clean up after their pets. On beaches located outside of Oregon State Park boundaries, dogs might be allowed off-leash and under direct voice control, please look for signs or postings. This park is located off U.S. Highway 101, 2 miles north of Bandon.

Seven Devils State Recreation Site
Highway 101
Bandon, OR
800-551-6949
oregonstateparks.org/park_69.php
Enjoy several miles of beach at this park. Picnic tables are available at this park. There are no day use fees. Dogs are allowed on the beach. They must be on a six foot or less leash at all times and people are required to clean up after their pets. On beaches located outside of Oregon State Park boundaries, dogs might be allowed off-leash and under direct voice control, please look for signs or postings. This park is located off U.S. Highway 101, 10 miles north of Bandon.

Harris Beach State Park
Highway 101

Brookings, OR
541-469-2021
oregonstateparks.org/park_79.php
The park offers sandy beaches for beachcombing, whale watching, and sunset viewing. Picnic tables, restrooms (including an ADA restroom) and shaded campsites are available at this park. There is a minimal day use fee. Leashed dogs are allowed on the beach. Dogs are also allowed at the campgrounds. They must be on a six foot or less leash at all times and people are required to clean up after their pets. On beaches located outside of Oregon State Park boundaries, dogs might be allowed off-leash and under direct voice control, please look for signs or postings. This park is located off U.S. Highway 101, just north of Brookings.

McVay Rock State Recreation Site
Highway 101
Brookings, OR
800-551-6949
oregonstateparks.org/park_75.php
This beach is a popular spot for clamming, whale watching and walking. Picnic tables and restrooms are available at this park. There are no day use fees. Dogs are allowed on the beach. They must be on a six foot or less leash at all times and people are required to clean up after their pets. On beaches located outside of Oregon State Park boundries, dogs might be allowed off-leash and under direct voice control, please look for signs or postings. This park is located off U.S. Highway 101, just south of Brookings.

Samuel H. Boardman State Scenic Corridor
Highway 101
Brookings, OR
800-551-6949
oregonstateparks.org/park_77.php
Steep coastline at this 12 mile long corridor is interrupted by small sandy beaches. Picnic tables, restrooms (including an ADA restroom), and a hiking trail are available at this park. There are no day use fees. Leashed dogs are allowed on the beach. Dogs are also allowed on the hiking trail. They must be on a six foot or less leash at all times and people are required to clean up after their pets. On beaches located outside of Oregon State Park boundaries, dogs might be allowed off-leash and under direct voice control, please look for signs or postings. This park

is located off U.S. Highway 101, 4 miles north of Brookings.

Arcadia Beach State Recreation Site
Highway 101
Cannon Beach, OR
800-551-6949
This sandy ocean beach is just a few feet from where you can park your car. Picnic tables and restrooms are available at this park. There are no day use fees. Dogs are allowed on the beach. They must be on a six foot or less leash at all times and people are required to clean up after their pets. On beaches located outside of Oregon State Park boundaries, dogs might be allowed off-leash and under direct voice control, please look for signs or postings. This park is located off U.S. Highway 101, 3 miles south of Cannon Beach.

Ecola State Park
Highway 101
Cannon Beach, OR
503-436-2844
According to the Oregon State Parks Division, this park is one of the most photographed locations in Oregon. To reach the beach, you will need to walk down a trail. Restrooms, hiking and primitive campgrounds are available at this park. There is a $3 day use fee. Leashed dogs are allowed on the beach. Dogs are also allowed on hiking trails and campgrounds. They must be on a six foot or less leash at all times and people are required to clean up after their pets. On beaches located outside of Oregon State Park boundaries, dogs might be allowed off-leash and under direct voice control, please look for signs or postings. This park is located off U.S. Highway 101, 2 miles north of Cannon Beach.

Hug Point State Recreation Site
Highway 101
Cannon Beach, OR
800-551-6949
According to the Oregon State Parks Division, people used to travel via stagecoach along this beach before the highway was built. Today you can walk along the original trail which was carved into the point by stagecoaches. The trail is located north of the parking area. Visitors can also explore two caves around the point, but be aware of high tide. Some people have become stranded at high tide when exploring the point! This beach is easily accessible from the parking area. Picnic tables and

restrooms are available at this park. There are no day use fees. Dogs are allowed on the beach. They must be on a six foot or less leash at all times and people are required to clean up after their pets. On beaches located outside of Oregon State Park boundaries, dogs might be allowed off-leash and under direct voice control, please look for signs or postings. This park is located off U.S. Highway 101, 5 miles south of Cannon Beach.

Tolovana Beach State Recreation Site
Highway 101
Cannon Beach, OR
800-551-6949
Indian Beach is popular with surfers. There is a short walk down to the beach. Picnic tables are available at this park. There are no day fees. Dogs are allowed on the beach. They must be on a six foot or less leash at all times and people are required to clean up after their pets. On beaches located outside of Oregon State Park boundaries, dogs might be allowed off-leash and under direct voice control, please look for signs or postings. This park is located off U.S. Highway 101, 1 mile south of Cannon Beach.

Sunset Bay State Park
89814 Cape Arrago H
Coos Bay, OR
541-888-4902
This scenic park's beautiful sandy beaches are protected by the towering sea cliffs surrounding them, and the day-use and picnic facilities are only a short walk from the beach allowing for easy access for beachcombing, fishing, swimming, and boating. There is a network of hiking trails that connect Sunset Bay with nearby Shore Acres and Cape Arago State Parks. These trails give the hiker opportunities to experience the pristine coastal forests, seasonal wildflowers, and the spectacular ocean vistas of the area. There is a fully enclosed observation building that has interpretive panels describing the history of the Simpson estate along the way. From points along the trail you can see views of Gregory Point and the Cape Arago lighthouse. The park is open year round from 8 a.m. until sunset. Dogs on lead at all times are allowed, and pets must be cleaned up after. Dogs may not be left unattended at any time. There is a campground here that offer a variety of activities and recreation.

Fogarty Creek State Recreation Area
Highway 101
Depoe Bay, OR
800-551-6949
This beach and park offer some of the best birdwatching and tidepooling. Picnic tables and hiking are available at this park. There is a $3 day use fees. Leashed dogs are allowed on the beach. Dogs are also allowed on hiking trails. They must be on a six foot or less leash at all times and people are required to clean up after their pets. On beaches located outside of Oregon State Park boundaries, dogs might be allowed off-leash and under direct voice control, please look for signs or postings. This park is located off U.S. Highway 101, 2 miles north of Depoe Bay.

Carl G. Washburne Memorial State Park
Highway 101
Florence, OR
541-547-3416
This park offers five miles of sandy beach. Picnic tables, restrooms, hiking and campgrounds are available at this park. There is a day use fee. Leashed dogs are allowed on the beach. Dogs are also allowed on hiking trails and campgrounds. They must be on a six foot or less leash at all times and people are required to clean up after their pets. On beaches located outside of Oregon State Park boundaries, dogs might be allowed off-leash and under direct voice control, please look for signs or postings. This park is located off U.S. Highway 101, 14 miles north of Florence.

Heceta Head Lighthouse State Scenic Viewpoint
Highway 101
Florence, OR
800-551-6949
Go for a walk above the beach or explore the natural caves and tidepools along the beach. This is a great spot for whale watching. According to the Oregon State Parks Division, the lighthouse located on the west side of 1,000-foot-high Heceta Head (205 feet above ocean) is one of the most photographed on the Oregon coast. Picnic tables, restrooms and hiking are available at this park. There is a $3 day use fee. Leashed dogs are allowed on the beach. Dogs are also allowed on hiking trails. They

must be on a six foot or less leash at all times and people are required to clean up after their pets. On beaches located outside of Oregon State Park boundaries, dogs might be allowed off-leash and under direct voice control, please look for signs or postings. This park is located off U.S. Highway 101, 13 miles north of Florence.

Pistol River State Scenic Viewpoint
Highway 101
Gold Beach, OR
800-551-6949
oregonstateparks.org/park_76.php
This beach is popular for ocean windsurfing. There has even been windsurfing national championships held at this beach. Picnic tables and restrooms are available here. There are no day use fees. Dogs are allowed on the beach. They must be on a six foot or less leash at all times and people are required to clean up after their pets. On beaches located outside of Oregon State Park boundaries, dogs might be allowed off-leash and under direct voice control, please look for signs or postings. This park is located off U.S. Highway 101, 11 miles south of Gold Beach.

D River State Recreation Site
Highway 101
Lincoln City, OR
800-551-6949
This beach, located right off the highway, is a popular and typically windy beach. According to the Oregon State Parks Division, this park is home to a pair of the world¹s largest kite festivals every spring and fall which gives Lincoln City the name Kite Capital of the World. Restrooms are available at the park. Dogs are allowed on the beach. They must be on a six foot or less leash at all times and people are required to clean up after their pets. On beaches located outside of Oregon State Park boundaries, dogs might be allowed off-leash and under direct voice control, please look for signs or postings. This park is located off U.S. Highway 101 in Lincoln City.

Roads End State Recreation Site
Highway 101
Lincoln City, OR
800-551-6949
There is a short trail here that leads down to the beach. Picnic tables are available at this park. There are no day use fees. Dogs are allowed on the beach. They must be on a six foot or less leash at all times and

people are required to clean up after their pets. On beaches located outside of Oregon State Park boundaries, dogs might be allowed off-leash and under direct voice control, please look for signs or postings. This park is located off U.S. Highway 101, 1 mile north of Lincoln City.

Nehalem Bay State Park
Highway 101
Manzanita, OR
503-368-5154
The beach can be reached by a short walk over the dunes. This park is a popular place for fishing and crabbing. Picnic tables, restrooms (including an ADA restroom), hiking and camping are available at this park. There is a $3 day use fee. Leashed dogs are allowed on the beach. Dogs are also allowed on hiking trails and campgrounds. They must be on a six foot or less leash at all times and people are required to clean up after their pets. On beaches located outside of Oregon State Park boundaries, dogs might be allowed off-leash and under direct voice control, please look for signs or postings. This park is located off U.S. Highway 101, 3 miles south of Manzanita Junction.

Oswald West State Park
Highway 101
Manzanita, OR
800-551-6949
The beach is located just a quarter of a mile from the parking areas. It is a popular beach that is frequented by windsurfers and boogie boarders. Picnic tables, restrooms, hiking, and campgrounds are available at this park. There are no day use fees. Leashed dogs are allowed on the beach. Dogs are also allowed on hiking trails and campgrounds. They must be on a six foot or less leash at all times and people are required to clean up after their pets. On beaches located outside of Oregon State Park boundaries, dogs might be allowed off-leash and under direct voice control, please look for signs or postings. This park is located off U.S. Highway 101, 10 miles south of Cannon Beach.

Neskowin Beach State Recreation Site
Highway 101
Neskowin, OR
800-551-6949
Not really any facilities (picnic tables, etc.) here, but a good place to enjoy the beach. Dogs are allowed on the

beach. They must be on a six foot or less leash at all times and people are required to clean up after their pets. On beaches located outside of Oregon State Park boundaries, dogs might be allowed off-leash and under direct voice control, please look for signs or postings. This park is located off U.S. Highway 101 in Neskowin.

Agate Beach State Recreation Site
Highway 101
Newport, OR
800-551-6949
This beach is popular with surfers. Walk through a tunnel to get to the beach. According to the Oregon State Parks Division, many years ago Newport farmers led cattle westward through the tunnel to the ocean salt. Picnic tables and restrooms are available at this park. There is no day use fees. Dogs are allowed on the beach. They must be on a six foot or less leash at all times and people are required to clean up after their pets. On beaches located outside of Oregon State Park boundaries, dogs might be allowed off-leash and under direct voice control, please look for signs or postings. This park is located off U.S. Highway 101, 1 mile north of Newport.

Beverly Beach State Park
Highway 101
Newport, OR
541-265-9278
To get to the beach, there is a walkway underneath the highway that leads to the ocean. Picnic tables, restrooms (including an ADA restroom), a walking trail and campgrounds are available at this park. There is a day use fee. Leashed dogs are allowed on the beach. Dogs are also allowed on the walking trail and campgrounds. They must be on a six foot or less leash at all times and people are required to clean up after their pets. On beaches located outside of Oregon State Park boundaries, dogs might be allowed off-leash and under direct voice control, please look for signs or postings. This park is located off U.S. Highway 101, 7 miles north of Newport.

Devils Punch Bowl State Natural Area
Highway 101
Newport, OR
800-551-6949
This is a popular beach for surfing. Picnic tables, restrooms and hiking

are available at this park. There are no day use fees. Leashed dogs are allowed on the beach. Dogs are also allowed on hiking trails. They must be on a six foot or less leash at all times and people are required to clean up after their pets. On beaches located outside of Oregon State Park boundaries, dogs might be allowed off-leash and under direct voice control, please look for signs or postings. This park is located off U.S. Highway 101, 8 miles north of Newport.

South Beach State Park
Highway 101
Newport, OR
541-867-4715
This beach offers many recreational opportunities like beachcombing, fishing, windsurfing and crabbing. Picnic tables, restrooms (including an ADA restroom), hiking (including an ADA hiking trail), and campgrounds are available at this park. There is a day use fee. Leashed dogs are allowed on the beach. Dogs are also allowed on hiking trails and campgrounds. They must be on a six foot or less leash at all times and people are required to clean up after their pets. On beaches located outside of Oregon State Park boundaries, dogs might be allowed off-leash and under direct voice control, please look for signs or postings. This park is located off U.S. Highway 101, 2 miles south of Newport.

Bob Straub State Park
Highway 101
Pacific City, OR
800-551-6949
This is a nice stretch of beach to walk along. Picnic tables and restrooms (including an ADA restroom) are available at this park. There are no day use fees. Dogs are allowed on the beach. They must be on a six foot or less leash at all times and people are required to clean up after their pets. On beaches located outside of Oregon State Park boundaries, dogs might be allowed off-leash and under direct voice control, please look for signs or postings. This park is located off U.S. Highway 101 in Pacific City.

Cape Kiwanda State Natural Area
Highway 101
Pacific City, OR
800-551-6949
This beach and park is a good spot for marine mammal watching, hang gliding and kite flying. Picnic tables

are available at this park. There are no day use fees. Dogs are allowed on the beach. They must be on a six foot or less leash at all times and people are required to clean up after their pets. On beaches located outside of Oregon State Park boundaries, dogs might be allowed off-leash and under direct voice control, please look for signs or postings. This park is located off U.S. Highway 101, 1 mile north of Pacific City.

Cape Blanco State Park
Highway 101
Port Orford, OR
541-332-6774
oregonstateparks.org/park_62.php
Take a stroll on the beach or hike on over eight miles of trails which offer spectacular ocean vistas. Picnic tables, restrooms, hiking and campgrounds are available at this park. There is a minimal day use fee. Leashed dogs are allowed on the beach. Dogs are also allowed on hiking trails and campgrounds. They must be on a six foot or less leash at all times and people are required to clean up after their pets. On beaches located outside of Oregon State Park boundaries, dogs might be allowed off-leash and under direct voice control, please look for signs or postings. This park is located off U.S. Highway 101, 9 miles north of Port Orford.

Humbug Mountain State Park
Highway 101
Port Orford, OR
541-332-6774
oregonstateparks.org/park_56.php
This beach is frequented by windsurfers and scuba divers. A popular activity at this park is hiking to the top of Humbug Mountain (elevation 1,756 feet) . Picnic tables, restrooms, hiking and campgrounds are available at this park. There is a minimal day use fee. Leashed dogs are allowed on the beach. Dogs are also allowed on hiking trails and campgrounds. They must be on a six foot or less leash at all times and people are required to clean up after their pets. On beaches located outside of Oregon State Park boundaries, dogs might be allowed off-leash and under direct voice control, please look for signs or postings. This park is located off U.S. Highway 101, 6 miles south of Port Orford.

Manhattan Beach State Recreation Site

Highway 101
Rockaway Beach, OR
800-551-6949
The beach is a short walk from the parking area. Picnic tables are available at this park. There are no day use fees. Dogs are allowed on the beach. They must be on a six foot or less leash at all times and people are required to clean up after their pets. On beaches located outside of Oregon State Park boundaries, dogs might be allowed off-leash and under direct voice control, please look for signs or postings. This park is located off U.S. Highway 101, 2 miles north of Rockaway Beach.

Del Rey Beach State Recreation Site
Highway 101
Seaside, OR
800-551-6949
There is a short trail to the beach. There is no day use fee. Dogs are allowed on the beach. They must be on a six foot or less leash at all times and people are required to clean up after their pets. On beaches located outside of Oregon State Park boundaries, dogs might be allowed off-leash and under direct voice control, please look for signs or postings. This park is located off U.S. Highway 101, 2 miles north of Gearhart.

Cape Lookout State Park
Highway 101
Tillamook, OR
503-842-4981
This is a popular beach during the summer. The beach is a short distance from the parking area. It is located about an hour and half west of Portland. Picnic tables, restrooms (including an ADA restroom), hiking trails and campgrounds are available at this park. There is a $3 day use fee. Leashed dogs are allowed on the beach. Dogs are also allowed on hiking trails and campgrounds. They must be on a six foot or less leash at all times and people are required to clean up after their pets. On beaches located outside of Oregon State Park boundaries, dogs might be allowed off-leash and under direct voice control, please look for signs or postings. This park is located off U.S. Highway 101, 12 miles southwest of Tillamook.

Cape Meares State Scenic Viewpoint
Highway 101

Tillamook, OR
800-551-6949
The beach is located south of the scenic viewpoint. The viewpoint is situated on a headland, about 200 feet above the ocean. According to the Oregon State Parks Division, bird watchers can view the largest colony of nesting common murres (this site is one of the most populous colonies of nesting sea birds on the continent). Bald eagles and a peregrine falcon have also been known to nest near here. In winter and spring, this park is an excellent location for viewing whale migrations. Picnic tables, restrooms and hiking are available at this park. There are no day use fees. Leashed dogs are allowed on the beach. Dogs are also allowed on hiking trails. They must be on a six foot or less leash at all times and people are required to clean up after their pets. On beaches located outside of Oregon State Park boundaries, dogs might be allowed off-leash and under direct voice control, please look for signs or postings. This park is located off U.S. Highway 101, 10 miles west of Tillamook.

Beachside State Recreation Site
Highway 101
Waldport, OR
541-563-3220
Enjoy miles of broad sandy beach at this park or stay at one of the campground sites that are located just seconds from the beach. Picnic tables, restrooms (including an ADA restroom), and hiking are also available at this park. There is a day use fees. Leashed dogs are allowed on the beach. Dogs are also allowed on hiking trails and campgrounds. They must be on a six foot or less leash at all times and people are required to clean up after their pets. On beaches located outside of Oregon State Park boundaries, dogs might be allowed off-leash and under direct voice control, please look for signs or postings. This park is located off U.S. Highway 101, 4 miles south of Waldport.

Governor Patterson Memorial State Recreation Site
Highway 101
Waldport, OR
800-551-6949
This park offers miles of flat, sandy beach. It is also an excellent location for whale watching. Picnic tables and restrooms are available at this park. There are no day use fees. Dogs are allowed on the beach. They must be

on a six foot or less leash at all times and people are required to clean up after their pets. On beaches located outside of Oregon State Park boundaries, dogs might be allowed off-leash and under direct voice control, please look for signs or postings. This park is located off U.S. Highway 101, 1 mile south of Waldport.

Fort Stevens State Park
Highway 101
Warrenton, OR
503-861-1671
oregonstate.org/park_179.php
There are miles of ocean beach. Picnic tables, restrooms (including an ADA restroom), hiking and campgrounds are available at this park. There is a $3 day use fee. Leashed dogs are allowed on the beach. Dogs are also allowed on hiking trails and campgrounds. They must be on a six foot or less leash at all times and people are required to clean up after their pets. On beaches located outside of Oregon State Park boundaries, dogs might be allowed off-leash and under direct voice control, please look for signs or postings. This park is located off U.S. Highway 101, 10 miles west of Astoria.

Neptune State Scenic Viewpoint
Highway 101
Yachats, OR
800-551-6949
During low tide at this beach you can walk south and visit a natural cave and tidepools. Or sit and relax at one of the picnic tables that overlooks the beach below. Restrooms (including an ADA restroom) are available at this park. There are no day use fees. Dogs are allowed on the beach. They must be on a six foot or less leash at all times and people are required to clean up after their pets. On beaches located outside of Oregon State Park boundaries, dogs might be allowed off-leash and under direct voice control, please look for signs or postings. This park is located off U.S. Highway 101,

Yachats State Recreation Area
Highway 101
Yachats, OR
800-551-6949
This beach is a popular spot for whale watching, salmon fishing, and exploring tidepools. Picnic tables and restrooms are available at this park. There are no day use fees. Dogs are allowed on the beach. They must be on a six foot or less leash at all times

and people are required to clean up after their pets. On beaches located outside of Oregon State Park boundaries, dogs might be allowed off-leash and under direct voice control, please look for signs or postings. This park is located off U.S. Highway 101 in Yachats.

Pennsylvania

Presque Isle State Park Beach
PA Route 832
Erie, PA
814-833-7424
This state park offers beaches and almost 11 miles of hiking trails. Popular activities at the park include surfing, swimming, boating, hiking, in-line skating and bicycling. Dogs are allowed on a 6 foot or less leash at the park including on the hiking trails and only on beaches that are not guarded by lifeguard staff. Dogs can go into the water, still on leash, but people can only wade in up to their knees since there are no lifeguards in those areas. The unguarded beaches are located throughout the park, but if you want to know exact locations, please stop at the park office for details. The park is located four miles west of downtown Erie, off Route 832.

Rhode Island

Block Island Beaches
Corn Neck Road
Block Island, RI
401-466-2982
Dogs are allowed year-round on the island beaches, but they must be leashed and people are required to clean up after their pets. To get to the beaches, take a right out of town and follow Corn Neck Road. To get to the island, you will need to take the Block Island Ferry which allows leashed dogs. The ferry from Port Judith, RI to Block Island operates daily. If you are taking the ferry from Newport, RI or New London, CT to the island, please note these ferries only operate during the summer. If you are bringing a vehicle on the ferry, reservations are required. Call the Block Island Ferry at 401-783-4613 for auto reservations.

East Beach State Beach
East Beach Road
Charlestown, RI
401-322-0450
riparks.com/misquamicut.htm
Dogs are only allowed on the beach during the off-season, from October 1 through March 31. Pets must be on leash and people are required to clean up after their pets. However, according to a representative at the Rhode Island State Parks Department, in a conversation with them July 2004, the rules may change in the future to have no dogs on the beach year round. To get there, take I-95 to Route 4 South. Then take Route 1 South to East Beach exit in Charlestown.

East Ferry
Conanicus Avenue
Jamestown, RI
401-849-2822
There is a nice green area with a memorial here, and benches placed to watch out over the busy harbor life. Leashed dogs are allowed on the wharf; they must be leashed and under their owner's control at all times. There is also dog friendly dining on the wharf.

Salty Brine State Beach
254 Great Road
Narragansett, RI
401-789-3563
riparks.com/saltybrine.htm
Dogs are only allowed on the beach during the off-season, from October 1 through March 31. Pets must be on leash and people are required to clean up after their pets. However, according to a representative at the Rhode Island State Parks Department, in a conversation with them July 2004, the rules may change in the future to have no dogs on the beach year round. To get there, take I-95 to Route 4 South. Then take Route 1 South to Route 108 South to Point Judith. If you are there during the summer, take the dog-friendly ferry at Pt. Judith to Block Island where leashed dogs are allowed year-round on the island beaches.

Easton's Beach
Memorial Blvd.
Newport, RI
401-847-6875
Dogs are only allowed on the beach during the off-season. They are not allowed on the beach from Memorial Day weekend through Labor Day weekend. Pets must be on leash and people need to clean up after their

pets. The beach is located off Route 138A (Memorial Blvd.). There is a parking fee.

Sandy Point Beach
Sandy Point Avenue
Portsmouth, RI
401-683-2101
portsmouthri.com/frames.htm
Located along the Sakonnet River, this beach area offers changing rooms, restrooms, and picnic tables. There are lifeguards on duty from Memorial Day to Labor Day. Free for residents, there is a fee for non-residents; non-resident season stickers are available at the Town Clerk's office at 2200 East Main Road. Dogs are allowed on the beach after the beach has closed at 5 pm. Dogs must be leashed and cleaned up after at all times.

Teddy's Beach
Park Avenue
Portsmouth, RI
401-683-7899
portsmouthri.com/frames.htm
Although located in Island Park, this is not a staffed town beach. There are no restrooms and it is a carry in/carries out facility. Dogs are allowed; they must be leashed and cleaned up after at all times.

East Matunuck State Beach
950 Succotash Road
South Kingston, RI
401-789-8585
riparks.com/eastmatunuck.htm
Dogs are only allowed on the beach during the off-season, from October 1 through March 31. Pets must be on leash and people are required to clean up after their pets. However, according to a representative at the Rhode Island State Parks Department, in a conversation with them July 2004, the rules may change in the future to have no dogs on the beach year round. To get there, take I-95 to Route 4 South. Then take Route 1 South to East Matunuck Exit and follow the signs to the state beach.

Misquamicut State Beach
257 Atlantic Avenue
Westerly, RI
401-596-9097
riparks.com/misquamicut.htm
Dogs are only allowed on the beach during the off-season, from October 1 through March 31. Pets must be on leash and people are required to clean up after their pets. However, according to a representative at the Rhode Island State Parks

Department, in a conversation to them July 2004, the rules may change in the future to have no dogs on the beach year round. To get there, take I-95 to Route 4 South. Then take Route 1 South to Westerly. Follow the signs to the state beach.

South Carolina

Edisto Beach State Park
8377 State Cabin Road
Edisto Island, SC
843-869-2756
Sunbathe, beachcomb or hunt for seashells on this 1.5 mile long beach. This park also has a 4 mile nature trail that winds through a maritime forest with great vistas that overlook the salt marsh. Dogs on a 6 foot or less leash are allowed on the beach and on the trails. People need to clean up after their pets.

Folly Beach County Park
Ashley Avenue
Folly Beach, SC
843-588-2426
beachparks.com/follybeach.htm
Dogs are only allowed during the off-season at this beach. They are not allowed from May 1 through September 30. But the rest of the year, dogs on leash are allowed on the beach during park hours. People are required to clean up after their pets. The park is located on the west end of Folly Island. On the island, turn right at Ashley Avenue stoplight and go to the end of the road.

Alder Lane Beach Access
S. Forest Beach Drive
Hilton Head Island, SC
843-341-4600
This beach has restricted seasons and hours for dogs. During the summertime, from the Friday before Memorial Day through the Tuesday after Labor Day, dogs can only be on the beach before 10am and then after 5pm (they are not allowed from 10am to 5pm). Pets must be leashed. During the off-season and winter months, from April 1 through the Thursday before Memorial Day, dogs must be on a leash between 10am and 5pm. From the Tuesday after Labor Day through September 30, dogs again must be on a leash between 10am and 5pm. At all other times, dogs may be off-leash,

but must be under direct, positive voice control. People are required to clean up after their pets. There are 22 metered spaces for beach parking. The cost is a quarter for each 15 minutes.

Coligny Beach Park
Coligny Circle
Hilton Head Island, SC
843-341-4600
This beach has restricted seasons and hours for dogs. During the summertime, from the Friday before Memorial Day through the Tuesday after Labor Day, dogs can only be on the beach before 10am and then after 5pm (they are not allowed from 10am to 5pm). Pets must be leashed. During the off-season and winter months, from April 1 through the Thursday before Memorial Day, dogs must be on a leash between 10am and 5pm. From the Tuesday after Labor Day through September 30, dogs again must be on a leash between 10am and 5pm. At all other times, dogs may be off-leash, but must be under direct, positive voice control. People are required to clean up after their pets. There are 30 metered spaces for beach parking. The cost is a quarter for each 15 minutes. A flat fee of $4 is charged at the parking lot on Fridays through Sundays and holidays.

Folly Field Beach Park
Folly Field Road
Hilton Head Island, SC
843-341-4600
This beach has restricted seasons and hours for dogs. During the summertime, from the Friday before Memorial Day through the Tuesday after Labor Day, dogs can only be on the beach before 10am and then after 5pm (they are not allowed from 10am to 5pm). Pets must be leashed. During the off-season and winter months, from April 1 through the Thursday before Memorial Day, dogs must be on a leash between 10am and 5pm. From the Tuesday after Labor Day through September 30, dogs again must be on a leash between 10am and 5pm. At all other times, dogs may be off-leash, but must be under direct, positive voice control. People are required to clean up after their pets. There are 52 metered spaces for beach parking. The cost is a quarter for each 15 minutes.

Hilton Head Island Beaches
Hilton Head Island, SC
800-523-3373

Dogs are welcome on the beaches of the island during certain times/days: They are not permitted on the beach between 10 AM and 5 PM from the Friday before Memorial Day through Labor Day; they may be on the beach between 10 AM and 5 PM from April 1st to the Thursday before Memorial Day, and between 10 AM and 5 PM the Tuesday after Labor Day through September 30th. Dogs must be leashed and picked up after at all times.

Hunting Island State Park
2555 Sea Island Parkway
Hunting Island, SC
843-838-2011
This park offers over 4 miles of beach. Dogs on a 6 foot or less leash are allowed on the beach and on the trails at this state park. People need to clean up after their pets.

Isle of Palms County Park Beach
14th Avenue
Isle of Palms, SC
843-886-3863
beachparks.com/isleofpalms.htm
Dogs on leash are allowed year-round at this beach. People are required to clean up after their pets. The park is located on the Isle of Palms, on 14th Ave., between Palm Blvd. and Ocean Blvd. Then coming to Isle of Palms from 517, continue straight at the Palm Blvd intersection and then take the next left at the park gate.

Beachwalker County Park
Beachwalker Drive
Kiawah, SC
843-768-2395
beachparks.com/beachwalker.htm
Dogs on leash are allowed year-round at this beach. People are required to clean up after their pets. The park is located on the west end of Kiawah Island. Take Bohicket Road to the island. Just before the island security gate, turn right on Beachwalker Drive. Follow the road to the park.

Huntington Beach State Park
16148 Ocean Highway
Murrells Inlet, SC
843-234-4440
This beach is the best preserved beach on the Grand Strand. Dogs on a 6 foot or less leash are allowed on the beach. People need to clean up after their pets.

Myrtle Beach City Beaches
off Interstate 73
Myrtle Beach, SC

843-281-2662
There are certain restrictions for pets on the beach. Dogs are not allowed on the right of way of Ocean Blvd. (part of I-73), between 21st Avenue North and 13th Avenue South during March 1 through September 30. From Memorial Day weekend through Labor Day weekend, leashed dogs are allowed on Myrtle Beach city beaches before 9am and after 5pm. During off-season, leashed dogs are allowed on the city beaches anytime during park hours. People need to clean up after their pets.

Myrtle Beach State Park
4401 South Kings Highway
Myrtle Beach, SC
843-238-5325
This is one of the most popluar public beaches on the South Carolina coast. It is located in the heart of the Grand Strand. During the summertime, dogs are only allowed during certain hours. From June through August, dogs are only allowed on the beach after 4pm. For all other months of the year, dogs are allowed on the beach anytime during park hours. Dogs must be on leash at all times. People are required to clean up after their pets.

Sullivan Island Beach
Atlantic Avenue
Sullivan's Island, SC
843-883-3198
sullivansisland-sc.com/
Dogs are allowed off leash on this barrier island beach from 5 AM to 10 AM April through October, and from 5 AM to 12 Noon November 1st to March 31st; this does not include walkways or access paths to the area where they must be leashed (no longer than 10 feet). A pet permit is required that can be obtained at the Town Hall at 1610 Middle Street-proof of vaccinations and rabies required. Dogs are NOT allowed on the beach, paths, or the adjacent waters at any time from 10 AM to 6 PM from April 1st to October 31st; however they are allowed at these areas on a leash from 6 PM to 5 AM, April 1st to October 31st, and from 12 Noon to 5 AM from November 1st to March 31st. Dogs must be under their owner's control at all times. Dogs must be leashed when not in designated off-lead areas.

Texas

Cole Park
Ocean Drive
Corpus Christi, TX
800-766-2322
Dogs on leash are allowed on the beach. People need to clean up after their pets.

Bryan Beach
Road 1495
Freeport, TX
979-233-3526
Pooches are allowed to come and frolic on this 3.5 mile long city beach or even primitive camp overnight; there are no facilities here. Dogs must be under their owner's immediate control at all times.

Big Reef Nature Park
Boddeker Drive
Galveston, TX
409-765-5023
Take a walkway to the beach which runs parallel to Bolivar Rd. Dogs on leash are allowed on the beach. People need to clean up after their pets. There are no day use fees. This park is part of East Beach which does not allow dogs on the pavilion. The beach is located on the east end of Galveston Isle, off Boddeker Drive.

Dellanera RV Park
FM 3005 at 7 Mile Rd.
Galveston, TX
409-740-0390
This RV park offers 1,000 feet of sandy beach. Dogs on leash are allowed on the beach and at the RV spaces. People need to clean up after their pets. There are over 60 full RV hookups, over 20 partial hookups and day parking. Picnic tables and restrooms are available at this park. There is a $5 day parking fee. RV spaces are about $25 and up.

Galveston Island State Park
14901 FM 3005
Galveston, TX
409-737-1222
Leashed dogs are allowed on the beach and at the campsites. There is a $3 per person (over 13 years old) day use fee. There is no charge for children 12 and under. The park can be reached from Interstate 45 by exiting right onto 61st Street and traveling south on 61st Street to its intersection with Seawall Boulevard

and then right (west) on Seawall (FM 3005) 10 miles to the park entrance.

Stewart Beach
6th and Seawall Boulevard
Galveston, TX
409-765-5023
This is one of the best family beaches in Galveston. Many family-oriented events including a sandcastle competition are held at this beach. Restrooms, umbrella and chair rentals, and volleyball courts are available. There is a $7 per car admission fee. Dogs on leash are allowed on the beach. People need to clean up after their pets. The beach is located at 6th Street and Seawall Blvd.

Padre Island National Seashore
Highway 22
Padre Island, TX
361-949-8068
nps.gov/pais/
Visitors to this beach can swim, sunbathe, hunt for shells or just enjoy a walk. About 800,000 visitors per year come to this park. Dogs on leash are allowed on the beach. People need to clean up after their pets. There is a minimal day use fee. The park is located on Padre Island, southeast of Corpus Christi.

Andy Bowie Park
Park Road 100
South Padre Island, TX
956-761-3704
co.cameron.tx.us
Dogs on leash are allowed on the beach. People need to clean up after their pets. There is a minimal day use fee. This park is located on the northern end of South Padre Island.

Edwin K. Atwood Park
Park Road 100
South Padre Island, TX
956-761-3704
co.cameron.tx.us
This beach offers 20 miles of beach driving. Dogs on leash are allowed on the beach. People need to clean up after their pets. There is a minimal day use fee. This park is located almost 1.5 miles north of Andy Bowie Park.

Isla Blanca Park
Park Road 100
South Padre Island, TX
956-761-5493
This popular beach offers about a mile of clean, white beach. Picnic tables, restrooms, and RV spaces are available at this park. Dogs on leash are allowed on the beach.

People need to clean up after their pets. There is a minimal day use fee. The park is located on the southern tip of South Padre Island.

Virginia

Back Bay National Wildlife Refuge
Sandpiper Road
Virginia Beach, VA
757-721-2412
backbay.fws.gov/
Dogs are only allowed on the beach during the off-season. Dogs are only allowed on the beach from October 1 through March 31. Pets must be leashed (on leashes up to 10 feet long) and people need to clean up after their pets. This park is located approximately 15 miles south of Virginia Beach. From I-64, exit to I-264 East (towards the oceanfront). Then take Birdneck Road Exit (Exit 22), turn right onto Birdneck Road. Go about 3-4 miles and then turn right on General Booth Blvd. Go about 5 miles. After crossing the Nimmo Parkway, pay attention to road signs. Get into the left lane so you can turn left at the next traffic light. Turn left onto Princess Anne Rd. The road turns into Sandbridge Rd. Keep driving and then turn right onto Sandpiper Road just past the fire station. Follow Sandpiper Road for about 4 miles to the end of the road.

First Landing State Park
2500 Shore Drive
Virginia Beach, VA
757-412-2300
Dogs on a 6 foot or less leash are allowed year-round on the beach. People need to clean up after their pet. All pets must have a rabies tag on their collar or proof of a rabies vaccine. To get there, take I-64. Then take the Northampton Blvd/US 13 North (Exit 282). You will pass eight lights and then turn right at the Shore Drive/US 60 exit. Turn right onto Shore Drive and go about 4.5 miles to the park entrance.

Virginia Beach Public Beaches
off Highway 60
Virginia Beach, VA
757-437-4919
Dogs are only allowed during off-season on Virginia Beach public beaches. From the Friday before Memorial Day through Labor Day

weekend, pets are not allowed on public sand beaches, the boardwalk or the grassy area west of the boardwalk, from Rudee Inlet to 42nd Street. People are required to clean up after their pets and dogs must be leashed.

Washington

Fay Bainbridge State Park
Sunset Drive NE
Bainbridge Island, WA
360-902-8844
This park is located on the northeast side of Bainbridge Island on Puget Sound. On a clear day, you can see Mt. Rainer and Mt. Baker from the beach. Picnic tables, restrooms and campgrounds are available at this park. Leashed dogs are allowed on the beach. Pets are not permitted on designated swimming beaches. However, there is usually a non-designated swimming beach area as well. Dogs are also allowed at the campgrounds. They must be on a eight foot or less leash at all times and people are required to clean up after their pets. To get there from From Poulsbo, take Hwy. 305 toward Bainbridge Island. Cross the Agate Pass Bridge. After three miles, come to stoplight and big brown sign with directions to park. Turn left at traffic light onto Day Rd. NE. Travel approximately two miles to a T-intersection. Turn left onto Sunrise Drive NE, and continue to park entrance, about two miles away.

Birch Bay State Park
Grandview
Blaine, WA
360-902-8844
This beach, located near the Canadian border, offers panoramic coastal views. Picnic tables, restrooms (including an ADA restroom), and campgrounds (including ADA campsites) are available at this park. Leashed dogs are allowed on the beach. Pets are not permitted on designated swimming beaches. However, there is usually a non-designated swimming beach area as well. Dogs are also allowed in the campgrounds. They must be on a eight foot or less leash at all times and people are required to clean up after their pets. This park is located 20 miles north of Bellingham and ten miles south of Blaine. From the south

take exit #266 off of I-5. Go left on Grandview for seven miles, then right on Jackson for one mile, then turn left onto Helweg. From the north take exit #266 off of I-5, and turn right onto Grandview.

Griffith-Priday State Park
State Route 109
Copalis Beach, WA
360-902-8844
This beach extends from the beach through low dunes to a river and then north to the river's mouth. Picnic tables and restrooms are available at this park. Dogs are allowed on the beach. They must be on a eight foot or less leash at all times and people are required to clean up after their pets. This park is located 21 miles northwest of Hoquiam. From Hoquiam, go north on SR 109 for 21 miles. At Copalis Beach, at the sign for Benner Rd., turn left (west).

Saltwater State Park
Marine View Drive
Des Moines, WA
360-902-8844
This state beach is located on Puget Sound, halfway between the cities of Tacoma and Seattle (near the Sea-Tac international airport). Picnic tables, restrooms and campgrounds are available at this park. Leashed dogs are allowed on the beach. Pets are not permitted on designated swimming beaches. However, there is usually a non-designated swimming beach area as well. Dogs are also allowed at the campgrounds. They must be on a eight foot or less leash at all times and people are required to clean up after their pets. To get there from the north, take exit #149 off of I-5. Go west, then turn south on Hwy. 99 (sign missing). Follow the signs into the park. Turn right on 240th at the Midway Drive-in. Turn left on Marine View Dr. and turn right into the park.

Off-Leash Area and Beach
498 Admiral Way
Edmonds, WA
425-771-0230
olae.org
The Off-leash area and beach in Edmonds gives dogs a place to run free, swim and meet other dogs. The area is maintained and supported by O.L.A.E. and overseen by the City of Edmonds Parks and Rec Dept. From I-5 follow signs to the Edmonds Ferry until Dayton Street. Turn west on Dayton Street and then south on Admiral Way. The off-leash area is south of Marina Beach.

Howarth Park Dog Beach
1127 Olympic Blvd.
Everett, WA
425-257-8300
Most of the park and beach areas require that dogs are on-leash and there are fines for violations. There is an off-leash beach area north of the pedestrian bridge that crosses the railroad tracks. Your dog should be under excellent voice control at this beach if it is off-leash due to the nearby train tracks. In addition, the train may spook a dog. There are also some trails for leashed dogs. The park is open from 6 am to 10 pm.

Dash Point State Park
Dash Point Rd.
Federal Way, WA
360-902-8844
This beach offers great views of Puget Sound. Picnic tables, restrooms, 11 miles of hiking trails and campgrounds are available at this park. Leashed dogs are allowed on the beach. Pets are not permitted on designated swimming beaches. However, there is usually a non-designated swimming beach area as well. Dogs are also allowed on hiking trails and campgrounds. They must be on a eight foot or less leash at all times and people are required to clean up after their pets. This park is located on the west side of Federal Way in the vicinity of Seattle. From Highway 5, exit at the 320th St. exit (exit #143). Take 320th St. west approximately four miles. When 320th St. ends at a T-intersection, make a right onto 47th St. When 47th St. ends at a T-intersection, turn left onto Hwy. 509/Dash Point Rd. Drive about two miles to the park. (West side of street is the campground side, and east side is the day-use area.)

Double Bluff Beach
6400 Double Bluff Road
Freeland, WA
360-321-4049
fetchparks.org
South of Freeland and on Whidbey Island, this unfenced off-leash area also includes a dog beach. This is one of the largest off-leash beaches in the U.S. The off-leash beach is about 2 miles long. On clear days you can see Mt Rainier, the Seattle skyline and many ships. The beach nearest the parking lot is an on-leash area and the off-leash beach starts about 500 feet from the lot. There will be steep fines for dogs

that are unleashed in an inappropriate area. From WA-525 watch for a sign for Double Bluff Road and it south. The road ends at the beach.

South Beach
125 Spring Street
Friday Harbor, WA
360-378-2902
nps.gov/sajh/
Dogs on leash are allowed at South Beach, which is located at the American Camp in the San Juan Island National Historic Park.

Grayland Beach State Park
Highway 105
Grayland, WA
360-902-8844
This 412 acre park offers beautiful ocean frontage and full hookup campsites (including ADA campsites). Leashed dogs are allowed on the beach. Dogs are also allowed at the campgrounds. They must be on a eight foot or less leash at all times and people are required to clean up after their pets. This park is located five miles south of Westport. From Aberdeen, drive 22 miles on Highway 105 south to Grayland. Traveling through the town, watch for park signs.

Cape Disappointment State Park
Highway 101
Ilwaco, WA
360-902-8844
This park offers 27 miles of ocean beach and 7 miles of hiking trails. Enjoy excellent views of the ocean, Columbia River and two lighthouses. Picnic tables, restrooms (including an ADA restroom), hiking and campgrounds (includes ADA campsites) are available at this park. Leashed dogs are allowed on the beach. Dogs are also allowed on hiking trails and campgrounds. They must be on a eight foot or less leash at all times and people are required to clean up after their pets. This park is located two miles southwest of Ilwaco.From Seattle, Take I-5 south to Olympia, SR 8 west to Montesano. From there, take U.S. Hwy. 101 south to Long Beach Peninsula.

Spencer Spit State Park
Bakerview Road
Lopez Island, WA
360-902-8844
Located in the San Juan Islands, this lagoon beach offers great crabbing, clamming and beachcombing. Picnic tables, restrooms, campgrounds and 2 miles of hiking trails are available

at this park. Leashed dogs are allowed on the beach. Pets are not permitted on designated swimming beaches. However, there is usually a non-designated swimming beach area as well. Dogs are also allowed on hiking trails and campgrounds. They must be on a eight foot or less leash at all times and people are required to clean up after their pets. This park is located on Lopez Island in the San Juan Islands. It is a 45-minute Washington State Ferry ride from Anacortes. Dogs are allowed on the ferry. Once on Lopez Island, follow Ferry Rd. Go left at Center Rd., then left at Cross Rd. Turn right at Port Stanley and left at Bakerview Rd. Follow Bakerview Rd. straight into park. For ferry rates and schedules, call 206-464-6400.

Fort Ebey State Park
Hill Valley Drive
Oak Harbor, WA
360-902-8844
This 600+ acre park is popular for hiking and camping, but also offers a saltwater beach. Picnic tables and restrooms (including an ADA restroom) are available at this park. Leashed dogs are allowed on the saltwater beach. Dogs are also allowed on hiking trails and campgrounds. They must be on a eight foot or less leash at all times and people are required to clean up after their pets. To get to the park from Seattle, take exit #189 off of I-5, just south of Everett. Follow signs for the Mukilteo/ Clinton ferry. Take the ferry to Clinton on Whidbey Island. Dogs are allowed on the ferry. Once on Whidbey Island, follow Hwy. 525 north, which becomes Hwy. 20. Two miles north of Coupeville, turn left on Libbey Rd. and follow it 1.5 miles to Hill Valley Dr. Turn left and enter park.

Joseph Whidbey State Park
Swantown Rd
Oak Harbor, WA
360-902-8844
This 112 acre park offers one of the best beaches on Whidbey Island. Picnic tables, restrooms, and several miles of hiking trails (including a half mile ADA hiking trail) are available at this park. Leashed dogs are allowed on the beach. Pets are not permitted on designated swimming beaches. However, there is usually a non-designated swimming beach area as well. Dogs are also allowed on hiking trails. They must be on a eight foot or less leash at all times and people are required to clean up after their pets.

To get there from the south, drive north on Hwy. 20. Just before Oak Harbor, turn left on Swantown Rd. and follow it about three miles.

Pacific Pines State Park
Highway 101
Ocean Park, WA
360-902-8844
Fishing, crabbing, clamming and beachcombing are popular activities at this beach. Picnic tables and a restroom are available at this park. Dogs are allowed on the beach. They must be on a eight foot or less leash at all times and people are required to clean up after their pets. This park is located approximately one mile north of Ocean Park. From north or south, take Hwy. 101 until you reach Ocean Park. Continue on Vernon St. until you reach 271st St.

Damon Point State Park
Point Brown Avenue
Ocean Shores, WA
360-902-8844
Located on the southeastern tip of the Ocean Shores Peninsula, this one mile long beach offers views of the Olympic Mountains, Mount Rainer, and Grays Harbor. Picnic tables are available at this park. Dogs are allowed on the beach. They must be on a eight foot or less leash at all times and people are required to clean up after their pets. To get there from From Hoquiam, take SR 109 and SR 115 to Point Brown Ave. in the town of Ocean Shores. Proceed south on Point Brown Ave. through town, approximately 4.5 miles. Just past the marina, turn left into park entrance.

Ocean City State Park
State Route 115
Ocean Shores, WA
360-902-8844
Beachcombing, clamming, surfing, bird watching, kite flying and winter storm watching are all popular activites at this beach. Picnic tables, restrooms, and campgrounds (including ADA campgrounds) are available at this park. Leashed dogs are allowed on the beach. Dogs are also allowed at the campgrounds. They must be on a eight foot or less leash at all times and people are required to clean up after their pets. This park is located on the coast one-and-a-half miles north of Ocean Shores on Hwy. 115. From Hoquiam, drive 16 miles west on SR 109, then turn south on SR 115 and drive 1.2 miles to the

park.

Pacific Beach State Park
State Route 109
Pacific Beach, WA
360-902-8844
The beach is the focal point at this 10 acre state park. This sandy ocean beach is great for beachcombing, wildlife watching, windy walks and kite flying. Picnic tables, restrooms (including an ADA restroom), and campgrounds (some are ADA accessible) are available at this park. Leashed dogs are allowed on the beach. Dogs are also allowed in the campgrounds. They must be on a eight foot or less leash at all times and people are required to clean up after their pets. This park is located 15 miles north of Ocean Shores, off SR 109. From Hoquiam, follow SR 109, 30 miles northwest to the town of Pacific Beach. The park is located in town.

Kalaloch Beach
Olympic National Park
Port Angeles, WA
360-962-2283
nps.gov/olym/
Dogs are allowed on leash, during daytime hours only, on Kalaloch Beach along the Pacific Ocean and from Rialto Beach north to Ellen Creek. These beaches are in Olympic National Park, but please note that pets are not permitted on this national park's trails, meadows, beaches (except Kalaloch and Rialto beaches) or in any undeveloped area of the park. For those folks and dogs who want to hike on a trail, try the adjacent dog-friendly Olympic National Forest. Kalaloch Beach is located off Highway 101 in Olympic National Park.

Sand Point Magnuson Park Dog Off-Leash Beach and Area
7400 Sand Point Way NE
Seattle, WA
206-684-4075
This leash free dog park covers about 9 acres and is the biggest fully fenced off-leash park in Seattle. It also offers an access point to the lake where your pooch is welcome to take a dip in the fresh lake water. To find the dog park, take Sand Point Way Northeast and enter the park at Northeast 74th Street. Go straight and park near the playground and sports fields. The main gate to the off-leash area is located at the southeast corner of the main parking lot. Dogs must be leashed until you enter the off-leash area.

Twin Harbors State Park
Highway 105
Westport, WA
360-902-8844
This beach is popular for beachcombing, bird watching, and fishing. Picnic tables, restrooms (including an ADA restroom), and campgrounds (includes ADA campgrounds) are available at this park. Leashed dogs are allowed on the beach. Dogs are also allowed at the campgrounds. They must be on a eight foot or less leash at all times and people are required to clean up after their pets. This park is located three miles south of Westport on Highway 105. From Aberdeen,

Westport Light State Park
Ocean Avenue
Westport, WA
360-902-8844
Enjoy the panoramic view at this park or take the easy access trail to the beach. Swimming in the ocean here is not advised because of variable currents or rip tides. Picnic tables, restrooms (including an ADA restroom), and a 1.3 mile paved trail (also an ADA trail) are available at this park. Leashed dogs are allowed on the beach. Dogs are also allowed on the paved trail. They must be on a eight foot or less leash at all times and people are required to clean up after their pets. This park is located on the Pacific Ocean at Westport, 22 miles southwest of Aberdeen. To get there from Westport, drive west on Ocean Ave. about one mile to park entrance.

Wisconsin

Apostle Islands National Lakeshore
Route 1
Bayfield, WI
715-779-3398
nps.gov/apis/pphtml/contact.html
You will pretty much need your own boat to access this park and beach as the boat cruise tours do not allow pets. If you do have a boat and can reach the islands, dogs are allowed on the trails, in the backcountry campgrounds and on the beaches but must be on a 6 foot or less leash at all times. People need to clean up after their pets.

Harrington Beach State Park
531 Highway D

Belgium, WI
262-285-3015
Pets are allowed only on part of South Beach. They must be leashed except while swimming in the water. But once out of the water, they need to be leashed. Pets are also allowed at one of the picnic areas and on all trails except for the nature trail. Please remember to clean up after your pet.

Kohler-Andrae State Park Beach
1020 Beach Park Lane
Sheboygan, WI
920-451-4080
Pets are not allowed on the swimming beaches but they are allowed only on the beach area north of the nature center. Pets must be on an 8 foot or less leash and cleaned up after. Pets can be off leash only in the water but if one paw hits the sand, he or she must be back on leash or you may get a citation from a park ranger. Dogs are also allowed at certain campsites and on the regular hiking trails but not on nature trails, in the picnic areas or the playground.

Potawatomi State Park Beach
3740 Park Drive
Sturgeon Bay, WI
920-746-2890
Dogs are allowed on the beach but must be leashed except when in the water. To get there from Green Bay, take Highway 57 north. Go about 37 miles to County Highway PD. Turn north onto Highway PD and go 2.4 miles to the park entrance.

Point Beach State Forest
9400 County Highway O
Two Rivers, WI
920-794-7480
Pets are allowed only on a certain part of the beach, located south of the lighthouse. Dogs must be leashed at all times including on the beach and are not allowed in the picnic areas except for the one near the beach that allows dogs. Pets are also allowed on some of the park trails. Please remember to clean up after your pet.

Canada

British Columbia

CRAB Park at Portside Off-Leash Dog Water Access and Dog Park
101 E Waterfront Road
Vancouver, BC
604-257-8400
The CRAB Park unfenced dog off-leash area and dog beach is available for off-leash play from 6 am to 10 am and 5 pm to 10 pm. The off-leash area is the east side of the park. Dogs are not allowed in the area of the playground. Dogs must be well-behaved, have a current license, leashed outside of the off-leash areas and cleaned up after.

Fraser River Park Off-Leash Dog Water Access and Dog Park
8705 Angus Drive
Vancouver, BC
604-257-8689
The Fraser River Park unfenced dog off-leash area and dog beach is available for off-leash play from 6 am to 10 am and 5 pm to 10 pm. Please see the signs outlining the off-leash area. Dogs must be well-behaved, have a current license, leashed outside of the off-leash areas and cleaned up after. The park is located at W 75th Avenue at Angus Drive.

John Hendry Park Off-Leash Dog Water Access and Dog Park
3300 Victoria Drive
Vancouver, BC
604-257-8613
The John Hendry Park unfenced dog off-leash area and dog beach is available for off-leash play from 5 am to 10 pm. Please see the signs outlining the off-leash area. Dogs must be well-behaved, have a current license, leashed outside of the off-leash areas and cleaned up after.

New Brighton Park Off-Leash Dog Water Access and Dog Park
8705 Angus Drive
Vancouver, BC
604-257-8613
The Fraser River Park unfenced dog off-leash area and dog beach is available for off-leash play from 5 am to 10 am from May 1 to September 30 and from 5 am to 10 pm during the rest of the year. Please see the signs outlining the off-leash area. Dogs must be well-behaved, have a

current license, leashed outside of the off-leash areas and cleaned up after.

Spanish Bank Beach Park Off-Leash Dog Water Access and Dog Park
4801 NW Marine Drive
Vancouver, BC
604-257-8689
The Spanish Bank Beach Park unfenced dog off-leash area and dog beach is available for off-leash play from 6 am to 10 pm. Please see the signs outlining the off-leash area. Dogs must be well-behaved, have a current license, leashed outside of the off-leash areas and cleaned up after. The park is located on NW Marine Drive at the entrance to Pacific Spirit Park.

Sunset Beach Park Off-Leash Dog Water Access and Dog Park
1204 Beach Avenue
Vancouver, BC
604-257-8400
The Sunset Beach Park unfenced dog off-leash area and dog beach is available for off-leash play from 6 am to 10 pm. Please see the signs outlining the off-leash area. Dogs must be well-behaved, have a current license, leashed outside of the off-leash areas and cleaned up after.

Vanier Park Off-Leash Dog Water Access and Dog Park
1000 Chestnut Street
Vancouver, BC
604-257-8689
The Vanier Park unfenced dog off-leash area and dog beach is available for off-leash play from 6 am to 10 am and 5 pm to 10 pm from May 1 to September 30 and from 6 am to 10 pm during the rest of the year. Please see the signs outlining the off-leash area. Dogs must be well-behaved, have a current license, leashed outside of the off-leash areas and cleaned up after. The park is located at Chestnut Street at English Bay.

Dallas Road Off-Leash Beach
Dallas Road at Douglass St
Victoria, BC
250-385-5711
victoria.ca/dogs/
Dogs are allowed off-leash year round at the gravel beach in Beacon Hill Park. People are required to clean up after their dogs. The beach is located in downtown Victoria, along Dallas Road, between Douglas Street and

Cook Street.

Gonzales Beach Off-Leash Area
South end of Foul Bay Rd
Victoria, BC
250-361-0600
victoria.ca/dogs/
Gonzales Beach is a large beach that circles Gonzales Bay in the south-eastern section of Victoria. Dogs are allowed on Gonzales Beach 24 hours a day except from June 1 to August 31 when they are not allowed on the beach at all. Dogs must be under control at all times, must be cleaned up after and must be on-leash whenever they are outside of the off-leash area.

Ontario

Dog Beach - Kew Gardens
2075 Queen Street
Toronto, ON
Located in The Beaches neighborhood, dogs are allowed to run leash-free on this section of the beach. Dogs can run leashless 24 hours a day. The dog beach area is located at the foot of Kew, on Beach, between snow fence and Lake.

Chapter 4

Off-Leash Dog Park Guide

United States

Alabama

Daphne Dog Park
Whispering Pines Road
Daphne, AL
251-621-3703
Located behind the Al Trione Sports Complex, this off lead doggy play area has a place for grooming, 3 poop-n-scoop areas, water fountains, small and large dog sections, a bench, and a water hose. Dogs must be sociable, current on all vaccinations and license, and under their owner's control at all times. Dogs must be leashed when not in designated off-lead areas.

Alaska

Conners Lake Park
Jewel Lake Road
Anchorage, AK
907-343-8118
muni.org/healthmsd/dogparks.cfm
With the exception of the winter months when trails are restricted and marked, dogs are allowed on all the trails. Dogs must be legally licensed, have a current rabies vaccination, and be leashed and cleaned up after. Owners must have total voice control of their pets in the off lead area.

Far North Bicentennial Park
Campbell Airstrip Road
Anchorage, AK
907-343-4355
A popular feature of this park is the variety of year round, multi-use trails (non-motored) with sections specified for skiing, skijoring, and dog mushing in the winter months. Dogs are allowed throughout the park and on the trails; they must be legally licensed, have a current rabies vaccination, and be leashed and cleaned up after. In the off-leash area dogs must be under their owner's control at all times. The off-leash area is on North Gasline Trail off Campbell Airstrip Road.

Russian Jack Springs Park
6th Avenue and Boniface Parkway
Anchorage, AK
907-343-8118
muni.org/healthmsd/dogparks.cfm
This park has a number of recreational areas and dogs are allowed throughout the park and on the trails (unless otherwise noted). Dogs must be legally licensed, have a current rabies vaccination, and be leashed and cleaned up after. The off-leash area is located in Lions Camper Park, and dogs must be under their owner's control at all times when in this area.

University Lake Park
Bragaw Street and University Lake Drive
Anchorage, AK
907-343-8118
muni.org/healthmsd/dogparks.cfm
A beautiful lake and great scenery accompany this off-leash area. Dogs are allowed throughout the park and on the trails (unless otherwise noted). Certain trails are off limits to dogs during grooming. Dogs must be legally licensed, have a current rabies vaccination, and be leashed and cleaned up after. In the off-leash area dogs must be under their owner's control at all times.

Arizona

Dog Park
12325 W McDowell Road
Avondale, AZ
623-333-2400
This off leash area is located at Friendship Park where there is also an abundance of recreational opportunities. Dogs must be sociable, current on all vaccinations, licensed, and cleaned up after at all times. Dogs must be leashed when not in designated off-lead areas.

Casa Grande Dog Park
Pinal Ave at Rodeo Rd
Casa Grande, AZ
520-421-8600
This off-leash dog park is located at the Paul Mason Sportsplex. It has two fenced areas. One is for larger dogs and one is for small dogs. Dogs must be spayed or neutered to use the park.

Shawnee Bark Park
1400 W. Mesquite
Chandler, AZ
480-782-2727
The Shawnee Bark Park is a fenced dog park. The park is open from 6:30 am to 10:30 pm daily. Children under 12 are not allowed in the dog park.

Snedigar Bark Park
4500 S. Basha Rd
Chandler, AZ
480-782-2727
The Snedigar Bark Park is a fenced dog park. Located at the Snedigar Sportsplex, the dog park is open from 6:30 am to 10:30 pm daily. Children under 12 are not allowed in the dog park.

West Chandler Bark Park
250 S. Kyrene Rd
Chandler, AZ
480-782-2727
The West Chandler Bark Park is a fenced dog park. Located in West Chandler Park, the dog park is open from 6:30 am to 10:30 pm daily. Children under 12 are not allowed in the dog park.

Bushmaster Dog Park
3150 N. Alta Vista
Flagstaff, AZ
This fenced dog park has separate areas for small and large dogs. It is about 1 1/2 acres in size. From I-40 exit at Country Club Drive, head north to Route 66 west. Immediately turn right onto Lockett to Bushmaster Park on your left.

Thorpe Park Bark Park
191 N. Thorpe Road
Flagstaff, AZ
928-779-7690
flagstaff.az.gov
This 1.5 acre dog park is double-gated and has benches, picnic tables, and a water fountain.

Desert Vista Off-Leash Dog Park
11800 North Desert Vista
Fountain Hills, AZ
480-816-5152
adog.org
This 12 acre park offers a dog park for off-leash romping. The area is fully fenced with multi-station watering fountains and shade structures. Paws in the Park, an annual dog festival, is held at this park. The park is located on Saguaro Blvd., between Tower Drive and Desert Vista. To get there, head east on Shea Blvd. Turn left onto Saguaro Blvd. Go 1.5 miles and turn right onto Desert Vista. Turn left immediately onto Saguaro Blvd. Go about .2 miles and then turn right onto Tower Drive. The park is on the right. Thanks to ADOG (Association of Dog Owners Group) for the directions. The hours are from sunrise to sunset.

Cosmo Dog Park
2502 E. Ray Road
Gilbert, AZ
480-503-6200
There are almost 4 acres at this off-leash park with separate sections for active and timid dogs, benches, tables, "mutt-mitt" stations, drinking fountains, and wash stations. Dogs must be sociable, current on all vaccinations, licensed, and under their owner's control at all times. Dogs must be leashed when not in designated off-lead areas.

Dog Park at Crossroads
2155 E. Knox Rd
Gilbert, AZ
480-503-6200
The Dog Park at Crossroads is open from 6 am to 10 pm daily. It is 2 acres and fenced. It is partially lit for night use. There are tables and benches. There are separate areas for large and small dogs. Crossroads Park is located on the west side of Greenfield Road, north of Ray. To get to the park go west on Knox Rd from Greenfield.

Foothills Park Dog Park
57th Avenue and Union Hills Drive
Glendale, AZ
623-930-2820
This fenced dog park is located in Foothills Park in Glendale. The dog park is located next to the Foothills Library parking lot.

Northern Horizon Dog Park
63rd and Northern Avenue
Glendale, AZ
623-930-2820
This dog park is located in Northern Horizon Park. It has a large fenced in area for larger dogs and a smaller play area for small dogs.

Saguaro Ranch Dog Park
63rd Avenue
Glendale, AZ
This fully fenced dog park has a large grassy area with trees, fire hydrants, benches and even a doggie drinking fountain. The park is located at 63rd Avenue and Mountain View Road. The off-leash area is just north of the west parking lot and just south of the softball complex. Thanks to one of our readers for recommending this dog park!

Goodyear Dog Park
15600 W Roeser
Goodyear, AZ

623-882-7537
There are 3 acres of safe doggy fun at this park that has separate areas for passive and active dogs, fountains for hounds and humans, benches, and restrooms. Dogs must be sociable, current on all vaccinations, licensed, and cleaned up after at all times. Dogs must be leashed when not in designated off-lead areas.

Lions Dog Park
1340 McCulloch Blvd.
Lake Havasu City, AZ
928-453-8686
This dog park is located with the London Bridge Beach park. The grassy off-leash area is completely fenced and offers a water feature, hydrants, benches, and shade. Dogs are not allowed along the Bridgewater Channel, parking lots or other areas of London Bridge Beach. Dogs must be on leash when outside the off-leash area.

Quail Run Park Dog Park
4155 E. Virginia
Mesa, AZ
480-644-2352
This park offers a completely fenced 3 acre dog park. Amenities include separate areas for timid and active dogs, park benches, water fountains for people and dogs, and doggie poop bags. The dog park is closed every Thursday for maintenance. Dogs must be on leash when outside the off-leash area.

Grovers Basin Dog Park
20th Street at Grovers Ave
Phoenix, AZ
602-262-6696
This dog park is 2.3 acres in total divided between a large and small dog area. Both areas are fenced. There are no dog water fountains at the park.

Mofford Sports Complex Dog Park
9833 N. 25th Avenue
Phoenix, AZ
602-261-8011
This fenced dog park is divided into separate areas for small dogs and large dogs. It is open from 6:30 am to 10 pm daily. The dog park may be closed in periods of heavy rain. There is water for dogs, shade trees and benches. The dog park is located on N. 25th Avenue just north of Dunlap.

Pecos Park Dog Park
48th Street

Phoenix, AZ
602-262-6862
phoenix.gov/PARKS/dogparks.html
This two acre dog park is fully fenced with double-gates and a separate area for small and large dogs. Pecos Park is located at 48th Street and Pecos Parkway. Enter from 48th Street via Chandler Blvd. The dog park is located at the southeast corner of the park.

PetsMart Dog Park
21st Avenue
Phoenix, AZ
602-262-6971
phoenix.gov/PARKS/dogparks.html
This fully fenced dog park has over 2.5 grassy acres. Amenities include a water fountain and two watering stations for dogs, benches, bag dispensers and garbage cans. This off-leash park is located in Washington Park on 21st Avenue north of Maryland (between Bethany Home and Glendale roads).

Steele Indian School Dog Park
7th Street at Indian School Road
Phoenix, AZ
602-495-0739
This off-leash dog park opened in June of 2006. The 2 acre park is divided between fenced areas for large and small dogs. Park in the parking lot on the west side of 7th Street just north of Indian School Rd.

Willow Creek Dog Park
Willow Creek Road
Prescott, AZ
928-777-1100
This completely fenced dog park offers a separate section for small and large dogs. Amenities include picnic tables, benches, water and shade. The dog park is located next to Willow Creek Park. The park is located just north of the junction of Willow Lake and Willow Creek Roads.

Anamax Off-Leash Dog Park
17501 S. Camino de las Quintas
Sahuarita, AZ
520-625-2731
This dog park opened in November, 2006. Located in Anamax Park the fenced dog park has seperate areas for large and small dogs. The dog park is one acre in size and is equipped with benches, water and dog clean up bags. To get to the dog park from I-19 take the Sahuarita Rd exit west and turn south onto N La Canada Dr. Turn left onto W. Camino Cuzco and take it to Camino De Las Quintas. Turn right and the park will

491

be on your left.

Chaparral Park Dog Park
5401 N. Hayden Road
Scottsdale, AZ
480-312-2353
This park offers a two acre fenced designated off-leash area for dogs. The temporary off-leash area is on Hayden Road, north of Jackrabbit. The permanent dog park will be located on the southeast corner of Hayden and McDonald Drives after the water treatment facility is completed. Dogs must be on leash when outside the dog park.

Horizon Park Dog Park
15444 N. 100th Street
Scottsdale, AZ
480-312-2650
This park offers a designated off-leash area for dogs. The park is located at 100th Street and Thompson Peak. Dogs must be on leash when outside the off-leash area.

Vista del Camino Park Dog Park
7700 E. Roosevelt Street
Scottsdale, AZ
480-312-2330
This park offers a designated off-leash area for dogs. The park is located at Hayden and Roosevelt. Dogs must be on leash when outside the off-leash area.

Sedona Dog Park
NW Corner of Carruth and Soldiers Pass Roads
Sedona, AZ
928-301-0226
sedonadogpark.org/design.html
Located in natural undisturbed terrain, this 1.9 acre site has 2 separate areas for large and small dogs, and sanitary stations on site. Parking is not permitted in the school parking lot. Dogs must be sociable, current on all vaccinations, licensed, and cleaned up after at all times. Dogs must be leashed when not in designated off-lead areas.

Surprise Dog Park
15930 N. Bullard Avenue
Surprise, AZ
623-266-4500
This 1.5 acre dog park is located in Community Park. It has a small dog area as well as a large dog area. The dog park is open from sun up until 10 pm and provides drinking fountains for dogs and people.

Creamery Park

8th Street and Una Avenue
Tempe, AZ
480-350-5200
This park offers a designated off-leash area for dogs. Dogs must be on leash when outside the off-leash area.

Jaycee Park
5th Street and Hardy Drive
Tempe, AZ
480-350-5200
This park offers a small designated off-leash area for dogs. Dogs must be on leash when outside the off-leash area.

Mitchell Park
Mitchell Drive and 9th Street
Tempe, AZ
480-350-5200
This park offers a designated off-leash area for dogs. Dogs must be on leash when outside the off-leash area.

Papago Park
Curry Road and College Avenue
Tempe, AZ
480-350-5200
This park offers a designated off-leash area for dogs. Dogs must be on leash when outside the off-leash area.

Tempe Sports Complex Dog Park
Warner Rd & Hardy Dr
Tempe, AZ
480-350-5200
This fenced dog park is open from 6 am to 10 pm. It is located at the Tempe Sports Complex.

Christopher Columbus Dog Park
4600 N. Silverbell
Tucson, AZ
520-791-4873x0
This dog park is fenced and is about 1/3 acre in size. It has lights and is open to about 2 or 3 hours after dark. There is a separate fenced area for small dogs. The park is located just south of the intersection of Silverbell and W El Camino Del Cerro and just west of I-10 at El Camino Del Cerro.

Gene C. Reid Park Off-Leash Area
900 S. Randolph Way
Tucson, AZ
520-791-3204
This park offers a designated off-leash area. It is located across from the Reid Park Zoo entrance on a converted Little League field. The one acre dog park is lighted and fenced. Amenities include water,

picnic tables, trees, and a separate area for small and large dogs. Dog park hours are from 7am to 9pm. Dogs must be on leash when outside the off-leash area.

Jacobs Dog Park
3300 N. Fairview Ave.
Tucson, AZ
520-791-4873x0
This dog park opened in Jacobs Park in 2005. The dog park is fenced and located on the west side of the park. It is open during daylight hours.

McDonald District Park Off-Leash Area
4100 N. Harrison Road
Tucson, AZ
520-877-6000
This park offers a designated off-leash area. Dogs must be on leash when outside the off-leash area.

Northwest Center Off-Leash Dog Park
2075 N. 6th Ave
Tucson, AZ
520-791-4873x0
This half an acre fenced off-leash dog park was opened in 2004. It is located across 6th Street from the Northwest Center. The park features double gates and tables. The park is open during daylight hours.

Palo Verde Park Off-Leash Area
300 S. Mann Avenue
Tucson, AZ
520-791-4873
This park offers a designated off-leash area. Amenities of this fenced and double-gated dog park include doggie drinking fountains, picnic tables and pooper scooper dispensers. Dogs must be on leash when outside the off-leash area. The park is located at 300 S. Mann Avenue, south of Broadway, west of Kolb, and directly between Langley and Mann Avenues.

Udall Dog Park
7290 E. Tanque Verde
Tucson, AZ
520-791-5930
This one acre, fenced dog park has lights and is open from 6 am to 10:30 pm. It has water for dogs. The dog park opened in 2004 in Udall Regional Park. The park is located south of E. Tanque Verde Road between N Sabino Canyon Rd and N. Pantano Rd.

California

Polo Grounds Dog Park
2255 Huntington Avenue
Aptos, CA
831-454-7900
scparks.com
This one acre off leash dog park is fenced and includes water and benches. The park is open during daylight hours. To get there, take Highway 1 and exit at Rio Del Mar. Go left over the freeway and turn right onto Monroe Avenue (second stop light). After Monroe turns into Wallace Avenue, look for Huntington Drive on the left. Turn left on Huntington and the park entrance will be on the left.

Arcadia Dog Park
Second Avenue and Colorado Blvd
Arcadia, CA
626-574-5400
The fenced dog park is located in Eisenhower Park in Arcadia. The park is open from 7 am to 10 pm daily. On even numbered days the park is reserved for small dogs. On odd numbered days it is open to large dogs. The park is near I-210 at the Santa Anita Ave exit. Go north on Santa Anita, turn right on E Foothill and go right on 2nd Ave to the park.

Heilmann Dog Park
Atascadero, CA
tcsn.net/parks4pups/
The Heilmann Dog Park is almost one acre in size, fenced, and has restrooms for people. From Highway 101 take the Santa Rosa Avenue exit east, turn right (south) on El Camino Real, and left (east) on El Bordo Avenue.

Ashley Memorial Dog Park
Auburn Ravine Road (back of Ashford Park)
Auburn, CA
530-887-9993
ashleydogpark.com/
A fairly new park, there will be more amenities/events to be added as time goes by. At present there are 2 sections for large and small dogs, water features, agility play areas, picnic areas, and lots of shade trees. Dogs must be sociable, current on all vaccinations and license, and under their owner's control at all times. Dogs must be leashed when not in designated off-lead areas.

Centennial Park Off-Leash Dog Park
On Montclair north of Stockdale Hwy
Bakersfield, CA
661-326-3866
Centennial Park off-leash dog park, close to Highway 99, is a fenced in dog park that is easily accessible to locals and travelers alike. From Highway 99, take the Stockdale Hwy exit west and turn right onto Montclair. The park is on the right.

Kroll Park Off-Leash Dog Park
Kroll Way and Montalvo Dr
Bakersfield, CA
661-326-3866
This large, fenced off-leash dog park is located near Stockdale Hwy and Gosford on the west side of Bakersfield. To get there from Highway 99, take Stockdale Hwy west to Gosford, turn left and then turn left onto Kroll Way.

University Park Off-Leash Dog Park
University Ave east of Columbus
Bakersfield, CA
661-326-3866
This fenced, off-leash dog park is located in University Park. The park is located on University Ave east of Columbus Street and between Camden and Mission Hills.

Wilson Park Off-Leash Dog Park
Wilson Road and Hughes Lane
Bakersfield, CA
661-326-3866
This fenced off-leash dog park is located in Wilson Park south of central Bakersfield. The park is located on Wilson Road at Hughes Lane. Wilson Road is one major block south of Ming Ave. You can exit and take Ming Avenue from Highway 99 and take the access roads to Wilson.

City of Belmont Dog Park
2525 Buena Vista Avenue
Belmont, CA
650-365-3524
This dog park is located at the Cipriani Elementary School.

Cesar Chavez Park Off-Leash Dog Area
11 Spinnaker Way
Berkeley, CA
510-981-6700
There is an off-leash dog area in the north side of the park. Your dog must be leashed while walking to and from this area, and dogs must be cleaned up after. Bags are available at the park. To get to the park from Berkeley go over I-80 on University Ave. From I-80 exit University Avenue and go west towards the bay. However, you will have to turn around on University Avenue if coming from the south.

Ohlone Dog Park
Hearst Avenue
Berkeley, CA
This is a relatively small dog park. At certain times, there can be lots of dogs here. The hours are 6am-10pm on weekdays and 9am-10pm on weekends. The park is located at Hearst Ave, just west of Martin Luther King Jr. Way. There is limited street parking.

Bayside Park Dog Park
1125 South Airport Blvd
Burlingame, CA
650-558-7300
This dog park is over 570 feet long. It is in the back of the parking area and then you have to walk about 1/8 mile down a path to the off-leash dog park.

Calabasas Bark Park
Las Virgines Road
Calabasas, CA
Thanks to one of our readers for recommending this dog park. It is located on Las Virgines Road, south of the Agoura Road and Las Virgines Road intersection. This fenced dog park is open from 5 am to 9 pm daily. There is a separate fenced children's play area next to the dog park.

Cambria Dog Park
Main Street - Santa Rosa Creek Rd
Cambria, CA
The fenced Cambria Dog Park is located south of the town center on Main Street. From Highway 1 North or South take Main Street to the dog park.

Los Gatos Creek County Dog Park
1250 Dell Avenue
Campbell, CA
408-866-2105
The dog park offers separate fenced off-leash areas for large and small dogs. Water for dogs, benches for people, and pooper scoopers are at the park. The dog park is located in Los Gatos Creek Park. If you park at the Dell Avenue parking area to access the park there is a $5 parking fee. Alternatively, you can walk in from Dell Avenue or by a pedestrian bridge over the 17 freeway. The location of the dog park is between the ponds and San Tomas Expressway, just east of 17.

Ann D. L'Heureaux Memorial Dog Park
Carlsbad Village Drive
Carlsbad, CA
760-434-2825
This memorial dog park offers over 13,000 square feet of fenced off lead area with shade trees, benches, a doggy sanitary station, and a pet drinking fountain. Dogs must be sociable, current on all vaccinations and license, and under their owner's control at all times. Dogs must be leashed when not in designated off-lead areas.

Carmichael Park and Dog Park
Fair Oaks Blvd & Grant Ave
Carmichael, CA
916-485-5322
This is a one acre off leash dog park. It is located in Carmichael Park which can be accessed from Fair Oaks Blvd in Carmichael. The rest of the park is nice for picnics and other activities. Dogs must be leashed when not inside the dog park.

Castro Valley Dog Park
4660 Crow Canyon
Castro Valley, CA
510-881-6700
geocities.com/cvdogpark/
The Castro Valley Dog Run has two fenced areas, one for larger dogs and one for small dogs. There are two parking lots, rest rooms, an open lawn area and picnic tables. The park is open during daylight hours daily. The dog park is located in Earl Warren Park. Exit I 580 at Crow Canyon and head north.

Dog Park at Otay Ranch Town Center
Eastlake Pkwy At Olympic Pkwy
Chula Vista, CA
619-656-9100
This dog park opened in Oct, 2006 in the new Otay Ranch Town Center which is also pet-friendly. The fenced, 10,000 square foot dog park is located next to the Macy's at the outdoor mall. To get to the mall and dog park from San Diego go south on the 805 Freeway to the Orange Avenue Exit. Head east on Orange Avenue which will become Olympic Parkway. Go 4 miles east to the mall.

Montevalle Park Dog Park
840 Duncan Ranch Road
Chula Vista, CA
619-691-5269
This dog park is fully fenced and is located in the 29 acre Montevalle Park. The park is grassy and there are separate areas for small dogs and large dogs. There are drinking fountains for dogs and cleanup bags are also available. From I-805 take H Street east for about 6 miles. It will become Proctor Valley Rd go an additional 1 mile and turn right onto Duncan Ranch Rd to the park.

P.O.O.C.H. Park of Citrus Heights
Oak Avenue east of Fair Oaks
Citrus Heights, CA
916-725-1585
poochdogpark.com/
The dog park is located in C-Bar-C Park on Oak Ave. east of Fair Oaks and West of Wachtel. The dog park is over 2 acres in size and fenced. Benches are available and there is shade in the park. There is drinking water for dogs and people. For your water loving pups there are hoses and small wading pools in the park. The park is host to a number of dog events annually.

Pooch Park
100 S. College Avenue
Claremont, CA
claremontpoochpark.org
This park has lots of grass and trees and a ravine for the dogs to climb up and down. There is a 3 foot fence around the park. The Pooch Park is located in College Park, just south of the Metrolink tracks on S. College Avenue.

Newhall Community Park Dog Park
Turtle Creek Road
Concord, CA
925-671-3329
Offering 126 acres along Galindo Creek, this park is mostly wide open spaces with picnic areas, gaming courts/fields, more than 2 miles of multi-use trails, a Vietnam War Memorial, great views, and an off leash, fenced doggy play area. Dogs must be sociable, current on all vaccinations and license, and under their owner's control at all times. Dogs must be leashed when not in designated off-lead areas.

Paw Patch in Newall Community Park
Clayton Rd & Newhall Pkwy
Concord, CA
925-671-3329
This fenced dog park is located in Newhall Community Park in Concord. To get to the park from Clayton Road or Turtle Creek Road head south on Newhall Parkway. Local dog groups frequently meet at the dog park.

Butterfield Park Dog Park
1886 Butterfield Drive
Corona, CA
909-736-2241
This .8 acre fenced off-leash dog area is located in Butterfield Park. The dog park is well-shaded with benches, a picnic table and a doggie drinking fountain. From the 91 Freeway, take the Maple Street exit and go north. Maple will dead end at Smith Street. Go left on Smith Street about .5 miles to Butterfield Drive. Then turn left to Butterfield Park just across the street from the airport. Thanks to one of our readers for recommending this dog park.

Corona Dog Park
Butterfield Drive and Smith Avenue
Corona, CA
888-636-7387
rcdas.org/parks.htm
This park is almost an acre of off leash doggy fun; there is a drinking fountain for pups and their owners. Dogs must be sociable, current on all vaccinations, and under their owner's control at all times. Dogs must be leashed when not in designated off-lead areas.

Harada Heritage Dogs Park
13100 65th Street
Corona, CA
888-636-7387
rcdas.org/parks.htm
One of the county's newest off lead areas, and it is located in the unincorporated town of Eastvale just north of Corona. Dogs must be sociable, current on all vaccinations, and under their owner's control at all times. Dogs must be leashed when not in designated off-lead areas.

Bark Park Dog Park
Arlington Dr
Costa Mesa, CA
949-73-4101
cmbarkpark.org
Located in TeWinkle Park, this two acre dog park is fully fenced. It is open from 7am until dusk every day except for Tuesday, which is clean-up day. The park is located near the Orange County Fairgrounds on Arlington Drive, between Junipero Drive and Newport Blvd.

Culver City Off-Leash Dog Park
Duquesne Ave near Jefferson Blvd
Culver City, CA
310-390-9114
culvercitydogpark.org
This new dog park opened in April, 2006. Known as the Boneyard to the locals, this one acre park has a large

dog and a small dog area. There are benches, trees, shade and water fountains. The park is located near Jefferson Blvd on Duquesne Ave in Culver City Park. It is about 3/4 miles east of Overland.

Toad Hollow Dog Park
1919 Second Street
Davis, CA
530-757-5656
Toad Hollow Dog Park is located in Davis on Second Street between L Street and the Pole Line Road bridge. The fenced park is large (about 2 1/2 acres). The dog park will be closed during periods of heavy rains. The dog park is run by the Davis Parks & Community Services Department.

Camarillo Grove Dog Park
off Camarillo Springs Road
East Camarillo, CA
805-482-1996
pvrpd.org
This fenced dog park is about one acre and double gated. Amenities include a water fountain for dogs and people, benches, and a fire hydrant. The dog park is located off Camarillo Springs Road, at the base of the Conejo Grade. Dogs are not allowed in other parts of the park except for the off-leash area.

Wells Park & Off-Leash Dog Park
1153 E. Madison Ave
El Cajon, CA
619-441-1680
This fenced dog park has two separate off-leash areas for large dogs and small dogs. Exit I-8 at Mollison Avenue and head south one block and then left on Madison Ave. The park will be on your right in a few blocks.

Elk Grove Dog Park
9950 Elk Grove Florin Rd
Elk Grove, CA
916-405-5600
egcsd.ca.gov/parks/parks_dog.asp
The fenced dog park is best accessed from the East Stockton Blvd side of Elk Grove Park.From 99 take Grant Line Rd east and go left on East Stockton. The Elk Grove dog parks are monitored and maintained by the Park department and W.O.O.F. (We Offer Off-leash Fun), a dog owners organization in Elk Grove.

Laguna Dog Park
9014 Bruceville Rd
Elk Grove, CA
916-405-5600

egcsd.ca.gov/parks/parks_dog.asp
The fenced Laguna Community Dog Park is located on the west side of Laguna Community Park. The small Laguna Community Park is located south of Big Horn Blvd and west of Brucevill Rd. The Elk Grove dog parks are monitored and maintained by the Park department and W.O.O.F. (We Offer Off-leash Fun), a dog owners organization in Elk Grove.

Encinitas Park
D Street
Encinitas, CA
Thanks to one of our readers who recommends the following two dog parks in Encinitas Park. Encinitas Viewpoint Park, on "D" Street at Cornish Drive, off-leash dogs permitted 6:00-7:30 AM and 4:00-6:00 PM on MWF only. Other days of the week, dogs must be on leash. Orpheus Park, on Orpheus Avenue at Union Street, off-leash dogs permitted 6:00-7:30 AM and 4:00-6:00 PM on MWF only. Other days of the week, dogs must be on leash.

Rancho Coastal Humane Society Dog Park
389 Requeza Street
Encinitas, CA
760-753-6413
The dog park at the humane society has limited hours. It is open on Tuesday and Thursdays from 2 pm to 5 pm and 11 am - 5 pm on Saturday and Sunday. The dog park is fenced, with separate areas for large and small dogs. There are benches and water for dogs and people. To get to the dog park from I-5 heading north take the Santa Fe Drive exit to Regal Rd and then left on Requeza Street. From I-5 south, exit Encinitas Blvd. Turn left onto Encinitas Blvd, right on Westlake and right onto Requeza Street.

Sepulveda Basin Dog Park
17550 Victory Blvd.
Encino, CA
818-756-7667
Sepulveda Basin Dog Park is located near the Sepulved Dam Rec Area. It consists of 5 acres of legal off-leash roaming that is fully fenced. There is a smaller area for small dogs that is about half an acre. The dog park is near the junction of I 405 with Highway 101. It is at the corner of White Oak Ave and Victory Blvd. There is parking for about 100 cars at the location.

Mayflower Dog Park

3420 Valley Center Road
Escondido, CA

Mayflower Dog Park is a 1.5 acre fenced area for off-leash dog play.

Phoenix Dog Park
9050 Sunset Ave
Fair Oaks, CA
916-966-1036
fordog.org
The Phoenix Dog Park is located in Phoenix Park in Fair Oaks. It is just under 2 acres in size and has three separate fenced areas. There is one area for large dogs, one area for small dogs and an area for shy dogs. There are shade structures, benches and a washoff pad just outside of the dog park. The park is sponsored by FORDOG which stands for Fair Oaks Responsible Dog Owners Group. The park is located on Sunset Avenue east of Hazel. To get to the dog park from Highway 50, take Hazel north to Sunset and turn right. The dog park will be on your right.

Foster City Dog Run
Foster City Blvd at Bounty
Foster City, CA
There is a separate dog area for small dogs and large dogs at this off leash dog park. The parks are about 1/2 an acre in size. There are tables and benches. The dog park is located in Boat Park at the corner of Bounty Drive and Foster City Blvd.

Central Park Dog Park
1110 Stevenson Blvd
Fremont, CA
510-494-4800
Thanks to one of our readers who writes: "Fenced, fresh water on demand, plenty of free parking, easy to find, all grass." Pet waste disposal bags are available at the park. The dog park is open from sunrise to 10 pm. The park is located on one acre, is adjacent to the Central Park Softball Complex with access off of Stevenson Blvd. To get there from I 680 head north on Mission Blvd and turn left on Stevenson Blvd. The park is on the left. From I 880 take Stevenson Blvd east to the park on the right.

Basin AH1 Dog Park and Pond
4257 W. Alamos
Fresno, CA
559-621-2900
This is a seasonal dog park which offers a wading pool for dogs to use during the summer. The park is open from May through November from 7 am to 10 pm daily. The dog park is

located at 4257 W. Alamos at El Capitan. To get to the dog park from Highway 99, exit at Shaw Avenue and head east. In about a mile turn right on El Capitan.

Woodward Park Dog Park
E. Audubon Drive
Fresno, CA
559-621-2900
Thanks to one of our readers who writes "Woodward Park now has a wonderful, enclosed area built specifically for dogs to play off-leash. It is located inside the park area and contains toys, water bowls and plastic bags."

Fullerton Pooch Park
S Basque Avenue
Fullerton, CA
714-738-6575
Located next to the library, this off leash area offers 2 sections; one for larger dogs, and one for small dogs. Water is available in the off lead area. Dogs must be sociable, current on all vaccinations, and under their owner's control at all times. Dogs must be leashed when not in designated off-lead areas.

Elizabeth Anne Perrone Dog Park
13630 Sonoma H/H 12
Glen Ellen, CA
707-565-2041
Located at the 162 acre Sonoma Valley Regional Park, this fenced 1 acre off leash area offers a drinking fountain for thirsty pooches, a gazebo, wooded areas and pathways. Dogs must be sociable, current on all vaccinations, and under their owner's control at all times. Dogs must be leashed on no more than a 6 foot leash when not in designated off-lead areas.

Coastside Dog Park
Wavecrest Road
Half Moon Bay, CA
650-726-8297
coastdogs.org
This fenced, public off-leash dog park is supported by citizen volunteers. The dog park is located at Smith Field, at the western end of Wavecrest Road. The organization that runs the park would appreciate a $20 annual membership from locals that use the park regularly but it is not mandatory.

Huntington Beach Dog Park
Edwards Street
Huntington Beach, CA
949-536-5672
hbdogpark.org/

This dog park has a small dog run for pups under 25 pounds and a separate dog run for the larger pooches. It's been open since 1995 and donations are always welcome. They have a coin meter at the entrance. The money is used to keep the park maintained and for doggie waste bags. If you want to go for a walk with your leashed pup afterwards, there many walking trails at the adjacent Huntington Central Park.

Central Bark
6405 Oak Canyon
Irvine, CA
949-724-7740
Thanks to one of our readers who writes: "Irvine's dog park is open daily from 6:30 am to 9 pm, closed Wednesdays." The dog park is located next to the Irvine Animal Care Center and is a 2.8 acre fenced dog park. There is a separate area for small dogs and water for your dog.

Harry Griffen Park
9550 Milden Street
La Mesa, CA
619-667-1307
Thanks to one of our readers who writes: "A leash-free dog area - very nice area of the park and no restrictions on dog size."

Laguna Beach Dog Park
Laguna Canyon Rd at El Toro Rd
Laguna Beach, CA
This dog park, known by the locals as Bark Park, is open six days a week and closed on Wednesdays for clean-up. The park is open from dawn to dusk. The park will be closed during and after heavy rains.

Laguna Niguel Pooch Park
Golden Latern
Laguna Niguel, CA
This fully enclosed dog park is located in the city of Laguna Niguel, which is between Laguna Beach and Dana Point. The park is operated by the City of Laguna Niguel's Parks and Recreation Department. It is located on Golden Latern, next to fire station 49. From the Pacific Coast Highway in Dana Point, go up Goldern Latern about 2 miles. Thanks to one of our readers for this information.

Canine Commons
Doherty, East of Magnolia
Larkspur, CA
415-927-5110
ci.larkspur.ca.us/3053.html

This fenced dog park is located in Piper Park. The park is run by the Larkspur Park and Recreation Department.

Lincoln Dog Park
Third Street
Lincoln, CA
916-624-6808
lincolndogpark.org/
The amenities at this dog park include 2.5 fenced acres for dogs to run off-leash, potable water, handicap accessible, parking, and limited seating. The park is open from dawn to dusk and is closed Wednesdays until 12pm. To get there, take Highway 65 (City of Lincoln) to Third Street. Go west on Third Street 1.8 miles to Santa Clara (just past the big oak tree).

Del Valle Dog Run
Del Valle Road
Livermore, CA
510-562-PARK
ebparks.org/parks/delval.htm
This dog run is located in Del Valle Regional Park. Here your dog can walk leash free along the trail with you. Del Valle Regional Park is over 3,997 acres of land and it includes a five mile long lake. To get there from Hwy 580 heading east, exit S. Vasco Road. Turn right onto Vasco and head south. When Vasco ends, turn right onto Tesla Rd. Then turn left onto Mines Rd. Turn right onto Del Valle Road. Follow Del Valle Rd to the park entrance. The dog run is to the right of the marina.

Livermore Canine Park
Murdell Lane
Livermore, CA
This dog park is located in Max Baer Park. It has several trees and a lawn. To get there from downtown Livermore, head west on Stanely Blvd. Turn left on Isabel Ave. Then turn left onto Concannon Blvd (if you reach Alden Ln, you've passed Concannon). Turn left on Murdell Lane and the park will be on the right.

Loma Linda Dog Park
Beaumont Ave and Mountain View Ave.
Loma Linda, CA
There are two fenced areas at this dog park. One is for large dogs and one is for small dogs. The dog park is open during daylight hours. The dog park is on the side of a hill so it can get slick after rain. From I-10 take Mountain View south to Beaumont. Turn left on Beaumont

and the park is on the right.

Recreation Park Dog Park
7th St & Federation Dr
Long Beach, CA
562-570-3100
geocities.com/lbdogpark/
Licensed dogs over four months are allowed to run leash-free in this area by the casting pond. As usual with all dog parks, owners are responsible for their dogs and must supervise them at all times. The Recreation Park Dog Park is located off 7th Street and Federation Drive behind the Casting Pond. It is open daily until 10 p.m. Thanks to one of our readers for recommending this park.

Barrington Dog Park
333 South Barrington Avenue
Los Angeles, CA
310-476-4866
Barrington Dog Park is located just west of the 405 Freeway at Sunset Blvd. Exit the 405 at Sunset, head west, and then south onto Barrington. This fenced 1 1/2 acre dog park is open during daylight hours.

Griffith Park Dog Park
North Zoo Drive
Los Angeles, CA
323-913-4688
This dog park is located 1/2 mile west of the 134 Fwy at the John Ferraro Soccer Field, next to the Autry Museum and across from the main zoo parking. There are two separate fenced areas, one for larger dogs and the other for small or timid dogs. There is a portable restroom for people.

Herman Park Dog Park
5566 Via Marisol
Los Angeles, CA
323-255-0370
Herman Park in the Arroyo Seco Dog Park is a 1 1/3 acre fenced dog park with separate areas for large and small dogs. The park is open during daylight hours. The park is located off of the 110 Freeway east on Via Marisol.

Laurel Canyon Park
8260 Mulholland Dr.
Los Angeles, CA
This nice dog park is located in the hills of Studio City. It is completely fenced with water and even a hot dog stand. To get there, take Laurel Canyon Blvd and go west on Mulholland Blvd. Go about a 1/4 mile and turn left. There is a parking lot below.

Runyon Canyon Park
Mulholland Hwy
Los Angeles, CA
323-666-5046
From this popular hiking trail and excellent off-leash area you can see views of Hollywood, the Wilshire District, and the skyscrapers of downtown L.A. This park has mostly off-leash and some on-leash hiking trails. It is about a 2 mile round-trip from end to end in the park. The top of the trail is located off Mulholland Hwy (about 2 miles east of Laurel Canyon Blvd) at Desmond Street in the Hollywood Hills. The bottom part of the trail is located at the end of Fuller Ave. Parking is available on the street. The trailhead might be kind of tricky to find from Fuller, but you'll probably see other people going to or coming from the trail.

Silverlake Dog Park
2000 West Silverlake Blvd.
Los Angeles, CA
This is one of the best dog parks in the Los Angeles area and it usually averages 30-40 dogs. It is located at approximately 2000 West Silverlake Blvd. It's on the south side of the reservoir in Silverlake, which is between Hollywood and downtown L.A. between Sunset Blvd. and the 5 Freeway. The easiest way to get there is to take the 101 Freeway to Silverlake Blvd. and go east. Be careful about street parking because they ticket in some areas. Thanks to one of our readers for recommending this dog park.

Mill Valley Dog Run
Sycamore Ave At Camino Alto
Mill Valley, CA
This large, 2 acre fenced dog park in Bayfront Park in Mill Valley even has drains installed. It is located on Sycamore, east of Camino Alto.

City of Milpitas Dog Park
3100 Calveras Blvd.
Milpitas, CA
408-262-6980
parkhere.org
This dog park has separate sections for small and large dogs. The dog park is run by the City of Milpitas, but it is located at Ed Levin County Park. The dog park is located off Calaveras Blvd. Turn onto Downing Road and head toward Sandy Wool Lake. Go uphill by the lake until you come to the dog park.

Morgan Hill Off-Leash Dog Park
Edumundson Avenue
Morgan Hill, CA
408-779-3451
morganhilldog.org/
This two acre off-leash dog park opened in January 2007 in Morgan Hill. It is managed by the Morgan Hill Dog Owner's Group. There is a separate area for small dogs and both areas have water faucets. Dogs must be licensed, vaccinated and not aggresive. The dog park is located in Community Park and is open during daylight hours.

Mountain View Dog Park
Shoreline Blvd at North Rd
Mountain View, CA
mvdp.org
This fenced, off leash dog park is located across from Shoreline Ampitheatre at the entrance to Shoreline Park. Dogs are not allowed in Shoreline Park itself.

Canine Commons Dog Park
Dry Creek Rd at Redwood Rd
Napa, CA
707-257-9529
This fenced 3 acre dog park has water, benches, and pooper scoopers. The dog park is located in Alston Park which has about 100 acres of dog-friendly on-leash trails and some off-leash trails. To get there from Napa, take Hwy 29 North and exit Redwood Rd. Turn left on Redwood Rd and then right on Dry Creek Rd. The park will be on the left.

Shurtleff Park Dog Park
Shetler Avenue
Napa, CA
707-257-9529
This park offers an off-leash exercise area. Dogs must be under voice control at all times. The park is located on Shetler Avenue, east of Shurtleff Avenue.

Whitnall Off-Leash Dog Park
5801 1/2 Whitnall Highway
North Hollywood, CA
818-756-8190
Whitnall Off-Leash Dog Park is located one block west of Cahuenga Blvd on Whitnall. The park has a 50,000 square foot fenced area for large dogs and a 22,000 square foot fenced area for small dogs. The park is open during daylight hours.

Ohair Park Dog Park
Novato Blvd at Sutro
Novato, CA
This no-frills fenced dog park is located in the Neil Ohair Park in

Novato. The park has been organized by the D.O.G.B.O.N.E. Dog Park Group which is looking to improve the park.

Hardy Dog Park
491 Hardy Street
Oakland, CA
510-238-PARK
This 2 acre dog park in fully fenced. Dogs must be on-leash outside of the park. The park is located on Hardy Street at Claremont Avenue in the Rockridge District. It is just under the 24 Freeway.

Dusty Rhodes Dog Park
Sunset Cliffs Blvd.
Ocean Beach, CA
619-236-5555
This dog park is located in Dusty Rhodes Neighborhood Park. The park is on Sunset Cliffs Blvd. between Nimitz and West Point Loma.

Oceanside Dog Park
2905 San Luis Rey Rd
Oceanside, CA
760-757-4357
nchumane.org/news/dogpark.php
The first off-leash dog park in Oceanside is located next to the North County Humane Society buiding. The fenced park is open from 7 am to 7 pm except for Wednesday when it is closed for maintenance.

Yorba Dog Park
190 S Yorba Street
Orange, CA
714-633-2980
orangedogpark.com/
There is a separate small dog section at this park, and until there are benches installed, lawn chairs may be brought into the park and set along the fence that separates the big dog/small dog areas. Chairs must be taken out each night. The park is closed for maintenance on Wednesdays.

Civic Center Dog Park
73-510 Fred Waring Dr
Palm Desert, CA
760-346-0611
The Civic Center Dog Park is open from Dawn to 11 pm and is lighted at night. It is about 3/4 acres in size and has two separate fenced areas for large and small dogs. The dog park is located in Civic Center Park on Fred Waring Drive between Monterey Avenue and Portola Ave.

Joe Mann Dog Park
California Drive
Palm Desert, CA
888-636-7387
rcdas.org/parks.htm
This off lead area is only a short distance from the Palm Desert Civic Center Park and offers 1/3 of an acre for pups to run and play. Dogs must be sociable, current on all vaccinations, and under their owner's control at all times. Dogs must be leashed when not in designated off-lead areas.

Palm Desert Civic Center Park
Fred Waring
Palm Desert, CA
888-636-7387
rcdas.org/parks.htm
Located at the 70 acre Palm Desert Civic Center Park is a ¾ acre section fenced as an off-leash area, and when the pups are through playing, there is a pathway around the park with artwork and a small lake. Dogs must be sociable, current on all vaccinations, and under their owner's control at all times. Dogs must be leashed when not in designated off-lead areas.

Palm Springs Dog Park
222 Civic Drive N
Palm Springs, CA
888-636-7387
rcdas.org/parks.htm
This green pooch oasis is open 24 hours and provides a smaller fenced area for little dogs, 11 antique-style fire hydrants, dual drinking fountains, benches, and pooper scoopers. Dogs must be sociable, current on all vaccinations, and under their owner's control at all times. Dogs must be leashed when not in designated off-lead areas.

Greer Dog Park
1098 Amarillo Avenue
Palo Alto, CA
650-329-2261
This is a fenced off leash dog exercise park. Dogs on leash are allowed in the rest of the park.

Hoover Park
2901 Cowper St
Palo Alto, CA
650-329-2261
This is a small off leash dog exercise area. Dogs on leash are allowed in the rest of the park.

Mitchell Park/Dog Run
3800 Middlefield Rd
Palo Alto, CA

650-329-2261
Located in Mitchell Park at 3800 Middlefield Rd (between E. Charleston and E. Meadow) Note: It can be tough to find at first. The dog run is closer to E. Charleston by the baseball fields and over a small hill.

Alice Frost Kennedy Off-Leash Dog Area
3026 East Orange Grove Blvd
Pasadena, CA
626-744-4321
The dog park is located in Vina Vieja Park. It is open during daylight hours and is 2.5 acres and fenced. There is a large dog area and a small dog area. The dog park has a grass surface with no herbicides used. The park is maintained by the City of Pasadena and capital improvements are done by POOCH, a dog group in Pasadena. To get to the dog park from I-210 exit at Sierra Madre Blvd and head east. Turn right onto Orange Grove Blvd to the dog park.

Rocky Memorial Dog Park
W. Casa Grande Road
Petaluma, CA
707-778-4380
Your dog can run leash-free in this 9 acre fenced dog park. To get there, take Lakeville Hwy. (Hwy 116) east, and turn west on Casa Grande Rd.

Muirwood Dog Exercise Area
4701 Muirwood Drive
Pleasanton, CA
925-931-5340
This 3/4 acre fenced dog park is located in Muirwood Community Park. To get to the park, exit I-680 at Stoneridge Dr and head west. Turn left on Springdale Avenue and left again on Muirwood Drive. The park will be on the left.

Poway Dog Park
13094 Civic Center Drive
Poway, CA
This 1 3/4 acre dog park is open from sunrise to 9:30 pm. The park is lighted at night. There are three separate fenced areas. From the I-15 freeway take Poway Rd east 3.9 miles. Turn right on Bowron and park at the lot at the end of the road.

Benton Dog Park
1700 Airpark Drive
Redding, CA
530-941-8200
bentondogpark.com/
This fenced off-lead dog park is located on 2.30 acres. Dogs of all sizes are welcome, they must be leashed when out of the off-lead

area, and please clean up after your pet.

Redondo Beach Dog Park
Flagler Lane and 190th
Redondo Beach, CA
310-376-9263
rbdogpark.com
This dog park is located next to Dominguez Park. Local dogs and vacationing dogs are welcome at the dog park. There is a separate section for small dogs and big dogs. It is completely fenced and has pooper scooper bags available. From the PCH take Herondo Street east which will become 190th Street.

Shores Dog Park
Radio Road
Redwood City, CA
shoredogs.org
This dog park (opened Nov/Dec 98) was funded by Redwood City residents. To get there from Hwy 101, take Holly/Redwood Shores Parkway Exit. Go east (Redwood Shore Parkway). Turn right on Radio Road (this is almost at the end of the street). The park will be on the right. Thanks to one of our readers for this information.

Point Isabel Regional Shoreline
Isabel Street
Richmond, CA
510-562-PARK
ebparks.org/parks/ptisable.htm
This 20 plus acre park is a dog park that is not completely fenced, but has paved paths, grass and beach access to the bay. If your pooch likes chasing birds, beware... dogs sometimes run over to the bird sanctuary which is close to the freeway. Other activities at this park include bay fishing, jogging and running trails, birdwatching, kite flying and picnicking. Thanks to one of our readers for providing us with this great information. From I-80 (the Eastshore Freeway) in Richmond, take Central Avenue west to Point Isabel, adjacent to the U.S. Postal Service Bulk Mail Center.

West Side Dog Park
810 Oak Lane
Rio Linda, CA
916) 991-5929
This one acre fenced dog park is located in Westside Park at 810 Oak Lane in Rio Linda.

Carlson Dog Park
At the foot of Mt. Rubidoux
Riverside, CA
888-636-7387

rcdas.org/parks.htm
In addition to providing 2 sections; one for large dogs, and one for the small pooches, this off leash area is also a good starting point to take a walk along the Santa Ana River trail or hike the paved trail up Mt. Rubidoux. Dogs must be sociable, current on all vaccinations, and under their owner's control at all times. Dogs must be leashed when not in designated off-lead areas.

Pat Merritt Dog Park
Limonite Frontage Road
Riverside, CA
888-636-7387
rcdas.org/parks.htm
This doggy free run area offers great views of the Santa Ana River and offer 2 sections; one for large dogs, and one for the small pooches. Dogs must be sociable, current on all vaccinations, and under their owner's control at all times. Dogs must be leashed when not in designated off-lead areas.

Riverwalk Dog Park
Pierce Street and Collett Avenue
Riverside, CA
951-358- 7387
rcdas.org/parks.htm
Riverwalk Dog Park is divided into two areas for large and small dogs. The park has water, cleanup bags and benches. There is not much shade in the park yet as the trees that have been planted there are still small. To get to the dog park from the 91 Freeway exit at Magnolia and head north on Pierce. Pierce will turn into Esplanade but Pierce will head off to the left. Follow Pierce by turning left to the dog park.

Marco Dog Park
1800 Sierra Gardens Drive
Roseville, CA
916-774-5950
RDOG (Roseville Dog Owners Group) helped to establish this 2 acre dog park which is Roseville's first off-leash dog park. This park was named Marco Dog Park in memory of a Roseville Police Department canine named Marco who was killed in the line of duty. The park has a large grassy area with a few trees and doggie fire hydrants. It is closed on Wednesdays from dawn until 3:30pm for weekly maintenance. Like other dog parks, it may also be closed some days during the winter due to mud. To get there from Hwy 80, exit Douglas Blvd. heading east.

Go about 1/2 mile and turn left on Sierra Gardens Drive. Marco Dog Park will be on the right.

Bannon Creek Dog Park
Bannon Creek Drive near West El Camino
Sacramento, CA
916-264-5200
sacto.org/parks/dogpark1.htm
This off leash dog park is in Bannon Creek Park. Its hours are 5am to 10 pm daily. The park is 0.6 acres in size.

Granite Park Dog Park
Ramona Avenue near Power Inn Rd
Sacramento, CA
916-264-5200
sacto.org/parks/dogpark1.htm
This dog park is in Granite Regional Park. Its hours are 5 am to 10 pm daily. It is 2 acres in size.

Howe Dog Park
2201 Cottage Way
Sacramento, CA
916-927-3802
Howe Dog Park is completely fenced and located in Howe Park. It has grass and several trees. To get there, take Business Route 80 and exit El Camino Ave. Head east on El Camino Ave. Turn right on Howe Ave. Howe Park will be on the left. Turn left onto Cottage Way and park in the lot. From the parking lot, the dog park is located to the right of the tennis courts.

Partner Park Dog Park
5699 South Land Park Drive
Sacramento, CA
916-264-5200
sacto.org/parks/dogpark1.htm
This dog park is located behind the Bell Cooledge Community Center. The park is 2.5 acres and its hours are 5 am to 10 pm daily. There are lights at the park.

Tanzanite Community Park Dog Park
Tanzanite Dr at Innovator Dr
Sacramento, CA
916-808-5200
Tanzanite Community Park Dog Park is located in the Tanzanite Community Park in North Natomas. This new two acre fenced dog park is scheduled to open by the Fall of 2006. The park is located east of Airport Road in the Tanzanite Community Park.

Wildwood Dog Park
536 E. 40th St
San Bernardino, CA

Thanks to one of our readers who writes: "We have 3.5 acres divided into 2 large areas & 1 smaller area just for little and older dogs. The larger areas are rotated to help reduce wear & tear on the turf. Amenities include: Fencing, Benches, Handicapped Access, Lighting, Parking, Poop Bags, Restrooms, Shelter, Trash Cans, Water Available. Current Shots & License Required. We are also double-gated for Safety."

San Bruno Dog Park
Commodore Lane and Cherry Ave
San Bruno, CA
650-877-8868
San Bruno moved its dog park to this new location. The dog park has two fenced areas for large and small dogs, water for dogs and people, benches, bags to clean up and shade. If your dog doesn't like loud noises, beware of the large jets taking off from San Francisco Airport less than 2 miles away. The dog park is located in Commodore Park the intersection of I-280 and I-380. Take the 280 San Bruno Avenue exit east and turn left on Cherry Avenue to the park.

Heather Dog Exercise Area
2757 Melendy Drive
San Carlos, CA
650-802-4382
This 1.5 acre park offers a small area where dogs can run off-leash as well as an on-leash hiking trail. Access the park through the Heather School parking lot.

Pulgas Ridge Off-Leash Dog Area
Edmonds Road and Crestview Drive
San Carlos, CA
650-691-1200
Most of Pulgas Ridge Open Space Preserve allows dogs on leash. There is a large, seventeen acre area in the center of the preserve that allows dogs off-leash under voice control. Please check the signs for the appropriate boundries of the off-leash area. To get to the preserve, take I-280 to Edgewood Rd. Head east on Edgewood and turn left on Crestview. Immediately after that turn, turn left onto Edmonds to the entrance to the preserve.

San Clemente Dog Park
310 Avenida La Pata
San Clemente, CA
San Clemente Dog Park has two fenced areas, one for large dogs and

one for small dogs. The park has benches and water for dogs.

Balboa Park Dog Run
Balboa Dr
San Diego, CA
619-235-1100
balboapark.org/rules.html
The dog-friendly Balboa Park has set aside a portion of land for an off leash dog run. It's not fenced, so make sure your pup listens to voice commands. It is located between Balboa Drive and Hwy 163.

Capehart Dog Park
Felspar at Soledad Mountain Rd
San Diego, CA
619-525-8212
This one acre fenced dog park has a separate area for large and small dogs. There is water for dogs and people and benches. The dog park is open 24 hours. It is located in Capehart Park at the corner of Felspar and Soledad Mountain Rd. This is just off the I-5 at Mission Bay Dr west toward Garnet Ave. Then turn right on Soledad Mountain Rd.

Doyle Community Park
8175 Regents Road
San Diego, CA
619-525-8212
This dog park offers two fenced areas for large and small dogs. It is open 24 hours but there are no lights. The park is located behind the Doyle Community Center. From I-5 take La Jolla Village Dr east to Regents Rd. Turn right on Regents to the park.

Grape Street Park Off-Leash Area
Grape Street at Granada Ave
San Diego, CA
619-525-8212
This is a non-fenced five acre legal off-leash area for certain hours. Currently, the hours are Monday thru Friday 7:30 am to 9 pm, and on weekends and holidays from 9 am to 9 pm. The Grape Street off-leash area is on the eastern boundry of Balboa Park. From Fern Street/30th Street go east on Grape Street to the street ends.

Kearny Mesa Dog Park
3170 Armstrong Street
San Diego, CA
619-525-8212
kmdogpark.com/
This dog park is fenced and is one acre in size. It is open 24 hours and there is some lighting from the nearby ball fields. Parking can be difficult during the day due to the

nearby Mesa College. The dog park can be accessed from the 163 freeway (south of 805) at Mesa College Dr. Go west on Mesa College Drive to Armstrong. Turn left on Armstrong to the park.

Maddox Dog Park
7815 Flanders Dr
San Diego, CA
619-525-8212
This 2/3 acre fenced dog park is located in Maddox Neighborhood Park. The park is located just south of Mira Mesa Blvd. Go south on Parkdale Ave and turn right onto Flanders.

Rancho Bernardo Off-Leash Park
18448 West Bernardo Drive
San Diego, CA
858-538-8129
ranchobernardodogpark.com/
The dog park is 2.66 acres divided into three separate fenced areas. There are benches, clean-up bags and shade in each area. To get to the park from I-15 take the West Bernardo/Pomerado Road exit. Go to the west and the park is on your right in about 1/4 mile. The dog park is in the southern end of the park.

Torrey Highlands Park
Landsdale Drive at Del Mar Heights Road
San Diego, CA
619-525-8212
ourdogpark.com/
This one acre dog park is located in Torrey Highlands Park. To get to the dog park from I-5 take Del Mar Heights Rd East 1.2 miles. Turn left on Lansdale and left immediately into the park.

San Dimas Dog Park
301 Horsethief Canyon Rd
San Dimas, CA
909-394-6230
sandimasdogpark.org/
The fenced dog park is open during daylight hours. The park is closed on Wednesday afternoons for cleaning. The dog park is located in the Horsethief Canyon Park which is one mile north of the 210 Freeway.

Alamo Square Off Leash Dog Park
Scott Street, between Hayes and Fulton Streets
San Francisco, CA
415-831-2084
Dogs may be off leash under voice control in the Western half of this 5 1/2 acre multi-use park; it is not fenced in. The Eastern half of the park is on-leash. This park offers

beautiful panoramic views and rolling hills, and is the second largest legal off-leash area in San Francisco.

Alta Plaza Off Leash Dog Park
Steiner and Clay Street
San Francisco, CA
415-831-2084
sfdog.org/do/city_ne.htm#ap
This many tiered, Pacific Heights park takes up one square block, and from the top of the park you can enjoy panoramic views of the city. It is bordered by Jackson, Clay, Steiner and Scott streets, and is across from the tennis courts. The first Sunday of every month is Pug Day at this park. It's a casual meeting of pug owners which takes place at the north end of park, usually between 3:30 - 5:00, weather permitting. At the gathering, there can be 20-50 pugs. The legal off-leash area is well marked with paint on the pathways. Dogs should be leashed when not in this area, and they must be cleaned up after at all times.

Bernal Heights Off Leash Dog Park
Bernal Heights and Esmerelda
San Francisco, CA
415-831-2084
This popular park is the largest official DPA/off-leash area in San Francisco. It is on a rocky steep hill, and is accessible via narrow, single track trails. They are situated such that you can walk for up to an hour without retracing any steps. There are also paved trails, an abundance of nature to enjoy, and great views of the city. You can enter either at the parking lot located at Folsom Street at Bernal Heights Ave or at the end of Bernal Heights Ave where the street dead-ends (on the South side of the hill). Dogs must be cleaned up after at all times.

Brotherhood Mini Off Leash Dog Park
Brotherhood Way
San Francisco, CA
415-831-2084
This small park is located on Public Works property along Brotherhood Way at Head Street, and covers about an 1/8 of an acre. Dogs can run off leash in the designated dog park. Please clean up after your pet.

Buena Vista Off Lead Dog Park
Buena Vista West at Central Avenue
San Francisco, CA
415-831-2084
sfdog.org/do/city_nw.htm#bv
This is the city's oldest park and is

basically a giant one acre hill offering expansive views at the top. It is a popular destination location because of its size and safety/isolation from traffic, for the most part. The legal off-leash area is hardly used by dog walkers because it is not safe being so close to the road and most would prefer the enjoyment of the fantastic trail experience Buena Vista offers. You can enter the park at the intersection of Buena Vista Ave. and Central St. or at any of the other park entrances along Buena Vista Ave. The off-leash area is located in a lower area, along the Western side of the park near Central Ave. Dogs must be leashed in the off leash areas, and please clean up after your pet.

Corona Heights
16th and Roosevelt
San Francisco, CA
415-831-2084
This park is for those who enjoy the climb as much as the view. To get there, go almost to the top of 17th Street and take a right on Roosevelt and follow it around to another right on Levant. It is located adjacent to the Field Museum. There is a green area used by local dog-walkers and pet owners in addition to the fenced-in area to allow the dogs to socialize and run off-leash. Extended walking is required and be prepared for dirt/off road and steep walks at this park. Dogs must be on leash when not in the off lead area, and always please clean up after your pet.

Crocker Amazon Off Leash Dog Park
At Geneva Avenue and Moscow Street
San Francisco, CA
415-831-2084
This 1.8 acre park is located in the northern part of the park, adjacent to the community garden. This is an unfenced area so dogs must be under firm voice control, and please clean up after your pet.

Delores Off Lead Dog Park
19th Street and Delores Street
San Francisco, CA
415-831-2084
This area is a large, grassy, gently sloping and sometimes hilly, mixed use park, with gorgeous views of the city from the top half. There are 6 tennis courts, a basketball court, 2 soccer fields, a playground, and a club house with public restrooms.

As a popular relaxation/recreation area, it does tend to be quite crowed on weekends. Also, since there is no fenced in off-lead area, it is a good idea to stay away from the streets, and please clean up after your pet.

Douglass Park, Upper Field Off Leash Dog Area
27th and Douglass Streets
San Francisco, CA
415-831
sfdog.org/do/city_se.htm
This great multi-use neighborhood park offers a wonderful, grassy place for dogs to play off-leash. Dogs must be under firm voice control as there are no fenced in areas, and please clean up after your pet.

Eureka Valley Off Leash Dog Park
100 Collingwood Street
San Francisco, CA
415-695-5012
This small neighborhood recreation park of 2 acres is known for its gymnasium, playground structure, athletic field, and excellent recreational programs. The fenced in off lead area is East of the baseball diamond and adjacent to the tennis courts. Dogs must be cleaned up after, and leashed when out of the fenced area.

Fort Miley Off Lead Dog Area
Point Lobos and 48th Avenues
San Francisco, CA
415-561-4700
Owned and operated by the Golden Gate National Recreation Area, this area is actually a combination of 3 parks entities, which are Land's End, Lincoln Park, and Fort Miley. There is a large parking and viewing area at the end of El Camino Del Mar off Point Lobos Avenue, and this is where you can take one of the paths to the above. An easier access from the Veteran's Administration Hospital parking lot is also available. Fort Miley is home to the historical ruins of a fully recessed military armament. A large open lawn encloses a recessed bunker that is sunny and has great views over the Ocean Beach and Richmond area. It is a nice place to picnic and is one of the only multi-use open field areas here. There are plenty of areas to explore, and your pet may be off lead, except where marked. Please be sure to clean up after your pet.

Glen Park Off Leash Dog Area
400 O'Shaughnessy Blvd
San Francisco, CA
415-337-4705

This large, natural canyon area is a well used neighborhood park with wonderful trails throughout where there are edible berries to find and a variety of naturescapes to enjoy. Although not an official DPA yet is a great place to walk your dog. They request that you keep the dogs out of the newly planted areas and the seasonal "creek". Enter the park at Bosworth and O'Shaughnessy Blvd. Please clean up after your pet.

Golden Gate Park Off Leash Dog Areas
Stanyan & Great Highway
San Francisco, CA
415-751-8987
Listed among the world's greatest urban parks at over 1,000 acres, there are grassy meadows, wooded trails, secluded lakes, open groves, gardens, museums, and four official, legal off leash dog areas. (1) The Southeast area is located in a wooded strip of land bounded by 3rd Ave., 7th Ave., North of Lincoln Way, and South of Martin Luther King Blvd. It is small, not well marked, with lots of traffic and foxtails in the spring, so the Big Rec locale is the de facto mixed-use off-leash area. Enter Lincoln Way at 7th or 9th Avenue, and the area used is located above/behind the athletic fields. This area is preferred because it is safer and easier to use. (2) The Northeast section is at Fulton and Willard in a Natural Area of 0 .2 acres. This park is near the intersection of Stanyan & Fulton Streets, and is a small, little used area with no fences and prone to heavy traffic. (3) The Southcentral area is bounded by Martin Luther King Drive, Middle Drive and 34th and 38th Avenues; 4.4 acres. This dog friendly knoll has become the last immediate off leash area for people in the outer district. (4) The Northcentral area near 38th Ave. and Fulton (Fenced, training area; 1.4 acres) is the bay areas largest, fenced, exclusive-use off-leash area. It is located behind the Bison pens and West of Spreckles Lake. You can walk in near 39th Avenue and Fulton, or drive in from 38th Ave. The area is surrounded by a low fence that larger dogs could jump and they suggest that this play area may be more suitable for dogs that are in training or not under voice control. Dogs under 4 months old are not allowed, and females in heat should be leashed, and they are not allowed in the single use areas. Dogs must be under control and cleaned up after at all times.

Jefferson Square Off Lead Dog Park
Eddy and Laguna Streets
San Francisco, CA
415-831-2084
The legal off-leash area is a gently sloping grassy park located on the Northwest side of Jefferson Square Park at the corner of Eddy and Laguna. Dogs must be cleaned up after at all times.

Lafayette Park
Washington/Clay/Laguna
San Francisco, CA
415-831-2084
The legal off-leash area at this park is quite small and located on a slope adjacent to a busy street, so dogs must be under firm voice control. It is near Sacramento Street between Octavia and Gough Streets, and offers beautiful views of downtown. It is suggested to use caution by the steep slope that leads down to heavy traffic on Sacramento Street. This large city park has lots of trees, hills, and is a great place for walking. Dogs must be leashed when not in the off-leash area, and they must be cleaned up after at all times.

McKinley Off Leash Dog Park
20th Street and Vermont
San Francisco, CA
415-666-7005
This park is a small neighborhood park with a playground, grassy areas- often frequented by dogs and their owners, walking paths, and great views of the city to the west and south. Dogs must be cleaned up after at all times.

McLaren Park Off Leash Dog Areas
1600 Geneva Avenue
San Francisco, CA
415-831-2084
This park of about 60 acres has two locations for off lead. The top section at the North end of the park is bounded by Shelly Drive with a fence at the roadway, trails, an open area, a natural area, and a reservoir. Dogs are not allowed at the group picnic or children's play area, and leash restrictions apply during performances at the Amphitheater. The South entrance is accessible via the 1600 block of Geneva or Sunnydale. Dogs are not allowed in sensitive habitat areas, they must be leashed when not in the off leash areas, and cleaned up after at all times.

Mountain Lake Off Leash Dog Park
12th Avenue and Lake Street
San Francisco, CA
415-666-7005
Although small, this popular park has a strong local dog community. The off-leash area is at the Eastern corner of the park on the opposite end of the lake area. You can enter at 8th Avenue and Lake Street, but for wheelchair access and the doggy water fountain, enter one block west at 9th Avenue. Dogs must be leashed when not in the off-leash area, and they must be cleaned up after at all times.

Pine Lake Off Leash Dog Park
Sloat Boulevard & Vale Street
San Francisco, CA
415-831-2700
This park's lake is one of only 3 natural lakes left in San Francisco. The off leash area is on the second terrace of the park, west, and shares a boundary with Stern Grove Park, which also has an off leash area. There is a 1/5 mile trail from the Pine Lake DPA to the Stern Grove DPA. Dogs must be on leash when not in off lead areas, and they must be cleaned up after at all times.

Pine Lake/Stern Grove Trail
Between H 1(Stern Grove) and Wawona (Pine Lake)
San Francisco, CA
415-252-6252
This off leash trail runs west from the Pine Lake Meadow DPA to the Stern Grove DPA. Dogs must be cleaned up after.

Portrero Hill Mini Off Leash Dog Park
22nd Street and Arkansas
San Francisco, CA
415-695-5009
This .04 acre park is located on 22nd Street between Arkansas and Connecticut Streets and offers a great view of the bay. The area is unfenced so dogs must be under firm voice control. Dogs must be leashed when not in the off leash area, and be cleaned up after at all times.

St Mary's Off Leash Dog Park
95 Justin Drive
San Francisco, CA
415-695-5006
This 3 tiered multi-use park offers a fenced-in dog park with grassy and paved areas on the lower level (below the playground), benches, and canine and human water fountains. It is frequently closed (locked shut) during rain or wet seasons. Dogs must be on leash

when not in off lead areas, and they must be cleaned up after at all times.

Stern Grove Off Leash Dog Park
19th Avenue and Wawona Avenue
San Francisco, CA
415-252-6252
Stern Grove is said to be one of the most peaceful getaways in the city. It's foggy sunsets and woodsy retreat belies being in a big city. There are picnic tables, horseshoe courts, walking trails, and it is surrounded by fir, redwood, and eucalyptus trees. There is also a 1/5 mile off leash trail that connects this park to the Pine Lake Park, and the 2 parks comprise an area of about 64 acres. Dogs must be leashed when not in off leash areas, and they must be cleaned up after at all times.

Upper Noe Off Lead Dog Park
30th and Church Street
San Francisco, CA
415-831-2084
This park is located at the eastern end of the Upper Noe Recreation Center behind and along the baseball field, and can be accessed at 30th Street between Church and Sanchez Streets. This is a rather small fenced in dog park with a dirt floor, and may not give the amenities or exercise room wanted, however it still gets a lot of use, and upgrades are planned for this area.

Walter Haas Playground and Dog Park
Diamond Heights and Addison Street
San Francisco, CA
415-831-2084
This 4 acre park offers great views of downtown and the East Bay, an open lawn, basketball court, playgrounds, and a fenced, off leash dog area located in the Northeast section on the upper terrace of the park. This area is accessed from Diamond Heights Blvd. Dogs must be leashed when not in the off-leash area, and they must be cleaned up after at all times.

West Pacific Avenue Park
Pacific Avenue and Lyon Street
San Francisco, CA
415-831-2084
Dogs can be off lead under voice control along the corridor from West Pacific Avenue at the Broadway Street entrance to the 14th Avenue gate. They must be leashed in the forest and fields east of Lover's Lane and North of the Ecology Trail. This is one of the only off leash trail experiences remaining in the

Presidio, however, it is adjacent to roads.

Butcher Dog Park
Camden Avenue at Lancaster Drive
San Jose, CA
408-277-2757
This entirely fenced and double gated off-leash dog park has benches, grass and water fountains for dogs. There is a separate area for small dogs as well.

Delmas Dog Park
Park Avenue and Delmas Avenue
San Jose, CA
408-535-3570
sjparks.org/dogparks.asp
Delmas Dog Park opened in February, 2006. It is completely fenced and nearly 1/2 an acre in size. The dog park is a joint venture between the City of San Jose and the Santa Clara Valley Transportation Authority. The dog park is located just under Highway 87 one block south of San Carlos Street on Dalmas Avenue just south of downtown.

Fontana Dog Park
Golden Oak Way at Castello Drive
San Jose, CA
408-535-3570
sjparks.org/dogparks.asp
Fontana Dog Park is a fenced dog park with two sections. It is closed on Tuesdays and some Fridays for maintainence. There are benches and bags provided to clean up after your dog.

Hellyer Park/Dog Run
Hellyer Ave
San Jose, CA
408-225-0225
This two acre dog park has a nice lawn and is completely fenced. It is closed Wednesdays for maintenance. The dog park is located at the northeast end of Hellyer Park, near the Shadowbluff group area. There is a minimal fee for parking. To get there, take Hwy 101 to Hellyer Ave. Exit and head west on Hellyer. Continue straight, pay at the booth and drive to the parking lot where the dog park is located.

Miyuki Dog Park
Santa Teresa Boulevard
San Jose, CA
408-277-4573
This dog park is almost one half acre. There is a rack where dog owners can leave spare toys for other pups to use. All dogs that use

this off-leash park must wear a current dog license and proof of the rabies vaccine. The park is open from sunrise to one hour after sunset.

Ryland Dog Park
First Street at Bassett Street
San Jose, CA
408-535-3570
sjparks.org/dogparks.asp
This dog park is located in Ryland Park which is a few blocks north of Julian Street on North First Street. The dog park is on the west side of Ryland Park and is under the Coleman Avenue overpass. This gives it shade and protection from rain. It has a gravel surface.

El Chorro Regional Park and Dog Park
Hwy 1
San Luis Obispo, CA
805-781-5930
This regional park offers hiking trails, a botanical garden, volleyball courts, softball fields, campground and a designated off-leash dog park. The hiking trails offer scenic views on Eagle Rock and a cool creek walk along Dairy Creek. The Eagle Rock trail is about .7 miles and is rated strenuous. There are two other trails including Dairy Creek that are about 1 to 2 miles long and rated easy. Dogs must be on leash at all times, except in the dog park. To get to the park from Highway 101, head south and then take the Santa Rosa St. exit. Turn left on Santa Rosa which will turn into Highway 1 after Highland Drive. Continue about 5 miles and the park will be on your left, across from Cuesta College.

Nipomo Park Off-Leash Area
W. Tefft St and Pomery Rd
San Luis Obispo, CA
805-781-5930
1nora.tripod.com/
This off-leash area in Nipoma Park is fully fenced and is open during daylight hours. There are two separate enclosed areas for large dogs and small dogs. The park is located 3/4 miles west of 101 on W. Tefft St.

Knoll Hill Off-Leash Dog Park
200 Knoll Drive
San Pedro, CA
310-514-0338
dogparks.org
This 2.5 acre off-leash dog park is open during daylight hours. This park is located at the south end of the 110 Freeway. Exit 110 at Highway 47

east and exit quickly at N. Front St/Harbor Blvd. Go north on N. Front St to Knoll Drive on the left. The dog park is managed by Peninsula Dog Parks, Inc.

Field of Dogs
Civic Center Drive behind the Marin County Civic Center
San Rafael, CA
fieldofdogs.org
The Field Of Dogs off-leash dog park is located behind the Marin County Civic Center. To get there from 101, take the N. San Pedro Road exit east. Turn left onto Civic Center Drive and the dog park is on the right. The park is open during daylight hours, is fenced and is 2/3 acres in size.

Del Mar Dog Park
Del Mar and Pine Valley
San Ramon, CA
925-973-3200
To get to this fenced dog park, take I-680 to Alcosta, exit east, and turn left onto Broadmoor. Turn left onto Pine Valley and left on Del Mar.

Memorial Park Dog Run
Bollinger Canyon Road at San Ramon Valley Blvd
San Ramon, CA
925-973-3200
This fenced dog park is just over one acre in size and is located within San Ramon's Memorial Park. It has shade and benches. From I-680 exit Bollinger Canyon Rd, go west and cross San Ramon Valley Blvd and park on the left.

Douglas Family Preserve
Linda Street
Santa Barbara, CA
805-564-5418
Once planned to support a major housing development, this beautiful, undeveloped stretch of property was rescued to be enjoyed by all. Features include spectacular ocean and beach views and a great walking path along the bluffs. Dogs are allowed throughout the park and on the trails. Dogs must be under their owner's immediate control at all times, and cleaned up after.

Santa Barbara Off-Leash Areas
Various
Santa Barbara, CA
805-564-5418
sbparks.org/DOCS/dogpark.html
Unlike almost all larger California cities, Santa Barbara does not have any fenced off-leash dog parks nor any off-leash unfenced dog runs that

are available throughout the day. However, they do have five unfenced park areas with very limited off-leash hours. Please check the signs to find the off-leash areas and the hours as they may change. The five parks are Toro Canyon Park Meadow, daily (8 am to 10 am, 4 pm - sunset), Patterson Open Space, M - F (8 am to 10 am), Tucker's Grove, M - F (8 am - 10 am, 4 pm - sunset), Tabano Hollow, daily (4 pm to sunset) and Isla Vista Park, M - F (8 am - 10 am, 4 pm - sunset). Please keep in mind that in winter there is not much time between 4 pm and sunset.

Santa Clara Dog Park
888 Reed Street
Santa Clara, CA
408-615-3140
Thanks to one of our readers for letting us know about this new dog park which replaces the Brookdale Dog Park which is now closed. The Reed Street Dog Park is 1 1/2 acres in size and has two separate fenced areas for larger and smaller dogs. The park is open during daylight hours except that it is closed on Thursdays for maintenance. The dog park is located about 4 blocks north of El Camino Real on Lafayette at Reed.

University Terrace Dog Run
Meder Street and Nobel Drive
Santa Cruz, CA
831-420-5270
Dogs are allowed off leash in University Terrace from sunrise to 10 am and from 4 pm to sunset. They are allowed on-leash from 10 am to 4 pm. The park is on the corner of Meder Street and Noble Drive. Please check the signs for the off-leash area in the park.

Woof-Pac Park
300 Goodwin Rd
Santa Maria, CA
805-896-2344
doggiedogood.com/woof/index.html
This three acre fenced dog park opened in 2006 in Waller Park. It is located next to the Hagerman Softball Complex. Its hours are dawn to dusk. From 101 take Betteravia Rd west and turn left onto Orcutt Expy. Turn right into Waller Park.

Joslyn Park Dog Park
633 Kensington Road
Santa Monica, CA
310-458-8974

The fenced Joslyn Park dog park includes two areas. One is for small dogs and the other for large dogs.

Memorial Park
1401 Olympic Blvd
Santa Monica, CA
310-450-1121
There is an off-leash dog run located in this park.

Dog Park-Deturk Park
819 Donahue Street
Santa Rosa, CA
707-543-3292
ci.santa-rosa.ca.us
This dog park is fully fenced.

Dolye Community Park Dog Park
700 Doyle Park Drive
Santa Rosa, CA
707-543-3292
ci.santa-rosa.ca.us
This dog park is fully fenced.

Galvin Community Park Dog Park
3330 Yulupa Avenue
Santa Rosa, CA
707-543-3292
ci.santa-rosa.ca.us
This dog park is fully fenced.

Northwest Community Dog Park
2620 W. Steele Lane
Santa Rosa, CA
707-543-3292
Thanks to one of our readers who writes "Wonderful dog park. 2 separately fenced areas (one for little dogs too... It's all grassy and some trees and right near the creek. Also a brand new childrens play area (one for big kids and one fenced for toddlers). This dog park is sponsored by the Peanut's comics creator Charles M. Schultz's estate."

Rincon Valley Community Park Dog Park
5108 Badger Road
Santa Rosa, CA
707-543-3292
ci.santa-rosa.ca.us
This dog park is fully fenced.

Sausalito Dog Park
Bridgeway and Ebbtide Avenues
Sausalito, CA
sausalitodogpark.org
This fenced dog park is 1.3 acres complete with lighting, picnic tables, benches, a dog drinking water area, and a scooper cleaning station. On some days, this very popular park has over 300 dogs per day.

Scotts Valley Dog Park

Bluebonnet Road
Scotts Valley, CA
831-438-3251
svdogpark.org
This off leash dog park is located in the Skypark complex next to the soccer fields. The dog park offers 1.2 fully enclosed acres which is divided into two sections. One section is for small dogs under 25 pounds, puppies or shy dogs. The other section is for all dogs but primarily for larger and more active dogs. Other amenities include water bowls, wading pools, tennis balls, other dog toys, drinking fountains, shaded seating, plastic bags and pooper scoopers. To get there from Highway 17, take the Mt. Hermon exit and follow Mt. Hermon Road straight. Pass two stoplights and take the second right into the shopping center at the movie theatre sign. Go about .1 miles and turn left on Bluebonnet Road. The dog park is on the left.

Arbor Dog Park
Lampson Avenue at Heather St.
Seal Beach, CA
562-799-9660
This entirely fenced dog park is 2 1/2 acres in size. It has a number of large shade trees. There is water for people and dogs. The dog park is open during all daylight hours weather permitting except that it is closed on Thursdays from 8 am until noon for maintenance. To get to the dog park, take Valley View Street from the 22 or 405 Freeways north. Turn left on Lampson Avenue. You will have to turn right to the dog park which is directly behind the building at 4665 Lampson Avenue.

Sebastopol Dog Park
500 Ragle Rd
Sebastopol, CA
707-823-7262
This off lead area is located at the 157 acre Ragle Ranch Regional recreational park that is also home to a peace garden with a sculpture by a famed artist and a nature trail leading to the Atascadero Creek. Dogs must be sociable, current on all vaccinations, and under their owner's control at all times. Dogs must be leashed on no more than a 6 foot leash when not in designated off-lead areas.

Ernie Smith Community Park Dog Park
18776 Gilman Drive
Sonoma, CA
707-539-8092
Located at the Ernest Maynard Smith

Park recreational park, this off lead area provides a pet drinking fountain and tables. Dogs must be sociable, current on all vaccinations, and under their owner's control at all times. Dogs must be leashed on no more than a 6 foot leash when not in designated off-lead areas.

Las Palmas Park/Dog Park
850 Russett Drive
Sunnyvale, CA
408-730-7506
After your pup finishes playing with other dogs at this dog park, you can both relax by the pond at one of the many picnic tables. It's located at 850 Russett Drive (by Remington Avenue and Saratoga-Sunnyvale Rd).

Temecula Dog Exercise Area
44747 Redhawk Parkway
Temecula, CA
951-694-6444
Tomecula's first dog park was opened in 2006 in the Redhawk Community Park. The fenced park is divided into two areas, one for large dogs and one for small dogs. To get to the dog park from Interstate 15 take Highway 79 east and turn right onto Redhawk Parkway.

Thousand Oaks Dog Park
Avenida de las Flores
Thousand Oaks, CA
805-495-6471
pvrpd.org
This 3.75 acre enclosed dog park has a separate section for large dogs and small dogs. Amenities include picnic tables and three drinking fountains. The dog park is located at Avenida de las Flores, at the northwest quadrant of Conejo Creek.

Drigon Dog Park
Mission Blvd at 7th Street
Union City, CA
510-471-3232x702
The Drigon Dog Park is open from 6 am to 10 pm except for Mondays. It is closed all day Monday for cleaning. The dog park has separate fenced areas for small and large dogs. There are agility tunnels and climbing items available at the park. The park is sometimes closed due to wet weather. To get to the park from I-880 take Decoto Road to Mission Blvd and head south on Mission to the park. From I-680 take Mission Blvd north to the park.

Baldy View Dog Park
11th Street at Mountain Ave.
Upland, CA
909-931-4280
uplanddogpark.com/
The 1.3 acre Baldy View Dog Park has two fenced areas for large and small dogs. To get to the dog park, which is in Baldy View Park, take the I-10 to Mountain Ave. Head north on Mountain Ave and turn right on 11th Street. The park will be on your left.

Wardlaw Dog Park
Redwood Pkwy at Ascot Pkwy
Vallejo, CA
wardlawdogpark.com/
Located in Blue Rock Springs Corridor Park, the dog park is 2.2 acres in size and fully fenced. There is a separate area for small, shy or older dogs. There is a 2 mile walking path in Blue Rock Springs Park where you can take your leashed dog. From I-80 take the Redwood Pkwy East exit. Turn right on Ascot Parkway to the park.

Westminster Dog Park
1234 Pacific Ave
Venice, CA
310-392-5566
The Westminster Dog Park is 0.8 acres in size and it is open daily from 6 am to 10 pm. There is a smaller fenced area for small dogs. The park is located one block south of Venice Blvd near Centinela Avenue.

Arroyo Verde Park, Parks and Recreation
Foothill and Day Road
Ventura, CA
805-658-4740
This park has a designated off-leash area for use at specific times. There are benches and drinking fountains for the dogs and their people. Only well-socialized, dogs are permitted in the off-leash areas. All dogs must be vaccinated for rabies and have a current license, and owners are expected to be responsible for their dogs including keeping them under voice control and cleaning up after them. Their hours are Tuesday through Sunday from 6 to 9 AM, excluding holidays and days reserved for special events.

Camino Real Park
At Dean Drive and Varsity Street
Ventura, CA
805-658-4740
This park has a fenced in area in the southwest corner of the park for dogs and their owners to socialize and exercise. Hours of the dog park are

from dawn to dusk, and amenities include drinking fountains for the dogs and their people, benches, and doggie-doo bags. Double gates allow both small and large dogs to come in and out of the area safely. All dogs must be vaccinated for rabies and have a current license, and owners are expected to be responsible for their dogs including keeping them under voice control and cleaning up after them.

Walnut Creek Dog Park
301 N San Carlos Drive
Walnut Creek, CA
925-671-3329
Located at the north end of Heather Farm Park, this off leash area offers an acre of running room for pooches, plus there is a section for small dogs 30 pounds or under. Restrooms are nearby. Dogs must be sociable, current on all vaccinations and license, and under their owner's control at all times. Dogs must be leashed when not in designated off-lead areas.

Watsonville Dog Park
757 Green Valley Road
Watsonville, CA
831-454-7900
Watsonville Dog Park is located in the Pinto Lake County Park off of Green Valley Rd at Dalton Lane. Head west on Dalton Lane until you reach the park. The fenced dog park is about 1/3 of an acre.

Sam Combs Dog Park
205 Stone Blvd
West Sacramento, CA
916-617-4620
This fenced off-leash dog park opened in early 2006. There is a separate area for large dogs and small dogs. Take Jefferson Blvd south from the I-80 Freeway, left on Stone Blvd to the park on the left.

Colorado

Arvada Dog Park
17975 West 64th Parkway
Arvada, CO
303-421-3487
This five acre fenced dog park has separate areas for small and large dogs. It is open during daylight hours. Dogs must be leashed when not in the off-leash area. The park is located about 1/2 mile east of Highway 93. There are still 15 acres

to develop as funds allow.

Grandview Park Dog Park
17500 E. Salida Street
Aurora, CO
303-739-7160
This park has a designated off-leash dog park. The 5 acre dog park is fenced. It is located at the west end of Quincy Reservoir, about a third of a mile east of Buckley on Quincy. Dogs must be leashed when outside of the off-leash area.

East Boulder Park
5660 Sioux Drive
Boulder, CO
303-413-7258
This three acre dog park has separate fenced areas for small and large dogs. There is limited water access to a small lake. The city warns to be careful as water quality can vary. People need to pick up after their pets, especially near the water because of water quality issues. The dog park is located near the East Boulder Community Center.

Foothills Park Dog Park
Cherry Ave at 7th St
Boulder, CO
303-413-7258
This 2 acre dog park is fully fenced. There are separate areas for small dogs and large dogs. The park is open during daylight hours. To get to the park from Broadway turn west onto Violet Ave, then right on 10th and left on Cherry Ave. The dog park is at the north end of Foothills Community Park.

Howard Hueston Dog Park
34th Street
Boulder, CO
303-413-7258
This 1.25 acre off-leash area (Voice and Sight area) is not fenced but is designated by yellow poles. Dogs must be leashed when outside the off-leash area. The park is located on 34th Street, south of Iris Avenue and east of 30th Street.

Valmont Dog Park
5275 Valmont Road
Boulder, CO
303-413-7258
This three acre dog park has separate fenced areas for small and large dogs. Water is available seasonally.

Happy Tails Dog Park

1111 Judicial Center Drive
Brighton, CO
303-655-2049
This dog park is fully fenced and is open during daylight hours daily. Dogs must be cleaned up after. From I-76 exit at E. 152nd Avenue and head west. Turn left onto Judicial Center Dr to the park.

Broomfield County Commons Dog Park
13th and Sheridan Blvd
Broomfield, CO
303-464-5509
Broomfield's first dog park is located at this temporary location. It is in the North Pod of the Broomfield County Commons. There are two separate fully fenced areas for large and small dogs. Dogs must be licensed and people must clean up after their dogs.

Glendale Open Space Dog Park
100 Third Street
Castle Rock, CO
303-660-7495
This area has a 5 acre off leash dog-park where you can really let them run. It is adjacent to a 1.6 mile natural multi-use trail area where dogs must be on lead because of the sensitive habitats. The Open Space area is on the east side of the highway down a short gravel drive, and the dog park area is just west of the main trailhead; southwest of the parking lot. Benches and port-a-potties are on site.

Cheyenne Meadows Dog Park
Charmwood Dr. and Canoe Creek Dr.
Colorado Springs, CO
719-385-2489
There is a fenced dog park in the southern portion of Cheyenne Meadows Park.

Garden of the Gods Park Off-Leash Area
Gateway Road
Colorado Springs, CO
719-385-2489
This park has a designated off-leash area which is not fenced. The area is located east of Rock Ledge Ranch and south of Gateway Road. Dogs must be leashed when outside the off-leash area.

Palmer Park Dog Park
3650 Maizeland Road
Colorado Springs, CO
719-385-2489
This park has a fenced off-leash area. It is located at the old baseball

field, .3 miles from the Maizeland entrance. There is also an off-leash area (Dog Run Area) in the park which is not fenced. Dogs must be leashed when outside the off-leash area.

Rampart Park Dog Park
8270 Lexington Drive
Colorado Springs, CO
719-385-2489
This park has a fenced off-leash area. It is located just east of the baseball diamond. Dogs must be leashed when outside the off-leash area. The area is located near Rampart High School, next to the running track.

Red Rock Canyon Off-Leash Dog Loops
31st Street at Highway 24
Colorado Springs, CO
719-385-2489
At Red Rock Canyon Open Space Reserve there are two dog loops on which dogs are allowed to be off-leash if they are under voice control. These trails total about 5/8 mile in length and are located just south of the main entrance to the park. Dogs on leash are allowed on the rest of the trails in the park. To get to the reserve take Highway 24 to High Street and head south into the reserve.

Beaver Ranch Bark Park
11369 Foxton Rd
Conifer, CO
303-829-1917
There is a 2 acre fenced dog park located in Conifer's Beach Ranch Community Park. The dog park is located at the top of the Tipi Loop Trail in the park.

Barnum Park Off-Leash Area
Hooker and West 5th
Denver, CO
720-913-0696
This park has a designated off-leash area which is located in the northeast area of the park. It borders the 6th Avenue Freeway. Enter from the parking lot on 5th. This off-leash area is part of a pilot program for the city and county of Denver. It is in place to test the feasibility of off-leash areas in Denver parks. Volunteers observe the conditions at the parks on a regular basis and the success and future of the program will be determined at the end of the pilot program.

Berkeley Park Dog Park
Sheridan and West 46th

Denver, CO
720-913-0696
This park has a designated fenced dog park which is located west of the lake. Enter from lake side. This dog park is part of a pilot program for the city and county of Denver. It is in place to test the feasibility of off-leash areas in Denver parks. Volunteers observe the conditions at the parks on a regular basis and the success and future of the program will be determined at the end of the pilot program.

Denver's Off Leash Dog Park
666 South Jason Street
Denver, CO
303-698-0076
This park is Denver's first off leash dog park. It is open from sunrise to sunset, seven days a week. The park is located directly behind the Denver Animal Control building.

Fuller Park Dog Park
Franklin and East 29th
Denver, CO
720-913-0696
This park has a designated fenced dog park which is located at the northwest part of the park. It is west of the basketball courts. Enter from 29th Avenue. This dog park is part of a pilot program for the city and county of Denver. It is in place to test the feasibility of off-leash areas in Denver parks. Volunteers observe the conditions at the parks on a regular basis and the success and future of the program will be determined at the end of the pilot program.

Green Valley Ranch East Off-Leash Area
Jebel and East 45th
Denver, CO
720-913-0696
This park has a designated off-leash area which is located at the southwest area of the park. This off-leash area is part of a pilot program for the city and county of Denver. It is in place to test the feasibility of off-leash areas in Denver parks. Volunteers observe the conditions at the parks on a regular basis and the success and future of the program will be determined at the end of the pilot program.

Kennedy Soccer Complex Off-Leash Area
Hampden and South Dayton
Denver, CO
720-913-0696
This park has a designated off-

leash area which is located at the southwest point of the park. Do not park inside the complex gate as it will be locked. This off-leash area is part of a pilot program for the city and county of Denver. It is in place to test the feasibility of off-leash areas in Denver parks. Volunteers observe the conditions at the parks on a regular basis and the success and future of the program will be determined at the end of the pilot program.

Durango Dog Park
Highway 160
Durango, CO
970-385-2950
This dog park is located off Highway 160 West, at the base of Smelter Mountain. The designated parking area is located at the first driveway located west of the off-leash area entrance on Highway 160.

Eagle Dog Park
Sylvan Lake Rd at Lime Park Dr
Eagle, CO
970-328-6354
townofeagle.org
The Eagle town off-leash area is located at the south end of Brush Creek Park. It is an unfenced area and is marked by signage. Dogs must be under clear and demonstratable voice control to be off-leash in the area. To get to the dog park from I-70 take the Eby Creek Rd exit south. Turn right onto Highway 6 past downtown Eagle and turn left on Sylvan Lake Rd. Follow Sylvan Lake Rd a few miles to the park.

Centennial Park Off-Leash Area
4630 S. Decatur
Englewood, CO
303-762-2300
There is an off-leash area in Centennial Park. The off-leash area is not fenced and dogs must be under good voice control.

Duncan Park Off-Leash Area
4800 S. Pennsylvania
Englewood, CO
303-762-2300
There is an off-leash area in Duncan Park. The off-leash area is not fenced and dogs must be under good voice control.

Englewood Canine Corral
4848 S. Windermere
Englewood, CO
303-762-2300
The one and 1/2 acre Englewood Canine Corral is a completely fenced

off-leash dog park. It has a number of benches and shade. The dog park is located on the west side of Belleview Park. To get to the dog park from Belleview Avenue head north on Windermere. The park will be on your right.

Jason Park Off-Leash Area
4200 S. Jason
Englewood, CO
303-762-2300
There is an off-leash area in Jason Park. The off-leash area is not fenced and dogs must be under good voice control.

Northwest Greenbelt Off-Leash Area
Tejon at W Baltic Pl
Englewood, CO
303-762-2300
The off-leash area is not fenced and dogs must be under good voice control. To get to the off-leash area from I-25 take the Colorado Blvd exit south to Evens. Turn west on Evans Avenue to Tejon and turn south on Tejon a few blocks to the off-leash area.

Estes Valley Dog Park
off Highway 36
Estes Park, CO
970-586-8191
estesvalleyrecreation.com/
The dog park is located off Highway 36. It is next to Fishcreek Road. This fenced off-leash area has lake access.

Fossil Creek Dog Park
5821 South Lemay Avenue
Fort Collins, CO
970-221-6618
fcgov.com/parks/
This one acre dog park has a separate fenced area for small and shy dogs. Amenities include a double-gated entry and a drinking fountain. The park is located at the entrance to Fossil Creek Community Park.

Soft Gold Dog Park
520 Hickory Street
Fort Collins, CO
970-221-6618
The one acre fenced park is located in Soft Gold Neighborhood Park. From North College Avenue turn west on Hickory Street to the park.

Spring Canyon Dog Park
Horsetooth Road
Fort Collins, CO
970-221-6618
fcgov.com/parks/

This 2 to 3 acre dog park has a separate fenced area for small and shy dogs. Amenities include water fountains, bags and trash cans. The dog park is located at the west end of Horsetooth Road. It is in the undeveloped Spring Canyon Community Park along Spring Creek.

Canyon View Dog Park
Interstate 70 at 24 Road
Grand Junction, CO
970-254-3846
The dog park is 3.2 acres and enclosed by a 6 foot fence. The dog park is open from 5 am to midnight daily. It is located in the northern most end of Canyon View park which is just south of Interstate 70. To get to the park from I-70, take 24 Road south and turn left into the Canyon View Park. Then turn left again on the park road to the dog park.

Longmont Dog Park #1
21st and Francis
Longmont, CO
303-651-8447
The fenced dog park is located at 21st and Francis Street. The city requests that dog park visitors park west of the dog park in Garden Acres Park or east of the dog park at Carr Park. From I-25 take the Ute Hwy (66) west to Francis Street and turn south to the dog park.

Longmont Dog Park #2
Airport Road at St Vrain Rd
Longmont, CO
303-651-8447
The fenced dog park is located at Airport Rd at the intersection with St Vrain Rd. This is just north of the Longmont Airport.

Louisville Community Park Dog Park
955 Bella Vista Drive
Louisville, CO
303-335-4735
The dog park is fully fenced and is open during daylight hours. There is a pond with reclaimed water in the dog pond. You may not want your dog to be drinking this water. You should be aware that Louisville and Denver have a complete Pit Bull ban. Boulder does not have such a ban.

Poudre Pooch Park
Eastman Park Dr at 7th Street
Windsor, CO
970-674-3500
This one acre fenced dog park is

located in the southwest corner of Poudre Natural Park. From I-25 take County Highway 68 east to 7th Street (County Highway 17). Head south on 7th Street to Eastman Park Dr. The park is to the west.

Connecticut

Granby D.O.G.G.S. Park
215 Salmon Brook Street/H 202
Granby, CT
860-653-0173
granbydogpark.com
D.O.G.G.S. (Dog Owners of Granby Getting Social) is a community volunteer organization that established this fenced-in off-leash recreation area within Salmon Brook Park. Dogs of all sizes are allowed, and there can be up to 3 dogs per person. All dogs must have current license and shot tags on their collar/harness; be accompanied and in sight of their owners/custodians at all times, and under voice control. Choke, prong, or spiked collars are not allowed inside the off-leash area. Owners/custodians must carry a leash at all times, and dogs must be leashed entering and exiting the dog park. If you have a small, older, infirmed, or a shy dog, use the small dog area. You must clean up after your pet immediately, dispose of their waste properly, and fill in any holes they may dig. Females in heat; unaltered males, sick, or aggressive dogs are prohibited in the park and for the safety of all, immediately leash your dog if it exhibits aggressive behavior and leave the dog park area. The picnic tables are for the dogs to play on, but feel free to have a seat; however, food or drink for humans is not allowed within the fenced area.

The Hamden Dog Park at Bassett
On Waite Street at Ridge Road
Hamden, CT
hamdenrdog.org
The Hamden Dog Park is completely fenced with a brick path and patio, a separate small dog area with separate entrance, benches and picnic tables (mostly for the dogs to play on or under), and a compressed gravel trail. It is wheelchair accessible. Dogs of all sizes are allowed, but owners/custodians must carry their leashes on them at all times. All dogs must have current license and shot tags on their

collar/harness; be accompanied and in sight of their owners/custodians at all times, and under voice control. If you have a small, older, infirmed, or a shy dog, use the SMALL DOG AREA. You must clean up after your pet immediately, dispose of their waste properly, and fill in any holes they may dig. Female dogs in heat, and aggressive dogs are prohibited in the park and for the safety of all, immediately leash your dog if it exhibits aggressive behavior and leave the dog park area. Dogs younger than four months should not be brought to the park.

Eisenhower Park Dog Run
North Street
Milford, CT
203-783-3280

Pawsitive Park Dog Park, Estelle Cohn Memorial Dog Park
261 Asylum Street
Norwich, CT
860-367-7271
pawsitivepark.com/
Dogs of all sizes are allowed at this beautiful off leash dog-park. There can be up to 3 dogs per person. All dogs must have current license and shot tags on their collar/harness; be accompanied and in sight of their owners/custodians at all times, and under voice control. If you have a small, older, infirmed, or a shy dog, use the SMALL DOG AREA. Choke, prong, or spiked collars are not allowed inside the off-leash area. Water is available for dogs to drink and for filling up the wading pools in both dog play areas. You must clean up after your pet immediately and dispose of their waste properly. Poop bags and pooper scoopers are always available for people who have forgotten to bring theirs. Females in heat; unaltered males and aggressive dogs are prohibited in the park and for the safety of all, immediately leash your dog if it exhibits aggressive behavior and leave the dog park area. There is also a dog-free zone that is a fenced in area for small children or for people who just want to come, sit, and watch the dogs in the park. There are also landscaped trails around the entire park that you can walk with your dog on lead.

Bark Park
Governor Street
Ridgefield, CT
There are two fenced parks, one for large dogs and one for small dogs. There is water at the park. From

Route 35 take Main Street. Turn right on Governor Street and proceed near the end of Governor Street. The park is on the right. At the stop sign past the police station turn right and then left onto Hampton Park Road to the dog park. The dog park is next to Scalzo Field at the back of the park.

Bark Park
Main Street N
Southbury, CT
860-274-0802
roar-ridgefield.org/park.html
This off lead area is fenced on 3 sides, and open to the river on the other side. Doggy play toys, table and chairs, and benches are on site. Dogs must be sociable, current on all vaccinations, licensed, and under their owner's control at all times. Dogs must be leashed when not in designated off-lead areas

Mill Woods Park Dog Park
154 Prospect St
Wethersfield, CT
860-721-2890
wethersfielddogpark.org
The one acre fenced dog park is located in Mill Woods Park. In all Connecticut parks dogs must display their license tags on their collars at all times.

Delaware

Lums Pond Dog Area
Bear, DE
302-368-698
destateparks.com/lpsp/lpsp.asp
This area is part of Lums Pond State Park. This is a place where you can take your dog to swim in Lums Pond. It does not have much area for running or play. To get to the off-leash area take Howell School Rd to Buck Jersey Road. At the end of Buck Jersey Road the parking lot will be on the left.

Brandywine Dog Park
North Park Drive at North Adams
Wilmington, DE
302-577-7020
This is an unfenced dog area. It is located in Brandywine Park along the Brandywine River in Wilmington and near the Wilimington Zoo.

Carousel Park Off-Leash Area
3700 Limestone Rd
Wilmington, DE

302-995-7670
This nearly 50 acre unfenced off-leash area for dogs includes a lake for swimming and lots of area for running. The park is often quite busy with dogs on weekends. Throughout the rest of Carousel Park dogs must be leashed. The park closes at dark.

Rockford Dog Park
Rockford Rd at Tower Road
Wilmington, DE
302-577-7020
This unfenced dog park is over ten acres in size. It has recently been officially recognized as an off-leash area after serving as an unofficial off-leash area for years. There are cleanup bags available. The park is open during daylight hours.

Talley Day Bark Park
1300 Foulk Road
Wilmington, DE
302-395-5654
rsweiner.com/photo_bark_park.asp
This was the first fenced dog park in the state of Delaware. There is a separate area for large dogs and small dogs. It is located off Foulk Rd at the back of the Talley-Day grounds behind the Brandywine Hundred Library. The address given to the park is that of the library.

Florida

Boca Raton Dog Park
751 Banyan Trail
Boca Raton, FL
561-393-7821
There are 3 separate sections at this park; 1 each for small, medium, and large dogs. Benches, water fountains, wash stations, and 6 doggie waste stations are on site. Dogs must be sociable, current on all vaccinations, licensed, and under their owner's control at all times. Dogs must be leashed when not in designated off-lead areas, and they must be cleaned up after at all times.

Dog Beach
County Road 865
Bonita Beach, FL
239-461-7400
Brought about by public demand, this off lead beach area is located at Lover's Key State Park, and only 2 dogs per person at a time are allowed. (Children under 15 are not allowed in off lead area at any time) Dogs must be friendly to other pets,

people, and wildlife. Dogs must be sociable, current on all vaccinations and license, and under their owner's control at all times. Sanitary stations are on site. Dogs must be leashed when not in designated off-lead areas.

Happy Trails Canine Park
5502 33rd Avenue Drive W
Bradenton, FL
941-742-5923
manateechamber.com/parks.asp
Located at one of the county's largest parks with 140 acres of recreational opportunities with an emphasis on sporting activities, this 3 acre, fenced doggy play area has a separate section for small dogs, a drinking fountain, and free waste disposal bags. Dogs must be sociable, current on all vaccinations, licensed, and under their owner's control at all times. Dogs must be leashed when not in designated off-lead areas.

Sand Key Park Paw Playground
1060 Gulf Blvd.
Clearwater, FL
727-588-4852
This leash free dog park is fully fenced with amenities like cooling stations complete with showers and dog-level water fountains. People need to clean up after their pets and all dogs must be on a leash when outside of the Paw Playground area. Sand Key Park is located south of Cleveland Street, on Gulf Blvd.

Dog Chow Dog Park
2400 S Bayshore Drive
Coconut Grove, FL
954-570-9507
Located at Kennedy Park, this off leash area offers human and canine visitors lots of shade trees, benches, and water; plus there is a separate section for small dogs, and restrooms are on site. Dogs must be sociable, current on all vaccinations, licensed, and under their owner's control at all times. Dogs must be leashed when not in designated off-lead areas.

Dr. Paul's Pet Care Center Dog Park
2575 Sportsplex Drive
Coral Springs, FL
954-346-4428
sportsplexatcs.com/
Located in a 180+ acre regional park, this 2 acre, fenced doggy play area offers large and small dog areas, an obstacle course, exercise and play equipment, benches, picnic shelters, water fountains, and asphalt

pathways. Dogs must be sociable, current on all vaccinations and license, and under their owner's control at all times. Dogs must be leashed when not in designated off-lead areas.

Sportsplex Dog Park
2575 Sportsplex Drive
Coral Springs, FL
954-346-4428
sportsplexatcs.com/
A major recreation destination with several attractions and recreational opportunities, this park also holds major community events and festivals here, plus there is a 2 acre, fenced off leash dog park on site. Dogs must be sociable, current on all vaccinations and license, and under their owner's control at all times. Dogs must be leashed when not in designated off-lead areas.

Gemini Springs Dog Park
37 Dirksen Drive
Debary, FL
386-736-5953
volusia.org/parks/geminidog.htm
There are 4.5 acres at this off lead area with separate areas for large and small dogs; there are shade trees, benches, watering stations, dog wash stations, and picnic tables. Dogs must be sociable, current on all vaccinations and license, and under their owner's control at all times. Dogs must be leashed when not in designated off-lead areas.

Barkley Square Dog Park
1010 N Ridgewood Avenue
Deland, FL
386-736-5953
volusia.org/parks/barkley.htm
There are 14 acres at this off lead area with separate areas for large and small dogs, training events, and time out spaces; there are shade trees and a pond in the large dog area, benches, watering stations, and restrooms. Dogs must be sociable, current on all vaccinations and license, and under their owner's control at all times. Dogs must be leashed when not in designated off-lead areas.

Lake Ida Dog Park
2929 Lake Ida Road
Delray Beach, FL
561-966-6600
Located in a park with a variety of land and water recreation, this doggy off leash park offers lots of play room, shaded areas, benches, waste bags/receptacles, and a

water fountain, plus they have a paved dog washing section. Dogs must be sociable, current on all vaccinations, licensed, and under their owner's control at all times. Dogs must be leashed when not in designated off-lead areas.

Estero Community Dog Park
9200 Corkscrew Palms Blvd
Estero, FL
239-498-0415
Although dogs are not allowed in the rest of the park, they can have a lot of fun at this fenced play area. There are separate sections for large and small dogs. Dogs must be sociable, current on all vaccinations, licensed, and cleaned up after at all times. Dogs must be leashed when not in designated off-lead areas.

K-9 Corral at Estero Park
9200 Corkscrew Palms Blvd
Estero, FL
239-498-0415
This fenced, 2 acre off lead area is located at the southeast corner of the park and there 2 separate areas for small and large dogs, water fountains, large trees for shade, and disposal stations. The dog park is open during regular park hours. Dogs must be sociable, current on all vaccinations and license, and under their owner's control at all times. Dogs must be leashed when not in designated off-lead areas.

Bark Park At Snyder Park
3299 S.W. 4th Avenue
Fort Lauderdale, FL
954-828-3647
This fully fenced dog park has separate areas for small dogs and large dogs. There are benches, water, and pickup bags. Dogs must be on leash when outside the Bark Park. To get to Bark Park from I-95, exit at State Road 84 and head east to S.W. 4th Avenue. Turn right into Snyder Park. The Bark Park will be on your right.

Barkingham Park
9800 Buckingham Road
Fort Myers, FL
239-338-3288
This is the county's first off lead dog park and there are 2 separate sections for large and small dogs, agility equipment, benches, watering holes, a cleaning/cooling off shower, sanitary stations, and back trails, plus they are open dawn to dusk 7 days a week. Dogs must be sociable, current on all vaccinations and license, and under their owner's

control at all times. Dogs must be leashed when not in designated off-lead areas.

Bark Park
401 E. 65th Street
Hialeah, FL
305-769-2693
Located in the Amelia Earhart Park, this off lead doggy play area offers lots of run room, shade trees, paved walkways, drinking fountains for hounds and humans, and waste dispenser stations. Dogs must be sociable, current on all vaccinations, licensed, and cleaned up after at all times. Dogs must be leashed when not in designated off-lead areas.

Poinciana Dog Park
1301 S 21st Avenue
Hollywood, FL
954-921-3404
This popular off lead area has plenty of grassy and treed places with lots of play room, a paved pathway, fountains, pools, and a dog wash area. Dogs must be sociable, current on all vaccinations, licensed, and under their owner's control at all times. Dogs must be leashed when not in designated off-lead areas.

Dogwood Park
7407 Salisbury Rd South
Jacksonville, FL
904-296-3636
jaxdogs.com
This dog park is great for any size canine. It has 25 fenced acres in a 42 acre park. Dogs can be off leash in any part of the park. The park offers picnic tables, a pond for small dogs, a pond for large dogs (Lake Bow Wow), shower for dogs, warm water for dog baths, tennis balls and toys for play, a playground with games for your dogs, trails to walk on, and bag stations for cleanup. Locals can become members for the year for about $24.00 per month or out-of-town visitors can pay about $11 for a one time visit.

Paws Park
Penman Road S
Jacksonville Beach, FL
904-513-9240
pawsparkjaxbeach.com/index.php
Open year round from dawn to dusk (except during maintenance on Thursdays), this off leash area has separate small/large dog areas, automatic watering bowls, benches, rinsing areas, clean up bag dispensers, and shaded areas. Dogs must be sociable, current on all vaccinations and license, and under

their owner's control at all times. Dogs must be leashed when not in designated off-lead areas.

Higgs Beach Dog Park
White Street and Atlantic Blvd
Key West, FL
305-809-3765
keywestdogpark.org/
Located across from Higgs Beach this off leash area offers pets a fenced area with plenty of shade, water fountains, 2 separate areas for large and small dogs, and lots of play room. Dogs must be sociable, current on all vaccinations and license, and under their owner's control at all times. Dogs must be leashed when not in designated off-lead areas.

Walsingham Park Paw Playground
12615 102nd Avenue North
Largo, FL
727-549-6142
This leash free dog park is fully fenced with amenities like cooling stations complete with showers and dog-level water fountains. People need to clean up after their pets and all dogs must be on a leash when outside of the Paw Playground area. Walsingham Park is located south of Highway 688, on 102nd Avenue N near 125th Street.

Amelia Earhart Park Bark Park
401 East 65th Street
Miami, FL
305-755-7800
geocities.com/ameliabarkpark/
This 5 acre dog park is completely fenced and has a separate area for small dogs. There are paved walkways, benches, shade, and water. The dog park is open from sunrise to sunset. The Bark Park is located in Amelia Earhart Park.

Flamingo Bark Park
13th Street and Michigan Avenue
Miami Beach, FL
305-673-7224
This popular pooch play yard offers landscaped grounds, skill and training equipment, water fountains for hounds and humans, and waste stations. Dogs must be sociable, current on all vaccinations, licensed, and cleaned up after at all times. Dogs must be leashed when not in designated off-lead areas.

Mount D.o.r.a. Dog Park
East end of 11th Avenue
Mount Dora, FL
352-735-7183
Located right past the Ice House

Theater, this large, fenced off-leash area has separate sections for small, medium, and large dogs, plus a water station with bowls, waste stations, and benches. Dogs must be sociable, current on all vaccinations, licensed, and cleaned up after at all times. Dogs must be leashed when not in designated off-lead areas.

Pooch Park
1297 Driftwood Drive
North Fort Myers, FL
239-656-7748
Located in Judd Park, this fenced off lead area has 2 separate areas for small and large dogs, water for hounds and humans, and disposal stations. The dog park is open during regular park hours. Dogs must be sociable, current on all vaccinations and license, and under their owner's control at all times. Dogs must be leashed when not in designated off-lead areas.

Downey Dog Park
10107 Flowers Avenue
Orlando, FL
407-249-6195
There are separate sections for large and small dogs, water fountains, and doggy sanitary stations. Dogs must be sociable, current on all vaccinations and license, and under their owner's control at all times. Dogs must be leashed when not in designated off-lead areas.

Dr. Phillips Dog Park
8249 Buenavista Woods Blvd
Orlando, FL
407-254-9037
This park is located off of S. Apopka-Vineland Road south of Sandlake Road. Dogs must be sociable, current on all vaccinations and license, and under their owner's control at all times. Dogs must be leashed when not in designated off-lead areas.

Chestnut Park Paw Playground
2200 East Lake Road
Palm Harbor, FL
727-669-1951
This leash free dog park is fully fenced with amenities like cooling stations complete with showers and dog-level water fountains. People need to clean up after their pets and all dogs must be on a leash when outside of the Paw Playground area. Chestnut Park is located on East Lake Road, between Keystone Road and Highway 580.

Pembroke Pines Dog Park

9751 Johnson Street
Pembroke Pines, FL
954-435-6525
There are large and small sections for pets at this off leash area; there are kiddie pools for the pooches, water, obstacles, and benches on site. Dogs must be sociable, current on all vaccinations and licensed, and under their owner's control at all times. Dogs must be leashed when not in designated off-lead areas.

Scott Complex Dog Park
Summit Blvd
Pensacola, FL
850-436-5511
About an acre in size, this off leash doggy play area offers water fountains for hounds and humans, a pooper scooper station, benches, and picnic tables. Dogs must be sociable, current on all vaccinations, licensed, and under their owner's control at all times. Dogs must be leashed when not in designated off-lead areas.

Happy Tails Dog Park at Seminole Park
6600 SW 16th Street
Plantation, FL
954-452-2510
Located in Seminole Park, this off lead 5 acre site has 3 separate sections; one each for large and small dogs, and an exercise area that can be used for agility training, plus they are home to a variety of canine happenings held throughout the year. A pavilion, picnic area, and restrooms are on site. Dogs must be sociable, current on all vaccinations and license, and under their owner's control at all times. Dogs must be leashed when not in designated off-lead areas.

Paw Park of Historic Sanford
427 S. French Avenue
Sanford, FL
407-330-5688
pawparksanford.org
This off-leash dog park is located in the historic district of Sanford. The fenced park has a dog water fountain and dog shower. It is located south of State Route 46, off Highway 17-92 at East 5th Street.

Satellite Beach Off-leash Dog Park
Satellite Beach Sports & Rec Park
Satellite Beach, FL
321-777-8004
satellitebeach.org/RCdogPrk.htm
The dog park is 1.5 acres and fully fenced. The park offers water, tables and benches. There is a separate

area for small dogs. The park is open daily from 8 am to 8 pm except for Mondays and Thursdays from 12 - 3 pm for maintenance. The park is next to the Satellite Beach Library which is at 751 Jamaica Blvd.

Mango Dog Park
11717 Claypit Road
Seffner, FL
813-975-2160
There are 5 acres at this off lead doggy play area offering lots of run room, shade trees, swim areas, picnic tables, 2 pavilions, a doggy wash station, drinking fountains for hounds and humans, and waste dispenser stations. Dogs must be sociable, current on all vaccinations, licensed, and cleaned up after at all times. Dogs must be leashed when not in designated off-lead areas.

Boca Ciega Park Paw Playground
12410 74th Ave. N
Seminole, FL
727-588-4882
This leash free dog park is fully fenced with amenities like cooling stations complete with showers and dog-level water fountains. People need to clean up after their pets and all dogs must be on a leash when outside of the Paw Playground area. Boca Ciega Park is located south of Park Blvd, on 74th Avenue N. near 125th Street N.

Barkham at Markham Park
16001 W H 84
Sunrise, FL
954-389-2000
broward.org/parks/dogpark.htm
Located in a large county park, this off leash area covers about 3 acres of landscaped grounds with divided sections for large and small pooches. Some of the amenities include lush Bermuda sod grass, wide walking paths, 3 shelter rest areas-2 have refrigerated water for pet owners, doggy watering fountains, a common wash area, plus an additional wash area in the large dog section. Dogs must be sociable, current on all vaccinations and license, and cleaned up after at all times. Dogs must be on no more than a 6 foot leash when not in designated off-lead areas.

Al Lopez Dog Park
4810 North Himes
Tampa, FL
813-274-8615
There is a 1.5 acre fenced dog park

for larger dogs and an 8000 square foot park for small dogs. There is a double gated entry area, benches, water and pickup bags are available. The dog park is located on the west side of Al Lopez Park.

Davis Islands Dog Park
1002 Severn
Tampa, FL
813-274-8615
There are two fenced dog parks at the south end of Davis Islands. One of the parks is entirely fenced and is about one acre. The other park is a 1 1/2 acre beach front park with over 200 feet of waterfront available for dogs. There is water, double gated entry, and pickup bags available.

Palma Ceia
San Miguel & Marti
Tampa, FL
813-274-8615
The dog park is about 3/4 acres and is entirely fenced. It has a double gated entry, water, and pickup bags available. The park is located on the northeast corner of the park at West San Miguel & Marti.

Anderson Park Paw Playground
39699 U.S. Highway 19 North
Tarpon Springs, FL
727-943-4085
This leash free dog park is fully fenced with amenities like cooling stations complete with showers and dog-level water fountains. People need to clean up after their pets and all dogs must be on a leash when outside of the Paw Playground area. Anderson Park is located off Highway 19, north of Klosterman Road.

Fort DeSoto Park Paw Playground
3500 Pinellas Bayway South
Tierra Verde, FL
727-582-2267
This leash free dog park is fully fenced with amenities like cooling stations complete with showers and dog-level water fountains. People need to clean up after their pets and all dogs must be on a leash when outside of the Paw Playground area. Fort DeSoto Park is located at the southern end of the Pinellas Bayway.

Dog Park
2975 Greenbriar Blvd
Wellington, FL
561-791-4005
Located at Greenbriar Park, this 3 acre dog park is open from dawn to dusk and gives plenty of run room. Dogs must be sociable, current on all

vaccinations, licensed, and under their owner's control at all times. Dogs must be leashed when not in designated off-lead areas.

Pooch Park
7715 Forest Hill Blvd/H 882
West Palm Beach, FL
561-966-6600
There are 5 acres of play area for pooches here with 2 large dog sections and 1 small dog section. A paved doggy wash station, fountains, dog bag dispensers, plenty of shady areas, and benches are on site. Dogs must be sociable, current on all vaccinations, licensed, and cleaned up after at all times. Dogs must be leashed when not in designated off-lead areas.

West Orange Dog Park
12400 Marshall Farms Road
Winter Garden, FL
407-656-3299
This off lead area can also be accessed through West Orange Park (150 Windermere Road). There are separate sections for large and small dogs, water fountains, and doggy sanitary stations. Dogs must be sociable, current on all vaccinations and license, and under their owner's control at all times. Dogs must be leashed when not in designated off-lead areas.

Fleet Peeples Park Dog Park
South Lakemont Avenue
Winter Park, FL
407-740-8897
ffpp.org/
This park is a fenced dog park with a pond for swimming. Dogs are allowed off-leash within the park. There is shade, water, and bags for cleanup. The park is open to Winter Park residents as well as the public at large. The dog park is located in Fleet Peeples Park on South Lakemont Avenue.

Georgia

Waggy World Dog Park
175 Roswell Street
Alpharetta, GA
678-297-6100
This 1.5 acre fenced off-leash dog park is managed by the city parks department. It is open 8 am to sunset daily. There are separate areas for large and small dogs. The park features water and benches.

Memorial Park Dog Park
293 Gran Ellen Drive
Athens, GA
706-613-3580
This fenced, 1.5 acre off-leash dog park is located on the hillside near the lake in the 72 acre park. Dogs must be leashed when outside of the off-leash area.

Sandy Creek Park Dog Parks
400 Bob Holman Rd
Athens, GA
706-613-3800
sandycreekpark.com
There are actually 4 two to three acre fenced off-leash areas in Sandy Creek Park. One is a standard dog park where anyone may bring their dogs free of charge. The other three are by reservation only and there is a charge for this reservation of $1.00 per hour per dog. They can be used for private groups, training and other purposes. Dogs must be leashed in the park outside of the off-leash areas.

Southeast Clarke Park Dog Park
4440 Lexington Road
Athens, GA
706-613-3871
This fenced, 2 acre off-leash dog park is located on the Whit Davis Rd side of the park. There are separate areas for small and large dogs. Dogs must be leashed when outside of the off-leash area.

Piedmont Park Off Leash Dog Park
Park Drive
Atlanta, GA
404-875-7275
Dogs can run leash-free only in this designated area of Piedmont Park. The dog park is just over 1.5 acres. To get there, take I-85/75 north and take exit 101 (10th Street). Go straight to the first light, then turn right on 10th Street. Go past Piedmont Park, then turn left onto Monroe Drive. At the first light, turn left onto Park Drive. The dog park is below the bridge on the north side.

Windermere Dog Park
3355 Windermere Parkway
Cumming, GA
770-781-2215
This fenced dog park is located in Windermere Park and is run by the County of Forsyth. There are separate areas for large and small dogs. The park is open from 8 am until sunset daily.

Henry Jones Dog Park
4770 N. Peachtree Rd
Dunwoody, GA
404-371-2631
This four acre and fenced dog park is located in Brook Run Park in the Atlanta/Dunwoody area on Peachtree and just south of Peeler Rd. There are no water fountains. The park is open during daylight hours.

Laurel Park Dog Park
3100 Old Cleveland Hwy
Gainesville, GA
770-535-8280
This fenced dog park has two areas; one for small dogs and one for large dogs. There are quite a few trees in the dog park.

Ronald Reagan Dog Park
2777 Five Forks Trickum Rd
Lawrenceville, GA
This is a two acre fenced dog park. It is managed by Gwinnett County and is located just north of Ronald Reagan Parkway on 5 Forks Trickum Rd.

Macon Dog Park
Chestnut and Adams
Macon, GA
478-742-5084
macondogpark.org
This fully fenced dog park is open from sunrise to sunset. The Dog Park is just off of I-75 at the Forsyth Street exit. It is located one block north of Tatnall Square at the corner of Chestnut Street and Adams Street.

Sweat Mountain Dog Park
4346 Steinhauer Road
Marietta, GA
770-591-3160
This off-leash park has separate fenced areas for small and large dogs. The park is open from dawn until dusk daily except for Wednesday mornings when it is closed for maintenance.

Wolf Brook Private Dog Park and Club
13665 New Providence Rd
Milton, GA
770-772-0440
wolfbrook.com
This private club requires a temperment test and prior approval. It has 8 acres of off-leash area, dog day care, a club building with dog supplies, dog sports and other activities.

513

Graves Dog Park
1540 Graves Rd
Norcross, GA
770-822-8840
This two acre fenced dog park has separate areas for large dogs and small dogs.

Leila Thompson Dog Park
1355 Woodstock Rd
Roswell, GA
770-641-3760
ci.roswell.ga.us
This fenced off-leash park is located near the Arts Center building in Leila Thompson Park. There is a second fenced area for smaller dogs.

Savannah Dog Park
41st and Drayton St
Savannah, GA
savannahdogpark.com/
This dog park is located in the Starland Area at 41st and Drayton St. The park is shaded and fenced.

Burger Dog Park
680 Glendale Pl
Smyrna, GA
770-431-2842
This off-leash park is fenced and has separate areas for small and large dogs. The park is located west of S. Cobb Drive and and south of WIndy Hill Rd.

Red Dog Park
3rd and 4th Streets
Stone Mountain, GA
770-879-4971
There are 2 separate sections for large and small dogs at this off lead area. There are benches and shady areas plus a pathway that leads from the off lead area into the Stone Mountain Park. Dogs must be sociable, current on all vaccinations and license, and under their owner's control at all times. Dogs must be leashed when not in designated off-lead areas.

City of Tybee Dog Park
Van Horne and Fort Streets
Tybee, GA
912-786-4573
There are 2 sections to this dog park; one for large dogs and one for dog 20 pounds or less. The park is open from dawn to dusk. Dogs must be sociable, current on all vaccinations and license, and under their owner's control at all times. Dogs must be leashed when not in designated off-lead areas. They ask that visitors park on Van Horn and not in the

police impound lot.

Hawaii

McInerny Dog Park
2700 Waialae Avenue
Honolulu, HI
808-946-2187
This dog park is 1/3 acre in size and is surrounded by a fence. It is open M-F from noon - 8 pm and 10 am - 4 pm on weekends and holidays. The dog park is at the Hawaiian Humane Society. Take the H-1 to the King Street exit.

Mililani Dog Park
95-1069 Ukuwai St
Honolulu, HI
808-946-2187
The fenced off-leash dog park is located at the Mililani Mauka District Park at the Park & Ride area. It is open daily during daylight hours except that it is closed on Wednesday mornings for maintenance.

Moanalua Dog Park
Moanalua Park Rd and Hahiole St
Honolulu, HI
moanaluadogpark.org/
This fenced dog park is located in the Moanalua Park. It is maintained by the Moanalua Gardens Community Association. The park is open during daylight hours daily except Tuesday when it is closed until noon for maintenance. Dog Park visitors are required to bring and use their own poop bags as none are provided at the park.

Oahu Dog-Friendly Parks (Leashes Required)
Various
Honolulu, HI
808-946-2187
Many of the parks on Oahu allow leashed dogs. Leash laws are strictly enforced. Dogs are only allowed off-leash in the off-leash dog parks. In all public places you are required to clean up after your dog. For a detailed list of parks on Oahu that allow leashed dogs see the Hawaiian Humane Societies website at:
http://www.hawaiianhumane.org/programs/dogparks/otherparks.html.

The Bark Park
Diamond Head Rd at 18th Avenue
Honolulu, HI

barkpark-honolulu.org/
This fenced dog park is open during daylight hours daily.

Ala Wai K9 Playground
Ala Wai Blvd
Waikiki, HI
alawaik9playground.com
This off leash area is presently located at the end of University Avenue on the gaming fields of the Ala Wai Community Park. Dogs must be sociable, current on all vaccinations, licensed, and under their owner's control at all times. Dogs must be leashed when not in designated off-lead areas.

Idaho

Military Reserve Off-Leash Park
Mountain Cove Road and Reserve St
Boise, ID
208-384-4240
cityofboise.org/parks
Dogs are allowed off-leash in this park. There is some shade and picnic tables.

Illinois

Challenger Playlot Park
1100 W. Irving Park Rd
Chicago, IL
312-742-PLAY
This is a fenced dog park. All dogs that use the Chicago dog parks are required to have an annual permit. The permits currently cost $5 per dog. You will have to visit an approved location to get a permit. Proof of certain vaccinations are also required.

Churchill Field Park Dog Park
1825 N. Damen Ave.
Chicago, IL
312-742-PLAY
This is one of a number of official off-leash areas in the city for dogs. There is a fenced off-leash dog area. Beginning in September, 2005 all dogs that use the dog parks are required to have an annual permit. The permits currently cost $5 per dog. You will have to visit an approved location to get a permit. Proof of certain vaccinations are also required.

Coliseum Park Dog Park

1466 S. Wabash Ave.
Chicago, IL
312-742-PLAY
This is one of a number of official off-leash areas in the city for dogs. There is a fenced off-leash dog area. Beginning in September, 2005 all dogs that use the dog parks are required to have an annual permit. The permits currently cost $5 per dog. You will have to visit an approved location to get a permit. Proof of certain vaccinations are also required.

Grant Park Bark Park
9th and Columbus
Chicago, IL
312-742-PLAY
southloopdogs.com
Grant Park Bark Park opened on July 15, 2006 and is located in the famous Grant Park along the lake in Chicago. It is fully fenced and is about 18,000 square feet in size. There is access to the dog park from Columbus Avenue and from the 11th Street bridge. The park is maintained by the South Loop Dog P.A.C. All dogs that use the Chicago dog parks are required to have an annual permit. The permits currently cost $5 per dog. You will have to visit an approved location to get a permit. Proof of certain vaccinations are also required.

Hamlin Park Dog Park
3035 N. Hoyne Ave.
Chicago, IL
312-742-PLAY
This is one of a number of official off-leash areas in the city for dogs. There is a fenced off-leash dog area. Beginning in September, 2005 all dogs that use the dog parks are required to have an annual permit. The permits currently cost $5 per dog. You will have to visit an approved location to get a permit. Proof of certain vaccinations are also required.

Margate Park Dog Park
4921 N. Marine Drive
Chicago, IL
312-742-PLAY
Also known as Puptown, this is one of a number of official off-leash areas in the city for dogs. There is a fenced off-leash dog area. Beginning in September, 2005 all dogs that use the dog parks are required to have an annual permit. The permits currently cost $5 per dog. You will have to visit an approved location to get a permit. Proof of certain vaccinations are also required.

Noethling (Grace) Park Dog Park
2645 N. Sheffield Ave.
Chicago, IL
312-742-PLAY
Also known as Wiggly Field, this is one of a number of official off-leash areas in the city for dogs. There is a fenced off-leash dog area. Beginning in September, 2005 all dogs that use the dog parks are required to have an annual permit. The permits currently cost $5 per dog. You will have to visit an approved location to get a permit. Proof of certain vaccinations are also required.

River Park Dog Park
5100 N. Francisco Ave
Chicago, IL
312-742-PLAY
This is a fenced dog park. All dogs that use the Chicago dog parks are required to have an annual permit. The permits currently cost $5 per dog. You will have to visit an approved location to get a permit. Proof of certain vaccinations are also required.

Walsh Park Dog Park
1722 N. Ashland Ave.
Chicago, IL
312-742-PLAY
This is one of a number of official off-leash areas in the city for dogs. There is a fenced off-leash dog area. Beginning in September, 2005 all dogs that use the dog parks are required to have an annual permit. The permits currently cost $5 per dog. You will have to visit an approved location to get a permit. Proof of certain vaccinations are also required.

Wicker Park Dog Park
1425 N. Damen Ave.
Chicago, IL
312-742-PLAY
This is one of a number of official off-leash areas in the city for dogs. There is a fenced off-leash dog area. Beginning in September, 2005 all dogs that use the dog parks are required to have an annual permit. The permits currently cost $5 per dog. You will have to visit an approved location to get a permit. Proof of certain vaccinations are also required.

Whalon Lake Dog Park
Royce Road
Naperville, IL
815-727-8700
fpdwc.org/whalon.cfm

Although there are plenty of recreational opportunities at this park with a scenic wetland, a large oak-savanna grove, an 80 acre man-made lake, and several trails, there are several improvements in the works to expand the facilities. This park is also home to an 8 acre fenced off-leash dog exercise area for large dogs and a 2.5 acre fenced park for dogs less than 30 pounds. Dogs must be leashed when not in the off-lead area. Annual permits are required and accessible through the website or at any of the Forest Preserve locations. Dogs must be under their owner's control at all times.

Vicary Bottoms Dog Exercise Area
Kickapoo Creek Road
Peoria, IL
309-682-6684
Only 2 healthy dogs are allowed per owner at this park, and because it is a non-fenced area only well-trained dogs should be brought here. There are no water or restroom facilities at this location. Dogs must be under their owner's control and leashed at all times.

Hammel Woods Dog Park
DuPage River Access on E Black Road
Shorewood, IL
815-727-8700
This 300 acre preserve sits along the DuPage River and offers a wide variety of recreational activities and miles of scenic trails with one leading to an observation deck with a view of the river and dam. This park is also home to a 7 acre fenced off-leash dog exercise area. Dogs must be leashed when not in the off-lead area. Annual permits are required and accessible through the website or at any of the Forest Preserve locations. Dogs must be under their owner's control at all times.

Urbana Park District Dog Park
1501 E. Perkins Rd.
Urbana, IL
217-344-9583
There are 10 fenced doggy running acres at this meadow park, including a small or timid dog area, plus there is a shady area toward the center of the park. There is a $3 daily registration fee or 1-year memberships are available. Dogs must be under their owner's control at all times.

Indiana

Dogwood Run at Lemon Lake County Park
6322 W. 133rd Avenue
Crown Point, IN
219-945-0543
This 14 acre dog park is divided into two 7 acre areas. Only one is open at a time. There is a $35 annual fee or a $2 per day pass. The single day pass is collected on the honor system. All users must have proof of vaccinations unless you have an annual pass.

Pawster Park Pooch Playground
Winchester Road and Bluffton Road
Fort Wayne, IN
260-427-6000
A Pooch Pass is required to use this fenced dog park. The park is open from 6 am to 10 pm daily. The annual Pooch Pass costs $25 for residents and $75 for non-residents. To obtain a Pooch Pass visit the Parks and Rec Dept office at 705 East State Street, Fort Wayne, IN 46805.

Robert Nelson Dog Park
60376 C.R. 13
Goshen, IN
This fenced dog park is open from sunrise to sunset daily. You must be a member in order to use the park. Membership is available at the Animal Aid Clinic South at 3718 Mishawaka Rd, Elkhart, IN. For more information about the membership call 574-875-5102.

Wicker Memorial Park
8554 Indianapolis Boulevard
Highland, IN
219-838-3420
This dog run is located at a 226 acre recreational park where there are also many miles of walking trails. Dogs must be sociable, current on all vaccinations, licensed, and cleaned up after at all times. Dogs must be leashed when not in designated off-lead areas.

Broad Ripple Park Bark Park
1550 Broad Ripple Avenue
Indianapolis, IN
317-327-7161
This fenced Bark Park requires an annual Pooch Pass. The cost of a pass is $75 annually. You may get the annual pass at the park office during business hours.

Eagle Creek Park Bark Park
7840 W 56th St
Indianapolis, IN
317-327-7110
This fenced Bark Park requires an annual Pooch Pass. The cost of a pass is $75 annually. You may get the annual pass at the park office during business hours.

Shamrock Park Dog Park
Wabash Avenue
Lafayette, IN
765-225-8388
dogparkinlafayette.org/
Yearly memberships are available for this off leash park or visitors can get a day pass at Buckles Feed Depot and Pet Supply at 220 S 4th Avenue. Owners must have proof of rabies and required vaccinations plus they are required to sign a hold-harness agreement. Dogs must be sociable, have a current license, and be under their owner's control at all times. Dogs must be leashed when not in designated off-lead areas.

Creek Ridge County Park Dog Park
7943 W 400 North
Michigan City, IN
219-325-8315
laportecountyparks.org/bark.html
This doggy play area offers drinking fountains, benches, fire hydrants, and exercise equipment. Dogs must have up-to-date vaccinations, and be registered with a daily or annual permit to use the park. Dogs may not be left unattended at any time, and they must be under their owner's control and cleaned up after at all times.

Canine Country Club
3556 Sturdy Road
Valparaiso, IN
219-548-3604
cccdogpark.com
Although a membership only park by the month or year, day passes are available during office hours. The entire park is closed on Monday, and the office is closed on Friday and Sundays. Visitors may utilize the park from 7 am until dusk year around. Dogs must be sociable, current on all vaccinations and license, and under their owner's control at all times. Dogs must be leashed when not in designated off-lead areas.

Bluhm County Park Dog Park
3855 South 1100 W
Westville, IN
219-325-8315

laportecountyparks.org/bark.html
This doggy park offers a variety of special fun features for some great exercise; there's a window jump, doggie crawl, tire jump, a pause table, hills, and more. Dogs must have up-to-date vaccinations, and be registered with a daily or annual permit to use the park. Dogs may not be left unattended at any time, and they must be under their owner's control and cleaned up after at all times.

Iowa

Crow Creek Dog Park
4800 N Devils Glen Road
Bettendorf, IA
563-344-4113
There are about 5 fenced areas that provide a safe off leash play area at this park; it is located at the north end of the park across from softball field #3. There are pet waste stations, restrooms, and a doggie drinking fountain on site. Dogs must be sociable, current and have proof of all vaccinations and license, and be under their owner's control at all times. Dogs must be leashed when not in designated off-lead areas.

Cedar Falls Paw Park
S Main and Hwy 58 Overpass
Cedar Falls, IA
319-273-8624
There are 3 acres for pooches to play and run at this off lead area. Dogs must be sociable, current on all vaccinations and license, and under their owner's control at all times. Dogs must be leashed when not in designated off-lead areas.

Cheyenne Park Off-Leash Area
1500 Cedar Bend Lane SW
Cedar Rapids, IA
319-286-5760
There is a 1 acre section for small dogs; a 1.5 acre section for individual or class training, and a full fenced 12 acres for plenty of roaming room at this off lead park. Permits are required; annual passes can be obtained at Animal Control (1401 Cedar Bend Lane) or daily passes on site. Dogs must be sociable, current on all vaccinations, licensed, and cleaned up after at all times. Dogs must be leashed when not in designated off-lead areas.

Prairie Pastures Dog Park at Soaring

Eagle Nature Center
3923 North 3rd Street
Clinton, IA
563-243-3022
soaringeagle.20m.com/index.html
This off leash area is available to members of the Soaring Eagle Nature Center-an environment education center; membership forms are available by calling the number above or at the park. Some of the area has been landscaped; there is a small dog area, nature trail, and benches dotted throughout. Dogs must be sociable, current on all vaccinations and license, and under their owner's control at all times. Dogs must be leashed when not in designated off-lead areas.

Indianola Off-Leash Dog Playground
S K Street and W 17th Avenue
Indianola, IA
515-480-0740
Located at Downey Park, this off lead play area offers grassy fields with big shade trees, large and small dog sections, watering stations, clean-up bag dispensers, and sheltered picnic tables; an agility area is soon to come as well. A daily pass or an annual permit is required to use the dog park, and can be obtained at the Parks and Recreation office at 2204 West 2nd Avenue. Permit tags must be visible on pets while in the park. Dogs must be sociable, have proof of current vaccinations and be licensed. Dogs are to be under their owner's control at all times, and leashed when not in designated off-lead areas.

Thornberry Off-Leash Dog Park
Foster Road
Iowa City, IA
319-356-5107
icgov.org/PR/parks/dogpark.asp
There are about 11 acres of fenced doggy play area with 3 separate sections that include a small dog yard, one for all dogs, and a training and agility area. A permit is required and can be obtained on line, at the Robert A. Lee Recreation Center or at the city's Animal Care and Adoption Center. Dogs must be sociable, current on all vaccinations, licensed, and cleaned up after at all times. Dogs must be leashed when not in designated off-lead areas.

Rover's Ranch Dog Park and Training Center
108th Street
Runnells, IA
515-967-6768
roversranch.com

In addition to having an off leash membership only dog-park, this privately owned center has several training opportunities available. Owners must schedule a 1st appointment for the membership; drop-ins are not accepted. Some of the amenities include 5 fenced acres, an agility practice area, water for hounds and humans, pet waste disposal stations, pools and sprinklers, benches, trails, lighting at night, and much more. Dogs must be current on all vaccinations and license.

Lewis and Clark Dog Park
5015 Correctionville Road
Sioux City, IA
712-279-6311
sola-sc.org/
This off lead area is located at the Bacon Creek Park. Dogs must be sociable, current and have proof of all vaccinations and license, and under their owner's control at all times. Dogs must be leashed when not in designated off-lead areas.

Washington Sunset Dog Park
915 W Main Street
Washington, IA
319-653-6584
Lots of grass, shade trees, a pavilion, a separate small dog area, water, and lights are some of the amenities at this off lead area. Dogs must be sociable, current and have proof of all vaccinations and license, and under their owner's control at all times. Dogs must be leashed when not in designated off-lead areas.

Racoon River Dog Park
2500 Grand Avenue
West Des Moines, IA
515-222-3444
This off lead area is located at the 631+ acre Raccoon River Park with a 232 acre lake. There are 10 fenced acres for pooches to run and play, and it is open from 6:30 am to dusk with separate areas for large and small dogs. A park dog permit is required and can be obtained at the Raccoon River Park Nature Lodge or at the Parks and Recreation Office. Dogs must be sociable, current on all vaccinations and license, and under their owner's control at all times. Dogs must be leashed when not in designated off-lead areas.

Kansas

Kill Creek Streamway Park
33460 West 95th St
De Soto, KS
913-831-3355
This park features on leash walking trails and 19 acres of fenced area for off leash dogs. Cleanup and water stations are provided.

Mutt Run
1330 East 902 Road
Lawrence, KS
785-832-3405
This 30 acre off-leash area has mowed paths through the fields and along wooded areas. Amenities include a drinking fountain and water for dogs, restrooms and a small parking lot. The off-leash area is about 30 minutes east of Topeka. From I-70, take the KS 10 Exit. Turn right on KS 10 and go about 3.5 miles. Take Clinton Parkway west to the Clinton Day road. Turn south on the dam road and take the first left onto 902 Road. Take 902 Road to the first left.

Heritage Park
16050 Pflumm
Olathe, KS
913-831-3355
This park features an offleash dog park that is fenced in. Water and cleanup stations are provided.

Thomas S. Stoll Memorial Dog Park
12500 W. 119th Street
Overland Park, KS
913-831-3355
There are almost 7 fenced acres of grassy fields set aside for pooches at this beautifully landscaped 79 acre park. Dogs must be sociable, current on all vaccinations, licensed, and cleaned up after at all times. Dogs must be leashed when not in designated off-lead areas.

Shawnee Mission Park
7900 Renner Rd/87th St
Shawnee, KS
913-831-3355
This off leash park provides water and cleanup stations in a fenced area. It is open to everyone with no fee. Dogpark is located at the 87th St parkway entrance. In the main park area, pets have to be leashed.

Bark Park (Gage Park)
10th and Gage St

Topeka, KS
785-368-3838
Dogs are allowed off leashed in the Bark Park section and leashed in the main park area. The dog park features water fountains, cleanup stations, and running areas in a fenced-in area.

Kentucky

Ashland Boyd County Dog Park
Fraley Field
Ashland, KY
This dog park is located near the West Virginia and Kentucky State line in Ashland, KY. The dog park is fully fenced and there are cleanup bags provided. From I-64, take exit 185 at Cannonsburg. Follow US 180 toward Ashland. US 180 will merge with US 60 - stay on US 60. Turn left at West Summit Rd. Turn left onto the road to Fraley Field just past Boyd County Middle School. From Ashland, take US 60 west from town and turn right at West Summit Rd.

Cochran Hill Dog Run
Cochran Hill Road
Louisville, KY
502-291-6873
Located at the 409 acre Cherokee Park, this doggy run area covers about 2 divided acres for large and small dogs. Usage is by permit only and can be obtained by the Louisville Dog Run Association either on line or at 291 N Hubbards Lane. Dogs must be sociable, current on all vaccinations, and under their owner's control at all times.

Sawyer Dog Park
Freys Hill Road
Louisville, KY
502-291-6873
Located at the 369 acre E.P. Sawyer State Park, this doggy play area covers 4 acres divided into 2 two acre sections; one for all dogs, and one for dogs under 30 pounds. Usage is by permit only and can be obtained by the Louisville Dog Run Association either on line or at 291 N Hubbards Lane. Dogs must be sociable, current on all vaccinations, and under their owner's control at all times.

Vettiner Dog Run
Mary Dell Road
Louisville, KY
502-291-6873

Located behind the tennis courts at the 283 acre Charlie Vettiner Park, this doggy play area offers 2 one acre sections; one for all dogs, and one for dogs under 30 pounds. Usage is by permit only and can be obtained by the Louisville Dog Run Association either on line or at 291 N Hubbards Lane. Dogs must be sociable, current on all vaccinations, and under their owner's control at all times.

Kennel Resorts
5825 Meadowview Drive
Milford, KY
kentonpawpark.com
There are 2 enclosed doggy areas at this park; they are open from sunrise to sunset with shade trees, water, benches, tables, litter bags, and a scenic creek setting. Dogs must be sociable, current on all vaccinations, and under their owner's control at all times.

Louisiana

Forest Park Dog Park
13950 Harrell's Ferry Road
Baton Rouge, LA
225-752-1853
There are separate areas here for small and large dogs with shaded park benches in both areas, and water for hounds and humans near the entrance. Dogs must be sociable, current on all vaccinations, licensed, and under their owner's control at all times. Dogs must be leashed when not in designated off-lead areas.

Raising Cane's Dog Park
1442 City Park Avenue
Baton Rouge, LA
225-272-9200
brec.org
Located at the City Brooks Community Park, this off leash area has separate sections for large and small dogs, and they are open from dawn to dusk. Dogs must be sociable, current on all vaccinations and license, and under their owner's control at all times. Dogs must be leashed when not in designated off-lead areas.

Calcasieu Parish Animal Control
Public Dog Park
5500-A Swift Plant Rd.
Lake Charles, LA
337-439-8879

This fenced off-leash dog park is open daily from dawn to dusk.

Maine

Little Long Pond Leash-Free Area
near Seal Harbor
Bar Harbor, ME
207-288-3338
This leash free area is a privately owned section of land bordering the Acadia National Park. The off-leash property is located near Seal Harbor on the east side of Long Pond. Pets must be leashed when on Acadia National Park property while accessing the leash-free area.

Kennebunk Dog Park
36 Sea Road
Kennebunk, ME
207-985-3244
This popular, fenced off leash area offers a natural environment setting, benches, and year round accessibility from dawn to dusk. Dogs must be sociable, current on all vaccinations and license, and under their owner's control at all times. Dogs must be leashed when not in designated off-lead areas.

Old Orchard Beach Dog Park
Memorial Park at 1st St.
Old Orchard Park, ME
207-934-0860
This fenced dog park is open 24 hours a day. It is located in Memorial Park.

Capisic Pond Park
Capisic Street
Portland, ME
207-874-8793
Dogs can be off-leash in this park but need to be under direct voice control. People need to make sure they pick up their dog's waste with a plastic bag and throw it away in a trash can. There is no fenced off-leash area in the park.

Eastern Promenade Park Off-Leash Area
Cutter Street
Portland, ME
207-874-8793
Dogs are allowed off-leash under direct voice control during certain hours and only within the perimeter bounded by the Portland House Property, the water side of the Eastern Prominade, and Cutter Street following the curve of the

parking lot. Fort Allen Park is not part of the off-leash area. Off-leash play is allowed from April 15 to October 15, from 5am to 9am and from 5pm to 10pm daily. From October 16 through April 14, the off-leash hours are from 5am to 10pm daily.

Hall School Woods
23 Orono Road
Portland, ME
207-874-8793
Dogs can be off-leash in the woods near this school, but need to be under direct voice control. Dogs need to be leashed except for when in this special area. People need to make sure they pick up their dog's waste with a plastic bag and throw it away in a trash can.

Jack School Dog Run
North St. and Washington Ave.
Portland, ME
207-874-8793
Dogs can be off-leash in this area, but need to be under direct voice control. The leash free area is located behind Jack School. Dogs need to be leashed except for when in this special area. People need to make sure they pick up their dog's waste with a plastic bag and throw it away in a trash can.

Pine Grove Park
Harpswell Road
Portland, ME
207-874-8793
Dogs can be off-leash in this park but need to be under direct voice control. People need to make sure they pick up their dog's waste with a plastic bag and throw it away in a trash can.

Portland Arts & Technology School Dog Run
196 Allen Avenue
Portland, ME
207-874-8793
Dogs can be off-leash in the woods behind this school, but need to be under direct voice control. Dogs need to be leashed except for when in this special area. People need to make sure they pick up their dog's waste with a plastic bag and throw it away in a trash can.

Riverton Park
Riverside Street
Portland, ME
207-874-8793
Dogs can be off-leash in this park but need to be under direct voice control. People need to make sure they pick up their dog's waste with a plastic bag and throw it away in a trash can.

University Park
Harvard Street
Portland, ME
207-874-8793
Dogs can be off-leash in this park but need to be under direct voice control. People need to make sure they pick up their dog's waste with a plastic bag and throw it away in a trash can.

Valley Street Park
Valley St.
Portland, ME
207-874-8793
Dogs can be off-leash in this park but need to be under direct voice control. People need to make sure they pick up their dog's waste with a plastic bag and throw it away in a trash can.

Maryland

Quiet Waters Dog Park
600 Quiet Waters Park Rd
Annapolis, MD
410-222-1777
friendsofquietwaterspark.org
This fenced off-leash dog park is located between the South River and Harness Creek in Quiet Waters Park. There is a separate fenced dog park for small and older dogs. The dog park is next to the dog beach (see separate listing).

Canton Dog Park
Clinton & Toone Streets
Baltimore, MD
410-396-7900
This fenced dog park has two areas. One is for small dogs and one is for larger dogs. Water is provided and the dog park is open during daylight hours. To get to the park, take the I-95 Boston Street Exit, then west to Clinton Street. Turn right on Clinton Street.

Bowie Dog Park
Northview Drive and Enfield Drive
Bowie, MD
This one acre fenced dog park has two areas, one for larger dogs and one for small or shy dogs.

Black Hills Regional Park Dog Park
20930 Lake Ridge Rd
Boyds, MD
301-972-9396
mc-dog.org/black_hill.html

This fenced dog park is located in the Black Hills Regional Park. The park also has over ten miles of trails to hike with your leashed dog.

Worthington Park
8170 Hillsborough Road
Ellicott City, MD
410-313-PARK (7275)
This 2.7 acre off-lead dog area has a separate section for smaller or older dogs. All users of the park must have a permit; daily permits can be obtained on site. Dogs must have current vaccine and license tags. Sanitary stations are available, and they suggest bringing a non-glass water bowl for your pet (water available on site 4-15/11-01). Dogs must be under their owner's control and cleaned up after at all times. Dogs must be on leash when out of the off-lead area. The inclement weather line is 410-313-4455.

Green Run Dog Park
Bickerstaff Rd and I-370
Gaithersburg, MD
This dog park is run by the city of Gaithersburg and charges a $25 fee for non-residents to use the park.

Ridge Road Recreational Dog Park
21155 Frederick Road
Germantown, MD
301-972-9396
mc-dog.org/ridge_rd.html
This is a fenced off-leash dog park.

Laurel Dog Park
Brock Bridge Road
Laurel, MD
410-222-7317
This fenced dog park has two areas, one for larger dogs and one for small or shy dogs.

Ocean City Dog Park
94th Street
Ocean City, MD
There is a fenced dog park with separate areas for larger and smaller dogs. This is the only area within Ocean City where dogs may be off-leash on public property. Dogs must be registered with the town before using the park. There is an annual pass for residents and a weekly pass for visitors.

Wheaton Regional Park Dog Exercise Area
11717 Orebaugh Ave
Silver Spring, MD
301-680-3803

mc-dog.org/wheaton_main.html
This fenced off-leash dog park is located in Wheaton Regional Park. Use the Orebaugh Ave entrance to the park.

Massachusetts

Boston Common Off-Leash Dog Hours
Beacon Street/H 2
Boston, MA
617-635-4505
Well-behaved dogs under solid verbal control are allowed off-leash in the Boston Common between the hours of 6 am to 9 am and 4 pm - 8 pm. Please observe any signs with areas where dogs are not allowed or must be on leash.

Peters Park Dog Run
E. Berkeley and Washington St.
Boston, MA
peterspark.org/
This off-leash dog park is located in South Boston on East Berkeley Street between Shawmut and Washington Streets.

Cambridge Dog Park
Mt. Auburn and Hawthorne
Cambridge, MA
617-349-4800
This dog park is located at Mount Auburn and Hawthorne Streets. Dogs need to be under voice control. Please remember to clean up after your dog.

Danehy Park
99 Sherman Street
Cambridge, MA
617-349-4800
This park is a 50 acre recreational facility that was built on a former city landfill. There is a unfenced leash free area located with this park. The park is located in North Cambridge, on Sherman Street, adjacent to Garden and New Streets.

Fort Washington Park
Waverly Street
Cambridge, MA
This park offers an off-leash dog run. Dogs need to be under voice control. The park is located on Waverly Street between Erie Street and Putnam Avenue. Please remember to clean up after your dog.

French Park Dog Park
Baldwin Hill Road

Egremont, MA
413-528-0182
This fenced, off-leash dog park is located in French Park. It is open during daylight hours.

Stoddard's Neck Dog Run
Route 3A
Hingham, MA
Stoddard's Neck is an unfenced, large off-leash park where dogs can run off-leash. It is surrounded on three sides by water and there is only one entrance from land. You can hike while your dog runs off-leash on the approximately one mile round trip path.There are swimming areas for your pup in the harbor. The park is located on the west side of Hingham on Route 3A. There is a gate at the entrance to the peninsula.

Henry Garnsey Canine Recreation Park
Cottage Street and Village Street
Medway, MA
medwaydogpark.com
This fenced off-leash dog park allows your dog to stretch his legs off-leash.

Pilgrim Bark Park
Corner of Shank Painter Road and H 6
Provincetown, MA
508-487-1325
provincetowndogpark.org/
Located next to the Cumberland Farms, this off leash park offers almost an acre of play area with 2 sections; one being for dogs less than 25 pounds. Dogs must be sociable, current on all vaccinations and license, and under their owner's control at all times. Dogs must be leashed when not in designated off-lead areas.

Sharon Dog Park
East Foxboro Street
Sharon, MA
sharondogpark.org
This dog park is fenced, and is about one acre in size. It is free to use and has water, benches and a few trees. The dog park is located on East Foxboro Street about 1/4 mile from Sharon Center near the skateboard park. Park near the skateboard park and follow the walking trail to the dog park.

Nunziato Field
22 Vinal Avenue
Somerville, MA
617-947-1191
This neighborhood doggy play area

offers a stone dust even surface, trees, and benches. Dogs must be sociable, current on all vaccinations, licensed, and under their owner's control at all times. Dogs must be leashed when not in designated off-lead areas.

Michigan

Shaggy Pines Dog Park
3895 Cherry Lane SE
Ada, MI
616-676-9464
shaggypines.com
This is a 20 acre private dog park featuring a fenced dog park, one mile jogging trail, a large sand pile for climbing, a dog swimming pond, and a small dog area. A membership is required to use the park. These fees are $24 and up per month for the first dog and $5 and up per month for each additional dog. Visitors to the area may use the park on Sundays from 10 to 5 for an $8 per day fee for the first dog and $2.50 per additional dog.

Clinton Township Dog Park
Romeo Plank Rd
Clinton Township, MI
586-286-9336
This fenced dog park is located at the Clinton Township Civic Center. There is a fee for non-residents to use the park.

Frankenmuth Hund Platz
624 E Tuscola
Frankenmuth, MI
989-652-3440
Located at Memorial Park, this off lead area offers benches, sun and shade, and dog agility equipment; visitors should bring their own water. Dogs must be sociable and current on all vaccinations.

E-Z Dog Park and Training Center
230 Norlynn Dr
Howell, MI
810-229-7353
ezdogpark.com/
This off-leash dog park is privately owned and includes a fenced dog park and an agility center. The agility center includes indoor facilities. Fees to use the dog park are $40 per month or $8 per visit per dog. The facility is open 24 hours a day every day of the year. The dog park is for dogs larger than about 25 pounds, smaller dogs may use the agility

center. From I-96 west take exit 145 (Grand River) and turn right at the exit. Turn right on Hacker in 7/10 mile, and go 3.3 miles to the facility. Hacker will become a gravel road before the facility.

Orion Oaks Dog Park
2301 Clarkston Road
Lake Orion, MI
248-858-0906
There are 14 fenced, doggy recreational acres at this 927 acre park that has a smaller section fenced for the little pooches, plenty of wide open spaces, two trails, lake access, and woods to explore. Benches, picnic tables, benches, water, and portable toilets are on site. A daily pass or annual vehicle permit is required, and although they can usually be purchased at the park, they suggest they be gotten prior to arrival (sometimes they run out). Dogs must be sociable, current on all vaccinations, licensed, and under their owner's control at all times. Dogs must be leashed on no more than a 6 foot leash when not in designated off-lead areas.

Soldan Dog Park
1601 East Cavanaugh Road
Lansing, MI
Located at the Hawk Island Park, there are more than 17 diverse acres for pooches to explore here. They have a large pond, a spacious open field, drinking fountains for hounds and humans, an enclosed area for small dogs, and sanitary stations. A variety of doggy events also happen here. Dogs must be sociable, current on all vaccinations and license, and under their owner's control at all times. Dogs must be leashed when not in designated off-lead areas.

Behnke Memorial Dog Park
300 N Groesbeck Highway
Mount Clemens, MI
This fully fenced dog park is open from 7 am to 11 pm. There are benches, tables and water.

Cummingston Park Dog Run
Torquay & Leafdale
Royal Oak, MI
248-246-3300
This is an unfenced dog run area located in part of Cummingston Park. Dogs must be on leash in all areas of the park that are not designated as off-leash. Dogs must be cleaned up after throughout the park.

Mark Twain Park Dog Run
Campbell Rd, South of 14 Mile

Royal Oak, MI
248-246-3300
This is an unfenced dog run area located in part of Mark Twain Park. Dogs must be on leash in all areas of the park that are not designated as off-leash. Dogs must be cleaned up after throughout the park.

Quickstad Park Dog Run
Marais between Normandy & Lexington
Royal Oak, MI
248-246-3300
This is an unfenced dog run area located in part of Quckstad Park. Dogs must be on leash in all areas of the park that are not designated as off-leash. Dogs must be cleaned up after throughout the park.

Wagner Park Dog Run
Detroit Ave, between Rochester and Main
Royal Oak, MI
248-246-3300
This is an unfenced dog run area located in part of Wagner Park. Dogs must be on leash in all areas of the park that are not designated as off-leash. Dogs must be cleaned up after throughout the park.

Saline Dog Park
W. Bennett St
Saline, MI
This dog park is fenced on 3 sides with a pond on the 4th side. Dogs may swim in the pond. From US-12 in Saline go north on Ann Arbor Street and left on W. Bennett St. The dog park is located in Mill Pond Park.

Hines Park Dog Park
Hawthorne Ridge west of Merriman
Westland, MI
This 3 acre dog park requires a registration and that you sign a waiver before using the park. You may register at Wayne County Administrative Offices at 33175 Ann Arbor Trl in Westland. The park is open from dawn to dusk year round.

Lyon Oaks Dog Park
52221 Pontiac Trail
Wixom, MI
248-437-7345
There are 13 fenced, doggy recreational acres at this 1, 043 acre park with a smaller section fenced for the little pooches. Benches, picnic tables, benches, a water fountain, and portable toilets are on site. A daily pass or annual vehicle permit is required, and although they can usually be

purchased at the park, they suggest they be gotten prior to arrival (sometimes they run out). Dogs must be sociable, current on all vaccinations, and under their owner's control at all times. Dogs must be leashed on no more than a 6 foot leash when not in designated off-lead areas. Dogs are not allowed on the nature trails or the golf course.

Minnesota

Bloomington Off-leash Recreation Area
111th Street
Bloomington, MN
952-563-8892
This huge fenced 25 acre dog park is located at 111th Street, between Nesbitt and Hampshire Ave. The site features a swimming pond for your dog, hills, trees and grass.

Alimagnet Dog Park
1200 Alimagnet Parkway
Burnsville, MN
alimagnetdogpark.org
This fenced dog park is fully fenced and lit for nighttime use. It is open daily from 5 am to 10 pm. There is a dog washing station, a pond, and a separate small and timid dog run. The dog park is located on County Road 11 two blocks north of County Road 42.

Dakota Woods Dog Park
16470 Blaine Ave.
Coates, MN
651-437-3191
This is a 16 acre, fenced and wooded dog park. From US 52 exit at County Rd 46 (160th St E) and head west one mile. Turn left on Blaine Ave to the dog park. The park is open daily from 5 am to 10 pm. There is a $40 fee for an annual pass or visitors can pay $5 for a daily pass which may be purchased at the park.

Bryant Lake Regional Park Dog Park
6800 Rowland Road
Eden Prairie, MN
763-694-7764
threeriversparkdistrict.org
This is a 9-acre fenced off-leash area with a pond and a separate space for small dogs. A daily or annual pass is required. A daily pass is $5 and can be purchased at the park. An annual pass is $30 and covers all persons and dogs in the household. If a

second pass is desired, it is $15. To purchase an annual pass, call 763-559-9000 or visit threeriversparkdistrict.org.

Crow-Hassan Park Reserve Off-Leash Area
11629 Crow-Hassan Park Road
Hanover, MN
763-694-7860
threeriversparkdistrict.org
The off-leash area is 40 acres, unfenced, with access to the Crow River. A daily or annual pass is required. A daily pass is $5 and can be purchased at the park. An annual pass is $30 and covers all persons and dogs in the household. If a second pass is desired, it is $15. To purchase an annual pass, call 763-559-9000 or visit threeriversparkdistrict.org .

Battle Creek Dog Park
Lower Afton Rd E at McKnight Rd S
Maplewood, MN
651-748-2500
This more than ten acre off-leash area is fenced along part of its perimeter but is not completely fenced. The off-leash park is located just north of Lower Afton and McKnight. There are no permit requirements at this off-leash park.

Franklin Terrace Off-Leash Rec Area
Franklin Terrace at SE Franklin Ave
Minneapolis, MN
612-230-6400
This 1.6 acre dog park is located just south of I-94 adjacent to Riverside Park. Enter from Franklin Terrace or W. River Parkway. An annual permit is required to use Minneapolis dog parks. The cost is $40 for city residents and $60 for non-residents. You can get the permit at the website, 212 17th Ave N. or by calling 612-348-4250.

Lake of the Isles Off-Leash Rec Area
Lake of the Isles Pkwy at W. 28th St
Minneapolis, MN
612-230-6400
This 3.6 acre dog park is located next to the soccer field on the south end of Lake of the Isles. Enter the park from Lake of the Isles Parkway. An annual permit is required to use Minneapolis dog parks. The cost is $40 for city residents and $60 for non-residents. You can get the permit at the website, 212 17th Ave N. or by calling 612-348-4250.

Loring Park Off-Leash Dog Park
Maple St at Harmon Place
Minneapolis, MN

This 10,000 square foot fenced dog park opened on June 27, 2007. Located in downtown Minneapolis, the park is noteworthy for art sculptures in the dogpark. An annual permit is required to use Minneapolis dog parks. The cost is $40 for city residents and $60 for non-residents. You can get the permit at the website, 212 17th Ave N. or by calling 612-348-4250.

Minnehaha Off-Leash Rec Area
54th St and Hiawatha Ave
Minneapolis, MN
612-230-6400
This 4.3 acre dog park is located on the south end of Minnehaha Park. There is a parking lot off of 54th Street and a walking path to the dog park. An annual permit is required to use Minneapolis dog parks. The cost is $40 for city residents and $60 for non-residents. You can get the permit at the website, 212 17th Ave N. or by calling 612-348-4250.

St. Anthony Parkway Off-Leash Rec Area
St. Anthony Parkway
Minneapolis, MN
612-230-6400
This 2.3 acre dog park is located south of St. Anthony Parkway between Central Ave NE and 5th St. NE. An annual permit is required to use Minneapolis dog parks. The cost is $40 for city residents and $60 for non-residents. You can get the permit at the website, 212 17th Ave N. or by calling 612-348-4250.

Elm Creek Park Reserve Off-Leash Area
Elm Creek Rd at Zachary Lane N
Osseo, MN
763-559-9000
This is a large and fenced 30 acre off-leash area with a pond. A daily or annual pass is required. A daily pass is $5 and can be purchased at the park. An annual pass is $30 and covers all persons and dogs in the household. If a second pass is desired, it is $15. To purchase an annual pass, call 763-559-9000 or visit www.threeriversparkdistrict.org.

Cleary Lake Regional Park Dog Park
Eagle Creek Ave SE at Texas Ave
Prior Lake, MN
763-559-9000
This is a large and fenced 28 acre off-leash area with a pond. A daily or annual pass is required. A daily pass is $5 and can be purchased at the park. An annual pass is $30 and

covers all persons and dogs in the household. If a second pass is desired, it is $15. To purchase an annual pass, call 763-559-9000 or visit www.threeriversparkdistrict.org. Outside of the off-leash area there is a 1.1 mile hiking trail for people with leashed dogs.

Lake Sarah Regional Park Off-Leash Area
S Lake Sarah Dr at W Lake Sarah Drive
Rockford, MN
763-559-9000
threeriversparkdistrict.org
The off-leash area is 40 acres. It is partially fenced. A daily or annual pass is required. A daily pass is $5 and can be purchased at the park. An annual pass is $30 and covers all persons and dogs in the household. If a second pass is desired, it is $15. To purchase an annual pass, call 763-559-9000 or visit threeriversparkdistrict.org .

Woodview Off-Leash Area
Kent St at Larpenteur Ave W
Roseville, MN
651-748-2500
This off-leash dog area is located north of Larpenteur between Dale and Rice. There is a partially fenced area for larger dogs and a fenced area for small dogs. Larpenteur is a busy street and the off-leash area is not fenced on this side. There are no permit requirements at this off-leash park.

Rice Creek North Trail Corridor Off-Leash Area
Lexington Avenue at County Road J
Shoreview, MN
651-748-2500
This large, unfenced off-leash area is 12 acres in size. There is a pond in the off-leash area. From Lexington Ave and County Road J go south to the park. There are no permit requirements at this off-leash park.

Arlington Arkwright Off-Leash Dog Area
Arlington Ave E at Arkwright St
St Paul, MN
651-266-8989
This 4.5 acre fenced dog park is maintained by Responsible Owners of Mannerly Pets of Ramsey County. It is open from sunrise to 9 pm daily. There is no water at the park so please bring your own water.

Carver Park Reserve Off-Leash Dog Park
7025 Victoria Drive

St. Louis

Victoria, MN
763-694-7650
threeriversparkdistrict.org
This is a 27-acre fenced off-leash area, including a separate space for small dogs. A daily or annual pass is required. A daily pass is $5 and can be purchased at the park. An annual pass is $30 and covers all persons and dogs in the household. If a second pass is desired, it is $15. To purchase an annual pass, call 763-559-9000 or visit threeriversparkdistrict.org.

Otter Lake Regional Park Dog Park
County Rd H2 E at Otter Lake Rd
White Bear, MN
651-748-2500
This ten acre off-leash area is fenced along part of its perimeter but is not completely fenced. There is a one acre fenced area for small dogs. The off-leash park is located just south of County Rd H2 and Otter Lake. There are no permit requirements at this off-leash park.

Missouri

Broemmelsiek Park
Schwede and Wilson Roads
Defiance, MO
636-949-7535
In the interest of preserving green space, this 494-acre park spotlights its natural features, and offers miles of trails, a fishing lake, and picnic areas in addition to the off-leash dog area. Natural, equestrian, and bike paths, as well as the off-leash dog park, are closed during inclement weather to preserve the areas; call 636-949-7475 to get park conditions. Dogs must be sociable, current on all vaccinations, and under their owner's control at all times. Dogs must be leashed when not in designated off-lead areas.

Penn Valley Off-Leash Park
Pershing Road and Main Street
Kansas City, MO
816-513-7500
In addition to the 2.7 acre, double gated dog park, this 130 acre recreation area also offers an exercise trail, playing fields, a 3 acre lake, the Liberty Memorial and the National WWII museum. Dogs are allowed throughout the park, and they must be leashed when not in the off-lead area. There are water fountains for hounds and humans,

and the dog park is open from dawn to 1 hour after dusk. Dogs must be under their owner's control at all times.

Wayside Waifs Bark Park
3901 Martha Truman Rd
Kansas City, MO
816-761-8151
waysidewaifs.org
This off leash park provides water and cleanup stations in a fenced area. This a private park that charges a fee for residents and non-residents.

DuSable Dog Park
2598 N Main Street
St Charles, MO
636-949-3372
This 2½ acre off lead area offers 2 equal sized play areas for large and small dogs. Restrooms are available here. Dogs must be sociable, current on all vaccinations, and under their owner's control at all times. Dogs must be leashed when not in designated off-lead areas.

Lister Dog Park
Taylor Rd and Olive St
St Louis, MO
stldogparks.org
This off leash dog park is located in Central West End for residents only. There are no day passes and there is an annual fee. The dog park offers a fenced in area, water and cleanup stations, and it is lighted in the evenings.

Shaw Neighborhood Dog Park
Thurman and Cleveland Ave
St Louis, MO
stldogparks.org
This fenced in area is an off-leash park for dogs. It is open 6am-10pm with lighting available in the evenings. The dog park offers water and cleanup stations. There are no day passes but there are annual passes for a fee to both residents and nonresidents.

Taylor Dog Park
Taylor Rd
St Louis, MO
stldogparks.org
This off leash dog park is located in the Central West End for residents only. There is an annual fee to use the park. No day passes are available. The park is fenced and lit in the evenings.

Quail Ridge Park

Quail Ridge Rd
Wentzville, MO
stldogparks.org
The dog park hours are from dawn until dusk. Dogs to have to be leashed outside of the fenced in off-leash area. This park features a six feet high fence, bathrooms, water fountains (for dogs and people) and cleanup stations. It is located in the suburbs of St Louis.

Montana

Bozeman Dog Park
Highland Blvd at Haggerty Lane
Bozeman, MT
406-582-3200
bozeman.net/parks/parks.aspx
There is a fenced dog park at the south end of the Softball Complex at Highland Blvd and Haggerty Lane.

Burke Park
S. Church and E. Story
Bozeman, MT
406-582-3200
bozeman.net/parks/parks.aspx
Dogs are allowed off-leash under voice control in Burke Park which offers trails for walking and running as well as great views of Bozeman.

Jacob's Island Park Dog Park
off VanBuren Street
Missoula, MT
406-721-7275
ci.missoula.mt.us/parksrec/
This park has a dog park located at the east end of the park. This six acre fenced off-leash area includes a double-gate.

Nebraska

Meadowlark North Dog Park
30th Avenue at 39th Street
Kearney, NE
308-237-4644
This fairly new, fenced doggy play area is open from 7 am to 10 pm (or as posted), and future plans for the park include watering stations, benches, tables, and shade structures. For now be sure to bring water to the park. Dogs must be sociable, current on all vaccinations, licensed, and cleaned up after at all times. Dogs must be leashed when not in designated off-lead areas. The

dog park is on the west side of 30th Avenue between 39th and 40th Streets.

Holmes Lake Dog Run
70th Street
Lincoln, NE
402-441-7847
This 3 to 4 acre off-leash area is located across the street from Holmes Lake.

Off-Leash Dog Recreation Area
2201 South 13th Street
Norfolk, NE
402-844-2000
Located at the TaHaZouka Park, this off lead area offers two fenced sections; a .38 acre for small dogs and a 1.68 acre for larger dogs. The dog park has water, benches, doggy waste bags, lots of shade and a fire hydrant. Dogs must be sociable, current on all vaccinations and license, and under their owner's control at all times. Dogs must be leashed when not in designated off-lead areas.

Waggin' Tails Dog Park
S McDonald Street
North Platte, NE
308-535-6772
Visitors can park at the recreation center (1300 S McDonald) and walk to the off lead area. There are 2.4 fenced acres with water for hounds and humans, benches, and 2 separate fenced areas for large and small pets. Dogs must be sociable, current on all vaccinations and license, and under their owner's control at all times. Dogs must be leashed when not in designated off-lead areas.

Hefelinger Park Dog Park
112th Street and West Maple Road
Omaha, NE
402-444-5900
omahadogpark.org/
Seven acres have been set aside at this 67 acre recreational park for pooches to run free. Five acres are for all dogs, and a separate 2 acre side is set aside for small dogs. Dogs must be sociable, current on all vaccinations and license, and under their owner's control at all times. Dogs must be leashed when not in designated off-lead areas.

Dog Park
Off S Beltline Road
Scottsbluff, NE
308-630-6238
Located at Riverside Park behind the zoo, this off lead park offers separate

areas for passive and active dogs. Dogs must be sociable, current on all vaccinations, licensed, and cleaned up after at all times. Dogs must be leashed when not in designated off-lead areas.

Scottsbluff Dog Park
S Beltline Road
Scottsbluff, NE
308-630-6238
Located in Riverside Park behind the zoo, this off leash park features two sections for large and small dogs. It is surrounded by a 6 foot fence and offers some play items. There is no water at the park, but there are water bowls. Dogs must be sociable, current on all vaccinations and license, and under their owner's control at all times. Dogs must be leashed when not in designated off-lead areas.

Nevada

Acacia Park Dog Park
S Gibson Road and Las Palmas Entrada
Henderson, NV
702-267-4000
This fenced dog park is open daily from 6 am to midnight. The park is just south of I-215 at Gibson Rd.

Dos Escuelas Park Dog Park
1 Golden View Street
Henderson, NV
702-267-4000
This fenced dog park is open daily from 6 am to midnight. To get to the park, which is just south of I-215, take the S. Green Valley Pkwy exit and head south. Turn left onto Paseo Verde Pkwy and make a left onto Desert Shadow Trail. Turn left onto Rainbow View Street and left again onto Golden View Street. The park will be on the left.

Desert Breeze Dog Run
8425 W. Spring Mtn. Road
Las Vegas, NV
This dog park is fully enclosed with benches, trees, trash cans and water. There are three dog runs available, one for small dogs, one for middle sized dogs and one for larger dogs over 30 pounds. The park is located approximately 5 miles west of downtown Las Vegas and the Strip. From Flamingo Road/589 in downtown, head west

and pass Hwy 15. Turn right on Durango Drive. Then turn right onto Spring Mountain Road. The dog park is located off Spring Mountain Rd., between the Community Center and Desert Breeze County Park.

Desert Inn Dog Park
3570 Vista del Monte
Las Vegas, NV
702-455-8200
This fenced dog park is open daily from 6 am to 11 pm. The park is located off of Boulder Highway east of the 515 freeway. From Boulder Highway take Indios Avenue east to Twain Ave. Turn right on Twain and go two blocks. Turn left on VIsta Del Monte Drive to the park.

Dog Fancier's Park
5800 E. Flamingo Rd.
Las Vegas, NV
702-455-8200
Dog Fancier's Park is a 12 acre park that allows canine enthusiasts to train their dogs off leash. Owner's must still have control over their dogs and may be cited if their dogs (while off leash) interfere with other animals training at the park. This dog park has benches, poop bags and water taps.

Molasky Park Dog Run
1065 E. Twain Ave
Las Vegas, NV
702-455-8200
This fenced dog park is open daily from 6 am to 11 pm. To get to the dog park from the Strip take Flamingo Rd east past Paradise. Turn left (north) on Cambridge St and east on Twain Ave. The dog park is located between Cambridge St and Maryland Parkway on Twain.

Shadow Rock Dog Run
2650 Los Feliz on Sunrise Mountain
Las Vegas, NV
702-455-8200
This is a 1.5 acre dog park with benches, poop bags and water taps.

Silverado Ranch Park Dog Park
9855 S. Gillespie
Las Vegas, NV
702-455-8200
This fenced dog park is open daily from 6 am to 11 pm. The park is south of the Strip off of Las Vegas Blvd. From the Strip head south on Las Vegas Blvd and turn left onto Silverado Ranch Blvd. Turn right onto Gillespie and the park will be on the right.

Sunset Park Dog Run
2601 E. Sunset Rd
Las Vegas, NV
702-455-8200
Located in Sunset Park, this dog park offers about 1.5 acres of land for your pooch to play. The dog park has benches, poop bags and water taps.

Rancho San Rafael Regional Park
1595 North Sierra Street
Reno, NV
775-785-4512
Home to the annual Great Reno Balloon races, this huge park covers almost 600 acres of manicured turf, natural desert and wetlands, and has the largest off-leash space in the area. There is a pond and creek for dogs to play in with a walking path that surrounds it. Some of the amenities include benches, picnic areas, restrooms, and clean-up stations. Dogs must be on lead when not in the off leash areas, and there is signage indicating the areas in the park where pets are not allowed. Dogs must be cleaned up after at all times.

Sparks Marina Park
300 Howard Drive
Reno, NV
775-353-2376
This park has a 77 acre lake offering a wide variety of land and water activities and recreational pursuits. They also have the only fenced, off-lead dog park in the Reno area where dogs can play in the water. The off lead area is almost an acre in size on the south side of the marina and features lots of grass, 150 feet of shoreline, clean-up stations, a fire hydrant, and a doggie drinking fountain. The marina is surrounded by a walking trail almost 2 miles long that is lighted for nighttime walks with your pet. Dogs must be on leash when not in the fenced, off-lead area, and they must be cleaned up after at all times. Dogs are not allowed on any of the beaches.

Virginia Lake Dog Park
Lakeside Drive
Reno, NV
775-334-2099
ci.reno.nv.us
This one acre dog park includes mitt dispensers. The park is located at Mountain View and Lakeside Drive, at the north field.

Whitaker Dog Park
550 University Terrace
Reno, NV

775-334-2099
ci.reno.nv.us
This fenced dog park is about .75 acres. Amenities include mitt dispensers.

New Hampshire

Town of Derry Dog Park
45 Fordway
Derry, NH
603-432-6100
This half acre dog park is adjacent to the Derry Animal Control office. To get there from I-93, take exit #4/Route 102 towards Derry(east). Go about 1.5 miles and turn right onto Fordway. Go about 1/2 mile and arrive at the dog park at 45 Fordway.

Portsmouth Dog Park
South Mill Pond
Portsmouth, NH
603-431-2000
cityofportsmouth.com
This fenced dog park is located at the South Mill Pond. The South Mill Pond is located near downtown Portsmouth, south of the Pleasant Street and Junkins Avenue intersection. From I-93, take exit #4.

New Jersey

Bayonne Dog Park
1st Street at Kennedy Blvd
Bayonne, NJ
201-858-7181
This small dog park located next to Kill Van Kull Park in Bayonne is fully fenced and has shade and benches. The dog park is located behind the baseball park. The dog park is open during daylight hours.

Bedminster Dog Park
River Road at Rt 206
Bedminster, NJ
908-212-7014
bedminster.us
This fenced dog park located in Bedminster's River Road Park. The dog park is open during daylight hours.

RJ Miller Airpark Dog Park
Route 530
Berkeley Township, NJ
732-506-9090

ocean.nj.us/parks/Dogpark.pdf
There is a fenced off-leash dog park in RJ Miller Airpark. There are separate areas for large and small dogs. Children under 8 are not allowed in the dog park. Dogs must receive an Ocean County annual permit to use the dog parks in the county. The fee is $20 for the first dog and $10 for each additional dog. Dogs must have a valid dog license to be registered and male dogs must be neutered. See the website at http://www.ocean.nj.us/parks/Dogpark.pdf or call the parks department at 732-506-9090 for locations to register.

Cooper River Dog Park
North Park Drive at Cuthbert Blvd
Cherry Hill, NJ
856-795-PARK
This dog park has separate areas for large dogs and small dogs. The dog park has benches and lighting. To get to the park take the Cuthbert Blvd South Jughandle and turn onto North Park Drive. The dog park is at the east end of North Park Drive.

Pooch Park (Cooper River Park)
North Park Drive
Cherry Hill, NJ
856-225-5431
camdencounty.com
The Pooch Park portion of the park allows dogs to be unleashed in the fenced in area. The dog park offers water and cleanup stations, tables, and lighting. It is open 6am-10pm with no fee.

The Hunterdon County Off-Leash Dog Area
1020 State Route 31
Flemington, NJ
908-782-1158
This off lead doggy area offers 1.75 fenced acres with a scattering of trees for shade. There is no water available here, so water for pets is highly recommended. Dogs must be leashed going into and out of the off-lead area, and cleaned up after at all times. Dogs must be spayed or neutered, and puppies under 6 months old are prohibited.

Veteran's Park Dog Park
Kuser Road
Hamilton, NJ
This fenced dog park is located in Veterans Park. Use the park entrance on Kuser Rd and go 1500 feet into the park to the dogpark on the right. There are separate areas for big dogs and little dogs.

Church Square Dog Run
4th and 5th, between Garden and Willow
Hoboken, NJ
There are two dog runs in Church Square Park. One is for larger dogs and another for small dogs only.

Elysian Park Dog Run
Hudson between 10th and 11th
Hoboken, NJ
There is an off-leash dog run in the park.

Stevens Park Dog Run
Hudson between 4th and 5th
Hoboken, NJ
There is an off-leash dog run in the park.

Van Vorst Dog Park
Jersrey Avenue and Montgomery Street
Jersey City, NJ
201-433-5127
stevenfulop.com/dogrun.htm
This nicely landscaped neighborhood dog park offers separate sections for large and small dogs, water spouts, and benches. Dogs must be sociable, current on all vaccinations, licensed, and cleaned up after at all times. Dogs must be leashed when not in designated off-lead areas.

Ocean County Park Dog Park
Route 88
Lakewood, NJ
732-506-9090
ocean.nj.us/parks/Dogpark.pdf
There is a clean, fenced off-leash dog park in Ocean County Park. There are separate areas for large and small dogs. Children under 8 are not allowed in the dog park. Dogs must receive an Ocean County annual permit to use the dog parks in the county. The fee is $20 for the first dog and $10 for each additional dog. Dogs must have a valid dog license to be registered and male dogs must be neutered. See the website at http://www.ocean.nj.us/parks/Dogpark.pdf or call the parks department at 732-506-9090 for locations to register.

Overpeck County Park Dog Run
Fort Lee Road
Leonia, NJ
201-336-7275
There is an official Bergen County off-leash dog run area in Overpeck County Park.

Thompson Park Dog Park
805 Newman Springs Road

Lincroft, NJ
732-842-4000x4256
This fenced off-leash dog park is located in Thompson Park adjacent to the Craft Center. Access the area using the park maintenance entrance which is west of the park gate and follow the road to the end and turn right.

Riverside County Park Dog Run
Riverside Ave
Lyndhurst, NJ
201-336-7275
There is an official Bergen County off-leash dog run area in Riverside County Park.

Freedom Park Dog Park
Union Street at Main Street
Medford, NJ
609-654-2512
This dog park is located in Medford's Freedom Park. It has benches, water and shade trees.

Essex County South Mountain Dog Park
Crest Drive
Millburn, NJ
973-268-3500
In addition to an honorary memorial to lost rescue dogs of 911, this 2 acre, 2 sectioned doggy park offers agility equipment, benches, drinking fountains for hounds and humans, a washing station, walking paths, and waste dispenser stations. Dogs must be sociable, current on all vaccinations, licensed, and cleaned up after at all times. Dogs must be leashed when not in designated off-lead areas.

Hudson County Park Dog Park
Bergenline Ave at 81st
North Bergen, NJ
201-915-1386
hudsoncountynj.org
This fenced dog park is lit for evening use and has trees and benches. Dogs must be on leash outside of the dog run area in the rest of the 170 acre park. The dog park is behind the North Bergen High School stadium.

Cape May County Dog Park
45th Street and Haven Avenue
Ocean City, NJ
oceancitydogpark.org/
This off lead area is by membership; yearly or weekly summer passes are available. Paw Passes can be obtained at the City Hall at 9th Street and Asbury Avenue or on-line. The park has 3

sections on about an acre, with benches, a shaded pavilion, drinking fountains for hounds and humans, and agility equipment. Dogs must be sociable, have proof of vaccinations, be licensed, and cleaned up after at all times. Dogs must be leashed when not in designated off-lead areas.

Rocky Top Private Dog Park
4106 Route 27
Princeton, NJ
732-297-6527
rockytopdogpark.com
This private dog park is located on 2 acres in Princeton. They offer weekly, monthly and yearly plans and also options for single visits. For non-members there is usually afternoon hours on weekends to visit the park. For details please check with the website at rockytopdogpark.com or call.

Mercer County Park
Old Trenton Road at Robbinsville Rd
West Windsor, NJ
609-448-1947
The dog park, located within the 2500 acre Mercer County Park, has separate areas for large and small dogs. It is open during daylight hours. Dogs must be on leash outside of the fenced dog park. The Trenton Kennel Dog Show is held in the park annually.

Echo Lake Dog Park
Rt 22
Westfield, NJ
908-527-4900
This 3 acre, fenced off-leash dog park is open during daylight hours. The park is located just off Rt 22 East on the Mountainside/Westfield border. The park is managed by the Union County Department of Parks.

Wood Dale County Park Dog Run
Prospect Avenue
Woodcliff Lake, NJ
201-336-7275
There is an official Bergen County off-leash dog run area in Wood Dale County Park.

New Mexico

Coronado Dog Park
301 McKnight Ave. NW
Albuquerque, NM
505-768-1975
cabq.gov/pets/dogpark.html

This fenced dog park is open from 6 am to 10 pm daily. It is located in Coronado Park. Please bring your own water for your dog as there is none at the park. From I-40 take Exit 159A (4th/2nd Street), head east on the frontage road and turn right onto 3rd Street to the park.

Los Altos Dog Park *Ok*
821 Eubank Blvd. NE
Albuquerque, NM
505-768-1975
cabq.gov/pets/dogpark.html
This fenced off-leash dog park is open from 6 am to 10 pm daily. The dog park is located in Los Altos Park. Please bring your own water for your dog as none is available at the park. From I-40 take Eubank Blvd (Exit 165). Head north on Eubank 1/4 mile and the park is on the left.

Homeless Here?

Montessa Park Off-Leash Area
3615 Los Picaros Rd SE
Albuquerque, NM
505-768-1975
cabq.gov/pets/dogpark.html
This unfenced off-leash area is located in Montessa Park. There is minimal shade here and you need to bring water for your dog as none is provided. From I-25 take the Rio Bravo Exit and go west. Turn left on Broadway, left on Bobby Foster and left on Los Picasos to the off-leash area.

Rio Grande Park Dog Park
Iron Avenue
Albuquerque, NM
505-873-6620
cabq.gov/gis/park.htm
Rio Grande Park offers a designated off-leash area for dogs. The dog park is located on Iron Avenue, between Alcalde Place and 14th Street.

Roosevelt Park Dog Park
Hazeldine Avenue
Albuquerque, NM
505-873-6620
cabq.gov/gis/park.htm
Roosevelt Park offers a designated off-leash area for dogs. The park is located off Hazeldine Avenue, between Cedar and Maple Streets.

Santa Fe Village Dog Park
5700 Bogart St. NW
Albuquerque, NM
505-768-1975
cabq.gov/pets/dogpark.html
This fenced dog park is open from 6 am to 10 pm daily. Please bring water for your dog as none is available at the dog park. To get to the dog park from I-40 take the

Unser exit (Exit 154) and go north on Unser. Turn left on Bogart to the park.

Tom Bolack Urban Forest Dog Park
Haines Avenue
Albuquerque, NM
505-873-6620
cabq.gov/gis/park.htm
Tom Bolack Park offers a designated off-leash area for dogs. The park is located near Haines Avenue and San Pedro Drive.

USS Bullhead Dog Park
1606 San Pedro SE
Albuquerque, NM
505-768-1975
cabq.gov/pets/dogpark.html
This Fenced off-leash dog park is located in USS Bullhead Park. Take I-25 to Gibson Blvd, head east on Gibson to San Pedro Blvd, and turn right to the park. There is no drinking water available at the park for dogs so please bring your own.

Rainbow Dog Park
Southern Blvd at Atlantic
Rio Rancho, NM
This fenced dog park is located in Rainbow Park. It has water for dogs and people and has limited shade. It can get extremely hot here in the summer. There is a separate small dog area. Rainbow Park is located on the far west side of Rio Rancho north of the Petroglyph National Monument west of Albuquerque.

Frank Ortiz Park Off-Leash Area
Camino Las Crucitas
Santa Fe, NM
505-955-2100
santafenm.gov/parks/index.asp
This off-leash area is located in Frank Ortiz park which used to be the old landfill. To get there from town, head west on Paseo De Paralta towards St. Francis. When you come to St. Francis, do not turn left or right, but instead go across to Camino Las Crucitas Street. Follow this road which takes you through the Casa Solana residential neighborhood. The park has a large field on the left where the off-leash area is located.

New York

Department of General Services Off Lead Area

Erie Blvd
Albany, NY
518-434-CITY (2489)
This off lead area sit just north of the I 90 bridge overpass. Dogs must be sociable, current on all vaccinations, and under their owner's control at all times. Dogs must be leashed when not in designated off-lead areas.

Hartman Road Dog Park
Hartman Road
Albany, NY
518-434-CITY (2489)
Only a ½ mile past the Thruway Bridge, this off lead area sits adjacent to the Community Garden. Dogs must be sociable, current on all vaccinations, and under their owner's control at all times. Dogs must be leashed when not in designated off-lead areas.

Normanskill Farm Dog Park
Mill Road/Delaware Avenue
Albany, NY
518-434-CITY (2489)
Off the beaten track a bit makes for a nice setting for an off leash area. Dogs must be sociable, current on all vaccinations, and under their owner's control at all times. Dogs must be leashed when not in designated off-lead areas.

Westland Hills Dog Park
Anthony Street
Albany, NY
518-434-CITY (2489)
This off lead area is located in Westland Hills Park. Dogs must be sociable, current on all vaccinations, and under their owner's control at all times. Dogs must be leashed when not in designated off-lead areas.

Kelly Park Dog Run
Ralph Street
Ballston Spa, NY
518-885-9220
There is a fenced dog run in Kelly Park. Kelly Park is located where Ralph Street intersects with Malta Avenue (Route 63).

Ewen Park Dog Run
Riverdale to Johnson Aves., South of West 232nd St.
Bronx, NY
212-NEW-YORK (311 in NYC)
This is an official off-leash dog run. All New York City Off-leash Dog Parks are run by the New York City Parks Department.

Frank S. Hackett Park Dog Run
Riverdale Ave. and W. 254th Street

Bronx, NY
212-NEW-YORK (311 in NYC)
This is an official off-leash dog run.
All New York City Off-leash Dog
Parks are run by the New York City
Parks Department.

Pelham Bay Park Dog Run
Middletown Rd. & Stadium Ave.,
Northwest of Parking Lot
Bronx, NY
212-NEW-YORK (311 in NYC)
This is an official off-leash dog run.
All New York City Off-leash Dog
Parks are run by the New York City
Parks Department.

Seton Park Dog Run
West 232nd St. & Independence
Ave.
Bronx, NY
212-NEW-YORK (311 in NYC)
This is an official off-leash dog run.
All New York City Off-leash Dog
Parks are run by the New York City
Parks Department.

Van Cortlandt Park Dog Run
West 251st Street & Broadway
Bronx, NY
212-NEW-YORK (311 in NYC)
This is an official off-leash dog run.
All New York City Off-leash Dog
Parks are run by the New York City
Parks Department.

Williamsbridge Oval Dog Run
3225 Reservoir Oval East
Bronx, NY
212-NEW-YORK (311 in NYC)
This is an official off-leash dog run.
All New York City Off-leash Dog
Parks are run by the New York City
Parks Department.

Brooklyn Bridge Park Dog Run
Adams Street and N/S Plymouth St
Brooklyn, NY
212-NEW-YORK (311 in NYC)
This is an official off-leash dog run.
All New York City Off-leash Dog
Parks are run by the New York City
Parks Department.

Cooper Park Dog Run
Olive St at Maspeth Ave
Brooklyn, NY
212-NEW-YORK (311 in NYC)
This is an official off-leash dog run.
All New York City Off-leash Dog
Parks are run by the New York City
Parks Department.

DiMattina Park Dog Run
Hicks, Coles and Woodhull Streets
Brooklyn, NY
212-NEW-YORK (311 in NYC)

There are two official off-leash dog
runs in DiMattina Park. All New
York City Off-leash Dog Parks are
run by the New York City Parks
Department.

Dyker Beach Park Dog Run
86th Street from 7th Ave to 14th
Ave
Brooklyn, NY
212-NEW-YORK (311 in NYC)
This is an official off-leash dog run.
All New York City Off-leash Dog
Parks are run by the New York City
Parks Department.

Hillside Park Dog Run
Columbia Heights & Vine Street
Brooklyn, NY
212-NEW-YORK (311 in NYC)
hillsidedogs.org
This is an official off-leash dog run.
All New York City Off-leash Dog
Parks are run by the New York City
Parks Department.

J J Byrne Memorial Park Dog Run
3rd to 4th Streets between 4th and
5th Ave
Brooklyn, NY
212-NEW-YORK (311 in NYC)
This is an official off-leash dog run.
All New York City Off-leash Dog
Parks are run by the New York City
Parks Department.

Manhattan Beach Dog Run
East of Ocean Avenue, North Shore
Rockaway inlet
Brooklyn, NY
212-NEW-YORK (311 in NYC)
This is an official off-leash dog run.
All New York City Off-leash Dog
Parks are run by the New York City
Parks Department.

McCarren Park Dog Run
Nassau Ave, Bayard, Leonard & N.
12th Sts
Brooklyn, NY
212-NEW-YORK (311 in NYC)
This is an official off-leash dog run.
All New York City Off-leash Dog
Parks are run by the New York City
Parks Department.

McGolrick Park Dog Run
North Henry Street at Driggs Ave
Brooklyn, NY
212-NEW-YORK (311 in NYC)
This is an official off-leash dog run.
All New York City Off-leash Dog
Parks are run by the New York City
Parks Department.

Owls Head Park Dog Run
Shore Pkwy, Shore Rd, Colonial

Rd, 68th Street
Brooklyn, NY
212-NEW-YORK (311 in NYC)
This is an official off-leash dog run.
All New York City Off-leash Dog
Parks are run by the New York City
Parks Department.

Palmetto Playground Dog Run
Atlantic Ave, Furman, Columbia,
State Streets
Brooklyn, NY
212-NEW-YORK (311 in NYC)
This is an official off-leash dog run.
All New York City Off-leash Dog
Parks are run by the New York City
Parks Department.

Prospect Park
Brooklyn, NY
212-NEW-YORK (311 in NYC)
Prospect Park, in Brooklyn, allows
dogs in much of the park on leash
has a number of large off-leash
areas during specified hours. Dogs
are allowed off-leash before 9 am
and after 9 pm in the summer and
after 5 pm in the winter in the Long
Meadow, Nethermead and the
Peninsula Meadow areas of the park.
Dogs are not allowed in the
children's playground or on the Bridle
paths. Owners must clean up after
their dogs. There's even a man made
dog beach in the park.

Seth Low Playground Dog Run
Avenue P, Bay Parkway, W. 12th
Street
Brooklyn, NY
212-NEW-YORK (311 in NYC)
This is an official off-leash dog area.
All New York City Off-leash Dog
Parks are run by the New York City
Parks Department.

Elmsford Dog Park
North Everts at Winthrop Avenue
Elmsford, NY
This 5000 square foot fenced dog-
park has two separate areas for
small dogs and larger dogs. The
surface is grass and dirt. Violent
dogs are not allowed and dogs must
have their vaccinations.

Forest Park Dog Run
Park Lane South & 85th Street
Forest Park, NY
212-NEW-YORK (311 in NYC)
This is an official off-leash dog area.
Its hours are 8 am to 8 pm seven
days a week. All New York City Off-
leash Dog Parks are run by the New
York City Parks Department.

West Hills County Park Dog Run
Sweet Hollow Rd at Old Country
Road
Huntington, NY
631-854-4423
lidog.org/li_dogparks.htm
There is a small fenced dog run in
West Hills County Park. This is an
over 700 acre park with nature trails
and hiking. Dogs must be on leash in
the park outside of the dog run.

Jamesville Beach Park Off-Leash
Area
South Street at Coye Rd
Jamesville, NY
There is a fenced off-leash dog park
in Jamesville Beach Park which
accesses the Jamesville Reservoir.
Proof of a current rabies vaccine
may be required on site.Dogs on
leash are allowed in the rest of the
park except that they are not allowed
in the beach areas during the
summer beach season. During the
winter dogs may use the beach
areas on leash. There is a disc golf
course in the park. Dogs must
always be cleaned up after
throughout the park. To get to the
park from I-81 take Route 173 east
to Jamesville, then head south on
South Stree to the park.

Nickerson Beach Park Dog Run
Merrick Road at Wantagh Avenue
Lido Beach, NY
516-571-7700
There is a fenced dog run in
Nickerson Beach Park across the
parking lot from the "Fun Zone"
playground area. There are two
areas, a larger area for large dogs
and a smaller area for smaller dogs.
During beach season there may be
fees to park at the dog park. To get
to the park take Meadowbrook Pkwy
South and look for signs to Lido and
Nickerson State Park.

Wegmans Good Dog Park
Route 370
Liverpool, NY
The first dog park in central New
York state is located in Onondaga
Lake Park. You should use the Cold
Springs entrance to the park. The
dog park is 40,000 square feet in
size and has a separate area for
small dogs. Proof of a current rabies
vaccine may be required on site.

Kakiat Park Dog Park
668 Haverstraw Road
Montebello, NY
845-364-2670
The fenced, off-leash dog park area
is located near the parking lot. In

addition to the dog park area, there
is significant hiking in the 370 acre
park. The trails from the park also
lead into the Harriman State Park.
There is a log cabin from 1922 and
a footbridge across the Mahwah
River.

Kennedy Dells Dog Park
355 North Main Street
New City, NY
845-364-2670
There is a fenced, off-leash area in
the nearly 200 acre Kennedy Dells
Park. Dogs must be leashed when
outside of the dog park area. In
addition to the dog park there is
also a parcourse fitness trail, ball
fields and hiking trails.

Ward Acres Park
Broadfield Rd at Quaker Ridge
Road
New Rochelle, NY
animal-link.org/parks.shtml
This non-fenced 62 acre park was
formerly the estate of the Ward
Family. Effective April, 2007 dogs
will be allowed off-leash in the
mornings until 10 am daily. From
November 15 to March 31 dogs
may also run unleashed from 4 pm
on on weekdays. During the rest of
the year dogs can run unleashed
starting again at 5 pm. Dogs may
not run off-leash in the afternoons
or evenings on weekends and
holidays. In order to use the park a
permit must be purchased. The cost
of the permit is $50 for city
residents and $250 for others. Dogs
will need to have proof of rabies
vaccinations. The park is
maintained by the Friends of Ward
Acres Park.

Carl Schurz Park Dog Run
East End Ave.between 84th and
89th Street
New York, NY
212-NEW-YORK (311 in NYC)
This is an official off-leash dog run.
All New York City Off-leash Dog
Parks are run by the New York City
Parks Department.

Central Park Off-Leash Hours and
Areas
New York, NY
212-NEW-YORK (311 in NYC)
Central Park is a designated off-
leash area for the hours of 9 pm
until 9 am daily. Dogs are allowed
off-leash in most of Central Park
during these hours. They are never
allowed at all in playgrounds,
display fountains, ballfields, Elm

Islands, Sheep Meadow, East Green
and Strawberry Fields. They must
always be leashed in the the
woodlands, Conservatory Garden,
Shakespeare Garden, Bridle Trail,
Cedar Hill, Kerbs Boathouse Plaza
and whereever signs are posted.
Between 9 am and 9 pm and in
areas where off-leash is not allowed
dog owners will be fined if their dogs
are off-leash. New York City Off-
leash Dog Parks are run by the New
York City Parks Department. They
can be reached at 212-NEW-YORK
(311 in NYC) or by calling 311 from a
phone in the city of New York.

Chelsea Waterside Park Dog Run
22nd St and 11th Avenue
New York, NY
212-627-2020
This fenced dog park is located in
the Hudson River Park on land
owned by the Hudson River Park
Trust which is a partnership between
New York State and the city. The dog
run is open from 6 am to 1 am. Dogs
are required to be on leash outside
of the dog run areas and are not
allowed on many of the lawns in the
park.

Coleman Oval Park Dog Run
Pike St at Monroe St
New York, NY
212-NEW-YORK (311 in NYC)
This is an official off-leash dog run.
All New York City Off-leash Dog
Parks are run by the New York City
Parks Department.

DeWitt Clinton Park Dog Run
Between 10th and 11th Ave at 52nd
and 54th
New York, NY
212-NEW-YORK (311 in NYC)
This is an official off-leash dog run.
All New York City Off-leash Dog
Parks are run by the New York City
Parks Department.

East River Esplanade Dog Run
East River at East 60th Street
New York, NY
212-NEW-YORK (311 in NYC)
This is an official off-leash dog run.
All New York City Off-leash Dog
Parks are run by the New York City
Parks Department.

Fish Bridge Park Dog Run
Dover St., between Pearl & Water St.
New York, NY
212-NEW-YORK (311 in NYC)
This is an official off-leash dog run.
All New York City Off-leash Dog
Parks are run by the New York City
Parks Department.

Fort Tryon Park Dog Run
Margaret Corbin Drive, Washington Heights
New York, NY
212-NEW-YORK (311 in NYC)
This is an official off-leash dog run. All New York City Off-leash Dog Parks are run by the New York City Parks Department.

Highbridge Park Dog Run
Amsterdam at Fort George Avenue
New York, NY
212-NEW-YORK (311 in NYC)
This is an official off-leash dog run. All New York City Off-leash Dog Parks are run by the New York City Parks Department.

Hudson River Park - Greenwich Village Dog Run
Leroy Street at Pier 40
New York, NY
212-NEW-YORK (311 in NYC)
This is an official off-leash dog run. All New York City Off-leash Dog Parks are run by the New York City Parks Department.

Hudson River Park - North Chelsea Dog Run
W 44th Street at Pier 84
New York, NY
212-NEW-YORK (311 in NYC)
This is an official off-leash dog run. All New York City Off-leash Dog Parks are run by the New York City Parks Department.

Inwood Hill Park Dog Run
Dyckman St and Payson Ave
New York, NY
212-NEW-YORK (311 in NYC)
This is an official off-leash dog run. All New York City Off-leash Dog Parks are run by the New York City Parks Department.

J. Hood Wright Dog Run
Fort Washington & Haven Aves., West 173rd St.
New York, NY
212-NEW-YORK (311 in NYC)
This is an official off-leash dog run. All New York City Off-leash Dog Parks are run by the New York City Parks Department.

Madison Square Park Dog Run
Madison Ave. To 5th Ave. between East 23rd St. & East 26th St.
New York, NY
212-NEW-YORK (311 in NYC)
This is an official off-leash dog run. All New York City Off-leash Dog Parks are run by the New York City

Parks Department.

Marcus Garvey Park Dog Run
Madison Ave at East 120th Street
New York, NY
212-NEW-YORK (311 in NYC)
This is an official off-leash dog run. All New York City Off-leash Dog Parks are run by the New York City Parks Department.

Morningside Park Dog Run
Morningside Avenue between 114th and 119th Streets
New York, NY
212-NEW-YORK (311 in NYC)
This is an official off-leash dog run. All New York City Off-leash Dog Parks are run by the New York City Parks Department.

Other New York City Off-Leash Areas
New York, NY
212-NEW-YORK (311 in NYC)
In addition to the off-leash dog runs listed, New York City allows dogs to be off-leash in designated areas of certain parks between the hours of 9 pm and 9 am during hours when the parks are open. There are many park areas that are designated this way in all boroughs. To find these designated parks, see the website http://www.nycgovparks.org/sub_thi ngs_to_do/facilities/af_dog_runs.ht ml. Please check this website for updates to the off-leash policies in New York. New York City Off-leash Dog Parks are run by the New York City Parks Department. They can be reached at 212-NEW-YORK (311 in NYC) or by calling 311 from a phone in the city of New York.

Peter Detmold Park Dog Run
West Side of FDR Drive between 49th and 51st
New York, NY
212-NEW-YORK (311 in NYC)
This is an official off-leash dog run. All New York City Off-leash Dog Parks are run by the New York City Parks Department.

Riverside Park Dog Runs
Riverside Dr at W 72nd,87th, and 105th
New York, NY
212-NEW-YORK (311 in NYC)
There are three official off-leash dog areas in Riverside Park. All New York City Off-leash Dog Parks are run by the New York City Parks Department.

Robert Moses Park Dog Run

41st Street and 1st Ave.
New York, NY
212-NEW-YORK (311 in NYC)
This is an official off-leash dog run. All New York City Off-leash Dog Parks are run by the New York City Parks Department.

Sirius Dog Run
Liberty St and South End Avenue
New York, NY
On September 8, 2005 this dog park was named for Sirius, a Police Labrador Retriever killed on September 11 in the World Trade Center. It is in the Kowsky Plaza and is run by the Port Authority of New York and New Jersey, not the park department.

St Nicholas Park Dog Run
St Nicholas Ave at 135th Street
New York, NY
212-NEW-YORK (311 in NYC)
This is an official off-leash dog area. It is located in the center of St Nicholas Park in Harlem between 135th and 137th Streets. All New York City Off-leash Dog Parks are run by the New York City Parks Department.

Theodore Roosevelt Park Dog Run
Central Park West and W 81st St.
New York, NY
212-NEW-YORK (311 in NYC)
This is an official off-leash dog run. All New York City Off-leash Dog Parks are run by the New York City Parks Department.

Thomas Jefferson Park Dog Run
East 112th Street at FDR Drive
New York, NY
212-NEW-YORK (311 in NYC)
This is an official off-leash dog run. All New York City Off-leash Dog Parks are run by the New York City Parks Department.

Tompkins Square Park Dog Run
1st Ave and Ave B between 7th and 10th
New York, NY
212-NEW-YORK (311 in NYC)
This is an official off-leash dog run. All New York City Off-leash Dog Parks are run by the New York City Parks Department.

Union Square Dog Run
Union Square
New York, NY
212-NEW-YORK (311 in NYC)
This is an official off-leash dog area located on 15th Street at Union Square. All New York City Off-leash

Dog Parks are run by the New York City Parks Department.

Washington Sq. Park Dog Run
Washington Sq. South
New York, NY
ci.nyc.ny.us/html/dpr/
This dog run is located in Washington Square Park in Greenwich Village. The run is located in the south side of the park near Thompson Street.

Cedar Lane Dog Park
235 Cedar Lane
Ossining, NY
914-941-3189
ossiningdogpark.com/
This free, fenced dog park has lights for night use and is open 24 hours. It was the first fenced off-leash park in Westchester County when it opened in 2003. The park has benches and tables and there is parking available. The There are various toys around for the dogs. The dog park is maintained by the Friends of Ossining Dog Park.

Alley Pond Park Dog Run
Alley Picnic Field Number 12
Queens, NY
212-NEW-YORK (311 in NYC)
This is an official off-leash dog area. All New York City Off-leash Dog Parks are run by the New York City Parks Department.

Cunningham Park Dog Run
193rd Street between Aberdeen Road and Radnor Road
Queens, NY
212-NEW-YORK (311 in NYC)
This is an official off-leash dog run. All New York City Off-leash Dog Parks are run by the New York City Parks Department.

K-9 Dog Run in Forest Park
Park Lane South at 85th Street
Queens, NY
212-NEW-YORK (311 in NYC)
This is an official off-leash dog run open from 8 am to 8 pm seven days a week. All New York City Off-leash Dog Parks are run by the New York City Parks Department.

Little Bay Dog Run
Cross Island Parkway between Clearview Expwy and Utopia Parkway
Queens, NY
212-NEW-YORK (311 in NYC)
This is an official off-leash dog run. All New York City Off-leash Dog Parks are run by the New York City

Parks Department.

Murray Playground Dog Run
21st Street & 45th Road on the SE side of park
Queens, NY
212-NEW-YORK (311 in NYC)
This is an official off-leash dog run. All New York City Off-leash Dog Parks are run by the New York City Parks Department.

Sherry Park Dog Run
Queens Boulevard, 65 Place and the BQE
Queens, NY
212-NEW-YORK (311 in NYC)
This is an official off-leash dog run. All New York City Off-leash Dog Parks are run by the New York City Parks Department.

Underbridge Playground Dog Run
64th Ave and 64th Road on Grand Central Parkway service road
Queens, NY
212-NEW-YORK (311 in NYC)
This is an official off-leash dog run. All New York City Off-leash Dog Parks are run by the New York City Parks Department.

Veteran's Grove Dog Run
Judge & Whitney on the south side of the park
Queens, NY
212-NEW-YORK (311 in NYC)
This is an official off-leash dog run. All New York City Off-leash Dog Parks are run by the New York City Parks Department.

Windmuller Park Dog Run
Woodside Ave., 54-56 Sts.
Queens, NY
212-NEW-YORK (311 in NYC)
This is an official off-leash dog run. All New York City Off-leash Dog Parks are run by the New York City Parks Department.

Bark Park
500 Chestnut Street
Rome, NY
315-339-7656
There is a two acre fenced dog park that opened in 2006. The park also features an agility course. In order to use the dog park, owners must fill out an application for each dog. To get a permit to use the dog park the dog is required to have a rabies shot and an DHLPPV vaccine. There is a $25 fee for the first year and a $15 renewal fee annually.

Christopher Morley Park Dog Run

Searingtown Road
Roslyn, NY
516-571-8113
There is a fenced dog run in Wantagh Park near the maintenance building. Dogs must be leashed while walking from your car to the dog run.

Cedar Creek Dog Run
Merrick Road at Wantagh Avenue
Seaford, NY
516-571-7470
There is a fenced dog run in Cedar Creek Park. Dogs are only allowed in the dog run area. They are not allowed to use the rest of the park.

Kingsland Point Park Dog Park
Palmer Ave at Munroe Ave
Sleepy Hollow, NY
914-366-5104
This dog park is located in Kingland Point Park which is located on the Hudson River just west of Route 9. Dogs must be licensed, vaccinated against rabies and must get a pass to use the park. The annual pass is $25 and you can call 914-366-5104 to get a pass, which also includes parking fees.

Blydenburgh County Park Dog Park
Veterans Memorial Highway
Smithtown, NY
631-854-4949
blydenburghdogpark.com
Located in the south area of the 627 acre Blydenburgh County Park, this 1.8 acre doggy play area offers open fields, woods, a separate large and small dog section, benches, waste bag dispensers, and water fountains for pooches and humans. Dogs must be sociable, current on all vaccinations, and under their owner's control at all times. Dogs must be leashed on no more than a 6 foot leash when not in designated off-lead areas.

Silver Lake Park Dog Run
Victory Blvd just within Silver Lake Park
Staten Island, NY
212-NEW-YORK (311 in NYC)
This is an fenced off-leash dog run. All New York City Off-leash Dog Parks are run by the New York City Parks Department.

Wolfe's Pond Park Dog Run
End of Huguenot & Chester Avenues
Staten Island, NY
212-NEW-YORK (311 in NYC)
This is an official off-leash dog run. All New York City Off-leash Dog Parks are run by the New York City Parks Department.

Wantagh Park Dog Run
Kings Road at Canal Place
Wantagh, NY
516-571-7460
There is a fenced dog run in
Wantagh Park near the maintenance
building. Dogs must be leashed while
walking from your car to the dog run.

White Plains Bark Park
Brockway Place at South Kensico
Road
White Plains, NY
914-422-1336
This 14,000 square foot fenced dog
park has two areas; one for large
dogs and one for small dogs. Its
surface is gravel.

North Carolina

Barkingham Park Dog Park - Reedy
Creek
2900 Rocky River Rd.
Charlotte, NC
704-336-3854
fidocarolina.org/
Reedy Creek Dog Park opened in
the Summer of 2003. It consists of 4
acres. Currently the park has an off-
leash dog park. Expected to be
added soon are a small dog area
and an agility playground. Charlotte
Dog Parks require a annual pooch
pass which you can get by signing a
liability form. Currently the fee is $35
per year for a pooch pass. More
information is available from
FidoCarolina at
http://www.fidocarolina.org.

Fetching Meadows Dog Park
McAlpine Park
Charlotte, NC
704-336-3854
fidocarolina.org/
Fetching Meadows Dog Park opened
in late 2002. Charlotte Dog Parks
require a annual pooch pass which
you can get by signing a liability
form. Currently the fee is $35 per
year for a pooch pass. More
information is available from
FidoCarolina at
http://www.fidocarolina.org.

Bark Park
3905 Nathaneal Greene Drive
Greensboro, NC
336-545-5343
gsobarkpark.org/
Located in the Country Park, there
are 3 separate fenced, off leash

areas to choose from-each with
their own features; Lot B is often
used for fund raising events. The
park is closed to vehicles on
weekends and holidays, but there is
a place to park and paths. Dogs
must be sociable, current on all
vaccinations and license, and under
their owner's control at all times.
Dogs must be leashed when not in
designated off-lead areas.

Millbrook Exchange Off Leash Dog
Park
1905 Spring Forest Road
Raleigh, NC
919-872-4156
This park is the home of the fenced
Millbrook Exchange Off Leash Dog
Park, and it is double-gated to
prevent dogs from wandering off.
When dogs are not in the off-leash
area they must be on lead.

Wilmington Dog Park at Empie
Independence Blvd at Park Avenue
Wilmington, NC
910-341-3237
This fenced dog park is located on
two acres in Empie Park. The dog
park is open during daylight hours.

North Dakota

Village West Dog Park
45th Street
Fargo, ND
This off-leash dog park has been
opened with fenced areas for both
small and large dogs. The dog park
is located in Village West Park. The
park is at 45th Street and 9th
Avenue.

Roaming Paws
Lincoln Drive
Grand Forks, ND
218-779-5037
roamingpaws.tripod.com/
This 2.75 acre off lead area is open
daily from 5 AM to 11 PM. Dogs
must be sociable, current on all
vaccinations, and under their
owner's control at all times. Dogs
must be leashed when not in
designated off-lead areas.

Ohio

Kellogg Park Dog Field

6701 Kellogg Avenue/H 52
Cincinnati, OH
513-357-6629 ext. 1
There is plenty of running room for
pups at this 5½ acre dog park with a
section for all-sized dogs and one for
small dogs. There are benches and a
grove of trees in the off-leash area,
and water is available at a nearby
concession /restroom area. To use
the dog park requires either an
annual pass or a $5 per dog day
pass. Dogs must be sociable, current
on all vaccinations, and under their
owner's control at all times.

Mt. Airy Forest Dog Park
Westwood Northern Blvd.
Cincinnati, OH
513-352-4080
cincinnati-oh.gov/parks/
The City of Cincinnati has
designated about 2 acres in the Mt.
Airy Forest for an off-leash dog park.
Dogs may run leash free when
accompanied by a person. The area
is fenced and the rules are posted on
site. The dog park is located at Mt.
Airy Forest's Highpoint Picnic Area
on Westwood Northern Blvd.
between Montana Avenue and North
Bend Road.

Big Walnut Dog
5000 E Livingston Avenue
Columbus, OH
614-645-3300
bigwalnutdogpark.com/home.htm
The first of the city's off-leash dog
parks, there are plans to have one in
each quadrant of the city. This park
is approximately 3 fenced-in acres
with 2 double-gated entrances and a
pond. Dogs must be well mannered,
remain leashed until inside the gates,
and be cleaned up after at all times.

Alum Creek Dog Park
Hollenback Road
Gahanna, OH
614-342-4250
This is a 4 acre fenced site along the
Alum Creek reservoir, and the
grounds include an area with water
access for dogs, 2 additional fenced
sites for small and large dogs,
drinking fountains, and restrooms.
Dogs must be well mannered, remain
leashed until inside the gates, and be
cleaned up after at all times.

Pooch Playground
6547 Clark State Road
Gahanna, OH
614-342-4250.
poochplayground.com/
This is the city's first public dog park,
and it covers 2.3 fenced-in acres with

a separate area for small dogs 25 pounds or less. There are water dishes and a few tables with benches inside the park, and porta-potties are available just outside of the fenced area. Dogs must be well mannered, remain leashed until inside the gates, and be cleaned up after at all times.

Schappacher Park Dog Run
4686 Old Irwin Simpson Road
Mason, OH
513-701-6958
Popular for its beauty, picnic, and playground areas, this 10 acre park adorned with old, large Oak trees is home to the city's 1st off-leash dog run area. Dogs must be sociable, current on all vaccinations, and under their owner's control at all times.

Wiggly Field
8070 Tylersville Road
West Chester, OH
513-759-7304
westchesteroh.org/
Located in the historical 330 acre Voice of America Park (also home to several nice walking paths and the Daisaku Ikeda Tree Grove) is a 3 acre off-lead area that can accommodate large or small dogs. Dogs must be sociable and current on all vaccinations.

Scout Burnell-Garbrecht Dog Park
210 Fairground Road
Xenia, OH
937-562-7440
Located at the Fairgrounds Recreation Center where there are several gaming areas, picnic spots, and paved walking trails, this dog play area offers a 2 acre fenced, off leash section and various doggy related events throughout the year. Dogs must be sociable, current on all vaccinations, and under their owner's control at all times.

Oklahoma

Norman Community Dog Park
Robinson and 12th St NE
Norman, OK
normandogpark.org/
This dog park has separate areas for large and small dogs. It is open 7 days a week from dawn to dusk. The park is located north of the intersection of Robinson and 12th Street NE.

Paw Park
Grand Blvd. and Lake Hefner Parkway
Oklahoma City, OK
405-782-4311
pawok.com
This two acre off-leash dog park is fenced and double-gated. Amenities include a small pond where dogs can swim or play in the water, separate areas for small or senior dogs and large dogs, trees, park benches and trash cans. Use of the dog park is free, but donations for keeping the park clean and in good condition are always appreciated. Envelopes and information forms are available at the park. The dog park is located in Lake Hefner Park. It is at the corner of North Grand Blvd. and Hefner Parkway in northwest Oklahoma City. Go north on the paved road east of the Grand Blvd/Hefner Parkway overpass. Continue north and park near the baseball fields. Thanks to PAW OK for the directions. Check out their web site at http://pawok.com for more details including photos of the park.

Pets and People Dog Park
701 Inla
Yukon, OK
This off-leash dog park is located west of Oklahoma City, in Yukon. From I-40, take the OK 92 exit towards Yukon. Turn right on Garth Brooks Blvd./S 11th Street and go about 1.4 miles. Continue on N 11th Street for .2 miles. Turn right on Inla Avenue and go for about .5 miles and you will reach the dog park.

Oregon

The Dog Park
Nevada and Helman Streets
Ashland, OR
541-488-6002
ashland.or.us
This 2 acre fenced dog park has picnic tables and drinking water. It is located behind the Ashland Greenhouse and Nursery, off Nevada, across from Helman Street.

Hazeldale Park Dog Park
Off 196th, N of Farmington
Beaverton, OR
thprd.org
This fenced dog park has a

separate section for small dogs and large dogs. Thanks to one of our readers for recommending this dog park.

Big Sky Dog Park
21690 NE Neff Road
Bend, OR
541-389-7275
The Big Sky Off-Leash Dog Park opened in 2005. It is 3 acres and completely fenced. There are picnic tables and water for your dog. You can walk your dog on leash outside of the dog park in the 90 acre Big Sky Park with walking trails, ponds and landscaping. The park is on the east side of town on Neff Rd east of Hamby Rd.

Molalla River State Park Off-Leash Area
Canby Ferry Road
Canby, OR
800-551-6949
This state park offers a designated off-leash exercise area. Dogs must be leashed in all other areas of the park. The park is located about 2 miles north of Canby.

Bald Hill Park Dog Park
Oak Creek Drive
Corvallis, OR
541-766-6918
ci.corvallis.or.us
There is a designated off-leash area located west of this park. People must clean up after their pets.

Chip Ross Park Dog Park
Lester Avenue
Corvallis, OR
541-766-6918
ci.corvallis.or.us
This park has a designated off-leash area. People must clean up after their pets. The park is located at the end of Lester Avenue.

Crystal Lake Sports Field Dog Park
Crystal Lake Drive
Corvallis, OR
541-766-6918
ci.corvallis.or.us
From March to November only, dogs can play off-leash at the non-improved turf areas. People must clean up after their pets. This sports field area is lcoated off Crystal Lake Drive, adjacent to Williamette Park.

Martin Luther King Jr Park Dog Park
Walnut Boulevard
Corvallis, OR
541-766-6918
ci.corvallis.or.us

This park has a designated off-leash area which is located in the southwest corner of the park. People must clean up after their pets.

Williamette Park Dog Park
SE Goodnight Avenue
Corvallis, OR
541-766-6918
ci.corvallis.or.us
This park has a designated off-leash area. People must clean up after their pets. The park is located southeast of Corvallis, off Highway 99W on southeast Goodnight Avenue.

Woodland Meadow Park Dog Park
Circle and Witham Hill Drive
Corvallis, OR
541-766-6918
ci.corvallis.or.us
This park has a designated off-leash area which is located in the upper portion of the park. People must clean up after their pets.

Milo McIver State Park Off-Leash Area
Springwater Road
Estacada, OR
503-630-7150
This state park offers a designated off-leash exercise area. Dogs must be leashed in all other areas of the park. The park is located on Springwater Road, 4 miles west of Estacada.

Alton Baker Park Off-Leash Area
Leo Harris Parkway
Eugene, OR
541-682-4800
This park offers a designated off-leash area. The dog park is located off Martin Luther King Jr. Boulevard on Leo Harris Parkway, behind Autzen Stadium. Park in lot 8.

Amazon Park Off-Leash Area
Amazon Parkway
Eugene, OR
541-682-4800
This park offers a designated off-leash area. The park is located off Amazon Parkway, at 29th Avenue.

Candlelight Park Off-Leash Area
Royal Avenue
Eugene, OR
541-682-4800
This park offers a designated off-leash area. The park is located off Royal Avenue, at Candlelight.

Morse Ranch Park Off-Leash Area
595 Crest Drive

Eugene, OR
541-682-4800
This park offers a designated off-leash area.

Bear Creek Park Dog Park
Highland Drive
Medford, OR
541-774-2400
ci.medford.or.us
This park offers a 2 acre fenced off-leash area. Amenities include water and a picnic table. Dogs must be on leash when not in the dog park. People must clean up after their pets. The park is located at the corner of Highland Drive and Barnett Road, near I-5, exit 27.

North Clackamas Park
5440 SE Kellog Ck Drive
Milwaukie, OR
503-794-8002
The North Clackamas Dog Park is fully fenced and open during daylight hours. There is water for your dog at the dog park. Dogs must be on-leash whenever they are outside of the fenced dog area.

Brentwood Park Dog Park
60th Street and Duke
Portland, OR
503-823-PLAY
This fenced off-leash dog park is next to the Joseph Lan School. There is some shade. The dog park hours are 5 am to 12 midnight daily. The dog park has been "adopted" and supported by the Friends of Brentwood Off-Leash Association.

Chimney Dog Park
9360 N. Columbia Blvd
Portland, OR
503-823-7529
This entire 16-acre park is designated as an off-leash area. The park has meadows and trails but is not fenced and no water is available. The park is open year-round and is located next to the City Archives Building.

East Delta Park Off-Leash Area
N. Union Court
Portland, OR
503-823-7529
This 5 acre off-leash fenced field has trees and benches, but no water. It is open during the dry season only, from May through October. Dogs are allowed off-leash, but not on the sports fields. The park is located off exit 307 on I-5 across from the East Delta Sports Complex.

Gabriel Park and Off-Leash Area
SW 45 Ave and Vermont
Portland, OR
503-823-7529
This popular regional park offers trails, a natural area and picnic tables. Dogs are not allowed on the playgrounds, sports fields, tennis courts, or in the wetlands and creeks. They are allowed in the rest of the park but must be leashed, except for the designated off-leash area. There is a 1.5 acre fenced dog park that has trees, picnic tables and water. The dog park is only open during the dry season, from May through October.

Normandale Off-Leash Dog Park
NE 57th Ave at Halsey St
Portland, OR
503-823-7529
This fenced dog park is located in Narmandale Park. It is open from 5 am to 12 midnight daily.

Portland's Unfenced Off-Leash Dog Areas
Various
Portland, OR
503-823-PLAY
Portland has a number of parks with unfenced off-leash dog areas. These parks are available for unleashed dogs from 5 am to 12 midnight daily. The parks are Alberta Park (NE 22 and Killingsworth), Cathedral Park (N. Edison and Pittsburg), Fernhill Park (NE 37 and Ainsworth), Lents Park (SE 92 and Holgate), Mt Tabor Park (SE Lincoln - east of SE 64), Portland International Raceway (N. Denver and Victory Blvd), Williamette Park (SW Macadam and Nebraska) and Wilshire Park (NE 33 and Skidmore). Portland has additional off-leash areas that have limited hours and other restrictions. Many of the limited off-leash hours at the additional parks are during the early morning and the evening hours. For a list of these parks you should check the Portland City Web Site at http://www.portlandonline.com/parks/index.cfm?c=39523. Most of the Portland Parks allow leashed dogs at all times.

Rooster Rock State Park Off-Leash Area
I-84
Portland, OR
503-695-2261
This state park offers a designated off-leash exercise area. Dogs must be leashed in all other areas of the park. The park is located on I-84, 22

miles east of Portland (exit 25).

West Delta Park Off-Leash Area
N. Expo Road & Broadacre
Portland, OR
503-823-7529
This 3 acre field has a portion which is fenced. No water is available. It is open year-round but the ground gets soggy after heavy rains. Dogs are allowed off-leash. The park is located off exit 306B on I-5 next to the entrance to Portland International Raceway (PIR).

Minto-Brown Island Park
2200 Minto Island Road
Salem, OR
503-588-6336
cityofsalem.net
This park offers a designated area for dogs to play off-leash. The area is not fenced. Dogs must be leashed when outside the off-leash area.

Orchard Heights Park
1165 Orchard Heights Road NW
Salem, OR
503-588-6336
cityofsalem.net
This park has a small designated area where dogs can play off-leash. Dogs must be leashed when outside the off-leash area.

Ash Street Dog Park
12770 SW Ash Avenue
Tigard, OR
503-639-4171
This small, 100x100 foot fenced dog park is located off of Burnham Street on Ash Avenue. There is limited parking. The dog park is open during daylight hours. From the 217 Freeway exit on 99W and head west. Turn left on SW Hall Blvd (south) and right on Burnham Street after crossing the train tracks. From I-5 North, take 217 and follow the above directions.

Potso Dog Park
Wall Street at Hunziker Street
Tigard, OR
503-639-4171
Potso Dog Park is named for the "first dog" of Coe Manufacturing which allowed the city to use a 4 acre site for the dog park. The fenced dog park has a separate, smaller area for small dogs. This dog park is open only on weekends in the fall and winter and daily during the summer.

Summerlake Park Dog Park
11450 SW Winterlake Drive

Tigard, OR
503-639-4171
The Summerlake Park Dog Park is 2/3 of an acre in size and fenced. It is open daily year round during daylight hours. From SW Scholls Ferry Rd take SW 130th Street to the park.

Mary S. Young Dog Park
Hwy 43
West Linn, OR
503-557-4700
This unfenced area in the Mary S. Young State Park is a designated off-leash area. It is about 9 miles from Portland on Highway 43 heading towards Lake Oswego/West Linn. The park has tables, benches, restrooms and water.

Memorial Park Off-Leash Dog Park
8100 SW Wilsonville Road
Wilsonville, OR
503-682-3727
The Memorial Park Dog Park is fully fenced and has a path around the perimeter for jogging. The dog park is open during daylight hours daily. From I-5 take the Wilsonville Rd exit. Go east on Wilsonville Road. Turn right onto Memorial Drive. The park is on the left.

Pennsylvania

Mondaug Bark Park
1130 Camphill Road
Fort Washington, PA
This park opened in July, 2005. It is a one acre fenced off-leash dog park. There is a separate dog park for small dogs and there is a double entry fence around the dog park. There are also trails around the dog park where you can walk your leashed dog. There is a stream where your leashed dog can play.

Buchanon Park Dog Park
Buchanan Avenue and Race Avenue
Lancaster, PA
fandm.edu/x2050.xml
This fenced off-leash dog park is in the 22 acre Buchanon Park. This city owned park is run by Franklin & Marshall University. The park is located at the F& M campus.

South Park Dog Park

Corrigan Drive at South Park
Library, PA
412-350-7275
This fenced dog park has drinking water, pickup bags and benches. Dogs on leash are allowed in most of the rest of this 2000 acre park.

White Oak Dog Park
Route 48
McKeesport, PA
412-350-7275
This fenced dog park in White Oak Park has water, pickup bags and benches. It is about 2 acres in size. The dog park can be accessed from Route 48. Take the White Oak Park entrance. Dogs are allowed on leash in most of the rest of this 810 acre park.

Heritage Park Dog Park
2364 Saunders Station Road
Monroeville, PA
412-350-7275
monroeville.pa.us/dogpark/
This fenced dog park has shade, water, and pickup bags. The park is open from sunrise to sunset.

Chester Avenue Dog Park
Chester Ave and 48th
Philadelphia, PA
215-748-3440
This nearly one acre park is a privately run dog park. Membership is required to use the park and runs $50 per year. For membership information, please contact Linda Amsterdam at 215-748-3440.

Eastern State Dog Pen
Corinthian Ave & Brown St
Philadelphia, PA
fairmountdog.org/
This is a fenced dog park. Barking in the park is prohibited between 9 pm and 9 am.

Orianna Hill Dog Park
North Orianna St, between Poplar and Wildey
Philadelphia, PA
215-423-4516
oriannahill.org
This is a privately owned fenced dog run. Dues are required and are $20 per year. To join, please call 215-423-4516.

Pretzel Park Dog Run
Cresson St
Philadelphia, PA
This is a fenced in dog park in the dog-friendly Manayunk region of Philadelphia.

Schuylkill River Park Dog Run
25th St between Pine and Locust
Philadelphia, PA
phillyfido.net
This fenced dog park is located near the Centre City across the Schuylkill River from the 30th Street Train Station.

Segar Dog Park
11th Street between Lombard and South St.
Philadelphia, PA
segerdogrunonline.org
Located in Segar Park, this is a fenced dog park with separate areas for small dogs and large dogs.

Frick Park
6750 Forbes Avenue
Pittsburgh, PA
412-255-2539
This off leash dog area is located in the city's largest park which is a popular area for its extensive trails, its historical and educational opportunities, and for the variety of recreation available. The off leash dog area is about a ½ mile past the Blue Slide Playground on Riverview Trail. Dogs must be kept leashed until in the fenced area, and they must be under their owner's control and cleaned up after at all times.

Hartwood Acres Off-Leash Park
Middle Road
Pittsburgh, PA
412-767-9200
This fenced, off leash dog area is located on a beautifully landscaped 629 acre historic country estate with more than 30 miles of hiking trails. Dogs are allowed throughout the park; they are not allowed in buildings. The off-leash dog area is off Middle Road behind the amphitheater. Dogs must remain on lead when not in this area, and they must be cleaned up after at all times.

Upper Frick Dog Park
Beechwood and Nicholson
Pittsburgh, PA
This fenced dog park has pickup bags. It is about one acre in size.

Op Barks Farm
2590 Schukraft Rd
Quakertown, PA
888-672-2757
opbarks.com/bark/index.cfm
In addition to providing training and behavior services, there are opportunities for lots of fun with 5 acres with nature trails, a creek,

wooded areas, and a dog and people friendly pool. There are also special events, an indoor training space, and a full agility course.

Rhode Island

Haines Park Dog Park
Rt 103
Barrington, RI
401-253-7482
riparks.com/haines.htm
This fenced dog park is located on the west side of the 100 acre Haines Memorial State Park in Barrington. Dogs must be on leash when outside of the off-leash area. The park is open during daylight hours. From East Providence exit I-195 at Route 103 and head south to the park.

Newport Dog Park
Connell Highway
Newport, RI
401-845-5800
This dog park is located on Connell Highway in Newport. It is a fenced dog park and is open from 6 am to 9 pm.

Gano Street Dog Park
Gano Street and Power
Providence, RI
401-785-9450
providencedogparkassociation.org
This fenced, off-leash dog park opened on June 14, 2006. It is Providence's first official off-leash area for dogs. The park is maintained by the Providence Dog Park Association which is looking to make some improvements to the park. To get to the dog park you can enter Gano Street Park at Gano and Power. Pass the Fox Point Community Garden and turn right. The dog park is behind the basketball courts.

Warwick Dog Park
40 Asylum Road
Warwick, RI
401-734-3690
This is a 33,000 square foot fenced dog park with grass, shade and benches. The dog park is open during daylight hours and is located in Warwick City Park at the end of Asylum Road.

South Carolina

Hampton Park Off-Leash Dog Park
corner of Rutledge and Grove
Charleston, SC
charlestoncity.info
This park has a fenced dog run for your pet. Dogs must be on leash when not in the dog run area.

James Island County Park Dog Park
871 Riverland Drive
Charleston, SC
843-795-PARK (7275)
Located in the 643 acre James Island County Park, this is the only off leash dog area that also has lake access. There is drinking water for humans and pooches, water hoses for cooling/cleaning off, and bag stations with collection cans on site. The dog park is closed here each Wednesday from 7 to 9 AM for regular maintenance. Dogs must be sociable, current on all vaccinations, and under their owner's control at all times. Dogs must be leashed when not in designated off-lead areas.

Sesqui Dog Park
9564 Two Notch Rd
Columbia, SC
803-788-2706
An annual permit of $25 per dog or a day permit of $4 per dog is required to use the dog park which is located in Sesquicentennial State Park. Contact the park office for additional information.

Cleveland Park Dog Park
Woodland Way
Greenville, SC
864-271-5333
greenvillesouth.com/animal.html
This is a fenced off-leash dog park. It is located in Cleveland Park across from the horse stables and the Cleveland Park Animal Hospital. The dog park is open during daylight hours. Small children are not permitted in the dog park.

Six Wags of Greer K-9 Fun Park
3669 North Highway 14
Greer, SC
upstatedogtraining.com
This is a private dog park with three play yards. Dogs are divided by how they get along with each other. There is also an area for people who want to run their dogs without other dogs and a one mile nature trail. Agility equipment is also available. There is

a $5 a day pass to use the facility. Kennel and training services are also available.

Best Friends Dog Park
Off Hwy 40
Hilton Head, SC
hiltonhead360.com
Dogs are allowed unleashed in the dog park and leashed outside on the beaches. There is a water and cleanup stations for your pets.

Isle of Palms Dog Park
29th Ave behind Rec Center
Isle of Palms, SC
843-886-8294
This fenced dog park is open from sunrise to sunset. The park is closed on Wednesdays from 10 am - 12 noon for cleaning. Children under 12 are not allowed into the dog park.

Palmetto Islands County Park Dog Park
444 Needlerush Parkway
Mount Pleasant, SC
843-572- PARK (7275)
This off lead area is located in the lush, tropical setting of the 943 acre Mount Pleasant Palmetto Islands County Park, and provides drinking water for humans and pooches, water hoses for cooling/cleaning off, and bag stations with collection cans. Dogs must be sociable, current on all vaccinations, and under their owner's control at all times. Dogs must be leashed when not in designated off-lead areas.

Myrtle Beach Barc Parc
Kings Hwy at Mallard Lake Drive
Myrtle Beach, SC
843-918-1000
This is an especially nice fenced dog park of 11 acres. There is a large pond in the park for swimming. There is even a doggy shower at the park. The park is located in the former Air Force Base area just south of the city. Take Kings Hwy south just out of the city and turn left on Mallard Lake Drive. The park is the only area in Myrtle Beach where a dog is allowed to be off-leash.

Wannamaker County Park Dog Park
8888 University Blvd
North Charleston, SC
843-572- PARK (7275)
Located in the 1,015 acre Wannamaker County Park, a scenic experience of woodlands and wetlands with miles of trails to enjoy the natural surroundings, this off lead area provides drinking water for humans and pooches, water hoses

for cooling/cleaning off, and bag stations with collection cans. Dogs must be sociable, current on all vaccinations, and under their owner's control at all times. Dogs must be leashed when not in designated off-lead areas.

South Dakota

Lien Park Off-Leash Area
North Cliff Avenue
Sioux Falls, SD
605-367-6076
siouxfalls.org/parks
This off-leash area is being run on a trial basis by the city of Sioux Falls. Amenities at the off-leash area include a picnic table, plastic bag dispenser and a trash can. The park is located on the east side of North Cliff Ave. at the Big Sioux River, about .25 miles north of the Rice Street and Cliff Avenue intersection. Off-street parking is available.

Spencer Park Off-Leash Area
3501 South Cliff Avenue
Sioux Falls, SD
siouxfalls.org/parks
This fenced off-leash area is being run on a trial basis by the city of Sioux Falls. Amenities at the off-leash area include a picnic table, plastic bag dispenser and a trash can. The park is located at 3501 S. Cliff Avenue, on the west side of Cliff Avenue near I-229. Off-street parking is available.

Tennessee

PetSafe Village Dog Park
10427 Electric Avenue
Knoxville, TN
865-777-DOGS (3647)
petsafevillage.com/
PetSafe introduced Knoxville to its first public dog park. It is situated on a little over an acre and offers a natural pond, a full set of agility equipment, park benches, picnic tables, walking trails, and a doggy water fountain. This is an on leash dog park; however, there are daily hours when dogs may be off leash when it is being supervised by PetSafe staff personnel. Off leash times are after 5 pm Monday

through Friday, and after 3 pm on the weekends. All dog park participants must sign a park usage agreement. Dogs of all sizes are allowed, and they must be well behaved, leashed (except during supervised hours), and cleaned up after at all times. Also on site is a boarding/grooming/training/24 hour pet care facility.

Centennial Dog Park
31st Avenue and Park Plaza
Nashville, TN
615-862-8400
Open from dawn until 8 PM, this off-lead area offers 2 separate areas for large and small dogs; there may only be 2 pets per person. Dogs must be sociable, current on all vaccinations and license, and under their owner's control at all times. Dogs must be leashed when not in designated off-lead areas. Parking is located of Parthenon Avenue.

Edwin Warner Dog Park
Vaughn Gap Road at Old Hickory Blvd
Nashville, TN
615-862-8400
Open from dawn to dusk, this off-lead park offers a large fenced area with benches, a water fountain, and disposal bags. Two dogs are allowed per person; they must be sociable, current on all vaccinations and license and under their owner's control at all times. Dogs must be leashed when not in designated off-lead areas.

Shelby Park
South 20th and Shelby
Nashville, TN
615-862-8400
Open from dawn to 8PM, this natural off-lead area offers 2 fenced acres with paved walkways, and they allow 2 dogs per person. Dogs must be sociable, current on all vaccinations and license, and under their owner's control at all times. Dogs must be leashed when not in designated off-lead areas. The park is located behind the Shelby Community Center.

Texas

Auditorium Shores Off-Leash Area
920 W. Riverside Drive
Austin, TX
512-974-6700

Austin

Off-Leash Dog Parks—Texas - Please call ahead to confirm an establishment is still dog-friendly.

Town Lake = No
mills Pond = No

This designated off-leash area is located between South First and Bouldin Avenue.

Bull Creek District Off-Leash Area
6701 Lakewood Drive
Austin, TX
512-974-6700
This dog park is not fenced. It has access to the creek for water-loving pooches. Well-behaved dogs can roam and play off-leash, but must be under verbal control and within your sight. The off-leash area is located behind the restrooms.

Emma Long Metro Park Off-Leash Area
1600 City Park Rd.
Austin, TX
512-974-6700
This park has a designated off-leash area. It is located between City Park Drive, the west park boundary fence, Turkey Creek and the top ridge of the bluff line overlooking Lake Austin.

Far West Off-Leash Area
Far West at Great Northern Blvd *OK*
Austin, TX
512-974-6700
This unfenced, off-leash dog run is located on Far West Blvd between Great Northern Blvd and Shoal Creek Blvd. Dogs must be leashed in the remainder of the park.

Northeast District Park Off-Leash Area
5909 Crystalbrook Drive
Austin, TX
512-974-6700
This park has a designated off-leash area. It is located between Crystalbrook Drive, the railroad right of way and Decker Lake Road.

OK Norwood Estate Off-Leash Area
I-35 and Riverside Drive
Austin, TX
512-974-6700
This is a fully fenced dog park. Well-behaved dogs can roam and play off-leash, but must be under verbal control and within your sight. The dog park is located on the north end of Travis Heights at the northwest corner of Riverside Drive and I-35.

Onion Creek District Park Off-Leash Area
6900 Onion Creek Drive
Austin, TX
512-974-6700
This off-leash dog park is located at the north end of the greenbelt.

Red Bud Isle Off-Leash Area
3401 Red Bud Trail Unit Circle
Austin, TX
512-974-6700
Dogs can play leash-free in this designated off-leash area.

Shoal Creek Greenbelt Off-Leash Area
2600-2799 Lamar Blvd.
Austin, TX
512-974-6700
This park has a designated off-leash area. It is located between 24th and 29th Streets.

Walnut Creek District Off-Leash Area
12138 North Lamar Blvd.
Austin, TX
512-974-6700
This park has a designated off-leash area. It is located between Old Cedar Lane, Walnut Creek and the east and west park fences.

West Austin Park Off-Leash Area
1317 W 10th Street
Austin, TX
512-974-6700
This fenced, off-leash dog run is located in the southwest area of the park; adjacent to W 9th Street. Dogs must be leashed in the remainder of West Austin Park.

Zilker Off-Leash Area
2100 Barton Springs Rd.
Austin, TX
512-974-6700
This dog park is not fenced. Well-behaved dogs can roam and play off-leash, but must be under verbal control and within your sight. The dog park is located in Zilker Metropolitan Park at 2100 Barton Springs Road. The leash free area is located near the soccer field area, between Great Northern Blvd. and Shoal Creek Blvd.

White Rock Lake Dog Park
8000 Mockingbird Lane
Dallas, TX
214-670-8895
dallasdogparks.org
Dogs are welcome to run leash-free at this dog park. The fully enclosed park offers a separate section for large dogs and small dogs. The dog park is closed on Mondays for maintenance. To get there from Central Expressway (75), go East on Mockingbird Lane. After you pass the West Lawther exit, begin looking for the parking lot. If you go

to Buckner Blvd., then you have passed the dog park. The dog park is located on Mockingbird Point.

Wiggly Field at Lake Forest Park
1400 E Ryan Road
Denton, TX
940-349-8731
Wiggly Field is Denton's 1st dog park, and they offer 3 fenced acres of running room. There is a large area for bigger dogs, and a separate section for small or shy dogs. They also offer a memorial brick commemorative program. The park is open 7 days a week, except on Wednesday-they are closed until 3:30 pm. Please clean up after your pet.

Fort Woof Off-Leash Dog Park
3500 Gateway Park Drive
Fort Worth, TX
817-871-7638
fortwoof.org/
Award winning Fort Woof, located at Gateway Park, is Fort Worth's first fenced, off-leash dog park. There are 2 large fenced areas for dogs; one is for dogs over 40 pounds or more, and a separate area for the smaller dogs. Each area has picnic tables (but no food-please), park benches for human visitors, a watering station for both, and several clean-up stations. The park is open from 5 am to 11:30 pm daily, and the park is lighted at night. They also host Barktoberfest, an annual fall festival to help raise money for Fort Woof. Dogs must be at least 4 months old and have had their rabies shots. Dogs must be leashed when entering and exiting the park, and they must be cleaned up after at all times.

Central Bark
2222 W Warrior Trail
Grand Prairie, TX
pawpalsofgrandprairie.org/
The off leash pet area covers more than 4 acres with a separate section for large and small dogs, shade trees, and shelters in both areas. Dogs must be sociable, current on all vaccinations, licensed, and under their owner's control at all times. Dogs must be leashed when not in designated off-lead areas.

Paw Pals of Grand Prairie Dog Park
2222 W Warrior Trl
Grand Prairie, TX
pawpalsofgrandprairie.org/
This fenced dog park opened in April 2007. The park is open during daylight hours.

Pease Dog Park
1100 Kingsbury St

Ervan Chew Park Dog Park
4502 Dunlavy
Houston, TX
713-845-1000
ci.houston.tx.us/pr/
This park has a designated dog park. The 9,000 square foot off-leash area is fully fenced. The dog park is located adjacent to the picnic area and swimming pool.

Maxey Park Dog Park
601 Maxey Road
Houston, TX
ci.houston.tx.us/pr/
This off-leash park is 12-13 acres with fencing, including an area for smaller dogs and doggie drinking fountains.

Millie Bush Dog Park
Westheimer Parkway
Houston, TX
713-755-6306
pct3.hctx.net/ParksMain.htm
This 15 acre dog park was named after Millie, the English Springer Spaniel who shared the White House with George and Barbara Bush. The park was dedicated and opened on April 2, 2004. The off-leash area is open from 7am to dusk. It is located in George Bush Park, on the south side of Westheimer Parkway, across from the American Shooting Center.

Hogans Run Dog Park
1201 E Wadley
Midland, TX
432-685-7424
This off lead area if open from dawn to dusk, and they are closed Monday morning for maintenance. Entrance to the off lead area is on Sibley Circle. Dogs must be sociable, current on all vaccinations, licensed, and cleaned up after at all times. Dogs must be leashed when not in designated off-lead areas.

Jack Carter Park Dog Park
Pleasant Valley Drive
Plano, TX
972-941-7250
planoparks.org/
This city park has a 2 acre designated dog park. The off-leash area is fenced and double-gated. Amenities include benches, picnic tables, drinking fountains for people and dogs and trash cans. The dog park is located in Jack Carter Park, along Bluebonnet Trail and near the intersection of Chisolm Trail. Parking is available west of the dog park. Go 1/2 block north on Pleasant Valley Drive, from the intersection of Spring Creek Parkway, west of Custer

Road.

Round Rock Dog Depot (Dog Park)
800 Deerfoot Drive
Round Rock, TX
512-218-5540
roundrocktexas.gov/dogpark
This 1.85 acre dog park opened in March, 2008 and has three fenced areas. One is for large dogs, one is for small dogs and the third is used to rotate use away from the primary areas to allow for growing the grass and other closures. The park's hours are 6 am to 8 pm from April through September and from 6 am to 6 pm from October through March.

McAllister Dog Park
13102 Jones-Maltsberger
San Antonio, TX
210-207-3000
sanantonio.gov/sapar/dogpark.asp
Located on the Starcrest side of the park, this off lead area offers about 1.5 acres, exercise equipment, plenty of fire hydrants, benches, a walking trail, a covered picnic area, water for hounds and humans, and restrooms. Dogs must be sociable, current on all vaccinations and license, and under their owner's control at all times. Dogs must be leashed when not in designated off-lead areas.

Pearsall Park Dog Park
4700 Old Pearsall Road
San Antonio, TX
210-207-3000
sanantonio.gov/sapar/dogpark.asp
This city park has a 1.5 acre designated dog park. The fenced in area has picnic tables, trash cans and play features. Dog park hours are from 5am to 11pm every day.

Utah

Herman Frank's Park
700 E 1300 S
Salt Lake City, UT
This park has a designated off-leash area. Dogs must be leashed when outside the leash free area.

Jordan Park
1060 South 900 West
Salt Lake City, UT
801-972-7800
This park has a designated off-leash area. Dogs must be leashed when outside the leash free area.

Lindsey Gardens
9th Avenue and M Street
Salt Lake City, UT
801-972-7800
This park has a designated off-leash area. Dogs must be leashed when outside the leash free area.

Memory Grove Park Off-Leash Park
485 N. Canyon Road
Salt Lake City, UT
801-972-7800
This park has a designated off-leash area which is located in the Freedom Trail area. Dogs must be leashed when outside the leashed area. The park is located east of the Utah State Capitol.

Parley's Gulch
2700 East Salt Lake City
Salt Lake City, UT
801-269-7499
The Parley's Gulch area behind Tanner Park is now an official off-leash area. However, Tanner Park is not and dogs must be leashed there. This is mostly an unfenced area. The off-leash dog area is around the intersection of the I-80 and I-215 freeways. There is a fence between the off-leash areas and the freeways.

Sandy City Dog Park
9980 South 300 East
Sandy, UT
801-568-2900
This fenced, one acre dog park has benches, trees for shade and a walking trail. From I-15 exit at S 106th. Head east to State Street and head north (left) on State Street to E Sego Lily Dr. Turn right on Sego Lily Dr. Turn right on South 300 East to the park.

Millrace Off-Leash Dog Park
5400 South at 1100 West
Taylorsville, UT
801-963-5400
The fenced, Millrace Park Dog Park is open during the summer from 7 am to 10 pm and during the winter from 7 am to 7 pm. The park will be closed during bad weather and possibly after bad weather. Beginning in July, 2006 the dog park requires an annual permit to use the park. It costs $10 for Taylorsville residents and $25 for non-residence. To get a tag call 801-269-7499 or visit
http://www.slcoanimalservices.org.

Vermont

Starr Farm Dog Park
Starr Farm Rd
Burlington, VT
802-864-0123
burlingtondogpark.org/
This off-leash dog park is fenced and offers separate large and small dogs sections. It is located west of the bike path and adjacent to the Starr Farm Community Garden. Parking is available. The dog park is open 8am to 8pm in April through October and 8am to 6pm in November through March. To get there from I-89, take exit #14w towards Burlington(west). The road becomes Main Street. Turn right on Route 127 and go about a half of a mile. Turn left on Sherman Street. Sherman St. becomes North Avenue. Go about 3 miles and turn left on Starr Farm Road. The park is located off Starr Farm Road, near Lake Champlain and adjacent to the community garden.

Waterfront Dog Park
near Moran Building
Burlington, VT
802-865-7247
This off-leash dog park is fenced and provides access to the lake. It is located about 1,000 feet north of the Moran Building (the old electric generating station). It is a walk-in area with parking at the north end of Waterfront Park or at North Beach. The park is open daily with no hour restrictions. To get there from I-89, take exit #14w towards Burlington (west). The road becomes Main Street. Main Street turns to the right (north) and becomes Lake Street. Park at the north end of Waterfront Park or at North Beach.

Virginia

Ben Brenman Dog Park
at Backlick Creek
Alexandria, VA
703-838-4343
This is an official off-leash dog area. The park is completely fenced. These parks are controlled by the Alexandria Department of Recreation, Parks and Cultural Activities.

Braddock Road Dog Run Area

SE Corner of Braddock Rd and Commonwealth
Alexandria, VA
703-838-4343
This is an unfenced official off-leash dog area. Alexandria Off-leash dog parks are controlled by the Alexandria Department of Recreation, Parks and Cultural Activities.

Chambliss Street Dog Run Area
Chambliss St
Alexandria, VA
703-838-4343
This is an unfenced official off-leash dog area. It is located south of the tennis courts. Alexandria Off-leash dog parks are controlled by the Alexandria Department of Recreation, Parks and Cultural Activities.

Chinquapin Park Dog Run Area
Chinquapin Park East of Loop
Alexandria, VA
703-838-4343
This is an unfenced official off-leash dog area. Alexandria Off-leash dog parks are controlled by the Alexandria Department of Recreation, Parks and Cultural Activities.

Duke Street Dog Park
5000 block of Duke Street
Alexandria, VA
703-838-4343
This is an official off-leash dog area. The park is completely fenced. The park is located east of the Beatley Library. These parks are controlled by the Alexandria Department of Recreation, Parks and Cultural Activities.

Fort Ward Park Offleash Dog Run
East of Park Road
Alexandria, VA
703-838-4343
This is an unfenced official off-leash dog area. Alexandria Off-leash dog parks are controlled by the Alexandria Department of Recreation, Parks and Cultural Activities.

Fort Williams Dog Run Area
Between Ft Wiliams and Ft Williams Parkway
Alexandria, VA
703-838-4343
This is an unfenced official off-leash dog area. Alexandria Off-leash dog parks are controlled by the Alexandria Department of Recreation, Parks and Cultural Activities.

Founders Park Dog Run Area
Oronoco St and Union St
Alexandria, VA
703-838-4343
This is an unfenced official off-leash dog area. Alexandria Off-leash dog parks are controlled by the Alexandria Department of Recreation, Parks and Cultural Activities.

Hooff's Run Dog Run Area
Commonwealth between Oak and Chapman St
Alexandria, VA
703-838-4343
This is an unfenced official off-leash dog area. Alexandria Off-leash dog parks are controlled by the Alexandria Department of Recreation, Parks and Cultural Activities.

Montgomery Park Dog Park
Fairfax and 1st Streets
Alexandria, VA
703-838-4343
This is an official off-leash dog area. The park is completely fenced. These parks are controlled by the Alexandria Department of Recreation, Parks and Cultural Activities.

Monticello Park Dog Run Area
Monticello Park
Alexandria, VA
703-838-4343
This is an unfenced official off-leash dog area. Alexandria Off-leash dog parks are controlled by the Alexandria Department of Recreation, Parks and Cultural Activities.

Simpson Stadium Dog Park
Monroe Avenue
Alexandria, VA
703-838-4343
This is an official off-leash dog area. The park is completely fenced. These parks are controlled by the Alexandria Department of Recreation, Parks and Cultural Activities.

Tarleton Park Dog Run Area
Old Mill Run west of Gordon St
Alexandria, VA
703-838-4343
This is an unfenced official off-leash dog area. Alexandria Off-leash dog parks are controlled by the Alexandria Department of Recreation, Parks and Cultural Activities.

W&OD Railroad Dog Run Area
Raymond Avenue
Alexandria, VA
703-838-4343
This is an unfenced official off-leash dog area. Alexandria Off-leash dog parks are controlled by the Alexandria Department of Recreation, Parks and Cultural Activities.

Windmill Hill Park Dog Run Area
Gibbon and Union Streets
Alexandria, VA
703-838-4343
This is an unfenced official off-leash dog area. Alexandria Off-leash dog parks are controlled by the Alexandria Department of Recreation, Parks and Cultural Activities.

Mason District
6621 Columbia Pike
Annandale, VA
This fenced dog park is open from dawn to dusk. The park is controlled by the Fairfax County Park Authority and sponsored by the Mason District Dog Opportunity Group.

Benjamin Banneker Park Dog Run
1600 Block North Sycamore
Arlington, VA
This partially fenced off-leash dog park is open during daylight hours. It is over eleven acres. This dog park is maintained by Banneker Dogs.

Fort Barnard Dog Run
Corner of South Pollard St and South Walter Reed Drive
Arlington, VA
This dog run is open from dawn to dusk. It is sponsored by Douglas Dogs.

Glencarlyn Park Dog Run
301 South Harrison St
Arlington, VA
This is an unfenced dog run area in Glencarlyn Park. The area is located near a creek. It is open during daylight hours.

Madison Community Center Dog Park
3829 North Stafford St
Arlington, VA
This 15 acre fully fenced dog park is located at the Madison Community Center. Please note that dogs are not allowed on the adjacent soccer field and that you need to park in the Community Center front lot and not

the back lot.

Shirlington Park Dog Run
2601 South Arlington Mill Drive
Arlington, VA
This unfenced dog park is located along the bicycle path between Shirlington Rd and South Walter Reed Dr. It is open during daylight hours.

Towers Park Dog Park
801 South Scott St
Arlington, VA
This fenced dog park is located in Towers Park behind the tennis courts. There is a separate fenced small dog off-leash area.

Darden Towe Park
1445 Darden Towe Park Road
Charlottesville, VA
434-296-5844
This 110 acre park is open from 7 am to dark year round offering gaming fields/courts, trails, picnic areas with grills, and a 1 acre fenced-in off leash dog area. Dogs are allowed throughout the rest of the park and on the trails as long as they are on leash and cleaned up after at all times. Dogs must be under good voice control when not on lead.

Chandon Dog Park
900 Palmer Drive
Herndon, VA
This fenced dog park is open from dawn to dusk. The park is controlled by the Fairfax County Park Authority and sponsored by Herndon Dogs, Inc.

Brambleton Dog Park
Booth Street and Malloy Ave
Norfolk, VA
757-441-2400
This off-leash dog park is not fenced. You must control your dog at all times.

Cambridge Dog Park
Cambridge Place and Cambridge Place
Norfolk, VA
757-441-2400
This off-leash dog park is not fenced. You must control your dog at all times.

Dune Street Dog Park
Dune St & Meadow Brook Lane
Norfolk, VA
757-441-2400
This off-leash dog park is not fenced. You must control your dog

at all times.

Blake Lane Dog Park
10033 Blake Lane
Oakton, VA
This fenced dog park is open from dawn to dusk. The park is controlled by the Fairfax County Park Authority and sponsored by OaktonDogs, Inc.

Baron Cameron Dog Park
11300 Baron Cameron Avenue
Reston, VA
This fenced dog park is open from dawn to dusk. The park is controlled by the Fairfax County Park Authority and sponsored by RestonDogs, Inc. This dog park has a separate area for small dogs and water for your dog.

South Run Dog Park
7550 Reservation Drive
Springfield, VA
This fenced dog park is open from dawn to dusk. The park is controlled by the Fairfax County Park Authority and sponsored by Lorton Dogs, Inc.

Red Wing Park Dog Park
1398 General Booth Blvd.
Virginia Beach, VA
757-563-1100
This is a one acre fenced dog park. The park is open from 7:30 am until sunset. There is a $5 annual fee. Dogs must also show proof of license and vaccination. You may get the annual pass at the Maintenance Office at the dog park.

Woodstock Park Dog Park
5709 Providence Rd.
Virginia Beach, VA
757-563-1100
This is a one acre fenced dog park. The park is open from 7:30 am until sunset. There is a $5 annual fee. Dogs must also show proof of license and vaccination. You may get the annual pass at the Maintenance Office at the dog park.

Washington

Eagledale Park Off-Leash Dog Park
5055 Rose Avenue NE
Bainbridge Island, WA
206-842-2306
This one acre dog park is located in Eagledale Park which is at Rose Avenue a few blocks south of Eagle Harbor Dr NE.

Golden Gardens Dog Park
8498 Seaview Place NW
Ballard, WA
206-684-4075
This 2.2 acre fenced dog park is in the upper part of Golden Gardens Park. The park is open from 6 am to 11:30 pm. To get to the park from I-5 take the 85 St exit and head west. When 85 Street ends turn right and go under the railroad tracks to the park.

Bremerton Bark Park
1199 Union Avenue
Bremerton, WA
360-473-5305
visitkitsap.com/kitsap.asp
This fenced off-leash dog park is located at Pendergast Park. It opened in November, 2005. To get to the park from Hwy 16 or Hwy 3, head towards Bremerton, take the Loxie Eagans Blvd exit off of Hwy 3 and go west onto Werner Road. Turn left on Union Street and the park will be on the right. This location is considered a temporary location for the park so check to see if it has moved.

Bandix Dog Park
Bandix Road SE at Burley-Olalla Rd
Burley, WA
visitkitsap.com/kitsap.asp
This very large 30 acre off-leash park opened in July, 2004. It is not fenced and dogs that use it should follow voice commands well. The dog park is located on Bandix Road SE south of Burley-Olalla Rd and North of Nelson (Stevens) Road near State Highway 16. From State Highway 16 take Burley-Olalla Rd east to Bandix Road SE and turn right. The park will be on the right. The dog park is sponsored and maintained by Kitsap Dog Parks, Inc.

Patmore Pit Off-Leash Area
Patmore Rd At Keystone Hill Rd
Coupeville, WA
360-321-4049
fetchparks.org
This large forty acre meadow is partially fenced. There is also a fenced agility area with toys, water and cleanup bags. To get to the park from SR 20 take Patmore Road west to Keystone Hill Rd. Turn left (south) on Keystone Hill to the park. It will be on the right side.

Loganberry Lane Off-Leash Area

18th Ave. W.
Everett, WA
425-257-8300
This is a small unfenced off-leash area which is about 1/2 acre in size. It is wooded with trails. The hours at the park are 6 am to 10 pm.

Lowell Park Off-Leash Area
46th St at S 3rd Ave.
Everett, WA
425-257-8300
This is a small but fenced off-leash area. The hours at the park are 6 am to 10 pm. The off-leash dog park is located north of the tennis courts in Lowell Park. From I-5 you can exit at 41st Street, head east and then turn south on 3rd Ave to the park.

French Lake Dog Park
31531 1st Ave S
Federal Way, WA
253-835-6901
The French Lake Dog Park is a large, 10 acre off-leash area. It has a pond and picnic benches. To get to the park take I-5 to the S. 320th Street exit. Head west on 320th Street to 1st Way and head north to the park.

Marguerite Brons Dog Park
WA 525 at Bayview Rd
Freeland, WA
360-321-4049
fetchparks.org
This large thirteen acre off-leash park is fully fenced. Most of the park is wooded with trails through the trees. Some of the park is an open meadow. To get to the park from Freeland take WA-525 south and turn right on Bayview Rd. The park is on the left in about 1/2 mile.

Luther Burbank Dog Park
2040 84th Avenue SE
Mercer Island, WA
206-236-3545
The unfenced, off-leash dog area is on the north side of the park on the shore of Lake Washington. There are places for your dog to take a dip in Lake Washington in the off-leash areas. Dogs are allowed on leash in the rest of the park. To get there from I-5, take I-90 East to Mercer Island and take the Island Crest Way exit (#7). At the top of the ramp, turn right on SE 26th Street. At the stop sign turn left on 84th Avenue SE and drive straight to the park after another stop sign at SE

24th Street.

Clover Valley Dog Park
Oak Harbor at Ault Field Rd
Oak Harbor, WA
360-321-4049
fetchparks.org
This two acre fenced dog park is located north of the city of Oak Harbor on Whidbey Island. The dog park is located next to the Clover Valley Baseball Park. From SR 20 head west about one mile on Ault Field Road to the park.

Oak Harbor Dog Park
Technical Park at Goldie Rd
Oak Harbor, WA
360-321-4049
fetchparks.org
This one acre fenced dog park is located north of the city of Oak Harbor on Whidbey Island. From SR 20 head west on Ault Field Rd. Turn left on Goldie Rd and turn left on Technical Drive. Follow Technical Drive to the park.

Howe Farm Historic Park and Off-Leash Dog Area
Long Lake Rd at Sedgwick Rd
Port Orchard, WA
360-337-5350
visitkitsap.com/kitsap.asp
Howe Farm County Park is a Historic Farm with Walking Trails. Dogs are allowed on leash at outside areas of the park. In addition, there is a 5.5 acre off-leash area. This area is not fenced and dogs should be under voice control and well-behaved. To get to Howe Farm take Hwy 16 to Sedgwick. Head east on Sedgwick for three miles to Long Lake Road. Turn left on Long Lake Rd to the park.

Raab Dog Park
18349 Caldart Ave
Poulsbo, WA
360-779-9898
The fenced, off-leash area is located in Raab Park. Raab Park overlooks downtown Poulsbo and also has a nature trail and a running or walking track. From Washington 305 Turn east on NE Hostmark St and then south on Caldart Ave to the park.

Marymoor Park Off-Leash Area
6046 West Lake
Redmond, WA
206-205-3661
This park has a designated off-leash area for dogs. The off-leash area is forty acres in size but most of the 640 acre park is not designated off-leash so check the signs. There are

a number of trails with bridges through the off-leash area and a stream for dogs to play in. To get to the park from I-5 or I-405, take State Route 520 east to the West Lake Sammamish Parkway exit. At the bottom of the ramp, go right/southbound on W. Lake Sammamish Parkway NE. The park entrance is the next left at the traffic light.

Grandview Park Dog Park
Seatac, WA
425-881-0148
soda.org
This is a very large 37 acre fenced dog park. There are picnic benches and, on nice days, you can see Mt Rainier. The park is mostly grassy fields. To get to the Grandview Dog Park take I-5 to Kent-Des Moines Rd (Route 516) and head east on 516. Turn north on Military Rd and east on S 228th Street to the park.

Genesee Park Dog Park
46th Avenue S & S Genesee Street
Seattle, WA
206-684-4075
This fully fenced dog park in Genesee Park has double gates, a drinking fountain for dogs and a kiosk for community notices.

I-5 Colonnade Dog Park
E. Howe Street at Lakeview Blvd
Seattle, WA
206-684-4075
There is a narrow but fenced off-leash dog park located underneath the I-5 Freeway. Since the dog park is under the freeway it stays dry during most rain. The dog park shares the 7 acre park sight with a mountain bike course. The park is open from 4 am to 11:30 pm. The park is located just beneath the I-5 Freeway at E. Howe Street between Lakeview Blvd and Franklin Ave E.

I-90 "Blue Dog Pond" Off-Leash Area
S Massachusetts
Seattle, WA
206-684-4075
This dog park is located at the northwest corner of the intersection of Martin Luther King Jr. Way S and S Massachusetts. The park has a large sculpture of a blue dog.

Jose Rizal Park Off-Leash Area
1008 12th Avenue S
Seattle, WA
206-684-4075
This park offers a designated off-leash area. The park is located at 1008 12th Avenue S on North

Beacon Hill. Parking is available on 12th South.

Northacres Park Off-Leash Area
North 130th Street
Seattle, WA
206-684-4075
This park is located west of I-5 at North 130th Street. The park is south of North 130th Street and the off-leash area is in the northeast corner of the park. Parking is available on the west side of the park on 1st NE and on the south side of the park on N 125th.

Plymouth Pillars Dog Park
Boren Avenue at Pike Street
Seattle, WA
206-684-4075
The off-leash dog park opened in January of 2006. The dog park is 10,000 square feet and is a narrow and curved design. The surface is rock. The park is located above the I-5 freeway. To get to the park from the freeway take exits 166 or 165. The park is located on Boren Avenue between Pike Street and Pine Street.

Regrade Park Off-Leash Area
2251 3rd Avenue
Seattle, WA
206-684-4075
This small off-leash area in Regrade Park is located in downtown at 2251 3rd Avenue at Bell Street.

Sand Point Magnuson Park Dog Off-Leash Area
7400 Sand Point Way NE
Seattle, WA
206-684-4946
This leash free dog park covers about 9 acres and is the biggest fully fenced off-leash park in Seattle. It also offers an access point to the lake where your pooch is welcome to take a dip in the fresh lake water. To find the dog park, take Sand Point Way Northeast and enter the park at Northeast 74th Street. Go straight and park near the playground and sports fields. The main gate to the off-leash area is located at the southeast corner of the main parking lot. Dogs must be leashed until you enter the off-leash area.

Westcrest Park
8806 8th Avenue SW
Seattle, WA
206-684-4075
This dog park in Westcrest Park is over 4 acres in size. It is located in

West Seattle.

Woodland Park Off-Leash Area
W Green Lake Way N
Seattle, WA
206-684-4075
This park has a designated off-leash area.

SCRAPS Dog Park
26715 E Spokane Bridge Rd
Spokane, WA
509-477-2532
spokanecounty.org/animal
This 3 1/2 acre fenced dog park is located in the new Gateway Park. It is the first off-leash dog park in Spokane County. Gateway Park is just north of I-90 at the Idaho state line. The Park was built on the abandoned rest area.

Rogers Park Off-Leash Dog Park
E L St At E Wright Ave
Tacoma, WA
253-305-1060
This fenced dog park is located in Rogers Park. From I-5 you can take the Portland Avenue Exit. Head east of E Wiley Ave (parallels the I-5 South) and turn south on E Valley View Terrace to the park on your left.

Ross Off-Leash Rec Area
NE Ross St at NE 18th St
Vancouver, WA
360-619-1111
This nearly 9 acre fenced dog park was a joint project between BPA (which donated land), DOGPAW and the city of Vancouver. It is Vancouver's first off-leash dog park. To get to the park, exit I-5 at Highway 99 and head north. Turn right onto NE Ross St to NE 18th St and the park.

Wisconsin

Brookfield Dog Park
River Rd
Brookfield, WI
This off-leash dog park is not fenced. Dogs must be leashed outside of the off-leash area. The park is located on the north side of River Rd between N. Barker Rd and N. Brookfield Rd.

Indian Lake Pet Exercise Area
Hwy 19
Cross Plains, WI
608-266-4711
The dog exercise areas in the park are posted on signs in the park. This

is a non-fenced dog exercise area. A permit is required to use the off-leash park. The permit allows use of all Madison and Dane County off-leash areas. An annual permit costs $20 per dog or you may opt for a daily fee of $3 per dog per day. Permits may be purchased at the parks department at 4318 Robertson Rd or at many places around the county. The pet exercise area is located north of Cross Plains on Hwy 19 in Indian Lake Park.

Eau Claire Dog Park
4503 House Rd
Eau Claire, WI
715-839-4923
ecdogpark.com/
This dog park requires a permit. You may purchase a day pass by depositing $2 per day in a drop box at the dog park or you may purchase an annual permit for $15 for residents or $20 for non-residents.

Muttland Meadows Dog Park
789 Green Bay Road
Grafton, WI
This is a 6.6 acre fenced dog park . It is located southwest of Lime Kiln Park on South Green Bay Road.

Brown County Park Pet Exercise Area
Highway 54
Green Bay, WI
920-448-4466
This fenced dog park is open from 8 am to sunset daily. You must have a permit to use the dog park. Annual permits cost $15 and are available at a number of Green Bay locations. Or you can call 920-448-6242 for an application. Visitors to Green Bay or residents may use the park for $2 for a one day pass. This may be purchased at the dog park. To get to the park from Green Bay take Highway 54 west. The park is located just east of the Brown County Golf Course.

Palmer Park Pet Exercise Area
Palmer Park
Janesville, WI
This off-leash dog exercise area is not fenced. Dogs may be off-leash in the area designated as off-leash. Outside of this area dogs must be on leash.

Rock River Parkway Pet Exercise Area
Rock River Parkway
Janesville, WI
This off-leash dog exercise area is not fenced. Dogs may be off-leash in the area designated as off-leash only. Outside of this area dogs must be on leash. The off-leash dog exercise area is located near the boat launch near Center Ave and Rockport Rd.

Jefferson County Dog Park
Hwy 26
Johnson Creek, WI
co.jefferson.wi.us/dogpark/
The Jefferson County Dog Park requires a permit in order to use the park. You may pay $2 at the dog park through a self-registration or purchase an annual permit at the Jefferson County Court House, Rm 204, 320 South Main St, Jefferson, WI.

Brittingham Park Dog Park
401 West Shore Dr
Madison, WI
608-266-4711
The dog exercise areas in the park are posted on signs in the park. This is a non-fenced dog exercise area. A permit is required to use the off-leash park. The permit allows use of all Madison and Dane County off-leash areas. An annual permit costs $20 per dog or you may opt for a daily fee of $3 per dog per day. Permits may be purchased at the parks department at 4318 Robertson Rd or at many places around the county.

Quann Park Dog Park
1802 Expo Drive
Madison, WI
608-266-4711
The dog exercise areas in the park are posted on signs in the park. This is a non-fenced dog exercise area. A permit is required to use the off-leash park. The permit allows use of all Madison and Dane County off-leash areas. An annual permit costs $20 per dog or you may opt for a daily fee of $3 per dog per day. Permits may be purchased at the parks department at 4318 Robertson Rd or at many places around the county.

Sycamore Park Dog Park
4517 Sycamore Park
Madison, WI
608-266-4711
The dog exercise areas in the park are posted on signs in the park. This is a non-fenced dog exercise area. A permit is required to use the off-leash park. The permit allows use of all Madison and Dane County off-leash areas. An annual permit costs $20 per dog or you

may opt for a daily fee of $3 per dog per day. Permits may be purchased at the parks department at 4318 Robertson Rd or at many places around the county.

Token Creek Park Pet Exercise Area
Hwy 51
Madison, WI
608-266-4711
The dog exercise areas in the park are posted on signs in the park. This is a non-fenced dog exercise area. A permit is required to use the off-leash park. The permit allows use of all Madison and Dane County off-leash areas. An annual permit costs $20 per dog or you may opt for a daily fee of $3 per dog per day. Permits may be purchased at the parks department at 4318 Robertson Rd or at many places around the county. The pet exercise area is located north of Madison on Hwy 51 in Token Creek Park.

Warner Park Dog Park
Sheridan Drive
Madison, WI
608-266-4711
The dog exercise areas in the park are posted on signs in the park. This is a non-fenced dog exercise area. A permit is required to use the off-leash park. The permit allows use of all Madison and Dane County off-leash areas. An annual permit costs $20 per dog or you may opt for a daily fee of $3 per dog per day. Permits may be purchased at the parks department at 4318 Robertson Rd or at many places around the county. The park is located on Sheridan Drive along Lagoon at the boat launch auxilary parking lot.

Yahara Heights Pet Exercise Area
5428 State Highway 113
Madison, WI
608-266-4711
The dog exercise areas in the park are posted on signs in the park. This is a non-fenced dog exercise area. A permit is required to use the off-leash park. The permit allows use of all Madison and Dane County off-leash areas. An annual permit costs $20 per dog or you may opt for a daily fee of $3 per dog per day. Permits may be purchased at the parks department at 4318 Robertson Rd or at many places around the county. The pet exercise area is located near the intersection of State Highway 113 and Highway M.

Katherin Kearny Carpenter Dog Run
N Katherine Dr

Mequon, WI
This park offers an off-leash dog run area. It is not fenced. Dogs must be on leash outside of the off-leash area. To get to the park from I-43 exit at N Port Washington Rd and head north. When the road curves to go over I-43, merge right on N. Katherine Dr.

Middleton Pet Exercise Area
County Highway Q S of Hwy K
Middleton, WI
608-266-4711
The dog exercise areas in the park are posted on signs in the park. This is a non-fenced dog exercise area. A permit is required to use the off-leash park. The permit allows use of all Madison and Dane County off-leash areas. An annual permit costs $20 per dog or you may opt for a daily fee of $3 per dog per day. Permits may be purchased at the parks department at 4318 Robertson Rd or at many places around the county. The pet exercise area is located north of Middleton on the left side of County Hwy Q, south of the County Hwy K intersection.

Runway Dog Exercise Area
1214 E Rawson Ave
Milwaukee, WI
This dog park opened in August, 2005. It is fully fenced with a double gate. A permit is required to use the dog park. See the website http://www.county.milwaukee.gov/display/router.asp?docid=11518 to download a permit application. An annual pass to the dogpark costs $20. You may also pay $5 at the dogpark for a day pass. The park is located on Rawson Avenue between Howell and Nicholson.

Winnebago County Community Park Dog Park
501 East County Road Y
Oshkosh, WI
920-232-1960
This dog park is located in the Winnebago County Community Park in Oshkosh. The park is open from dawn to dusk daily.

Standings Rock Park Dog Exercise Area
Standing Rocks Road
Portage, WI
715-346-1433
The dog exercise area is located in Standing Rocks Road between Custer Road and Bear Lake Rd.

Viking Park Pet Exercise Area
Highway N

Stoughton, WI
608-266-4711
The dog exercise areas in the park are posted on signs in the park. This is a non-fenced dog exercise area. A permit is required to use the off-leash park. The permit allows use of all Madison and Dane County off-leash areas. An annual permit costs $20 per dog or you may opt for a daily fee of $3 per dog per day. Permits may be purchased at the parks department at 4318 Robertson Rd or at many places around the county. The pet exercise area is located north of Stoughton on Hwy N.

Sun Praire Pet Exercise Area
S. Bird Street
Sun Prairie, WI
608-266-4711
The dog exercise areas in the park are posted on signs in the park. This is a non-fenced dog exercise area. A permit is required to use the off-leash park. The permit allows use of all Madison and Dane County off-leash areas. An annual permit costs $20 per dog or you may opt for a daily fee of $3 per dog per day. Permits may be purchased at the parks department at 4318 Robertson Rd or at many places around the county. The pet exercise area is located south of Sheehan Park on S. Bird Street, over the railroad tracks and hill.

Praire Moraine Parkway Pet Exercise Area
County Hwy PB
Verona, WI
608-266-4711
The dog exercise areas in the park are posted on signs in the park. This is a non-fenced dog exercise area. A permit is required to use the off-leash park. The permit allows use of all Madison and Dane County off-leash areas. An annual permit costs $20 per dog or you may opt for a daily fee of $3 per dog per day. Permits may be purchased at the parks department at 4318 Robertson Rd or at many places around the county.

Waupaca County Dog Park
Hwy K
Waupaca, WI
715-258-6243
The dog park is located on Hwy K, south of Waupaca. It is next to the Waupaca Regional Recycling and Composting Center.

Canada

Alberta

Acadia Off-Leash Areas
Various
Acadia, AB
403-268-2489
Calgary's off-leash parks have unfenced areas authorized for off-leash play. However, please check for signs as policies may have changed. The off-leash park is Southland Dog Run at 9800 Blackfoot Tr SE.

Altadore Off-Leash Areas
Various
Altadore, AB
403-268-2489
Calgary's off-leash parks have unfenced areas authorized for off-leash play. However, please check for signs as policies may have changed. The off-leash park is at 4500 14A St SW.

Bankview Off-Leash Areas
Various
Bankview, AB
403-268-2489
Calgary's off-leash parks have unfenced areas authorized for off-leash play. However, please check for signs as policies may have changed. The off-leash park is at 1815 23 Av SW.

Beaverdam Off-Leash Areas
Various
Beaverdam, AB
403-268-2489
Calgary's off-leash parks have unfenced areas authorized for off-leash play. However, please check for signs as policies may have changed. The off-leash park is at 750 Blackthorn Rd NE.

Beddington Heights Off-Leash Areas
Various
Beddington Heights, AB
403-268-2489
Calgary's off-leash parks have unfenced areas authorized for off-leash play. However, please check for signs as policies may have changed. The off-leash parks are at 52 Berkley Wy NW, 172 Bermuda Dr NW, and 1051 Berkley Dr NW.

Belgravia Off-Leash Area
Saskatchewan Dr at University Ave
Belgravia, AB

780-496-1475
This narrow, unfenced dog park parallels the North Saskatchewan River on the west side of Saskatchewan Drive. Dogs using this off-leash area should be under very good control as it is a narrow area near the road. Dogs must be licensed and you must carry a leash with you even in the off-leash area. For detailed rules please see the Edmonton city website.

Bowness Off-Leash Areas
Various
Bowness, AB
403-268-2489
Calgary's off-leash parks have unfenced areas authorized for off-leash play. However, please check for signs as policies may have changed. The off-leash parks are at 160R Bow Green Cr NW, 7135 34 AveTr.

Braeside Off-Leash Areas
Various
Braeside, AB
403-268-2489
Calgary's off-leash parks have unfenced areas authorized for off-leash play. However, please check for signs as policies may have changed. The off-leash park is at 14 St and Anderson Rd SW.

Brentwood Off-Leash Areas
Various
Brentwood, AB
403-268-2489
Calgary's off-leash parks have unfenced areas authorized for off-leash play. However, please check for signs as policies may have changed. The off-leash park is at 3387R Breton Cl NW.

Briar Hill Off-Leash Areas
Various
Briar Hill, AB
403-268-2489
Calgary's off-leash parks have unfenced areas authorized for off-leash play. However, please check for signs as policies may have changed. The off-leash park is at 1025 19 St NW.

Bridgeland Off-Leash Areas
Various
Bridgeland, AB
403-268-2489
Calgary's off-leash parks have unfenced areas authorized for off-leash play. However, please check for signs as policies may have changed. The off-leash park is at 25 St. Georges Dr NE.

Britannia Off-Leash Areas
Various
Britannia, AB
403-268-2489
Calgary's off-leash parks have unfenced areas authorized for off-leash play. However, please check for signs as policies may have changed. The off-leash park is at 1120 50 Ave SW.

Bowmont Park Home Road Off-Leash Area
Home Road at 52 St NW
Calgary, AB
403-268-2489
There are two off-leash areas in Bowmont Park. The areas are not fenced and Calgary has very strict rules about the control and behavior of off-leash dogs and they do issue fines. For all rules see the Calgary city website. Dogs are not allowed in the Bowmont Park children's playgrounds at all and must be on-leash in all areas of the park outside of the off-leash areas. The Home Road off-leash area is accessible from Home Road at 52 St NW and extends to the west end of the Klippert Gravel Pit. Please check signs for exact areas.

Bowmont Park Silver Springs Gate Off-Leash Area
SilverView Dr and SilverView Way NW
Calgary, AB
403-268-2489
There are two off-leash areas in Bowmont Park. The areas are not fenced and Calgary has very strict rules about the control and behavior of off-leash dogs and they do issue fines. For all rules see the Calgary city website. Dogs are not allowed in the Bowmont Park children's playgrounds at all and must be on-leash in all areas of the park outside of the off-leash areas. The Silver Springs Gate off-leash area is at the south end of SilverSprings Gate NW. Please check signs for exact areas.

West Jasper Place Park Off-Leash Area
69 Ave at 172 St
Callingwood North, AB
780-496-1475
This non-fenced off-leash area is within West Jasper Place Park. The off-leash area is on the east side of the park at 172 Street from 70 Ave to 73 Av. Dogs must be licensed and you must have a leash with you even in the off-leash area. For detailed rules please see the Edmonton city

website.

Cambrian Heights Off-Leash Areas
Various
Cambrian Heights, AB
403-268-2489
Calgary's off-leash parks have unfenced areas authorized for off-leash play. However, please check for signs as policies may have changed. The off-leash parks are at 1407 John Laurie BV NW and 3425 10 St NW.

Coach Hill Off-Leash Areas
Various
Coach Hill, AB
403-268-2489
Calgary's off-leash parks have unfenced areas authorized for off-leash play. However, please check for signs as policies may have changed. The off-leash park is at 6204 Coach Hill Rd SW.

Collingwood Off-Leash Areas
Various
Collingwood, AB
403-268-2489
Calgary's off-leash parks have unfenced areas authorized for off-leash play. However, please check for signs as policies may have changed. The off-leash parks are at 1924 Canberra Rd NW and 1612 Cayuga Dr NW.

Crescent Heights Off-Leash Areas
Various
Crescent Heights, AB
403-268-2489
Calgary's off-leash parks have unfenced areas authorized for off-leash play. However, please check for signs as policies may have changed. The off-leash park is at Rotary Park at 617 1 St NE.

Cromdale Off-Leash Area
Kinnard Ravine at 78 St.
Cromdale, AB
780-496-1475
This non-fenced off-leash area is on the north side of Kinnard Ravine from 78 St to 79 St. You can access the area off of 112 Ave. Dogs must be licensed and you must carry a leash with you even in the off-leash area. For detailed rules please see the Edmonton city website.

Deer Ridge Off-Leash Areas
Various
Deer Ridge, AB
403-268-2489
Calgary's off-leash parks have unfenced areas authorized for off-

leash play. However, please check for signs as policies may have changed. The off-leash park is at 151 Deerfield Dr SE.

Diamond Cove Off-Leash Areas
Various
Diamond Cove, AB
403-268-2489
Calgary's off-leash parks have unfenced areas authorized for off-leash play. However, please check for signs as policies may have changed. The off-leash parks are at 247 Queensland Pl SE between Diamond Cove and Queensland and at 11404 Bow Bottom Tr SE east of the river.

Orval Allen Park Off-Leash Area
127 St South of 162 Ave
Dunluce, AB
780-496-1475
This non-fenced off-leash area includes Orval Allen Park as well as some narrow road right-of-way. Dogs must be licensed and you must have a leash with you even in the off-leash area. For detailed rules please see the Edmonton city website.

Eagleridge Off-Leash Areas
Various
Eagleridge, AB
403-268-2489
Calgary's off-leash parks have unfenced areas authorized for off-leash play. However, please check for signs as policies may have changed. The off-leash park is at 52 Eagle Crest Pl SW.

East Village Off-Leash Areas
Various
East Village, AB
403-268-2489
Calgary's off-leash parks have unfenced areas authorized for off-leash play. However, please check for signs as policies may have changed. The off-leash park is at 610 5 Ave SE.

Edgemont Off-Leash Areas
Various
Edgemont, AB
403-268-2489
Calgary's off-leash parks have unfenced areas authorized for off-leash play. However, please check for signs as policies may have changed. The off-leash parks are at 47 Edgepark Blvd NW, 175 Edgedale Dr NW and 124 Edendale Cr NW.

Buena Vista Great Meadow Off-Leash Area
Buena Vista Dr and Valleyview Cres NW
Edmonton, AB
780-496-1475
The large, unfenced off-leash area covers much of Laurier Park. This is a balloon launching area so dogs should be leashed when balloons are taking off. Dogs must be licensed and you must carry a leash with you even in the off-leash area. For detailed rules please see the Edmonton city website.

Jackie Parker Park Off-Leash Area
Whitemud Dr and 50 St.
Edmonton, AB
780-496-1475
The large, unfenced off-leash area covers areas of Jackie Parker Park. It does not include the golf course. Dogs must be licensed and you must carry a leash with you even in the off-leash area. For detailed rules please see the Edmonton city website.

Elbow Park Off-Leash Areas
Various
Elbow Park, AB
403-268-2489
Calgary's off-leash parks have unfenced areas authorized for off-leash play. However, please check for signs as policies may have changed. The off-leash park is at 3029 8 St SW.

Elboya Off-Leash Areas
Various
Elboya, AB
403-268-2489
Calgary's off-leash parks have unfenced areas authorized for off-leash play. However, please check for signs as policies may have changed. The off-leash park is at 521 Lansdowne Ave SW.

Fairview Off-Leash Areas
Various
Fairview, AB
403-268-2489
Calgary's off-leash parks have unfenced areas authorized for off-leash play. However, please check for signs as policies may have changed. The off-leash parks are at 7510 Flint Rd SE and 450 71 Ave SE.

Falconridge Off-Leash Areas
Various
Falconridge, AB
403-268-2489
Calgary's off-leash parks have unfenced areas authorized for off-

leash play. However, please check for signs as policies may have changed. The off-leash park is at Falwood Wy NE from Falconridge Cr to Falbury Cr NE.

Forest Lawn Off-Leash Areas
Various
Forest Lawn Industrial, AB
403-268-2489
Calgary's off-leash parks have unfenced areas authorized for off-leash play. However, please check for signs as policies may have changed. The off-leash park is at 1827 68 St SE south of Elliston Park.

Glenbrook Off-Leash Areas
Various
Glenbrook, AB
403-268-2489
Calgary's off-leash parks have unfenced areas authorized for off-leash play. However, please check for signs as policies may have changed. The off-leash park is at 5302 32 Ave SW.

Greenview Off-Leash Areas
Various
Greenview, AB
403-268-2489
Calgary's off-leash parks have unfenced areas authorized for off-leash play. However, please check for signs as policies may have changed. The off-leash park is at 4307 Edmonton Tr NE.

Hawkwood Off-Leash Areas
Various
Hawkwood, AB
403-268-2489
Calgary's off-leash parks have unfenced areas authorized for off-leash play. However, please check for signs as policies may have changed. The off-leash parks are at 164 Hawkview Manor Cl NW, 100 Hawkwood Hill NW and 243 Hawkcliff Way NW.

Haysboro Off-Leash Areas
Various
Haysboro, AB
403-268-2489
Calgary's off-leash parks have unfenced areas authorized for off-leash play. However, please check for signs as policies may have changed. The off-leash parks are at 328 Haddon Rd SW and 1438 Heritage Dr SW.

Hidden Valley Off-Leash Areas
Various
Hidden Valley, AB

403-268-2489
Calgary's off-leash parks have unfenced areas authorized for off-leash play. However, please check for signs as policies may have changed. The off-leash park is at Hidden Valley Dr at Shaganappi Tr NW.

Huntington Hills Off-Leash Areas
Various
Huntington Hills, AB
403-268-2489
Calgary's off-leash parks have unfenced areas authorized for off-leash play. However, please check for signs as policies may have changed. The off-leash parks are at 520 78 Ave NW, 1135 78 Ave NW, 105 Huntstrom Dr and 8068 Huntington Rd NE.

Inglewood Off-Leash Areas
Various
Inglewood, AB
403-268-2489
Calgary's off-leash parks have unfenced areas authorized for off-leash play. However, please check for signs as policies may have changed. The off-leash park is at 620 12 St SE south of the Zoo Bridge.

Lake Bonavista Off-Leash Areas
Various
Lake Bonavista, AB
403-268-2489
Calgary's off-leash parks have unfenced areas authorized for off-leash play. However, please check for signs as policies may have changed. The off-leash parks are at 227 Lake Willow Rd SE, 1172R Lake Huron Cr SE, 289 129 Ave SE and 11904 Bonaventure Dr SE.

Lakeview Off-Leash Areas
Various
Lakeview, AB
403-268-2489
Calgary's off-leash parks have unfenced areas authorized for off-leash play. However, please check for signs as policies may have changed. The off-leash park is at 3129 Glenmore Tr SW.

Grand Trunk Park Off-Leash Area
127 Ave at 109 St
Lauderdale, AB
780-496-1475
The south end of Grand Trunk Park is an unfenced off-leash area. Dogs must be licensed and you must carry a leash with you even in the off-leash area. For detailed rules please see the Edmonton city

website.

Lynnwood Ridge Off-Leash Areas
Various
Lynnwood Ridge, AB
403-268-2489
Calgary's off-leash parks have unfenced areas authorized for off-leash play. However, please check for signs as policies may have changed. The off-leash parks are at 1003 Lysander Dr SE and 171R Lynnview Rd SE.

Mapleridge Off-Leash Areas
Various
Mapleridge, AB
403-268-2489
Calgary's off-leash parks have unfenced areas authorized for off-leash play. However, please check for signs as policies may have changed. The off-leash park is at 56 Mapleglade Cl SE.

Marlborough Off-Leash Areas
Various
Marlborough, AB
403-268-2489
Calgary's off-leash parks have unfenced areas authorized for off-leash play. However, please check for signs as policies may have changed. The off-leash park is at Marlborough Park Buffer from 52 St to 68 St NE.

Martindale Off-Leash Areas
Various
Martindale, AB
403-268-2489
Calgary's off-leash parks have unfenced areas authorized for off-leash play. However, please check for signs as policies may have changed. The off-leash park is at 199 Martindale BV NE.

Mayland Heights Off-Leash Areas
Various
Mayland Heights, AB
403-268-2489
Calgary's off-leash parks have unfenced areas authorized for off-leash play. However, please check for signs as policies may have changed. The off-leash parks are at 325 19 St NE, 320 19 St NE and 116 Mckinnon Cr NE.

Montgomery Off-Leash Areas
Various
Montgomery, AB
403-268-2489
Calgary's off-leash parks have unfenced areas authorized for off-leash play. However, please check

for signs as policies may have changed. The off-leash park is at 4707 Montalban Dr NW.

North Haven Off-Leash Areas
Various
North Haven, AB
403-268-2489
Calgary's off-leash parks have unfenced areas authorized for off-leash play. However, please check for signs as policies may have changed. The off-leash parks are at 314 Norsemand Rd NW, John Laurie Blvd NW behind Namaka Cr NW and 4827R Niven Rd NW.

Ogden Off-Leash Areas
Various
Ogden, AB
403-268-2489
Calgary's off-leash parks have unfenced areas authorized for off-leash play. However, please check for signs as policies may have changed. The off-leash parks are at 6030 18A St SE, 7231 20A St SE and 7120 20A St SE.

Parkland Off-Leash Areas
Various
Parkland, AB
403-268-2489
Calgary's off-leash parks have unfenced areas authorized for off-leash play. However, please check for signs as policies may have changed. The off-leash park is at 14220 Parkland Blvd SE.

Pineridge Off-Leash Areas
Various
Pineridge, AB
403-268-2489
Calgary's off-leash parks have unfenced areas authorized for off-leash play. However, please check for signs as policies may have changed. The off-leash park is at 2115 68 St NE.

Pumphill Off-Leash Areas
Various
Pumphill, AB
403-268-2489
Calgary's off-leash parks have unfenced areas authorized for off-leash play. However, please check for signs as policies may have changed. The off-leash park is at 2001 22 St SW.

Queensland Off-Leash Areas
Various
Queensland, AB
403-268-2489
Calgary's off-leash parks have

unfenced areas authorized for off-leash play. However, please check for signs as policies may have changed. The off-leash parks are at 48R Queen Alexandra Cl SE and 247 Queensland Pl SE.

Ramsay Off-Leash Areas
Various
Ramsay, AB
403-268-2489
Calgary's off-leash parks have unfenced areas authorized for off-leash play. However, please check for signs as policies may have changed. The off-leash park is at 2015 Salisbury St SE.

Ranchlands Off-Leash Areas
Various
Ranchlands, AB
403-268-2489
Calgary's off-leash parks have unfenced areas authorized for off-leash play. However, please check for signs as policies may have changed. The off-leash parks are at 200 Ranch Estates Dr NW, 239 Ranch Estates Dr NW and 655 Ranchlands Blvd NW.

Renfrew Off-Leash Areas
Various
Renfrew, AB
403-268-2489
Calgary's off-leash parks have unfenced areas authorized for off-leash play. However, please check for signs as policies may have changed. The off-leash park is at 936 Robert Rd NE.

Riverbend Off-Leash Areas
Various
Riverbend, AB
403-268-2489
Calgary's off-leash parks have unfenced areas authorized for off-leash play. However, please check for signs as policies may have changed. The off-leash parks are at 8925 Riverview Dr SE and 171 Riverbend Dr SE.

Riverdale Off-Leash Areas
Various
Riverdale, AB
403-268-2489
Calgary's off-leash parks have unfenced areas authorized for off-leash play. However, please check for signs as policies may have changed. The off-leash park is at 521 and 625 Landsdowne Ave SW.

Rosedale Off-Leash Areas
Various

Rosedale, AB
403-268-2489
Calgary's off-leash parks have unfenced areas authorized for off-leash play. However, please check for signs as policies may have changed. The off-leash parks are at 1101 Crescent Rd NW and 625 Crescent Rd NW.

Roxboro Off-Leash Areas
Various
Roxboro, AB
403-268-2489
Calgary's off-leash parks have unfenced areas authorized for off-leash play. However, please check for signs as policies may have changed. The off-leash parks are at 300 33 Av SW and 3010 Roxboro Glen Rd SW.

Rundle Off-Leash Areas
Various
Rundle, AB
403-268-2489
Calgary's off-leash parks have unfenced areas authorized for off-leash play. However, please check for signs as policies may have changed. The off-leash park is along 16 Ave from Rundlecairn Way to Rundleridge Dr NE.

Sandstone Off-Leash Areas
Various
Sandstone, AB
403-268-2489
Calgary's off-leash parks have unfenced areas authorized for off-leash play. However, please check for signs as policies may have changed. The off-leash parks are at 99 Sandstone Dr NW and 98 Sandringham Way NW.

Scarboro Off-Leash Areas
Various
Scarboro, AB
403-268-2489
Calgary's off-leash parks have unfenced areas authorized for off-leash play. However, please check for signs as policies may have changed. The off-leash parks are at 1616 22 st SW and 1521 Summit St SW.

Scenic Acres Off-Leash Areas
Various
Scenic Acres, AB
403-268-2489
Calgary's off-leash parks have unfenced areas authorized for off-leash play. However, please check for signs as policies may have changed. The off-leash parks are at 8611 Crowchild Tr NW between

Scenic View GA and Schubert GA and at 61 Scotia Pt NW.

Shaganappi Off-Leash Areas
Various
Shaganappi, AB
403-268-2489
Calgary's off-leash parks have unfenced areas authorized for off-leash play. However, please check for signs as policies may have changed. The off-leash park is at 2608 14 Ave W north of the Community Assocation.

Silver Springs Off-Leash Areas
Various
Silver Springs, AB
403-268-2489
Calgary's off-leash parks have unfenced areas authorized for off-leash play. However, please check for signs as policies may have changed. The off-leash park is at 5420 Silver Springs Blvd NW.

Southwood Off-Leash Areas
Various
Southwood, AB
403-268-2489
Calgary's off-leash parks have unfenced areas authorized for off-leash play. However, please check for signs as policies may have changed. The off-leash park is on the Northside of Anderson Rd from Macleod Trail to Elbow Drive SW.

Spruce Cliff Off-Leash Areas
Various
Spruce Cliff, AB
403-268-2489
Calgary's off-leash parks have unfenced areas authorized for off-leash play. However, please check for signs as policies may have changed. The off-leash parks are at 5050 Spruce Dr SW and at Edworthy Park east of the Lawrey Gardens, north of the train tracks and along the river.

Strathcona Off-Leash Areas
Various
Strathcona, AB
403-268-2489
Calgary's off-leash parks have unfenced areas authorized for off-leash play. However, please check for signs as policies may have changed. The off-leash parks are at 795 Strathcona Dr SW and 111 Stratton Cr SW.

Sunalta Off-Leash Areas
Various
Sunalta, AB

403-268-2489
Calgary's off-leash parks have unfenced areas authorized for off-leash play. However, please check for signs as policies may have changed. The off-leash park is at 2240 Pumphouse Ave SW.

Thorncliffe Off-Leash Areas
Various
Thorncliffe, AB
403-268-2489
Calgary's off-leash parks have unfenced areas authorized for off-leash play. However, please check for signs as policies may have changed. The off-leash parks are at 280 Northmount Dr NW, 628 63 Ave NW, 6227 Touchwood Dr NW and 421 60 Ave NE.

Varsity Off-Leash Areas
Various
Varsity, AB
403-268-2489
Calgary's off-leash parks have unfenced areas authorized for off-leash play. However, please check for signs as policies may have changed. The off-leash parks are at 4120 37 St NW, 4001 36 St NW, 37 St NW and Crowchild Tr NW and at Vienna Dr NW and Crowchild Tr NW.

Wellington Off-Leash Area
West of 141 St from 137 Ave to 132 Ave
Wellington, AB
780-496-1475
This is a narrow non-fenced off-leash area that includes a strip on the west side of 141 Street between 137 Ave and 132 Ave. It also includes the south side of 132 Ave from to 135 St. Dogs using this area should be very well behaved off-leash. Dogs must be licensed and you must carry a leash with you even in the off-leash area. For detailed rules please see the Edmonton city website.

Willowpark Off-Leash Areas
Various
Willowpark, AB
403-268-2489
Calgary's off-leash parks have unfenced areas authorized for off-leash play. However, please check for signs as policies may have changed. The off-leash park is at 809 Willingdon BV SE.

Woodbine Off-Leash Areas
Various
Woodbine, AB
403-268-2489

Calgary's off-leash parks have unfenced areas authorized for off-leash play. However, please check for signs as policies may have changed. The off-leash park is at 37 St SW from Anderson Rd to 130 Ave SW.

British Columbia

Confederation Park Off-Leash Area
Willingdon Avenue
Burnaby, BC
604-294-7450
Dogs are allowed off-leash year-round in a designated area. The area is located north of Penzance Drive, roughly between Willingdon and Gamma Avenues. There will be signs posted indicating the off-leash area. The following off-leash codes apply: clean up after your pet, you must be present and in verbal control of your dog at all times, dogs must wear a valid rabies tag, no aggressive dogs allowed, and dogs must be leashed before and after using the off-leash area. Dogs on leash are allowed throughout Confederation Park.

Burnaby Fraser Foreshore Park Off-Leash Area
Byrne Road
South Burnaby, BC
604-294-7450
From October through March, dogs are allowed off-leash in a designated area near the Fraser River. The area is located near the end of Byrne Road. The following off-leash codes apply: clean up after your pet, you must be present and in verbal control of your dog at all times, dogs must wear a valid rabies tag, no aggressive dogs allowed, and dogs must be leashed before and after using the off-leash area. Dogs on leash are allowed in the rest of the park, but not on the banks of the Fraser River.

37th and Oak Park Off-Leash Dog Park
West 37th Avenue at Oak Street
Vancouver, BC
604-257-8689
The unfenced dog off-leash area is available for off-leash play from 6 am to 10 pm. Please see the signs outlining the off-leash area. Dogs must be well-behaved, have a current license, leashed outside of the off-leash areas and cleaned up after.

Balaclava Park Off-Leash Dog Park
4594 Balaclava Street
Vancouver, BC
604-257-8689
The unfenced dog off-leash area is available for off-leash play from 7 am to 10 am and 5 pm to 10 pm. Please see the signs outlining the off-leash area. Dogs must be well-behaved, have a current license, leashed outside of the off-leash areas and cleaned up after. The park is located at Carnarvon and Balaclava Streets at West 29th and West 31st Avenues.

Charleston Park Off-Leash Dog Park
999 Charleson Street
Vancouver, BC
604-257-8400
The grass bowl area is off-leash from 6 am to 10 pm year round. The waterfall pond is off-leash from October thru May only. Please see the signs outlining the off-leash areas. Dogs must be well-behaved, have a current license, leashed outside of the off-leash areas and cleaned up after.

Cooper's Park Off-Leash Dog Park
1020 Marinaside Crescent
Vancouver, BC
604-257-8400
The unfenced dog off-leash area is the grass field east of the Cambie Street Bridge and is available for off-leash play from 6 am to 10 pm. Please see the signs outlining the off-leash area. Dogs must be well-behaved, have a current license, leashed outside of the off-leash areas and cleaned up after.

Dusty Greenwell Park Off-Leash Dog Park
2799 Wall Street
Vancouver, BC
604-257-8613
This unfenced park is available for off-leash play from 5 am to 10 am and 5 pm to 10 pm. Please see the signs outlining the off-leash areas. Dogs must be well-behaved, have a current license, leashed outside of the off-leash areas and cleaned up after.

Falaise Park Off-Leash Dog Park
3434 Falaise Avenue
Vancouver, BC
604-257-8613
The unfenced dog off-leash area is available for off-leash play from 5 am to 10 am and 5 pm to 10 pm. However, the area closest to the neighboring school is only off-leash from 5 am to 8 am. Please see the signs outlining the off-leash areas. Dogs must be well-behaved, have a current license, leashed outside of the off-leash areas and cleaned up after.

Fraserview Golf Course Off-Leash Dog Park
8101 Kerr Street
Vancouver, BC
604-257-8613
The unfenced dog off-leash area is available for off-leash play from 5 am to 10 am and 5 pm to 10 pm. Please see the signs outlining the off-leash area which is located only around the north and west sides of the golf course and is near major roads. Dogs must be well-behaved, have a current license, leashed outside of the off-leash areas and cleaned up after.

George Park Off-Leash Dog Park
500 E 63rd Avenue
Vancouver, BC
604-257-8689
The unfenced off-leash park is available for off-leash play from 6 am to 10 am and 5 pm to 10 pm. Please see the signs outlining the off-leash area. No dogs are allowed near the playground area. Dogs must be well-behaved, have a current license, leashed outside of the off-leash areas and cleaned up after.

Jones Park Off-Leash Dog Park
5350 Commercial Street
Vancouver, BC
604-257-8613
The unfenced off-leash area is available for off-leash play from 5 am to 10 am and 5 pm to 10 pm. Please see the signs outlining the off-leash area. Dogs must be well-behaved, have a current license, leashed outside of the off-leash areas and cleaned up after.

Killarney Park Off-Leash Dog Park
6205 Kerr Street
Vancouver, BC
604-257-8613
The unfenced off-leash area is available for off-leash play from 5 am to 10 am and 5 pm - 10 pm. However, during the summer dogs are allowed off-leash from 5 am to 10 pm. Please see the signs outlining the off-leash area. Dogs must be well-behaved, have a current license, leashed outside of the off-leash areas and cleaned up after.

Kingcrest Park Off-Leash Dog Park
4150 Knight Street
Vancouver, BC
604-257-8613
The unfenced off-leash area is available for off-leash play from 5 am to 10 am and 5 pm - 10 pm. Please see the signs outlining the off-leash area. Dogs must be well-behaved, have a current license, leashed outside of the off-leash areas and cleaned up after.

Locarno Park Off-Leash Dog Park
NW Marine Drive and Trimble Street
Vancouver, BC
604-257-8689
The unfenced dog off-leash area is available for off-leash play from 6 am to 10 pm. Please see the signs outlining the off-leash area. Dogs must be well-behaved, have a current license, leashed outside of the off-leash areas and cleaned up after. The park is located 1 block south of the beach between Trimble and Sasamat Streets. Dogs are not allowed near the playground.

Musqueam Park Off-Leash Dog Park
4000 SW Marine Drive
Vancouver, BC
604-257-8689
The unfenced off-leash area is available for off-leash play from 6 am to 10 pm. Please see the signs outlining the off-leash area. Dogs must be well-behaved, have a current license, leashed outside of the off-leash areas and cleaned up after.

Nat Bailey Stadium Off-Leash Dog Park
4601 Ontario Street
Vancouver, BC
604-257-8689
The unfenced off-leash area is available for off-leash play from 6 am to 10 pm. Please see the signs outlining the off-leash area. Dogs must be well-behaved, have a current license, leashed outside of the off-leash areas and cleaned up after. The park is located one block north of E 33rd Avenue and on the west side of Ontario Street.

Nelson Park Off-Leash Dog Park
1030 Bute Street
Vancouver, BC
604-257-8400
The unfenced off-leash park is available for off-leash play from 6 am to 8 am and 5 pm to 10 pm. Dogs are not allowed inside the school fence. Dogs must be well-behaved, have a current license, leashed

outside of the off-leash areas and cleaned up after.

Queen Elizabeth Park Off-Leash Dog Park
4600 Cambie Street
Vancouver, BC
604-257-8689
The unfenced off-leash area is available for off-leash play from 6 am to 10 pm. Please see the signs outlining the off-leash area. Dogs must be well-behaved, have a current license, leashed outside of the off-leash areas and cleaned up after. The off-leash park is located off East 37th Avenue and Columbia Street.

Quilchena Park Off-Leash Dog Park
4590 Magnolia Street
Vancouver, BC
604-257-8689
The unfenced off-leash area is available for off-leash play from 6 am to 10 pm. Please see the signs outlining the off-leash area. Dogs must be well-behaved, have a current license, leashed outside of the off-leash areas and cleaned up after.

Sparwood Park Off-Leash Dog Park
6998 Arlington Street
Vancouver, BC
604-257-8613
The unfenced off-leash area is available for off-leash play from 5 am to 10 am and 5 pm to 10 pm. Please see the signs outlining the off-leash area. Dogs must be well-behaved, have a current license, leashed outside of the off-leash areas and cleaned up after.

Stanley Park Dog Park for Small Dogs Only
Stanley Park Shuffleboard Court Area
Vancouver, BC
604-257-8400
The fully fenced off-leash area is available for off-leash play from 7 am to 9 pm for SMALL DOGS only. Please see the signs outlining the off-leash area. Dogs must be well-behaved, have a current license, leashed outside of the off-leash areas and cleaned up after.

Strathcona Park Off-Leash Dog Park
857 Malkin Avenue
Vancouver, BC
604-257-8613
The unfenced off-leash area is available for off-leash play from 5 am to 10 am and 5 pm to 10 pm. Please see the signs outlining the off-leash

area. Dogs must be well-behaved, have a current license, leashed outside of the off-leash areas and cleaned up after.

Sunrise Park Off-Leash Dog Park
1950 Windermere Street
Vancouver, BC
604-257-8613
The unfenced off-leash area is available for off-leash play from 5 am to 10 am and 5 pm to 10 pm. Dogs are not allowed on the sports fields or the playground but the rest of the park is off-leash during off-leash hours. Dogs must be well-behaved, have a current license, leashed outside of the off-leash areas and cleaned up after.

Sunset Park Off-Leash Dog Park
300 E 53rd Avenue
Vancouver, BC
604-257-8689
The unfenced off-leash park is available for off-leash play from 6 am to 10 pm. Dogs must be well-behaved, have a current license, leashed outside of the off-leash areas and cleaned up after. The park is located at Prince Edward Street and East 53rd Avenue.

Tecumseh Park Off-Leash Dog Park
1751 E 45th Avenue
Vancouver, BC
604-257-8613
The unfenced off-leash area is available for off-leash play from 5 am to 10 am and 5 pm to 10 pm. Dogs are not allowed in the playground but the rest of the park is off-leash during off-leash hours. Dogs must be well-behaved, have a current license, leashed outside of the off-leash areas and cleaned up after.

Valdez Park
3210 W 22nd Avenue
Vancouver, BC
604-257-8689
The unfenced off-leash park is available for off-leash play from 6 am to 10 am and 5 pm to 10 pm. Dogs must be well-behaved, have a current license, leashed outside of the off-leash areas and cleaned up after. The park is located at Balaclava Street and West 22nd Avenue.

Alexander Park Off-Leash Area
Victoria, BC
250-361-0600
victoria.ca/dogs/
There is an official off-leash area

during limited hours in Alexander Park. The summer hours are 6 am - 9 am and 6 pm - 9 pm. The hours from October through March are 6 am - 10 am and 4 pm - 9 pm. Dogs are not allowed in any playground areas either on-leash or off-leash, dogs must be under control at all times, must be cleaned up after and must be on-leash whenever they are outside of the off-leash area.

Arbutus Park Off-Leash Area
Washington Street
Victoria, BC
250-361-0600
victoria.ca/dogs/
There is an official off-leash area during limited hours in Arbutus Park. The daily off-leash hours are 6 - 10 am and 3 - 9 pm year round. Dogs are not allowed in any playground areas either on-leash or off-leash, dogs must be under control at all times, must be cleaned up after and must be on-leash whenever they are outside of the off-leash area.

Oswald Park Off-Leash Area
Stroud Rd at Gosworth Rd
Victoria, BC
250-361-0600
victoria.ca/dogs/
There is an official off-leash area during limited hours in Oswald Park. In the summer the off-leash hours are 6 am - 9 pm and 6 pm - 9 pm. From October through March the hours are 6 am - 10 am and 4 pm - 9 pm. Dogs are not allowed in any playground areas either on-leash or off-leash, dogs must be under control at all times, must be cleaned up after and must be on-leash whenever they are outside of the off-leash area.

Redfern Park Off-Leash Area
Redfern St at Leighton Ave
Victoria, BC
250-361-0600
victoria.ca/dogs/
There is an official off-leash area during limited hours in the park. The summer hours are 6 am - 8 am and 6 pm - 9 pm. The hours from October through March are 6 am - 8 am and 4 pm - 9 pm. Dogs are not allowed in any playground areas either on-leash or off-leash, dogs must be under control at all times, must be cleaned up after and must be on-leash whenever they are outside of the off-leash area.

Topaz Park Off-Leash Area
Topaz at Blanshard
Victoria, BC
250-361-0600

victoria.ca/dogs/
There is an official off-leash area during limited hours in Topaz Park. The hours vary by season and differ on weekdays and weekends. On weekends the off-leash hours are 6 -8 am and 5 - 9 pm year round. On weekdays the off-leash hours are 6 - 10 am and 5 - 9 pm during the summer. From October to March the evening offleash hours go from 4 pm to 9 pm. Dogs are not allowed in any playground areas either on-leash or off-leash, dogs must be under control at all times, must be cleaned up after and must be on-leash whenever they are outside of the off-leash area.

Victoria West Park Off-Leash Area
Wilson St at Bay St
Victoria, BC
250-361-0600
victoria.ca/dogs/
There is an official off-leash area during limited hours in Victoria West Park. The daily off-leash hours are 6 am - 9 am and 6 pm - 9 pm year roung. Dogs are not allowed in any playground areas either on-leash or off-leash, dogs must be under control at all times, must be cleaned up after and must be on-leash whenever they are outside of the off-leash area.

Manitoba

Bourkevale Park Off-Leash Area
100 Ferry Rd
Winnipeg, MB
204-986-7623
This unfenced, off-leash area is located in Bourkevale Park in the area south of the dike and along the riverbank. Dogs must be cleaned up after and dogs must be under voice control. Dogs must be licensed as well. Other rules are posted at each of the off-leash sites in Winnipeg.

Juba Park Off-Leash Area
Bannatyne Ave at Ship St.
Winnipeg, MB
204-986-7623
This unfenced, off-leash area is located next to Juba Park at Pioneer Avenue. The off-leash area consists of the vacant land west of the walkway that enters Juba Park. Dogs must be cleaned up after and dogs must be under voice control. Dogs must be licensed as well. Other rules are posted at each of the off-leash sites in Winnipeg.

Kilcona Park Off-Leash Area
Lagimodiere Blvd at Springfield Road
Winnipeg, MB
204-986-7623
This unfenced, off-leash area is located in Kilcona Park north of the west parking lot. Dogs must be cleaned up after and dogs must be under voice control. Dogs must be licensed as well. Other rules are posted at each of the off-leash sites in Winnipeg.

King's Park Park Off-Leash Area
King's Drive at Kilkenny Drive
Winnipeg, MB
204-986-7623
This unfenced, off-leash area is located in King's Park at the south end of the park south of the lake. Dogs must be cleaned up after and dogs must be under voice control. Dogs must be licensed as well. Other rules are posted at each of the off-leash sites in Winnipeg.

Little Mountain Park Off-Leash Area
Klimpke Road at Farmers Rd
Winnipeg, MB
204-986-7623
This unfenced, off-leash area is located in Little Mountain Park on the west side of the park near the Klimpke Road entrance. Dogs must be cleaned up after and dogs must be under voice control. Dogs must be licensed as well. Other rules are posted at each of the off-leash sites in Winnipeg.

Maple Grove Park Off-Leash Area
190 Frobisher Road
Winnipeg, MB
204-986-7623
This unfenced, off-leash area is located in the north end of the park and is bounded on most sides by the river. The park is located south of the University of Manitoba on the north side of the Perimeter Hwy (100) south of the city. Dogs must be cleaned up after and dogs must be under voice control. Dogs must be licensed as well. Other rules are posted at each of the off-leash sites in Winnipeg.

St. Boniface Industrial Park Off-Leash Area
Mazenod Rd at Camile Sys
Winnipeg, MB
204-986-7623
This unfenced, off-leash area is located in the St. Boniface Industrial Park and consists of the area surrounding the retention pond. The area is bounded by Mazenod Rd,

Camiel Sys Street and Beghin Street. To get to the park turn south from Dugald Rd onto Mazenod Rd. Dogs must be cleaned up after and dogs must be under voice control. Dogs must be licensed as well. Other rules are posted at each of the off-leash sites in Winnipeg.

Sturgeon Road Off-Leash Area
Sturgeon Rd at Silver Avenue
Winnipeg, MB
204-986-7623
There is an unfenced off-leash area on the northeast side of Sturgeon Rd and Silver Avenue. Dogs must be cleaned up after and dogs must be under voice control. Dogs must be licensed as well. Other rules are posted at each of the off-leash sites in Winnipeg.

Westview Park Off-Leash Area
Midland Street and Saskatchewan Avenue
Winnipeg, MB
204-986-7623
This entire Westview Park is an unfenced off-leash area. The park is located in the north part of the city at Midland and Saskatchewan. From the Trans-Canada Highway 1 head north on Century Street past the Airport. Turn right on Saskatchewan Avenue and the park will be on your right in about 3 blocks. Dogs must be cleaned up after and dogs must be under voice control. Dogs must be licensed as well. Other rules are posted at each of the off-leash sites in Winnipeg.

Woodsworth Park Off-Leash Area
King Edward Ave at Park Lane
Winnipeg, MB
204-986-7623
This unfenced, off-leash area is located in Woodsworth Park northeast of King Edward Avenue and Park Lane. Dogs must be cleaned up after and dogs must be under voice control. Dogs must be licensed as well. Other rules are posted at each of the off-leash sites in Winnipeg.

Nova Scotia

Point Pleasant Park Off-Leash Area
Point Pleasant Dr at Tower Rd
Halifax, NS

This 185 acre park allows dogs off-leash in sections of the park. After 10 am dogs are not allowed at all along Shore Road at the park. There are signs indicating the off-leash areas in the park and the park is monitored for violations.

Seaview Park Off-Leash Area
North end of Barrington Street below the A.Murray MacKay Bridge
Halifax, NS
Dogs are allowed off-leash in parts of Seaview Park. This park is the former site of Africville, a black community that was relocated in the 1960s. There are signs indicating the off-leash areas in the park and the park is monitored for violations.

Ontario

Greenway Off-Leash Dog Park
Springbank Dr at Greenside Ave
London, ON
This fenced off-leash dog park has one area for larger dogs and another area for small dogs. The dog park is open from 6 am to 10 pm daily.

Pottersburg Dog Park
Hamilton Rd at Gore Rd
London, ON
This fenced off-leash dog park has one area for larger dogs and another area for small dogs. The dog park is open from 6 am to 10 pm daily. The dog park is located on the south side of the intersection.

Stoney Creek Off-Leash Dog Park
Adelaide St N. at Windermere
London, ON
This fenced off-leash dog park has one area for larger dogs and another area for small dogs. The dog park is open from 6 am to 10 pm daily. The dog park is located on the west side of Adelaide.

Totoredaca Leash Free Park
2715 Meadowvale Blvd
Mississauga, ON
totoredaca.org/park.htm
This off leash park features a wading pool, tables, and cleanup stations in 3 fenced-in acres. There is a fee for use of the park.

Dog Park - High Park
1873 Bloor Street
Toronto, ON
416-397-8186
Dogs can run leash-free at the open area located west of the Dream Site and the allotment Gardens, and

northeast of the Grenadier Restaurant. The dog park area is open 24 hours a day, except for 6pm to 10pm during stage productions at the Dream Site. The park is located at Bloor Street and Parkside Drive.

Quebec

Autoroute 20 at 55e Avenue Off-Leash Area
Autoroute 20 at 55e Avenue
Lachine Borrough, PQ
514-637-7587
This is one of several parks that have off-leash areas. Dogs are not allowed at all in other Lachine Borrough parks except for these dog parks. You must clean up after your dog. The park is located at Autoroute 20 and 55e Avenue.

Promendade du rail Off-Leash Area
rue Victoria between 10e and 15e
Lachine Borrough, PQ
514-637-7587
This is one of several parks that have off-leash areas. Dogs are not allowed at all in other Lachine Borrough parks except for these dog parks. You must clean up after your dog. The park is located at Promenade du rail between 10e and 15e Avenues and between rue Victoria and rue William-MacDonald.

Rue Victoria and 28e Avenue Off-Leash Area
Rue Victoria and 28e Avenue
Lachine Borrough, PQ
514-637-7587
This is one of several parks that have off-leash areas. Dogs are not allowed at all in other Lachine Borrough parks except for these dog parks. You must clean up after your dog.

Rue Victoria and 40e Avenue Off-Leash Area
Rue Victoria and 40e Avenue
Lachine Borrough, PQ
514-637-7587
This is one of several parks that have off-leash areas. Dogs are not allowed at all in other Lachine Borrough parks except for these dog parks. You must clean up after your dog.

Rue des Erables Off-Leash Area
Rue des Erables at Rue Emile-

Pominville
Lachine Borrough, PQ
514-637-7587
This is one of several parks that have off-leash areas. Dogs are not allowed at all in other Lachine Borrough parks except for these dog parks. You must clean up after your dog.

Stoney Point River Park Off-Leash Area
Between 45e and 56e Avenues
Lachine Borrough, PQ
514-637-7587
This is one of several parks that have off-leash areas. Dogs are not allowed at all in other Lachine Borrough parks except for these dog parks. You must clean up after your dog. The off-leash hours are from 6 am to 10 am and from 6 pm to 10 pm. The area that allows dogs off-leash is from 45e to 56e Avenues in the park.

Notre-Dame-de-Grace Park
Girouard and Sherbrooke West
Montreal, PQ
514-637-7587
This off-leash dog run is open from 7 am to 10 pm on weekdays and on weekends from 9 am to 10 pm.

King George Park Off-Leash Area
Cote St. Antoine and Murray
Westmount, PQ
514-989-5200
This off-leash dog run is located east of the tennis courts in King George Park. The area is off-leash 24 hours a day.

Saskatchewan

Off Leash Dog Parks
Various sites
Saskatoon, SK
306-975-2611
The city of Saskatoon offers several off leash areas with more being planned; some of them are located at: South of Glasgow Street and Yorath Avenue in Avalon; 11th Street W from Crerar Drive to Crescent Blvd in Montgomery; along the riverbank near Silverwood adjacent to the end of the golf course, and just north of 8th street on the east side of McOrmond Drive near Briarwood. Dogs must be licensed, leashed, and under their owner's control at all times.

Chapter 5

Dog-Friendly Highway Campground Guide

Interstate 5 Dog-Friendly Campgrounds and RV Parks

Washington   (Interstate 5)   Dogs per Site

Blaine
Birch Bay State Park	360-371-2800	5105 Helwig - Exit Grandview Road Blaine WA	3+

Bellingham
Bellingham RV Park	360-752-1224	3939 Bennett Drive - Exit 258 Bellingham WA	3+
Larrabee State Park	360-676-2093	245 Chuckanut Drive - Exit 250 Bellingham WA	3+
Lynden/Bellingham KOA	360-354-4772	8717 Line Road - Exit H 539 Lynden WA	3+

Burlington
Burlington/Anacortes KOA	360-724-5511	6397 N Green Road - Exit Bow Hill Burlington WA	3+

Everett
Lakeside Park	425-347-2970	12321 H 99S Everett WA	2
Maple Grove RV Resort	425-423-9608	12417 H 99 Everett WA	2

Seattle
Blake Island State Park	360-731-8330	P.O. Box 42650 Seattle WA	2
Blue Sky RV Park	425-222-7910	9002 302nd Avenue SE Seattle WA	3+

Kent
Seattle/Tacoma KOA	253-872-8652	5801 S 212th Street - Exit 152 Kent WA	3+

Federal Way
Dash Point State Park	253-661-4955	5700 SW Dash Point Road - Exit 320th Federal Way WA	3+

Olympia
Olympic National Forest	360-956-23300	1835 Black Lk Blvd SW - Exit H 101 Olympia WA	3+

Rochester
Outback RV Park	360-273-0585	19100 Huntington - Exit 88 Rochester WA	2

Chehalis
Scotts RV Park	360-262-9220	118 h 12 - Exit 68 Chehalis WA	2

Castle Rock
Seaquest State Park	206-274-8633	Spirit Lake H Castle Rock WA	1+

Vancouver
Gifford Pinchot National Forest	360-891-5000	10600 N.E. 51st Circle Vancouver WA	3+
Vancouver RV Park	360-695-1158	7603 NE 13th Avenue - Exit 4 Vancouver WA	2

Woodland
Columbia Riverfront RV Park	360-225-8051	1881Pike Road - Exit 22 Woodland WA	2

Oregon   (Interstate 5)   Dogs per Site

Portland
Portland Fairview RV Park	503-661-1047	21401 NE Sandy Blvd Fairview OR	3+
Rolling Hills RV Park	503-666-7282	20145 NE Sandy Blvd Fairview OR	3+
Jantzen Beach RV Park	503-289-7626	1503 N Hayden Island Drive - Exit Jantzen Beach Portland OR	1
RV Park of Portland	503-692-0225	6645 SW Nyberg Road - Exit 289 E Tualatin OR	1+

Salem
Premier RV Resorts	503-364-7714	4700 H 22 Salem OR	3+
Salem Campground	503-581-6736	3700 Hager's Grove Road - Exit H 22E Salem OR	2

Albany
Albany/Corvallis KOA	541-967-8521	33775 Oakville Road S - Exit 228/W on H 34 Albany OR	1+

Eugene
Premier RV Resorts	541-686-3152	33022 Van Duyn Road - Exit 199 Eugene OR	3+
Shamrock RV Village	541-747-7473	4531 Franklin Blvd - Exit 189 Eugene OR	3+

Roseburg
Rising River RV Park	541-679-7256	5579 Grange Road - Exit H 42 Roseburg OR	2
Umpqua National Forest	541-750-7000	2900 Stewart Parkway Roseburg OR	3+

Myrtle Creek
On the River Golf & RV Resort	541-679-3505	111 Whitson Lane - Exit H 99 Myrtle Creek OR	3+

Grants Pass
Jack's Landing RV Resort	541-472-1144	247 NE Morgan Lane - Exit 58 Grants Pass OR	3+
Siskiyou National Forest	541-471-6500	2164 NE Spalding Avenue - Exit 55 Grants Pass OR	3+

Medford
Rogue River National Forest	541-858-2200	333 W 8th Street - Exit H 99 Medford OR	3+

Hornbrook
Blue Heron RV Park	530-475-3270	6930 Copco Road - Exit 789 Hornbrook OR	3+

California   (Interstate 5)   Dogs per Site

Yreka

Tree of Heaven Campground, Klamath National Forest	530-468-5351	1312 Fairlane Road - Exit H 96 Yreka CA	3+
Mount Shasta			
Railroad Park Resort	530-235-4440	100 Railroad Park Road - Exit 728/Railroad Park Road Dunsmuir CA	3+
Fowlers Campground	530-964-2184	H 89 McCloud CA	3+
Lake Siskiyou Camp Resort	530-926-2618	4239 W. A. Barr Rd - Exit Central Mount Shasta CA	3+
Mount Shasta KOA	530-926-4029	900 N Mt Shasta Blvd - Exit Central/Mt Shasta Shasta City CA	3+
Redding			
Mountain Gate RV Park	530-283-0769	14161 Holiday Road - Exit Mountaingate/Wonderland Blvd to 1st R Redding CA	3+
Redding RV Park	530-241-0707	11075 Campers Court - Exit 680/Lake Blvd Redding CA	3+
Sacramento River RV Resort	530-365-6402	6596 Riverland Drive - Exit 673 Redding CA	1+
Corning			
Rolling Hills Casino	530-528-3500	2657 Barham Avenue - Exit 628 Corning CA	3+
Woodson Bridge State Recreation Area	530-839-2112	25340 South Avenue - Exit Corning Corning CA	3+
Orland			
Black Butte Lake Recreation Area	530-865-4781	19225 Newville Road - Exit Orland Orland CA	3+
Buckhorn Recreation Area	530-865-4781	19225 Newville Road - Exit Black Butte Lake Orland CA	3+
Sacramento			
Beals Point Campground	916-988-0205	7806 Folsom-Auburn Road Folsom CA	3+
Cal Expo RV Park	916-263-3000	1600 Exposition Blvd Sacramento CA	2
Sacramento Metropolitan KOA	916-371-6771	3951 Lake Road West Sacramento CA	1+
Stockton			
Stockton/Lodi (formally KOA)	209-334-0309	2851 East Eight Mile Road - Exit Eight Mile Road Lodi CA	3+
Lost Hills			
Lost Hills RV Park (formally KOA)	661-797-2719	14831 Warren Street - Exit H 46 Lost Hills CA	3+
Castaic			
Valencia Travel Resort	661-257-3333	27946 Henry Mayo Drive (H 126) - Exit H 126/Henry Mayo Drive Castaic CA	3+
Los Angeles			
Kenneth Hahn State Rec Area	323-298-3660	4100 S La Cienega Los Angeles CA	3+
Anaheim Resort Area			
Canyon RV Park at Featherly	714-637-0210	24001 Santa Ana Canyon Road Anaheim CA	3+
Orange County South			
Doheny State Beach Park	949-496-6172	25300 Dana Point Harbor Drive - Exit Camino Del Los Mares Dana Point CA	3+
San Clemente State Beach	949-492-3156	3030 El Avenida Del Presidente - Exit Avendia Calalia San Clemente CA	3+
San Diego County North			
San Elijio State Beach Campground	760-753-5091	2050 Coast H - Exit Encinitas Blvd Cardiff CA	2
Guajome County Park	858-565-3600	3000 Guajome Lake Road Oceanside CA	3+
Paradise by the Sea RV Resort	760-439-1376	1537 S Coast H Oceanside CA	3+
San Diego			
Sweetwater Summit Regional Park	619-472-7572	3218 Summit Meadow Road Bonita CA	3+
San Diego Metro	619-427-3601	111 N 2nd Avenue - Exit E Street Chula Vista CA	3+
Sunland RV Resort - San Diego	619-469-4697	7407 Alvarado Road La Mesa CA	2
Lake Jennings County Park	619-443-2004	10108 Bass Road Lakeside CA	3+
Campland on the Bay	800-422-9386	2211 Pacific Beach Drive - Exit Mission Bay Drive to Garnet & Balboa Avenues San Diego CA	2
Santee Lakes Recreation Preserve	619-596-3141	9310 Fanita Parkway - Exit H 52E San Diego CA	2

Interstate 10 Dog-Friendly Campgrounds and RV Parks

California   (Interstate 10)   Dogs per Site

Los Angeles			
Kenneth Hahn State Rec Area	323-298-3660	4100 S La Cienega - Exit S La Cienega Los Angeles CA	3+
Pomona - Ontario			
East Shore RV Park	909-599-8355	1440 Camper View Road - Exit Fairplex Road N to Via Verde San Dimas CA	3+
Banning			
Banning Stagecoach KOA	951-849-7513	1455 S San Gorgonio - Exit 8th Street Banning CA	3+
Palm Springs			
Palm Springs Oasis RV Resort	800-680-0144	36-100 Date Palm Drive Cathedral City CA	3+
Indian Wells RV Resort	800-789-0895	47-340 Jefferson Street - Exit Jefferson Street Indio CA	3+
Blythe			
Blythe / Colorado River KOA	760-922-5350	14100 Riviera Drive Blythe CA	3+
Collis Mayflower Park	760-922-4665	4980 Colorado River Road Blythe CA	3+

| Reynolds Riviera Resort | 760-922-5350 | 14100 Riviera Drive - Exit Riviera Drive Blythe CA | 3+ |

Arizona (Interstate 10)
Dogs per Site

Quartzsite
| B-10 Campground | 928-927-4393 | 615 Main - Exit 17 Quartzsite AZ | 3+ |

Phoenix
Covered Wagon RV Park	602-242-2500	6540 N Black Canyon H Phoenix AZ	3+
Desert Sands RV Park	623-869-8186	22036 N 27th Avenue Phoenix AZ	3+
Desert Shadows RV Resort	623-869-8178	19203 N 29th Avenue Phoenix AZ	2
Destiny RV Resort	623-853-0537	416 N Citrus Road - Exit 124 Phoenix AZ	1+
Pioneer RV Resort	800-658-5895	36408 N Black Canyon H Phoenix AZ	2
Tonto National Forest	602-225-5200	2324 E. McDowell Road Phoenix AZ	3+

Phoenix Area
| Mesa Spirit | 480-832-1770 | 3020 E Main Street Mesa AZ | 2 |
| Silveridge RV Resort | 480-373-7000 | 8265 E Southern Mesa AZ | 3+ |

Apache Junction
La Hacienda RV Resort	480-982-2808	1797 W 28th Avenue Apache Junction AZ	1+
Lost Dutchman State Park	480-982-4485	6109 N. Apache Trail Apache Junction AZ	3+
Mesa/Apache Junction KOA	480-982-4015	1540 S Tomahawk Road - Exit H 60E Apache Junction AZ	3+
Superstition Sunrise	480-986-4524	702 S Meridian Apache Junction AZ	3+
Weaver's Needle Travel Trailor Resort	480-982-3683	250 S Tomahawk Road Apache Junction AZ	1+

Casa Grande
| Buena Tierra RV Park and Campground | 520-836-3500 | 1995 S Cox Road Casa Grande AZ | 3+ |
| Palm Creek Golf and RV Resort | 800-421-7004 | 1110 N Hennes Road - Exit 194 Casa Grande AZ | 2 |

Tucson
Catalina State Park	520-628-5798	11570 N Oracle Road Tucson AZ	3+
Coronado National Forest	520-388-8300	5700 N Sabino Canyon Road - Exit Grant Road Tucson AZ	3+
Crazy Horse RV Park	520-574-0157	6660 S Craycroft - Exit S Craycroft Tucson AZ	2
Prince of Tucson RV Park	520-887-3501	3501 N Freeway - Exit Prince Road Tucson AZ	3+

Benson
Benson KOA	520-586-3977	180 W Four Feathers - Exit 304 N Benson AZ	2
Butterfield RV Resort and Observatory	520-586-4400	251 S Ocotillo - Exit 204 Benson AZ	3+
Kartchner Caverns State Park	520-586-2283	2980 S H 90 - Exit H 90 Benson AZ	3+

New Mexico (Interstate 10)
Dogs per Site

Deming
Little Vineyard	505-546-3560	2901 E Pine - Exit 85 Deming NM	3+
Roadrunner RV Park	505-546-6960	2849 E Pine Street - Exit 85 Deming NM	3+
Rockhound State Park	505-546-6182	P. O. Box 1064 Deming NM	3+

Las Cruces
| Hacienda RV and Rally Resort | 888-686-9090 | 740 Stern Drive - Exit 140 Las Cruces NM | 3+ |
| The Coachlight Inn and RV Park | 505-526-3301 | 301 S Motel Blvd - Exit 139 Las Cruces NM | 1+ |

Texas (Interstate 10)
Dogs per Site

El Paso
El Paso Roadrunner RV Park	915-598-4469	1212 LaFayette - Exit 28B El Paso TX	3+
Franklin Mountains State Park	915-566-6441	1331 McKelligon Canyon Road El Paso TX	3+
Sampson RV Park	915-859-8383	11300 Gateway Blvd - Exit 351/East Lake El Paso TX	3+

Van Horn
| Van Horn KOA | 432-283-2728 | 10 Kamper's Lane - Exit 140A Van Horn TX | 3+ |

Sonora
| Caverns of Sonora | 325-387-3105 | Private Road 4468 - Exit 392 Sonora TX | 2 |

Junction
| Junction KOA | 325-446-3138 | 2145 Main Street - Exit 456 Junction TX | 3+ |

Fredericksburg
Enchanted Rock State Natural Area	830-685-3636	16710 Ranch Road 965 Fredericksburg TX	3+
Fredericksburg	830-997-4796	5681 H 290E Fredericksburg TX	1+
Oakwood RV Resort	830-997-9817	#78 FM 2093 - Exit Kerriville to Tivydale Road Fredericksburg TX	1+

Kerrville
| Kerrville KOA | 830-895-1665 | 2950 Goat Creek Road - Exit 501 Kerrville TX | 3+ |

San Antonio
Pioneer Rivers Resort	830-796-3751	1203 Maple Bandera TX	3+
Jellystone Park	830-964-3731	12915 Hwy 306 Canyon Lake TX	1+
Admiralty RV Resort	800-999-7872	1485 N Ellison Drive San Antonio TX	3+
Blazing Star RV Resort	210-680-7827	1120 W H 1604N San Antonio TX	2
San Antonio KOA	210-224-9296	602 Gembler Road - Exit 580 San Antonio TX	2
Traveler's World RV Resort	210-532-8310	2617 Roosevelt Avenue San Antonio TX	3+

Stone Creek RV Park	830-609-7759	18905 IH 35N Schertz TX	3+
Guadalupe River State Park	830-438-2656	3350 Park Road 31 Spring Branch TX	3+
Houston			
Houston East/Baytown KOA	281-383-3618	11810 I-10E - Exit H 146 Baytown TX	3+
Houston West/Brookshire KOA	281-375-5678	35303 Cooper Road - Exit 731 Brookshire TX	3+
All Star RV Resort	713-981-6814	10650 SW Plaza Court Houston TX	3+
Houston Central KOA	281-442-3700	1620 Peachleaf Houston TX	3+
Houston Leisure RV Resort	281-426-3576	1601 S Main Street - Exit 787 Houston TX	3+
Lake Houston Park	713-845-1000	22031 Baptist Encampment Road Houston TX	3+
Trader's Village	281-890-5500	7979 N Eldridge Road Houston TX	3+
Brazos Bend State Park	979-553-5101	21901 FM 762/Crab River Road Needville TX	3+
Jellystone Park	979-826-4111	34843 Betka Road Waller TX	2
Beaumont			
Big Thicket National Preserve	409-951-6725	6044 H 420 Kountze TX	3+
Village Creek State Park	409-755-7322	8854 Park Road 74 Lumberton TX	3+

Louisiana   (Interstate 10)   Dogs per Site

Lake Charles			
Jellystone Park	337-433-1114	4200 Luke Powers Road - Exit 36 Lake Charles LA	3+
Sam Houston Jones State Park	337-855-2665	107 Sutherland Road Lake Charles LA	3+
Hidden Ponds RV Park	337-583-4709	1207 Ravia Road Sulphur LA	3+
Lafayette			
Bayou Wilderness RV Resort	337-896-0598	201 St Claire Road Carencro LA	3+
Acadian Village RV Park	337-981-2364	200 Greenleaf Drive Lafayette LA	2
Lafayette KOA	337-235-2739	537 Apollo Road - Exit 97 Scott LA	3+
Fausse Point State Park and Canoe Trail	337-229-4764	5400 Levee Road/PR-169 St Martinville LA	3+
Baton Rouge			
Baton Rouge KOA	225-664-7281	7628 Vincent Road Denham Springs LA	3+
Cajun Country Campground	800-264-8554	4667 Relle Lane - Exit 151 Port Allen LA	3+
New Orleans			
St. Bernard State Park	504-682-2101	501 St. Bernard Parkway Braithwaite LA	3+

Alabama   (Interstate 10)   Dogs per Site

Mobile			
Shady Acres Campground	251-478-0013	2500 Old Military Road - Exit 22 Mobile AL	3+
Gulf Shores			
Fort Morgan RV Park	251-540-2416	10397 2nd Street Gulf Shores AL	3+
Gulf Breeze Resort	251-968-8884	19800 Oak Road W - Exit H 59 Gulf Shores AL	3+
Gulf State Park	251-948-7275	20115 H 135 Gulf Shores AL	3+
Luxury RV Resort	251-948-5444	590 Gulf Shores Parkway - Exit H 59 Gulf Shores AL	3+

Florida   (Interstate 10)   Dogs per Site

Holt			
Blackwater River State Park	850-983-5363	7720 Deaton Bridge Road - Exit 31/H 87N Holt FL	3+
Chipley			
Falling Waters State Rec Area	850-638-6130	1130 State Park Road - Exit 121/H77 Chipley FL	3+
Marianna			
Florida Caverns State Park	850-482-9598	3345 Caverns Road (H 166) Marianna FL	3+
Chattahoochee			
Chattahoochee/Tallahassee W KOA	850-442-6657	2309 Flat Circle Road - Exit 166/H270A Chattahoochee FL	
Tallahassee			
Apalachicola National Forest	850-643-2282	11152 NW State Road 20 Tallahassee FL	3+
Big Oak RV Park	850-562-4660	4024 N Monroe Street - Exit 199 Tallahassee FL	3+
Madison			
Jellystone Park	800-347-0174	1051 SW Old St. Augustine Road - Exit 258 Madison FL	3+
Live Oak			
Suwannee River State Park	386-362-2746	20185 County Road 132 - Exit H 90 Live Oak FL	3+
Lake City			
Stephen Foster Folk Culture Center State Park	386-397-2733	P. O. Drawer G/ US 41 N White Springs FL	3+
Suwannee Valley Campground	866-397-1667	786 N W Street White Springs FL	2
Jacksonville			
Little Talbot Island State Park	904-251-2320	12157 Heckscher Drive Jacksonville FL	3+
Flamingo Lake RV Resort	904-766-0672	3640 Newcomb Road N Jacksonville FL	3+

Interstate 15 Dog-Friendly Campgrounds and RV Parks

Montana   (Interstate 15)   Dogs per Site

Shelby

Lewis and Clark RV Park	406-434-2710	Box 369, Front Street - Exit 364 Shelby MT	2

Great Falls

Acklley Lake State Park	406-454-5840	4600 Giant Srings Road Great Falls MT	3+
Dick's RV Park	406-452-0333	1403 11th Street SW - Exit 278 to Exit '0' Great Falls MT	3+
Great Falls KOA	406-727-3191	1500 51st Street S - Exit 278 go E Great Falls MT	3+
Lewis and Clark National Forest	406-791-7700	1101 15th Street N. Great Falls MT	3+

Wolf Creek

Holter Lake Recreation Area	406-494-5059	Recreation Road - Exit 226 Left on Missouri River Road Wolf Creek MT	3+

Helena

Helena Campground	406-458-4714	5820 N Montana Avenue Helena MT	2
Helena National Forest	406-449-5201	2880 Skyway Drive - Exit H 12 Helena MT	3+

Butte

Butte KOA	406-782-8080	1601 Kaw Avenue Butte MT	3+

Dillon

Bannack State Park	406-834-3413	4200 Bannack Road - Exit 59/H 278 Dillon MT	3+
Deerlodge (Beaverhead) National Forest	406-683-3900	420 Barrett Street - Exit Barrett Street Dillon MT	3+
Dillon KOA	406-683-2749	735 Park Street - Exit 62 Dillon MT	3+

Idaho   (Interstate 15)   Dogs per Site

Idaho Falls

Caribou-Targhee National Forest	208-524-7500	3659 East Ririe Highway Idaho Falls ID	3+
Targhee-Caribou National Forest	208-524-7500	1405 Hollipark Drive Idaho Falls ID	3+

Pocatello

Pocatello KOA	208-233-6851	9815 W Pocatello Creek Road - Exit 71 Pocatello ID	3+

Utah   (Interstate 15)   Dogs per Site

Ogden

Cherry Hill RV Resort	801-451-5379	1325 S Main - Exit 324/H 89 Kaysville UT	3+

Salt Lake City

Sunset Campground	877-444-6777	Farmington Canyon Farmington City UT	1+
Salt Lake City KOA	801-355-1214	1400 W North Temple - Exit 311 Salt Lake City UT	3+
Wasatch -Cache National Forest	801-466-6411	3285 East 3800 S Salt Lake City UT	3+
Quail Run RV Park	801-255-9300	9230 S State Street - Exit 295 Sandy UT	3+

Provo

Lakeside RV Campground	801-373-5267	4000 W Center Street - Exit 265 or 265B Provo UT	3+
Provo KOA	801-375-2994	320N 2050 W - Exit 265 Provo UT	3+
Uinta National Forest	801-377-5780	88 W 100 N - Exit W 100 N Provo UT	3+
Utah Lake State Park	801-375-0733	4400 West Center Street - Exit 268 Provo UT	3+

Fillmore

Fillmore KOA	435-743-4420	900 S 410 W - Exit 163 Fillmore UT	1+

Beaver

Beaver KOA	435-438-2924	1428 Manderfield Road - Exit 112 Beaver UT	3+

Cedar City

Cedar City KOA	435-586-9872	1121 N Main - Exit 57 Cedar City UT	1+
Dixie National Forest	435-865-3700	1789 N Wedgewood Lane - Exit 57 (H 14-goes into the forest) Cedar City UT	3+

St George

Snow Canyon State Park	435-628-2255	1002 Snow Canyon Drive (H 18) St George UT	3+
Templeview RV Resort	800-381-0321	975 S Main - Exit 6 St George UT	2

Nevada   (Interstate 15)   Dogs per Site

Overton

Valley of Fire State Park	702-397-2088	P. O. Box 515/ Valley of Fire Road - Exit 75/Old State Route 169 Overton NV	3+

Las Vegas

Las Vegas KOA at Circus Circus	702-733-9707	500 Circus Circus Drive - Exit Sahara Avenue Las Vegas NV	3+
Oasis Las Vegas RV Resort	800-566-4707	2711 W Windmill Lane - Exit Blue Diamond Las Vegas NV	2

California   (Interstate 15)   Dogs per Site

Baker

Hole in the Wall Campground	760-928-2562	Black Canyon Road - Exit Cima Rd to Kelso Cima Rd Baker CA	3+

Highway Guides - Please always call ahead to make sure an establishment is still dog-friendly.

Mohave National Preserve Campgrounds	760-252-6101	Black Canyon Road - Exit Cima Road Baker CA	3+
Barstow			
Rainbow Basin Natural Area	760-252-6060	Fossil Bed Road Barstow CA	3+
Barstow/Calico KOA	760-254-2311	35250 Outer H 15 - Exit Ghost Town Road Yermo CA	3+
Barstow/Calico KOA	760-254-2311	35250 Outer H 15 - Exit Ghost Town Road Yermo CA	3+
Victorville			
Victorville/Inland Empire KOA	760-245-6867	16530 Stoddard Wells Road - Exit 2nd Stoddard Wells Road Victorville CA	1+
Temecula			
Pechanga RV Resort	951-587-0484	45000 Pechanga Parkway Temecula CA	2
Vail Lake Wine Country RV Resort	951-303-0173	38000 H 79 S - Exit H 79S Temecula CA	2
San Diego I-15 Corridor			
Sunland RV Resorts	760-740-5000	1740 Seven Oaks Road Escondido CA	2
San Diego County North			
San Elijo State Beach Campground	760-753-5091	2050 Coast H Cardiff CA	2
Guajome County Park	858-565-3600	3000 Guajome Lake Road Oceanside CA	3+
Paradise by the Sea RV Resort	760-439-1376	1537 S Coast H Oceanside CA	3+
San Diego			
Sweetwater Summit Regional Park	619-472-7572	3218 Summit Meadow Road Bonita CA	3+
San Diego Metro	619-427-3601	111 N 2nd Avenue Chula Vista CA	3+
Sunland RV Resort - San Diego	619-469-4697	7407 Alvarado Road La Mesa CA	2
Lake Jennings County Park	619-443-2004	10108 Bass Road Lakeside CA	3+
Campland on the Bay	800-422-9386	2211 Pacific Beach Drive San Diego CA	2
Santee Lakes Recreation Preserve	619-596-3141	9310 Fanita Parkway - Exit H 52E San Diego CA	2

Interstate 20 Dog-Friendly Campgrounds and RV Parks

Texas   (Interstate 20)   Dogs per Site

Monahans			
Monahans Sandhills State Park	432-943-2092	Park Road 41 - Exit 86 Monahans TX	3+
Abilene			
Abilene KOA	915-672-3681	4851 W Stamford Street - Exit 282 Abilene TX	3+
Abilene State Park	325-572-3204	150 Park Road 32 Tuscola TX	3+
Fort Worth			
Treetops RV Village	817-467-7943	1901 W Arbrook - Exit H 157 Arlington TX	1+
RV Ranch	888-855-9091	2301 S I 35W Burleson TX	3+
Caddo-LBJ National Grasslands	940-627-5475	1400 H 81/287 Decatur TX	3+
Dallas			
Cedar Hill State Park	972-291-3900	1570 W FM 1382 Cedar Hill TX	3+
Trader's Village	972-647-8205	2602 Mayfield Road - Exit N360 Grand Prairie TX	2

Louisiana   (Interstate 20)   Dogs per Site

Shreveport			
Cypress Black Bayou Recreation Area	318-965-0007	135 Cypress Park Dr - Exit Airline Drive Benton LA	3+
Cash Point Landing	318-742-4999	215 Cash Point Landing Bossier City LA	3+
Shreveport/Bossier KOA	318-687-1010	6510 W 70th Street - Exit 10 S to W 70th Shreveport LA	3+
Minden			
Caney Lakes Rec Area	318-927-2061	194 Caney Lake Road Minden LA	3+
Monroe			
Bayou Boeuf RV Park	318-665-2405	11791 H 165 N Sterlington LA	3+
Cheniere Lake Park	318-387-2383	104 Cheniere Lake Road West Monroe LA	3+
Delhi			
Poverty Point Reservoir State Park	318-878-7536	1500 Poverty Point Parkway - Exit Delhi Delhi LA	3+

Mississippi   (Interstate 20)   Dogs per Site

Vicksburg			
Rivertown Campground	601-630-9995	5900 H 61S - Exit H 61S Vicksburg MS	3+
Vicksburg Battlefield	601-636-2025	4407 N Frontage Road - Exit 4B Vicksburg MS	3+
Jackson			
Swinging Bridge RV Park	800-297-9127	100 Holiday Rambler Lane Bryam MS	3+
Holly Springs National Forest	662-236-6550	100 W Capital Street, Suite 1141 Jackson MS	3+
LeFleur's Bluff State Park	601-987-3923	2140 Riverside Drive Jackson MS	3+
Meridian			

Twitley Branch Camping Area	601-626-8068	9200 Hamrick Road Collinsville MS	3+
Nanabe Creek Campground	601-485-4711	1933 Russell Mount Gilliad Road - Exit 160 Meridian MS	3+

Alabama   (Interstate 20)   Dogs per Site

Knoxville			
Knox Hill RV Park	205-372-3911	252 Old Patton Road - Exit 52 Knoxville AL	3+
Birmingham			
Cherokee Campground	205-428-8339	2800 H 93 Helena AL	3+
Tannehill Ironworks Historical State Park	205-477-5711	12632 Confederate Parkway McCalla AL	3+
Birmingham South Campground	205-664-8832	222 H 33 Pelham AL	3+
Oak Mountain State Park	800-ALAPARK (252-7275)	200 Terrace Drive Pelham AL	3+

Georgia   (Interstate 20)   Dogs per Site

Atlanta			
Stone Mountain Park	800-385-9807	H 78E Stone Mountain GA	3+
Atlanta Area			
Brookwood RV Park	877-727-5787	1031 Wylie Road SE Marietta GA	3+
Atlanta South RV Resort	770-957-2610	281 Mount Olive Road McDonough GA	3+

South Carolina   (Interstate 20)   Dogs per Site

Columbia			
Francis Marion and Sumter National Forests	803-561-4000	4931 Broad River Road Columbia SC	3+
Sesquicentennial State Park	803-788-2706	9564 Two Notch Road - Exit 74/Two Notch Road Columbia SC	3+
Barnyard RV Park	803-957-1238	201 Oak Drive - Exit 58 Lexington SC	3+
River Bottom Farms	803-568-4182	357 Cedar Creek Road Swansea SC	3+
Florence			
Florence KOA	843-665-7007	1115 E Campground Road Florence SC	3+

Interstate 25 Dog-Friendly Campgrounds and RV Parks

Wyoming   (Interstate 25)   Dogs per Site

Buffalo			
Buffalo KOA	307-684-5423	87 H 16E - Exit 299 Buffalo WY	3+
Deer Park RV Park	307-684-5722	Box 568, On H 16E Buffalo WY	3+
Indian Campground	307-684-9601	660 E Hart Street - Exit 299 Buffalo WY	1+
Casper			
Casper KOA	307-577-1664	1101 Prairie Lane - Exit 191 Casper WY	3+
Fort Casper Campground	888-243-7709	4205 Fort Caspar Road Casper WY	2
Douglas			
Douglas KOA	307-358-2164	168 H 91 - Exit 146 Douglas WY	3+
Cheyenne			
Cheyenne KOA	307-638-8840	8800 Archer Frontage Road Cheyenne WY	3+
Curt Gowdy State Park	307-632-7946	1319 Hynds Lodge Road Cheyenne WY	3+
Terry Bison Ranch	307-634-4171	51 I 25 Service Road E - Exit 2 Cheyenne WY	3+

Colorado   (Interstate 25)   Dogs per Site

Wellington			
Fort Collins North/Wellington KOA	970-568-7486	4821 E County Road 70/Owl Canyon Road - Exit 281 Wellington CO	3+
Fort Collins			
Arapaho Roosevelt National Forest	970-498-2770	2150 Center Avenue, Building E - Exit Prospect Road Fort Collins CO	3+
Fort Collins KOA Lakeside	970-484-9880	1910 N Taft Hill - Exit 269B Fort Collins CO	3+
Loveland			
Johnson's Corner RV Retreat	970-669-8400	3618 SE Frontage Road - Exit 254 Loveland CO	3+
Longmont			
St. Vrain State Park	303-678-9402	3525 H 119 Longmont CO	3+
Denver			
Denver Meadows RV Park	303-364-9483	2075 Potomac Street Aurora CO	3+
Dakota Ridge RV Park	800-398-1625	17800 W Colfax Golden CO	3+
Genesee Park/Chief Hosa Campground	303-526-1324	27661 Genesee Drive Golden CO	3+

Chatfield State Park	303-791-7275	11500 N Roxborough Park Road Littleton CO	3+
Prospect RV Park	303-424-4414	11600 W 44th Avenue Wheat Ridge CO	3+
Castle Rock			
Castle Rock Campground	303-681-3169	6527 S I 25 - Exit 174 Castle Rock CO	3+
Colorado Springs			
Fountain Creek RV Park	719-633-2192	3023 W Colorado Avenue - Exit 141 Colorado Springs CO	3+
Garden of the Gods Campground	719-475-9450	3704 W Colorado Avenue Colorado Springs CO	3+
Pueblo			
Lake Pueblo	719-561-9320	640 Reservoir Road Pueblo CO	3+
Pike and San Isabel National Forests	719-545-8737	2840 Kachina Drive Pueblo CO	3+
Pueblo KOA	719-542-2273	4131 I 25N - Exit 108 Pueblo CO	3+

New Mexico   (Interstate 25) Dogs per Site

Raton			
Sugarlite Canyon State Park	505-445-5607	HCR 63, Box 386 - Exit H 72 Raton NM	3+
Las Vegas			
Storrie Lake State Park	505-425-7278	HC 33, Box 109 #2 Las Vegas NM	3+
Santa Fe			
Hyde Memorial State Park	505-983-7175	740 Hyde Park Road Santa Fe NM	3+
Rancheros de Santa Fe	800-426-9259	736 Old Las Vegas H - Exit 290 Santa Fe NM	3+
Santa Fe National Forest	505-438-7840	1474 Rodeo Road Santa Fe NM	3+
Santa Fe Skies RV Park	505-473-5946	14 Browncastle Ranch - Exit 276 Santa Fe NM	3+
Trailer Ranch RV Resort	505-471-9970	3471 Cerrillos - Exit 278 Santa Fe NM	3+
Albuquerque			
Albuquerque Central KOA	505-296-2729	12400 Skyline Road NE Albuquerque NM	3+
Enchanted Trails	505-831-6317	14305 Central Albuquerque NM	3+
High Desert RV Park	866-839-9035	13000 W Frontage Road SW Albuquerque NM	3+
Albuquerque N/Bernalillo KOA	505-867-5227	555 S Hill Road - Exit 240 Bernalillo NM	3+
Coronado State Park	505-980-8256	106 Monument Road Bernalillo NM	3+
Truth or Consequences			
Cielo Vista RV Resort	505-894-3738	501 S Broadway - Exit 75 Truth or Consequences NM	3+
Caballo			
Caballo Lake State Park	505-743-3942	Box 32; On H 187 - Exit 59 N Caballo NM	3+
Percha Dam State Park	505-743-3942	Box 32; on H 187 - Exit 59 S Caballo NM	3+
Las Cruces			
Hacienda RV and Rally Resort	888-686-9090	740 Stern Drive Las Cruces NM	3+
The Coachlight Inn and RV Park	505-526-3301	301 S Motel Blvd Las Cruces NM	1+

Interstate 35 Dog-Friendly Campgrounds and RV Parks

Minnesota   (Interstate 35) Dogs per Site

Duluth			
Jay Cooke State Park	218-384-4610	500 E H 210 Carlton MN	3+
Cloquet/Duluth KOA	218-879-5726	1381 Carlton Road Cloquet MN	2
Indian Point Campground	218-628-4977	7000 Polaski Street - Exit Grand Avenue Duluth MN	3+
Superior National Forest	218-626-4300	8901 Grand Avenue Place Duluth MN	3+
Hinckley			
St Croix State Park	320-384-6591	30065 St Croix Park Road - Exit Hinckley to H 48 Hinckley MN	3+
Minneapolis - St Paul			
Greenwood Campground	651-437-5269	13797 190th Street E Hastings MN	2
Minneapolis Northwest KOA	763-420-2255	10410 Brockton Maple Grove MN	2
Dakotah Meadows RV Park	952-445-8800	2341 Park Place Prior Lake MN	3+
St Paul East KOA	651-436-6436	568 Cottage Grove Woodbury MN	3+
Owatonna			
Hope Oak Knoll Campground	507-451-2998	9545 County Road 3 - Exit 32 Owatonna MN	3+
Kiesler's Campground	800-533-4642	14360 H 14E Waseca MN	3+
Albert Lea			
Big Island State Park	507-379-3403	19499 780th Avenue - Exit 11 Albert Lea MN	3+
Albert Lea/Austin KOA	507-373-5170	84259 County Road 46 Hayward MN	3+

Iowa   (Interstate 35) Dogs per Site

Des Moines			
Des Moines West KOA	515-834-2729	3418 L Avenue Adel IA	3+
Adventureland Campground	512-265-7384	2600 Adventureland Drive Altoona IA	2

Iowa State Fair Campground	515-262-3111 ext. 284	E 30th Street and University Avenue Des Moines IA	3+
Ledges State Park	515-432-1852	1515 P Avenue Madrid IA	3+
Rolling Acres RV Park	641-792-2428	1601 E 36th Street Newton IA	3+
Walnut Woods State Park	515-285-4502	3155 Walnut Woods Drive - Exit Grand Avenue West Des Moines IA	3+
Osceola			
Terribles Lakeside Casino	541-342-9511	777 Casino Drive - Exit Clay Street Osceola IA	2

Missouri   (Interstate 35)   Dogs per Site

Kansas City			
Trailside RV Park	816-229-2267	1000 R.D. Mize Road Grain Valley MO	3+
Basswood Country RV Resort	816-858-5556	15880 Inter Urban Road Platte City MO	3+

Kansas   (Interstate 35)   Dogs per Site

Kansas City			
Rutlader Outpost and RV Park	866-888-6779	33565 Metcalf Louisburg KS	3+
Emporia			
Emporia RV Park	620-343-3422	1601 W H 50 Emporia KS	3+
Wichita			
Deer Grove RV Park	316-321-6272	2873 SE H 54 El Dorado KS	3+
El Dorado State Park	316-321-7180	618 NE Bluestem Road El Dorado KS	3+
All Seasons RV Campground	316-722-1154	15520 W Maple Street Goddard KS	2
USI RV Park	316-838-8699	2920 E 33rd Wichita KS	3+

Oklahoma   (Interstate 35)   Dogs per Site

Oklahoma City			
Oklahoma City East KOA	405-391-5000	6200 S Choctaw Road Choctaw OK	3+
Lake Thunderbird State Park	405-360-3572	13101 Alameda Drive Norman OK	3+
Abe's RV Park	405-478-0278	12115 N I 35 Service Road - Exit 137 Oklahoma City OK	3+
Rockwell RV Park	405-787-5992	720 S Rockwell Oklahoma City OK	3+
Ardmore			
Lake Murray State Park/Tucker Tower Nature Center	580-223-6600	3323 Lodge Road - Exit 24 or 29 Ardmore OK	3+

Texas   (Interstate 35)   Dogs per Site

Dallas			
Cedar Hill State Park	972-291-3900	1570 W FM 1382 Cedar Hill TX	3+
Trader's Village	972-647-8205	2602 Mayfield Road Grand Prairie TX	2
Fort Worth			
Treetops RV Village	817-467-7943	1901 W Arbrook Arlington TX	1+
RV Ranch	888-855-9091	2301 S I 35W Burleson TX	3+
Caddo-LBJ National Grasslands	940-627-5475	1400 H 81/287 Decatur TX	3+
Hillsboro			
Meridian State Park	254-435-2536	173 Park Road 7 Meridian TX	3+
Lake Whitney State Park	254-694-3793	Box 1175; (on FM-1244) Whitney TX	3+
Waco			
Waco North KOA	254-826-3869	24132 N I 35 - Exit 355 Waco TX	3+
i 35 RV Park	254-829-0698	1513 N I 35 - Exit 345 or 346 Waco TX	2
Austin			
Austin Lone Star RV Resort	512-444-6322	7009 S IH 35 Austin TX	3+
Oak Forest RV Park	800-478-7275	8207 Canoga Avenue - Exit H 290E Austin TX	3+
Bastrop State Park	512-321-2101	3005 H 21 Bastrop TX	3+
San Antonio			
Pioneer Rivers Resort	830-796-3751	1203 Maple Bandera TX	3+
Jellystone Park	830-964-3731	12915 Hwy 306 - Exit 191 Canyon Lake TX	1+
Admiralty RV Resort	800-999-7872	1485 N Ellison Drive San Antonio TX	3+
Blazing Star RV Resort	210-680-7827	1120 W H 1604N San Antonio TX	2
San Antonio KOA	210-224-9296	602 Gembler Road - Exit 160 San Antonio TX	2
Traveler's World RV Resort	210-532-8310	2617 Roosevelt Avenue - Exit Military Drive San Antonio TX	3+
Stone Creek RV Park	830-609-7759	18905 IH 35N Schertz TX	3+
Guadalupe River State Park	830-438-2656	3350 Park Road 31 Spring Branch TX	3+

Interstate 40 Dog-Friendly Campgrounds and RV Parks

California   (Interstate 40)   Dogs per Site

Barstow			
Rainbow Basin Natural Area	760-252-6060	Fossil Bed Road Barstow CA	3+
Barstow/Calico KOA	760-254-2311	35250 Outer H 15 - Exit Daggett N Yermo CA	3+
Barstow/Calico KOA	760-254-2311	35250 Outer H 15 - Exit Daggett Yermo CA	3+
Needles			
Moabi Regional Park Campgrounds	760-326-3831	Park Moabi Road - Exit Park Moabi Needles CA	3+
Needles KOA	760-326-4207	5400 National Old Trails H - Exit W Broadway Needles CA	3+

Arizona   (Interstate 40)   Dogs per Site

Kingman			
Kingman KOA	928-757-4397	3820 N Roosevelt - Exit 51N Kingman AZ	3+
Grand Canyon			
Ash Fork RV Park	928-637-2521	783 W Old Route 66 - Exit Old H 66 Ash Fork AZ	3+
Grand Canyon National Park	928-638-7888	Hwy 64 Grand Canyon AZ	1+
Supai and the Havasupai Reservation	928-448-2141	P. O. Box 10/Indian Road 18 - Exit Old Route 66 Supai AZ	2
Flintstones Bedrock City	928-635-2600	Junction 64 and 180 Williams AZ	3+
Grand Canyon/Williams KOA	928-635-2307	5333 H 64 - Exit 165 N Williams AZ	3+
Kaibab National Forest	928-635-8200	Railroad Blvd - Exit H 66 Williams AZ	3+
Williams/Circle Pines KOA	928-635-2626	1000 Circle Pines Road - Exit 167 Williams AZ	3+
Flagstaff			
Coconino National Forest	928-527-3600	1824 S Thompson Street - Exit H 66 Flagstaff AZ	3+
Flagstaff KOA	928-526-9926	5803 N H 89 - Exit 201 Flagstaff AZ	3+
Woody Mountain Campground and RV Park	928-774-7727	2727 W H 66 - Exit 191/H 66 Flagstaff AZ	2
Winslow			
Homolovi Ruins State Park	928-289-4106	Honahanie Road Winslow AZ	3+

New Mexico   (Interstate 40)   Dogs per Site

Grants			
Coal Mine Canyon Campground	505-287-8833	1800 Lobo CanyonRoad Grants NM	3+
Albuquerque			
Albuquerque Central KOA	505-296-2729	12400 Skyline Road NE - Exit 166 Albuquerque NM	3+
Enchanted Trails	505-831-6317	14305 Central - Exit 149 Albuquerque NM	3+
High Desert RV Park	866-839-9035	13000 W Frontage Road SW - Exit 149 Albuquerque NM	3+
Albuquerque N/Bernalillo KOA	505-867-5227	555 S Hill Road Bernalillo NM	3+
Coronado State Park	505-980-8256	106 Monument Road Bernalillo NM	3+
Santa Rosa			
Santa Rosa Campground	505-472-3126	2136 Historic H 66 - Exit 277 Santa Rosa NM	3+
Santa Rosa Lake State Park	505-472-3110	P.O. Box 384 Santa Rosa NM	3+
Tucumcari			
Mountain Road RV Park	505-461-9628	1700 Mountain Road - Exit 333 Tucumcari NM	3+

Texas   (Interstate 40)   Dogs per Site

Amarillo			
Amarillo KOA	806-335-1762	1100 Folsom Road - Exit 75/H60 Amarillo TX	3+
Amarillo Ranch	806-373-4962	1414 Sunrise - Exit 74 Amarillo TX	3+
Fort Amarillo RV Resort	806-331-1700	10101 Amarillo Blvd - Exit Soncy Amarillo TX	3+
Palo Duro Canyon State Park	806-488-2227	11450 Park Road 5 Canyon TX	3+
Lake Meridith National Rec Area	806-857-3151	419 E. Broadway/H 136 (park headquarters) Fritch TX	3+
Caprock Canyons State Park	806-455-1492	850 Caprock Canyons Park Road Quitaque TX	3+

Oklahoma   (Interstate 40)   Dogs per Site

Elk City			
Elk City/Clinton KOA	580-592-4409	Clinton Lake Road - Exit 50 Canute OK	3+
Elk Creek RV Park	580-225-7865	317 E 20th - Exit 38 Elk City OK	3+
El Reno			
El Reno West KOA	405-884-2595	301 S Walbaum Road - Exit 108 Calumet OK	3+
Oklahoma City			
Oklahoma City East KOA	405-391-5000	6200 S Choctaw Road - Exit 166 Choctaw OK	3+
Lake Thunderbird State Park	405-360-3572	13101 Alameda Drive Norman OK	3+
Abe's RV Park	405-478-0278	12115 N I 35 Service Road Oklahoma City OK	3+
Rockwell RV Park	405-787-5992	720 S Rockwell - Exit S. Rockwell Oklahoma City OK	3+
Checotah			
Checotah/Henryetta KOA	918-473-6511	On I 40 @Pierce Road (HC 68, Box750) - Exit 255/Pierce Road Checotah OK	3+

Sallisaw

Sallisaw KOA	918-775-2792	1908 Power Drive - Exit 308/H 59 Sallisaw OK	3+

Arkansas   (Interstate 40)   Dogs per Site

Fort Smith

Fort Smith/Alma KOA	479-632-2704	3539 N H 71 - Exit 13/H 71 Alma AR	1+

Russellville

Ozark-St. Francis National Forest	479-964-7200	605 W Main Street Russellville AR	3+

Morrilton

Morrilton/Conway KOA	501-354-8262	30 Kamper Lane - Exit 107 N/H 95 Morrilton AR	3+
Petit Jean State Park	501-727-5441	1285 Petit Jean Mountain Road - Exit 108/H 9 Morrilton AR	1+

Little Rock

Burns Park Campground	501-771-0702	4101 Arlene Laman Drive - Exit 150 North Little Rock AR	3+
Little Rock North/Jct I 40 KOA	501-758-4598	7820 Crystal Hill Road - Exit 148/Crystal Hill Road North Little Rock AR	3+

West Memphis

America's Best Campground	870-739-4801	7037 I 55 Marion AR	3+
Memphis KOA	870-739-4801	7037 I-55 Marion Marion AR	1+
Tom Sawyer's Mississippi River RV Park	870-735-9770	1286 S 8th Street - Exit I 55 West Memphis AR	3+

Tennessee   (Interstate 40)   Dogs per Site

Memphis

Memphis Graceland RV Park and Campground	901-396-7125	3691 Elvis Presley Blvd Memphis TN	3+
T. O. Fuller State Park	901-543-7581	1500 W Mitchell Road Memphis TN	3+
Meeman-Shelby Forest State Park	901-876-5215	910 Riddick Road Millington TN	3+
Tom Sawyer's Mississippi River RV Park	870-735-9770	1286 S 8th Street - Exit I 55 West Memphis AR	3+

Hurricane Mills

Buffalo/I-40/Exit 143 KOA	931-296-1306	473 Barren Hollow Road - Exit 143 Hurricane Mills TN	1+
Loretta Lynn's Ranch	931-296-7700	44 Hurricane Mills - Exit 143 Hurricane Mills TN	3+

Dickson

Montgomery Bell State Park	615-797-9052	1020 Jackson Hill Road Burns TN	3+

Nashville

Jellystone Park	615-889-4225	2572 Music Valley Drive - Exit Briley Parkway to exit 12 Nashville TN	3+
Two Rivers Campground	615-883-8559	2616 Music Valley Drive Nashville TN	3+

Lebanon

Cedars of Lebanon State Park	615-443-2769	328 Cedar Forest Road - Exit H 231S Lebanon TN	3+
Countryside RV Resort	615-449-5527	2100 Safari Camp Road - Exit 232/L. on H 109 Lebanon TN	3+

Crossville

Ballyhoo Campground	931-484-0860	256 Werthwyle Drive - Exit 322 Crossville TN	1+
Cumberland Mountain State Park	931-484-6138	24 Office Dirve Crossville TN	3+
Roam and Roost RV Campground	931-707-1414	255 Fairview Drive - Exit 322 Crossville TN	2

Knoxville

Southlake RV Park	865-573-1837	3730 Maryville Pike Knoxville TN	3+

Kodak

Knoxville East KOA	865-933-6393	241 KOA Way - Exit 407 Kodak TN	3+

North Carolina   (Interstate 40)   Dogs per Site

Asheville

Bear Creek RV Park	828-253-0798	81 S Bear Creek Road - Exit 47/Farmer's Market Asheville NC	3+
Pisgah National Forest	828-877-3350	1001 Pisgah H (H276) Asheville NC	3+
Creekside Mountain Camping	800-248-8118	24 Chimney View Road - Exit H 74A Bat Cave NC	2
Asheville West KOA	828-665-7015	309 Wiggins Road - Exit 37 R Candler NC	3+
Jellystone Park	828-654-7873	170 Rutledge Road Fletcher NC	2

Marion

Buck Creek Campground	828-724-4888	2576 Toms Creek Road - Exit 86 Marion NC	3+
Jellystone Park at Hidden Valley Campground	828-652-7208	1210 Deacon Drive - Exit 86/H 226 Marion NC	3+

Raleigh

Jordan Lake State Park	919-362-0586	280 State Park Road Apex NC	3+
William B. Umstead State Park	919-571-4170	8801 Glenwood Avenue - Exit Harrison Avenue Raleigh NC	3+
Falls Lake State Park	919-676-1027	13304 Creedmoor Road (H 50) Wake Forest NC	3+

Smithfield

Selma/Smithfield KOA	919-965-5923	428 Campground Road Selma NC	3+

Interstate 55 Dog-Friendly Campgrounds and RV Parks

Illinois   (Interstate 55)   Dogs per Site

Chicago Area - West			
Double J Campground	217-483-9998	9683 Palm Road Chatham IL	3+
Burnidge and Paul Wolff Forest Preserve	630-232-5980	38W235 Big Timber Road Elgin IL	3+
Jellystone Park	800-438-9644	8574 Millbrook Road Millbrook IL	3+
Hide-A-Way Lakes	630-553-6323	8045 Van Emmons Road Yorkville IL	3+
Chicago Area - South			
Windy City Campground	708-720-0030	18701 S 80th Avenue Tinley Park IL	2
Springfield			
Lincoln's New Salem State Historic Site	217-632-4000	15588 History Lane Petersburg IL	2
Springfield KOA	217-498-7002	4320 KOA Road - Exit 94 Rochester IL	1+
St Louis Area			
MGM Lakeside Campground	618-797-2820	3133 W Chain of Rocks Granite City IL	3+
Northeast/I 270/Granite City KOA	618-931-5160	3157 Chain of Rocks Road Granite City IL	3+

Missouri   (Interstate 55)   Dogs per Site

St Louis			
St Louis West KOA	636-257-3018	18475 Old H 66 Eureka MO	3+
Sundermeier RV Park	636-940-0111	111 Transit Street St Charles MO	3+
Beacon RV Park	816-279-5417	822 S Belt H St Joseph MO	3+
Pin Oak Creek RV Park	636-451-5656	1302 H 8AT Villa Ridge MO	3+
Perryville			
Perryville/Cape Girardeau KOA	573-547-8303	89 KOA Lane - Exit 129 Perryville MO	2
Cape Girardeau			
Trail of Tear State Park	573-334-1711	429 Moccasin Springs - Exit 105/H 61 Jackson MO	3+
Hayti			
Hayti/Portageville KOA	573-359-1580	2824 MO State E Outer Road - Exit 19 Portageville MO	3+

Arkansas   (Interstate 55)   Dogs per Site

West Memphis			
America's Best Campground	870-739-4801	7037 I 55 - Exit 14 Marion AR	3+
Memphis KOA	870-739-4801	7037 I-55 Marion - Exit 14 Marion AR	1+
Tom Sawyer's Mississippi River RV Park	870-735-9770	1286 S 8th Street - Exit 4 West Memphis AR	3+

Tennessee   (Interstate 55)   Dogs per Site

Memphis			
Memphis Graceland RV Park and Campground	901-396-7125	3691 Elvis Presley Blvd Memphis TN	3+
T. O. Fuller State Park	901-543-7581	1500 W Mitchell Road - Exit 9/Mallory onto Riverport Memphis TN	3+
Meeman-Shelby Forest State Park	901-876-5215	910 Riddick Road Millington TN	3+
Tom Sawyer's Mississippi River RV Park	870-735-9770	1286 S 8th Street - Exit 4 West Memphis AR	3+

Mississippi   (Interstate 55)   Dogs per Site

Sardis			
John W Kyle State Park	662-487-1345	4235 State Park Road - Exit 252 Sardis MS	3+
Canton			
Movietown RV Park	601-859-7990	109 Movietown Drive - Exit 119/H 22 Canton MS	3+
Jackson			
Swinging Bridge RV Park	800-297-9127	100 Holiday Rambler Lane - Exit 85 Bryam MS	3+
Holly Springs National Forest	662-236-6550	100 W Capital Street, Suite 1141 Jackson MS	3+
LeFleur's Bluff State Park	601-987-3923	2140 Riverside Drive Jackson MS	3+
Brookhaven			
Lake Lincoln State Park	601-643-9044	2573 Sunset Road - Exit 42 to H 51N Wesson MS	3+

Louisiana   (Interstate 55)   Dogs per Site

New Orleans			
St. Bernard State Park	504-682-2101	501 St. Bernard Parkway Braithwaite LA	3+

Interstate 59 Dog-Friendly Campgrounds and RV Parks

Georgia   (Interstate 59)   Dogs per Site

Trenton

Lookout Mountain/Chattanooga West KOA	706-657-6815	930 Mountain Shadows Drive - Exit 17/Slygo Road Trenton GA	3+

Alabama   (Interstate 59)   Dogs per Site

Fort Payne

DeSoto Resort State Park	256-845-0051	13883 H 89 Fort Payne AL	3+
Gadsden			
Noccalula Falls Park and Campground	256-543-7412	1600 Noccalula Road - Exit 188 Gadsden AL	3+
River Country Campground	256-543-7111	1 River Road Gadsden AL	2
Birmingham			
Cherokee Campground	205-428-8339	2800 H 93 Helena AL	3+
Tannehill Ironworks Historical State Park	205-477-5711	12632 Confederate Parkway - Exit 100 McCalla AL	3+
Birmingham South Campground	205-664-8832	222 H 33 Pelham AL	3+
Oak Mountain State Park	800-ALAPARK (252-7275)	200 Terrace Drive Pelham AL	3+
Knoxville			
Knox Hill RV Park	205-372-3911	252 Old Patton Road Knoxville AL	3+

Mississippi   (Interstate 59)   Dogs per Site

Meridian

Twitley Branch Camping Area	601-626-8068	9200 Hamrick Road Collinsville MS	3+
Nanabe Creek Campground	601-485-4711	1933 Russell Mount Gilliad Road Meridian MS	3+
Hattiesburg			
Paul B Johnson State Park	601-582-7721	319 Geiger Lake Road Hattiesburg MS	3+

Interstate 64 Dog-Friendly Campgrounds and RV Parks

Missouri   (Interstate 64)   Dogs per Site

St Louis

St Louis West KOA	636-257-3018	18475 Old H 66 Eureka MO	3+
Sundermeier RV Park	636-940-0111	111 Transit Street St Charles MO	3+
Beacon RV Park	816-279-5417	822 S Belt H St Joseph MO	3+
Pin Oak Creek RV Park	636-451-5656	1302 H 8AT Villa Ridge MO	3+

Illinois   (Interstate 64)   Dogs per Site

St Louis Area

MGM Lakeside Campground	618-797-2820	3133 W Chain of Rocks Granite City IL	3+
Northeast/I 270/Granite City KOA	618-931-5160	3157 Chain of Rocks Road Granite City IL	3+

Indiana   (Interstate 64)   Dogs per Site

Dale

Lincoln State Park	812-937-4710	On H 162 3 miles W of Santa Claus Lincoln City IN	3+
Lake Rudolph Campground	877-478-3657	78 N Holiday Blvd - Exit 63 Santa Claus IN	3+
Corydon			
O'Bannon Woods State Park	812-738-8232	7240 Old Forest Road - Exit 105 Corydon IN	3+

Kentucky   (Interstate 64)   Dogs per Site

Louisville

Louisville Metro KOA	812-282-4474	900 Marriott Drive - Exit I 65N to Exit 1 Clarksville IN	3+
Grand Trails RV Park	812-738-9077	205 S Mulberry Corydon IN	3+
Lexington			
Elkhorn Campground	502-695-9154	165 N Scruggs Lane - Exit 58 Frankfort KY	3+

Kentucky Horse Park Campground	859-259-4257	4089 Iron Works Parkway Lexington KY	3+
Winchester			
Daniel Boone National Forest	859-745-3100	1700 Bypass Road/H 1958 Winchester KY	3+
Morehead - Cave Run Lake			
Poppy Mountain Campground	606-780-4192	8030 H 60E Morehead KY	3+
Twin Knobs Rec Area	606-784-6428	2375 Kentucky H - Exit 133/Farmers (H801) Morehead KY	3+

West Virginia   (Interstate 64)   Dogs per Site

Huntington			
Beech Fork State Park	304-528-5794	5601 Long Branch Road Barboursville WV	2
Fox Fire Resort	304-743-5622	Route 2, Box 655 - Exit 20A Milton WV	2
Huntington / Fox Fire KOA	304-743-5622	290 Fox Fire Road Milton WV	3+
Charleston			
Kanawha State Forest	304-558-3500	Rt. 2 Box 285 - Exit 58A/H 119S Charleston WV	3+
Beckley			
Babcock State Park	304-438-3004	HC 35, Box 150 Clifftop WV	2
New River Gorge National River	304-465-0508	104 Main Street Glen Jean WV	3+
The Gauley River National Recreation Area	304-465-0508	H 129/ P. O. Box 246 Glen Jean WV	3+
Bluestone State Park	304-466-2805	HC 78 Box 3/H 20 - Exit 139 (Sandstone/Hinton) /H 20 S Hinton WV	2
Twin Falls Resort State Park	304-294-4000	Route 97, Box 667 Mullens WV	2
Plum Orchard Lake Wildlife Management Area	304-469-9905	Plum Orchard Lake Road Scarbro WV	3+
Lake Stephens Park	304-256-1747	1400 Lake Stephens Road/H 3 Surveyor WV	3+
Lewisburg			
Greenbrier State Forest	304-536-1944	HC 30 Box 154/Harts Run Road - Exit 175/White Sulphur Springs Caldwell WV	2

Virginia   (Interstate 64)   Dogs per Site

Covington			
Douthat State Park	540-862-8100	Rt 1, Box 212 Clifton Forge VA	3+
Staunton			
Staunton/Verona KOA	540-248-2746	296 Riner Lane Verona VA	3+
Charlottesville			
Charlottesville KOA	434-296-9881	3825 Red Hill Lane Charlottesville VA	3+
Misty Mountain Campground	888-647-8900	56 Misty Mountain Road - Exit H 250/ Crozet VA	3+
Richmond			
Pocohontas State Park	804-796-4255	10301 State Park Road Chesterfield VA	3+
Williamsburg			
Chippokes Plantation	757-294-3625	695 Chippokes Park Road Surry VA	3+
Pottery Campground	757-565-2101	Lightfoot Road/H 646 Williamsburg VA	3+
Williamsburg KOA	757-565-2907	5210 Newman Road - Exit 234B Williamsburg VA	3+
Williamsburg/Colonial KOA	757-565-2734	4000 Newman Road - exit 234B Williamsburg VA	3+
Virginia Beach Area			
False Cape State Park	757-426-3657	4001 Sandpiper Road - Exit Indian River Road East Virginia Beach VA	2
First Landing State Park	757-412-2320	2500 Shore DriveH 60 Virginia Beach VA	2
Holiday Trav-L-Park	757-425-0249	1075 General Booth Blvd Virginia Beach VA	2
Virginia Beach KOA	757-428-1444	1240 General Booth Blvd Virginia Beach VA	3+
Virginia Beach KOA	757-428-1444	1240 General Booth Blvd Virginia Beach VA	3+

Interstate 65 Dog-Friendly Campgrounds and RV Parks

Indiana   (Interstate 65)   Dogs per Site

Remington			
Caboose Lake Campground	877-600-CAMP (2267)	3657 H 24 - Exit H 24 Remington IN	3+
Lafayette			
Prophetstown State Park	765-567-4919	4112 E State Road 4 - Exit 178/H 43 Battle Ground IN	3+
Indianapolis			
Broadview Lake Campground	765-324-2622	4850 Broadview Road Colfax IN	3+
Heartland Resort	317-326-3181	1613 W 300N Greenfield IN	2
Indianapolis KOA	317-894-1397	5896 W 200 N Greenfield IN	3+
S & H Campground	317-326-3208	2573 W 100N Greenfield IN	3+
Columbus			
Woods N Waters Kampground	812-342-1619	8855 S 300 W - Exit 64 Columbus IN	3+

Scottsburg

| Jellystone Park | 812-752-4062 | 4577 W H 56 Scottsburg IN | 3+ |

Kentucky   (Interstate 65)

Dogs per Site

Louisville

| Louisville Metro KOA | 812-282-4474 | 900 Marriott Drive Clarksville IN | 3+ |
| Grand Trails RV Park | 812-738-9077 | 205 S Mulberry Corydon IN | 3+ |

Cave City

| Crystal Onyx Cave and Campground Resort | 270-773-2359 | 363 Prewitts Knob Road - Exit 53 Cave City KY | 2 |
| Jellystone Park | 270-773-3840 | 1002 Mammoth Cave Road - Exit 53 Cave City KY | 3+ |

Bowling Green

| Beech Bend Park & Splash Lagoon Family Campground | 270-781-7634 | 798 Beech Bend Road - Exit 28 Bowling Green KY | 3+ |
| Bowling Green KOA | 270-843-1919 | 1960 Three Springs Road - Exit 22 Bowling Green KY | 3+ |

Franklin

| Franklin KOA | 270-586-5622 | 2889 Scottsville Road Franklin KY | 3+ |

Tennessee   (Interstate 65)

Dogs per Site

Nashville

| Jellystone Park | 615-889-4225 | 2572 Music Valley Drive Nashville TN | 3+ |
| Two Rivers Campground | 615-883-8559 | 2616 Music Valley Drive Nashville TN | 3+ |

Alabama   (Interstate 65)

Dogs per Site

Decatur

| Point Mallard Campground | 256-351-7772 | 2600-C Point Mallard Drive Decatur AL | 3+ |

Cullman

| Good Hope Campground | 256-739-1319 | 330 Super Saver Road - Exit 304 Cullman AL | 3+ |

Birmingham

Cherokee Campground	205-428-8339	2800 H 93 Helena AL	3+
Tannehill Ironworks Historical State Park	205-477-5711	12632 Confederate Parkway McCalla AL	3+
Birmingham South Campground	205-664-8832	222 H 33 Pelham AL	3+
Oak Mountain State Park	800-ALAPARK (252-7275)	200 Terrace Drive - Exit H 119/Cahaba Valley Road Pelham AL	3+

Montgomery

| Capital City RV Park | 877-271-8026 | 4655 Old Wetumpka H (H 231N) - Exit 173/H 231N Montgomery AL | 3+ |

Mobile

| Shady Acres Campground | 251-478-0013 | 2500 Old Military Road Mobile AL | 3+ |

Interstate 70 Dog-Friendly Campgrounds and RV Parks

Utah   (Interstate 70)

Dogs per Site

Sevier

| Fremont Indian State Park | 435-527-4631 | 3820 W Clear Creek Canyon Road - Exit 17 Sevier UT | 3+ |

Richfield

| Fishlake National Forest | 435-896-9233 | 115 East 900 North Richfield UT | 3+ |
| Richfield KOA | 435-896-6674 | 600 W 600 S - Exit 37 or 40 Richfield UT | 2 |

Green River

Goblin Valley State Park	435-564-3633	P.O. Box 637 - Exit 147 Green River UT	3+
Green River KOA	435-564-8195	235 S 1780 E - Exit 164 Green River UT	3+
Green River State Park	435-564-3633	125 Fairway Avenue - Exit Green River Green River UT	3+
United Campground of Green River	435-564-8195	910 E Main Street - Exit 164 Green River UT	3+

Colorado   (Interstate 70)

Dogs per Site

Clifton

| Colorado River State Park | 970-434-3388 | 700 32 Road Clifton CO | 3+ |
| RV Ranch at Grand Junction | 970-434-6644 | 3238 E I 70 Business Loop Clifton CO | 1 |

Rifle

| Rifle Falls State Park | 970-625-1607 | 575 H 325 - Exit H 13 Rifle CO | 3+ |

Glenwood Springs

| Glenwood Canyon Resort | 970-945-6737 | 1308 County Road 129 - Exit 119/No Name Glenwood Springs CO | 3+ |

Rock Gardens RV Resort and Campground	800-958-6737	1308 County Road 129 - Exit 119 Glenwood Springs CO	3+
White River Naional Forest	970-945-2521	900 Grand Avenue Glenwood Springs CO	3+

Denver

Denver Meadows RV Park	303-364-9483	2075 Potomac Street Aurora CO	3+
Dakota Ridge RV Park	800-398-1625	17800 W Colfax - Exit 259 Golden CO	3+
Genesee Park/Chief Hosa Campground	303-526-1324	27661 Genesee Drive - Exit 253 Golden CO	3+
Chatfield State Park	303-791-7275	11500 N Roxborough Park Road Littleton CO	3+
Prospect RV Park	303-424-4414	11600 W 44th Avenue - Exit 266 Wheat Ridge CO	3+

Strasburg

Denver East/Strasburg KOA	303-622-9274	1312 Monroe - Exit 310 Strasburg CO	3+

Limon

Limon KOA	719-775-2151	575 Colorado Avenue - Exit 361 Limon CO	3+

Burlington

Bonny Lake State Park	970-354-7306	32300 Yuma County Road 2 - Exit H 385 Burlington CO	3+

Kansas   (Interstate 70)   Dogs per Site

Goodland

Goodland KOA	785-890-5701	1114 E H 24 - Exit 19 Goodland KS	3+

Colby

Bourquin's RV Park	785-462-3300	155 E Willow - Exit 54 Colby KS	3+

WaKeeney

WaKeeney KOA	785-743-5612	I 70 S. Frontage Road, Box 170 - Exit 127 WaKeeney KS	3+

Salina

Salina KOA	785-827-3182	1109 W Diamond Drive - Exit 252 Salina KS	1+

Abilene

Covered Wagon RV Resort	785-263-2343	803 Buckeye - Exit 275 Abilene KS	3+

Junction City

Owl's Nest RV Campground	785-238-0778	1912 Old H 40 Junction City KS	3+
Milford State Park	785-238-3014	8811 State Park Road Milford KS	3+

Manhattan

Tuttle Creek State Park	785-539-7941	5800A River Pond Road Manhattan KS	3+

Topeka

Topeka KOA	785-246-3419	3366 KOA Road Grantville KS	3+
Capital City RV Park	785-862-5267	1949 SW 49th Street Topeka KS	3+

Lawrence

Lawrence/Kansas City KOA	785-842-3877	1473 H 40 - Exit 204 N Lawrence KS	3+

Kansas City

Rutlader Outpost and RV Park	866-888-6779	33565 Metcalf Louisburg KS	3+

Missouri   (Interstate 70)   Dogs per Site

Kansas City

Trailside RV Park	816-229-2267	1000 R.D. Mize Road - Exit 24 Grain Valley MO	3+
Basswood Country RV Resort	816-858-5556	15880 Inter Urban Road Platte City MO	3+

Oak Grove

Kansas City East/Oak Grove KOA	816-690-6660	303 NE 3rd - Exit 28 Oak Grove MO	3+

Higginsville

Interstate RV Park	800-690-2267	On Old H 40 - Exit 49 Higginsville MO	3+

Columbia

Cottonwoods RV Park	573-474-2747	5170 Oakland Gravel Road Columbia MO	3+
Finger Lakes State Park	573-443-5315	1505 E Peabody Road - Exit 128A/H 63 Columbia MO	3+

Fulton

Lazy Day Campground	573-564-2949	214 H J Montgomery City MO	1+

St Louis

St Louis West KOA	636-257-3018	18475 Old H 66 Eureka MO	3+
Sundermeier RV Park	636-940-0111	111 Transit Street St Charles MO	3+
Beacon RV Park	816-279-5417	822 S Belt H St Joseph MO	3+
Pin Oak Creek RV Park	636-451-5656	1302 H 8AT Villa Ridge MO	3+

Illinois   (Interstate 70)   Dogs per Site

St Louis Area

MGM Lakeside Campground	618-797-2820	3133 W Chain of Rocks Granite City IL	3+
Northeast/I 270/Granite City KOA	618-931-5160	3157 Chain of Rocks Road Granite City IL	3+

Effingham

Camp Lakewood	217-342-6233	1217 W Rickelman Effingham IL	3+

Casey

Casey KOA	217-932-5319	1248 E 1250th Road - Exit 129 Casey IL	3+

Marshall

Lincoln Trail State Park	217-826-2222	1685 1350th Road Marshall IL	3+

Indiana   (Interstate 70)

Dogs per Site

Terre Haute

Terre Haute KOA	812-232-2457	5995 E Sony Drive - Exit 11/H46 Terre Haute IN	3+

Indianapolis

Broadview Lake Campground	765-324-2622	4850 Broadview Road Colfax IN	3+
Heartland Resort	317-326-3181	1613 W 300N - Exit 96 Greenfield IN	2
Indianapolis KOA	317-894-1397	5896 W 200 N - Exit 96 Greenfield IN	3+
S & H Campground	317-326-3208	2573 W 100N - Exit 96 Greenfield IN	3+

Knightstown

Yogi Bear Campground	765-737-6585	5964 S H 109 - Exit Knightstown/Wilkenson (H 109) Knightstown IN	3+

New Castle

Summit Lake State Park	765-766-5873	5993 N Messick Road New Castle IN	3+
Walnut Ridge Campground	877-619-2559	408 County Road 300W New Castle IN	3+

Richmond

Whitewater Memorial Park	765-458-5565	1418 S State Road 101 Liberty IN	1+
Richmond KOA	756-962-1219	3101 Cart Road - Exit 151 or 151B Richmond IN	1+

Ohio   (Interstate 70)

Dogs per Site

Springfield

Buck Creek State Park	937-322-5284	1901 Buck Creek Lane - Exit 64 Springfield OH	2
Enon Beach Campground	937-882-6431	2401 Enon Road - Exit 48 Springfield OH	3+

Columbus

Crosscreek Camping Resort	740-549-2267	3190 S Old State Delaware OH	3+

Buckeye Lake

Buckeye Lake/Columbus East KOA	740-928-0706	4460 Walnut Road Buckeye Lake OH	2

Cambridge

Hillview Acres Campground	740-439-3348	66271 Wolfs Den Road Cambridge OH	1+
Spring Valley Campground	740-439-9291	8000 Dozer Road - Exit 178 Cambridge OH	3+

Pennsylvania   (Interstate 70)

Dogs per Site

Washington

Washington KOA	724-225-7590	7 KOA Road - Exit 20 Washington PA	1+

Somerset

Kooser State Park	814-445-7725	934 Glades Pike Somerset PA	2

Maryland   (Interstate 70)

Dogs per Site

Hagerstown

Fort Frederick State Park	301-842-2155	11100 Fort Frederick Road Big Pool MD	3+
KOA Hagerstown/Snug Harbor	301-223-7571	11759 Snug Harbor Lane Williamsport MD	3+
Yogi Bear Jellystone Park	800-421-7116	16519 Lappans Road Williamsport MD	2

Interstate 75 Dog-Friendly Campgrounds and RV Parks

Michigan   (Interstate 75)

Dogs per Site

Sault Ste Marie

Brimley State Park	906-248-3422	9200 W 6 Mile Road - Exit H 28 Brimley MI	3+

Mackinaw City

Mackinaw City/Mackinac Island KOA	231-436-5643	566 Trailsend Road - Exit H 108 Mackinaw City MI	1+
Mackinaw Mill Creek Camping	231-436-5584	9730 H 23 Mackinaw City MI	3+
St. Ignace/Mackinac Island KOA	906-643-9303	1242 H 2 W - Exit H 2W St Ignace MI	3+

Indian River

Jellystone Park	231-238-8259	2201 E H 68 - Exit 310/H 68 Indian River MI	3+

Gaylord

Gaylord KOA	989-939-8723	5101 Campfires Parkway - Exit 279 Gaylord MI	3+

Grayling

Hartwick Pines State Park	989-348-7068	4216 Ranger Road Grayling MI	3+
Jellystone Park	989-348-2157	370 W 4 Mile Road - Exit 251 Grayling MI	3+
Higgins Lake / Roscommon KOA	989-275-8151	3800 W. Federal H - Exit 244 Roscommon MI	3+

North Higgins Lake State Park	989-821-6125	11747 N Higgins Lake Drive - Exit 244 Roscommon MI	3+
Standish			
Au Gres City Park	989-876-8310	522 Park Street Au Gres MI	3+
Big Bend Family Campground	989-653-2267	513 Conrad Road Standish MI	3+
Saginaw			
Bay City State Recreation Area	989-684-3020	3582 State Park Drive - Exit 168/Beaver Road Bay City MI	3+
Frankenmuth Jellystone Park	989-652-6668	1339 Weiss Street - Exit 136 Frankenmuth MI	3+
Hoyles Marina and Campground	989-697-3153	135 S Linwood Beach Road - Exit 173/Linwood Linwood MI	3+
Valley Plaza Resort	989-496-2159	5215 Bay City Road Midland MI	1
Flint			
Walnut Hills	989-634-9782	7685 Lehring Durand MI	3+
Detroit			
Wayne County Fairgrounds and RV Park	734-697-7002	10871 Quirk Road Belleville MI	3+
Highland Recreation Area	248-889-3750	5200 E Highland Road White Lake MI	3+

Ohio   (Interstate 75)   Dogs per Site

Toledo			
Maumee Bay State Park Campground	419-836-7758	1400 State Park Road Oregon OH	1+
Toledo East/Stony Ridge KOA	419-837-6848	24787 Luckey Road Perrysburg OH	3+
Findlay			
Pleasant View	419-299-3897	12611 Township Road 218 Van Buren OH	3+
Van Buren State Park Campgrounds	419-832-7662	12259 Township Rd. 218 Van Buren OH	1+
Wapakoneta			
Wapakoneta/Lima S KOA	419-738-6016	14719 Cemetery Road - Exit 111 Wapakoneta OH	3+
Cincinnati			
Miami Whitewater Forest Campground	513-521-PARK	various entrances Crosby OH	1+
Indian Springs Campground	513-353-9244	3306 Stateline Road N Bend OH	2
Winton Woods Campground	513-521-PARK	Winton Road Springfield Township OH	1+

Kentucky   (Interstate 75)   Dogs per Site

Lexington			
Elkhorn Campground	502-695-9154	165 N Scruggs Lane Frankfort KY	3+
Kentucky Horse Park Campground	859-259-4257	4089 Iron Works Parkway - Exit Iron Works Parkway Lexington KY	3+
Richmond			
Ft. Boonesborough State Park	859-527-3131	4375 Boonesborough Road/H 627 - Exit H 627/Boonesborough Road Richmond KY	3+
Berea			
Old Kentucky RV Park	859-986-1150	1142 Paint Lick Road Berea KY	3+
Renfro Valley			
Renfro Valley KOA	606-256-2474	Red Foley Road, H 25 - Exit 62 Renfro Valley KY	1+
Renfro Valley RV Park	606-256-2638	Renfro Valley Entertainment Center - Exit 62 Renfro Valley KY	3+
Corbin			
Corbin KOA	806-528-1534	171 E City Dam Road - Exit 29 Corbin KY	1+
Cumberland Falls State Resort Park	606-528-4121	7351 H 90 Corbin KY	3+

Tennessee   (Interstate 75)   Dogs per Site

Jellico			
Indian Mountain State Park	423-784-7958	143 State Park Circle - Exit 160/H 25W Jellico TN	3+
Caryville			
Cove Lake State Park	423-566-9701	110 Cove Lake Lane - Exit H 25W Caryville TN	3+
Royal Blue RV Resort	423-566-4847	305 Luther Seiber Road - Exit 141 Caryville TN	3+
Knoxville			
Southlake RV Park	865-573-1837	3730 Maryville Pike Knoxville TN	3+
Cleveland			
Chattanooga North/Cleveland KOA	423-472-8928	648 Pleasant Grove Road - Exit 20 McDonald TN	1+
Chattanooga			
Cherokee National Forest/Ocoee / Hiwassee Ranger District	423-476-9700	3171 Highway 64 Benton TN	3+
Raccoon Mountain Caverns/RV Park and Campground	423-821-9403	319 W Hills Road Chattanooga TN	3+
Harrison Bay State Park	423-344-2272	8411 Harrison Bay Road Harrison TN	3+

Georgia   (Interstate 75)   Dogs per Site

Dalton			

Fort Mountain State Park	706-422-1932	181 Fort Mountain Park Road Chatsworth GA	1+
Calhoun			
Calhoun KOA	706-629-7511	2523 Redbud Road NE - Exit 315/Redbud Road E Calhoun GA	3+
Adairsville			
Harvest Moon RV Park	770-773-7320	1001 Poplar Springs Road - Exit 306 Adairsville GA	2
Atlanta Area			
Brookwood RV Park	877-727-5787	1031 Wylie Road SE Marietta GA	3+
Atlanta South RV Resort	770-957-2610	281 Mount Olive Road - Exit 222 McDonough GA	3+
Atlanta			
Stone Mountain Park	800-385-9807	H 78E Stone Mountain GA	3+
Forsyth			
Forsyth KOA	478-994-2019	414 S Frontage Road - Exit 186 Forsyth GA	3+
Cordele			
Cordele KOA	229-273-5454	373 Rockhouse Road E - Exit 97 Cordele GA	1+
Veterans Memorial State Park	229-276-2371	2459A H 280W - Exit 101/H 280W Cordele GA	3+
Tifton			
Agirama RV Park	229-386-3344	1392 Windmill Road - Exit 63b Tifton GA	2
Amy's South Georgia RV Park	229-386-8441	4632 Union Road - Exit 60 Tifton GA	3+
Lake Park			
Eagle's Roost RV Resort	229-559-5192	5465 Mill Store Road - Exit 5 Lake Park GA	3+
Valdosta/Lake Park KOA	229-559-9738	5300 Jewel Futch Road - Exit 5 Lake Park GA	3+

Florida   (Interstate 75)   Dogs per Site

Lake City			
Stephen Foster Folk Culture Center State Park	386-397-2733	P. O. Drawer G/ US 41 N - Exit H 136 White Springs FL	3+
Suwannee Valley Campground	866-397-1667	786 N W Street - Exit 439/H 136 White Springs FL	2
Reddick			
Encore RV Resort	352-591-1723	16905 NW H 225 - Exit H 368 Reddick FL	3+
Ocala			
Silver River State Park	352-236-7148	1425 NE 58th Avenue - Exit 352 onto H 40 E Ocala FL	3+
Ocala National Forest	352-625-2520	17147 E H 40 Silver Springs FL	3+
Tampa Bay			
Oscar Scherer State Park	941-483-5956	1843 S Tamiami Trail - Exit Laurel Road Osprey FL	3+
Clearwater/Tarpon Springs KOA	727-937-8412	37061 H 19N Palm Harbor FL	2
Hillsborough River State Park	813-987-6771	15402 H 301 N Thonotosassa FL	3+
Sarasota			
Horseshoe Cove RV Resort	941-758-5335	5100 60th Street & Caruso Road - Exit 217/70th Street Bradenton FL	2
Lake Manatee State Park	941-741-3028	20007 H 64E - Exit 220 Bradenton FL	3+
Sarasota North Resort	800-678-2131	800 K Road - Exit 220 Bradenton FL	3+
Fort Myers			
Koreshan State Historic Site	239-992-0311	Corner of H 41 and Corkscrew Road Estero FL	3+
Indian Creek RV Resort	800-828-6992	17340 San Carlos Blvd - Exit 131 Fort Myers Beach FL	2
North Fort Myers RV Resort (Pioneer Village)	239-543-3303	7974 Samville Road - Exit 26 North Fort Myers FL	3+
Fort Myers/Pine Island KOA	239-283-2415	5120 Stringfellow Road - Exit W H 78 St James City FL	3+
Naples			
Collier-Seminole State Park	239-394-3397	20200 E Tamiami Trail Naples FL	3+
Hitching Post RV Resort	239-774-1259	100 Barefoot Williams Road Naples FL	3+
Lake San Marino RV Resort	239-597-4202	1000 Wiggins Pass Naples FL	2
South Florida			
Juno Ocean Walk RV Resort	561-622-7500	900 Juno Ocean Walk Juno Beach FL	3+
Paradise Island RV Resort	954-485-1150	2121 NW 29th Court Oakland Park FL	3+
Highland Woods	866-340-0649	850/900 NE 48th Street Pompano Beach FL	3+
Markham Park	954-389-2000	16001 W H 84 Sunrise FL	2

Interstate 77 Dog-Friendly Campgrounds and RV Parks

Ohio   (Interstate 77)   Dogs per Site

Cleveland			
Kool Lakes Family RV park	440-548-8436	12990 H 282 Parkman OH	3+
Country Acres Campground	866-813-4321	9850 Minyoung Road Ravenna OH	3+
Akron			
Portage Lakes State Park Campground	330-644-2220	5031 Manchester Road Akron OH	1+
Canton			

Canton/East Sparta KOA	330-484-3901	3232 Downing Street SW East Sparta OH	1+
Cambridge			
Hillview Acres Campground	740-439-3348	66271 Wolfs Den Road Cambridge OH	1+
Spring Valley Campground	740-439-9291	8000 Dozer Road Cambridge OH	3+

West Virginia   (Interstate 77)   Dogs per Site

Charleston			
Kanawha State Forest	304-558-3500	Rt. 2 Box 285 Charleston WV	3+
Beckley			
Babcock State Park	304-438-3004	HC 35, Box 150 Clifftop WV	2
New River Gorge National River	304-465-0508	104 Main Street Glen Jean WV	3+
The Gauley River National Recreation Area	304-465-0508	H 129/ P. O. Box 246 Glen Jean WV	3+
Bluestone State Park	304-466-2805	HC 78 Box 3/H 20 Hinton WV	2
Twin Falls Resort State Park	304-294-4000	Route 97, Box 667 Mullens WV	2
Plum Orchard Lake Wildlife Management Area	304-469-9905	Plum Orchard Lake Road - Exit Pax (Exit 54) or Mossy (Exit 60) Scarbro WV	3+
Lake Stephens Park	304-256-1747	1400 Lake Stephens Road/H 3 Surveyor WV	3+

Virginia   (Interstate 77)   Dogs per Site

Wytheville			
Whtheville KOA	276-228-2601	231 KOA Road - Exit Bluesky Drive Wytheville VA	3+

North Carolina   (Interstate 77)   Dogs per Site

Charlotte			
Carowinds Camp Wilderness Resort	704-588-2600	14523 Carowinds Blvd - Exit SC 90 Charlotte NC	3+
McDowell Nature Preserve Campground	704-583-1284	15222 York Road - Exit 90 Charlotte NC	3+
Fleetwood RV Racing Camping Resort	704-455-4445	6600 Speedway Blvd Concord NC	3+
Charlotte/Fort Mill KOA	803-548-1148	940 Gold Hill Road - Exit 88 Fort Mill NC	3+

South Carolina   (Interstate 77)   Dogs per Site

Winnsboro			
Lake Wateree State Rec Area	803-482-6401	881 State Park Road - Exit H 41 Winnsboro SC	3+
Columbia			
Francis Marion and Sumter National Forests	803-561-4000	4931 Broad River Road Columbia SC	3+
Sesquicentennial State Park	803-788-2706	9564 Two Notch Road Columbia SC	3+
Barnyard RV Park	803-957-1238	201 Oak Drive Lexington SC	3+
River Bottom Farms	803-568-4182	357 Cedar Creek Road Swansea SC	3+

Interstate 80 Dog-Friendly Campgrounds and RV Parks

California   (Interstate 80)   Dogs per Site

San Francisco			
Candlestick RV Park	415-822-2299	650 Gilman Avenue San Francisco CA	3+
Vacaville			
Midway RV Park	707-446-7679	4933 Midway Road Vacaville CA	3+
Vineyard RV Park	707-693-8797	4985 Midway Road Vacaville CA	2
Sacramento			
Beals Point Campground	916-988-0205	7806 Folsom-Auburn Road Folsom CA	3+
Cal Expo RV Park	916-263-3000	1600 Exposition Blvd Sacramento CA	2
Sacramento Metropolitan KOA	916-371-6771	3951 Lake Road - Exit W Capitol Avenue West Sacramento CA	1+
Auburn - Gold Country North			
Auburn Gold Country RV (formally KOA)	530-885-0990	3550 KOA Way Auburn CA	3+
Rocky Rest Campground	530-288-3231	H 49 Downieville CA	3+
French Meadows Reservoir Campground	530-367-2224	Mosquito Ridge Road - Exit Foresthill Road Foresthill CA	3+
Robinson Flat Campground	530-367-2224	Foresthill Divide Road - Exit H 49 to Foresthill Foresthill CA	3+
Lodgepole Campground	916-386-5164	Lake Valley Reservoir - Exit Yuba Gap Nevada City CA	2
South Yuba Campground	916-985-4474	North Bloomfield Road - Exit H 49N Nevada City CA	3+
South Yuba Campground	919-985-4474	North Bloomfield Road Nevada City CA	3+

Lake Tahoe

D. L. Bliss State Park	530-525-9529	H 89 South Lake Tahoe CA	3+
Encore Tahoe Valley RV Resort	877-717-8737	1175 Melba Drive South Lake Tahoe CA	3+
Fallen Leaf Campground	530-543-2600	Fallen Leaf Lake Road South Lake Tahoe CA	3+
Lake Tahoe-South Shore KOA	530-577-3693	760 North Highway 50 South Lake Tahoe CA	3+
Meeks Bay Campground	530-543-2600	H 89 Tahoe City CA	3+
D. L. Bliss State Park	530-525-7277	H 89/South Lake Tahoe Tahoma CA	3+
Emerald Bay State Park	530-541-3030	H 89/South Lake Tahoe Tahoma CA	3+
General Creek Campground	530-525-7982	West Shore Lake Tahoe Tahoma CA	3+
Lakeside Campground	530-587-3558	Off H 89 - Exit H 89N Truckee CA	2
Logger Campground, Truckee District	530-587-3558	9646 Donner Pass Road - Exit Hirschdale Road AKA-Stampede Dam Road Truckee CA	3+
Camp at the Cove	775-589-4907	760 H 50 Zephyr Cove NV	3+
Zephyr Cove RV Park and Campground	775-589-4922	760 H 50 Zephyr Cove NV	3+

Nevada   (Interstate 80)

Dogs per Site

Reno

Bonanza Terrace RV Park	775-329-9624	4800 Stoltz Road Reno NV	3+
Reno RV Park	775-323-3381	735 Mill Street - Exit Wells Avenue Reno NV	3+
Rivers Edge RV Park	775-358-8533	1405 S Rock Blvd - Exit 17/S Rock Blvd Sparks NV	3+
Gold Ranch Casino and RV Resort	877-792-6789	320 Gold Ranch Road - Exit Old H 40/Verdi Verdi NV	1+
Reno / Boomtown KOA	775-345-2444	2100 I-80 W Garson Road - Exit 4 Verdi NV	3+

Lovelock

Rye Patch State Recreation Area	775-538-7321	2505 Rye Patch Reservoir Road - Exit 22 miles N of Lovelock Lovelock NV	3+

Winnemucca

Model T RV Park	775-623-2588	1130 W Winnemucca Blvd - Exit 176/E on Winnemucca Blvd Winnemucca NV	3+

Elko

Double Dice RV Park	775-738-5642	3730 Idaho Street Elko NV	3+
Wild Horse State Recreation Area	775-758-6493	HC 31, Box 26/H 225 - Exit H 225 Elko NV	3+

Wendover

Wendover KOA	775-664-3221	651 N Camper Drive - Exit 410/Wendover Blvd West Wendover NV	3+

Utah   (Interstate 80)

Dogs per Site

Salt Lake City

Sunset Campground	877-444-6777	Farmington Canyon Farmington City UT	1+
Salt Lake City KOA	801-355-1214	1400 W North Temple - Exit 115 Salt Lake City UT	3+
Wasatch -Cache National Forest	801-466-6411	3285 East 3800 S Salt Lake City UT	3+
Quail Run RV Park	801-255-9300	9230 S State Street Sandy UT	3+

Park City

Park City RV Resort	435-649-2535	2200 Rasmussen Road - Exit 145 Park City UT	3+

Wyoming   (Interstate 80)

Dogs per Site

Fort Bridger

Fort Bridger RV Camp	307-782-3150	64 Groshon Rd - Exit 34 Fort Bridger WY	2

Green River

Buckboard Marina	307-875-6927	H 530/Flaming Gorge Lake (HCR 65, Box 100) - Exit 91 Green River WY	2

Rock Springs

Rock Springs KOA	307-362-3063	86 Foothill Blvd - Exit 99 Rock Springs WY	3+

Rawlins

RV World Campground	307-328-1091	3101 Wagon Circle Road - Exit 209 Rawlins WY	3+
Rawlins KOA	307-328-2021	205 E H 71 - Exit 214 Rawlins WY	3+
Western Hills Campground	888-568-3040	2500 Wagon Circle Road - Exit 211 Rawlins WY	3+

Laramie

Laramie KOA	307-742-6553	1271 W Baker Street - Exit 310 Laramie WY	1+
Medicine Bow-Routt National Forests and Thunder Basin National Grassland	307-745-2300	2468 Jackson Street Laramie WY	3+
Vedauwoo Recreation Area	307-745-2300	Verdauwoo Glen Road - Exit 329/Vedauwoo Glen Road Laramie WY	3+

Cheyenne

Cheyenne KOA	307-638-8840	8800 Archer Frontage Road - Exit 367/Campstool Road Cheyenne WY	3+
Curt Gowdy State Park	307-632-7946	1319 Hynds Lodge Road Cheyenne WY	3+
Terry Bison Ranch	307-634-4171	51 I 25 Service Road E Cheyenne WY	3+

Nebraska   (Interstate 80)

Dogs per Site

Highway Guides - Please always call ahead to make sure an establishment is still dog-friendly.

Kimball

Kimball KOA	308-235-4404	4334 Link 53E Kimball NE	3+
Twin Pines RV Camp	308-235-3231	1508 S H 71 - Exit 20 Kimball NE	3+

Ogallala

Lake Ogallala State Rec Area	308-284-8800	1475 H 61N - Exit 126 Ogallala NE	3+

North Platte

Holiday Trav-L-Park	308-534-2265	601 Halligan Drive - Exit 177/H 83 North Platte NE	3+
Lake Maloney State Rec Area	308-535-8025	301 E State Farm Road North Platte NE	3+

Gothenburg

Gothenburhg KOA	308-537-7387	1102 S Lake Avenue - Exit H 47S Gothenburg NE	3+

Grand Island

Grand Island KOA	402-886-2249	904 South B Road - Exit 318 Doniphan NE	3+
Mormon Island State Rec Area	308-385-6211	7425 S H 281 - Exit 312/Grand Island Interchange Doniphan NE	3+
Wood River Motel and RV Park	308-583-2256	11774 S H 11 - Exit 300 Wood River NE	3+

Lincoln

Camp A Way	866-719-2267	200 Camper's Circle - Exit 401 Lincoln NE	3+
Conestoga State Recreation Area	402-796-2362	SW 98th Street and W Pioneers Blvd Lincoln NE	3+
Pawnee State Recreation Area	402-796-2362	3800 NW 105th Street Lincoln NE	3+
Rockford State Recreation Area	402-471-5566	3019 Apple Street Lincoln NE	3+

Omaha

Eugene T. Mahoney State Park	402-944-2523	28500 W Park H - Exit 426 Ashland NE	3+
Linoma Beach Resort	402-332-4500	17106 S 255th Street - Exit 420E or 432W to H 6 Gretna NE	2
West Omaha KOA	402-332-3010	14601 H 6 Gretna NE	3+
Memphis State Recreation Area	402-471-5566	County Road D Memphis NE	3+
Glenn Cunningham Lake Park	402-444-4FUN (4386)	8660 Lake Cunningham Road Omaha NE	3+
Two Rivers State Recreation Area	402-359-5165	27702 F Street Waterloo NE	3+

Iowa   (Interstate 80)   Dogs per Site

Des Moines

Des Moines West KOA	515-834-2729	3418 L Avenue - Exit 106 Adel IA	3+
Adventureland Campground	512-265-7384	2600 Adventureland Drive - Exit 142 or 142A Altoona IA	2
Iowa State Fair Campground	515-262-3111 ext. 284	E 30th Street and University Avenue Des Moines IA	3+
Ledges State Park	515-432-1852	1515 P Avenue Madrid IA	3+
Rolling Acres RV Park	641-792-2428	1601 E 36th Street - Exit 168 Newton IA	3+
Walnut Woods State Park	515-285-4502	3155 Walnut Woods Drive West Des Moines IA	3+

Newton

Kellogg RV Park	641-526-8535	1570 H 224 - Exit 173/Kellogg Kellogg IA	3+
Rock Creek State Park	641-236-3722	5628 Rock Creek E - Exit 173 Kellogg IA	3+

Amana Colonies

Amana Colonies RV Park	319-622-7622	3890 C Street - Exit 225 Amana IA	3+
Amana Colony RV Park	319-622-7616	#39 38th Avenue - Exit 225 Amana IA	3+

Iowa City

Devonian Fossil Gorge	319-338-3543 ext. 6300	2850 Prairie Du Chien Road NE - Exit 244 Iowa City IA	3+
Colony Country Campground	319-626-2221	1275 Forever Green Road - Exit 240/Coroville North Liberty IA	3+

Quad Cities

Interstate RV Park	563-386-7292	8448 Fairmont - Exit 292 Davenport IA	3+

Illinois   (Interstate 80)   Dogs per Site

Chicago Area - South

Windy City Campground	708-720-0030	18701 S 80th Avenue - Exit Harlem Tinley Park IL	2

Indiana   (Interstate 80)   Dogs per Site

South Bend

South Bend East KOA	574-277-1335	50707 Princess Way - Exit 83 Granger IN	3+
Mini Mountain Campground	574-654-3307	32351 H 2 New Carlisle IN	3+
Potato Creek State Park	574-656-8186	25601 H 4 North Liberty IN	3+

Elkhart

Elkhart Campground	574-264-2914	25608 County Road 4 Elkhart IN	2
Elkhart Co/Middlebury Exit KOA	574-825-5932	52867 H 13 - Exit 107 Middlebury IN	3+
Natural Springs Resort	888-330-5771	500 S Washington Street New Paris IN	3+

Howe

Twin Mills Camping Resort	260-562-3212	1675 W H 120 Howe IN	1+

Ohio   (Interstate 80)   Dogs per Site

Toledo

Maumee Bay State Park Campground	419-836-7758	1400 State Park Road Oregon OH	1+
Toledo East/Stony Ridge KOA	419-837-6848	24787 Luckey Road Perrysburg OH	3+
Lake Erie Island Region			
Kelleys Island State Park Campground	419-746-2546	Division Street Kelleys Island OH	1+
Cedarlane RV Park	419-797-9907	2926 NE Catawba Road Port Clinton OH	2
East Harbor State Park Campground	419-734-4424	Route 269 Port Clinton OH	1+
Shade Acres RV Campground	419-797-4681	1810 W. Catawba Road Port Clinton OH	1+
Sleepy Hollows Family Camping	419-734-3556	2817 E. Harbor Road Port Clinton OH	1+
Camper Village RV Park	419-627-2106	One Cedar Point Drive Sandusky OH	1+
South Bass Island State Park Campground	419-285-2112	Catawba Avenue South Bass Island OH	1+
Cleveland			
Kool Lakes Family RV park	440-548-8436	12990 H 282 Parkman OH	3+
Country Acres Campground	866-813-4321	9850 Minyoung Road - Exit 209/H 209W Ravenna OH	3+
Akron			
Portage Lakes State Park Campground	330-644-2220	5031 Manchester Road Akron OH	1+

Pennsylvania   (Interstate 80)   Dogs per Site

Milton			
Jellystone Park	570-524-4561	670 Hidden Paradise Road - Exit 212S Milton PA	1+
Bloomsburg			
Lackawanan State Park	570-945-3239	N Abington Road/H 407 Benton PA	2
Knoebel's Campground	800-ITS-4FUN	Route 487 Elysburg PA	1+
Hazleton			
Locust Lake State Park	570-467-2404	Burma Road/H 1006 Barnesville PA	1+
Poconos - Stroudsburg Area			
Delaware Water Gap KOA	570-223-8000	233 Hollow Road - Exit 309 E Stroudsburg PA	3+
Mountain Vista Campground	570-223-0111	50 Taylor Drive - Exit 309 E Stroudsburg PA	3+
Otter Lake Camp Resort	570-223-0123	4805 Marshall's Creek Road - Exit 309 E Stroudsburg PA	3+
Tobyhanna State Park	570-894-8336	On H 423 Tobyhanna PA	2
Hickory Run State Park	570-443-0400	H 534 White Haven PA	2

New Jersey   (Interstate 80)   Dogs per Site

Newark - NYC Area			
Liberty Harbor RV Park	201-387-7500	11 Marin Blvd Jersey City NJ	3+

Interstate 81 Dog-Friendly Campgrounds and RV Parks

New York   (Interstate 81)   Dogs per Site

Watertown			
Black River Bay Campground	315-639-3735	16129 Foster Park Road (Box541) - Exit 46 Dexter NY	1+
KOA Natural Bridge/Watertown	315-644-4880	6081 State H 3 Natural Bridge NY	3+
Long Point State Park-Thousand Islands	315-649-5258	7495 State Park Road Three Mile Bay NY	3+
Finger Lakes			
Hickory Hill Farm Camping Resort	607-776-4345	7531 H 13/Mitchellsville Road Bath NY	1+
Letchworth State Park	585-493-3600	1 Letchworth State Park Castile NY	3+
Spruce Row Campground and RV Resort	607-387-9225	2271 Kraft Road Ithaca NY	3+
Cayuga Lake State Park	315-568-5163	2678 Lower Lake Road Seneca Falls NY	3+
Taughannock Falls State Park	607-387-6739	2221 Taughannock Park Road Trumansburg NY	2
KOA Watkins Glen/Corning	607-535-7404	1710 H 414 Watkins Glen NY	2
Watkins Glen State Park	607-535-4511	South end of Seneca Lake Watkins Glen NY	3+
Binghamton			
Chenango Valley State Park	607-648-5251	153 State Park Road Chenango Forks NY	3+
Kellystone Park	607-639-1090	51 Hawkins Road Nineveh NY	3+

Pennsylvania   (Interstate 81)   Dogs per Site

Hazleton			
Locust Lake State Park	570-467-2404	Burma Road/H 1006 - Exit H 1008/Morea Road Barnesville PA	1+
Jonestown			

Jonestown/I-81,78 KOA	717-865-2526	145 Old Route 22 - Exit 90 Jonestown PA	1+
Chambersburg			
Twin Bridge Meadow Campground	717-369-2216	1345 Twin Bridges Road Chambersburg PA	2

Maryland   (Interstate 81)   Dogs per Site

Hagerstown			
Fort Frederick State Park	301-842-2155	11100 Fort Frederick Road Big Pool MD	3+
KOA Hagerstown/Snug Harbor	301-223-7571	11759 Snug Harbor Lane Williamsport MD	3+
Yogi Bear Jellystone Park	800-421-7116	16519 Lappans Road - Exit 1 in Maryland Williamsport MD	2

Virginia   (Interstate 81)   Dogs per Site

Harrisonburg			
Harrisonburg/New Market	540-896-8929	12480 Mountain Valley Road - Exit 257 Broadway VA	1+
Staunton			
Staunton/Verona KOA	540-248-2746	296 Riner Lane - Exit 227 Verona VA	3+
Natural Bridge			
Natural Bridge/Lexington KOA	540-291-2770	214 Killdeer Lane - Exit 180B Natural Bridge VA	1+
Yogi Bear at Natural Bridge	540-291-2727	16 Recreation Lane - Exit 175 NB; 180A SB Natural Bridge Station VA	2
Roanoke			
George Washington and Jefferson National Forests	540-265-5100	5162 Valleypointe Parkway/S area Forest HQ Roanoke VA	3+
Pulaski			
Bluecat on the New Camping	276-766-3729	2800 Wysor H (100) Draper VA	3+
New River Trail State Park	276-699-6778	176 Orphanage Drive Foster Falls VA	2
Wytheville			
Whtheville KOA	276-228-2601	231 KOA Road Wytheville VA	3+
Marion			
Hungry Mother State Park	276-781-7400	2854 Park Blvd - Exit 47/H 11 Marion VA	3+
Mount Rogers National Rec Area	540-265-5100	3714 H 16 Marion VA	3+

Tennessee   (Interstate 81)   Dogs per Site

Kingsport			
Warriors Path State Park	423-239-8531	490 Hemlock Road - Exit 59/H 36 Kingsport TN	3+
Morristown			
Panther Creek State Park	423-587-7046	2010 Panther Creek Road Morristown TN	3+

Interstate 84 Dog-Friendly Campgrounds and RV Parks

Oregon   (Interstate 84)   Dogs per Site

Portland			
Portland Fairview RV Park	503-661-1047	21401 NE Sandy Blvd - Exit 14 Fairview OR	3+
Rolling Hills RV Park	503-666-7282	20145 NE Sandy Blvd - Exit 14 Fairview OR	3+
Jantzen Beach RV Park	503-289-7626	1503 N Hayden Island Drive Portland OR	1
RV Park of Portland	503-692-0225	6645 SW Nyberg Road Tualatin OR	1+
Cascade Locks			
Cascade Locks/Portland East KOA	541-374-8668	841 NW Forest Lane - Exit 44 Cascade Locks OR	3+
Port of Cascade Locks and Marine Park	541-374-8619	355 WaNaPa Street - Exit 44 Cascade Locks OR	2
Pendleton			
Umatilla National Forest	541-278-3716	2517 SW Hailey Avenue - Exit 209 Pendleton OR	3+
Baker City			
Oregon Trails West RV Park	888-523-3236	42534 N Cedar Road - Exit 302 Baker City OR	3+
Wallowa-Whitman National Forest	541-523-6391	1550 Dewey Avenue - Exit Campbell Street Baker City OR	3+

Idaho   (Interstate 84)   Dogs per Site

Caldwell			
Ambassador RV Resort	888-877-8307	615 S Mead Parkway - Exit 29 Caldwell ID	3+
Boise			
On the River RV Park	208-375-7432	6000 Glenwood - Exit Eagle Road Boise ID	3+
Mountain Home			
Bruneau Dunes State Park	208-366-7919	27608 Sand Dunes Road - Exit 112 to H 78 Mountain Home ID	3+

Mountain Home KOA	208-587-5111	220 E 10th N Mountain Home ID	3+
Mountain Home RV Park	208-890-4100	2295 American Legion Blvd - Exit 95 Mountain Home ID	3+
Jerome			
Twin Falls/Jerome KOA	208-324-4169	5431 H 93 Jerome ID	3+
Twin Falls			
Anderson Camp	888-480-9400	S Tipperary - Exit 182 Eden ID	3+
Sawthooth National Forest	208-737-3200	2647 Kimberly Road E. Twin Falls ID	3+

Utah   (Interstate 84) Dogs per Site

Ogden			
Cherry Hill RV Resort	801-451-5379	1325 S Main Kaysville UT	3+

Interstate 85 Dog-Friendly Campgrounds and RV Parks

Virginia   (Interstate 85) Dogs per Site

Petersburg			
Petersburg KOA	804-732-8345	2809 Cortland Road Petersburg VA	3+

North Carolina   (Interstate 85) Dogs per Site

Henderson			
Kerr Lake State Rec Area	252-438-7791	6254 Satterwhite Point Road - Exit 217 Henderson NC	3+
Charlotte			
Carowinds Camp Wilderness Resort	704-588-2600	14523 Carowinds Blvd Charlotte NC	3+
McDowell Nature Preserve Campground	704-583-1284	15222 York Road Charlotte NC	3+
Fleetwood RV Racing Camping Resort	704-455-4445	6600 Speedway Blvd - Exit 49 Concord NC	3+
Charlotte/Fort Mill KOA	803-548-1148	940 Gold Hill Road Fort Mill NC	3+

South Carolina   (Interstate 85) Dogs per Site

Gaffney			
Kings Mountain State Park	803-222-3209	1277 Park Road - Exit 8 Blacksburg SC	3+
Greenville			
Table Rock State Park	864-878-9813	158 E Ellison Lane Pickens SC	3+
Scuffletown USA	864-967-2276	603 Scuffletown Road Simpsonville SC	3+
Anderson			
Anderson/Lake Hartwell KOA	864-287-3161	200 Wham Road - Exit 14S Anderson SC	3+

Georgia   (Interstate 85) Dogs per Site

Atlanta			
Stone Mountain Park	800-385-9807	H 78E Stone Mountain GA	3+
Atlanta Area			
Brookwood RV Park	877-727-5787	1031 Wylie Road SE Marietta GA	3+
Atlanta South RV Resort	770-957-2610	281 Mount Olive Road McDonough GA	3+

Alabama   (Interstate 85) Dogs per Site

Opelika			
Leisure Time Campground	334-821-2267	2670 S College Street Auburn AL	3+
Tuskegee			
Tuskegee National Forest	334-727-2652	125 National Forest Road, Bldg 949 Tuskegee AL	3+
Montgomery			
Capital City RV Park	877-271-8026	4655 Old Wetumpka H (H 231N) Montgomery AL	3+

Interstate 90 Dog-Friendly Campgrounds and RV Parks
(From Chicago to Cleveland see Highway 80)

Highway Guides - Please always call ahead to make sure an establishment is still dog-friendly.

Washington   (Interstate 90)

Dogs per Site

Seattle
Blake Island State Park	360-731-8330	P.O. Box 42650 Seattle WA	2
Blue Sky RV Park	425-222-7910	9002 302nd Avenue SE - Exit 22 Seattle WA	3+

Ellensburg
Ellensburg KOA	509-925-9319	32 Thorp H S - Exit 106 Ellensburg WA	3+

Vantage
Iron Horse State Park	509-856-2700	P. O. Box 1203 - Exit 38 or 101 Vantage WA	3+

Spokane
Alderwood RV Resort	509-467-5320	14007 N Newport H Spokane WA	3+

Spokane Valley
Trailer Inns RV Park	509-535-1811	6021 E 4th - Exit 285 Spokane Valley WA	3+

Idaho   (Interstate 90)

Dogs per Site

Post Falls
Suntree RV Park	208-773-9982	350 N Idahline Road - Exit 2/Pleasant View Road Post Falls ID	2

Coeur D'Alene
Coeur D'Alene KOA	208-664-4471	10588 E Wolf Lodge Bay Road - Exit 22 Coeur D'Alene ID	3+
Blackwell Island RV Resort	208-665-1300	800 S Marina Way Coeur d'Alene ID	3+
Idaho Panhandle National Forest	208-765-7223	3815 Schreiber Street - Exit H 95N Coeur d'Alene ID	3+

Montana   (Interstate 90)

Dogs per Site

St Regis
Campground St Regis	406-649-2470	44 Frontage Road - Exit 33 St Regis MT	3+
Nugget Campground	888-800-0125	E of Stop Sign on Main Street - Exit 33/St Regis St Regis MT	3+

Missoula
Beavertail Hill State Park	406-542-5500	3201 Spurgin Road - Exit 130/Beavertail S Missoula MT	3+
Jellystone Park	406-543-9400	9900 Jellystone Drive Missoula MT	2
Lolo National Forest	406-329-3750	Building 24, Fort Missoula - Exit Missoula Missoula MT	3+
Missoula KOA	406-549-0881	3450 Tina Avenue - Exit 101 Missoula MT	3+
Painted Rocks State Park	406-542-5500	Secondary H 473 Missoula MT	1+

Deer Lodge
Deer Lodge KOA	406-846-1629	330 Park Street - Exit at either end of town Deer Lodge MT	3+

Butte
Butte KOA	406-782-8080	1601 Kaw Avenue - Exit 126 Butte MT	3+

Whitehall
Lewis and Clark Caverns State Park	406-287-3541	1455 H 2E - Exit Three Forks to H 2E Whitehall MT	3+
Pipestone RV Park	406-287-5224	41 Bluebird Lane - Exit 241 Whitehall MT	3+

Bozeman
Bozeman KOA	406-587-3030	81123 Gallatin Road - Exit 298 at Belgrade Bozeman MT	3+
Sunrise Campground	877-437-2095	31842 Frontage Road - Exit 309 Bozeman MT	3+

Livingston
Livingston/Paradise Valley KOA	406-222-0992	163 Pine Creek Road Livingston MT	3+

Big Timber
Big Timber KOA	406-932-6569	693 H 10 East - Exit 377 Big Timber MT	1+

Billings
Billings KOA	406-252-3104	547 Garden Avenue - Exit 447 or 450 Billings MT	3+
Custer National Forest	406-657-6200	1310 Main Street Billings MT	3+
Yellowstone River Campground	406-259-0878	309 Garden Avenue - Exit 450 Billings MT	3+
Cooney State Park	406-445-2326	Boyd County Road Joliet MT	3+
Pelican RV Park	406-628-4324	11360 S Frontage - Exit 437 Laurel MT	3+

Hardin
7th Ranch RV Camp	800-371-7963	7th Ranch & Reno Creek Road Garryowen MT	3+
Hardin KOA	406-665-1635	RR 1 - Exit 495 Hardin MT	3+

Wyoming   (Interstate 90)

Dogs per Site

Sheridan
Conner Battlefield State Historic Site	307-684-7629	Off H 67 - Exit H 14 Ranchester WY	3+
Bighorn National Forest	307-674-2600	2013 Eastside 2nd Street/H 16 Sheridan WY	3+
Sheridan/Big Horn Mountains KOA	307-674-8766	63 Decker Road - Exit 20 Sheridan WY	3+

Buffalo
Buffalo KOA	307-684-5423	87 H 16E - Exit 56A or 56B Buffalo WY	3+
Deer Park RV Park	307-684-5722	Box 568, On H 16E Buffalo WY	3+
Indian Campground	307-684-9601	660 E Hart Street - Exit 56b Buffalo WY	1+

Gillette
High Plains Campground	307-687-7339	1500 S Garner Lake Road Gillette WY	3+

Moorcroft

Keyhole State Park	307-756-3596	353 McKean Road Moorcroft WY	3+

South Dakota   (Interstate 90)   Dogs per Site

Mount Rushmore - Black Hills

Big Pine Campground	800-235-3981	12084 Big Pine Road Custer SD	3+
Black Hills National Forest	605-673-9200	25041 N H 16 Custer SD	3+
Crazy Horse Kampground	605-673-2565	1116 N 5th Street Custer SD	3+
Custer State Park	605-255-4515	13329 H 16A Custer SD	3+
Fort WeLikit Family Campground	605-673-3600	24992 Sylvan Lake Road/H 89 Custer SD	3+
KOA Campground	605-673-4304	U.S. Highway 16 Custer SD	1+
The Flintstones Bedrock City Campground	605-673-4079	US Highways 16 and 385 Custer SD	1+
The Roost Resort	605-673-2326	12462 H 16 A Custer SD	3+
Crooked Creek Resort	800-252-8486	24184 S H 385/16 Hill City SD	2
Horsethief Campground	605-574-2668	24391 H 87 Hill City SD	3+
KOA Campground and Resort	605-574-2525	12620 Highway 244 Hill City SD	1+
Rafter J Bar Ranch	605-574-2527	12325 Rafter J Road Hill City SD	3+
Angostura Recreation Area	605-745-6996	13157 N Angostura Road Hot Springs SD	3+
Elk Mountain Campground/Wind Cave National ParkHot	605-745-4600	26611 H 385 (Visitor Ctr) Hot Springs SD	3+
Hot Springs KOA	605-745-6449	HCR 52, Box 112-C Hot Springs SD	3+
Elk Creek Lodge and Resort	605-787-4884	8220 Elk Creek Road - Exit 46 Piedmont SD	3+
Elk Creek Resort and RV Park	800-846-2267	8220 Elk Creek Road - Exit 46 Piedmont SD	3+
Berry Patch Campground	800-658-4566	1860 E North Street - Exit 60 Rapid City SD	3+
Happy Holiday Resort	605-342-7365	8990 H 16S Rapid City SD	3+
KOA Campground	605-348-2111	P.O. Box 2592 Rapid City SD	1+
Rushmore Shadows	800-231-0425	23645 Clubhouse Drive Rapid City SD	3+
Kennebec			
Kennebec KOA	605-869-2300	311 S H 273 - Exit 235 Kennebec SD	3+
Chamberlain			
Oasis Campground	605-734-6959	1003 H 16 - Exit 260 Oacoma SD	3+
Mitchell			
Dakota Campground	605-996-9432	1800 Spruce - Exit 330 Mitchell SD	3+
Mitchell KOA	605-996-1131	41244 H 38 - Exit 335 N Mitchell SD	3+
Rondees Campground	605-996-0769	911 East K - Exit 332 Mitchell SD	3+
Sioux Falls			
Big Sioux Recreation Area	605-582-7243	410 Park Street Brandon SD	3+
Yogi Bear Jellystone Park	605-332-2233	26014 478th Avenue - Exit 402 Brandon SD	3+
Newton Hills State Park	605-987-2263	28767 482nd Avenue/H 135 Canton SD	3+
Palisades State Park	605-594-3824	25495 485th Avenue Garretson SD	3+
Sioux Falls KOA	605-332-9987	1401 E Robur Drive - Exit 399/Cliff Avenue Sioux Falls SD	3+
Red Barn RV Park	605-368-2268	47003 272nd Street Tea SD	3+

Minnesota   (Interstate 90)   Dogs per Site

Fairmont

Flying Goose Campground	507-235-3458	2521 115th Street - Exit 107 Fairmont MN	3+
Albert Lea			
Big Island State Park	507-379-3403	19499 780th Avenue Albert Lea MN	3+
Albert Lea/Austin KOA	507-373-5170	84259 County Road 46 Hayward MN	3+
Austin			
Beaver Trails Campground and RV Park	507-584-6611	21943 630th Avenue - Exit 187 Austin MN	3+
Rochester			
Chester Woods Campground	507-285-7050	8378 H 14 E Eyota MN	3+
Rochester/Marion KOA	507-288-0785	5232 65th Avenue SE Rochester MN	3+

Wisconsin   (Interstate 90)   Dogs per Site

La Crosse

Goose Island Campground	608-788-7018	H 35 La Crosse WI	3+
Neshonoc Lakeside Camp Resort	608-786-1792	N4668 H 16 West Salem WI	2
Wisconsin Dells			
Arrowhead Resort Campground	608-254-7244	W1530 Arrowhead Road Wisconsin Dells WI	2
Wisconsin Dells KOA	608-254-4177	S 235 Stand Rock Road - Exit 87 Wisconsin Dells WI	3+
Madison			
Blue Mound State Park	608-437-5711	4350 Mounds Park Road Blue Mounds WI	3+
Madison KOA	608-846-4528	4859 CTH-V - Exit 126 DeForest WI	3+
Yogi Bear's Waterpark Camp Resort	608-254-2568	S 1915 Ishnala Road Lake Delton WI	3+
Crystal Lake Campground	608-592-5607	N550 Gannon Road Lodi WI	3+
Lake Kegonsa State Park	608-873-9695	2405 Door Creek Road Stoughton WI	1+

Highway Guides - Please always call ahead to make sure an establishment is still dog-friendly.

Illinois   (Interstate 90)   Dogs per Site

Rockford
Rock Cut State Park	815-885-3311	7318 Harlem Road - Exit Riverside to Perryville Road Loves Park IL	3+
River's Edge Campground	815-629-2526	12626 N Meridian Rockton IL	3+

Ohio   (Interstate 90)   Dogs per Site

Cleveland
Kool Lakes Family RV park	440-548-8436	12990 H 282 Parkman OH	3+
Country Acres Campground	866-813-4321	9850 Minyoung Road Ravenna OH	3+

Conneaut
Evergreen Lake Park Campground	440-599-8802	703 Center Road Conneaut OH	1+

Pennsylvania   (Interstate 90)   Dogs per Site

Erie
Erie KOA	814-476-7706	6645 West Road - Exit 18 McKean PA	3+

New York   (Interstate 90)   Dogs per Site

Westfield
KOA Westfield/Lake Erie	716-326-3573	8001 H 5 Westfield NY	3+

Brocton
Lake Erie State Park	716-792-9214	5905 Lake Road - Exit 59/H 60N Brocton NY	3+

Buffalo
Jellystone Park	585-457-9644	5204 Youngers Road North Java NY	2

Rochester
Genesee Country Campgrounds	585-538-4200	40 Flinthill Road Caledonia NY	2

Rome
Delta Lake State Park	315-337-04670	8797 H 46 Rome NY	3+
Verona Beach State Park	315-762-4463	6541 Lakeshore Road S - Exit 34/Canastota Verona Beach NY	3+

Utica
Turning Stone RV Park	315-361-7275	5065 State H 365 Verona NY	3+

Massachusetts   (Interstate 90)   Dogs per Site

Springfield
Prospect Mountain Campground	888-550-4PMC (762)	1349 Main Road (H 57) Granville MA	3+
Sunset View Farms	413-267-9269	57 Town Farm Road Monson MA	2

Sturbridge
Jellystone Park	508-347-9570	30 River Road Sturbridge MA	3+
Wells State Park	508-347-9257	159 Walker Pond Road Sturbridge MA	3+
Oak Haven Family Campground	413-245-7148	22 Main Street Wales MA	2
The Old Sawmill Campground	508-867-2427	Box 377 Longhill Road West Brookfield MA	2

Worcester
KOA-Webster/Sturbridge	508-943-1895	106 Douglas Road Webster MA	3+

Boston Area
Circle Farm	508-966-1136	131 Main Street Bellingham MA	3+
Normandy Farms	508-543-7600	72 West Street Foxboro MA	3+
Wompatuck State Park	781-749-7160	Union Street Hingham MA	3+
Boston Minuteman Campground	877-677-0042	264 Ayer Road Littleton MA	3+
KOA	508-947-6435	438 Plymouth Street Middleboro MA	3+
Winter Island Park	978-745-9430	50 Winter Island Road Salem MA	2
Rusnik Campground	978-462-9551	115 Lafayette Road Salisbury MA	3+

Interstate 94 Dog-Friendly Campgrounds and RV Parks

Montana   (Interstate 94)   Dogs per Site

Billings
Billings KOA	406-252-3104	547 Garden Avenue Billings MT	3+
Custer National Forest	406-657-6200	1310 Main Street Billings MT	3+
Yellowstone River Campground	406-259-0878	309 Garden Avenue Billings MT	3+
Cooney State Park	406-445-2326	Boyd County Road Joliet MT	3+
Pelican RV Park	406-628-4324	11360 S Frontage Laurel MT	3+

Miles City

Medicine Rocks State Park	406-234-0900	1 Mile west on County Road from Milepost 10/H 7 Miles City MT	3+
Miles City KOA	406-232-3991	1 Palmer Street - Exit 135 Miles City MT	3+

Glendive

Makoshika State Park	406-542-5500	1301 Synder Avenue Glendive MT	3+

North Dakota   (Interstate 94)   Dogs per Site

Dickinson

Patterson Lake Recreation Area	701-456-2056	H 10 - Exit 59 Dickinson ND	2

Bismarck

Bismarck KOA	701-222-2662	3720 Centennial Road - Exit 161 Bismarck ND	3+
Fort Abraham Lincoln State Park	701-667-6340	4480 Ft. Lincoln Road Mandan ND	3+

Jamestown

Frontier Fort Campground	701-252-7492	1838 3rd Avenue SE - Exit 258 Jamestown ND	3+
Jamestown Campground	701-252-6262	3605 80th Avenue - Exit 256 Jamestown ND	3+
Lakeside Marina	701-252-1183	223 E Lakeside Road Jamestown ND	3+
Pelican Point	701-252-1451	8310 28th Street SE Jamestown ND	3+

Fargo

Governor's RV Park and Campground	701-347-4524	2050 Governor's Drive - Exit 331 Casselton ND	2
Lindenwood Campground	701-232-3987	1905 Roger Maris Drive S - Exit 1A or 351 Fargo ND	3+
Campground at Red River Valley Fair	701-282-2200	1201 Main Ave W - Exit 343 West Fargo ND	3+

Minnesota   (Interstate 94)   Dogs per Site

Moorhead

Moorhead/Fargo KOA	218-233-0671	4396 28th Avenue S - Exit 2 Moorhead MN	3+

St Cloud

St Cloud Campground	320-251-4463	2491 2nd Street SE/H 8/47 St Cloud MN	2

Minneapolis - St Paul

Greenwood Campground	651-437-5269	13797 190th Street E Hastings MN	2
Minneapolis Northwest KOA	763-420-2255	10410 Brockton Maple Grove MN	2
Dakotah Meadows RV Park	952-445-8800	2341 Park Place Prior Lake MN	3+
St Paul East KOA	651-436-6436	568 Cottage Grove - Exit 253 Woodbury MN	3+

Wisconsin   (Interstate 94)   Dogs per Site

Black River Falls

Hixton/Alma Center KOA	715-964-2508	N9657 H 95 Alma Center WI	1+
Black River State Forest	715-284-4103	10325 H 12 E - Exit H 5 4E Black River Falls WI	3+

Madison

Blue Mound State Park	608-437-5711	4350 Mounds Park Road Blue Mounds WI	3+
Madison KOA	608-846-4528	4859 CTH-V DeForest WI	3+
Yogi Bear's Waterpark Camp Resort	608-254-2568	S 1915 Ishnala Road Lake Delton WI	3+
Crystal Lake Campground	608-592-5607	N550 Gannon Road Lodi WI	3+
Lake Kegonsa State Park	608-873-9695	2405 Door Creek Road Stoughton WI	1+

Delafield

Lapham Peak Unit, Kettle Moraine State Forest	262-646-3025	W 329 N 846 County Road C - Exit Lapham Peak State Park Delafield WI	3+

Milwaukee

Wisconsin State Fair RV Park	414-266-7035	601 S 76th Street - Exit 68th or 70th Street Milwaukee WI	3+

Indiana   (Interstate 94)   Dogs per Site

Michigan City

Indiana Dunes State Park	219-926-1952	1600 North 25 E Chesterton IN	3+
Michigan City Campground	800-813-2267	601 N H 421 Michigan City IN	2

Michigan   (Interstate 94)   Dogs per Site

Benton Harbor

House of David Travel Trailer Park	269-927-3302	1019 E Empire - Exit 28 Benton Harbor MI	2
Coloma/St Joseph KOA	269-849-3333	3527 Coloma Road Riverside MI	2

Kalamazoo

Hungry Horse Campground	616-681-9843	2016 142nd Avenue Allegan MI	3+
Fort Custer Recreation Area	269-731-4200	5163 Fort Custer Drive Augusta MI	3+
Oak Shores Campground	269-423-7370	86882 County Road 215 Decatur MI	3+

Battle Creek

Tri-Lakes Trails Campground	269-781-2297	219 Perrett Road Marshall MI	3+

Jackson

Irish Hills Campground	517-592-6751	16230 US H 12 Cement City MI	3+
Apple Creek Campground	517-522-3467	11185 Orban Road Grass Lake MI	3+
Greenwood Campgrounds	517-522-8600	2401 Hilton Road - Exit 147 Jackson MI	3+
Moscow Maples RV Park	517-688-9853	8291 E Chicago Moscow MI	3+
Pleasant Lake County Park & Campground	517-467-2300	1000 Styles Road Pleasant Lake MI	2
Ann Arbor			
Waterloo Recreation Area	734-475-8307	16345 McClure Road - Exit 153/Clearlake (Sugarloaf) Chelsea MI	3+
Pinckney Recreation Area	734-426-4913	8555 Silver Hill Road Pinckney MI	3+
Detroit/Greenfield KOA	734-482-7222	6680 Bunton Road - Exit 187 Ypsilanti MI	3+
Detroit			
Wayne County Fairgrounds and RV Park	734-697-7002	10871 Quirk Road - Exit 190 Belleville MI	3+
Highland Recreation Area	248-889-3750	5200 E Highland Road White Lake MI	3+
Port Huron			
Emmett KOA	810-395-7042	3864 Breen Road Emmett MI	3+
Lakeport State Park	810-327-6765	7605 Lakeshore Road - Exit H 25 Lakeport MI	3+

Interstate 95 Dog-Friendly Campgrounds and RV Parks

Maine   (Interstate 95)

Dogs per Site

Bangor			
Paul Bunyan Campground	207-941-1177	1862 Union Street - Exit 184 Bangor ME	1+
Paul Bunyan's Wheeler Stream Campground	207-848-7877	2202 H 2 Hermon ME	3+
Pumpkin Patch	207-848-2231	149 Billings Road - Exit 180 Hermon ME	3+
Red Barn Campground	207-843-6011	602 Main Road Holden ME	3+
Augusta			
Augusta West Lakeside Resort	207-377-9993	183 Holmes Brook Lane Winthrop ME	2
Portland			
Bayley's Camping Resort	207-883-6043	275 Pine Point Road Scarborough ME	3+
Wassamki Springs	207-839-4276	56 Soco Street Scarborough ME	2
Kennebunk			
Hemlock Grove Campground	207-985-0398	1299 Portland Road Arundel ME	2
Red Apple Campground	207-967-4927	111 Sinnott Road Kennebunkport ME	3+
Sea-Vu Campground	207-646-7732	1733 Post Road Wells ME	3+
Well Beach Resort	207-646-7570	1000 Post Road Wells ME	3+

New Hampshire   (Interstate 95)

Dogs per Site

Portsmouth			
Wakeda Campground	603-772-5274	294 Exeter Road Hampton Falls NH	3+

Massachusetts   (Interstate 95)

Dogs per Site

Boston Area			
Circle Farm	508-966-1136	131 Main Street Bellingham MA	3+
Normandy Farms	508-543-7600	72 West Street Foxboro MA	3+
Wompatuck State Park	781-749-7160	Union Street Hingham MA	3+
Boston Minuteman Campground	877-677-0042	264 Ayer Road Littleton MA	3+
KOA	508-947-6435	438 Plymouth Street Middleboro MA	3+
Winter Island Park	978-745-9430	50 Winter Island Road Salem MA	2
Rusnik Campground	978-462-9551	115 Lafayette Road Salisbury MA	3+

Rhode Island   (Interstate 95)

Dogs per Site

Providence			
Bowdish Lake	401-568-8890	40 Safari Road Glocester RI	3+
Holiday Acres Camping Resort	401-934-0780	591 Snakehill Road N Scituate RI	2

Connecticut   (Interstate 95)

Dogs per Site

Stonington			
Mystic KOA	860-599-5101	118 Pendleton Hill Road - Exit 92 North Stonington CT	3+
Pachaug State Forest Chapman Area	860-376-4075	H 49/ P. O. Box 5 Voluntown CT	1+
New London - Mystic			
Aces High RV Park	860-739-8858	301 Chesterfield Road East Lyme CT	3+

Seaport Campground	860-536-4044	Old Campground Road Old Mystic CT	2

New Jersey   (Interstate 95)   Dogs per Site

Newark - NYC Area
Liberty Harbor RV Park	201-387-7500	11 Marin Blvd - Exit 14C/Jersey City-Grand Street Jersey City NJ	3+

Camden Area
Timberlane Campground	856-423-6677	117 Timberlane Road Clarksboro NJ	3+

Delaware Bridge Area
Four Seasons Family Campground	856-769-3635	158 Woodstown Road Pilesgrove NJ	3+

Delaware   (Interstate 95)   Dogs per Site

Wilmington
Delaware Motel and RV Park	302-328-3114	235 S. Dupont Highway New Castle DE	3+

Newark
Lums Pond State Park	302-368-6989	1068 Howell School Road Bear DE	3+

Maryland   (Interstate 95)   Dogs per Site

North East
Elk Neck State Park	410-287-5333	4395 Turkey Point Road North East MD	3+

Aberdeen - Havre de Grace
Susquehanna State Park	410-557-7994	4122 Wilkinson Road Havre de Grace MD	2

Washington Suburbs
Cherry Hill Park	800-801-6449	9800 Cherry Hill Road - Exit 25 College Park MD	3+
Duncan's Family Campground	410-741-9558	5381 Sands Beach Road Lothian MD	3+

Virginia   (Interstate 95)   Dogs per Site

Northern Virginia
Bull Run Regional Park	703-631-0550	7700 Bull Run Drive Centreville VA	3+
Pohick Bay Park	703-352-5900	6501 Pohick Bay Drive - Exit Hwy 1 Lorton VA	3+
Lake Fairfax Park	703-471-5415	1400 Lake Fairfax Drive Reston VA	3+

Fredericksburg
Fredericksburg/Washington DC S KOA	540-898-7252	7400 Brookside Lane - Exit H 607 Fredericksburg VA	2
Prince William Forest Park	703-221-7181	18100 Park Headquarters Road Triangle VA	3+

Richmond
Pocohontas State Park	804-796-4255	10301 State Park Road Chesterfield VA	3+

Petersburg
Petersburg KOA	804-732-8345	2809 Cortland Road - Exit 41 Petersburg VA	3+

Emporia
Jellystone Park	434-634-3115	2940 Sussex Drive - Exit 17 Emporia VA	3+

North Carolina   (Interstate 95)   Dogs per Site

Enfield
Enfield/Rocky Mount KOA	252-445-5925	101 Bell Acres - Exit 154/Enfield Enfield NC	3+

Hollister
Medoc Mountain State Park	252-586-6588	1541 Medoc State Park Road/ H 1322 - Exit 160/H 561W Hollister NC	3+

Smithfield
Selma/Smithfield KOA	919-965-5923	428 Campground Road - Exit 98 Selma NC	3+

Fayetteville
Fayetteville/Wade KOA	910-484-5500	6250 Wade Stedman Road - Exit 61 Wade NC	3+

South Carolina   (Interstate 95)   Dogs per Site

Dillon
Little Pee Dee State Park	843-774-8872	1298 State Park Road Dillon SC	3+
South of the Border Campgrounds	843-774-2411	H 301/501 - Exit 1/H 301/501 Dillon SC	3+

Florence
Florence KOA	843-665-7007	1115 E Campground Road - Exit 169 Florence SC	3+

Santee
Santee State Park	803-854-2408	251 State Park Road Santee SC	3+

Yemassee
Point South KOA	843-726-5733	14 Campground Road - Exit 33 to H 17 Yemassee SC	3+

Georgia   (Interstate 95)   Dogs per Site

Savannah

Brookwood RV Park	888-636-4616	Rt 5, Box 3107; on Pulaski Excelsior Metter GA	3+
Fort McAllister State Historic Park	912-727-2339	3894 Fort McAllister Road - Exit 90 to H 144 Richmond Hill GA	3+
Savannah South KOA	912-765-3396	4915 H 17 - Exit 87 @ Richmond Hill Richmond Hill GA	3+
Waterway RV Park	912-756-2296	70 H 17 Richmond Hill GA	2
Skidaway Island State Park	912-598-2300	52 Diamond Causeway Savannah GA	3+

Brunswick

Blythe Island Regional Park	912-279-2812	6616 Blythe Island H (H 303) Brunswick GA	3+

St Marys

Jacksonville N/Kingsland KOA	912-729-3232	2970 Scrubby Buff Road - Exit 1 Kingsland GA	3+

Florida   (Interstate 95)   Dogs per Site

Jacksonville

Little Talbot Island State Park	904-251-2320	12157 Heckscher Drive Jacksonville FL	3+
Flamingo Lake RV Resort	904-766-0672	3640 Newcomb Road N Jacksonville FL	3+

St Augustine

Anastasia State Park Campgrounds	904-461-2033	Anastasia Park Drive St Augustine FL	1+
St. Augustine Beach KOA	904-471-3113	525 West Pope Road St Augustine FL	1+
Stagecoach RV Park	904-824-2319	2711 County Road 208 - Exit H 16W St Augustine FL	3+

Daytona Beach

Bulow Plantation RV Resort	800-782-8569	3345 Old Kings Road S - Exit 278 Flagler Beach FL	3+
Daytona North RV Resort	877-277-8737	1701 H 1 - Exit H 1 Ormond Beach FL	3+
Tomoka State Park	386-676-4050	2099 N Beach Street - Exit 268 Ormond Beach FL	3+
Daytona Beach Campground	386-761-2663	4601 Clyde Morris Blvd - Exit 256 Port Orange FL	3+

South Florida

Juno Ocean Walk RV Resort	561-622-7500	900 Juno Ocean Walk Juno Beach FL	3+
Paradise Island RV Resort	954-485-1150	2121 NW 29th Court - Exit 33311 Oakland Park FL	3+
Highland Woods	866-340-0649	850/900 NE 48th Street - Exit 39/Sample Road Pompano Beach FL	3+
Markham Park	954-389-2000	16001 W H 84 Sunrise FL	2

Highway 101 Dog-Friendly Campgrounds and RV Parks

Washington   (Highway 101)   Dogs per Site

Olympia

Olympic National Forest	360-956-23300	1835 Black Lk Blvd SW Olympia WA	3+

Sequim

Rainbows End RV Park	360-683-3863	261831 H 101 Sequim WA	2

Port Angeles

Log Cabin Resort	360-928-3325	3183E Beach Road - Exit E Beach Road Port Angeles WA	3+
Olympia National Park	360-452-4501	600 East Park Avenue - Exit Race Street Port Angeles WA	3+
Port Angeles/Swquim KOA	360-457-5916	80 O'Brien Road - Exit O'Brien Road Port Angeles WA	2

Ilwaco

Ilwaco/Long Beach KOA	360-642-3292	1509 H 101 Ilwaco WA	2

Oregon   (Highway 101)   Dogs per Site

Cannon Beach

Cannon Beach RV Resort	800-847-2231	340 Elk Creek Road Cannon Beach OR	3+
Sea Ranch RV Park and Stables	503-436-2815	415 1st Street - Exit Cannon Beach Cannon Beach OR	3+

Tillamook

Cape Lookout State Park	503-842-4981	13000 Whiskey Creek Road W Tillamook OR	3+

Newport

Beverly Beach State Park	541-265-9278	198 NE 123rd Street Newport OR	3+

Florence

Jessie M Honeyman Memorial State Park	541-997-3641	84505 H 101S Florence OR	3+
Mercer Lake Resort	800-355-3633	88875 Bay Berry Lane - Exit Mercer Lake Road Florence OR	2

North Bend

Oregon Dunes KOA	541-756-4851	68632 H 101 North Bend OR	3+

Coos Bay

Lucky Loggers RV Park	541-267-6003	250 E Johnson - Exit E Johnson Coos Bay OR	3+
Sunset Bay State Park	541-888-4902	89814 Cape Arago - Exit Central Avenue Coos Bay OR	3+

Bandon

Bandon by the Sea RV Park	541-347-5155	49612 H 101 Bandon OR	3+
Bullards Beach State Park	541-347-2209	52470 H 101 Bandon OR	3+

Langlois

| Bandon/Port Orford KOA | 541-348-2358 | 46612 H 101   Langlois OR | 2 |

Port Orford

| Port Orford RV Village | 541-332-1041 | 2855 Port Orford Loop - Exit Port Orford Loop Port Orford OR | 3+ |

Brookings

At Rivers Edge RV Park	541-469-3356	98203 S Bank Chetco River Road - Exit S Bank Chetco RiverRoad Brookings OR	2
Harris Beach State Park	541-469-2021	1655 H 101N Brookings OR	3+
Whaleshead Beach Resort	541-469-7446	19921 Whaleshead Road - Exit Whaleshead Road Brookings OR	3+

California   (Highway 101)   Dogs per Site

Crescent City

Crescent City KOA	707-464-5744	4241 H 101N Crescent City CA	3+
De Norte Coast Redwoods State Park	707-464-6101, ext. 5064	7 miles S of Crescent City off H 101 Crescent City CA	3+
Jedediah Smith Campground	707-464-6101	1440 H 199 Crescent City CA	3+
Jedediah Smith Redwoods State Park	707-464-6101, ext. 5112	9 miles east of Crescent City on Highway 199. - Exit H 199 Crescent City CA	1+
Mill Creek Campground	707-464-9533	1375 Elk Valley Road - Exit Campground Road Crescent City CA	3+
Panther Flat Campground	707-457-3131	mile post 16.75 on Highway 199 Gasquet CA	3+
Panther Flat Campground	707-442-1721	Mile Post 16.75 H 199 Gasquet CA	3+

Eureka

| Eureka KOA | 707-822-4243 | 4050 N H 101 - Exit at KOA Drive Eureka CA | 3+ |

Ukiah

| Cow Mountain Recreation Area/Ukiah Field Office | 707-468-4000 | 2550 North State Street - Exit Talmage Road Ukiah CA | 3+ |
| Lake Mendocino Recreation Area | 707-462-7581 | 1160 Lake Mendocino Drive - Exit Lake Mendocino Drive Ukiah CA | 3+ |

Marin - North Bay

Bodega Bay RV Park	707-875-3701	2001 H 1 Bodega Bay CA	2
Bodega Dunes Campground	707-875-3483	3095 H 1 Bodega Bay CA	3+
Doran Regional Park Campgrounds	707-875-3540	201 Doran Beach Road Bodega Bay CA	3+
Porto Bodega Marina and RV Park	707-875-2354	1500 Bay Flat Road Bodega Bay CA	3+
Westside Regional Park Campground	707-875-3540	2400 Westshore Road Bodega Bay CA	3+
Lawsons Landing Campground	707-878-2726	137 Marine View Dr Dillon Beach CA	1+
Samuel P. Taylor State Park	415-488-9897	8889 Sir Francis Drake Blvd Lagunitas CA	3+
Novato RV Park	415-897-1271	1530 Armstrong Avenue - Exit Atherton Novato CA	3+
Olema Ranch Campground	415-663-8001	10155 H 1 Olema CA	3+
San Francisco North/Petaluma KOA	707-763-1492	20 Rainsville Road - Exit Penngrove Petaluma CA	3+

San Francisco

| Candlestick RV Park | 415-822-2299 | 650 Gilman Avenue - Exit 429A San Francisco CA | 3+ |

Palo Alto - Peninsula

| Butano State Park Campground | 650-879-2040 | Off H 1 4.5 miles SE of Pescadero Pescadero CA | 3+ |

San Juan Bautista

| Betabel RV Park | 831-623-2202 | 9664 Betabel Road - Exit Betabel Road San Juan Bautista CA | 2 |
| Mission Farms RV Park & Campground | 831-623-4456 | 400 San Juan Hollister Road - Exit H 156W San Juan Bautista CA | 3+ |

Salinas

| Laguna Seca Campground | 831-755-4895 | 1025 Monterey H 68 - Exit San Born Left on Main/H 68 Salinas CA | 2 |

King City

| San Lorenzo Campground and RV Park | 831-385-5964 | 1160 Broadway - Exit Broadway King City CA | 2 |

San Luis Obispo

Lake Lopez Recreation Area Campground	805-788-2381	6820 Lopez Drive - Exit Grand Avenue Arroyo Grande CA	3+
Lake San Antonio Campground	805-472-2311	2610 San Antonio Road - Exit Jolon Road (G-14) 27 miles to Pleyto Rd Rt Bradley CA	2
North Beach Campground, Pismo State Beach Park	805-489-1869	555 Pier Avenue Oceano CA	3+
Pacific Dunes RV Resort	760-328-4813	1025 Silver Spur Place Oceano CA	3+
Lake Nacimiento Resort RV and Campgrounds	805-238-3256	10625 Nacimiento Lake Drive Paso Robles CA	3+
Pismo Coast Village RV Park	805-773-1811	165 S Dolliver Street - Exit S H 1 Pismo Beach CA	3+
El Chorro Regional Park Campground	805-781-5930	H 1 - Exit Santa Rosa Street to H 1 San Luis Obispo CA	3+
Santa Margarita KOA	805-438-5618	4765 Santa Margarita Lake Road - Exit Santa Margarita Lake Santa Margarita CA	2
Santa Margarita Lake Regional Park Camping	805-781-5930	4695 Santa Margarita Lake Road Santa Margarita CA	3+

Solvang

| Flying Flags RV Park and Campground | 805-688-3716 | 180 Avenue of the Flags - Exit 246 Buellton CA | 1+ |

Santa Barbara			
El Capitan State Beach	805-968-1033	10 Refugio Beach Road Goleta CA	2
Cachuma Lake Rec Area	805-686-5054	H 154 - Exit H 154E Santa Barbara CA	3+
Ventura - Oxnard			
Evergreen RV Park	805-485-1936	2135 N Oxnard Blvd - Exit Oxnard Blvd Oxnard CA	3+
Lake Casitas Recreation Area	805-649-2233	11311 Santa Ana Road Ventura CA	3+
Ventura Beach RV Resort	805-643-9137	800 W Main Street - Exit California Street Ventura CA	3+

Canadian Highway 1 and 5 (West) and Highway 17 (East)
Dog-Friendly Campgrounds and RV Parks

British Columbia   (Trans-Canada)

Dogs per Site

Surrey			
Dogwood Campground and RV Park	604-583-5585	15151 112th Avenue - Exit 50 Surrey BC	2
Hazelmere RV Park	877-501-5007	18843 8th Avenue Surrey BC	1+
Chilliwack			
Cottonwood Meadows RV Country Club	604-824-7275	44280 Luckakuck Way - Exit 116/Lickman Road Chilliwack BC	3+
Vedder River Campground	604-823-6012	5215 Giesbrecht Road - Exit 119/Vedder Road Chilliwack BC	2
Sunnyside Campground	604-858-5253	3405 Columbia Valley H Cultus Lake BC	2
Camperland	604-794-7361	53730 Bridal Falls Road - Exit 138 Rosedale BC	2
Hope			
Hope Valley Campground	604-869-9857	62280 Flood Hope Road - Exit Flood Hope Road Hope BC	3+
Othello Tunnels Campground and RV Park	604-869-9448	67851 Othello Road - Exit Othello Road Hope BC	3+
Wild Rose Campground	604-867-9734	62030 Flood Hope Road - Exit 165 Hope BC	3+
Sicamous			
Sicamous KOA	250-836-2507	3250 Oxboro Road Sicamous BC	3+
Revelstoke			
Canyon Hot Springs Resort	250-837-2420	35 KM E of Revelstoke on H 1 Revelstoke BC	1
Glacier National Park of Canada	250-837-7500	P.O. Box 350 Revelstoke BC	3+
Lamplighter Campground	250-837-3385	1760 Nixon - Exit 23S Revelstoke BC	3+
Revelstoke KOA	250-837-2085	2411 KOA Road - Exit "S" Revelstoke BC	2
Williamson's Lake Campground	250-837-5512	1816 Williamson Lake Road Revelstoke BC	3+
Field			
Yoho National Park of Canada	250-343-6783	P. O. Box 99/H 1 - Exit H 1 Field BC	3+

Alberta   (Trans-Canada)

Dogs per Site

Banff			
Banff National Park of Canada	403-762-1550	224 Banff Avenue Banff AB	1+
Canmore			
Spring Creek Mountain Village	403-678-5111	502 3rd Avenue - Exit Town Center Canmore AB	3+
Calgary			
Calaway Park	403-240-3822	245033 Range Road 33 - Exit Range Road 33 Calgary AB	2
Hinton/Jasper KOA	403-288-8351	4720 Vegas Road NW Calgary AB	2
Pine Creek RV Campground	403-256-3002	On McCloud Trail Calgary AB	2
Symon's Valley RV Park	403-274-4574	260011 Symon's Valley Road NW Calgary AB	2
Brooks			
Dinosaur Provincial Park	403-378-3700	Prairie Road 30 - Exit Patricia Brooks AB	3+
Medicine Hat			
Wild Rose Trailer Park	403-526-2248	28B Camp Drive SW Medicine Hat AB	3+

Saskatchewan   (Trans-Canada)

Dogs per Site

Swift Current			
Ponderosa Campground	306-773-5000	On H 1 a quarter mile E of Swift Current SK	3+
Trail Campground	306-773-8088	701 11th Avenue NW - Exit 11th Avenue NW Swift Current SK	3+
Chaplin			
Silver Dollar RV Park and Campground	306-395-2332	Corner of H 1 and H 19 Chaplin SK	3+
Moose Jaw			
Besant Trans-Canada Campground	306-756-2700	25 miles W of Moose Jaw on H 1 Moose Jaw SK	3+
Prairie Oasis Campground and Motel	306-693-8888	955 Thatcher - Exit Thatcher Moose Jaw SK	2
River Park Campground	306-692-5474	300 River Drive Moose Jaw SK	3+

Regina

Buffalo Lookout Campground	306-525-1448	2 miles E of Regina on H 1 Regina SK	3+
Kings Acres Campground	306-522-1619	l km E of Regina on H 1, N service road Regina SK	3+
Sherwood Forest Country Club	306-545-0330	RR 2 Box 16 - Exit Grand Clouee Regina SK	3+

Grenfell

Grenfell Regional Park	306-697-3055	709 Lake Street - Exit West Access Road Grenfell SK	3+

Moosomin

Fieldstone Campground	306-435-2677	Box 1524 - Exit H 8N 2 km Moosomin SK	1+

Manitoba   (Trans-Canada)   Dogs per Site

Virden

Virden's Lion's Campground	204-748-6393	Corner &th and H 257 Virden MB	3+

Brandon

Curran Park Campground	204-571-0750	Box 6, 305 RR 3 - Exit Grand Valley Road Brandon MB	3+
Meadowlark Campground	204-728-7205	1629 Middleton Brandon MB	3+

Portage la Prairie

Miller's Camping Resort	204-857-4255	6 miles E of Portage on H 1 Portage la Prairie MB	3+
Portage Campground	204-267-2191	8 miles E of Portage on H 1 Portage la Prairie MB	2

Winnipeg

Bird's Hill Provincial Park	888-482-2267	On Lagimodiere/H 59 Winnipeg MB	3+
Northgate Trailer Park	204-339-6631	2695 Main - Exit H 52 Winnipeg MB	3+
Traveller's RV Resort	204-256-2186	56001 Murdock Road - Exit Murdock Road Winnipeg MB	3+

Richer

Rock Garden Campground	204-422-5441	Provincial Road #302 - Exit 302 Richer MB	3+

Hadashville

Whitemouth River RV Park and Campground	204-392-7110	On Government Jet Road - Exit H 43N Hadashville MB	1

Falcon Lake

Whiteshell Provincial Park	888-482-CAMP (2267)	H 1 and H 44 - Exit H 44 Falcon Lake MB	3+

West Hawk Lake

Whitelshell Provincial Park	204-349-2245	P. O. Box 119 West Hawk Lake MB	3+

Ontario   (Trans-Canada)   Dogs per Site

Kenora

Anicinabe Park	807-467-2700	955 Golf Course Road - Exit Miikana Way Kenora ON	3+

Thunder Bay

Thunder Bay KOA	807-683-6221	162 Spruce River Road - Exit Spruce River Road Thunder Bay ON	3+

North Bay

Champlain Tent and Trailer Park	705-474-4669	1202 Premier Road - Exit 338/Lakeshore Drive North Bay ON	3+

Renfrew

Renfrew KOA	613-432-6280	2826 Johnston Road - Exit Storyland Road Renfrew ON	3+

Ottawa

Poplar Grove Tourist Camp	613-821-2973	6154 Bank Street Ottawa ON	2
Rec-Land	613-833-2974	1566 Canaan Road - Exit Canaan Road Ottawa ON	3+

Canadian Highway 16
Dog-Friendly Campgrounds and RV Parks

Alberta   (Highway 16)   Dogs per Site

Hinton

Best Canadian Motor Inn and RV Park	780-865-5099	386 Smith Street Hinton AB	1+

Edson

East of Eden Campground and RV Park	780-723-2287	162 Range Road - Exit Range Road Edson AB	2

Edmonton

Glowing Embers RV Park	877-785-7275	26309 Acheson Edmonton AB	3+
Whitemud Creek Gold and RV Park	780-988-6800	3428 156th Street SW Edmonton AB	2

Vermilion

Vermilion Campground	780-853-4372	5301 48th Street Vermilion AB	3+

Saskatchewan   (Highway 16)

Dogs per Site

Lloydminster

Weaver Park Campground	306-825-3726	On H 16 at Bar Colony Museum Lloydminster SK	3+

Battleford

Eiling Kramer Campground	306-937-6212	15th Street E and Central Avenue Battleford SK	3+

North Battleford

David Laird Campground	306-445-3552	Box 1383 North Battleford SK	3+

Saskatoon

Gordon Howe Campground	306-975-3328	Avenue P South Saskatoon SK	3+
Saskatoon 16 West RV Park	306-931-8905	Corner of 71st Street and H 16 Saskatoon SK	3+

Yorkton

Yorkton City Campground	306-786-1757	On H 16 W of Yorkton Yorkton SK	3+

Canadian Highway 401 (Ontario) and Highway 20 (Quebec)
Dog-Friendly Campgrounds and RV Parks

Ontario   (Highways 401 and 20)

Dogs per Site

London

London/401 KOA	519-644-0222	136 Cromarty Drive London ON	2

Cambridge

Valens Conservation Area	905-525-2183	1691 Regional Park Road 97 Cambridge ON	3+

Toronto Area

Indian Line Campground	905-678-1233	7625 Finch Avenue W Brampton ON	3+
Milton Heights Campground	905-878-6781	8690 Tremaine Road Milton ON	3+

Toronto

Glen Rouge Campground	416-338-2267	7450 Kingston Road - Exit 390 Toronto ON	3+

Kingston

1000 Islands/Kingston KOA	613-546-6140	2039 Cordukes Road Kingston ON	3+
Lake Ontario Park	613-542-6574	1000 King Street W - Exit 615 Kingston ON	3+
Rideau Acres	613-546-2711	1014 Cunningham Road - Exit H 15 Kingston ON	3+

Cardinal

Cardinal KOA	613-657-4536	609 Pittston Road - Exit 730 Cardinal ON	3+

Quebec   (Highways 401 and 20)

Dogs per Site

Montreal

Camping de Compton	800-563-5277	24 Chemin De La Station Compton PQ	3+
Montreal West KOA	450-763-5625	171 H 338 Coteau du Lac PQ	3+
Camping Lac LaFontaine	450-431-7373	110 Boul Grand Heron PQ	2
Camping Alouette	450-464-1661	3449 L'Industrie Saint-Mathieu-de-beloeil PQ	3+

Drummondville

Camping La Detente	819-478-0651	1580 Fontaine Bleau Drummondville PQ	3+

Quebec

Camping Plage Fortier	888-226-7387	1400 Lucen Francoes L'ange-Gardien PQ	3+
Camping Aeroport	800-294-1574	2050 Aeroport Quebec City PQ	3+
Camping Parc Beaumont	418-837-3787	432 Fleuve Quebec City PQ	2

Alaska Highway Western Route
Dog-Friendly Campgrounds and RV Parks

Washington   (Alaska Highway Western Route)

Dogs per Site

Bellingham

Bellingham RV Park	360-752-1224	3939 Bennett Drive Bellingham WA	3+
Larrabee State Park	360-676-2093	245 Chuckanut Drive Bellingham WA	3+
Lynden/Bellingham KOA	360-354-4772	8717 Line Road - Exit 546 Lynden WA	3+

British Columbia   (Alaska Highway Western Route)

Dogs per Site

Highway Guides - Please always call ahead to make sure an establishment is still dog-friendly.

Chilliwack

Cottonwood Meadows RV Country Club	604-824-7275	44280 Luckakuck Way - Exit 116/Lickman Road Chilliwack BC	3+
Vedder River Campground	604-823-6012	5215 Giesbrecht Road - Exit 119/Vedder Road Chilliwack BC	2
Sunnyside Campground	604-858-5253	3405 Columbia Valley H Cultus Lake BC	2
Camperland	604-794-7361	53730 Bridal Falls Road - Exit 138 Rosedale BC	2

Hope

Hope Valley Campground	604-869-9857	62280 Flood Hope Road - Exit Flood Hope Road Hope BC	3+
Othello Tunnels Campground and RV Park	604-869-9448	67851 Othello Road - Exit Othello Road Hope BC	3+
Wild Rose Campground	604-867-9734	62030 Flood Hope Road - Exit 165 Hope BC	3+

Cache Creek

Brookside Campsite	250-457-6633	1621 E Trans Canada H Cache Creek BC	3+
Evergreen Fishing Resort	250-459-2372	1820 Loon Lake Road - Exit H 97 Cache Creek BC	3+
Historic Hat Creek Ranch	250-457-9722	Junction of Highway 97 and 99, 11 km north of Cache Creek Cache Creek BC	2

Clinton

Clinton Pines	250-459-0030	1204 Cariboo Ave Box 759 Clinton BC	3+

Lac La Hache

Fir Crest Resort	250-396-7337	Fir Crest Road Lac La Hache BC	2

Williams Lake

Big Bar Lake Provincial Park	250-398-4414	181 1st Avenue Williams Lake BC	2
Springhouse Trails Ranch	250-392-4780	3067 Dog Creek Road Williams Lake BC	2
Williams Lake Stampede	250-369-6718	850 McKinsey Avenue Williams Lake BC	3+

Quesnel

Lazy Daze	250-992-6700	714 Ritchie Road Quesnel BC	3+

Prince George

Bee Lazee RV Park and Campground	250-963-7263	15910 H 97 S - Exit H 97S Prince George BC	3+
Blue Spruce RV Park and Campground	250-964-7272	4433 Kimball Road - Exit Kimball Road Prince George BC	3+
Hartway RV Park	250-962-8848	7729 S Kelly Road Prince George BC	3+
Sintich Trailer Park	250-963-9862	7817 H 97 Prince George BC	3+
Stone Creek RV Park and Campground	250-330-4321	31605 H 97 S Prince George BC	3+

Chetwynd

Caron Creek RV Park	250-788-2522	7537 H 97S Chetwynd BC	3+
Westwind RV Park	250-788-2190	4401 53rd Avenue Chetwynd BC	3+

Dawson Creek

Alahart RV Park	250-782-4702	1725 Alaska Avenue/H 49E Dawson Creek BC	3+
Mile Zero Park and Campground	250-782-2590	1901 Alaska Avenue Dawson Creek BC	3+
Northern Lights RV Park	250-782-9433	9636 Friesen Sub-division Dawson Creek BC	3+
Tubby's RV Park	250-782-2584	1913 96th Avenue Dawson Creek BC	3+

Fort St John

Ross H. Maclean Rotary RV Park	250-785-1700	13016 Lakeshore Drive Fort St John BC	3+

Pink Mountain

Pink Mountain	250-772-5133	Mile 143 Alaska Hwy Pink Mountain BC	2

Fort Nelson

Fort Nelson Truck Stop and RV Park	250-774-7270	Mile 293 Alaska Hwy Fort Nelson BC	3+
Westend RV Campground	250-774-2340	5651 Alaska Hwy Fort Nelson BC	3+

Toad River

Poplars Campground and Cafe	250-232-5465	Mile 426 Alaska Hwy Toad River BC	3+
Toad River RV Camp and Lodge	250-232-5401	Mile 422 Alaska Hwy Toad River BC	3+

Muncho Lake

J and H Wilderness Resort and RV Park	250-776-3453	M.P. 463 Alaska Hwy Muncho Lake BC	3+
Northern Rockies Lodge	250-776-3481	M.P. 462 Alaska Hwy Muncho Lake BC	2

Coal River

Coal River Lodge and RV Park	250-776-7306	Mile 533 Alaska Hwy Coal River BC	3+

Yukon (Alaska Highway Western Route)   Dogs per Site

Watson Lake

Baby Nugget RV Park	867-536-2307	1003 Alaska H Watson Lake YU	3+
Campground Services Campground	867-536-7448	18 Adela Trail Watson Lake YU	3+
Downtown RV Park	867-536-2646	Mile 635 Alaska H Watson Lake YU	3+
Racheria RV Park	867-851-6456	M.M. 710 Alaska Hwy (70 miles past Watson Lake) Watson Lake YU	3+
Tetlin National Wildlife Refuge	907-883-5312	Mile 1229 Alaska H Watson Lake YU	3+

Teslin

Dawson Peaks Resort	867-390-2244	Km 1232 Alaska H Teslin YU	1+

Whitehorse

Caribou RV Park	867-668-2961	Km 1403 Alaska H Whitehorse YU	3+

Hi Country RV Park	867-667-7445	91374 Alaska H Whitehorse YU	3+
Pioneer Park	867-668-5944	91091 Alaska H (Km 1414.7) Whitehorse YU	3+
Haines Junction			
Haines Junction	867-634-2505	1016 Alaska H Haines Junction YU	3+
Kluane National Park and Reserve of Canada	867-634-7250	P. O. Box 5495/ 117 Logan Street Haines Junction YU	3+
Kluane RV Campground	867-634-2709	Km 1635.9 Alaska H Haines Junction YU	3+
Otter Falls Cutoff	867-634-2812	1546 Alaska H Haines Junction YU	2
Destruction Bay			
Cottonwood Park Campground	867-841-4066	Km 717 Alaska H Destruction Bay YU	3+
Destruction Bay Lodge	867-841-5332	M.M. 1083 Alaska Hwy Destruction Bay YU	3+
Beaver Creek			
1202 RV Park and Motor Inn	867-862-7600	Mile 1202 Alaska H Beaver Creek YU	1+
Westmark RV Park	867-862-7501	M.P. 1202 Alaska Hwy Beaver Creek YU	1+

Alaska   (Alaska Highway Western Route)   Dogs per Site

Border City			
Border City Motel and RV Park	907-774-2205	Mile 1225 Alaska H Border City AK	1+
Tok			
Gateway Salmon Bake and RV Park	907-883-5555	1313.1 Alaska H Tok AK	3+
Sourdough Campground	907-883-5543	Mile 122.8 Glen H Tok AK	3+
Tundra Lodge and RV Park	907-883-7875	M.P. 1315 Alaska Hwy Tok AK	3+
Delta Junction			
Big Delta State Historical Park	907-269-8400	Mile 274.5 Richardson Highway Delta Junction AK	3+
Smith's Green Acres	907-895-4369	Mile 268 Richardson Highway Delta Junction AK	2
Fairbanks			
Chena Hot Springs	907-451-8104	56.5 Chena Hot Springs Road Fairbanks AK	3+
Pioneer Park	907-459-1087	2300 Airport Way Fairbanks AK	3+
Pioneer Park and RV	907-459-1059	2300 Airport Way Fairbanks AK	3+
River's Edge Resort and RV Park	907-474-0286	4200 Boat Street Fairbanks AK	3+
Riverview RV Park	888-488-6392	1316 Badger Road Fairbanks AK	3+

Alaska Highway Eastern Route
Dog-Friendly Campgrounds and RV Parks

Montana   (Alaska Highway Eastern Route)   Dogs per Site

Great Falls			
Acklley Lake State Park	406-454-5840	4600 Giant Srings Road Great Falls MT	3+
Dick's RV Park	406-452-0333	1403 11th Street SW Great Falls MT	3+
Great Falls KOA	406-727-3191	1500 51st Street S Great Falls MT	3+
Lewis and Clark National Forest	406-791-7700	1101 15th Street N. Great Falls MT	3+
Shelby			
Lewis and Clark RV Park	406-434-2710	Box 369, Front Street Shelby MT	2

Alberta   (Alaska Highway Eastern Route)   Dogs per Site

Milk River			
Writing on Stone Provincial Park	403-647-2364	H 4/P. O. Box 297 - Exit 32 km East of Milk River Milk River AB	3+
Lethbridge			
Bridgeview RV Resort	403-381-2357	1501 2nd Avenue W Lethbridge AB	3+
Henderson Lake Campground	403-328-5452	3419 Parkside Drive S Lethbridge AB	2
Calgary			
Calaway Park	403-240-3822	245033 Range Road 33 - Exit Range Road 33 Calgary AB	2
Hinton/Jasper KOA	403-288-8351	4720 Vegas Road NW Calgary AB	2
Pine Creek RV Campground	403-256-3002	On McCloud Trail Calgary AB	2
Symon's Valley RV Park	403-274-4574	260011 Symon's Valley Road NW Calgary AB	2
Balzac			
Whispering Spruce Campground	403-226-0097	Range Road 10, 262195 Balzac AB	3+
Red Deer			
Lions Campground	403-342-8183	4759 Riverside Drive Red Deer AB	3+
Westerner Campground	403-352-8801	4847-D 19th Street Red Deer AB	3+
Edmonton			
Glowing Embers RV Park	877-785-7275	26309 Acheson Edmonton AB	3+
Whitemud Creek Gold and RV Park	780-988-6800	3428 156th Street SW Edmonton AB	2
Whitecourt			
Sagitawah RV Park	780-778-3734	43 Whitecourt Avenue Whitecourt AB	3+

Highway Guides - Please always call ahead to make sure an establishment is still dog-friendly.

Valleyview

| Sherks RV Park | 780-524-4949 | 38th Avenue/ P. O. Box Box 765   Valleyview AB | 3+ |

Beaverlodge

| Pioneer Campground | 780-354-2201 | H 43   Beaverlodge AB | 3+ |

British Columbia   (Alaska Highway Eastern Route)   Dogs per Site

Dawson Creek

Alahart RV Park	250-782-4702	1725 Alaska Avenue/H 49E Dawson Creek BC	3+
Mile Zero Park and Campground	250-782-2590	1901 Alaska Avenue Dawson Creek BC	3+
Northern Lights RV Park	250-782-9433	9636 Friesen Sub-division Dawson Creek BC	3+
Tubby's RV Park	250-782-2584	1913 96th Avenue Dawson Creek BC	3+

Chapter 6

United States National Park Guide

DogFriendly.com's Top 5 National Parks
(Ratings based on sights to see and places to walk or hike with dogs)

1. Grand Canyon National Park, Arizona, 928-638-7888

You and your dog can view the popular Grand Canyon along the South Rim where millions of visitors come every year. Dogs are allowed on the South Rim trails which includes a 2.7 mile scenic walk along the rim. And, well-behaved pooches are allowed on the Geology Walk, a one hour park ranger guided tour which consists of a leisurely walk along a 3/4 mile paved rim trail. The following is the remainder of the doggie regulations. Dogs are not allowed in park lodging, or on park buses. Pets are not permitted at all on North Rim trails with the exception of a bridle path which connects the lodge with the North Kaibab Trail.

2. Acadia National Park, Maine, 207-288-3338

Dogs are allowed on most of the trails and carriage roads. There is even an off-leash area within the park at Little Long Pond. Pets are not allowed on sand beaches or on the steeper hiking trails. Pets must be on a 6 foot or less leash at all times, except for the above mentioned off-leash area.

3. Shenandoah National Park, Virginia, 540-999-3500

This national park, located along a section of the Blue Ridge Parkway, offers miles and miles of dog-friendly hiking trails. There are some trails where dogs are not allowed, but your pooch is allowed on the majority of trails in this park. Pets must be on a 6 foot or less leash at all times, and are allowed in campgrounds, and picnic areas.

4.Yosemite National Park, California, 209-372-0200

Dogs are allowed on the paved trails throughout the Yosemite Valley. The valley is where the majority of tourists visit and you can see most of the popular landmarks and sights from the valley floor, with your pet. Dogs are not allowed on other trails, in wilderness areas, or on the shuttle buses. Owners must clean up after their pets.

5. North Cascades National Park, Washington, 360-856-5700

Dogs are allowed on one of the hiking trails, the Pacific Crest Trail. This scenic hiking trail runs through the park and is rated moderate to difficult. The trail is located off Highway 20, about one mile east of Rainy Pass. At the Bridge Creek Trailhead, park on the north side of the highway and then hike north (uphill) or south (downhill). A Northwest Forest Pass is required to park at the trailhead. The cost is about $5 and can be purchased at the Visitor's Center in Newhalem. For a larger variety of trails, including a less strenuous hike, dogs are also allowed on trails at the adjacent Ross Lake National Recreation Area and the Lake Chelan National Recreation Area. Both recreation areas are managed by the national park.

Author Tara Kain and her dog Java at the Grand Canyon.

National Parks - Please call ahead to confirm an establishment is still dog-friendly.

Alaska

Wrangell-St Elias National Park and Preserve
PO Box 439
Copper Center, AK
907-822-5234
nps.gov/wrst/index.htm
Dogs on leash are allowed in the park. They are not allowed in buildings. The park features camping, hiking, auto touring, and more.

Denali National Park and Preserve
PO Box 9
Denali Park, AK
907-683-2294
nps.gov/dena/index.htm
Dogs must be on leash and must be cleaned up after in Denali National Park. Dogs are only allowed on the paved roads and dirt roads. One place to walk is on the road to Savage after mile 15, which is a dirt road and only the park buses are allowed. Access is by car depending on weather. Dogs on leash are allowed in the Denali National Park campgrounds, but they may not be left unattended in the campgrounds. The park features auto touring, camping, and scenery.

Gates of the Arctic National Park and Preserve
201 First Avenue
Fairbanks, AK
907-692-5494
nps.gov/gaar/index.htm
Dogs must be on leash and must be cleaned up after in the park. The park is accessed by plane, foot and car depending on weather. Dogs are allowed in the backcountry of the park but there are no man-made trails. It is a wilderness park. There are no campgrounds in the park and there are no facilities in the park.

Glacier Bay National Park
1 Park Road
Gustavus, AK
907-697-2230
nps.gov/glba
This national park offers coastal beaches and high mountains. The way to arrive at this park is by plane, boat, or ferry, usually from Juneau. The Glacier Bay Visitor Center is open daily from May 27 to September 11, from noon to 8:45 p.m. Dogs are not allowed to be off the road more than 100 feet, and they are not allowed on any of the trails into the back country. They are also not allowed on the Barlett Trail

or on the Forest Loop Trail, or in any of the camp buildings. The Visitor Information Station for boaters and campers, is open May through June from 8 to 5 p.m.; June, July, and August from 7 to 9 p.m., and September 8 to 5 p.m. Dogs are allowed at no additional fee, and they can be in the developed Barlett Cove area, or on any of the marked trails. Dogs may not be left unattended at any time, and they must be leashed at all times, and cleaned up after.

Katmai National Park and Preserve
PO Box 7
King Salmon, AK
907-246-3305
nps.gov/katm/index.htm
Dogs on leash are allowed only in developed areas. They are not allowed in the Brooks camping area. The park is accessed by plane or dogsled only.

Kobuk Valley National Park
PO Box 1029
Kotzebue, AK
907-442-3760
nps.gov/kova/index.htm
Dogs on leash are allowed in the park. The park is accessed by plane, foot, or dogsled only.

Western Arctic National Parklands
PO Box 1029
Kotzebue, AK
907-442-3760
nps.gov/nwak/index.htm
Pets are allowed. There is not an official pet policy. The park is accessed by plane and dogsledding.

Lake Clark National Park and Preserve
1 Park Place
Port Alsworth, AK
907-781-2218
nps.gov/lacl/index.htm
Dogs on leash are allowed in the park area. The park is accessed by plane or dogsled only. The park features boating, camping, fishing, hiking, and more.

Kenai Fjords National Park
PO Box 1727
Seward, AK
907-224-2132
nps.gov/klgo/index.htm
Dogs on leash are only allowed in the parking lot area and along roads. They are not allowed in buildings, on trails, or in the back country.

Arizona

Grand Canyon National Park
Hwy 64
Grand Canyon, AZ
928-638-7888
nps.gov/grca/
The Grand Canyon, located in the northwest corner of Arizona, is considered to be one of the most impressive natural splendors in the world. It is 277 miles long, 18 miles wide, and at its deepest point, is 6000 vertical feet (more than 1 mile) from rim to river. The Grand Canyon has several entrance areas, but the most popular is the South Rim. Dogs are not allowed in most areas of the North Rim of the Park. On the North Rim, the only trail that dogs are allowed on is the bridle trail from the lodge to the North Kaibab Trail (but not on the North Kaibab Trail). Dogs are not allowed on any trails below the rim, but leashed dogs are allowed on the paved rim trail. This dog-friendly trail is about 2.7 miles each way and offers excellent views of the Grand Canyon. Remember that the elevation at the rim is 7,000 feet, so you or your pup may need to rest more often than usual. Also, the weather can be very hot during the summer and can be snowing during the winter, so plan accordingly. And be sure you or your pup do not get too close to the edge! Feel like taking a tour? Well-behaved dogs are allowed on the Geology Walk. This is a one hour park ranger guided tour and consists of a leisurely walk along a 3/4 mile paved rim trail. They discuss how the Grand Canyon was created and more. The tour departs at 11am daily (weather permitting) from the Yavapai Observation Station. Pets are allowed in the Grand Canyon's Mather Campground in Grand Canyon Village, the Desert View Campground 26 miles east of the village, and, for RVs, the Trailer Village in Grand Canyon Village. Dogs must be leashed at all times in the campgrounds and may not be left unattended. There are kennels available at the South Rim. Its hours are 7:30 am to 5 pm. To make kennel reservations or for other kennel information call 928-638-0534. The Grand Canyon park entrance fee is currently $25.00 per private vehicle, payable upon entry to the park. Admission tickets are for 7 days.

Petrified Forest National Park
Entrances on Hwy 40 and Hwy 180
Petrified Forest National Park, AZ
928-524-6228
nps.gov/pefo/
The Petrified Forest is located in northeastern Arizona and features one of the world's largest and most colorful concentrations of petrified wood. Also included in the park's 93,533 acres are the multi-hued badlands of the Painted Desert, archeological sites and displays of 225 million year old fossils. Your leashed dog is welcome on all of the paved trails and scenic overlooks. Take a walk on the self-guided Giant Logs trail or view ancient petroglyphs from an overlook. The entrance fee is $10 per private vehicle.

Saguaro National Park
3693 South Old Spanish Trail
Tucson, AZ
520-733-5100
nps.gov/sagu/index.htm
Dogs must be on leash and must be cleaned up after on roadways and picnic areas. They are not allowed on any trails or buildings.

Arkansas

Hot Springs National Park
369 Central Avenue
Hot Springs, AR
501-624-2701
nps.gov/hosp
There are 47 hot springs here, and this reserve was established in 1832 to protect them. That makes this park our oldest national park. The park is open daily from 9:00 a.m. to 5:00 p.m., except in the summer from May 28 to August 12, when they stay open until 6:00 p.m. Dogs are allowed at no additional fee at the park and in the campground, which does not have hookups. Dogs may not be left unattended, they must be leashed, and cleaned up after. Dogs are allowed throughout the park, trails and in the camp area.

California

Death Valley National Park
Highway 190
Death Valley, CA
760-786-2331
nps.gov/deva
TDeath Valley is one of the hottest places on Earth, with summer temperatures averaging well over 100 degrees Fahrenheit. It is also the lowest point on the Western Hemisphere at 282 feet below sea level. Average rainfall here sets yet another record. With an average of only 1.96 inches per year, this valley is the driest place in North America. Because of the high summer heat, the best time to visit the park is during the winter. Even though dogs are not allowed on any trails, you will still be able to see the majority of the sights and attractions from your car. There are several scenic drives that are popular with all visitors, with or without dogs. Dante's View is a 52 mile round trip drive that takes about 2 hours or longer. Some parts of the road are graded dirt roads and no trailers or RVs are allowed. On this drive you will view scenic mudstone hills which are made of 7 to 9 million year old lakebed sediments. You will also get a great view from the top of Dantes View. Another scenic drive is called Badwater. It is located about 18 miles from the Visitor Center and can take about 1.5 to 2 hours or longer. On this drive you will view the Devil's Golf Course where there are almost pure table salt crystals from an ancient lake. You will also drive to Badwater which is the lowest point in the Western Hemisphere at 282 feet below sea level. Dogs are allowed at view points which are about 200 yards or less from roads or parking lots. Pets must be leashed and attended at all times. Please clean up after your pets. While dogs are not allowed on any trails in the park, they can walk along roads. Pets are allowed up to a few hundred yards from the paved and dirt roads. Stop at the Furnance Creek Visitor Center to pick up a brochure and more information. The visitor center is located on Highway 190, north of the lowest point..

Lassen Volcanic National Park
PO Box 100
Mineral, CA
530-595-4444
nps.gov/lavo/
This national park does not really have much to see or do if you bring your pooch, except for staying overnight at the campgrounds. However, the dog-friendly Lassen National Forest surrounds the national park. At the national forest you will be able to find dog-friendly hiking, sightseeing and camping. Pets must be leashed and attended at all times. Please clean up after your pet.

Sequoia and Kings Canyon National Park
47050 General Highway
Three Rivers, CA
559-565-3341
nps.gov/seki/
This national park does not really have much to see or do if you bring your pooch, except for driving through a giant redwood forest in your car and staying overnight at the campgrounds. However, located to the west and south of this national park is the dog-friendly Giant National Sequoia Monument. There you will be able to find dog-friendly hiking, sightseeing and camping. Pets must be leashed and attended at all times. Please clean up after your pet.

Joshua Tree National Park
74485 National Park Drive
Twentynine Palms, CA
760-367-5500
nps.gov/jotr
Dogs are not allowed on the trails, cannot be left unattended, and must be on leash. However, they are allowed on dirt and paved roads including the Geology Tour Road. This is actually a driving tour, but you'll be able to see the park's most fascinating landscapes from this road. It is an 18 mile tour with 16 stops. The park recommends taking about 2 hours for the round trip. At stop #9, about 5 miles out, there is room to turnaround if you do not want to complete the whole tour.

Channel Islands National Park
Ventura, CA
805-658-5730
nps.gov/jotr
Dogs are not allowed.

Yosemite National Park
PO Box 577
Yosemite, CA
209-372-0200
nps.gov/yose
Yosemite's geology is world famous for its granite cliffs, tall waterfalls and giant sequoia groves. As with most national parks, pets have limited access within the park. Pets are not allowed on unpaved or poorly paved trails, in wilderness areas including hiking trails, in park lodging (except for some campgrounds) and on shuttle buses. However, there are still several nice areas to walk with your pooch and you will be able to see the majority of sights and points of interest that most visitors see. Dogs are allowed in developed

areas and on fully paved trails, include Yosemite Valley which offers about 2 miles of paved trails. From these trails you can view El Capitan, Half Dome and Yosemite Falls. You can also take the .5 mile paved trail right up to the base of Bridalveil Fall which is a 620 foot year round waterfall. In general dogs are not allowed on unpaved trails, but this park does make the following exceptions. Dogs are allowed on the Meadow Loop and Four Mile fire roads in Wawona. They are also allowed on the Carlon Road and on the Old Big Oak Flat Road between Hodgdon Meadow and Hazel Green Creek. Dogs must be on a 6 foot or less leash and attended at all times. People must also clean up after their pets. There are four main entrances to the park and all four lead to the Yosemite Valley. The park entrance fees are as follows: $20 per vehicle, $40 annual pass or $10 per individual on foot. The pass is good for 7 days. Prices are subject to change. Yosemite Valley may be reached via Highway 41 from Fresno, Highway 140 from Merced, Highway 120 from Manteca and in late spring through late fall via the Tioga Road (Highway 120 East) from Lee Vining. From November through March, all park roads are subject to snow chain control .

Colorado

Rocky Mountain National Park
1000 Highway 36
Estes Park, CO
970-586-1206
nps.gov/romo/
Dogs cannot really do much in this park, but as you drive through the park, you will find some spectacular scenery and possibly some sightings of wildlife. Pets are not allowed on trails, or in the backcountry. Pets are allowed in your car, along the road, in parking lots, at picnic areas and campgrounds. Dogs must be on a 6 foot or less leash. You can still take your dog for a hike, not in the national park, but in the adjacent Arapaho-Roosevelt National Forest.

Black Canyon of the Gunnison National Park
102 Elk Creek
Gunnison, CO
970-641-2337
nps.gov/blca/index.htm
This unique canyon in the Rockies is narrow and deep. Dogs may view the

Canyon with you from the Rim Rock Trail. Dogs on leash are allowed on roads, campgrounds, overlooks, the Rim Rock trail, Cedar Point Nature trail, and North Rim Chasm View Nature trail. They are not allowed on other hiking trails, inner canyon routes, or in the wilderness area within the park. Dogs on leash are permitted throughout the Curecanti National Recreation Area nearby.

Mesa Verde National Park
PO Box 8
Mesa Verde, CO
970-529-4465
nps.gov/meve/index.htm
Dogs on leash are allowed in the campgrounds and parking lots only. Dogs are not allowed on hiking trails or archaeological sites. Pets cannot be left alone or in vehicles.

Great Sand Dunes National Park and Preserve
11999 Highway 150
Mosca, CO
719-378-6300
nps.gov/grsa/index.htm
The dunes of Great Sand Dunes National Park rise over 750 feet high. Dogs are allowed throughout the park and must be on leash. You must clean up after your dog and dogs may not be left unattended in the park. Leashed dogs are also welcome in the campgrounds. The park features auto touring, camping fishing, hiking, and more.

Florida

Biscayne National Park
9700 SW 328 Street
Homestead, FL
305-230-7275
nps.gov/bisc/
In addition to providing protection for and educating visitors of the 4 primary ecosystems that this park maintains, it also shares a long cultural history with evidence of human occupation of more than 10,000 years. Guests will also find a wide variety of planned Ranger activities and plenty of land and water recreation. Dogs are allowed for no additional fee; they must be leashed and cleaned up after at all times. They are only allowed at the Elliot campground, and they are allowed on the trails unless otherwise marked. Multiple dogs may be allowed.

Everglades National Park

40001 H 9336/Main Park Road
Homestead, FL
305-242-7700 (800/365-CAMP (2267))
nps.gov/ever/
Home to many rare and endangered species, this park is also the country's largest subtropical wilderness - now designated a World Heritage Site, a Wetland of International Importance site, and an International Biosphere Reserve. Dogs are allowed for no additional fee; they may only be in the campground, picnic areas, in the parking lots and on paved roads. Dogs may not be left unattended at any time, and they must be leashed and cleaned up after. Multiple dogs may be allowed.

Dry Tortugas National Park
PO Box 6208
Key West, FL
305-242-7700
nps.gov/drto/index.htm
This set of Islands is 70 miles west of Key West in the Gulf of Mexico. Dogs must be on leash and must be cleaned up after on this island. Dogs are not allowed on the ferry but they can come over by private boat or charter from Key West. The park features picnicking, camping, fishing, swimming and more. It is open year round.

Hawaii

Haleakala National Park
It is located off Hana Highway
Hawaii, HI
808-572-4400
nps.gov/hale
Dogs are not allowed on the trails or in any wilderness area. They are allowed in the campgrounds. There are no water or bathroom facilities at this park, so be sure to bring enough for you and your pet.

Hawaii Volcanoes National Park
MM 31.5 H 11
Hawaii National Park, HI
808-985-6000
nps.gov/havo
This park covers the top of earth's most massive volcano the Mauna Loa at almost 14,000 feet. The park is open 7 days a week year round. Dogs are allowed at no additional fee, but they may only be on paved roads, the developed areas, and the campgrounds. They are not allowed on any of the trails or off the roads. Dogs may not be left unattended at

any time, and they must be leashed and cleaned up after.

Kentucky

Mammoth Cave National Park
off Interstate 65
Mammoth Cave, KY
270-758-2251
nps.gov/maca/
At this national park, leashed dogs are allowed on hiking trails and in campgrounds. There are over 70 miles of hiking trails which go through valleys, up into hills, and next to rivers, lakes and waterfalls. However, dogs are not allowed in the cave, which is the main attraction at this park. The park does offer kennels that are located near the Mammoth Cave Hotel. The kennels are outdoor and not heated or air-conditioned. If you want to try the kennels at Mammoth Cave, be sure to check them out first. You will need to make a reservation for the kennels and there is a $5 key deposit fee for the cage lock and a $2.50 fee for half a day or a $5.00 fee for the entire day. To make kennel reservations, call the Mammoth Cave Hotel directly at 270-758-2225.

Maine

Acadia National Park
Eagle Lake Road
Bar Harbor, ME
207-288-3338
nps.gov/acad/
This National Park ranks high on the tail wagging meter. Dogs are allowed on most of the hiking trails, which is unusual for a national park. There are miles and miles of both hiking trails and carriage roads. Pets are also allowed at the campgrounds, but must be attended at all times. They are not allowed on sand beaches during the summer or on the steeper hiking trails year-round. Pets must be on a 6 foot or less leash at all times. There is one exception to the leash rule. There is an area in the park that is privately owned where dogs are allowed to run leash-free. It is called Little Long Pond and is located near Seal Harbor. Don't miss the awe-inspiring view from the top of Cadillac Mountain in the park. Overall, this is a pretty popular national park for dogs and their dog-loving owners. There is a $10 entrance fee into the park, which is good for 7 days. You

can also purchase an audio tape tour of the Park Loop Road which is a self-guided auto tour. The driving tour is about 27 miles and takes 3 to 4 hours including stops. Audio tapes are available at the Hulls Cove Visitor Center.

Michigan

Isle Royale National Park
800 East Lakeshore Drive
Houghton, MI
906) 482-0984
nps.gov/isro
No dogs are allowed within the park.

Minnesota

Voyageurs National Park
3131 H 53S
International Falls, MN
218-283-9821
nps.gov/voya
Voyageurs is a water based park located on the northern edge of Minnesota, and has some of the oldest exposed rock formations in the world. The park can also be accessed on Highway 11 from the west. There is camping, but a boat is required to access the trailheads to get there. There is another camping area just outside of the park as well. Dogs are allowed in developed areas of the park, outside visitor centers, at boat ramps, picnic areas, at tent camping areas, houseboats, and day use sites on the four main lakes. There are no additional pet fees. Dogs may not be left unattended at any time, they must be on no more than a 6 foot leash, and be cleaned up after. Pets are not allowed on park trails or in the backcountry.

Montana

Glacier National Park
PO Box 128
West Glacier, MT
406-888-7800
nps.gov/glac/index.htm
Dogs must be on leash and must be cleaned up after in the park area. Dogs are not allowed on the hiking trails. They are allowed in the camping, picnic areas and along roadways and parking lots.

Nevada

Great Basin National Park
100 Great Basin
Baker, NV
775-234-7331
nps.gov/grba
The Great Basin Park rises to over 13,000 feet and hosts the Lehman Caves and an abundant variety of wildlife, plants, and waterways. They are open year round for tent and RV camping with no hook ups. There is no additional fee for dogs, but they may not be left unattended, they must be on no more than a 6 foot leash, and be cleaned up after. Dogs are not allowed on any of the trails.

New Mexico

Carlsbad Canyon National Park
727 Carlsbad Canyon H 62/180
Carlsbad, NM
505-785-2232
nps.gov/cave/
This national park was established to preserve the Carlsbad Caverns, and over 100 other caves housed within a fossil reef. It is also home to America's deepest and 4th longest limestone cave. Dogs are not allowed at the park, except in the parking lot and at the kennel that is on site, and they must be on leash and cleaned up after.

North Carolina

Great Smoky Mountains National Park
107 Park Headquarters Road
Cherokee, NC
865-436-1200
(http://www.nps.gov/grsm/)
Great Smoky Mountains National Park is located both in Tennessee and North Carolina and is one of the most popular of the National Parks. Pets must be leashed or restrained at all times within the park and are not allowed on most of the hiking trails. They can accompany you in your car and at lookouts and stops near the road. However, there are two trails in Great Smoky Mountains National Park that will allow leashed dogs. The Gatlinburg Trail is a 1.9 mile trail from the Sugarland's Visitor Center to the outskirts of Gatlinburg; it runs along the forest with beautiful river views and it passes old homesteads along the way. It follows a creek a good portion of the way.

The Oconaluftee River Trail follows along the river for a 1.5 mile

North Dakota

Theodore Roosevelt National Park
On I 94 at Exits 25 or 27 (South Unit)
Medora, ND
701-623-4466
nps.gov/thro
This Park is located in the North Dakota Badlands. It is named after the 26th president, Theodore Roosevelt. He was a great conservationist, who, out of concern for the future of our lands, established the National Forest Service in 1906. The park is open all year although some roads close at times due to snow. The campgrounds are also open all year (no hookups). Dogs are allowed in the park and the campgrounds at no additional fee, but dogs may not be left unattended at any time, and they are not allowed in any of the buildings, or on any of the trails. However, there are trails just outside the park where dogs are allowed. One of the trails is the Maahdaahhey Trail.

Ohio

Cuyahoga Valley National Park
Canal Road
Brecksville, OH
216-524-1497
nps.gov/cuva/
This national park consists of 33,000 acres along the banks of the Cuyahoga River. Scenery and terrain varies from a rolling floodplain to steep valley walls, ravines and lush upland forests. Popular activities at this park include hiking, bicycling, birdwatching and picnicking. Dogs are allowed at the park including the hiking trails. Pets must be leashed and cleaned up after. Pets are not allowed inside any buildings. The park is open daily and can be accessed by many different highways, including I-77, I-271, I-80/Ohio Turnpike, and State Route 8. To get to Canal Visitor Center, exit I-77 at Rockside Road. Go approximately 1 mile east to Canal Road and turn right. The visitor center is about 1.5 miles on the right. To get to Happy Days Visitor Center, take State Route 8 to west State Route 303. The visitor center is about 1 mile on the left. There is no park entrance fee.

Oregon

Crater Lake National Park
PO Box 7
Crater Lake, OR
541-594-3100
nps.gov/crla/index.htm
Dogs must be on leash and must be cleaned up after in park. Dogs must remain in the developed portions of the park and are not allowed on the dirt trails or in the backcountry. They are allowed on the roads and the sidewalks. There is a road and sidewalk surrounding Crater Lake so you and your dog may view the lake and walk quite a ways around it. Dogs are not allowed in any buildings. Dogs are allowed in the campgrounds on leash in the park.

South Carolina

Congaree National Park
48 Old Bluff Road
Columbia, SC
803-776-4396
nps.gov/cosw
This 22,200-acre park protects the largest contiguous tract of old-growth bottomland hardwood forest still in the US. The park's floodplain forest has one of the highest canopies and some of the tallest trees in the eastern US. Enjoy hiking, primitive camping, birdwatching, picnicking, canoeing, kayaking, Ranger guided interpretive walks, canoe tours, nature study, and environmental education programs. Open all year; Monday to Thursday from 8:30 am to 5 pm, and Friday to Sunday from 8 am to 7 pm. To walk the trails after hours park outside the gate. Well behaved dogs on leash are allowed on the trails and the outside guided tours, but they are not allowed on the Boardwalk or in the buildings.

South Dakota

Wind Cave National Park
26611 H 385
Hot Springs, SD
605-745-4600
nps.gov/wica
This park is home to one of the world's longest and most complex caves. The park is open year round from 8 to 5 pm during summer

hours and until 4:30 pm winter hours. Dogs are allowed at the park and at the campground (no hookups) for no additional fee, but basically they can only go where your car can go. The campground is open year round except when it snows and they have to close the roads to the camping areas. Dogs are not allowed on the trails, they may not be left unattended, they must be leashed at all times, and cleaned up after.

Badlands National Park
25216 Ben Reifel Rd
Interior, SD
605-433-5361
nps.gov/badl/
This park covers 160 square acres, has America's largest mixed grass prairies, and is home to the Badlands National Monument. Highway 240 is the Badlands Loop Scenic Byway and is 31 1/2 miles long with 14 lookouts. Dogs are not allowed on any of the trails in the park. They are allowed only at the campground or the parking lots. The contact station for the Cedar Pass Campground is on Highway 240, and this campground has an amphitheater. The other campground, White River, has a visitor's center on Highway 27. The campgrounds are open year round, and there are no hook-ups at either camp. Dogs of all sizes are allowed in the campgrounds. There are no additional fees. Dogs may not be left unattended outside, and only inside if it creates no danger to the pet. Dog must be leashed and cleaned up after.

Tennessee

Great Smoky Mountains National Park
107 Park Headquarters Road
Gatlinburg, TN
865-436-1200
(http://www.nps.gov/grsm/)
Greate Smoky Mountains National Park is located both in Tennessee and North Carolina and is one of the most popular of the National Parks. Pets must be leashed or restrained at all times within the park and are not allowed on most of the hiking trails. They can accompany you in your car and at lookouts and stops near the road. However, there are two trails in Great Smoky Mountains National Park that will allow leashed dogs. The Gatlinburg Trail is a 1.9 mile trail from the Sugarland's Visitor Center to the outskirts of Gatlinburg;

it runs along the forest with beautiful river views and it passes old homesteads along the way. It follows a creek a good portion of the way. The Oconaluftee River Trail follows along the river for a 1.5 mile

Texas

Big Bend National Park
P.O. Box 129
Big Bend National Park, TX
432-477-2251
nps.gov/bibe/
This park is at the big bend of the Rio Grande, and there are 2 entrances; in the North on Highway 118, and in the West on Highway 385. Dogs are not allowed anywhere in the back country, on any of the trails, at the river, or off any of the roads.There are 3 campgrounds, and an RV park. The RV park is the only camp area with full hookups. It is concession operated, sites are on a first come/ first served basis, and full hookup capability is required. Dogs may not be left unattended at any time, they must be leashed or crated at all times, and be cleaned up after.

Guadalupe Mountains National Park
H 62/180
Pine Springs, TX
915-828-3251
nps.gov/gumo
This parks hosts an extensive Permisan Limestone fossil reef. The park is open year-round; visitor center hours are from 8:00 a.m. to 4:30 p.m., and a bit longer in summer. Dogs on lead are allowed to go to the Sitting Bull Falls and the Last Chance Canyon. Dogs are not allowed on any of the other trails, but they are allowed on the trails in the neighboring Lincoln National Forest. This forest is very rugged, and pets must be watched very closely that they do not step on the plant called Letchigia Cactus. It may even go through tires and must be removed only by surgical means. Dogs are allowed at no additional fee at either of the campgrounds, and the campsites do not have hookups. Dogs may not be left unattended, they must be leashed, and cleaned up after. This park can also be accessed from the New Mexico side on Highway 137.

Utah

Bryce Canyon National Park

PO Box 640201/ On H 63
Bryce, UT
435-834-5322
nps.gov/brca/
This park is famous for it's unique geology, creating vast and unusual limestone formations throughout the region. Dogs are not allowed on any of the trails, the shuttle, the viewpoints, or the visitor's center. The park is open 24 hours a day year round. There are 2 campgrounds; Loop A, the north campground, is open all year, and the Sunset campground is only open for the season. There are no hookups at either campground. Dogs can walk along the road in the campground. There are no additional fees for the dogs. Dogs may not be left unattended, they must be leashed at all times, and cleaned up after.

Arches National Park
PO Box 907
Moab, UT
435-719-2299
nps.gov/arch/index.htm
Pets on leash with cleanup are allowed in the campsites and paved areas of the parks. Dogs are not allowed on any trails or backcountry. They are allowed unattended if well-behaved in the Devil's Garden campground.

Canyonlands National Park
2282 SW Resource Blvd
Moab, UT
435-719-2313
nps.gov/cany/index.htm
Pets on leash are allowed in developed areas, such as campgrounds, paved roads, and the Potash/Shafer Canyon road between Moab and the Island in the Sky. They are not allowed on hiking trails or in the backcountry.

Zion National Park
State Route 9
Springdale, UT
435-772-3256
nps.gov/zion/
Dogs are allowed on one walking trail at this national park. Dogs on a 6 foot or less leash are allowed on the Pa'rus Trail which is a 1.5 mile long trail that runs from the South Campground to Canyon Junction. You and your pooch can also enjoy a 10-12 mile scenic drive on the Zion-Mount Carmel Highway which goes through the park. If you are there from November through March, you can also take your car on the Zion Canyon Scenic Drive. If

you arrive during the summer months, the Zion Canyon Scenic Drive is closed and only allows park shuttle buses. Other pet rules include no pets on shuttle buses, in the backcountry, or in public buildings. Pets are allowed in the campgrounds and along roadways.

Capitol Reef National Park
HC 70 Box 15
Torrey, UT
435-425-3791
nps.gov/care/index.htm
Dogs on leash are allowed in campsites and on paved road areas. Dogs are not allowed on hiking trails or in the backcountry.

Virgin Islands

Virgin Islands National Park
1300 Cruz Bay Creek
St John, VI
340-776-6201
nps.gov/viis
The Virgin Islands National Park is one of breathtaking beauty offering white sandy beaches, tropical forests, and coral reefs. The visitor center is open daily from 8 to 4:30pm. Park areas are open 24 hours a day year-round. Dogs are allowed in the park and on the trails. They are not allowed at the campground, or at Trunk Bay. Dogs must be leashed, cleaned up after, and under owners control at all times.

Virginia

Shenandoah National Park
3655 U.S. Highway 211 East
Luray, VA
540-999-3500
nps.gov/shen/
Shenandoah National Park is one of the most dog-friendly National Parks, with dogs allowed on most of the trails. Covering 300 mostly forested square miles of the Blue Ridge Mountains the park provides many diverse habitats for thousands of birds and wildlife. The park also provides a wide range of recreational opportunities. There are more than 500 miles of trails, including 101 miles of the Appalachian Trail, summer and fall festivals/reenactments, a rich cultural history to share, interpretive programs, and breathtaking natural beauty. There are several highlights along the 105 mile long, 35 MPH,

Skyline Drive (the only public road through the park), such as 75 scenic overlooks and Mary's Rock Tunnel at milepost 32. The 610 foot-long tunnel was considered an engineering feet in 1932; just note that the clearance for the tunnel is 12'8". Dogs of all sizes are allowed for no additional fee. Dogs must be under their owner's control, on no more than a 6 foot leash or securely crated, cleaned up after at all times, and are not to be left unattended. Dogs are not allowed in buildings or on about 14 miles of the trails; please ask the attendant at the gate for a list of the trails.

Washington

Mount Rainer National Park
Tahoma Woods State Route
Ashford, WA
360-569-2211
nps.gov/mora/index.htm
Dogs must be on leash where they are allowed. Dogs are only allowed on roads, parking lots, and campgrounds. They are not allowed on trails, snow, in buildings, or any wilderness areas. There is a small portion of Pacific Crest Trail near the park's eastern boundary that allows pets on leash.

North Cascades National Park
State Route 20
Newhalem, WA
360-856-5700
nps.gov/noca
Dogs are allowed on one of the hiking trails, the Pacific Crest Trail. This scenic hiking trail runs through the park and is rated moderate to difficult. The trail is located off Highway 20, about one mile east of Rainy Pass. At the Bridge Creek Trailhead, park on the north side of the highway and then hike north (uphill) or south (downhill). A Northwest Forest Pass is required to park at the trailhead. The cost is about $5 and can be purchased at the Visitor's Center in Newhalem. For a larger variety of trails, including a less strenuous hike, dogs are also allowed on trails at the adjacent Ross Lake National Recreation Area and the Lake Chelan National Recreation Area. Both recreation areas are managed by the national park.

Olympic National Park
600 East Park Avenue
Port Angeles, WA

360-565-3130
nps.gov/olym/
Pets are not permitted on park trails, meadows, beaches or in any undeveloped area of the park. There is one exception. Dogs are allowed on leash, during daytime hours only, on Kalaloch Beach along the Pacific Ocean and from Rialto Beach north to Ellen Creek. For those folks and dogs who want to hike on a trail, try the adjacent dog-friendly Olympic National Forest.

Wyoming

Grand Teton National Park
Moose, WY
307-739-3300
nps.gov/grte/
Grand Teton National Park offers spectacular views of the jagged Teton Range, meadows, pine trees and beautiful blue lakes. This national park limits pets mostly to where cars can go. Pets are allowed in your car, on roads and within 50 feet of any road, campgrounds, picnic areas and parking lots. Pets are not allowed on any hiking trails, in the backcountry, on swimming beaches, or in any visitor centers. However, dogs are allowed on paths in the campgrounds, and can ride in a boat on Jackson Lake only. Dogs must be on a 6 foot leash or less, caged, crated, or in your car at all times. Pets cannot be left unattended or tied to an object. An activity you can do with your pet is to take a scenic drive. There are three scenic drives in the park. Many turnouts along the road offer exhibits on park geology, wildlife and plants. The Teton Park Road follows along the base of the Teton Range from Moose to Jackson Lake Junction. The Jenny Lake Scenic Drive skirts along Jenny Lake and offers great views of the Grand Teton peaks. This drive is one-way and starts just south of String Lake. You can reach this scenic drive by driving south at the North Jenny Lake Junction. Another scenic drive is the Signal Mountain Summit Road which climbs 800 feet to offer panoramic views of the Teton Range, Jackson Hole valley and Jackson Lake. For accommodations within the park, dogs are welcome in some of the Colter Bay Cabins and in some rooms at the Jackson Lake Lodge. For hiking trails that are dog-friendly, try the nearby

Bridger-Teton National Forest.

Yellowstone National Park
various
Yellowstone National Park, WY
307-344-7381
nps.gov/yell
Yellowstone National Park was established in 1872 and is America's first national park. Most of the park is at a high altitude of 7,500 feet or greater. The park is home to a wide variety of wildlife including grizzly bears, wolves, bison, elk, deer, coyotes and more. Yellowstone is also host to many natural scenic attractions including the popular Old Faithful geyser. There are numerous other geysers, hot springs, mudpots, and fumaroles which are all evidence of ongoing volcanic activity. Included in this park is Yellowstone Lake, which is the largest high-altitude lake in North America. While the lake looks stunning with its brilliantly blue water, it does have many hot hydrothermal spots, so people are advised not to swim in most of the lake areas and pets are prohibited from swimming. Traveling to Yellowstone Park with a pet can be pretty restrictive, but you will still be able to view most of the popular sights that tourists without pets usually come to see. While pets are not allowed on the trails, in the backcountry, in thermal areas, or on the boardwalks, you will still be able to view Old Faithful from about 200 feet back. Even at that distance, Old Faithful can look pretty spectacular. And if you drive the Grand Loop Road, you will be able to view some points of interest and perhaps see some wildlife including black bears, grizzly bears, bison and elk. Dogs are allowed in parking areas, campgrounds and within 100 feet of roads. Pets must be on a 6 foot or less leash or crated or caged at all times. Pets are not allowed to be left unattended and tied to an object. However, they can remain in your car while you view attractions near roads and parking areas. The park officials do require that you provide sufficient ventilation in the car for your pet's comfort and survival. For accommodations within the park, dogs are welcome in some of the park's cabins. There are some dog-friendly cabins within easy walking distance of Old Faithful. If you are looking for some dog-friendly hiking trails, there are numerous dog-friendly trails in the nearby Shoshone National Forest, located between the Cody and Yellowstone.